The Baseball *Autograph* Collector's Handbook

Number 14

BY JACK SMALLING

The Baseball Autograph Collector's Handbook

Number 14

Contents

ISBN-10: 1-932391-22-3 ISBN-13: 978-1-932391-22-0

Cover Design: Linwood Webb. **Production:** Phillip Daquila, Linwood Webb.

SMALLING FAMILY *AUTOGRAPHS*

HALL OF FAME SIGNATURES

PLAYER	A 3x5	B 3x5	C 3x5	D 3x5	CUT	G.P.
ANDERSON	10.00	8.00	7.00			
APPLING	10.00					$30
ASHBURN	15.00	12.00	10.50	9.00		
AVERILL	15.00	12.00	10.50			
BARLICK	15,00	12.00	10.50	9.00		$15
BELL	20.00	16.00		12.00		
BERRA	20.00	16.00	14.00			$20
BOUDREAU	8.00	6.40	5.60		5.00	$6
BUNNING					6.00	
CAREY	40.00	32.00				
CEPEDA	25.00					
CHANDLER	15.00	12.00	10.50	9.00	7.50	$15
COMBS						
CONLAN	10.00				5.00	$20
COVELESKI	8.00	6.40			4.00	$20
CRONIN	40.00	32.00	28.00		20.00	
DICKEY	50.00	40.00		30.00	25.00	$40
DOBY				12.00	10.00	
DOERR	5.00	4.00	3.50		1.00	$8
DUROCHER	40.00		28.00	24.00	20.00	
FABER	60.00					
FELLER	8.00		5.60		4.00	$12
FERRELL	8.00		5.60		4.00	$15
FISK	20.00					
FORD	20.00		14.00		10.00	
GEHRINGER	8.00	6.40	5.60			$30
GOMEZ	30.00	24.00	21.00		15.00	
GREENBERG					30.00	
GRIMES	30.00	24.00	21.00			$40
GROVE	60.00					
HAINES	40.00	32.00	28.00			
HERMAN	8.00	6.40	5.60			$20
HOOPER	50.00					
HOYT	10.00					
HUBBELL	10.00	8.00	7.00			
HUNTER	15.00					$20
IRVIN	15.00	12.00	10.50	9.00	7.50	
T. JACKSON	15.00	12.00	10.50		7.50	
JENKINS	20.00				10.00	
J. JOHNSON	20.00	16.00	14.00	12.00		
KALINE				15.00		$20
KELL	6.00	4.80	4.20	3.60	3.00	$8
G. KELLY	15.00	12.00	10.50	9.00		$25
KILLEBREW			10.50	9.00	7.50	
KINER	20.00		14.00	12.00		$25
LEMON	8.00	6.40	5.60			$10
LEONARD	15.00		10.50			$15
LINDSTROM	40.00	32.00	28.00		20.00	
LOMBARDI	60.00				30.00	
LOPEZ	20.00		14.00	12.00	7.50	$30
LYONS	15.00		10.50		7.50	
MACPHAIL	20.00		14.00		10.00	$20
MARQUARD	40.00	32.00			20.00	
MATHEWS	20.00	16.00	14.00			$30
MCCARTHY	30.00	24.00	21.00	18.00	15.00	
MARICHAL	25.00				10.00	
MEDWICK	60.00	48.00			30.00	
MIZE	20.00	16.00	14.00		10.00	$30
MUSIAL	25.00	20.00	17.50	15.00	12.50	$25
NEWHOUSER	20.00	16.00	14.00		10.00	
NIEKRO	20.00	16.00	14.00		10.00	
PEREZ	12.00					
PERRY	20.00	16.00			10.00	
RIZZUTO	25.00	20.00	17.5	15.00	12.50	
ROBERTS	10.00	8.00	7.00		5.00	$15
B.ROBINSON	10.00	8.00	7.00		5.00	$15
ROUSH	15.00	12.00	10.50		7.50	$40
RUFFING	50.00					
RYAN	30.00				15.00	
SCHOENDIENST	25.00	20.00	17.50		12.50	
SEWELL	12.00	9.60	8.40		6.00	$30
SISLER	60.00					
SLAUGHTER	6.00	4.80	4.20		3.00	$10
SNIDER	15.00		10.50			$20
SPAHN	15.00	12.00	10.50		7.50	$25
SEAVER					10.00	
TERRY	15.00	12.00	10.50			$30
L. WANER	25.00	20.00			12.50	$30
WEAVER	15.00	12.00	10.5		7.50	
B.WILLIAMS	12.00					
WYNN						$30

KEY

A 3x5 Blank side signed, no other marks
B 3x5 Lined side signed, no other marks
D 3x5 Dedicated to some particular person
C 3x5 Lined or blank side with typing or other marks

Cut A signature from a letter, sheet of paper, return address, etc.

Add shipping to above prices

Smalling Family Autographs
R.J. "Jack" Smalling
2308 Van Buren Avenue
Ames, Iowa 50010-4598

Phone: 515-232-7599
Fax: 515-232-7746
E-mail: jack@baseballaddresses.com
http://www.baseballaddresses.com

DAVID SMALLING AUTOGRAPHS

Hi, I'm Jack's son, David, and I live in Olathe, Kansas (a southwest suburb of Kansas City) with my wife, Kristin. I have helped my dad sort autographs, fill orders, and compile his price list since I was about 8 years old. I share my dad's passion for collecting autographs and look forward to doing business with you!

SELLING

My autographs were obtained from buying collections, mail requests, in-person signings, and some from my dad years ago. Primarily, I have signed baseball cards and signed baseball 3″x5″ index cards for sale.

I accept payment with credit card via PayPal.

In addition to including my price list with my dad's price list (sent US mail), I will be emailing 2 or 3 updates to my price list as an Adobe Acrobat Document (.pdf). You can view and search for items right on your computer. However, if you'd don't have email, I can send a hard copy.

SEND YOUR EMAIL ADDRESS

BUYING

Buying Collections - I am interested in buying baseball autograph collections. If you really want to sell, give me a call. Then send your collection along with your phone number and email address. I'm particularly looking for collections of signed baseball cards, and signed baseball 3″x5″ index cards.

Buying Lots - I will also buy in lots. For signed baseball 3″x5″ index cards, I'll pay $20 per 100 cards. For signed baseball cards, I'll pay $30 per 100 cards. They must be signed on the front. Please do not send minor league or personalized cards.

I seldom have to return collections, the collector and I generally agree on a fair price.

DAVID SMALLING AUTOGRAPHS

David Smalling

15863 West 158th Street

Olathe, KS 66062

Phone: 913-829-9360 / Email: dksmalling@sbcglobal.net

Preface

This book concentrates on the personal signatures or autographs of baseball players. It attempts to provide the background, explanations, and wherewithal for a collector to begin or augment his collection. Many illustrations are taken from what are believed authentic signatures. Some helpful hints are provided so that your autograph hunting pursuits may be simplified and fruitful.

When reading and using this book, please keep in mind the moral and legal rights of the ballplayers. Some are more cooperative than others, some have more time to comply with your requests than others, but all are entitled to respect, privacy and the right to affix or not affix his signature based on his own personal thoughts or moods.

There might be nothing more distinctive and personal that a person may do throughout his life than write his own name. This signature, how it changes from childhood to senility, its thin or broad stroke, its clarity, neatness and readability is a reflection of the character, mood and personality of the signer. Perhaps for these reasons, a person's signature has become his universally accepted mark for identification, acknowledgment and legal contractual agreement.

As these addresses are under constant update because of the transient nature of the society in which we live, I would appreciate any information you can provide concerning the validity of the information and addresses contained herein. Please send all correspondence concerning address corrections, changes of address or death notices to:

R.J. "Jack" Smalling
2308 Van Buren Avenue
Ames, IA 50010

Special thanks to Jim Hoekstra from Iowa State University for file preparation.

I hope this edition of *The Baseball Autograph Collector's Handbook* provides a useful, interesting and enjoyable tool for your autograph and baseball historical pursuits.

Sincerely,

Jack Smalling

Authenticity

One of the enjoyable features of collecting autographs is knowing that one possesses an original mark made by another human being, who for one reason or another has distinguished him or herself in the eyes of the collector. Facsimile autographs, autographs signed by someone other than the one whose name appears on the autograph or photographs or copies of autographs do not comply with the definition of a true autograph; hence, they are of no value to the collector.

The only way one can be absolutely sure that an autograph is authentic is to personally witness the signer as he affixes his autograph. Practically speaking, were directly obtained autographs the only ones collected, logistic problems would prevent anyone from having but a modest collection. While authenticity can only be assured by directly obtaining autographs, many sources offer a high probability that an autograph is valid.

Knowing how a person's signature is supposed to look is a first step toward ascertaining authenticity. Facsimile autographs to compare with ones you are attempting to validate can be found on baseball cards, in books or magazines, or quite possibly, from the many facsimile autographs found in the text of this book. The reputation of the secondary source (dealer, friend, other collector) from whom you are obtaining the autograph is of utmost importance. Unfortunately, even the most reputable source may be unaware that he possesses a non-legitimate autograph.

Obtaining an autograph from a logical source increases the probability that an autograph is authentic. Other variables being equal, a resident of Boston is more likely to have a valid autograph of a Red Sox player than is a resident of Butte, Mont. A 70-year old is much more likely to possess an autographed Babe Ruth ball than is a 12-year old. Autographs obtained from the estate or from personal friends of the autographer are highly likely to be authentic. Autographs from financial or legal documents, such as cancelled checks or contracts, or any notarized communications can be considered authentic.

How To Obtain Autographs

Although the text of this book is intended to provide the information necessary to obtain autographs through the mail, there are other ways to obtain autographs of ballplayers. There are basically two general categories by which you can obtain an autograph–firsthand or directly, where you actually watch the ballplayer affix his signature, and secondhand or indirectly, where you are not present at the time the ballplayer signs the autograph. As autograph collectors place such a high concern on authenticity, obtaining autographs firsthand is preferential. Practically speaking, some autographs are impossible to obtain firsthand, while many others are near impossible or at best very difficult to obtain firsthand; hence, most collectors obtain a considerable portion of their collections via the indirect method.

Obtaining Autographs Firsthand

The most obvious place to obtain a ballplayer's autograph is at the ballpark. The traditional crowd around the clubhouse awaiting the departure of their favorite players after the game, pens and papers in hand, is still perhaps the most viable means to obtain autographs. Many clubs provide special nights at the ballpark where, before the game, fans are encouraged to chat, photograph and obtain autographs from the local team members who are available for these activities for the time periods specified.

Local merchants sometimes sponsor promotional activities at their establishments and feature a ballplayer as the guest celebrity. The ballplayer is normally available to sign autographs, and the merchants might well provide a medium (photo, postcard, etc.) for obtaining the autograph.

Other opportunities arise at hotels, airports, celebrity dinners or other public places where a ballplayer might chance to be during the course of his normal routine. However, I must emphasize again the necessity for patience and politeness when requesting an autograph in person from a ballplayer. Quite often, time may allow only a few or no signatures to be signed before the ballplayer's schedule requires him to halt the autograph activities.

More and more over the past few years, the many sports collectibles conventions and shows held across the country have been featuring guest baseball players. These shows provide excellent opportunities for obtaining autographs from some of the most popular ballplayers.

Each year the Baseball Hall of Fame in Cooperstown, NY, holds induction ceremonies for newly elected members. Not only do the newly elected members attend, but also many of the members who have been previously elected are in attendance. There is probably no other time or place during the year when one can obtain, in person, as many living HOFer autographs as on induction day in Cooperstown.

Obtaining Autographs Indirectly

Most collectors, by necessity, obtain the bulk of their collections indirectly. Trading with other collectors, purchasing from dealers, purchasing from private parties, bidding at auction from estate liquidations, hobby paper ads, or sports collectibles conventions are the most prevalent methods which do not involve the sports personality himself. The most common way to obtain an autograph from the sports personality without the presence of the sports personality is through the mail. It is for this purpose that *The Baseball Autograph Collector's Handbook* is most useful.

Autograph collecting is a reasonably popular hobby. It is not uncommon to find other collectors with autograph interests similar to yours. It is also not uncommon to find collectors who possess, more than one autograph of the same player; a duplicate which they can be convinced to part with in exchange for an autograph which they desire but do not possess - one which you yourself may have in duplicate. These conditions form the basis for trade negotiations from which both parties can obtain satisfaction. Most trading is not quite this simple; however, the underlying motives of all tradings are to obtain something you do not possess and desire to have, for something you have but do not place such a high value on as you do the item you desire to obtain.

Dealers in autographed material exist just as they do for any collectible. Many specialize in particular types of autographs. In any event, these dealers have acquired autograph material and are willing to sell it at a given price (a price which may or may not be negotiable). These dealers can be found at sports collectibles conventions, at local flea markets and from advertisements in the hobby papers or autograph oriented periodicals (including this book).

A check of your local newspaper, particularly the auction section of the Sunday edition, is an excellent way to become aware of estate and private party autograph sales and auctions. The auction method offers you the opportunity to obtain autographs you desire for amounts less than you might pay to a dealer. In fact, because of the scarcity of certain autographs, the auction method may be the only available way to obtain a particular autograph. In such cases a fair market value might not be known, and the auction offers a means to arrive at a price based on the value of the autograph to the collector.

Obtaining Autographs Through the Mail

A large number of active and retired baseball players honor autograph requests made through the mail. One of the prime purposes of compiling this book is to provide the collector with the wherewithal to obtain autographs he or she desires through the mail. The author does not profess to know all players who will comply with your autograph requests, nor those who will not comply. The author does not promote or sanction any harassment or excessive requests on your part of the ballplayers contacted through the addresses found in this Address List. To the contrary, I emphatically suggest a polite, patient and respectful course in obtaining autographs through the mail.

Ballplayers, particularly active players during the baseball season, have schedules much tighter and more regimented than the normal 9 to 5 worker. Mail they receive may not be opened for lengthy periods. Many schedule limited time periods that they devote to autograph requests. Quite possibly, dependent on the number of autograph requests a particular player receives, your autograph request might not be answered for a considerable period of time. Be patient. The author knows of cases where years have elapsed before an autograph request was returned.

Like everyone else, ballplayers are human beings and appreciate politeness. Words such as "please" and "thank you" are as pleasantly received and as revered by ballplayers as they are by parents of teenagers (fortunately, ballplayers hear them much more often). Excessive requests, imperative tones and impoliteness are justifiably scorned.

Some ballplayers do not honor autograph requests, either in person or through the mail. Some do not even accept mail, and your letter may come back marked "refused." Some change their autographing philosophies over the years, becoming more liberal or conservative in their autographing habits. Whatever a player's thoughts or ideas are on accepting or refusing autograph requests, they should be respected.

The mechanics of obtaining autographs through the mail are quite simple. Send the request, postpaid, to the ballplayer, including a politely written request outlining what you are asking of the ballplayer, any material that you wish to have autographed and an SASE (self-addressed stamped envelope) large enough to contain the material you wish to be autographed and returned to you. Never send an autograph request postage due. To do so is presumptuous, in poor taste and completely uncalled for.

Do not send an unreasonable amount of material for autographing. A limit of three items per request has become the accepted practice of collectors. An exception to this limit is considered permissible if you have duplicates of the item you wish to have autographed, and you would like to give the ballplayer the opportunity to keep one of the duplicates for his own enjoyment. Ballplayers, like most of us, enjoy seeing and having interesting photos or other material concerning themselves, particularly if the item is novel or the ballplayer has never before seen it. Many collectors use this method as a gesture of good faith and intent when requesting autographs through the mail. However, the limit of three items you wish to have signed and returned to you, exclusive of the items you wish to present to the ballplayer at his option to keep, is still the accepted standard.

It is not considered unreasonable to request a short personalization with an autograph; for example, "To John from . . . ," or "Best Wishes to Gayle from . . . ," etc. Requesting a two-page letter or an answer to a question that requires a dissertation is unreasonable. Do not do it.

Always include an SASE with sufficient postage to cover the material you expect might be returned to you. The SASE alleviates the need for the ballplayer to package and address your reply himself; it enables you to pay, as you should, for return postage; and it assures that the reply will be sent to the party requesting it (assuming you can competently write your own address on an envelope).

Values

Like other collectibles, there is a definite price structure for the autographs of ballplayers. I would like to present a discussion of values within a context of scarcity and desirability, which, when all results are in, are the prime determinants of value for any collectible.

Living or Deceased

Like artists and martyrs, the values of whose accomplishments during their lifetimes are magnified and glorified after death, the value of ballplayers' autographs increases considerably after death. The deceased ballplayer can no longer, of course, sign autographs; hence, the supply of the autographs of this ballplayer ceases at this point in time. All autographs of deceased ballplayers must be obtained secondhand after death, making authenticity questionable.

Hall of Fame Members

The pinnacle of success for a ballplayer is election to baseball's Hall of Fame. This honor is limited to the most skillful and proficient players and those others who have made the most significant contributions to the game. The autographs of these men are among the most desirable and have, other factors being equal, the highest value to collectors.

Popularity and Notoriety

While popularity can generally be measured by ballplaying skills, there are certainly exceptions. Many ballplayers whose skills on the field were limited have achieved success and notoriety in other walks of life (William A. "Billy" Sunday, Joe Garagiola, Chuck Connors, Jim Thorpe, to name a few). The more popular the ballplayer, whether his popularity was derived by playing skills or by some other means, the higher the value placed on his autograph.

Condition and Type of Autograph

Autographs, like other collectibles, exist in various physical conditions - from the weakest, broken pencil autograph to the boldest, unbroken, indelible ink signature. The higher value is placed on the better condition autograph of the same person. Many types of media are available on which to obtain autographs. There are the relatively bland cuts and 3 x 5 varieties at one end of the spectrum and the most elaborate pieces of one-of-a-kind items autographed by the player at the other end. In between there are myriad possible forms and designs that the autograph medium may take. The same autograph has a higher value based on the more interesting, enjoyable and attractive medium on which the autograph is written.

New in this Edition of the Address List

The Address List contains nearly 12,600 entries. The players new to the big leagues in 2005 and 2006 have been added with their corresponding debut years and numbers. Address corrections have been made and obituary data have been supplied for those who have died since the last edition. In total, more than 4,000 additions or corrections have been made.

How To Use The Baseball Autograph Collector's Handbook

The Handbook is composed of four sections:

1. Players in the Baseball Hall of Fame
2. Players who debuted from 1920 to 2006
3. Coaches with no major league playing or managerial experience who debuted from 1930 to 2006
4. Umpires who debuted from 1930 to 2006

The address portion of the listing contains the known current address of the player if the player is now living or other information as follows:

DEBUT YEAR **PLAYER'S NAME** **ADDRESS OR DEATH DATA**

DEBUT YEAR NUMBER

1944-048	GILLESPIE, ROBERT WILLIAM	D. NOVEMBER 4, 2001, WINSTON-SALEM, N.C.
1953-028	GILLIAM, JAMES WILLIAM 'JUNIOR'	D. OCTOBER 8, 1978, INGLEWOOD, CALIF.
1967-039	GILLIFORD, PAUL GANT	7 WOODLAND DR, MALVERN PA 19355
1927-040	GILLIS, GRANT	D. FEBRUARY 4, 1981, THOMASVILLE, ALA.
1944-049	GILMORE, LEONARD PRESTON	7500 NE 102ND STREET, JONES OK 73049
1968-027	GILSON, HAROLD	7243 NORTH 8TH WAY, PHOENIX AZ 85020
2006-056	GIMENEZ, HECTOR C.	OLD ADD: SAN FELIPE VENEZ
1948-040	GINSBERG, MYRON NATHAN 'JOE'	12635 SW KINGSWAY CIRCLE #D1, LAKE SUZY FL 33821
2000-067	GINTER, KEITH MICHAEL	1531 EAST HORSESHOE DRIVE, CHANDLER AZ 85249
2000-068	GINTER, MATTHEW SHANE	3325 NEW BOONESBORO, WINCHESTER KY 40391
1944-050	GIONFRIDDO, ALBERT FRANCIS	D. MARCH 14, 2003, SOLVANG, CALIF.
1953-029	GIORDANO, THOMAS ARTHUR	176 RIVERSIDE AVENUE, AMITYVILLE NY 11701
1995-083	GIOVANALA, EDWARD THOMAS	1741 NOMARK COURT, SAN JOSE CA 95125
1998-066	GIPSON, CHARLES WELLS	632 SOUTH EARLHAM STREET, ORANGE CA 92869
1989-042	GIRARDI, JOSEPH ELLIOTT	1845 SOUTH JAMES COURT NORTH, LAKE FOREST IL 60045
2004-073	GISSELL, CHRISTOPHER ODELL	305 NE 107TH STREET, VANCOUVER WA 98685
1936-031	GIULIANI, ANGELO JOHN	D. OCTOBER 8, 2004, SAINT PAUL, MINN.
1962-048	GIUSTI, DAVID JOHN	524 CLAIR DR, PITTSBURGH PA 15241
1995-084	GIVENS, BRIAN	719 STONEMONT COURT, CASTLE ROCK CO 80104

ADDRESS NOT KNOWN — An old address is given for players for whom a current address is not known. In many cases, the year the address was last valid is shown in the data. Birth information is given if no other data is available. If no information is known about a player except his name, a blank space will appear in the address portion of the listing.

DECEASED PLAYERS — The date and place of a player's death will be listed for deceased players. Incomplete death data is given for some players because complete information is not known. The abbreviation D. with no other information in the address portion of the listing indicates that a player is reportedly deceased, but that no other data is available.

PLEASE NOTE:

■ Managers who never appeared as a player in a big league game are listed with the year they first managed in the big leagues.

■ Only those coaches who never appeared as a player in a big league game are listed in the coaches section.

■ The abbreviations used for states on addresses are standard U.S. Postal Service abbreviations.

■ B. indicates born, D. indicates deceased and other abbreviations are self-explanatory as they are used in normal written communications.

As this is a nation of transients, one can expect that the addresses of a considerable number of the ballplayers listed will become invalid over the next year or two.

GLOSSARY

The definitions presented in this glossary are definitions as they are interpreted by autograph collectors. For example, **PHOTO** refers to an autographed photo and **HOFer** refers to the autograph of a Hall of Famer. Some of the definitions may appear self-explanatory and hence unnecessary; however, they are included for completeness.

ALL-STAR BALL
A ball autographed by most or all members of a particular baseball all-star game.

AUTOPEN
A mechanical device used to affix a signature on a document, letter or other paper medium. Autopen autographs are not considered collectible.

BALL POINT
A type of pen through which the ink is delivered by means of a revolving ball tip.

BASEBALL COMMEMORATIVE ENVELOPE
A stamped envelope postmarked on the date of a significant event in baseball history. The envelope contains some graphic or illustrative identification of the event.

CARD
A card autographed by the player portrayed on the card. Cards are normally autographed on the front; however, cards autographed on the back still qualify under this definition.

CHECK
A cancelled check or bank note containing the autograph of a ballplayer. Checks are quite often obtained from the estate of deceased ballplayers. Official ballclub checks in many cases contain more than one autograph.

CLUB ISSUED POSTCARDS
Postcard size pictures of ballplayers, the older ones normally being in black and white, with modern postcards being predominantly in color. They are usually blank backed, sold at ballparks and make excellent autograph media. Many players send autographed copies of these postcards to fans requesting autographs.

CONTRACT
A legal document, for any purpose, including agreements concerning players and management, equipment or other product manufacturers, or personal agreements signed by the sports personality.

CUT
An autograph that has been "cut" from a larger piece of paper, photo, letter or other written or printed matter.

DATED
An autograph which contains both the signature and the date when the signature was written.

DEBUT YEAR
The year in which a player first appeared in a game in the big leagues. For a manager or coach with no player experience, the debut year refers to the year he first appeared as manager or coach.

DEBUT YEAR NUMBER
Within a particular debut year the number for a player is obtained by placing in alphabetical order all players who debuted that particular year and placing a number on each, from 1 to "the total number of players debuting that year," based on this alphabetical order.

FACSIMILE
A copy of an original signature. Facsimile autographs are not considered collectible.

FELT TIP
A type of pen which has a felt tip and which provides a smooth unbroken signature.

HOFer
The autograph of a member of baseball's Hall of Fame.

LETTER
A typed or handwritten communication with a heading listing to whom the letter is written and a closing autographed by a sports personality.

ORIGINAL ART
A unique drawing, painting or other piece of artwork portraying a personality or an event and bearing the signature of a participant of the event or the personality portrayed.

PENCIL
A signature in pencil by a sports personality. Pencil signatures predominated during the early parts of the century and are sometimes the only types of signatures available of certain sports personalities. Care should be taken with pencil signatures as they smear quite easily.

PLAQUE
Postcard pictures of the bronzed plaques of Hall of Fame baseball players in the Baseball Hall

of Fame in Cooperstown, NY. Through the years there have been several different color plaques issued by the Hall of Fame, including black and white types.

PERSONALIZED
An autograph which contains a reference to the person for whom the autograph was written.

PHOTO
A glossy picture, normally 5" x 7" or 8" x 10", which contains an autograph of the player portrayed on the photo.

SASE
Self-addressed stamped envelope. When requesting autographs, SASEs should be sent to ensure that returned autographs will be sent to the proper place and to provide the autograph giver a convenient means of returning autographed material.

SHARPIE
A brand of ink pen very popular with autograph collectors because of its broad stroke and its rapid drying characteristics on almost any surface.

STAMP
A signature affixed by means of a rubber or wooden device that contains a facsimile of the sports personality's autograph. Stamped signatures are not considered collectible.

TEAM BALL
A ball autographed by most or all members of a particular team.

TEAM SHEET
A single sheet of paper containing the autographs of most or all members of a particular team during a particular year. Many team sheets are on club stationery.

3 x 5
An index card, either lined or unlined, which many collectors use for obtaining autographs. The 3 x 5 refers to the approximate dimensions of the card. 3 x 5s usually contain only one signature.

BASEBALL HALL OF FAME MEMBERS

BBHOF177	AARON, HENRY LOUIS	1611 ADAMS DRIVE SW, ATLANTA GA 30311
BBHOF014	ALEXANDER, GROVER CLEVELAND	D. NOVEMBER 4, 1950, SAINT PAUL, NEB.
BBHOF181	ALSTON, WALTER EMMONS 'SMOKEY'	D. OCTOBER 1, 1984, OXFORD, OHIO
BBHOF245	ANDERSON, GEORGE LEE 'SPARKY'	PO BOX 6415, THOUSAND OAKS CA 91360
BBHOF017	ANSON, ADRIAN CONSTANTINE 'CAP'	D. APRIL 14, 1922, CHICAGO, ILL.
BBHOF185	APARICIO, LUIS ERNEST	OLD ADD: CALLE 67 #26-82, MARACAIBO, VENEZ
BBHOF095	APPLING, LUCIUS BENJAMIN 'LUKE'	D. JANUARY 3, 1991, CUMMING, GA.
BBHOF221	ASHBURN, RICH	D. SEPTEMBER 9, 1997, NEW YORK, N.Y.
BBHOF147	AVERILL, HOWARD EARL 'EARL'	D. AUGUST 16, 1983, EVERETT, WASH.
BBHOF074	BAKER, JOHN FRANKLIN 'HOME RUN'	D. JUNE 28, 1963, TRAPPE, MD.
BBHOF119	BANCROFT, DAVID JAMES	D. OCTOBER 9, 1972, SUPERIOR, WISC.
BBHOF158	BANKS, ERNEST 'ERNIE'	578 WASHINGTON BLVD #284, MARINA DEL REY CA 90292
BBHOF203	BARLICK, ALBERT JOSEPH	D. DECEMBER 27, 1995, SPRINGFIELD, ILL.
BBHOF063	BARROW, EDWARD GRANT	D. DECEMBER 15, 1953, PORT CHESTER, N.Y.
BBHOF120	BECKLEY, JACOB PETER	D. JUNE 25, 1918, KANSAS CITY, MO.
BBHOF141	BELL, JAMES 'COOL PAPA'	D. MARCH 7, 1991, ST. LOUIS, MO.
BBHOF201	BENCH, JOHN LEE	528 4 MILE ROAD, CINCINNATI OH 45230
BBHOF064	BENDER, CHARLES ALBERT 'CHIEF'	D. MAY 22, 1954, PHILADELPHIA, PA.
BBHOF127	BERRA, LAWRENCE PETER 'YOGI'	19 HIGHLAND AVENUE, MONTCLAIR NJ 07042
BBHOF259	BOGGS, WADE ANTHONY	6006 WINDHAM PLACE, TAMPA FL 33647
BBHOF142	BOTTOMLEY, JAMES LEROY	D. DECEMBER 11, 1959, SAINT LOUIS, MO.
BBHOF115	BOUDREAU, LOUIS	D. AUGUST 10, 2001, OLYMPIA FIELDS, ILL.
BBHOF029	BRESNAHAN, ROGER PATRICK	D. DECEMBER 4, 1944, TOLEDO, OHIO
BBHOF238	BRETT, GEORGE HOWARD	6512 GRANADA DRIVE, PRAIRIE VILLAGE KS 66208
BBHOF190	BROCK, LOUIS CLARK	61 BARKLEY PLACE, SAINT CHARLES MO 63301
BBHOF030	BROUTHERS, DENNIS 'DAN'	D. AUGUST 3, 1932, EAST ORANGE, N.J.
BBHOF056	BROWN, MORDECAI PETER CENTENNIAL	D. FEBRUARY 14, 1948, TERRE HAUTE, IND.
BBHOF262	BROWN, RAYMOND	D. FEBRUARY 8, 1965, DAYTON, OHIO
BBHOF263	BROWN, WILLARD JESSE	D. AUGUST 4, 1996, HOUSTON, TEXAS
BBHOF006	BULKELEY, MORGAN G.	D. NOVEMBER 6, 1922, HARTFORD, CONN.
BBHOF225	BUNNING, JAMES PAUL DAVID	1717 DIXIE HIGHWAY #180, FORT WRIGHT KY 41011
BBHOF039	BURKETT, JESSE CAIL	D. MAY 27, 1953, WORCESTER, MASS.
BBHOF111	CAMPANELLA, ROY	D. JUNE 26, 1993, WOODLAND HILLS, CALIF.
BBHOF207	CAREW, RODNEY CLINE	1171 VIA SANTIAGO, CORONA CA 92882
BBHOF085	CAREY, MAX GEORGE	D. MAY 30, 1976, MIAMI, FLA.
BBHOF217	CARLTON, STEVEN NORMAN	555 SOUTH CAMINO DEL RIO #B2, DURANGO CO 81303
BBHOF255	CARTER, GARY EDMUND	560 VILLAGE BLVD #260, WEST PALM BEACH FL 33409
BBHOF015	CARTWRIGHT, ALEXANDER JOY	D. JULY 12, 1892, HONOLULU, HAWAII
BBHOF239	CEPEDA, ORLANDO MANUEL	2305 PALMER CIRCLE, FAIRFIELD CA 94533
BBHOF016	CHADWICK, HENRY	D. APRIL 20, 1908, BROOKLYN, N.Y.
BBHOF040	CHANCE, FRANK LEROY	D. SEPTEMBER 15, 1924, LOS ANGELES, CALIF.
BBHOF178	CHANDLER, ALBERT BENJAMIN 'HAPPY'	D. JUNE 15, 1991, VERSAILLES, KY.
BBHOF152	CHARLESTON, OSCAR MCKINLEY	D. OCTOBER 11, 1954, PHILADELPHIA, PA.
BBHOF041	CHESBRO, JOHN DWIGHT 'JACK'	D. NOVEMBER 6, 1931, CONWAY, MASS.
BBHOF240	CHYLAK, NESTOR	D. FEBRUARY 17, 1982, DUNMORE, PA.
BBHOF031	CLARKE, FRED CLIFFORD	D. AUGUST 14, 1960, WINFIELD, KAN.
BBHOF091	CLARKSON, JOHN GIBSON	D. FEBRUARY 4, 1909, CAMBRIDGE, MASS.
BBHOF135	CLEMENTE, ROBERTO WALKER	D. DECEMBER 31, 1972, SAN JUAN, P.R.
BBHOF001	COBB, TYRUS RAYMOND	D. JULY 17, 1961, ATLANTA, GA.
BBHOF050	COCHRANE, GORDON STANLEY 'MICKEY'	D. JUNE 28, 1962, LAKE FOREST, ILL.
BBHOF018	COLLINS, EDWARD TROWBRIDGE	D. MARCH 25, 1951, BOSTON, MASS.
BBHOF032	COLLINS, JAMES JOSEPH	D. MARCH 6, 1943, BUFFALO, N.Y.
BBHOF116	COMBS, EARLE BRYAN	D. JULY 21, 1976, RICHMOND, KY.
BBHOF019	COMISKEY, CHARLES ALBERT	D. OCTOBER 26, 1931, EAGLE RIVER, WISC.
BBHOF143	CONLAN, JOHN BERTRAND 'JOCKO'	D. APRIL 16, 1989, SCOTTSDALE, ARIZ.
BBHOF065	CONNOLLY, THOMAS HENRY	D. APRIL 28, 1961, NATICK, MASS.
BBHOF153	CONNOR, ROGER	D. JANUARY 4, 1931, WATERBURY, CONN.
BBHOF264	COOPER, ANDREW LEWIS	D. JUNE 3, 1941, WACO, TEXAS
BBHOF112	COVELESKI, STANLEY ANTHONY	D. MARCH 20, 1984, SOUTH BEND, IND.
BBHOF082	CRAWFORD, SAMUEL EARL	D. JUNE 15, 1968, HOLLYWOOD, CALIF.
BBHOF080	CRONIN, JOSEPH EDWARD	D. SEPTEMBER 7, 1984, OSTERVILLE, MASS.
BBHOF020	CUMMINGS, WIILLIAM ARTHUR 'CANDY'	D. MAY 17, 1924, TOLEDO, OHIO
BBHOF108	CUYLER, HAZEN SHIRLEY 'KIKI'	D. FEBRUARY 11, 1950, ANN ARBOR, MICH.
BBHOF199	DANDRIDGE, RAYMOND	D. FEBRUARY 12, 1994, PALM BAY, FLA.
BBHOF233	DAVIS, GEORGE STACEY	D. OCTOBER 17, 1940, PHILADELPHIA, PA.
BBHOF222	DAY, LEON	D. MARCH 13, 1995, BALTIMORE, MD.
BBHOF066	DEAN, JAY HANNA 'DIZZY'	D. JULY 17, 1974, RENO, NEV.
BBHOF033	DELAHANTY, EDWARD JAMES	D. JULY 2, 1903, FORT ERIE, ONT.
BBHOF071	DICKEY, WILLIAM MALCOLM	D. NOVEMBER 12, 1993, LITTLE ROCK, ARK.
BBHOF159	DIHIGO, MARTIN	D. MAY 22, 1971, CIENFUEGOS, CUBA
BBHOF075	DIMAGGIO, JOSEPH PAUL	D. MARCH 8, 1999, HOLLYWOOD, FLA.
BBHOF234	DOBY, LAWRENCE EUGENE	D. JUNE 18, 2003, MONTCALIR, N.J.
BBHOF194	DOERR, ROBERT PERSHING	37705 AGNESS ILLAHE ROAD, AGNESS OR 97406
BBHOF186	DRYSDALE, DONALD SCOTT	D. JULY 3, 1993, MONTREAL, QUE.
BBHOF034	DUFFY, HUGH	D. OCTOBER 19, 1954, BOSTON, MASS.
BBHOF218	DUROCHER, LEO ERNEST	D. OCTOBER 7, 1991, PALM SPRINGS, CALIF.
BBHOF257	ECKERSLEY, DENNIS LEE	6 MACY LANE, IPSWICH MA 01938
BBHOF136	EVANS, WILLIAM GEORGE 'BILLY'	D. JANUARY 23, 1956, MIAMI, FLA.
BBHOF042	EVERS, JOHN JOSEPH	D. MARCH 28, 1947, ALBANY, N.Y.
BBHOF021	EWING, WILLIAM BUCKINGHAM 'BUCK'	D. OCTOBER 20, 1906, CINCINNATI, OHIO

BBHOF096	FABER, URBAN CHARLES 'RED'	D. SEPTEMBER 25, 1976, CHICAGO, ILL.
BBHOF087	FELLER, ROBERT WILLIAM ANDREW	PO BOX 157, GATES MILLS OH 44040
BBHOF187	FERRELL, RICHARD BENJAMIN 'RICK'	D. JULY 27, 1995, BLOOMFIELD HILLS, MICH.
BBHOF212	FINGERS, ROLAND GLEN 'ROLLIE'	PO BOX 230729, LAS VEGAS NV 89123
BBHOF246	FISK, CARLTON ERNEST	18705 63RD AVENUE EAST, BRADENTON FL 34202
BBHOF092	FLICK, ELMER HARRISON	D. JANUARY 9, 1971, BEDFORD, OHIO
BBHOF144	FORD, EDWARD CHARLES 'WHITEY'	3750 GALT OCEAN DRIVE #1411, FORT LAUDERDALE FL 33308
BBHOF174	FOSTER, ANDREW 'RUBE'	D. DECEMBER 9, 1930, KANKAKEE, ILL.
BBHOF226	FOSTER, WILLIAM HENDRICK	D. SEPTEMBER 16, 1978, LORMAN, MISS.
BBHOF229	FOX, JACOB NELSON 'NELLIE'	D. DECEMBER 1, 1975, BALTIMORE, MD.
BBHOF059	FOXX, JAMES EMORY	D. JULY 21, 1967, MIAMI, FLA.
BBHOF117	FRICK, FORD CHRISTOPHER	D. APRIL 8, 1978, BRONXVILLE, N.Y.
BBHOF051	FRISCH, FRANK FRANCIS	D. MARCH 12, 1973, WILMINGTON, DEL.
BBHOF102	GALVIN, JAMES F. 'PUD'	D. MARCH 7, 1902, PITTSBURGH, PA.
BBHOF022	GEHRIG, HENRY LOUIS 'LOU'	D. JUNE 2, 1941, RIVERDALE, N.Y.
BBHOF057	GEHRINGER, CHARLES LEONARD	D. JANUARY 21, 1993, BLOOMFIELD HILLS, MICH.
BBHOF128	GIBSON, JOSH	D. JANUARY 20, 1947, PITTSBURGH, PA.
BBHOF175	GIBSON, ROBERT	215 BELLEVIEW BLVD SOUTH, BELLEVUE NE 68005
BBHOF167	GILES, WARREN CHRISTOPHER	D. FEBRUARY 7, 1979, CINCINNATI, OHIO
BBHOF129	GOMEZ, VERNON LOUIS 'LEFTY'	D. FEBRUARY 17, 1989, GREENBRAE, CALIF.
BBHOF109	GOSLIN, LEON ALLEN 'GOOSE'	D. MAY 15, 1971, BRIDGETON, N.J.
BBHOF265	GRANT, ULYSSES F. 'FRANK'	D. MAY 27, 1937, NEW YORK, N.Y.
BBHOF081	GREENBERG, HENRY BENJAMIN 'HANK'	D. SEPTEMBER 4, 1986, BEVERLY HILLS, CALIF.
BBHOF043	GRIFFITH, CLARK CALVIN	D. OCTOBER 27, 1955, WASHINGTON, D.C.
BBHOF097	GRIMES, BURLEIGH ARLAND	D. DECEMBER 6, 1985, CLEAR LAKE, WISC.
BBHOF052	GROVE, ROBERT MOSES 'LEFTY'	D. MAY 22, 1975, NORWALK, OHIO
BBHOF279	GWYNN, ANTHONY KEITH	15643 BOULDER RIDGE LANE, POWAY CA 92064
BBHOF121	HAFEY, CHARLES JAMES 'CHICK'	D. JULY 2, 1973, CALISTOGA, CALIF.
BBHOF118	HAINES, JESSE JOSEPH 'POP'	D. AUGUST 5, 1978, DAYTON, OHIO
BBHOF086	HAMILTON, WILLIAM ROBERT	D. DECEMBER 16, 1940, WORCESTER, MASS.
BBHOF227	HANLON, EDWARD HUGH 'NED'	D. APRIL 14, 1937, BALTIMORE, MD.
BBHOF130	HARRIDGE, WILLIAM	D. APRIL 9, 1971, EVANSTON, ILL.
BBHOF148	HARRIS, STANLEY RAYMOND 'BUCKY'	D. NOVEMBER 8, 1977, BETHESDA, MD.
BBHOF076	HARTNETT, CHARLES LEO 'GABBY'	D. DECEMBER 20, 1972, PARK RIDGE, ILL.
BBHOF061	HEILMANN, HARRY EDWIN	D. JULY 9, 1951, DETROIT, MICH.
BBHOF149	HERMAN, WILLIAM JENNINGS BRYAN 'BILLY'	D. SEPTEMBER 5, 1992, WEST PALM BEACH, FLA.
BBHOF266	HILL, JOSEPH PRESTON 'PETE'	D. NOVEMBER 26, 1951, BUFFALO, N.Y.
BBHOF122	HOOPER, HARRY BARTHOLOMEW	D. DECEMBER 18, 1974, SANTA CRUZ, CALIF.
BBHOF027	HORNSBY, ROGERS	D. JANUARY 5, 1963, CHICAGO, ILL.
BBHOF113	HOYT, WAITE CHARLES	D. AUGUST 25, 1984, CINCINNATI, OHIO
BBHOF154	HUBBARD, ROBERT CAL 'CAL'	D. OCTOBER 16, 1977, ST. PETERSBURG, FLA.
BBHOF053	HUBBELL, CARL OWEN	D. NOVEMBER 21, 1988, SCOTTSDALE, ARIZ.
BBHOF098	HUGGINS, MILLER JAMES	D. SEPTEMBER 25, 1929, NEW YORK, N.Y.
BBHOF223	HULBERT, WILLIAM AMBROSE	D. APRIL 10, 1882, CHICAGO, ILL.
BBHOF197	HUNTER, JAMES AUGUSTUS 'CATFISH'	D. SEPTEMBER 9, 1999, HERTFORD, N.C.
BBHOF137	IRVIN, MONFORD MERRILL 'MONTE'	1815 ENCLAVE PKWY #6111, HOUSTON TX 77077
BBHOF216	JACKSON, REGINALD MARTINEZ 'REGGIE'	305 AMADOR AVENUE, SEASIDE CA 93955
BBHOF179	JACKSON, TRAVIS CALVIN	D. JULY 27, 1987, WALDO, ARK.
BBHOF208	JENKINS, FERGUSON ARTHUR	41913 NORTH SIGNAL HILL COURT, PHOENIX AZ 85086
BBHOF035	JENNINGS, HUGH AMBROSE	D. FEBRUARY 1, 1928, SCRANTON, PA.
BBHOF007	JOHNSON, BYRON BANCROFT 'BAN'	D. MARCH 28, 1931, SAINT LOUIS, MO.
BBHOF002	JOHNSON, WALTER PERRY 'BIG TRAIN'	D. DECEMBER 10, 1946, WASHINGTON, D.C.
BBHOF150	JOHNSON, WILLIAM JULIUS 'JUDY'	D. JUNE 14, 1989, WILMINGTON, DEL.
BBHOF164	JOSS, ADRIAN 'ADDIE'	D. APRIL 14, 1911, TOLEDO, OHIO
BBHOF170	KALINE, ALBERT WILLIAM	3613 YORK COURT, BLOOMFIELD HILLS MI 48302
BBHOF099	KEEFE, TIMOTHY J.	D. APRIL 23, 1933, CAMBRIDGE, MASS.
BBHOF023	KEELER, WILLIAM HENRY 'WEE WILLIE'	D. JANUARY 1, 1923, BROOKLYN, N.Y.
BBHOF182	KELL, GEORGE CLYDE	PO BOX 70, SWIFTON AR 72471
BBHOF123	KELLEY, JOSEPH JAMES	D. AUGUST 14, 1943, BALTIMORE, MD.
BBHOF138	KELLY, GEORGE LANGE	D. OCTOBER 13, 1984, BURLINGAME, CALIF.
BBHOF036	KELLY, MICHAEL JOSEPH	D. NOVEMBER 8, 1894, BOSTON, MASS.
BBHOF188	KILLEBREW, HARMON CLAYTON	PO BOX 14550, SCOTTSDALE AZ 85267
BBHOF151	KINER, RALPH MCPHERRAN	200 BRADLEY PLACE #204, PALM BEACH FL 33480
BBHOF171	KLEIN, CHARLES HERBERT 'CHUCK'	D. MARCH 28, 1958, INDIANAPOLIS, IND.
BBHOF067	KLEM, WILLIAM J. 'BILL'	D. SEPTEMBER 16, 1951, MIAMI, FLA.
BBHOF131	KOUFAX, SANFORD 'SANDY'	OLD ADD: 160 AMY LANE, VERO BEACH FL 32963
BBHOF008	LAJOIE, NAPOLEON 'NAP'	D. FEBRUARY 7, 1959, DAYTONA BEACH, FLA.
BBHOF028	LANDIS, KENESAW MOUNTAIN	D. NOVEMBER 25, 1944, CHICAGO, ILL.
BBHOF230	LASORDA, THOMAS CHARLES	1473 WEST MAXZIM, FULLERTON CA 92633
BBHOF209	LAZZERI, ANTHONY MICHAEL 'TONY'	D. AUGUST 6, 1946, SAN FRANCISCO, CALIF.
BBHOF155	LEMON, ROBERT GRANVILLE	D. JANUARY 11, 2000, LONG BEACH, CALIF.
BBHOF132	LEONARD, WALTER FENNER 'BUCK'	D. NOVEMBER 27, 1997, ROCKY MOUNT, N.C.
BBHOF156	LINDSTROM, FRED CHARLES	D. OCTOBER 4, 1981, CHICAGO, ILL.
BBHOF160	LLOYD, JOHN HENRY	D. MARCH 19, 1964
BBHOF195	LOMBARDI, ERNEST NATALI	D. SEPTEMBER 26, 1977, SANTA CRUZ, CALIF.
BBHOF161	LOPEZ, ALFONSO RAMON	D. OCTOBER 30, 2005, TAMPA, FLA.
BBHOF077	LYONS, THEODORE AMAR	D. JULY 25, 1986, SULPHUR, LA.
BBHOF009	MACK, CORNELIUS ALEXANDER 'CONNIE'	D. FEBRUARY 8, 1956, GERMANTOWN, PA.
BBHOF267	MACKEY, JAMES RALEIGH 'BIZ'	D. SEPTEMBER 22, 1965, LOS ANGELES, CALIF.
BBHOF165	MACPHAIL, LELAND STANFORD 'LARRY'	D. OCTOBER 1, 1975, MIAMI, FLA.
BBHOF235	MACPHAIL, LELAND STANFORD, JR. 'LEE'	100 REDDING ROAD #1421, REDDING CT 06896
BBHOF268	MANLEY, EFFA	D. APRIL 16, 1981, LOS ANGELES, CALIF.
BBHOF145	MANTLE, MICKEY CHARLES	D. AUGUST 13, 1995, DALLAS, TEXAS

BBHOF100	MANUSH, HENRY EMMETT 'HEINIE'	D. MAY 12, 1971, SARASOTA, FLA.
BBHOF072	MARANVILLE, WALTER JAMES VINCENT 'RABBIT'	D. JANUARY 5, 1954, NEW YORK, N.Y.
BBHOF183	MARICHAL, JUAN ANTONIO SANCHEZ	9458 NW 54 DORAL CIRCLE LANE, MIAMI FL 33128
BBHOF124	MARQUARD, RICHARD WILLIAM 'RUBE'	D. JUNE 1, 1980, BALTIMORE, MD.
BBHOF166	MATHEWS, EDWIN LEE	D. FEBRUARY 18, 2001, LAJOLLA, CALIF.
BBHOF003	MATHEWSON, CHRISTOPHER 'CHRISTY'	D. OCTOBER 7, 1925, SARANAC LAKE, N.Y.
BBHOF168	MAYS, WILLIE HOWARD	51 MOUNT VERNON LANE, ATHERTON CA 94025
BBHOF252	MAZEROSKI, WILLIAM STANLEY	281 WALTON TEA ROOM ROAD, GREENSBURG PA 15601
BBHOF083	MCCARTHY, JOSEPH VINCENT	D. JANUARY 13, 1978, BUFFALO, N.Y.
BBHOF044	MCCARTHY, THOMAS FRANCIS MICHAEL	D. AUGUST 5, 1922, BOSTON, MASS.
BBHOF196	MCCOVEY, WILLIE LEE	PO BOX 620342, WOODSIDE CA 94062
BBHOF045	MCGINNITY, JOSEPH JEROME	D. NOVEMBER 14, 1929, BROOKLYN, N.Y.
BBHOF213	MCGOWAN, WILLIAM ALOYSIUS 'BILL'	D. DECEMBER 9, 1954, SILVER SPRING, MD.
BBHOF010	MCGRAW, JOHN JOSEPH	D. FEBRUARY 25, 1934, NEW ROCHELLE, N.Y.
BBHOF088	MCKECHNIE, WILLIAM BOYD	D. OCTOBER 29, 1965, BRADENTON, FLA.
BBHOF247	MCPHEE, JOHN ALEXANDER 'BID'	D. JANUARY 3, 1943, SAN DIEGO, CALIF.
BBHOF110	MEDWICK, JOSEPH MICHAEL 'DUCKY'	D. MARCH 21, 1975, ST. PETERSBURG, FLA.
BBHOF269	MENDEZ, JOSE	D. OCTOBER 31, 1928, HAVANA, CUBA
BBHOF176	MIZE, JOHN ROBERT	D. JUNE 2, 1993, DEMOREST, GA.
BBHOF258	MOLITOR, PAUL LEO	748 LAKE POINT DRIVE, CHANHASSEN MN 55317
BBHOF205	MORGAN, JOSEPH LEONARD	3239 DANVILLE BLVD #A, ALAMO CA 94507
BBHOF256	MURRAY, EDDIE CLARENCE	26911 TRIUMPH AVENUE, CANYON COUNTRY CA 91351
BBHOF114	MUSIAL, STANLEY FRANK	85 TRENT DRIVE, LADUE MO 63124
BBHOF214	NEWHOUSER, HAROLD	D. NOVEMBER 10, 1998, DETROIT, MICH.
BBHOF058	NICHOLS, CHARLES AUGUSTUS 'KID'	D. APRIL 11, 1953, KANSAS CITY, MO.
BBHOF231	NIEKRO, PHILIP HENRY	6382 NICHOLS ROAD, FLOWERY BRANCH GA 30542
BBHOF037	OROURKE, JAMES HENRY	D. JANUARY 8, 1919, BRIDGEPORT, CONN.
BBHOF060	OTT, MELVIN THOMAS	D. NOVEMBER 21, 1958, NEW ORLEANS, LA.
BBHOF125	PAIGE, LEROY 'SATCHEL'	D. JUNE 8, 1982, KANSAS CITY, MO.
BBHOF206	PALMER, JAMES ALVIN	239 SANFORD AVENUE, PALM BEACH FL 33480
BBHOF054	PENNOCK, HERBERT JEFFERIS	D. JANUARY 30, 1948, NEW YORK, N.Y.
BBHOF248	PEREZ, ATANASIO RIGAL 'TONY'	LAS FLORES 113, SANTURCE PR 00911
BBHOF210	PERRY, GAYLORD JACKSON	PO BOX 489, SPRUCE PINE NC 28777
BBHOF046	PLANK, EDWARD STEWART	D. FEBRUARY 24, 1926, GETTYSBURG, PA.
BBHOF270	POMPEZ, ALEJANDRO 'ALEX'	D. MARCH 14, 1974, NEW YORK, N.Y.
BBHOF271	POSEY, CUMBERLAND WILLIS	D. MARCH 28, 1946, PITTSBURGH, PA.
BBHOF250	PUCKETT, KIRBY	D. MARCH 6, 2006, PHOENIX, ARIZ.
BBHOF024	RADBOURN, CHARLES 'HOSS'	D. FEBRUARY 5, 1897, BLOOMINGTON, ILL.
BBHOF189	REESE, HAROLD HENRY 'PEEWEE'	D. AUGUST 14, 1999, LOUISVILLE, KY.
BBHOF093	RICE, EDGAR CHARLES 'SAM'	D. OCTOBER 13, 1974, ROSSMOR, MD.
BBHOF105	RICKEY, WESLEY BRANCH 'BRANCH'	D. DECEMBER 9, 1965, COLUMBIA, MO.
BBHOF280	RIPKEN, CALVIN EDWIN, JR.	OLD ADD: 2330 WEST JOPPA ROAD #333, LUTHERVILLE MD 21093
BBHOF094	RIXEY, EPPA	D. FEBRUARY 28, 1963, TERRACE PARK, OHIO
BBHOF219	RIZZUTO, PHILIP FRANCIS 'SCOOTER'	912 WESTMINSTER AVENUE, HILLSIDE NJ 07205
BBHOF157	ROBERTS, ROBIN EVAN	504 TERRACE HILL DRIVE, TEMPLE TERRACE FL 33617
BBHOF184	ROBINSON, BROOKS CALBERT	PO BOX 1168, BALTIMORE MD 21203
BBHOF180	ROBINSON, FRANK	15557 AQUA VERDE DRIVE, LOS ANGLES CA 90077
BBHOF089	ROBINSON, JACK ROOSEVELT	D. OCTOBER 24, 1972, STAMFORD, CONN.
BBHOF038	ROBINSON, WILBERT	D. AUGUST 8, 1934, ATLANTA, GA.
BBHOF236	ROGAN, WILBUR 'BULLET JOE'	D. MARCH 4, 1967, KANSAS CITY, MO.
BBHOF090	ROUSH, EDD	D. MARCH 21, 1988, BRADENTON, FLA.
BBHOF106	RUFFING, CHARLES HERBERT 'RED'	D. FEBRUARY 17, 1986, MAYFIELD HEIGHTS, OHIO
BBHOF162	RUSIE, AMOS WILSON	D. DECEMBER 6, 1942, SEATTLE, WASH.
BBHOF004	RUTH, GEORGE HERMAN 'BABE'	D. AUGUST 16, 1948, NEW YORK, N.Y.
BBHOF241	RYAN, LYNN NOLAN 'NOLAN'	2925 SOUTH LOOP 35, ALVIN TX 77511
BBHOF260	SANDBERG, RYNE DEE	26 BILTMORE ESTATES, PHOENIX AZ 85016
BBHOF272	SANTOP, LOUIS	D. JANUARY 22, 1942, PHILADELPHIA, PA.
BBHOF078	SCHALK, RAYMOND WILLIAM 'CRACKER'	D. MAY 19, 1970, CHICAGO, ILL.
BBHOF220	SCHMIDT, MICHAEL JACK	373 EAGLE DRIVE, JUPITER FL 33477
BBHOF204	SCHOENDIENST, ALBERT FRED 'RED'	1105 JO CARR DRIVE, TOWN AND COUNTRY MO 63017
BBHOF215	SEAVER, GEORGE THOMAS 'TOM'	1761 DIAMOND MOUNTAIN ROAD, CALISTOGA CA 94515
BBHOF242	SELEE, FRANK GIBSON	D. JULY 5, 1909, DENVER, COLO.
BBHOF163	SEWELL, JOSEPH WHEELER	D. MARCH 6, 1990, MOBILE, ALA.
BBHOF068	SIMMONS, ALOYSIUS HARRY	D. MAY 26, 1956, MILWAUKEE, WISC.
BBHOF025	SISLER, GEORGE HAROLD	D. MARCH 26, 1973, SAINT LOUIS, MO.
BBHOF191	SLAUGHTER, ENOS BRADSHER	D. AUGUST 12, 2002, DURHAM, N.C.
BBHOF253	SMITH, HILTON	D. NOVEMBER 18, 1983, KANSAS CITY, MO.
BBHOF254	SMITH, OSBORNE EARL 'OZZIE'	PO BOX 164, SAINT ALBANS MO 63073
BBHOF172	SNIDER, EDWIN DONALD 'DUKE'	3037 LAKEMONT DRIVE, FALLBROOK CA 92028
BBHOF139	SPAHN, WARREN EDWARD	D. NOVEMBER 24, 2003, BROKEN ARROW, OKLA.
BBHOF026	SPALDING, ALBERT GOODWILL	D. SEPTEMBER 9, 1915, SAN DIEGO, CALIF.
BBHOF011	SPEAKER, TRISTRAM E.	D. DECEMBER 8, 1958, LAKE WHITNEY, TEXAS
BBHOF200	STARGELL, WILVER DORNEL 'WILLIE'	D. APRIL 9, 2001, WILMINGTON, N.C.
BBHOF249	STEARNES, NORMAN THOMAS 'TURKEY'	D. SEPTEMBER 4, 1979, DETROIT, MICH.
BBHOF103	STENGEL, CHARLES DILLON 'CASEY'	D. SEPTEMBER 29, 1975, GLENDALE, CALIF.
BBHOF261	SUTTER, HOWARD BRUCE 'BRUCE'	510 SADDLE BROOKE DRIVE, DALLAS GA 30132
BBHOF273	SUTTLES, GEORGE 'MULE'	D. JULY 9, 1966, NEWARK, N.J.
BBHOF237	SUTTON, DONALD HOWARD	120 CALLE DE LAS ROSAS, RANCHO MIRAGE CA 92270
BBHOF274	TAYLOR, BENJAMIN HARRISON	D. JANUARY 24, 1953, BALTIMORE, MD.
BBHOF073	TERRY, WILLIAM HAROLD	D. JANUARY 9, 1989, JACKSONVILLE, FLA.
BBHOF146	THOMPSON, SAMUEL L.	D. NOVEMBER 7, 1922, DETROIT, MICH.
BBHOF047	TINKER, JOSEPH BERT	D. JULY 27, 1948, ORLANDO, FLA.
BBHOF275	TORRIENTE, CRISTOBAL	D. APRIL 11, 1938, NEW YORK, N.Y.

BBHOF055	TRAYNOR, HAROLD JOSEPH 'PIE'	D. MARCH 16, 1972, PITTSBURGH, PA.
BBHOF079	VANCE, CLARENCE ARTHUR 'DAZZY'	D. FEBRUARY 16, 1961, HOMOSASSA SPRINGS, FLA.
BBHOF192	VAUGHAN, JOSEPH FLOYD 'ARKY'	D. AUGUST 30, 1952, EAGLEVILLE, CALIF.
BBHOF211	VEECK, WILLIAM L. 'BILL'	D. JANUARY 2, 1986, CHICAGO, ILL.
BBHOF048	WADDELL, GEORGE EDWARD 'RUBE'	D. APRIL 1, 1914, SAN ANTONIO, TEXAS
BBHOF005	WAGNER, JOHN PETER 'HONUS'	D. DECEMBER 6, 1955, CARNEGIE, PA.
BBHOF069	WALLACE, RHODERICK JOHN 'BOBBY'	D. NOVEMBER 3, 1960, TORRANCE, CALIF.
BBHOF049	WALSH, EDWARD AUGUSTIN	D. MAY 26, 1959, POMPANO BEACH, FLA.
BBHOF107	WANER, LLOYD JAMES	D. JULY 22, 1982, OKLAHOMA CITY, OKLA.
BBHOF062	WANER, PAUL GLEE	D. AUGUST 29, 1965, SARASOTA, FLA.
BBHOF101	WARD, JOHN MONTGOMERY	D. MARCH 4, 1925, AUGUSTA, GA.
BBHOF228	WEAVER, EARL SIDNEY	501 CYPRESS POINTE DRIVE WEST, PEMBROKE PINES FL 33027
BBHOF126	WEISS, GEORGE MARTIN	D. AUGUST 13, 1972, GREENWICH, CONN.
BBHOF140	WELCH, MICHAEL FRANCIS 'MICKEY'	D. JULY 30, 1941, NASHUA, N.H.
BBHOF232	WELLS, WILLIE JAMES	D. JANUARY 22, 1989, AUSTIN, TEXAS
BBHOF084	WHEAT, ZACHARY DAVIS	D. MARCH 11, 1972, SEDALIA, MO.
BBHOF276	WHITE, KING SOLOMON	D. AUGUST 26, 1955, CENTRAL ISLIP, N.Y.
BBHOF193	WILHELM, JAMES HOYT 'HOYT'	D. AUGUST 23, 2002, SARASOTA, FLA.
BBHOF277	WILKINSON, J. LESLIE	D. AUGUST 21, 1964, KANSAS CITY, MO.
BBHOF198	WILLIAMS, BILLY LEO	586 PRINCE EDWARD ROAD, GLEN ELLYN IL 60137
BBHOF243	WILLIAMS, JOE 'SMOKEY'	D. MARCH 12, 1946, NEW YORK, N.Y.
BBHOF104	WILLIAMS, THEODORE SAMUEL	D. JULY 5, 2002, INVERNESS, FLA.
BBHOF224	WILLIS, VICTOR GAZAWAY	D. AUGUST 2, 1947, ELKTON, MD.
BBHOF278	WILSON, ERNEST JUDSON 'JUD'	D. JUNE 24, 1963, WASHINGTON, D.C.
BBHOF169	WILSON, LEWIS ROBERT 'HACK'	D. NOVEMBER 23, 1948, BALTIMORE, MD.
BBHOF251	WINFIELD, DAVID MARK	2235 STRATFORD CIRCLE, LOS ANGELES CA 90077
BBHOF012	WRIGHT, GEORGE	D. AUGUST 31, 1937, BOSTON, MASS.
BBHOF070	WRIGHT, WILLIAM HENRY 'HARRY'	D. OCTOBER 3, 1895, ATLANTIC CITY, N.J.
BBHOF133	WYNN, EARLY	D. APRIL 4, 1999, VENICE, FLA.
BBHOF202	YASTRZEMSKI, CARL MICHAEL	255 STATE STREET, BOSTON MA 02109
BBHOF173	YAWKEY, THOMAS AUSTIN	D. JULY 9, 1976, BOSTON, MASS.
BBHOF013	YOUNG, DENTON TRUE 'CY'	D. NOVEMBER 4, 1955, NEWCOMERSTOWN, OHIO
BBHOF134	YOUNGS, ROSS MIDDLEBROOK	D. OCTOBER 22, 1927, SAN ANTONIO, TEXAS
BBHOF244	YOUNT, ROBIN R.	5001 EAST ARABIAN WAY, PARADISE VALLEY AZ 85253

PLAYERS DEBUTING FROM 1920 TO 2006

A

2004-001	AARDSMA, DAVID ALLAN	22 GROGANS POINT ROAD, THE WOODLANDS TX 77380
1954-001	AARON, HENRY LOUIS	1611 ADAMS DRIVE SW, ATLANTA GA 30311
1962-001	AARON, TOMMIE LEE	D. AUGUST 16, 1984, ATLANTA, GA.
1977-001	AASE, DONALD WILLIAM	5055 VIA RICARDO, YORBA LINDA CA 92686
2001-001	ABAD, FAUSTO ANDREW 'ANDY'	118 BONAIRE LANE, JUPITER FL 33458
1989-001	ABBOTT, JAMES ANTHONY	3449 QUIET COVE, CORONA DEL MAR CA 92625
1997-001	ABBOTT, JEFFREY WILLIAM	805 GLEN ROYAL DRIVE, ROSWELL GA 30076
1993-001	ABBOTT, KURT THOMAS	613 HOWARD CREEK LANE, STUART FL 34994
1991-001	ABBOTT, LAWRENCE KYLE 'KYLE'	332 SPRINGFIELD BEND, ARGYLE TX 76226
1990-001	ABBOTT, PAUL DAVID	1945 DANA PLACE, FULLERTON CA 92831
1973-001	ABBOTT, WILLIAM GLENN 'GLENN'	4413 DAWSON, NORTH LITTLE ROCK AR 72116
1950-001	ABER, ALBERT JULIUS	D. MAY 20, 1993, GARFIELD HEIGHTS, OHIO
2006-001	ABERCROMBIE, REGINALD DAMASCUS	5920 BUXTON DRIVE, COLUMBUS GA 31907
1952-001	ABERNATHIE, WILLIAM EDWARD	D. FEBRUARY 19, 2006, YUCAIPA, CALIF.
2001-002	ABERNATHY, MICHAEL BRENT 'BRENT'	3721 FARNHAM COURT, PALM HARBOR FL 34684
1942-001	ABERNATHY, TALMADGE LAFAYETTE 'TAL'	D. NOVEMBER 16, 2001, CHARLOTTE, N.C.
1955-001	ABERNATHY, THEODORE WADE 'TED'	D. DECEMBER 16, 2004, GASTONIA, N.C.
1946-001	ABERNATHY, VIRGIL WOODROW 'WOODY'	D. DECEMBER 5, 1994, LOUISVILLE, KY.
1947-001	ABERSON, CLIFFORD ALEXANDER	D. JUNE 23, 1973, VALLEJO, CALIF.
1987-001	ABNER, SHAWN WESLEY	OLD ADD: 539 BRIGHTON PLACE, MECHANICSBURG PA 17055
1949-001	ABRAMS, CALVIN ROSS	D. FEBRUARY 25, 1997, FORT LAUDERDALE, FLA.
1923-001	ABRAMS, GEORGE ALLEN	D. DECEMBER 5, 1986, CLEARWATER, FLA.
1985-001	ABREGO, JOHNNY RAY	PO BOX 680801, SAN ANTONIO TX 78268
1996-001	ABREU, BOB KELLY	3933 194TH LANE, NORTH MIAMI BEACH FL 33160
1942-002	ABREU, JOSEPH LAWRENCE	D. MARCH 17, 1993, HAYWARD, CALIF.
2006-002	ABREU, WINSTON LEONARDO	112 BONNIE WOODS DRIVE, GREENVILLE SC 29605
2005-001	ACCARDO, JEREMY LEE	3306 EAST JUANITA AVENUE, MESA AZ 85204
2001-003	ACEVEDO, JOSE OMAR	OLD ADD: SANTIAGO DOM REP
1995-001	ACEVEDO, JUAN CARLOS	143 MADERA CIRCLE, CARPENTERSVILLE IL 60110
1983-001	ACKER, JAMES JUSTIN	PO BOX 214, FREER TX 78357
1956-001	ACKER, THOMAS JAMES	118 GLOUCESTER ROAD, STUARTS DRAFT VA 24477
1963-001	ACKLEY, FLORIAN FREDERICK 'FRITZ'	D. MAY 22, 2002, DULUTH, MINN.
1972-001	ACOSTA, CECILIO 'CY'	AUG RAMIREZ 1420,COL GAB LEYVA CULIACAN SINALOA, MEXICO
1970-001	ACOSTA, EDUARDO ELIXBET	22822 BOLTANA, MISSION VIEJO CA 92675
1920-001	ACOSTA, JOSE	D. NOVEMBER 16, 1977, HAVANA, CUBA
1994-001	ACRE, MARK ROBERT	1588 WEST YOSEMITE PLACE, CHANDLER AZ 85248
1931-001	ADAIR, JAMES AUBREY	D. DECEMBER 9, 1982, DALLAS, TEXAS
1958-001	ADAIR, KENNETH JERRY 'JERRY'	D. MAY 31, 1987, TULSA, OKLA.
1970-002	ADAIR, MARION DANNE 'BILL'	D. JUNE 17, 2002, MINETTE, ALA.
1941-001	ADAMS, ACE TOWNSEND	D. FEBRUARY 26, 2006, ALBANY, GA.
1946-002	ADAMS, CHARLES DWIGHT 'RED'	6058 PUERTO DRIVE, RANCHO MURIETA CA 95683
1922-001	ADAMS, EARL JOHN 'SPARKY'	D. FEBRUARY 24, 1989, POTTVILLE, PA.
1939-001	ADAMS, ELVIN CLARK 'BUSTER'	D. SEPTEMBER 1, 1990, RANCHO MIRAGE, CALIF.
1975-001	ADAMS, GLENN CHARLES	916 CALLIS ROAD, SEDAN NM 88436
1969-001	ADAMS, HAROLD DOUGLAS 'DOUG'	1129 HARMONY CIR NE, JANESVILLE WI 53545
1948-001	ADAMS, HERBERT LOREN	4021 EAST 84TH STREET, TULSA OK 74137
2004-002	ADAMS, JON MICHAEL 'MIKE'	800 BOOTY, SINTON TX 78387
1947-002	ADAMS, RICHARD LEROY	4650 DULIN ROAD #136, FALLBROOK CA 92028
1982-001	ADAMS, RICKY LEE	6437 GARRET STREET, ALTA LOMA CA 91701
1931-002	ADAMS, ROBERT ANDREW	D. MARCH 6, 1970, JACKSONVILLE, FLA.
1925-001	ADAMS, ROBERT BURDETTE	D. OCTOBER 17, 1996, LEMOYNE, PA.
1946-003	ADAMS, ROBERT HENRY	D. FEBRUARY 13, 1997, GIG HARBOR, WASH.
1977-002	ADAMS, ROBERT MELVIN	31713 157TH STREET EAST, LLANO CA 93544
1972-002	ADAMS, ROBERT MICHAEL 'MIKE'	13205 JO LANE NE, ALBUQUERQUE NM 87111
2004-003	ADAMS, RUSS MOORE	2342 LAKE HEATHER HTS COURT NORTH, DUNEDIN FL 34698
1923-002	ADAMS, SPENCER DEWEY	D. NOVEMBER 25, 1970, FT. LAUDERDALE, FLA.
1995-002	ADAMS, TERRY WAYNE	11315 HOWELL'S FERRY ROAD, SEMMES AL 36575
1996-002	ADAMS, WILLIAM EDWARD 'WILLIE'	11903 KIBBEE AVENUE, LAMIRADA CA 90638
1996-003	ADAMSON, JOEL LEE	14832 SOUTH 46TH PLACE, PHOENIX AZ 85044
1967-001	ADAMSON, JOHN MICHAEL 'MIKE'	17610 CANTERBURY DRIVE, MONUMENT CO 80132
1950-002	ADCOCK, JOSEPH WILBUR	D. MAY 3, 1999, COUSHATTA, LA.
1950-003	ADDIS, ROBERT GORDON	7466 HOLLYCROFT LANE, MENTOR OH 44060
1983-002	ADDUCI, JAMES DAVID	10429 SOUTH LAMON, OAK LAWN IL 60453
1939-002	ADERHOLT, MORRIS WOODROW 'MOE'	D. MARCH 18, 1955, SARASOTA, FLA.
1928-001	ADKINS, GRADY EMMETT	D. MARCH 31, 1966, LITTLE ROCK, ARK.
1942-003	ADKINS, JOHN DEWEY 'DEWEY'	D. DECEMBER 26, 1998, SANTA MONICA, CALIF.
2003-001	ADKINS, JONATHAN SCOTT	OLD ADD: WAYNE WV 25570
1942-004	ADKINS, RICHARD EARL	D. SEPTEMBER 12, 1955, ELECTRA, TEXAS
1990-002	ADKINS, STEVEN THOMAS	5001 DERRY WAY, TAMPA FL 33647
1963-002	ADLESH, DAVID GEORGE	9770 AVENIDA MONTEREY, CYPRESS CA 90630
1987-002	AFENIR, MICHAEL TROY	459 OLD VIA RANCHO PKWY, ESCONDIDO CA 92029
2002-001	AFFELDT, JEREMY DAVID	10111 SOUTH GREEN GATE LANE, MEDICAL LAKE WA 99022
1998-001	AGBAYANI, BENNY PETER	66-948 KOLU PLACE, WAIALUA HI 96791
1962-002	AGEE, TOMMIE LEE	D. JANUARY 22, 2001, NEW YORK, N.Y.
1954-002	AGGANIS, HARRY	D. JUNE 27, 1955, CAMBRIDGE, MASS.
1981-001	AGOSTO, JUAN ROBERTO	3815 65TH STREET EAST #175, BRADENTON FL 34208
1980-001	AGUAYO, LUIS	OLD ADD: DORADO DEL MAR LIRIOS #C23, DORADO PR 00646
2004-004	AGUILA, CHRISTOPHER LOUIS	2011 BRITTANY MEADOWS DRIVE, RENO NV 89521
1985-002	AGUILERA, RICHARD WARREN 'RICK'	PO BOX 174, RANCHO SANTA FE CA 92067

1955-002	AGUIRRE, HENRY JOHN 'HANK'	D. SEPTEMBER 5, 1994, BLOOMFIELD HILLS, MICH.
1995-003	AHEARNE, PATRICK HOWARD	246 MILAM LANE, BASTROP TX 78602
1977-003	AIKENS, WILLIE MAYS	610 MCDONOUGH BLVD SE #BM101454, ATLANTA GA 30315
1979-001	AINGE, DANIEL RAY	140 WELLESLEY AVENUE, WELLESLEY HILLS MA 02481
2001-004	AINSWORTH, KURT HAROLD	15220 MEMORIAL TOWER DRIVE, BATON ROUGE LA 70810
1964-001	AKER, JACK DELANE	38 PICADILLY ROAD, GREAT NECK NY 11023
1986-001	AKERFELDS, DARREL WAYNE	12834 WEST ROSEWOOD DRIVE, EL MIRAGE AZ 85335
1929-001	AKERS, THOMAS ERNEST 'BILL'	D. APRIL 13, 1962, CHATTANOOGA, TENN.
1988-001	ALBA, GIBSON ROBERTO	87 EAST 17TH STREET, PATERSON NJ 07524
1958-002	ALBANESE, JOSEPH PETER	D. JUNE 17, 2000, NEW YORK, N.Y.
1995-004	ALBERRO, JOSE EDGARDO	OLD ADD: SAN JUAN PR
2006-003	ALBERS, MATTHEW JAMES	OLD ADD: SUGAR LAND TX
1978-001	ALBERTS, FRANCIS BURT 'BUTCH'	3063 AMBERLEA LN, BALDWINSVILLE NY 13027
1941-002	ALBOSTA, EDWARD JOHN	D. JANUARY 7, 2003, SAGINAW, MICH.
1949-002	ALBRECHT, EDWARD ARTHUR	D. DECEMBER 29, 1979, CAHOKIA, ILL.
1947-003	ALBRIGHT, JOHN HAROLD	D. JULY 22, 1991, SAN DIEGO, CALIF.
1973-002	ALBURY, VICTOR	OLD ADD: 1200 SOUTH MIAMI #30, FORT LAUDERDALE FL 33316
1976-001	ALCALA, SANTO	RAMON MOTA 18 SAN PEDRO DE MACORIS, DOM REP
2000-001	ALCANTARA, ISRAEL CHRISTOSOMO	OLD ADD: SANTO DOMINGO DOM REP
1967-002	ALCARAZ, ANGEL LUIS 'LUIS'	CALLE CHIHUAHUA 679 VENUS GARDENS, RIO PIEDRAS PR 00926
1943-001	ALDERSON, DALE LEONARD	D. FEBRUARY 12, 1982, GARDEN GROVE, CALIF.
1990-003	ALDRED, SCOTT WILLIAM	3508 MALACHITE DRIVE, ZEPHYRHILLS FL 33540
1986-002	ALDRETE, MICHAEL PETER	22160 TORO HILLS DRIVE, SALINAS CA 93908
1987-003	ALDRICH, JAY ROBERT	9209 SOUTH 51ST STREET, FRANKLIN WI 53132
2001-005	ALDRIDGE, CORY JEROME	417 PENROSE, ABILENE TX 79601
1941-003	ALENO, CHARLES	D. FEBRUARY 10, 2003, DELAND, FLA.
1929-002	ALEXANDER, DAVID DALE 'DALE'	D. MARCH 2, 1979, GREENEVILLE, TENN.
1971-001	ALEXANDER, DOYLE LAFAYETTE	5416 HUNTER PARK COURT, ARLINGTON TX 76017
1975-002	ALEXANDER, GARY WAYNE	5420 SENFORD AVENUE, LOS ANGELES CA 90056
1990-004	ALEXANDER, GERALD PAUL	307 WOODLAND DRIVE, DONALDSONVILLE LA 70346
1937-001	ALEXANDER, HUGH	D. NOVEMBER 25, 2000, OKLAHOMA CITY, OKLA.
1992-001	ALEXANDER, MANUEL DEJESUS	OLD ADD: CALLE D.BAFRRIO REST. CASA #20, SAN PEDRO DE MACORIS DOM REP
1973-003	ALEXANDER, MATTHEW	2419 STONEWALL, SHREVEPORT LA 71103
1955-003	ALEXANDER, ROBERT SOMERVILLE	D. APRIL 7, 1993, OCEANSIDE, CALIF.
2004-005	ALFARO, JASON	7409 PENSACOLA, FORT WORTH TX 76116
1997-002	ALFONSECA, ANTONIO	2655 LEJUENE ROAD, MIAMI FL 33134
1995-005	ALFONZO, EDGARDO ANTONIO	8035 SPENDTHRIFT LANE, PORT SAINT LUCIE FL 34986
2006-004	ALFONZO, ELIEZER JESUS	OLD ADD: PUERTO LA CRUZ VENEZ
1988-002	ALICEA, LUIS RENE	2140 C ROAD, LOXAHATCHEE FL 33470
1986-003	ALLANSON, ANDREW NEAL	1337 CHEETAH WAY, PALMDALE CA 93551
1979-002	ALLARD, BRIAN MARSHALL	22102 NORTH PERRY ROAD, COLBERT WA 99005
1962-003	ALLEN, BERNARD KEITH	3725 COVENTRY WAY, CARMEL IN 46033
2000-002	ALLEN, DUSTIN R. 'DUSTY'	913 ESTRELLA VISTA STREET, LAS VEGAS NV 89138
1926-001	ALLEN, ETHAN NATHAN	D. SEPTEMBER 15, 1993, BROOKINGS, ORE.
1966-001	ALLEN, HAROLD ANDREW 'HANK'	PO BOX 4612, UPPER MARLBORO MD 20775
1983-003	ALLEN, JAMES BRADLEY 'BRAD'	1920 EAST BELLMONT DRIVE, TEMPE AZ 85284
1999-001	ALLEN, JOHN CHAD 'CHAD'	7152 BLACKWOOD DRIVE, DALLAS TX 75231
1932-001	ALLEN, JOHN THOMAS	D. MARCH 29, 1959, ST. PETERSBURG, FLA.
1980-002	ALLEN, KIM BRYANT	2705 LAPRAIX STREET, HIGHLAND CA 92346
1969-002	ALLEN, LLOYD CECIL	OLD ADD: 1678 MARGUERITE AVENUE, CORONA DEL MAR CA 92625
2002-002	ALLEN, LUCAS G.	282 COOPER ROAD, SOCIAL CIRCLE GA 30025
1979-003	ALLEN, NEIL PATRICK	3619 TORREY PINES BLVD, SARASOTA FL 34238
1963-003	ALLEN, RICHARD ANTHONY 'RICHIE'	PO BOX 254, WAMPUM PA 16157
1937-002	ALLEN, ROBERT EARL 'EARL'	D. OCTOBER 30, 2005, CHESAPEAKE, VA.
1961-001	ALLEN, ROBERT GRAY	PO BOX 677, TATUM TX 75691
1983-004	ALLEN, RODERICK BERNET	3150 EAST WOODLAND, PHOENIX AZ 85048
1972-003	ALLEN, RONALD FREDRICK	917 WINONA DR, YOUNGSTOWN OH 44511
1979-004	ALLENSON, GARY MARTIN	711 SE 34TH STREET, CAPE CORAL FL 33904
1996-004	ALLENSWORTH, JERMAINE LAMONT	1824 EUCLID DRIVE, ANDERSON IN 46011
1963-004	ALLEY, LEONARD EUGENE 'GENE'	10236 STEUBEN DRIVE, GLEN ALLEN VA 23060
1954-003	ALLIE, GAIR ROOSEVELT	11818 BUTTON WILLOW COVE, SAN ANTONIO TX 78213
1975-003	ALLIETTA, ROBERT GEORGE	25 ROBINSON RD, FALMOUTH MA 02540
1991-002	ALLISON, DANA ERIC	322 THOMAS DRIVE, MIDDLETOWN VA 22645
1958-003	ALLISON, WILLIAM ROBERT 'BOB'	D. APRIL 9, 1995, RIO VERDE, ARIZ.
1989-002	ALLRED, DALE LEBEAU 'BEAU'	2094 SOUTH SHANNON ROAD, SAFFORD AZ 85546
1933-001	ALMADA, MELO BALDOMERO	D. AUGUST 13, 1988, HERMOSILLO, SONORA MEXICO
1999-002	ALMANZA, ARMANDO N.	7804 SANTA MARIA COURT, EL PASO TX 79915
1997-003	ALMANZAR, CARLOS MANUEL	OLD ADD: SANTO DOMINGO DOM REP
1974-001	ALMON, WILLIAM FRANCIS	35 SARAHS TRACE, EAST GREENWICH RI 02818
2003-002	ALMONTE, EDWIN	OLD ADD: NEW YORK NY 10001
2001-006	ALMONTE, ERICK R.	OLD ADD: SANTO DOMINGO DOM REP
1999-003	ALMONTE, HECTOR RADHAMES	16742 SW 12TH STREET, PEMBROKE PINES FL 33027
1950-004	ALOMA, LUIS BARBA	D. APRIL 7, 1997, PARK RIDGE, ILL.
1988-003	ALOMAR, ROBERTO VELAZQUEZ	URB. MONSERRATE B-56, BOX 367, SALINAS PR 00751
1988-004	ALOMAR, SANTOS 'SANDY'	URB. MONSERRATE B-56, BOX 367, SALINAS PR 00751
1964 002	ALOMAR, SANTOS CONDES 'SANDY'	PO BOX 367, SALINAS PR 00751
1958-004	ALOU, FELIPE ROJAS	6891 COBIA CIRCLE, BOYNTON BEACH FL 33437
1963-005	ALOU, JESUS MARIA	APARTADO POSTAL 539/2 LAFARIA SANTO DOMINGO, DOM REP
1960-001	ALOU, MATEO ROJAS 'MATTY'	PO BOX 30063 MANUEL DE JESUS TRONCOSO #16, PARAISO, SANTO DOMINGO DOM REP
1990-005	ALOU, MOISES ROJAS	13095 NW 13TH STREET, PEMBROKE PINES FL 33028
1996-005	ALSTON, GARVIN JAMES	4705 EAST THUNDERHILL PLACE, PHOENIX AZ 85044
1954-004	ALSTON, THOMAS EDISON	D. DECEMBER 30, 1993, WINSTON-SALEM, N.C.
1936-001	ALSTON, WALTER EMMONS 'SMOKEY'	D. OCTOBER 1, 1984, OXFORD, OHIO
1977-004	ALSTON, WENDELL 'DEL'	1524 KIRKWOOD AVENUE, BALTIMORE MD 21207
1982-002	ALTAMARINO, PORFIRIO	OLD ADD: CARACAS VENEZUELA
1920-002	ALTEN, ERNEST MATTHIAS	D. SEPTEMBER 9, 1981, NAPA, CALIF.

1959-001	ALTMAN, GEORGE LEE	915 MID POINT DRIVE, O'FALLON MO 63366
1955-004	ALTOBELLI, JOSEPH	10 STOWELL DRIVE #3, ROCHESTER NY 14616
1958-005	ALUSIK, GEORGE JOSEPH	PO BOX 454, WOODBRIDGE NJ 07095
1968-001	ALVARADO, LUIS CESAR	D. MARCH 20, 2001, LAJAS. P. R.
2004-006	ALVAREZ, ABRAHAM	OLD ADD: FONTANA CA
2002-003	ALVAREZ, ANTONIO ENRIQUE	OLD ADD: LOS TEQUES VENEZUELA
1995-006	ALVAREZ, CESAR OCTAVIO 'TAVO'	OLD ADD: PO BOX 51813, PHOENIX AZ 85076
2000-003	ALVAREZ, CLEMENTE RAFAEL	18711 NW 46TH AVENUE, MIAMI FL 33126
1998-002	ALVAREZ, GABRIEL DEJESUS 'GABE'	4401 LAMADERA AVENUE, EL MONTE CA 91732
1973-004	ALVAREZ, JESUS ORLANDO	COMMUNIDAD DOLORES 37, RIO GRANDE PR 00745
1981-002	ALVAREZ, JOSE LINO	210 MURPHY LANE, GREENVILLE SC 29607
1999-004	ALVAREZ, JUAN M.	10995 SW 107TH AVENUE, MIAMI FL 33176
1958-006	ALVAREZ, OSWALDO GONZALES 'OSSIE'	SANTUARIO 3137, COL. CHAPALITA GUADALAJARA JALISCO, MEXICO
1960-002	ALVAREZ, ROGELIO	5010 NW 183RD ST, CAROL CITY FL 33055
2002-004	ALVAREZ, VICTOR AURELIO	OLD ADD: CULIACAN MEXICO
1989-003	ALVAREZ, WILSON EDUARDO	6927 WESTCHESTER CIRCLE, BRADENTON FL 34202
1962-004	ALVIS, ROY MAXWELL 'MAX'	806 HUNTERWOOD DR, JASPER TX 75951
1965-001	ALYEA, BRANT RYERSON	119 LOCKHART ROAD, TRYON NC 28782
1954-005	AMALFITANO, JOHN JOSEPH	265 BOWSTRING DRIVE, SEDONA AZ 86336
1991-003	AMARAL, RICHARD LOUIS	3122 COUNTRY CLUB DRIVE, COSTA MESA CA 92626
1958-007	AMARO, RUBEN	4098 CINNAMON WAY, WESTON FL 33331
1991-004	AMARO, RUBEN JR	2661 WOODSVIEW DRIVE, BENSALEM PA 19020
1937-003	AMBLER, WAYNE HARPER	D. JANUARY 3, 1998, PONTE VEDRA BEACH, FLA.
2005-002	AMBRES, RAYMOND PAYNE 'CHIP'	4460 BEALE STREET, BEAUMONT TX 77705
1984-001	AMELUNG, EDWARD ALLEN	16681 CEDAR CIRCLE, FOUNTAIN VALLEY CA 92708
2002-005	AMEZAGA, ALFREDO DELGADO	OLD ADD: OBREGON MEXICO
1955-005	AMOR, VINCENTE ALVAREZ	13871 SW 52ND STREET, MIRAMAR FL 33027
1952-002	AMOROS, EDMUNDO ISASI 'SANDY'	D. JUNE 27, 1992, MIAMI, FLA.
1975-004	ANDERSEN, LARRY EUGENE	102 DICKINSON STREET, PHILADELPHIA PA 19147
1941-004	ANDERSON, ALFRED WALTON	D. JUNE 23, 1985, ALBANY, GA.
1986-004	ANDERSON, ALLAN LEE	1491 LANCASTER KIRKERVILLE RD, LANCASTER OH 43130
1948-002	ANDERSON, ANDY HOLM	D. JULY 18, 1982, SEATTLE, WASH.
1937-004	ANDERSON, ARNOLD REVOLA 'RED'	D. AUGUST 7, 1972, SIOUX CITY, IOWA
1988-005	ANDERSON, BRADY KEVIN	17736 ST. ANDREWS DRIVE, POWAY CA 92064
1993-002	ANDERSON, BRIAN JAMES	3571 NORTH MEYERS ROAD, GENEVA OH 44041
2005-003	ANDERSON, BRIAN NIKOLA	9553 NORTH CORTE ROCA DE PLATA, TUCSON AZ 85704
1983-005	ANDERSON, DAVID CARTER	207 ATHLETIC OFFICE BLDG, MEMPHIS TN 38152
2006-005	ANDERSON, DREW THOMAS	1607 WEST 36TH STREET, KEARNEY NE 68845
1971-002	ANDERSON, DWAIN CLEAVEN	1807 FALLBROOK DRIVE, ALAMO CA 94507
1946-004	ANDERSON, FERRELL JACK 'ANDY'	D. MARCH 12, 1978, JOPLIN, MO.
1994-002	ANDERSON, GARRET JOSEPH	34 VERNAL SPRING, IRVINE CA 92603
1959-002	ANDERSON, GEORGE LEE 'SPARKY'	PO BOX 6415, THOUSAND OAKS CA 91360
1932-002	ANDERSON, HAROLD	D. MAY 1, 1974, ST. LOUIS, MO.
1957-001	ANDERSON, HARRY WALTER	D. JUNE 11, 1998, GREENVILLE, DEL.
1999-005	ANDERSON, JAMES DREW	4507 MCRAE CLOSE, CHESAPEAKE VA 23321
1978-002	ANDERSON, JAMES LEA	21301 BOTTLETREE LANE #203, NEWHALL CA 91321
2003-003	ANDERSON, JASON R	14 EAST NINTH STREET, DANVILLE IL 61832
1958-008	ANDERSON, JOHN CHARLES	D. DECEMBER 20, 1998, HOUSTON, TEXAS
1982-003	ANDERSON, KARL ADAM 'BUD'	240 TWIN LANE, EAST WANEAUGH NY 11793
1989-004	ANDERSON, KENT MCKAY	925 EAST TWIN CHURCH ROAD, TIMMONSVILLE SC 29161
1974-002	ANDERSON, LAWRENCE DENNIS	477 PEANUT WAY, ARROYO GRANDE CA 93420
1998-003	ANDERSON, MARLON ORDELL	2643 GULF TO BAY BLVD #1560, CLEARWATER FL 33759
1998-004	ANDERSON, MATTHEW JASON	14626 ANDERSON WOODS TRAIL, LOUISVILLE KY 40245
1971-003	ANDERSON, MICHAEL ALLEN	OLD ADD: RURAL ROUTE 1, TIMMONSVILLE SC 29261
1993-003	ANDERSON, MICHAEL JAMES	140 CLEAR SPRING, GEORGETOWN TX 78628
1961-002	ANDERSON, NORMAN CRAIG 'CRAIG'	19217 SW 96TH LOOP, DUNNELLON FL 34432
1986-005	ANDERSON, RICHARD ARLEN	3929 BENJAMIN DRIVE, SAINT PAUL MN 55125
1979-005	ANDERSON, RICHARD LEE	D. JUNE 23, 1989, WILMINGTON, CALIF.
1957-002	ANDERSON, ROBERT CARL	4209 EAST 104TH, TULSA OK 74137
1987-004	ANDERSON, SCOTT RICHARD	13555 FIELDING ROAD, LAKE OSWEGO OR 97034
1925-002	ANDERSON, WILLIAM EDWARD	D. MARCH 13, 1983, MEDFORD, MASS.
2005-004	ANDINO, ROBERT LAZARO	4811 129TH AVENUE NORTH, WEST PALM BEACH FL 33411
2006-006	ANDRADE, STEPHEN MICHAEL	1360 WALDEN ROAD, WALNUT CREEK CA 94597
1955-006	ANDRE, JOHN EDWARD	D. NOVEMBER 25, 1976, CENTERVILLE, MASS.
1946-005	ANDRES, ERNEST HENRY	5714 GARDEN LAKES DRIVE, BRADENTON FL 34203
1975-005	ANDREW, KIM DARRELL	10052 DENSMORE AVE, SEPULVEDA CA 91343
2000-004	ANDREWS, CLAYTON JOHN	12800 VONN ROAD #9901, LARGO FL 33774
1995-007	ANDREWS, DARRELL SHANE 'SHANE'	1818 NORTH GUADALUPE STREET, CARLSBAD NM 88226
1925-003	ANDREWS, ELBERT DEVORE 'DEVORE'	D. NOVEMBER 25, 1979, GREENWOOD, S.C.
1976-002	ANDREWS, FRED	PO BOX 898, WEDOWEE AL 36278
1947-004	ANDREWS, HERBERT CARL 'HUB'	2305 2ND STREET, DODGE CITY KS 67801
1931-003	ANDREWS, IVY PAUL	D. NOVEMBER 23, 1970, DORA, ALA.
1973-005	ANDREWS, JOHN RICHARD	9292 GORDON AVE, LAHABRA CA 90631
1966-002	ANDREWS, MICHAEL JAY	375 LONGWOOD AVENUE, BOSTON MA 02215
1937-005	ANDREWS, NATHAN HARDY	D. APRIL 26, 1991, WINSTON-SALEM, N.C.
1975-006	ANDREWS, ROBERT PATRICK	1280 MOUNTBATTEN CT, CONCORD CA 94518
1939-003	ANDREWS, STANLEY JOSEPH	D. JUNE 10, 1995, BRADENTON, FLA.
1931-004	ANDRUS, WILLIAM MORGAN	D. MARCH 12, 1982, WASHINGTON, D.C.
1976-003	ANDUJAR, JOAQUIN	AVE. L. AMIAMA TIO #47 SAN PEDRO DE MACORIS, DOM REP
1995-008	ANDUJAR, LUIS SANCHEZ	OLD ADD: BANI DOMINICAN REPUBLIC
1972-004	ANGELINI, NORMAN STANLEY	15063 EAST CHENANGO PLACE, AURORA CO 80015
1929-003	ANGLEY, THOMAS SAMUEL	D. OCTOBER 26, 1952, WICHITA, KAN.
1936-002	ANKENMAN, FRED NORMAN 'PAT'	D. JANUARY 13, 1989, HOUSTON, TEXAS
1999-006	ANKIEL, RICHARD ALEXANDER 'RICK'	126 SANDPIPER LANE, JUPITER FL 33458
1989-005	ANTHONY, ERIC TODD	42 FOSTERS GLEN, SUGAR LAND TX 77479
1944-001	ANTOLICK, JOSEPH	D. JUNE 25, 2002, CATASAQUA, PA.

1948-003	ANTONELLI, JOHN AUGUST	18 TOBEY COURT, PITTSFORD NY 14534
1944-002	ANTONELLI, JOHN LAWRENCE	D. APRIL 18, 1990, MEMPHIS, TENN.
1953-001	ANTONELLO, WILLIAM JAMES	D. MARCH 4, 1993, FRIDLEY, MINN.
1956-002	APARICIO, LUIS ERNEST	OLD ADD: CALLE 67 #26-82, MARACAIBO VENEZUELA
1973-006	APODACA, ROBERT JOHN	2999 SW VAN BUREN TERRACE, PORT SAINT LUCIE FL 34953
1980-003	APONTE, LUIS EDUARDO	OLD ADD: RES LAS GIRASOLES #17A,ST ELENA, BARQUISIMETO LARA VENEZ
1989-006	APPIER, ROBERT KEVIN 'KEVIN'	30743 VICTORY ROAD, PAOLA KS 66071
1927-001	APPLETON, PETER WILLIAM	D. JANUARY 18, 1974, TRENTON, N.J.
1930-001	APPLING, LUCIUS BENJAMIN 'LUKE'	D. JANUARY 3, 1991, CUMMING, GA.
2004-007	AQUINO, GREGORI EMILIO	OLD ADD: PALENQUE DOM REP
1986-006	AQUINO, LUIS ANTONIO COLON	6917 COLLINS AVENUE #1612, MIAMI BEACH FL 33141
1941-005	ARAGON, ANGEL VALDES, JR. 'JACK'	D. APRIL 4, 1988, CLEARWATER, FLA.
1923-003	ARCHDEACON, MAURICE BRUCE	D. SEPTEMBER 5, 1954, ST. LOUIS, MO.
1936-003	ARCHER, FREDERICK MARVIN	D. OCTOBER 31, 1981, CHARLOTTE, N.C.
1961-003	ARCHER, JAMES WILLIAM	1414 OLEANDER DR, TARPON SPRINGS FL 33589
1938-001	ARCHIE, GEORGE ALBERT	D. SEPTEMBER 20, 2001, NASHVILLE, TENN.
1968-002	ARCIA, JOSE RAIMUNDO	7325 NW 3RD ST, MIAMI FL 33126
1961-004	ARDELL, DANIEL MIERS	554 HAZEL DRIVE, CORONA DEL MAR CA 92625
1947-005	ARDIZOIA, RINALDO JOSEPH 'RUGGER'	130 SANTA ROSA AVENUE, SAN FRANCISCO CA 94112
2000-005	ARDOIN, DANIEL WAYNE	1524 LEE ROAD, VILLE PLATTE LA 70586
1948-004	ARFT, HENRY IRVIN 'HANK'	D. DECEMBER 14, 2002, ST. LOUIS, MO.
1992-002	ARIAS, ALEJANDRO	37 EDMUND ROAD, HOLLYWOOD FL 33023
1996-006	ARIAS, GEORGE ALBERT	4343 WEST TELLURITE DRIVE, TUCSON AZ 85745
2006-007	ARIAS, JOAQUIN	OLD ADD: SANTO DOMINGO DUM REP
1959-003	ARIAS, RODOLFO MARTINEZ 'RUDY'	3911 NW 11TH ST, MIAMI FL 33126
1931-005	ARLETT, RUSSELL LORIS 'BUZZ'	D. MAY 16, 1964, MINNEAPOLIS, MINN.
1965-002	ARLICH, DONALD LOUIS	7877 SOUTH 73RD ST, COTTAGE GROVE MN 55016
1969-003	ARLIN, STEPHEN RALPH	6819 CLAREMORE AVENUE, SAN DIEGO CA 92120
1999-007	ARMAS, ANTONIO JOSE	OLD ADD: PUERTO PIRITU VENEZUELA
1976-004	ARMAS, ANTONIO RAFAEL	CALLE LOS MERCEDES #37 PUERTO PIRITU, VENEZUELA
1993-004	ARMAS, MARCOS RAFAEL (RUIZ)	CALLE LOS MERCEDES #37 PUERTO PIRITU, VENEZUELA
1973-007	ARMBRISTER, EDISON ROSANDER	MCQUAY ST, BOX 2003 NASSAU BAHAMAS, WEST INDIES
1934-001	ARMBRUST, ORVILLE MARTIN	D. OCTOBER 2, 1967, MOBILE, ALA.
1946-006	ARMSTRONG, GEORGE NOBLE	D. JULY 24, 1993, ORANGE, N.J.
1988-006	ARMSTRONG, JACK WILLIAM	272 EAST RIVER PARK DRIVE, JUPITER FL 33477
1980-004	ARMSTRONG, MICHAEL DENNIS	525 ASHBROOK COURT, ATHENS GA 30605
1989-007	ARNDT, LARRY WAYNE	5970 EAST WEST MIRAMAR DRIVE, TUCSON AZ 85715
1971-004	ARNOLD, CHRISTOPHER PAUL	2219 EL CAPITAN, ARCADIA CA 91006
1999-008	ARNOLD, JAMES LEE	17216 WEST BANFF LANE, SURPRISE AZ 85388
1988-007	ARNOLD, SCOTT GENTRY	3282 GONDOLA DRIVE, LEXINGTON KY 40513
1986-007	ARNOLD, TONY DALE	5708 VINEYARD LANE, MCKINNEY TX 75070
1936-004	ARNOVICH, MORRIS 'MOE'	D. JULY 20, 1959, SUPERIOR, WISC.
1986-008	ARNSBERG, BRADLEY JEFF	706 CHAFFEE COURT, ARLINGTON TX 76006
1943-002	ARNTZEN, ORIE EDGAR	D. JANUARY 28, 1970, CEDAR RAPIDS, IOWA
1993-005	AROCHA, RENE	14273 SW 24TH STREET, MIAMI FL 33175
1961-005	ARRIGO, GERALD WILLIAM	3740 REDTHORNE DR, AMELIA OH 45102
1998-005	ARROJO, LUIS ROLANDO 'ROLANDO'	5955 BAYVIEW CIRCLE SOUTH, SAINT PETERSBURG FL 33707
2000-006	ARROYO, BRONSON ANTHONY	PO BOX 281, BROOKSVILLE FL 34601
1975-007	ARROYO, FERNANDO	5232 EAST INGRAM STREET, MESA AZ 85205
1955-007	ARROYO, LUIS ENRIQUE	BOX 354, PENUELAS PR 00724
1971-005	ARROYO, RUDOLPH	828 SIERRA VISTA, MOUNTAIN VIEW CA 94040
1986-009	ASADOOR, RANDALL CARL	4857 EAST RICHWOOD AVENUE, CLOVIS CA 93611
1938-002	ASBELL, JAMES MARION	D. JULY 6, 1967, SAN MATEO, CALIF.
1928-002	ASBJORNSON, ROBERT ANTHONY	D. JANUARY 21, 1970, WILLIAMSPORT, PA.
2002-006	ASENCIO, MIGUEL DEPAULA	OLD ADD: LAVICTORIA DOM REP
1925-004	ASH, KENNETH LOWTHER	D. NOVEMBER 15, 1979, CLARKSBURG, W.VA.
1948-005	ASHBURN, RICH	D. SEPTEMBER 9, 1997, NEW YORK, N.Y.
1973-008	ASHBY, ALAN DEAN	12011 CYPRESS CREEK LAKES DRIVE, CYPRESS TX 77433
1991-005	ASHBY, ANDREW JASON	2 OSBORNE DRIVE, PITTSTON PA 18640
1976-005	ASHFORD, THOMAS STEVEN 'TUCKER'	502 MAPLE ST, COVINGTON TN 38019
1992-003	ASHLEY, BILLY MANUAL	2787 AUTUMN RIDGE DRIVE, THOUSAND OAKS CA 91362
1957-003	ASPROMONTE, KENNETH JOSEPH	2 DERHAM PARC STREET, HOUSTON TX 77024
1956-003	ASPROMONTE, ROBERT THOMAS	1000 UPTOWN PARK BLVD #241, HOUSTON TX 77056
1976-006	ASSELSTINE, BRIAN HANLY	1488 COUNTRY CT, SANTA YNEZ CA 93460
1986-010	ASSENMACHER, PAUL ANDRE	500 COVINGTON COVE, ALPHARETTA GA 30022
2005-005	ASTACIO, EZEQUIEL F	OLD ADD: HATO MAYOT DOM REP
1992-004	ASTACIO, PEDRO JULIO	666 DUNDEE ROAD #704, NORTHBROOK IL 60062
1945-001	ASTROTH, JOSEPH HENRY	151 SOUTH MOYER ROAD, CHALFONT PA 18914
2004-008	ATCHISON, SCOTT BARHAM	9732 MERIBEE DRIVE, KELLER TX 76248
2001-007	ATCHLEY, JUSTIN SCOTT	17958 COVE LANE, MOUNT VERNON WA 98274
1983-006	ATHERTON, KEITH ROWE	PO BOX 571, COBBS CREEK VA 23035
2003-004	ATKINS, GARRETT BERNARD	31 CEZANNE, IRVINE CA 92603
1950-005	ATKINS, JAMES CURTIS	1030 COUNTY ROAD 1518, CULLMAN AL 35055
1927-002	ATKINSON, HUBERT BURLEY 'LEFTY'	D. FEBRUARY 12, 1961, CHICAGO, ILL.
1976-007	ATKINSON, WILLIAM CECIL GLENN	15 ARGYLE CRESCENT CHATHAM ON, N7L 4T7 CANADA
1926-002	ATTREAU, RICHARD GILBERT	D. JULY 5, 1964, CHICAGO, ILL.
1952-003	ATWELL, MAURICE DAILEY 'TOBY'	D. JANUARY 25, 2003, PURCELLVILLE, VA.
1936-005	ATWOOD, WILLIAM FRANKLIN	D. SEPTEMBER 14, 1993, SNYDER, TEXAS
1996-007	AUCOIN, DEREK ALFRED	OLD ADD: 719 SANCTUARY COVE DRIVE, WEST PALM BEACH FL 33410
1993-006	AUDE, RICHARD THOMAS	4817 NATOMA AVENUE, WOODLAND HILLS CA 91364
1971-006	AUERBACH, FREDERICK STEVEN 'RICK'	2139 NORTH STUNT ROAD, CALABASAS CA 91302
1988-008	AUGUST, DONALD GLENN	28372 LORENTE, MISSION VIEJO CA 92692
1973-009	AUGUSTINE, DAVID RALPH	PO BOX 1114, SAINT ALBANS WV 25177
1975-008	AUGUSTINE, GERALD LEE	574W13490 COURTLAND LANE, MUSKEGO WI 53150
1933-002	AUKER, ELDEN LEROY	D. AUGUST 4, 2006, VERO BEACH, FLA.
1947-006	AULDS, LESLIE DOYLE 'TEX'	D. OCTOBER 13, 1999, HONDO, TEXAS

1976-008	AULT, DOUGLAS REAGAN	D. DECEMBER 22, 2004, TARPON SPRINGS, FLA.
1995-009	AURILIA, RICHARD SANTO	5448 EAST MARIPOSA STREET, PHOENIX AZ 85018
1994-003	AUSANIO, JOSEPH JOHN	646 DELAWARE AVENUE, KINGSTON NY 12401
1993-007	AUSMUS, BRADLEY DAVID	1644 STRATFORD WAY, DEL MAR CA 92014
1965-003	AUST, DENNIS RAY	16252 ESTUARY COURT, BOKEELIA FL 33922
1991-006	AUSTIN, JAMES PARKER	OLD ADD: 5252 MAIN STREET, STEPHENS CITY VA 22655
2001-008	AUSTIN, JEFFREY WELLINGTON	1943 RIVER FALLS DRIVE, HUMBLE TX 77339
1970-003	AUSTIN, RICK GERALD	BOX 347, BROOKFIELD MO 64628
1976-009	AUTRY, ALBERT	319 HOGANS VALLEY WAY, CARY NC 27513
1924-001	AUTRY, MARTIN GORDON	D. JANUARY 26, 1950, SAVANNAH, GA.
1997-004	AVEN, DAVID BRUCE 'BRUCE'	1097 NW 167TH AVENUE, HOLLYWOOD FL 33028
1956-004	AVERILL, EARL DOUGLAS	1806 19TH DR NE, AUBURN WA 98002
1929-004	AVERILL, HOWARD EARL 'EARL'	D. AUGUST 16, 1983, EVERETT, WASH.
1990-006	AVERY, STEVEN THOMAS	2 GLENEAGLES COURT, DEARBORN MI 48120
1949-003	AVILA, ROBERTO FRANCISCO GONZALEZ 'BOBBY'	D. OCTOBER 26, 2004, VERACRUZ, MEXICO
1977-005	AVILES, RAMON ANTONIO	JARDINES DEMONICO,CALLE 2 C19, MANATI PR 00701
1950-006	AVREA, JAMES EPHERIUM	D. JUNE 26, 1987, DALLAS, TEXAS
1974-003	AYALA, BENIGNO 'BENNIE'	PO BOX 1483, TOA BAJA PR 00951
2003-005	AYALA, LUIS IGNACIO	OLD ADD: LOS MOCHIS MEXICO
1992-005	AYALA, ROBERT JOSEPH	OLD ADD: 158 SYCAMORE STREET, OXNARD CA 93030
2006-008	AYBAR, ERICK JOHAN	OLD ADD: BANI DOM REP
1997-005	AYBAR, MANUEL ANTONIO	OLD ADD: BANI DOM REP
2005-006	AYBAR, WILLY JESUS	OLD ADD: BANI DOM REP
1947-007	AYERS, WILLIAM OSCAR	D. SEPTEMBER 24, 1980, NEWNAN, GA.
1953-002	AYLWARD, RICHARD JOHN	D. JUNE 11, 1983, SPRING VALLEY, CALIF.
1996-008	AYRAULT, JOSEPH ALLEN	2338 VINTAGE STREET, SARASOTA FL 34240
1992-006	AYRAULT, ROBERT CUNNINGHAM	2395 SOUTH ARLINGTON AVRNUE, RENO NV 89509
1960-003	AZCUE, JOSE JOAQUIN	7609 WEST 115TH ST, OVERLAND PARK KS 66210
1990-007	AZOCAR, OSCAR GREGORIO	OLD ADD: 6650 N. ANDREWS AVE, FT. LAUDERDALE FL 33309

B

1979-006	BABCOCK, ROBERT ERNEST	623 PINE TRACT ROAD, WEST SUNBURY PA 16061
1952-004	BABE, LOREN ROLLAND	D. FEBRUARY 14, 1984, OMAHA, NEB.
1934-002	BABICH, JOHN CHARLES	D. JANUARY 19, 2001, RICHMOND, CALIF.
1981-003	BABITT, MACK N. 'SHOOTY'	4912 PLAZA CIRCLE, RICHMOND CA 94804
2002-007	BACKE, BRANDON ALLEN	2550 QUAKER DRIVE, TEXAS CITY TX 77590
1980-005	BACKMAN, WALTER WAYNE 'WALLY'	421 NORTH MAIN STREET, PRINEVILLE OR 97754
1975-009	BACSIK, MICHAEL JAMES	4014 FALCON LAKE DRIVE, ARLINGTON TX 76016
2001-009	BACSIK, MICHAEL JOSEPH	4014 FALCON LAKE DRIVE, ARLINGTON TX 76016
1953-003	BACZEWSKI, FREDERICK JOHN	D. NOVEMBER 14, 1976, CULVER CITY, CALIF.
1929-005	BADGRO, MORRIS HIRAM 'RED'	D. JULY 13, 1998, KENT, WASH.
1926-003	BAECHT, EDWARD JOSEPH	D. AUGUST 15, 1957, QUARRY TWP., ILL.
2004-009	BAEK, CHA-SEUNG	2331 CEDAR PARK LOOP SE, OLYMPIA WA 98501
1990-008	BAERGA, CARLOS OBED (ORTIZ)	OLD ADD: RUTA RURAL, 142 BUZON 181G, CAGUAS PR 00625
2001-010	BAEZ, BENITO (CERI)	OLD ADD: BONAO DOM REP
2001-011	BAEZ, DANYS	6190 SW 114TH STREET, MIAMI FL 33156
1977-006	BAEZ, JOSE ANTONIO	1028 EAST JERSEY STREET #2, ELIZABETH NJ 07201
1990-009	BAEZ, KEVIN RICHARD	110 SPRUCE DRIVE, HOLBROOK NY 11741
1938-003	BAGBY, JAMES CHARLES JACOB, JR.	D. SEPTEMBER 2, 1988, MARIETTA, GA.
1991-007	BAGWELL, JEFFREY ROBERT	4 SADDLE CREEK, HOUSTON TX 77024
1923-004	BAGWELL, WILLIAM MALLORY	D. OCTOBER 5, 1976, CHOUDRANT, LA.
1966-003	BAHNSEN, STANLEY RAYMOND	3500 BLUE LAKE DRIVE #C402, POMPANO BEACH FL 33064
1946-007	BAHR, EDSON GARFIELD	D. APRIL 6, 2007, SEATTLE, WASH.
1986-011	BAILES, SCOTT ALAN	2415 EAST EDGEWOOD STREET, SPRINGFIELD MO 65804
1995-010	BAILEY, CHARLES ROGER 'ROGER'	11045 SOUTH PUMA RUN, LITTLETON CO 80124
1981-004	BAILEY, HOWARD L.	11674 156TH AVENUE, WEST OLIVE MI 49460
1959-004	BAILEY, JAMES HOPKINS	250 CADE ROAD, TEN MILE TN 37880
1984-002	BAILEY, JOHN MARK 'MARK'	32703 WALTHAM CROSSING, FULSHEAR TX 77441
1953-004	BAILEY, LONAS EDGAR 'ED'	D. MARCH 29, 2007, KNOXVILLE, TENN.
1993-008	BAILEY, PHILIP CORY 'CORY'	19752 GALATIA POST ROAD, MARION IL 62959
1962-005	BAILEY, ROBERT SHERWOOD	3180 LIDO ISLE COURT, LAS VEGAS NV 89117
1967-003	BAILEY, STEVEN JOHN	4600 QUEEN ANNE AVENUE, LORAIN OH 44052
1975-010	BAILOR, ROBERT MICHAEL	1950 SWAN LANE, PALM HARBOR FL 34683
1945-002	BAIN, HERBERT LOREN 'LOREN'	D. NOVEMBER 24, 1996, CHETEK, WISC.
1980-006	BAINES, HAROLD DOUGLAS	PO BOX 10, SAINT MICHAELS MD 21663
1976-010	BAIR, CHARLES DOUGLAS 'DOUG'	560 OHIO PIKE, CINCINNATI OH 45255
1962-006	BAIRD, ROBERT ALLEN	D. APRIL 11, 1974, CHATTANOOGA, TENN.
2004-010	BAJENARU, JEFFREY MICHAEL	12953 E. DOUGLAS CAMP SPRING DRIVE, VAIL AZ 85641
1964-003	BAKENHASTER, DAVID LEE	3710 ROME CORNERS ROAD, GALENA OH 43021
1938-004	BAKER, ALBERT JONES	D. NOVEMBER 6, 1982, KENEDY, TEXAS
1978-003	BAKER, CHARLES JOSEPH	3035 MESCALERO DRIVE, LAKE HAVASU CITY AZ 86404
1982-004	BAKER, DAVID GLENN	22234 523 HWY, LACONA IA 50139
1984-003	BAKER, DOUGLAS LEE	2454 HEYNEMAN HOLLOW, FALLBROOK CA 92028
1953-005	BAKER, EUGENE WALTER	D. DECEMBER 1, 1999, DAVENPORT, IOWA
1943-003	BAKER, FLOYD WILSON	D. NOVEMBER 16, 2004, YOUNGSTOWN, OHIO
1969-004	BAKER, FRANK	OLD ADD: 383 GIRARD AVENUE, SOMERSET NJ 08873
1970-004	BAKER, FRANK WATTS	BOX 3066, MERIDIAN MS 39301
1976-011	BAKER, JACK EDWARD	5513 HUNTER'S HILL ROAD, IRONDALE AL 35210
2005-007	BAKER, JEFFREY GLEN	4747 TIMBER RIDGE DRIVE, DUMFRIES VA 22025
1968-003	BAKER, JOHNNIE B. 'DUSTY'	40 LIVINGSTON TERRACE DRIVE, SAN BRUNO CA 94066
1927-003	BAKER, NEAL VERNON	D. JANUARY 5, 1982, HOUSTON, TEXAS
1995-011	BAKER, SCOTT	OLD ADD: 7424 CYPRESS GROVE COURT, LAS VEGAS NV 89127
1978-004	BAKER, STEVEN BYRNE	27527 EASY ACRES DRIVE, EUGENE OR 97405
1935-001	BAKER, THOMAS CALVIN	D. JANUARY 3, 1991, FORT WORTH, TEXAS

1963-006 BAKER, THOMAS HENRY..........D. MARCH 9, 1980, PORT TOWNSEND, WASH.
2005-008 BAKER, TIMOTHY SCOTT 'SCOTT'..........9785 BAYOU BEND DRIVE, SHREVEPORT LA 71115
1940-001 BAKER, WILLIAM PRESLEY..........D. APRIL 13, 2006, MYRTLE BEACH, S.C.
1998-006 BAKO, GABOR PAUL 'PAUL'..........330 ACORN DRIVE, LAFAYETTE LA 70507
1938-005 BALAS, MITCHELL FRANCIS..........D. OCTOBER 15, 1996, WESTFORD, MASS.
1974-004 BALAZ, JOHN LARRY..........3757 UDALL STREET #301, SAN DIEGO CA 92107
1981-005 BALBONI, STEPHEN CHARLES..........117 BURLINGTON ROAD, MURRAY HILL NJ 07974
1956-005 BALCENA, ROBERT RUDOLPH..........D. JANUARY 4, 1990, SAN PEDRO, CALIF.
2003-006 BALDELLI, ROCCO DANIEL..........45 WINDSONG DRIVE, CUMBERLAND RI 02864
1961-006 BALDSCHUN, JACK EDWARD..........311 ERIE ROAD, GREEN BAY WI 54311
1966-004 BALDWIN, DAVID GEORGE..........PO BOX 190, YACHATS OR 97498
1953-006 BALDWIN, FRANK DEWITT..........D. NOVEMBER 18, 2004, BEAVER, ORE.
1927-004 BALDWIN, HENRY CLAY..........D. FEBRUARY 24, 1964, PHILADELPHIA, PA.
1924-002 BALDWIN, HOWARD EDWARD 'HARRY'..........D. JANUARY 23, 1958, BALTIMORE, MD.
1995-012 BALDWIN, JAMES..........18 MONTEITH PLACE, PINEHURST NC 28374
1990-010 BALDWIN, JEFFREY ALLEN..........1209 PINE STREET, KENOVA WV 25530
1978-005 BALDWIN, REGINALD CONRAD..........763 LIEBOLD, DETROIT MI 48217
1975-011 BALDWIN, RICK ALAN..........PO BOX 1068, SALIDA CA 95368
1975-012 BALDWIN, ROBERT HARVEY 'BILLY'..........878 PACKARD DR, AKRON OH 44320
1999-009 BALE, JOHN ROBERT..........PO BOX 806, CRESTVIEW FL 32536
1966-005 BALES, WESLEY OWEN 'LEE'..........7422 GREATWOOD LAKE DRIVE, SUGARLAND TX 77479
2001-012 BALFOUR, GRANT ROBERT..........OLD ADD: SYDNEY AUSTRALIA
1998-007 BALL, JEFFERY D...........1166 6TH AVENUE, VERO BEACH FL 32960
1987-005 BALLARD, JEFFREY SCOTT..........4828 RIMROCK ROAD, BILLINGS MT 59102
1928-003 BALLENGER, PELHAM ASHBY..........D. DECEMBER 8, 1948, GREENVILLE COUNTY, S.C.
1982-005 BALLER, JAY SCOT..........303 SPRING VALLEY ROAD, READING PA 19605
1971-007 BALLINGER, MARK ALAN..........1212 SW 5TH AVENUE, OKEECHOBEE FL 34974
1925-005 BALLOU, NOBLE WINFRED 'WIN'..........D. JANUARY 30, 1963, SAN FRANCISCO, CALIF.
1962-007 BALSAMO, ANTHONY FRED..........15 DORAL LANE, BAY SHORE NY 11706
1951-001 BAMBERGER, GEORGE IRVIN..........D. APRIL 4, 2004, NORTH REDINGTON BEACH, FLA.
1948-006 BAMBERGER, HAROLD EARL..........480 MOUNTZ ROAD, BIRDSBORO PA 19508
1981-006 BANDO, CHRISTOPHER MICHAEL..........3926 EAST AUGUSTA AVENUE, QUEEN CREEK AZ 85242
1966-006 BANDO, SALVATORE LEONARD..........6173 NORTH 28TH PLACE, PHOENIX AZ 85016
1973-010 BANE, EDWARD NORMAN..........598 PALOMA COURT, ENCINITAS CA 92024
1969-005 BANEY, RICHARD LEE..........2231 NORTHUP DRIVE, TUSTIN CA 92782
1991-008 BANISTER, JEFFERY TODD..........5228 HIDDEN BROOK LANE, LEAGUE CITY TX 77573
1947-008 BANKHEAD, DANIEL ROBERT..........D. MAY 2, 1976, HOUSTON, TEXAS
1986-012 BANKHEAD, MICHAEL SCOTT 'SCOTT'..........1236 IDLEWOOD, ASHEBORO NC 27203
1996-009 BANKS, BRIAN GLEN..........1053 NORTH ALBA CIRCLE, MESA AZ 85213
1953-007 BANKS, ERNEST 'ERNIE'..........578 WASHINGTON BLVD #284, MARINA DEL REY CA 90292
1962-008 BANKS, GEORGE EDWARD..........D. MARCH 1, 1985, SPARTANBURG, S.C.
1991-009 BANKS, WILLIE ANTHONY..........99B OLD BERGEN ROAD, JERSEY CITY NJ 07305
1974-005 BANNISTER, ALAN..........6730 NORTH SCOTTSDALE ROAD #150, SCOTTSDALE AZ 85253
2006-009 BANNISTER, BRIAN P...........OLD ADD: PARADISE VALLEY AZ
1977-007 BANNISTER, FLOYD FRANKLIN..........6701 EAST CABALLO DRIVE, PARADISE VALLEY AZ 85253
1947-009 BANTA, JOHN KAY..........D. SEPTEMBER 17, 2006, HUTCHINSON, KAN.
1998-008 BAPTIST, TRAVIS STEVEN..........21405 SW ROCK ROAD, BEAVERTON OR 97006
1999-010 BARAJAS, RODRIGO RICHARD..........8533 NORTH 50TH PLACE, PARADISE VALLEY AZ 85253
1943-004 BARBARY, DONALD ODELL 'RED'..........D. SEPTEMBER 27, 2003, SIMPSONVILLE, S.C.
1926-004 BARBEE, DAVID MONROE..........D. JULY 1, 1968, ALBEMARLE, N.C.
1995-013 BARBER, BRIAN SCOTT..........347 BLUE STONE CIRCLE, WINTER GARDEN FL 34787
1960-004 BARBER, STEPHEN DAVID..........D. FEBRUARY 4, 2007, HENDERSON, NEV.
1970-005 BARBER, STEVEN LEE..........902 SAN EDUARDO AVENUE, HENDERSON NV 89015
1991-010 BARBERIE, BRET EDWARD..........11607 BOS STREET, CERRITOS CA 90701
1966-007 BARBIERI, JAMES PATRICK..........13619 EAST 5TH AVE, SPOKANE WA 99216
2000-007 BARCELO, LORENZO ANTHONY..........1520 NORTH BLACKLAWN AVENUE, TUCSON AZ 85745
1957-004 BARCLAY, CURTIS CORDELL..........D. MARCH 27, 1985, MISSOULA, MONT.
2002-008 BARD, JOSHUA DAVID..........2505 AKRON STREET, DENVER CO 80238
1972-005 BARE, RAYMOND DOUGLAS..........D. MARCH 29, 1994, MIAMI, FLA.
1981-007 BARFIELD, JESSE LEE..........5814 SPANISH MOSS COURT, SPRING TX 77379
1989-008 BARFIELD, JOHN DAVID..........OLD ADD: 6262 MCPHERSON ROAD, LAREDO TX 78041
2006-010 BARFIELD, JOSHUA LAROY..........5814 SPANISH MOSS COURT, SPRING TX 77379
1922-002 BARFOOT, CLYDE RAYMOND..........D. MARCH 11, 1971, HIGHLAND PARK, CALIF.
1983-007 BARGAR, GREG ROBERT..........902 FELBAR AVENUE, TORRANCE CA 90503
1995-014 BARK, BRIAN STUART..........5051 SW HAMMOCK CREEK DRIVE, PALM CITY FL 34990
1999-011 BARKER, GLEN F...........10 PROVIDENCE PLACE, ALBANY NY 12202
1999-012 BARKER, KEVIN STEWART..........OLD ADD: MENDOTA VA 24270
1976-012 BARKER, LEONARD HAROLD..........10690 LOCUST GROVE DRIVE, CHARDON OH 44024
1960-005 BARKER, RAYMOND HAROLD..........303 GREENBRIAR ROAD, MARTINSBURG WV 25401
1999-013 BARKER, RICHARD FRANK 'RICHIE'..........17 LANDERS ROAD, STONEHAM MA 02180
2001-013 BARKETT, ANDREW JON..........OLD ADD: 11121 NORTH KENDALL DRIVE, MIAMI FL 33176
1998-009 BARKLEY, BRIAN EDWARD..........9208 SPRING RIDGE CIRCLE, WACO TX 76712
1984-004 BARKLEY, JEFFREY CARVER..........264 THIRD AVE NE, HICKORY NC 28601
1937-006 BARKLEY, JOHN DUNCAN 'RED'..........D. DECEMBER 12, 2000, WACO, TEXAS
1975-013 BARLOW, MICHAEL ROSWELL..........C/O SHEFTIC, 4524 FRANCIS ROAD, CAZENOVIA NY 13035
1953-008 BARMES, BRUCE RAYMOND..........509 MCDONALD AVENUE, CHARLOTTE NC 28203
2003-007 BARMES, CLINT HAROLD..........OLD ADD: VINCENNES IN 47591
1937-007 BARNA, HERBERT PAUL 'BABE'..........D. MAY 18, 1972, CHARLESTON, W.VA.
1927-005 BARNABE, CHARLES EDWARD..........D. AUGUST 16, 1977, WACO, TEXAS
1990-011 BARNES, BRIAN KEITH..........860 RAVENCOVE DRIVE, DACULA GA 30019
1927-006 BARNES, EMILE DEERING 'RED'..........D. JULY 3, 1959, MOBILE, ALA.
1923-005 BARNES, EVERETT DUANE 'EPPIE'..........D. NOVEMBER 17, 1980, MINEOLA, N.Y.
1957-005 BARNES, FRANK..........1508 BRAZIL, GREENVILLE MS 38701
1929-006 BARNES, FRANK SAMUEL 'LEFTY'..........D. SEPTEMBER 27, 1967, HOUSTON, TEXAS
2000-008 BARNES, JOHN DELBERT..........9 BROWN DRIVE, NOVATO CA 94647
1926-005 BARNES, JOHN FRANCIS 'HONEY'..........D. JUNE 18, 1981, LOCKPORT, N.Y.

1934-003	BARNES, JUNIE SHOAF	D. DECEMBER 31, 1963, JACKSONVILLE, N.C.
2001-014	BARNES, LARRY RICHARD	11906 CROCKETT COURT, BAKERSFIELD CA 93312
1972-006	BARNES, LUTHER OWEN	35911 DONNY CIRCLE, PALM DESERT CA 92211
1982-006	BARNES, RICHARD MONROE 'RICH'	2845 WILDERNESS ROAD, WEST PALM BEACH FL 33409
1924-003	BARNES, ROBERT AVERY	D. DECEMBER 8, 1993, PEORIA, ILL.
1921-001	BARNES, SAMUEL THOMAS	D. FEBRUARY 19, 1981, MONTGOMERY, ALA.
1983-008	BARNES, WILLIAM HENRY 'SKEETER'	11544 WINDING WOOD DRIVE, INDIANAPOLIS IN 46235
1943-005	BARNEY, REX EDWARD	D. AUGUST 12, 1997, BALTIMORE, MD.
1920-003	BARNHART, CLYDE LEE	D. JANUARY 21, 1980, HAGERSTOWN, MD.
1924-004	BARNHART, EDGAR VERNON	D. SEPTEMBER 14, 1984, COLUMBIA, MO.
1928-004	BARNHART, LESLIE EARL	D. OCTOBER 7, 1971, SCOTTSDALE, ARIZ.
1944-003	BARNHART, VICTOR DEE	13102 UNGER ROAD, HAGERSTOWN MD 21741
1939-004	BARNICLE, GEORGE BERNARD	D. OCTOBER 10, 1990, LARGO, FLA.
1965-004	BARNOWSKI, EDWARD ANTHONY	2380 LAKE LUCY ROAD, CHANHASSEN MN 55317
2006-011	BARNWELL, CHRISTOPHER EDWARD	1442 FRUIT COVE ROAD NORTH, JACKSONVILLE FL 32259
1982-007	BAROJAS, SALOME ROMERO	OLD ADD: MEXICO CITY MEXICO
1960-006	BARONE, RICHARD ANTHONY	1220 HEATHER GLEN CIRCLE, HOLLISTER CA 95023
1971-008	BARR, JAMES LELAND	6335 OAK HILL DRIVE, ROSEVILLE CA 95661
1935-002	BARR, ROBERT ALEXANDER	D. JUNE 25, 2002, DOVER, N.H.
1974-006	BARR, STEVEN CHARLES	260 WEST VAN FLEET DRIVE #59, BARTOW FL 33830
1961-007	BARRAGAN, FACUNDO ANTHONY 'CUNO'	1824 ST. ANN COURT, CARMICHAEL CA 95608
1979-007	BARRANCA, GERMAN	199 KREIDLER AVENUE, YORK PA 17402
1937-008	BARRETT, CHARLES HENRY 'RED'	D. JULY 28, 1990, WILSON, N.C.
1939-005	BARRETT, FRANCIS JOSEPH	D. MARCH 8, 1998, LEESBURG, FLA.
1942-005	BARRETT, JOHN JOSEPH	D. AUGUST 17, 1974, SEABROOK BEACH, N.H.
1982-008	BARRETT, MARTIN GLENN	2731 SOUTH MCCLELLAND PLACE, CHANDLER AZ 85248
1998-010	BARRETT, MICHAEL PATRICK	8010 HENDERSON COURT, ALPHARETTA GA 30004
1923-006	BARRETT, ROBERT SCHLEY	D. JANUARY 18, 1982, ATLANTA, GA.
1988-009	BARRETT, THOMAS LOREN	5306 WEST JUPITER WAY, CHANDLER AZ 85226
1988-010	BARRETT, TIMOTHY WAYNE	5588 JANDEL DRIVE, AURORA IN 47001
1933-003	BARRETT, TRACEY SOUTER 'DICK'	D. NOVEMBER 7, 1966, SEATTLE, WASH.
1921-002	BARRETT, WILLIAM JOSEPH	D. JANUARY 26, 1951, CAMBRIDGE, MASS.
1974-007	BARRIOS, FRANCISCO XAVIER	D. APRIL 9, 1982, HERMOSILLO SONORA MEXICO
1982-009	BARRIOS, JOSE MANUEL	6484 SW 25TH ST, MIAMI FL 33155
1997-006	BARRIOS, MANUEL ANTONIO	OLD ADD: CABECERA PANAMA
1996-010	BARRON, ANTHONY DIRK 'TONY'	12312 172ND STREET EAST #E103, PUYALLUP WA 98374
1929-007	BARRON, DAVID IRENUS 'RED'	D. OCTOBER 4, 1982, ATLANTA, GA.
1995-015	BARRY, JEFFREY FINAS	430 GOLD TERRACE, JACKSONVILLE OR 97530
2006-012	BARRY, KEVIN THOMAS	PO BOX 822, OLD FORGE NY 13420
1969-006	BARRY, RICHARD DONOVAN	12020 HOFFMAN STREET #K, STUDIO CITY CA 91604
1996-011	BARTEE, KIMERA ANOTCHI	10808 NORTH 57TH DRIVE, GLENDALE AZ 85304
1927-007	BARTELL, RICHARD WILLIAM	D. AUGUST 4, 1995, ALAMEDA, CALIF.
1944-004	BARTHELSON, ROBERT EDWARD	D. APRIL 14, 2000, BRANFORD, CONN.
1928-005	BARTHOLOMEW, LESTER JUSTIN	D. SEPTEMBER 19, 1972, MADISON, WISC.
1952-005	BARTIROME, ANTHONY JOSEPH	1104 PALMA SOLA BLVD, BRADENTON FL 34209
2004-011	BARTLETT, JASON ALAN	248 RIVER OAKS DRIVE, LODI CA 95240
1943-006	BARTLEY, BOYD OWEN	7500 NOREAST DRIVE, FORT WORTH TX 76180
1938-006	BARTLING, IRVING HENRY	D. JUNE 12, 1973, WESTLAND, MICH.
1965-005	BARTON, ROBERT WILBUR	37193 STARDUST WAY, MURRIETA CA 92563
1992-007	BARTON, SHAWN EDWARD	4012 HILLTOP AVENUE, READING PA 19605
1931-006	BARTON, VINCENT DAVID	D. SEPTEMBER 13, 1973, TORONTO, ONT.
2004-012	BARTOSCH, CLIFFORD PAUL	939 FAIRLAWN, DUNCANVILLE TX 75116
1945-003	BARTOSCH, DAVID ROBERT	D. APRIL 30, 2006, NASHVILLE, TENN.
2006-013	BARZILLA, PHILIP JOSEPH	3310 CRYSTAL CREEK DRIVE, SUGARLAND TX 77478
1948-007	BASGALL, ROMANUS 'MONTY'	D. SEPTEMBER 22, 2005, SIERRA VISTA, ARIZ.
1936-006	BASHORE, WALTER FRANKLIN	D. SEPTEMBER 26, 1984, SEBRING, FLA.
1944-005	BASINSKI, EDWIN FRANK	4110 SE JACKSON, MILWAUKIE OR 97222
1982-010	BASS, KEVIN CHARLES	3630 MARANATHA, SUGAR LAND TX 77479
1961-008	BASS, NORMAN DELANEY	8814 THIRD AVE, INGLEWOOD CA 90305
1977-008	BASS, RANDY WILLIAM	2709 SW COOMBS ROAD, LAWTON OK 73501
1939-006	BASS, RICHARD WILLIAM	D. FEBRUARY 3, 1989, GRACEVILLE, FLA.
1923-007	BATCHELDER, JOSEPH EDMUND	D. MAY 5, 1989, BEVERLY, MASS.
1993-009	BATCHELOR, RICHARD ANTHONY	1004 PINENEEDLE ROAD, HARTSVILLE SC 29550
1963-007	BATEMAN, JOHN ALVIN	D. DECEMBER 3, 1996, SAND SPRINGS, OKLA.
1969-007	BATES, CHARLES RICHARD 'DICK'	5859 WEST CIELO GRANDE, GLENDALE AZ 85310
1927-008	BATES, CHARLES WILLIAM	D. JANUARY 29, 1980, TOPEKA, KAN.
1970-006	BATES, DELBERT OAKLEY	8213 NE 115TH WAY, KIRKLAND WA 98034
1939-007	BATES, HUBERT EDGAR	D. APRIL 29, 1987, LONG BEACH, CALIF.
1995-016	BATES, JASON CHARLES	OLD ADD: 15832 CRESTROCK CIRCLE, PARKER CO 80134
1989-009	BATES, WILLIAM DERRICK	2606 SHADY BAYOU LANE, SPRING TX 77373
1986-013	BATHE, WILLIAM DAVID	4530 NORTH MOUNTAIN QUAIL ROAD, TUCSON AZ 85750
1996-012	BATISTA, LEOCADIO FRANCISCO 'TONY'	141 SUNRIDGE WOODS COURT, DAVENPORT FL 33837
1992-008	BATISTA, MIGUEL JEREZ DESCARTES	30 DE MARZOH #31 SAN PEDRO DE MACORIS, DOM REP
1973-011	BATISTA, RAFAEL	BOX 211 SAN PEDRO DE MACORIS, DOM REP
1989-010	BATISTE, KEVIN WADE	3624 AVENUE M, GALVESTON TX 77550
1991-011	BATISTE, KIMOTHY EMIL	16163 AIKENS ROAD, PRAIRIEVILLE LA 70769
1955-008	BATTEY, EARL JESSE	D. NOVEMBER 15, 2003, OCALA, FLA.
1995-017	BATTLE, ALLEN ZELMO	106 DONETTE LOOP, DAPHNE AL 36526
1995-018	BATTLE, HOWARD DEAN	420 FAYARD STREET, BILOXI MS 39530
1927-009	BATTLE, JAMES MILTON	D. SEPTEMBER 30, 1965, CHICO, CALIF.
1976-013	BATTON, CHRISTOPHER SEAN	23546 UNDERWOOD CIRCLE, MURRIETA CA 92562
1947-010	BATTS, MATTHEW DANIEL	17927 SILVER CREEK COURT, BATON ROUGE LA 70810
1948-008	BAUER, HENRY ALBERT 'HANK'	D. FEBRUARY 9, 2007, KANSAS CITY, MO.
2001-015	BAUER, RICHARD EDWARD	5312 YGNACIO DRIVE, SACRAMENTO CA 95842
1936-007	BAUERS, RUSSELL LEE	D. JANUARY 21, 1995, HINES, ILL.
1998-011	BAUGHMAN, JUSTIN REIS	4052 NE 21ST AVENUE, PORTLAND OR 97212

1955-009	BAUMANN, FRANK MATTHEW	7712 SUNRAY LN, SAINT LOUIS MO 63123
1949-004	BAUMER, JAMES SLOAN	D. JULY 8, 1996, PAOLI, PA.
1978-006	BAUMGARTEN, ROSS	1020 BLUFF RD, GLENCOE IL 60022
1920-004	BAUMGARTNER, HARRY E.	D. DECEMBER 3, 1930, AUGUSTA, GA.
1953-009	BAUMGARTNER, JOHN EDWARD	1215 OXFORD COURT, BIRMINGHAM AL 35242
1947-011	BAUMHOLTZ, FRANK CONRAD	D. DECEMBER 14, 1997, WINTER SPRINGS, FLA.
1960-007	BAUTA, EDUARDO GALVEZ	1400 SOUTH NOVA ROAD #107, DAYTONA BEACH FL 32114
1993-010	BAUTISTA, DANIEL	OLD ADD: FRANCISCO DEL ROSARIO #65, SANTO DOMINGO DOM REP
2004-013	BAUTISTA, DENNY M.	OLD ADD: SANTO DOMINGO DOM REP
2004-014	BAUTISTA, JOSE ANTONIO	OLD ADD: SANTO DOMINGO DOM REP
1988-011	BAUTISTA, JOSE JOAQUIN	1000 ST. CHARLES PLACE, HOLLYWOOD FL 33026
1959-005	BAXES, DIMITRIOS SPEROS 'JIM'	D. NOVEMBER 14, 1996, GARDEN GROVE, CALIF.
1956-006	BAXES, MICHAEL	303 WICKMAN DR, MILL VALLEY CA 94941
2003-008	BAY, JASON RAYMOND	OLD ADD: TRAIL BC CANADA
2005-009	BAYLISS, JONAH JAMES	370 COLE AVENUE, WILLIAMSTOWN MA 01267
1970-007	BAYLOR, DON EDWARD	56325 RIVIERA, LAQUINTA CA 92253
2005-010	BAZARDO, YORMAN MICHAEL	OLD ADD: MARACAY VENEZ
1975-014	BEALL, ROBERT BROOKS	513 BIRCHWOOD RD, HILLSBORO OR 97123
1924-005	BEALL, WALTER ESAU	D. JANUARY 28, 1959, SUITLAND, MD.
2006-014	BEAM, THEODORE LESTER 'T.J.'	8731 EAST TURNEY AVENUE, SCOTTSDALE AZ 85251
1978-007	BEAMON, CHARLES ALONZO	OLD ADD: 1690 164TH AVENUE #3, SAN LEANDRO CA 94578
1956-007	BEAMON, CHARLES ALONZO, SR.	1717 WOODLAND AVE #313, EAST PALO ALTO CA 94303
1996-013	BEAMON, CLIFFORD 'TREY'	9730 WHITEHURST #51, DALLAS TX 75243
1930-002	BEAN, BEVERIC BENTON 'BELVE'	D. JUNE 1, 1988, COMANCHE, TEXAS
2005-011	BEAN, RANDALL COLTER 'COLTER'	2116 SHADES CREST ROAD, BIRMINGHAM AL 35216
1987-006	BEAN, WILLIAM DARO	OLD ADD: 12934 CARMEL CREEK ROAD, SAN DIEGO CA 92130
1984-005	BEANE, WILLIAM LAMAR	1720 KNOLL FIELD WAY, ENCINITAS CA 92024
1980-007	BEARD, CHARLES DAVID 'DAVE'	5325 DERBY CHASE COURT, ALPHARETTA GA 30202
1948-009	BEARD, CRAMER THEODORE 'TED'	10517 STELORS COURT, FISHERS IN 46038
1974-008	BEARD, MICHAEL RICHARD	400 WALNUT STREET, LITTLE ROCK AR 72205
1954-006	BEARD, RALPH WILLIAM	D. FEBRUARY 10, 2003, WEST PALM BEACH, FLA.
1947-012	BEARDEN, HENRY EUGENE 'GENE'	D. MARCH 18, 2004, ALEXANDER CITY, ALA.
1976-014	BEARE, GARY RAY	12718 SHADOWLINE STREET, POWAY CA 92064
1963-008	BEARNARTH, LAWRENCE DONALD	D. DECEMBER 31, 1999, ST. PETERSBURG, FLA.
1990-012	BEARSE, KEVIN GERARD	36 SARAH LANE, HOWELL NJ 07731
1991-012	BEASLEY, CHRISTOPHER CHARLES	OLD ADD: 9410 ALEXANDER AVENUE, SOUTH GATE CA 90280
1977-009	BEASLEY, LEWIS PAIGE	24653 NEWTON ROAD, BOWLING GREEN VA 22427
1978-008	BEATTIE, JAMES LOUIS	1 KENWOOD ROAD, BALTIMORE MD 21210
1989-011	BEATTY, GORDON BLAINE 'BLAINE'	867 KOLODZEY ROAD, VICTORIA TX 77905
1963-009	BEAUCHAMP, JAMES EDWARD	105 PAULA DRIVE, TYRONE GA 30290
1941-006	BEAZLEY, JOHN ANDREW	D. APRIL 21, 1990, NASHVILLE, TENN.
2002-009	BECHLER, STEVEN SCOTT	D. FEBRUARY 17, 2003, FORT LAUDERDALE, FLA.
1926-006	BECK, CLYDE EUGENE	D. JULY 15, 1988, TEMPLE CITY, CALIF.
1965-006	BECK, RICHARD HENRY	8218 NORTH SUMTER COURT, SPOKANE WA 99208
1991-013	BECK, RODNEY ROY	5928 EAST LUDLOW DRIVE, SCOTTSDALE AZ 85254
1924-006	BECK, WALTER WILLIAM 'BOOM BOOM'	D. MAY 7, 1987, CHAMPAIGN, ILL.
1943-007	BECKER, HEINZ REINHARD	D. NOVEMBER 11, 1991, DALLAS, TEXAS
1936-008	BECKER, JOSEPH EDWARD	D. JANUARY 11, 1998, SUNSET HILLS, MO.
1993-011	BECKER, RICHARD GODHARD 'RICH'	210 MARY SENICA COURT, LASALLE IL 61301
1965-007	BECKERT, GLENN ALFRED	1953 ARKANSAS AVENUE, ENGLEWOOD FL 34224
2001-016	BECKETT, JOSHUA PATRICK	3610 OTTO ROAD, SPRING TX 77373
1996-014	BECKETT, ROBERT JOSEPH 'ROBBIE'	20822 JUMPERS DELIGHT, PFLUGERVILLE TX 78660
1927-010	BECKMAN, JAMES JOSEPH	D. DECEMBER 5, 1974, CINCINNATI, OHIO
1939-008	BECKMANN, WILLIAM ALOYSIUS	D. JANUARY 2, 1990, FLORISSANT, MO.
1979-008	BECKWITH, THOMAS JOSEPH 'JOE'	859 ANNABROOK DRIVE, AUBURN AL 36830
1955-010	BECQUER, JULIO VELLEGAS	829 VINCENT AVE, MINNEAPOLIS MN 55411
2002-010	BEDARD, ERIK JOSEPH	OLD ADD: NAVON ONTARIO
1962-009	BEDELL, HOWARD WILLIAM	1187 CRESTWOOD DR, POTTSTOWN PA 19464
1925-006	BEDFORD, WILLIAM EUGENE	D. OCTOBER 6, 1977, SAN ANTONIO, TEXAS
1922-003	BEDGOOD, PHILIP BURLETTE	D. NOVEMBER 8, 1927, FORT PIERCE, FLA.
1930-003	BEDNAR, ANDREW JACKSON	D. NOVEMBER 26, 1937, GRAHAM, TEXAS
1981-008	BEDROSIAN, STEPHEN WAYNE	3915 GORDON ROAD, SENOIA GA 30276
1996-015	BEECH, LUCAS MATTHEW 'MATT'	516 SHEFFIELD DRIVE, RICHARDSON TX 75081
1944-006	BEELER, JOSEPH SAM 'JODIE '	D. OCTOBER 8, 2002, MESQUITE, TEXAS
1968-004	BEENE, FREDERICK RAY	BOX 143, OAKHURST TX 77359
1983-009	BEENE, RAMON ANDREW 'ANDY'	124 UPPER MASON CREEK EAST, CENTER POINT TX 78010
1948-010	BEERS, CLARENCE SCOTT	D. DECEMBER 16, 2002, TUCSON, ARIZ.
1938-007	BEGGS, JOSEPH STANLEY	D. JULY 19, 1983, INDIANAPOLIS, IND.
1924-007	BEGLEY, JAMES LAWRENCE	D. FEBRUARY 22, 1957, SAN FRANCISCO, CALIF.
1921-003	BEHAN, CHARLES FREDERICK 'PETIE'	D. JANUARY 21, 1957, BRADFORD, PA.
1983-010	BEHENNA, RICHARD KIPP	164 BRADFORD STATION DRIVE, SHARPSBURG GA 30277
1970-008	BEHNEY, MELVIN BRIAN	6286 MISTY WAY, LONGMONT CO 80503
1946-008	BEHRMAN, HENRY BERNARD	D. JANUARY 20, 1987, NEW YORK, N.Y.
2001-017	BEIMEL, JOSEPH RONALD	107 BEACON HILL DRIVE, CRANBERRY TWP PA 16066
2000-009	BEIRNE, KEVIN PATRICK	2 CEDAR CHASE PLACE, SPRING TX 77381
1934-004	BEJMA, ALOYSIUS FRANK 'OLLIE'	D. JANUARY 3, 1995, SOUTH BEND, IND.
1965-008	BELANGER, MARK HENRY	D. OCTOBER 6, 1998, NEW YORK, N.Y.
1950-007	BELARDI, CARROLL WAYNE 'WAYNE'	D. OCTOBER 21, 1993, SANTA CRUZ, CALIF.
1990-013	BELCHER, KEVIN DONNELL	OLD ADD: 8620 PARK LANE #204, DALLAS TX 75231
1987-007	BELCHER, TIMOTHY WAYNE	1830 STATE ROUTE 314, MARENGO OH 43334
1989-012	BELINDA, STANLEY PETER	454 SYLVAN DRIVE, STATE COLLEGE PA 16803
1962-010	BELINSKY, ROBERT 'BO'	D. NOVEMBER 23, 2001, LAS VEGAS, NEV.
2003-009	BELISLE, MATTHEW THOMAS	4009 SIERRA DRIVE, AUSTIN TX 78731
2000-010	BELITZ, TODD STEPHEN	17901 NORTH COLTON COURT, COLBERT WA 99005
1996-016	BELK, TIMOTHY WILLIAM	10608 HAZELHURST DRIVE, HOUSTON TX 77043
1972-007	BELL, DAVID GUS 'BUDDY'	PO BOX 11718, CHANDLER AZ 85248

1995-019 BELL, DAVID MICHAEL .... PO BOX 11718, CHANDLER AZ 85248
1950-008 BELL, DAVID RUSSELL 'GUS' .... D. MAY 7, 1995, CINCINNATI, OHIO
1991-014 BELL, DEREK NATHANIEL .... OLD ADD: 10005 MARATHON COURT, TAMPA FL 33615
1985-003 BELL, ERIC ALVIN .... 1140 SOUTH 124TH STREET, CHANDLER AZ 85249
1939-009 BELL, FERNANDO JEROME LEE 'FERN' .... D. AUGUST 29, 2000, RANCHO MIRAGE, CALIF.
2004-015 BELL, HEATH JUSTIN .... 665 SE STRAIT AVENUE, PORT SAINT LUCIE FL 34983
1924-008 BELL, HERMAN S. 'HI' .... D. JUNE 7, 1949, GLENDALE, CALIF.
1986-014 BELL, JAY STUART .... PO BOX 50249, PHOENIX AZ 85076
1971-009 BELL, JERRY HOUSTON .... 631 AUDREY ROAD, MOUNT JULIET TN 37122
1981-009 BELL, JORGE ANTONIO 'GEORGE' .... L.AMIAMA #14, BELL SEGUNDA PLANTOR, SAN PEDRO DE MACORIS, DOM REP
1989-013 BELL, JUAN MATHEY .... OLD ADD: CALLE T174 BO RESTAURACION, SAN PEDRO DE MAC, DOM REP
1976-015 BELL, KEVIN ROBERT .... OLD ADD: 2341 ALGONQUIN PKWY, ROLLING MEADOWS IL 60008
1923-008 BELL, LESTER ROWLAND .... D. NOVEMBER 26, 1985, HARRISBURG, PA.
1990-014 BELL, MICHAEL ALLEN .... 1331 NOAH AVENUE, SPRING HILL FL 34608
2000-011 BELL, MICHAEL JOHN .... OLD ADD: 12014 MAXIM AVENUE, COLUMBUS OH 45249
2000-012 BELL, ROBERT ALLEN .... 28 BLOSSOM HILL DRIVE, MARLBORO NY 12542
1935-003 BELL, ROY CHESTER 'BEAU' .... D. SEPTEMBER 14, 1977, COLLEGE STATION, TEXAS
1986-015 BELL, TERENCE WILLIAM .... 8352 NORMANDY CREEK DRIVE, DAYTON OH 45458
1958-009 BELL, WILBUR GARY 'GARY' .... 2107 OAK RANCH, SAN ANTONIO TX 78259
1952-006 BELL, WILLIAM SAMUEL .... D. OCTOBER 11, 1962, DURHAM, N.C.
1957-006 BELLA, JOHN 'ZEKE' .... 409 CYPRESS DRIVE #7, TEQUESTA FL 33469
1989-014 BELLE, ALBERT JOJUAN .... 9574 EAST ANN WAY, SCOTTSDALE AZ 85260
1997-007 BELLHORN, MARK CHRISTIAN .... 1447 PALOMINO WAY, OVIEDO FL 32765
1982-011 BELLIARD, RAFAEL LEONIDAS .... 10846 KING BAY DRIVE, BOCA RATON FL 33498
1998-012 BELLIARD, RONALD .... 2999 NW 96TH STREET, MIAMI FL 33147
1999-014 BELLINGER, CLAYTON DANIEL .... 1390 EAST HORSESHOE DRIVE, CHANDLER AZ 85149
1975-015 BELLOIR, ROBERT EDWARD .... PO BOX 2933, SAVANNAH GA 31402
1998-013 BELTRAN, CARLOS IVAN .... OLD ADD: 6624 ROSE QUEEN COURT, ORLANDO FL 32807
2002-011 BELTRAN, FRANCIS LEBRON .... OLD ADD: SANTO DOMINGO DOM REP
1997-008 BELTRAN, RIGOBERTO .... 3950 LAURELWOOD LANE, DELRAY BEACH FL 33445
1998-014 BELTRE, ADRIAN PEREZ .... 345 WEST LONGDEN AVENUE, ARCADIA CA 91007
1991-015 BELTRE, ESTEBAN (VALERA) .... 15 #28 LALOMA SAN PEDRO DE MACORIS, DOM REP
1995-020 BENARD, MARVIN LARRY .... 30405 SOUTH 903 PR SE, KENNEWICK WA 99338
1991-016 BENAVIDES, ALFREDO 'FREDDIE' .... 2502 GARFIELD, LAREDO TX 78040
1967-004 BENCH, JOHN LEE .... 528 4 MILE ROAD, CINCINNATI OH 45230
1978-009 BENEDICT, BRUCE EDWIN .... OLD ADD: 8505 WEST BRONSON HWY, KISSIMMEE FL 34747
1995-021 BENES, ALAN PAUL .... 13005 WHEATFIELD FARM ROAD, SAINT LOUIS MO 63141
1989-015 BENES, ANDREW CHARLES .... 1127 HIGHLAND POINT DRIVE, SAINT LOUIS MO 63131
1931-007 BENES, JOSEPH ANTHONY .... D. MARCH 7, 1975, ELMHURST N.Y.
1925-007 BENGE, RAYMOND ADELPHIA .... D. JUNE 27, 1997, CENTERVILLE, TEXAS
1923-009 BENGOUGH, BERNARD OLIVER 'BENNY' .... D. DECEMBER 22, 1968, PHILADELPHIA, PA.
1971-010 BENIQUEZ, JUAN JOSE .... CALLE 99A BLK.87 #12, CAROLINA PR 00630
1994-004 BENITEZ, ARMANDO GERMAN .... BATEY EL SOCO RAMON SANTANA, DOM REP
1995-022 BENITEZ, YAMIL ANTONIO .... CALLE 13 BO. 918 CAPERRA TERRACE, RIO PIEDRAS PR 00921
1939-010 BENJAMIN, ALFRED STANLEY 'STAN' .... 15 SPEAK WAY, HARWICH MA 02645
1989-016 BENJAMIN, MICHAEL PAUL .... 25608 SOUTH 182ND PLACE, QUEEN CREEK AZ 85242
1964-004 BENNETT, DAVID HANS .... PO BOX 884, YREKA CA 96097
2004-016 BENNETT, DAVID JEFFREY 'JEFF' .... 18 BLUEBIRD DRIVE, BRUSH CREEK TN 38547
1962-011 BENNETT, DENNIS JOHN .... 630 NORTH 5TH, KLAMATH FALLS OR 97601
1995-023 BENNETT, ERIK HANS .... PO BOX 884, YREKA CA 96097
1927-011 BENNETT, FRANCIS ALLEN .... D. MARCH 18, 1966, WILMINGTON, DEL.
1995-024 BENNETT, GARY DAVID .... 1403 WEST BEACH ROAD, WAUKEGAN IL 60087
1923-010 BENNETT, HERSCHELL EMMETT .... D. SEPTEMBER 9, 1964, SPRINGFIELD, MO.
1928-006 BENNETT, JAMES FRED .... D. MAY 12, 1957, ATKINS, ARK.
1998-015 BENNETT, JOEL TODD .... 401 RILEY ROAD, WINDSOR NY 13865
1923-011 BENNETT, JOSEPH ROSENBLUM .... D. JULY 11, 1987, MORRO BAY, CALIF.
1997-009 BENNETT, SHAYNE ANTHONY .... OLD ADD: 99 CHERRY HILL ROAD, PARSIPPANY NJ 07054
2001-018 BENOIT, JOAQUIN ANTONIO (PENA) .... OLD ADD: SANTIAGO DOM REP
1934-005 BENSON, ALLEN WILBERT .... D. NOVEMBER 16, 1999, VIBORG, S.D.
1999-015 BENSON, KRISTEN JAMES .... 5550 CLAIRE ROSE LANE NW, ATLANTA GA 30327
1943-008 BENSON, VERNON ADAIR .... PO BOX 127, GRANITE QUARRY NC 28072
1978-010 BENTON, ALFRED LEE 'BUTCH' .... 12314 SW 60TH AVENUE, BELLEVIEW FL 34420
1934-006 BENTON, JOHN ALTON 'AL' .... D. APRIL 14, 1968, LYNWOOD, CALIF.
1923-012 BENTON, LAWRENCE JAMES .... D. APRIL 3, 1953, CINCINNATI, OHIO
1922-004 BENTON, SIDNEY WRIGHT .... D. MARCH 8, 1977, FAYETTEVILLE, ARK.
1922-005 BENTON, STANLEY 'RABBIT' .... D. JUNE 7, 1984, DALLAS, TEXAS
2004-017 BENTZ, CHAD ROBERT .... 150 HOLLY STREET, RUTLAND VT 05701
1987-008 BENZINGER, TODD ERIC .... 6527 ORISKANY DRIVE, LOVELAND OH 45140
1939-011 BERARDINO, JOHN .... D. MAY 19, 1996, LOS ANGELES, CALIF.
1954-007 BERBERET, LOUIS JOSEPH .... D. APRIL 6, 2004, LAS VEGAS, NEV.
1997-010 BERBLINGER, JEFFREY JAMES .... 102 SWANEE STREET, GODDARD KS 67052
1993-012 BERE, JASON PHILLIP .... 40 BERRINGTON PLACE, NORTH ANDOVER MA 01845
1978-011 BERENGUER, JUAN BAUTISTA .... 8616 ALISA COURT, CHANHASSEN MN 55317
1980-008 BERENYI, BRUCE MICHAEL .... PMB 131 2940 NE 188TH STREET, AVENTURA FL 33180
1998-016 BERG, DAVID SCOTT .... 1917 STONECASTLE DRIVE, ROANOKE TX 76262
1923-013 BERG, MORRIS 'MOE' .... D. MAY 29, 1972, BELLEVILLE, N.J.
1944-007 BERGAMO, AUGUST SAMUEL .... D. AUGUST 19, 1974, GROSSE POINTE CITY, MICH.
2001-019 BERGER, BRANDON CHARLES .... 2172 GLENVIEW DRIVE, HEBRON KY 41048
1922-006 BERGER, JOHN HENNE .... D. MAY 7, 1979, LAKE CHARLES, LA.
1932-003 BERGER, LOUIS WILLIAM 'BOZE' .... D. NOVEMBER 3, 1992, BETHESDA, MD.
1930-004 BERGER, WALTER ANTON 'WALLY' .... D. NOVEMBER 30, 1988, REDONDO BEACH, CALIF.
1999-016 BERGERON, PETER FRANCIS .... 3495 MANATEE DRIVE SE, SAINT PETERSBURG FL 33705
1975-016 BERGMAN, DAVID BRUCE .... 728 CANTERBURY COURT, GROSSE POINTE WOODS MI 48236
2004-018 BERGMAN, DUSTIN MICHAEL .... 41884 NORTH SUNLAND DRIVE, MARICOPA AZ 85239
1993-013 BERGMAN, SEAN FREDERICK .... 14421 SCOTT ROAD, BRYAN OH 43506
2005-012 BERGMANN, JASON CHRIS 'JAY' .... 13 ABILENE LANE, ENGLISHTOWN NJ 07726

2005-013	BERGOLLA, WILLIAM JOSE	OLD ADD: VALENCIA VENEZ
1999-017	BERKMAN, WILLIAM LANCE 'LANCE'	285 BRYN MAWR CIRCLE, HOUSTON TX 77024
1924-009	BERLY, JOHN CHAMBERS	D. JUNE 26, 1977, HOUSTON, TEXAS
1977-010	BERNAL, VICTOR HUGO	D. SEPTEMBER 2, 2006, ARCADIA, CALIF.
1978-012	BERNARD, DWIGHT VERN	728 CANTERBURY COURT, BELLE RIVE IL 62810
1979-009	BERNAZARD, ANTONIO (GARCIA)	SANTA AV D-25, URB SANTA ELVIRA, CAGUAS PR 00625
2000-013	BERNERO, ADAM GINO	19391 TITLEIST WAY, REDDING CA 96003
1976-016	BERNHARDT, JUAN RAMON	OLD ADD: EDUARDO BRITO 13, SAN PEDRO DE MACORIS DOM REP
1953-010	BERNIER, CARLOS RODRIGUEZ	D. APRIL 6, 1989, JUANA DIAZ, P.R.
1948-011	BERO, JOHN GEORGE	D. MAY 11, 1985, GARDENA, CALIF.
1977-011	BERRA, DALE ANTHONY	19 HIGHLAND AVENUE, MONTCLAIR NJ 07042
1946-009	BERRA, LAWRENCE PETER 'YOGI'	19 HIGHLAND AVENUE, MONTCLAIR NJ 07042
1934-007	BERRES, RAYMOND	D. FEBRUARY 1, 2007, KENOSHA, WISC.
2001-020	BERROA, ANGEL MARIA (SELMO)	OLD ADD: SANTO DOMINGO DOM REP
1989-017	BERROA, GERONIMO EMILIANO	3681 BROADWAY #23, NEW YORK NY 10031
1962-012	BERRY, ALLEN KENNETH 'KEN'	1131 SW CAMDEN LANE, TOPEKA KS 66604
1925-008	BERRY, CHARLES FRANCIS	D. SEPTEMBER 6, 1972, EVANSTON, ILL.
1948-012	BERRY, CORNELIUS JOHN 'NEIL'	407 INKSTER AVENUE, KALAMAZOO MI 49001
1942-006	BERRY, JONAS ARTHUR	D. SEPTEMBER 27, 1958, ANAHEIM, CALIF.
1921-004	BERRY, JOSEPH HOWARD, JR.	D. APRIL 29, 1976, PHILADELPHIA, PA.
1990-015	BERRY, SEAN ROBERT	2330 EAST ASHLAN AVENUE #104, FRESNO CA 93726
1987-009	BERRYHILL, DAMON SCOTT	11 SPRINGBROOK ROAD, LAGUNA NIGUEL CA 92677
1964-005	BERTAINA, FRANK LOUIS	OLD ADD: SUGARLOAF LODGE, KEY WEST FL 33040
1960-008	BERTELL, RICHARD GEORGE	D. DECEMBER 20, 1999, MISSION VIEJO, CALIF.
1953-011	BERTOIA, RENO PETER	705-5125 RIVERSIDE DRIVE EAST WINDSOR ON, N8S 4L8 CANADA
1995-025	BERTOTTI, MICHAEL DAVID	JUPITER ROAD, HIGHLAND MILLS NY 10930
1936-009	BERTRAND, ROMAN MATHIAS	D. MARCH 17, 2002, THE DALLES, ORE.
1995-026	BERUMEN, ANDRES	PO BOX 1436, BANNING CA 92220
1956-008	BESANA, FREDERICK CYRIL	222 DIAMOND OAKS DR, ROSEVILLE CA 95678
1940-002	BESSE, HERMAN	D. AUGUST 13, 1972, LOS ANGELES, CALIF.
1955-011	BESSENT, FRED DONALD 'DON'	D. JULY 7, 1990, JACKSONVILLE, FLA.
1983-011	BEST, KARL JOHN	PO BOX 1790, SNOHOMISH WA 98291
1978-013	BESWICK, JAMES WILLIAM	6911 BUCKHORN DRIVE, COLUMBUS GA 31904
2003-010	BETANCOURT, RAFAEL JOSE	OLD ADD: CUMANA VENEZUELA
2005-014	BETANCOURT, YUNIESKY	9500 SW 146TH STREET, MIAMI FL 33176
2001-021	BETEMIT, WILSON	OLD ADD: SANTO DOMINGO DOM REP
1964-006	BETHEA, WILLIAM LAMAR	ATH. DEPT., ARKANSAS STATE, PO BOX 1000, JONESBORO AR 72467
1965-009	BETHKE, JAMES CHARLES	6209 NORTH ROBINHOOD LANE, KANSAS CITY MO 64151
1928-007	BETTENCOURT, LAWRENCE JOSEPH	D. SEPTEMBER 15, 1978, NEW ORLEANS, LA.
1984-006	BETTENDORF, JEFFREY ALLEN	10349 SE NICOLE LOOP, HAPPY VALLEY OR 97086
1920-005	BETTS, WALTER MCKINLEY 'HUCK'	D. JUNE 13, 1987, MILLSBORO, DEL.
1971-011	BEVACQUA, KURT ANTHONY	7679 SITIO MANANA, CARLSBAD CA 92009
1952-007	BEVAN, HAROLD JOSEPH	D. OCTOBER 5, 1968, NEW ORLEANS, LA.
1944-008	BEVENS, FLOYD CLIFFORD 'BILL'	D. OCTOBER 26, 1991, SALEM, ORE.
2002-012	BEVERLIN, JASON ROBERT	83 OCTOBER SCENIC ROAD, WAYNESVILLE NC 28785
1996-017	BEVIL, BRIAN SCOTT	12655 KUYKENDAHL ROAD #7108, HOUSTON TX 77090
1942-007	BEVIL, LOUIS EUGENE	D. FEBRUARY 1, 1973, DIXON, ILL.
1995-027	BEVINGTON, TERRY PAUL	2600 HALLE PKWY, COLLIERVILLE TN 38017
1982-012	BIANCALANA, ROLAND AMERICO 'BUDDY'	304 EAST LOWE AVENUE, FAIRFIELD IA 52556
1975-017	BIANCO, THOMAS ANTHONY	12 KNOLLTOP DRIVE, NESCONSET NY 11767
1949-005	BIASATTI, HENRY ARCADO	D. APRIL 20, 1996, DEARBORN, MICH.
1972-008	BIBBY, JAMES BLAIR	1826 SOUTH COOLWELL ROAD, MADISON HEIGHTS VA 24572
1988-012	BICHETTE, ALPHONSE DANTE 'DANTE'	1830 GIPSON GREEN LANE, WINTER PARK FL 32789
1948-013	BICKFORD, VERNON EDGELL	D. MAY 8, 1960, RICHMOND, VA.
1948-014	BICKNELL, CHARLES STEPHEN	109 CREEKSIDE LANE, CHAPEL HILL TN 37034
2000-014	BIDDLE, LEE FRANCIS 'ROCKY'	2031 EAST RANCHO CULEBRA DRIVE, COVINA CA 91724
1984-007	BIELECKI, MICHAEL JOSEPH	1505 HABERSHAM PLACE, CROWNSVILLE MD 21032
1920-006	BIEMILLER, HARRY LEE	D. MAY 25, 1965, ORLANDO, FLA.
2001-022	BIERBRODT, NICHOLAS RAYMOND	390 PINELLAS BAYWAY SOUTH #C, SAINT PETERSBURG FL 33715
1997-011	BIESER, STEVEN RAY	11770 ROYAL OAK COURT, SAINTE GENEVIEVE MO 63670
1920-007	BIGBEE, LYLE RANDOLPH	D. AUGUST 5, 1942, PORTLAND, ORE.
2001-023	BIGBIE, LARRY R.	2250 EAST 61ST AVENUE, HOBART IN 46342
1929-008	BIGELOW, ELLIOT ALLARDICE	D. AUGUST 13, 1933, TAMPA, FLA.
1988-013	BIGGIO, CRAIG ALAN	6520 BELMONT STREET, HOUSTON TX 77005
1932-004	BIGGS, CHARLES ORVAL	D. MAY 24, 1954, FRENCH LICK, IND.
1970-009	BIITTNER, LARRY DAVID	915 3RD AVENUE NW, POCAHONTAS IA 50574
1983-012	BILARDELLO, DANN JAMES	560 ALEXANDRA AVENUE SW, VERO BEACH FL 32968
1949-006	BILBREY, JAMES MELVIN	D. DECEMBER 26, 1985, TOLEDO, OHIO
1937-009	BILDILLI, EMIL	D. SEPTEMBER 16, 1946, HARTFORD CITY, IND.
1949-007	BILKO, STEPHEN THOMAS	D. MARCH 7, 1978, WILKES-BARRE, PA.
1968-005	BILLINGHAM, JOHN EUGENE 'JACK'	625 FAULKNER STREET, NEW SMYRNA FL 32168
1927-012	BILLINGS, HASKELL CLARK	D. DECEMBER 26, 1983, GREENBRAE, CALIF.
1968-006	BILLINGS, RICHARD ARLIN	1917 CREEKWOOD DR, ARLINGTON TX 76010
1999-018	BILLINGSLEY, BRETT AARON	16112 MEDLAR LANE, CHINO HILLS CA 91709
2006-015	BILLINGSLEY, CHAD RYAN	1085 OAKDALE LANE, LEMOORE CA 93245
1944-009	BINKS, GEORGE EUGENE	4803 BELMONT ROAD, DOWNERS GROVE IL 60515
1944-010	BIRAS, STEPHEN ALEXANDER	D. APRIL 21, 1965, ST. LOUIS, MO.
1973-012	BIRD, JAMES DOUGLAS 'DOUG'	11821 LADY ANNE CIRCLE, CAPE CORAL FL 33991
1921-005	BIRD, JAMES EDWARD 'RED'	D. MARCH 23, 1972, MURFREESBORO, ARK.
1986-016	BIRKBECK, MICHAEL LAURENCE	1705 WEST HILL DRIVE, ORRVILLE OH 44667
2006-016	BIRKINS, KURT DANIEL	24106 VANOWEN STREET, WEST HILLS CA 91307
1933-004	BIRKOFER, RALPH JOSEPH	D. MARCH 16, 1971, CINCINNATI, OHIO
1955-012	BIRRER, WERNER JOSEPH 'BABE'	8455 CLARENCE CENTER ROAD, CLARENCE CENTER NY 14032
1985-004	BIRTSAS, TIMOTHY DEAN	43 ROBERTSON COURT, CLARKSTON MI 48346
1942-008	BISCAN, FRANK STEPHEN	D. MAY 22, 1959, ST. LOUIS, MO.
1925-009	BISCHOFF, JOHN GEORGE 'GEORGE'	D. DECEMBER 28, 1981, GRANITE CITY, ILL.

1952-008	BISHOP, CHARLES TULLER	D. JULY 5, 1993, LAWRENCEVILLE, GA.
1923-014	BISHOP, JAMES MORTON	D. SEPTEMBER 20, 1973, MEXICO, MO.
1924-010	BISHOP, MAX FREDERICK	D. FEBRUARY 4, 1962, WAYNESBORO, PA.
1983-013	BISHOP, MICHAEL DAVID	3119 HAMPTON DRIVE, SANTA MARIA CA 93455
1921-006	BISHOP, WILLIAM HENRY	D. FEBRUARY 14, 1956, ST. JOSEPH, MO.
1928-008	BISSONETTE, DELPHIA LOUIS	D. JUNE 9, 1972, AUGUSTA, MAINE
1942-009	BITHORN, HIRAM GABRIEL	D. JANUARY 1, 1952, EL MANTE, MEXICO
1990-016	BITKER, JOSEPH ANTHONY	39 BLACKSTONE COURT, CHICO CA 95928
1986-017	BITTIGER, JEFFREY SCOTT	PO BOX 896, SAYLORSBURG PA 18353
1935-004	BIVIN, JAMES NATHANIEL	D. NOVEMBER 7, 1982, PUEBLO, COLO.
1983-014	BJORKMAN, GEORGE ANTON	3525 TEAKWOOD LANE, PLANO TX 75075
1943-009	BLACK, DONALD PAUL	D. APRIL 21, 1959, CUYAHOGA FALLS, OHIO
1981-010	BLACK, HARRY RALSTON 'BUD'	PO BOX 2133, RANCHO SANTA FE CA 92067
1924-011	BLACK, JOHN WILLIAM 'BILL'	D. JANUARY 14, 1968, PHILADELPHIA, PA.
1952-009	BLACK, JOSEPH	D. MAY 17, 2002, PHOENIX, ARIZ.
1952-010	BLACK, WILLIAM CARROLL	D. OCTOBER 2, 2005, ST. LOUIS, MO.
1962-013	BLACKABY, ETHAN ALLEN	2308 EAST ORANGEWOOD, PHOENIX AZ 85020
1948-015	BLACKBURN, JAMES RAY	D. OCTOBER 26, 1969, CINCINNATI, OHIO
1958-010	BLACKBURN, RONALD HAMILTON	D. APRIL 29, 1998, MORGANTON, N.C.
1928-009	BLACKERBY, GEORGE FRANKLIN	D. MARCH 30, 1987, WICHITA FALLS, TEXAS
2004-019	BLACKLEY, TRAVIS JARROD	OLD ADD: CHELIENHAM AUSTRALIA
1942-010	BLACKWELL, EWELL 'THE WHIP'	D. OCTOBER 29, 1996, HENDERSONVILLE, N.C.
1974-009	BLACKWELL, TIMOTHY P.	8854 WHITEPORT LANE, SAN DIEGO CA 92119
1922-007	BLADES, FRANCIS RAYMOND 'RAY'	D. MAY 18, 1979, LINCOLN, ILL.
1969-008	BLADT, RICHARD ALAN	525 MAPLE STREET, MOUNT ANGEL OR 97362
1925-010	BLAEHOLDER, GEORGE FRANKLIN	D. DECEMBER 29, 1947, GARDEN GROVE, CALIF.
1941-007	BLAEMIRE, RAE BERTRUM	D. DECEMBER 23, 1975, CHAMPAIGN, ILL.
1929-009	BLAIR, CLARENCE VICK	D. JULY 1, 1982, TEXARKANA, TEXAS
1974-010	BLAIR, DENNIS HERMAN	1706 AURORA DRIVE, RICHARDSON TX 75081
1942-011	BLAIR, LOUIS NATHAN	D. JUNE 7, 1996, MONROE, LA.
1964-007	BLAIR, PAUL L. D.	10829 SHERWOOD HILL ROAD, OWINGS MILLS MD 21117
1990-017	BLAIR, WILLIAM ALLEN 'WIILIE'	62 ELDER LANE, PIKEVILLE KY 41501
1951-002	BLAKE, EDWARD JAMES	208 WILLOW CREEK COURT, BELLEVILLE IL 62223
1920-008	BLAKE, JOHN FREDERICK 'HUCK'	D. OCTOBER 31, 1982, BECKLEY, W.VA.
1999-019	BLAKE, WILLIAM CASEY 'CASEY'	1801 COUNTRY CLUB ROAD, INDIANOLA IA 50125
1934-008	BLAKELY, LINCOLN HOWARD 'LINK'	D. SEPTEMBER 28, 1976, OAKLAND, CALIF.
2002-013	BLALOCK, HANK JOE	408 COUNTRY PLACE, COLLEYVILLE TX 76034
1955-013	BLANCHARD, JOHN EDWIN	230 CENTRAL AVENUE NORTH #306, WAYZATA MN 55391
1935-005	BLANCHE, PROSPER ALBERT 'AL'	D. APRIL 2, 1997, MELROSE, MASS.
2004-020	BLANCO, ANDRES ELOY	OLD ADD: MORON VENEZ
1972-009	BLANCO, DAMASO	OLD ADD: 659 CATAMARAN ST #2, FOSTER CITY CA
1965-010	BLANCO, GILBERT HENRY	18403 NORTH 16TH PLACE, PHOENIX AZ 85022
1997-012	BLANCO, HENRY RAMON	14450 WEST LEXINGTON AVENUE, GOODYEAR AZ 85338
1970-010	BLANCO, OSVALDO CARLOS	OLD ADD: DE LOZADA B1 E16, SAN JOSE DE AVILA, VENEZUELA
2005-015	BLANCO, TONY HEMIPHERE	OLD ADD: HAINA DOM REP
2003-011	BLAND, NATHAN GARRETT	OLD ADD: BIRMINGHAM AL 35201
2000-015	BLANK, CLARENCE MATTHEW 'MATT'	13706 KELLERTON LANE, CYPRESS TX 77429
1922-008	BLANKENSHIP, HOMER	D. JUNE 22, 1974, LONGVIEW, TEXAS
1988-014	BLANKENSHIP, KEVIN DEWAYNE	5014 REGENCY DRIVE, ROCKLIN CA 95677
1988-015	BLANKENSHIP, LANCE ROBERT	340 KIMBERWICKE COURT, ALAMO CA 94507
1922-009	BLANKENSHIP, THEODORE	D. JANUARY 14, 1945, ATOKA, OKLA.
1972-010	BLANKS, LARVELL	3825 EAST CARSON ROAD, PHOENIX AZ 85042
1934-009	BLANTON, DARRELL ELIJAH 'CY'	D. SEPTEMBER 13, 1945, NORMAN, OKLA.
2004-021	BLANTON, JOSEPH MATTHEW	3860 OTTER GAP ROAD, BOWLING GREEN KY 42101
1955-014	BLASINGAME, DONALD LEE	D. APRIL 13, 2005, FOUNTAIN HILLS, ARIZ.
1963-010	BLASINGAME, WADE ALLEN	5207 RIVERHILL RD NE, MARIETTA GA 30067
1964-008	BLASS, STEPHEN ROBERT	1756 QUIGG DRIVE, PITTSBURGH PA 15241
1971-012	BLATERIC, STEPHEN LAWRENCE	1662 SOUTH UTICA, DENVER CO 80219
1948-016	BLATNIK, JOHN LOUIS	D. JANUARY 21, 2004, LANSING, OHIO
1942-012	BLATTNER, ROBERT GARNETT 'BUDDY'	2335 MANOR GROVE DRIVE #2, CHESTERFIELD MO 63017
1987-010	BLAUSER, JEFFREY MICHAEL	OLD ADD: 3005 COMPTON COURT, ALPHARETTA GA 30202
1959-006	BLAYLOCK, GARY NELSON	BOX 241, MALDEN MO 63863
1950-009	BLAYLOCK, MARVIN EDWARD	D. OCTOBER 23, 1993, CONWAY, ARK.
1956-009	BLAYLOCK, ROBERT EDWARD	472933 EAST 1122 ROAD, MULDROW OK 74948
1996-018	BLAZIER, RONALD PATRICK	610 NORTH NINTH STREET, BELLWOOD PA 16617
1965-011	BLEFARY, CURTIS LEROY	D. JANUARY 28, 2001, POMPANO BEACH, CALIF.
1960-009	BLEMKER, RAYMOND 'BUDDY'	D. FEBRUARY 15, 1994, EVANSVILLE, IND.
1972-011	BLESSITT, ISAIAH 'IKE'	19712 ANGLIN, DETROIT MI 48234
1923-015	BLETHEN, CLARENCE WALDO	D. APRIL 11, 1973, FREDERICK, MD.
1942-013	BLOCK, SEYMOUR 'CY'	D. SEPTEMBER 22, 2004, MANHASSET, N.Y.
1985-005	BLOCKER, TERRY FENNELL	745 GUIDE POST LANE, STONE MOUNTAIN GA 30086
1969-009	BLOMBERG, RONALD MARK	11660 MOUNTAIN LAUREL DRIVE, ROSWELL GA 30075
1995-028	BLOMDAHL, BENJAMIN EARL	5370 NOTTINGHAM ROAD, RIVERSIDE CA 92506
1937-010	BLOODWORTH, JAMES HENRY	D. AUGUST 17, 2002, APALACHICOLA, FLA.
1963-011	BLOOMFIELD, CLYDE STALCUP 'BUD'	14250 STATE HWY 180, GULF SHORES AL 36542
2002-014	BLOOMQUIST, WILLIAM PAUL 'WILLIE'	9676 WEST OBERLIN WAY, PEORIA AZ 85383
1993-014	BLOSSER, GREGORY BRENT	PO BOX 50425, SARASOTA FL 34232
1924-012	BLOTT, JACK LEONARD	D. JUNE 11, 1964, ANN ARBOR, MICH.
1989-018	BLOWERS, MICHAEL ROY	22211 42ND AVENUE EAST, SPANAWAY WA 98387
1921-007	BLUE, LUZERNE ATWELL	D. JULY 28, 1958, ALEXANDRIA, VA.
1969-010	BLUE, VIDA	PO BOX 1449, PLEASANTON CA 94556
1922-010	BLUEGE, OSWALD LOUIS	D. OCTOBER 15, 1985, EDINA, MINN.
1932-005	BLUEGE, OTTO ADAM	D. JUNE 28, 1977, CHICAGO, ILL.
1999-020	BLUM, GEOFFREY EDWARD	9723 LAJOLLA DRIVE #C, ALTA LOMA CA 91701
1996-019	BLUMA, JAMES ANDREW 'JAIME'	15219 REEDS, OVERLAND PARK KS 66223
1922-011	BLUME, CLINTON WILLIS	D. JUNE 12, 1973, ISLIP, N.Y.

1970-011	BLYLEVEN, RIKALBERT BERT 'BERT'	PO BOX 2308, FORT MYERS FL 33902
1953-012	BLYZKA, MICHAEL JOHN	D. OCTOBER 13, 2004, CHEYENNE, WYO.
1960-010	BOAK, CHESTER ROBERT 'CHET'	D. NOVEMBER 28, 1983, EMPORIUM, PA.
1968-007	BOBB, MARK RANDALL 'RANDY'	D. JUNE 13, 1982, CARNELIAN BAY, CALIF.
2000-016	BOCACHICA, HIRAM COLON	PO BOX 364951, SAN JUAN PR 00936
1963-012	BOCCABELLA, JOHN DOMINIC	1035 LEA DR, SAN RAFAEL CA 94903
1933-005	BOCEK, MILTON FRANK	D. APRIL 29, 2007, BROOKFIELD, ILL.
1974-011	BOCHTE, BRUCE ANTON	3688 HASTINGS COURT, LAFAYETTE CA 94549
1995-029	BOCHTLER, DOUGLAS EUGENE	154 NARROW GATE ROAD, MARYVILLE TN 37801
1978-014	BOCHY, BRUCE DOUGLAS	16144 BRITTANY PARK LANE, POWAY CA 92064
1946-010	BOCKMAN, JOSEPH EDWARD 'EDDIE'	1400 MILBRAE AVENUE #2, MILLBRAE CA 94030
1986-018	BOCKUS, RANDY WALTER	560 HELENA DRIVE, TALLMADGE OH 44278
1980-009	BODDICKER, MICHAEL JAMES	11324 WEST 121ST STREET, OVERLAND PARK KS 66213
1967-005	BOEHMER, LEONARD JOSEPH	206 TOWNVIEW COURT, WENTZVILLE MO 63385
1995-030	BOEHRINGER, BRIAN EDWARD	10 SUNSET DRIVE, FENTON MO 63026
1932-006	BOERNER, LAWRENCE HYER	D. OCTOBER 16, 1969, STAUNTON, VA.
1985-006	BOEVER, JOSEPH MARTIN	13085 MORRIS ROAD #11112, ALPHARETTA GA 30004
1993-015	BOGAR, TIMOTHY PAUL	12343 NORTH 1200 EAST ROAD, PONTIAC IL 61764
1920-009	BOGART, JOHN RENZIE	D. DECEMBER 7, 1986, CLARENCE, N.Y.
1982-013	BOGENER, TERRY WAYNE	411 MCCABE, PALMYRA MO 63461
1928-010	BOGGS, RAYMOND JOSEPH	D. NOVEMBER 27, 1989, GRAND JUNCTION, COLO.
1976-017	BOGGS, THOMAS WINSTON	11401 PARKFIELD DRIVE, AUSTIN TX 78758
1982-014	BOGGS, WADE ANTHONY	6006 WINDHAM PLACE, TAMPA FL 33647
1968-008	BOGLE, WARREN FREDERICK	11605 SW 103RD AVE, MIAMI FL 33156
1990-018	BOHANON, BRIAN EDWARD	243 WEST THORN WAY, HOUSTON TX 77015
2006-017	BOHN, THOMAS JOSEPH T.J.	7090 QUARRY AVENUE NE, ELK RIVER MN 55345
1982-015	BOHNET, JOHN KELLY	224 PANORAMA DR, BENICIA CA 94510
1974-012	BOISCLAIR, BRUCE ARMAND	5532 JON DODSON DRIVE, AGOURA CA 91301
1978-015	BOITANO, DANNY JON	15400 WINCHESTER BLVD #43, LOS GATOS CA 95030
1951-003	BOKELMANN, RICHARD WERNER	629 NORTH BELMONT AVENUE, ARLINGTON HEIGHTS IL 60004
1933-006	BOKEN, ROBERT ANTHONY	D. OCTOBER 6, 1988, LAS VEGAS, NEV.
1936-010	BOKINA, JOSEPH	D. OCTOBER 25, 1991, CHATTANOOGA, TENN.
1934-010	BOLAND, EDWARD JOHN	D. FEBRUARY 5, 1993, CLEARWATER, FLA.
1926-007	BOLEN, STEWART O'NEAL	D. AUGUST 30, 1969, JACKSON, ALA.
1962-014	BOLES, CARL THEODORE	3618 PINE BAY DRIVE, TAMPA FL 33625
1996-020	BOLES, JOHN EGAN	7901 TIMBERLAKE DRIVE, WEST MELBOURNE FL 32904
1927-013	BOLEY, JOHN PETER 'JOE'	D. DECEMBER 30, 1962, MAHANOY CITY, PA.
1950-010	BOLGER, JAMES CYRIL	5524 SIDNEY ROAD, CINCINNATI OH 45238
1993-016	BOLICK, FRANK CHARLES	RURAL ROUTE 2 BOX 98E, PAICINES PA 17860
1961-009	BOLIN, BOBBY DONALD	PO BOX 1948, EASLEY SC 29641
1954-008	BOLLING, FRANK ELMORE	171 FENWICK RD, MOBILE AL 36608
1939-012	BOLLING, JOHN EDWARD 'JACK'	D. APRIL 13, 1998, PANAMA CITY, FLA.
1952-011	BOLLING, MILTON JOSEPH	4009 OLD SHELL ROAD #C14, MOBILE AL 36608
1965-012	BOLLO, GREGORY GENE	29970 BAYVIEW DRIVE, GROSSE ILE MI 48138
1950-011	BOLLWEG, DONALD RAYMOND	D. MAY 26, 1996, WHEATON, ILL.
1928-011	BOLTON, CECIL GLENFORD	D. AUGUST 25, 1993, JACKSON, MISS.
1993-017	BOLTON, RODNEY EARL	2195 OOLTEWAH RINGGOLD ROAD, OOLTEWAH TN 37363
1987-011	BOLTON, THOMAS EDWARD	2288 ROLLING HILLS DRIVE, NOLENSVILLE TN 37135
1931-008	BOLTON, WILLIAM CLIFTON 'CLIFF'	D. APRIL 21, 1979, LEXINGTON, N.C.
1978-016	BOMBACK, MARK VINCENT	2482 RIVERSIDE AVENUE, SOMERSET MA 02726
1960-011	BOND, WALTER FRANKLIN	D. SEPTEMBER 14, 1967, HOUSTON, TEXAS
2003-012	BONDERMAN, JEREMY ALLEN	3703 VERBENA COURT, PASCO WA 99301
1986-019	BONDS, BARRY LAMAR	OLD ADD: 235 WEST PLEASANT AVENUE, TULARE CA 93274
1968-009	BONDS, BOBBY LEE	D. AUGUST 23, 2003, SAN FRANCISCO, CALIF.
1991-017	BONES, RICARDO 'RICKY'	VILLA ROSA 2 A19, GUAYAMA PR 00654
1937-011	BONETTI, JULIO	D. JUNE 17, 1952, BELMONT, CALIF.
1927-014	BONEY, HENRY TATE	D. JUNE 12, 2002, LAKE WORTH, FLA.
2002-015	BONG, JUNG KEUN	OLD ADD: 3805 BROCKETT TRAIL, CLARKSTON GA 30021
1938-008	BONGIOVANNI, ANTHONY THOMAS 'NINO'	416 ROSEWOOD AVENUE, SAN JOSE CA 95117
1940-003	BONHAM, ERNEST EDWARD 'TINY'	D. SEPTEMBER 15, 1949, PITTSBURGH, PA.
1971-013	BONHAM, WILLIAM GORDON	2135 HOLLY LANE, SOLVANG CA 93463
1962-015	BONIKOWSKI, JOSEPH PETER	6701 OLD REID RD, CHARLOTTE NC 28210
1981-011	BONILLA, JUAN GUILLERMO	2902 ORCHIDCREST DRIVE, CRESTVIEW FL 32539
1986-020	BONILLA, ROBERTO MARTIN ANTONIO	390 ROUND HILL ROAD, GREENWICH CT 06831
1977-012	BONNELL, ROBERT BARRY 'BARRY'	2102 179TH COURT NE, REDMOND WA 98052
1980-010	BONNER, ROBERT AVERILL	923 FOXTAIL DRIVE, GRAIN VALLEY MO 64029
1944-011	BONNESS, WILLIAM JOHN	D. DECEMBER 3, 1977, CLEVELAND, OHIO
1920-010	BONO, ADLAI WENDELL 'GUS'	D. DECEMBER 3, 1948, DEARBORN, MICH.
2006-018	BONSER, BOOF	4510 67TH AVENUE, PINELLAS PARK FL 33781
1934-011	BONURA, HENRY JOHN 'ZEKE'	D. MARCH 9, 1987, NEW ORLEANS, LA.
2005-016	BOOKER, CHRISTOPHER SCOTT	OLD ADD: MONROEVILLE AL
1983-015	BOOKER, GREGORY SCOTT	1535 CHARLEIGH COURT, ELON COLLEGE NC 27244
1966-008	BOOKER, RICHARD LEE	BOX 59, BROOKNEAL VA 24528
1987-012	BOOKER, RODERICK STEWART	526 WEST ALTADENA DRIVE, ALTADENA CA 91001
1928-012	BOOL, ALBERT	D. SEPTEMBER 27, 1981, LINCOLN, NEB.
1997-013	BOONE, AARON JOHN	9701 EAST HAPPY VALLEY ROAD #5, SCOTTSDALE AZ 85255
1992-009	BOONE, BRET ROBERT	18305 CALLE STELLING, RANCHO SANTA FE CA 92091
1981-012	BOONE, DANIEL HUGH	320 MINNESOTA, EL CAJON CA 92020
1922-012	BOONE, ISAAC MORGAN 'IKE'	D. AUGUST 1, 1958, NORTHPORT, ALA.
1948-017	BOONE, RAYMOND OTIS	D. OCTOBER 17, 2004, SAN DIEGO, CALIF.
1972-012	BOONE, ROBERT RAYMOND	18571 VILLA DRIVE, VILLA PARK CA 92667
2003-013	BOOTCHECK, CHRISTOPHER BRANDON	1308 WEST DEER CREEK ROAD, PHOENIX AZ 85045
1996-021	BOOTY, JOSHUA GIBSON	65 PALATINE #132, IRVINE CA 92612
1962-016	BOOZER, JOHN MORGAN	D. JANUARY 24, 1986, LEXINGTON, S.C.
1992-010	BORBON, PEDRO FELIX	4303 SWEET CICELY COURT, HOUSTON TX 77059
1969-011	BORBON, PEDRO RODRIGUEZ	OLD ADD: URB LAS PALMAS, SANTO DOMINGO DOM REP

2002-016 BORCHARD, JOSEPH EDWARD............................791 LEMON DRIVE, CAMARILLO CA 93010
1934-012 BORDAGARAY, STANLEY GEORGE 'FRENCHY'....D. APRIL 13, 2000, VENTURA, CALIF.
1988-016 BORDERS, PATRICK LANCE..................................1135 SOUTH LAKESHORE BLVD, LAKE WALES FL 33853
1980-011 BORDI, RICHARD ALBERT 'RICH'........................1301 MICHELE COURT, ROHNERT PARK CA 94928
1990-019 BORDICK, MICHAEL TODD..................................1302 LOCUST AVENUE, BALTIMORE MD 21204
1980-012 BORDLEY, WILLIAM CLARKE..............................39 MOCCASIN LANE, PALOS VERDES PENINSULA CA 90274
1972-013 BORGMANN, GLENN DENNIS..............................16 LUNDY TER, BUTLER NJ 07405
1982-016 BORIS, PAUL STANLEY.......................................28 SUNNYSIDE LANE, HILLSBOROUGH NJ 08876
1964-009 BORK, FRANK BERNARD.....................................8488 DUNSINANNE LANE, DUBLIN OH 43017
1999-021 BORKOWSKI, DAVID RICHARD............................35308 MONZA COURT, STERLING HEIGHTS MI 48312
1950-012 BORKOWSKI, ROBERT VILARIAN.........................1031 GERHARD STREET, DAYTON OH 45404
1960-012 BORLAND, THOMAS BRUCE...............................624 CHEROKEE DR, STILLWATER OK 74074
1994-005 BORLAND, TOBY SHAWN.....................................8659 QUITMAN HWY, QUITMAN LA 71268
1944-012 BOROM, EDWARD JONES 'RED'..........................827 HIGHLAND OAKS, DALLAS TX 75232
1957-007 BOROS, STEPHEN..401 HERON POINT WAY, DELAND FL 32724
1995-031 BOROWSKI, JOSEPH THOMAS............................14672 EAST LARKSPUR DRIVE, SCOTTSDALE AZ 85259
1942-014 BOROWY, HENRY LUDWIG 'HANK '....................D. AUGUST 23, 2004, BRICK, N.J.
1966-009 BOSCH, DONALD JOHN.......................................PO BOX 25, FORT JONES CA 96032
1976-018 BOSETTI, RICHARD ALAN..................................1471 ARROYO MANOR DRIVE, REDDING CA 96003
1986-021 BOSIO, CHRISTOPHER LOUIS............................10425 AMBASSADOR DRIVE, RANCHO CORDOVA CA 95670
1990-020 BOSKIE, SHAWN KEALOHA...............................10220 NORTH 55TH STREET, SCOTTSDALE AZ 85253
1977-013 BOSLEY, THADDIS...19440 AMHERST COURT, CERRITOS CA 90703
1966-010 BOSMAN, RICHARD ALLAN................................3113 LANDMARK TRAIL, PALM HARBOR FL 34684
1928-013 BOSS, ELMER HARLEY.......................................D. MAY 15, 1964, NASHVILLE, TENN.
1945-004 BOSSER, MELVIN EDWARD.................................D. MARCH 26, 1986, CROSSVILLE, TENN.
1975-018 BOSTOCK, LYMAN WESLEY...............................D. SEPTEMBER 24, 1978, GARY, IND.
1984-008 BOSTON, DARYL LAMONT.................................3136 NORTHCHESTER PLACE, LITHONIA GA 30038
1964-010 BOSWELL, DAVID WILSON................................309 ROXBURY CT, JOPPA MD 21085
1967-006 BOSWELL, KENNETH GEORGE..........................PO BOX 1244, JOHNSON CITY TX 78636
1982-017 BOTELHO, DEREK WAYNE.................................1819 ORCHARD STREET, BURLINGTON IA 52601
1994-006 BOTTALICO, RICHARD PAUL 'RICKY'.................71 MURPHY DRIVE, ROCKY HILL CT 06067
1937-012 BOTTARINI, JOHN CHARLES.............................D. OCTOBER 8, 1976, SPRING, N.M.
1992-011 BOTTENFIELD, KENT DENNIS............................1142 NORTH KEYSTONE DRIVE #2028, JUPITER FL 33477
1979-010 BOTTING, RALPH WAYNE..................................7 SOMERSET, DOVE CANYON CA 92679
1922-013 BOTTOMLEY, JAMES LEROY.............................D. DECEMBER 11, 1959, SAINT LOUIS, MO.
2005-017 BOTTS, JASON CARL..OLD ADD: PASO ROBLES CA
1962-017 BOTZ, ROBERT ALLEN..14229 DESERT FIRE COURT, EL PASO TX 79928
1956-010 BOUCHEE, EDWARD FRANCIS...........................1621 EAST TREMAINE AVENUE, GILBERT AZ 85234
1991-018 BOUCHER, DENIS...644 36TH AVENUE #201 LACHINE QC, H8T 3M1 CANADA
1938-009 BOUDREAU, LOUIS...D. AUGUST 10, 2001, OLYMPIA FIELDS, ILL.
1961-010 BOULDIN, CARL EDWARD.................................53 WESLEY DRIVE, WILDER KY 41076
1996-022 BOURGEOIS, STEVEN JAMES...........................PO BOX 143, PAULINA LA 70763
1980-013 BOURJOS, CHRISTOPHER.................................10345 EAST DREYFUS AVENUE, SCOTTSDALE AZ 85260
2006-019 BOURN, MICHAEL RAY.......................................20718 BEIGEWOOD DRIVE, HUMBLE TX 77338
1992-012 BOURNIGAL, RAFAEL ANTONIO.........................630 CRESCENT HILLS DRIVE, LAKELAND FL 33813
1971-014 BOURQUE, PATRICK DANIEL.............................2350 NORTH AUGUSTA DRIVE, FLAGSTAFF AZ 86004
1962-018 BOUTON, JAMES ALAN..PO BOX 188, NORTH EDGEMONT MA 01252
1997-014 BOVEE, MICHAEL CRAIG...................................9088 SOUTH PELICAN WAY, LITTLETON CO 80126
1970-012 BOWA, LAWRENCE ROBERT 'LARRY'.................129 UPPER GULPH ROAD, RADNOR PA 19087
2003-014 BOWEN, ROBERT MCCLURE..............................OLD ADD: 14571 GRANDE CAY CIRCLE #3207, FORT MYERS FL 33908
1991-019 BOWEN, RYAN EUGENE......................................2806 MARYLAND AVENUE, DALLAS TX 75216
1977-014 BOWEN, SAMUEL THOMAS................................8219 VICTORY TRAIL, BRENTWOOD TN 37027
1963-013 BOWENS, SAMUEL EDWARD.............................D. MARCH 28, 2003, WILMINGTON, N.C.
1996-023 BOWERS, BRENT RAYMOND..............................19257 MANCHESTER DRIVE, MOKENA IL 60448
1949-008 BOWERS, GROVER BILL....................................D. SEPTEMBER 17, 1996, WYNNE, ARK.
1997-015 BOWERS, SHANE PATRICK...............................792 RANCHO SIMI DRIVE, COVINA CA 91724
1935-006 BOWERS, STEWART COLE 'DOC'......................D. DECEMBER 14, 2005, HAVERTOWN, PA.
1994-007 BOWIE, JAMES R..620 SUISUN STREET, SUISUN CITY CA 94585
1999-022 BOWIE, MICAH ANDREW...................................2039 MSLL TOWN DRIVE, NEW BRAUNFELS TX 78130
1931-009 BOWLER, GRANT TIERNEY...............................D. JUNE 25, 1968, DENVER, COLO.
2001-024 BOWLES, BRIAN CHRISTOPHER.......................2001 FLOURNOY ROAD, MANHATTAN BEACH CA 90266
1943-010 BOWLES, CHARLES JAMES..............................D. DECEMBER 23, 2003, HICKORY, N.C.
1922-014 BOWLES, EMMETT JEROME...............................D. SEPTEMBER 3, 1959, FLAGSTAFF, ARIZ.
1967-007 BOWLIN, LOIS WELDON 'HOSS'.........................BOX 1026, LIVINGSTON AL 35470
1976-019 BOWLING, STEPHEN SHADDON........................524 EAST 117TH, JENKS OK 74037
1920-011 BOWMAN, ELMER WILHELM.............................D. DECEMBER 17, 1985, LOS ANGELES, CALIF.
1961-011 BOWMAN, ERNEST FERRELL 'BUDDY'...............ROUTE 17, EAST SHORE APTS. #8, JOHNSON CITY TN 37601
1932-007 BOWMAN, JOSEPH EMIL....................................D. NOVEMBER 22, 1990, KANSAS CITY, MO.
1939-013 BOWMAN, ROBERT JAMES...............................D. SEPTEMBER 4, 1972, BLUEFIELD, W.VA.
1955-015 BOWMAN, ROBERT LEROY..............................702 WEST MOUNTAIN RIDGE ROAD, LAKE ALMANOR CA 96137
1949-009 BOWMAN, ROGER CLINTON.............................D. JULY 21, 1997, LOS ANGELES, CALIF.
1958-011 BOWSFIELD, EDWARD OLIVER 'TED'..................PO BOX 1492, NIPOMO CA 93444
2005-018 BOWYER, TRAVIS CARLTON..............................2483 CHARLEMONT ROAD, BIG ISLAND VA 24526
1982-018 BOYD, DENNIS RAY 'OIL CAN'............................1611 20TH STREET, MERIDIAN MS 39301
1969-012 BOYD, GARY LEE..15308 HAAS, GARDENA CA 90249
1999-023 BOYD, JASON PERNELL.....................................412 HILLSBORO AVENUE, EDWARDSVILLE IL 62025
1951-004 BOYD, ROBERT RICHARD.................................D. SEPTEMBER 7, 2004, WICHITA, KAN.
2005-019 BOYER, BLAINE THOMAS..................................105 LAKESHORE CIRCLE NE, MARIETTA GA 30067
1955-016 BOYER, CLETIS LEROY......................................2034 20TH AVENUE PKWY, INDIAN ROCK BEACH FL 33785
1949-010 BOYER, CLOYD VICTOR.....................................14528 COUNTRY ROAD 210, JASPER MO 64755
1955-017 BOYER, KENTON LLOYD....................................D. SEPTEMBER 7, 1982, ST. LOUIS, MO.
1978-017 BOYLAND, DORIAN SCOTT 'DOE'......................15570 SW CYNTHIA LANE, BEAVERTON OR 97007
1926-008 BOYLE, JAMES JOHN...D. DECEMBER 24, 1958, CINCINNATI, OHIO
1929-010 BOYLE, RALPH FRANCIS 'BUZZ'........................D. NOVEMBER 12, 1978, CINCINNATI, OHIO
1938-010 BOYLES, HARRY...D. JANUARY 7, 2005, MCALLEN, TEXAS
1996-024 BOZE, MARSHALL WAYNE.................................4 WILSON PLACE, PALM COAST FL 32164

1966-011	BRABENDER, EUGENE MATHEW	D. DECEMBER 27, 1996, MADISON, WISC.
1937-013	BRACK, GILBERT HERMAN 'GIB'	D. JANUARY 20, 1960, GREENVILLE, TEXAS
1964-011	BRADEY, DONALD EUGENE	330 COUNCIL BLUFF PKWY, MURFREESBORO TN 37127
1998-017	BRADFORD, CHADWICK LEE	3867 BILL DOWNING ROAD, RAYMOND MS 39154
1966-012	BRADFORD, CHARLES WILLIAM 'BUDDY'	6440 SPRING PARK AVE, LADERA HEIGHTS CA 90056
1943-011	BRADFORD, HENRY VICTOR 'VIC'	D. JUNE 10, 1994, PARIS, KY.
1977-015	BRADFORD, LARRY	D. SEPTEMBER 11, 1998, ATLANTA, GA.
1956-011	BRADFORD, WILLIAM	D. AUGUST 22, 2000, FAIRFIELD BAY, ALA.
1948-018	BRADLEY, FREDERICK LANGDON	4540 SOUTH LAYMAN AVENUE, PICO RIVERA CA 90660
1946-011	BRADLEY, GEORGE WASHINGTON	D. OCTOBER 19, 1982, LAWRENCEBURG, TENN.
1927-015	BRADLEY, HERBERT THEODORE	D. OCTOBER 16, 1959, CLAY CENTER, KAN.
1981-013	BRADLEY, MARK ALLEN	PO BOX 27, WATER VALLEY KY 42085
2000-017	BRADLEY, MILTON OBELLE	801 NORTH MARIA AVENUE, REDONDO BEACH CA 90277
1983-016	BRADLEY, PHILIP POOLE	6950 SEMINOLE COURT, COLUMBIA MO 65203
1998-018	BRADLEY, RYAN JAMES	3454 ALDER PLACE, CHINO HILLS CA 91709
1984-009	BRADLEY, SCOTT WILLIAM	43 CHICORY LANE, PENNINGTON NJ 08534
1983-017	BRADLEY, STEVEN BERT 'BERT'	6039 OLD STATE ROAD, MATTOON IL 61938
1969-013	BRADLEY, THOMAS WILLIAM	4104 WOODBERRY STREET, HYATTSVILLE MD 20782
1952-012	BRADSHAW, GEORGE THOMAS	D. NOVEMBER 4, 1994, HENDERSONVILLE, N.C.
1929-011	BRADSHAW, JOE SIAH	D. JANUARY 30, 1985, TAVARES, FLA.
1995-032	BRADSHAW, TERRY LEON	6605 SNOW GEESE LANE, PRINCE GEORGE VA 23875
1989-019	BRADY, BRIAN PHELAN	920 WEST 23RD STREET, ODESSA TX 79763
1920-012	BRADY, CLIFFORD FRANCIS	D. SEPTEMBER 25, 1974, BELLEVILLE, ILL.
1956-012	BRADY, JAMES JOSEPH	1072 MEADOW VIEW LANE, SAINT AUGUSTINE FL 32092
1946-012	BRADY, ROBERT JAY	D. APRIL 22, 1996, MANCHESTER, CONN.
1995-033	BRADY, STEPHEN DOUGLAS 'DOUG'	1494 VASEY LANE, JACKSONVILLE IL 62650
1940-004	BRAGAN, ROBERT RANDALL	5312 COLLINWOOD AVENUE, FORT WORTH TX 76107
1994-008	BRAGG, DARREN WILLIAM	14150 OLD COURSE DRIVE, ROSWELL GA 30075
1986-022	BRAGGS, GLENN ERICK	4827 AZUCENA ROAD, WOODLAND HILLS CA 91364
1928-014	BRAME, ERVIN BECKHAM	D. NOVEMBER 22, 1949, HOPKINSVILLE, KY.
1935-007	BRAMHALL, ARTHUR WASHINGTON	D. SEPTEMBER 4, 1985, MADISON, WISC.
1944-013	BRANCA, RALPH THEODORE JOSEPH	WESTCHESTER COUNTRY CLUB, RYE NY 10580
1939-014	BRANCATO, ALBERT	108 GREEN VALLEY ROAD, UPPER DARBY PA 19082
1962-019	BRANCH, HARVEY ALFRED	4995 JOLLY DR, MEMPHIS TN 38101
1941-008	BRANCH, NORMAN DOWNS	D. NOVEMBER 21, 1971, NAVASOTA, TEXAS
1979-011	BRANCH, ROY	5322 TERRY AVENUE, SAINT LOUIS MO 63120
1963-014	BRAND, RONALD GEORGE	4421 STATE ISLAND DRIVE, PLANO TX 75024
1995-034	BRANDENBURG, MARK CLAY	C/O D. BRANDENBURG, 9801 CANTERTROT, HUMBLE TX 77338
1966-013	BRANDON, DARRELL	12 SOUTHCLIFF DRIVE, PLYMOUTH MA 02360
1928-015	BRANDT, EDWARD ARTHUR	D. NOVEMBER 1, 1944, SPOKANE, WASH.
1956-013	BRANDT, JOHN GEORGE	5 RABBIT TRAIL, WILDWOOD FL 34785
1941-009	BRANDT, WILLIAM GEORGE	D. MAY 16, 1968, FORT WAYNE, IND.
1928-016	BRANNAN, OTIS OWEN	D. JUNE 6, 1967, LITTLE ROCK, ARK.
1927-016	BRANOM, EDGAR DUDLEY 'DUD'	D. FEBRUARY 4, 1980, SUN CITY, ARIZ.
1992-013	BRANSON, JEFFREY GLENN	10749 SPOKANE COURT, UNION KY 41091
1980-014	BRANT, MARSHALL LEE	604 SCOTLAND DRIVE, SANTA ROSA CA 95409
1991-020	BRANTLEY, CLIFFORD	90 GRANDVIEW AVENUE, STATEN ISLAND NY 10303
1988-017	BRANTLEY, JEFFREY HOKE	2 ST. CHARLES PLACE, CLINTON MS 39056
1986-023	BRANTLEY, MICHAEL CHARLES 'MICKEY'	3089 SOUTHWEST VENTURA STREET, PORT SAINT LUCIE FL 34953
1998-019	BRANYAN, RUSSELL OLES	13400 OSMUND ROAD, BURTON OH 44021
1921-008	BRATCHE, FREDERICK OSCAR	D. JANUARY 7, 1962, MASSILLON, OHIO
1924-013	BRATCHER, JOSEPH WARLICK	D. OCTOBER 13, 1977, FORT WORTH, TEXAS
1964-012	BRAUN, JOHN PAUL	4711 WESTERLY COURT, OCEANSIDE CA 92056
2006-020	BRAUN, RYAN ZACHARY	173 WEST MARANTA ROAD, MOORESVILLE NC 28117
1971-015	BRAUN, STEPHEN RUSSELL	30 HAWTHORNE AVENUE, TRENTON NJ 08638
1969-014	BRAVO, ANGEL ALFONSO	OLD ADD: CALLE CAMINO NUEVO #208, ARACAIBO, VENEZUELA
1921-009	BRAXTON, EDGAR GARLAND 'GARLAND'	D. FEBRUARY 25, 1966, NORFLOK, VA.
1941-010	BRAY, CLARENCE WILBUR 'BUSTER'	D. SEPTEMBER 4, 1982, EVANSVILLE, IND.
2006-021	BRAY, WILLIAM PAUL	411 SOUTH BENGE STREET, MCKINNEY TX 75069
2004-022	BRAZELL, CRAIG WALTER	6118 MARGO PLACE, MONTGOMERY AL 36117
2002-017	BRAZELTON, DEWON CORTEZ	107 SCENIC DRIVE, TULLAHOMA TN 37388
1921-010	BRAZILL, FRANK LEO	D. NOVEMBER 3, 1976, OAKLAND, CALIF.
1943-012	BRAZLE, ALPHA EUGENE	D. OCTOBER 24, 1973, GRAND JUNCTION , COLO.
2004-023	BRAZOBAN, YHENCY JOSE	OLD ADD: SANTO DOMINGO DOM REP
2000-018	BREA, LESLIE GUILLERMO	OLD ADD: 1949 EAST SALTSAGE DRIVE, PHOENIX AZ 85048
1983-018	BREAM, SIDNEY EUGENE	115 SABLE RUN, ZELIENOPE PA 16063
1969-015	BREAZEALE, JAMES LEO	790 COUNTY ROAD 297, BAY CITY TX 77414
1940-005	BRECHEEN, HARRY DAVID 'THE CAT'	D. JANUARY 17, 2004, ADA, OKLA.
1929-012	BRECKINRIDGE, WILLIAM ROBERTSON	D. AUGUST 23, 1958, TULSA, OKLA.
1996-025	BREDE, BRENT DAVID	1891 J ROCK ROAD, TRENTON IL 62293
1969-016	BREEDEN, DANNY RICHARD	5111 B AVENUE, LOXLEY AL 36551
1971-016	BREEDEN, HAROLD NOEL	665 MIDDLE ROAD SOUTH, LEESBURG GA 31763
1960-013	BREEDING, MARVIN EUGENE	D. DECEMBER 30, 2006, DECATUR, ALA.
1980-015	BREINING, FRED LAWRENCE	2120 TICONDEROGA DRIVE, SAN MATEO CA 94402
1937-014	BREMER, HERBERT FREDERICK	D. NOVEMBER 28, 1979, COLUMBUS, GA.
1981-014	BRENLY, ROBERT EARL	9726 EAST LAUREL LANE, SCOTTSDALE AZ 85260
1933-007	BRENNAN, JAMES DONALD 'DON'	D. APRIL 26, 1953, BOSTON, MASS.
1981-015	BRENNAN, THOMAS MARTIN	8204 MILLBANK DRIVE, ORLAND PARK IL 60462
1988-018	BRENNAN, WILLIAM RAYMOND	802 COTTAGE HILL DRIVE, MACON GA 31210
1965-013	BRENNEMAN, JAMES LEROY	D. MARCH 10, 1994, PEARL, MISS.
1932-008	BRENZEL, WILLIAM RICHARD	D. JUNE 12, 1979, OAKLAND, CALIF.
2005-020	BRESLOW, CRAIG ANDREW	26 FINCHWOOD DRIVE, TRUMBULL CT 06611
1956-014	BRESSOUD, EDWARD FRANCIS	515 MARBLE CANYON LANE, SAN RAMON CA 94583
1973-013	BRETT, GEORGE HOWARD	6512 GRANADA DRIVE, PRAIRIE VILLAGE KS 66208
1924-014	BRETT, HERBERT JAMES	D. NOVEMBER 25, 1974, ST PETERSBURG, FLA.
1967-008	BRETT, KENNETH ALLEN	D. NOVEMBER 18, 2003, SPOKANE, WASH.

1939-015	BREUER, MARVIN HOWARD	D. JANUARY 17, 1991, ROLLA, MO.
1984-010	BREWER, ANTHONY BRUCE	9911 MURRAY LANDING, MISSOURI CITY TX 77459
1944-014	BREWER, JACK HERNDON	D. NOVEMBER 30, 2003, SUN CITY, CALIF.
1960-014	BREWER, JAMES THOMAS	D. NOVEMBER 16, 1987, TYLER, TEXAS
1986-024	BREWER, MICHAEL QUINN	40 ARMHURST, MENLO PARK CA 94025
1990-021	BREWER, RODNEY LEE	OLD ADD: 1201 LAVANHAM COURT, APOPKA FL 32712
1954-009	BREWER, THOMAS AUSTIN	409 STATE RD, CHERAW SC 29520
1993-018	BREWER, WILLIAM ROBERT 'BILLY'	7405 WOODWAY DRIVE, WACO TX 76712
1995-035	BREWINGTON, JAMIE CHANCELLOR	2490 EAST STEPHENS PLACE, CHANDLER AZ 85225
1943-013	BREWSTER, CHARLES LAWRENCE	D. OCTOBER 1, 2000, ALMA, GA.
1961-012	BRICE, ALAN HEALEY	6726 71ST STREET EAST, BRADENTON FL 34203
1958-012	BRICKELL, FRITZ DARRELL	D. OCTOBER 15, 1965, WICHITA, KAN.
1926-009	BRICKELL, GEORGE FREDERICK 'FRED'	D. APRIL 8, 1961, WICHITA, KAN.
1952-013	BRICKNER, RALPH HAROLD	D. MAY 9, 1994, BRIDGETOWN, OHIO
1951-005	BRIDEWESER, JAMES EHRENFELD	D. AUGUST 25, 1989, EL TORO, CALIF.
1951-006	BRIDGES, EVERETT LAMAR 'ROCKY'	2927 JULIA STREET #59, COEUR D'ALENE ID 83814
1959-007	BRIDGES, MARSHALL	D. SEPTEMBER 3, 1990, JACKSON, MISS.
1930-005	BRIDGES, THOMAS JEFFERSON DAVIS	D. APRIL 19, 1968, NASHVILLE, TENN.
1975-019	BRIGGS, DANIEL LEE	231 FRANCE ST, SONOMA CA 95476
1964-013	BRIGGS, JOHN EDWARD	238 WALL AVENUE, PATERSON NJ 07504
1956-015	BRIGGS, JOHN TIFT	PO BOX 4025, CAMP CONNELL CA 95223
1958-013	BRIGHT, HARRY JAMES	D. MARCH 13, 2000, SACRAMENTO, CALIF.
1965-014	BRILES, NELSON KELLEY	D. FEBRUARY 13, 2005, ORLANDO, FLA.
1988-019	BRILEY, GREGORY	2170 SUNNYBROOK ROAD, GREENVILLE NC 27834
1922-015	BRILLHEART, JAMES BENSON	D. SEPTEMBER 2, 1972, RADFORD, VA.
1992-014	BRINK, BRADFORD ALBERT	2628 SURREY AVENUE, MODESTO CA 95355
1969-017	BRINKMAN, CHARLES ERNEST	11849 WILLIAMS COUNTY ROAD, BRYAN OH 43506
1961-013	BRINKMAN, EDWIN ALBERT	4510 CLEARWATER PLACE #7, CINCINNATI OH 45248
1952-014	BRINKOPF, LEON CLARENCE	D. JULY 2, 1998, CAPE GIRARDEAU, MO.
1991-021	BRISCOE, JOHN ERIC	6815 CASA LOMA AVENUE, DALLAS TX 75214
1947-013	BRISSIE, LELAND VICTOR 'LOU'	1908 WHITEPINE DRIVE, NORTH AUGUSTA SC 29841
1966-014	BRISTOL, JAMES DAVID 'DAVE'	1748 FAIRVIEW ROAD, ANDREWS NC 28901
1992-015	BRITO, BERNARDO (PEREZ)	B #90 SABANA PALENQUE, DOM REP
2005-021	BRITO, EUDE EZEQUIEL	OLD ADD: SABANA DE LA MAR DOM REP
1995-036	BRITO, JORGE MICHAEL	C/O TOMAS BRITO 308 MART ST SW, DECATUR AL 35601
2002-018	BRITO, JUAN RAMON	OLD ADD: SANTIAGO DOM REP
1996-026	BRITO, TILSON MANUEL	OLD ADD: 6809 FISHERS FARM LANE, CHARLOTTE NC 28277
1937-015	BRITTAIN, AUGUST SCHUSTER 'GUS'	D. FEBRUARY 16, 1974, WILMINGTON, N.C.
1950-013	BRITTIN, JOHN ALBERT	D. JANUARY 5, 1994, SPRINGFIELD, ILL.
2006-022	BRITTON, CHRISTOPHER DANIEL	7481 NW ELEVENTH COURT, FORT LAUDERDALE FL 33313
1967-009	BRITTON, JAMES ALAN	825 FORESTWALK DRIVE, SUWANEE GA 30174
1979-012	BRIZZOLARA, ANTHONY JOHN	1638 PRINCESS CIR NE, ATLANTA GA 30345
1934-013	BROACA, JOHN JOSEPH	D. MAY 16, 1985, LAWRENCE, MASS.
1971-017	BROBERG, PETER SVEN	220 MONTEREY RD, PALM BEACH FL 33480
1992-016	BROCAIL, DOUGLAS KEITH	253 WEST HAHNS PEAK AVENUE, PUEBLO WEST CO 81007
1982-019	BROCK, GREGORY ALLEN	3727 VALLEY OAKS DRIVE, LOVELAND CO 80538
1961-014	BROCK, LOUIS CLARK	61 BARKLEY PLACE, SAINT CHARLES MO 63301
2000-019	BROCK, TARRIK JUMAAN	8111 FAIRCHILD AVENUE, WINNETKA CA 91306
1997-016	BROCK, TERRENCE CHRISTOPHER 'CHRIS'	7684 MARKHAM BEND PLACE, SANFORD FL 32771
1952-015	BRODOWSKI, RICHARD STANLEY	120 PINE STREET, MANCHESTER MA 01944
1959-008	BROGLIO, ERNEST GILBERT	2838 VIA CARMEN, SAN JOSE CA 95124
1992-017	BROGNA, RICO JOSEPH	110 WOODBURY ROAD, WATERTOWN CT 06795
1972-014	BROHAMER, JOHN ANTHONY 'JACK'	39017 NARCISSUS DRIVE, PALM DESERT CA 92211
2001-025	BROHAWN, MICHAEL TROY	1719 TAYLORS ISLAND, WOOLFORD MD 21677
1944-015	BRONDELL, KENNETH LEROY	D. OCTOBER 3, 2004, VAN NUYS, CALIF.
1993-019	BRONKEY, JACOB JEFFREY 'JEFF'	622 SUNNY BROOK DRIVE, EDMOND OK 73034
1959-009	BRONSTAD, JAMES WARREN	63 ONE MAIN PLACE, FORT WORTH TX 76126
1975-020	BROOKENS, EDWARD DWAIN 'IKE'	1053 BROOKENS ROAD, FAYETTEVILLE PA 17222
1979-013	BROOKENS, THOMAS DALE	488 BLACK GAP ROAD, FAYETTEVILLE PA 17222
2004-024	BROOKS, FRANK J.	115 BOULDER STREET, STATEN ISLAND NY 10312
1980-016	BROOKS, HUBERT	15001 OLIVE STREET, HESPERIA CA 92345
1993-020	BROOKS, JEROME EDWARD	12152 MOUNTAIN VIEW LANE, FRISCO TX 75035
1925-011	BROOKS, JONATHAN JOSEPH 'MANDY'	D. JUNE 17, 1962, KIRKWOOD, MO.
1969-018	BROOKS, ROBERT	D. OCTOBER 11, 1994, HARBOR CITY, CALIF.
1991-022	BROSIUS, SCOTT DAVID	3270 NW WESTSIDE ROAD, MCMINNVILLE OR 97128
1940-006	BROSKIE, SIGMUND THEODORE	D. MAY 17, 1975, CANTON, OHIO
1954-010	BROSNAN, JAMES PATRICK	7742 WEST CHURCHILL STREET, MORTON GROVE IL 60053
1991-023	BROSS, TERRANCE PAUL	7952 EAST CAMINO REAL, SCOTTSDALE AZ 85255
1969-019	BROSSEAU, FRANKLIN LEE	41 ISLAND ROAD, SAINT PAUL MN 55127
1980-017	BROUHARD, MARK STEVEN	6289 JACKIE AVE, WOODLAND HILLS CA 91367
2002-019	BROUSSARD, BENJAMIN ISAAC	4340 WESTRIDGE LANE #207, BEAUMONT TX 77706
1955-018	BROVIA, JOSEPH JOHN	D. AUGUST 15, 1994, SANTA CRUZ, CALIF.
1993-021	BROW, SCOTT JOHN	1194 WEST REMINGTON DRIVE, CHANDLER AZ 85248
1920-013	BROWER, FRANK WILLARD	D. NOVEMBER 20, 1960, BALTIMORE, MD.
1999-024	BROWER, JAMES ROBERT	4644 SOUTH LOCKWOOD RIDGE ROAD, SARASOTA FL 34231
1931-010	BROWER, LOUIS LESTER	D. MARCH 4, 1994, TYLER, TEXAS
1986-025	BROWER, ROBERT RICHARD	2703 NORTH VAN BUREN STREET, HUTCHINSON KS 67502
1997-017	BROWN, ADRIAN DEMOND	609 GARDEN CITY ROAD SW, ROXIE MS 39661
1951-007	BROWN, ALTON LEO	253 CONSUL AVENUE, VIRGINIA BEACH VA 23462
2006-023	BROWN, ANDREW AARON	1417 NE OLD MILL DRIVE, DELTONA FL 32725
1996-027	BROWN, BRANT MICHAEL	1612 FIELDSPRING DRIVE, BAKERSFIELD CA 93311
1928-017	BROWN, CLINTON HAROLD	D. DECEMBER 31, 1955, ROCKY RIVER, OHIO
1973-014	BROWN, CURTIS	3200 CLOUDVIEW DRIVE, SACRAMENTO CA 95833
1983-019	BROWN, CURTIS STEVEN	5130 NW 15TH STREET, POMPANO BEACH FL 33063
1981-016	BROWN, DARRELL WAYNE	OLD ADD: 5843 FIFTH AVENUE, LOS ANGELES CA 90043
1998-020	BROWN, DERMAL BRAM	2626 BALMORAL COURT, KISSIMMEE FL 34744

1920-014	BROWN, EDWARD WILLIAM	D. SEPTEMBER 10, 1956, VALLEJO, CALIF.
1969-020	BROWN, EDWIN RANDOLPH 'RANDY'	2317 NORTH DEPAUW AVENUE, ORLANDO FL 32804
1997-018	BROWN, EMIL QUINCY	12210 SOUTH STATE, CHICAGO IL 60629
1951-008	BROWN, HECTOR HAROLD 'HAL'	4216 HENDERSON ROAD, GREENSBORO NC 27410
1969-021	BROWN, ISAAC 'IKE'	D. MAY 17, 2001, MEMPHIS, TENN.
1970-013	BROWN, JACKIE GENE	7337 EAST 136 ROAD, HOLDENVILLE OK 74848
1986-026	BROWN, JAMES KEVIN 'KEVIN'	105 BROWNS RIDGE, MACON GA 31210
1937-016	BROWN, JAMES ROBERSON	D. DECEMBER 29, 1977, BATH, N.C.
2004-025	BROWN, JAMIE MONROE	7891 HWY 19 NORTH, COLLINSVILLE MS 39325
1991-024	BROWN, JARVIS ARDEL	1412 85TH STREET, KENOSHA WI 53143
1975-021	BROWN, JERALD RAY 'JAKE'	D. DECEMBER 18, 1981, HOUSTON, TEXAS
2006-024	BROWN, JEREMY SCOTT	OLD ADD: HUEYTOWN AL
1984-011	BROWN, JOHN CHRISTOPHER 'CHRIS'	D. DECEMBER 26, 2006, HOUSTON, TEXAS
1937-017	BROWN, JOHN LINDSAY	D. JANUARY 1, 1967, SAN ANTONIO, TEXAS
1968-010	BROWN, JOPHERY CLIFFORD	3008 WEST 81ST ST, INGLEWOOD CA 90305
1927-017	BROWN, JOSEPH HENRY	D. MARCH 7, 1950, LOS ANGELES, CALIF.
1988-020	BROWN, KEITH EDWARD	6313 WILLOW OAK DRIVE, NASHVILLE TN 37221
1990-022	BROWN, KEVIN DEWAYNE	OLD ADD: 8022 NORTHERN OAK CIRCLE, SACRAMENTO CA 95828
1996-028	BROWN, KEVIN LEE	4333 BELL ROAD #102, NEWBURGH IN 47630
1963-015	BROWN, LARRY LESLEY	13158 LAMIRADA CIRCLE, WEST PALM BEACH FL 33414
1976-020	BROWN, LEON	7537 SOUTH LAROSA, TEMPE AZ 85283
1925-012	BROWN, LLOYD ANDREW	D. JANUARY 14, 1974, OPALOCKA, FLA.
1935-008	BROWN, MACE STANLEY	D. MARCH 24, 2002, GREENSBORO, N.C.
1984-012	BROWN, MARK ANTHONY	108 NE FIRST TERRACE, BLUE SPRINGS MO 64014
1988-021	BROWN, MARTY LEO	4425 BENT TREE BLVD, SARASOTA FL 34241
1983-020	BROWN, MICHAEL CHARLES	OLD ADD: 312 COPCO LANE, SAN JOSE CA 95123
1982-020	BROWN, MICHAEL GARY	710 95TH AVENUE NORTH, NAPLES FL 34108
1922-016	BROWN, MYRL LINCOLN	D. FEBRUARY 23, 1981, HARRISBURG, PA.
1943-014	BROWN, NORMAN	D. MAY 31, 1995, BENNETTSVILLE, S.C.
1965-015	BROWN, OLLIE LEE	8462 COUNTRY CLUB DR, BUENA PARK CA 90621
1969-022	BROWN, OSCAR LEE	19113 GUNLOCK AVE, CARSON CA 90746
1961-015	BROWN, PAUL DWAYNE	3617 HWY 75, HOLDENVILLE OK 74848
1957-008	BROWN, RICHARD ERNEST	D. APRIL 12, 1970, BALTIMORE, MD.
1930-006	BROWN, ROBERT MURRAY	D. AUGUST 3, 1990, PEMBROKE, MASS.
1946-013	BROWN, ROBERT WILLIAM	4100 CLARK AVENUE, FORT WORTH TX 76107
1979-014	BROWN, ROGERS LEE 'BOBBY'	700 PLEASANT RIDGE COURT, CHESAPEAKE VA 23322
1999-025	BROWN, ROOSEVELT LAWAYNE	308 NEWIT VICK DRIVE, VICKSBURG MS 39183
1981-017	BROWN, SCOTT EDWARD	1238 ALTON PIERCE ROAD, DEQUINCY LA 70633
1983-021	BROWN, STEPHEN ELBERT	4428 OLD DAIRY DRIVE, ANTELOPE CA 95843
1978-018	BROWN, THOMAS DALE	17414 SHARPSBURG AVENUE, BATON ROUGE LA 70817
1944-016	BROWN, THOMAS MICHAEL	8119 SHADY PLACE, BRENTWOOD TN 37027
1963-016	BROWN, THOMAS WILLIAM	27981 NANTICOKE ROAD, SALISBURY MD 21801
1925-013	BROWN, WALTER GEORGE 'JUMBO'	D. OCTOBER 2, 1966, FREEPORT, N.Y.
1947-014	BROWN, WALTER IRVING	D. FEBRUARY 3, 1991, WESTFIELD, N.Y.
1947-015	BROWN, WILLARD JESSE	D. AUGUST 4, 1996, HOUSTON, TEXAS
1963-017	BROWN, WILLIAM JAMES 'GATES'	17206 SANTA BARBARA, DETROIT MI 48221
1965-016	BROWNE, BYRON ELLIS	9708 WEST RIVERSIDE AVENUE, TOLLESON AZ 85353
1935-009	BROWNE, EARL JAMES	D. JANUARY 12, 1993, WHITTIER, CALIF.
1986-027	BROWNE, JEROME AUSTIN	2A PRINCE STREET, CHRISTIANSTED VI 00820
1962-020	BROWNE, PRENTICE ALMONT 'PIDGE'	D. JUNE 3, 1997, HOUSTON, TEXAS
1960-015	BROWNING, CALVIN DUANE	111 BUCKNER DRIVE, RUIDOSO NM 88345
1984-013	BROWNING, THOMAS LEO	3094 FRIARS LANE, EDGEWOOD KY 41017
1998-021	BROWNSON, MARK PHILLIP	13992 ASTER AVENUE, WELLINGTON FL 33414
2005-022	BROXTON, JONATHAN ROY	1284 PORTER CARSWELL ROAD, WAYNESBORO GA 30830
1967-010	BRUBAKER, BRUCE ELLSWORTH	C/O CHAMPION FORD 140 SOUTHTOWN BLVD, OWENSBORO KY 42303
1932-009	BRUBAKER, WILBUR LEE 'BILL'	D. APRIL 2, 1978, LAGUNA HILLS, CALIF.
1959-010	BRUCE, ROBERT JAMES	25830 WHATA VIEW, SAN ANTONIO TX 78258
1961-016	BRUCKBAUER, FRED JOHN	7673 COLINIAL COURT, NAPLES FL 34112
1948-019	BRUCKER, EARLE FRANCIS	629 MUNDY TERRACE, EL CAJON CA 92020
1937-018	BRUCKER, EARLE FRANCIS, SR.	D. MAY 8, 1981, SAN DIEGO, CALIF.
1992-018	BRUETT, JOSEPH TIMOTHY 'J.T.'	ILLINOIS-CHICAGO BASEBALL 901 WEST ROOSEVELT ROAD, CHICAGO IL 60608
1921-011	BRUGGY, FRANK LEO	D. APRIL 5, 1959, ELIZABETH, N.J.
1978-019	BRUHERT, MICHAEL EDWIN	907 CENTER DRIVE, FRANKLIN SQUARE NY 11010
2001-026	BRUMBAUGH, CLIFFORD MICHAEL	PO BOX 303, NORTH EAST MD 21901
1992-019	BRUMFIELD, JACOB DARNELL	43275 TILLMAN DRIVE, HAMMOND LA 70403
1987-013	BRUMLEY, ANTHONY MICHAEL 'MIKE'	112 CORRAL DRIVE, KELLER TX 76248
1994-009	BRUMLEY, DUFF LECHAUN	230 CG EARNEST ROAD NW, CHARLESTON TN 37310
1964-014	BRUMLEY, TONY MIKE 'MIKE'	1020 WESTERN TRAIL, KELLER TX 76248
1981-018	BRUMMER, GLENN EDWARD	2243 SPRINGRAIN DRIVE, CLEARWATER FL 34623
1993-022	BRUMMETT, GREGORY SCOTT	605 WEST 10TH STREET, CONCORDIA KS 66901
1981-019	BRUNANSKY, THOMAS ANDREW	13411 SUMMIT CIRCLE, POWAY CA 92064
1949-011	BRUNER, JACK RAYMOND	D. JUNE 24, 2003, LINCOLN, NEB.
1939-016	BRUNER, WALTER ROY 'ROY'	D. NOVEMBER 30, 1986, ST. MATTHEWS, KY.
1956-016	BRUNET, GEORGE STUART	D. OCTOBER 25, 1991, POZA RICA, MEXICO
2000-020	BRUNETTE, JUSTIN THOMAS	11 ATHERTON, IRVINE CA 92620
2004-020	BRUNEY, BRIAN ANTHONY	13450 CHEROKEE TRAIL, NORTHPORT AL 35475
1976-021	BRUNO, THOMAS MICHAEL	316 FORT SULLY TRAIL, PIERRE SD 57501
1966-015	BRUNSBERG, ARLO ADOLPH	083 104TH LANE NW, COON RAPIDS MN 55433
1998-022	BRUNSON, WILLIAM DONALD 'WILL'	13992 ASTER AVENUE, WEST PALM BEACH FL 33414
2003-015	BRUNTLETT, ERIC KEVIN	3903 EAST 200 NORTH, LAFAYETTE IN 47905
1995-037	BRUSKE, JAMES SCOTT	5242 NORTH QUAIL RUN PLACE, PARADISE VALLEY AZ 85253
1977-016	BRUSSTAR, WARREN SCOTT	3320 REDWOOD RD, NAPA CA 94558
1953-013	BRUTON, WILLIAM HARON	D. DECEMBER 5, 1995, WILMINGTON, DEL.
1961-017	BRYAN, BILLY RONALD	3001 HICKORY LANE, OPELIKA AL 36801
1935-010	BRYANT, CLAIBORNE HENRY	D. APRIL 9, 1999, FORT LAUDERDALE, FLA.
1979-015	BRYANT, DEREK RUSSELL	OLD ADD: C-12 COOPERSTOWN, LEXINGTON KY 40508

1966-016	BRYANT, DONALD RAY	1844 SWISS OAKS STREET, JACKSONVILLE FL 32259
1985-007	BRYANT, RALPH WENDELL	367 SPRUILL BRIDGE ROAD, TEMPLE GA 30179
1967-011	BRYANT, RONALD RAYMOND	4050 GODLEY ROAD, LINCOLN CA 95648
1986-028	BRYDEN, THOMAS RAY 'T.R.'	1021 NINTH STREET, CLARKSTON WA 99403
1970-014	BRYE, STEPHEN ROBERT	2200 GOLDEN RAIN ROAD, WALNUT CREEK CA 94595
2005-023	BUBELA, JAIME L	14927 ROYAL BIRKDALE STREET, HOUSTON TX 77095
1922-017	BUBSER, HAROLD FREDERICK	D. JUNE 22, 1959, MELROSE PARK, ILL.
1948-020	BUCHA, JOHN GEORGE	D. APRIL 28, 1996, BETHLEHEM, PA.
2000-021	BUCHANAN, BRIAN JAMES	8600 EL MIRASOL COURT, FORT MYERS FL 33967
1985-008	BUCHANAN, ROBERT GORDON	2035 BEVER AVENUE SE, CEDAR RAPIDS IA 52403
1961-018	BUCHEK, GERALD PETER	349 PORT DRIVE #1, KIMBERLING CITY MO 65686
1934-014	BUCHER, JAMES QUINTER	D. OCTOBER 21, 2004, ELIZABETHTOWN, PA.
2006-025	BUCHHOLZ, TAYLOR	321 SOUTHCROFT ROAD, SPRINGFIELD PA 19064
2004-027	BUCK, JOHNATHAN R	OLD ADD: SALT LAKE CITY UT
1994-010	BUCKELS, GARY SCOTT	3510 EAST LONGRIDGE DRIVE, ORANGE CA 92867
1984-014	BUCKLEY, KEVIN JOHN	34 CALVIN ST, BRAINTREE MA 02184
1969-023	BUCKNER, WILLIAM JOSEPH	4405 EAST WILD HORSE LANE, BOISE ID 83712
1978-020	BUDASKA, MARK DAVID	15025 WEST BUTTONWOOD DRIVE, SUN CITY WEST AZ 85375
1998-023	BUDDIE, MICHAEL JOSEPH	157 SCOTTSDALE DRIVE, ADVANCE NC 27006
1956-017	BUDDIN, DONALD THOMAS	27 HARVEST COURT, GREENVILLE SC 29601
1946-014	BUDNICK, MICHAEL JOE	D. DECEMBER 2, 1999, SEATTLE, WASH.
2003-016	BUDZINSKI, MARK JOSEPH	4919 PACKARD ROAD, GLEN ALLEN VA 23060
1985-009	BUECHELE, STEVEN BERNARD	2600 ROYAL GLEN DRIVE, ARLINGTON TX 76012
2000-022	BUEHRLE, MARK A.	1837 PRESCOTT RIDGE, SAINT CHARLES MO 63303
1993-023	BUFORD, DAMON JACKSON	15412 VALLEY VISTA BLVD, SHERMAN OAKS CA 91403
1963-018	BUFORD, DONALD ALVIN	13331 BRANFORD STREET, PACOIMA CA 91331
1953-014	BUHL, ROBERT RAY	D. FEBRUARY 16, 2001, TITUSVILLE, FLA.
1987-014	BUHNER, JAY CAMPBELL	1420 NW GILMAN BLVD #2666, ISSAQUAH WA 98027
1987-015	BUICE, DEWAYNE ALLISON	PO BOX 5185, INCLINE VILLAGE NV 89450
1945-005	BUKER, CYRIL OWEN	108 CENTRAL AVENUE, GREENWOOD WI 54437
2002-020	BUKVICH, RYAN ADRIEN	1923 SPILLWAY ROAD, BRANDON MS 39047
2005-024	BULGER, JASON PATRICK	1898 HARBOUR OAKS DRIVE, SNELLVILLE GA 30078
1954-011	BULLARD, GEORGE DONALD	D. DECEMBER 23, 2002, LYNN, MASS.
1991-025	BULLETT, SCOTT DOUGLAS	218 VICKY BULLETT STREET, MARTINSBURG WV 25401
1977-017	BULLING, TERRY CHARLES 'BUD'	405 WEST WALNUT STREET, NEWPORT WA 99156
1992-020	BULLINGER, JAMES ERIC	2504 ELISE AVENUE, METAIRIE LA 70003
1998-024	BULLINGER, KIRK MATTHEW	3608 DAVID DRIVE, METAIRIE LA 70003
2005-025	BULLINGTON, BRYAN PAUL	OLD ADD: INDIANAPOLIS IN
1985-010	BULLOCK, ERIC JERALD	17503 HARWICK COURT, CARSON CA 90746
1936-011	BULLOCK, MALTON JOSEPH	D. JUNE 27, 1988, PASCAGOULA, MISS.
1972-015	BUMBRY, ALONZO BENJAMIN	28 TREMBLANT CT, LUTHERVILLE MD 21093
2003-017	BUMP, NATHAN LOUIS	274 CARAVELLE DRIVE, JUPITER FL 33458
1995-038	BUNCH, MELVIN LYNN	HORSELOOP LOOP ROUTE, TEXARKANA TX 75501
1963-019	BUNKER, WALLACE EDWARD	330 COOSAW WAY #38, RIDGELAND SC 29936
1955-019	BUNNING, JAMES PAUL DAVID	1717 DIXIE HIGHWAY #180, FORT WRIGHT KY 41011
1990-023	BURBA, DAVID ALLEN	378 NORTH SHORE LANE, GILBERT AZ 85233
1969-024	BURBACH, WILLIAM DAVID	147 SHENANDOAH DRIVE, JOHNSON CITY TN 37601
1955-020	BURBRINK, NELSON EDWARD	D. APRIL 12, 2001, LARGO, FLA.
1969-025	BURCHART, LARRY WAYNE	5310 EAST 94TH STREET, TULSA OK 74137
1962-021	BURDA, EDWARD ROBERT 'BOB'	4502 EAST CAROL AVENUE #14, MESA AZ 85253
1962-022	BURDETTE, FREDDIE THOMASON	1200 KINGSTON CT #G5, ALBANY GA 31707
1950-014	BURDETTE, SELVA LEWIS 'LOU'	D. FEBRUARY 6, 2007, WINTER GARDEN, FLA.
1949-012	BURGESS, FORREST HARRILL 'SMOKY'	D. SEPTEMBER 15, 1991, ASHEVILLE, N.C.
1954-012	BURGESS, THOMAS ROLAND	97 SUNRAY AVENUE LONDON ON, N6P 1C6 CANADA
1968-011	BURGMEIER, THOMAS HENRY	13118 WALMER, OVERLAND PARK KS 66209
1943-015	BURGO, WILLIAM ROSS	D. OCTOBER 19, 1988, MORGAN CITY, LA.
2005-026	BURGOS, AMBIORIX	OLD ADD: NAGUA DOM REP
1993-024	BURGOS, ENRIQUE	OLD ADD: CALLE QUINTA VISTA ALEGRE, ARRAJIAN, PANAMA CITY, PANAMA
1942-015	BURICH, WILLIAM MAX	1175 LAMOREE ROAD #62, SAN MARCOS CA 92069
1956-018	BURK, MACK EDWIN	5710 GLEN PINES, HOUSTON TX 77069
1936-012	BURKART, ELMER ROBERT	D. FEBRUARY 6, 1995, BALTIMORE, MD.
2004-028	BURKE, CHRISTOPHER ALLEN	15415 CRYSTAL SPRINGS WAY, LOUISVILLE KY 40245
1976-022	BURKE, GLENN LAWRENCE	D. MAY 30, 1995, OAKLAND, CALIF.
2001-027	BURKE, JAMES EUGENE	2204 EDNA AVENUE, ROSEBURG OR 97470
1996-029	BURKE, JOHN C.	3490 WESTBROOK LANE, LITTLETON CO 80129
1958-014	BURKE, LEO PATRICK	3395 TORREY PINES CIRCLE, RINER VA 24149
1923-016	BURKE, LESLIE KINGSTON	D. MAY 6, 1975, DANVERS, MASS.
1924-015	BURKE, PATRICK EDWARD	D. JULY 7, 1965, ST. LOUIS, MO.
1927-018	BURKE, ROBERT JAMES	D. FEBRUARY 8, 1971, JOLIET, ILL.
1977-018	BURKE, STEVEN MICHAEL	1812 AMBER LEAF WAY, LODI CA 95242
1985-011	BURKE, TIMOTHY PHILIP	5016 SOUTH NELSON STREET #D, LITTLETON CO 80127
1987-016	BURKETT, JOHN DAVID	104 CRANDON CIRCLE, BEAVER PA 15009
2000-023	BURKHART, MORGAN	105 TURTLE ROCK COURT, SAINT CHARLES MO 63304
1945-006	BURKHART, WILLIAM KENNETH 'KEN'	D. DECEMBER 29, 2004, KNOXVILLE, TENN.
1987-017	BURKS, ELLIS RENA	115 SOUTH LANE, CHAGRIN FALLS OH 44022
1974-013	BURLESON, RICHARD PAUL 'RICK'	241 EAST COUNTRY HILLS DRIVE, LAHABRA CA 90631
1999-026	BURNETT, ALLAN JAMES 'A.J.'	15208 JARRETTSVILLE PIKE, MONKTON MD 21111
1927-019	BURNETT, JOHN HENDERSON	D. AUGUST 12, 1959, TAMPA, FLA.
2004-029	BURNETT, SEAN RICHARD	14016 ASTER AVENUE, WELLINGTON FL 33414
1956-019	BURNETTE, WALLACE HARPER	D. FEBRUARY 12, 2003, DANVILLE, VA.
1993-025	BURNITZ, JEROMY NEAL	18520 OLD COACH DRIVE, POWAY CA 92064
1923-017	BURNS, DENNIS	D. MAY 21, 1969, TULSA, OKLA.
1930-007	BURNS, JOHN IRVING 'JACK'	D. APRIL 18, 1975, BOSTON, MASS.
1924-016	BURNS, JOSEPH FRANCIS	D. JANUARY 7, 1986, TRENTON, N.J.
1943-016	BURNS, JOSEPH JAMES	D. JUNE 24, 1974, BRYN MAWR, PA.
2005-027	BURNS, MICHAEL JOHN	1729 REDGATE CIRCLE, DIAMOND BAR CA 91765

1978-021 BURNS, ROBERT BRITT 'BRITT'....847 BLACK BIRD COURT, ROCKLEDGE FL 32955
1988-022 BURNS, TODD ERIC....PO BOX 111, PRINCETON AL 35766
1955-021 BURNSIDE, PETER WILLITS....1945 CHESTNUT, WILMETTE IL 60091
1978-022 BURNSIDE, SHELDON JOHN....7519 WYNFORD CIRCLE, MONTGOMERY AL 36117
1946-015 BURPO, GEORGE HARVIE....8981 EAST PALMS DRIVE, TUCSON AZ 85715
2000-024 BURRELL, PATRICK BRIAN....PO BOX 1770, BOULDER CREEK CA 95006
2006-026 BURRES, BRIAN JAMES....OLD ADD: 14820 SE WAY EAST AVENUE, CLACKAMAS OR 97015
1962-023 BURRIGHT, LARRY ALLEN....1239 EAST PALM DR, GLENDORA CA 91740
1973-015 BURRIS, BERTRAM RAY 'RAY'....2422 GRAVEL DRIVE, FORT WORTH TX 76118
1948-021 BURRIS, PAUL ROBERT....D. OCTOBER 3, 1999, CHARLOTTE, N.C.
1970-015 BURROUGHS, JEFFREY ALAN....6155 LAGUNA CT, LONG BEACH CA 90803
2002-021 BURROUGHS, SEAN PATRICK....935 ARMADA TERRACE, SAN DIEGO CA 92106
1943-017 BURROWS, JOHN....D. APRIL 27, 1987, COAL RUN, OHIO
1994-011 BURROWS, TERRY DALE....7019 BURGUNDY DRIVE, LAKE CHARLES LA 70605
1958-015 BURTON, ELLIS NARRINGTON....15621 BEACH BLVD #7, WESTMINSTER CA 92683
1975-022 BURTON, JIM SCOTT....PO BOX 240385, CHARLOTTE NC 28224
1950-015 BURTSCHY, EDWARD FRANK....D. MAY 2, 2004, CINCINNATI, OHIO
1985-012 BURTT, DENNIS ALLEN....135 WEST STADIUM DRIVE, STOCKTON CA 95204
1960-016 BURWELL, RICHARD MATTHEW....PO BOX 9486, SCOTTSDALE AZ 85252
1920-015 BURWELL, WILLIAM EDWIN....D. JUNE 11, 1973, ORMOND BEACH, FLA.
1950-016 BUSBY, JAMES FRANKLIN....D. JULY 8, 1996, AUGUSTA, GA.
1996-030 BUSBY, MICHAEL J....OLD ADD: WILMINGTON CA 90744
1941-011 BUSBY, PAUL MILLER....2011 35TH AVENUE, MERIDIAN MS 39301
1972-016 BUSBY, STEVEN LEE....2701 BRITTANY LANE, GRAPEVINE TX 76051
1943-018 BUSCH, EDGAR JOHN....D. JANUARY 17, 1987, SHILOH VALLEY TWP., ST. CLAIR CO., ILL.
1995-039 BUSCH, MICHAEL ANTHONY....PO BOX 273, ELDON IA 52554
1965-017 BUSCHHORN, DONALD LEE....17804 EAST 26TH ST, INDEPENDENCE MO 64057
2004-030 BUSH, DAVID T....518 DELANCY CIRCLE, DEVON PA 19333
1923-018 BUSH, GUY TERRELL....D. JULY 2, 1985, SHANNON, MISS.
1997-019 BUSH, HOMER GILES....3600 SHERIDEN AVENUE, BELLEVILLE IL 62226
1982-021 BUSH, ROBERT RANDALL 'RANDY'....NEW ORLEANS BASEBALL LAKEFRONT ARENA, NEW ORLEANS LA 70148
1927-020 BUSHEY, FRANCIS CLYDE....D. MARCH 18, 1972, TOPEKA, KAN.
1993-026 BUSHING, CHRISTOPHER SHAWN....12830 NW 21ST STREET, PEMBROKE PINES FL 33028
1926-010 BUSKEY, JOSEPH HENRY....D. APRIL 11, 1949, CUMBERLAND, MD.
1977-019 BUSKEY, MICHAEL T....117 CEDAR WOODS TRAIL, CANTON GA 30114
1973-016 BUSKEY, THOMAS WILLIAM....D. JUNE 7, 1998, HARRISBURG, PA.
1971-018 BUSSE, RAYMOND EDWARD....4265 LEMON STREET, COCOA FL 32926
1936-013 BUTCHER, ALBERT MAXWELL 'MAX'....D. SEPTEMBER 15, 1957, LOGAN, W.VA.
1980-018 BUTCHER, JOHN DANIEL....820 WOODRIDGE DRIVE SOUTH, CHASKA MN 55318
1992-021 BUTCHER, MICHAEL DANA....2585 CAMINO DEL RIO, BULLHEAD CITY AZ 86442
1980-019 BUTERA, SALVATORE PHILIP....324 TERSAS COURT, LAKE MARY FL 32746
1943-019 BUTKA, EDWARD LUKE....D. APRIL 21, 2005, PITTSBURGH, PA.
1940-007 BUTLAND, WILBURN RUE 'BILL'....D. SEPTEMBER 19, 1997, TERRE HAUTE, IND.
1998-025 BUTLER, ADAM CHRISTOPHER....OLD ADD: BURKE VA 22015
1981-020 BUTLER, BRETT MORGAN....4488 EAST THOMAS ROAD #2012, PHOENIX AZ 85018
1962-024 BUTLER, CECIL DEAN....5126 HICKORY GAP, DALLAS GA 30132
1933-008 BUTLER, CHARLES THOMAS....D. MAY 10, 1964, BRUNSWICK, GA.
1926-011 BUTLER, JOHN STEPHEN....D. APRIL 29, 1967, LONG BEACH, CALIF.
2001-028 BUTLER, JUSTIN BRENT 'BRENT'....10441 SCOTLAND FARMS ROAD, LAURINBURG NC 28352
1997-020 BUTLER, RICHARD DWIGHT....OLD ADD: TORONTO ONTARIO
1993-027 BUTLER, ROBERT FRANK JOHN 'ROB'....OLD ADD: 27 BARRINGTON AVE, TORONTO ONTARIO M4C 4Y6
1969-026 BUTLER, WILLIAM FRANKLIN....141 BUCKSKIN LANE, BERKELEY SPRINGS WV 25411
1962-025 BUTTERS, THOMAS ARDEN....4 TURNBERRY COURT, DURHAM NC 27712
1938-011 BUXTON, RALPH STANLEY....D. JANUARY 6, 1988, SAN LEANDRO, CALIF.
1945-007 BUZAS, JOSEPH JOHN....D. MARCH 19, 2003, SALT LAKE CITY, UTAH
1958-016 BUZHARDT, JOHN WILLIAM....37 BRINTON HITE ROAD, PROSPERITY SC 29127
1943-020 BYERLY, ELDRED WILLIAM 'BUD'....8611 SAPPINGTON ROAD, SAINT LOUIS MO 63126
1987-018 BYERS, RANDELL PARKER....15 LONGVIEW DRIVE, BRIDGETON NJ 08302
2005-028 BYNUM, FREDDIE LEE....2987 POPE FARM ROAD, STANTONSBURG NC 27883
2002-022 BYNUM, MICHAEL ALAN....4576 JUNCTION DRIVE, MIDDLEBURG FL 32068
1950-017 BYRD, HARRY GLADWIN....D. MAY 14, 1985, DARLINGTON, S.C.
1993-028 BYRD, JAMES EDWARD....511 WOODRIDGE DRIVE, LAWTON OK 73507
1977-020 BYRD, JEFFREY ALAN....39376 OPALOCKA ROAD, BOULEVARD CA 91905
2002-023 BYRD, MARLON JERRARD....3252 ALLEGHENY DRIVE, MARIETTA GA 30066
1995-040 BYRD, PAUL GREGORY 'GREG'....910 FOXHOLLOW RUN, ALPHARETTA GA 30004
1929-013 BYRD, SAMUEL DEWEY....D. MAY 11, 1981, MESA, ARIZ.
1998-026 BYRDAK, TIMOTHY CHRISTOPHER....16721 WEST SENECA DRIVE, LOCKPORT IL 60441
1929-014 BYRNE, GERALD WILFORD....D. AUGUST 11, 1955, LANSING, MICH.
1943-021 BYRNE, THOMAS JOSEPH....1108 FAIRWAY VILLAS DRIVE, WAKE FOREST NC 27587
2000-025 BYRNES, ERIC JAMES....17530 VENTURA BLVD #201, ENCINO CA 91316
1943-022 BYRNES, MILTON JOHN....D. FEBRUARY 1, 1979, ST. LOUIS, MO.
1980-020 BYSTROM, MARTIN EUGENE....PO BOX 89, GEIGERTOWN PA 19523

C

1944-017 CABALLERO, RALPH JOSEPH 'PUTSY'....1120 SHIRLEY DRIVE, METAIRIE LA 70001
1972-017 CABELL, ENOS MILTON....4103 FROST LAKE COURT, MISSOURI CITY TX 77459
2000-026 CABRERA, ALEXANDER ALBERTO....OLD ADD: EL TIGRE VENEZUELA
2004-031 CABRERA, DANIEL ALBERTO....OLD ADD: SAN PEDRO DE MACORIS DOM REP
2004-032 CABRERA, FERNANDO JOSE....OLD ADD: TOA BAJA PR
1989-020 CABRERA, FRANCISCO (PAULINO)....OLD ADD: 250 STADIUM PLAZA, SAINT LOUIS MO 63102
1998-027 CABRERA, JOLBERT ALEXIS....OLD ADD: CARTAGENA COLOMBIA
1997-021 CABRERA, JOSE ALBERTO....OLD ADD: SANTIAGO DOM REP
2003-018 CABRERA, JOSE MIGUEL (TORRES) 'MIGUEL'....OLD ADD: MARACAY VENEZ
2005-029 CABRERA, MELKY....OLD ADD: SANTO DOMINGO DOM REP

1997-022	CABRERA, ORLANDO LUIS	9248 SCARLETTE OAK AVENUE, FORT MYERS FL 33912
1977-021	CACEK, CRAIG THOMAS	909 6TH STREET #3, SANTA MONICA CA 90403
1995-041	CACERES, EDGAR FIDEL	2575 51ST STREET, SARASOTA FL 34234
1987-019	CADARET, GREGORY JAMES	22636 BRIDLEWOOD LANE, PALO CEDRO CA 96073
1937-019	CAFEGO, THOMAS	D. OCTOBER 29, 1961, DETROIT, MICH.
1956-020	CAFFIE, JOSEPH CLIFFORD	PO BOX 1932, WARREN OH 44482
1978-023	CAGE, WAYNE LEVELL	1305 DAVIS BLVE, RUSTON LA 71270
1968-012	CAIN, LESLIE	31 CUTTING COURT, RICHMOND CA 94804
2005-030	CAIN, MATTHEW T	OLD ADD: COLLIERVILLE TN
1932-010	CAIN, MERRITT PATRICK 'SUGAR'	D. APRIL 3, 1975, ATLANTA, GA.
1949-013	CAIN, ROBERT MAX	D. APRIL 8, 1997, CLEVELAND, OHIO
2000-027	CAIRNCROSS, CAMERON	OLD ADD: 1758 TREETOP TRAIL, AKRON OH 44313
1996-031	CAIRO, MIGUEL JESUS	513 REDWING AVENUE, BAKERSFIELD CA 93309
1934-015	CAITHAMER, GEORGE THEODORE	D. JUNE 1, 1954, CHICAGO, ILL.
1984-015	CALDERON, IVAN	D. DECEMBER 27, 2003, LOIZA, P.R.
1950-018	CALDERONE, SAMUEL FRANCIS	D. NOVEMBER 28, 2006, BEVERLY, N.J.
1928-018	CALDWELL, BRUCE	D. FEBRUARY 15, 1959, WEST HAVEN, CONN.
1925-014	CALDWELL, CHARLES WILLIAM	D. NOVEMBER 1, 1957, PRINCETON, N.J.
1928-019	CALDWELL, EARL WELTON	D. SEPTEMBER 15, 1981, MISSION, TEXAS
1971-019	CALDWELL, RALPH MICHAEL 'MIKE'	1645 BROOK RUN DR, RALEIGH NC 27614
2003-019	CALERO, ENRIQUE NOMAR 'KIKO'	18 DANSON DRIVE, SAINT PETERS MO 63376
1984-016	CALHOUN, JEFFREY WILTON	10002 SPRINGWOOD FOREST DRIVE, HOUSTON TX 77080
2004-033	CALI, CARMEN S	5751 COPPER LEAF LANE, NAPLES FL 34116
1941-012	CALIGIURI, FREDERICK JOHN	100 BAKER STREET, RIMERSBURG PA 16248
1922-018	CALLAGHAN, MARTIN FRANCIS	D. JUNE 24, 1975, NORWOOD, MASS.
1983-022	CALLAHAN, BENJAMIN FRANKLIN	1140 ASHFORD GREEN DRIVE, CONCORD NC 28027
1939-017	CALLAHAN, JOSEPH THOMAS	D. MAY 24, 1949, SOUTH BOSTON, MASS.
2006-027	CALLASPO, ALBERTO JOSE	OLD ADD: MARACAY ARAGUA VENEZ
1921-012	CALLAWAY, FRANK BURNETT	D. AUGUST 21, 1987, KNOXVILLE, TENN.
1999-027	CALLAWAY, MICHAEL CHRISTOPHER 'MICKEY'	1008 ISLAND PARK DRIVE, MEMPHIS TN 38103
1958-017	CALLISON, JOHN WESLEY	D. OCTOBER 12, 2006, ABINGTON, PA.
2003-020	CALLOWAY, RONALD ISIAH	PO BOX 13345, LAS CRUCES NM 88013
1963-020	CALMUS, RICHARD LEE	3823 SOUTH 28TH WEST AVENUE, TULSA OK 74107
1983-023	CALVERT, MARK	908 WEST WACO STREET, BROKEN ARROW OK 74011
1942-016	CALVERT, PAUL LEO EMILE	D. FEBRUARY 1, 1999, SHERBROOKE, QUE.
2005-031	CALZADO, NAPOLEON	OLD ADD: SANTO DOMINGO DOM REP
1980-021	CAMACHO, ERNIE CARLOS	746 ST. REGIS, SALINAS CA 93905
1970-016	CAMBRIA, FREDERICK DENNIS	12 IRIS CT, NORTHPORT NY 11768
1943-023	CAMELLI, HENRY RICHARD	D. JULY 14, 1996, WELLESLEY, MASS.
1995-042	CAMERON, MICHAEL TERRANCE	165 JACKSON LAKE ROAD, JACKSON GA 30233
1933-009	CAMILLI, ADOLF LOUIS 'DOLPH'	D. OCTOBER 21, 1997, SAN MATEO, CALIF.
1960-017	CAMILLI, DOUGLAS JOSEPH	4245 61ST AVENUE, VERO BEACH FL 32967
1969-027	CAMILLI, LOUIS STEVEN	1314 SIGMA CHI ROAD NE, ALBUQUERQUE NM 87106
1987-020	CAMINITI, KENNETH GENE	D. OCTOBER 10, 2004, BRONX, N.Y.
2000-028	CAMMACK, ERIC WADE	2136 WALKER LANE, NEDERLAND TX 77627
1976-023	CAMP, RICK LAMAR	OLD ADD: 1223 DEFOOR FERRY COURT, ATLANTA GA 30318
2004-034	CAMP, SHAWN ANTHONY	5415 LEEWAY COURT, FAIRFAX VA 22032
1948-022	CAMPANELLA, ROY	D. JUNE 26, 1993, WOODLAND HILLS, CALIF.
1964-015	CAMPANERIS, DAGOBERTO 'BERT'	9797 NORTH 105TH PLACE, SCOTTSDALE AZ 85258
1943-024	CAMPANIS, ALEXANDER SEBASTIAN	D. JUNE 21, 1998, FULLERTON, CALIF.
1966-017	CAMPANIS, JAMES ALEXANDER	17082 CASCADES AVE, YORBA LINDA CA 92686
1928-020	CAMPBELL, ARCHIBALD STEWART	D. DECEMBER 22, 1989, SPARKS, NEV.
1930-008	CAMPBELL, BRUCE DOUGLAS	D. JUNE 17, 1995, FORT MYERS BEACH, FLA.
1940-008	CAMPBELL, CLARENCE 'SOUP'	D. FEBRUARY 16, 2000, SPARTA, VA.
1977-022	CAMPBELL, DAVID ALLEN	878 AMIDON STREET, DELTONA FL 32725
1967-012	CAMPBELL, DAVID WILSON	726 DUNDEE DRIVE, POST FALLS ID 83854
1990-024	CAMPBELL, JAMES MARCUS	1671 SIXTH STREET, OROVILLE CA 95965
1962-026	CAMPBELL, JAMES ROBERT	1924 KNOLLWOOD LN, LOS ALTOS CA 94022
1970-017	CAMPBELL, JAMES ROBERT	209 WEST SEVEN PINES, LAMAR SC 29069
1933-010	CAMPBELL, JOHN MILLARD	D. APRIL 24, 1995, DAYTONA BEACH, FLA.
1967-013	CAMPBELL, JOSEPH EARL	330 LEGENDS COURT, BOWLING GREEN KY 42103
1991-026	CAMPBELL, KEVIN WADE	207 RIDOUT DRIVE, DES ARC AR 72040
1987-021	CAMPBELL, MICHAEL THOMAS	4500 36TH AVENUE SW #12, SEATTLE WA 98126
1941-013	CAMPBELL, PAUL MCLAUGHLIN	D. JUNE 22, 2006, CHARLOTTE, N.C.
2006-028	CAMPBELL, RICHARD BRETT	OLD ADD: DOUGLASVILLE GA
1964-016	CAMPBELL, RONALD THOMAS	1104 SWEETBRIAR AVENUE NW, CLEVELAND TN 37311
1933-011	CAMPBELL, WILLIAM GILTHORPE 'GILLY'	D. FEBRUARY 21, 1973, LOS ANGELES, CALIF.
1973-017	CAMPBELL, WILLIAM RICHARD	133 SOUTH HALE STREET, PALATINE IL 60067
1977-023	CAMPER, CARDELL	1611 WASHINGTON AVENUE, SAN JACINTO CA 92583
2005-032	CAMPILLO, JORGE HIDALGO	9644 WEST MARY ANN DRIVE, PEORIA AZ 85382
1969-028	CAMPISI, SALVATORE JOHN	644 77TH AVENUE, SAINT PETERSBURG BEACH FL 33706
1951-009	CAMPOS, FRANCISCO JOSE LOPEZ 'FRANK'	D. JANUARY 28, 2006, MIAMI, FLA.
1988-023	CAMPUSANO, SILVESTRE	C. GUZMAN #5 CASA 19,MANOGUAYABO SANTO DOMINGO, DOM REP
1989-021	CANALE, GEORGE ANTHONY	7333 OLD MILL ROAD, ROANOKE VA 24018
1993-029	CANATE, WILLIAM EMISAEL	OLD ADD: 963 MANZANITA AVE, PASADENA CA 91103
1999-028	CANCEL, ROBINSON CASTRO	OLD ADD: 2811 WEST LOOP 250 NORTH, MIDLAND TX 79705
1986-029	CANDAELE, CASEY TODD	251 BROAD STREET, SAN LUIS OBISPO CA 93405
1975-023	CANDELARIA, JOHN ROBERT	606 WINGSPREAD, PEACHTREE CITY GA 30269
1943-025	CANDINI, MILO CAIN	D. MARCH 17, 1998, MANTECA, CALIF.
1983-024	CANDIOTTI, THOMAS CAESER	6061 EAST JENAN DRIVE, SCOTTSDALE AZ 85254
1977-024	CANEIRA, JOHN CASCAES	18 SPRUCE ST, NAUGATUCK CT 06770
1985-013	CANGELOSI, JOHN ANTHONY	10914 CARIBOU LANE, ORLAND PARK IL 60467
1996-032	CANIZARO, JASON KYLE 'JAY'	19523 PINEY LAKE DRIVE, SPRING TX 77388
2006-029	CANNIZARO, ANDREW LEE	968 NANCY STREET, MANDEVILLE LA 70448
1960-018	CANNIZZARO, CHRISTOPHER JOHN	13597 GRAIN LANE, SAN DIEGO CA 92129
1977-025	CANNON, JOSEPH JEROME 'J.J.'	3017 CEDARWOOD VILLAGE, PENSACOLA FL 32514

1989-022	CANO, JOSELITO SORIANO	OLD ADD: VILA DOLORES 2DA #41, SAN PEDRO DE MACORIS DOM REP
2005-033	CANO, ROBINSON JOSE	OLD ADD: SAN PEDRO DE MACORIS DOM REP
1985-014	CANSECO, JOSE	9200 WEST SUNSET BLVD, WEST HOLLYWOOD CA 90069
1990-025	CANSECO, OSVALDO	OLD ADD: 2539 SOUTH BAYSHORE DRIVE, MIAMI FL 33133
1925-015	CANTRELL, DEWEY GUY 'GUY'	D. JANUARY 31, 1961, MCALESTER, OKLA.
2004-035	CANTU, JORGE LUIS	1006 MIRACLE LANE, MISSION TX 78572
1927-021	CANTWELL, BENJAMIN CALDWELL	D. DECEMBER 4, 1962, SALEM, MO.
1988-024	CAPEL, MICHAEL LEE	4911 BRIDGE CREEK LANE, KATY TX 77494
2004-036	CAPELLAN, JOSE FRANCISCO	OLD ADD: COTUI DOM REP
1976-024	CAPILLA, DOUGLAS EDMOND	PO BOX 54053, SAN JOSE CA 95154
2005-034	CAPPS, MATTHEW DICUS	OLD ADD: DOUGLASVILLE GA
1981-021	CAPPUZZELLO, GEORGE ANGELO	2024 STILLWOOD PLACE, WINDERMERE FL 34786
1971-020	CAPRA, LEE WILLIAM 'BUZZ'	2061 EAST PARKVIEW CIRCLE, HOFFMAN ESTATES IL 60169
1982-022	CAPRA, NICK LEE	300 TOWN PARK ROAD, NORMAN OK 73072
1944-018	CAPRI, PATRICK NICHOLAS	D. JUNE 14, 1989, NEW YORK, N.Y.
2003-021	CAPUANO, CHRISTOPHER FRANK	35 WOODBROOK TERRACE, WEST SPRINGFIELD MA 01089
1993-030	CARABALLO, RAMON SANCHEZ	OLD ADD: SANTO DOMINGO DOM REP
1930-009	CARAWAY, CECIL BRADFORD PATRICK 'PAT'	D. JUNE 9, 1974, EL PASO, TEXAS
1969-029	CARBO, BERNARDO	6352 WOODSIDE DRIVE SOUTH, THEODORE AL 36582
1946-016	CARDEN, JOHN BRUTON	D. FEBRUARY 8, 1949, MEXIA, TEXAS
1963-021	CARDENAL, JOSE DOMEC	118 BRIDGEWATER COURT, BRADENTON FL 34212
1960-019	CARDENAS, LEONARDO LAZARO 'CHICO'	5412 RAVENNA STREET, CINCINNATI OH 45227
1963-022	CARDINAL, CONRAD SETH 'RANDY'	3601 URANUS DRIVE, NORTH LAS VEGAS NV 89031
2000-029	CARDONA, JAVIER PETERSON	OLD ADD: DORADO PR
1943-026	CARDONI, ARMAND JOSEPH 'BEN'	D. APRIL 2, 1969, JESSUP, PA.
1957-009	CARDWELL, DONALD EUGENE	PO BOX 454, CLEMMONS NC 27012
1967-014	CAREW, RODNEY CLINE	1171 VIA SANTIAGO, CORONA CA 92882
1952-016	CAREY, ANDREW ARTHUR	575 PROMONTORY DRIVE WEST, LIDO ISLE CA 92663
1993-031	CAREY, PAUL STEPHEN	5334 OLIVE AVENUE, SARASOTA FL 34231
1935-011	CAREY, THOMAS FRANCIS ALOYSIUS	D. FEBRUARY 21, 1970, ROCHESTER, N.Y.
1932-011	CARLETON, JAMES OTTO 'TEX'	D. JANUARY 11, 1977, FORT WORTH, TEXAS
1941-014	CARLIN, JAMES ARTHUR	D. NOVEMBER 29, 2003, BIRMINGHAM, ALA.
1967-015	CARLOS, FRANCISCO MANUEL 'CISCO'	6027 NORTH 7TH STREET, PHOENIX AZ 85014
1948-023	CARLSEN, DONALD HERBERT	D. SEPTEMBER 22, 2002, DENVER, COLO.
1996-033	CARLSON, DAN SCOTT	3004 SW PHYLLIS DRIVE, GRESHAM OR 97080
1920-016	CARLSON, LEON ALTON	D. SEPTEMBER 15, 1961, JAMESTOWN, N.Y.
1965-018	CARLTON, STEVEN NORMAN	555 SOUTH CAMINO DEL EIO #B2, DURANGO CO 81302
1999-029	CARLYLE, EARL L. 'BUDDY'	1205 WEST 16TH AVENUE, BELLEVUE NE 68005
1927-022	CARLYLE, HIRAM CLEO 'CLEO'	D. NOVEMBER 12, 1967, LOS ANGELES, CALIF.
1925-016	CARLYLE, ROY EDWARD	D. NOVEMBER 22, 1956, NORCROSS, GA.
1983-025	CARMAN, DONALD WAYNE	555 MUREX DRIVE, NAPLES FL 34102
1959-011	CARMEL, LEON JAMES 'DUKE'	10 PHEASANT VALLEY DRIVE, CORAM NY 11727
2006-030	CARMONA, FAUSTO C.	OLD ADD: SANTO DOMINGO DOM REP
1995-043	CARMONA, RAFAEL	OLD ADD: COMERIO PR 00782
1941-015	CARNETT, EDWIN ELLIOTT	2639 RIDGEVIEW DRIVE, LEBANON MO 65536
2000-030	CARPENTER, CHARLES SIDNEY 'BUBBA'	4601 SADDLEBROOK AVENUE, SPRINGDALE AR 72762
1997-023	CARPENTER, CHRISTOPHER JOHN	2 DONNA LANE, RAYMOND NH 03077
1988-025	CARPENTER, CRIS HOWELL	1760 LAKEVIEW CIRCLE, GAINESVILLE GA 30501
1943-027	CARPENTER, LEWIS EMMETT	D. APRIL 25, 1979, MARIETTA, GA.
1940-009	CARPENTER, ROBERT LOUIS	D. OCTOBER 19, 2005, EVERGREEN PARK, ILL.
1965-019	CARPIN, FRANK DOMINIC	C/O CAROLYN TAYLOR PO BOX 18235, RICHMOND VA 23226
1990-026	CARR, CHARLES LEE GLENN	OLD ADD: 16607 REED STREET, FONTANA CA 92335
1995-044	CARRARA, GIOVANNI JIMINEZ	SANTA ROSA CAR. 3 CASA #1-52 BARQUISIMETO, VENEZUELA
2003-022	CARRASCO, DANIEL 'D.J.'	1891 WEST 45TH STREET, SAFFORD AZ 85546
1994-012	CARRASCO, HECTOR (PACHECO)	CLE L. VALERA #42 MIRAMAR SAN PEDRO DE MACORIS, DOM REP
1939-018	CARRASQUEL, ALEJANDRO ALEXANDER 'ALEX'	D. AUGUST 19, 1969, CARACAS, VENEZUELA
1950-019	CARRASQUEL, ALFONSO COLON 'CHICO'	D. MAY 26, 2005, CARACAS, VENEZ.
1991-027	CARRENO, AMALIO RAFAEL (ADRIAN)	CALLE LA PLAYA, EDO NUA CHACACHACARE,ESPARTA, VENEZUELA
1959-012	CARREON, CAMILO GARCIA	D. SEPTEMBER 2, 1987, TUCSON, ARIZ.
1987-022	CARREON, MARK STEVEN	1034 HUTSON CIRCLE, SUMMIT MS 39666
1991-028	CARRILLO, MATIAS GARCIA	COLONIA LAS VILLAS #95 GUAYMAS SONORA, MEXICO
1970-018	CARRITHERS, DONALD GEORGE	9367 SUNNY GLADE COURT, ELK GROVE CA 95624
1964-017	CARROLL, CLAY PALMER	3052 22ND STREET, SARASOTA FL 34234
1929-015	CARROLL, EDGAR FLEISCHER	D. OCTOBER 13, 1984, ROSSVILLE, MD.
2002-024	CARROLL, JAMEY BLAKE	2301 VOGEL ROAD, EVANSVILLE IN 47711
1925-017	CARROLL, OWEN THOMAS	D. JUNE 8, 1975, ORANGE, N.J.
1955-022	CARROLL, THOMAS EDWARD	304 SONNET COURT, PEACHTREE CITY GA 30269
1974-014	CARROLL, THOMAS MICHAEL	38572 PHEASANT HILL LANE, HAMILTON VA 20158
1934-016	CARSON, WALTER LLOYD 'KIT'	D. JUNE 21, 1983, LONG BEACH, CALIF.
1953-015	CARSWELL, FRANK WILLIS	D. OCTOBER 16, 1998, HOUSTON, TEXAS
1994-013	CARTER, ANDREW GODFREY	106 MONTGOMERY AVENUE, GLENSIDE PA 19038
1944-019	CARTER, ARNOLD LEE	D. APRIL 12, 1989, LOUISVILLE, KY.
1974-015	CARTER, GARY EDMUND	560 VILLAGE BLVD #260, WEST PALM BEACH FL 33409
1991-029	CARTER, JEFFREY ALLEN	4625 RIVER OVERLOOK DRIVE, VALRICO FL 33594
1926-012	CARTER, JOHN HOWARD 'HOWIE'	D. JULY 24, 1991, NEW YORK, N.Y.
1983-026	CARTER, JOSEPH CHRIS	OLD ADD: 12609 ALHAMBRA, LEAWOOD KS 66209
1999-030	CARTER, LANCE DAVID	306 74TH STREET COURT NW, BRADENTON FL 34209
1992-022	CARTER, LARRY GENE	4305 WILMETTE DRIVE, DENTON TX 76208
1925-018	CARTER, OTIS LEONARD 'BLACKIE'	D. SEPTEMBER 10, 1978, GREENVILLE, S.C.
1931-011	CARTER, SOLOMON MOBLEY	D. DECEMBER 23, 2006, EL DORADO, ARK.
1989-023	CARTER, STEVEN JEROME	13006 INNISBROOK DRIVE, BELTSVILLE MD 20705
1963-023	CARTY, RICARDO ADOLFO JACABO 'RICO'	5 ENS ENRIQUILLO SAN PEDRO DE MACORIS, DOM REP
1998-028	CARUSO, MICHAEL J	OLD ADD: CORAL SPRINGS FL 33077
2005-035	CARVAJAL, MARCOS JOSE	OLD ADD: BOLIVAR VENEZ
1985-015	CARY, CHARLES DOUGLAS	484 BAYSHORE DRIVE, MIRAMAR BEACH FL 32550
1947-016	CARY, SCOTT RUSSELL	926 BLOCK ROAD BOX 205, BRONSON MI 49028

1958-018	CASALE, JERRY JOSEPH	358 WASHINGTON AVENUE, BEACON NY 12508
1965-020	CASANOVA, ORTIZ PAULINO 'PAUL'	5040 WESLEYAN DRIVE, WOODSTOCK GA 30189
1996-034	CASANOVA, RAUL	820 NW 87TH AVENUE #313, MIAMI FL 33172
1934-017	CASCARELLA, JOSEPH THOMAS	D. MAY 22, 2002, BALTIMORE, MD.
1937-020	CASE, GEORGE WASHINGTON	D. JANUARY 23, 1989, TRENTON, N.J.
1935-012	CASEY, HUGH THOMAS	D. JULY 3, 1951, ATLANTA, GA.
1997-024	CASEY, SEAN THOMAS	271 TROTWOOD DRIVE, PITTSBURGH PA 15241
1969-030	CASH, DAVID	16308 BIRKDALE DRIVE, ODESSA FL 33556
2002-025	CASH, KEVIN FORREST	848 NICKAJACK ROAD, FRANKLIN NC 28734
1958-019	CASH, NORMAN DALTON	D. OCTOBER 12, 1986, BEAVER ISLAND, MICH.
1973-018	CASH, RONALD FOREST	5418 DEERBROOKE CREEK CIRCLE #4, TAMPA FL 33624
1990-027	CASIAN, LAWRENCE PAUL	1939 POPCORN STREET NW, SALEM OR 97304
2006-031	CASILLA, ALEXIS (LORA)	OLD ADD: SAN CRISTOBAL DOM REP
2000-031	CASIMIRO, CARLOS RAFAEL	OLD ADD: SAN PEDRO DE MACORIS DOM REP
1973-019	CASKEY, CRAIG DOUGLAS	17422 PALOMINO DRIVE, BOTHELL WA 98012
2002-026	CASSIDY, SCOTT ROBERT	4203 HUNTING CREEK DRIVE, CLAY NY 13041
1949-014	CASSINI, JACK DEMPSEY	2498 LEISURE WORLD, MESA AZ 85206
1993-032	CASTELLANO, PEDRO ORLANDO (ARRIETA)	PARCELA 63 #63-6, CABUDARE LARA, VENEZUELA
1934-018	CASTER, GEORGE JASPER	D. DECEMBER 18, 1955, LAKEWOOD, CALIF.
1942-017	CASTIGLIA, JAMES VINCENT	5301 WESTBARD CIRCLE #313, BETHESDA MD 20816
1947-017	CASTIGLIONE, PETER PAUL	1320 NE 26TH TERRACE, POMPANO BEACH FL 33062
1991-030	CASTILLA, VINICIO (SORIA) 'VINNY'	7680 POLO RIDGE DRIVE, LITTLETON CO 80128
1995-045	CASTILLO, ALBERTO TERRERO	513 NW BISCAYNE DRIVE, PORT SAINT LUCIE FL 34983
1978-024	CASTILLO, ANTHONY BELTRAN	6402 SILVERWOOD DRIVE, HUNTINGTON BEACH CA 92647
1988-026	CASTILLO, ANTONIO JOSE	EL MOLINO VIA SANARE QUIBOR LARA, VENEZUELA
1991-031	CASTILLO, BRAULIO ROBINSON MEDRANO	OLD ADD: CASTELLANO #259,LUPERON, ANTO DOMINGO DOM REP
1997-025	CASTILLO, CARLOS	OLD ADD: MIAMI FL 33101
1980-022	CASTILLO, ESTEBAN MANUEL 'MANNY'	COSTA RICA 112,ENS. OZAMA SANTO DOMINGO, DOM REP
1991-032	CASTILLO, FRANK ANTHONY	15560 NORTH FRANK L. WRIGHT BLVD, SCOTTSDALE AZ 85260
2004-037	CASTILLO, JOSE	OLD ADD: LAS MERCEDES VENEZ
1986-030	CASTILLO, JUAN	CALLE ELIA CAMARENA 100 SAN PEDRO DE MACORIS, DOM REP
1994-014	CASTILLO, JUAN FRANCISCO	AVE 4, QUINTA, SANTA ANA LA BOYERA CARACAS, VENEZUELA
1996-035	CASTILLO, LUIS ANTONIO DONATO	OLD ADD: SAN PEDRO DE MAC. DOM REP
1981-022	CASTILLO, MARTIN HORACE	2118 SE 14TH STREET, CAPE CORAL FL 33990
1982-023	CASTILLO, MONTE CARMELO 'CARMELO'	OLD ADD: 495 DEKALB AVENUE, BROOKLYN NY 11205
1977-026	CASTILLO, ROBERT ERNIE	2837 SIERRA ST, LOS ANGELES CA 90031
1979-016	CASTINO, JOHN ANTHONY	6290 BLUESTEM ROAD SOUTH, HAZEL MN 55340
1943-028	CASTINO, VINCENT CHARLES	D. MARCH 6, 1967, SACRAMENTO, CALIF.
1973-020	CASTLE, DONALD HARDY	560 COUNTRY CLUB DRIVE, SENATOBIA MS 38668
1934-019	CASTLEMAN, CLYDELL	D. MARCH 2, 1998, NASHVILLE, TENN.
1954-013	CASTLEMAN, FOSTER EPHRAIM	8250 GRAVES ROAD, CINCINNATI OH 45243
1923-019	CASTNER, PAUL HENRY	D. MARCH 3, 1986, ST. PAUL, MINN.
2004-038	CASTRO, ALFREDO RAMON 'RAMON'	OLD ADD: VALENCIA VENEZ
2005-036	CASTRO, BERNABEL 'BERNIE'	4121 58TH STREET, WOODSIDE NY 11377
2006-032	CASTRO, FABIO ENRIQUE	OLD ADD: MONTE CRISTI DOM REP
1995-046	CASTRO, JUAN C.	OLD ADD: LOS MOCHIS MEXICO
1999-031	CASTRO, RAMON ABRAHAM	OLD ADD: VEGA BAJA PR 00743
1974-016	CASTRO, WILLIAMS RADHAMES	5217 WEST HARVARD DRIVE, FRANKLIN WI 53132
1997-026	CATALANATTO, FRANK JOHN	OLD ADD: SMITHTOWN NY 11787
1964-018	CATER, DANNY ANDERSON	3268 CANDLEWOOD TRAIL, PLANO TX 75023
1997-027	CATHER, MICHAEL PETER	104 GRASSWOOD COURT, FOLSOM CA 95630
1942-018	CATHEY, HARDIN	D. JULY 27, 1997, NASHVILLE, TENN.
1983-027	CATO, JOHN KEEFE 'KEEFE'	98 MARYTON ROAD, WHITE PLAINS NY 10603
1979-017	CAUDILL, WILLIAM HOLLAND	11605 NE 41ST STREET, KIRKLAND WA 98033
1946-017	CAULFIELD, JOHN JOSEPH	D. DECEMBER 16, 1986, SAN FRANCISCO, CALIF.
1955-023	CAUSEY, JAMES WAYNE 'WAYNE'	2905 PAYNTER DR, RUSTON LA 71270
1934-020	CAVARRETTA, PHILIP JOSEPH	4037 KELLOGG DRIVE SW, LILBURN GA 30047
1922-019	CAVENEY, JAMES CHRISTOPHER 'IKE'	D. JULY 6, 1949, SAN FRANCISCO, CALIF.
1955-024	CECCARELLI, ARTHUR EDWARD	63 HALL DRIVE, ORANGE CT 06477
1988-027	CECENA, JOSE ISABEL	OLD ADD: CD. OBREGON SONORA MEXICO
1944-020	CECIL, REX HOLSTON	D. OCTOBER 30, 1966, LONG BEACH, CALIF.
1990-028	CEDENO, ANDUJAR	D. OCTOBER 28, 2000, LAROMANA, DOMINICAN REPUBLIC
1970-019	CEDENO, CESAR EUGENITO	2112 MARISOLLOOP, KISSIMMEE FL 34743
1993-033	CEDENO, DOMINGO (DOMASTORG)	AVE. PADRE ABREU #13 LAROMANA, DOM REP
1995-047	CEDENO, ROGER LEONARD	OLD ADD: 7595 PLANTATION CIRCLE, BRADENTON FL 34201
2005-037	CEDENO, RONNY ALEXANDER	1725 NORTH CIRCLE DRIVE, TEMPE AZ 85281
1942-019	CENTER, MARVIN EARL 'PETE'	D. AUGUST 8, 2004, CAMPTON, KY.
1958-020	CEPEDA, ORLANDO MANUEL	2305 PALMER CIRCLE, FAIRFIELD CA 94533
2002-027	CEPICKY, MATTHEW WILLIAM	7 UPPER BLUFFS VIEW COURT, EUREKA MO 63025
2002-028	CERDA, JAIME M.	2707 NORTHILL STREET, SELMA CA 93662
1975-025	CERONE, RICHARD 'RICK'	34 WINDING WAY, WEST PATERSON NJ 07424
2003-023	CERROS, R. JUAN 'JUAN'	OLD ADD: MONTERREY MEX
1985-016	CERUTTI, JOHN JOSEPH	D. OCTOBER 3, 2004, TORONTO, ONT.
1951-010	CERV, ROBERT HENRY	1620 AVENUE M, HAWARDEN IA 51023
1971-021	CEY, RONALD CHARLES	22714 CREOLE RD, WOODLAND HILLS CA 91364
2004-039	CHACIN, GUSTAVO ADOLFO	OLD ADD: MARACAIBO VENEZ
1960-020	CHACON, ELIO RODRIGUEZ	D. APRIL 24, 1992, CARACAS, VENEZUELA
2001-029	CHACON, SHAWN ANTHONY	2907 WEST 17TH STREET, GREELEY CO 80631
1986-031	CHADWICK, RAY CHARLES	607 GADDIS STREET, DURHAM NC 27702
1929-016	CHAGNON, LEON WILBUR	D. JULY 30, 1953, AMESBURY, MASS.
1951-011	CHAKALES, ROBERT EDWARD	8916 RIVER ROAD, RICHMOND VA 23229
1973-021	CHALK, DAVID LEE	137 CROSS TIMBERS TRAIL, COPPELL TX 75019
1979-018	CHAMBERLAIN, CRAIG PHILIP	PO BOX 473, SURFSIDE CA 90743
1990-029	CHAMBERLAIN, WESLEY POLK	PO BOX 1358, HOMEWOOD IL 60430
1932-012	CHAMBERLAIN, WILLIAM VINCENT	D. FEBRUARY 6, 1994, BROCKTON, MASS.
1934-021	CHAMBERLIN, JOSEPH JEREMIAH	D. JANUARY 28, 1983, SAN FRANCISCO, CALIF.

1983-028	CHAMBERS, ALBERT EUGENE	1303 NORTH 14TH ST, HARRISBURG PA 17103
1948-024	CHAMBERS, CLIFFORD DAY	749 NORTH EAGLE ROAD, EAGLE ID 83616
1937-021	CHAMBERS, JOHNNIE MONROE	D. MAY 11, 1977, PALATKA, FLA.
2003-024	CHAMBLEE, JAMES NATHANIEL	1408 BROADWAY, DENTON TX 76201
1971-022	CHAMBLISS, CARROLL CHRISTOPHER 'CHRIS'	12755 WYNGATE TRAIL, ALPHARETTA GA 30005
1969-031	CHAMPION, BUFORD BILLY 'BILLY'	240 TRIPLE H FARM ROAD, INMAN SC 29349
1976-025	CHAMPION, ROBERT MICHAEL 'MIKE'	28952 MODJESKA CANYON ROAD, SILVERADO CA 92679
1963-024	CHANCE, ROBERT	2258 OAKRIDGE DRIVE, CHARLESTON WV 25311
1961-019	CHANCE, WILMER DEAN 'DEAN'	9505 W. SMITHVILLE WESTERN, WOOSTER OH 44691
1947-018	CHANDLER, EDWARD OLIVER	D. JULY 6, 2003, LAS VEGAS, NEV.
1937-022	CHANDLER, SPURGEON FERDINAND 'SPUD'	D. JANUARY 9, 1990, ST. PETERSBURG, FLA.
1969-032	CHANEY, DARREL LEE	289 SKYLAKE ROAD, SAUTEE NACOOCHEE GA 30571
1975-024	CHANT, CHARLES JOSEPH	7831 SYCAMORE AVENUE, RIVERSIDE CA 92504
1991-033	CHAPIN, DARRIN JOHN	328 PORTAGE EASTERLY, CORTLAND OH 44410
1920-017	CHAPLIN, BERT EDGAR	D. AUGUST 15, 1978, SANFORD, FLA.
1928-021	CHAPLIN, JAMES BAILEY 'TINY'	D. MARCH 25, 1939, NATIONAL CITY, CALIF.
1935-013	CHAPMAN, CALVIN LOUIS	D. APRIL 1, 1983, BATESVILLE, MISS.
1933-012	CHAPMAN, EDWIN VOLNEY	D. MAY 3, 2000, CLARKSDALE, MISS.
1939-019	CHAPMAN, FREDERICK WILLIAM	D. MARCH 27, 1997, KANNAPOLIS, N.C.
1934-022	CHAPMAN, GLENN JUSTICE	D. NOVEMBER 5, 1988, RICHMOND, IND.
1924-017	CHAPMAN, JOHN JOSEPH	D. NOVEMBER 3, 1953, PHILADELPHIA, PA.
1979-019	CHAPMAN, KELVIN KEITH	9301 LAUGHLIN WAY, REDWOOD VALLEY CA 94570
1938-012	CHAPMAN, SAMUEL BLAKE	D. DECEMBER 22, 2006, TIBURON, CALIF.
2003-025	CHAPMAN, TRAVIS ADRIAN	OLD ADD: JACKSONVILLE FL 32203
1930-010	CHAPMAN, WILLIAM BENJAMIN 'BEN'	D. JULY 7, 1993, HOOVER, ALA.
1978-025	CHAPPAS, HARRY PERRY	22 SE FIRST AVENUE, DANIA FL 33004
1980-023	CHARBONEAU, JOSEPH	33020 LEAFY MILL LANE, NORTH RIDGEVILLE OH 44039
1962-027	CHARLES, EDWIN DOUGLAS	57 PARK TERRACE EAST #B58, NEW YORK NY 10034
2000-032	CHARLES, FRANKLIN SCOTT	7703 RIO ESTRADA WAY, SACRAMENTO CA 95831
1988-028	CHARLTON, NORMAN WOOD	312 ESTES DRIVE, ROCKPORT TX 78382
1940-010	CHARTAK, MICHAEL GEORGE	D. JULY 25, 1967, OAKDALE, IOWA
1964-019	CHARTON, FRANK LANE 'PETE'	27 VINCINDA LN, HARRIMAN TN 37748
1936-014	CHASE, KENDALL FAY	D. JANUARY 16, 1985, ONEONTA, N.Y.
1930-011	CHATHAM, CHARLES L. 'BUSTER'	D. DECEMBER 15, 1975, WACO, TEXAS
1966-018	CHAVARRIA, OSWALDO QUIJANO 'OSSIE'	9061 HORNER STREET #201 BURNABY BC, V3N 4L2 CANADA
2005-038	CHAVEZ, ANGEL ARISTIDES	OLD ADD: DAVID PANAMA
1997-028	CHAVEZ, ANTHONY FRANCISCO 'TONY'	OLD ADD: MERCED CA 95340
2001-030	CHAVEZ, EDDY DEJESUS	OLD ADD: VALENCIA VENEZ
1998-029	CHAVEZ, ERIC CESAR	6635 NORTH 66TH PLACE, PARADISE VALLEY AZ 85253
1967-016	CHAVEZ, NESTOR ISAIAS SILVA	D. MARCH 16, 1969, MARACAIBO, VENEZ.
1996-036	CHAVEZ, RAUL ALEXANDER	OLD ADD: VALENCIA VENEZUELA
1973-022	CHEADLE, DAVID BAIRD	77 ANDORA STREET, SAINT AUGUSTINE FL 32086
1997-029	CHECO, ROBINSON PEREZ	OLD ADD: 95 ARTHUR STREET, PAWTUCKET RI 02860
1920-018	CHEEVES, VIRGIL EARL 'CHIEF'	D. MAY 5, 1979, DALLAS, TEXAS
1935-014	CHELINI, ITALO VINCENT	D. AUGUST 25, 1972, SAN FRANCISCO, CALIF.
1998-030	CHEN, BRUCE KASTULO	114 DUTCHFORK CREEK TRAIL, IRMO SC 29063
2002-029	CHEN, CHIN-FENG	OLD ADD: TAINAN CITY TAIWAN
1957-010	CHENEY, THOMAS EDGAR	D. NOVEMBER 1, 2001, ROME, GA.
1937-023	CHERVINKO, PAUL	D. JUNE 3, 1976, DANVILLE, ILL.
1948-025	CHESNES, ROBERT VINCENT	D. MAY 23, 1979, EVERETT, WASH.
1945-008	CHETKOVICH, MITCHELL	D. AUGUST 24, 1971, GRASS VALLEY, CALIF.
1977-027	CHEVEZ, ANTONIO SILVIO	TELIA D PTO. LEON, NICARAGUA
1990-030	CHIAMPARINO, SCOTT MICHAEL	179 ORTEGA AVENUE, MOUNTAIN VIEW CA 94040
2001-031	CHIASSON, SCOTT CHRISTOPHER	25 OAKWOOD ROAD, NIANTIC CT 06357
2006-033	CHICK, TRAVIS COLE	2201 VILLA DRIVE, TYLER TX 75703
1982-024	CHIFFER, FLOYD JOHN	4325 LEVELSIDE AVE, LAKEWOOD CA 90712
1930-012	CHILD, HARRY PATRICK	D. NOVEMBER 8, 1972, ALEXANDRIA, VA.
2006-034	CHILDERS, JASON LEE	702 FOREST CIRCLE, DOUGLAS GA 31533
2002-030	CHILDERS, MATTHEW WILKIE	2015 HOPETOWN DRIVE, AUGUSTA GA 30909
1985-017	CHILDRESS, RODNEY OSBORNE 'ROCKY'	5 MEADOWGLEN COURT, SANTA ROSA CA 95404
1971-023	CHILES, RICHARD FRANCIS 'RICH'	4501 SAN RAMON DR, DAVIS CA 95616
1935-015	CHIOZZA, DINO JOSEPH	D. APRIL 23, 1972, MEMPHIS, TENN.
1934-023	CHIOZZA, LOUIS PEO	D. FEBRUARY 28, 1971, MEMPHIS, TENN.
1941-016	CHIPMAN, ROBERT HOWARD	D. NOVEMBER 8, 1973, HUNTINGTON, N.Y.
1945-009	CHIPPLE, WALTER JOHN	D. JUNE 8, 1988, TONAWANDA, N.Y.
1979-020	CHISM, THOMAS RAYMOND	532 WEST BROOKHAVEN ROAD #F1, BROOKHAVEN PA 19015
1950-020	CHITI, HARRY	D. JANUARY 31, 2002, HAINES CITY, FLA.
1990-031	CHITREN, STEPHEN VINCENT	10417 SMOKEMONT COURT, LAS VEGAS NV 89129
1958-021	CHITTUM, NELSON BOYD	616 BONITA PARKWAY, HENDERSONVILLE TN 37075
1970-020	CHLUPSA, ROBERT JOSEPH	55 WILLOW STREET, GARDEN CITY NY 11530
1998-031	CHO, JIN HO	OLD ADD: JUN JU CITY KOREA
1960-021	CHOATE, DONALD LEE	9506 MARY ANN DRIVE, FAIRVIEW HEIGHTS IL 62208
2000-033	CHOATE, RANDOL DOYLE	20818 LAKE VIENNA DRIVE, LAND O'LAKES FL 34638
2002-031	CHOI, HEE SEOP	14310 SE 29TH CIRCLE, VANCOUVER WA 98683
2005-039	CHOO, SHIN-SOO	OLD ADD: PUSAN SOUTH KOREA
1996-037	CHOUINARD, ROBERT WILLIAM	6024 SOUTH PARIS PLACE, ENGLEWOOD CO 80111
1937-024	CHOZEN, HARRY KENNETH	D. SEPTEMBER 16, 1994, HOUSTON, TEXAS
1979-021	CHRIS, MICHAEL	12437 WOODGREEN ST, LOS ANGELES CA 90066
1957-011	CHRISLEY, BARBRA O'NEIL 'NEIL'	395 MYRTLE GREEN DRIVE, CONWAY SC 29526
1971-024	CHRISTENSEN, BRUCE RAY	BOX 178, MORONI UT 84646
1984-017	CHRISTENSEN, JOHN LAWRENCE	2931 YUMA DRIVE, LAKE HAVASU CITY AZ 86406
1999-032	CHRISTENSEN, MCKAY A	2288 NEW HARVEST LANE, LEHI UT 84043
1926-013	CHRISTENSEN, WALTER NIELS 'CUCKOO'	D. DECEMBER 20, 1984, MENLO PARK, CALIF.
1979-022	CHRISTENSON, GARY RICHARD	436 EAST TREMAINE AVENUE, GILBERT AZ 85234
1973-023	CHRISTENSON, LARRY ROBERT	1465 LEBOUTILLIER ROAD, MALVERN PA 19358
1998-032	CHRISTENSON, RYAN ALAN	4021 ONTARIO STREET #136, CARLSBAD CA 92008

1968-013	CHRISTIAN, ROBERT CHARLES	D. FEBRUARY 20, 1974, SAN DIEGO, CALIF.
1984-018	CHRISTIANSEN, CLAY C.	RURAL ROUTE 3, COLUMBUS KS 66725
1995-048	CHRISTIANSEN, JASON SAMUEL	3428 EAST JASMINE CIRCLE, MESA AZ 85213
1938-013	CHRISTMAN, MARQUETTE JOSEPH 'MARK'	D. OCTOBER 9, 1976, ST. LOUIS, MO.
2001-032	CHRISTMAN, TIMOTHY ARTHUR	16 PARISH AVENUE, ONEONTA NY 13820
1983-029	CHRISTMAS, STEPHEN RANDALL	600 BENTLEY STREET, OVIEDO FL 32765
1959-013	CHRISTOPHER, JOSEPH O'NEAL	PO BOX 65240, BALTIMORE MD 21209
1945-010	CHRISTOPHER, LOYD EUGENE	D. SEPTEMBER 5, 1991, RICHMOND, CALIF.
1991-034	CHRISTOPHER, MICHAEL WAYNE	RURAL ROUTE 1 BOX 445, CHURCH ROAD VA 23833
1942-020	CHRISTOPHER, RUSSELL ORMAND	D. DECEMBER 5, 1954, POINT RICHMOND, CALIF.
2003-026	CHULK, CHARLES VINCENT 'VINNY'	10062 SW 223RD TERRACE, MIAMI FL 33190
1950-021	CHURCH, EMORY NICHOLAS 'BUBBA'	D. SEPTEMBER 17, 2001, BIRMINGHAM, ALA.
1966-019	CHURCH, LEONARD	D. APRIL 22, 1988, RICHARDSON, TEXAS
2004-040	CHURCH, RYAN MATTHEW	625 NORTH FIFTH STREET, LOMPOC CA 93436
1957-012	CHURN, CLARENCE NOTTINGHAM 'CHUCK'	733 TREVINO DRIVE, LADY LAKE FL 32159
1924-018	CHURRY, JOHN	D. FEBRUARY 8, 1970, ZANESVILLE, OHIO
1951-012	CIAFFONE, LAWRENCE THOMAS	D. DECEMBER 14, 1991, BROOKLYN, N.Y.
1992-023	CIANFROCCO, ANGELO DOMINIC 'ARCHIE'	12424 ADDAX COURT, SAN DIEGO CA 92129
1987-023	CIARDI, MARK THOMAS	21 MITCHELL AVENUE, PISCATAWAY NJ 08854
1983-030	CIAS, DARRYL RICHARD	12330 LITHUANIA ST, GRANADA HILLS CA 91344
1929-017	CICERO, JOSEPH FRANCIS	D. MARCH 30, 1983, CLEARWATER, FLA.
1957-013	CICOTTE, ALVA WARREN	D. NOVEMBER 29, 1982, WESTLAND, MICH.
1944-021	CIESLAK, THADDEUS WALTER 'TED'	D. MAY 9, 1993, MILWAUKEE, WISC.
1945-011	CIHOCKI, ALBERT JOSEPH	43 COCHISE CIRCLE, MEDFORD LAKES NJ 08055
1932-013	CIHOCKI, EDWARD JOSEPH	D. NOVEMBER 9, 1987, NEWARK, DEL.
1965-021	CIMINO, PETER WILLIAM	14 FILLMORE ST, BRISTOL PA 19007
1956-021	CIMOLI, GINO NICHOLAS	2409 GREENWICH STREET, SAN FRANCISCO CA 94123
1994-015	CIMORELLI, FRANK THOMAS	2448 NORTH 112TH STREET, MILWAUKEE WI 53226
2001-033	CINTRON, ALEXANDER	OLD ADD: YABUCAO PR
1943-029	CIOLA, LOUIS ALEXANDER	D. OCTOBER 18, 1981, AUSTIN, MINN.
1961-020	CIPRIANI, FRANK DOMINICK	14 OAKHILL DRIVE, WEST SENECA NY 14224
1994-016	CIRILLO, JEFFREY HOWARD	OLD ADD: 58 GLENMOOR CIRCLE, ENGLEWOOD CO 80110
1937-025	CISAR, GEORGE JOSEPH	9026 WEST 24TH STREET, NORTH RIVERSIDE IL 60546
1961-021	CISCO, GALEN BERNARD	604 ELMWOOD LANE, CELINA OH 45822
1928-022	CISSELL, CHALMER WILLIAM 'BILL'	D. MARCH 15, 1949, CHICAGO, ILL.
1983-031	CITARELLA, RALPH ALEXANDER	29 EAST SHERMAN AVE, COLONIA NJ 07067
1926-014	CLABAUGH, JOHN WILLIAM 'MOOSE'	D. JULY 11, 1984, TUCSON, ARIZ.
1920-019	CLAIRE, DAVID MATTHEW	D. JANUARY 7, 1956, LAS VEGAS, NEV.
1977-028	CLANCY, JAMES	PO BOX 148, TWIN LAKES WI 53181
1924-019	CLANCY, JOHN WILLIAM 'BUD'	D. SEPTEMBER 26, 1968, OTTUMWA, IOWA
1922-020	CLANTON, UCAL CURT	D. FEBRUARY 24, 1960, ANTLERS, OKLA.
1999-033	CLAPINSKI, CHRISTOPHER ALAN	178 COVE LOOP DRIVE, MERRITT ISLAND FL 32953
2001-034	CLAPP, RICHARD KEITH 'STUBBY'	OLD ADD: 1298 ARMAND DRIVE, MEMPHIS TN 38103
1976-026	CLAREY, DOUGLAS WILLIAM	2116 HILLHURST AVENUE, LOS ANGELES CA 90027
1947-019	CLARK, ALFRED ALOYSIUS 'ALLIE'	250 NORTH STEVENS AVENUE, SOUTH AMBOY NJ 08879
1995-049	CLARK, ANTHONY CHRISTOPHER	11084 1/2 CAMINO PLAYA CARMEL, SAN DIEGO CA 92124
1927-023	CLARK, BAILEY EARL 'EARL'	D. JANUARY 16, 1938, WASHINGTON, D.C.
2000-034	CLARK, BRADY WILLIAM	PO BOX 638, WALTERVILLE OR 97489
1981-023	CLARK, BRYAN DONALD	508 NORTH CLARK STREET, MADERA CA 93637
1922-021	CLARK, DANIEL CURRAN	D. MAY 23, 1937, MERIDIAN, MISS.
1986-032	CLARK, DAVID EARL	4842 MAYFIELD ROAD WEST, COLLIERVILLE TN 38017
2005-040	CLARK, DOUGLAS DWYER	OLD ADD: SPRINGFIELD MA
1967-017	CLARK, GLEN ESTER	5605 MARBLEHEAD, DALLAS TX 75232
2002-032	CLARK, HOWARD RODDY	5564 CHUCK DRIVE, LAKE CHARLES LA 70605
1975-026	CLARK, JACK ANTHONY	6541 SCOTTSDALE WAY, FRISCO TX 75034
1948-026	CLARK, JAMES	D. OCTOBER 24, 1990, SANTA MONICA, CALIF.
1971-025	CLARK, JAMES	659 SOUTH INDIAN HILL BLVD #C, CLAREMONT CA 91711
1988-029	CLARK, JERALD DWAYNE	OLD ADD: 618 SOUTH SYCAMORE STREET, CROCKETT TX 75835
2001-035	CLARK, JERMAINE MARCEL	2325 GOLDEN GATE #302, SAN FRANCISCO CA 94118
1938-014	CLARK, JOHN CARROLL 'CAP'	D. FEBRUARY 16, 1957, FAYETTEVILLE, N.C.
1991-035	CLARK, MARK WILLARD	18262 EAST CR 520N, KILBOURNE IL 62655
1951-013	CLARK, MELVIN EARL	PO BOX 97, WEST COLUMBIA WV 25287
1952-017	CLARK, MICHAEL JOHN	D. JANUARY 15, 1996, CAMDEN, N.J.
1958-022	CLARK, PHILIP JAMES	OLD ADD: 112 HICKS ROAD, SASSER GA 39885
1992-024	CLARK, PHILLIP BENJAMIN	9062 DANCY TREE COURT, ORLANDO FL 32836
1967-018	CLARK, RICKEY CHARLES	8953 EMERALD WATER COURT, LAS VEGAS NV 89147
1979-023	CLARK, ROBERT CALE	1030 PERRISITO ST, PERRIS CA 92570
1920-020	CLARK, ROBERT WILLIAM	D. MAY 18, 1944, CARLSBAD, N.M.
1966-020	CLARK, RONALD BRUCE	700 STARKEY RD #511, LARGO FL 33541
1988-030	CLARK, TERRY LEE	OLD ADD: PO BOX 1357, NILES OH 44446
1986-033	CLARK, WILLIAM NUSCHLER 'WILL'	36170 PLEASANT HILL COURT, PRAIRIEVILLE LA 70769
1945-012	CLARK, WILLIAM OTIS 'OTEY'	601 LABELLE STREET, BOSCOBEL WI 53805
1924-020	CLARK, WILLIAM WATSON 'WATTY'	D. MARCH 4, 1972, CLEARWATER, FLA.
1921-013	CLARKE, ALAN THOMAS	D. MARCH 11, 1975, CHEVERLY, MD.
1965-022	CLARKE, HORACE MEREDITH	BOX 891, FREDERIKSTED VI 00840
1944-022	CLARKE, RICHARD GREY 'GREY'	D. NOVEMBER 25, 1993, KANNAPOLIS, N.C.
1923-020	CLARKE, RUFUS RIVERS	D. FEBRUARY 8, 1983, COLUMBIA, S.C.
1983-032	CLARKE, STANLEY MARTEN	5533 SANDERS DRIVE, TOLEDO OH 43615
1920-021	CLARKE, SUMPTER MILLS	D. MARCH 16, 1962, KNOXVILLE, TENN.
1955-025	CLARKE, VIBERT ERNESTO 'WEBBO'	D. JUNE 14, 1970, CRISTOBAL, CANAL ZONE
1929-018	CLARKE, WILLIAM STUART 'STU'	D. AUGUST 26, 1985, HAYWARD, CALIF.
1952-018	CLARKSON, JAMES BUSTER 'BUS'	D. JANUARY 18, 1989, JEANNETTE, PA.
1927-024	CLARKSON, WILLIAM HENRY	D. AUGUST 27, 1971, RALEIGH, N.C.
1942-021	CLARY, ELLIS	D. JUNE 2, 2000, VALDOSTA, GA.
1987-024	CLARY, MARTIN KEITH	205 YORKTOWN COURT, EASLEY SC 29642
1933-013	CLASET, GOWELL SYLVESTER	D. MARCH 8, 1981, ST. PETERSBURG, FLA.

2003-027	CLAUSSEN, BRANDON ALLEN	5129 NORTH JA ROB LANE, HOBBS NM 88242
1943-030	CLAY, DAIN ELMER	D. AUGUST 28, 1994, CHULA VISTA, CALIF.
1988-031	CLAY, DANNY BRUCE	5392 GRACEWOOD COURT, COLUMBUS OH 43229
1977-029	CLAY, KENNETH EARL	4523 60TH STREET COURT, BRADENTON FL 34210
1991-036	CLAYTON, ROYCE SPENCER	6035 DEBUTTS TERRACE, MALIBU CA 90265
1979-024	CLEAR, MARK ALAN	3229 ARMSLEY DRIVE, CHINO HILLS CA 91709
1945-013	CLEARY, JOSEPH CHRISTOPHER	D. JUNE 3, 2004, YONKERS, N.Y.
1939-020	CLEMENS, CHESTER SPURGEON	D. FEBRUARY 10, 2002, SAN CLEMENTE, CALIF.
1960-022	CLEMENS, DOUGLAS HORACE	4799 LOWER MOUNTAIN ROAD, NEW HOPE PA 18938
1984-019	CLEMENS, WILLIAM ROGER 'ROGER'	11535 QUAIL HOLLOW, HOUSTON TX 77024
1939-021	CLEMENSEN, WILLIAM MELVILLE	D. FEBRUARY 18, 1994, ALTA, CALIF.
1998-033	CLEMENT, MATTHEW PAUL	210 CAMELOT DRIVE, BUTLER PA 16001
1998-034	CLEMENTE, EDGARD ALEXIS	PO BOX 4, BURLINGAME CA 94011
1955-026	CLEMENTE, ROBERTO WALKER	D. DECEMBER 31, 1972, SAN JUAN, P.R.
1985-018	CLEMENTS, PATRICK BRIAN	166 LAZY SOUTH LANE, CHICO CA 95926
1997-030	CLEMONS, CHRISTOPHER HALE	490 KIOWA CIRCLE, ROBINSON TX 76706
1971-026	CLEMONS, LANCE LEVIS	4516 GOLF CLUB LANE, BROOKSVILLE FL 34609
1961-022	CLENDENON, DONN ALVIN	D. SEPTEMBER 17, 2005, SIOUX FALLS, S.D.
1969-033	CLEVELAND, REGINALD LESLIE	202 CREEKVIEW DRIVE, ANNA TX 75409
1954-014	CLEVENGER, TRUMAN EUGENE 'TEX'	31727 COUNTRY CLUB DRIVE, PORTERVILLE CA 93257
2006-035	CLEVLEN, BRENT AARON	2019 SPYGLASS HILL, LEANDER TX 78641
1980-024	CLIBURN, STANLEY GENE	4807 HIGHWAY 80, JACKSON MS 39209
1984-020	CLIBURN, STEWART WALKER	12831 EAGLE POINTE CIRCLE, FORT MYERS FL 33913
1934-024	CLIFT, HARLOND BENTON	D. APRIL 27, 1992, YAKIMA, WASH.
1934-025	CLIFTON, HERMAN EARL 'FLEA'	D. DECEMBER 22, 1997, CINCINNATI, OHIO
1960-023	CLINE, TYRONE ALEXANDER	676 AYERS, CHARLESTON SC 29412
1970-021	CLINES, EUGENE ANTHONY	5303 9TH AVENUE DRIVE WEST, BRADENTON FL 34209
1960-024	CLINTON, LUCIEAN LOUIS 'LOU'	D. DECEMBER 6, 1997, WICHITA, KAN.
1961-023	CLONINGER, TONY LEE	PO BOX 1500, DENVER NC 28037
1995-050	CLONTZ, JOHN BRADLEY 'BRAD'	1367 SPRING ROAD, PATRICK SPRINGS VA 24133
2004-041	CLOSSER, JEFFREY DARRIN 'J.D.'	417 EAST 1100 NORTH, ALEXANDRIA IN 46001
1966-021	CLOSTER, ALAN EDWARD	4103 HICKORY ROAD, RICHMOND VA 23235
1997-031	CLOUDE, KENNETH BRIAN	1605 STONEWOOD ROAD, BALTIMORE MD 21239
1924-021	CLOUGH, EDGAR GEORGE	D. JANUARY 30, 1944, HARRISBURG, PA.
1926-015	CLOWERS, WILLIAM PERRY	D. JANUARY 13, 1978, SWEENY, TEXAS
1986-034	CLUTTERBUCK, BRYAN RICHARD	C/O MM CLUTTERBUCK, 1986 LOVELL, MILFORD MI 48381
1997-032	CLYBURN, DANNY	148 EAST BROOKLYN AVENUE, LANCASTER SC 29720
1973-024	CLYDE, DAVID EUGENE	C/O MCCAULEY LUMBER, 27210 FM 149, TOMBALL TX 77375
1943-031	CLYDE, THOMAS KNOX	D. OCTOBER 1, 2005, DALLAS, TEXAS
1990-032	COACHMAN, BOBBY DEAN 'PETE'	PO BOX 44, COTTONWOOD AL 36320
1946-018	COAN, GILBERT FITZGERALD	PO BOX 558, BREVARD NC 28712
1956-022	COATES, JAMES ALTON	1098 OAK HILL ROAD, LANCASTER VA 22503
2006-036	COATS, BUCK	OLD ADD: HAHIRA GA
1929-019	COBB, HERBERT EDWARD	D. JANUARY 8, 1980, TARBORO, N.C.
1939-022	COBLE, DAVID LAMAR	D. OCTOBER 15, 1971, ORLANDO, FLA.
1983-033	COCANOWER, JAMES STANLEY 'JAIME'	10777 GRAM B CIRCLE, LOWELL AR 72745
1986-035	COCHRANE, DAVID CARTER	11 MUIRFIELD, DOVE CANYON CA 92679
1925-019	COCHRANE, GORDON STANLEY 'MICKEY'	D. JUNE 28, 1962, LAKE FOREST, ILL.
1996-038	COCKRELL, ATLEE ALAN 'ALAN'	605 COOPER AVENUE, COLORADO SPRINGS CO 80905
2000-035	COCO, PASQUAL REYNOSO	OLD ADD: SANTO DOMINGO DOM REP
1982-025	CODIROLI, CHRISTOPHER ALLEN	2700 HILLCREST DRIVE, CAMERON PARK CA 95682
2005-041	COFFEY, JUSTIN TODD 'TODD'	OLD ADD: 174 OAKLAND HEIGHTS ROAD, FOREST CITY NC 28043
2000-036	COFFIE, IVANON ANGELINO	OLD ADD: CURACAO NETHERLANDS ANTILLES
1937-026	COFFMAN, GEORGE DAVID	D. MAY 8, 2003, BIRMINGHAM, ALA.
1987-025	COFFMAN, KEVIN REESE	313 KELLY DRIVE, VICTORIA TX 77904
1927-025	COFFMAN, SAMUEL RICHARD 'DICK'	D. MARCH 24, 1972, ATHENS, ALA.
2001-036	COGAN, ANTHONY MICHAEL	151 PINE POINT DRIVE, HIGHLAND PARK IL 60035
2000-037	COGGIN, DAVID RAYMOND	861 EMERSON STREET, UPLAND CA 91784
1967-019	COGGINS, FRANKLIN	2937 NELSON DRIVE, DULUTH GA 30096
1972-018	COGGINS, RICHARD ALLEN	OLD ADD: 3801 PARKVIEW, IRVINE CA 92713
1931-012	COHEN, ALTA ALBERT	D. MARCH 11, 2003, MAPLEWOOD, N.J.
1926-016	COHEN, ANDREW HOWARD	D. OCTOBER 29, 1988, EL PASO, TEXAS
1955-027	COHEN, HYMAN	35734 DONNY CIRCLE, PALM DESERT CA 92211
1934-026	COHEN, SYDNEY HARRY	D. APRIL 9, 1988, EL PASO, TEXAS
1958-023	COKER, JIMMIE GOODWIN	D. OCTOBER 29, 1991, THROCKMORTON, TEXAS
1999-034	COLANGELO, MICHAEL GUS	5751 FINCASTLE DRIVE, MANASSAS VA 20112
1955-028	COLAVITO, ROCCO DOMENICO 'ROCKY'	OLD ADD: ORWIGSBURG PA 17961
1978-026	COLBERN, MICHAEL MALLOY	5120 EAST TANO STREET, PHOENIX AZ 85044
1992-025	COLBERT, CRAIG CHARLES	2000 JASPER BLUFF STREET, LAS VEGAS NV 89117
1966-022	COLBERT, NATHAN	2756 GREEN VALLEY PKWY #3, HENDERSON NV 89014
1970-022	COLBERT, VINCENT NORMAN	18071 BLANDFORD ROAD, CLEVELAND OH 44121
1969-034	COLBORN, JAMES WILLIAM	2932 SOLIMAR BEACH DRIVE, VENTURA CA 93001
1992-026	COLBRUNN, GREGORY JOSEPH	3196 PIGNATELLI CRESCENT, MOUNT PLEASANT SC 29466
1921-014	COLE, ALBERT GEORGE 'BERT'	D. MAY 30, 1975, SAN MATEO, CALIF.
1990-033	COLE, ALEXANDER	OLD ADD: 1071 ROBMONT DRIVE, RICHMOND VA 23236
1950-022	COLE, DAVID BRUCE	2072 PEBBLE BEACH BLVD, ORLANDO FL 32826
1938-015	COLE, EDWARD WILLIAM	D. JULY 28, 1999, NASHVILLE, TENN.
1951-014	COLE, RICHARD ROY	3149 MEDEIRA AVENUE, COSTA MESA CA 92626
1991-037	COLE, STEWART BRYAN	6527 WILLOW GATE LANE, CHARLOTTE NC 28215
1992-027	COLE, VICTOR ALEXANDER	138 ESTONALIE ROAD, MERCER TN 38392
1961-024	COLEMAN, CLARENCE 'CHOO CHOO'	127 EAST 13TH STREET, APOPKA FL 32703
1977-030	COLEMAN, DAVID LEE	4303 DELHI DR, DAYTON OH 45432
1949-015	COLEMAN, GERALD FRANCIS 'JERRY'	1004 HAVENHURST DRIVE, LAJOLLA CA 92037
1959-014	COLEMAN, GORDON CALVIN	D. MARCH 12, 1994, CINCINNATI, OHIO
1965-023	COLEMAN, JOSEPH HOWARD	17851 EAGLE VIEW LANE, CAPE CORAL FL 33909
1942-022	COLEMAN, JOSEPH PATRICK	D. APRIL 9, 1997, FORT MYERS, FLA.

1997-033	COLEMAN, MICHAEL DONNELL	3700 FREE FERRY ROAD, FORT SMITH AR 72903
1932-014	COLEMAN, PARKE EDWARD 'ED'	D. AUGUST 5, 1964, OREGON CITY, ORE.
1947-020	COLEMAN, RAYMOND LEROY	PO BOX 8, HORNBROOK CA 96044
1985-019	COLEMAN, VINCENT MAURICE	12936 NORTH 137TH STREET, SCOTTSDALE AZ 85259
1955-029	COLEMAN, WALTER GARY 'RIP'	D. MAY 14, 2004, WOLFEBORO, N.H.
1958-024	COLES, CHARLES EDWARD	D. JANUARY 25, 1996, MYRTLE BEACH, S.C.
1983-034	COLES, DARNELL	306 SIGNATURE TERRACE, SAFETY HARBOR FL 34695
1972-019	COLETTA, CHRISTOPHER MICHAEL	206 SW 45TH STREET, CAPE CORAL FL 33914
2006-037	COLINA, ALVIN ENRIQUE	OLD ADD: PUERTO CABELLO VENEZ
1927-026	COLLARD, EARL CLINTON 'HAP'	D. JULY 14, 1968, JAMESTOWN, CALIF.
1997-034	COLLIER, LOUIS KEITH	6409 SOUTH KENWOOD AVENUE, CHICAGO IL 60637
1931-013	COLLIER, ORLIN EDWARD	D. SEPTEMBER 9, 1944, MEMPHIS, TENN.
1975-027	COLLINS, DAVID SCOTT	4813 AUDUBON ROAD, DETROIT MI 48224
1977-031	COLLINS, DONALD EDWARD	127 DEERWOOD TRAIL, SHARPSBURG GA 30277
1939-023	COLLINS, EDWARD TROWBRIDGE	D. NOVEMBER 2, 2000, KENNETT SQUARE, PA.
1920-022	COLLINS, HARRY WARREN 'RIP'	D. MAY 27, 1968, BRYAN, TEXAS
1931-014	COLLINS, JAMES ANTHONY 'RIP'	D. APRIL 16, 1970, NEW HAVEN, N.Y.
1948-027	COLLINS, JOSEPH EDWARD	D. AUGUST 30, 1989, UNION, N.J.
1965-024	COLLINS, KEVIN MICHAEL	9121 POINT CHARITY DRIVE, PIGEON MI 48755
1923-021	COLLINS, PHILIP EUGENE	D. AUGUST 14, 1948, CHICAGO, ILL.
1940-011	COLLINS, ROBERT JOSEPH	D. APRIL 19, 1969, PITTSBURGH, PA.
1994-017	COLLINS, TERRY LEE	40992 HOLLYDALE, NOVI MI 40375
1951-015	COLLUM, JACK DEAN	PO BOX 82, GRINNELL IA 50112
1942-023	COLMAN, FRANK LOYD	D. FEBRUARY 19, 1983, LONDON, ONT.
2001-037	COLOME, JESUS (DE LA CRUZ)	OLD ADD: SAN PEDRO DE MACORIS DR
1997-035	COLON, BARTOLO	3308 ISLEWOOD AVENUE, WESTON FL 33332
1992-028	COLON, CRISTOBAL (MARTINEZ)	OLD ADD: CASA ANNA AVENUE, ALAMO, LAGUIRA, VENEZ
2004-042	COLON, ROMAN BENEDICTO	OLD ADD: MONTE CRISTI DOM REP
1970-023	COLPAERT, RICHARD CHARLES	47412 ELDON, UTICA MI 48317
1970-024	COLSON, LOYD ALBERT	PO BOX 128, HOLLIS OK 73550
1968-014	COLTON, LAWRENCE ROBERT	3027 NE 68TH AVENUE, PORTLAND OR 97213
1973-025	COLUCCIO, ROBERT PASQUALI	369 FLOWER STREET, COSTA MESA CA 92627
2003-028	COLYER, STEPHEN EDWARD	104 LAURA HILL ROAD, SAINT PETERS MO 63376
1980-025	COMBE, GEOFFREY WADE	743 TUDOR CIRCLE, THOUSAND OAKS CA 91360
1924-022	COMBS, EARLE BRYAN	D. JULY 21, 1976, RICHMOND, KY.
1947-021	COMBS, MERRILL RUSSELL	D. JULY 8, 1981, RIVERSIDE, CALIF.
1989-024	COMBS, PATRICK DENNIS	2219 SPANISH FOREST LANE, RICHMOND TX 77469
1945-014	COMELLAS, JORGE	D. SEPTEMBER 13, 2001, MIAMI, FLA.
1967-020	COMER, HARRY WAYNE 'WAYNE'	145 MARCUS STREET, SHENANDOAH VA 22849
1978-027	COMER, STEVEN MICHAEL	2029 STAHLKE WAY, CHASKA MN 55318
1954-015	COMMAND, JAMES DALTON	2136 CRANBROOK DRIVE NE, GRAND RAPIDS MI 49505
1926-017	COMORSKY, ADAM ANTHONY	D. MARCH 2, 1951, SWOYERSVILLE, PA.
1970-025	COMPTON, MICHAEL LYNN	8624 LEIGHTON DRIVE, TAMPA FL 33614
1972-020	COMPTON, ROBERT CLINTON 'CLINT'	4600 KELLY ANNE COURT, MONTGOMERY AL 36109
1984-021	COMSTOCK, KEITH MARTIN	9615 EAST DESERT TRAIL, SCOTTSDALE AZ 85260
1948-028	CONATSER, CLINTON ASTOR	26701 QUAIL STREET #191, LAGUNA HILLS CA 92653
1970-026	CONCEPCION, DAVID ISMAEL	URB. LOS CAOBOS BOTALON 5D, 5 PISO, MARACAY, VENEZUELA
1980-026	CONCEPCION, ONIX (CARDONA)	1486 STEEPLECHASE LANE, DELTONA FL 32725
1962-028	CONDE, RAMON LUIS	BOX 57, JUANA DIAZ PR 00665
2002-033	CONDREY, CLAYTON LEE	412 EIGHTH STREET, NAVASOTA TX 77868
1986-036	CONE, DAVID BRIAN	13735 PEMBROKE CIRCLE, OVERLAND PARK KS 66224
1940-012	CONGER, RICHARD	D. FEBRUARY 16, 1970, LOS ANGELES, CALIF.
1964-020	CONIGLIARO, ANTHONY RICHARD	D. FEBRUARY 24, 1990, SALEM, MASS.
1969-035	CONIGLIARO, WILLIAM MICHAEL	144 RIVER STREET, MIDDLETON MA 01949
1990-034	CONINE, JEFFREY GUY	3166 INVERNESS, FORT LAUDERDALE FL 33332
1920-023	CONKWRIGHT, ALLEN HOWARD	D. JULY 30, 1991, LAMESA, CALIF.
1934-027	CONLAN, JOHN BERTRAND 'JOCKO'	D. APRIL 16, 1989, SCOTTSDALE, ARIZ.
1952-019	CONLEY, DONALD EUGENE 'GENE'	2105 GRAFTON AVENUE, CLERMONT FL 34711
1958-025	CONLEY, ROBERT BURNS	16A CANTON DRIVE, WHITING NJ 08759
1923-022	CONLON, ARTHUR JOSEPH	D. AUGUST 5, 1987, FALMOUTH, MASS.
1983-035	CONNALLY, FRITZIE LEE	615 PORTOFINO DRIVE, ARLINGTON TX 76012
1921-015	CONNALLY, GEORGE WALTER 'SARGE'	D. JANUARY 27, 1978, TEMPLE, TEXAS
1925-020	CONNALLY, MERVIN THOMAS	D. JUNE 12, 1964, BERKELEY, CALIF.
1931-015	CONNATSER, BROADUS MILBURN 'BRUCE'	D. JANUARY 27, 1971, TERRE HAUTE, IND.
1931-016	CONNELL, EUGENE JOSEPH	D. AUGUST 31, 1937, WAVERLY, N.Y.
1926-018	CONNELL, JOSEPH BERNARD	D. SEPTEMBER 21, 1977, TREXLERTOWN, PA.
1998-035	CONNELLY, STEVEN LEE	1863 LITCHFIELD AVENUE, LONG BEACH CA 90815
1920-024	CONNELLY, THOMAS MARTIN	D. FEBRUARY 18, 1941, HINES, ILL.
1945-015	CONNELLY, WILLIAM WIRT	D. NOVEMBER 27, 1980, RICHMOND, VA.
1929-020	CONNOLLY, EDWARD JOSEPH	D. NOVEMBER 14, 1963, PITTSFIELD, MASS.
1964-021	CONNOLLY, EDWARD JOSEPH	D. JULY 1, 1998, NEW CANAAN, CONN.
1921-016	CONNOLLY, JOSEPH GEORGE	D. MARCH 30, 1960, SAN FRANCISCO, CALIF.
1949-016	CONNORS, KEVIN JOSEPH 'CHUCK'	D. NOVEMBER 10, 1992, LOS ANGELES, CALIF.
1937-027	CONNORS, MERVYN JAMES	D. JANUARY 8, 2006, SAN FRANCISCO, CALIF.
1966-023	CONNORS, WILLIAM JOSEPH	3329 ENTERPRISE ROAD EAST, SAFETY HARBOR FL 34695
1978-028	CONROY, TIMOTHY JAMES	109 MOONLIGHT DRIVE, MONROEVILLE PA 15146
1923-023	CONROY, WILLIAM FREDERICK 'PEP'	D. JANUARY 23, 1970, CHICAGO, ILL.
1935-016	CONROY, WILLIAM GORDON	D. NOVEMBER 13, 1997, BLOOMINGTON, ILL.
1953-016	CONSOLO, WILLIAM ANGELO	1266 WILLSBROOK COURT, WESTLAKE VILLAGE CA 91360
1956-023	CONSTABLE, JAMES LEE	D. SEPTEMBER 4, 2002, JOHNSON CITY, TENN.
1950-023	CONSUEGRA, SANDALIO SIMEON 'SANDY'	D. NOVEMBER 16, 2005, MIAMI, FLA.
2000-038	CONTI, STANLEY JASON 'JASON'	740 NORTH APRIL DRIVE, CHANDLER AZ 85226
1980-027	CONTRERAS, ARNALDO JUAN 'NARDIE'	17546 WILLOW POND DRIVE, LUTZ FL 33549
2003-029	CONTRERAS, JOSE ARIEL	OLD ADD: LA MARTINAS CUBA
1993-034	CONVERSE, JAMES DANIEL	11865 COBBLE BROOK DRIVE, RANCHO CORDOVA CA 95742
1941-017	CONWAY, JACK CLEMENTS	D. JUNE 11, 1993, WACO, TEXAS

1920-025	CONWAY, JEROME PATRICK	D. APRIL 16, 1980, HOLYOKE, MASS.
1950-024	CONYERS, HERBERT LEROY	D. SEPTEMBER 16, 1964, CLEVELAND, OHIO
1950-025	COOGAN, DALE ROGER	D. MARCH 8, 1989, MISSION VIEJO CALIF.
2002-034	COOK, AARON LANE	6113 LIBERTY FAIRCHILD ROAD, HAMILTON OH 45011
1993-035	COOK, ANDREW BERNARD	3312 CENTRAL AVENUE, MEMPHIS TN 38111
1988-032	COOK, DENNIS BRYAN	5017 CEDAR CREEK, DICKINSON TX 77539
1941-018	COOK, EARL DAVIS	D. NOVEMBER 21, 1996, MARKHAM, ONT.
1985-020	COOK, GLEN PATRICK	424 SCARLET SAGE DRIVE, LEAGUE CITY TX 77573
1986-037	COOK, MICHAEL HORACE	OLD ADD: 1618 POINSETTIA ROAD #2, CHARLESTON SC 29407
1959-015	COOK, RAYMOND CLIFFORD 'CLIFF'	605 WILLIAMSBURG MANOR, ARLINGTON TX 76044
1970-027	COOK, RONALD WAYNE	1918 FRANKLIN DRIVE, LONGVIEW TX 75601
1930-013	COOKE, ALLEN LINDSEY 'DUSTY'	D. NOVEMBER 21, 1987, RALEIGH, N.C.
1992-029	COOKE, STEVEN MONTAGUE	1 SW BOWERMAN DRIVE, BEAVERTON OR 97005
1995-051	COOKSON, BRENT ADAM	1232 MANZANITA DRIVE, SANTA PAULA CA 93060
2001-038	COOLBAUGH, MICHAEL ROBERT	12146 APRICOT DRIVE, SAN ANTONIO TX 78247
1989-025	COOLBAUGH, SCOTT RICHARD	6078 CARRIAGE LANE, COLLEYSVILLE TX 76034
1963-025	COOMBS, DANIEL BERNARD	14130 CLEOBROOK, HOUSTON TX 77070
1933-014	COOMBS, RAYMOND FRANK 'BOBBY'	D. OCTOBER 21, 1991, OGUNQUIT, MAINE
1995-052	COOMER, RONALD BRYAN	7021 HOWARD LANE, EDEN PRAIRIE MN 55346
1921-017	COONEY, JOHN WALTER	D. JULY 8, 1986, SARASOTA, FLA.
1931-017	COONEY, ROBERT DANIEL	D. MAY 4, 1976, GLEN FALLS, N.Y.
1999-035	COOPER, BRIAN JOHN	346 WEST ADA AVENUE, GLENDORA CA 91741
1948-029	COOPER, CALVIN ASA	D. JULY 4, 1994, CLINTON, S.C.
1971-027	COOPER, CECIL CELESTER	24802 BOULDER LAKE COURT, KATY TX 77494
1981-024	COOPER, DONALD JAMES	2320 ARBORFIELD LANE, SARASOTA FL 34235
1991-038	COOPER, GARY CLIFTON	1136 BIRCH CIRCLE, ALPINE UT 84004
1980-028	COOPER, GARY NATHANIEL	4309 AUGUSTA ROAD #109B, SAVANNAH GA 31408
1938-016	COOPER, MORTON CECIL	D. NOVEMBER 17, 1958, LITTLE ROCK, ARK.
1946-019	COOPER, ORGE PATTERSON 'PAT'	D. MARCH 15, 1993, CHARLOTTE, N.C.
1990-035	COOPER, SCOTT KENDRICK	7 FAIRWAY CIRCLE #F, SAINT CHARLES MO 63303
1940-013	COOPER, WILLIAM WALKER 'WALKER'	D. APRIL 11, 1991, SCOTTSDALE, ARIZ.
1935-017	COPELAND, MAYS	D. NOVEMBER 29, 1982, INDIO, CALIF.
1996-039	COPPINGER, JOHN THOMAS 'ROCKY'	7208 ALTO REY AVENUE, EL PASO TX 79912
1935-018	COPPOLA, HENRY PETER	D. JULY 10, 1990, NORFOLK, MASS.
1999-036	COQUILLETTE, TRACE ROBERT	5200 MISSISSIPPI BAR DRIVE, ORANGEVALE CA 95662
1998-036	CORA, JOSE ALEXANDER 'ALEX'	OLD ADD: 2105 31ST AVENUE, VERO BEACH FL 32960
1987-026	CORA, JOSE MANUEL	CALLE 17, F12 VILLA NUEVA, CAGUAS PR 00625
1980-029	CORBETT, DOUGLAS MITCHELL	861214 NORTH HAMPTON CLUB WAY, FERNANDINA FL 32034
1936-015	CORBETT, EUGENE LOUIS	1109 SOUTH SCHUMAKER DRIVE #204, SALISBURY MD 21804
1988-033	CORBETT, SHERMAN STANLEY	7031 WASHITA WAY, SAN ANTONIO TX 78256
1971-028	CORBIN, ALTON RAY 'RAY'	65 MOORE STREET, FRANKLIN NC 28734
1991-039	CORBIN, ARCHIE RAY 'RAY'	7525 TRAM ROAD, BEAUMONT TX 77713
1945-016	CORBITT, CLAUDE ELLIOTT	D. MAY 1, 1978, CINCINNATI, OHIO
2003-030	CORCORAN, ROY ELLIOT	PO BOX 173, SLAUGHTER LA 70777
2005-042	CORCORAN, TIMOTHY HUGH	PO BOX 173, SLAUGHTER LA 70777
1977-032	CORCORAN, TIMOTHY MICHAEL	4349 FRIAR CIRCLE, LAVERNE CA 91750
2003-031	CORDERO, CHAD P	OLD ADD: UPLAND CA
1999-037	CORDERO, FRANCISCO JAVIER	OLD ADD: SANTO DOMINGO DOM REP
1992-030	CORDERO, WILFREDO NIEVA	OLD ADD: 25844 KENSINGTON DRIVE, WESTLAKE OH 44145
1996-040	CORDOVA, FRANCISCO	OLD ADD: VERACRUZ MEXICO
1995-053	CORDOVA, MARTIN KEEVIN	448 TATUM RIDGE STREET, HENDERSON NV 89012
1998-037	COREY, BRYAN SCOTT	3060 NORTH RIDGECREST, MESA AZ 85207
2001-039	COREY, MARK FRANKLIN	PO BOX 113, AUSTIN PA 16720
1979-025	COREY, MARK MUNDELL	9321 SOUTH CORNELL CIRCLE, HIGHLANDS RANCH CO 80126
1925-021	CORGAN, CHARLES HOWARD	D. JUNE 13, 1928, WAGONER, OKLA.
1969-036	CORKINS, MICHAEL PATRICK	3760 CHEMEHUEVI BLVD, LAKE HAVASU CITY AZ 86406
2004-043	CORMIER, LANCE ROBERT	502 DOWNING STREET, LAFAYETTE LA 70506
1991-040	CORMIER, RHEAL PAUL	15711 CEDAR GROVE LANE, WELLINGTON FL 33414
2001-040	CORNEJO, NATHAN J.	512 NORTH WASHINGTON AVENUE, WELLINGTON KS 67152
1978-029	CORNEJO, NEIVES MARDIE 'MARDIE'	321 EAST THIRD STREET, WELLINGTON KS 67152
1995-054	CORNELIUS, JONATHAN REID 'REID'	10117 HUNT CLUB LANE, PALM BEACH GARDENS FL 33418
1984-022	CORNELL, JEFFERY RAY	1644 SW JEFFREY CIRCLE, LEES SUMMIT MO 64081
1994-018	CORNETT, BRAD BYRON	1301 EAST 63RD, ODESSA TX 79762
1977-033	CORNUTT, TERRY STANTON	179 WEST HAZEL, ROSEBURG OR 97470
2006-038	CORPAS, MANUEL	OLD ADD: PANAMA CITY PANAMA
1964-022	CORRALES, PATRICK	2 WEST WESLEY ROAD NW, ATLANTA GA 30305
1985-021	CORREA, EDWIN JOSEPH	MILAGROS CABEZAS A-2 CAROLINA ALTA, CAROLINA PR 00987
2003-032	CORREIA, KEVIN JOHN	2752 PIANFINO CIRCLE, SAN DIEGO CA 92108
1993-036	CORREIA, RONALD DOUGLAS 'ROD'	24 SOUTH BULFINCH STREET #102, NORTH ATTLEBORO MA 02760
1972-021	CORRELL, VICTOR CROSBY	119 KENTUCKY DOWNS, PERRY GA 31069
1946-020	CORRIDEN, JOHN MICHAEL	D. JUNE 4, 2001, INDIANAPOLIS, IND.
1988-034	CORSI, JAMES BERNARD	48 EASTVIEW ROAD, HOPKINTON MA 01748
1977-034	CORT, BARRY LEE	201 WEST LAUREL STREET #404, TAMPA FL 33602
1923-024	CORTAZZO, JOHN FRANK 'SHINE'	D. MARCH 4, 1963, PITTSBURGH, PA.
1999-038	CORTES, DAVID C	OLD ADD: 427 EAST BRIGHTON AVE, EL CENTRO CA 92243
2005-043	CORTEZ, FERNANDO	OLD ADD: 1581 BLACK EAGLE DRIVE, SAN DIEGO CA 92126
1951-016	CORWIN, ELMER NATHAN 'AL'	D. OCTOBER 23, 2003, GENEVA, ILL.
1935-019	COSCARART, JOSEPH MARVIN	D. APRIL 5, 1993, SEQUIM, WASH.
1938-017	COSCARART, PETER JOSEPH	D. JULY 24, 2002, ESCONDIDO, CALIF.
1980-030	COSEY, DONALD RAY	139 BYXBEE ST, SAN FRANCISCO CA 94132
1972-022	COSGROVE, MICHAEL JOHN	8813 WEST CORRINE DRIVE, PEORIA AZ 85381
1966-024	COSMAN, JAMES HARRY	BLACKBURN ROAD, SEWICKLEY PA 15143
2005-044	COSTA, SHANE JEREMY	1747 NORTH COTTA COURT, VISALIA CA 93292
2006-039	COSTE, CHRISTOPHER ROBERT	515 21ST AVENUE SOUTH, FARGO ND 58103
1988-035	COSTELLO, JOHN REILLY	68 ROYAL OAK COURT #206, VERO BEACH FL 32962
1992-031	COSTO, TIMOTHY ROGER	3107 PINTAIL LANE, SIGNAL MOUNTAIN TN 37377

2001-041	COTA, HUMBERTO FIGUEROA	OLD ADD: SAN LUIS RIO MEX
1926-019	COTE, WARREN PETER 'PETE'	D. OCTOBER 17, 1987, MIDDLETON, MASS.
1926-020	COTTER, EDWARD CHRISTOPHER	D. JUNE 14, 1959, HARTFORD, CONN.
1922-022	COTTER, HARVEY LOUIS	D. AUGUST 6, 1955, LOS ANGELES, CALIF.
1959-016	COTTIER, CHARLES KEITH	7129 LAKE BALLINGER WAY, EDMONDS WA 98026
1984-023	COTTO, HENRY	OLD ADD: 2659 MEADOWOOD COURT, FORT LAUDERDALE FL 33932
2003-033	COTTS, NEAL JAMES	506 WEST SCHUETZ STREET, LEBANON IL 62254
1983-036	COUCHEE, MICHAEL EUGENE	3060 NORTH RIDGECREST #155, MESA AZ 85207
1960-025	COUGHTRY, JAMES MARLAN 'MARLAN'	9113 NE 65TH STREET, VANCOUVER WA 98662
1969-037	COULTER, THOMAS LEE 'CHIP'	718 TRENTON STREET, TORONTO OH 43964
1995-055	COUNSELL, CRAIG JOHN	992 EAST CIRCLE DRIVE, MILWAUKEE WI 53217
1951-017	COURTNEY, CLINTON DAWSON	D. JUNE 16, 1985, ROCHESTER, N.Y.
1995-056	COURTRIGHT, JOHN CHARLES	316 SOUTH ROOSEVELT AVENUE, COLUMBUS OH 43209
1923-025	COUSINEAU, ED 'D'	D. JULY 14, 1951, WATERTOWN, MASS.
1944-023	COVINGTON, CHESTER ROGERS	D. JUNE 11, 1976, PEMBROKE PARK, FLA.
1956-024	COVINGTON, JOHN WESLEY 'WES'	905 10145 119TH STREET, EDMONTON AB, T5K 1Z2 CANADA
1963-026	COWAN, BILLY ROLAND	1539 VIA CORONEL, PALOS VERDES ESTATES CA 90274
1974-017	COWENS, ALFRED EDWARD	D. MARCH 11, 2002, DOWNEY, CALIF.
1982-026	COWLEY, JOSEPH ALAN	102 SUMMERTREE DRIVE, NICHOLASVILLE KY 40356
1999-039	COX, CHARLES STEVEN 'STEVE'	22678 AVENUE 188, STRATHMORE CA 93267
1983-037	COX, DANNY BRADFORD	306 FEAGIN MILL RD, WARNER ROBINS GA 31093
1925-022	COX, ELMER JOSEPH 'DICK'	D. JUNE 1, 1966, MORRO BAY, CALIF.
1922-023	COX, ERNEST THOMPSON	D. APRIL 29, 1974, BIRMINGHAM, ALA.
1928-023	COX, GEORGE MELVIN	D. DECEMBER 17, 1995, BEDFORD, TEXAS
1955-030	COX, GLENN MELVIN	PO BOX 432, LOS MOLINOS CA 96055
1973-026	COX, JAMES CHARLES	8370 EAST CHARTER OAK DRIVE, SCOTTSDALE AZ 85260
1999-040	COX, JAMES DARRON 'DARRON'	2708 EAST 148TH DRIVE, THORNTON CO 80602
1980-031	COX, JEFFREY LINDON	2727 VANDERHOOF DR, WEST COVINA CA 91791
1966-025	COX, JOSEPH CASEY 'CASEY'	2840 LA CONCHA DRIVE, CLEARWATER FL 33762
1973-027	COX, LARRY EUGENE	D. FEBRUARY 17, 1990, BELLEFONTAINE, OHIO
1926-021	COX, LESLIE WARREN	D. OCTOBER 14, 1934, SAN ANGELO, TEXAS
1920-026	COX, PLATEAU REX	D. OCTOBER 15, 1984, ROANOKE, VA.
1968-015	COX, ROBERT JOSEPH 'BOBBY'	2938 WINDSTONE CIRCLE, MARIETTA GA 30062
1970-028	COX, TERRY LEE	6666 SOUTH NOTTINGHAM CIRCLE, WEST JORDAN UT 84084
1936-016	COX, WILLIAM DONALD	D. FEBRUARY 16, 1988, CHARLESTON, ILL.
1941-019	COX, WILLIAM RICHARD	D. MARCH 30, 1978, HARRISBURG, PA.
1977-035	COX, WILLIAM TED 'TED'	5117 KENNINGTON LANE, OKLAHOMA CITY OK 73150
1945-017	COZART, CHARLES RHUBIN	D. DECEMBER 31, 2004, LENOIR, N.C.
1929-021	CRABTREE, ESTEL CRAYTON	D. JANUARY 4, 1967, LOGAN, OHIO
1995-057	CRABTREE, TIMOTHY LYLE	1503 KINGSWOOD LANE, COLLEYVILLE TX 76034
1955-031	CRADDOCK, WALTER ANDERSON	D. JULY 6, 1980, PARMA HEIGHTS OHIO
1998-038	CRADLE, RICKEY NELSON	1311 DRY GAP PIKE, KNOXVILLE TN 37918
1937-028	CRAFT, HARRY FRANCIS	D. AUGUST 3, 1995, CONROE, TEXAS
1931-018	CRAGHEAD, HOWARD OLIVER	D. JULY 15, 1962, SAN ZIELOE, CALIF.
1964-023	CRAIG, PETER JOEL	5915 CARMEL LANE, RALEIGH NC 27609
1979-026	CRAIG, RODNEY PAUL 'ROCKY'	OLD ADD: 23230 SESAME STREET, TORRANCE CA 90504
1955-032	CRAIG, ROGER LEE	PO BOX 2174, BORREGO SPRINGS CA 92004
2004-044	CRAIN, JESSE ALAN	4025 FREDERICK CIRCLE, LONGMONT CO 80503
1969-038	CRAM, GERALD ALLEN	33015 VICTORIA BROOKE LANE, LAKE ELSINORE CA 92530
1929-022	CRAMER, ROGER MAXWELL 'DOC'	D. SEPTEMBER 9, 1990, MANAHAWKIN, N.J.
1949-017	CRANDALL, DELMAR WESLEY	OLD ADD: 807 AZALEA LANE, VERO BEACH FL 32963
2002-035	CRAWFORD, CARL DEMONTE	12515 SILVERGLEN ESTATES DRIVE, HOUSTON TX 77014
1996-041	CRAWFORD, CARLOS LAMONTE	1851 ATLANTIC DRIVE, RUSKIN FL 33570
1937-029	CRAWFORD, CHARLES LOWRIE 'LARRY'	D. DECEMBER 20, 1994, HANOVER, PA.
1929-023	CRAWFORD, CLIFFORD RANKIN 'PAT'	D. JANUARY 25, 1994, KINSTON, N.C.
1945-018	CRAWFORD, GLENN MARTIN	D. JANUARY 2, 1972, SAGINAW, MICH.
1973-028	CRAWFORD, JAMES FREDERICK	OLD ADD: 2202 NORTH INDIAN RUINS ROAD, TUCSON AZ 85715
1997-036	CRAWFORD, JOSEPH RANDOL	5428 US 50, HILLSBORO OH 45133
2000-039	CRAWFORD, PAXTON KEITH	OLD ADD: MORILLTON AR
1952-020	CRAWFORD, RUFUS 'JAKE '	7800 MOCKINGBIRD LANE #52, NORTH RICHLAND HILLS TX 76180
1980-032	CRAWFORD, STEVE RAY	6532 ANGUS DRIVE, LAKELAND FL 33810
1964-024	CRAWFORD, WILLIE MURPHY	D. AUGUST 27, 2004, LOS ANGELES, CALIF.
2000-040	CREDE, JOSEPH	HC 65, WESTPHALIA MO 65085
1943-032	CREEDEN, CORNELIUS STEPHEN	D. NOVEMBER 30, 1969, SANTA ANA, CALIF.
1931-019	CREEDEN, PATRICK FRANCIS	D. APRIL 20, 1992, BROCKTON, MASS.
1995-058	CREEK, PAUL DOUGLAS 'DOUG'	8048 SYCAMORE DRIVE, NEW PORT RICHEY FL 34654
1945-019	CREEL, JACK DALTON	D. AUGUST 13, 2002, HOUSTON, TEXAS
1982-027	CREEL, STEVEN KEITH 'KEITH'	527 TRAIL RIDGE DRIVE, DUNCANVILLE TX 75116
1947-022	CREGER, BERNARD ODELL	D. NOVEMBER 30, 1997, LYNCHBURG, VA.
1927-027	CREMINS, ROBERT ANTHONY	D. MARCH 27, 2004, PELHAM, N.Y.
1938-018	CRESPI, FRANK ANGELO JOSEPH 'CREEPY'	D. MARCH 1, 1990, FLORISSANT, MO.
2001-042	CRESPO, CESAR ANTONIO (CLAUDIO)	OLD ADD: CAGUAS PR
1996-042	CRESPO, FELIPE JAVIER CLAUSO	1798 PAM CIRCLE, ORLANDO FL 32809
1948-030	CRESS, WALKER JAMES	D. APRIL 21, 1996, BATON ROUGE, LA.
2000-041	CRESSEND, JOHN BAPTISTE 'JACK'	525 TANAGER DRIVE, MANDEVILLE LA 70448
1987-027	CREWS, STANLEY TIMOTHY 'TIM'	D. MARCH 23, 1993, ORLANDO, FLA.
1969-039	CRIDER, JERRY STEPHEN	OLD ADD: 821 KENSINGTON DRIVE, ORLANDO FL 32808
1987-028	CRIM, CHARLES ROBERT 'CHUCK'	25800 SAND CANYON ROAD, SANTA CLARITA CA 91350
1951-018	CRIMIAN, JOHN MELVIN	3012 GREEN STREET, CLAYMONT DE 19703
1978-030	CRIPE, DAVID GORDON	1835 MONTARA WAY, SAN JACINTO CA 92583
1977-036	CRISCIONE, DAVID GERALD	87 HAMLET ST, FREDONIA NY 14063
1942-024	CRISCOLA, ANTHONY PAUL	D. JULY 10, 2001, LAJOLLA, CALIF.
2002-036	CRISP, COVELLI LOYCE	9949 WARWICK DRIVE, DESERT HOT SPRINGS CA 92240
1951-019	CRISTANTE, LEO DANTE	D. AUGUST 24, 1977, DEARBORN, MICH.
1924-023	CRITZ, HUGH MELVILLE	D. JANUARY 10, 1980, GREENWOOD, MISS.
1944-024	CROCKER, CLAUDE ARTHUR	D. DECEMBER 19, 2002, CLINTON, S.C.

1974-018	CROMARTIE, WARREN LIVINGSTON	PO BOX 601802, NORTH MIAMI BEACH FL 33160
2000-042	CROMER, DAVID THOMAS 'D.T.'	142 STERLING LAKE DRIVE, LEXINGTON SC 29072
1993-037	CROMER, ROY BUNYAN 'TRIPP'	32 WEST TOMBEE LANE, COLUMBIA SC 29209
1937-030	CROMPTON, HERBERT BRYAN	D. AUGUST 5, 1963, MOLINE, ILL.
1991-041	CRON, CHRISTOPHER JOHN	14879 SOUTH 43RD PLACE, PHOENIX AZ 85044
1954-016	CRONE, RAYMOND HAYES	508 PANORAMA, WAXAHACHIE TX 75165
1929-024	CRONIN, JAMES JOHN	D. JUNE 10, 1983, RICHMOND, CALIF.
1926-022	CRONIN, JOSEPH EDWARD	D. SEPTEMBER 7, 1984, OSTERVILLE, MASS.
1928-024	CRONIN, WILLIAM PATRICK	D. OCTOBER 26, 1966, NEWTON, MASS.
1970-029	CROSBY, EDWARD CARLTON	6952 BRIGHTWOOD LANE #9, GARDEN GROVE CA 92645
1975-028	CROSBY, KENNETH STEWART	BOX 680306, PARK CITY UT 84068
2003-034	CROSBY, RICHARD STEPHEN 'BUBBA'	5217 BRAEBURN DRIVE, BELLAIRE TX 77401
2003-035	CROSBY, ROBERT EDWARD 'BOBBY'	11463 ANTICOST WAY, CYPRESS CA 90630
1932-015	CROSETTI, FRANK PETER JOSEPH	D. FEBRUARY 11, 2002, COMPTON, CALIF.
1942-025	CROSS, JOFFRE JAMES 'JEFF'	D. JULY 23, 1997, HUNTSVILLE, TEXAS
1930-014	CROUCH, JACK ALBERT	D. AUGUST 25, 1972, LEESBURG, FLA.
1939-024	CROUCH, WILLIAM ELMER	D. DECEMBER 26, 1980, HOWELL, MICH.
1988-036	CROUCH, ZACHARY QUINN	3122 TORY, SACRAMENTO CA 95827
1939-025	CROUCHER, FRANK DONALD	D. MAY 21, 1980, HOUSTON, TEXAS
1923-026	CROUSE, CLYDE ELLSWORTH 'BUCK'	D. OCTOBER 23, 1983, MUNCIE, IND.
1998-039	CROUSHORE, RICHARD STEVEN 'RICK'	3110 BASTOGNE WAY, BENTON AR 72015
1982-028	CROW, DONALD LEROY	1554 BROOK DRIVE, FORT MILL SC 29708
1998-040	CROW, PAUL DEAN 'DEAN'	11507 WICKCHESTER LANE, HOUSTON TX 77043
1926-023	CROWDER, ALVIN FLOYD 'GEN'	D. APRIL 3, 1972, WINSTON-SALEM, N.C.
1952-021	CROWE, GEORGE DANIEL	1955 D O MILLS COURT, GOLD RIVER CA 95670
1997-037	CROWELL, JAMES E.	4003 SLEIGHBELL LANE, VALPARAISO IN 46383
1928-025	CROWLEY, EDGAR JEWEL	D. APRIL 14, 1970, BIRMINGHAM, ALA.
1969-040	CROWLEY, TERRENCE MICHAEL	10626 ANGLOHILL RD, COCKEYSVILLE MD 21030
1945-020	CROWSON, THOMAS WOODROW WILSON 'WOODY'	D. AUGUST 14, 1947, MAYODAN, N.C.
2004-045	CROZIER, ERIC LE ROI	3142 CLERMONT ROAD, COLUMBUS OH 43227
2004-046	CRUCETA, FRANCISCO ALBERTO	OLD ADD: LA VEGA DOM REP
2002-037	CRUDALE, MICHAEL CHRISTOPHER	2319 TREE CREEK PLACE, DANVILLE CA 94506
1945-021	CRUMLING, EUGENE LEON	135 LISA CIRCLE, YORK PA 17406
1924-024	CRUMP, ARTHUR ELLIOTT	D. SEPTEMBER 26, 1976, RALEIGH, N.C.
1920-027	CRUMPLER, RAY MAXTON	D. OCTOBER 6, 1969, FAYETTEVILLE, N.C.
1973-029	CRUZ, CIRILO 'TOMMY'	URB. JARDINES DE ARROYO CALLE EE C 104, ARROYO PR 00714
1997-038	CRUZ, DEIVI GARCIA	OLD ADD: BANI DOM REP
2003-036	CRUZ, ENRIQUE MICHAEL	OLD ADD: SANTO DOMINGO DOM REP
1994-019	CRUZ, FAUSTO SANTIAGO	FEDERICO DE JESUS GARCIA #112 VILLA VASQUEZ, DOM REP
1973-030	CRUZ, HECTOR LUIS 'TOMMY'	CALLE H-E-8, ARROYO PR 00615
1975-029	CRUZ, HENRY ACOSTA	T-0-6 URB MONTE BRISAS, FAJARDO PR 00738
1996-043	CRUZ, JACOB	979 EAST STRORBE STREET, OXNARD CA 93030
1970-030	CRUZ, JOSE DELAN	2309 DELTA BRIDGE DRIVE, PEARLAND TX 77584
1997-039	CRUZ, JOSE LUIS	2309 DELTA BRIDGE DRIVE, PEARLAND TX 77584
2001-043	CRUZ, JUAN CARLOS	OLD ADD: BANAO DOM REP
1977-037	CRUZ, JULIO LOUIS	2260 95TH AVENUE, CLYDE HILL WA 98004
1997-040	CRUZ, LUIS IVAN 'IVAN'	OLD ADD: FAJARDO PR 00738
1997-041	CRUZ, NELSON	2920 14TH COURT, MIAMI FL 33142
2005-045	CRUZ, NELSON RAMON	OLD ADD: MONTE CRISTI DOM REP
1978-031	CRUZ, TODD RUBEN	15655 REED DRIVE, FONTANA CA 92336
1978-032	CRUZ, VICTOR MANUEL	D. SEPTEMBER 26, 2004, SANTO DOMINGO, DOM REP
1974-019	CUBBAGE, MICHAEL LEE	3349 CARROLL CREEK ROAD, KESWICK VA 22947
2000-043	CUBILLAN, DARWIN HARRIKSON	OLD ADD: BOBURE VENEZUELA
1935-020	CUCCINELLO, ALFRED EDWARD	D. MARCH 29, 2004, MALVERNE, N.Y.
1930-015	CUCCINELLO, ANTHONY FRANCIS 'TONY'	D. SEPTEMBER 21, 1995, TAMPA, FLA.
1943-033	CUCCURULLO, ARTHUR JOSEPH 'COOKIE'	D. JANUARY 23, 1983, WEST ORANGE, N.J.
2001-044	CUDDYER, MICHAEL BRENT	522 JOHN ETHERIDGE ROAD, CHESAPEAKE VA 23322
1977-038	CUELLAR, BOBBY	705 EAST SIXTH STREET, ALICE TX 78332
1950-026	CUELLAR, JESUS PATRACIS 'CHARLIE'	D. OCTOBER 11, 1994, TAMPA, FLA.
1959-017	CUELLAR, MIGUEL SANTANA 'MIKE'	1046 HEATHER GLENN DRIVE, MINNEOLA FL 34715
1961-025	CUETO, DAGOBERTO CONCEPCION 'BERT'	540 CROCUS COURT, CHARLOTTE NC 28217
1943-034	CULBERSON, DELBERT LEON 'LEON'	D. SEPTEMBER 17, 1989, ROME, GA.
1962-029	CULLEN, JOHN PATRICK	164 ALEXANDER AVE, NUTLEY NJ 07110
1966-026	CULLEN, TIMOTHY LEO	159 WEST G STREET, BENICIA CA 94510
1938-019	CULLENBINE, ROY JOSEPH	D. MAY 28, 1991, MOUNT CLEMENS, MICH.
1936-017	CULLER, RICHARD BROADUS	D. JUNE 16, 1964, CHAPEL HILL, N.C.
1926-024	CULLOP, HENRY 'NICK'	D. DECEMBER 8, 1978, WESTERVILLE, OHIO
1925-023	CULLOTON, BERNARD ALOYSIUS 'BUD'	D. NOVEMBER 9, 1976, KINGSTON, N.Y.
1983-038	CULMER, WILFRED HILLARD 'WIL'	D. OCTOBER 14, 2003, NASSAU, BAHAMAS
1942-026	CULP, BENJAMIN BALDY	D. OCTOBER 23, 2000, PHILADELPHIA, PA.
1963-027	CULP, RAY LEONARD	7400 WATERLINE, AUSTIN TX 78731
1966-027	CULVER, GEORGE RICHARD	5409 RUSTIC CANYON STREET, BAKERSFIELD CA 93306
1968-016	CUMBERLAND, JOHN SHELDON	19417 GOLDEN SLIPPER PLACE, LUTZ FL 33548
1993-038	CUMMINGS, JOHN RUSSELL	21 PARK PASEO, LAGUNA NIGUEL CA 92677
1926-025	CUMMINGS, JOHN WILLIAM	D. OCTOBER 5, 1962, WEST MIFFLIN, PA.
1993-039	CUMMINGS, MIDRE ALMERIC	408 DENISE STREET, TARPON SPRINGS FL 34689
1989-026	CUMMINGS, STEVEN BRENT	11010 SAGECREST, HOUSTON TX 77089
1997-042	CUNNANE, WILLIAM JOSEPH 'WILL'	352 STRAWTOWN ROAD, WEST NYACK NY 10994
1929-025	CUNNINGHAM, BRUCE LEE	D. MARCH 8, 1984, HAYWARD, CALIF.
1954-017	CUNNINGHAM, JOSEPH ROBERT	RURAL ROUTE 1 BOX 80A, KOSHKONONG MO 65692
1931-020	CUNNINGHAM, RAYMOND LEE	D. JULY 30, 2005, PEARLAND, TEXAS
1921-018	CUNNINGHAM, WILLIAM ALOYSIUS	D. SEPTEMBER 26, 1953, COLUSA, CALIF.
1975-030	CURRENCE, DELANCY LAFAYETTE 'LAFAYETTE'	523 NEVILLE STREET, ROCK HILL SC 29730
1955-033	CURRIE, WILLIAM CLEVELAND	125 LAKE SIDE DRIVE, ARLINGTON GA 31713
1947-023	CURRIN, PERRY GILMORE	818 AMBERSTONE DRIVE, SAN ANTONIO TX 78258
1960-026	CURRY, GEORGE ANTHONY 'TONY'	D. OCTOBER 16, 2006, NASSAU, BAHAMAS

1988-037	CURRY, STEPHEN THOMAS	OLD ADD: 1711 21ST AVENUE WEST, BRADENTON FL 34205
1992-032	CURTIS, CHAD DAVID	1221 OLD OAK HILL DRIVE, ADA MI 49301
1961-026	CURTIS, JACK PATRICK	4949 IKE STARNES ROAD, GRANITE FALLS NC 28630
1970-031	CURTIS, JOHN DUFFIELD	1800 ROUNDHILL ROAD #1207, CHARLESTON WV 25314
1943-035	CURTIS, VERNON EUGENE	D. JUNE 24, 1992, CAIRO, ILL.
1943-036	CURTRIGHT, GUY PAXTON	D. AUGUST 23, 1997, SUN CITY CENTER, FLA.
1951-020	CUSICK, JOHN PETER 'JACK'	D. NOVEMBER 17, 1989, ENGLEWOOD, N.J.
2001-045	CUST, JOHN JOSEPH	PO BOX 372, FLEMINGTON NJ 08822
1921-019	CUYLER, HAZEN SHIRLEY 'KIKI'	D. FEBRUARY 11, 1950, ANN ARBOR, MICH.
1990-036	CUYLER, MILTON	4360 ARIAN AVENUE, FORT MYERS FL 33916
1922-024	CVENGROS, MICHAEL JOHN	D. AUGUST 2, 1970, HOT SPRINGS, ARK.
2002-038	CYR, ERIC	OLD ADD: 1766 GRISSO DRIVE, SEMINOLE OK 74868
1994-020	CZAJKOWSKI, JAMES MARK	1648 RIVERGATE DRIVE, SEVIERVILLE TN 37862

D

1993-040	DAAL, OMAR JOSE (CORDERO)	2458 PROVENCE COURT, WESTON FL 33327
1973-031	DACQUISTO, JOHN FRANCIS	600 PALM AVENUE, LOS ALTOS CA 94022
1975-031	DADE, LONNIE PAUL 'PAUL'	5212 66TH STREET COURT WEST, UNIVERSITY PLACE WA 98467
1943-037	DAGENHARD, JOHN DOUGLAS	D. JULY 16, 2001, BOLIVAR, OHIO
1932-016	DAGLIA, PETER GEORGE	D. MARCH 11, 1952, WILLITS, CALIF.
1955-034	DAGRES, ANGELO GEORGE	PO BOX 27, ROWLEY MA 01969
1963-028	DAHL, JAY STEVEN	D. JUNE 20, 1965, SALISBURY, N.C.
1935-021	DAHLGREN, ELLSWORTH TENNEY 'BABE'	D. SEPTEMBER 4, 1996, BRADBURY, CALIF.
1956-025	DAHLKE, JEROME ALEXANDER	D. SEPTEMBER 2, 2006, BATESVILLE, MISS.
2004-047	DAIGLE, SEAN CASEY 'CASEY'	2607 WPA ROAD, SULPHUR LA 70663
1929-026	DAILEY, SAMUEL LAURENCE	D. DECEMBER 2, 1979, COLUMBIA, MO.
1961-027	DAILEY, WILLIAM GARLAND	5019 MEADOW WAY, DUBLIN VA 24084
1967-021	DAL CANTON, JOHN BRUCE 'BRUCE'	624 RAY DR, CARNEGIE PA 15106
1999-041	DALE, JAMES CARL 'CARL'	3358 OAK TRAIL, COOKEVILLE TN 38506
1989-027	DALENA, PETER MARTIN	4951 NORTH THORNE, FRESNO CA 93704
1994-021	DALESANDRO, MARK ANTHONY	1908 ARBOR FIELDS DRIVE, PLAINFIELD IL 60431
1955-035	DALEY, BUDDY LEO	3607 MAPLE PASS COURT, KATY TX 77449
1955-036	DALEY, PETER HARVEY	4019 CALLE MIRA MONTE, NEWBURY PARK CA 91320
1937-031	DALLESSANDRO, NICHOLAS DOMINIC 'DOM'	D. APRIL 29, 1988, INDIANAPOLIS, IND.
2004-048	DALLIMORE, BRIAN SCOTT	10531 HAYWOOD DRIVE, LAS VEGAS NV 89135
1960-027	DALRYMPLE, CLAYTON ERROL	28248 MATEER ROAD, GOLD BEACH OR 97444
1991-042	DALTON, MICHAEL EDWARD	354 FLYNN AVENUE, MOUNTAIN VIEW CA 94043
1963-029	DAMASKA, JACK LLOYD	252 BLACKHAWK RD, BEAVER FALLS PA 15010
1996-044	DAMICO, JEFFREY CHARLES	2223 MUIRFIELD WAY, OLDSMAR FL 34677
2000-044	DAMICO, JEFFREY MICHAEL	9567 NE NORTHOWN LOOP, BAINBRIDGE ISLAND WA 98110
1995-059	DAMON, JOHNNY DAVID	904 MAIN STREET, WINDERMERE FL 34786
1999-042	DANEKER, PATRICK REES	1419 RITCHEY STREET, WILLIAMSPORT PA 17701
1928-026	DANEY, ARTHUR LEE	D. MARCH 11, 1988, SCOTTSDALE, ARIZ.
1957-014	DANIEL, CHARLES EDWARD	59 JILGUERO WAY, HOT SPRINGS AR 71909
1937-032	DANIEL, HANDLEY JACOB 'JAKE'	D. APRIL 23, 1996, LAGRANGE, GA.
1957-015	DANIELS, BENNIE	938 WEST 156TH STREET, COMPTON CA 90220
1945-022	DANIELS, FREDERICK CLINTON	D. JULY 23, 2005, STATESVILLE, N.C.
1952-022	DANIELS, HAROLD JACK 'JACK'	3715 ELMRIDGE DRIVE, EVANSVILLE IN 47711
1986-038	DANIELS, KALVOSKI 'KAL'	PO BOX 9632, WARNER ROBINS GA 31095
1933-015	DANNING, HARRY	D. NOVEMBER 29, 2004, VALPARAISO, IND.
1928-027	DANNING, ISAAC 'IKE'	D. MARCH 28, 1983, SANTA MONICA, CALIF.
1944-025	DANTONIO, JOHN JAMES	D. MAY 28, 1993, NEW ORLEANS, LA.
1942-027	DAPPER, CLIFFORD ROLAND	733 BURMA ROAD, FALLBROOK CA 92028
1974-020	DARCY, PATRICK LEONARD	515 SOUTH COLUMBUS BLVD, TUCSON AZ 85711
1998-041	DARENSBOURG, VICTOR ANTHONY	4151 ABERNATHY FOREST PLACE, LAS VEGAS NV 89141
1946-021	DARK, ALVIN RALPH	103 CRANBERRY WAY, EASLEY SC 29642
1983-039	DARLING, RONALD MAURICE	19 WOODLAND STREET, MILLBURY MA 01527
1954-018	DARNELL, ROBERT JACK	D. JANUARY 1, 1995, FREDERICKSBURG, TEXAS
1999-043	DARR, MICHAEL CURTIS	D. FEBRUARY 15, 2002, PEORIA, ARIZ.
1977-039	DARR, MICHAEL EDWARD	1461 MAPLEBROOK LANE, CORONA CA 92881
1934-028	DARROW, GEORGE OLIVER 'LEFTY'	D. MARCH 24, 1983, SUN CITY, ARIZ.
1962-030	DARWIN, ARTHUR BOBBY LEE	17509 ALORA STREET, CERRITOS CA 90701
1978-033	DARWIN, DANIEL WAYNE	6489 STAGS LEAP RAOD, SANGER TX 76266
1994-022	DARWIN, JEFFREY SCOTT	1010 RUSSELL AVENUE, BONHAM TX 75418
1988-038	DASCENZO, DOUGLAS CRAIG	PO BOX 7, HILLER PA 15444
1924-025	DASHIELL, JOHN WALLACE 'WALLY'	D. MAY 20, 1972, PENSACOLA, FLA.
1945-023	DASSO, FRANCIS JOSEPH NICHOLAS	1413 MADISON, WENATCHEE WA 98801
1989-028	DATZ, JEFFREY WILLIAM	867 LONGBROOK DRIVE, WADSWORTH OH 44281
1998-042	DAUBACH, BRIAN MICHAEL	2059 BOWLER ROAD, O'FALLON IL 62269
1976-027	DAUER, RICHARD FREMONT	2510 BROOK HAVEN LANE, HINCKLEY OH 44233
1951-021	DAUGHERTY, HAROLD RAY	314 SUMMERS DRIVE, LANCASTER PA 17601
1987-029	DAUGHERTY, JOHN MICHAEL 'JACK'	20360 NORTH 95TH PLACE, SCOTTSDALE AZ 85255
1937-033	DAUGHTERS, ROBERT FRANCIS	D. AUGUST 22, 1988, SOUTHBURY, CONN.
1983-040	DAULTON, DARREN ARTHUR	5 MEADOW LANE, ARKANSAS CITY KS 67005
1953-017	DAVALILLO, POMPEYO ROMERO 'YOYO'	OLD ADD: LISTA DE CORREO, NUEVA, GRANDA, CARACAS, VENEZUELA
1963-030	DAVALILLO, VICTOR JOSE	CALLE TRUJILLO 7, MARIPEREZ, Q.V, CARACAS, VENEZUELA
1969-041	DAVANON, FRANK GERALD 'JERRY'	5323 HIDALGO STREET, HOUSTON TX 77056
1999-044	DAVANON, JEFFREY GRAHAM	731 EAST BUENA VISTA DRIVE, CHANDLER AZ 95249
1920-028	DAVENPORT, CLAUDE EDWIN	D. JUNE 13, 1976, CORPUS CHRISTI, TEXAS
1958-026	DAVENPORT, JAMES HOUSTON	1016 HEWITT DR, SAN CARLOS CA 94070
1999-045	DAVENPORT, JOSEPH JONATHAN	10102 WYCLIFFE STREET, SANTEE CA 92071
1921-020	DAVENPORT, JOUBERT LUM	D. APRIL 21, 1961, DALLAS, TEXAS
1977-040	DAVEY, MICHAEL GERARD	902 WEST MELINDA LANE, SPOKANE WA 99203
1999-046	DAVEY, THOMAS JOSEPH	13125 ANDOVER DRIVE, PLYMOUTH MI 48170

1962-031	DAVIAULT, RAYMOND JOSEPH ROBERT	12116 ONTARIO EAST, POINTES AUX TREMBLES QC, H1B 1L4 CANADA
1984-024	DAVID, ANDRE ANTER	17341 WEST BANFF LANE, SURPRISE AZ 85379
1999-047	DAVIDSON, CLEATUS LAVON	2560 POSSUM TROT AVENUE, HAINES CITY FL 33844
1986-039	DAVIDSON, JOHN MARK	996 OLD MOUNTAIN ROAD, STATESVILLE NC 28677
1989-029	DAVIDSON, ROBERT BRUCE	OLD ADD: 402 BASHFORD DRIVE, RALEIGH NC 27606
1965-025	DAVIDSON, THOMAS EUGENE 'TED'	D. SEPTEMBER 1, 2006, BULLHEAD CITY, ARIZ.
1959-018	DAVIE, GERALD LEE	3377 NASSER ROAD, FAIRVIEW MI 48621
2005-046	DAVIES, HIRAM KYLE 'KYLE'	5436 GLENRIDGE VIEW NE, ATLANTA GA 30342
1984-025	DAVIS, ALVIN GLENN	7983 ARMAGOSA DRIVE, RIVERSIDE CA 92508
1965-026	DAVIS, ARTHUR WILLARD 'BILL'	6638 KNOX AVE SOUTH, MINNEAPOLIS MN 55423
1963-031	DAVIS, BRYSHEAR BARNETT 'BROCK'	2080 WEST ONTARIO AVENUE, CORONA CA 91720
1981-025	DAVIS, CHARLES THEODORE 'CHILI'	4625 LAKE WASHINGTON BLVD, BELLEVUE WA 98006
1934-029	DAVIS, CURTIS BENTON	D. OCTOBER 12, 1965, COVINA, CALIF.
1999-048	DAVIS, DOUGLAS P	1524 FIELDCREST DRIVE, PLEASANT HILL CA 94523
1988-039	DAVIS, DOUGLAS RAYMOND	279 WHITES CHURCH ROAD, BLOOMSBURG PA 17815
1984-026	DAVIS, ERIC KEITH	5334 COLLINGWOOD CIRCLE, CALABASAS CA 91302
1982-029	DAVIS, GEORGE EARL 'STORM'	2792 EUNICE HOLCOMB CIRCLE, DACULA GA 30019
1926-026	DAVIS, GEORGE WILLIS 'KIDDO'	D. MARCH 4, 1983, BRIDGEPORT, CONN.
1983-041	DAVIS, GERALD EDWARD	72 THERESA STREET, TRENTON NJ 08618
1984-027	DAVIS, GLENN EARLE	45 CASCADE ROAD, COLUMBUS GA 31904
1932-017	DAVIS, HARRY ALBERT	D. MARCH 3, 1997, SHREVEPORT, LA.
1959-019	DAVIS, HERMAN THOMAS 'TOMMY'	9767 WHIRLAWAY, ALTA LOMA CA 91701
1962-032	DAVIS, JACKE SYLVESTA	815 UNIVERSITY DRIVE, CARTHAGE TX 75633
1954-019	DAVIS, JAMES BENNETT	D. DECEMBER 6, 1995, SAN MATEO, CALIF.
2002-039	DAVIS, JASON THOMAS	161 POTTER PLACE ROAD NW, CHARLESTON TN 37310
2002-040	DAVIS, JERRY C 'J.J.'	OLD ADD: 2333 PINEVIEW LANE, GASTONIA NC 28054
1981-026	DAVIS, JODY RICHARD	4445 SHIRLEY ROAD, GAINESVILLE GA 30506
1985-022	DAVIS, JOEL CLARK	609 MATTERHORN ROAD, JACKSONVILLE FL 32216
1941-020	DAVIS, JOHN HUMPHREY 'RED'	D. APRIL 26, 2002, LAUREL, MISS.
1987-030	DAVIS, JOHN KIRK	343 MILL RUN, SHEPHERDVILLE KY 40165
2001-046	DAVIS, JOHNNY LANCE 'LANCE'	5845 OLD BERKEY ROAD, AUBURNDALE FL 33823
2000-045	DAVIS, KANE THOMAS	4794 RIPLEY ROAD, REEDY WV 25270
1940-014	DAVIS, LAWRENCE COLUMBUS 'CRASH'	D. AUGUST 31, 2001, GREENSBORO, N.C.
1991-043	DAVIS, MARK ANTHONY	1672 EAST MOUNTAIN STREET, PASADENA CA 91104
1998-043	DAVIS, MARK CHRISTOPHER 'BEN'	416 HOMESTEAD DRIVE, WEST CHESTER PA 19382
1980-033	DAVIS, MARK WILLIAM	8867 EAST SIERRA PINTA DRIVE, SCOTTSDALE AZ 85255
1980-034	DAVIS, MICHAEL DWAYNE	2491 SAN RAMON VALLEY #1407, SAN RAMON CA 94583
1980-035	DAVIS, ODIE ERNEST	1014 MONTANA ST, SAN ANTONIO TX 78203
1946-022	DAVIS, OTIS ALLEN	1115 ROYAL TROON COURT, TARPON SPRINGS FL 34688
2006-040	DAVIS, RAJAI LAVAE	OLD ADD: NEW LONDON CT
1936-018	DAVIS, RAY THOMAS 'PEACHES'	D. APRIL 28, 1995, DUNCAN, OKLA.
1977-041	DAVIS, RICHARD EARL	2415 WEST ALONDRA, COMPTON CA 90220
1952-023	DAVIS, ROBERT BRANDON 'BRANDY'	D. JUNE 12, 2005, NEWARK, DEL.
1958-027	DAVIS, ROBERT EDWARD	D. DECEMBER 22, 2001, NEW YORK, N.Y.
1973-032	DAVIS, ROBERT JOHN EUGENE	BOX 198, LOCUST GROVE OK 74352
1962-033	DAVIS, RONALD EVERETTE	D. SEPTEMBER 5, 1992, HOUSTON, TEXAS
1978-034	DAVIS, RONALD GENE	10869 NORTH SCOTTSDALE ROAD #107, SCOTTSDALE AZ 85254
1994-023	DAVIS, RUSSELL STUART	3351 CRESCENT DRIVE, HUEYTOWN AL 35025
1985-023	DAVIS, STEVEN KENNON	OLD ADD: 3500 SOUTH HIWASSEE RD, CHOCTAW OK 73020
1979-027	DAVIS, STEVEN MICHAEL	2266 FAIR VALLEY COURT, SAN JOSE CA 95125
1999-049	DAVIS, THOMAS JAMES	4685 CAVALIER DRIVE, SEMMES AL 36575
1949-018	DAVIS, THOMAS OSCAR 'TOD'	D. DECEMBER 31, 1978, WEST COVINA, CALIF.
1994-024	DAVIS, TIMOTHY HOWARD	RURAL ROUTE 1 BOX 1223, BRISTOL FL 32321
1985-024	DAVIS, TRENCH NEAL	306 40TH STREET CIRCLE WEST, PALMETTO FL 34221
1928-028	DAVIS, VIRGIL LAWRENCE 'SPUD'	D. AUGUST 14, 1984, BIRMINGHAM, ALA.
1983-042	DAVIS, WALLACE MCARTHUR 'BUTCH'	1108 BRUCEMONT DRIVE, GARNER NC 27529
1960-028	DAVIS, WILLIAM HENRY 'WILLIE'	1916 WEST VICTORY BLVD #5, BURBANK CA 91506
1938-020	DAVIS, WOODROW WILSON	D. JULY 18, 1999, JESUP, GA.
1969-042	DAVISON, MICHAEL LYNN	578 PROSPECT, HUTCHINSON MN 55350
1995-060	DAVISON, SCOTTY RAY	4507 SHARYNNE LANE, TORRANCE CA 90505
1999-050	DAWKINS, TRAVIS SENTELL 'GOOKIE'	PO BOX 81325, CONYERS GA 30013
2002-041	DAWLEY, JOSEPH THOMAS	27951 CACTUS AVENUE #A, MORENO VALLEY CA 92555
1983-043	DAWLEY, WILLIAM CHESTER	RR 2, KENDALL ROAD EXT, LISBON CT 06417
1976-028	DAWSON, ANDRE NOLAN	10601 SW 74TH AVENUE, MIAMI FL 33156
1924-026	DAWSON, RALPH FENTON 'JOE'	D. JANUARY 4, 1978, LONGVIEW, TEXAS
1969-043	DAY, CHARLES FREDERICK 'BOOTS'	OLD ADD: 12639 WESTPORT DRIVE, SAINT LOUIS MO 63146
1924-027	DAY, CLYDE HENRY 'PEA RIDGE'	D. MARCH 21, 1934, KANSAS CITY, MO.
2002-042	DAY, STEPHEN ZACHARY 'ZACH'	1154 CAROLINA TRACE ROAD, WEST HARRISON IN 47060
1983-044	DAYETT, BRIAN KELLY	10 HEMLOCK TERRACE EXT, DEEP RIVER CT 06417
1982-030	DAYLEY, KENNETH GRANT	1300 WINDGATE WAY COURT, CHESTERFIELD MO 63005
2002-043	DE LOS SANTOS, LUIS	OLD ADD: SAN PEDRO DE MACORIS DR
2003-037	DEAGO, ROGER I. (VILLARREAL)	OLD ADD: MONAGRILLO PANAMA
1947-024	DEAL, ELLIS FERGUSON 'COT '	9009 NORTH MAY AVENUE #164, OKLAHOMA CITY OK 73120
1939-026	DEAL, LINDSAY FRED	D. APRIL 18, 1979, LITTLE ROCK, ARK.
1936-019	DEAN, ALFRED LOVILL 'CHUBBY'	D. DECEMBER 21, 1970, RIVERSIDE, N.J.
1941-021	DEAN, JAMES HARRY	D. JUNE 1, 1960, ROCKMART, GA.
1930-016	DEAN, JAY HANNA 'DIZZY'	D. JULY 17, 1974, RENO, NEV.
1934-030	DEAN, PAUL DEE	D. MARCH 17, 1981, SPRINGDALE, ARK.
1967-022	DEAN, TOMMY DOUGLAS	268 COUNTY ROAD 238 PMB 1014, IUKA MS 38852
1924-028	DEAN, WAYLAND OGDEN	D. APRIL 11, 1930, HUNTINGTON, W.VA.
1927-028	DEAR, PAUL STANFORD 'BUDDY'	D. AUGUST 29, 1989, RADFORD, VA.
1977-042	DEBARR, DENNIS LEE	33843 JULIET CIRCLE, FREMONT CA 94555
1920-029	DEBERRY, JOSEPH GADDY	D. OCTOBER 9, 1944, SOUTHERN PINES, N.C.
1962-034	DEBUSSCHERE, DAVID ALBERT	D. MAY 14, 2003, NEW YORK, N.Y.
2006-041	DECASTER, YURENDELL EITHEL	OLD ADD: CURACAO NETA. ANTILLES
1922-025	DECATUR, ARTHUR RUE	D. APRIL 25, 1966, TALLADEGA, ALA.

1973-033	DECINCES, DOUGLAS VERNON	124 RIVIERA WAY, LAGUNA BEACH CA 92651
1983-045	DECKER, DEE MARTIN 'MARTY'	1630 YOUNGS LANE, YUBA CITY CA 95991
1969-044	DECKER, GEORGE HENRY 'JOE'	D. MARCH 2, 2003, FRASER, MICH.
1990-037	DECKER, STEVEN MICHAEL	1024 LAURELRIDGE STREET NE, KEIZER OR 97303
1935-022	DEDEAUX, RAOUL MARTIAL 'ROD'	D. JANUARY 5, 2006, GLENDALE, CALIF.
1983-046	DEDMON, JEFFREY LINDEN	21102 SOUTH BROADWELL, TORRANCE CA 90502
1995-061	DEDRICK, JAMES MICHAEL	630 HOYT AVENUE, EVERETT WA 98201
1984-028	DEER, ROBERT GEORGE 'ROB'	27030 NORTH 70TH PLACE, SCOTTSDALE AZ 85262
1963-032	DEES, CHARLES HENRY	1064 ALLISON WOODS COURT, LAWRENCEVILLE GA 30043
1978-035	DEFREITES, ARTURO SIMON	PO BOX 161, SAN PEDRO DE MACORIS, DOM REP
1961-028	DEGERICK, MICHAEL ARTHUR	2702 OSBORNE DRIVE, LAKE WORTH FL 33461
2000-046	DEHAAN, KORWIN JAY 'KORY'	19040 EAST SUPERSTITION DRIVE, QUEEN CREEK AZ 85242
1997-043	DEHART, RICHARD ALLEN	811 NE WABASH AVENUE, TOPEKA KS 66616
1974-021	DEIDEL, JAMES LAWRENCE	14312 WRIGHT WAY, BROOMFIELD CO 80020
1940-015	DEJAN, MIKE DAN	D. FEBRUARY 2, 1953, WEST LOS ANGELES, CALIF.
1997-044	DEJEAN, MICHAEL DWAIN	9430 PRINCE CHARLES STREET, DENHAM SPRINGS LA 70726
2003-038	DEJESUS, DAVID CHRISTOPHER	46 GUILDEN STREET, NEW BRUNSWICK NJ 08901
1974-022	DEJESUS, IVAN	14608 VELLEUX DRIVE, ORLANDO FL 32837
1988-040	DEJESUS, JOSE LUIS	7E6 VILLA DEL CARMEN, CIDRA PR 00639
1982-031	DEJOHN, MARK STEPHEN	24 NEW HAMPSHIRE DRIVE #1C, NEW BRITAIN CT 06052
1945-024	DEKONING, WILLIAM CALLAHAN	D. JULY 26, 1979, PALM HARBOR, FLA.
1944-026	DELACRUZ, TOMAS	D. SEPTEMBER 6, 1958, HAVANA, CUBA
1960-029	DELAHOZ, MIGUEL ANGEL	PO BOX 441233, MIAMI FL 33144
1997-045	DELAMAZA, ROLAND ROBERT	28533 SILVERKING TRAIL, SANTA CLARITA CA 91350
1932-018	DELANCEY, WILLIAM PINKNEY	D. NOVEMBER 28, 1946, PHOENIX, ARIZ.
1924-029	DELANEY, ARTHUR DEWEY	D. MAY 2, 1970, HAYWARD, CALIF.
1991-044	DELAROSA, FRANCISCO	OLD ADD: QUISQUEYA PROJECTO KENNEDY, SAN PEDRO DE MACORIS DOM REP
1975-032	DELAROSA, JESUS	20 #28 LOS MINOS SANTO DOMINGO, DOM REP
2004-049	DELAROSA, JORGE ALBERTO	OLD ADD: SAN NICOLAS MEX
2000-047	DELAROSA, TOMAS	OLD ADD: LA VICTORIA DOM REP
2005-047	DELCARMEN, MANUEL	23 ROXANA STREET, HYDE PARK MA 02136
1983-047	DELEON, JOSE	OLD ADD: 207 PATTERSON, PERTH AMBOY NJ 08861
1981-027	DELEON, LUIS ANTONIO	OLD ADD: SAN ANTON #120, PONCE PR 00731
1996-045	DELGADO, ALEXANDER	OLD ADD: 20425 RIMROCK ROAD, APPLE VALLEY CA 92307
1993-041	DELGADO, CARLOS JUAN (HERNANDEZ)	RPTO RAMOS #9, BO. BORINQUER, AGUADILLO PR 00605
1977-043	DELGADO, LUIS FELIPE	OLD ADD: CARR. 492, KM D 1, HATILLO PR 00659
1996-046	DELGADO, WILSON DURAN	OLD ADD: SAN CRISTOBAL DOM REP
1952-024	DELGRECO, ROBERT GEORGE	625 SOUTHVIEW DRIVE, PITTSBURGH PA 15226
1955-037	DELIS, JUAN FRANCISCO	D. DECEMBER 1, 2003, HAVANA, CUBA
1929-027	DELKER, EDWARD ALBERT	D. MAY 14, 1997, POTTSVILLE, PA.
1999-051	DELLAERO, JASON CHRISTOPHER	7413 SKYLINE DRIVE #2, HUDSON FL 34667
1997-046	DELLUCCI, DAVID MICHAEL	18489 LAKE TULIP AVENUE, BATON ROUGE LA 70817
1933-016	DELMAS, ALBERT CHARLES 'BERT'	D. DECEMBER 4, 1979, HUNTINGTON BEACH, CALIF.
1952-025	DELOCK, IVAN MARTIN 'IKE'	433 CYPRESS WAY EAST, NAPLES FL 34110
1988-041	DELOSSANTOS, LUIS MANUEL	OLD ADD: 535 WEST 162ND STREET, NEW YORK NY 10032
1974-023	DELOSSANTOS, RAMON	CALLE ACTIVO 20-30 112-B #3 ALMA ROSA, SANTO DOMINGO, DOM REP
1998-044	DELOSSANTOS, VALERIO LORENZO	9838 NORTH 119TH PLACE, SCOTTSDALE AZ 85259
1943-038	DELSAVIO, GARTON ORVILLE 'GAR'	D. NOVEMBER 9, 2006, BLAUVELT, N.Y.
1948-031	DELSING, JAMES HENRY	D. MAY 4, 2006, CHESTERFIELD, MO.
1999-052	DELTORO, MIGUEL ALFONSO	D. OCTOBER 6, 2001, OBREGON, MEXICO
1990-038	DELUCIA, RICHARD ANTHONY 'RICH'	4 RICK ROAD, READING PA 19607
1951-022	DEMAESTRI, JOSEPH PAUL	50 FAIRWAY, NOVATO CA 94947
1932-019	DEMAREE, JOSEPH FRANKLIN	D. AUGUST 30, 1958, LOS ANGELES, CALIF.
2005-048	DEMARIA, CHRIS NEAL	4214 WEST 172ND STREET, TORRANCE CA 90504
1948-032	DEMARS, WILLIAM LESTER	770 ISLAND WAY #305, CLEARWATER FL 34630
1957-016	DEMERIT, JOHN STEPHEN	550 WEST WALTERS ST, PORT WASHINGTON WI 53074
1974-024	DEMERY, LAWRENCE CALVIN	10719 PETALO DRIVE, BAKERSFIELD CA 93311
1956-026	DEMETER, DONALD LEE	6240 SOUTH COUNTRY CLUB DRIVE, OKLAHOMA CITY OK 73159
1959-020	DEMETER, STEVEN	6032 RAVINE BLVD, CLEVELAND OH 44134
1974-025	DEMOLA, DONALD JOHN	352 VILLAGE DRIVE, HAUPPAUGE NY 11788
1951-023	DEMPSEY, CORNELIUS FRANCIS 'CON'	D. AUGUST 5, 2006, REDWOOD CITY, CALIF.
1969-045	DEMPSEY, JOHN RIKARD 'RICK'	1673 CROWN RIDGE COURT, WESTLAKE VILLAGE CA 91362
1982-032	DEMPSEY, MARK STEVEN	673 WEST MARTINDALE, UNION OH 45322
1998-045	DEMPSTER, RYAN SCOTT	3638 NORTH WAYNE AVENUE, CHICAGO IL 60613
1967-023	DENEHY, WILLIAM FRANCIS	OLD ADD: 5008 EASTWINDS DRIVE, ORLANDO FL 32819
1982-033	DENMAN, BRIAN JOHN	16 CINDY DRIVE, BUFFALO NY 14221
1923-027	DENNEHEY, THOMAS FRANCIS 'TOD'	D. AUGUST 8, 1977, PHILADELPHIA, PA.
2004-050	DENNEY, KYLE DEAN	PO BOX 300, PRAGUE OK 74864
1942-028	DENNING, OTTO GEORGE	D. MAY 25, 1992, CHICAGO, ILL.
1965-027	DENNIS, DONALD RAY	D. MARCH 22, 2007, FORT SCOTT, KAN.
1974-026	DENNY, JOHN ALLEN	111 SOUTH HIGHLAND STREET #279, MEMPHIS TN 38111
2005-049	DENORFIA, CHRISTOPHER ANTHONY	137 WILLIAMSBURG DRIVE, SOUTHINGTON CT 06489
1989-030	DENSON, ANDREW	1718 AVONLEA AVENUE, CINCINNATI OH 45237
1973-034	DENT, RUSSELL EARL 'BUCKY'	8895 INDIAN RIVER RUN, BOYNTON BEACH FL 33437
1947-025	DENTE, SAMUEL JOSEPH	D. APRIL 21, 2002, MONTCLAIR, N.J.
2003-039	DEPASTINO, JOSEPH BERNARD	12853 SHERINGHAM WAY, SARASOTA FL 34240
2003-040	DEPAULA, JORGE	OLD ADD: SABANA GRANDE, DOM REP.
1999-053	DEPAULA, SEAN MICHAEL	2 THOMAS STREET, DERRY NH 03038
1943-039	DEPHILLIPS, ANTHONY ANDREW	D. MAY 5, 1994, PORT JEFFERSON, N.Y.
1980-036	DERNIER, ROBERT EUGENE	1242 SW ARBORMILL TERRACE, LEES SUMMIT MO 64082
1998-046	DEROSA, MARK THOMAS	626 EIGHTH STREET, CARLSTADT NJ 07072
1970-032	DERRICK, JAMES MICHAEL	340 CEDAR VALE DRIVE, LEXINGTON SC 29073
1931-021	DERRINGER, PAUL	D. NOVEMBER 17, 1987, SARASOTA, FLA.
1956-027	DERRINGTON, CHARLES JAMES 'JIM'	711 SANDLEWOOD AVENUE, LA HABRA CA 90631
1944-027	DERRY, ALVA RUSSELL 'RUSS'	D. OCTOBER 26, 2004, KANSAS CITY, MO.
1980-037	DESA, JOSEPH	D. DECEMBER 20, 1986, SAN JUAN, P.R.

1930-017	DESAUTELS, EUGENE ABRAHAM	D. NOVEMBER 5, 1994, FLINT, MICH.
1984-029	DESHAIES, JAMES JOSEPH	151 NORTH TAYLOR POINT DRIVE, THE WOODLANDS TX 77382
1990-039	DESHIELDS, DELINO LAMONT	100 SHADY BROOK WALK, FAIRBURN GA 30213
1932-020	DESHONG, JAMES BROOKLYN	D. OCTOBER 16, 1993, LOWER PAXSON TWP., PA.
1993-042	DESILVA, JOHN REED	32750 AIRPORT ROAD, FORT BRAGG CA 95437
1996-047	DESSENS, ELMER (JUSAINO)	5104 NORTH 32ND STREET, PHOENIX AZ 85018
1987-031	DESTRADE, ORESTES	9218 SYDNEY LANE, BRENTWOOD TN 37027
1980-038	DETHERAGE, ROBERT WAYNE	322 TURF STREET, CARL JUNCTION MO 64834
1930-018	DETORE, GEORGE FRANCIS	D. FEBRUARY 7, 1991, UTICA, N.Y.
1994-025	DETTMER, JOHN FRANKLIN	549 HICKORY VIEW LANE, BALLWIN MO 63011
1973-035	DETTORE, THOMAS ANTHONY	1120 MCEWEN AVE, CANONSBURG PA 15317
1942-029	DETWEILER, ROBERT STERLING 'DUCKY'	312 HOLT STREET, FEDERALSBURG MD 21632
1946-023	DEUTSCH, MELVIN ELLIOTT	D. NOVEMBER 18, 2001, AUSTIN, TEXAS
1995-062	DEVAREZ, CESAR SALVATORE	OLD ADD: 3730 42ND WAY SOUTH, SAINT PETERSBURG FL 33711
1932-021	DEVENS, CHARLES	D. AUGUST 13, 2003, MILTON, MASS.
1987-032	DEVEREAUX, MICHAEL	2236 WEST DOUBLEGROVE STREET, WEST COVINA CA 91790
2005-050	DEVINE, JOSEPH	2014 MCFARLAND ROAD, JUNCTION CITY KS 66441
1973-036	DEVINE, PAUL ADRIAN 'ADRIAN'	271 TIMBER LAUREL LANE, LAWRENCEVILLE GA 30245
1920-030	DEVINEY, JOHN HAROLD 'HAL'	D. JANUARY 4, 1933, WESTWOOD, MASS.
1924-030	DEVIVEIROS, BERNARD JOHN	D. JULY 5, 1994, OAKLAND, CALIF.
1944-028	DEVLIN, JAMES RAYMOND	D. JANUARY 15, 2004, DANVILLE, PA.
2004-051	DEVORE, DOUG RINEHART	5247 WILLOW GROVE PLACE SOUTH, DUBLIN OH 43017
1990-040	DEWEY, MARK ALAN	PO BOX 14, NEW ERA MI 49446
1987-033	DEWILLIS, JEFFREY ALLEN	OLD ADD: 2929 HAYES ROAD, HOUSTON TX 77082
2000-048	DEWITT, MATTHEW BRIAN	7177 SIXSHOOTER DRIVE, LAS VEGAS NV 89119
1992-033	DIAZ, ALEXIS	OLD ADD: CALLE 10-R-4, SAN SEBASTIAN PR 00685
1977-044	DIAZ, BAUDILIO JOSE 'BO'	D. NOVEMBER 23, 1990, CARACAS, VENEZUELA
1982-034	DIAZ, CARLOS ANTHONY	47-709 WAIOHIA STREET, KANEOHE HI 96744
1990-041	DIAZ, CARLOS FRANCISCO	730 DEL ORO DRIVE, SAFETY HARBOR FL 34695
1997-047	DIAZ, EDDY JAVIER	11492 NW 87TH PLACE, HIALEAH FL 33018
1986-040	DIAZ, EDGAR SERRANO	OLD ADD: CLE DIAMANTE #32 V. BLANCA, CAGUAS PR 00625
1998-047	DIAZ, EDWIN	OLD ADD: VEGA ALTA PR 00762
1996-048	DIAZ, EINAR ANTONIO	9518 OLD HYDE PARK PLACE, BRADENTON FL 34202
2004-052	DIAZ, FELIX	OLD ADD: LA MARAS DOM REP
2006-042	DIAZ, JOSELO SORIANO	OLD ADD: SAN PERRO DE MACORIS
2002-044	DIAZ, JUAN CARLOS	OLD ADD: SANTO DOMINGO DOM REP
1987-034	DIAZ, MARIO RAFAEL	OLD ADD: 275 WASHINGTON STREET, BUFFALO NY 14205
2003-041	DIAZ, MATTHEW E.	1124 AFTON STREET, LAKELAND FL 33803
1983-048	DIAZ, MICHAEL ANTHONY	703 LUNDY WAY, PACIFICA CA 94044
2004-053	DIAZ, VICTOR ISRAEL	2107 NORTH AVERS, CHICAGO IL 60647
1988-042	DIBBLE, ROBERT KEITH	250 DINO ROAD, BRISTOL CT 06010
1924-031	DIBUT, PEDRO	D. DECEMBER 4, 1979, HIALEAH, FLA.
1964-025	DICKEN, PAUL FRANKLIN	8409 NW 121ST AVENUE, OCALA FL 34482
1923-028	DICKERMAN, LEO LOUIS	D. APRIL 30, 1982, ATKINS, ARK.
1935-023	DICKEY, GEORGE WILLARD 'SKEETS'	D. JUNE 16, 1976, DEWITT, ARK.
2001-047	DICKEY, ROBERT ALAN 'R. A.'	701 CANTRELL AVENUE, NASHVILLE TN 37215
1928-029	DICKEY, WILLIAM MALCOLM	D. NOVEMBER 12, 1993, LITTLE ROCK, ARK.
1936-020	DICKMAN, GEORGE EMERSON 'EMERSON'	D. APRIL 27, 1981, NEW YORK, N.Y.
1936-021	DICKSHOT, JOHN OSCAR	D. NOVEMBER 4, 1997, WAUKEGAN, ILL.
1963-033	DICKSON, JAMES EDWARD	90580 SUNSET LAKE ROAD #1, WARRENTON OR 97146
1996-049	DICKSON, JASON ROYCE	OLD ADD: 281 NORTH NAPAN ROAD, CHATHAM NEW BRUNSWICK E1N 3A3
1990-042	DICKSON, LANCE MICHAEL	4615 NORTH PLACITA ROCA BLANCA, TUCSON AZ 85718
1939-027	DICKSON, MURRY MONROE	D. SEPTEMBER 21, 1989, KANSAS CITY, KAN.
1969-046	DIDIER, ROBERT DANIEL	544 SW 335TH STREET, FEDERAL WAY WA 98023
1942-030	DIEHL, GEORGE KRAUSE	D. AUGUST 24, 1986, KINGSPORT, TENN.
1947-026	DIERING, CHARLES EDWARD ALLEN	1 NOB HILL DRIVE, SAINT LOUIS MO 63138
1964-026	DIERKER, LAWRENCE EDWARDS	8318 NORTH TAHOE, HOUSTON TX 77040
1933-017	DIETRICH, WILLIAM JOHN	D. JUNE 20, 1978, PHILADELPHIA, PA.
1927-029	DIETRICK, WILLIAM ALEXANDER	D. MAY 6, 1946, BETHESDA, MD.
1940-016	DIETZ, LLOYD ARTHUR 'DUTCH'	D. OCTOBER 29, 1972, BEAUMONT, TEXAS
1966-028	DIETZ, RICHARD ALLEN	D. JUNE 28, 2005, DILLARD, GA.
1954-020	DIETZEL, LEROY LOUIS	8421 COULWOOD OAK LANE, CHARLOTTE NC 28214
1948-033	DIFANI, CLARENCE JOSEPH 'JAY'	D. DECEMBER 3, 2003, CRYSTAL CITY, MO.
1996-050	DIFELICE, MICHAEL WILLIAM	3980 MIMOSA PLACE, PALM HARBOR FL 34685
2002-045	DIGGINS, BENJAMIN HOWARD	4804 EAST MERRELL STREET, PHOENIX AZ 85018
1934-031	DIGGS, REESE WILSON	D. OCTOBER 30, 1978, BALTIMORE, MD.
1969-047	DILAURO, JACK EDWARD	168 EAST MOHAWK, MALVERN OH 44644
1959-021	DILLARD, DAVID DONALD 'DON'	45 BREAM LANE, WATERLOO SC 29384
1988-043	DILLARD, GORDON LEE	840 VIA MANZANA, AROMAS CA 95004
1975-033	DILLARD, STEPHEN BRADLEY	154 DRIVE 841, SALTILLO MS 38866
1946-024	DILLINGER, ROBERT BERNARD	15380 RHODODENDRON DRIVE, CANYON COUNTRY CA 91351
1967-024	DILLMAN, WILLIAM HOWARD	PO BOX 5167, WINTER PARK FL 32793
2005-051	DILLON, JOSEPH WILLIAM	OLD ADD: ROCKLIN CA
1963-034	DILLON, STEPHEN EDWARD	110 HYATT AVENUE, YONKERS NY 10704
1974-027	DILONE, MIGUEL ANGEL	CALLE EL SOL #190 SANTIAGO, DOM REP
1940-017	DIMAGGIO, DOMINIC PAUL	6110 NORTH OCEAN BLVD #24, OCEAN RIDGE FL 33435
1936-022	DIMAGGIO, JOSEPH PAUL	D. MARCH 8, 1999, HOLLYWOOD, FLA.
1937-034	DIMAGGIO, VINCENT PAUL	D. OCTOBER 3, 1986, NORTH HOLLYWOOD, CALIF.
1988-044	DIMICHELE, FRANK LAWRENCE	812 TASKER STREET, PHILADELPHIA PA 19148
1977-045	DIMMEL, MICHAEL WAYNE	100 CRESCENT COURT #600, DALLAS TX 75201
2004-054	DINARDO, LEONARD EDWARD 'LENNY'	23015 NW 227TH DRIVE, HIGH SPRINGS FL 32543
1975-034	DINEEN, KERRY MICHAEL	2155 ARROWHEAD DRIVE, SANTA MARIA CA 93455
1945-025	DINGES, VANCE GEORGE	D. OCTOBER 4, 1990, HARRISONBURG, VA.
2000-049	DINGMAN, CRAIG ALLEN	3573 DEL SIENNO STREET, WICHITA KS 67203
1973-037	DIORIO, RONALD MICHAEL	2 WHITE OAK LN, WATERBURY CT 06705
1951-024	DIPIETRO, ROBERT LOUIS PAUL	909 CARRIAGE HILL DRIVE, YAKIMA WA 98902

1981-028	DIPINO, FRANK MICHAEL	5238 EAST FOXHILL LANE, CAMILLUS NY 13031
1993-043	DIPOTO, GERARD PETER 'JERRY'	9947 FOUNTAIN CIRCLE, LENEXA KS 60220
1989-031	DISARCINA, GARY THOMAS	6 PATRICK AVENUE, BILLERICA MA 01866
1995-063	DISHMAN, GLENEIG EDWARD	OLD ADD: 1200 BROOKDALE DRIVE, BRENTWOOD CA 94513
1969-048	DISTASO, ALEC JOHN	PO BOX 721, MACOMB IL 61455
1984-030	DISTEFANO, BENITO JAMES	9911 MURRAY LANDING, MISSOURI CITY TX 77459
1954-021	DITMAR, ARTHUR JOHN	6687 WISTERIA DRIVE, MYRTLE BEACH SC 29575
1952-026	DITTMER, JOHN DOUGLAS 'JACK'	200 NORTH MAIN STREET, ELKADER IA 52043
1953-018	DIXON, JOHN CRAIG 'SONNY'	2912 IRON GATE LANE, CHARLOTTE NC 28212
1984-031	DIXON, KENNETH JOHN	OLD ADD: 3043 NORTH 37TH ST, MILWAUKEE WI 53210
1925-024	DIXON, LEO MOSES	D. APRIL 11, 1984, CHICAGO, ILL.
1993-044	DIXON, STEVEN ROSS	6510 HOLLOW TREE ROAD, LOUISVILLE KY 40228
1977-046	DIXON, THOMAS EARL	2945 SOUTH DELANEY STREET, ORLANDO FL 32806
1924-032	DOBB, JOHN KENNETH	D. JULY 31, 1991, MUSKEGON, MICH.
1959-022	DOBBEK, DANIEL JOHN	4042 SE YAMHILL, PORTLAND OR 97214
2004-055	DOBBS, GREGORY STUART	OLD ADD: MORENO VALLEY CA
1929-028	DOBENS, RAYMOND JOSEPH	D. APRIL 21, 1980, STUART, FLA.
1939-028	DOBERNIC, ANDREW JOSEPH 'JESS'	D. JULY 16, 1998, SAINT LOUIS, ILL.
1966-029	DOBSON, CHARLES THOMAS	4208 LOCUST STREET, KANSAS CITY MO 64110
1939-029	DOBSON, JOSEPH GORDON	D. JUNE 23, 1994, JACKSONVILLE, FLA.
1967-025	DOBSON, PATRICK EDWARD	D. NOVEMBER 22, 2006, SAN DIEGO, CALIF.
1947-027	DOBY, LAWRENCE EUGENE	D. JUNE 18, 2003, MONTCLAIR, N.J.
1945-026	DOCKINS, GEORGE WOODROW	D. JANUARY 22, 1997, CLYDE, KAN.
1998-048	DODD, ROBERT WAYNE	3467 OVERHILL DRIVE, FRISCO TX 75034
1986-041	DODD, THOMAS MARION	3735 NORTHEAST SHAVER, PORTLAND OR 97212
1921-021	DODGE, SAMUEL EDWARD	D. APRIL 5, 1966, UTICA, N.Y.
1986-042	DODSON, PATRICK NEAL	1034 HILLSIDE ROAD, GROVE OK 74344
1937-035	DOERR, ROBERT PERSHING	37705 AGNESS ILLAHE ROAD, AGNESS OR 97406
1992-034	DOHERTY, JOHN HAROLD	202 ALPINE PLACE, TUCKAHOE NY 10707
1974-028	DOHERTY, JOHN MICHAEL	109 WAKEFIELD ST, READING MA 01867
2004-056	DOHMANN, CHRISTOPHER SCOTT 'SCOTT'	1142 OAK HARBOR DRIVE, MORGAN CITY LA 70380
1930-019	DOLJACK, FRANK JOSEPH	D. JANUARY 23, 1948, CLEVELAND, OHIO
1935-024	DOLL, ARTHUR JAMES	D. APRIL 28, 1978, CALUMET CITY, ILL.
2003-042	DOMINGUEZ, JUAN RAMON	OLD ADD: SANCHEZ RAMIREZ, DOM REP
2004-057	DOMINIQUE, ANDREW JOHN	OLD ADD: 12421 HENZIE PLACE, GRANADA HILLS CA 91344
1923-029	DONAHUE, JOHN FREDERICK	D. OCTOBER 3, 1949, BOSTON, MASS.
1943-040	DONAHUE, JOHN STEPHEN MICHEAL	812 NORTH SALEM LANE, CARPENTERSVILLE IL 60110
1938-021	DONALD, RICHARD ATLEY 'ATLEY'	D. OCTOBER 19, 1992, WEST MONROE, LA.
1966-030	DONALDSON, JOHN DAVID	3913 YATES COURT, CHARLOTTE NC 28215
1929-029	DONDERO, LEONARD PETER	D. JANUARY 1, 1999, FREMONT, CALIF.
2002-046	DONNELLY, BRENDAN KEVIN	4149 EAST PEACH TREE DRIVE, CHANDLER AZ 85249
1959-023	DONNELLY, EDWARD VINCENT	D. DECEMBER 25, 1992, HOUSTON, TEXAS
1944-029	DONNELLY, SYLVESTER URBAN 'BLIX'	D. JUNE 20, 1976, OLIVIA, MINN.
1991-045	DONNELS, CHRIS BARTON	21256 OAKRIDGE LANE, TRABUCO CANYON CA 92679
1961-029	DONOHUE, JAMES THOMAS	16 HUNTLEIGH DOWNS, SAINT LOUIS MO 63131
1921-022	DONOHUE, PETER JOSEPH	D. FEBRUARY 23, 1988, FORT WORTH, TEXAS
1979-028	DONOHUE, THOMAS JAMES	29 RUSBY ROAD, WESTBURY NY 11590
1955-038	DONOSO, LINO GALATA	D. OCTOBER 13, 1990, VERA CRUZ, MEXICO
1950-027	DONOVAN, RICHARD EDWARD	D. JANUARY 6, 1997, WEYMOUTH, MASS.
1942-031	DONOVAN, WILLARD EARL 'BILL'	D. SEPTEMBER 25, 1997, MAYWOOD, ILL.
1985-025	DOPSON, JOHN ROBERT	3337 OLD GAMBER ROAD, FINKSBURG MD 21048
1982-035	DORAN, WILLIAM DONALD	5720 GRAND LEGACY DRIVE, MAINEVILLE OH 45039
1922-026	DORAN, WILLIAM JAMES	D. MARCH 9, 1978, SANTA MONICA, CALIF.
1947-028	DORISH, HARRY	D. DECEMBER 31, 2000, WILKES-BARRE, PA.
1923-030	DORMAN, CHARLES WILLIAM	D. NOVEMBER 15, 1928, SAN FRANCISCO, CALIF.
1928-030	DORMAN, DWIGHT DEXTER	D. DECEMBER 7, 1974, ANAHEIM, CALIF.
1987-035	DORSETT, BRIAN RICHARD	700 SOUTH DOBBS GLEN STREET, TERRE HAUTE IN 47803
1940-018	DORSETT, CALVIN LEAVELLE	D. OCTOBER 22, 1970, ELK CITY, OKLA.
1980-039	DORSEY, JAMES EDWARD	335 ELM STREET, SEEKONK MA 02771
2006-043	DORTA, MELVIN A.	314 EAST BROAD STREET, PALMYRA PA 17078
1996-051	DOSTER, DAVID ERIC	9320 OLD GRIST MILL PLACE, FORT WAYNE IN 46835
1999-054	DOTEL, OCTAVIO EDUARDO	8012 WILES ROAD #7, POMPANO BEACH FL 33067
1979-029	DOTSON, RICHARD ELLIOTT	7 COLONEL WATSON, NEW RICHMOND OH 45157
1961-030	DOTTER, GARY RICHARD	17 EDGEMERE DRIVE, ROANOKE TX 76262
1957-017	DOTTERER, HENRY JOHN 'DUTCH'	D. OCTOBER 9, 1999, SYRACUSE, N.Y.
1995-064	DOUGHERTY, JAMES E.	OLD ADD: 952 ANGLER WAY, KITTY HAWK NC 27949
1921-023	DOUGLAS, ASTYANAX SAUNDERS	D. JANUARY 26, 1975, EL PASO, TEXAS
1957-018	DOUGLAS, CHARLES WILLIAM 'WHAMMY'	PO BOX 231, HUBERT NC 28539
1945-027	DOUGLAS, JOHN FRANKLIN	D. FEBRUARY 11, 1984, MIAMI, FLA.
2001-048	DOUGLASS, SEAN R.	OLD ADD: 43956 JOHNS COURT, LANCASTER CA 93536
2005-052	DOUMIT, RYAN MATTHEW	34819 NORTH 30TH DRIVE, PHOENIX AZ 85086
1923-031	DOUTHIT, TAYLOR LEE	D. MAY 28, 1986, FREMONT, CALIF.
1987-036	DOWELL, KENNETH ALLEN	5221 HELEN WAY, SACRAMENTO CA 95822
1964-027	DOWLING, DAVID BARCLAY	6131 WEST ROSE GARDEN LANE, GLENDALE AZ 85308
1961-031	DOWNING, ALPHONSO ERWIN	25343 SILVER ASPEN WAY #735, VALENCIA CA 91381
1973-038	DOWNING, BRIAN JAY	8095 COUNTY ROAD 135, CELINA TX 75009
1972-023	DOWNS, DAVID RALPH	925 EAST 1050 NORTH, BOUNTIFUL UT 84010
1986-043	DOWNS, KELLY ROBERT	244 WEST 1750 NORTH, CENTERVILLE UT 84014
2000-050	DOWNS, SCOTT JEREMY	6814 BARBROOK ROAD, LOUISVILLE KY 40258
1978-036	DOYLE, BRIAN REED	PO BOX 9156, WINTER HAVEN FL 33880
1943-041	DOYLE, HOWARD JAMES 'DANNY'	D. DECEMBER 14, 2004, STILLWATER, OKLA.
1983-049	DOYLE, JEFFREY DONALD	5940 SW BANYON CIRCLE, CORVALLIS OR 97333
1925-025	DOYLE, JESSE HERBERT	D. APRIL 15, 1961, BELLEVILLE, ILL.
1969-049	DOYLE, PAUL SINNOTT	5832 WOODBORO DR, HUNTINGTON BEACH CA 92649
1970-033	DOYLE, ROBERT DENNIS 'DENNY'	PO BOX 9156, WINTER HAVEN FL 33880
1935-025	DOYLE, WILLIAM CARL	D. SEPTEMBER 4, 1951, KNOXVILLE, TENN.

1986-044	DOZIER, THOMAS DEAN	1231 WILLOW AVENUE #D7, HERCULES CA 94547
1992-035	DOZIER, WILLIAM HENRY 'D.J.'	5242 DARTMOUTH DRIVE, MACENGIE PA 18062
1947-029	DOZIER, WILLIAM JOSEPH 'BUZZ'	D. NOVEMBER 24, 2005, WACO, TEXAS
1986-045	DRABEK, DOUGLAS DEAN	15 IVY POND PLACE, THE WOODLANDS TX 77381
1956-028	DRABOWSKY, MYRON WALTER 'MOE'	D. JUNE 10, 2006, LITTLE ROCK, ARK.
1969-050	DRAGO, RICHARD ANTHONY	7257 RANGER DRIVE, FORT COLLINS CO 80526
1991-046	DRAHMAN, BRIAN STACY	1405 SNOWY CLOUD WAY, SANTA ROSA CA 95409
1945-028	DRAKE, LARRY FRANCIS	D. JULY 14, 1985, HOUSTON, TEXAS
1922-027	DRAKE, LOGAN GAFFNEY	D. JUNE 1, 1940, COLUMBIA, S.C.
1960-030	DRAKE, SAMUEL HARRISON	4415 SPRINGDALE DRIVE, LOS ANGELES CA 90043
1956-029	DRAKE, SOLOMON LOUIS	1732 CORNING ST, LOS ANGELES CA 90035
1939-030	DRAKE, THOMAS KENDALL	D. JULY 2, 1988, BIRMINGHAM, ALA.
1999-055	DRANSFELDT, KELLY DANIEL	1207 LAKEWOOD DRIVE, MORRIS IL 60450
1993-045	DRAPER, MICHAEL ANTHONY	18317 MANOR CHURCH ROAD, BOONSBORO MD 21713
1982-036	DRAVECKY, DAVID FRANCIS	13840 GLENEAGLE DRIVE, COLORADO SPRINGS CO 80921
1991-047	DREES, THOMAS KENT	14723 BOULDER POINT ROAD, EDEN PRAIRIE MN 55347
1931-022	DREESEN, WILLIAM RICHARD	D. NOVEMBER 9, 1971, MOUNT VERNON, N.Y.
1994-026	DREIFORT, DARREN JOHN	821 ALMA REAL DRIVE, PACIFIC PALISADES CA 90272
1944-030	DREISEWERD, CLEMENT JOHN	D. SEPTEMBER 11, 2001, OCEAN SPRINGS, MISS.
1944-031	DRESCHER, WILLIAM CLAYTON	D. MAY 15, 1968, CONGERS, N.Y.
2001-049	DRESE, RYAN THOMAS	311 OAK STREET #304, OAKLAND CA 94607
1925-026	DRESSEN, CHARLES WALTER	D. AUGUST 10, 1966, DETROIT, MICH.
1991-048	DRESSENDORFER, KIRK RICHARD	1403 ROY COURT, PEARLAND TX 77581
1975-035	DRESSLER, ROBERT ALAN	2037 17TH AVENUE, FOREST GROVE OR 97116
1988-045	DREW, CAMERON STEWARD	31 HIGHBRIDGE ROAD, YARDVILLE NJ 08620
1998-049	DREW, DAVID JONATHAN 'J.D.'	5006 OLD US HWY N, HAHIRA GA 31632
2006-044	DREW, STEPHEN ORIS	5006 OLD US HWY N, HAHIRA GA 31632
2000-051	DREW, TIMOTHY ANDREW	5006 OLD US HWY N, HAHIRA GA 31632
1944-032	DREWS, FRANK JOHN	D. APRIL 22, 1972, BUFFALO, N.Y.
1946-025	DREWS, KARL AUGUST	D. AUGUST 15, 1963, DANIA, FLA.
1993-046	DREYER, STEVEN WILLIAM	6018 GREYWOOD CIRCLE, JOHNSTON IA 50131
1973-039	DRIESSEN, DANIEL	97 WILLIAM HILTON PKWY, HILTON HEAD ISLAND SC 29926
1970-034	DRISCOLL, JAMES BERNARD	8145 EAST CAMELBACK ROAD #140, SCOTTSDALE AZ 85251
2002-047	DRISKILL, TRAVIS COREY	800 BLUE SPRING CIRCLE, ROUND ROCK TX 78681
1949-019	DROPO, WALTER	104 BROOKSBY VILLAGE DRIVE #104, PEABODY MA 01960
1957-019	DROTT, RICHARD FRED	D. AUGUST 16, 1985, GLENDALE HEIGHTS, ILL.
1987-037	DRUMMOND, TIMOTHY DARNELL	102 HALDONE COURT, LAPLATA MD 20646
1978-037	DRUMRIGHT, KEITH ALAN	1333 WEST LINDBERG, SPRINGFIELD MO 65807
1956-030	DRYSDALE, DONALD SCOTT	D. JULY 3, 1993, MONTREAL, QUE.
1944-033	DUBIEL, WALTER JOHN 'MONK'	D. OCTOBER 25, 1969, HARTFORD, CONN.
1989-032	DUBOIS, BRIAN ANDREW	359 EAST RIDGE STREET, BRAIDWOOD IL 60408
2004-058	DUBOIS, JASON BRADFORD	2204 LORD SEATON CIRCLE, VIRGINIA BEACH VA 23454
2002-048	DUBOSE, ERIC LADELL	16315 LOCKE HAVEN DRIVE, HOUSTON TX 77059
1987-038	DUCEY, ROBERT THOMAS 'ROB'	699 RICHMOND CLOSE, TARPON SPRINGS FL 34689
2001-050	DUCHSCHERER, JUSTIN CRAIG	4700 GREEN OAKS DRIVE, COLLEYVILLE TX 76034
2001-051	DUCKWORTH, BRANDON J.	4460 WEST 6095 SOUTH, KEARNS UT 84118
1963-035	DUCKWORTH, JAMES RAYMOND	405 ESTHER COURT, FORT MILL SC 29708
1929-030	DUDLEY, ELISE CLISE	D. JANUARY 12, 1989, MONCKS CORNER, S.C.
1941-022	DUDRA, JOHN JOSEPH	D. OCTOBER 24, 1965, PANA, ILL.
1977-047	DUES, HAL JOSEPH	DRAWER R, DICKINSON TX 77539
1922-028	DUFF, CECIL ELBA 'LARRY'	D. NOVEMBER 10, 1969, BEND, ORE.
2002-049	DUFF, MATTHEW CLARK	PO BOX 8, ALLIGATOR MS 38720
1961-032	DUFFALO, JAMES FRANCIS	C/O JOSEPH DUFFALO, PO BOX 1082, DUBOIS PA 15801
1967-026	DUFFIE, JOHN BROWN	177 LAKESIDE CIRCLE, DOUGLAS GA 31535
2005-053	DUFFY, CHRISTOPHER ELLIS	6724 WEST BEHREND DRIVE, GLENDALE AZ 85308
1970-035	DUFFY, FRANK THOMAS	1740 EAST SILVER STREET, TUCSON AZ 85719
1928-031	DUGAN, DANIEL PHILLIP	D. JUNE 25, 1968, GREEN BROOK, N.J.
1930-020	DUGAS, AUGUSTIN JOSEPH 'GUS'	D. APRIL 14, 1997, COLCHESTER, CONN.
2005-054	DUKE, ZACHARY THOMAS	OLD ADD: WACO TX
1969-051	DUKES, JAN NOBLE	959 HELENA DRIVE, SUNNYVALE CA 94087
1967-027	DUKES, THOMAS EARL	325 MONTE VISTA RD, ARCADIA CA 91007
1959-024	DULIBA, ROBERT JOHN	327 PHILADELPHIA AVENUE, WEST PITTSTON PA 18643
1977-048	DUMOULIN, DANIEL LYNN	2545 EAST COUNTY ROAD 100 NORTH, KOKOMO IN 46901
1923-032	DUMOVICH, NICHOLAS	D. DECEMBER 12, 1979, LAGUNA HILLS, CALIF.
1995-065	DUNBAR, MATTHEW MARSHALL	6328 COUNTY DONEGAL COURT, CHARLOTTE NC 28277
1983-050	DUNBAR, THOMAS JEROME	558 SOUTH PALM DRIVE, AIKEN SC 29801
2005-055	DUNCAN, CHRISTOPHER EDWARD	OLD ADD: 1511 EAST SOLEDAD VIA, TUCSON AZ 85718
2001-052	DUNCAN, COURTNEY DEMOND	121 ADALENE LANE, MADISON AL 35757
1964-028	DUNCAN, DAVID EDWIN	205 HUNTERS GLENN LANE, KIMBERLING CITY MO 65686
2003-043	DUNCAN, JEFFREY MATTHEW	825 LINCOLN LANE, FRANKFORT IL 60423
1985-026	DUNCAN, MARIANO	INGENIO ANGELINA #137 SAN PEDRO DE MACORIS, DOM REP
1977-049	DUNCAN, TAYLOR MCDOWELL	D. JANUARY 3, 2004, ASHEVILLE, N.C.
1970-036	DUNEGAN, JAMES WILLIAM	20246 180TH STREET, NEW LONDON IA 52645
1926-027	DUNHAM, LELAND HUFFIELD	D. MAY 11, 1961, ATLANTA, ILL.
1953-019	DUNLAP, GRANT LESTER	1431 ALGA COURT, VISTA CA 92083
1929-031	DUNLAP, WILLIAM JAMES	D. NOVEMBER 29, 1980, READING, PA.
2001-053	DUNN, ADAM TROY	OLD ADD: 23494 DUNN LANE, PORTER TX 77365
1952-027	DUNN, JAMES WILLIAM 'BILL'	D. JANUARY 6, 1999, GADSDEN, ALA.
1974-029	DUNN, RONALD RAY	1161 HUSTED AVENUE, SAN JOSE CA 95125
2004-059	DUNN, SCOTT ALLEN	1331 ARIZONA ASH, SAN ANTONIO TX 78232
1994-027	DUNN, STEVEN ROBERT	OLD ADD: 49 SPRUCE STREET, HAMPTON VA 23665
1996-052	DUNN, TODD KENT	12030 LONDON LAKE DRIVE WEST, JACKSONVILLE FL 32258
1987-039	DUNNE, MICHAEL DENNIS	5115 WEST ANCIENT OAK DRIVE, PEORIA IL 61615
1970-037	DUNNING, STEVEN JOHN	12437 HIGHLAND DRIVE, TUSTIN CA 92680
1985-027	DUNSTON, SHAWON DONNELL	594-3 LOUISIANA AVENUE, BROOKLYN NY 11239
1997-048	DUNWOODY, TODD FRANKLIN	1704 KING EIDER DRIVE, WEST LAFAYETTE IN 47906

1976-029 DUPREE, MICHAEL DENNIS ....5164 E. ASHLAN #129, FRESNO CA 93727
1981-029 DURAN, DANIEL JAMES ....1311 HAPPY VALLEY AVENUE, SAN JOSE CA 95129
1997-049 DURAN, ROBERTO ALEJANDRO..........OLD ADD: MOCA DOMINICAN REPUBLIC
1996-053 DURANT, MICHAEL JOSEPH..........7520 MARSTON LANE, DUBLIN OH 43016
1999-056 DURAZO, ERUBIEL CARDENAS ....OLD ADD: 901 EAST VAN BUREN STREET, PHOENIX AZ 85006
1999-057 DURBIN, CHAD GRIFFIN..........17918 JEFFERSON RIDGE DRIVE, BATON ROUGE LA 70817
2004-060 DURBIN, JOSEPH ADAM 'J.D.' ....1913 EAST PINTO DRIVE, GILBERT AZ 85296
1954-022 DUREN, RINOLD GEORGE 'RYNE' ....4068 DUNMORE ROAD, LAKE WALES FL 33859
1972-024 DURHAM, DONALD GARY ....2627 PENNINGTON BEND ROAD, NASHVILLE TN 37214
1929-032 DURHAM, EDWARD FANT..........D. APRIL 27, 1976, CHESTER, S.C.
1954-023 DURHAM, JOSEPH VANN ....9715 MENDOZA RD, RANDALLSTOWN MD 21133
1980-040 DURHAM, LEON..........3932 DICKSON AVE, CINCINNATI OH 45229
1995-066 DURHAM, RAY 'SUGAR RAY'..........1815 LAKE DRIVE, CHARLOTTE NC 28214
1957-020 DURNBAUGH, ROBERT EUGENE ....1638 NORTH CENTRAL DRIVE, DAYTON OH 45432
1925-027 DURNING, GEORGE DEWEY ....D. APRIL 18, 1986, TAMPA, FLA.
2002-050 DUROCHER, JAYSON PAUL..........[illegible] NORTH 43RD STREET, CAVE CREEK AZ 85331
1925-028 DUROCHER, LEO ERNEST ....D. OCTOBER 7, 1991, PALM SPRINGS, CALIF.
[illegible]-034 DURRETT, ELMER CHARLES 'RED' ....D. JANUARY 17, 1992, WAXAHACHIE, TEXAS
1999-058 DURRINGTON, TRENT JOHN ....499 NORTH CAON DRIVE, BEVERLY HILLS CA 90210
1922-029 DURST, CEDRIC MONTGOMERY..........D. FEBRUARY 16, 1971, SAN DIEGO, CALIF.
1941-023 DUSAK, ERVIN FRANK..........D. NOVEMBER 6, 1994, GLENDALE HEIGHTS, ILL.
1956-031 DUSER, CARL ROBERT..........3021 CORMWALL RD, BETHLEHEM PA 18017
1963-036 DUSTAL, ROBERT ANDREW ....2704 ROXIE AVENUE, LAKELAND FL 33801
1998-050 DUVALL, MICHAEL ALAN..........2743 NATURE POINTE LOOP, FORT MYERS FL 33905
1973-040 DWYER, JAMES EDWARD ....826 HANCOCK BRIDGE PKWY, CAPE CORAL FL 33990
1937-036 DWYER, JOSEPH MICHAEL ....D. OCTOBER 21, 1992, GLEN RIDGE, N.J.
1980-041 DYBZINSKI, JEROME MATTHEW ....1626 HAYWOOD PLACE, FORT COLLINS CO 80526
1951-025 DYCK, JAMES ROBERT..........D. JANUARY 10, 1998, CHENEY, WASH.
1996-054 DYE, JERMAINE TERRELL ....6655 NORTH 66TH PLACE, PARADISE VALLEY AZ 85253
1968-017 DYER, DONALD ROBERT 'DUFFY'..........742 WEST LAS PALMARITAS, PHOENIX AZ 85021
1922-030 DYER, EDWIN HAWLEY ....D. APRIL 20, 1964, HOUSTON, TEXAS
1989-033 DYER, MICHAEL LAWRENCE..........22392 MANACOR, MISSION VIEJO CA 92692
1998-051 DYKHOFF, RADHAMES ALVIRO..........OLD ADD: ORANJESTAD, ARUBA, NETHERLAND ANTILLES
1985-028 DYKSTRA, LENNY KYLE ....2672 LADBROOK WAY, THOUSAND OAKS CA 91361

E

1959-025 EADDY, DONALD JOHNSON..........2276 SOUTHGATE DRIVE SE, KENTWOOD MI 49508
1984-032 EARL, WILLIAM SCOTT 'SCOTT'..........9798 MIRAFIELD LANE, MCCORDSVILLE IN 46055
1960-031 EARLEY, ARNOLD CARL ....D. SEPTEMBER 29, 1999, FLINT, MICH.
1938-022 EARLEY, THOMAS FRANCIS ALOYSIUS ....D. APRIL 5, 1988, NANTUCKET ISLAND, MASS.
1986-046 EARLEY, WILLIAM ALBERT..........112 CARRUTHERS POND DRIVE, CINCINNATI OH 45246
1939-031 EARLY, JACOB WILLARD ....D. MAY 31, 1985, MELBOURNE, FLA.
1928-032 EARNSHAW, GEORGE LIVINGSTON..........D. DECEMBER 1, 1976, LITTLE ROCK, ARK.
1973-041 EASLER, MICHAEL ANTHONY..........5650 RED ROOF STREET, NORTH LAS VEGAS NV 89081
1992-036 EASLEY, DAMION JACINTO..........14125 NORTH 65TH AVENUE, GLENDALE AZ 85306
1987-040 EASLEY, KENNETH LOGAN 'LOGAN' ....555 WILDROSE LOOP, TWIN FALLS ID 83301
1941-024 EAST, GORDON HUGH 'HUGH'..........D. NOVEMBER 2, 1981, CHARLESTON, S.C.
1949-020 EASTER, LUSCIOUS 'LUKE' ....D. MARCH 29, 1979, EUCLID, OHIO
1928-033 EASTERLING, PAUL ....D. MARCH 15, 1993, REIDSVILLE, GA.
1974-030 EASTERLY, JAMES MORRIS 'JAMIE' ....1306 PLANTATION, CROCKETT TX 75835
1944-035 EASTERWOOD, ROY CHARLES..........D. AUGUST 24, 1984, GRAHAM, TEXAS
1955-039 EASTON, JOHN DAVID ....D. JULY 28, 2001, PRINCETON, N.J.
1974-031 EASTWICK, RAWLINS JACKSON ....10 RIVER MEADOW DRIVE, WEST NEWBURY MA 01985
2000-052 EATON, ADAM THOMAS ....401 NORTH ANGFORD DRIVE, ELLENSBURG WA 98226
1979-030 EATON, CRAIG..........3307 BALTUSROL LN, LAKE WORTH FL 33467
1944-036 EATON, ZEBULON VANCE ....D. DECEMBER 17, 1989, WEST PALM BEACH, FLA.
1988-046 EAVE, GARY LOUIS ....1601 KING AVENUE, BASTROP LA 71220
1935-026 EAVES, VALLIE ENNIS..........D. APRIL 19, 1960, NORMAN, OKLA.
1999-059 EBERT, DERRIN LEE..........13785 WEST ACAPULCO LANE, SURPRISE AZ 85379
1996-055 ECHEVARRIA, ANGEL SANTOS..........OLD ADD: BRIDGEPORT CT 06602
1939-032 ECHOLS, JOHN GRESHAM ....D. NOVEMBER 13, 1972, ATLANTA, GA.
2002-051 ECKENSTAHLER, ERIC RYAN..........24250 ALPINE COURT, LAKE VILLA IL 60046
1975-036 ECKERSLEY, DENNIS LEE..........6 MACY LANE, IPSWICH MA 01938
1930-021 ECKERT, ALBERT GEORGE..........D. APRIL 20, 1974, MILWAUKEE, WISC.
1932-022 ECKHARDT, OSCAR GEORGE 'OX' ....D. APRIL 22, 1951, YORKTOWN, TEXAS
2001-054 ECKSTEIN, DAVID MARK ....103 ALDEAN DRIVE, SANFORD FL 32771
1995-067 EDDY, CHRISTOPHER MARK..........47 WINTERBURY CIRCXLE, WILMINGTON DE 19808
1970-038 EDDY, DONALD EUGENE..........BOX 537, ROCKWELL IA 50469
1979-031 EDDY, STEVEN ALLEN..........700 NORTH DOBSON #38, CHANDLER AZ 85224
1981-030 EDELEN, BENNY JOE 'JOE' ....PO BOX 38, WASHINGTON OK 73038
1932-023 EDELEN, EDWARD JOSEPH ....D. FEBRUARY 1, 1982, LAPLATA, MD.
1955-040 EDELMAN, JOHN ROGERS ....922 MONTE VISTA DRIVE, WEST CHESTER PA 19380
1976-030 EDEN, EDWARD MICHAEL 'MIKE'..........11531 FOREST HILLS DRIVE, TAMPA FL 33612
1995-068 EDENFIELD, KENNETH EDWARD ....4407 BARBARA DRIVE, KNOXVILLE TN 37918
1987-041 EDENS, THOMAS PATRICK..........2033 QUAILRIDGE COURT, CLARKSTON WA 99403
1979-032 EDGE, CLAUDE LEE 'BUTCH' ....PO BOX 601414, SACRAMENTO CA 95860
1966-031 EDGERTON, WILLIAM ALBERT..........1725 EAST JEFFERSON BLVD, MISHAWAKA IN 46545
1980-042 EDLER, DAVID DELMAR ....1504 SOUTH 34TH AVE, YAKIMA WA 98902
1993-047 EDMONDS, JAMES PATRICK ....114 HUNTERS GROVE DRIVE, SAINT LOUIS MO 63141
1998-052 EDMONDSON, BRIAN CHRISTOPHER ....304 RIDGEVIEW TRACE, CANTON GA 30114
1922-031 EDMONDSON, GEORGE HENDERSON ....D. JULY 11, 1973, WACO, TEXAS
1969-052 EDMONDSON, PAUL MICHAEL..........D. FEBRUARY 13, 1970, SANTA BARBARA, CALIF.
1946-026 EDWARDS, CHARLES BRUCE 'BRUCE'..........D. APRIL 25, 1975, SACRAMENTO, CALIF.
1978-038 EDWARDS, DAVID LEONARD ....5059 QUAIL RUN ROAD #75, RIVERSIDE CA 92507

1925-029	EDWARDS, FOSTER HAMILTON	D. JANUARY 4, 1980, ORLEANS, MASS.
1941-025	EDWARDS, HENRY ALBERT	D. JUNE 22, 1988, SANTA ANA, CALIF.
1962-035	EDWARDS, HOWARD RODNEY 'DOC'	3706 DRIFTWOOD DRIVE, SAN ANGELO TX 76904
1922-032	EDWARDS, JAMES CORBETTE 'JIM JOE'	D. JANUARY 19, 1965, CALHOUN COUNTY, MISS.
1961-033	EDWARDS, JOHN ALBAN	2511 EAST BLUE LAKE DRIVE, MAGNOLIA TX 77354
1981-031	EDWARDS, MARSHALL LYNN	5059 QUAIL RUN ROAD #75, RIVERSIDE CA 92507
2003-044	EDWARDS, MICHAEL DONALD	502 SHARON AVENUE, MECHANICSBURG PA 17055
1977-050	EDWARDS, MICHAEL LEWIS	11370 MORENO BEACH DRIVE, MORENO VALLEY CA 92555
1934-032	EDWARDS, SHERMAN STANLEY	D. MARCH 8, 1992, EL DORADO, ARK.
1989-034	EDWARDS, WAYNE MAURICE	9738 AQUEDUCT AVENUE, SEPULVEDA CA 91343
1994-028	EENHOORN, ROBERT FRANCISCUS	ZERMILIEPLAATS 15 3068J ROTTERDAM, NETHERLANDS
1963-037	EGAN, RICHARD WALLIS	1611 WEST THUNDERHILL DRIVE, PHOENIX AZ 85045
1965-028	EGAN, THOMAS PATRICK	184 EAST MYRNA LANE, TEMPE AZ 85284
1927-030	EGGERT, ELMER ALBERT	D. APRIL 9, 1971, ROCHESTER, N.Y.
1991-049	EGLOFF, BRUCE EDWARD	3136 SOUTH EMPORIA COURT, DENVER CO 80231
1924-033	EHRHARDT, WELTON CLAUDE 'RUBE'	D. APRIL 27, 1980, CHICAGO HEIGHTS, ILL.
1978-039	EICHELBERGER, JUAN TYRONE	14674 SILVERSET ST, POWAY CA 92064
1982-037	EICHHORN, MARK ANTHONY	147 NORMA COURT, APTOS CA 95003
1925-030	EICHRODT, FREDERICK GEORGE	D. JULY 14, 1965, INDIANAPOLIS, IND.
1988-047	EILAND, DAVID WILLIAM	2824 BLUE SPRINGS PLACE, WESLEY CHAPEL FL 33543
1964-029	EILERS, DAVID LOUIS	602 PERKINS LANE, BRENHAM TX 77833
2000-053	EINERTSON, DARRELL LEE	5205 SE 26TH COURT, DES MOINES IA 50320
1994-029	EISCHEN, JOSEPH RAYMOND 'JOEY'	14 FAIRWAY ROAD, ROTUNDA WEST FL 33947
1944-037	EISENHART, JACOB HENRY 'HANK'	D. DECEMBER 20, 1987, HUNTINGDON, PA.
1982-038	EISENREICH, JAMES MICHAEL	21300 EAST 34TH STREET SOUTH, INDEPENDENCE MO 64057
1935-027	EISENSTAT, HARRY	D. MARCH 21, 2003, BEACHWOOD, OHIO
1998-053	ELARTON, VINCENT SCOTT 'SCOTT'	PO BOX 5, VILLA GROVE CO 81155
2002-052	ELDER, DAVID MATTHEW	2642 HIGH STREET SOUTHWEST, CONYERS GA 30094
1949-021	ELDER, GEORGE REZIN	423 AMETHYST DRIVE, FRUITA CO 81521
2005-056	ELDRED, BRADLEY ROSS	OLD ADD: COCONUT CREEK FL
1991-050	ELDRED, CALVIN JOHN	170 ABBOTSFORD ROAD, CEDAR RAPIDS IA 52403
1966-032	ELIA, LEE CONSTANTINE	11613 INNFIELDS DRIVE, ODESSA FL 33556
1943-042	ELKO, PETER	D. SEPTEMBER 17, 1993, WILKES-BARRE, PA.
1974-032	ELLINGSEN, HAROLD BRUCE 'BRUCE'	5873 DANELAND, LAKEWOOD CA 90713
1962-036	ELLIOT, LAWRENCE LEE	13010 CAMINITO BRACHO, SAN DIEGO CA 92128
1923-033	ELLIOTT, ALLEN CLIFFORD	D. MAY 6, 1979, ST. LOUIS, MO.
1921-024	ELLIOTT, CARTER WARD	D. MAY 21, 1959, PALM SPRINGS, CALIF.
1994-030	ELLIOTT, DONALD GLENN 'DONNIE'	1206 BAYOU VISTA, DEER PARK TX 77536
1929-033	ELLIOTT, HAROLD WILLIAM	D. APRIL 25, 1963, HONOLULU, HAWAII
1953-020	ELLIOTT, HARRY LEWIS	1154 RANDOM, EL CAJON CA 92020
1947-030	ELLIOTT, HERBERT GLENN	D. JULY 27, 1969, PORTLAND, ORE.
1923-034	ELLIOTT, JAMES THOMPSON	D. JANUARY 7, 1970, TERRE HAUTE, IND.
1972-025	ELLIOTT, RANDY LEE	PO BOX 834, SOMIS CA 93066
1939-033	ELLIOTT, ROBERT IRVING	D. MAY 4, 1966, SAN DIEGO, CALIF.
1968-018	ELLIS, DOCK PHILIP	121 E. 139TH ST, LOS ANGELES CA 90061
1967-028	ELLIS, JAMES RUSSELL	13608 AVE 224, TULARE CA 93274
1969-053	ELLIS, JOHN CHARLES	24 SALTUS DRIVE, OLD SAYBROOK CT 06475
2002-053	ELLIS, MARK WILLIAM	318 KINNEY AVENUE, RAPID CITY SD 57702
1996-056	ELLIS, ROBERT RANDOLPH	2066 75TH AVENUE, BATON ROUGE LA 70807
1971-029	ELLIS, ROBERT WALTER	2020 KRISLIN DRIVE NE, GRAND RAPIDS MI 49505
1962-037	ELLIS, SAMUEL JOSEPH	12511 FOREST HIGHLANDS DRIVE, DADE CITY FL 33525
1920-031	ELLISON, GEORGE RUSSELL	D. JANUARY 20, 1978, SAN FRANCISCO, CALIF.
2003-045	ELLISON, JASON JEROME	3745 248TH AVENUE SE, ISSAQUAH WA 98029
1958-028	ELLSWORTH, RICHARD CLARK	1099 WEST MORRIS, FRESNO CA 93705
1988-048	ELLSWORTH, STEVEN CLARK	OLD ADD: 8215 NORTH CHANCE AVENUE, FRESNO CA 93720
1924-034	ELMORE, VERDO WILSON	D. AUGUST 5, 1969, BIRMINGHAM, ALA.
1923-035	ELSH, EUGENE RAYBOLD 'ROY'	D. NOVEMBER 12, 1978, PENNS GROVE NJ
1986-047	ELSTER, KEVIN DANIEL	5801 MARSHALL DRIVE, HUNTINGTON BEACH CA 92649
1953-021	ELSTON, DONALD RAY	D. JANUARY 2, 1995, ARLINGTON HEIGHTS, ILL.
1990-043	ELVIRA, NARCISCO DELGADO	DOM CONOCIDA, EL COCUITE MUN TLALIX VERACRUZ VERACRUZ, MEXICO
1992-037	EMBREE, ALAN DUANE	29400 NE 70TH CIRCLE, CAMAS WA 98607
1941-026	EMBREE, CHARLES WILLIAM 'RED'	D. SEPTEMBER 24, 1996, EUGENE, ORE.
1923-036	EMBRY, CHARLES AKIN 'SLIM'	D. OCTOBER 10, 1947, NASHVILLE, TENN.
1963-038	EMERY, CALVIN WAYNE	4817 SOUTH 195TH EAST AVENUE, BROKEN ARROW OK 74014
1924-035	EMERY, HERRICK SMITH 'SPOKE'	D. JUNE 2, 1975, CAPE CANAVERAL, FLA.
1923-037	EMMERICH, ROBERT GEORGE	D. NOVEMBER 22, 1948, BRIDGEPORT, CONN.
1945-029	EMMERICH, WILLIAM PETER 'SLIM'	D. SEPTEMBER 17, 1998, ALLENTOWN, PA.
1995-069	ENCARNACION, ANGELO BENJAMIN	OLD ADD: SANTO DOMINGO DOM REP
2005-057	ENCARNACION, EDWIN ELPIDIO	OLD ADD: LA ROMANA DOM REP
1997-050	ENCARNACION, JUAN DEDIOS	OLD ADD: LAS MATAS DE FARAN DOM REP
1990-044	ENCARNACION, LUIS MARTIN	MANZ 9 #6 LAS CAOBOS DE HERRERA SANTO DOMINGO, DOM REP
2001-055	ENCARNACION, MARIO (GONZALEZ)	D. OCTOBER 3, 2005, DANSHUEI TAIWAN
2000-054	ENDERS, TREVOR HALE	450 WEST SUNWEST DRIVE #57, CASA GRANDE AZ 85222
1946-027	ENDICOTT, WILLIAM FRANKLIN	14219 OAK KNOLL ROAD, SONORA CA 95370
1985-029	ENGEL, STEVEN MICHAEL	6212 OLD STONE COURT, HAMILTON OH 45011
1925-031	ENGLE, CHARLES AUGUST	D. OCTOBER 12, 1983, SAN ANTONIO, TEXAS
1981-032	ENGLE, RALPH DAVID 'DAVE'	5343 CASTLE HILLS DRIVE, SAN DIEGO CA 92109
1981-033	ENGLE, RICHARD DOUGLAS 'DOUG'	6413 SENECA TRAIL, MENTOR OH 44060
1932-024	ENGLISH, CHARLES DEWIE	D. JUNE 25, 1999, PASADENA, CALIF.
1927-031	ENGLISH, ELWOOD GEORGE 'WOODY'	D. SEPTEMBER 26, 1997, NEWARK, OHIO
1931-023	ENGLISH, GILBERT RAYMOND	D. AUGUST 31, 1996, TRINITY, N.C.
1946-028	ENNIS, DELMAR	D. FEBRUARY 8, 1996, HUNTINGDON VALLEY, PA.
2002-054	ENNIS, JOHN WAYNE	OLD ADD: PANORAMA CITY CA 91402
1926-028	ENNIS, RUSSELL ELWOOD	D. JANUARY 29, 1949, SUPERIOR, WISC.
1976-031	ENRIGHT, GEORGE ALBERT	3075 STRAWFLOWER WAY, LAKE WORTH FL 33467
1922-033	ENS, JEWEL WINKLEMEYER	D. JANUARY 17, 1950, SYRACUSE, N.Y.

2000-055	ENSBERG, MORGAN P.	1132 THIRD STREET, HERMOSA BEACH CA 90254
1974-033	ENYART, TERRY GENE	3444 FOXWOOD BLVD, ZEPHYRHILLS FL 33543
1987-042	EPPARD, JAMES GERHARD	320 ASHBY STREET, AZUSA CA 91702
1938-023	EPPERLY, ALBERT PAUL	D. APRIL 14, 2003, MCFARLAND, WISC.
1935-028	EPPS, AUBREY LEE	D. NOVEMBER 13, 1984, ACKERMAN, MISS.
1938-024	EPPS, HAROLD FRANKLIN	D. AUGUST 25, 2004, HOUSTON, TEXAS
1966-033	EPSTEIN, MICHAEL PETER	6384 SOUTH BLACKHAWK WAY, AURORA CO 80016
1977-051	ERARDI, JOSEPH GREGORY 'GREG'	42 WESTGATE ROAD, MASSAPEQUA PARK NY 11762
1947-031	ERAUTT, EDWARD LORENZ SEBASTIAN	7252 WAITE DRIVE, LAMESA CA 91941
1950-028	ERAUTT, JOSEPH MICHAEL	D. OCTOBER 6, 1976, PORTLAND, ORE.
1997-051	ERDOS, TODD MICHAEL	118 WINSLOW COURT, CRANBERRY TWP PA 16066
1995-070	ERICKS, JOHN EDWARD	17000 OKETO AVENUE, TINLEY PARK IL 60477
1958-029	ERICKSON, DON LEE	1929 MONTANA DRIVE, SPRINGFIELD IL 62704
1953-022	ERICKSON, HAROLD JAMES	2674 FOOTHILL DRIVE, OGDEN UT 84403
1935-029	ERICKSON, HENRY NELS	D. DECEMBER 13, 1964, LOUISVILLE, KY.
2004-061	ERICKSON, MATT E.	OLD ADD: 5000 NORTH BALLARD ROAD, APPLETON WI 54913
1941-027	ERICKSON, PAUL WALFORD	D. APRIL 5, 2002, FOND DU LAC, WISC.
1929-034	ERICKSON, RALPH LIEF	D. JUNE 27, 2002, CHANDLER, ARIZ.
1978-040	ERICKSON, ROGER FARRELL	2647 DELAWARE DRIVE, SPRINGFIELD IL 62702
1990-045	ERICKSON, SCOTT GAVIN	1183 CORRAL AVENUE, SUNNYVALE CA 94088
1947-032	ERMER, CALVIN COOLIDGE	1009 PANORAMA DRIVE, CHATTANOOGA TN 37421
1957-021	ERNAGA, FRANK JOHN	50 NORTH ROOP ST, SUSANVILLE CA 96130
1938-025	ERRICKSON, RICHARD MERRIWELL	D. NOVEMBER 28, 1999, VINELAND, N.J.
1948-034	ERSKINE, CARL DANIEL	4031 FALLBROOK LANE, ANDERSON IN 46011
1996-057	ERSTAD, DARIN CHARLES	3224 35 1/2 COURT AVENUE SOUTH, FARGO ND 58104
1983-051	ESASKY, NICHOLAS ANDREW	1779 STARLIGHT DRIVE NE, MARIETTA GA 30062
1954-024	ESCALERA, SATURNINO CUADRADO 'NINO'	OLD ADD: DC-20 STREET 201, CAROLINA PR 00983
2002-055	ESCALONA, FELIX EDUARDO	OLD ADD: PUERTO VALLERTO VENEZ
1982-039	ESCARREGA, ERNESTO	OLD ADD: APARTADO POSTAL 48G, LOS MOCHIS MEXICO
1942-032	ESCHEN, LAWRENCE EDWARD	3649 GARDEN BLVD, GAINESVILLE GA 30503
2001-056	ESCOBAR, ALEXANDER JOSE	OLD ADD: VALENCIA VENEZ
1988-049	ESCOBAR, ANGEL RUBEN	OLD ADD: CARICUAO, CARACAS VENEZUELA
1991-051	ESCOBAR, JOSE ELIAS (SANCHEZ)	OLD ADD: LASABANA,DPT. VARGAS, CALLE LAS FLORES VENEZ
1997-052	ESCOBAR, KELVIM JOSE BOLIVAR	OLD ADD: 4775 COLLINS AVENUE #3503, MIAMI BEACH FL 33140
1995-071	ESHELMAN, VAUGHN MICHAEL	30106 FALHER DRIVE, SPRING TX 77386
1982-040	ESPINO, JUAN	EUGENIO M. DE CESTOS #50 BONAO, DOM REP
1974-034	ESPINOSA, ARNULFO ACEVEDO 'NINO'	D. DECEMBER 25, 1987, VILLA ALTAGRACIA, DOM REP
1984-033	ESPINOZA, ALVARO ALBERTO	1601 SE AIROSO BLVD, PORT SAINT LUCIE FL 34984
2005-058	ESPOSITO, MICHAEL ANTHONY	OLD ADD: LAS VEGAS NV
1952-028	ESPOSITO, SAMUEL	8303 AMBER LEAF COURT, RALEIGH NC 27612
1983-052	ESPY, CECIL EDWARD	5480 ENCINA DRIVE, SAN DIEGO CA 92114
1958-030	ESSEGIAN, CHARLES ABRAHAM	15639 BRONCO DRIVE, CANYON COUNTRY CA 91351
1979-033	ESSER, MARK GERALD	208 RIDGE ROAD, JUPITER FL 33477
1973-042	ESSIAN, JAMES SARKIS	134 ECKFORD, TROY MI 48098
1996-058	ESTALELLA, ROBERT M.	OLD ADD: 2210 NW 94TH AVENUE, HOLLYWOOD FL 33024
1935-030	ESTALELLA, ROBERTO MENDEZ	D. JANUARY 6, 1991, HIALEAH, FLA.
1964-030	ESTELLE, RICHARD HARRY	2221 TAYLOR AVE, POINT PLEASANT NJ 08742
1995-072	ESTES, AARON SHAWN 'SHAWN'	6659 EAST MAEDOWLARK LANE, PARADISE VALLEY AZ 85253
1951-026	ESTOCK, GEORGE JOHN	595 RAY STREET, SEBASTIAN FL 32958
1960-032	ESTRADA, CHARLES LEONARD	1289 MANZANITA WAY, SAN LUIS OBISPO CA 93401
1971-030	ESTRADA, FRANCISCO (SOTO)	MANUEL DOBLADO PTE 605-A NAVAJOA SONORA, MEXICO C.P. 85800
1999-060	ESTRADA, HORACIO	OLD ADD: SAN JOAQUIN VENEZUELA
2001-057	ESTRADA, JOHNNY PULADO	4343 EAST FLORENCE AVENUE, FRESNO CA 93725
1929-035	ESTRADA, OSCAR	D. JANUARY 2, 1978, HAVANA, CUBA
2000-056	ESTRELLA, LEONCIO RAMIREZ	5462 NW BODOGA AVENUE, PORT SAINT LUCIE FL 34986
1962-038	ETCHEBARREN, ANDREW AUGUSTE	188 VERMEER DRIVE, NOKOMIS FL 34275
1943-043	ETCHISON, CLARENCE HAMPTON 'BUCK'	D. JANUARY 24, 1980, CAMBRIDGE, MD.
1967-029	ETHERIDGE, BOBBY LAMAR	118 PORTLAND ROAD, EUDORA AR 71640
2000-057	ETHERTON, SETH MICHAEL	32651 SEVEN SEAS DRIVE, DANA POINT CA 92629
2006-045	ETHIER, ANDRE EVERETT	324 WEST THOMPSON PLACE, CHANDLER AZ 85240
1938-026	ETTEN, NICHOLAS RAYMOND THOMAS	D. OCTOBER 18, 1990, HINSDALE, ILL.
1993-048	ETTLES, MARK EDWARD	3-10 ROSE AVENUE SOUTH PERTH, WESTERN AUSTRALIA 6151
1922-034	EUBANKS, UEL MELVIN	D. NOVEMBER 21, 1954, DALLAS, TEXAS
1985-030	EUFEMIA, FRANK ANTHONY	433 6TH AVENUE, SEASIDE HEIGHTS NJ 08751
1991-052	EUSEBIO, RAUL ANTONIO 'TONY'	2078 SHANNON LAKES BLVD, KISSIMMEE FL 34743
1939-034	EVANS, ALFRED HUBERT	D. APRIL 6, 1979, WILSON, N.C.
1978-041	EVANS, BARRY STEVEN	8303 SEVEN OAKS DRIVE, JONESBORO GA 30236
1998-054	EVANS, BART STEVEN	8323 ROLLING HILLS DRIVE, NIXA MO 65714
1969-054	EVANS, DARRELL WAYNE	1900 EAST OCEAN BLVD #901, LONG BEACH CA 90802
1972-026	EVANS, DWIGHT MICHAEL	15881 GREY FRIARS COURT, FORT MYERS FL 33912
1936-023	EVANS, RUSSELL EDISON 'RED'	D. JUNE 14, 1982, LAKEVIEW, ARK.
1997-053	EVANS, THOMAS JOHN	32533 SE 68TH STREET, ISSAQUAH WA 98027
1932-025	EVANS, WILLIAM ARTHUR	D. JANUARY 8, 1952, WICHITA, KAN.
1949-022	EVANS, WILLIAM LAWRENCE	D. NOVEMBER 30, 1983, GRAND JUNCTION, COLO.
2005-059	EVELAND, DANA JAMES	37816 SULPHUR SPRINGS ROAD, PALMDALE CA 93552
1993-049	EVERETT, CARL EDWARD	19108 HARBORBRIDGE LANE, LUTZ FL 33558
2001-058	EVERETT, JEFFREY ADAM 'ADAM'	959 FAIRLONG DRIVE NW, ACWORTH GA 30101
1969-055	EVERITT, EDWARD LEON	OLD ADD: 6257 SOUTH LABREA AVENUE, LOS ANGELES CA 90056
1941-028	EVERS, WALTER ARTHUR 'HOOT'	D. JANUARY 25, 1991, HOUSTON, TEXAS
1994-031	EVERSGERD, BRYAN DAVID	211 EAST 2ND STREET, HOFFMAN IL 62250
1921-025	EWING, REUBEN	D. OCTOBER 5, 1970, WEST HARTFORD, CONN.
1973-043	EWING, SAMUEL JAMES	1048 CEDARVIEW LANE, FRANKLIN TN 37067
1997-054	EYRE, SCOTT ALAN	7010 190TH STREET EAST, BRADENTON FL 34201
2006-046	EYRE, WILLIAM MAYS	42 NORTH 200 WEST, PAROWAN UT 84101
1943-044	EYRICH, GEORGE LINCOLN	D. JUNE 25, 2006, READING, PA.
1923-038	EZZELL, HOMER ESTELL	D. AUGUST 3, 1976, SAN ANTONIO, TEXAS

1994-032	FABREGAS, JORGE	4936 SOUTHWEST 6TH STREET, MIAMI FL 33134
1953-023	FACE, ELROY LEON	608 DELLA DRIVE #5F, NORTH VERSAILLES PA 15137
1980-043	FAEDO, LEONARDO LAGO 'LENNY'	2920 COLLINS ST, TAMPA FL 33607
1943-045	FAGAN, EVERETT JOSEPH	D. FEBRUARY 16, 1983, MORRISTOWN, N.J.
2006-047	FAHEY, BRANDON WADE	5740 MONA LANE, DALLAS TX 75236
1971-031	FAHEY, WILLIAM ROGER	5740 MONA LANE, DALLAS TX 75236
1951-027	FAHR, GERALD WARREN 'RED'	7749 HIGHWAY 49 NORTH, MARMADUKE AR 72443
1947-033	FAIN, FERRIS ROY	D. OCTOBER 18, 2001, GEORGETOWN, CALIF.
1968-019	FAIREY, JAMES BURKE	218 STRAWBERRY ST, CLEMSON SC 29361
1958-031	FAIRLY, RONALD RAY	75369 SPYGLASS DRIVE, INDIAN WELLS CA 92210
1991-053	FAJARDO, HECTOR (NAVARRETE)	OLD ADD: SAHUAYO MICHOACAN MEXICO
1975-037	FALCONE, PETER FRANK	2232 THORNTON COURT, ALEXANDRIA LA 71301
1920-032	FALK, BIBB AUGUST	D. JUNE 8, 1989, AUSTIN, TEXAS
1925-032	FALK, CHESTER EMANUEL 'CHET'	D. JANUARY 7, 1982, AUSTIN, TEXAS
1999-061	FALKENBORG, BRIAN THOMAS	3135 NORTH 155TH LANE, GOODYEAR AZ 85338
1931-024	FALLENSTIN, EDWARD JOSEPH	D. NOVEMBER 24, 1971, ORANGE, N.J.
1937-037	FALLON, GEORGE DECATUR	D. OCTOBER 25, 1994, LAKE WORTH, FLA.
1984-034	FALLON, ROBERT JOSEPH	1830 SW 81ST AVENUE #4416, NORTH LAUDERDALE FL 33068
1997-055	FALTEISEK, STEVEN JAMES	540 WEST IRIS DRIVE, CHANDLER AZ 85248
1993-050	FANEYTE, RIKKERT	C/O M. FANEYTE, J. FRANKLIN STRATT 26 III, 1056 TC AMSTERDAM, NETHERLANDS
1945-030	FANNIN, CLIFFORD BRYSON	D. DECEMBER 11, 1966, SANDUSKY, OHIO
1954-025	FANNING, WILLIAM JAMES 'JIM'	154 TINER AVENUE DORCHESTER ON, N0L 1G2 CANADA
1963-039	FANOK, HARRY MICHAEL	12373 OLD STATE ROAD, CHARDON OH 44024
1949-023	FANOVICH, FRANK JOSEPH	3 FAIRGREEN AVENUE, NEW SMYRNA BEACH FL 32168
1986-048	FANSLER, STANLEY ROBERT	RURAL ROUTE 2 BOX 55901, ELKINS WV 26241
1970-039	FANZONE, CARMEN	5114 RANCHITA AVENUE, SHERMAN OAKS CA 91423
1990-046	FARIES, PAUL TYRELL	3299 BEECHWOOD DRIVE, LAFAYETTE CA 94549
1991-054	FARISS, MONTY TED	PO BOX 249, LEEDEY OK 73654
1961-034	FARLEY, ROBERT JACOB	1325 SYCAMORE ROAD, MONTOURSVILLE PA 17754
1971-032	FARMER, EDWARD JOSEPH	333 WEST 35TH STREET, CHICAGO IL 60616
1990-047	FARMER, HOWARD EARL	1675 WEST 10TH PLACE, GARY IN 46404
1996-059	FARMER, MICHAEL ANTHONY	OLD ADD: GARY IN 46401
2002-056	FARNSWORTH, JEFFREY ELLIS	OLD ADD: PENSACOLA FL 32502
1999-062	FARNSWORTH, KYLE LYNN	1400 STICKLEY AVENUE, KISSIMMEE FL 34747
1982-041	FARR, JAMES ALFRED	3 TYNDAL COURT, WILLIAMSBURG VA 23188
1984-035	FARR, STEVEN MICHAEL	6032 CURRITUCK ROAD, KITTY HAWK NC 27949
1925-033	FARRELL, EDWARD STEPHEN 'DOC'	D. DECEMBER 20, 1966, LIVINGSTON, N.J.
1987-043	FARRELL, JOHN EDWARD	31009 WILDERNESS TRAIL, CLEVELAND OH 44145
1943-046	FARRELL, MAJOR KERBY 'KERBY'	D. DECEMBER 17, 1975, NASHVILLE, TENN.
1956-032	FARRELL, RICHARD JOSEPH 'DICK'	D. JUNE 11, 1977, GREAT YARMOUTH, ENGLAND
1996-060	FASANO, SALVATORE FRANK	3202 ERNST STREET, FRANKLIN PARK IL 60131
1991-055	FASSERO, JEFFREY JOSEPH	9841 NORTH 56TH STREET, PARADISE VALLEY AZ 85253
1968-020	FAST, DARCY RAE	2981 HARRISON AVENUE, CENTRALIA WA 98531
1953-024	FASZHOLZ, JOHN EDWARD 'JACK'	18338 MARIES ROAD 308, BELLE MO 65013
1962-039	FAUL, WILLIAM ALVAN	D. FEBRUARY 21, 2002, CINCINNATI, OHIO
1927-032	FAULKNER, JAMES LEROY	D. JUNE 2, 1962, WEST PALM BEACH, FLA.
1944-038	FAUSETT, ROBERT SHAW	D. MAY 2, 1994, COLLEGE STATION, TEXAS
1962-040	FAZIO, ERNEST JOSEPH	2310 ROYAL OAKS DRIVE, ALAMO CA 94507
1952-029	FEAR, LUVERN CARL	D. SEPTEMBER 6, 1976, SPENCER, IOWA
1998-055	FEBLES, CARLOS MANUEL	OLD ADD: 7000 WEST 124TH STREET, LEAWOOD KS 66209
1951-028	FEDEROFF, ALFRED	10150 MORTONVIEW, TAYLOR MI 48180
1934-033	FEHRING, WILLIAM PAUL 'DUTCH'	D. APRIL 14, 2006, PALO ALTO, CALIF.
2006-048	FEIERABEND, RYAN ROBERT	6230 STATE HIGHWAY 534, WEST FARMINGTON OH 44491
1938-027	FEINBERG, EDWARD	D. APRIL 20, 1986, HOLLYWOOD, FLA.
1985-031	FELDER, MICHAEL OTIS	3033 ELLIS STREET #B, BERKELEY CA 94703
1942-033	FELDERMAN, MARVIN WILFRED 'COONEY'	D. AUGUST 6, 2000, RIVERSIDE, CALIF.
1941-029	FELDMAN, HARRY	D. MARCH 16, 1962, FORT SMITH, ARK.
2005-060	FELDMAN, SCOTT WAYNE	OLD ADD: BURLINGTON CA
2002-057	FELICIANO, PEDRO JUAN MOLINA	OLD ADD: DORADO PR 00646
1923-039	FELIX, AUGUST GUENTHER 'GUS'	D. MAY 12, 1960, MONTGOMERY, ALA.
1989-035	FELIX, JUNIOR FRANCISCO	DONA ANTONIA #42, VILLA ELINA GUAYUBIN, DOM REP
2000-058	FELIZ, PEDRO JULIO	OLD ADD: AZUA DOM REP
1958-032	FELLER, JACK LELAND	145 OAKWOOD DRIVE, COLDWATER MI 49035
1936-024	FELLER, ROBERT WILLIAM ANDREW	PO BOX 157, GATES MILLS OH 44040
1968-021	FELSKE, JOHN FREDRICK	3804 RIDGE ROAD, SPRING GROVE IL 60081
1979-034	FELTON, TERRY LANE	1253 CORDOBA DRIVE, ZACHARY LA 70791
1921-026	FENNER, HORACE ALFRED 'HOD'	D. NOVEMBER 20, 1954, DETROIT, MICH.
1972-027	FENWICK, ROBERT RICHARD	51201 HUTCHINSON ROAD, THREE RIVERS MI 49093
1942-034	FERENS, STANLEY	D. OCTOBER 7, 1994, HEMPFIELD TWP., PA.
1970-040	FERGUSON, JOSEPH VANCE	OLD ADD: 1095 WEST EL CAMINO REAL, SUNNYVALE CA 94087
1944-039	FERGUSON, ROBERT LESTER	26 WETUMPKA GARDEN APTS, WETUMPKA AL 36092
1987-044	FERMIN, FELIX JOSE	CALLE K - ESQ. MIRADOR, CERRO ALTO SANTIAGO, DOM REP
1995-073	FERMIN, RAMON ANTONIO	PRO YECTO AGUAYO CLE F #4 SAN FRANCISCO DE MACORIS, DOM REP
1940-019	FERNANDES, EDWARD PAUL	D. NOVEMBER 27, 1968, HAYWARD, CALIF.
1990-048	FERNANDEZ, ALEXANDER	12323 SW 55TH STREET #1007, COOPER CITY FL 33330
1983-053	FERNANDEZ, CHARLES SIDNEY 'SID'	543 PUNAA STREET, KAILUA HI 96734
1967-030	FERNANDEZ, FRANK	37 COUGHLAN AVE, STATEN ISLAND NY 10310
1942-035	FERNANDEZ, FROILAN 'NANNY'	D. SEPTEMBER 19, 1996, HARBOR CITY, CALIF.
1956-033	FERNANDEZ, HUMBERTO PEREZ 'CHICO'	8401 NW 40TH COURT, SUNRISE FL 33351
2001-059	FERNANDEZ, JARED WADE	4298 SOUTH 4625 WEST, WEST VALLEY UT 84120
1999-063	FERNANDEZ, JOSE MAYOBANEX ROJAS	OLD ADD: SANTIAGO DOM REP
1968-022	FERNANDEZ, LORENZO MARTO 'CHICO'	1310 SW 97TH AVE, MIAMI FL 33175
1983-054	FERNANDEZ, OCTAVIO ANTONIO 'TONY'	950 PENINSULA CORPORATE CIR #2000, BOCA RATON FL 33487
1996-061	FERNANDEZ, OSVALDO X.	OLD ADD: SANTO DOMINGO DOM REP

1963-040	FERRARA, ALFRED JOHN	OLD ADD: 6125 EAST INDIAN SCHOOL RD, SCOTTSDALE AZ 85251
1955-041	FERRARESE, DONALD HUGH	15290 MYALON ROAD, APPLE VALLEY CA 92307
2003-046	FERRARI, ANTHONY MICHAEL	17 BRETANO WAY, GREENBRAE CA 94904
1966-034	FERRARO, MICHAEL DENNIS	5201 RIM VIEW LANE, LAS VEGAS NV 89130
1935-031	FERRAZZI, WILLIAM JOSEPH	D. AUGUST 10, 1993, KEYSTONE HEIGHTS, FLA.
1985-032	FERREIRA, ANTHONY ROSS	22111 NEWPORT AVENUE #30, GRAND TERRACE CA 92313
1929-036	FERRELL, RICHARD BENJAMIN 'RICK'	D. JULY 27, 1995, BLOOMFIELD HILLS, MICH.
1927-033	FERRELL, WESLEY CHEEK	D. DECEMBER 9, 1976, SARASOTA, FLA.
1974-035	FERRER, SERGIO	OLD ADD: PEDRO AREILAGE HX, LEVITTOWN LAKES PR 00632
1941-030	FERRICK, THOMAS JEROME	D. OCTOBER 15, 1996, LIMA, PA.
1979-035	FERRIS, ROBERT EUGENE	18259 GLEN OAK WAY, LEESBURG VA 20176
1945-031	FERRISS, DAVID MEADOW 'BOO'	510 ROBINSON DRIVE, CLEVELAND MS 38732
1937-038	FETTE, LOUIS HENRY WILLIAM	D. JANUARY 3, 1981, WARRENSBURG, MO.
1989-036	FETTERS, MICHAEL LEE	2411 EAST CEDAR PLACE, CHANDLER AZ 85249
1981-034	FIALA, NEAL STEPHEN	BELLEVILLE AREA CC BASEBALL 2500 CARLYLE ROAD, BELLEVILLE IL 62221
1944-040	FICK, JOHN RALPH	D. JUNE 9, 1950, [illegible] POINT, N.J.
1998-056	FICK, ROBERT CHARLES	887 CALLE JON, THOUSAND OAKS CA 91360
1970-032	FIDRYCH, MARK STEVEN	260 WEST STREET, NORTHBORO MA 01532
1932-026	FIEBER, CLARENCE THOMAS 'LEFTY'	D. AUGUST 20, 1985, REDWOOD CITY, CALIF.
2002-058	FIELD, NATHAN PATRICK	PO BOX 120, HOLSINGTON KS 67544
1985-033	FIELDER, CECIL GRANT	OLD ADD: PO BOX 110278, ATLANTA GA 30311
2005-061	FIELDER, PRINCE SEMIEN	6907 SMOKEY BROOK LANE, KATY TX 77494
1986-049	FIELDS, BRUCE ALAN	20160 RENFREW, DETROIT MI 48221
2006-049	FIELDS, JOSHUA DEAN	OLD ADD: 1815 NORTH BOOMER ROAD, STILLWATER OK 74074
1973-044	FIFE, DANNY WAYNE	5854 MISTY HILL DRIVE, CLARKSTON MI 48346
1997-056	FIGGA, MICHAEL ANTHONY	6513 ALTA MONTE DRIVE, TAMPA FL 33634
2002-059	FIGGINS, DESMOND DECHONE 'CHONE'	208 RAVEN WAY DRIVE, SEFFNER FL 33584
1992-038	FIGUEROA, BIENVENIDO (DELEON) 'BIEN'	3909 RESERVE DRIVE #1522, TALLAHASSEE FL 32311
1974-036	FIGUEROA, EDUARDO	CALLE 41 A-N15, SANTA JUANITA PR 00619
1980-044	FIGUEROA, JESUS MARIA	OLD ADD: #23 AVE MIRABEL, SANTO DOMINGO DOM REP
2001-060	FIGUEROA, LUIS R.	OLD ADD: VEGA ALTA PR
2000-059	FIGUEROA, NELSON	OLD ADD: 2937 WEST 33RD STREET #16E, BROOKLYN NY 11224
2001-061	FIKAC, JEREMY JOSEPH	1456 DAVID CURRY DRIVE, ROUND ROCK TX 78664
1940-020	FILE, LAWRENCE SAMUEL	264 WINDJAMMER ROAD, BERLIN MD 21811
2001-062	FILE, ROBERT MICHAEL	6412 RIVERFRONT DRIVE, PALMYRA NJ 08065
1982-042	FILER, THOMAS CARSON	425 FOX HOLLOW DRIVE, LANGHORNE PA 19053
1944-041	FILIPOWICZ, STEPHEN CHARLES	D. FEBRUARY 21, 1975, WILKES-BARRE, PA.
1934-034	FILLEY, MARCUS LUCIUS	D. JANUARY 20, 1995, YARMOUTH, MAINE
1982-043	FILSON, WILLIAM PETER 'PETE'	1034 TENTH AVENUE, FOLSOM PA 19033
1983-055	FIMPLE, JOHN JOSEPH 'JACK'	8012 CLIFTROSE STREET, WINDSOR CA 95492
1979-036	FINCH, JOEL	68571 OAK SPRING RD, EDWARDSBURG MI 49112
1947-034	FINE, THOMAS MORGAN	D. JANUARY 10, 2005, LITTLE ELM, TEXAS
1968-023	FINGERS, ROLAND GLEN 'ROLLIE'	PO BOX 230729, LAS VEGAS NV 89123
1954-026	FINIGAN, JAMES LEROY	D. MAY 16, 1981, QUINCY, ILL.
1935-032	FINK, HERMAN ADAM	D. AUGUST 24, 1980, SALISBURY, N.C.
1986-050	FINLEY, CHARLES EDWARD	OLD ADD: 1601 KINGS ROAD, NEWPORT BEACH CA 92663
1943-047	FINLEY, ROBERT EDWARD	D. JANUARY 2, 1986, WEST COVINA, CALIF.
1989-037	FINLEY, STEVEN ALLEN	PO BOX 2101, RANCHO SANTA FE CA 92067
1930-022	FINN, CORNELIUS FRANCIS 'MICKEY'	D. JULY 7, 1933, ALTOONA, PA.
1931-025	FINNEY, HAROLD WILSON 'HAL'	D. DECEMBER 20, 1991, LAFAYETTE, ALA.
1931-026	FINNEY, LOUIS KLOPSCHE	D. APRIL 22, 1966, LAFAYETTE, ALA.
1994-033	FINNVOLD, ANDERS GAR 'GAR'	830 SOUTHWEST 15TH STREET, BOCA RATON FL 33432
2000-060	FIORE, ANTHONY JAMES	19021 FISHERMENS BEND DRIVE, LUTZ FL 33558
1968-024	FIORE, MICHAEL GARY JOSEPH	17 SILVER ST, MALVERNE NY 11565
2005-062	FIORENTINO, JEFFREY PHILIP	4200 CHARDONNAY DRIVE, ROCKLEDGE FL 32955
1981-035	FIREOVID, STEPHEN JOHN	1408 WOODSTREAM AVENUE, BRYAN OH 43506
1981-036	FIROVA, DANIEL MICHAEL	202 SAINT JOHN, REFUGIO TX 78377
1930-023	FISCHER, CHARLES WILLIAM 'CARL'	D. DECEMBER 10, 1963, MEDINA, N.Y.
1962-041	FISCHER, HENRY WILLIAM	10367 BIG CANOE, JASPER GA 30143
1987-045	FISCHER, JEFFREY THOMAS	215 WORTH COURT NORTH, WEST PALM BEACH FL 33405
1941-031	FISCHER, REUBEN WALTER 'RUBE'	D. JULY 16, 1997, GREEN BAY, WISC.
1986-051	FISCHER, TODD RICHARD	12734 NEWTOWN ROAD, UNIONVILLE TN 37180
1956-034	FISCHER, WILLIAM CHARLES	139 UPLAND DRIVE, COUNCIL BLUFFS IA 51501
1977-052	FISCHLIN, MICHAEL	1020 BILLY MANTLE LANE, GREENSBORO GA 30642
1988-050	FISHEL, JOHN ALAN	329 MARJORAM DRIVE, GAHANNA OH 43230
1985-034	FISHER, BRIAN KEVIN	3660 SOUTH URAVEN STREET, AURORA CO 80013
1945-032	FISHER, DONALD RAYMOND	D. JULY 29, 1973, MAYFIELD HEIGHTS, OHIO
1959-026	FISHER, EDDIE GENE	408 CARDINAL CIRCLE SOUTH, ALTUS OK 73521
1964-031	FISHER, FREDERICK BROWN 'FRITZ'	3703 BARCELONA DRIVE, TOLEDO OH 43615
1923-040	FISHER, GEORGE ALOYS	D. MAY 15, 1994, ST. CLOUD, MINN.
1951-029	FISHER, HARRY DEVEREAUX	D. SEPTEMBER 20, 1981, WATERLOO, ONT.
1959-027	FISHER, JOHN HOWARD 'JACK'	4407 NICHOLAS STREET, EASTON PA 18045
1955-042	FISHER, MAURICE WAYNE	15920 LUCERNE RD, FREDERICKTOWN OH 43019
1967-031	FISHER, THOMAS GENE	OLD ADD: 4561 TURNEY, CLEVELAND OH 44105
1969-056	FISK, CARLTON ERNEST	18705 63RD AVENUE EAST, BRADENTON FL 34202
1928-034	FITZBERGER, CHARLES CASPAR	D. JANUARY 25, 1965, BALTIMORE, MD.
2002-060	FITZGERALD, BRIAN MICHAEL	7226 JOHN TAYLOR MEWS, RUTHER GLEN VA 22546
1948-035	FITZGERALD, EDWARD RAYMOND	431 CHRISTOPHER STREET, FOLSOM CA 95630
1922-035	FITZGERALD, HOWARD CHUMNEY	D. FEBRUARY 26, 1959, EAGLE FALLS, TEXAS
1958-033	FITZGERALD, JOHN FRANCIS	1913 GREVE AVENUE #I, SPRING LAKE NJ 07762
1988-051	FITZGERALD, MICHAEL PATRICK	OLD ADD: 10412 INDIGO ROAD, SAVANNAH GA 31406
1983-056	FITZGERALD, MICHAEL ROY	502 FLINT AVENUE, LONG BEACH CA 90814
1931-027	FITZGERALD, RAYMOND FRANCIS	D. SEPTEMBER 6, 1977, WESTFIELD, MASS.
1924-036	FITZKE, PAUL FREDERICK HERMAN	D. JUNE 30, 1950, SACRAMENTO, CALIF.
1966-035	FITZMAURICE, SHAUN EARLE	1911 NORMANDSTONE DRIVE, MIDLOTHIAN VA 23113
1969-057	FITZMORRIS, ALAN JAMES	17512 WEST 159TH TERRACE, OLATHE KS 66062

1925-034	FITZSIMMONS, FREDERICK LANDIS	D. NOVEMBER 18, 1979, YUCCA VALLEY, CALIF.
1945-033	FLAGER, WALTER LEONARD	D. DECEMBER 16, 1990, KEIZER, ORE.
1992-039	FLAHERTY, JOHN TIMOTHY	66 MINUTEMAN CIRCLE, ORANGEBURG NY 10962
1941-032	FLAIR, ALBERT DELL	D. JULY 25, 1988, NEW ORLEANS, LA.
1975-038	FLANAGAN, MICHAEL KENDALL	15010 YORK ROAD, SPARKS MD 21152
1946-029	FLANIGAN, RAYMOND ARTHUR	D. MARCH 28, 1993, BALTIMORE, MD.
1954-027	FLANIGAN, THOMAS ANTHONY	114 EAST 40TH, COVINGTON KY 41015
1977-053	FLANNERY, JOHN MICHAEL	9002 SCOTTISH PASTURES DRIVE, AUSTIN TX 78750
1979-037	FLANNERY, TIMOTHY EARL	715 HYMATTUS AVENUE, LEUCADIA CA 92024
1927-034	FLASKAMPER, RAYMOND HAROLD	D. FEBRUARY 3, 1978, SAN ANTONIO, TEXAS
1964-032	FLAVIN, JOHN THOMAS	23060 16TH STREET, NEWHALL CA 91321
1948-036	FLEITAS, ANGEL FELIX HUSTA	D. JULY 10, 2006, MIAMI, FLA.
1991-056	FLEMING, DAVID ANTHONY	37 LAUREL WOODS LANE, SOUTHBURY CT 06488
1940-021	FLEMING, LESLIE FLETCHERD 'BILL'	D. JUNE 4, 2006, RENO, NEV.
1939-035	FLEMING, LESLIE HARVEY 'LES'	D. MARCH 5, 1980, CLEVELAND, TEXAS
1993-051	FLENER, GREGORY ALAN 'HUCK'	2012 BLACKRIDGE AVENUE, SACRAMENTO CA 95835
1989-038	FLETCHER, DARRIN GLEN	PO BOX 73, FITHIAN IL 61844
1993-052	FLETCHER, EDWARD PAUL 'PAUL'	548 MOCKINGBIRD WAY, WARRINGTON PA 18976
1934-035	FLETCHER, ELBURT PRESTON 'ELBIE'	D. MARCH 9, 1994, MILTON, MASS.
1981-037	FLETCHER, SCOTT BRIAN	300 BIRKDALE DRIVE, FAYETTEVILLE GA 30215
1962-042	FLETCHER, THOMAS WAYNE	9287 EAST 2085 NORTH ROAD, OAKWOOD IL 61858
1955-043	FLETCHER, VANOIDE 'VAN'	2404 WHITAKER ROAD, BOONVILLE NC 27011
1943-048	FLICK, LEWIS MILLER	D. DECEMBER 7, 1990, WEBER CITY, VA.
1978-042	FLINN, JOHN RICHARD	6221 LAKE PROVIDENCE LANE, CHARLOTTE NC 28277
1942-036	FLITCRAFT, HILDRETH MILTON 'HILLY'	D. APRIL 2, 2003, BOULDER, COLO.
1934-036	FLOHR, MORITZ HERMAN 'MORT'	D. JUNE 2, 1994, HORNELL, N.Y.
1956-035	FLOOD, CURTIS CHARLES	D. JANUARY 10, 1997, LOS ANGELES, CALIF.
1991-057	FLORA, KEVIN SCOT	11 SPRINGSIDE, TRABUCO CANYON CA 92679
1995-074	FLORENCE, DONALD EMERY	144 BEDFORD ROAD, NEW BOSTON NH 03070
1926-029	FLORENCE, PAUL ROBERT	D. MAY 28, 1986, GAINESVILLE, FLA.
1977-054	FLORES, GILBERTO	OLD ADD: BDA SALAZAR 1 #38, PONCE PR 00731
1942-037	FLORES, JESSE SANDOVAL	D. DECEMBER 17, 1991, ORANGE, CALIF.
2002-061	FLORES, JOSE CARLOS	2460 CRICKET HOLLOW STREET, CORPUS CHRISTI TX 78414
2002-062	FLORES, RANDY ALAN	7513 MOONLIGHT VIEW COURT, LAS VEGAS NV 89129
2005-063	FLORES, RONALD JOEL	7313 MOONLIGHT VIEW COURT, LAS VEGAS NV 89129
1994-034	FLORIE, BRYCE BETTENCOURT	3356 QUEENSGATE WAY, MOUNT PLEASANT SC 29466
1951-030	FLOWERS, BENNETT	901 TREMONT ROAD NW, WILSON NC 27895
1940-022	FLOWERS, CHARLES WESLEY 'WES'	D. DECEMBER 31, 1988, WYNNE, ARK.
1923-041	FLOWERS, D'ARCY RAYMOND 'JAKE'	D. DECEMBER 27, 1962, CLEARWATER, FLA.
1993-053	FLOYD, CORNELIUS CLIFFORD 'CLIFF'	3283 BIRCH TERRACE, DAVIE FL 33330
2004-062	FLOYD, GAVIN CHRISTOPHER	473 YORKSHIRE DRIVE, SEVERNA PARK MD 21146
1944-042	FLOYD, LESLIE ROE 'BUBBA'	D. DECEMBER 15, 2000, DALLAS, TEXAS
1968-025	FLOYD, ROBERT NATHAN	1757 SE DOMINIC AVENUE, PORT SAINT LUCIE FL 34952
1975-039	FLYNN, ROBERT DOUGLAS 'DOUG'	2465 VALE DRIVE, LEXINGTON KY 40514
1936-025	FLYTHE, STUART MCGUIRE	D. OCTOBER 18, 1963, DURHAM, N.C.
1958-034	FODGE, EUGENE ARLEN	1505 NORTH CHICAGO STREET, SOUTH BEND IN 46628
2001-063	FOGG, JOSHUA SMITH	4910 SOUTH QUINCY STREET, TAMPA FL 33611
1953-025	FOILES, HENRY LEE 'HANK'	4333 SILVERLEAF COURT, VIRGINIA BEACH VA 23462
1978-043	FOLEY, MARVIS EDWIN	4970 COUNTRY MEADOWS BLVD, SARASOTA FL 34235
1928-035	FOLEY, RAYMOND KIRWIN	D. MARCH 22, 1980, VERO BEACH, FLA.
1983-057	FOLEY, THOMAS MICHAEL	5237 KARLSBURG PLACE, PALM HARBOR FL 34685
1970-041	FOLI, TIMOTHY JOHN	525 TIMBERLINE DRIVE, LENOIR CITY TN 37772
1970-042	FOLKERS, RICHARD NEVIN 'RICH'	7100 3RD AVENUE NORTH, SAINT PETERSBURG FL 33710
1951-031	FONDY, DEE VIRGIL	D. AUGUST 19, 1999, REDLANDS, CALIF.
1921-027	FONSECA, LEWIS ALBERT	D. NOVEMBER 26, 1989, ELY, IOWA
1998-057	FONTENOT, JOSEPH D	115 LOGAN STREET, LAFAYETTE LA 70506
2005-064	FONTENOT, MICHAEL EUGENE	1436 CONSTITUTION DRIVE, SLIDELL LA 70458
1983-058	FONTENOT, SILTON RAY 'RAY'	1674 NORTH CRESTVIEW DRIVE, LAKE CHARLES LA 70605
1995-075	FONVILLE, CHAD EVERETTE	2338 PINEY GREEN ROAD, MIDWAY PARK NC 28544
1971-033	FOOR, JAMES EMERSON	2018 BOLSOVER STREET, HOUSTON TX 77005
1973-045	FOOTE, BARRY CLIFTON	2705 MIDDLE SOUND LOOP ROAD, WILMINGTON NC 28411
2003-047	FOPPERT, JESSE WILLIAM	PO BOX 150682, SAN RAFAEL CA 94915
1998-058	FORBES, PATRICK JOSEPH 'P.J.'	9017 CHARTWELL CIRCLE, WICHITA KS 67205
1998-059	FORD, BENJAMIN COOPER	1717 APPLEWOOD PLACE NE, CEDAR RAPIDS IA 52402
1985-035	FORD, CURTIS GLENN	6306 SPRIG OAK COURT #B, SAINT LOUIS MO 63128
1975-040	FORD, DARNELL GLENN 'DAN'	8807 DIGGER PINE DRIVE, RIVERSIDE CA 92508
1978-044	FORD, DAVID ALAN	19523 NORTH SAGAMORE ROAD, CLEVELAND OH 44126
1950-029	FORD, EDWARD CHARLES 'WHITEY'	3750 GALT OCEAN DRIVE DRIVE #1411, FORT LAUDERDALE FL 33308
1936-026	FORD, EUGENE MATTHEW	D. SEPTEMBER 7, 1970, EMMETSBURG, IOWA
2003-048	FORD, JON LEWIS 'LEW'	1109 DAMSEL GINGER LANE, LEWISVILLE TX 75056
2003-049	FORD, MATTHEW LEE	10837 CYPRESS GLEN DRIVE, CORAL SPRINGS FL 33071
1973-046	FORD, PERCIVAL EDMUND WENTWORTH 'WENTY'	D. JULY 8, 1980, NASSAU BAHAMAS
1970-043	FORD, THEODORE HENRY	OLD ADD: 430 NORTH 4TH STREET, VINELAND NJ 08360
1997-057	FORDHAM, THOMAS JAMES	14559 MIGUEL LANE, EL CAJON CA 92021
1995-076	FORDYCE, BROOK ALEXANDER	5 RIVER CREST COURT, STUART FL 34996
1924-037	FOREMAN, AUGUST	D. FEBRUARY 13, 1953, NEW YORK, N.Y.
1952-030	FORNIELES, JOSE MIGUEL 'MIKE'	D. FEBRUARY 11, 1998, ST. PETERSBURG, FLA.
1970-044	FORSCH, KENNETH ROTH	881 SOUTH COUNTRY GLEN WAY, ANAHEIM CA 92808
1974-037	FORSCH, ROBERT HERBERT	8349 FAIRHILL DRIVE, BROOKSVILLE FL 34613
2000-061	FORSTER, SCOTT CHRISTIAN	17 ROSE LANE, FLOURTOWN PA 19031
1971-034	FORSTER, TERRY JAY	PO BOX 711658, SANTEE CA 92071
1992-040	FORTUGNO, TIMOTHY SHAWN	3604 BABSON DRIVE, ELK GROVE CA 95758
2004-063	FORTUNATO, BARTOLOME	OLD ADD: SANTO DOMINGO DOM REP
1964-033	FOSNOW, GERALD EUGENE	369 CADDIE, DEBARY FL 32713
1921-028	FOSS, GEORGE DUEWARD	D. NOVEMBER 10, 1969, MIAMI, FLA.
1961-035	FOSS, LAWRENCE CURTIS	4303 EAST ENGLISH STREET, WICHITA KS 67218

1988-052	FOSSAS, EMILIO ANTHONY 'TONY'	11302 NW 9TH STREET, PLANTATION FL 33325
1967-032	FOSSE, RAYMOND EARL	PO BOX 567, DIABLO CA 94528
2001-064	FOSSUM, CASEY PAUL	209 10TH AVENUE #405, NASHVILLE TN 37203
1967-033	FOSTER, ALAN BENTON	10330 GRANDVIEW DRIVE, LAMESA CA 91941
1969-058	FOSTER, GEORGE ARTHUR	15 EAST PUTNAM AVENUE #320, GREENWICH CT 06830
2001-065	FOSTER, JOHN KRISTIAN 'KRIS'	116 JOHNS AVENUE, LEHIGH ACRES FL 33972
2002-063	FOSTER, JOHN NORMAN	519 AIRWAY AVENUE, LEWISTON ID 83501
1993-054	FOSTER, KEVIN CHRISTOPHER	2323 GREENLEAF, EVANSTON IL 60202
1963-041	FOSTER, LARRY LYNN	205 WEST OBELL STREET, WHITEHALL MI 49461
1971-035	FOSTER, LEONARD NORRIS 'LEO'	699 GLENSPRINGS DRIVE, CINCINNATI OH 45246
1970-045	FOSTER, ROY	32020 SOUTH 627 ROAD, GROVE OK 74344
1991-058	FOSTER, STEPHEN EUGENE	1201 HILLVIEW, WAXAHACHIE TX 75165
1922-036	FOTHERGILL, ROBERT ROY 'FATTY'	D. MARCH 20, 1938, DETROIT, MICH.
1973-047	FOUCAULT, STEVEN RAYMOND	109 TROPIC PLACE, ROCKLEDGE FL 32955
1997-058	FOULKE, KEITH CHARLES	4944 WEST ELECTRA LANE, GLENDALE AZ 85310
1924-038	FOWLER, JESSE 'PETE'	D. SEPTEMBER [illegible], COLUMBIA, S.C.
1954-028	FOWLER, JOHN ARTHUR [illegible]	D. JANUARY 29, 2007, SPARTANBURG, S.C.
[illegible]	FOWLER, JOSEPH CHESTER 'CHET'	D. OCTOBER 8, 1988, DALLAS, TEXAS
1941-033	FOWLER, RICHARD JOHN	D. MAY 22, 1972, ONEONTA, N.Y.
1982-044	FOWLKES, ALAN KIM	405 EMERALD LAKE DRIVE, LUMBERTON NC 28358
1996-062	FOX, ANDREW JUNIPERO	8008 SACRAMENTO STREET, FAIR OAKS CA 95826
1997-059	FOX, CHAD DOUGLAS	20146 PINEHAVEN LANE, SPRING TX 77379
1942-038	FOX, CHARLES FRANCIS	D. FEBRUARY 17, 2004, PALO ALTO, CALIF.
1992-041	FOX, ERIC HOLLIS	OLD ADD: CRESTON STAR ROUTE, PASO ROBLES CA 93446
1933-018	FOX, ERVIN 'PETE'	D. JULY 5, 1966, DETROIT, MICH.
1944-043	FOX, HOWARD FRANCIS	D. OCTOBER 9, 1955, SAN ANTONIO, TEXAS
1947-035	FOX, JACOB NELSON 'NELLIE'	D. DECEMBER 1, 1975, BALTIMORE, MD.
1960-033	FOX, TERRENCE EDWARD	2312 SUGAR MILL ROAD, NEW IBERIA LA 70560
1925-035	FOXX, JAMES EMORY 'JIMMIE'	D. JULY 21, 1967, MIAMI, FLA.
1966-036	FOY, JOSEPH	D. OCTOBER 12, 1989, BRONX, N.Y.
1953-026	FOYTACK, PAUL EUGENE	1910 PORTVIEW DRIVE, SPRING HILL TN 37174
1972-028	FRAILING, KENNETH DOUGLAS	2150 SHADOW OAK ROAD, SARASOTA FL 34240
1960-034	FRANCIS, EARL COLEMAN	D. JULY 3, 2002, PITTSBURGH, PA.
2004-064	FRANCIS, JEFFREY WILLIAM	OLD ADD: 4719 226TH COURT SE, SAMMAMISH WA 98075
1922-037	FRANCIS, RAY JAMES	D. JULY 14, 1932, ATLANTA, GA.
2004-065	FRANCISCO, FRANKLIN	OLD ADD: SANTO DOMINGO DOM REP
1984-036	FRANCO, JOHN ANTHONY	111 HELENA ROAD, STATEN ISLAND NY 10304
1982-045	FRANCO, JULIO CESAR	OLD ADD: 1269 CEDARLAND PLAZA DRIVE, ARLINGTON TX 76011
1995-077	FRANCO, MATTHEW NEIL	1008 CLEAR SKY PLACE, SIMI VALLEY CA 93065
2005-065	FRANCOEUR, JEFFREY BRONDAN	5219 BEECH FOREST DRIVE SW, LILBURN GA 30047
1956-036	FRANCONA, JOHN PATSY 'TITO'	1109 PENN AVENUE, NEW BRIGHTON PA 15066
1981-038	FRANCONA, TERRY JON	750 NEWTON STREET, CHESTNUT HILL MA 02467
2006-050	FRANDSEN, KEVIN VINCENT	OLD ADD: SAN JOSE CA
1998-060	FRANK, STEPHEN MICHAEL 'MIKE'	1343 WEST 19TH STREET, UPLAND CA 91784
1927-035	FRANKHOUSE, FREDERICK MELOY	D. AUGUST 17, 1989, PORT ROYAL, PA.
2000-062	FRANKLIN, GARY WAYNE 'WAYNE'	24342 SARAGOSSA LANE, PUNTA GORDA FL 33955
1944-044	FRANKLIN, JAMES WILFORD 'JACK'	D. NOVEMBER 15, 1991, PANAMA CITY, FLA.
1971-036	FRANKLIN, JOHN WILLIAM 'JAY'	C/O TRUDY FANKLIN-CAHOON, 7208 WOODS EDGE COURT, WARRENTON VA 20187
1997-060	FRANKLIN, MICAH ISHANTI	533 FLOOD AVENUE, SAN FRANCISCO CA 94112
1941-034	FRANKLIN, MURRAY ASHER	D. MARCH 16, 1978, HARBOR CITY, CALIF.
1999-064	FRANKLIN, RYAN RAY	PO BOX 321, SHAWNEE OK 74802
1939-036	FRANKS, HERMAN LOUIS	2745 COMANCHE DRIVE, SALT LAKE CITY UT 84108
1994-035	FRASCATORE, JOHN VINCENT	3121 SATURN ROAD, BROOKSVILLE FL 34604
1986-052	FRASER, WILLIAM PATRICK 'WILLIE'	3908 PLANTATION BLVD, LEESBURG FL 34748
1931-028	FRASIER, VICTOR PATRICK	D. JANUARY 10, 1977, JACKSONVILLE, TEXAS
2004-066	FRASOR, JASON ANDREW	15043 LANDINGS LANE, OAK FOREST IL 60425
1993-055	FRAZIER, ARTHUR LOUIS 'LOU'	1371 NORTH CONCORD AVENUE, CHANDLER AZ 85225
1978-045	FRAZIER, GEORGE ALLEN	2011 WEST G STREET, JENKS OK 74037
1947-036	FRAZIER, JOSEPH FILMORE	519 FAIRWAY DRIVE, BROKEN ARROW OK 74012
1929-037	FREDERICK, JOHN HENRY	D. JUNE 18, 1977, TIGARD, ORE.
2002-064	FREDERICK, KEVIN ALBERT FRANCIS	20512 NORTH CLARICE AVENUE, PRAIRIE VIEW IL 60069
1993-056	FREDRICKSON, SCOTT ERIC	12637 KING OAKS, SAN ANTONIO TX 78233
1942-039	FREED, EDWIN CHARLES	D. NOVEMBER 15, 2002, ROCK HILL, S.C.
1970-046	FREED, ROGER VERNON	D. JANUARY 9, 1996, CHINO, CALIF.
1961-036	FREEHAN, WILLIAM ASHLEY	6999 INDIAN GARDEN ROAD, PETOSKEY MI 49770
2001-066	FREEL, RYAN PAUL	12107 RED BARN COURT, JACKSONVILLE FL 32226
1921-029	FREEMAN, ALEXANDER VERNON 'BUCK'	D. FEBRUARY 21, 1953, FORT SAM HOUSTON, TEXAS
1921-030	FREEMAN, HARVEY BAYARD	D. JANUARY 10, 1970, KALAMAZOO, MICH.
1952-031	FREEMAN, HERSHELL BASKIN	D. JANUARY 17, 2004, ORLANDO, FLA.
1972-029	FREEMAN, JIMMY LEE	4716 EAST 106TH STREET, TULSA OK 74137
1927-036	FREEMAN, JOHN EDWARD	D. APRIL 14, 1958, WASHINGTON, D.C.
1989-039	FREEMAN, LAVEL MAURICE	2501 GARDENDALE ROAD, SACRAMENTO CA 95822
1959-028	FREEMAN, MARK PRICE	D. FEBRUARY 21, 2006, RANCHO MIRAGE, CALIF.
1986-053	FREEMAN, MARVIN	20135 MOHAWK TRAIL, OLYMPIA FIELDS IL 60461
2004-067	FREEMAN, RAPHAEL 'CHOO'	720 NORTH JOE WILSON ROAD #1521, CEDAR HILL TX 75104
1955-044	FREESE, EUGENE LEWIS	6504 GLENDALE, METAIRIE LA 70003
1953-027	FREESE, GEORGE WALTER	3341 SW MARIGOLD STREET, PORTLAND OR 97219
1925-036	FREEZE, CARL ALEXANDER 'JAKE'	D. APRIL 9, 1983, SAN ANGELO, TEXAS
1961-037	FREGOSI, JAMES LOUIS	1092 COPELAND CT, TARPON SPRINGS FL 34689
1941-035	FREIBURGER, VERNON DONALD	D. FEBRUARY 27, 1990, PALM SPRINGS, CALIF.
1922-038	FREIGAU, HOWARD EARL	D. JULY 18, 1932, CHATTANOOGA, TENN.
2005-066	FREIRE, ALEJANDRO	OLD ADD: CARACAS VENEZUELA
1974-038	FREISLEBEN, DAVID JAMES	2119 PEACH LN, PASADENA TX 77502
1932-027	FREITAS, ANTONIO	D. MARCH 13, 1994, ORANGEVALE, CALIF.
1929-038	FRENCH, LAWRENCE ROBERT 'LARRY'	D. FEBRUARY 9, 1987, SAN DIEGO, CALIF.
1920-033	FRENCH, RAYMOND EDWARD	D. APRIL 3, 1978, ALAMEDA, CALIF.

1965-029	FRENCH, RICHARD JAMES 'JIM'	PO BOX 6551, CHICAGO IL 60680
1923-043	FRENCH, WALTER EDWARD	D. MAY 13, 1984, MOUNTAIN HOME, ARK.
1929-039	FREY, BENJAMIN RUDOLPH	D. NOVEMBER 1, 1937, JACKSON, MICH.
1980-045	FREY, JAMES GOTTFRIED	20297 WILDCAT RUN DRIVE, ESTERO FL 33928
1933-019	FREY, LINUS REINHARD 'LONNY'	995 WEST WOODLAWN DRIVE, HAYDEN ID 83835
1989-040	FREY, STEVEN FRANCIS	1414 SECOND STREET PIKE, SOUTHAMPTON PA 18966
1997-061	FRIAS, HANLEY ACEVEDO	OLD ADD: 135 HOLYOKE STREET, ROCHESTER NY 14615
1973-048	FRIAS, JESUS MARIA 'PEPE'	OLD ADD: CLE 4 CASA 9 ING CONSUELO, SAN PEDRO DE MAC DOM REP
1952-032	FRICANO, MARION JOHN	D. MAY 18, 1976, TIJUANA, MEXICO
1923-044	FRIDAY, GRIER WILLIAM 'SKIPPER'	D. AUGUST 25, 1962, GASTONIA, N.C.
1952-033	FRIDLEY, JAMES RILEY	D. FEBRUARY 28, 2003, PORT CHARLOTTE, FLA.
1920-034	FRIED, ARTHUR EDWIN 'CY'	D. OCTOBER 10, 1970, SAN ANTONIO, TEXAS
1932-028	FRIEDRICHS, ROBERT GEORGE	D. APRIL 15, 1997, JASPER, IND.
1949-024	FRIEND, OWEN LACEY	2055 PORTER STREET #103, WICHITA KS 67203
1951-032	FRIEND, ROBERT BARTMESS	4 SALEM CIRCLE, FOX CHAPEL PA 15238
1941-036	FRIERSON, ROBERT LAWRENCE 'BUCK'	D. JUNE 26, 1996, PARIS, TEXAS
1934-037	FRINK, FREDERICK FERDINAND	D. MAY 19, 1995, MIAMI SPRINGS, FLA.
1967-034	FRISELLA, DANIEL VINCENT	D. JANUARY 1, 1977, PHOENIX, ARIZ.
1975-041	FRITZ, LAURENCE JOSEPH	2632 SCHRAGE AVE, WHITING IN 46394
1955-045	FROATS, WILLIAM JOHN	D. FEBRUARY 9, 1998, MINNEAPOLIS, MINN.
1982-046	FROBEL, DOUGLAS STEPHEN	37 WILLOW CROSSING ROAD, GREENSBURG PA 15601
1987-046	FROHWIRTH, TODD GERARD	566 W 24360 SKYLINE AVENUE, WAUKESHA WI 53189
1977-055	FROST, CARL DAVID 'DAVE'	2206 OCANA DR, LONG BEACH CA 90815
2006-051	FRUTO, EMILIANO RICARDO	OLD ADD: BOLIVAR COLOMBIA
1978-046	FRY, JERRY RAY	3300 STANTON STREET, SPRINGFIELD IL 62703
1923-045	FRY, JOHNSON	D. APRIL 7, 1959, CARMI, ILL.
1940-023	FRYE, CHARLES ANDREW	D. MAY 25, 1945, HICKORY, N.C.
1992-042	FRYE, JEFFREY DUSTIN	6833 LAHONTAN DRIVE, FORT WORTH TX 76132
1990-049	FRYMAN, DAVID TRAVIS 'TRAVIS'	2600 BARRINEAU PARK ROAD, MOLINO FL 32577
1966-037	FRYMAN, WOODROW THOMPSON	RR 1 BOX 21, EWING KY 41039
1942-040	FUCHS, CHARLES RUDOLPH	D. JUNE 10, 1969, WEEHAWKEN, N.J.
1929-040	FUCHS, EMIL EDWIN	D. DECEMBER 5, 1961, BOSTON, MASS.
2001-067	FUENTES, BRIAN CHRISTOPHER	2787 ELM AVENUE, MERCED CA 95348
1983-059	FUENTES, MICHAEL JAY	3160 PEACHTREE CIRCLE, DAVIE FL 33329
1969-059	FUENTES, MIGUEL	D. JANUARY 29, 1970, LOIZA ALDEA, P.R.
1965-030	FUENTES, ROGOBERTO PEAT 'TITO'	61 SOUTH MADDUX DRIVE, RENO NV 89512
1921-031	FUHR, OSCAR LAWRENCE	D. MARCH 27, 1975, DALLAS, TEXAS
1922-039	FUHRMAN, ALFRED GEORGE 'OLLIE'	D. JANUARY 11, 1969, PEORIA, ILL.
2006-052	FULCHINO, JEFFREY JOSEPH	178 PINE HILL ROAD, HOLLIS NH 03049
1921-032	FULGHUM, JAMES LAVOISIER 'DOT'	D. NOVEMBER 2, 1947, MIAMI, FLA.
1979-038	FULGHUM, JOHN THOMAS	OLD ADD: 7361 AIRLINE, BATON ROUGE LA 70805
1973-049	FULLER, JAMES	5107 BUR OAK DRIVE, PASADENA TX 77505
1974-039	FULLER, JOHN EDWARD	31912 PASEO TERRAZA, SAN JUAN CAPISTRANO CA 92675
1964-034	FULLER, VERN GORDON	155 IRONWOOD CIRCLE, AURORA OH 44202
1921-033	FULLERTON, CURTIS HOOPER	D. JANUARY 2, 1975, WINTHROP, MASS.
1928-036	FULLIS, CHARLES PHILIP 'CHICK'	D. MARCH 28, 1946, ASHLAND, PA.
1997-062	FULLMER, BRADLEY RYAN	860 HAVERFORD AVENUE #503, PACIFIC PALISADES CA 90272
1987-047	FULTON, WILLIAM DAVID	3001 LEXINGTON DRIVE, EXPORT PA 15632
2000-063	FULTZ, RICHARD AARON 'AARON'	2344 2ND AVENUE NW, FAYETTE AL 35555
1981-039	FUNDERBURK, MARK CLIFFORD	6924 OLD PROVIDENCE ROAD, CHARLOTTE NC 28226
1929-041	FUNK, ELIAS CALVIN 'LIZ'	D. JANUARY 17, 1968, OKLAHOMA CITY, OKLA.
1960-035	FUNK, FRANKLIN RAY	4022 SOUTH ALAMANDAS WAY, GOLD CANYON AZ 85218
1986-054	FUNK, THOMAS JAMES	6952 NORTH OLIVE STREET, KANSAS CITY MO 64118
2000-064	FURCAL, RAFAEL ANTONI	4820 SPANISH OAK ROAD, DOUGLASVILLE GA 30135
1946-030	FURILLO, CARL ANTHONY	D. JANUARY 21, 1989, STONY CREEK MILLS, PA.
2005-067	FURMANIAK, JASON JOSEPH 'J.J.'	184 NOTTINGHAM DRIVE, BOLINGBROOK IL 60440
1998-061	FUSSELL, CHRISTOPHER WREN	OLD ADD: 644 ANSONIA STREET, OREGON OH 43016
1922-040	FUSSELL, FREDERICK MORRIS	D. OCTOBER 23, 1966, SYRACUSE, N.Y.
1952-034	FUSSELMAN, LESTER LEROY	D. MAY 21, 1970, CLEVELAND, OHIO
1996-063	FYHRIE, MICHAEL EDWIN	4 WELLESLEY COURT, TRABUCO CANYON CA 92679

G

2006-053	GABBARD, KASON RONALD	4534 SEVENTH PLACE SW, VERO BEACH FL 32968
1935-033	GABLER, FRANK HAROLD	D. NOVEMBER 1, 1967, LONG BEACH, CALIF.
1959-029	GABLER, JOHN RICHARD	8606 WEST 81ST ST, OVERLAND PARK KS 66204
1958-035	GABLER, WILLIAM LOUIS	3227 BAYSHORE PKWY, ARNOLD MO 63010
1945-034	GABLES, KENNETH HARLIN	D. JANUARY 2, 1960, WALNUT GROVE, MO.
1960-036	GABRIELSON, LEONARD GARY	24230 HILLVIEW ROAD, LOS ALTOS HILLS CA 94024
1939-037	GABRIELSON, LEONARD HILBOURNE	D. NOVEMBER 14, 2000, STANFORD, CALIF.
1938-028	GADDY, JOHN WILSON	D. MAY 3, 1966, ALBEMARLE, N.C.
1951-033	GAEDEL, EDWARD CARL	D. JUNE 19, 1961, CHICAGO, ILL.
1981-040	GAETTI, GARY JOSEPH	OLD ADD: 78255 HIGHWAY 1082, COVINGTON LA 70435
1982-047	GAFF, BRENT ALLEN	5925 SOUTH STATE ROAD #9, ALBION IN 46701
1936-027	GAFFKE, FABIAN SEBASTIAN 'FABE'	D. FEBRUARY 8, 1992, MILWAUKEE, WISC.
1963-042	GAGLIANO, PHILIP JOSEPH	1095 CRESCENT DRIVE, HOLLISTER MO 65672
1965-031	GAGLIANO, RALPH MICHAEL	1756 OVERTON PARK AVENUE, MEMPHIS TN 38112
1999-065	GAGNE, ERIC SERGE	8502 NORTH 58TH PLACE, PARADISE VALLEY AZ 85253
1983-060	GAGNE, GREGORY CARPENTER	746 WHETSTONE HILL ROAD, SOMERSET MA 02726
1922-041	GAGNON, HAROLD DENNIS 'CHICK'	D. APRIL 30, 1970, WILMINGTON, DEL.
1997-063	GAILLARD, JULIAN EDWARD 'EDDIE'	6113 PALM HARBOR DRIVE, LAKE WORTH FL 33462
1993-057	GAINER, JONATHAN KEITH 'JAY'	1035 EAST 8TH STREET, PANAMA CITY FL 32401
1960-037	GAINES, ARNESTA JOE 'JOE'	77 ANAIR WAY, OAKLAND CA 94605
1921-034	GAINES, WILLARD ROLAND 'NEMO'	D. JANUARY 26, 1979, WARRENTON, VA.
1985-036	GAINEY, TELMANCH 'TY'	3040 WEST MARKET STREET EXT, CHERAW SC 29520

1998-062	GAJKOWSKI, STEPHEN ROBERT	416 TURNER STREET NE, OLYMPIA WA 98506
1991-059	GAKELER, DANIEL MICHAEL	3501 TERRAULT DRIVE, GREENSBORO NC 27410
1934-038	GALAN, AUGUST JOHN 'AUGIE'	D. DECEMBER 28, 1993, FAIRFIELD, CALIF.
1999-066	GALANTE, MATTHEW JOSEPH	22 ROSE LANE, STATEN ISLAND NY 10312
1985-037	GALARRAGA, ANDRES JOSE PADOVANI	1933 FLAGLER ESTATES DRIVE, WEST PALM BEACH FL 33411
1977-056	GALASSO, ROBERT JOSE	267 ADELAIDE ROAD, CONNELLSVILLE PA 15425
1933-020	GALATZER, MILTON	D. JANUARY 29, 1976, SAN FRANCISCO, CALIF.
1978-047	GALE, RICHARD BLACKWELL 'RICH'	869 CENTER PARK STREET, DANIEL ISLAND SC 29492
1934-039	GALEHOUSE, DENNIS WARD	D. OCTOBER 12, 1998, DOYLESTOWN, OHIO
2005-068	GALL, JOHN CHRISTOPHER	147 CRESCENT AVENUE, PORTOLA VALLEY CA 94028
1970-047	GALLAGHER, ALAN MITCHELL EDWARD	OLD ADD: 2047 EAST PIONEER ROAD, DULUTH MN 55804
1987-048	GALLAGHER, DAVID THOMAS	29 CARRS TAVERN ROAD, CLARKSBURG NJ 08510
1962-043	GALLAGHER, DOUGLAS EUGENE	1690 MAPLE LN, FREMONT OH 43420
1932-029	GALLAGHER, EDWARD MICHAEL	D. DECEMBER 22, 1981, HYANNIS PORT, MASS.
1923-046	GALLAGHER, JOHN LAURENCE 'JACKIE'	D. SEPTEMBER 10, 1984, GLADWYN, PA
1939-038	GALLAGHER, JOSEPH EMMETT	D. FEBRUARY [illegible], HOUSTON, TEXAS
1922-042	GALLAGHER, [illegible]	D. JANUARY 6, 1957, WASHINGTON, D.C.
[illegible]	GALLAGHER, ROBERT COLLINS	315 FAIR AVE, SANTA CRUZ CA 95060
1942-041	GALLE, STANLEY JOSEPH	D. JANUARY 28, 2006, MOBILE, ALA.
1985-038	GALLEGO, MICHAEL ANTHONY	20205 CHANDLER DRIVE, YORBA LINDA CA 92887
1931-029	GALLIVAN, PHILIP JOSEPH	D. NOVEMBER 24, 1969, ST. PAUL, MINN.
2003-050	GALLO, MICHAEL DWAIN	4121 HATHAWAY STREET #1, LONG BEACH CA 90802
1986-055	GALVEZ, BALVINO	3986 SW 190TH AVENUE, HOLLYWOOD FL 33029
1930-024	GALVIN, JAMES JOSEPH	D. SEPTEMBER 30, 1969, MARIETTA, GA.
1972-031	GAMBLE, JOHN ROBERT	369 CALIENTE STREET, RENO NV 89509
1935-034	GAMBLE, LEE JESSE	D. OCTOBER 5, 1994, PUNXSUTAWNEY, PA.
1969-060	GAMBLE, OSCAR CHARLES	9705 BENT BROOK DRIVE, MONTGOMERY AL 36117
2001-068	GANDARILLAS, GUSTAVO	6320 NW 114TH STREET, HIALEAH FL 33012
1987-049	GANT, RONALD EDWIN	1090 OLD TOWNE LANE, WOODSTOCK GA 30189
1939-039	GANTENBEIN, JOSEPH STEPHEN	D. AUGUST 2, 1993, SAN FRANCISCO, CALIF.
1976-033	GANTNER, JAMES ELMER	BOX 156, EDEN WI 53019
1927-037	GANZEL, FOSTER PIRIE 'BABE'	D. FEBRUARY 6, 1978, JACKSONVILLE FLA.
2005-069	GARABITO, EDDY JORGE	OLD ADD: MANRREZA DOM REP
1946-031	GARAGIOLA, JOSEPH HENRY	401 EAST JEFFERSON STREET, PHOENIX AZ 85001
1994-036	GARAGOZZO, KEITH JOHN	16 FOX CROFT WAY, MOUNT LAUREL NJ 08054
1944-045	GARBARK, NATHANIEL MICHAEL 'MIKE'	D. AUGUST 31, 1994, CHARLOTTE, N.C.
1934-040	GARBARK, ROBERT MICHAEL	D. AUGUST 15, 1990, MEADVILLE, PA.
1969-061	GARBER, HENRY EUGENE 'GENE'	771 STONEMILL DRIVE, ELIZABETHTOWN PA 17022
1956-037	GARBER, ROBERT MITCHELL	D. JUNE 7, 1999, REDWOOD, CALIF.
1984-037	GARBEY, BARBARO GARBEY	730 SW JEFFERSON, PEORIA IL 61602
1952-035	GARBOWSKI, ALEXANDER	100 OAKRIDGE DRIVE, PUTNAM VALLEY NY 10579
1990-050	GARCES, RICHARD ARON	SECTOR 2, CALLE 2 NO. 2 MARACAY ARAGUA, VENEZUELA
1976-034	GARCIA, ALFONSO RAFAEL 'KIKO'	526 TRAILVIEW CIRCLE, MARTINEZ CA 94553
1999-067	GARCIA, AMAURY MIGUEL	OLD ADD: SANTO DOMINGO DOM REP
1990-051	GARCIA, CARLOS JESUS	207 ENCHANTED FOREST NORTH, DEPEW NY 14043
1978-048	GARCIA, DAMASO DOMINGO	SANCHEZ NO. 104 MOCA, DOM REP
2003-051	GARCIA, DANIEL JOSEPH	35210 PERSIMMON AVENUE, YUCAIPA CA 92399
1981-041	GARCIA, DANIEL RAPHAEL	274 FAIRHAVEN MALL #A8, JERICHO NY 11753
1977-057	GARCIA, DAVID	17842 AVENIDA CORDILLERA #28, SAN DIEGO CA 92128
1948-037	GARCIA, EDWARD MIGUEL 'MIKE'	D. JANUARY 13, 1986, FAIRVIEW PARK, OHIO
1995-078	GARCIA, FREDDY ADRIAN	QUISQUELLA GTA ETAPA M22 #52 LA RAMONA, DOM REP
1999-068	GARCIA, FREDDY ANTONIO	OLD ADD: BARUTA VENEZUELA
1998-063	GARCIA, GUILLERMO ANTONIO	3806 SHOMA DRIVE, WEST PALM BEACH FL 33414
1995-079	GARCIA, GUSTAVO KARIM 'KARIM'	38 AGNEW FARM ROAD, ARMONK NY 10504
2004-068	GARCIA, JAIRO	OLD ADD: JUAN BARON DOM REP
1999-069	GARCIA, JESUS JESSE 'JESSE'	115 WEST LIGUSTRUM, ROBSTOWN TX 78380
2006-054	GARCIA, JOSE LUIS	OLD ADD: DE JABON DOM REP
1987-050	GARCIA, LEONARDO ANTONIO	5416 WEST SUNLAND AVENUE, LAVEEN AZ 85339
2002-065	GARCIA, LUIS CARLOS	OLD ADD: HERMOSILLO MEX
1999-070	GARCIA, LUIS RAFAEL	OLD ADD: SAN FRANCISCO DE MACORIS DOM RP
1999-071	GARCIA, MICHAEL R.	28428 EAGLE STREET, MORENO VALLEY CA 92555
1987-051	GARCIA, MIGUEL ANGEL	CARLOS DELGADO CHALBAUD BLQ6 LETRA C #6, CARACAS, VENEZUELA
1973-050	GARCIA, PEDRO MODESTO	PARQUE DEL CONDADO L-4, B.PARK, CAGUAS PR 00725
1972-032	GARCIA, RALPH	7441 BRIAN LANE, LAPALMA CA 90623
1991-060	GARCIA, RAMON ANTONIO	BO. COLOMBIA N. CALLEJON 2 GAUNARE EDO.PORTYGUESA, VENEZUELA
1948-038	GARCIA, RAMON GARCIA	HATUEY 259 E. ORIENTE Y CAMAGUEY ARROYO, HAVANA CUBA
2002-066	GARCIA, REYNALDO	OLD ADD: SANTO DOMINGO DOM REP
2003-052	GARCIA, ROSMAN J.	OLD ADD: SAN JOAQUIN VZ
1954-029	GARCIA, VINICIO UZCANGA	R. CAMPOAMOR 805, COLANAHUAC MONTERREY NUEVO LAREDO, MEXICO
1996-064	GARCIAPARRA, ANTHONY NOMAR 'NOMAR'	120 16TH STREET, MANHATTAN BEACH CA 90266
1945-035	GARDELLA, ALFRED STEVE	D. SEPTEMBER 10, 2006, CORAL SPRINGS, FLA.
1944-046	GARDELLA, DANIEL LEWIS	D. MARCH 6, 2005, YONKERS, N.Y.
1981-042	GARDENHIRE, RONALD CLYDE	668 COUNTY ROAD B2 EAST, LITTLE CANADA MN 55117
1923-047	GARDINER, ARTHUR CECIL	D. OCTOBER 21, 1954, COPIAGUE, N.Y.
1990-052	GARDINER, MICHAEL JAMES	26 READ DRIVE, HANOVER MA 02339
1975-042	GARDNER, ARTHUR JUNIOR	1963 HWY 35 SOUTH, WALNUT GROVE MS 39189
1991-061	GARDNER, CHRISTOPHER JOHN	2304 SW ABALON CIRCLE, PORT SAINT LUCIE FL 34953
1945-036	GARDNER, GLENN MILESO	D. JULY 7, 1964, ROCHESTER, N.Y.
1991-062	GARDNER, JEFFREY SCOTT	1906 PORT WEYBRIDGE PLACE, NEWPORT BEACH CA 92660
1989-041	GARDNER, MARK ALLAN	15216 MESA VIEW AVENUE, FRIANT CA 93626
1929-042	GARDNER, RAYMOND VINCENT	D. MAY 3, 1968, FREDERICK, MD.
1965-032	GARDNER, RICHARD FRANK 'ROB'	OLD ADD: 1318 WESLEY DRIVE, PUNTA GORDA FL 33950
2002-067	GARDNER, TERRENCE LEE 'LEE'	2215 FENTON ROAD, HARTLAND MI 48353
1984-038	GARDNER, WESLEY BRIAN	305 RUTH STREET, BENTON AR 72015
1954-030	GARDNER, WILLIAM FREDERICK	35 DAYTON RD, WATERFORD CT 06385
1936-028	GARIBALDI, ARTHUR EDWARD	D. OCTOBER 20, 1967, SACRAMENTO, CALIF.

1962-044	GARIBALDI, BOB ROY	2143 OREGON AVENUE, STOCKTON CA 95204
2000-065	GARIBAY, DANIEL	OLD ADD: MANEADERO MEXICO
2005-070	GARKO, RYAN F	20430 PRESTINA WAY, WALNUT CA 91789
2000-066	GARLAND, JON STEVEN	8329 LEWIS AVENUE, ANTELOPE CA 95843
1931-030	GARLAND, LOUIS LYMAN	D. AUGUST 30, 1990, IDAHO FALLS, IND.
1973-051	GARLAND, MARCUS WAYNE 'WAYNE'	9115 IVYBRIDGE STREET, LAS VEGAS NV 89123
1969-062	GARMAN, MICHAEL DOUGLAS	15144 KINGS ROW ROAD, CALDWELL ID 83605
1932-030	GARMS, DEBS C.	D. DECEMBER 16, 1984, GLEN ROSE, TEXAS
1973-052	GARNER, PHILIP MASON	7503 PRAIRIE OAK TRAIL, HUMBLE TX 77346
1968-026	GARR, RALPH ALLAN	6702 BURKETT STREET, HOUSTON TX 77021
1982-048	GARRELTS, SCOTT WILLIAM	11070 ASHLAND WAY, SHREVEPORT LA 71106
1970-048	GARRETT, GREGORY	D. JUNE 7, 2003, NEWHALL, CALIF.
1966-038	GARRETT, HENRY ADRIAN 'ADRIAN'	PO BOX 201, MANCHACA TX 78652
1969-063	GARRETT, RONALD WAYNE 'WAYNE'	4331 LINWOOD STREET, SARASOTA FL 34232
1964-035	GARRIDO, GIL GONZALO	PO BOX 527948, MIAMI FL 33152
1946-032	GARRIOTT, CECIL VIRGIL	D. FEBRUARY 20, 1990, LAKE ELSINORE, CALIF.
1928-037	GARRISON, CLIFFORD WILLIAM	D. AUGUST 25, 1994, WOODLAND, CALIF.
1943-049	GARRISON, ROBERT FORD 'FORD'	D. JUNE 6, 2001, LARGO, FLA.
1996-065	GARRISON, WEBSTER LEOTIS	OLD ADD: 3502 VESPASIAN BLVD #154, NEW ORLEANS LA 70114
1931-031	GARRITY, FRANCIS JOSEPH 'HANK'	D. SEPTEMBER 3, 1962, BOSTON, MASS.
1948-039	GARVER, NED FRANKLIN	1121 TOWNLINE ROAD #164, BRYAN OH 43506
1969-064	GARVEY, STEVEN PATRICK	74-923 HWY 111, INDIAN WELLS CA 92210
1977-058	GARVIN, THEODORE JARED 'JERRY'	1082 PERAZZO CIRCLE, FOLSOM CA 95630
2006-055	GARZA, MATTHEW SCOTT	OLD ADD: 416 WEST K STREET, LOS BANOS CA 93635
1969-065	GASPAR, RODNEY EARL	28771 PEACH BLOSSOM, MISSION VIEJO CA 92692
1944-047	GASSAWAY, CHARLES CASON	D. JANUARY 15, 1992, MIAMI, FLA.
2005-071	GASSNER, DAVID KENNETH	2932 WEST GLENPARK DRIVE, APPLETON WI 54914
1955-046	GASTALL, THOMAS EVERETT	D. SEPTEMBER 20, 1956, CHESAPEAKE BAY, MD.
1920-035	GASTON, ALEXANDER NATHANIEL	D. FEBRUARY 8, 1979, SANTA MONICA, CALIF.
1967-035	GASTON, CLARENCE EDWIN 'CITO'	2 BLYTHDALE ROAD TORONTO ON, M4N 3M2 CANADA
1924-039	GASTON, NATHANIEL MILTON 'MILT'	D. APRIL 26, 1996, HYANNIS, MASS.
1993-058	GATES, BRENT ROBERT	234 GRAYFIELD COURT SE, ADA MI 49301
1978-049	GATES, JOSEPH DANIEL	1517 EAST NINETEENTH AVE, GARY IN 46407
1981-043	GATES, MICHAEL GRANT	HC 075 BOX 45C, KOOSKIA ID 83539
1963-043	GATEWOOD, AUBREY LEE	5 PINE TREE LOOP, NORTH LITTLE ROCK AR 72116
2004-069	GATHRIGHT, JOEY RENARD	625 BENJAMIN COURT, LA PLACE LA 70068
1978-050	GAUDET, JAMES JENNINGS	3336 VINEVILLE AVENUE, MACON GA 31204
2003-053	GAUDIN, CHAD EDWARD	108 CITRUS ROAD, NEW ORLEANS LA 70123
1925-037	GAUTREAU, WALTER PAUL 'DOC'	D. AUGUST 23, 1970, SALT LAKE CITY, UTAH
1936-029	GAUTREAUX, SIDNEY ALLEN	D. APRIL 19, 1980, MORGAN CITY, LA.
1920-036	GAW, GEORGE JOSEPH 'CHIPPY'	D. MAY 26, 1968, BOSTON, MASS.
1923-048	GAZELLA, MICHAEL	D. SEPTEMBER 11, 1978, ODESSA, TEXAS
1947-037	GEARHART, LLOYD WILLIAM	D. APRIL 2, 2001, DAYTON, OHIO
1923-049	GEARIN, DENNIS JOHN 'DINTY'	D. MARCH 11, 1959, PROVIDENCE, R.I.
1942-042	GEARY, EUGENE FRANCIS JOSEPH 'HUCK'	D. JANUARY 27, 1981, CUBA, N.Y.
2003-054	GEARY, GEOFFREY MICHAEL	1060 RIPPEY STREET, EL CAJON CA 92020
1971-037	GEBHARD, ROBERT HENRY	5242 EAST OTERO PLACE, LITTLETON CO 80123
1947-038	GEBRIAN, PETER	D. MAY 6, 2005, STUART, FLA.
1972-033	GEDDES, JAMES LEE	6738 HARRISBURG LONDON ROAD, ORIENT OH 43146
1939-040	GEDEON, ELMER JOHN	D. APRIL 20, 1944, SAINT POL, FRANCE
1980-046	GEDMAN, RICHARD LEO 'RICH'	10 PARMENTER ROAD, FRAMINGHAM MA 01701
1939-041	GEE, JOHN ALEXANDER	D. JANUARY 23, 1988, CORTLAND, N.Y.
1923-050	GEHRIG, HENRY LOUIS 'LOU'	D. JUNE 2, 1941, RIVERDALE, N.Y.
1924-040	GEHRINGER, CHARLES LEONARD	D. JANUARY 21, 1993, BLOOMFIELD HILLS, MICH.
1937-039	GEHRMAN, PAUL ARTHUR	D. OCTOBER 23, 1986, BEND, ORE.
1958-036	GEIGER, GARY MERLE	D. APRIL 24, 1996, MURPHYSBORO, ILL.
1978-051	GEISEL, JOHN DAVID 'DAVE'	4 BLACKSMITH LANE, MEDIA PA 19063
1969-066	GEISHERT, VERNON WILLIAM	984 NORTH PARK STREET, RICHLAND CENTER WI 53581
1929-043	GELBERT, CHARLES MAGNUS	D. JANUARY 13, 1967, EASTON, PA.
1964-036	GELNAR, JOHN RICHARD	300 NORTH HITCHCOCK, HOBART OK 73651
1922-043	GENEWICH, JOSEPH EDWARD	D. DECEMBER 21, 1985, LOCKPORT, N.Y.
1950-030	GENOVESE, GEORGE MICHAEL	11474 ERWIN STREET, HOLLYWOOD CA 91606
1957-022	GENTILE, JAMES EDWARD	1016 NEPTUNE, EDMOND OK 73034
1943-050	GENTILE, SAMUEL CHRISTOPHER	D. MAY 4, 1998, EVERETT, MASS.
1969-067	GENTRY, GARY EDWARD	301 WEST LAWRENCE LANE, PHOENIX AZ 85021
1954-031	GENTRY, HARVEY WILLIAM	109 EATON LN, BRISTOL TN 37620
1943-051	GENTRY, JAMES RUFFUS 'RUFE'	D. JULY 3, 1997, WINSTON-SALEM, N.C.
1955-047	GEORGE, ALEX THOMAS	8432 LINDEN DRIVE, PRAIRIE VILLAGE KS 66207
1935-035	GEORGE, CHARLES PETER 'GREEK'	D. AUGUST 15, 1999, METAIRIE, LA.
2001-069	GEORGE, CHRISTOPHER COLEMAN	7703 GOLDENGROVE DRIVE, SPRING TX 77379
1991-063	GEORGE, CHRISTOPHER SEAN	428 KATHY LYNN DRIVE, PITTSBURGH PA 15239
1938-029	GEORGY, OSCAR JOHN	D. JANUARY 15, 1999, NEW ORLEANS, LA.
1936-030	GERAGHTY, BENJAMIN RAYMOND	D. JUNE 18, 1963, JACKSONVILLE, FLA.
1962-045	GERARD, DAVID FREDERICK	D. OCTOBER 10, 2001, NEWTOWN, PA.
1985-039	GERBER, CRAIG STUART	4297 PERSHING AVENUE, SAN BERNARDINO CA 92407
1962-046	GERBERMAN, GEORGE ALOIS	1501 MICHAEL, EL CAMPO TX 77437
1988-053	GEREN, ROBERT PETER	16032 SOUTH FIRST AVENUE, PHOENIX AZ 85045
1974-040	GERHARDT, ALLEN RUSSELL 'RUSTY'	PO BOX 426, NEW LONDON TX 75682
1986-056	GERHART, HAROLD KENNETH 'KEN'	1603 ASHFORD COURT, MURFREESBORO TN 37129
1943-052	GERHEAUSER, ALBERT	D. MAY 28, 1972, SPRINGFIELD, MO.
1927-038	GERKEN, GEORGE HERBERT	D. OCTOBER 23, 1977, ARCAIDA, CALIF.
1945-037	GERKIN, STEPHEN PAUL	D. NOVEMBER 8, 1978, BAY PINES, FLA.
1938-030	GERLACH, JOHN GLENN	D. AUGUST 28, 1999, MADISON, WISC.
2002-068	GERMAN, ESTEBAN GURIDI	OLD ADD: SANTO DOMINGO DOM REP
2002-069	GERMAN, FRANKLYN MIGUEL MADE	OLD ADD: SAN CRISTOBAL DOM REP
2004-070	GERMANO, JUSTIN WILLIAM	1250 NORTH INDIAN HILL BLVD #10, CLAREMONT CA 91711

1952-036	GERNERT, RICHARD EDWARD	1420 ROSE VIRGINIA ROAD, READING PA 19615
1969-068	GERONIMO, CESAR FRANCISCO	OLD ADD: 120 W. 97TH #9E, NEW YORK NY 10025
2003-055	GERUT, JOSEPH DIEGO 'JODY'	623 ROCHDALE CIRCLE, LOMBARD IL 60198
1945-038	GETTEL, ALLEN JAMES	D. APRIL 8, 2005, NORFOLK, VA.
2004-071	GETTIS, BYRON EARL	907 NORTH 87TH STREET, EAST SAINT LOUIS IL 62203
1924-041	GEYGAN, JAMES EDWARD 'CHAPPIE'	D. MARCH 16, 1966, COLUMBUS, OHIO
1983-061	GHELFI, ANTHONY PAUL	3414 GENEVA LANE, LACROSSE WI 54601
1958-037	GIALLOMBARDO, ROBERT PAUL	7903 ANTIQUE CIRCLE, WAXHAW NC 28173
1995-080	GIAMBI, JASON GILBERT	1034 EAST BELMONT ABBEY LANE, CLAREMONT CA 91711
1998-064	GIAMBI, JEREMY DEAN	1034 EAST BELMONT ABBEY LANE, CLAREMONT CA 91711
1991-064	GIANNELLI, RAYMOND JOHN	56 EAST SALTAIRE ROAD, LINDENHURST NY 11757
1925-038	GIARD, JOSEPH OSCAR	D. JULY 10, 1956, WORCESTER, MASS.
2005-072	GIARRATANO, ANTHONY J	OLD ADD: 9 OLD MATAWAN ROAD, OLD BRIDGE NJ 08857
1960-038	GIBBON, JOSEPH CHARLES	26 COUNTY ROAD 24142, NEWTON MS 39345
2001-070	GIBBONS, JAY JONATHAN	6 SPRING FOREST COURT, OWINGS MILLS MD 21117
1984-039	GIBBONS, JOHN MICHAEL	13530 CHARTER BEND DRIVE, SAN ANTONIO TX 78231
1962-047	GIBBS, JERRY DEAN 'JAKE'	225 ST. ANDREWS CIRCLE, OXFORD MS 38655
1995-081	GIBRALTER, STEPHEN BENSON	3651 ASBURY STREET, DALLAS TX 75205
1924-042	GIBSON, CHARLES GRIFFIN	D. DECEMBER 18, 1990, LAGRANGE, GA.
1998-065	GIBSON, DERRICK LAMONT	303 AVENUE O NW, WINTER HAVEN FL 33881
1967-036	GIBSON, JOHN RUSSELL 'RUSS'	924 GARDNERS NECK ROAD #12, SWANSEA MA 02777
1979-039	GIBSON, KIRK HAROLD	15135 CHARLEROIX STREET, GROSSE POINTE MI 48230
1988-054	GIBSON, PAUL MARSHALL	PO BOX 354, CENTER MORICHES NY 11934
1959-030	GIBSON, ROBERT	215 BELLEVIEW BLVD SOUTH, BELLEVUE NE 68005
1983-062	GIBSON, ROBERT LOUIS	751 WEST ROLLING ROAD, SPRINGFIELD PA 19064
1926-030	GIBSON, SAMUEL BRAXTON	D. JANUARY 31, 1983, HIGH POINT, N.C.
1937-040	GICK, GEORGE EDWARD	875 ELSTON ROAD, LAFAYETTE IN 47909
1987-052	GIDEON, BYRON BRETT	PO BOX 822, GEORGETOWN TX 78627
1975-043	GIDEON, JAMES LESLIE	2509 MCCALLUM, AUSTIN TX 78703
1939-042	GIEBELL, FLOYD GEORGE	D. APRIL 28, 2004, WILKESBORO, N.C.
1954-032	GIEL, PAUL ROBERT	D. MAY 23, 2002, MINNEAPOLIS, MINN.
1959-031	GIGGIE, ROBERT THOMAS	89 MCANDREW RD, BRAINTREE MA 02184
1967-037	GIGON, NORMAN PHILLIP	2503 RIO VISTA DRIVE, MAHWAH NJ 07430
2001-071	GIL, GERONIMO	OLD ADD: 7115 MILWOOD AVENUE, CANOGA PARK CA 91303
2004-072	GIL, JERRY BIENBENIDO	OLD ADD: SANTO DOMINGO DOM REP
1993-059	GIL, ROMAR BENJAMIN 'BENJI'	504 UNBRIDLED LANE, KELLER TX 76248
1967-038	GIL, TOMAS GUSTAVO 'GUS'	2240 SW 42ND TERRACE, FORT LAUDERDALE FL 33317
1997-064	GILBERT, ALBERT SHAWN 'SHAWN'	1644 WEST WRENWOOD AVENUE, FRESNO CA 93711
1942-043	GILBERT, ANDREW	D. AUGUST 29, 1992, DAVIS, CALIF.
1940-024	GILBERT, CHARLES MADER	D. AUGUST 13, 1983, NEW ORLEANS, LA.
1959-032	GILBERT, DREW EDWARD 'BUDDY'	1913 BELCARO DR, KNOXVILLE TN 37918
1950-031	GILBERT, HAROLD JOSEPH 'TOOKIE'	D. JUNE 23, 1967, NEW ORLEANS, LA.
1972-034	GILBERT, JOE DENNIS	1952 NORTH BOWIE ST, JASPER TX 75951
1985-040	GILBERT, MARK DAVID	2340 NW 45TH STREET, BOCA RATON FL 33431
1928-038	GILBERT, WALTER JOHN	D. SEPTEMBER 8, 1959, DULUTH, MINN.
1972-035	GILBREATH, RODNEY JOE	1438 RIDGELAND WAY, LILBURN GA 30247
1971-038	GILBRETH, WILLIAM FREEMAN	709 GARY LANE, ABILENE TX 79601
1959-033	GILE, DONALD LOREN	570 SEAHORSE LANE, REDWOOD CITY CA 94065
1981-044	GILES, BRIAN JEFFREY	1907 DEERPARK DRIVE #430, FULLERTON CA 92831
1995-082	GILES, BRIAN STEPHEN	4130 RANCHO LAS BRISAS TRAIL, SAN DIEGO CA 92130
2001-072	GILES, MARCUS WILLIAM	2940 VIA ASOLEADO, ALPINE CA 91901
2003-056	GILFILLAN, JASON EDWARD	153 GILFILLAN ROAD, BLACKSBURG SC 29702
1920-037	GILHAM, GEORGE LEWIS	D. APRIL 25, 1937, LANSDOWNE, PA.
1990-053	GILKEY, OTIS BERNARD 'BERNARD'	2200 DUNHILL WAY COURT, CHESTERFIELD MO 63005
1937-041	GILL, GEORGE LLOYD	D. FEBRUARY 21, 1999, JACKSON, MISS.
1923-051	GILL, HAROLD EDWARD	D. AUGUST 1, 1932, BROCKTON, MASS.
1927-039	GILL, JOHN WESLEY	D. DECEMBER 26, 1984, NASHVILLE, TENN.
1940-025	GILLENWATER, CARDEN EDISON	D. MAY 10, 2000, LARGO, FLA.
1923-052	GILLENWATER, CLARAL LEWIS	D. FEBRUARY 26, 1978, PENSACOLA, FLA.
1990-054	GILLES, THOMAS BRADFORD	3116 NORTH EMERY AVENUE, PEORIA IL 61604
1922-044	GILLESPIE, JOHN PATRICK	D. FEBRUARY 15, 1954, VALLEJO, CALIF.
1942-044	GILLESPIE, PAUL ALLEN	D. AUGUST 11, 1970, ANNISTON, ALA.
1944-048	GILLESPIE, ROBERT WILLIAM	D. NOVEMBER 4, 2001, WINSTON-SALEM, N.C.
1953-028	GILLIAM, JAMES WILLIAM 'JUNIOR'	D. OCTOBER 8, 1978, INGLEWOOD, CALIF.
1967-039	GILLIFORD, PAUL GANT	7 WOODLAND DR, MALVERN PA 19355
1927-040	GILLIS, GRANT	D. FEBRUARY 4, 1981, THOMASVILLE, ALA.
1944-049	GILMORE, LEONARD PRESTON	7500 NE 102ND STREET, JONES OK 73049
1968-027	GILSON, HAROLD	7243 NORTH 8TH WAY, PHOENIX AZ 85020
2006-056	GIMENEZ, HECTOR C.	OLD ADD: SAN FELIPE VENEZ
1948-040	GINSBERG, MYRON NATHAN 'JOE'	12635 SW KINGSWAY CIRCLE #D1, LAKE SUZY FL 33821
2000-067	GINTER, KEITH MICHAEL	1531 EAST HORSESHOE DRIVE, CHANDLER AZ 85249
2000-068	GINTER, MATTHEW SHANE	3325 NEW BOONESBORO, WINCHESTER KY 40391
1944-050	GIONFRIDDO, ALBERT FRANCIS	D. MARCH 14, 2003, SOLVANG, CALIF.
1953-029	GIORDANO, THOMAS ARTHUR	176 RIVERSIDE AVENUE, AMITYVILLE NY 11701
1995-083	GIOVANALA, EDWARD THOMAS	1741 NOMARK COURT, SAN JOSE CA 95125
1998-066	GIPSON, CHARLES WELLS	632 SOUTH EARLHAM STREET, ORANGE CA 92869
1989-042	GIRARDI, JOSEPH ELLIOTT	1845 SOUTH JAMES COURT NORTH, LAKE FOREST IL 60045
2004-073	GISSELL, CHRISTOPHER ODELL	305 NE 107TH STREET, VANCOUVER WA 98685
1936-031	GIULIANI, ANGELO JOHN	D. OCTOBER 8, 2004, SAINT PAUL, MINN.
1962-048	GIUSTI, DAVID JOHN	524 CLAIR DR, PITTSBURGH PA 15241
1995-084	GIVENS, BRIAN	719 STONEMONT COURT, CASTLE ROCK CO 80104
1946-033	GLADD, JAMES WALTER	D. NOVEMBER 8, 1977, LONG BEACH, CALIF.
1983-063	GLADDEN, CLIFTON DANIEL 'DAN'	6543 PINNACLE DRIVE, EDEN PRAIRIE MN 55346
1961-038	GLADDING, FRED EARL	4721 MACMONT CIR, POWELL TN 37819
1944-051	GLADU, ROLAND EDWIN	D. JULY 26, 1994, MONTREAL, QUE.
1920-038	GLAISER, JOHN BURKE	D. MARCH 7, 1959, HOUSTON, TEXAS

1996-066	GLANVILLE, DOUGLAS MATUNWA	2043 WEST MCLEAN AVENUE, CHICAGO IL 60647
1925-039	GLASS, THOMAS JOSEPH	D. DECEMBER 15, 1981, GREENSBORO, N.C.
1998-067	GLAUBER, KEITH H	20 HIGHLAND COURT, FREEHOLD NJ 07728
1998-068	GLAUS, TROY EDWARD	PMB 332 1240 EAST ONTARIO AVENUE #102, CORONA CA 92881
1949-025	GLAVIANO, THOMAS GIATANO	D. JANUARY 19, 2004, SACRAMENTO, CALIF.
2003-057	GLAVINE, MICHAEL PATRICK	89 TREBLE COVE ROAD, NORTH BILLERICA MA 01862
1987-053	GLAVINE, THOMAS MICHAEL	3050 COMPTON COURT, ALPHARETTA GA 30002
1920-039	GLAZNER, CHARLES FRANKLIN 'WHITEY'	D. JUNE 6, 1989, ORLANDO, FLA.
1920-040	GLEASON, JOSEPH PAUL	D. SEPTEMBER 8, 1990, PHELPS, N.Y.
1963-044	GLEASON, ROY WILLIAM	41770 MARGARITA ROAD #1043, TEMECULA CA 92591
1979-040	GLEATON, JERRY DON	129 MISTY LANE, EARLY TX 76802
1936-032	GLEESON, JAMES JOSEPH	D. MAY 1, 1996, KANSAS CITY, MO.
1920-041	GLENN, BURDETTE 'BOB'	D. JUNE 3, 1977, RICHMOND, CALIF.
1960-039	GLENN, JOHN	1317 PERRY AVENUE, AUGUSTA GA 30901
1932-031	GLENN, JOSEPH CHARLES	D. MAY 6, 1985, TUNKHANNOCK, PA.
1930-025	GLIATTO, SALVADOR MICHAEL	D. NOVEMBER 2, 1995, TYLER, TEXAS
1994-037	GLINATSIS, GEORGE	1670 SOUTH DEFRAME STREET #C1, LAKEWOOD CO 80228
2000-069	GLOAD, ROSS P.	23 HARRISON AVENUE, EAST HAMPTON NY 11937
1939-043	GLOSSOP, ALBAN	D. JULY 2, 1991, WALNUT CREEK, CALIF.
1999-072	GLOVER, JOHN GARY 'GARY'	2135 PENNSYLVANIA DRIVE, DELAND FL 32724
1975-044	GLYNN, EDWARD PAUL	157 SAN CARLOS STREET, TOMS RIVER NJ 08757
1999-073	GLYNN, RYAN DAVID	OLD ADD: 6329 LIBERTY LANE, GOSHEN OH 45122
1949-026	GLYNN, WILLIAM VINCENT	6916 51ST, SAN DIEGO CA 92120
2003-058	GOBBLE, BILLY JAMES 'JIMMY'	150 LAKE VIEW ESTATES DRIVE, BRISTOL TN 37620
1974-041	GODBY, DANNY RAY	RURAL ROUTE 2 BOX 17A, CHAPMANVILLE WV 25508
1972-036	GODDARD, JOSEPH HAROLD	304 RIDGEPARK DRIVE, BECKLEY WV 25801
2005-073	GODWIN, CARLTON TYRELL	PO BOX 14, COUNCIL NC 28434
1922-045	GOEBEL, WILBUR EDWIN 'EDWIN'	D. AUGUST 12, 1959, BROOKLYN, N.Y.
1960-040	GOETZ, JOHN HARDY	3253 MYDDLETON, TROY MI 48084
1990-055	GOFF, JERRY LEE	3 OAK VALLEY DRIVE, NOVATO CA 94947
1972-037	GOGGIN, CHARLES FRANCIS	158 CHEROKEE ROAD, HENDERSONVILLE TN 37075
1970-049	GOGOLEWSKI, WILLIAM JOSEPH	1522 GRAHAM AVE, OSHKOSH WI 54901
1993-060	GOHR, GREGORY JAMES	77 SCOTLAND ROAD, READING MA 01867
1960-041	GOLDEN, JAMES EDWARD	8630 SW 10TH, TOPEKA KS 66606
1928-039	GOLDMAN, JONAH JOHN	D. AUGUST 17, 1980, PALM BEACH, FLA.
1949-027	GOLDSBERRY, GORDON FREDERICK	D. FEBRUARY 23, 1996, LAKE FOREST, ILL.
1926-031	GOLDSMITH, HAROLD EUGENE	D. OCTOBER 20, 1985, RIVERHEAD, N.Y.
1932-032	GOLDSTEIN, ISADORE	D. SEPTEMBER 24, 1993, DELRAY BEACH, FLA.
1943-053	GOLDSTEIN, LESLIE ELMER 'LONNIE'	6799 GRANBURY ROAD #108, FORT WORTH TX 76133
1962-049	GOLDY, PURNAL WILLIAM	1318 CHERRYVILLE RD, LITTLETON CO 80120
1941-037	GOLETZ, STANLEY	D. JULY 7, 1997, TEMPLE, TEXAS
1949-028	GOLIAT, MIKE MITCHEL	D. JANUARY 14, 2004, SEVEN HILLS, OHIO
1972-038	GOLTZ, DAVID ALLAN	1009 STONYBROOK MANOR, FERGUS FALLS MN 56537
1922-046	GOLVIN, WALTER GEORGE	D. JUNE 11, 1973, GARDENA, CALIF.
2003-059	GOMES, JONNY JOHNSON	OLD ADD: PETALUMA CA 94952
1997-065	GOMES, WAYNE MAURICE	4 BOYKIN LANE, HAMPTON VA 23663
2002-070	GOMEZ, ALEXIS DEJESUS	OLD ADD: LOMA DE CABRERA DOM REP
1993-061	GOMEZ, CHRIS CORY	8 VERNAL SPRING, IRVINE CA 92603
1935-036	GOMEZ, JOSE LUIS RODRIGUEZ	D. DECEMBER 1, 1992, NUEVO LAREDO, MEXICO
1990-056	GOMEZ, LEONARDO	OLD ADD: PO BOX 1630-542, CANOVANOS PR 00729
1974-042	GOMEZ, LUIS JOSE	676 CHESTERFIELD DRIVE, LAWRENCEVILLE GA 30245
1993-062	GOMEZ, PATRICK ALEXANDER	7217 OAKBERRY WAY, CITRUS HEIGHTS CA 95621
1944-052	GOMEZ, PRESTON MARTINEZ	15765 SLEEPY OAK ROAD, CHINO HILLS CA 91709
1984-040	GOMEZ, RANDALL SCOTT 'ROCKY'	7400 FILICE DRIVE, GILROY CA 95020
1953-030	GOMEZ, RUBEN COLON	D. JULY 26, 2004, CAROLINA, P.R.
1930-026	GOMEZ, VERNON LOUIS 'LEFTY'	D. FEBRUARY 17, 1989, GREENBRAE, CALIF.
1960-042	GONDER, JESSE LEMAR	D. NOVEMBER 14, 2004, OAKLAND, CALIF.
1979-041	GONZALES, DANIEL DAVID	7758 BIRCHLEAF AVENUE, PICO RIVERA CA 90660
1937-042	GONZALES, JOE MADRID	D. NOVEMBER 16, 1996, TORRANCE, CALIF.
1977-059	GONZALES, JULIO C.	OLD ADD: PO BOX 75755, CAGUAS PR 00725
1949-029	GONZALES, JULIO ENRIQUE	D. FEBRUARY 15, 1991, BANES, CUBA
1993-063	GONZALES, LAWRENCE CHRISTOPHER 'LARRY'	OLD ADD: WEST COVINA CA
1984-041	GONZALES, RENE ADRIAN	755 ORANGEWOOD, COVINA CA 91723
1955-048	GONZALES, WENCESLAO O'REILLY 'VINCE'	D. MARCH 11, 1981, CIUDAD DEL CARMEN, CAMP. MEXICO
2004-074	GONZALEZ, ADRIAN	11307 NORTH 152ND DRIVE, SURPRISE AZ 85379
1998-069	GONZALEZ, ALEXANDER	OLD ADD: TUMERO VENEZUELA
1994-038	GONZALEZ, ALEXANDER SCOTT	385 SOLANO PRADO, MIAMI FL 33156
1960-043	GONZALEZ, ANDRES ANTONIO 'TONY'	8011 SW 196TH TER, MIAMI FL 33189
1984-042	GONZALEZ, DENIO MARIANO	CALLE SAN LUIS #131, GUALEY SANTO DOMINGO, DOM REP
2001-073	GONZALEZ, DICKY ANGEL	OLD ADD: BAYAMON PR
2003-060	GONZALEZ, EDGAR GERALDO (ELIZONDO)	OLD ADD: SAN NICOLAS MEX
2006-057	GONZALEZ, ENRIQUE CESAR	OLD ADD: BOLIVAR VENEZ
1998-070	GONZALEZ, GABRIEL	920 CERRITOS AVENUE, LONG BEACH CA 90813
1997-066	GONZALEZ, GEREMI SEGUNDO 'JEREMI'	OLD ADD: 287 SOUTH TAMPA AVENUE, ORLANDO FL 32805
1988-055	GONZALEZ, GERMAN JOSE	OLD ADD: RIO CARIBE VENEZUELA
1972-039	GONZALEZ, JOSE FERNANDO 'FERNANDO'	OLD ADD: BO HATO VIEJO BOX 611, ARECIBO PR 00612
1985-041	GONZALEZ, JOSE RAFAEL	CALLE ANTERA MOTA #35 PUERTO PLATA, DOM REP
1989-043	GONZALEZ, JUAN ALBERTO	EXT. CATONI A-9, VEGA BAJA PR 00763
1998-071	GONZALEZ, LARIEL ALFONSO	OLD ADD: SAN CRISTOBAL DOM REP
2004-075	GONZALEZ, LUIS A	OLD ADD: EL TIGRE VENEZ
1990-057	GONZALEZ, LUIS EMILIO	OLD ADD: 8021 WEST BEARDSLEY ROAD, PEORIA AZ 85382
2003-061	GONZALEZ, MICHAEL VELA	2414 PINE BROOK COURT, DEER PARK TX 77536
1976-035	GONZALEZ, ORLANDO EUGENE	12460 NW 11TH LANE, MIAMI FL 33182
1963-045	GONZALEZ, PEDRO	104 GEN CABRAL SAN PEDRO DE MACORIS, DOM REP
2000-070	GONZALEZ, VICTOR RAUL 'RAUL'	OLD ADD: VILLA CAROLINA PR
1999-074	GONZALEZ, WIKLERMAN VICENTE 'WIKI'	OLD ADD: PALO NEGRO VENEZUELA

1929-044	GOOCH, CHARLES FURMAN	D. MAY 30, 1982, LANHAM, MD.
1921-035	GOOCH, JOHN BEVERLEY	D. MAY 15, 1975, NASHVILLE, TENN.
2003-062	GOOD, ANDREW RICHARD	1433 SOUTH BELCHER ROAD #G4, CLEARWATER FL 33764
1928-040	GOODELL, JOHN HENRY WILLIAM 'BILL'	D. SEPTEMBER 21, 1993, MESQUITE, TEXAS
1984-043	GOODEN, DWIGHT EUGENE	8349 GOLDEN PRAIRIE DRIVE, TAMPA FL 33647
1935-037	GOODMAN, IVAL RICHARD	D. NOVEMBER 25, 1984, CINCINNATI, OHIO
1947-039	GOODMAN, WILLIAM DALE	D. OCTOBER 1, 1984, SARASOTA, FLA.
1970-050	GOODSON, JAMES EDWARD 'ED'	2330 COLD SPRING LANE, GALAX VA 24333
1995-085	GOODWIN, CURTIS LAMAR	14939 WESTERN AVENUE, SAN LEANDRO CA 94578
1975-045	GOODWIN, DANNY KAY	1555 LINKSVIEW CIRCLE, STONE MOUNTAIN GA 30088
1948-041	GOODWIN, JAMES PATRICK	11533 FRANCETTA LANE, SAINT LOUIS MO 63138
1991-065	GOODWIN, THOMAS JONES	6480 POOL ROAD, GRAPEVINE TX 76051
1946-034	GOOLSBY, RAYMOND DANIEL	D. NOVEMBER 13, 1999, APOPKA, FLA.
1965-033	GOOSSEN, GREGORY BRYANT	4555 FULTON AVENUE #204, SHERMAN OAKS CA 91423
1955-049	GORBOUS, GLEN EDWARD	D. JUNE 12, 1990, CALGARY, ALTA.
1986-057	GORDON, DONALD THOMAS	3861 SOUTH BARBERRY PLACE, CHANDLER AZ 85248
1938-031	GORDON, JOSEPH LOWELL	D. APRIL 14, 1978, SACRAMENTO, CALIF.
1993-064	GORDON, KEITH BRADLEY	4601 THORNHURST DRIVE, OLNEY MD 20832
1977-060	GORDON, MICHAEL WILLIAM	35 LONGVIEW ROAD, BROCKTON MA 02401
1941-038	GORDON, SIDNEY	D. JUNE 17, 1975, NEW YORK, N.Y.
1988-056	GORDON, THOMAS	2006 LAKE LOTEWLA DRIVE, AVON PARK FL 33825
1921-036	GORDONIER, RAYMOND CHARLES	D. NOVEMBER 15, 1960, ROCHESTER, N.Y.
1997-067	GORECKI, RICHARD JOHN 'RICK'	16210 RIDGEWOOD DRIVE, LOCKPORT IL 60441
1954-033	GORIN, CHARLES PERRY	2617 FISET DR, AUSTIN TX 78731
1977-061	GORINSKI, ROBERT JOHN	BOX 133, CALUMET PA 15621
1952-037	GORMAN, HERBERT ALLEN	D. APRIL 5, 1953, SAN DIEGO, CALIF.
1937-043	GORMAN, HOWARD PAUL	D. APRIL 29, 1984, HARRISBURG, PA.
1952-038	GORMAN, THOMAS ALOYSIUS	D. DECEMBER 26, 1992, VALLEY STREAM, N.Y.
1939-044	GORMAN, THOMAS DAVID	D. AUGUST 11, 1986, CLOSTER, N.J.
1981-045	GORMAN, THOMAS PATRICK	1615 SW 5TH, PORTLAND OR 97201
1941-039	GORNICKI, HENRY FRANK	D. FEBRUARY 16, 1996, RIVIERA BEACH, FLA.
1940-026	GORSICA, JOHN JOSEPH PERRY	D. DECEMBER 16, 1998, CHARLOTTESVILLE, VA.
1957-023	GORYL, JOHN ALBERT	1888 CRANBERRY ISLES WAY, APOPKA FL 32712
2005-074	GORZELANNY, THOMAS STEPHEN	8320 EAGLE ISLES PLACE, BRADENTON FL 34212
1963-046	GOSGER, JAMES CHARLES	1823 7TH STREET, PORT HURON MI 48060
1921-037	GOSLIN, LEON ALLEN 'GOOSE'	D. MAY 15, 1971, BRIDGETON, N.J.
2004-076	GOSLING, MICHAEL F.	OLD ADD: 8604 FESTIVAL DRIVE, LAS VEGAS NV 89134
1962-050	GOSS, HOWARD WAYNE	D. JULY 31, 1996, RENO, NEV.
1972-040	GOSSAGE, RICHARD MICHAEL 'GOOSE'	35 MARLAND DRIVE, COLORADO SPRINGS CO 80906
1960-044	GOTAY, JULIO ENRIQUE	OLD ADD: JUAN JOSE CARTAGENA #34, PONCE PR 06713
2004-077	GOTAY, RUBEN A.	OLD ADD: FAJARDO PR
1982-049	GOTT, JAMES WILLIAM	1739 WINDSOR ROAD, SAN MARINO CA 91108
1944-053	GOULISH, NICHOLAS EDWARD	D. MAY 15, 1984, YOUNGSTOWN, OHIO
1972-041	GOWELL, LAWRENCE CLYDE	4 CARSON STREET, AUBURN ME 04210
1989-044	GOZZO, MAURO PAUL	956 COLD CREEK COVE, COLLIERVILLE TN 38017
1969-069	GRABARKEWITZ, BILLY CORDELL	2205 COPPER RIDGE ROAD, ARLINGTON TX 76006
1958-038	GRABER, RODNEY BLAINE	4674 MOUNT ARMET DR, SAN DIEGO CA 92117
2003-063	GRABOW, JOHN WILLIAM	114 NORTH FRANKLIN AVENUE, SAN GABRIEL CA 91778
1929-045	GRABOWSKI, ALFONS FRANCIS	D. OCTOBER 29, 1966, MEMPHIS, N.Y.
2002-071	GRABOWSKI, JASON WILLIAM	465 NORTH SUPERSTITION BLVD, NORWALK CT 06850
1924-043	GRABOWSKI, JOHN PATRICK	D. MAY 23, 1946, ALBANY, N.Y.
1932-033	GRABOWSKI, REGINALD JOHN	D. APRIL 2, 1955, SYRACUSE, N.Y.
1938-032	GRACE, JOSEPH LAVERNE	D. SEPTEMBER 18, 1969, MURPHYSBORO, ILL.
1988-057	GRACE, MARK EUGENE	5624 EAST BUENA VISTA, PARADISE VALLEY AZ 85253
1995-086	GRACE, MICHAEL JAMES	1156 BUELL AVENUE, JOLIET IL 60435
1978-052	GRACE, MICHAEL LEE	12791 BIG LAKE ROAD, DAVISBURG MI 48019
1929-046	GRACE, ROBERT EARL 'EARL'	D. DECEMBER 22, 1980, PHOENIX, ARIZ.
2004-078	GRACESQUI, FRANKLYN BENJAMIN	OLD ADD: 2064 DALY AVENUE, BRONX NY 10460
1957-024	GRAFF, MILTON EDWARD	D. AUGUST 2, 2005, ROCKDALE, TEXAS
1996-067	GRAFFANINO, ANTHONY JOSEPH	104 WARDEL ROAD, WILMINGTON DE 19804
1934-041	GRAHAM, ARTHUR WILLIAM 'SKINNY'	D. JULY 10, 1967, ARLINGTON, MASS.
1979-042	GRAHAM, DANIEL JAY	225 STANDAGE #33, MESA AZ 85201
1946-035	GRAHAM, JOHN BERNARD 'JACK'	D. DECEMBER 30, 1998, LOS ALAMITOS, CALIF.
1924-044	GRAHAM, KYLE	D. DECEMBER 1, 1973, OAK GROVE, ALA.
1983-064	GRAHAM, LEE WILLIAM	3201 137TH STREET, CLEVELAND OH 44120
1922-047	GRAHAM, ROY VINCENT	D. APRIL 26, 1933, MANILLA, PHILLIPINES
1963-047	GRAHAM, WAYNE LEON	RICE UNIV. BASEBALL 6100 SOUTH MAIN, HOUSTON TX 77005
1966-039	GRAHAM, WILLIAM ALBERT	D. OCTOBER 26, 2006, FLEMINGSBURG, KY.
1990-058	GRAHE, JOSEPH MILTON	2317 NORTH WALLEN DRIVE, LAKE PARK FL 33410
2004-079	GRAMAN, ALEX JOSEPH	10444 CUMBERLAND POINT BLVD, NOBLESVILLE IN 46060
1968-028	GRAMLY, BERT THOMAS 'TOM'	16485 RED WOOD CIRCLE, MCKINNEY TX 75069
1954-034	GRAMMAS, ALEXANDER PETER	3432 OAKDALE DR, BIRMINGHAM AL 35223
1927-041	GRAMPP, HENRY ECKHARD	D. MARCH 24, 1986, NEW YORK, N.Y.
2004-080	GRANDERSON, CURTIS	20485 TYLER DRIVE, CHICAGO HEIGHTS IL 60411
1993-065	GRANGER, JEFFREY ADAM	2905 GLASGOW DRIVE, ARLINGTON TX 76015
1968-029	GRANGER, WAYNE ALLEN	BOX 134, ALDRICH AVE, HUNTINGTON MA 01050
1923-053	GRANT, GEORGE ADDISON	D. MARCH 25, 1986, MONTGOMERY, ALA.
1942-045	GRANT, JAMES CHARLES	D. JULY 8, 1970, ROCHESTER, MINN.
1923-054	GRANT, JAMES RONALD	D. NOVEMBER 30, 1985, DES MOINES, IOWA
1958-039	GRANT, JAMES TIMOTHY 'MUDCAT'	1020 SOUTH DUNSMUIR, LOS ANGELES CA 90019
1984-044	GRANT, MARK ANDREW	123 FAIRLANE DRIVE, JOLIET IL 60435
1983-065	GRANT, THOMAS RAYMOND	36 MILLVILLE ROAD, MENDON MA 01756
1922-048	GRANTHAM, GEORGE FARLEY	D. MARCH 16, 1954, KINGMAN, ARIZ.
1983-066	GRAPENTHIN, RICHARD RAY	500 ARGYLLS CREST, ALPHARETTA GA 30202
1948-042	GRASMICK, LOUIS JUNIOR	6715 QUAD AVENUE, BALTIMORE MD 21237
1946-036	GRASSO, NEWTON MICHAEL 'MICKEY'	D. OCTOBER 15, 1975, MIAMI FLA.

1945-039	GRATE, DONALD	1245 NW 203RD STREET, MIAMI FL 33169
1991-066	GRATER, MARK ANTHONY	1136 INDIANA AVENUE, MONACA PA 15061
1999-075	GRATEROL, BEIKER	OLD ADD: 1504 TWIN OAKS DRIVE, TOLEDO OH 43615
1996-068	GRAVES, DANIEL PETER 'DANNY'	1204 BRANDON LAKES CIRCLE, VALRICO FL 33594
1926-032	GRAVES, JOSEPH EBENEZER	D. DECEMBER 22, 1980, SALEM, MASS.
1927-042	GRAVES, SAMUEL SIDNEY 'SID'	D. DECEMBER 26, 1983, BIDDEFORD, MAINE
1964-037	GRAY, DAVID ALEXANDER	OLD ADD: 1051 26TH STREET, OGDEN UT 84401
1977-062	GRAY, GARY GEORGE	BOX 98, LA PLACE LA 70068
1988-058	GRAY, JEFFREY EDWARD	17634 ESPRIT DRIVE, TAMPA FL 33647
1954-035	GRAY, JOHN LEONARD	10645 GREENBRIAR COURT, BOCA RATON FL 33498
1982-050	GRAY, LORENZO	912 NORTH PANNES AVENUE, COMPTON CA 90221
1937-044	GRAY, MILTON MARSHALL	D. JUNE 30, 1969, QUINCY, FLA.
1945-040	GRAY, PETER	D. JUNE 30, 2002, NANTICOKE, PA.
1958-040	GRAY, RICHARD BENJAMIN	503 SOUTH HAMPTON, ANAHEIM CA 92804
1924-045	GRAY, SAMUEL DAVID	D. APRIL 16, 1953, MCKINNEY, TEXAS
1946-037	GRAY, THEODORE GLENN	401 EAST LINTON BLVD #469, DELRAY BEACH FL 33483
1959-034	GRBA, ELI	106 FOX RUN, FLORENCE AL 35633
1954-036	GREASON, WILLIAM HENRY	PO BOX 7972, BIRMINGHAM AL 35228
1990-059	GREBECK, CRAIG ALLEN	27856 HOMESTEAD ROAD, LAGUNA NIGUEL CA 92677
2004-081	GREEN, ANDREW MULLIGAN	161 CHENAULT ROAD, LEXINGTON KY 40502
1997-068	GREEN, BERTRUM SCARBOROUGH 'SCARBOROUGH'	2020 CRIMSON MEADOWS DRIVE, O'FALLON MO 63366
1984-045	GREEN, CHRISTOPHER DEWAYNE	3417 59TH AVENUE WEST, BRADENTON FL 34210
1981-046	GREEN, DAVID ALEJANDRO	COLINIA MANAGUA GRUPO H#47 MANAGUA, NICARAGUA
2000-071	GREEN, DAVID JASON 'JASON'	OLD ADD: PORT HOPE ONTARIO
1959-035	GREEN, ELIJAH JERRY 'PUMPSIE'	PO BOX 1627, EL CERRITO CA 94530
1959-036	GREEN, FRED ALLEN	D. DECEMBER 22, 1996, TITUSVILLE, N.J.
1986-058	GREEN, GARY ALLEN	939 KENNEBEC STREET, PITTSBURGH PA 15217
1957-025	GREEN, GENE LEROY	D. MAY 23, 1981, ST. LOUIS, MO.
1960-045	GREEN, GEORGE DALLAS 'DALLAS'	846 CONOWINGO ROAD, CONOWINGO MD 21918
1935-038	GREEN, HARVEY GEORGE	D. JULY 24, 1970, FRANKLIN, LA.
1924-046	GREEN, JOSEPH HENRY	D. FEBRUARY 4, 1972, BRYN MAWR, PA.
1928-041	GREEN, JULIUS FOUST 'JUNE'	D. MARCH 19, 1974, GLENDORA, CALIF.
1957-026	GREEN, LEONARD CHARLES 'LENNY'	OLD ADD: 18693 SUNSET STREET, DETROIT MI 48234
2004-082	GREEN, NICHOLAS ANTHONY	1380 LAKE WASHINGTON CIRCLE, LAWRENCEVILLE GA 30043
1963-048	GREEN, RICHARD LARRY	3924 RIDGEMOOR DRIVE, RAPID CITY SD 57702
2006-058	GREEN, SEAN WILLIAM	2600 AUTUMN LAKE DRIVE, LOUISVILLE KY 40272
1993-066	GREEN, SHAWN DAVID	14755 PRESTON ROAD #830, DALLAS TX 75254
2001-074	GREEN, STEVE	OLD ADD: LONGUEUIL QUE
1993-067	GREEN, TYLER SCOTT	OLD ADD: 5558 SOUTH LANSING CT, ENGLEWOOD CO 80111
2005-075	GREENBERG, ADAM DANIEL	1350 BOSTON POST ROAD, GUILFORD CT 06437
1930-027	GREENBERG, HENRY BENJAMIN 'HANK'	D. SEPTEMBER 4, 1986, BEVERLY HILLS, CALIF.
1979-043	GREENE, ALTAR ALPHONSE	18294 MARLOWE, DETROIT MI 48235
1996-069	GREENE, CHARLES PATRICK	1449 OLDFIELD DRIVE, TALLAHASSEE FL 32308
1989-045	GREENE, IRA THOMAS 'TOMMY'	6001 DALECROSS WAY, GLEN ALLEN VA 23059
2003-064	GREENE, KHALIL THABIT	911 ABNER CREEK ROAD, GREER SC 29651
1924-047	GREENE, NELSON GEORGE	D. APRIL 6, 1983, LEBANON, PA.
1999-076	GREENE, RICHARD DOUGLAS 'RICK'	OLD ADD: MIAMI FL 33101
1996-070	GREENE, TODD ANTHONY	725 PINELEAF COURT, ALPHARETTA GA 30022
1992-043	GREENE, WILLIAM LOUIS 'WILLIE'	OLD ADD: RR 1 BOX 440, HADDOCK GA 31033
1924-048	GREENFIELD, KENT	D. MARCH 14, 1978, GUTHRIE, KY.
1952-039	GREENGRASS, JAMES RAYMOND	232 TALKING ROCK CREEK PKWY DR, CHATSWORTH GA 30705
1985-042	GREENWELL, MICHAEL LEWIS	12250 NORTH RIVER ROAD, ALVA FL 33920
1954-037	GREENWOOD, ROBERT CHANDLER	D. SEPTEMBER 1, 1994, HAYWARD, CALIF.
1977-063	GREER, BRIAN	307 BAGNALL, PLACENTIA CA 92670
1993-068	GREER, KENNETH WILLIAM	OLD ADD: 64 HILLSIDE DRIVE, PORTSMOUTH NH 03801
1994-039	GREER, THURMAN CLYDE 'RUSTY'	4703 PATTERSON LANE, COLLEYVILLE TX 76034
1943-054	GREGG, HAROLD DANA 'HAL'	D. MAY 13, 1991, BISHOP, CALIF.
2003-065	GREGG, KEVIN MARSCHALL	2860 NW HIGHLAND DRIVE, CORVALLIS OR 97330
1987-054	GREGG, WILLIAM THOMAS 'TOMMY'	10 CAMBRIDGE LANE, SHARPSBURG GA 30277
2003-066	GREGORIO, THOMAS ANDREW	66 MACARTHUR AVENUE, STATEN ISLAND NY 10312
1964-038	GREGORY, GROVER LEROY 'LEE'	6456 NORTH TEILMAN, FRESNO CA 93705
1932-034	GREGORY, PAUL EDWIN	D. SEPTEMBER 16, 1999, TUPELO, MISS.
1971-039	GREIF, WILLIAM BRILEY	807 EAST 31ST, AUSTIN TX 78705
2004-083	GREINKE, DONALD ZACKARY 'ZACK'	8629 VISTA PINE COURT, ORLANDO FL 32836
1998-072	GREISINGER, SETH ADAM	6460 OVERBROOK STREET, FALLS CHURCH VA 22043
1940-027	GREMP, LOUIS EDWARD	D. JANUARY 30, 1995, MANTECA, CALIF.
1970-051	GRICH, ROBERT ANTHONY	31 MADISON LANE, COTO DE CAZA CA 92679
1920-042	GRIESENBECK, CARLOS PHILIPPE TIMOTHY	D. MARCH 25, 1953, SAN ANTONIO, TEXAS
1997-069	GRIEVE, BENJAMIN	15 TULIP LANE, SAN CARLOS CA 94070
1970-052	GRIEVE, THOMAS ALAN	4107 CARNATION DRIVE, ARLINGTON TX 76016
1946-038	GRIFFETH, LEON CLIFFORD	PO BOX 51641, DURHAM NC 27717
1989-046	GRIFFEY, GEORGE KENNETH 'JUNIOR'	8815 CONROY ROAD, ORLANDO FL 32835
1973-053	GRIFFEY, GEORGE KENNETH 'KEN'	1102 PORT MOOR WAY, WINTER GARDENS FL 34787
1976-036	GRIFFIN, ALFREDO CLAUDINO	9731 NW 41ST STREET, MIAMI FL 33178
1970-053	GRIFFIN, DOUGLAS LEE	43 HIGHLAND VIEW, IRVINE CA 92715
2005-076	GRIFFIN, JOHN-FORD DAVID	OLD ADD: SARASOTA FL
1928-042	GRIFFIN, MARTIN JOHN	D. NOVEMBER 19, 1951, LOS ANGELES, CALIF.
1979-044	GRIFFIN, MICHAEL LEROY	1620 GROVE AVENUE, WOODLAND CA 95695
1969-070	GRIFFIN, THOMAS JAMES	13147 AVENIDA LA VELENCIA, POWAY CA 92064
1922-049	GRIFFITH, BARTHOLOMEW JOSEPH	D. MAY 5, 1973, BISHOP, CALIF.
1963-049	GRIFFITH, ROBERT DERRELL 'DERRELL'	201 EAST CENTRAL, ANADARKO OK 73005
2003-067	GRIFFITHS, JEREMY RICHARD	120 BEACHDALE DRIVE, AVON LAKE OH 44012
1956-038	GRIGGS, HAROLD LLOYD	D. MAY 10, 2005, TUCSON, ARIZ.
1923-055	GRIGSBY, DENVER CLARENCE	D. NOVEMBER 10, 1973, SAPULPA, OKLA.
1966-040	GRILLI, GUIDO JOHN	250 SLOAN LANE, LOCUST GROVE AR 72550
2000-072	GRILLI, JASON MICHAEL	9037 POINT CYPRESS DRIVE, ORLANDO FL 32836

1975-046 GRILLI, STEPHEN JOSEPH ....8637 BRIAR PATCH, BALDWINSVILLE NY 13027
1954-038 GRIM, ROBERT ANTON....................................D. OCTOBER 23, 1996, SHAWNEE, KAN.
1931-032 GRIMES, EDWARD ADELBERT ....D. OCTOBER 4, 1974, CHICAGO, ILL.
1938-033 GRIMES, OSCAR RAY, JR. ....D. MAY 19, 1993, WESTLAKE, OHIO
1920-043 GRIMES, OSCAR RAY, SR. ....D. MAY 25, 1953, MINERVA, OHIO
1920-044 GRIMES, ROY AUSTIN....................................D. SEPTEMBER 13, 1954, HANOVERTON, OHIO
1989-047 GRIMSLEY, JASON ALAN....................................500 WATERSIDE DRIVE, LAFAYETTE LA 70503
1951-034 GRIMSLEY, ROSS ALBERT....................................D. FEBRUARY 6, 1994, MEMPHIS, TENN.
1971-040 GRIMSLEY, ROSS ALBERT....................................92 CONEWANGO COURT, OWINGS MILLS MD 21117
1934-042 GRISSOM, LEO THEO ....D. OCTOBER 4, 1998, CORNING, CALIF.
1989-048 GRISSOM, MARQUIS DEAN....................................110 FIDDLERS RIDGE, FAIRBURN GA 30213
1946-039 GRISSOM, MARVIN EDWARD ....D. SEPTEMBER 19, 2005, RED BLUFF, CALIF.
1952-040 GROAT, RICHARD MORROW ....133 ROBERT DRIVE, BOLIVAR PA 15923
1956-039 GROB, CONRAD GEORGE ....D. SEPTEMBER 28, 1997, MADISON, WISC.
1941-040 GRODZICKI, JOHN ....D. MAY 2, 1998, DAYTONA BEACH, FLA.
1941-041 GROMEK, STEPHEN JOSEPH....................................D. MARCH 12, 2002, CLINTON TWP., MACOMB CO., MICH.
1992-044 GROOM, WEDSEL GARY 'BUDDY'....................................1991 SAINT ANDREWS DRIVE, OVILLA TX 75154
1930-028 GROSKLOSS, HOWARD HOFFMAN 'HOWDIE'.....D. JULY 15, 2006, VERO BEACH, FLA.
1955-050 GROSS, DONALD JOHN....................................1299 EAST FARRAND ROAD, CLIO MI 48420
1925-040 GROSS, EWELL 'TURKEY'....................................D. JANUARY 22, 1936, DALLAS, TEXAS
2004-084 GROSS, GABRIEL JORDAN....................................754 BERRY LANE, AUBURN AL 36830
1973-054 GROSS, GREGORY EUGENE ....802 HALLOWELL DRIVE, WEST CHESTER PA 19382
1983-067 GROSS, KEVIN FRANK....................................2058 NORTH MILLS AVENUE PMB 144, CLAREMONT CA 91711
1990-060 GROSS, KIP LEE ....2015 RIDGEVIEW COURT, REDLANDS CA 92373
1976-037 GROSS, WAYNE DALE ....45 LEONARD COURT, DANVILLE CA 94526
1952-041 GROSSMAN, HARLEY JOSEPH....................................D. SEPTEMBER 5, 2003, EVANSVILLE, IND.
1963-050 GROTE, GERALD WAYNE 'JERRY' ....5807 BABCOCK ROAD #215, SAN ANTONIO TX 78240
1992-045 GROTEWOLD, JEFFREY SCOTT ....PO BOX 3469, CRESTLINE CA 92325
1947-040 GROTH, ERNEST WILLIAM ....D. DECEMBER 27, 2004, BEAVER, PA.
1946-040 GROTH, JOHN THOMAS ....170 NORTH OCEAN BLVD #307, PALM BEACH FL 33480
1995-087 GROTT, MATTHEW ALAN....................................19431 NORTH CONCHO CIRCLE, SUN CITY AZ 85373
1940-028 GROVE, ORVAL LEROY....................................D. APRIL 20, 1992, CARMICHAEL, CALIF.
1925-041 GROVE, ROBERT MOSES 'LEFTY'....................................D. MAY 22, 1975, NORWALK, OHIO
1972-042 GRUBB, JOHN RAYMOND....................................6618 BEL LAC DRIVE, CHESTER VA 23831
1920-045 GRUBBS, THOMAS DILLARD....................................D. JANUARY 28, 1986, LEXINGTON, KY.
1931-033 GRUBE, FRANKLIN THOMAS ....D. JULY 2, 1945, NEW YORK, N.Y.
1984-046 GRUBER, KELLY WAYNE....................................3300 BEE CAVE ROAD #650-227, AUSTIN TX 78746
1995-088 GRUDZIELANEK, MARK JAMES....................................PO BOX 1581, RANCHO SANTA FE CA 92067
1996-071 GRUNDT, KENNETH ALLAN ....4814 WEST PARKER AVENUE, CHICAGO IL 60639
1955-051 GRUNWALD, ALFRED HENRY....................................21001 PLUMMER STREET #11, CHATSWORTH CA 91311
2002-072 GRYBOSKI, KEVIN JOHN ....130 MAFFETT STREET, WILKES-BARRE PA 18705
1938-034 GRYSKA, SIGMUND STANLEY....................................D. AUGUST 27, 1994, HINES, ILL.
1998-073 GRZANICH, MICHAEL EDWARD....................................170 HIGHLAND COVE, JACKSON MS 39212
1961-039 GRZENDA, JOSEPH CHARLES ....202 HILLCREST DRIVE, GOULDSBORO PA 18424
1982-051 GUANTE, CECILIO (MAGALLANE)....................................JALISCO 67 SIMON BOLIVAR SANTO DOMINGO, DOM REP
1993-069 GUARDADO, EDWARD ADRIAN....................................11268 OVERLOOK POINT, TUSTIN CA 92782
1999-077 GUBANICH, CREIGHTON WADE....................................10 GALICIA DRIVE, PHOENIXVILLE PA 19460
1984-047 GUBICZA, MARK STEVEN ....11808 MACODA LANE, CHATSWORTH CA 91311
1929-047 GUDAT, MARVIN JOHN ....D. MARCH 2, 1954, LOS ANGELES, CALIF.
1937-045 GUERRA, FERMIN ROMERO 'MICKEY' ....D. OCTOBER 9, 1992, MIAMI BEACH, FLA.
1992-046 GUERRERO, JUAN ANTONIO ....LAS PALMAS 22, PARTE ATRAS BO. GRINGO HAINA, DOM REP
1973-055 GUERRERO, MARIO MIGUEL....................................OLD ADD: CALLE DUARTE #450, SANTO DOMINGO DOM REP
1978-053 GUERRERO, PEDRO....................................OLD ADD: 10720 NW 66TH STREET #408, MIAMI FL 33178
1996-072 GUERRERO, VLADIMIR....................................OLD ADD: NIZAO BANI DOM REP
1996-073 GUERRERO, WILTON ....OLD ADD: NIZAO BANI DOM REP
2004-085 GUERRIER, MATTHEW OLSON....................................1018 FAIRMONT CIRCLE, BIRMINGHAM AL 35242
1984-048 GUETTERMAN, ARTHUR LEE 'LEE'....................................108 1/2 EAST BROADWAY STREET, LENOIR CITY TN 37771
1997-070 GUEVARA, GIOMAR ANTONIO ....OLD ADD: MIRANDA VENEZUELA
1975-047 GUIDRY, RONALD AMES....................................PO BOX 666, SCOTT LA 70583
2002-073 GUIEL, AARON COLIN....................................OLD ADD: LANGLEY BC
1998-074 GUILLEN, CARLOS ALFONSO ....OLD ADD: ARAGUA VENEZUELA
1997-071 GUILLEN, JOSE MANUEL....................................OLD ADD: SAN CRISTOBAL DOM REP
1985-043 GUILLEN, OSWALDO JOSE 'OZZIE' ....19485 40TH COURT, GOLDEN BEACH FL 33160
1964-039 GUINDON, ROBERT JOSEPH ....437 MARSH CREEK ROAD, VENICE FL 34292
1968-030 GUINN, DRANNON EUGENE 'SKIP'....................................RURAL ROUTE 3 BOX 790, STILWELL OK 74960
1946-041 GUINTINI, BENJAMIN JOHN ....D. DECEMBER 2, 1998, ROSEVILLE, CALIF.
1940-029 GUISE, WITT ORISON....................................D. AUGUST 13, 1968, NORTH LITTLE ROCK, ARK.
1997-072 GULAN, MICHAEL WATTS....................................4409 FAIRWAY DRIVE, STEUBENVILLE OH 43952
1978-054 GULDEN, BRADLEY LEE ....15820 LUNDSTEAD, CARVER MN 55315
1970-054 GULLETT, DONALD EDWARD ....194 KINGSWAY DRIVE, SOUTH SHORE KY 41175
1923-056 GULLEY, THOMAS JEFFERSON....................................D. NOVEMBER 24, 1966, ST. CHARLES, ARK.
1930-029 GULLIC, TEDD JASPER....................................D. JANUARY 28, 2000, WEST PLAINS, MO.
1979-045 GULLICKSON, WILLIAM LEE ....3 BANCHARY COURT, PALM BEACH GARDENS FL 33418
1982-052 GULLIVER, GLENN JAMES ....8123 CORTLAND, ALLEN PARK MI 48101
1935-039 GUMBERT, HARRY EDWARD....................................D. JANUARY 4, 1995, WIMBERLEY, TEXAS
1982-053 GUMPERT, DAVID LAWRENCE....................................68371 FLEETWOOD DRIVE, SOUTH HAVEN MI 49090
1936-033 GUMPERT, RANDALL PENNINGTON....................................49 SCHOOL STREET, DOUGLASSVILLE PA 19518
1990-061 GUNDERSON, ERIC ANDREW....................................19809 SE 10TH STREET, CAMAS WA 98607
1970-055 GURA, LARRY CYRIL....................................PO BOX 94, LITCHFIELD PARK AZ 85340
1939-045 GUSTINE, FRANK WILLIAM ....D. APRIL 1, 1991, DAVENPORT, IOWA
1972-043 GUTH, CHARLES HENRY 'BUCKY' ....202 MORRIS DR, SALISBURY MD 21801
2004-086 GUTHRIE, JEREMY ....OLD ADD: LAS VEGAS NV
1989-049 GUTHRIE, MARK ANDREW....................................4710 HIDDEN FOREST LANE, SARASOTA FL 34235
1967-040 GUTIERREZ, CESAR DARIO ....D. JANUARY 22, 2005, MARACAIBO, VENEZUELA
2005-077 GUTIERREZ, FRANKLIN RAFAEL....................................OLD ADD: CARACAS VENEZUELA
1983-068 GUTIERREZ, JOAQUIN FERNANDO....................................OLD ADD: 631 126TH COURT, MIAMI FL 33182

1993-070	GUTIERREZ, RICARDO 'RICKY'	1355 NW 143RD AVENUE, PEMBROKE PINES FL 33028
1936-034	GUTTERIDGE, DONALD JOSEPH	804 LAKEVIEW DRIVE, PITTSBURG KS 66762
2006-059	GUZMAN, ANGEL MOISES	OLD ADD: CARACAS VENEZ
1999-078	GUZMAN, CRISTIAN ANTONIO	OLD ADD: SANTO DOMINGO DOM REP
1991-067	GUZMAN, DIONINI RAMON 'JOHNNY'	HATILLO PALMA #215, MONTECRISTI, DOM REP
1999-079	GUZMAN, DOMINGO SERRANO	OLD ADD: SAN CRISTOBAL DOM REP
1999-080	GUZMAN, EDWARDS	OLD ADD: 1150 EAST HERNDON AVENUE, FRESNO CA 93720
2004-087	GUZMAN, FREDDY ANTONIO	OLD ADD: SANTO DOMINGO DOM REP
2000-073	GUZMAN, GERALDO MORENO	OLD ADD: TENARES DOMINICAN REP
2006-060	GUZMAN, IRVIN JOEL VIGO	OLD ADD: SAN PEDRO DE MACORIS DOM REP
1985-044	GUZMAN, JOSE ALBERTO	OLD ADD: 990 N. LAKE SHORE DR #5C, CHICAGO IL 60611
1991-068	GUZMAN, JUAN ANDRES	176 DOCKSIDE CIRCLE, WESTON FL 33327
1969-071	GUZMAN, SANTIAGO DONOVAN	OLD ADD: ENS REST. M4TA #12, SAN PEDRO DE MAC DOM REP
1981-047	GWOSDZ, DOUGLAS WAYNE	2108 ROSE ROAD, PEARLAND TX 77581
1982-054	GWYNN, ANTHONY KEITH	15643 BOULDER RIDGE LANE, POWAY CA 92064
2006-061	GWYNN, ANTHONY KEITH, JR.	15643 BOULDER RIDGE LANE, POWAY CA 92064
1987-055	GWYNN, CHRISTOPHER KARLTON	10975 HILLSIDE ROAD, ALTA LOMA CA 91737
1933-021	GYSELMAN, RICHARD REYNALD	D. SEPTEMBER 20, 1990, SEATTLE, WASH.

H

1999-081	HAAD, YAMID SALCEDO	5704 NW 24TH STREET, MARGATE FL 33063
1937-046	HAAS, BERTHOLD JOHN	D. JUNE 23, 1999, TAMPA, FLA.
1976-038	HAAS, BRYAN EDMOND 'MOOSE'	4351 EAST LARIAT LANE, PHOENIX AZ 85024
1957-027	HAAS, GEORGE EDWIN 'EDDIE'	4025 OLD US HIGHWAY45 SOUTH, PADUCAH KY 42003
1925-042	HAAS, GEORGE WILLIAM 'MULE'	D. JUNE 30, 1974, NEW ORLEANS, LA.
1991-069	HAAS, ROBERT DAVID 'DAVE'	PO BOX 5770, MESA AZ 85211
1951-035	HABENICHT, ROBERT JULIUS	D. DECEMBER 24, 1980, RICHMOND, VA.
1985-045	HABYAN, JOHN GABRIEL	4 DORFER LANE, NESCONSET NY 11767
1932-035	HACK, STANLEY CAMFIELD	D. DECEMBER 15, 1979, DIXON, ILL.
1971-041	HACKER, RICHARD WARREN 'RICH'	2400 18TH FAIRWAY, BELLEVILLE IL 62221
1948-043	HACKER, WARREN LOUIS	D. MAY 22, 2002, LENZBURG, ILL.
1999-082	HACKMAN, LUTHER GEAN	1406 12TH AVENUE NORTH, COLUMBUS MS 39701
1952-042	HADDIX, HARVEY	D. JANUARY 8, 1994, SPRINGFIELD, OHIO
1926-033	HADLEY, IRVING DARIUS 'BUMP'	D. FEBRUARY 15, 1963, LYNN, MASS.
1958-041	HADLEY, KENT WILLIAM	D. MARCH 10, 2005, POCATELLO. IDAHO
1943-055	HAEFNER, MILTON ARNOLD 'MICKEY'	D. JANUARY 3, 1995, NEW ATHENS, ILL.
2006-062	HAEGER, CHARLES WALLIS	9575 JESSICA J LANE, PLYMOUTH MI 48170
1924-049	HAFEY, CHARLES JAMES 'CHICK'	D. JULY 2, 1973, CALISTOGA, CALIF.
1935-040	HAFEY, DANIEL ALBERT 'BUD'	D. JULY 27, 1986, SACRAMENTO, CALIF.
1939-046	HAFEY, THOMAS FRANCIS	D. OCTOBER 2, 1996, EL CERRITO, CALIF.
2002-074	HAFNER, TRAVIS LEE	5133 HIGHWAY 200, SYKESTON ND 58486
1983-069	HAGEN, KEVIN EUGENE	24826 SOUTHEAST 164TH AVENUE, KENT WA 98042
1968-031	HAGUE, JOE CLARENCE	D. NOVEMBER 5, 1994, SAN ANTONIO, TEXAS
1969-072	HAHN, DONALD ANTONE	1046 BOISE DR, CAMPBELL CA 95008
1952-043	HAHN, FREDERICK ALOYS	D. AUGUST 16, 1984, VALHALLA, N.Y.
1940-030	HAHN, RICHARD FREDERICK	D. NOVEMBER 5, 1992, ORLANDO, FLA.
1923-057	HAINES, HENRY LUTHER 'HINKEY'	D. JANUARY 9, 1979, SHARON HILL, PA.
1973-056	HAIRSTON, JERRY WAYNE	7831 WEST PEACE PIPE ROAD, TUCSON AZ 85743
1998-075	HAIRSTON, JERRY WAYNE	7831 WEST PEACE PIPE ROAD, TUCSON AZ 85743
1969-073	HAIRSTON, JOHN LOUIS	4226 NE 22ND STREET, PORTLAND OR 97211
1951-036	HAIRSTON, SAMUEL HARDING	D. OCTOBER 31, 1997, BIRMINGHAM, ALA.
2004-088	HAIRSTON, SCOTT ALEXANDER	7831 WEST PEACE PIPE ROAD, TUCSON AZ 85743
1941-042	HAJDUK, CHESTER	D. JULY 4, 2006, CHICAGO, ILL.
1995-089	HAJEK, DAVID VINCENT	5190 BITTERWEED LANE, COLORADO SPRINGS CO 80917
1998-076	HALAMA, JOHN THADEUZ	6711 EIGHTH AVENUE, BROOKLYN NY 11220
1931-034	HALE, ARVEL ODELL 'ODELL'	D. JUNE 9, 1980, EL DORADO, ARK.
1974-043	HALE, JOHN STEVEN	2200 PINE STREET, BAKERSFIELD CA 93301
1955-052	HALE, ROBERT HOUSTON	616 OVERHILL AVENUE, PARK RIDGE IL 60068
1920-046	HALE, SAMUEL DOUGLAS	D. SEPTEMBER 6, 1974, WHEELER, TEXAS
1989-050	HALE, WALTER WILLIAM 'CHIP'	190 DRIFTWOOD COURT, APTOS CA 95003
1974-044	HALICKI, EDWARD LOUIS	19605 PADDLE WHEEL LANE, RENO NV 89511
1981-048	HALL, ALBERT	1628 SPAULDING RD, BIRMINGHAM AL 35211
1986-059	HALL, ANDREW CLARK 'DREW'	11105 SUCCESS LANE, LOUISVILLE KY 40229
1943-056	HALL, IRVIN GLADSTONE	D. DECEMBER 12, 2006, BALTIMORE, MD.
1963-051	HALL, JIMMIE RANDOLPH	8622 CARTER GROVE DRIVE, ELM CITY NC 27822
1948-044	HALL, JOHN SYLVESTER	D. JANUARY 17, 1995, MIDWEST CITY, OKLA.
1994-040	HALL, JOSEPH GEROY	OLD ADD: 1034 DUNDALE ROAD, PADUCAH KY 42003
2003-068	HALL, JOSHUA ALAN	3512 HAWKINS MILL ROAD, LYNCHBURG VA 24503
1981-049	HALL, MELVIN	OLD ADD: RURAL ROUTE 1 ROUTE 90, CAYAGA NY 13034
1994-041	HALL, MICHAEL DARREN 'DARREN'	3028 MONET COURT, FLOWER MOUND TX 75028
1952-044	HALL, RICHARD WALLACE	403 PLUMBRIDGE COURT #202, TIMONIUM MD 21093
1949-030	HALL, ROBERT LOUIS	D. MARCH 12, 1983, ST. PETERSBURG, FLA.
1968-032	HALL, THOMAS EDWARD	3592 LILLIAN AVENUE, RIVERSIDE CA 92504
2000-074	HALL, TOBY JASON	17209 JOURNEYS END DRIVE, ODESSA FL 33556
2002-075	HALL, WILLIAM	1850 HIGHWAY 371 SOUTH, NETTLETON MS 38801
1954-039	HALL, WILLIAM LEE	D. JANUARY 1, 1986, MOULTRIE, GA.
1998-077	HALLADAY, HARRY LEROY 'ROY'	4624 SYLVIA LANE, ERIE CO 80516
1925-043	HALLAHAN, WILLIAM ANTHONY	D. JULY 8, 1981, BINGHAMTON, N.Y.
1961-040	HALLER, THOMAS FRANK	D. NOVEMBER 26, 2004, LOS ANGELES, CALIF.
1940-031	HALLETT, JACK PRICE	D. JUNE 11, 1982, TOLEDO, OHIO
2004-089	HALSEY, BRADFORD A.	OLD ADD: AUSTIN TX
1997-073	HALTER, SHANE DAVID	2701 WEST 140TH STREET, LEAWOOD KS 66224
1922-050	HAMANN, ELMER JOSEPH 'DOC'	D. JANUARY 11, 1973, MILWAUKEE, WISC.
1971-042	HAMBRIGHT, ROGER DEE	8709 NE 37TH AVENUE, VANCOUVER WA 98665

1926-034	HAMBY, JAMES SANFORD 'SANDY'	D. OCTOBER 21, 1991, SPRINGFIELD, ILL.
1993-071	HAMELIN, ROBERT JAMES	51 PATTON COURT, CONCORD NC 28025
2006-063	HAMELS, COLBERT RICHARD	13235 MIDBLUFF AVENUE, SAN DIEGO CA 92128
1988-059	HAMILTON, DARRYL QUINN	4721 SOUTHWIND DRIVE, BATON ROUGE LA 70816
1972-044	HAMILTON, DAVID EDWARD	9464 CHERRY HILLS LN, SAN RAMON CA 94583
1962-051	HAMILTON, JACK EDWIN	109 ROCKY ROAD, RIDGEDALE MO 65739
1986-060	HAMILTON, JEFFREY ROBERT	2485 GOLFVIEW CIRCLE, FENTON MI 48430
1994-042	HAMILTON, JOHNS JOSEPH 'JOEY'	4035 WELLINGTON MIST POINT, DULUTH GA 30097
1961-041	HAMILTON, STEVE ABSHER	D. DECEMBER 2, 1997, MOREHEAD, KY.
1952-045	HAMILTON, THOMAS BALL	D. NOVEMBER 29, 1973, TYLER, TEXAS
1957-028	HAMLIN, KENNETH LEE	5242 COUNTY ROAD 413, MCMILLAN MI 49853
1933-022	HAMLIN, LUKE DANIEL 'HOT POTATO'	D. FEBRUARY 18, 1978, CLARE, MICH.
1970-056	HAMM, PETER WHITFIELD	525 LOCKHART GULCH ROAD, SANTA CRUZ CA 95060
1981-050	HAMMAKER, CHARLTON ATLEE 'ATLEE'	2739 STUBB BLUFF RD, KNOXVILLE TN 37932
2006-064	HAMMEL, JASON AARON	3925 RED FOX PLACE SE, PORT ORCHARD WA 98366
2003-069	HAMMOCK, ROBERT WADE 'ROB'	4200 CHATHAM VIEW DRIVE, BUFORD GA 30518
1990-062	HAMMOND, CHRISTOPHER ANDREW	908 OLD HWY 431, WEDOWEE AL 36278
1982-055	HAMMOND, STEVEN BEN	11104 LAKE BUTLER BLVD, WINDERMERE FL 34786
1993-072	HAMMONDS, JEFFREY BRYAN	2950 MEADOW LANE, FORT LAUDERDALE FL 33331
1944-054	HAMNER, GRANVILLE WILBUR 'GRANNY'	D. SEPTEMBER 12, 1993, PHILADELPHIA, PA.
1946-042	HAMNER, RALPH CONANT	D. MAY 22, 2001, LITTLE ROCK, ARK.
1945-041	HAMNER, WESLEY GARVIN 'GAR'	D. DECEMBER 15, 2003, RICHMOND, VA.
2006-065	HAMPSON, JUSTIN MICHAEL	6982 EAST FRONTAGE ROAD, WORDEN IL 62097
1974-045	HAMPTON, ISAAC BERNARD 'IKE'	2 WALDEN, LADERA RANCH CA 94028
1993-073	HAMPTON, MICHAEL WILLIAM	5410 SOUTH MAGNOLIA AVENUE, HOMOSASSA FL 34448
1955-053	HAMRIC, ODBERT HERMAN 'BERT'	D. AUGUST 8, 1984, SPRINGBORO, OHIO
1943-057	HAMRICK, RAYMOND BERNARD	349 ST. ANDREWS DRIVE, FRANKLIN TN 37069
2005-078	HAMULACK, TIMOTHY WILLIAM A.	530 CAMPBELL ROAD, YORK PA 17402
1940-032	HANCKEN, MORRIS MEDLOCK 'BUDDY'	D. FEBRUARY 15, 2007, ORANGE, TEXAS
1949-031	HANCOCK, FRED JAMES	D. MARCH 12, 1986, CLEARWATER, FLA.
2002-076	HANCOCK, JOSHUA MORGAN	D. APRIL 29, 2007, SAINT LOUIS, MO.
1995-090	HANCOCK, LELAND DAVID	8338 BRENTWOOD BLVD, BRENTWOOD CA 94513
1978-055	HANCOCK, RONALD GARRY	2217 GREEN HILLS DR, VALRICO FL 33594
1996-074	HANCOCK, RYAN LEE 'LEE'	637 EAST 12860 SOUTH, DRAPER UT 84020
1970-057	HAND, RICHARD ALLEN 'RICH'	3824 BAY COURT, FORT WORTH TX 76179
1946-043	HANDLEY, EUGENE LOUIS	393 HOSPITAL ROAD #16, NEWPORT BEACH CA 92663
1936-035	HANDLEY, LEE ELMER	D. APRIL 8, 1970, PITTSBURGH, PA.
1964-040	HANDRAHAN, JAMES VERNON 'VERN'	36 NEWLAND CRESCENT CHARLOTTETOWN PE, C1A 4H5 CANADA
1965-034	HANDS, WILLIAM ALFRED	PO BOX 334, ORIENT NY 11957
1953-031	HANEBRINK, HARRY ALOYSIUS	D. SEPTEMBER 9, 1996, BRIDGETON, MO.
1991-070	HANEY, CHRISTOPHER DEANE	PO BOX 135, BARBOURSVILLE VA 22923
1922-051	HANEY, FRED GIRARD	D. NOVEMBER 9, 1977, BEVERLY HILLS, CALIF.
1992-047	HANEY, TODD MICHAEL	5404 POINTWOOD CIRCLE, WACO TX 76710
1966-041	HANEY, WALLACE LARRY 'LARRY'	PO BOX 157, BARBOURSVILLE VA 22923
1927-043	HANKINS, DONALD WAYNE	D. MAY 16, 1963, WINSTON-SALEM, N.C.
1961-042	HANKINS, JAY NELSON	26509 EAST 150 HWY, GREENWOOD MO 64034
1975-048	HANNA, PRESTON LEE	5555 MAYFAIR DR, PENSACOLA FL 32506
2006-066	HANNAHAN, JOHN JOSEPH JACK	1995 BAYARD AVENUE, SAINT PAUL MN 55116
1976-039	HANNAHS, GERALD ELLIS	1411 ANDOVER RIDGE, LITTLE ROCK AR 72227
1962-052	HANNAN, JAMES JOHN	3907 CHERRY HILL WAY, ANNANDALE VA 22003
1939-047	HANNING, LOY VERNON	D. JULY 8, 1986, ANACONDA, MO.
2006-067	HANSACK, DEVERN M.	OLD ADD: PEARL LAGOON NICARAGUA
1995-091	HANSELL, GREGORY MICHAEL	1791 WEST PRESCOTT DRIVE, CHANDLER AZ 85248
1944-055	HANSEN, ANDREW VIGGO	D. FEBRUARY 2, 2002, LAKE WORTH, FLA.
2005-079	HANSEN, CRAIG R	OLD ADD: GLEN COVE NY
1990-063	HANSEN, DAVID ANDREW	9852 ORCHARD LANE, VILLA PARK CA 92861
1951-037	HANSEN, DOUGLAS WILLIAM	D. SEPTEMBER 16, 1999, OREM, UTAH
1997-074	HANSEN, JED RAMON	1534 12TH LANE FI, FOX ISLAND WA 98333
1974-046	HANSEN, ROBERT JOSEPH	19 NORTH KELSEY AVE, EVANSVILLE IN 47711
1958-042	HANSEN, RONALD LAVERN	13602 ALLISTON DRIVE, BALDWIN MD 21013
1930-030	HANSEN, ROY EMIL FREDERICK 'SNIPE'	D. SEPTEMBER 11, 1978, CHICAGO, ILL.
1943-058	HANSKI, DONALD THOMAS	D. SEPTEMBER 2, 1957, WORTH, ILL.
1921-038	HANSON, EARL SYLVESTER 'OLLIE'	D. AUGUST 19, 1951, CLIFTON, N.J.
1988-060	HANSON, ERIK BRIAN	3939 ERIE AVENUE #4020, CINCINNATI OH 45208
1942-046	HANYZEWSKI, EDWARD MICHAEL	D. OCTOBER 8, 1991, FARGO, N.D.
1923-058	HAPPENNY, JOHN CLIFFORD	D. DECEMBER 29, 1988, CORAL SPRINGS, FLA.
2002-077	HARANG, AARON MICHAEL	6411 GLENROY STREET, SAN DIEGO CA 92120
2003-070	HARDEN, JAMES RICHARD 'RICH'	OLD ADD: VICTORIA BC
1928-043	HARDER, MELVIN LEROY	D. OCTOBER 20, 2002, CHARDON, OHIO
1967-041	HARDIN, JAMES WARREN	D. MARCH 9, 1991, KEY WEST, FLA.
1952-046	HARDIN, WILLIAM EDGAR 'BUD'	D. JULY 28, 1997, RANCHO SANTA FE, CALIF.
1996-075	HARDTKE, JASON ROBERT	20052 LOWER SKYRIDGE DRIVE, GROVELAND CA 95321
1958-043	HARDY, CARROLL WILLIAM	1514 WHITEHALL DRIVE, LONGMONT CO 80501
1951-038	HARDY, FRANCIS JOSEPH 'RED'	D. AUGUST 15, 2003, PHOENIX, ARIZ.
1974-047	HARDY, HOWARD LAWRENCE 'LARRY'	7 JENNIFER COURT, TROPHY CLUB TX 76262
2005-080	HARDY, JAMES JERRY 'J.J.'	6202 EAST 25TH STREET, TUCSON AZ 85711
1989-051	HARDY, JOHN GRAYDON	1260 NW 192ND LANE, PEMBROKE PINES FL 33029
1991-071	HARE, SHAWN ROBERT	1975 DEER PATH TRAIL, OXFORD MI 48371
2003-071	HAREN, DANIEL JOHN	1217 WALNUT AVENUE, WEST COVINA CA 91790
1965-035	HARGAN, STEVEN LOWELL	2502 MORONGO TRAIL, PALM SPRINGS CA 92264
1980-047	HARGESHEIMER, ALAN HERBERT	107 NORTH EVANSTON, ARLINGTON HEIGHTS IL 60004
1979-046	HARGIS, GARY LYNN	157 GEMINI AVE, LOMPOC CA 93436
1923-059	HARGRAVE, WILLIAM MCKINLEY 'PINKY'	D. OCTOBER 3, 1942, FT. WAYNE, IND.
1923-060	HARGREAVES, CHARLES RUSSELL	D. MAY 9, 1979, NEPTUNE, N.J.
1974-048	HARGROVE, DUDLEY MICHAEL 'MIKE'	3925 RAMBLEWOOD ROAD, RICHFIELD OH 44286
1995-092	HARIKKALA, TIMOTHY ALAN	W6132 EVERGLADE ROAD, GREENVILLE WI 54942

1988-061	HARKEY, MICHAEL ANTHONY	23930 STRANGE CREEK DRIVE, DIAMOND BAR CA 91765
1961-043	HARKNESS, THOMAS WILLIAM 'TIM'	OLD ADD: 15095 12TH CONCESSION, NOBLETON ON CANADA
1975-049	HARLOW, LARRY DUANE	2880 BROKEN ARROW, NORCO CA 92860
1941-043	HARMAN, WILLIAM BELL	9 GUYENNE ROAD, WILMINGTON DE 19807
1954-040	HARMON, CHARLES BYRON	6035A RIDGEACRE DR, CINCINNATI OH 45237
1967-042	HARMON, TERRY WALTER	OAKWOOD DR, MEDFORD NJ 08055
1988-062	HARNISCH, PETER THOMAS	96 HOMINY HILL ROAD, COLTS NECK NJ 07722
2006-068	HARPER, BRANDON SCOTT	1601 NORTH VEGA DRIVE, HOBBS NM 88240
1979-047	HARPER, BRIAN DAVID	8319 EAST SHETLAND TRAIL, SCOTTSDALE AZ 85258
1980-048	HARPER, TERRY JOE	4225 JAILETTE ROAD, COLLEGE PARK GA 30349
1962-053	HARPER, THOMAS	5 COW HILL ROAD, SHARON MA 02067
2000-075	HARPER, TRAVIS BOYD	4209 MIDWAY ROAD, YAWKEY WV 25573
1969-074	HARRAH, COLBERT DALE 'TOBY'	316 LEEWOOD CIRCLE, AZLE TX 76020
1969-075	HARRELL, JOHN ROBERT	756 ERIE CIR, MILPITAS CA 95035
1935-041	HARRELL, RAYMOND JAMES	D. JANUARY 28, 1984, ALEXANDRIAS, LA.
1955-054	HARRELL, WILLIAM	253 MOUNT HOPE DRIVE, ALBANY NY 12202
1965-036	HARRELSON, DERREL MCKINLEY 'BUD'	357 RIDGEFIELD DRIVE, HAUPPAUGE NY 11788
1963-052	HARRELSON, KENNETH SMITH 'HAWK'	OLD ADD: 9006 SHAWN PARK PLACE, ORLANDO FL 32819
1968-033	HARRELSON, WILLIAM CHARLES	6900 KIMBERLY AVENUE, BAKERSFIELD CA 93308
1998-078	HARRIGER, DENNIS SCOTT	902 NORTH WATER STREET, KITTANNING PA 16201
1925-044	HARRINGTON, ANDREW MATTHEW	D. JANUARY 26, 1979, BOISE, IDAHO
1963-053	HARRINGTON, CHARLES MICHAEL 'MIKE'	135 SCENIC DRIVE, HATTIESBURG MS 39401
1953-032	HARRINGTON, WILLIAM WOMBLE	7219 CLEVELAND SCHOOL ROAD, GARNER NC 27529
1967-043	HARRIS, ALONZO	7378 TYLER LANE, FONTANA CA 92336
1925-046	HARRIS, ANTHONY SPENCER	D. JULY 3, 1982, MINNEAPOLIS, MINN.
1955-055	HARRIS, BOYD GAIL 'GAIL'	9008 WEIR STREET, MANASSAS VA 20110
2004-090	HARRIS, BRENDAN MICHAEL	30 FOX HOLLOW LANE, QUEENSBURY NY 12804
1941-044	HARRIS, CHALMER LUMAN 'LUM'	D. NOVEMBER 11, 1996, PELL CITY, ALA.
1948-045	HARRIS, CHARLES 'BUBBA'	PO BOX 159, NOBLETON FL 34263
1925-045	HARRIS, DAVID STANLEY	D. SEPTEMBER 18, 1973, ATLANTA, GA.
1991-072	HARRIS, DONALD	916 HUBERT, WACO TX 76704
1981-051	HARRIS, GREG ALLEN	PO BOX 2665, ORLEANS MA 02653
1988-063	HARRIS, GREGORY WADE	OLD ADD: 180 2ND AVENUE SE, ST. PETERSBURG FL 33701
1936-036	HARRIS, HERBERT BENJAMIN	D. JANUARY 18, 1991, CRYSTAL LAKE, ILL.
1996-076	HARRIS, HERNANDO PETROCELLI 'PEP'	995 TEN OAKS DRIVE, LANCASTER SC 29720
1968-034	HARRIS, JAMES WILLIAM 'BILLY'	114 WEST BRANDYWINE CIRCLE, WILMINGTON NC 28403
2005-081	HARRIS, JEFFREY AUSTIN	OLD ADD: SAN PABLO CA
1979-048	HARRIS, JOHN THOMAS	OLD ADD: 1720 SHELDON STREET, CLOVIS NM 88101
1988-064	HARRIS, LEONARD ANTHONY 'LENNY'	7435 NORTH AUGUSTA DRIVE, HIALEAH FL 33015
1940-033	HARRIS, MAURICE CHARLES 'MICKEY'	D. APRIL 15, 1971, FARMINGTON, MICH.
1990-064	HARRIS, REGINALD ALLEN	35 ASHLEIGH DRIVE, WAYNESBORO VA 22980
1938-035	HARRIS, ROBERT ARTHUR	D. AUGUST 8, 1989, NORTH PLATTE, NEB.
1941-045	HARRIS, ROBERT NED	D. DECEMBER 18, 1976, WEST PALM BEACH, FLA.
1989-052	HARRIS, TYRONE EUGENE 'GENE'	OLD ADD: 1267 NE 16TH AVENUE, OKEECHOBEE FL 33472
1972-045	HARRIS, VICTOR LANIER	5420 GARTH AVENUE, LOS ANGELES CA 90056
1970-058	HARRIS, WALTER FRANCIS 'BUDDY'	2305 CAROL LANE, NORRISTOWN PA 19401
2001-075	HARRIS, WILLIAM CHARLES 'WILLIE'	OLD ADD: CAIRO GA
1923-061	HARRIS, WILLIAM MILTON	D. AUGUST 21, 1965, INDIAN TRAIL, N.C.
1957-029	HARRIS, WILLIAM THOMAS	322 SOUTH REED, KENNEWICK WA 99336
1965-037	HARRISON, CHARLES WILLIAM	222 BUCKSKIN ROAD, ABILENE TX 79602
1955-056	HARRISON, ROBERT LEE	253 BRIERLEY WAY, INDIANAPOLIS IN 46032
1972-046	HARRISON, RORIC EDWARD	1 OCEAN HEIGHTS DRIVE, NEWPORT COAST CA 92657
1965-038	HARRISON, THOMAS JAMES	2932 CHANNING WAY, LOS ALAMITOS CA 90720
1920-047	HARRISS, WILLIAM JENNINGS BRYAN 'SLIM'	D. SEPTEMBER 19, 1963, TEMPLE, TEXAS
1945-042	HARRIST, EARL	D. SEPTEMBER 7, 1998, SIMSBORO, LA.
1937-047	HARSHANEY, SAMUEL	D. FEBRUARY 1, 2001, SAN ANTONIO, TEXAS
1948-046	HARSHMAN, JOHN ELVIN 'JACK'	320 YUKON TERRACE, GEORGETOWN TX 78628
2003-072	HART, BODHI J.	181 CRESTVIEW COURT, WATSONVILLE CA 95076
1980-049	HART, JAMES MICHAEL 'MIKE'	4395 18TH STREET NE, NAPLES FL 34120
1963-054	HART, JAMES RAY 'JIM RAY'	17074 TEMPLETON LANE, LATHROP CA 95330
2002-078	HART, JASON WYATT	3202 SOUTH WESTWARD AVENUE, SPRINGFIELD MO 65807
1989-053	HART, JOHN HENRY	5205 LATROBE DRIVE, WINDERMERE FL 34786
2004-091	HART, JON COREY 'COREY'	PO BOX 1245, VICTORVILLE CA 92393
1984-049	HART, MICHAEL LAWRENCE	16552 WEST CRESCENT DR, NEW BERLIN WI 53151
1943-059	HART, WILLIAM WOODROW	D. JULY 29, 1968, LYKINS, PA.
1965-039	HARTENSTEIN, CHARLES OSCAR	10735 CASSIA DRIVE, AUSTIN TX 78759
1995-093	HARTGRAVES, DEAN CHARLES	1741 SOUTH SIERRA VISTA DRIVE, TEMPE AZ 85281
1939-048	HARTJE, CHRISTIAN HENRY	D. JUNE 26, 1946, SEATTLE, WASH.
1989-054	HARTLEY, MICHAEL EDWARD	9485 QUAIL CANYON ROAD, EL CAJON CA 92021
1962-054	HARTMAN, J. C.	3425 ROSEDALE ST, HOUSTON TX 77004
1959-037	HARTMAN, ROBERT LOUIS	2580 18TH STREET #1, KENOSHA WI 53140
1922-052	HARTNETT, CHARLES LEO 'GABBY'	D. DECEMBER 20, 1972, PARK RIDGE, ILL.
1973-057	HARTS, GREGORY RUDOLPH	829 HUMPHRUES STREET SW, ATLANTA GA 30310
1950-032	HARTSFIELD, ROY THOMAS	PO BOX 236 WHITEPATH ROAD, EAST ELLIJAY GA 30539
1992-048	HARTSOCK, JEFFREY ROGER	1720 SWANNANO DRIVE, GREENSBORO NC 27410
1947-041	HARTUNG, CLINTON 'HONDO'	1018 EAST FULTON, SINTON TX 78387
1976-040	HARTZELL, PAUL FRANKLIN	PO BOX 2860, HAILEY ID 83333
1928-044	HARVEL, LUTHER RAYMOND 'RED'	D. APRIL 10, 1986, KANSAS CITY, MO.
1987-056	HARVEY, BRYAN STANLEY	1224 ASTORIA PKWY, CATAWBA NC 28609
2001-076	HARVEY, KENNETH EUGENE	OLD ADD: 1849 NORTH FREEDOM BLVD #321, PROVO UT 84604
1999-083	HARVILLE, CHAD ASHLEY	172 ELLIS STREET, BEAN STATION TN 37708
1997-075	HASEGAWA, SHIGETOSHI	110 NEWPORT CENTER DRIVE #200, NEWPORT BEACH CA 92660
1990-065	HASELMAN, WILLIAM JOSEPH	14501 SE 85TH STREET, RENTON WA 98059
1945-043	HASENMAYER, DONALD IRVIN	721 GOLF DRIVE, WARRINGTON PA 18976
1940-034	HASH, HERBERT HOWARD	PO BOX 191, CULPEPER VA 22701
1933-023	HASLIN, MICHAEL JOSEPH 'MICKEY'	D. MARCH 7, 2001, WILKES-BARRE, PA.

1936-037	HASSETT, JOHN ALOYSIUS 'BUDDY'	D. AUGUST 23, 1997, WESTWOOD, N.J.
1978-056	HASSEY, RONALD WILLIAM	6330 NORTH CALLE TREGUA SERENA, TUCSON AZ 85750
1971-043	HASSLER, ANDREW EARL	OLD ADD: PO BOX 85060, PHOENIX AZ 85060
1928-045	HASSLER, JOSEPH FREDERICK	D. SEPTEMBER 4, 1971, DUNCAN, OKLA.
1937-048	HASSON, CHARLES EUGENE 'GENE'	D. JULY 30, 2003, POMONA, CALIF.
1998-079	HATCHER, CHRISTOPHER KENNETH	1406 250TH STREET, AUDUBON IA 50025
1979-049	HATCHER, MICHAEL VAUGHN 'MICKEY'	2 BLUSAIL COVE, BUENA PARK CA 90621
1984-050	HATCHER, WILLIAM AUGUSTUS	5096 ROLLMAN ESTATES DRIVE, CINCINNATI OH 45236
1950-033	HATFIELD, FRED JAMES	D. MAY 22, 1998, TALLAHASSEE, FLA.
1992-049	HATHAWAY, HILLARY HOUSTON 'HILLY'	2672 FOREST BLVD, JACKSONVILLE FL 32216
1945-044	HATHAWAY, RAY WILSON	25 LEISURE MOUNT ROAD, ASHEVILLE NC 28804
1995-094	HATTEBERG, SCOTT ALLEN	802 BERG COURT NW, GIG HARBOR WA 98335
1946-044	HATTEN, JOSEPH HILARIAN	D. DECEMBER 16, 1988, REDDING, CALIF.
1935-042	HATTER, CLYDE MELNO	D. OCTOBER 16, 1937, YOSEMITE, KY.
2006-069	HATTIG, JOHN DUANE	OLD ADD: DEDEDO GUAM
1946-045	HATTON, GRADY EDGEBERT	PO BOX 97, WARREN TX 77664
1943-060	HAUGHEY, CHRISTOPHER FRANCIS	4141 STEVENSON BLVD #202, FREMONT CA 94538
1997-076	HAUGHT, GARY ALLEN	16445 LYNN DRIVE, CHOCTAW OK 73020
1947-042	HAUGSTAD, PHILIP DONALD	D. OCTOBER 21, 1998, BLACK RIVER FALLS, WISC.
1922-053	HAUSER, JOSEPH JOHN	D. JULY 11, 1997, SHEBOYGAN, WISC.
1975-050	HAUSMAN, THOMAS MATTHEW	3165 WESTFIELD CIR, LAS VEGAS NV 89121
1944-056	HAUSMANN, CLEMENS RAYMOND	D. AUGUST 29, 1972, BAYTOWN, TEXAS
1944-057	HAUSMANN, GEORGE JOHN	D. JUNE 16, 2004, BOERNE, TEXAS
1981-052	HAVENS, BRADLEY DAVID	2341 NORTH MAIN STREET, ROYAL OAK MI 48073
1996-077	HAWBLITZEL, RYAN WADE	7972 SOUTH FOUR OAKS POINT, FLORAL CITY FL 34436
1951-039	HAWES, ROY LEE	PO BOX 854, RINGGOLD GA 30736
1995-095	HAWKINS, LATROY	9802 HONEYSUCKLE DRIVE, FRISCO TX 75035
1982-056	HAWKINS, MELTON ANDREW 'ANDY'	PO BOX 1595, BRUCEVILLE TX 76630
1960-046	HAWKINS, WYNN FIRTH	5326 COTTAGE LN, CORTLAND OH 44410
1921-039	HAWKS, NELSON LOUIS 'CHICK'	D. MAY 26, 1973, SAN RAFAEL, CALIF.
2004-092	HAWPE, BRADLEY BONTE	PO BOX 136909, FORT WORTH TX 76136
1970-059	HAYDEL, JOHN HAROLD 'HAL'	304 LYNWOOD DR, HOUMA LA 70360
1958-044	HAYDEN, EUGENE FRANKLIN	D. JUNE 13, 2003, LODI, CALIF.
1982-057	HAYES, BEN JOSEPH	3501 10TH ST NE, SAINT PETERSBURG FL 33704
1988-065	HAYES, CHARLES DEWAYNE	22503 HOLLY CREEK TRAIL, TOMBALL TX 77375
1933-024	HAYES, FRANKLIN WITMAN	D. JUNE 22, 1955, POINT PLEASANT, N.J.
1935-043	HAYES, JAMES MILLARD	D. NOVEMBER 26, 1993, LITHONIA, GA.
1927-044	HAYES, MINTER CARNEY 'JACKIE'	D. FEBRUARY 9, 1983, BIRMINGHAM, ALA.
1981-053	HAYES, VON FRANK	819 15TH AVENUE NE, SAINT PETERSBURG FL 33704
1980-050	HAYES, WILLIAM ERNEST	4602 EAST EARLL DRIVE, PHOENIX AZ 85018
1994-043	HAYNES, HEATH BURNETT	2425 OLYMPIC BLVD, SANTA MONICA CA 90401
1995-096	HAYNES, JIMMY WAYNE	156 RIVERSIDE DRIVE, LA GRANGE GA 30240
1939-049	HAYNES, JOSEPH WALTER	D. JANUARY 6, 1967, HOPKINS, MINN.
1986-061	HAYWARD, RAYMOND ALTON	5113 DEERHURST DRIVE, NORMAN OK 73072
1968-035	HAYWOOD, WILLIAM KIERNAN	867 VILLA DRIVE, NORTH MYRTLE BEACH SC 29582
1944-058	HAYWORTH, MYRON CLAUDE 'RED'	D. NOVEMBER 2, 2006, HIGH POINT, N.C.
1926-035	HAYWORTH, RAYMOND HALL	D. SEPTEMBER 25, 2002, SALISBURY, N.C.
1980-051	HAZEWOOD, DRUNGO LARUE	7991 WESTBORO WAY, SACRAMENTO CA 95823
1955-057	HAZLE, ROBERT SIDNEY	D. APRIL 25, 1992, COLUMBIA, S.C.
1940-035	HEAD, EDWARD MARVIN	D. JANUARY 31, 1980, BASTROP, LA.
1923-062	HEAD, RALPH	D. OCTOBER 8, 1962, MUSCADINE, ALA.
1969-076	HEALY, FRANCIS XAVIER	1 PRIMROSE LN, HOLYOKE MA 01040
1930-031	HEALY, FRANCIS XAVIER PAUL	D. FEBRUARY 12, 1997, SPRINGFIELD, MASS.
1954-041	HEARD, JEHOSIE	D. NOVEMBER 18, 1999, BIRMINGHAM, ALA.
1986-062	HEARN, EDWARD JOHN	5737 THEDEN STREET, SHAWNEE KS 66218
1926-036	HEARN, ELMER LAFAYETTE 'BUNNY'	D. MARCH 31, 1974, VENICE, FLA.
1947-043	HEARN, JAMES TOLBERT	D. JUNE 10, 1998, BOCA GRANDE, FLA.
1985-046	HEARRON, JEFFREY VERNON	322 IVY MANOR DRIVE NW, MARIETTA GA 30064
1936-038	HEATH, JOHN GEOFFREY 'JEFF'	D. DECEMBER 9, 1975, SEATTLE, WASH.
1982-058	HEATH, KELLY MARK	2249 PORTAFINO PLACE #2222, PALM HARBOR FL 34683
1978-057	HEATH, MICHAEL THOMAS	1107 SWEETBREEZE DRIVE, VALRICO FL 33594
1931-035	HEATH, MINOR WILSON 'MICKEY'	D. JULY 30, 1986, DALLAS, TEXAS
1920-048	HEATH, SPENCER PAUL	D. JANUARY 25, 1930, CHICAGO, ILL.
1935-044	HEATH, THOMAS GEORGE	D. FEBRUARY 26, 1967, LOS GATOS, CALIF.
1965-040	HEATH, WILLIAM CHRIS	1626 LAKE CHARLOTTE LANE, RICHMOND TX 77469
1983-070	HEATHCOCK, RONALD JEFFREY 'JEFF'	24962 CALLE VENCINDAD, LAKE FOREST CA 92630
1998-080	HEATHCOTT, MICHAEL JOSEPH	OLD ADD: 3490 NEWPORT WAY, ARLINGTON HEIGHTS IL 60004
1982-059	HEATON, NEAL	3 NURSERY COURT, EAST PATCHOGUE NY 11772
1975-051	HEAVERLO, DAVID WALLACE	3720 WEST LAKESHORE DRIVE, MOSES LAKE WA 98837
1931-036	HEBERT, WALLACE ANDREW	D. DECEMBER 8, 1999, WESTLAKE, LA.
1968-036	HEBNER, RICHARD JOSEPH 'RICHIE'	6 TETREAULT STREET, WALPOLE MA 02081
2003-073	HEBSON, BRYAN MCCALL	OLD ADD: 2506 40TH STREET, PHENIX CITY AL 36887
1965-041	HEDLUND, MICHAEL DAVID	2412 KLINGER RD, ARLINGTON TX 76016
1979-050	HEEP, DANIEL WILLIAM	327 TEAKWOOD LN, SAN ANTONIO TX 78216
1992-050	HEFFERNAN, BERTRAM ALEXANDER	130 EAGLE COURT, LOCUST GROVE VA 22508
1934-043	HEFFNER, DONALD HENRY	D. AUGUST 1, 1989, PASADENA, CALIF.
1963-055	HEFFNER, ROBERT FREDERICK	910 NORTH TWELFTH, ALLENTOWN PA 18102
1996-078	HEFLIN, BRONSON WADE	108 RIVERS EDGE COURT, NASHVILLE TN 37214
1945-045	HEFLIN, RANDOLPH RUTHERFORD	D. AUGUST 17, 1999, FREDERICKSBURG, VA.
1941-046	HEGAN, JAMES EDWARD	D. JUNE 17, 1984, SWAMPSCOTT, MASS.
1964-041	HEGAN, JAMES MICHAEL 'MIKE'	7 WILD TURKEY RUN, HILTON HEAD ISLAND SC 29926
1985-047	HEGMAN, ROBERT HILMER	3529 NW WINDING WOODS DRIVE, LEES SUMMIT MO 64064
1969-077	HEIDEMANN, JACK SEALE	1816 SOUTH SALIDA DEL SOL CIR, MESA AZ 85202
2003-074	HEILMAN, AARON MICHAEL	4231 LEXINGTON ROAD, LOGANSPORT IN 46947
1942-047	HEIM, VAL RAYMOND	PO BOX 423, SUPERIOR NE 68978
1920-049	HEIMACH, FRED AMOS	D. JUNE 1, 1973, FORT MYERS, FLA.

1983-071	HEIMUELLER, GORMAN JOHN	2148 GLEN AVENUE, RIVERTON UT 84065
1921-040	HEINE, WILLIAM HENRY 'BUD'	D. SEPTEMBER 2, 1976, FORT LAUDERDALE, FLA.
1988-066	HEINKEL, DONALD ELLIOTT	22207 NICK DAVIS ROAD, ATHENS AL 35613
2005-082	HEINTZ, CHRISTOPHER JOHN	OLD ADD: CLEARWATER FL
1937-049	HEINTZELMAN, KENNETH ALPHONSE	D. AUGUST 24, 2000, SAINT PETERS, MO.
1973-058	HEINTZELMAN, THOMAS KENNETH	1500 WEST 8TH STREET, MESA AZ 85201
1934-044	HEISE, CLARENCE EDWARD 'LEFTY'	D. MAY 30, 1999, WINTER PARK, FLA.
1957-030	HEISE, JAMES EDWARD	2425 ALBION AVENUE, ORLANDO FL 32833
1967-044	HEISE, ROBERT LOWELL	537 LIVE OAK COURT, ANGELS CAMP CA 95222
1961-044	HEISER, LEROY BARTON	1038 GROVE HILL RD, BALTIMORE MD 21227
1999-084	HEISERMAN, RICHARD MICHAEL 'RICK'	17252 ADAMS STREET, OMAHA NE 68135
1960-047	HEIST, ALFRED MICHAEL	D. OCTOBER 2, 2006, TAHLEQUAH, OKLA.
1956-040	HELD, MELVIN NICHOLAS	103 HOGAN LANE, BRYAN OH 43506
1954-042	HELD, WOODSON GEORGE 'WOODIE'	BIG DIAMOND RANCH, DUBOIS WY 82513
1938-036	HELF, HENRY HARTZ	D. OCTOBER 27, 1984, AUSTIN, TEXAS
1993-074	HELFAND, ERIC JAMES	8679 CIRCLE R VALLEY LANE, ESCONDIDO CA 92026
1994-044	HELLING, RICKY ALLEN	3672 LAMDINGS DRIVE, EXCELSIOR MN 55331
1964-042	HELMS, TOMMY VANN	5427 BLUE SKY DR, CINCINNATI OH 45247
1998-081	HELMS, WESLEY RAY	1287 LAKE TRACE COVE, BIRMINGHAM AL 35244
1997-077	HELTON, TODD LYNN	8720 EAST 127TH COURT, BRIGHTON CO 80602
1943-061	HELTZEL, WILLIAM WADE 'HEINIE'	D. MAY 1, 1998, YORK, PA.
1961-045	HEMAN, RUSSELL FREDERICK	5555 CANYON CREST DRIVE #30, RIVERSIDE CA 92507
1989-055	HEMOND, SCOTT MATHEW	265 SPEARS DYKES ROAD, GREENEVILLE TN 37745
1999-085	HEMPHILL, BRET RYAN	1273 TREHOWELL DRIVE, ROSEVILLE CA 95678
1928-046	HEMSLEY, RALSTON BURDETT 'ROLLIE'	D. JULY 31, 1972, WASHINGTON, D.C.
1949-032	HEMUS, SOLOMON JOSEPH 'SOLLY'	6565 WEST LOOP SOUTH #555, BELLAIRE TX 77401
1921-041	HENDERSON, BERNARD	D. JUNE 4, 1966, LINDEN, TEXAS
1981-054	HENDERSON, DAVID LEE	6004 142ND COURT SE, BELLEVUE WA 98006
1974-049	HENDERSON, JOSEPH LEE	OLD ADD:125 INQUERO LN #38, EL PASO TX
1965-042	HENDERSON, KENNETH JOSEPH	182 LAMONTAGNE COURT, LOS GATOS CA 95032
1979-051	HENDERSON, RICKEY HENLEY	10561 ENGLEWOOD DR, OAKLAND CA 94621
1994-045	HENDERSON, RODNEY WOOD	3641 FAIR RIDGE DRIVE, LEXINGTON KY 40509
1977-064	HENDERSON, STEPHEN CURTIS	10509 GRETNA GREEN DRIVE, TAMPA FL 33626
1930-032	HENDERSON, WILLIAM MAXWELL	D. OCTOBER 6, 1966, PENSACOLA, FLA.
1961-046	HENDLEY, CHARLES ROBERT 'BOB'	645 WIMBISH, MACON GA 31204
1971-044	HENDRICK, GEORGE ANDREW	10672 BLUE NILE COURT, LAS VEGAS NV 89144
1923-063	HENDRICK, HARVEY LEE	D. OCTOBER 29, 1941, COVINGTON, TENN.
1968-037	HENDRICKS, ELROD JEROME	D. DECEMBER 21, 2005, GLEN BURNIE, MD.
2004-093	HENDRICKSON, BENJAMIN JOHN	2700 ROSALYN COURT, NEW HOPE MN 55427
1945-046	HENDRICKSON, DONALD WILLIAM	D. JANUARY 19, 1977, NORFOLK, VA.
2002-079	HENDRICKSON, MARK ALLAN	17289 DUNBAR ROAD, MOUNT VERNON WA 98273
1986-063	HENGEL, DAVID LEE	2642 KINGFISHER LANE, LINCOLN CA 95648
1982-060	HENKE, THOMAS ANTHONY	RR SIX, JEFFERSON CITY MO 65101
1954-043	HENLEY, GAIL CURTICE	7338 ALTA VISTA, LAVERNE CA 91750
1998-082	HENLEY, ROBERT CLIFTON	11050 MORELAND DRIVE, GRAND BAY AL 36541
1921-042	HENLINE, WALTER JOHN 'BUTCH'	D. OCTOBER 9, 1957, SARASOTA, FLA.
2005-083	HENN, SEAN MICHAEL	3658 SNOW CREEK DRIVE, ALEDO TX 76008
1987-057	HENNEMAN, MICHAEL ALAN	7002 OXFORD COURT, MCKINNEY TX 75070
2004-094	HENNESSEY, BRAD MARTIN	6657 BRENTRIDGE LANE, LAMBERTVILLE MI 48144
1937-050	HENNESSEY, GEORGE	D. JANUARY 15, 1988, PRINCETON, N.J.
1969-078	HENNIGAN, PHILLIP WINSTON	PO BOX 1212, CENTER TX 75935
1973-059	HENNINGER, RICHARD LEE	373 MAPLE DRIVE, POTTSBORO TX 75076
1990-066	HENNIS, RANDALL PHILIP	1747 SIENNA DRIVE, MELBOURNE FL 32934
1924-050	HENRICH, FRANK WILDE 'FRITZ'	D. MAY 1, 1959, PHILADELPHIA, PA.
1957-031	HENRICH, ROBERT EDWARD	1531 VIA LOS COYOTES, LAHABRA CA 90631
1937-051	HENRICH, THOMAS DAVID	3801 WOODBINE AVENUE, DAYTON OH 45420
1997-078	HENRIQUEZ, OSCAR EDUARDO	OLD ADD: LAGUAIRA VENEZUELA
1984-051	HENRY, DWAYNE ALLEN	502 HAMPSTEAD ROAD, MIDDLETOWN DE 19709
1944-059	HENRY, EARL CLIFFORD	D. DECEMBER 10, 2002, ZANESVILLE, OHIO
1992-051	HENRY, FLOYD BUFORD 'BUTCH'	10144 SUEZ, EL PASO TX 79925
1921-043	HENRY, FRANK JOHN 'DUTCH'	D. AUGUST 23, 1968, EAST CLEVELAND, OHIO
1922-054	HENRY, FREDERICK MARSHALL	D. OCTOBER 12, 1987, WENDELL, N.C.
1936-039	HENRY, JAMES FRANCIS	D. AUGUST 15, 1976, MEMPHIS, TENN.
1991-073	HENRY, RICHARD DOUGLAS 'DOUG'	2816 BURRIES ROAD, HARTLAND WI 53029
1961-047	HENRY, RONALD BAXTER	1708 MYSTIC DRIVE, DURHAM NC 27712
1966-042	HENRY, WILLIAM FRANCIS	26 STONEY CREEK ROAD, HILTON HEAD ISLAND SC 29928
1952-047	HENRY, WILLIAM RODMAN	2313 KILKENNY LANE, DEER PARK TX 77536
1933-025	HENSHAW, ROY KNIKELBINE	D. JUNE 8, 1993, LAGRANGE, ILL.
1935-045	HENSIEK, PHILIP FRANK	D. FEBRUARY 21, 1972, ST. LOUIS, MO.
1986-064	HENSLEY, CHARLES FLOYD	259 BONANZA DRIVE, ERIE CO 80516
2005-084	HENSLEY, CLAYTON ALLEN	3601 DOGWOOD BLOSSOM COURT, PEARLAND TX 77581
2004-095	HENSLEY, MATTHEW DAVIS	6407 EAST LAKE DRIVE, SAN DIEGO CA 92119
2002-080	HENSON, DREW DANIEL	2931 MAGNOLIA HILL COURT, DALLAS TX 75201
1991-074	HENTGEN, PATRICK GEORGE	14451 KNIGHTBRIDGE DRIVE, UTICA MI 48315
1966-043	HEPLER, WILLIAM LEWIS	12518 FORT KING ROAD, DADE CITY FL 33525
1963-056	HERBEL, RONALD SAMUEL	D. JANUARY 20, 2000, TADCOMA, WASH.
1950-034	HERBERT, RAYMOND ERNEST	9360 TAYLORS TURN, STANWOOD MI 49346
1996-079	HEREDIA, FELIX PEREZ	PO BOX 4842, HIALEAH FL 33014
1991-075	HEREDIA, GILBERT	12914 EAST CAMINO REMUDA, TUCSON AZ 85749
1987-058	HEREDIA, UBALDO JOSE	AVE. FUERZAS AMADOS SAN FRANCISCO PISO APT 21, CARACAS, VENEZUELA
1995-097	HEREDIA, WILSON	ENS. LA HOS NO. 47 ALTOS LA ROMANA, DOM REP
1999-086	HERGES, MATTHEW TYLER	2406 PRAIRIERIDGE PLACE, CHAMPAIGN IL 61822
1926-037	HERMAN, FLOYD CAVES 'BABE'	D. NOVEMBER 27, 1987, GLENDALE, CALIF.
1931-037	HERMAN, WILLIAM JENNINGS BRYAN	D. SEPTEMBER 5, 1992, WEST PALM BEACH, FLA.
1923-064	HERMANN, ALBERT BARTEL	D. AUGUST 20, 1980, LEWES, DEL.
1999-087	HERMANSEN, CHAD BRUCE	1835 RUBY LANE, HENDERSON NV 89014

1943-062 HERMANSKI, EUGENE VICTOR............................1 FAIRWOODS COURT, HOMOSASSA FL 34446
1995-098 HERMANSON, DUSTIN MICHAEL........................9002 EAST RIMROCK DRIVE, SCOTTSDALE AZ 85255
2005-085 HERMIDA, JEREMY RYAN..................................2827 LAKE MICHAELA BLVD, VALRICO FL 33594
1967-045 HERMOSO, ANGEL REMIGIO..............................OLD ADD: RES. DORADOTORRE DE PISO 6,#63D, CARACAS VENEZUELA
1974-050 HERNAIZ, JESUS RAFAEL..................................24 STREET BLOCK 76 #47 VILLA, CAROLINA PR 00630
2001-077 HERNANDEZ, ADRIAN.......................................OLD ADD: 14200 BRUCE B. DOWNS BLVD, TAMPA FL 33613
2000-076 HERNANDEZ, ALEXANDER VARGAS....................OLD ADD: LEVITTOWN PR
2005-086 HERNANDEZ, ANDERSON.................................OLD ADD: SANTO DOMINGO DOM REP
1990-067 HERNANDEZ, CARLOS ALBERTO........................ALFINGER MANZANA 16 #5 SAN FELIX BOLIVAR, VENEZUELA
2001-078 HERNANDEZ, CARLOS E....................................OLD ADD: YAGUA VENEZ
1999-088 HERNANDEZ, CARLOS EDUARDO........................OLD ADD: CARACAS VENEZUELA
1992-052 HERNANDEZ, CESAR DARIO (PREZ)...................OLD ADD: 13 #19 ENSANCHE CAPITILLO, SANTO DOMINGO DOM REP
1996-080 HERNANDEZ, EISLER LIVAN 'LIVAN'...................2655 SOUTH LEJEUNE ROAD, MIAMI FL 33134
1971-045 HERNANDEZ, ENZO OCTAVIO.............................VEREDA NORTH 5E-4, GUANTRA PUERTA LACRUZ ANZ, VENEZUELA
2005-087 HERNANDEZ, FELIX ABRAHAM...........................OLD ADD: VALENCIA VENEZUELA
1997-079 HERNANDEZ, FERNANDO..................................OLD ADD: SANTIAGO DOM REP
1989-056 HERNANDEZ, FRANCIS XAVIER 'XAVIER'............3002 EAST AUTUMN RUN CIRCLE, SUGAR LAND TX 77479
1956-041 HERNANDEZ, GREGORIO EVELIO 'EVELIO'.........3004 SW 113TH AVE, MIAMI FL 33165
1977-065 HERNANDEZ, GUILLERMO 'WILLIE'....................BO ESPINA, CALLE C BUZON 125, AGUADA PR 00602
1965-043 HERNANDEZ, JACINTO ZULUETA 'JACKIE'..........13390 7TH AVENUE, MIAMI FL 33161
1991-076 HERNANDEZ, JEREMY STUART..........................13611 BRANFORD STREET, ARLETA CA 91331
1991-077 HERNANDEZ, JOSE ANTONIO (FIGUEROA).........CALLE SUR #22, VEGA ALTA PR 00762
1974-051 HERNANDEZ, KEITH...255 EAST 49TH #28D, NEW YORK NY 10017
1982-061 HERNANDEZ, LEONARDO JESUS.......................1352 SW 75TH AVENUE, MIAMI FL 33144
1986-065 HERNANDEZ, MANUEL ANTONIO.......................EUGENIO A. ALFIONADA, #35 LAROMANA, DOM REP
2003-075 HERNANDEZ, MICHEL.......................................OLD ADD: CARACAS VZ
1998-083 HERNANDEZ, ORLANDO P.................................OLD ADD: MIAMI FL 33101
1979-052 HERNANDEZ, PEDRO JULIO...............................10413 91ST AVENUE, JAMAICA NY 11418
1967-046 HERNANDEZ, RAMON GONZALEZ.......................OLD ADD: REP. ROSEMARIA CALLE 5F-19, CAROLINA PR 00630
1999-089 HERNANDEZ, RAMON JOSE..............................OLD ADD: CARACAS VENEZUELA
1991-078 HERNANDEZ, ROBERTO MANUEL.......................5965 BAYVIEW CIRCLE SOUTH, GULFPORT FL 33707
1972-047 HERNANDEZ, RODOLFO...................................605 R AVENUE #11, NATIONAL CITY CA 91950
1960-048 HERNANDEZ, RUDOLPH ALBERT........................OLD ADD: 8 CALLE RODRIGUEZ SERRA, CONDADO PR 00907
2002-081 HERNANDEZ, RUNELVYS ANTONIO....................18717 EAST 24TH STREET CT SOUTH, INDEPENDENCE MO 64057
1942-048 HERNANDEZ, SALVADOR JOSE RAMOS.............D. JANUARY 3, 1986, HAVANA, CUBA
1984-052 HERNANDEZ, TOBIAS RAFAEL..........................IRA CALLE GUAMACHITO #47-49 CALABOZO, GUARICO, VENEZUELA
2001-079 HERNDON, HARRY FRANCIS 'JUNIOR'...............1477 SEQUOIA AVENUE, CRAIG CO 81625
1974-052 HERNDON, LARRY DARNELL............................6149 BRUNSWICK ROAD, ARLINGTON TN 38002
1979-053 HERR, THOMAS MITCHELL...............................1077 OLDE FORGE CROSSING, LANCASTER PA 17601
2002-082 HERRERA, ALEXANDER J.................................OLD ADD: MARACAIBO VENEZ
1967-047 HERRERA, JOSE CONCEPCION..........................MARAVEN ADRI 12 CEN.COM. LAGUNILLAS E. ZULIA, VENEZUELA
1995-099 HERRERA, JOSE RAMON CATALINO...................OLD ADD: SANTO DOMINGO DOM REP
1958-045 HERRERA, JUAN FRANCISCO 'FRANK'................D. APRIL 28, 2005, MIAMI, FLA.
1951-040 HERRERA, PROCOPIO RODRIGUEZ 'TITO'..........OLD ADD: APDO POSTAL 257, CD. SATELITE EDO MEXICO
1925-047 HERRERA, RAMON 'MIKE'...............................D. FEBRUARY 3, 1978, HAVANA, CUBA
1956-042 HERRIAGE, WILLIAM TROY 'TROY'....................238 CALIFORNIA AVENUE, OAKDALE CA 95361
1954-044 HERRIN, THOMAS EDWARD..............................D. NOVEMBER 29, 1999, HOMER, LA.
1929-048 HERRING, ARTHUR L..D. DECEMBER 2, 1995, MARION, IND.
1967-048 HERRMANN, EDWARD MARTIN.........................13153 TOBIASSON ROAD, POWAY CA 92064
1932-036 HERRMANN, LEROY GEORGE...........................D. JULY 3, 1972, LIVERMORE, CALIF.
1962-055 HERRNSTEIN, JOHN ELLETT..............................603 SEMINOLE RD, CHILLICOTHE OH 45602
1962-056 HERRSCHER, RICHARD FRANKLIN 'RICK'..........7714 MARQUETTE, DALLAS TX 75225
1956-043 HERSH, EARL WALTER.....................................3201 MURKLE RD, WESTMINSTER MD 21157
1961-048 HERSHBERGER, NORMAN MICHAEL 'MIKE'.......2887 CARRIE HILL CIRCLE NW, MASSILLON OH 44646
1938-037 HERSHBERGER, WILLARD MCKEE.....................D. AUGUST 3, 1940, BOSTON, MASS.
1983-072 HERSHISER, OREL LEONARD QUINTON.............7163 HELSEM BLVD, DALLAS TX 75230
1952-048 HERTWECK, NEAL CHARLES.............................111 LEESBURG LANE, TROUTMAN NC 28166
1964-043 HERTZ, STEPHEN ALLAN..................................10211 SW 96TH TERRACE, MIAMI FL 33156
1956-044 HERZOG, DORREL NORMAN ELVERT 'WHITEY'..9426 SAPPINGTON ESTATES DRIVE, SAINT LOUIS MO 63127
1984-053 HESKETH, JOSEPH THOMAS.............................202 GLENRIDGE ROAD, EAST AURORA NY 14052
2003-076 HESSMAN, MICHAEL STEVEN............................15861 KING CIRCLE, WESTMINSTER CA 92683
1945-047 HETKI, JOHN EDWARD.....................................4004 STARY DRIVE, PARMA OH 44134
1989-057 HETZEL, ERIC PAUL...2271 HETZEL ROAD, CROWLEY LA 70526
1935-046 HEUSSER, EDWARD BURLETON........................D. MARCH 1, 1956, AURORA, COLO.
1920-050 HEVING, JOHN ALOYSIUS.................................D. DECEMBER 24, 1968, SALISBURY, N.C.
1930-033 HEVING, JOSEPH WILLIAM...............................D. APRIL 11, 1970, COVINGTON, KY.
1973-060 HEYDEMAN, GREGORY GEORGE........................702 ROMONA AVENUE, MONTEREY CA 93940
1964-044 HIATT, JACK E...715 EAST FIRST STREET, COQUILLE OR 97423
1993-075 HIATT, PHILIP FARRELL...................................30 LITTLETON, CANTONMENT FL 32533
1989-058 HIBBARD, JAMES GREGORY 'GREG'..................1957 ARDEN LANDING COVE SOUTH, GERMANTOWN TN 38139
1967-049 HIBBS, JAMES KERR.......................................4659 FOOTHILL ROAD, VENTURA CA 93003
1991-079 HICKERSON, BRYAN DAVID...............................275 SOUTH HUNTERS RIDGE, WARSAW IN 46582
1942-049 HICKEY, JAMES ROBERT..................................D. SEPTEMBER 20, 1997, MANCHESTER, CONN.
1981-055 HICKEY, KEVIN JOHN.......................................5715 SOUTH MASON, CHICAGO IL 60638
1962-057 HICKMAN, JAMES LUCIUS................................PO BOX 455, HENNING TN 38041
1965-044 HICKMAN, JESSE OWENS................................1801 JEWEL STREET, PINEVILLE LA 71360
1956-045 HICKS, CLARENCE WALTER 'BUDDY'.................1526 NORTH DIXIE DOWNS #26, SAINT GEORGE UT 84770
1964-045 HICKS, JAMES EDWARD...................................9331 POSTAL DRIVE, HOUSTON TX 77031
1959-038 HICKS, WILLIAM JOSEPH 'JOE'.........................2707 BROOKMERE RD, CHARLOTTESVILLE VA 22901
1997-080 HIDALGO, RICHARD JOSE................................OLD ADD: GUARENAS VENEZUELA
2004-096 HIETPAS, JOSEPH CARL...................................611 TIMBERLINE DRIVE, APPLETON WI 54915
1937-052 HIGBE, WALTER KIRBY 'KIRBY'.........................D. MAY 6, 1985, COLUMBIA, S.C.
1922-055 HIGBEE, MAHLON JESSE..................................D. APRIL 7, 1968, DEPAUW, IND.
1949-033 HIGDON, WILLIAM TRAVIS...............................D. AUGUST 30, 1986, PASCAGOULA, MISS.
1966-044 HIGGINS, DENNIS DEAN..................................1123 BOONVILLE ROAD, JEFFERSON CITY MO 65109
1993-076 HIGGINS, KEVIN WAYNE..................................10551 HAYWOOD DRIVE, LAS VEGAS NV 89135

1989-059	HIGGINS, MARK DOUGLAS	2999 ABBOTTS OAK WAY, DULUTH GA 30097
1930-034	HIGGINS, MICHAEL FRANKLIN 'PINKY'	D. MARCH 21, 1969, DALLAS, TEXAS
1995-100	HIGGINSON, ROBERT LEIGH 'BOBBY'	3300 CHICKERING LANE, BLOOMFIELD HILLS MI 48302
1922-056	HIGH, ANDREW AIRD	D. FEBRUARY 22, 1981, TOLEDO, OHIO
1985-048	HIGUERA, TEODORO VALENZUELA	1567 SOUTH SYCAMORE PLACE, CHANDLER AZ 85248
1931-038	HILCHER, WALTER FRANK	D. NOVEMBER 21, 1962, MINNEAPOLIS, MINN.
1931-039	HILDEBRAND, ORAL CLYDE	D. SEPTEMBER 8, 1977, SOUTHPORT, IND.
1969-079	HILGENDORF, THOMAS EUGENE	PO BOX 124, CAMANCHE IA 52730
1999-090	HILJUS, ERIK KRISTIAN	10915 INDEPENDENCE AVENUE, CHATSWORTH CA 91311
2005-088	HILL, AARON WALTER	4741 WEST ADDISYN COURT, VISALIA CA 93291
1957-032	HILL, DAVID BURNHAM	125 JENNY LIND DRIVE, HENDERSONVILLE NC 27891
1983-073	HILL, DONALD EARL	6 KNOB HILL, LAGUNA NIGUEL CA 92677
1969-080	HILL, GARRY ALTON	9602 WILLOWGLEN TRAIL, CHARLOTTE NC 28215
1989-060	HILL, GLENALLEN	108 CALVIN PLACE, SANTA CRUZ CA 95060
1969-081	HILL, HERMAN ALEXANDER	D. DECEMBER 14, 1970, MAGALLANES, VENEZ.
2002-083	HILL, JEREMY DEE	10050 GOODING, DALLAS TX 75029
1935-047	HILL, JESSE TERRILL	D. AUGUST 31, 1993, PASADENA, CALIF.
1939-050	HILL, JOHN CLINTON	D. SEPTEMBER 20, 1970, DECATUR, GA.
1988-067	HILL, KENNETH WADE	1360 SHADY OAKS DRIVE, SOUTHLAKE TX 76092
2003-077	HILL, KOYIE DOLAN	3595 NORTH WEBB ROAD, WICHITA KS 67226
1973-061	HILL, MARC KEVIN	203 MAPLE STREET, ELSBERRY MO 63343
1991-080	HILL, MILTON GILES	8401 AVALON COURT, CUMMING GA 30041
2005-089	HILL, RICHARD JOSEPH 'RICH'	17 SPAFFORD ROAD, MILTON MA 02186
2004-097	HILL, SHAWN RICHARD	OLD ADD: GEORGETOWN ONT
2002-084	HILL, WILLIAM ROBERT 'BOBBY'	OLD ADD: SAN JOSE CA 95113
1987-059	HILLEGAS, SHAWN PATRICK	870 ROCKVILLE ROAD, SOUTH FORK PA 15956
2001-080	HILLENBRAND, SHEA MATTHEW	2614 EAST VIA DE PALMAS, GILBERT AZ 85297
1961-049	HILLER, CHARLES JOSEPH	D. OCTOBER 20, 2004, SAINT PETERSBURG BEACH, FLA.
1946-046	HILLER, FRANK WALTER	D. JANUARY 8, 1987, WEST CHESTER, PA.
1920-051	HILLER, HARVEY MAX 'HOB'	D. DECEMBER 27, 1956, LEHIGHTON, PA.
1965-045	HILLER, JOHN FREDERICK	WEST 8085 BECKER DRIVE, IRON MOUNTAIN MI 49801
1924-051	HILLIS, MALCOLM DAVID 'MACK'	D. JUNE 16, 1961, CAMBRIDGE, MASS.
1955-058	HILLMAN, DARIUS DUTTON 'DAVE'	849 MIMOSA DR, KINGSPORT TN 37660
1992-053	HILLMAN, JOHN ERIC 'ERIC'	157 BELLAIRE STREET, DENVER CO 80220
1990-068	HILTON, HOWARD JAMES	3139 SOUTH 'N' STREET, OXNARD CA 93030
1972-048	HILTON, JOHN DAVID 'DAVE'	4910 EAST SUNNYSIDE DRIVE, SCOTTSDALE AZ 85254
1961-050	HIMSL, AVITUS BERNARD 'VEDIE'	D. MARCH 15, 2004, CHICAGO, ILL.
1998-084	HINCH, ANDREW JAY 'A.J.'	16406 NORTH 106TH WAY, SCOTTSDALE AZ 85255
1999-091	HINCHCLIFFE, BRETT	87 CHARLEVOIX STREET, CLAWSON MI 48017
1977-066	HINDS, SAMUEL RUSSELL	6905 EAST LANE, FRESNO CA 93727
1934-045	HINKLE, DANIEL GORDON 'GORDIE'	D. MARCH 19, 1972, HOUSTON, TEXAS
1951-041	HINRICHS, PAUL EDWIN	1982 BRETT DRIVE, MADISONVILLE KY 42431
1982-062	HINSHAW, GEORGE ADDISON	1240 EAST ONTARIO #123, CORONA CA 91719
2002-085	HINSKE, ERIC SCOTT	631 EIGHTH STREET, MENASHA WI 54952
1964-046	HINSLEY, JERRY DEAN	4255 HOLIDAY LANE, LAS CRUCES NM 88005
1928-047	HINSON, JAMES PAUL	D. SEPTEMBER 23, 1960, MUSKOGEE, OKLA.
1961-051	HINTON, CHARLES EDWARD	6330 16TH ST NW, WASHINGTON DC 20011
1971-046	HINTON, RICHARD MICHAEL 'RICH'	7447 HAWKINS ROAD, SARASOTA FL 34241
1987-060	HINZO, THOMAS LEE	1030 NORTH IVY STREET, ESCONDIDO CA 92026
1966-045	HIPPAUF, HERBERT AUGUST	D. JULY 17, 1995, SANTA CLARA, CALIF.
2006-070	HIRSH, JASON MICHAEL	517 INDIAN BLUFF STREET, LAS VEGAS NV 89145
1971-047	HISER, GENE TAYLOR	1450 CALDWELL LANE, HOFFMAN ESTATES IL 60194
1968-038	HISLE, LARRY EUGENE	312 SADDLEWORTH COURT WEST, MEQUON WI 53092
1951-042	HISNER, HARLEY PARNELL	14322 MONROEVILLE ROAD, MONROEVILLE IN 46773
1938-038	HITCHCOCK, JAMES FRANKLIN	D. JUNE 23, 1959, MONTGOMERY, ALA.
1992-054	HITCHCOCK, STERLING ALEX	11101 US HIGHWAY 92 EAST, SEFFNER FL 33584
1942-050	HITCHCOCK, WILLIAM CLYDE	D. APRIL 9, 2006, OPELIKA AL
1949-034	HITTLE, LLOYD ELDON	2031 WEST ELM STREET, LODI CA 95242
1931-040	HOAG, MYRIL OLIVER	D. JULY 28, 1971, HIGH SPRINGS, FLA.
1954-045	HOAK, DONALD ALBERT	D. OCTOBER 9, 1969, PITTSBURGH, PA.
1961-052	HOBAUGH, EDWARD RUSSELL	527 5TH AVE, FORD CITY PA 16226
1957-033	HOBBIE, GLEN FREDERICK	RURAL ROUTE 2 BOX 234A, RAMSEY IL 62080
1981-056	HOBBS, JOHN DOUGLAS	3 WADE DR, CHERRY HILL NJ 08034
1975-052	HOBSON, CLELL LAVERN 'BUTCH'	12502 CRYSTAL COVE AVENUE, BAKERSFIELD CA 93311
1920-052	HOCK, EDWARD FRANCIS	D. NOVEMBER 21, 1963, PORTSMOUTH, OHIO
1975-053	HOCKENBERY, CHARLES MARION	1546 BIRKA LANE, ONALASKA WI 54650
1938-039	HOCKETT, ORIS LEON	D. MARCH 23, 1969, HAWTHORNE, CALIF.
1934-046	HOCKETTE, GEORGE EDWARD	D. JANUARY 20, 1974, PLANTATION, FLA.
1993-077	HOCKING, DENNIS LEE	2592 NORTH FALCONER WAY, ORANGE CA 92867
1925-048	HODAPP, URBAN JOHN 'JOHNNY'	D. JUNE 14, 1980, CINCINNATI, OHIO
1951-043	HODERLEIN, MELVIN ANTHONY	D. MAY 21, 2001, MOUNT CARMEL, OHIO
1920-053	HODGE, CLARENCE CLEMET 'SHOVEL'	D. DECEMBER 31, 1967, FORT WALTON BEACH, FLA.
1984-054	HODGE, ED OLIVER	127 JEWELL STREET, JOHNSON CITY TN 37601
1942-051	HODGE, EDWARD BURTON 'BERT'	D. JANUARY 8, 2001, KNOXVILLE, TENN.
1971-048	HODGE, HAROLD MORRIS 'GOMER'	PO BOX 1715, RUTHERFORDTON NC 28139
1943-063	HODGES, GILBERT RAYMOND	D. APRIL 2, 1972, WEST PALM BEACH, FLA.
2000-077	HODGES, KEVIN JON	19506 KUYKENDAHL ROAD, SPRING TX 77373
1973-062	HODGES, RONALD WRAY	3190 RAKES ROAD, ROCKY MOUNT VA 24151
2002-086	HODGES, TREY ALAN	19506 KUYKENDAHL ROAD, SPRING TX 77379
1939-051	HODGIN, ELMER RALPH 'RALPH'	3203 FARMINGTON DRIVE, GREENSBORO NC 27407
1980-052	HODGSON, PAUL JOSEPH DENIS	OLD ADD: 5 MCGLOIN STREET, FREDERICTON NB CANADA E3A 4J9
1946-047	HODKEY, ALOYSIUS JOSEPH 'ELI'	D. AUGUST 30, 2005, LORAIN, OHIO
1952-049	HOEFT, WILLIAM FREDERICK	9965 LOST CANYON DRIVE, STANWOOD MI 49346
1963-057	HOERNER, JOSEPH WALTER	D. OCTOBER 4, 1996, HERMANN, MO.
1940-036	HOERST, FRANK JOSEPH	D. FEBRUARY 18, 2000, MAPLE SHADE, N.J.
2006-071	HOEY, JAMES URBAN	1983 ARENA DRIVE, TRENTON NJ 08610

1944-060	HOFFERTH, STEWART EDWARD	D. MARCH 7, 1994, VALPARAISO, IND.
1929-049	HOFFMAN, CLARENCE CASPER 'DUTCH'	D. DECEMBER 6, 1962, BELLEVILLE, ILL.
1980-053	HOFFMAN, GLENN EDWARD	210 SOUTH OLD BRIDGE ROAD, ANAHEIM CA 92808
1979-054	HOFFMAN, GUY ALAN	1016 CROOKED STICK LANE, NORMAL IL 61761
1964-047	HOFFMAN, JOHN EDWARD	D. DECEMBER 27, 2001, SEATTLE, WASH.
1942-052	HOFFMAN, RAYMOND LAMONT	14475 THOMPSON ROAD, ALPHARETTA GA 30201
1993-078	HOFFMAN, TREVOR WILLIAM	2220 OCEAN, DEL MAR CA 92014
1939-052	HOFFMAN, WILLIAM JOSEPH	2 ROBIN LANE, LAFAYETTE HILL PA 19444
1949-035	HOFMAN, ROBERT GEORGE	D. APRIL 5, 1994, CHESTERFIELD, MO.
1925-049	HOGAN, JAMES FRANCIS 'SHANTY'	D. APRIL 7, 1967, BOSTON, MASS.
1921-044	HOGAN, KENNETH SYLVESTER	D. JANUARY 2, 1980, CLEVELAND, OHIO
1934-047	HOGG, WILBERT GEORGE 'BERT'	D. NOVEMBER 5, 1973, DETROIT, MICH.
1929-050	HOGSETT, ELON CHESTER 'CHIEF'	D. JULY 17, 2001, HAYS, KAN.
1952-050	HOGUE, CALVIN GREY	D. AUGUST 5, 2005, KETTERING, OHIO
1948-047	HOGUE, ROBERT CLINTON	D. DECEMBER 22, 1987, MIAMI, FLA.
1927-045	HOHMAN, WILLIAM HENRY	D. OCTOBER 29, 1968, BALTIMORE, MD.
1989-061	HOILES, CHRISTOPHER ALLEN	6556 ROSEDALE ROAD, WAYNE OH 43466
1996-081	HOLBERT, AARON KEITH	1040 54TH AVENUE SOUTH, SAINT PETERSBURG FL 33705
1994-046	HOLBERT, RAY ARTHUR	13981 WEST DESERT COVE ROAD, SURPRISE AZ 85379
1944-061	HOLBOROW, WALTER ALBERT	D. JULY 14, 1986, FORT LAUDERDALE, FLA.
1935-048	HOLBROOK, JAMES MARBURY 'SAMMY'	D. APRIL 10, 1991, JACKSON, MISS.
1945-048	HOLCOMBE, KENNETH EDWARD	32 BOTANY DRIVE, ASHEVILLE NC 28805
1934-048	HOLDEN, JOSEPH FRANCIS 'SOCKS'	D. MAY 10, 1996, SAINT CLAIR, PA.
1998-085	HOLDRIDGE, DAVID ALLEN	39512 NORTH LAURA AVENUE, QUEEN CREEK AZ 85242
1972-049	HOLDSWORTH, FREDRICK WILLIAM	LASALLE BASEBALL, 1900 WEST OLNEY AVENUE, PHILADELPHIA PA 19141
1920-054	HOLLAHAN, WILLIAM JAMES	D. NOVEMBER 27, 1965, NEW YORK, N.Y.
1977-067	HOLLAND, ALFRED WILLIS	4443 LEWISTON STREET NW, ROANOKE VA 24017
1926-038	HOLLAND, HOWARD ARTHUR 'MUL'	D. FEBRUARY 16, 1969, WESTCHESTER, VA.
1932-037	HOLLAND, ROBERT CLYDE 'DUTCH'	D. JUNE 16, 1967, LUMBERTON, N.C.
1939-053	HOLLAND, WILLIAM DAVID	D. APRIL 5, 1997, GOLDSBORO, N.C.
1995-101	HOLLANDSWORTH, TODD MATHEW	1310 MACALPIN DRIVE, INVERNESS IL 60010
1979-055	HOLLE, GARY CHARLES	820 FIFTH AVE, WATERVLIET NY 12189
1928-048	HOLLEY, EDWARD EDGAR	D. OCTOBER 26, 1986, PADUCAH, KY.
2004-098	HOLLIDAY, MATTHEW THOMAS	OLD ADD: 823 SOUTH SHUMARD STREET, STILLWATER OK 74074
1921-045	HOLLING, CARL	D. JULY 28, 1962, SONOMA, CALIF.
1935-049	HOLLINGSWORTH, ALBERT WAYNE 'BOOTS'	D. APRIL 28, 1996, AUSTIN, TEXAS
1922-057	HOLLINGSWORTH, JOHN BURNETT 'BONNIE'	D. JANUARY 4, 1990, SHANNONDALE, TENN.
1998-086	HOLLINS, DAMON JAMALL	112 EL CAMPO COURT, VALLEJO CA 94589
1990-069	HOLLINS, DAVID MICHAEL	20 LAKERIDGE DRIVE SOUTH, ORCHARD PARK NY 14127
1992-055	HOLLINS, JESSIE EDWARD	608 WEST STEWART STREET, WILLIS TX 77378
1949-036	HOLLMIG, STANLEY ERNEST	D. DECEMBER 4, 1981, SAN ANTONIO, TEXAS
1953-033	HOLLOMAN, ALVA LEE 'BOBO'	D. MAY 1, 1987, ATHENS, GA.
1929-051	HOLLOWAY, JAMES MADISON	D. APRIL 15, 1997, BATON ROUGE, LA.
1922-058	HOLLOWAY, KENNETH EUGENE	D. SEPTEMBER 25, 1968, THOMASVILLE, GA.
1977-068	HOLLY, JEFFREY OWEN	502 VILLAGE ROAD, PORT HUENEME CA 93041
1924-052	HOLM, ROSCOE ALBERT 'WATTIE'	D. MAY 19, 1950, EVERLY, IOWA
1943-064	HOLM, WILLIAM FRED	D. JULY 27, 1977, EAST CHICAGO, IND.
1993-079	HOLMAN, BRADLEY THOMAS	4720 NORTH RIDGE ROAD, WICHITA KS 67205
1988-068	HOLMAN, BRIAN SCOTT	22232 17TH AVENUE SE #312, BOTHELL WA 98021
1968-039	HOLMAN, GARY RICHARD	PO BOX 923, AGUANGA CA 92536
1980-054	HOLMAN, RANDY SCOTT 'SCOTT'	215 DUBLIN COURT, BRANDON MS 39047
1989-062	HOLMAN, SHAWN LEROY	ROUTE 3, EDGEWOOD ROAD, SEWICKLEY PA 15143
1990-070	HOLMES, DARREN LEE	1 EMERALD COURT, ARDEN NC 28704
1942-053	HOLMES, THOMAS FRANCIS	22601 CAMINO DEL MAR #2130, BOCA RATON FL 33433
1930-035	HOLSHOUSER, HERMAN ALEXANDER	D. JULY 26, 1994, CONCORD, N.C.
1996-082	HOLT, CHRISTOPHER MICHAEL	413 WATERVIEW DRIVE, COPPELL TX 75019
1925-050	HOLT, JAMES EMMETT MADISON 'RED'	D. FEBRUARY 2, 1961, BIRMINGHAM, ALA.
1968-040	HOLT, JAMES WILLIAM	170 JUDGE SHARPE ROAD, GRAHAM NC 27253
1980-055	HOLT, ROGER BOYD	804 HILL TOP STREET, FRUITLAND PARK FL 32731
1965-046	HOLTGRAVE, LAVERN GEORGE 'VERN'	389 NORTH 8TH ST, BREESE IL 62230
1985-049	HOLTON, BRIAN JOHN	831 STANISLAUS CIRCLE, CLAREMONT CA 91711
1996-083	HOLTZ, MICHAEL JAMES	243 GOODRIDGE ROAD, NORTHERN CAMBRIA PA 15714
1965-047	HOLTZMAN, KENNETH DALE	256 WATERSIDE DRIVE, GROVER MO 63040
1993-080	HOLZEMER, MARK HAROLD	10044 SOUTH MACALISTER TRAIL, HIGHLANDS RANCH CO 80126
1977-069	HONEYCUTT, FREDERICK WAYNE 'RICK'	207 FORREST ROAD, FORT OGLETHORPE GA 30742
1925-051	HOOD, ALBIE LARRISON	D. OCTOBER 14, 1988, CHESAPEAKE, VA.
1973-063	HOOD, DONALD HARRIS	708 FIRESTONE DR, FLORENCE SC 29501
1949-037	HOOD, WALLACE JAMES	D. JUNE 16, 2001, GLENDALE, CALIF.
1920-055	HOOD, WALLACE JAMES, SR.	D. MAY 2, 1965, HOLLYWOOD, CALIF.
1995-102	HOOK, CHRISTOPHER WAYNE	30 NORTHFIELD DRIVE, FLORENCE KY 41042
1957-034	HOOK, JAMES WESLEY 'JAY'	PO BOX 90, MAPLE CITY MI 49664
1935-050	HOOKS, ALEXANDER MARCUS	D. JUNE 19, 1993, EDGEWOOD, TEXAS
2005-090	HOOPER, KEVIN JAMES	2253 NORTH COVINGTON COURT, WICHITA KS 67205
1950-035	HOOPER, ROBERT NELSON	D. MARCH 17, 1980, NEW BRUNSWICK, N.J.
1974-053	HOOTEN, MICHAEL LEON 'LEON'	PO BOX 1481, COOS BAY OR 97420
1971-049	HOOTON, BURT CARLTON	3619 GRANBY COURT, SAN ANTONIO TX 78217
1990-071	HOOVER, JOHN NICKLAUS	1615 WEST FOUNTAIN, FRESNO CA 93705
2001-081	HOOVER, PAUL CHESTER	2320 ANDERSON ROAD, CUYAHOGA FALLS OH 44221
1952-051	HOOVER, RICHARD LLOYD	D. APRIL 12, 1981, LAKE PLACID, FLA.
1943-065	HOOVER, ROBERT JOSEPH 'JOE'	D. SEPTEMBER 2, 1965, LOS ANGELES, CALIF.
1993-081	HOPE, JOHN ALAN	835 SW 13TH STREET, FORT LAUDERDALE FL 33315
1975-054	HOPKINS, DONALD	PO BOX 8817, BENTON HARBOR MI 49023
1968-041	HOPKINS, GAIL EASON	120 CANTERBURY DRIVE, PARKERSBURG WV 26104
1934-049	HOPKINS, MEREDITH HILLIARD 'MARTY'	D. NOVEMBER 20, 1963
1927-046	HOPKINS, PAUL HENRY	D. JANUARY 2, 2004, DEEP RIVER, CONN.
1939-054	HOPP, JOHN LEONARD	D. JUNE 1, 2003, SCOTTSBLUFF, NEB.

1946-048	HOPPER, JAMES MCDANIEL	D. JANUARY 23, 1982, CHARLOTTE, N.C.
2006-072	HOPPER, NORRIS STEPHEN	OLD ADD: PASSAIC NY
1924-053	HORAN, JOSEPH PATRICK 'SHAGS'	D. FEBRUARY 13, 1969, LOS ANGELES, CALIF.
2004-099	HORGAN, JOSEPH PAUL	2039 KELLOGG WAY, RANCHO CORDOVA CA 95670
1961-053	HORLEN, JOEL EDWARD	3718 CHARTWELL DRIVE, SAN ANTONIO TX 78230
1987-061	HORN, SAMUEL LEE	5625 IMPERIAL AVENUE #420, SAN DIEGO CA 92114
1929-052	HORNE, BERLYN DALE 'TRADER'	D. FEBRUARY 3, 1983, FRANKLIN, OHIO
1978-058	HORNER, JAMES ROBERT 'BOB'	209 STEEPLECHASE DRIVE, IRVING TX 75062
1991-081	HORSMAN, VINCENT STANLEY JOSEPH	1941 PINEHURST DRIVE, CLEARWATER FL 33763
1964-048	HORTON, ANTHONY DARRIN	17001 LIVORNO DR, PACIFIC PALISADES CA 90272
1984-055	HORTON, RICKY NEAL	16026 ASTON COURT, CHESTERFIELD MO 63005
1963-058	HORTON, WILLIAM WATTISON 'WILLIE'	5655 WOODLAND PASS, BLOOMFIELD HILLS MI 48301
1995-103	HOSEY, DWAYNE SAMUEL	10950 CHURCH STREET #R101, RANCHO CUCAMONGA CA 91730
1992-056	HOSEY, STEVEN BERNARD	6445 NORTH LEAD AVENUE, FRESNO CA 93711
1953-034	HOSKINS, DAVID TAYLOR	D. APRIL 2, 1970, FLINT, MICH.
1970-060	HOSLEY, TIMOTHY KENNETH	112 ELENA DRIVE, MOORE SC 29369
1956-046	HOST, EUGENE EARL	D. AUGUST 20, 1998, NASHVILLE, TENN.
1944-062	HOSTETLER, CHARLES CLOYD	D. FEBRUARY 18, 1971, FORT COLLINS, COLO.
1981-057	HOSTETLER, DAVID ALAN	3404 STEEPLECHASE TRAIL, ARLINGTON TX 76016
1971-050	HOTTMAN, KENNETH	9537 SECOND AVENUE, ELK GROVE CA 95624
1970-061	HOUGH, CHARLES OLIVER	2266 SHADE TREE CIR, BREA CA 92621
1947-044	HOUK, RALPH GEORGE	3000 PLANTATION ROAD, WINTER HAVEN FL 33884
2005-091	HOULTON, DENNIS SEAN 'D.J.'	85 ORANGE BLOSSOM CIRCLE, LADERA RANCH CA 92694
2000-078	HOUSE, CRAIG MICHAEL	8845 PATRICIA ELLEN COVE, MEMPHIS TN 38133
1950-036	HOUSE, HENRY FRANKLIN 'FRANK'	D. MARCH 13, 2005, BIRMINGHAM, ALA.
2003-078	HOUSE, JAMES RODGER 'J.R.'	34 RIVER RIDGE TRAIL, ORMOND BEACH FL 32174
1967-050	HOUSE, PATRICK LORY	2554 WEST PENICK POINT COURT, MERIDIAN ID 83642
1971-051	HOUSE, THOMAS ROSS	12794 VIA FELINO, DEL MAR CA 92014
1980-056	HOUSEHOLDER, PAUL WESLEY	521 NORTH SWINTON, DELRAY BEACH FL 33444
1991-082	HOUSIE, WAYNE TYRONE	5180 TYLER STREET #23, RIVERSIDE CA 92503
1996-084	HOUSTON, TYLER SAM	325 PLEASANT SUMMIT DRIVE, HENDERSON NV 89012
1945-049	HOUTTEMAN, ARTHUR JOSEPH	D. MAY 6, 2003, ROCHESTER HILLS, MICH.
1969-082	HOVLEY, STEPHEN EUGENE	PO BOX 655, OAK VIEW CA 93022
2002-087	HOWARD, BENJAMIN RICHARD	45 CROSS BROOK COVE, JACKSON TN 38305
1963-059	HOWARD, BRUCE ERNEST	8705 MISTY CREEK DRIVE, SARASOTA FL 34241
1993-082	HOWARD, CHRISTIAN	17 SEA VIEW AVENUE, NAHANT MA 01908
1991-083	HOWARD, CHRISTOPHER HUGH	8655 JONES ROAD #301, HOUSTON TX 77065
1991-084	HOWARD, DAVID WAYNE	4720 FORGE ACRE DRIVE, PERRY HALL MD 21128
1972-050	HOWARD, DOUGLAS LYNN	8038 DEER CREEK ROAD, SALT LAKE CITY UT 84121
1955-059	HOWARD, ELSTON GENE	D. DECEMBER 14, 1980, NEW YORK, N.Y.
1958-046	HOWARD, FRANK OLIVER	24178 LENAH WOODS PLACE, ALDIE VA 20105
1979-056	HOWARD, FRED IRVING	250 LAKE LULU DRIVE, WINTER HAVEN FL 33880
1970-062	HOWARD, LARRY RAYFORD	OLD ADD: 40005 HERITAGE HOLLOW, GEORGETOWN TX 78628
1946-049	HOWARD, LEE VINCENT	4650 DULIN ROAD #203, FALLBROOK CA 92028
1996-085	HOWARD, MATTHEW CHRISTOPHER	37168 DELGADO WAY, TEMECULA CA 92592
1981-058	HOWARD, MICHAEL FREDRIC	OLD ADD: 4981 46TH ST, SACRAMENTO CA 95820
2004-100	HOWARD, RYAN JAMES	OLD ADD: WILDWOOD MO
1990-072	HOWARD, STEVEN BERNARD	4712 SHETLAND AVENUE, OAKLAND CA 94605
1990-073	HOWARD, THOMAS SYLVESTER	822 8TH AVENUE, MIDDLETOWN OH 45044
1973-064	HOWARD, WILBUR LEON	643 WALSTON LANE, HOUSTON TX 77060
1971-052	HOWARTH, JAMES EUGENE	PO BOX 4019 ONE HANCOCK PLACE, GULFPORT MS 39502
1974-054	HOWE, ARTHUR HENRY	711 KAHLDON COURT, HOUSTON TX 77079
1952-052	HOWE, CALVIN EARL	7450 BOULDER BLUFF DRIVE #51, JENISON MI 49428
1923-065	HOWE, LESTER CURTIS	D. JULY 16, 1976, WOODMERE, N.Y.
1980-057	HOWE, STEVEN ROY	D. APRIL 28, 2006, COACHELLA, CALIF.
1947-045	HOWELL, HOMER ELLIOTT 'DIXIE'	D. OCTOBER 5, 1990, BINGHAMTON, N.Y.
1985-050	HOWELL, JACK ROBERT	822 SOUTH LEHIGH DRIVE, TUCSON AZ 85710
2005-092	HOWELL, JAMES PHILLIP 'J.P.'	808 46TH STREET, SACRAMENTO CA 95819
1980-058	HOWELL, JAY CANFIELD	260 SCALE LANE, ALPHARETTA GA 30022
1984-056	HOWELL, KENNETH	22090 BUCKINGHAM DRIVE, FARMINGTON MI 48335
1940-037	HOWELL, MILLARD FILLMORE 'DIXIE'	D. MARCH 18, 1960, HOLLYWOOD, FLA.
1941-047	HOWELL, MURRAY DONALD 'RED'	D. OCTOBER 1, 1950, GREENVILLE, S.C.
1992-057	HOWELL, PATRICK O'NEAL	5228 WILHELM DRIVE, MOBILE AL 36618
1974-055	HOWELL, ROY LEE	276 EL PORTAL DRIVE, PISMO BEACH CA 93449
1949-038	HOWERTON, WILLIAM RAY	D. DECEMBER 18, 2001, BLAKELY, PA.
1989-063	HOWITT, DANN PAUL JOHN	63 ALLISON DRIVE, BATTLE CREEK MI 49017
1998-087	HOWRY, BOBBY DEAN	5440 WEST PARK VIEW LANE, GLENDALE AZ 85310
1961-054	HOWSER, RICHARD DALTON	D. JUNE 17, 1987, KANSAS CITY, MO.
1992-058	HOY, PETER ALEXANDER	770 LAMBERT STREET CARDINAL ON, K0E 1E0 CANADA
1952-053	HOYLE, ROLAND EDISON	D. JULY 4, 1994, CARBONDALE, PA.
1979-057	HOYT, DEWEY LAMARR 'LAMARR'	1594 LOST CREEK DRIVE, COLUMBIA SC 29212
1970-063	HRABOSKY, ALAN THOMAS	9 FRONTENAC ESTATES DRIVE, SAINT LOUIS MO 63131
1981-059	HRBEK, KENT ALAN	2611 WEST 112TH STREET, BLOOMINGTON MN 55431
1968-042	HRINIAK, WALTER JOHN	18 STACY DRIVE, NORTH ANDOVER MA 01845
1978-059	HUBBARD, GLENN DEE	1515 KING'S CROSSING, STONE MOUNTAIN GA 30087
1995-104	HUBBARD, MICHAEL WAYNE	2552 BROOKSTONE LANE, RICHMOND VA 23233
1994-047	HUBBARD, TRENIDAD AVIEL	17206 HILLSIDE AVENUE, HAZEL CREST IL 60429
1928-049	HUBBELL, CARL OWEN	D. NOVEMBER 21, 1988, SCOTTSDALE, ARIZ.
1961-055	HUBBS, KENNETH DOUGLASS	D. FEBRUARY 15, 1964, UTAH LAKE, UTAH
1920-056	HUBER, CLARENCE BILL	D. FEBRUARY 22, 1965, LAREDO, TEXAS
2006-073	HUBER, JONATHON LLOYD	OLD ADD: NORTH FORT MYERS FL
2005-093	HUBER, JUSTIN PATRICK	OLD ADD: EMERALD AUSTRALIA
1939-055	HUBER, OTTO	D. APRIL 9, 1989, PASSAIC, N.J.
2001-082	HUCKABY, KENNETH PAUL	4490 SOUTH RIO DRIVE, CHANDLER AZ 85249
1935-051	HUCKLEBERRY, EARL EUGENE	D. FEBRUARY 25, 1999, SEMINOLE, OKLA.
1994-048	HUDEK, JOHN RAYMOND	7603 SHADY WAY DRIVE, SUGAR LAND TX 77479

1983-074	HUDGENS, DAVID MARK	5802 EAST WINDSOR AVENUE, SCOTTSDALE AZ 85257
1923-066	HUDGENS, JAMES PRICE	D. AUGUST 26, 1955, ST. LOUIS, MO.
1984-057	HUDLER, REX ALLEN	11745 RIEHL AVENUE, TUSTIN CA 92782
1926-039	HUDLIN, GEORGE WILLIS 'WILLIS'	D. AUGUST 5, 2002, LITTLE ROCK, ARK.
1972-051	HUDSON, CHARLES	RURAL ROUTE 5 BOX 570, COALGATE OK 74538
1983-075	HUDSON, CHARLES LYNN	PO BOX 56, OAKWOOD TX 75055
1952-054	HUDSON, HAL CAMPBELL	422 SANDPIPER DRIVE #C, FORT PIERCE FL 34982
1969-083	HUDSON, JESSIE JAMES	PO BOX 1052, MANSFIELD LA 71052
1936-040	HUDSON, JOHN WILSON	D. NOVEMBER 7, 1970, BRYAN, TEXAS
1995-105	HUDSON, JOSEPH PAUL	109 PINE VALLEY DRIVE, MEDFORD NJ 08055
2002-088	HUDSON, LUKE STEPHEN	9912 ASTER CIRCLE, FOUNTAIN VALLEY CA 92708
2002-089	HUDSON, ORLANDO THILL	1554 POCKET ROAD, DARLINGTON SC 29532
1974-056	HUDSON, REX HAUGHTON	4704 SPRING MOWS, MIDLAND TX 79705
1940-038	HUDSON, SIDNEY CHARLES	1309 WESTWOOD DRIVE, WACO TX 76710
1999-092	HUDSON, TIMOTHY ADAM	600 GRYASTON COURT, PEACHTREE CITY GA 30269
2000-079	HUFF, AUBREY LEWIS	11831 94TH STREET, LARGO FL 33773
1989-064	HUFF, MICHAEL KALE	PO BOX 92385, SOUTHLAKE TX 76092
1937-053	HUFFMAN, BENNIE FRANKLIN	D. FEBRUARY 22, 2005, LURAY, VA.
1979-058	HUFFMAN, PHILLIP LEE	OLD ADD: 1101 CHERYL DRIVE, BURKBURNETT TX 76354
1974-057	HUGHES, JAMES MICHAEL	7526 EL MANOR AVENUE, LOS ANGELES CA 90045
1952-055	HUGHES, JAMES ROBERT	D. AUGUST 13, 2001, CHICAGO, ILL.
1987-062	HUGHES, KEITH WILLS	176 SYCAMORE ROAD, HAVERTOWN PA 19083
1966-046	HUGHES, RICHARD HENRY	BOX 598, STEPHENS AR 71764
1998-088	HUGHES, ROBERT E	OLD ADD: 8425 EAST VIA RUIDOSA, SCOTTSDALE AZ 85258
1935-052	HUGHES, ROY JOHN	D. MARCH 5, 1995, ASHEVILLE, N.C.
1970-064	HUGHES, TERRY WAYNE	532 PIERPONT AVENUE EXT., SPARTANBURG SC 29303
1959-039	HUGHES, THOMAS EDWARD	610 KIMSWICK COURT, DEER PARK TX 77536
1930-036	HUGHES, THOMAS FRANKLIN	D. AUGUST 10, 1989, BEAUMONT, TEXAS
1941-048	HUGHES, THOMAS OWEN	D. NOVEMBER 28, 1990, WILKES-BARRE, PA.
2004-101	HUGHES, TRAVIS WADE	70525 HIGHWAY 283, BEAVER CITY NE 68926
1921-046	HUGHES, WILLIAM NESBERT	D. FEBRUARY 25, 1963, BIRMINGHAM, ALA.
1941-049	HUGHSON, CECIL CARLTON 'TEX'	D. AUGUST 6, 1993, AUSTIN, TEXAS
2004-102	HUISMAN, JUSTIN RAY	1274 RIDGE FIELD RUN, SCHERERVILLE IN 46375
1995-106	HUISMAN, RICHARD ALLEN 'RICK'	17W25 OAK LANE, BENSENVILLE IL 60106
1983-076	HUISMANN, MARK LAWRENCE	705 NE LAKE POINTE DRIVE, LEES SUMMIT MO 64064
1983-077	HULETT, TIMOTHY CRAIG	6154 BUNCOMBE ROAD, SHREVEPORT LA 71129
1922-059	HULIHAN, HARRY JOSEPH	D. SEPTEMBER 11, 1980, RUTLAND, VT.
1992-059	HULSE, DAVID LINDSEY	1301 KENWOOD DRIVE, SAN ANGELO TX 76903
1923-067	HULVEY, JAMES HENSEL 'HANK'	D. APRIL 9, 1982, MOUNT SIDNEY, VA.
2006-074	HUMBER, PHILIP GREGORY	COUNTY ROAD 114, CARTHAGE TX 75633
1977-070	HUME, THOMAS HUBERT	3810 REDFISH COURT, PALMETTO FL 34221
2003-079	HUMMEL, TIMOTHY ROBERT	38 GROVE STREET, MONTGOMERY NY 12549
1938-040	HUMPHREY, BYRON WILLIAM	D. FEBRUARY 13, 1992, SPRINGFIELD, MO.
1971-053	HUMPHREY, TERRYAL GENE	7 OAKMONT, TRABUCO CANYON CA 92679
1991-085	HUMPHREYS, MICHAEL BUTLER	1402 LOST CREEK, DESOTO TX 75115
1962-058	HUMPHREYS, ROBERT WILLIAM	1803 OAKWOOD STREET, BEDFORD VA 24523
1938-041	HUMPHRIES, JOHN WILLIAM	D. JUNE 24, 1965, NEW ORLEANS, LA.
1964-049	HUNDLEY, CECIL RANDOLPH 'RANDY'	122 EAST FOREST LN, PALATINE IL 60067
1990-074	HUNDLEY, TODD RANDOLPH	830 RALEIGH ROAD, GLENVIEW IL 60025
1922-060	HUNGLING, BERNARD HERMAN	D. MARCH 30, 1968, DAYTON, OHIO
1926-040	HUNNEFIELD, WILLIAM FENTON	D. AUGUST 28, 1976, NANTUCKET, MASS.
1985-051	HUNT, JAMES RANDALL 'RANDY'	324 HOLLY RIDGE DRIVE, MONTGOMERY AL 36109
1959-040	HUNT, KENNETH LAWRENCE	D. JUNE 8, 1997, GARDENA, CALIF.
1961-056	HUNT, KENNETH RAYMOND	268 EAST 300 NORTH, MORGAN UT 84050
1931-041	HUNT, OLIVER JOEL 'JOEL'	D. JULY 24, 1978, TEAGUE, TEXAS
1963-060	HUNT, RONALD KENNETH	2806 JACKSON RD, WENTZVILLE MO 63385
1994-049	HUNTER, BRIAN LEE	31203 NE 49TH STREET, CAMAS WA 98607
1991-086	HUNTER, BRIAN RAYNOLD	12141 CENTRALIA #219, LAKEWOOD CA 90715
1933-026	HUNTER, EDISON FRANKLIN	D. MARCH 14, 1967, COLERAIN TWP., OHIO
1953-035	HUNTER, GORDON WILLIAM 'BILLY'	104 EAST SEMINARY AVENUE, LUTHERVILLE MD 21093
1971-054	HUNTER, HAROLD JAMES	14616 FIR CIRCLE, PLATTSMOUTH NE 68048
1965-048	HUNTER, JAMES AUGUSTUS 'CATFISH'	D. SEPTEMBER 9, 1999, HERTFORD, N.C.
1991-087	HUNTER, JAMES MACGREGOR	108 TINDALL ROAD, MIDDLETOWN NJ 07748
1996-086	HUNTER, RICHARD THOMAS 'RICH'	OLD ADD: 1931 WEST COAST HWY, NEWPORT BEACH CA 92663
1997-081	HUNTER, TORII KEDAR	PO BOX 1357, PROSPER TX 75078
1962-059	HUNTER, WILLARD MITCHELL 'BILL'	2562 POPPLETON AVE, OMAHA NE 68105
1967-051	HUNTZ, STEPHEN MICHAEL	2788 WOOSTER ROAD, ROCKY RIVER OH 44116
1923-068	HUNTZINGER, WALTER HENRY	D. AUGUST 11, 1981, UPPER DARBY, PA.
1983-078	HUPPERT, DAVID BLAINE	6732 STEPHENS PATH, ZEPHYRHILLS FL 33541
1954-046	HURD, THOMAS CARR	D. SEPTEMBER 5, 1982, WATERLOO, IOWA
1977-071	HURDLE, CLINTON MERRICK	9068 STURBRIDGE PLACE, LITTLETON CO 80129
1980-059	HURST, BRUCE VEE	1080 NORTH RIATA STREET, GILBERT AZ 85234
1928-050	HURST, FRANK O 'DONNELL 'DON'	D. DECEMBER 6, 1952, LOS ANGELES, CALIF.
1994-050	HURST, JAMES LAVON	1413 VAN PELT ROAD, SEBRING FL 33870
1997-082	HURST, JIMMY ONEAL	OLD ADD: 1310 37TH STREET EAST, TUSCALOOSA AL 35405
1992-060	HURST, JONATHAN	308 WOODBURN CREEK ROAD, SPARTANBURG SC 29302
1996-087	HURST, WILLIAM HANSEL	13327 SW 112TH COURT, MIAMI FL 33176
1995-107	HURTADO, EDWIN AMILGAR	OLD ADD: 221 N. LASALLE ST, CHICAGO IL 60601
1993-083	HUSKEY, ROBERT LEON	PO BOX 996, APACHE OK 73006
1988-069	HUSON, JEFFREY KENT	10340 ROWLOCK WAY, PARKER CO 80134
1925-052	HUSTA, CARL LAWRENCE	D. NOVEMBER 6, 1951, KINGSTON, N.Y.
1937-054	HUSTON, WARREN LLEWELLYN	D. AUGUST 30, 1999, WAREHAM, MASS.
1933-027	HUTCHESON, JOSEPH JOHNSON	D. FEBRUARY 23, 1993, TYLER, TEXAS
1940-039	HUTCHINGS, JOHN RICHARD JOSEPH	D. APRIL 27, 1963, INDIANAPOLIS, IND.
2001-083	HUTCHINSON, CHAD MARTIN	OLD ADD: 1801 NORTH GREEN VALLEY PKWY, LAS VEGAS NV 89074
1939-056	HUTCHINSON, FREDERICK CHARLES	D. NOVEMBER 12, 1964, BRADENTON, FLA.

1933-028 HUTCHINSON, IRA KENDALL ....D. AUGUST 21, 1973, CHICAGO, ILL.
1974-058 HUTSON, GEORGE HERBERT 'HERB'..................7203 WEST SUGARTREE COURT, SAVANNAH GA 31410
1925-053 HUTSON, ROY LEE..D. MAY 20, 1957, LAMESA, CALIF.
1970-065 HUTTO, JAMES NEAMON ....1317 JOHN CARROLL DRIVE, PENSACOLA FL 32504
1993-084 HUTTON, MARK STEVEN ....6 CORFU COURT, WESTLAKES ADELAIDE, AUSTRALIA 5021
1966-047 HUTTON, THOMAS GEORGE.................................18 HUNTLY DRIVE, PALM BEACH GARDENS FL 33410
1955-060 HYDE, RICHARD ELDE...1506 CAMBRIDGE DRIVE, CHAMPAIGN IL 61821
1994-051 HYERS, TIMOTHY JAMES......................................241 RIDGE ROAD, COVINGTON GA 30209
2000-080 HYZDU, ADAM DAVIS ....7823 EAST RED HAWK CIRCLE, MESA AZ 85207

I

2006-075 IANNETTA, CHRISTOPHER DOMENIC..................120 LANGDON STREET, PROVIDENCE RI 02904
1996-088 IBANEZ, RAUL JAVIER ....5601 ARBOR LANE, CORAL GABLES FL 33156
1973-065 IGNASIAK, GARY RAYMOND ....3084 ANGELOS DRIVE, WATERFORD MI 48329
1991-088 IGNASIAK, MICHAEL JAMES ....5821 SALINE ANN ARBOR ROAD, SALINE MI 48176
2005-094 IGUCHI, TADAHITO ....OLD ADD: TOKYO JAPAN
1994-052 ILSLEY, BLAISE FRANCIS ....2415 TIMBERLANE DRIVE, ALPENA MI 49707
1986-066 INCAVIGLIA, PETER JOSEPH ....PO BOX 526, PEBBLE BEACH CA 93953
1987-063 INFANTE, FERMIN ALEXIS ....URB. COLINAS DE LA ROSALEDA CALLE 4 CASA #20, BARQUISIMETO VENEZUELA
2002-090 INFANTE, OMAR R ....OLD ADD: GUANTE VENEZUELA
2001-084 INGE, CHARLES BRANDON 'BRANDON'.............832 UPPER SCOTSBOROUGH WAY, BLOOMFIELD HILLS MI 48304
2006-076 INGLETT, JOSEPH STEVEN ....7141 MARIPOSA AVENUE, CITRUS HEIGHTS CA 95610
1994-053 INGRAM, GAREY LAMAR.....................................2901 GATEWOOD DRIVE, PHENIX CITY AL 36870
1929-053 INGRAM, MELVIN DAVID ....D. OCTOBER 28, 1979, MEDFORD, ORE.
1994-054 INGRAM, RICCARDO BENAY...............................5720 MARTIN GROVE DRIVE NW, LILBURN GA 30047
1987-064 INNIS, JEFFREY DAVID ....4920 WOODLONG LANE, CUMMING GA 30130
1977-072 IORG, DANE CHARLES...928 SAGE DRIVE, PLEASANT GROVE UT 84062
1978-060 IORG, GARTH RAY ....OLD ADD: 1224 WALLINGFORD ROAD, KNOXVILLE TN 37923
1941-050 IOTT, CLARENCE EUGENE 'HOOKS' ....D. AUGUST 17, 1980, ST. PETERSBURG, FLA.
1997-083 IRABU, HIDEKI ....2212 VIA VELARDO, RANCHO PALOS VERDES CA 90275
1981-060 IRELAND, TIMOTHY NEAL ....20932 TIMES AVE, HAYWARD CA 94541
1949-039 IRVIN, MONFORD MERRILL 'MONTE ' ....1815 ENCLAVE PKWY #6111, HOUSTON TX 77077
1990-075 IRVINE, DARYL KEITH ....OLD ADD: 237 INGLEWOOD COURT, MCGAHEYSVILLE 22840
1938-042 IRWIN, THOMAS ANDREW..................................D. APRIL 25, 1996, ALTOONA, PA.
1921-047 IRWIN, WALTER KINGSLEY................................D. AUGUST 18, 1976, SPRING LAKE, MICH.
1980-060 ISALES, ORLANDO...14710 SW 106TH AVENUE, MIAMI FL 33176
2002-091 ISHII, KAZUHISA..OLD ADD: CHIBA JAPAN
2006-077 ISHIKAWA, TRAVIS TAKASHI...............................3714 48TH AVENUE NE, TACOMA WA 98422
1995-108 ISRINGHAUSEN, JASON DERIK...........................550 LAKE ROAD NORTH, TARPON SPRINGS FL 34688
1971-055 IVIE, MICHAEL WILSON.......................................894 ROCKER ROAD, CRAWFORDSVILLE GA 30631
1967-052 IZQUIERDO, ENRIQUE ROBERTO 'HANK' ....12458 71ST PLACE NORTH, WEST PALM BEACH FL 33412
2002-092 IZQUIERDO, HANSEL...8420 SW 154TH CIRCLE COURT, MIAMI FL 33193
2001-085 IZTURIS, CESAR D...OLD ADD: BARQUISIMETO VENEZ
2004-103 IZTURIS, MAICER ....OLD ADD: BARQUISIMETO VENEZ

J

1953-036 JABLONSKI, RAYMOND LEO...............................D. NOVEMBER 25, 1985, CHICAGO, ILL.
1959-041 JACKSON, ALVIN NEILL.......................................3321 SE MORNINGSIDE BLVD, PORT SAINT LUCIE FL 34952
1987-065 JACKSON, CHARLES LEO ....15821 SE 175TH PLACE, RENTON WA 98058
2005-095 JACKSON, CONOR S..7301 EAST THIRD AVENUE, SCOTTSDALE AZ 85251
1996-089 JACKSON, DAMIAN JACQUES ....2038 AMPARO COURT, ESCONDIDO CA 92025
1983-079 JACKSON, DANNY LYNN......................................13730 GOODMAN STREET, SHAWNEE MISSION KS 66223
1978-061 JACKSON, DARRELL PRESTON..........................PO BOX 4424, DOWNEY CA 90241
1985-052 JACKSON, DARRIN JAY ....16029 WEST MADISON STREET, GOODYEAR AZ 85338
2003-080 JACKSON, EDWIN...6955 SETTER DRIVE, COLUMBUS GA 31909
1965-049 JACKSON, GRANT DWIGHT................................212 MESA CIRCLE, UPPER SAINT CLAIR PA 15241
1933-029 JACKSON, JOHN LEWIS ....D. OCTOBER 24, 1956, SOMERS POINT, N.J.
1987-066 JACKSON, KENNETH BERNARD ....PO BOX 613, WASKOM TX 75692
1955-061 JACKSON, LAWRENCE CURTIS ....D. AUGUST 28, 1990, BOISE, IDAHO
1958-047 JACKSON, LOUIS CLARENCE ....D. MAY 27, 1969, TOKYO, JAPAN
1986-067 JACKSON, MICHAEL RAY ....PO BOX 6046, SAN RAMON CA 94583
1970-066 JACKSON, MICHAEL WARREN ....805 11TH AVENUE #2H, PATERSON NJ 07514
1950-037 JACKSON, RANSOM JOSEPH 'RANDY'...............250 HUNNICUT DRIVE, ATHENS GA 30601
1967-053 JACKSON, REGINALD MARTINEZ 'REGGIE'.........305 AMADOR AVENUE, SEASIDE CA 93955
1963-061 JACKSON, ROLAND THOMAS 'SONNY' ....117 PALM BAY #B, PALM BAY GARDENS FL 33418
1954-047 JACKSON, RONALD ALLEN.................................210 RAINTREE CIRCLE, KALAMAZOO MI 49007
1975-055 JACKSON, RONNIE ....515 WHITE ROAD, FAYETTEVILLE GA 30214
1977-073 JACKSON, ROY LEE ....8269 COUNTY ROAD 54, AUBURN AL 36830
1998-089 JACKSON, RYAN DEWITTE ....2335 ALPINE AVENUE, SARASOTA FL 34239
1922-061 JACKSON, TRAVIS CALVIN ....D. JULY 27, 1987, WALDO, ARK.
1986-068 JACKSON, VINCENT EDWARD 'BO' ....100 OAK RIDGE DRIVE WEST, BURR RIDGE IL 60521
2006-078 JACKSON, ZACHARY THOMAS..........................313 HILLCREST DRIVE, CRANBERRY TWP PA 16066
1948-048 JACOBS, ANTHONY ROBERT 'TONY'..................D. DECEMBER 21, 1980, NASHVILLE, TENN.
1939-057 JACOBS, ARTHUR EVAN.....................................D. JUNE 8, 1967, INGLEWOOD, CALIF.
1954-048 JACOBS, FORREST VANDERGRIFT 'SPOOK' ....BOX 66, MILFORD DE 19963
1960-049 JACOBS, LAMAR GARY 'JAKE'............................1626 TERRA CEIA BAY CIRCLE, PALMETTO FL 34221
2005-096 JACOBS, MICHAEL JAMES ....7448 GORGE VIEW TERRACE, SAN DIEGO CA 92120
1937-055 JACOBS, NEWTON SMITH 'BUCKY'.....................D. JUNE 15, 1990, RICHMOND, VA.
1928-051 JACOBS, RAYMOND FREDERICK.........................D. APRIL 5, 1952, LOS ANGELES, CALIF.
2004-104 JACOBSEN, LARRY WILLIAM 'BUCKY'................785 WEST DIV ISION AVENUE, HERMISTON OR 97838
1981-061 JACOBY, BROOK WALLACE ....21825 NORTH DOBSON ROAD, SCOTTSDALE AZ 85255
1994-055 JACOME, JASON JAMES.....................................5115 NORTH CAMINO ESPLENDORA, TUCSON AZ 85718

1971-056	JACQUEZ, PATRICK THOMAS	4430 ANNADALE DRIVE, STOCKTON CA 95219
2000-081	JACQUEZ, THOMAS PATRICK	4430 ANNADALE DRIVE, STOCKTON CA 95219
1964-050	JAECKEL, PAUL HENRY	328 WEST 7TH STREET, CLAREMONT CA 91711
1920-057	JAEGER, JOSEPH PETER	D. DECEMBER 13, 1963, HAMPTON, IOWA
1992-061	JAHA, JOHN EMILE	2506 NW 24TH CIRCLE, CAMAS WA 98607
1925-054	JAHN, ARTHUR CHARLES	D. JANUARY 9, 1948, LITTLE ROCK, ARK.
1936-041	JAKUCKI, SIGMUND	D. MAY 28, 1979, GALVESTON, TEXAS
1924-054	JAMERSON, CHARLEY DEWEY	D. AUGUST 4, 1980, MOCKSVILLE, N.C.
1975-056	JAMES, ARTHUR	139 HARMON STREET, DETROIT MI 48202
2005-097	JAMES, CHARLES HAMILTON 'CHUCK'	4870 GOLDEN CIRCLE SW, MABLETON GA 30126
1960-050	JAMES, CHARLES WESLEY	3303 TANGLEWOOD WAY, FULTON MO 65251
1968-043	JAMES, CLEO JOEL	PO BOX 9970, MORENO VALLEY CA 92552
2002-093	JAMES, DELVIN DEWAYNE	13355 FM 1878, NACOGDOCHES TX 75961
1983-080	JAMES, DION	5 SHELTER POINT COURT, SACRAMENTO CA 95831
1986-069	JAMES, DONALD CHRISTOPHER 'CHRIS'	1040 COUNTY ROAD 2707, ALTO TX 75925
1968-044	JAMES, JEFFREY LYNN	D. MAY 7, 2006, INDIANAPOLIS, IND.
1958-048	JAMES, JOHN PHILLIP	6037 EAST LARKSPUR, SCOTTSDALE AZ 85254
1995-109	JAMES, MICHAEL ELMO	115 AUSTIN COURT, MARY ESTHER FL 32569
1977-074	JAMES, PHILIP ROBERT 'SKIP'	7716 WEST 72ND TERRACE, OVERLAND PARK KS 66204
1967-054	JAMES, RICHARD LEE	OLD ADD: 508 AIRPORT ROAD, PANAMA CITY FL 32405
1929-054	JAMES, ROBERT BYRNE 'BERNIE'	D. AUGUST 1, 1994, SAN ANTONIO, TEXAS
1978-062	JAMES, ROBERT HARVEY	15844 CINDY COURT, CANYON COUNTRY CA 91351
1970-067	JANESKI, GERALD JOSEPH 'JERRY'	28901 VIA BUENA VIS, SAN JUAN CAPISTRANO CA 92675
1953-037	JANOWICZ, VICTOR FELIX	D. FEBRUARY 27, 1996, COLUMBUS, OHIO
1947-046	JANSEN, LAWRENCE JOSEPH 'LARRY'	3207 NW HIGHWAY 47, FOREST GROVE OR 97116
2006-079	JANSSEN, ROBERT CASEY	OLD ADD: HUNTINGTON BEACH CA
1996-090	JANZEN, MARTIN THOMAS	OLD ADD: 9483 SW 32ND LANE, GAINESVILLE FL 32608
1994-056	JARVIS, KEVIN THOMAS	1486 WILLOWBROOKE CIRCLE, FRANKLIN TN 37069
1944-063	JARVIS, LEROY GILBERT 'ROY'	D. JANUARY 13, 1990, OKLAHOMA CITY, OKLA.
1969-084	JARVIS, RAYMOND ARNOLD	15 HIGGINS STREET #106, SMITHFIELD RI 02917
1966-048	JARVIS, ROBERT PATRICK 'PAT'	4201 PROVIDENCE LANE, TUCKER GA 30084
1965-050	JASTER, LARRY EDWARD	1105 MILLCREEK DRIVE, JACKSONVILLE FL 32259
1972-052	JATA, PAUL	9276 SE 130TH LOOP, SUMMERFIELD FL 34491
1940-040	JAVERY, ALVA WILLIAM	D. SEPTEMBER 13, 1977, WOODSTOCK, CONN.
1976-041	JAVIER, IGNACIO ALFREDO 'ALFREDO'	BARRIO LIBRE #96 INGCON SAN PEDRO DE MACORIS, DOM REP
1960-051	JAVIER, MANUEL JULIAN 'JULIAN'	680 SECOND AVENUE NORTH, NAPLES FL 34102
1984-058	JAVIER, STANLEY JULIAN ANTONIO	B12 URB. PINA SAN FRANCISCO DE MACORIS, DOM REP
1953-038	JAY, JOSEPH RICHARD 'JOEY'	7209 BATTENWOOD COURT, TAMPA FL 33615
1993-085	JEAN, DOMINGO	CALLE E PUEBLO NUEVO #12 SAN PEDRO DE MACORIS, DOM REP
1921-048	JEANES, ERNEST LEE 'TEX'	D. APRIL 5, 1973, LONGVIEW, TEXAS
1936-042	JEFFCOAT, GEORGE EDWARD	D. OCTOBER 13, 1978, LEESVILLE, S.C.
1948-049	JEFFCOAT, HAROLD BENTLEY 'HAL'	4016 WISCONSIN AVENUE, TAMPA FL 33616
1983-081	JEFFCOAT, JAMES MICHAEL 'MIKE'	4224 OAK SPRINGS DRIVE, ARLINGTON TX 76016
1987-067	JEFFERIES, GREGORY SCOTT	70 DUMONT COURT, MILLBRAE CA 94030
1973-066	JEFFERSON, JESSE HARRISON	1421 RAILROAD AVE, MIDLOTHIAN VA 23113
1991-089	JEFFERSON, REGINALD JIROD	2693 MICCOSUKEE ROAD, TALLAHASSEE FL 32308
1986-070	JEFFERSON, STANLEY	2420-3E HUNTER AVENUE, BRONX NY 10475
1930-037	JEFFRIES, IRVINE FRANKLIN	D. JUNE 8, 1982, LOUISVILLE, KY.
1990-076	JELIC, CHRISTOPHER JOHN	33 ALLEGHENY AVENUE #5, CUDDY PA 15031
1941-051	JELINCICH, FRANK ANTHONY	D. JUNE 27, 1992, ROCHESTER, MINN.
1987-068	JELKS, GREGORY DION	615 BAY SPRINGS ROAD, CENTRE AL 35960
1983-082	JELTZ, LARRY STEVEN 'STEVE'	608 WEST 28TH PLACE, LAWRENCE KS 66046
1965-051	JENKINS, FERGUSON ARTHUR	41913 NORTH SIGNAL HILL COURT, PHOENIX AZ 85086
1998-090	JENKINS, GEOFFREY SCOTT	6683 EAST JUDSON ROAD, PARADISE VALLEY AZ 85253
1922-062	JENKINS, JOHN ROBERT	D. AUGUST 3, 1968, COLUMBIA, MO.
1925-055	JENKINS, THOMAS GRIFFIN	D. MAY 3, 1979, WEYMOUTH, MASS.
1962-060	JENKINS, WARREN WASHINGTON 'JACK'	D. JUNE 18, 2002, TAMPA, FLA.
2005-098	JENKS, ROBERT SCOTT	OLD ADD: 6224 226TH STREET SE, BOTHELL WA 98021
1988-070	JENNINGS, JAMES DOUGLAS 'DOUG'	1660 SW 14TH DRIVE, BOCA RATON FL 33486
2001-086	JENNINGS, JASON RYAN	4851 PALOS VERDES DRIVE, MESQUITE TX 75150
1996-091	JENNINGS, ROBIN CHRISTOPHER	6052 NORTH KINGSFORD AVENUE, PARK CITY UT 84098
1951-044	JENNINGS, WILLIAM LEE	7065 FOXCROFORT DRIVE, AFFTON MO 63123
1931-042	JENSEN, FORREST DUCENUS 'WOODY'	D. OCTOBER 5, 2001, WICHITA, KAN.
1950-038	JENSEN, JACK EUGENE 'JACKIE'	D. JULY 14, 1982, CHARLOTTESVILLE, VA.
2001-087	JENSEN, LARRY RYAN 'RYAN'	3059 SOUTH LARKSPUR STREET, GILBERT AZ 85296
1996-092	JENSEN, MARCUS CHRISTIAN	19550 NORTH GRAYHAWK DR #1134, SCOTTSDALE AZ 85255
1998-091	JERZEMBECK, MICHAEL JOSEPH	22011 HARTLAND AVENUE, QUEENS VILLAGE NY 11427
1929-055	JESSEE, DANIEL EDWARD	D. APRIL 30, 1970, VENICE, FLA.
1969-085	JESTADT, GARRY ARTHUR	9495 EAST SAN SALVADOR DR #100, SCOTTSDALE AZ 85258
1952-056	JESTER, VIRGIL MILTON	8130 RALEIGH PLACE, WESTMINSTER CO 80030
1995-110	JETER, DEREK SANDERSON	845 UNITED NATIONS PLAZA #88B, NEW YORK NY 10017
1969-086	JETER, JOHN	2725 SOUTHERN AVENUE, SHREVEPORT LA 71104
1992-062	JETER, SHAWN DARRELL	4287 WALFORD STREET, COLUMBUS OH 43224
1950-039	JETHROE, SAMUEL	D. JUNE 16, 2001, ERIE, PA.
1983-083	JIMENEZ, ALFONSO 'HOUSTON'	EXP. DE LA CD. DEPORTIVA COL. ATASTA DE SERRA, CP 86100, VILLAHERMOSA, MEXICO
2006-080	JIMENEZ, CESAR ENRIQUE	OLD ADD: CUMANA SUCRE VENEZ
1999-093	JIMENEZ, DANGELO	OLD ADD: SANTO DOMINGO DOM REP
1964-051	JIMENEZ, FELIX ELVIO 'ELVIO'	MANZANA A, ED. 19 #1B CANSINO SEGUNDO, SANTO DOMINGO, DOM REP
2002-094	JIMENEZ, JASON JON	9537 SECOND AVENUE, ELK GROVE CA 95624
1998-092	JIMENEZ, JOSE	OLD ADD: SAN PEDRO DE MACORIS DOM REP
1962-061	JIMENEZ, MANUEL EMILIO	OLD ADD: 24 SIMON BOLIVAR, SAN PEDRO DE MACORIS DOM REP
2006-081	JIMENEZ, UBALDO	OLD ADD: SAN CRISTOBAL DOM REP
2005-099	JIMERSON, CHARLTON MAXWELL	31880 CHICIONE AVENUE, HAYWARD CA 94544
1988-071	JIMINEZ, GERMAN	CALLE JUSTO SIERRA #118 SANTIAGO, IXCUINTIA, MEXICO
1974-059	JIMINEZ, JUAN ANTONIO	CALLE 9, CASA 1N EL ENSUENO SANTIAGO, DOM REP
1993-086	JIMINEZ, MIGUEL ANTHONY	OLD ADD: 943 FENWOOD DRIVE, VALLEY STREAM NY 11580

2001-088	JODIE, BRETT PAUL	1359 CORLEY MILL ROAD, LEXINGTON SC 29072
2006-082	JOHJIMA, KENJI	OLD ADD: SASEBO JAPAN
1963-062	JOHN, THOMAS EDWARD	6202 SETON HOUSE LANE, CHARLOTTE NC 28277
1926-041	JOHNS, AUGUSTUS FRANCIS	D. SEPTEMBER 12, 1975, SAN ANTONIO, TEXAS
1995-111	JOHNS, DOUGLAS ALAN	1131 SOUTHWEST 72ND AVENUE, PLANTATION FL 33317
1998-093	JOHNS, ROBERT KEITH 'KEITH'	16444 GREEN PINES DRIVE, BALLWIN MO 63011
2001-089	JOHNSON, ADAM BRYANT	7335 HERITAGE PALMS ESTATE DRIVE, FORT MYERS FL 33912
1941-052	JOHNSON, ADAM RANKIN 'RANK '	D. FEBRUARY 11, 2006, WILLIAMSPORT, PA.
1964-052	JOHNSON, ALEXANDER	18425 BRETTON DRIVE, DETROIT MI 48223
1981-062	JOHNSON, ANTHONY CLAIR	OLD ADD: 3351 DAWN DRIVE, MEMPHIS TH 38127
1927-047	JOHNSON, ARTHUR GILBERT	D. JUNE 7, 1982, SARASOTA, FLA.
1940-041	JOHNSON, ARTHUR HENRY	23 HEMLOCK DRIVE, HOLDEN MA 01520
1959-042	JOHNSON, BENJAMIN FRANKLIN	112 LOCKSLEY DR, GREENWOOD SC 29646
2005-100	JOHNSON, BENJAMIN JOSEPH	OLD ADD: 3583 PARK LANE DRIVE, MEMPHIS TN 38118
1981-063	JOHNSON, BOBBY EARL	265 QUARI STREET, AURORA CO 80011
1994-057	JOHNSON, BRIAN DAVID	7595 E. PALCITA VIS DEL BOSQUE, TUCSON AZ 85715
1994-058	JOHNSON, CHARLES EDWARD	12301 NW 7TH STREET, PLANTATION FL 33325
1946-050	JOHNSON, CHESTER LILLIS	D. APRIL 10, 1983, SEATTLE, WASH.
1969-087	JOHNSON, CLAIR BARTH 'BART'	9800 SOUTH 49TH AVENUE, OAKLAWN IL 60453
1972-053	JOHNSON, CLIFFORD	9618 MEDINTOR PASS, CONVERSE TX 78109
1953-039	JOHNSON, CLIFFORD 'CONNIE'	D. NOVEMBER 25, 2004, KANSAS CITY, MO.
1994-059	JOHNSON, DANE EDWARD	2652 BIG PINE DRIVE, HOLIDAY FL 34691
2005-101	JOHNSON, DANIEL RYAN	OLD ADD: 11901 SILVEROD STREET NW, COON RAPIDS MN 55433
1952-057	JOHNSON, DARRELL DEAN	D. MAY 3, 2004, FAIRFIELD, CALIF.
1965-052	JOHNSON, DAVID ALLEN	1064 HOWELL ROAD, WINTER PARK FL 32789
1974-060	JOHNSON, DAVID CHARLES	3202 WOODHOLLOW CIRCLE, ABILENE TX 79606
1987-069	JOHNSON, DAVID WAYNE	7101 MOUNT VISTA ROAD, KINGSVILLE MD 21087
1960-052	JOHNSON, DERON ROGER	D. APRIL 23, 1992, POWAY, CALIF.
1947-047	JOHNSON, DONALD ROY	1529 NE 21ST AVENUE #205, PORTLAND OR 97232
1943-066	JOHNSON, DONALD SPORE	D. APRIL 6, 2000, LAGUNA BEACH, CALIF.
1940-042	JOHNSON, EARL DOUGLAS	D. DECEMBER 3, 1994, SEATTLE, WASH.
1920-058	JOHNSON, EDWIN CYRIL	D. JULY 3, 1975, MORGANFIELD, KY.
1993-087	JOHNSON, ERIK ANTHONY	PO BOX 2989, SAN RAMON CA 94583
1950-040	JOHNSON, ERNEST THORWALD	6350 POLO CLUB DRIVE, CUMMING GA 30040
1966-049	JOHNSON, FRANK HERBERT	1151 CYPRESS HILL LANE, STOCKTON CA 95027
1922-063	JOHNSON, FREDERICK EDWARD	D. JUNE 14, 1973, KERRVILLE, TEXAS
2003-081	JOHNSON, GERALD CLYDE 'GARY'	50 TALLWOOD COURT, ATHERTON CA 94027
1925-056	JOHNSON, HENRY WARD	D. AUGUST 20, 1982, BRADENTON, FLA.
1982-063	JOHNSON, HOWARD MICHAEL 'HOJO'	8597 SE COCONUT STREET, HOBE SOUND FL 33455
1970-068	JOHNSON, JAMES BRIAN 'BRIAN'	D. DECEMBER 6, 1987, NORTH MUSKEGON, MICH.
2006-083	JOHNSON, JAMES ROBERT	OLD ADD: ENDICOTT NY
1997-084	JOHNSON, JASON MICHAEL	PO BOX 238, SANTA CLARA UT 84765
1968-045	JOHNSON, JERRY MICHAEL	16670 ESPOLA ROAD, POWAY CA 92064
1944-064	JOHNSON, JOHN CLIFFORD	D. JUNE 26, 1991, IRON MOUNTAIN, MICH.
1978-063	JOHNSON, JOHN HENRY	3345 DELNA, SPARKS NV 89431
1998-094	JOHNSON, JONATHAN KENT	7 ALVERSTON COURT, IRMO SC 29063
1985-053	JOHNSON, JOSEPH RICHARD	14 EVERGREEN ROAD, PLAINVILLE MA 02762
2005-102	JOHNSON, JOSHUA MICHAEL	OLD ADD: JUPITER FL
2000-082	JOHNSON, KEITH	256 SOUTH ANTHONY AVENUE, STOCKTON CA 95215
2005-103	JOHNSON, KELLY ANDREW	OLD ADD: AUSTIN TX
1987-070	JOHNSON, KENNETH LANCE 'LANCE'	5712 FOXFIRE ROAD, MOBILE AL 36618
1958-049	JOHNSON, KENNETH TRAVIS	121 MYRTLEWOOD DR, PINEVILLE LA 71360
1947-048	JOHNSON, KENNETH WANDERSEE	D. APRIL 6, 2004, WICHITA, KAN.
1974-061	JOHNSON, LAMAR	4105 SANGRE TRAIL, ARLINGTON TX 76016
1972-054	JOHNSON, LARRY DOBY	1905 EAST JEAN STREET, TAMPA FL 33610
1934-050	JOHNSON, LLOYD WILLIAM	D. OCTOBER 8, 1980, STOCKTON, CALIF.
1960-053	JOHNSON, LOUIS BROWN	4532 VALLEY RIDGE AVENUE, LOS ANGELES CA 90008
2000-083	JOHNSON, MARK J.	444 LUNALILO HOME ROAD #701, HONOLULU HI 96825
1998-095	JOHNSON, MARK LANDON	109 JAMESTOWN DRIVE, WARNER ROBINS GA 31088
1995-112	JOHNSON, MARK PATRICK	40 HELEN AVENUE, RYE NY 10580
1997-085	JOHNSON, MICHAEL KEITH	165 ST. MI9CHAEL COURT, JUPITER FL 33458
1974-062	JOHNSON, MICHAEL NORTON	OLD ADD: RURAL ROUTE 1, FARIBAULT MN 55021
2001-090	JOHNSON, NICHOLAS ROBERT	1201 NEVIS COURT, SACRAMENTO CA 95822
1920-136	JOHNSON, PAUL OSCAR	D. FEBRUARY 14, 1973, MCALLEN, TEXAS
1988-072	JOHNSON, RANDALL DAVID	10645 NORTH TATUM BLVD #200-203, PHOENIX AZ 85028
1982-064	JOHNSON, RANDALL GLENN	2427 TIMBER CREEK LANE, ESCONDIDO CA 92027
1980-061	JOHNSON, RANDALL SCOTT	18433 SW 88TH PLACE, MIAMI FL 33157
2003-082	JOHNSON, REED CAMERON	30137 MIRA LOMA DRIVE, TEMECULA CA 92592
1958-050	JOHNSON, RICHARD ALLAN	5001 EAST MAIN STREET #762, MESA AZ 85205
1969-088	JOHNSON, ROBERT DALE	650 CAVES HWY, CAVE JUNCTION OR 97523
1933-030	JOHNSON, ROBERT LEE	D. JULY 6, 1982, TACOMA, WASH.
1960-054	JOHNSON, ROBERT WALLACE	1474 BARCLAY STREET, SAINT PAUL MN 55106
1982-065	JOHNSON, RONALD DAVID	428 SOUTH MAIE, COMPTON CA 90220
1986-071	JOHNSON, RONDIN ALLEN	1025 SOUTH 324TH PLACE, FEDERAL WAY WA 98003
2003-083	JOHNSON, RONTREZ DEMON	1426 SE 18TH STREET, CAPE CORAL FL 33990
1929-056	JOHNSON, ROY CLEVELAND	D. SEPTEMBER 10, 1973, TACOMA, WASH.
1982-066	JOHNSON, ROY EDWARD	OLD ADD: 902 NORTH ST. LOUIS, CHICAGO IL 60651
1928-052	JOHNSON, SILAS KENNETH	D. MAY 12, 1994, SHERIDAN, ILL.
1960-055	JOHNSON, STANLEY LUCIUS	56 MORNINGSIDE DR, DALY CITY CA 94015
1922-064	JOHNSON, SYLVESTER	D. FEBRUARY 20, 1985, PORTLAND, ORE.
1974-063	JOHNSON, THOMAS RAYMOND	2200 MIDLAND GROVE #109, SAINT PAUL MN 55113
1973-067	JOHNSON, TIMOTHY EVALD	2505 ANTHEM VILLAGE DRIVE PMB 615, HENDERSON NV 89052
2005-104	JOHNSON, TYLER JAMES	507 HIGHVIEW STREET, NEWBURY PARK CA 91320
1944-065	JOHNSON, VICTOR OSCAR	D. MAY 10, 2005, EAU CLAIRE, WISC.
1981-064	JOHNSON, WALLACE DARNELL	PO BOX M618, GARY IN 46401
1983-084	JOHNSON, WILLIAM CHARLES	OLD ADD: 1701 NORTH LINCOLN ST, WILMINGTON DE 19806

1991-090	JOHNSON, WILLIAM JEFFREY 'JEFF'	OLD ADD: 424 NORTH HARDEE STREET, DURHAM NC 27703
1943-067	JOHNSON, WILLIAM RUSSEL	D. JUNE 20, 2006, AUGUSTA, GA.
1997-086	JOHNSON, WILLIAM RUSSELL 'RUSS'	33230 BEVERLY DRIVE, DENHAM SPRINGS LA 70726
1979-059	JOHNSTON, GREGORY BERNARD	OLD ADD: 4926 NORTHVIEW LANE, BURLINGTON IA 52601
1991-091	JOHNSTON, JOEL RAYMOND	1318 MEADOWVIEW DRIVE, POTTSTOWN PA 19464
2004-105	JOHNSTON, MICHAEL CHARLES	115 QUAIL DRIVE, LINCOLN UNIVERSITY PA 19252
1964-053	JOHNSTON, REX DAVID	11372 WEATHERBY ROAD, LOS ALAMITOS CA 90720
1924-055	JOHNSTON, WILFRED IVEY 'FRED'	D. JULY 14, 1959, TYLER, TEXAS
1993-088	JOHNSTONE, JOHN WILLIAM	9330 CLUBSIDE CIRCLE #3305, SARASOTA FL 34238
1966-050	JOHNSTONE, JOHN WILLIAM 'JAY'	853 CHAPEA, PASADENA CA 91107
1934-051	JOINER, ROY MERRILL 'POP'	D. DECEMBER 26, 1989, RED BLUFF, CALIF.
1954-049	JOK, STANLEY EDWARD	D. MARCH 6, 1972, BUFFALO, N.Y.
1930-038	JOLLEY, SMEAD POWELL	D. NOVEMBER 17, 1991, ALAMEDA, CALIF.
1953-040	JOLLY, DAVID	D. MAY 27, 1963, DURHAM, N.C.
2006-084	JONES, ADAM LA MARQUE	OLD ADD: SAN DIEGO CA
1983-085	JONES, ALFORNIA	1339 BRUSSELS STREET, SAN FRANCISCO CA 94134
1996-093	JONES, ANDRUW RUDOLF	7801 NW 42ND COURT, HOLLYWOOD FL 33024
1932-038	JONES, ARTHUR LENOX	D. NOVEMBER 25, 1980, COLUMBIA, S.C.
1986-072	JONES, BARRY LOUIS	411 SOUTH MORTON AVENUE, CENTERVILLE IN 47330
1991-092	JONES, CALVIN DOUGLAS	PO BOX 294679, LEWISVILLE TX 75029
1991-093	JONES, CHRISTOPHER CARLOS	1312 EAST THUNDERHILL PLACE, PHOENIX AZ 85048
1985-054	JONES, CHRISTOPHER DALE	1821 WESTWARD HO CIR, EL CAJON CA 92021
1967-055	JONES, CLARENCE WOODROW	26303 PLANTATION DRIVE NE, ATLANTA GA 30324
1963-063	JONES, CLEON JOSEPH	751 EDWARD ST, MOBILE AL 36610
1928-053	JONES, COBURN DYAS	D. JUNE 3, 1969, DENVER, COLO.
1941-053	JONES, DALE ELDON	D. NOVEMBER 8, 1980, ORLANDO, FLA.
1979-060	JONES, DARRYL LEE	15628 KINGS DRIVE, MEADVILLE PA 16335
1996-094	JONES, DAX XENOS	OLD ADD: 9078 EAST SHEENA DRIVE, SCOTTSDALE AZ 85260
1926-042	JONES, DECTAUR POINDEXTER 'DICK'	D. AUGUST 2, 1994, BURLINGAME, CALIF.
1982-067	JONES, DOUGLAS REID	129 EAST NAVILLA PLACE, COVINA CA 91723
1945-050	JONES, EARL LESLIE	D. JANUARY 14, 1989, FRESNO, CALIF.
1970-069	JONES, GARY HOWELL	475 S. WESTRIDGE CIR, ANAHEIM HILLS CA 92807
1954-050	JONES, GORDON BASSETT	D. APRIL 25, 1994, LODI, CALIF.
2003-084	JONES, GREG ALAN	14260 PASSAGE WAY, SEMINOLE FL 33776
1962-062	JONES, GROVER WILLIAM 'DEACON'	1015 GOLDFINCH, SUGARLAND TX 77478
1961-057	JONES, HAROLD MARION	4125 PALMYRA RD, LOS ANGELES CA 90008
1921-049	JONES, HOWARD	D. JULY 15, 1972, JEANNETTE, PA.
1999-094	JONES, JACQUE DEWAYNE	347 SAINT RITA COURT, SAN DIEGO CA 92113
1986-073	JONES, JAMES CONDIA	3054 NEWCASTLE DRIVE, DALLAS TX 75220
1964-054	JONES, JAMES DALTON 'DALTON'	4688 SOUTH DIXON LANE, LIBERTY MS 39643
1941-054	JONES, JAMES MURRELL 'JAKE'	D. DECEMBER 13, 2000, DELHI, LA.
2003-085	JONES, JASON DEWEY	1125 OAKVIEW DRIVE SE, SMYRNA GA 30080
1983-086	JONES, JEFFERY RAYMOND	311 WHITE HORSE PL, HADDON HEIGHTS NJ 08035
1980-062	JONES, JEFFREY ALLEN	51 EMMONS COURT, WYANDOTTE MI 48192
1923-069	JONES, JESSE F. 'BROADWAY'	D. SEPTEMBER 7, 1977, LEWES, DEL.
1924-056	JONES, JOHN JOSEPH 'BINKY'	D. MAY 13, 1961, ST. LOUIS, MO.
1923-070	JONES, JOHN WILLIAM	D. NOVEMBER 3, 1956, BALTIMORE, MD.
1991-094	JONES, JOSEPH STACY 'STACY'	1777 PONDEROSA ROAD, ATTALIA AL 35954
1924-057	JONES, KENNETH FREDERICK	D. MAY 15, 1991, HARTFORD, CONN.
1993-089	JONES, LARRY WAYNE 'CHIPPER'	217 CHEYENNE STREET, CARRIZO SPRINGS TX 78834
1979-061	JONES, LYNN MORRIS	9959 DICKSONBURG ROAD, CONNEAUTVILLE PA 16406
1961-058	JONES, MACK F.	D. JUNE 8, 2004, ATLANTA, GA.
2000-084	JONES, MARCUS RAY	20612 SMOKETREE AVENUE, YORBA LINDA CA 92686
1980-063	JONES, MICHAEL CARL	44 ALMERIA AVENUE, JACKSONVILLE FL 32211
1940-043	JONES, MORRIS E. 'RED'	D. JUNE 30, 1975, LINCOLN, CALIF.
1975-057	JONES, ODELL	5831 OPAL AVENUE, PALMDALE CA 93552
1920-059	JONES, PERCY LEE	D. MARCH 18, 1979, DALLAS, TEXAS
1973-068	JONES, RANDALL LEO	2638 CRANSTON DRIVE, ESCONDIDO CA 92025
1986-074	JONES, RICKY MIRON	109 ONYX PLACE, ATHENS GA 30605
1993-090	JONES, ROBERT JOSEPH	10222 NORTH WHITNEY, FRESNO CA 93720
1997-087	JONES, ROBERT MITCHELL	32 ELM STREET, RUTHERFORD NJ 07070
1974-064	JONES, ROBERT OLIVER	413 SOUTH ZURICH, TULSA OK 74112
1988-073	JONES, RONALD GLEN	D. JUNE 4, 2006, HOUSTON, TEXAS
1984-059	JONES, ROSS A.	1277 CAMELLIA CIRCLE, WESTON FL 33326
1976-042	JONES, RUPPERT SANDERSON	16766 BERNARDO CENTER DR #114A, SAN DIEGO CA 92128
1951-045	JONES, SAMUEL 'TOOTHPICK'	D. NOVEMBER 5, 1971, MORGANTOWN, W.VA.
1946-051	JONES, SHELDON LESLIE 'AVAILABLE'	D. APRIL 18, 1991, GREENVILLE, N.C.
1960-056	JONES, SHERMAN JARVIS	D. FEBRUARY 21, 2007, KANSAS CITY, KAN.
1967-056	JONES, STEVEN HOWELL	8116 KINGSDALE DR, KNOXVILLE TN 37919
1996-095	JONES, TERRY LEE	OLD ADD: 1836 COPPERFIELD LANE, BIRMINGHAM AL 35215
1976-043	JONES, THOMAS FREDERICK 'RICK'	6319 NANCY DRIVE, JACKSONVILLE FL 32244
1977-075	JONES, TIMOTHY BYRON	6204 GREENEYES WAY, ORANGEVALE CA 95662
1993-091	JONES, TODD BARTON GIVIN	421 EAGLE POINT DRIVE, PELL CITY AL 35128
1986-075	JONES, TRACY DONALD	101 HARBOR GREEN DRIVE #602, BELLEVUE KY 41073
1946-052	JONES, VERNAL LEROY 'NIPPY'	D. OCTOBER 3, 1995, SACRAMENTO, CALIF.
1988-074	JONES, WILLIAM TIMOTHY 'TIM'	30 CHICOT DRIVE, MAUMELLE AR 72113
1947-049	JONES, WILLIE EDWARD 'PUDDIN-HEAD'	D. OCTOBER 18, 1983, CINCINNATI, OHIO
1920-060	JONNARD, CLARENCE JAMES 'BUBBER'	D. AUGUST 23, 1977, NEW YORK, N.Y.
1921-050	JONNARD, CLAUDE ALFRED	D. AUGUST 27, 1959, NASHVILLE, TENN.
1936-043	JOOST, EDWIN DAVID	303 BELHAVEN CIRCLE, SANTA ROSA CA 95409
1927-048	JORDAN, BAXTER BYERLY 'BUCK'	D. MARCH 18, 1993, SALISBURY, N.C.
1992-063	JORDAN, BRIAN O'NEAL	1050 BEDFORD GARDENS DRIVE, ALPHARETTA GA 30202
1933-031	JORDAN, JAMES WILLIAM	D. DECEMBER 4, 1957, GASTONIA, N.C.
1995-113	JORDAN, KEVIN WAYNE	678 CHERRYDLAE DRIVE, LAFAYETTE HILL PA 19444
1953-041	JORDAN, MILTON MIGNOT	D. MAY 13, 1993, ITHACA, N.Y.
1951-046	JORDAN, NILES CHAPMAN	1114 METCALF, SEDRO-WOOLLEY WA 98284

1988-075	JORDAN, PAUL SCOTT 'RICKY'	5691A POWER INN ROAD, SACRAMENTO CA 95824
1995-114	JORDAN, RICARDO	OLD ADD: 249 COUNTRYSIDE KEY BLVD, OLDSMAR FL 34677
1988-076	JORDAN, SCOTT ALLAN	1530 CARROLL DRIVE NW #103, ATLANTA GA 30318
1944-066	JORDAN, THOMAS JEFFERSON	2909 SOUTH WYOMING, ROSWELL NM 88201
1929-057	JORGENS, ARNDT LUDWIG 'ART'	D. MARCH 1, 1980, WILMETTE, ILL.
1935-053	JORGENS, ORVILLE EDWARD	D. JANUARY 11, 1992, COLORADO SPRINGS, COLO.
1937-056	JORGENSEN, CARL 'PINKY'	D. MAY 2, 1996, SANTA CRUZ, CALIF.
1947-050	JORGENSEN, JOHN DONALD 'SPIDER'	D. NOVEMBER 6, 2003, RANCHO CUCAMONGA, CALIF.
1968-046	JORGENSEN, MICHAEL	1820 HARBOR MILL DRIVE, FENTON MO 63026
2005-105	JORGENSEN, RYAN WAYNE	1202 GOLDEN BEAR LANE, KINGWOOD TX 77339
1989-065	JORGENSEN, TERRY ALLEN	1493 SOUTH SUGAR BUSH ROAD, LUXEMBURG WI 54217
1988-077	JOSE, DOMINGO FELIX 'FELIX'	CALLE 30 DE MAYO #7A ING. OZAMA SAN LUIS, DOM REP
2002-095	JOSEPH, KEVIN JOHN	8826 LACROSSE DRIVE, DALLAS TX 75231
1964-055	JOSEPH, RICARDO EMELINDO	D. SEPTEMBER 8, 1979, SANTIAGO, DOM .REP.
1965-053	JOSEPHSON, DUANE CHARLES	D. JANUARY 30, 1997, NEW HAMPTON, IOWA
1969-089	JOSHUA, VON EVERETT	22580 INDIANWOOD DRIVE, SOUTH LYON MI 48178
2003-086	JOURNELL, JAMES RICHARD	1511 EASTGATE ROAD, SPRINGFIELD OH 45503
1962-063	JOYCE, MICHAEL LEWIS	1609 WHITMAN LN, WHEATON IL 60187
1965-054	JOYCE, RICHARD EDWARD	D. JANUARY 23, 2007, CARY, N.C.
1939-058	JOYCE, ROBERT EMMETT	D. DECEMBER 10, 1981, SAN FRANCISCO, CALIF.
1986-076	JOYNER, WALLACE KEITH	516 EAST 2800 SOUTH, MAPLETON UT 84664
1997-088	JUDD, MICHAEL GALEN	9805 SHADOWN ROAD, LAMESA CA 91941
1927-049	JUDD, RALPH WESLEY	D. MAY 6, 1957, LAPEER, MICH.
1941-055	JUDD, THOMAS WILLIAM OSCAR 'OSCAR'	D. DECEMBER 27, 1995, INGERSOLL, ONT.
1991-095	JUDEN, JEFFREY DANIEL	350 SE 2ND STREET #2260, FORT LAUDERDALE FL 33301
1940-044	JUDNICH, WALTER FRANKLIN	D. JULY 12, 1971, GLENDALE, CALIF.
1948-050	JUDSON, HOWARD KOLLS	239 FAIRWAY CIRCLE NE, WINTER HAVEN FL 33881
1935-054	JUDY, LYLE LEROY	D. JANUARY 15, 1991, ORMOND BEACH, FLA.
1939-059	JUELICH, JOHN WALTER	D. DECEMBER 25, 1970, ST. LOUIS, MO.
2001-091	JULIO, JORGE DANDYS	OLD ADD: CARACAS VENEZ
1940-045	JUMONVILLE, GEORGE BENEDICT	D. DECEMBER 12, 1996, MOBILE, ALA.
2002-096	JUNGE, ERIC DEBARI	27 CLAREMONT AVENUE, RYE NY 10580
1937-057	JUNGELS, KENNETH PETER	D. SEPTEMBER 9, 1975, WEST BEND, WISC.
1982-068	JURAK, EDWARD JAMES	3650 SOUTH WALKER AVE, SAN PEDRO CA 90731
1965-055	JUREWICZ, MICHAEL ALLEN	13804 EVREGREEN COURT, APPLE VALLEY MN 55124
1931-043	JURGES, WILLIAM FREDERICK	D. MARCH 3, 1997, CLEARWATER, FLA.
1944-067	JURISICH, ALVIN JOSEPH	D. NOVEMBER 3, 1981, NEW ORLEANS, LA.
1944-068	JUST, JOSEPH ERWIN	D. NOVEMBER 22, 2003, FRANKLIN, WISC.
1989-066	JUSTICE, DAVID CHRISTOPHER	15260 VENTURA BLVD #2100, SHERMAN OAKS CA 91403
1972-055	JUTZE, ALFRED HENRY 'SKIP'	3395 ZEPHYR CT, WHEAT RIDGE CO 80033

K

1959-043	KAAT, JAMES LEE	PO BOX 1130, PORT SALERNO FL 34992
1922-065	KAHDOT, ISAAC LEONARD 'IKE'	D. MARCH 31, 1999, OKLAHOMA CITY, OKLA.
1938-043	KAHLE, ROBERT WAYNE	D. DECEMBER 16, 1988, INGLEWOOD, CALIF.
1930-039	KAHN, OWEN EARLE 'JACK'	D. JANUARY 17, 1981, RICHMOND, VA.
1980-064	KAINER, DONALD WAYNE	1923 SIEBER, HOUSTON TX 77017
1955-062	KAISER, CLYDE DONALD 'DON'	2901 EAST 12TH, ADA OK 74820
1985-055	KAISER, JEFFREY PATRICK	26227 JAMES DRIVE, GROSSE ILE MI 48138
1971-057	KAISER, ROBERT THOMAS 'TOM'	OLD ADD: 2807 VIA TOPACIO, CARLSBAD CA 92068
1937-058	KALFASS, WILLIAM PHILIP	D. SEPTEMBER 8, 1968, BROOKLYN, N.Y.
1940-046	KALIN, FRANK BRUNO	D. JANUARY 12, 1975, WEIRTON, W.VA.
1953-042	KALINE, ALBERT WILLIAM	3613 YORK COURT, BLOOMFIELD HILLS MI 48302
1991-096	KAMIENIECKI, SCOTT ANDREW	10532 PINE TREE LANE, GOODRICH MI 48438
1923-071	KAMM, WILLIAM EDWARD 'WILLIE'	D. DECEMBER 21, 1988, BELMONT, CALIF.
1978-064	KAMMEYER, ROBERT LYNN	D. JANUARY 27, 2003, SACRAMENTO, CALIF.
1924-058	KAMP, ALPHONSE FRANCIS	D. FEBRUARY 25, 1955, BOSTON, MASS.
1934-052	KAMPOURIS, ALEXIS WILLIAM	D. MAY 29, 1993, SACRAMENTO, CALIF.
1925-057	KANE, JOHN FRANCIS	D. JULY 25, 1956, CHICAGO, ILL.
1938-044	KANE, THOMAS JOSEPH	D. NOVEMBER 26, 1973, CHICAGO, ILL.
1962-064	KANEHL, RODERICK EDWIN	D. DECEMBER 14, 2004, PALM SPRINGS, CALIF.
1998-096	KAPLER, GABRIEL STEFAN	OLD ADD: 14647 DICKENS STREET, SHERMAN OAKS CA 91403
1995-115	KARCHNER, MATTHEW DEAN	C/O MARL.KARCHNER 211 DUVAL STREET, BERWICK PA 18603
1936-044	KARDOW, PAUL OTTO	D. APRIL 27, 1968, SAN ANTONIO, TEXAS
1986-077	KARKOVICE, RONALD JOSEPH	108 GRACE AVENUE, KISSIMMEE FL 34747
1943-068	KARL, ANTON ANDREW	D. APRIL 8, 1989, LAJOLLA, CALIF.
1995-116	KARL, RANDALL SCOTT 'SCOTT'	C/O JOHN KARL 4503 SALISBURY DRIVE, CARLSBAD CA 92008
1930-040	KARLON, WILLIAM JOHN 'JACK'	D. DECEMBER 7, 1964, WARE, MASS.
2001-092	KARNUTH, JASON ANDRE	4994 NORMANDY LANE, MEMPHIS TN 38117
1927-050	KAROW, MARTIN GREGORY	D. APRIL 27, 1986, BRYAN, TEXAS
1995-117	KARP, RYAN JASON	10 WASHINGTON DRIVE, CRANBURY NJ 08512
1946-053	KARPEL, HERBERT	D. JANUARY 24, 1995, SAN DIEGO, CALIF.
1920-061	KARR, BENJAMIN JOYCE	D. DECEMBER 8, 1968, MEMPHIS, TENN.
1991-097	KARROS, ERIC PETER	6212 MADRA AVENUE, SAN DIEGO CA 92120
1993-092	KARSAY, STEFAN ANDREW 'STEVE'	11 SAN GABRIEL LANE, PALM COAST FL 32137
2006-085	KARSTENS, JEFFREY WAYNE	OLD ADD: SAN DIEGO CA
1997-089	KASHIWADA, TAKASHI	OLD ADD: TOKYO JAPAN
1957-035	KASKO, EDWARD MICHAEL	32 MAJOR GINTER COURT, RICHMOND VA 23227
2003-087	KATA, MATTHEW JOHN	2 STAFFORD PLACE, YARDLEY PA 19067
1952-058	KATT, RAYMOND FREDERICK	D. OCTOBER 19, 1999, NEW BRAUNFELS, TEXAS
1944-069	KATZ, ROBERT CLYDE	D. DECEMBER 14, 1962, ST. JOSEPH, MICH.
1921-051	KAUFMAN, ANTHONY CHARLES	D. JUNE 4, 1982, ELGIN, ILL.
1982-069	KAUFMAN, CURT GERRARD	308 HILLWAY DRIVE, GLENWOOD IA 51534
2002-097	KAYE, JUSTIN MALCOLM	7082 PARASOL, LAS VEGAS NV 89147

1948-051	KAZAK, EDWARD TERRANCE	D. DECEMBER 15, 1999, AUSTIN, TEXAS
1953-043	KAZANSKI, THEODORE STANLEY	1544 DORMIE DRIVE, GLADWIN MI 48624
2004-106	KAZMIR, SCOTT E.	PO BOX 99, CYPRESS TX 77410
1996-096	KEAGLE, GREGORY CHARLES	11 WOLCOTT DRIVE, HORSEHEADS NY 14845
1968-047	KEALEY, STEVEN WILLIAM	1080 1700 AVENUE, ABILENE KS 67410
1961-059	KEANE, JOHN JOSEPH	D. JANUARY 6, 1967, HOUSTON, TEXAS
1979-062	KEARNEY, ROBERT HENRY	11611 PICCADILLY CIRCLE, SAN ANTONIO TX 78251
2002-098	KEARNS, AUSTIN RYAN	719 HAVERHILL DRIVE, LEXINGTON KY 40503
1920-064	KEARNS, EDWARD JOSEPH	D. DECEMBER 21, 1949, TRENTON, N.J.
1942-054	KEARSE, EDWARD PAUL	D. JULY 15, 1968, EUREKA, CALIF.
1981-065	KEATLEY, GREGORY STEVEN	140 ROCKRIDGE COURT, LEXINGTON SC 29022
1922-066	KECK, FRANK JOSEPH 'CACTUS'	D. FEBRUARY 6, 1981, ST. LOUIS, MO.
1985-056	KEEDY, CHARLES PATRICK 'PAT'	6308 MOUNTAINVIEW CIRCLE, GARDENDALE AL 35071
1959-044	KEEGAN, EDWARD CHARLES	54 ARBOUR LANE, SEWELL NJ 08080
1953-044	KEEGAN, ROBERT CHARLES	D. JUNE 20, 2001, ROCHESTER, N.Y.
1944-070	KEELY, ROBERT WILLIAM	D. MAY 20, 2001, SARASOTA, FLA.
1920-062	KEENAN, JAMES WILLIAM	D. JUNE 5, 1980, SEMINOLE, FLA.
1982-070	KEENER, JEFFREY BRUCE	2107 DEWEY STREET, MURPHYSBORO IL 62966
1976-044	KEENER, JOSEPH DONALD	43025 LEMMING STREET, NEWBERRY SPRINGS CA 92365
1925-058	KEESEY, JAMES WARD	D. SEPTEMBER 5, 1951, BOISE, IDAHO
1980-065	KEETON, RICKEY	3433 STATHEM AVENUE, CINCINNATI OH 45211
1942-055	KEHN, CHESTER LAURENCE	D. APRIL 5, 1984, SAN DIEGO, CALIF.
2000-085	KEISLER, RANDY DEAN	312 HAWK DRIVE, SLIDELL LA 70461
1965-056	KEKICH, MICHAEL DENNIS	5314 CANADA VISTA PLACE NW, ALBUQUERQUE NM 87120
1952-059	KELL, EVERETT LEE 'SKEETER'	PO BOX 10113, CONWAY AR 72034
1943-069	KELL, GEORGE CLYDE	PO BOX 70, SWIFTON AR 72471
1942-056	KELLEHER, FRANCIS EUGENE	D. APRIL 13, 1979, STOCKTON, CALIF.
1935-055	KELLEHER, HAROLD JOSEPH	D. AUGUST 27, 1989, CAPE MAY COURT HOUSE, N.J.
1972-056	KELLEHER, MICHAEL DENNIS 'MICK'	1451 ALAMO PINTADO ROAD, SOLVANG CA 93463
1939-060	KELLER, CHARLES ERNEST	D. MAY 23, 1990, FREDERICK, MD.
1949-040	KELLER, HAROLD KEFAUVER	241 MADRONA TERRACE, SEQUIM WA 98382
2002-099	KELLER, KRISTOPHER SHANE	1074 GALLANT FOX CIRCLE SOUTH, JACKSONVILLE FL 32218
1966-051	KELLER, RONALD LEE	PO BOX 3267, CASHIERS NC 28717
1953-045	KELLERT, FRANK WILLIAM	D. NOVEMBER 19, 1976, OKLAHOMA CITY, OKLA.
1923-072	KELLETT, ALFRED HENRY 'RED'	D. JULY 14, 1960, NEW YORK, N.Y.
1934-053	KELLETT, DONALD STAFFORD 'RED'	D. NOVEMBER 5, 1970, FT. LAUDERDALE, ALA.
1925-059	KELLEY, HARRY LEROY	D. MARCH 23, 1958, PARKIN, ARK.
1964-056	KELLEY, RICHARD ANTHONY	D. DECEMBER 12, 1991, NORTHRIDGE, CALIF.
1964-057	KELLEY, THOMAS HENRY	OLD ADD: 7036 NORTHWAY DR NW, ROANOKE VA 24019
1948-052	KELLNER, ALEXANDER RAYMOND	D. MAY 3, 1996, TUCSON, ARIZ.
1952-060	KELLNER, WALTER JOSEPH	D. JUNE 19, 2006, TUCSON, ARIZ.
1986-078	KELLY, BRYAN KEITH	486 NORTH SUNSET DRIVE, MOUNT DORA FL 32757
1980-066	KELLY, DALE PATRICK 'PAT'	6748 FRIENDSHIP DRIVE, SARASOTA FL 34241
1967-057	KELLY, HAROLD PATRICK 'PAT'	D. OCTOBER 2, 2005, CHAMBERSBURG, PA.
1975-058	KELLY, JAY THOMAS 'TOM'	1643 CARRIE STREET, MAPLEWOOD MN 55119
1926-043	KELLY, JOSEPH JAMES	D. NOVEMBER 24, 1967, LYNBROOK, N.Y.
2000-086	KELLY, KENNETH ALPHONSO	5408 GARDEN ARBOR DRIVE, LUTZ FL 33558
1926-044	KELLY, MICHAEL J.	D. APRIL 26, 1982, MODESTO, CALIF.
1994-060	KELLY, MICHAEL RAYMOND	400 EAST VAN BUREN STREET, PHOENIX AZ 85004
1991-098	KELLY, PATRICK FRANKLIN	1131 HOWERTOWN ROAD, CATASAUQUA PA 18032
1923-073	KELLY, REYNOLDS JOSEPH 'REN'	D. AUGUST 24, 1963, MILLBRAE, CALIF.
1951-047	KELLY, ROBERT EDWARD	9 MOHAWK DRIVE, NIANTIC CT 06359
1987-071	KELLY, ROBERTO CONRADO	510 FRANKLIN DRIVE, ARLINGTON TX 76011
1969-090	KELLY, VAN HOWARD	11 BEAUREGARD DR, SPENCER NC 28159
1920-063	KELLY, WILLIAM HENRY	D. APRIL 8, 1990, SYRACUSE, N.Y.
1964-058	KELSO, WILLIAM EUGENE	136 NE BRIARCLIFF ROAD, KANSAS CITY MO 64116
1937-059	KELTNER, KENNETH FREDERICK	D. DECEMBER 12, 1991, NEW BERLIN, WISC.
2003-088	KELTON, DAVID WAYNE	515 RIVERSIDE DRIVE, LA GRANGE GA 30240
1954-051	KEMMERER, RUSSELL PAUL	6335 COLEBROOK DRIVE, INDIANAPOLIS IN 46220
1929-058	KEMNER, HERMAN JOHN 'DUTCH'	D. JANUARY 16, 1988, QUINCY, ILL.
2006-086	KEMP, MATTHEW RYAN	OLD ADD: MIDWEST CITY OK
1977-076	KEMP, STEVE F.	27150 PACIFIC HEIGHTS DRIVE, MISSION VIEJO CA 92692
1969-091	KENDALL, FRED LYNN	612 JOHN STREET, MANHATTAN BEACH CA 90266
1996-097	KENDALL, JASON DANIEL	692 CHAUTAUQUA BLVD, PACIFIC PALISADES CA 90272
1961-060	KENDERS, ALBERT DANIEL GEORGE	8744 MATILIJA AVE, VAN NUYS CA 91402
2006-087	KENDRICK, HOWARD JOSEPH	OLD ADD: CALLAHAN FL
1928-054	KENNA, EDWARD ALOYSIUS	D. AUGUST 21, 1972, SAN FRANCISCO, CALIF.
1999-095	KENNEDY, ADAM THOMAS	5025 WINDHILL DRIVE, RIVERSIDE CA 92507
1970-070	KENNEDY, JAMES EARL	13940 SW LISA LANE, BAEVERTON OR 97005
1962-065	KENNEDY, JOHN EDWARD	2 RODNEY ROAD, WEST PEABODY MA 01960
1957-036	KENNEDY, JOHN IRVIN	D. APRIL 27, 1998, JACKSONVILLE, FLA.
2001-093	KENNEDY, JOSEPH DARLEY	20260 NORTH AVENUE, BATTLE CREEK MI 49017
1974-065	KENNEDY, JUNIOR RAYMOND	6001 EUCALYPTUS #215, BAKERSFIELD CA 93306
1993-093	KENNEDY, KEVIN CURTIS	C/O FOX SPORTS, 1211 AVE OF THE AMERICAS, 2ND FLR, NEW YORK NY 10036
1934-054	KENNEDY, LLOYD VERNON 'VERN'	D. JANUARY 28, 1993, MENDON, MO.
1946-054	KENNEDY, MONTIA CALVIN	D. MARCH 1, 1997, MIDLOTHIAN, VA.
1939-061	KENNEDY, ROBERT DANIEL	D. APRIL 7, 2005, MESA, ARIZ.
1978-065	KENNEDY, TERRENCE EDWARD	333 NORTH PENNINGTON DRIVE #23, CHANDLER AZ 85224
1948-053	KENNEDY, WILLIAM AULTON	D. APRIL 8, 1983, SEATTLE, WASH.
1942-057	KENNEDY, WILLIAM GORMAN	D. AUGUST 20, 1995, ALEXANDRIA, VA.
1938-045	KENNEY, ARTHUR JOSEPH	3 TIMBER LANE, NORTH READING MA 01864
1967-058	KENNEY, GERALD	1980 HARRISON, BELOIT WI 53511
2004-107	KENSING, LOGAN FRENCH	208 EAST BANDERA ROAD, BOERNE TX 78006
1992-064	KENT, JEFFREY FRANKLIN	OLD ADD: 504 ST. THOMAS LANE, SAN MATEO CA 94404
2002-100	KENT, STEVEN PATRICK	3118 MINTHORN DRIVE, KILLEEN TX 76542
1962-066	KENWORTHY, RICHARD LEE	5551 RUE ROYALE #D, INDIANAPOLIS IN 46227

1968-048	KEOUGH, JOSEPH WILLIAM	110 BINHAM HEIGHTS, SHAVANO PARK TX 78249
1977-077	KEOUGH, MATTHEW LON	12 SHIRE, TRABUCO CANYON CA 92679
1956-047	KEOUGH, RICHARD MARTIN 'MARTY'	6874 EAST NIGHTINGALE STAR CIR, SCOTTSDALE AZ 85262
2006-088	KEPPEL, ROBERT GRIFFIN	127 LAGORCE DRIVE, CHESTERFIELD MO 63017
2004-108	KEPPINGER, JEFFREY SCOTT	1321 CENTER DRIVE, AUBURN GA 30011
1984-060	KEPSHIRE, KURT DAVID	45 STONEBRIDGE ROAD, OXFORD CT 06478
1985-057	KERFELD, CHARLES PATRICK	165 FALCON POINTE DRIVE, CHICO CA 95928
1950-041	KERIAZAKOS, CONSTANTINE NICHOLAS 'GUS'	D. MAY 4, 1996, HILTON HEAD, S.C.
1939-062	KERKSIECK, WAYMAN WILLIAM 'BILL'	D. MARCH 11, 1970, LITTLE ROCK, ARK.
1974-066	KERN, JAMES LESTER	6009 AMBERWOOD CT, ARLINGTON TX 76016
1962-067	KERN, WILLIAM GEORGE	625 GREEN ST, ALLENTOWN PA 18102
1965-057	KERNEK, GEORGE BOYD	16423 COTTON GIN AVENUE, WAYNE OK 73095
1945-051	KERNS, RUSSELL ELDON	D. AUGUST 21, 2000, HUMBLE, TEXAS
1923-074	KERR, JOHN FRANCIS	D. OCTOBER 19, 1993, LONG BEACH, CALIF.
1943-070	KERR, JOHN JOSEPH 'BUDDY'	D. NOVEMBER 7, 2006, NEW YORK, N.Y.
1925-060	KERR, JOHN MELVILLE 'MEL'	D. AUGUST 9, 1980, VERO BEACH, FLA.
1976-045	KERRIGAN, JOSEPH THOMAS	5148 LEIPER STREET, PHILADELPHIA PA 19124
2002-101	KERSHNER, JASON ASHLEY	4200 NORTH 82ND STREET #2019, SCOTTSDALE AZ 85251
1964-059	KESSINGER, DONALD EULON	907 CUMBERLAND RIDGE, OXFORD MS 38655
1993-094	KESSINGER, ROBERT KEITH 'KEITH'	3405 OLD DORNICK DRIVE, JONESBORO AR 72401
1968-049	KESTER, RICHARD LEE	BOX 623, GARDNERVILLE NV 89410
1922-067	KETCHUM, AUGUST FRANKLIN 'GUS'	D. SEPTEMBER 10, 1980, OKLAHOMA CITY, OKLA.
1984-061	KEY, JAMES EDWARD	128 TALAVERA PLACE, PALM BEACH GARDENS FL 33418
1995-118	KEYSER, BRIAN LEE	1030 EL MONTE AVENUE, MOUNTAIN VIEW CA 94040
1985-058	KHALIFA, SAM	741 EAST SIXTH STREET, TUCSON AZ 85719
1925-061	KIBBIE, HORACE KENT 'HOD'	D. OCTOBER 19, 1975, FORT WORTH, TEXAS
1999-096	KIDA, MASAO	OLD ADD: TOKYO JAPAN
1990-077	KIECKER, DANA ERVIN	4104 PRAIRIE RIDGE ROAD, EAGAN MN 55123
1920-065	KIEFER, JOSEPH WILLIAM	D. JULY 5, 1975, UTICA, N.Y.
1993-095	KIEFER, MARK ANDREW	11822 OLD FASHION, GARDEN GROVE CA 92640
1984-062	KIEFER, STEVEN GEORGE	11822 OLD FASHION, GARDEN GROVE CA 92640
2001-094	KIELTY, ROBERT MICHAEL 'BOBBY'	10001 THORNBIRD COURT, MORENO VALLEY CA 92557
1991-099	KIELY, JOHN FRANCIS	84 BROWN STREET, BROCKTON MA 02401
1951-048	KIELY, LEO PATRICK	D. JANUARY 18, 1984, GLEN RIDGE, N.J.
1996-098	KIESCHNICK, MICHAEL BROOKS 'BROOKS'	5150 BROADWAY STREET #255, SAN ANTONIO TX 78209
2006-089	KIGER, MARK WINSTON	OLD ADD: SAN DIEGO CA
1991-100	KILE, DARRYL ANDREW	D. JUNE 22, 2002, CHICAGO, ILL.
1987-072	KILGUS, PAUL NELSON	2102 SMALLHOUSE ROAD, BOWLING GREEN KY 42101
1969-092	KILKENNY, MICHAEL DAVID	OLD ADD: 5310 HURON LINE ROAD, WINDSOR ONT
1954-052	KILLEBREW, HARMON CLAYTON	PO BOX 14550, SCOTTSDALE AZ 85267
1959-045	KILLEEN, EVANS HENRY	PO BOX 885, WESTHAMPTON BEACH NY 11978
1999-097	KIM, BYUNG-HYUN	2037 NORTH CHESTNUT, MESA AZ 85213
2001-095	KIM, SUN-WOO	OLD ADD: SEOUL KOREA
1937-060	KIMBALL, NEWELL W. 'NEWT'	D. MARCH 22, 2001, LAS VEGAS, NEV.
1936-045	KIMBERLIN, HARRY LYDLE	D. DECEMBER 31, 1999, POPLAR BLUFF, MO.
1945-052	KIMBLE, RICHARD LOUIS	D. MAY 7, 2001, TOLEDO, OHIO
1920-066	KIME, HAROLD LEE	D. MAY 16, 1939, COLUMBUS, OHIO
1976-046	KIMM, BRUCE EDWARD	3168 121ST STREET, AMANA IA 52203
1929-059	KIMSEY, CLYDE ELIAS 'CHAD'	D. DECEMBER 3, 1942, PRYOR, OKLA.
1956-048	KINDALL, GERALD DONALD 'JERRY'	7220 EAST GREY FOX LANE, TUCSON AZ 85715
1946-055	KINDER, ELLIS RAYMOND	D. OCTOBER 16, 1968, JACKSON, TENN.
1946-056	KINER, RALPH MCPHERRAN	200 BRADLEY PLACE #204, PALM BEACH FL 33480
1954-053	KING, CHARLES GILBERT 'CHICK'	4036 HIGHWAY 54, PARIS TN 38242
1944-071	KING, CLYDE EDWARD	103 STRATFORD ROAD, GOLDSBORO NC 27530
1997-090	KING, CURTIS ALBERT	OLD ADD: PLYMOUTH MEETING PA 19462
1986-079	KING, ERIC STEVEN	1063 STANFORD DRIVE, SIMI VALLEY CA 93065
1967-059	KING, HAROLD 'HAL'	828 GENEVA DRIVE, OVIEDO FL 32765
1955-063	KING, JAMES HUBERT	720 STOKENBURY ROAD, ELKINS AR 72727
1989-067	KING, JEFFREY WAYNE	HC 66, WISDOM MT 59761
1993-096	KING, KEVIN RAY	RURAL ROUTE 1 BOX 107, BRAGGS OK 74423
1935-056	KING, LYNN PAUL	D. MAY 11, 1972, ATLANTIC, IOWA
1954-054	KING, NELSON JOSEPH	3890 BIGELOW BLVD #405, PITTSBURGH PA 15213
1999-098	KING, RAYMOND KEITH	290 EAST CERCADO LANE, LITCHFIELD PARK AZ 85340
1932-039	KINGDON, WESCOTT WILLIAM	D. APRIL 19, 1975, CAPISTRANO, CALIF.
1986-080	KINGERY, MICHAEL SCOTT	51923 298TH STREET, GROVE CITY MN 56243
1979-063	KINGMAN, BRIAN PAUL	14804 HILLSTONE STREET, FONTANA CA 92336
1971-058	KINGMAN, DAVID ARTHUR	PO BOX 209, GLENBROOK NV 89413
1996-099	KINGSALE, EUGENE HUMPHREY	105 ANGELFISH, JUPITER FL 33477
1998-097	KINKADE, MICHAEL A.	8845 SW 82ND AVENUE, PORTLAND OR 97223
1978-066	KINNEY, DENNIS PAUL	PO BOX 304, SCHNECKSVILLE PA 18078
2006-090	KINNEY, JOSHUA THOMAS	OLD ADD: PORT ALLEGHANY PA
2000-087	KINNEY, MATTHEW JOHN	23 FIELDSTONE DRIVE, BANGOR ME 04401
1980-067	KINNUNEN, MICHAEL JOHN	5818 MCKINLEY PLACE NORTH, SEATTLE WA 98103
2006-091	KINSLER, IAN MICHAEL	1549 WEST OAK SHADOWS DRIVE, TUCSON AZ 85737
1989-068	KINZER, MATTHEW ROY	6717 SWEETBRIER DRIVE, FORT WAYNE IN 46814
1934-055	KINZY, HENRY HENSEL 'HARRY'	D. JUNE 22, 2003, FORT WORTH, TEXAS
1957-037	KIPP, FRED LEO	C/O KLC, 6613 WEST 126TH TERRACE, OVERLAND PARK KS 66209
1985-059	KIPPER, ROBERT WAYNE	117 TUSCANY WAY, GREER SC 29650
1953-046	KIPPER, THORNTON JOHN	D. MARCH 29, 2006, SCOTTSDALE, ARIZ.
1969-093	KIRBY, CLAYTON LAWS	D. OCTOBER 11, 1991, ARLINGTON, VA.
1949-041	KIRBY, JAMES HERSCHEL	520 LOHMAN ROAD, MOUNT JULIET TN 37122
1991-101	KIRBY, WAYNE LEONARD	320 KENYA ROAD, LAS VEGAS NV 89123
1947-051	KIRK, THOMAS DANIEL	D. AUGUST 1, 1974, PHILADELPHIA, PA.
1961-061	KIRK, WILLIAM PARTHEMORE	16 TIMBER VILLA, ELIZABETHTOWN PA 17022
1958-051	KIRKLAND, WILLIE CHARLES	19375 NORTHRUP STREET, DETROIT MI 48219
1962-068	KIRKPATRICK, EDGAR LEON	24791 VIA LARGA, LAGUNA NIGUEL CA 92677

1974-067	KIRKWOOD, DONALD PAUL	455 WEST ELMWOOD, CLAWSON MI 48017
1950-042	KIRRENE, JOSEPH JOHN	2557 KILPATRICK COURT, SAN RAMON CA 94583
1991-102	KISER, GARLAND ROUTHARD	267 CARR DRIVE, BLOUNTVILLE TN 37617
1945-053	KISH, ERNEST ALEXANDER	D. DECEMBER 21, 1993, KIRTLAND, OHIO
1971-059	KISON, BRUCE EUGENE	1403 RIVERVIEW CIRCLE, BRADENTON FL 33529
1954-055	KITSOS, CHRISTOPHER ANESTOS	D. JUNE 7, 2004, MOBILE, ALA.
1982-071	KITTLE, RONALD DALE	1840 TOUR TRACE, CHESTERTON IN 46304
1934-056	KLAERNER, HUGO EMIL	D. JANUARY 3, 1982, FREDERICKSBURG, TEXAS
1966-052	KLAGES, FRED ANTHONY	2813 CROSSVINE CIRCLE, SPRING TX 77380
1998-098	KLASSEN, DANIEL VICTOR	8072 KIAWAH TRACE, PORT SAINT LUCIE FL 34986
1964-060	KLAUS, ROBERT FRANCIS	10661 GABACHO DR, SAN DIEGO CA 92124
1952-061	KLAUS, WILLIAM JOSEPH	D. DECEMBER 3, 2006, SARASOTA, FLA.
1985-060	KLAWITTER, THOMAS CARL	OLD ADD: 3220 DOVER COURT, JANESVILLE WI 53546
1925-062	KLEE, OLLIE CHESTER	D. FEBRUARY 9, 1977, TOLEDO, OHIO
1928-055	KLEIN, CHARLES HERBERT 'CHUCK'	D. MARCH 28, 1958, INDIANAPOLIS, IND.
1944-072	KLEIN, HAROLD JOHN	D. DECEMBER 10, 1957, ST. LOUIS, MO.
1943-071	KLEIN, LOUIS FRANK	D. JUNE 20, 1976, METAIRIE, LA.
1934-057	KLEINHANS, THEODORE OTTO	D. JULY 24, 1985, REDINGTON BEACH, FLA.
1935-057	KLEINKE, NORBERT GEORGE	D. MARCH 16, 1950, MARIN, CALIF.
1992-065	KLESKO, RYAN ANTHONY	735 HENDERSON MILL ROAD, COVINGTON GA 30014
1976-047	KLEVEN, JAY ALLEN	118 VIA BOLSA, SAN LORENZO CA 94580
1943-072	KLIEMAN, EDWARD FREDERICK	D. NOVEMBER 15, 1979, HOMOS ASSA, FLA.
1958-052	KLIMCHOCK, LOUIS STEPHEN	8876 SOUTH MYRTLE AVENUE, TEMPE AZ 85284
1969-094	KLIMKOWSKI, RONALD BERNARDO	117 CANDY LANE, SYOSSET NY 11791
1955-064	KLINE, JOHN ROBERT 'BOBBY'	6656 31ST WAY, SAINT PETERSBURG FL 33712
1930-041	KLINE, ROBERT GEORGE	D. MARCH 16, 1987, WESTERVILLE, OHIO
1952-062	KLINE, RONALD LEE	D. JUNE 22, 2002, CALLERY, PA.
1970-071	KLINE, STEVEN JACK	532 NORTH KNIGHTS BRIDGE ROAD, CANBY OR 97013
1997-091	KLINE, STEVEN JAMES	OLD ADD: 2518 DELOAK DRIVE, SAINT LOUIS MO 63129
1994-061	KLINGENBECK, SCOTT EDWARD	6230 KINGORA COURT, CINCINNATI OH 45233
1927-051	KLINGER, JOSEPH JOHN	D. JULY 31, 1960, LITTLE ROCK, ARK.
1938-046	KLINGER, ROBERT HAROLD	D. AUGUST 19, 1977, VILLA RIDGE, MO.
1987-073	KLINK, JOSEPH CHARLES	3300 ATLANTA STREET #F, HOLLYWOOD FL 33021
1950-043	KLIPPSTEIN, JOHN CALVIN	D. OCTOBER 10, 2003, CHICAGO, ILL.
1944-073	KLOPP, STANLEY HAROLD	D. MARCH 11, 1980, ROBESONIA, PA.
1931-044	KLOZA, JOHN CLARENCE 'NAP'	D. JUNE 11, 1962, MILWAUKEE, WISC.
1921-052	KLUGMANN, JOSIE	D. JULY 18, 1951, MOBERLY, MO.
1934-058	KLUMPP, ELMER EDWARD	D. OCTOBER 18, 1996, MENOMONEE FALLS, WISC.
1947-052	KLUSZEWSKI, THEODORE BERNARD	D. MARCH 29, 1988, CINCINNATI, OHIO
1976-048	KLUTTS, GENE ELLIS 'MICKEY'	6136 MAPLE AVENUE, LAKE ISABELLA CA 93240
1942-058	KLUTTZ, CLYDE FRANKLIN	D. MAY 12, 1979, SALISBURY, N.C.
1993-097	KMAK, JOSEPH ROBERT	1021 HATTERAS, FOSTER CITY CA 94404
1990-078	KNACKERT, BRENT BRADLEY	16802 LEAFWOOD CIRCLE, HUNTINGTON BEACH CA 92647
1975-059	KNAPP, ROBERT CHRISTIAN 'CHRIS'	1415 CASTLE CT, SAINT JOSEPH MI 49085
1926-045	KNEISCH, RUDOLPH FRANK	D. APRIL 6, 1965, BALTIMORE, MD.
1976-049	KNEPPER, ROBERT WESLEY	OLD ADD: 9400 WADE BLVD #1515, FRISCO TX 75035
1945-054	KNERR, WALLACE LUTHER 'LOU'	D. MARCH 23, 1980, LANCASTER, PA.
1979-064	KNICELY, ALAN LEE	BOX 433, DAYTON VA 22821
1947-053	KNICKERBOCKER, AUSTIN JAY	D. FEBRUARY 18, 1997, CLINTON CORNERS, N.Y.
1933-032	KNICKERBOCKER, WILLIAM HART	D. SEPTEMBER 8, 1963, SEBASTOPOL, CALIF.
2001-096	KNIGHT, BRANDON MICHAEL	191 SOUTH PACIFIC AVENUE #B, VENTURA CA 93001
1974-068	KNIGHT, CHARLES RAY 'RAY'	2308 TARA DRIVE, ALBANY GA 31707
1922-068	KNIGHT, ELMA RUSSELL 'JACK'	D. JULY 30, 1976, SAN ANTONIO, TEXAS
1991-103	KNOBLAUCH, EDWARD CHARLES 'CHUCK'	239 BYRONDALE AVENUE, WAYZATA MN 55391
1920-067	KNODE, KENNETH THOMSON 'MIKE'	D. DECEMBER 20, 1980, SOUTH BEND, IND.
1923-075	KNODE, ROBERT TROXELL 'RAY'	D. APRIL 13, 1982, BATTLE CREEK, MICH.
2004-109	KNOEDLER, JUSTIN JOSEPH	136 NORTH STATE STREET, SPRINGFIELD IL 62702
1964-061	KNOOP, ROBERT FRANK	2543 EAST MOUNTAIN SKY AVENUE, PHOENIX AZ 85044
1991-104	KNORR, RANDY DUANE	12134 BISHOPSFORD DRIVE, TAMPA FL 33626
1932-040	KNOTHE, GEORGE BERTRAM	D. JULY 3, 1981, DOVER, N.J.
1932-041	KNOTHE, WILFRED EDGAR 'FRITZ'	D. MARCH 22, 1963, PASSAIC, N.J.
2001-097	KNOTT, ERIC JAMES	1107 HYACINTH AVENUE, SEBRING FL 33875
1933-033	KNOTT, JOHN HENRY	D. OCTOBER 13, 1981, BROWNWOOD, TEXAS
2004-110	KNOTT, JONATHAN DAVID	951 SHIRE STREET, NOKOMIS FL 34275
2001-098	KNOTTS, GARY EVERETT	18 COVEY ROAD, DECATUR AL 35603
1965-058	KNOWLES, DAROLD DUANE	2322 DORA DRIVE, CLEARWATER FL 33765
1920-068	KNOWLTON, WILLIAM YOUNG	D. FEBRUARY 25, 1944, PHILADELPHIA, PA.
1924-060	KNOX, CLIFFORD HIRAM 'BUD'	D. SEPTEMBER 24, 1965, OSKALOOSA, IOWA
1972-057	KNOX, JOHN CLINTON	1413 THAMES DRIVE, PLANO TX 75075
1992-066	KNUDSEN, KURT DAVID	5155 PATTI JO DRIVE, CARMICHAEL CA 95608
1985-061	KNUDSON, MARK RICHARD	881 WEST 100TH AVE, NORTHGLENN CO 80221
1953-047	KOBACK, NICHOLAS NICHOLIA	71 HOPMEADOW STREET #9A1, SIMSBURY CT 06070
1973-069	KOBEL, KEVIN RICHARD	7650 EAST WILLIAMS DRIVE #1072, SCOTTSDALE AZ 85255
1963-064	KOCH, ALAN GOODMAN	1714 PEBBLE CREEK DRIVE, PRATTVILLE AL 36066
1944-074	KOCH, BARNETT	D. JUNE 6, 1987, TACOMA, WASH.
1999-099	KOCH, WILLIAM CHRISTOPHER	217 WINDWARD PASSAGE, CLEARWATER FL 33767
1946-057	KOECHER, RICHARD FINLEY	3310 GRAND CYPRESS DRIVE #102, NAPLES FL 34119
1970-072	KOEGEL, PETER JOHN	301 THE BIRCHES, SAUGERTIES NY 12477
1925-063	KOEHLER, HORACE LEVERING 'POP'	D. DECEMBER 8, 1986, TACOMA, WASH.
1993-098	KOELLING, BRIAN WAYNE	20230 AUGUSTA DRIVE, LAWRENCEBURG IN 47025
1932-042	KOENECKE, LEONARD GEORGE	D. SEPTEMBER 17, 1935, TORONTO, ONT.
1925-064	KOENIG, MARK ANTHONY	D. APRIL 22, 1993, WILLOWS, CALIF.
1937-061	KOHLMAN, JOSEPH JAMES	D. MARCH 16, 1974, PHILADELPHIA, PA.
2000-088	KOHLMEIER, RYAN LYLE	PO BOX 92, COTTONWOOD FALLS KS 66845
1948-054	KOKOS, RICHARD JEROME	D. APRIL 9, 1986, CHICAGO, ILL.
2000-089	KOLB, BRANDON CHARLES	2043 PIN OAK PLACE, DANVILLE CA 94506

1999-100	KOLB, DANIEL LEE	1501 51ST DRIVE, UNION GROVE WI 53182
1960-057	KOLB, GARY ALAN	5143 HOPEWELL DRIVE, CROSS LANES WV 25313
1940-047	KOLLOWAY, DONALD MARTIN	D. JUNE 30, 1994, BLUE ISLAND, ILL.
1921-053	KOLP, RAYMOND CARL	D. JULY 29, 1967, CINCINNATI, OHIO
1962-069	KOLSTAD, HAROLD EVERETTE	15149 BEL ESCOU DR, SAN JOSE CA 95124
2006-092	KOMINE, SHANE KENJI	641 EIGHTH AVENUE, HONOLULU HI 96816
2002-102	KOMIYAMA, SATORU	OLD ADD: CHIBA JAPAN
1983-087	KOMMINSK, BRAD LYNN	688 FALLSIDE LANE, WESTERVILLE OH 43081
1997-092	KONERKO, PAUL HENRY	11623 EAST BLOOMFIELD DRIVE, SCOTTSDALE AZ 85259
1973-070	KONIECZNY, DOUGLAS JAMES	9503 DUNDALK, SPRING TX 77379
1948-055	KONIKOWSKI, ALEXANDER JAMES 'WHITEY'	D. SEPTEMBER 28, 1997, SEYMOUR, CONN.
1942-059	KONOPKA, BRUCE BRUNO	D. SEPTEMBER 27, 1996, DENVER, COLO.
1944-075	KONSTANTY, CASIMIR JAMES 'JIM'	D. JUNE 11, 1976, ONEONTA, N.Y.
1995-119	KONUSZEWSKI, DENNIS JOHN	3054 YORKSHIRE DRIVE, BAY CITY MI 48706
2005-106	KOO, DAE-SUNG	OLD ADD: SEOUL SOUTH KOREA
1962-070	KOONCE, CALVIN LEE	D. OCTOBER 28, 1993, WINSTON-SALEM, N.C.
2003-089	KOONCE, GRAHAM CLINTON	2474 PIMLICO PLACE, ALPINE CA 91901
1967-060	KOOSMAN, JERRY MARTIN	2483 STATE ROAD 35, OSCEOLA WI 54020
1966-053	KOPACZ, GEORGE FELIX	14150 SOMERSET COURT, ORLAND PARK IL 60462
1921-054	KOPF, WALTER HENRY	D. APRIL 30, 1979, CINCINNATI, OHIO
1961-062	KOPLITZ, HOWARD DEAN	623 BOYD ST, OSHKOSH WI 54901
2001-099	KOPLOVE, MICHAEL PAUL	39 FESTIVAL DRIVE, VOORHEES NJ 08043
1958-053	KOPPE, JOSEPH	D. SEPTEMBER 27, 2006, ANN ARBOR, MICH.
1923-076	KOPSHAW, GEORGE KARL	D. DECEMBER 26, 1934, LYNCHBURG, VA.
1954-056	KORCHECK, STEPHEN JOSEPH	6424 FOX HUNT LANE, BRADENTON FL 34202
1966-054	KORINCE, GEORGE EUGENE	3033 TOWNLINE ROAD STEVENSVILLE ON, L0S 1S1 CANADA
2005-107	KORONKA, JOHN VINCENT	3957 BEACON RIDGE WAY, CLERMONT FL 34711
1965-059	KOSCO, ANDREW JOHN	9329 NEW SPRINGFIELD ROAD, POLAND OH 44514
1952-063	KOSHOREK, CLEMENT JOHN 'SCOOTER'	D. SEPTEMBER 8, 1991, ROYAL OAK, MICH.
1951-049	KOSKI, WILLIAM JOHN	1120 VALENCIA DRIVE, MODESTO CA 95350
1998-099	KOSKIE, CORDEL LEONARD 'COREY'	161 PRIMROSE LANE, MEDINA MN 55340
1941-056	KOSLO, GEORGE BERNARD 'DAVE'	D. DECEMBER 1, 1975, MENASHA, WISC.
1992-067	KOSLOFSKI, KEVIN CRAIG	1910 SHORE OAK DRIVE, DECATUR IL 62521
1944-076	KOSMAN, MICHAEL THOMAS	D. DECEMBER 10, 2002, LAFAYETTE, IND.
1931-045	KOSTER, FREDERICK CHARLES	D. APRIL 24, 1979, SAINT MATTHEWS, KY.
1962-071	KOSTRO, FRANK JERRY	36 STEELE STREET #20, DENVER CO 80206
2004-111	KOTCHMAN, CASEY JOHN	8442 125TH COURT, SEMINOLE FL 33776
1997-093	KOTSAY, MARK STEVEN	2947 FLINT RIDGE COURT, RENO NV 89511
1955-065	KOUFAX, SANFORD 'SANDY'	OLD ADD: 160 AMY LANE, VERO BEACH FL 32963
1925-065	KOUPAL, LOUIS LADDIE	D. DECEMBER 8, 1961, SAN GABRIEL, CALIF.
2006-093	KOUZMANOFF, KEVIN	28606 EVERGREEN MANOR DRIVE, EVERGREEN CO 80439
1932-043	KOWALIK, FABIAN LORENZ	D. AUGUST 14, 1954, KARNES CITY, TEXAS
1995-120	KOWITZ, BRIAN MARK	1657 BULLOCK CIRCLE, OWINGS MILLS MD 21117
1938-047	KOY, ERNEST ANYZ	D. JANUARY 1, 2007, BELLVILLE, TEXAS
1948-056	KOZAR, ALBERT KENNETH	5966 BAY HILL CIRCLE, LAKE WORTH FL 33463
2002-103	KOZLOWSKI, BENJAMIN ANTHONY	12550 81ST TERRACE, SEMINOLE FL 33776
1939-063	KRACHER, JOSEPH PETER	D. DECEMBER 25, 1981, SAN ANGELO, TEXAS
1989-069	KRAEMER, JOSEPH WAYNE	3212 NE 401ST CIRCLE, LA CENTER WA 98629
1937-062	KRAKAUSKAS, JOSEPH VICTOR LAWRENCE	D. DECEMBER 8, 1960, HAMILTON, ONT.
1959-046	KRALICK, JOHN FRANCIS 'JACK'	OLD ADD: 505 WEST 5TH STREET, LONG BEACH CA 90802
1953-048	KRALY, STEVEN CHARLES	12 DAVIS AVENUE, JOHNSON CITY NY 13790
1939-064	KRAMER, JOHN HENRY 'JACK'	D. MAY 18, 1995, METAIRIE, LA.
1988-078	KRAMER, RANDALL JOHN	304 BOWSPRIT DRIVE, APTOS CA 95003
1991-105	KRAMER, THOMAS JOSEPH	10665 HAMILTON AVENUE, CINCINNATI OH 45231
1962-072	KRANEPOOL, EDWARD EMIL	C/O MONICA KRANEPOOL, 177 HIGH POND DRIVE, JERICHO NY 11753
1943-073	KRAUS, JOHN WILLIAM 'TEX'	D. JANUARY 2, 1976, SAN ANTONIO, TEXAS
1961-063	KRAUSSE, LEWIS BERNARD	12811 NE 186TH, HOLT MO 64048
1931-046	KRAUSSE, LEWIS BERNARD, SR.	D. SEPTEMBER 6, 1988, SARASOTA, FLA.
1975-060	KRAVEC, KENNETH PETER	6752 TAEDA DRIVE, SARASOTA FL 34241
1956-049	KRAVITZ, DANIEL	RURAL ROUTE 1 BOX 1119, DUSHORE PA 18614
1984-063	KRAWCZYK, RAYMOND ALLEN	67 CLOUDCREST, ALISO VIEJO CA 92656
1931-047	KREEVICH, MICHAEL ANDREAS	D. APRIL 25, 1994, PANA, ILL.
1943-074	KREITNER, ALBERT JOSEPH 'MICKEY'	D. MARCH 6, 2003, NASHVILLE, TENN.
1924-061	KREMER, REMY PETER 'RAY'	D. FEBRUARY 8, 1965, PINOLE, CALIF.
1990-079	KREMERS, JAMES EDWARD 'JIMMY'	9525 SOUTH 95TH EAST AVENUE, TULSA OK 74133
1973-071	KREMMEL, JAMES LOUIS	W524 18TH AVENUE, SPOKANE WA 99203
1979-065	KRENCHICKI, WAYNE RICHARD	2524 HAWTHORNE DRIVE, BELOIT WI 53511
1947-054	KRESS, CHARLES STEVEN	1705 WEST PINE STREET #112, SANDPOINT ID 83864
1927-052	KRESS, RALPH 'RED'	D. NOVEMBER 29, 1962, LOS ANGELES, CALIF.
1946-058	KRETLOW, LOUIS HENRY	3302 GOLDFINCH, ENID OK 73701
1975-061	KREUGER, RICHARD ALLEN	7269 21ST AVENUE, JENISON MI 49428
1988-079	KREUTER, CHAD MICHAEL	22837 MARKET STREET, NEWHALL CA 91321
1962-073	KREUTZER, FRANKLIN JAMES	921 WINDWHISPER LANE, ANNAPOLIS MD 21403
1949-042	KRIEGER, KURT FERDINAND	D. AUGUST 16, 1970, ST. LOUIS, MO.
1937-063	KRIST, HOWARD WILBUR	D. APRIL 23, 1989, DELAVAN, N.Y.
1995-121	KRIVDA, RICK MICHAEL	112 DOLORES DRIVE, IRWIN PA 15642
2004-112	KROEGER, JOSHUA J.	10007 WILDLIFE ROAD, SAN DIEGO CA 92131
1978-067	KROL, JOHN THOMAS 'JACK'	D. MAY 30, 1994, WINSTON-SALEM, N.C.
1964-062	KROLL, GARY MELVIN	9038 EAST 40TH ST, TULSA OK 74145
1935-058	KRONER, JOHN HAROLD	D. AUGUST 26, 1968, ST. LOUIS, MO.
1995-122	KROON, MARC JASON	4817 EAST CROCUS DRIVE, SCOTTSDALE AZ 85254
1960-058	KRSNICH, MICHAEL	2137 SOUTH 102ND STREET, MILWAUKEE WI 53227
1949-043	KRSNICH, ROCCO PETER	5701 WEST 92ND STREET, OVERLAND PARK KS 66207
1983-088	KRUEGER, WILLIAM CULP	30132 SE REDMOND FALL CITY RD, FALL CITY WA 98024
1965-060	KRUG, EVERETT BEN 'CHRIS'	PO BOX 1350, WILDOMAR CA 92595
1981-066	KRUG, GARY EUGENE	1327 BAYLOR DR, COLORADO SPRINGS CO 80909

1986-081	KRUK, JOHN MARTIN	RURAL ROUTE BOX 3360, KEYSER WV 26726
1976-050	KRUKOW, MICHAEL EDWARD	6094 MADBURY COURT, SAN LUIS OBISPO CA 93401
1949-044	KRYHOSKI, RICHARD DAVID	D. APRIL 10, 2007, BEVERLY HILLS, MICH.
2004-113	KRYNZEL, DAVID BENJAMIN	4065 EAST WOODLAND DRIVE, PHOENIX AZ 85048
1957-038	KUBEK, ANTHONY CHRISTOPHER 'TONY'	121 EAST WATER STREET #120, APPLETON WI 54911
2004-114	KUBEL, JASON JAMES	39259 WILLOWVALE ROAD, PALMDALE CA 93551
1998-100	KUBENKA, JEFFREY S	6935 FARM 957, SCHULENBERG TX 78956
1967-061	KUBIAK, THEODORE ROGER	16443 MOUNT SHADOW LANE, RAMONA CA 92065
1997-094	KUBINSKI, TIMOTHY MARK	1839 CONEJO AVENUE, SAN LUIS OBISPO CA 93401
1961-064	KUBISZYN, JACK JOSEPH	2306 UNIVERSITY BLVD, TUSCALOOSA AL 35401
1980-068	KUBSKI, GILBERT THOMAS	4542 SCENARIO DRIVE, HUNTINGTON BEACH CA 92649
1950-044	KUCAB, JOHN ALBERT	D. MAY 26, 1977, YOUNGSTOWN, OHIO
1974-069	KUCEK, JOHN ANDREW CHARLES	8220 BLUE HERON LANE, CANFIELD OH 44406
1955-066	KUCKS, JOHN CHARLES	15 OAKLAND ST, HILLSDALE NJ 07642
1949-045	KUCZEK, STANISLAW LEO 'STEVE'	769 SACANDAGA ROAD, SCOTIA NY 12302
1943-075	KUCZYNSKI, BERNARD CARL 'BARNEY'	D. JANUARY 19, 1997, ALLENTOWN, PA.
1976-051	KUEHL, KARL OTTO	PO BOX 17017, FOUNTAIN HILLS AZ 85269
1952-064	KUENN, HARVEY EDWARD	D. FEBRUARY 18, 1988, PEORIA, ARIZ.
1977-078	KUHAULUA, FRED MAHELE	89-203 NALAKAHIKI PL, NANAKULI HI 96792
1930-042	KUHEL, JOSEPH ANTHONY	D. FEBRUARY 26, 1984, KANSAS CITY, KAN.
1924-062	KUHN, BERNARD DANIEL 'BUB'	D. NOVEMBER 20, 1956, LANSING, MICH.
1955-067	KUHN, KENNETH HAROLD	280 PANORAMIC HWY, MILL VALLEY CA 94941
1974-070	KUIPER, DUANE EUGENE	3665 DEER TRAIL DRIVE, DANVILLE CA 94506
1955-068	KUME, JOHN MICHAEL 'MIKE'	6810 WOODARD RD, ANDOVER OH 44003
1984-064	KUNKEL, JEFFREY WILLIAM	4921 COUNTY ROAD 605, BURLESON TX 76028
1961-065	KUNKEL, WILLIAM GUSTAVE JAMES	D. MAY 4, 1985, RED BANK, N.J.
1979-066	KUNTZ, RUSSELL JAY 'RUSTY'	6541 EAST 83RD PLACE, TULSA OK 74133
1923-077	KUNZ, EARL DEWEY	D. APRIL 14, 1963, SACRAMENTO, CALIF.
2005-108	KUO, HONG-CHIH	OLD ADD: TAINAN CITY TAIWAN
1975-062	KUROSAKI, RYAN YOSHITOMO	2024 FAIRMONT DRIVE, BENTON AR 72015
1941-057	KUROWSKI, GEORGE JOHN 'WHITEY'	D. DECEMBER 9, 1999, SHILLINGTON, PA.
1968-050	KURTZ, HAROLD JAMES	511 FLAT IRON SQUARE ROAD, CHURCH HILL MD 21623
1941-058	KUSH, EMIL BENEDICT	D. NOVEMBER 26, 1969, RIVER GROVE, ILL.
1973-072	KUSICK, CRAIG ROBERT	D. SEPTEMBER 27, 2006, SAINT PAUL. MINN.
1970-073	KUSNYER, ARTHUR WILLIAM	6598 TAEDA DRIVE, SARASOTA FL 34241
1986-082	KUTCHER, RANDY SCOTT	3016 PURPLE SAGE LANE, PALMDALE CA 93550
1959-047	KUTYNA, MARION JOHN 'MARTY'	2255 NW 14TH STREET, DELRAY BEACH FL 33445
1990-080	KUTZLER, JERRY SCOTT	8415 27TH AVENUE, KENOSHA WI 53143
1946-059	KUZAVA, ROBERT LEROY	1118 VINEWOOD AVENUE, WYANDOTTE MI 48192
1942-060	KVASNAK, ALEXANDER	D. SEPTEMBER 26, 2002, ARCADIA. CALIF.

L

1937-064	LAABS, CHESTER PETER	D. JANUARY 26, 1983, WARREN, MICH.
2004-115	LABANDEIRA, JOHN JOSHUA 'JOSH'	2166 WEST CRICKLEWOOD COURT, PORTERVILLE CA 93257
1950-045	LABINE, CLEMENT WALTER	D. MARCH 2, 2007, VERO BEACH, FLA.
1969-095	LABOY, JOSE ALBERTO 'COCO'	19TH STREET B20 #24 SABANA GARDENS, CAROLINA PR 00630
1977-079	LACEY, ROBERT JOSEPH	7623 EAST DECATUR STREET, MESA AZ 85207
1969-096	LACHEMANN, MARCEL ERNEST	PO BOX 587, PENRYN CA 95663
1965-061	LACHEMANN, RENE GEORGE	7500 EAST BOULDERS PKWY #66, SCOTTSDALE AZ 85262
1983-089	LACHOWICZ, ALLEN ROBERT	908 MUIRFIELD DRIVE, MANSFIELD TX 76063
2002-104	LACKEY, JOHN DARREN	1940 NORTH FIRST STREET, ABILENE TX 79603
1972-058	LACOCK, RALPH PIERRE 'PETE'	10019 MACKEY CIRCLE, SHAWNEE MISSION KS 66212
1975-063	LACORTE, FRANK JOSEPH	1667 EL DORADO DR, GILROY CA 95020
1978-068	LACOSS, MICHAEL JAMES	PO BOX 44033, LEMON COVE CA 93244
1996-100	LACY, KERRY ARDEEN	124 COUNTY ROAD 713, HIGDON AL 35479
1972-059	LACY, LEONDAUS 'LEE'	4424 WEBSTER STREET, OAKLAND CA 94609
1926-046	LACY, OSCEOLA GUY 'GUY'	D. NOVEMBER 19, 1953, CLEVELAND, TENN.
1979-067	LADD, PETER LINWOOD	299 BEECH RIDGE ROAD, SCARBOROUGH ME 04074
1946-060	LADE, DOYLE MARION	D. MAY 18, 2000, LINCOLN, NEB.
1947-055	LAFATA, JOSEPH JOSEPH	D. MAY 6, 2004, ROSEVILLE, MICH.
1945-055	LAFOREST, BYRON JOSEPH 'TY'	D. MAY 5, 1947, ARLINGTON, MASS.
2003-090	LAFOREST, PIERRE LUC 'PETE'	OLD ADD: MONTEBELLO QUE
1982-072	LAFRANCOIS, ROGER VICTOR	64 ASPINOOK ST, JEWETT CITY CT 06351
1982-073	LAGA, MICHAEL RUSSELL	838 ROUTE 6, SHOHOLA PA 18458
1934-059	LAGGER, EDWIN JOSEPH	D. NOVEMBER 10, 1981, JOLIET, ILL.
1970-074	LAGROW, LERRIN HARRIS	12271 EAST TURQUOISE, SCOTTSDALE AZ 85259
1968-051	LAHOUD, JOSEPH MICHAEL	90 TINKER HILL ROAD, NEW PRESTON CT 06777
1982-074	LAHTI, JEFFREY ALLEN	4632 TYLER DRIVE, HOOD RIVER OR 97031
2003-091	LAIRD, GERALD LEE	8891 MACALPINE ROAD, GARDEN GROVE CA 92641
1946-061	LAJESKIE, RICHARD EDWARD	D. AUGUST 15, 1976, RAMSEY, N.J.
1939-065	LAKE, EDWARD ERVING	D. JUNE 7, 1995, CASTRO VALLEY, CALIF.
1983-090	LAKE, STEPHEN MICHAEL	7402 NORTH 177TH AVENUE, WADDELL AZ 85355
1942-061	LAKEMAN, ALBERT WESLEY	D. MAY 25, 1976, SPARTANBURG, S.C.
1992-068	LAKER, TIMOTHY JOHN	673 AZURE HILLS DRIVE, SIMI VALLEY CA 93065
1962-074	LAMABE, JOHN ALEXANDER 'JACK'	16224 ANTIETAM AVE, BATON ROUGE LA 70816
1943-076	LAMACCHIA, ALFRED ANTHONY	13515 VISTA BONITA, SAN ANTONIO TX 78216
1940-048	LAMANNA, FRANK	D. SEPTEMBER 1, 1980, SYRACUSE, N.Y.
1941-059	LAMANNO, RAYMOND SIMON	D. FEBRUARY 9, 1994, BERKELEY, CALIF.
1935-059	LAMANSKE, FRANK JAMES	D. AUGUST 4, 1971, OLNEY, ILL.
1937-065	LAMASTER, NOBLE WAYNE 'WAYNE'	D. AUGUST 4, 1989, NEW ALBANY, IND.
1999-101	LAMB, DAVID CHRISTIAN	3287 ERINLEA AVENUE, NEWBURY PARK CA 91320
1970-075	LAMB, JOHN ANDREW	SHARON VALLEY RD, SHARON CT 06069
1920-069	LAMB, LAYMAN RAYMOND	D. OCTOBER 5, 1955, FAYETTEVILLE, ARK.
2000-090	LAMB, MICHAEL ROBERT	OLD ADD: 1346 HARTVIEW AVENUE, LA PUENTE CA 91744

1969-097	LAMB, RAYMOND RICHARD	3 CORTE TALLISTA, SAN CLEMENTE CA 92673
1946-062	LAMBERT, CLAYTON PATRICK	D. APRIL 3, 1981, OGDEN, UTAH
1941-060	LAMBERT, EUGENE MARION	D. FEBRUARY 10, 2000, GERMANTOWN, TENN.
1970-076	LAMONT, GENE WILLIAM	5194 SIESTA WOODS DRIVE, SARASOTA FL 34242
1920-070	LAMOTTE, ROBERT EUGENE	D. NOVEMBER 2, 1970, CHATHAM, GA.
1977-080	LAMP, DENNIS PATRICK	22751 EL PRADO #4303, RANCHO SANTA MARGARITA CA 92688
1969-098	LAMPARD, CHRISTOPHER KEITH	6124 HWY 6 NORTH, HOUSTON TX 77084
1988-080	LAMPKIN, THOMAS MICHAEL	OLD ADD: 3810 SE 153RD COURT, VANCOUVER WA 98683
1935-060	LANAHAN, RICHARD ANTHONY	D. MARCH 12, 1975, ROCHESTER, MINN.
1987-074	LANCASTER, LESTER WAYNE	OLD ADD: 105 EAST EIGHTH, IRVING TX 75060
1977-081	LANCE, GARY DEAN	207 SUNSET CIRCLE, PROSPERITY SC 29127
1982-075	LANCELLOTTI, RICHARD ANTHONY 'RICK'	5190 THOMPSON ROAD, CLARENCE NY 14031
1929-060	LAND, WILLIAM GILBERT 'DOC'	D. APRIL 14, 1986, LIVINGSTON, ALA.
1952-065	LANDENBERGER, KENNETH HENRY	D. JULY 28, 1960, CLEVELAND, OHIO
1977-082	LANDESTOY, RAFAEL SIVIALDO CAMILO	3121 SW 140TH AVENUE, MIAMI FL 33175
1957-039	LANDIS, JAMES HENRY	2350 LOUISA STREET, NAPA CA 94558
1963-065	LANDIS, WILLIAM HENRY	525 SYCAMORE, HANFORD CA 93230
1977-083	LANDREAUX, KENNETH FRANCIS	1510 NORTH SIESTA AVENUE, LAPUENTE CA 91746
1976-052	LANDRETH, LARRY ROBERT	116 ST. VINCENTS STREET SOUTH STRATFORD ON, N5A 2W8 CANADA
1950-046	LANDRITH, HOBERT NEAL 'HOBIE'	1462 NOME COURT, SUNNYVALE CA 94087
1991-106	LANDRUM, CEDRIC BERNARD	5207 NOCONA LANE, ARLINGTON TX 76018
1957-040	LANDRUM, DONALD LEROY	D. JANUARY 9, 2003, PITTSBURG, CALIF.
1938-048	LANDRUM, JESSE GLENN	D. JUNE 27, 1983, BEAUMONT, TEXAS
1950-047	LANDRUM, JOSEPH BUTLER	715 SHARPE ROAD, COLUMBIA SC 29203
1980-069	LANDRUM, TERRY LEE 'TITO'	1121 KENTUCKY SE, ALBUQUERQUE NM 87108
1986-083	LANDRUM, THOMAS WILLIAM 'BILL'	715 SHARPE ROAD, COLUMBIA SC 29203
1924-063	LANE, JAMES HUNTER 'HUNTER'	D. SEPTEMBER 12, 1994, MEMPHIS, TENN.
2002-105	LANE, JASON DEAN	8930 OAKGROVE AVENUE, SEBASTOPOL CA 95472
1953-049	LANE, JERALD HAL	D. JULY 24, 1988, CHATTANOOGA, TENN.
1971-060	LANE, MARVIN	40164 GULLIVER DRIVE, STERLING HEIGHTS MI 48310
1949-046	LANE, RICHARD HARRISON	2717 LEGEND DRIVE, LAS VEGAS NV 89134
1941-061	LANFRANCONI, WALTER OSWALD	D. AUGUST 18, 1986, BARRE, VT.
1938-049	LANG, DONALD CHARLES	150 SHELLEY CIRCLE, VENTURA CA 93005
1930-043	LANG, MARTIN JOHN	D. JANUARY 13, 1968, LAKEWOOD, COLO.
1975-064	LANG, ROBERT DAVID 'CHIP'	985 HOMER AVE, PITTSBURGH PA 15237
1972-060	LANGE, RICHARD OTTO	39744 SALVATORE DRIVE, STERLING HEIGHTS MI 48313
2002-106	LANGERHANS, RYAN DAVID	2311 FALCON DRIVE, ROUND ROCK TX 78681
1926-047	LANGFORD, ELTON 'SAM'	D. JULY 31, 1993, PLAINVIEW, TEXAS
1976-053	LANGFORD, JAMES RICK 'RICK'	2209 51ST AVENUE WEST, BRADENTON FL 34209
1984-065	LANGSTON, MARK EDWARD	56 GOLDEN EAGLE, IRVINE CA 92603
1964-063	LANIER, HAROLD CLIFTON	3270 COUNTRYSIDE VIEW DRIVE, SAINT CLOUD FL 34772
1938-050	LANIER, HUBERT MAX 'MAX'	D. JANUARY 30, 2007, LOCANTO, FLA.
1971-061	LANIER, LORENZO	4515 EAST FRONTENAC DRIVE, CLEVELAND OH 44128
1998-101	LANKFORD, FRANK GREENFIELD	104 LAKEVIEW AVENUE NE, ATLANTA GA 30305
1990-081	LANKFORD, RAYMOND LEWIS	15 TERRY HILL LANE, SAINT LOUIS MO 63131
1936-046	LANNING, JOHN YOUNG	D. NOVEMBER 8, 1989, ASHEVILLE, N.C.
1938-051	LANNING, THOMAS NEWTON	D. NOVEMBER 4, 1967, MARIETTA, GA.
1978-069	LANSFORD, CARNEY RAY	43736 POCAHONTAS ROAD, BAKER OR 97814
1982-076	LANSFORD, JOSEPH DALE 'JODY'	3691 WARBLER AVENUE, SANTA CLARA CA 95051
1922-069	LANSING, EUGENE HEWETT	D. JANUARY 18, 1945, RENSSELAER, N.Y.
1993-099	LANSING, MICHAEL THOMAS	9691 SOUTH SUN MEADOWS STREET, HIGHLANDS RANCH CO 80126
1951-050	LAPALME, PAUL EDMORE	167 SMITH STREET, LEOMINSTER MA 01453
1922-070	LAPAN, PETER NELSON	D. JANUARY 5, 1953, NORWALK, CALIF.
1942-062	LAPIHUSKA, ANDREW	D. FEBRUARY 17, 1996, MILLVILLE, R.I.
1980-070	LAPOINT, DAVID JEFFREY	5 QUEENSWAY, QUEENSBURY NY 12804
1947-056	LAPOINTE, RALPH JOHN	D. SEPTEMBER 13, 1967, BURLINGTON, VT.
2006-094	LARA, JUAN MANUEL	OLD ADD: BANI DOM REP
2000-091	LARA, YOVANNY B	OLD ADD: SAN CRISTOBAL DOM REP
1958-054	LARKER, NORMAN HOWARD	D. MARCH 12, 2007, LONG BEACH, CALIF.
1996-101	LARKIN, ANDREW DANE	5600 STADIUM PKWY, MELBOURNE FL 32940
1986-084	LARKIN, BARRY LOUIS	5410 OSPREY ISLE LANE, ORLANDO FL 32819
1987-075	LARKIN, EUGENE THOMAS	9496 ABBOT COURT, EDEN PRAIRIE MN 55347
1983-091	LARKIN, PATRICK CLIBURN	1346 SUN DIAL DRIVE, TUSTIN CA 92782
1998-102	LARKIN, STEPHEN KARARI	9178 SOLON DRIVE, CINCINNATI OH 45242
1934-060	LARKIN, STEPHEN PATRICK	D. MAY 2, 1969, NORRISTOWN, PA.
2000-092	LAROCCA, GREGORY MARK	3344 MORETOWN COMMONS ROAD, MORETOWN VT 05660
2004-116	LAROCHE, DAVID ADAM 'ADAM'	1735 EAST OAK STRET, FORT SCOTT KS 66701
1970-077	LAROCHE, DAVID EUGENE	RURAL ROUTE 4 BOX 3, FORT SCOTT KS 66701
1978-070	LAROSE, HENRY JOHN 'JOHN'	99 ROLAND, CUMBERLAND RI 02864
1968-052	LAROSE, VICTOR RAYMOND	2823 EAST TURQUOISE AVENUE, PHOENIX AZ 85028
1953-050	LARSEN, DON JAMES	PO BOX 2863, HAYDEN LAKE ID 83835
1936-047	LARSEN, ERLING ADELI	D. OCTOBER 8, 2005, TUCSON, ARIZ.
2001-100	LARSON, BRANDON JOHN	8922 RICHWAY, SAN ANTONIO TX 78251
1976-054	LARSON, DANIEL JAMES	797 OXEN STREET, PASO ROBLES CA 93446
1999-102	LARUE, MICHAEL JASON 'JASON'	3237 HAWTHORNE, SPRING BRANCH TX 78070
1963-066	LARUSSA, ANTHONY 'TONY'	338 GOLDEN MEADOW PLACE, ALAMO CA 94507
1954-057	LARY, ALFRED ALLEN	D. JULY 10, 2001, NORTHPORT, ALA.
1954-058	LARY, FRANK STRONG	11813 BASEBALL DRIVE, NORTHPORT AL 35475
1929-061	LARY, LYNFORD HOBART	D. JANUARY 9, 1973, DOWNEY, CALIF.
1963-067	LASHER, FREDERICK WALTER	N9596 COUNTY ROAD K, MERRILLAN WI 54754
1982-077	LASKEY, WILLIAM ALAN	4312 N. HOLLAND SYLVANIA RD #203, TOLEDO OH 43623
1924-064	LASLEY, WILLARD ALMOND	D. AUGUST 21, 1990, SEATTLE, WASH.
1954-059	LASORDA, THOMAS CHARLES	1473 WEST MAXZIM, FULLERTON CA 92633
1957-041	LASSETTER, DONALD ONEAL	PO BOX 326, LYON MS 38645
1997-095	LATHAM, CHRISTOPHER JOSEPH	6331 BUZZ ALDRIN DRIVE, LAS VEGAS NV 89149
1985-062	LATHAM, WILLIAM CAROL	211 MAGNOLIA, TRUSSVILLE AL 35173

1957-042 LATMAN, ARNOLD BARRY 'BARRY' .... 1206 SAN JULIAN DRIVE, SAN MARCOS CA 92069
1956-050 LAU, CHARLES RICHARD .... D. MARCH 18, 1984, KEY COLONY BEACH, FLA.
1981-067 LAUDNER, TIMOTHY JON .... PO BOX 10, HAMEL MN 55340
1967-062 LAUZERIQUE, GEORGE .... 601 OLEASTER AVE, WEST PALM BEACH FL 33414
1934-061 LAVAGETTO, HARRY ARTHUR 'COOKIE' .... D. AUGUST 10, 1990, ORINDA, CALIF.
1984-066 LAVALLIERE, MICHAEL EUGENE .... 216 81ST STREET WEST, BRADENTON FL 34209
1974-071 LAVELLE, GARY ROBERT .... 1100 WORTHINGTON CIRCLE, VIRGINIA BEACH VA 23464
1969-099 LAW, RONALD DAVID .... OLD ADD: 9000 YUCCA WAY, THORNTON CO 80229
1978-071 LAW, RUDY KARL .... 4626 BROADWAY, HAWTHORNE CA 90250
1980-071 LAW, VANCE AARON .... 1682 NORTH 1950 WEST, PROVO UT 84604
1950-048 LAW, VERNON SANDERS .... 1718 NORTH 1050 WEST, PROVO UT 84604
1946-063 LAWING, GARLAND FREDERICK .... D. SEPTEMBER 27, 1996, MURRELLS INLET, S.C.
1982-078 LAWLESS, THOMAS JAMES 'TIM' .... 16619 EVERGREEN FOREST DRIVE, BALLWIN MO 63011
2001-101 LAWRENCE, BRIAN MICHAEL .... 3379 COUNTY ROAD 1132, LINDEN TX 75563
1954-060 LAWRENCE, BROOKS ULYSSES .... D. APRIL 27, 2000, SPRINGFIELD, OHIO
1963-068 LAWRENCE, JAMES ROSS .... 225 HADDINGTON STREET CALEDONIA ON, N3W 1G1 CANADA
2002-107 LAWRENCE, JOSEPH DUDLEY .... 4839 TAIMER STREET, LAKE CHARLES LA 70605
1924-065 LAWRENCE, ROBERT ANDREW .... D. NOVEMBER 6, 1983, JAMAICA, N.Y.
1998-103 LAWRENCE, SEAN CHRISTOPHER .... 194 SOUTH CORAL HILL ROAD, EPHRAIM WI 54211
1932-044 LAWRENCE, WILLIAM HENRY .... D. JUNE 15, 1997, REDWOOD CITY, CALIF.
1930-044 LAWSON, ALFRED VOYLE 'ROXIE' .... D. APRIL 9, 1977, STOCKPORT, IOWA
1972-061 LAWSON, STEVEN GEORGE .... PO BOX 5630, BROOKINGS SD 97415
1989-070 LAWTON, MARCUS DWAYNE .... 110 CONNIE DRIVE, GULFPORT MS 39503
1995-123 LAWTON, MATTHEW .... PO BOX 101, SAUCIER MS 39574
1999-103 LAXTON, BRETT WILLIAM .... 6922 SPRINGWOOD BLVD, DENHAM SPRINGS LA 70726
1970-078 LAXTON, WILLIAM HARRY .... 261 MANSION AVE, AUDUBON NJ 08106
1990-082 LAYANA, TIMOTHY JOSEPH .... D. JUNE 26, 1999, BAKERSFIELD, CALIF.
1948-057 LAYDEN, PETER JOHN .... D. JULY 18, 1982, EDNA, TEXAS
1927-053 LAYNE, HERMAN .... D. AUGUST 27, 1973, GALLIPOLIS, OHIO
1941-062 LAYNE, IVORIA HILLIS 'HILLY' .... 101 WOODCLIFF CIRCLE, SIGNAL MOUNTAIN TN 37377
1948-058 LAYTON, LESTER LEE .... 8780 EAST MCKELLIPS ROAD #27, SCOTTSDALE AZ 85257
1968-053 LAZAR, JOHN DAN 'DAN' .... 8444 OAKWOOD AVE, MUNSTER IN 46321
1943-077 LAZOR, JOHN PAUL .... D. DECEMBER 9, 2002, RENTON, WASH.
1984-067 LAZORKO, JACK THOMAS .... 1360 MEANDERING WAY, ROCKWALL TX 75087
1926-048 LAZZERI, ANTHONY MICHAEL .... D. AUGUST 6, 1946, SAN FRANCISCO, CALIF.
1980-072 LEA, CHARLES WILLIAM .... 3064 MISTWOOD COVE SOUTH, COLLIERVILLE TN 38017
1923-078 LEACH, FREDERICK .... D. DECEMBER 10, 1981, HAGERMAN, IND.
2001-102 LEACH, JALAL DONNELL .... 3718 PHILLIP ISLAND ROAD, WEST SACRAMENTO CA 95691
1981-068 LEACH, RICHARD MAX 'RICK' .... 593 LAYMAN CREEK CIRCLE, GRAND BLANC MI 48439
1981-069 LEACH, TERRY HESTER .... 2135 SW LOCKS ROAD, STUART FL 34997
2004-117 LEAGUE, BRANDON PAUL .... 2034 SCOTT STREET #A, SAN FRANCISCO CA 94115
1980-073 LEAL, LUIS ENRIQUE .... CALLE 28 #30-60 BARQUISIMETO LARA, VENEZUELA
1981-070 LEARY, TIMOTHY JAMES .... 17020 WEST SUNSET BLVD #8, PACIFIC PALISADES CA 90272
1920-071 LEATHERS, HAROLD LANGFORD .... D. APRIL 12, 1977, MODESTO, CALIF.
2000-093 LECROY, MATTHEW HANKS .... 410 BROWN AVENUE, BELTON SC 29627
1998-104 LEDEE, RICARDO CHRISTOPHER 'RICKY' .... 6832 SE 12TH TERRACE, OCALA FL 34480
1995-124 LEDESMA, AARON DAVID .... 2446 DOUGLAS STREET, UNION CITY CA 94587
2003-092 LEDEZMA, WILFREDO JOSE 'WIL' .... OLD ADD: MARACAY VENEZUELA
1999-104 LEE, CARLOS NORIEL .... OLD ADD: AGUADULCE PANAMA
2002-108 LEE, CLIFTON PHIFER .... 3712 HAZELWOOD DRIVE, BENTON AR 72015
1999-105 LEE, COREY WAYNE .... 278 LANCASHIRE RUN, SMITHFIELD NC 27577
1999-106 LEE, DAVID EMMER .... 56 TERRACE DRIVE, PITTSBURGH PA 15205
1993-100 LEE, DEREK GERALD .... 8834 LIATRIS DRIVE, FRANKFORT IL 60423
1997-096 LEE, DERREK LEON .... 3576 BRITTANY WAY, EL DORADO HILLS CA 95762
1957-043 LEE, DONALD EDWARD .... 9101 PALM TREE DR, TUCSON AZ 85710
1920-072 LEE, ERNEST DUDLEY 'DUD' .... D. JANUARY 7, 1971, DENVER, COLO.
1930-045 LEE, HAROLD BURNHAM .... D. SEPTEMBER 4, 1989, PASCAGOULA, MISS.
1969-100 LEE, LERON .... 8159 WARREN COURT, GRANITE BAY CA 95746
1985-063 LEE, MANUEL LORA .... OLD ADD: 1310 GULF BLVD, CLEARWATER BEACH FL 33767
1978-072 LEE, MARK LINDEN .... 130 NORTH ROSEMOUNT STREET, AMARILLO TX 79106
1988-081 LEE, MARK OWEN .... 3580 BRUNSWICK DRIVE, COLORADO SPRINGS CO 80920
1960-059 LEE, MICHAEL RANDALL .... 1790 CALMIN DRIVE, FALLBROOK CA 92028
1964-064 LEE, ROBERT DEAN .... 2110 CASPAR DRIVE, LAKE HAVASU CITY AZ 86406
1945-056 LEE, ROY EDWIN .... D. NOVEMBER 11, 1985, ST. LOUIS, MO.
2000-094 LEE, SANG-HOON .... OLD ADD: SEOUL KOREA
1990-083 LEE, TERRY JAMES .... 4650 WENDOVER STREET, EUGENE OR 97404
1933-034 LEE, THORNTON STARR .... D. JUNE 9, 1997, TUCSON, ARIZ.
1998-105 LEE, TRAVIS REYNOLDS .... 1200 MARTINI DRIVE, HENDERSON NV 89052
1934-062 LEE, WILLIAM CRUTCHER .... D. JUNE 15, 1977, PLAQUEMINE, LA.
1969-101 LEE, WILLIAM FRANCIS .... 305 COMMON VIEW DRIVE, CRAFTSBURY VT 05826
1959-048 LEEK, EUGENE HAROLD .... 2722 EAST PACKER COURT, VISALIA CA 93292
1984-068 LEEPER, DAVID DALE .... 20309 SOUTH WESTERN AVENUE, TORRANCE CA 90501
1921-055 LEES, GEORGE EDWARD .... D. JANUARY 2, 1980, MECHANICSBURG, PA.
1965-062 LEFEBVRE, JAMES KENNETH .... 10160 EAST WHISPERING WIND DRIVE, SCOTTSDALE AZ 85255
1980-074 LEFEBVRE, JOSEPH HENRY .... 1701 HOOKSETT ROAD #111, HOOKSETT NH 03106
1938-052 LEFEBVRE, WILFRID HENRY 'BILL' .... D. JANUARY 19, 2007, LARGO, FLA.
1920-073 LEFEVRE, ALFREDO MODESTO .... D. JANUARY 21, 1982, GLEN COVE, N.Y.
1983-092 LEFFERTS, CRAIG LINDSAY .... OLD ADD: 12100 TRAVERTINE COURT, POWAY CA 92064
1924-066 LEFLER, WADE HAMPTON .... D. MARCH 6, 1981, HICKORY, N.C.
1974-072 LEFLORE, RONALD .... 6263 93RD TERRACE #4206, PINELLAS PARK FL 33782
1993-101 LEFTWICH, PHILLIP DALE .... 15819 SOUTH 31ST STREET, PHOENIX AZ 85048
1929-062 LEGETT, LOUIS ALFRED 'DOC' .... D. MARCH 6, 1988, NEW ORLEANS, LA.
1986-085 LEGG, GREGORY LYNN .... 412 JENNA KAY DRIVE, ARCHBALD PA 18403
1932-045 LEHENY, REGIS FRANCIS .... D. NOVEMBER 2, 1976, PITTSBURGH, PA.
1961-066 LEHEW, JAMES ANTHONY .... 3086 FAIRVIEW ROAD, GRANTVILLE MD 21536
1952-066 LEHMAN, KENNETH KARL .... 3463 RENEE DRIVE, SEDRO-WOOLLEY WA 98284

1946-064	LEHNER, PAUL EUGENE	D. DECEMBER 27, 1967, BIRMINGHAM, ALA.
2004-118	LEHR, CHARLES LARRY 'JUSTIN'	946 SOUTH FIRCROFT STREET, WEST COVINA CA 91791
1926-049	LEHR, NORMAN CARL MICHAEL	D. JULY 17, 1968, CONESUS LAKE, N.Y.
1933-035	LEIBER, HENRY EDWARD	D. NOVEMBER 8, 1993, TUCSON, ARIZ.
1979-068	LEIBRANDT, CHARLES LOUIS	1235 STUART RIDGE, ALPHARETTA GA 30202
2004-119	LEICESTER, JONATHAN DAVID	17151 CORBINA LANE #112, HUNTINGTON BEACH CA 92649
1921-056	LEIFER, ELMER EDWIN	D. SEPTEMBER 26, 1948, EVERETT, WASH.
1999-107	LEIFER, JEFFREY DAVID	OLD ADD: 1726 NEW HAMPSHIRE DRIVE, COSTA MESA CA 92626
1939-066	LEIP, EDGAR ELLSWORTH	D. NOVEMBER 24, 1983, ZEPHYRHILLS, FLA.
1984-069	LEIPER, DAVID PAUL	13082 NORTH 103RD STREET, SCOTTSDALE AZ 85268
1987-076	LEISTER, JOHN WILLIAM	304 DEVON DRIVE, SAINT LOUIS MI 48880
1987-077	LEITER, ALOIS TERRY	2660 RIVIERA MANOR, WESTON FL 33332
1990-084	LEITER, MARK EDWARD	721 PRINCETON ROAD, LANOKA HARBOR NJ 08734
1990-085	LEIUS, SCOTT THOMAS	12620 42ND PLACE NORTH, MINNEAPOLIS MN 55442
1954-061	LEJA, FRANK JOHN	D. MAY 3, 1991, BOSTON, MASS.
1965-063	LEJOHN, DONALD EVERETT	D. FEBRUARY 25, 2005, CALIFORNIA, PA.
1973-073	LEMANCZYK, DAVID LAWRENCE	24 LEHIGH CT, ROCKVILLE CENTRE NY 11570
1962-075	LEMASTER, DENVER CLAYTON	4833 CARLENE WAY SE, LILBURN GA 30247
1975-065	LEMASTER, JOHNNIE LEE	PIKEVILLE BASEBALL 147 SYCAMORE STREET, PIKEVILLE KY 41501
1961-067	LEMAY, RICHARD PAUL	1741 HOLLAND LANE, WICHITA KS 67212
1950-049	LEMBO, STEPHEN NEAL	D. DECEMBER 4, 1989, FLUSHING, N.Y.
1988-082	LEMKE, MARK ALAN	3 OLENA DRIVE, WHITESBORO NY 13492
1975-066	LEMON, CHESTER EARL	38150 TIMBERLANE DRIVE, UMATILLA FL 32784
1950-050	LEMON, JAMES ROBERT	D. MAY 14, 2006, BRANDON, MISS.
1941-063	LEMON, ROBERT GRANVILLE	D. JANUARY 11, 2000, LONG BEACH, CALIF.
1969-102	LEMONDS, DAVID LEE	3533 ARBORHILL ROAD, CHARLOTTE NC 28270
1976-055	LEMONGELLO, MARK	OLD ADD: 3201 WEST FRANKFORT DRIVE, CHANDLER AZ 85226
1950-051	LENHARDT, DONALD EUGENE	13317 WOODLAKE VILLAGE CT, SAINT LOUIS MO 63141
1928-056	LENNON, EDWARD FRANCIS	D. SEPTEMBER 13, 1947, PHILADELPHIA, PA.
1991-107	LENNON, PATRICK ORLANDO	OLD ADD: PINEWOOD DRIVE, WHITEVILLE NC 28472
1954-062	LENNON, ROBERT ALBERT	D. JUNE 14, 2005, DIX HILLS, N.Y.
1978-073	LENTINE, JAMES MATTHEW	1066 CALLE DEL CERRO #1411, SAN CLEMENTE CA 92672
1992-069	LEON, DANILO ENRIQUE	OLD ADD: CALLE 8 CASA 33-63, MARACAIBO VENEZ
1968-054	LEON, EDUARDO ANTONIO	6241 EAST VISTA DEL CANON, TUCSON AZ 85715
1945-057	LEON, ISIDORE JUAN	D. JULY 25, 2002, MIAMI, FLA.
2002-109	LEON, JOSE GERALDO VEGA	OLD ADD: CAYEY PR 00737
1973-074	LEON, MAXIMINO (MEDINA)	CERRADA DE SAN FERNANDO 3ERA SECCIN #68, HERMOSILLO MEXICO
1974-073	LEONARD, DENNIS PATRICK	4102 EVERGREEN LN, BLUE SPRINGS MO 64015
1933-036	LEONARD, EMIL JOHN 'DUTCH'	D. APRIL 17, 1983, SPRINGFIELD, ILL.
1977-084	LEONARD, JEFFREY	1626 NORTH FELTON STREET, PHILADELPHIA PA 19151
1990-086	LEONARD, MARK DAVID	22042 HIBISCUS DRIVE, CUPERTINO CA 95014
2004-120	LEONE, JUSTIN PAUL	OLD ADD: 6358 BREA, LAS VEGAS NV 89118
1967-063	LEONHARD, DAVID PAUL	87 CORNING ST, BEVERLY MA 01915
1928-057	LEOPOLD, RUDOLPH MATAS	D. SEPTEMBER 3, 1965, BATON ROUGE, LA.
1941-064	LEOVICH, JOHN JOSEPH	D. FEBRUARY 3, 2000, LINCOLN CITY, ORE.
1952-067	LEPCIO, THADDEUS STANLEY 'TED'	263 GREENLODGE STREET, DEDHAM MA 02026
1955-069	LEPPERT, DON EUGENE	1630 EPPING FOREST DRIVE, SOUTHAVEN MS 38671
1961-068	LEPPERT, DONALD GEORGE	317 SUNRISE CAY #201, NAPLES FL 34114
1975-067	LERCH, RANDY LOUIS	19490 MONTEREY STREET, MORGAN HILL CA 95037
1952-068	LERCHEN, GEORGE EDWARD	354 EAST ROSE, GARDEN CITY MI 48135
2005-109	LEREW, ANTHONY ALLEN	6 SUMMER DRIVE, DILLSBURG PA 17019
1928-058	LERIAN, WALTER IRVIN	D. OCTOBER 22, 1929, BALTIMORE, MD.
1997-097	LEROY, JOHN MICHAEL	D. JUNE 26, 2001, SIOUX CITY, IOWA
1969-103	LERSCH, BARRY LEE	2280 SOUTH JASPER WAY #B, AURORA CO 80013
1996-102	LESHER, BRIAN HERBERT	217 VASSAR DRIVE, NEWARK DE 19711
1972-062	LESHNOCK, DONALD LEE	289 CARLIN COURT, COLUMBUS OH 43230
1993-102	LESKANIC, CURTIS JOHN	2032 ALAQUA DRIVE, LONGWOOD FL 32779
1982-079	LESLEY, BRADLEY JAY	5235 KESTER AVENUE #207, SHERMAN OAKS CA 91411
1929-063	LESLIE, SAMUEL ANDREW	D. JANUARY 21, 1979, PASCAGOULA, MISS.
2006-095	LESTER, JONATHAN TYLER	8905 106TH STREET EAST, PUYALLUP WA 98373
1939-067	LETCHAS, CHARLIE	D. MARCH 14, 1995, TAMPA, FLA.
1947-057	LEVAN, JESSE ROY	D. NOVEMBER 30, 1998, READING, PA.
1922-071	LEVERETT, GORHAM VANCE 'DIXIE'	D. FEBRUARY 20, 1957, BEAVERTON, ORE.
1920-074	LEVERETTE, HORACE WILBUR 'HOD'	D. APRIL 10, 1958, ST. PETERSBURG, FLA.
1930-046	LEVEY, JAMES JULIUS	D. MARCH 14, 1970, DALLAS, TEXAS
1996-103	LEVINE, ALAN BRIAN	1004 HAMPTON COURT, BELLEVILLE IL 62223
1992-070	LEVIS, JESSE	1219 HIGHLAND AVENUE, FORT WASHINGTON PA 19034
2000-095	LEVRAULT, ALLEN HARRY	PO BOX 1316, WESTPORT MA 02790
1923-079	LEVSEN, EMIL HENRY 'DUTCH'	D. MARCH 12, 1972, MINNEAPOLIS, MINN.
1940-049	LEVY, EDWARD CLARENCE	5701 PINE ISLAND ROAD #360, TAMARAC FL 33321
1975-068	LEWALLYN, DENNIS DALE	2900 BRECKENRIDGE DR, PENSACOLA FL 32506
1951-051	LEWANDOWSKI, DANIEL WILLIAM	D. JULY 19, 1996, HAMILTON, ONT.
1967-064	LEWIS, ALLAN SYDNEY	URB. LA FLORIDA R-15, DAVID CHIRIQUI, PANAMA
2002-110	LEWIS, COLBY PRESTON	5731 MEDIO LUNA AVENUE, BAKERSFIELD CA 93306
1990-087	LEWIS, DARREN JOEL	OLD ADD: 1154 WASHINGTON STREET, BOSTON MA 02118
2006-096	LEWIS, FREDERICK DESHAUN	OLD ADD: WIGGINS MS
1979-069	LEWIS, JAMES MARTIN	5311 HANSEL AVENUE #D12, ORLANDO FL 32809
1991-108	LEWIS, JAMES STEVEN	OLD ADD: 5119 NORTH OLD RANCH RD, LAVERNE CA 91750
1935-061	LEWIS, JOHN KELLY 'BUDDY'	PO BOX 788, GASTONIA NC 28053
1964-065	LEWIS, JOHNNY JOE	810 TARA, CANTONMENT FL 32533
1991-109	LEWIS, MARK DAVID	1753 CLEVELAND AVENUE, HAMILTON OH 45313
1992-071	LEWIS, RICHIE TODD	13209 COUNTY ROAD EAST #7005, LOSANTVILLE IN 47354
1990-088	LEWIS, SCOTT ALLEN	2584 FAIRWAY DRIVE, COSTA MESA CA 92627
1924-067	LEWIS, WILLIAM BURTON	D. MARCH 24, 1950, TONAWANDA, N.Y.
1933-037	LEWIS, WILLIAM HENRY 'BUDDY'	D. OCTOBER 24, 1977, MEMPHIS, TENN.
1971-062	LEY, TERRENCE RICHARD	2620 FIRST STREET, BAKER CITY OR 97814

1986-086	LEYLAND, JAMES RICHARD	261 TECH ROAD, PITTSBURGH PA 15205
1990-089	LEYRITZ, JAMES JOSEPH	11020 SW 42ND COURT, DAVIE FL 33328
1989-071	LEYVA, NICHOLAS TOMAS	1098 TILGHMAN ROAD, WAYNE PA 19087
1980-075	LEZCANO, CARLOS MANUEL	415 WEST BOX ELDER PLACE, CHANDLER AZ 85225
1974-074	LEZCANO, SIXTO JOAQUIN	7828 BARDMOOR HILL CIRCLE, ORLANDO FL 32835
1945-058	LIBKE, ALBERT WALTER	D. MARCH 7, 2003, WENATCHEE, WASH.
1969-104	LIBRAN, FRANCISCO	OLD ADD: CALLE DR. ESCADE #202, MAYAGUEZ PR 00708
1981-071	LICKERT, JOHN WILBUR	PO BOX 279, NORTH SCITUATE RI 02857
1990-090	LIDDELL, DAVID ALEXANDER	17 MEADOW WOOD, COTO DE CAZA CA 92679
1953-051	LIDDLE, DONALD EUGENE	D. JUNE 5, 2000, MOUNT CARMEL, ILL.
2002-111	LIDGE, BRADLEY THOMAS	1274 LAURENWOOD WAY, HIGHLANDS RANCH CO 80129
1997-098	LIDLE, CORY FULTON	D. OCTOBER 11, 2006, NEW YORK, N.Y.
1935-062	LIEBER, CHARLES EDWIN 'DUTCH'	D. DECEMBER 31, 1961, LOS ANGELES, CALIF.
1994-062	LIEBER, JONATHAN RAY	3060 ISLE OF PALMS DRIVE WEST, MOBILE AL 36695
1994-063	LIEBERTHAL, MICHAEL SCOTT	1740 LARKFIELD AVENUE, THOUSAND OAKS CA 91362
1930-047	LIEBHARDT, GLENN IGNATIUS	D. MARCH 14, 1992, WINSTON-SALEM, N.C.
1997-099	LIGTENBERG, KERRY DALE	9274 ALBRIGHT COURT, INVER GROVE HEIGHTS MN 55077
1936-048	LILLARD, ROBERT EUGENE 'GENE'	D. APRIL 12, 1991, GOLETA, CALIF.
1939-068	LILLARD, WILLIAM BEVERLY	750 BLACK OAK LANE, NIPOMO CA 93944
1989-072	LILLIQUIST, DEREK JANSEN	226 10TH AVENUE, VERO BEACH FL 32962
1958-055	LILLIS, ROBERT PERRY	5107 CHERRY TREE LANE, ORLANDO FL 32819
1999-108	LILLY, THEODORE ROOSEVELT	PO BOX 257, BASS LAKE CA 93604
1994-064	LIMA, JOSE DESIDERIO RODRIGUEZ	OLD ADD: 3435 EAST CEDAR HOLLOW DRIVE, PEARLAND TX 77584
1951-052	LIMMER, LOUIS	D. APRIL 1, 2007, BOCA RATON, FLA.
1981-072	LINARES, RUFINO DELACRUZ	D. MAY 16, 1998, SAN PEDRO DE MACORIS, DOM REP
1999-109	LINCOLN, MICHAEL GEORGE	8269 MOSS OAK AVENUE, CITRUS HEIGHTS CA 95610
2006-097	LIND, ADAM ALAN	2123 TARTAN ROAD, ANDERSON IN 46012
1927-054	LIND, HENRY CARL	D. AUGUST 2, 1946, NEW YORK, N.Y.
1974-075	LIND, JACKSON HUGH	6132 EAST REDMONT DRIVE, MESA AZ 85215
1987-078	LIND, JOSE	VILLA CAITO #18, DORADO PR 00646
1960-060	LINDBECK, EMERIT DESMOND 'EM'	210 HILLCREST DRIVE, KEWANEE IL 61443
1965-064	LINDBLAD, PAUL ANTON	D. JANUARY 1, 2006, ARLINGTON, TEXAS
1947-058	LINDE, LYMAN GILBERT	D. OCTOBER 14, 1995, BEAVER DAM, WISC.
1941-065	LINDELL, JOHN HARLAN	D. AUGUST 27, 1985, NEWPORT BEACH, CALIF.
1986-087	LINDEMAN, JAMES WILLIAM	2278 SCOTT STREET, DES PLAINES IL 60018
2003-093	LINDEN, TODD ANTHONY	6465 TRACYTON BLVD, BREMERTON WA 98311
1950-052	LINDEN, WALTER CHARLES	4432 HARVEY AVENUE, WESTERN SPRINGS IL 60558
1943-078	LINDQUIST, CARL EMIL	D. SEPTEMBER 3, 2001, BLOSSBURG, PA.
1922-072	LINDSEY, JAMES KENDRICK	D. OCTOBER 25, 1963, JACKSON, LA.
1991-110	LINDSEY, MICHAEL DOUGLAS	OLD ADD: 2104 LONG HUNTER LANE, NASHVILLE TN 37217
2000-096	LINDSEY, RODNEY LEE	610 COMANCHEE DRIVE #43, OPELIKA AL 36804
1987-079	LINDSEY, WILLIAM DONALD	OLD ADD: 645 NORTH STATE ROAD, POMPANO BEACH FL 33063
1958-056	LINDSTROM, CHARLES WILLIAM	PO BOX 486, ATLANTA IL 61723
1924-068	LINDSTROM, FRED CHARLES	D. OCTOBER 4, 1981, CHICAGO, ILL.
2000-097	LINEBRINK, SCOTT CAMERON	PO BOX 862, TAYLOR TX 76574
1966-055	LINES, RICHARD GEORGE	1716 PEBBLE BEACH LANE, THE VILLAGES FL 32159
1952-069	LINHART, CARL JAMES	2647 DELMAR AVENUE, GRANITE CITY IL 62040
1999-110	LINIAK, COLE EDWARD	1752 MORGANS AVENUE, SAN MARCOS CA 92078
1933-038	LINKE, EDWARD KARL	D. JUNE 21, 1988, CHICAGO, ILL.
1954-063	LINT, ROYCE JAMES	D. APRIL 3, 2006, PORTLAND, ORE.
1929-064	LINTON, CLAUD CLARENCE 'BOB'	D. APRIL 3, 1980, DESTIN, FLA.
1992-072	LINTON, DOUGLAS WARREN	201 ELLISON STREET, ROCHESTER NY 14609
1973-075	LINTZ, LARRY	PO BOX 231854, SACRAMENTO CA 95823
1962-076	LINZ, PHILIP FRANCIS	20 ROCKY RAPIDS ROAD, STAMFORD CT 06903
1963-069	LINZY, FRANK ALFRED	38947 EAST 151ST SOUTH, COWETA OK 74429
1956-051	LIPETRI, MICHAEL ANGELO 'ANGELO'	150 YOAKUM AVENUE, FARMINGDALE NY 11735
1942-063	LIPON, JOHN JOSEPH	D. AUGUST 17, 1998, HOUSTON, TEXAS
1937-066	LIPSCOMB, GERARD 'NIG'	D. FEBRUARY 27, 1978, HUNTERSVILLE, N.C.
1963-070	LIPSKI, ROBERT PETER	1 SNOOK ST, SCRANTON PA 18505
1995-125	LIRA, ANTONIO FELIPE 'FELIPE'	OLD ADD: 2770 N. OLD LAKE WILSON ROAD, KISSIMMEE FL 34747
2005-110	LIRIANO, FRANCISCO CASILLAS	OLD ADD: SAN CRISTOBAL DOM REP
1987-080	LIRIANO, NELSON ARTURO	MARTIRES 19 DE NOV. #7, ENS LUPERON PUERTO PLATA, DOM REP
2004-121	LIRIANO, PEDRO ANTONIO	OLD ADD: COTUI DOM REP
1970-079	LIS, JOSEPH ANTHONY	4055 SECRETARIAT DRIVE, NEWBURGH IN 47630
1927-055	LISENBEE, HORACE MILTON 'HOD'	D. NOVEMBER 14, 1987, CLARKSVILLE, TENN.
1981-073	LISI, RICCARDO PATRICK EMILIO	1207 NORTH WREN DRIVE, ROGERS AR 72756
1929-065	LISKA, ADOLPH JAMES 'AD'	D. NOVEMBER 30, 1998, PORTLAND, ORE.
1992-073	LISTACH, PATRICK ALAN	PO BOX 2012, NATCHITOCHES LA 71457
1973-076	LITTELL, MARK ALAN	27358 NORTH 88TH LANE, PEORIA AZ 85383
1989-073	LITTLE, DENNIS SCOTT 'SCOTT'	1321 ROSEBUD LANE, JACKSON MO 63755
1980-076	LITTLE, DONALD JEFFREY 'JEFF'	5711 C.R. 169, GENOA OH 43430
1998-106	LITTLE, MARK TRAVIS	2105 APPOMATTOX COURT, EDWARDSVILLE IL 62025
1982-080	LITTLE, RICHARD BRYAN 'BRYAN'	4766 TIFFANY PARK CIRCLE, BRYAN TX 77802
2002-112	LITTLE, WILLIAM GRADY 'GRADY'	278 EAST COLORADO BLVD #1604, PASADENA CA 91101
1980-077	LITTLEFIELD, JOHN ANDREW	1214 NORTH ALAMEDA STREET, AZUSA CA 91702
1950-053	LITTLEFIELD, RICHARD BERNARD	D. NOVEMBER 20, 1997, DETROIT, MICH.
1927-056	LITTLEJOHN, CHARLES CARLISLE	D. OCTOBER 27, 1977, KANSAS CITY, MO.
1978-074	LITTLEJOHN, DENNIS GERALD	6813 KLAMATH WAY #D, BAKERSFIELD CA 93309
1981-074	LITTLETON, LARRY MARVIN	5718 LITTLE OAK TRAIL, STONE MOUNTAIN GA 30087
2006-098	LITTLETON, WES AVI	1885 AVENIDA SEGOVIA, OCEANSIDE CA 92056
1989-074	LITTON, JON GREGORY 'GREG'	4296 BRIGHTON DRIVE, PENSACOLA FL 32504
1952-070	LITTRELL, JACK NAPIER	7510 FLOYDSBURG ROAD, CRESTWOOD KY 40014
1940-050	LITWHILER, DANIEL WEBSTER	12805 ASTONWOOD DRIVE #304, TAMPA FL 33626
1947-059	LIVELY, EVERETT ADRIAN 'BUD'	8605 ESSLINGER COURT, HUNTSVILLE AL 35802
1939-069	LIVENGOOD, WESLEY AMOS	D. SEPTEMBER 2, 1996, WINSTON-SALEM, N.C.
2006-099	LIVINGSTON, ROBERT JAMES	OLD ADD: 3009 58TH STREET, LUBBOCK TX 79413

1938-053	LIVINGSTON, THOMPSON ORVILLE 'MICKEY'	D. APRIL 3, 1983, HOUSTON TX
1991-111	LIVINGSTONE, SCOTT LOUIS	1303 PECOS DRIVE, SOUTHLAKE TX 76092
1968-055	LLENAS, WINSTON ENRIQUILLO	APARTADO #92 SANTIAGO, DOM REP
1922-073	LLEWELLYN, CLEMENT MANLEY	D. NOVEMBER 27, 1969, CHARLOTTE, N.C.
1993-103	LLOYD, GRAEME JOHN	455 OCEANVIEW AVENUE, PALM HARBOR FL 34683
1995-126	LOAIZA, ESTEBAN ANTONIO	1404 LANDS END COURT, SOUTHLAKE TX 76092
1939-070	LOANE, ROBERT KENNETH	D. DECEMBER 11, 2002, MONTEREY, CALIF.
1962-077	LOCK, DONALD WILSON	1330 NORTH WALNUT, KINGMAN KS 67068
1955-070	LOCKE, CHARLES EDWARD	1560 HAVEN HILLS ROAD, POPLAR BLUFF MO 63901
1959-049	LOCKE, LAWRENCE DONALD 'BOBBY'	194 EIGHTY ACRES ROAD, DUNBAR PA 15431
1964-066	LOCKE, RONALD THOMAS	15 LEWISTON AVENUE, WEST KINGSTON RI 02892
1965-065	LOCKER, ROBERT AWTRY	1561 RANCHO VIEW ROAD, LAFAYETTE CA 94549
1994-065	LOCKHART, KEITH VIRGIL	3330 MCKINLEY POINT DRIVE, DACULA GA 30019
1973-077	LOCKLEAR, GENE	1811 PENASCO ROAD, EL CAJON CA 92019
1955-071	LOCKLIN, STUART CARLTON	224 PASEO DEL VOLCAN SW #43, ALBUQUERQUE NM 87121
1945-059	LOCKMAN, CARROLL WALTER 'WHITEY'	8787 EAST MOUNTAIN VIEW RD #1106, SCOTTSDALE AZ 85258
1965-066	LOCKWOOD, CLAUDE EDWARD 'SKIP'	47 JOHN DRUCE LANE, WRENTHAM MA 02093
1938-054	LODIGIANI, DARIO ANTHONY	745 LATHROP STREET, NAPA CA 94558
1998-107	LODUCA, PAUL ANTHONY	267 BENTLEY MANOR, SAN ANTONIO TX 78249
2004-122	LOE, KAMERON D.	20132 MARILLA STREET, CHATSWORTH CA 91311
1928-059	LOEPP, GEORGE HERBERT	D. SEPTEMBER 4, 1967, LOS ANGELES, CALIF.
1950-054	LOES, WILLIAM 'BILLY'	OLD ADD: 5054 NORTH ORACLE ROAD, TUCSON AZ 85705
2006-100	LOEWEN, ADAM A.	OLD ADD: SURREY BC
1998-108	LOEWER, CARLTON EDWARD	188 HAWETHORN DRIVE, ALPINE WY 83128
2001-103	LOFTON, JAMES O'NEAL	7616 SOUTH WESTERN AVENUE, LOS ANGELES CA 90047
1991-112	LOFTON, KENNETH	PO BOX 68473, TUCSON AZ 85737
1926-050	LOFTUS, FRANCIS PATRICK 'FRANK'	D. OCTOBER 27, 1980, BELCHERTOWN, MASS.
1924-069	LOFTUS, RICHARD JOSEPH	D. JANUARY 21, 1972, CONCORD, MASS.
2006-101	LOGAN, BOONE	OLD ADD: HELOTES TX
2004-123	LOGAN, EXAVIER PRENTE 'NOOK'	OLD ADD: NATCHEZ MS
1951-053	LOGAN, JOHN	6115 WEST CLEVELAND AVENUE, MILWAUKEE WI 53219
1935-063	LOGAN, ROBERT DEAN 'LEFTY'	D. MAY 20, 1978, INDIANAPOLIS, IND.
1947-060	LOHRKE, JACK WAYNE 'LUCKY'	2817 LUCENA DRIVE, SAN JOSE CA 95132
1934-063	LOHRMAN, WILLIAM LEROY	D. SEPTEMBER 13, 1999, POUGHKEEPSIE, N.Y.
2001-104	LOHSE, KYLE MATTHEW	1276 LUCKY LADY LANE, PARADISE CA 95969
1978-075	LOIS, ALBERTO	INGENIO CONSUELO CALLE 5, SAN PEDRO DE MACORIS, DOM REP
1996-104	LOISELLE, RICHARD FRANK 'RICH'	560 TIMBER DRIVE, HARVARD IL 60033
1963-071	LOLICH, MICHAEL STEPHEN 'MICKEY'	6252 ROBINHILL, WASHINGTON MI 48094
1971-063	LOLICH, RONALD JOHN	3225 SW 78TH AVENUE, PORTLAND OR 97225
1946-065	LOLLAR, JOHN SHERMAN 'SHERM'	D. SEPTEMBER 24, 1977, SPRINGFIELD, MO.
1980-078	LOLLAR, WILLIAM TIMOTHY 'TIM'	16626 WEST BAYARD DRIVE, GOLDEN CO 80401
1984-070	LOMAN, DOUGLAS EDWARD	25 LINCOLN STREET, BAKERSFIELD CA 93305
1999-111	LOMASNEY, STEVEN JAMES	620 SE 21ST TERRACE, CAPE CORAL FL 33990
1998-109	LOMBARD, GEORGE PAUL	2275 RHINEHILL ROAD NE, ATLANTA GA 30315
1931-048	LOMBARDI, ERNEST NATALI	D. SEPTEMBER 26, 1977, SANTA CRUZ, CALIF.
1986-088	LOMBARDI, PHILIP ARDEN	9640 ETIWANDA AVENUE, NORTHRIDGE CA 91325
1945-060	LOMBARDI, VICTOR ALVIN	D. DECEMBER 3, 1997, FRESNO, CALIF.
1948-059	LOMBARDO, LOUIS	D. JUNE 11, 2001, FORT MILL, S.C.
1985-064	LOMBARDOZZI, STEPHEN PAUL	64 WILLOWBROOK DRIVE, AUBURN NY 13021
1995-127	LOMON, KEVIN DALE	24955 BLAYLOCK LANE, CAMERON OK 74932
1965-067	LONBORG, JAMES REYNOLD	498 FIRST PARISH RD, SCITUATE MA 02066
2006-102	LONEY, JAMES ANTHONY	4926 BIRDSONG LANE, MISSOURI CITY TX 77459
1922-074	LONG, JAMES ALBERT	D. SEPTEMBER 14, 1970, FORT DODGE, IOWA
1963-072	LONG, JEOFFREY KEITH	11 FLOWER COURT, LAKSIDE PARK KY 41017
1997-100	LONG, JOEY J.	5541 KISER LAKE ROAD, CONOVER OH 45317
1951-054	LONG, RICHARD DALE 'DALE'	D. JANUARY 27, 1991, PALM COAST, FLA.
1981-075	LONG, ROBERT EARL	OLD ADD: 3560 NOHAVE DRIVE, GRANDVILLE MI 49418
1997-101	LONG, RYAN MARCUS	2021 STONECREST WAY, PEARLAND TX 77581
1999-112	LONG, TERRENCE DEON	4351 FAIRMEADOW LANE, PIKE ROAD AL 36064
1924-070	LONG, THOMAS FRANCIS	D. SEPTEMBER 16, 1973, LOUISVILLE, KY.
1985-065	LONG, WILLIAM DOUGLAS	7699 DIMMICK ROAD, CINCINNATI OH 45241
1993-104	LONGMIRE, ANTHONY EUGENE	OLD ADD: 1067 CRYSTAL SPRINGS DRIVE, VACAVILLE CA 95688
1956-052	LONNETT, JOSEPH PAUL	126 DUNCAN CIR, BEAVER PA 15009
1968-056	LOOK, BRUCE MICHAEL	4298 MAITLAND ROAD, WILLIAMSBURG MI 49690
1961-069	LOOK, DEAN ZACHARY	80 VICTORIAN HILLS DRIVE, OKEMOS MI 48864
1993-105	LOONEY, BRIAN JAMES	10525 WINE PALM ROAD, FORT MYERS FL 33912
2003-094	LOOPER, AARON JOSEPH	1510 NORTH MINNESOTA AVENUE, SHAWNEE OK 74804
1998-110	LOOPER, BRADEN LAVERN	442 SHADOW CREEK DRIVE, PALOS HEIGHTS IL 60463
1944-077	LOPAT, EDMUND WALTER	D. JUNE 15, 1992, DARIEN, CONN.
1948-060	LOPATA, STANLEY EDWARD	LEISURE WORLD MANOR #2239, MESA AZ 85206
1945-061	LOPATKA, ARTHUR JOSEPH	D. MARCH 10, 2007, ELK GROVE VILLAGE, ILL.
1972-063	LOPES, DAVID EARL 'DAVEY'	8 RACHEL STREET, PROVIDENCE RI 02905
1993-106	LOPEZ, ALBERT ANTHONY 'ALBIE'	2887 EAST PALO VERDE COURT, GILBERT AZ 85234
1928-060	LOPEZ, ALFONSO RAMON	D. OCTOBER 30, 2005, TAMPA, FLA.
2003-095	LOPEZ, AQUILINO (ROA)	OLD ADD: ALTAGRACIA DOM REP
1965-068	LOPEZ, ARTURO	16056 ENGLISH OAKS AVENUE #C, BOWIE MD 20716
1974-076	LOPEZ, AURELIO RIOS	D. SEPTEMBER 22, 1992, MATEHUALA, MEXICO
1976-056	LOPEZ, CARLOS ANTONIO	MEXICI #33A, POINTE MAZATLAN SINALOA, MEXICO
2001-105	LOPEZ, FELIPE	1204 SUNCAST LANE #2, EL DORADO HILLS CA 95762
1955-072	LOPEZ, HECTOR HEADLEY	11415 FALDO COURT, HUDSON FL 34667
1992-074	LOPEZ, JAVIER (TORRES) 'JAVY'	OLD ADD: 410 CLUB PLACE, DULUTH GA 30096
2003-096	LOPEZ, JAVIER ALFONSO	OLD ADD: FAIRFAX VA 22030
2004-124	LOPEZ, JOSE CELESTINO	OLD ADD: BARCELONA VENEZ
1966-056	LOPEZ, JOSE RAMON	D. SEPTEMBER 4, 1982, MIAMI, FLA.
2001-106	LOPEZ, LUIS	OLD ADD: BROOKLYN NY
1990-091	LOPEZ, LUIS ANTONIO	636 40TH STREET, BROOKLYN NY 11232

1993-107	LOPEZ, LUIS SANTOS	OLD ADD: CIDRA PR 00639
1963-073	LOPEZ, MARCELINO PONS	D. NOVEMBER 29, 2001, HIALEAH, FLA.
1998-111	LOPEZ, MENDY AUDE	OLD ADD: SANTO DOMINGO DOM REP
2005-111	LOPEZ, PEDRO MICHEL	OLD ADD: MOCA DOM REP
2004-125	LOPEZ, RAYMOND MICHAEL 'MICKEY'	17430 SW 117TH AVENUE, MIAMI FL 33177
2000-098	LOPEZ, RODRIGO MUNOZ	OLD ADD: MEXICO CITY MEX
1923-080	LORD, WILLIAM CARLTON 'CARL'	D. AUGUST 15, 1947, CHESTER, PA.
1995-128	LORETTA, MARK DAVID	PO BOX 9505, RANCHO SANTA FE CA 92067
1994-066	LORRAINE, ANDREW JASON	24015 MILL VALLEY ROAD, VALENCIA CA 91355
1980-079	LOUCKS, SCOTT GREGORY	1801 VIOLA DR, SIERRA VISTA AZ 85635
1967-065	LOUGHLIN, LAWRENCE JOHN	D. JANUARY 26, 1999, DENVER, COLO.
1964-067	LOUN, DONALD NELSON	9095 WEXFORD DR, VIENNA VA 22180
2002-113	LOUX, SHANE A	1201 EAST MINERAL ROAD, GILBERT AZ 85234
1922-075	LOVELACE, THOMAS RIVERS	D. JULY 12, 1979, DALLAS, TEXAS
1988-083	LOVELACE, VANCE ODELL	5608 TWELFTH AVENUE, TAMPA FL 33610
1955-073	LOVENGUTH, LYNN RICHARD	D. SEPTEMBER 29, 2000, BEAVERTON, ORE.
1933-039	LOVETT, MERRITT MARWOOD 'MEM'	D. SEPTEMBER 19, 1995, DOWNERS GROVE, ILL.
1980-080	LOVIGLIO, JOHN PAUL 'JAY'	23 THIRD AVENUE, EAST ISLIP NY 11730
1972-064	LOVITTO, JOSEPH	D. MAY 19, 2001, ARLINGTON, TEXAS
1963-074	LOVRICH, PETER	19626 BEECHNUT DR, MOKENA IL 60448
1988-084	LOVULLO, SALVATORE ANTHONY	16825 BAJIO ROAD, ENCINO CA 91436
1997-102	LOWE, DEREK CHRISTOPHER	15401 OLD WEDGEWOOD COURT, FORT MYERS FL 33908
1920-075	LOWE, GEORGE WESLEY	D. SEPTEMBER 2, 1981, SOMERS POINT, N.J.
1997-103	LOWE, JONATHAN SEAN 'SEAN'	802 OAK DRIVE, MESQUITE TX 75149
2006-103	LOWE, MARK CHRISTOPHER	OLD ADD: MISSOURI CITY TX
1998-112	LOWELL, MICHAEL AVERETT	620 SANTURCE AVENUE, MIAMI FL 33143
1970-080	LOWENSTEIN, JOHN LEE	7017 VIA LOCANDA AVENUE, LAS VEGAS NV 89131
1997-104	LOWERY, QUENTON TERRELL 'TERRELL'	3565 ANTIGUA PLACE, WEST SACRAMENTO CA 95691
1951-055	LOWN, OMAR JOSEPH 'TURK'	1106 VAN BUREN, PUEBLO CO 81004
1942-064	LOWREY, HARRY LEE 'PEANUTS'	D. JULY 2, 1986, INGLEWOOD, CALIF.
1984-071	LOWRY, DWIGHT	D. JULY 10, 1997, JAMESTOWN, N.Y.
2003-097	LOWRY, NOAH RYAN	181 NORTH ENCINAL AVENUE, OJAI CA 92023
1942-065	LOWRY, SAMUEL JOSEPH	D. DECEMBER 1, 1992, PHILADELPHIA, PA.
1986-089	LOYND, MICHAEL WALLACE	19 RANDALL DRIVE, SHORT HILLS NJ 07078
1984-072	LOZADO, WILLIAM 'WILLIE'	4407 SUNRISE COURT, SELLERSBURG IN 47172
1981-076	LUBRATICH, STEVEN GEORGE	24 SACKETT ROAD, LEE NH 03824
1936-049	LUBY, HUGH MAX 'MAX'	D. MAY 4, 1986, EUGENE, ORE.
1938-055	LUCADELLO, JOHN	D. OCTOBER 30, 2001, SAN ANTONIO, TEXAS
1923-081	LUCAS, CHARLES FREDERICK 'RED'	D. JULY 9, 1986, NASHVILLE, TENN.
1935-064	LUCAS, FREDERICK WARRINGTON	D. MARCH 11, 1987, CAMBRIDGE, MD.
1980-081	LUCAS, GARY PAUL	1511 HIGH STREET, RICE LAKE WI 54868
1931-049	LUCAS, JOHN CHARLES	D. OCTOBER 31, 1970, MARYVILLE, ILL.
1929-066	LUCAS, RAY WESLEY	D. OCTOBER 9, 1969, HARRISON, MICH.
1970-081	LUCCHESI, FRANK JOSEPH	4703 MILL CREEK DRIVE, COLLEYVILLE TX 76034
1923-082	LUCE, FRANK EDWARD	D. FEBRUARY 3, 1942, MILWAUKEE, WISC.
1920-076	LUCEY, JOSEPH EARL	D. JULY 30, 1980, HOLYOKE, MASS.
1943-079	LUCIER, LOUIS JOSEPH	579 HIGHLAND STREET, NORTHBRIDGE MA 01534
1924-071	LUDOLPH, WILLIAM FRANCIS	D. APRIL 8, 1952, OAKLAND, CALIF.
1996-105	LUDWICK, ERIC DAVIS	746 SAMUEL CHASE LANE, MELBOURNE FL 32904
2002-114	LUDWICK, RYAN ANDREW	10183 WHISPY WILLOW WAY, LAS VEGAS NV 89135
1925-066	LUEBBE, ROY JOHN	D. AUGUST 21, 1985, PAPILLION, NEB.
1971-064	LUEBBER, STEPHEN LEE	PO BOX 2841, JOPLIN MO 64803
1993-108	LUEBBERS, LARRY CHRISTOPHER	844 ISAAC SHELBY CIRCLE EAST, FRANKFORT KY 40601
1962-078	LUEBKE, RICHARD RAYMOND	D. DECEMBER 4, 1974, SAN DIEGO, CALIF.
1989-075	LUECKEN, RICHARD FRED	2902 FONTANA DRIVE, HOUSTON TX 77043
2000-099	LUGO, JULIO CESAR	1555 GANTS CIRCLE, KISSIMMEE FL 34744
2006-104	LUGO, RUDDY JORAIDER	OLD ADD: BROOKLYN NY
1985-066	LUGO, URBANO RAFAEL	ROOSEVELT RES. TIUNA ENT BPH 44 ROSALES CARACAS, VENEZUELA
1996-106	LUKACHYK, ROBERT JAMES	1 PATRIOTS PARK, BRIDGEWATER NJ 08807
2001-107	LUKASIEWICZ, MARK FRANCIS	8035 FIR DRIVE, CLAY NY 13041
1996-107	LUKE, MATTHEW CLIFFORD	5262 EUCALYPTUS HILL ROAD, YORBA LINDA CA 92886
1941-066	LUKON, EDWARD PAUL	D. NOVEMBER 7, 1996, CANONSBURG, PA.
1967-066	LUM, MICHAEL KEN-WAI	3476 COCHISE DRIVE NW, ATLANTA GA 30339
1957-044	LUMENTI, RAPHAEL ANTHONY 'RALPH'	9 TOMASSO, MILFORD MA 01757
1956-053	LUMPE, JERRY DEAN	732 PEARSON DRIVE, SPRINGFIELD MO 65804
1954-064	LUNA, GUILLERMO ROMERO 'MEMO'	CARDENAS 50 ORIENTE LOS MOCHIS SINALOA, MEXICO
2004-126	LUNA, HECTOR R.	OLD ADD: MONTE CRISTI DOM REP
2000-100	LUNAR, FERNANDO JOSE	OLD ADD: ANACO VENEZUELA
1945-062	LUND, DONALD ANDREW	1000 SOUTH STATE STREET, ANN ARBOR MI 48109
1967-067	LUND, GORDON THOMAS	1602 SOUTH HARVARD AVENUE, ARLINGTON HEIGHTS IL 60005
1924-072	LUNDGREN, EBIN DELMAR 'DEL'	D. OCTOBER 19, 1984, LINDSBORG, KAN.
1999-113	LUNDQUIST, DAVID BRUCE	714 12TH AVENUE NE, HICKORY NC 28601
1973-078	LUNDSTEDT, THOMAS ROBERT	PO BOX 409, EPHRAIM WI 54211
2002-115	LUNSFORD, JAMES LEWIS 'TREY'	3955 NAIL ROAD, SOUTHHAVEN MS 38672
1940-051	LUPIEN, ULYSSES JOHN 'TONY'	D. JULY 9, 2004, NORWICH, VT.
1961-070	LUPLOW, ALVIN DAVID	4250 LAKE CRESS DRIVE EAST, SAGINAW MI 48603
1987-081	LUSADER, SCOTT EDWARD	4169 BAD MEADOWS, OAKLAND TOWNSHIP MI 48306
1956-054	LUTTRELL, LYLE KENNETH	D. JULY 11, 1984, CHATTANOOGA, TENN.
1922-076	LUTZ, LOUIS WILLIAM	D. FEBRUARY 22, 1984, CINCINNATI, OHIO
1951-056	LUTZ, ROLLIN JOSEPH 'JOE'	1411 QUAIL DRIVE, SARASOTA FL 33581
1923-083	LUTZKE, WALTER JOHN 'RUBE'	D. MARCH 6, 1938, MILWAUKEE, WISC.
2000-101	LUULOA, KEITH H. M.	29890 MORNING BREEZE DRIVE, MENIFEE CA 92584
1970-082	LUZINSKI, GREGORY MICHAEL	25680 STREAMLET COURT, BONITA SPRINGS FL 34135
1993-109	LYDEN, MITCHELL SCOTT	227 SHORE COURT, FORT LAUDERDALE FL 33308
1993-110	LYDY, DONALD SCOTT 'SCOTT'	4464 SOUTH COBBLESTONE STREET, GILBERT AZ 85296
1967-068	LYLE, ALBERT WALTER 'SPARKY'	17 SIGNAL HILL DR, VOORHEES NJ 08043

1925-067 LYLE, JAMES CHARLES..D. OCTOBER 10, 1977, WILLIAMSPORT, PA.
1920-077 LYNCH, ADRIAN RYAN..D. MARCH 16, 1934, DAVENPORT, IOWA
1980-082 LYNCH, EDWARD FRANCIS..................................7832 EAST PARKVIEW LANE, SCOTTSDALE AZ 85255
1954-065 LYNCH, GERALD THOMAS..................................4840 CHAMBLEE DUNWOODY ROAD, DUNWOODY GA 30338
1948-061 LYNCH, MATT DANNY 'DUMMY'...........................D. JUNE 30, 1978, PLANO, TEXAS
1922-077 LYNCH, WALTER EDWARD..................................D. DECEMBER 21, 1976, DAYTONA BEACH, CALIF.
1974-077 LYNN, FREDRIC MICHAEL...................................7336 EL FUERTE STREET, CARLSBAD CA 92009
1939-071 LYNN, JAPHET MONROE 'RED'............................D. OCTOBER 27, 1977, BELLVILLE, TEXAS
1937-067 LYNN, JEROME EDWARD...................................D. SEPTEMBER 25, 1972, SCRANTON, PA.
2001-108 LYON, BRANDON JAMES....................................610 CYNTHIA LANE, SANTA CLARA UT 84765
1944-078 LYON, RUSSELL MAYO.......................................D. DECEMBER 24, 1975, CALHOUN FALLS, S.C.
1944-079 LYONS, ALBERT HAROLD...................................D. DECEMBER 20, 1965, INGLEWOOD, CALIF.
1986-090 LYONS, BARRY STEPHEN...................................1079 FRANK P. CORSO STREET, BILOXI MS 39530
1996-108 LYONS, CURT RUSSELL.....................................OLD ADD: 202 FLINT LOCK ROAD, CHARLESTON WV 25314
1947-061 LYONS, EDWARD HOYT......................................8799 CENTER GROVE CHURCH ROAD, CLEMMONS NC 27012
1920-078 LYONS, GEORGE TONY.......................................D. AUGUST 12, 1981, NEVADA, MO.
1941-067 LYONS, HERSCHEL...7900 DUNBARTON AVENUE, LOS ANGELES CA 90045
1985-067 LYONS, STEPHEN JOHN......................................301 2ND STREET, HERMOSA BEACH CA 90254
1929-067 LYONS, TERENCE HILBERT.................................D. SEPTEMBER 9, 1959, DAYTON, OHIO
1923-084 LYONS, THEODORE AMAR...................................D. JULY 25, 1986, SULPHUR, LA.
1983-093 LYONS, WILLIAMS ALLEN...................................811 TOMAHAWK COURT, HEYWORTH IL 61745
1980-083 LYSANDER, RICHARD EUGENE............................12667 GALLION COURT, SAN DIEGO CA 92128
1969-105 LYTTLE, JAMES LAWRENCE................................751 CAMINO LAKE CIR, BOCA RATON FL 33432

M

1955-074 MAAS, DUANE FREDRICK 'DUKE'..........................D. DECEMBER 7, 1976, MOUNT CLEMENS, MICH.
1990-092 MAAS, KEVIN CHRISTIAN....................................PO BOX 21019, CASTRO VALLEY CA 94546
1958-057 MABE, ROBERT LEE...D. JANUARY 9, 2005, DANVILLE, VA.
2006-105 MABEUS, CHRISTOPHER EUGENE........................151 SHADY LANE, SOLDOTNA AK 99669
1994-067 MABRY, JOHN STEVEN...715 BELLERIVE MANOR DRIVE, SAINT LOUIS MO 63141
1976-057 MACCORMACK, FRANK LOUIS.............................2 SCHMIDT PLACE, SECAUCUS NJ 07094
1928-061 MACDONALD, HARVEY FORSYTH.........................D. OCTOBER 4, 1965, MANOA, PA.
1990-093 MACDONALD, ROBERT JOSEPH...........................522 HARBOR GROVE CIRCLE, SAFETY HARBOR FL 34695
1950-055 MACDONALD, WILLIAM PAUL..............................D. MAY 4, 1991, SHASTA LAKE, CALIF.
2001-109 MACDOUGAL, ROBERT MICHAEL 'MIKE'.............9353 EAST LAUREL CIRCLE, MESA AZ 85207
1987-082 MACFARLANE, MICHAEL ANDREW......................8875 ROCKHILL AVENUE #M, LENEXA KS 66215
1926-051 MACFAYDEN, DANIEL KNOWLES..........................D. AUGUST 26, 1972, BRUNSWICK, MAINE
1974-078 MACHA, KENNETH EDWARD...............................6934 BERKSHIRE DRIVE, EXPORT PA 15632
1979-070 MACHA, MICHAEL WILLIAM...............................PO BOX 3844, VICTORIA TX 77903
2005-112 MACHADO, ALEJANDRO JOSE...........................OLD ADD: CARACAS VENEZUELA
2003-098 MACHADO, ANDERSON JAVIER..........................OLD ADD: CARACAS, VENEZUELA
1989-076 MACHADO, JULIO S...AV 2 CON C/19 #17-95, P DEL SUR L'CANADA, MARACAIBO, VENEZUELA
1996-109 MACHADO, ROBERT ALEXIS...............................OLD ADD: CARACAS VENEZUELA
1971-065 MACHEMEHL, CHARLES WALTER........................2005 MACHEMEHL ROAD, BRENHAM TX 77833
1978-076 MACHEMER, DAVID RITCHIE..............................2159 ALPINE COURT, STEVENSVILLE MI 49127
1999-114 MACIAS, JOSE PRADE...OLD ADD: PANAMA CITY PANAMA
1922-078 MACK, FRANK GEORGE..D. JULY 2, 1971, CLEARWATER, FLA.
1945-063 MACK, JOSEPH JOHN..D. DECEMBER 19, 1998, ATLANTA, GA.
1994-068 MACK, QUINN DAVID...OLD ADD: 5631 LOCKHAVEN DRIVE, BUENA PARK CA 90621
1938-056 MACK, RAYMOND JAMES....................................D. MAY 7, 1969, BUCYRUS, OHIO
1987-083 MACK, SHANE LEE..35324 MARSH LANE, WILDOMAR CA 92595
1985-068 MACK, TONY LYNN...1044 ARMSTRONG MILL ROAD #A, LEXINGTON KY 40517
1973-079 MACKANIN, PETER...6735 TAILFEATHER WAY, BRADENTON FL 34203
1955-075 MACKENZIE, ERIC HUGH....................................2002 JAMES EAST BRIGHT GROVE ON, N0N 1C0 CANADA
1961-071 MACKENZIE, HENRY GORDON 'GORDY'.............36535 MICRO RACETRACK ROAD, FRUITLAND PARK FL 32817
1960-061 MACKENZIE, KENNETH PURVIS.........................15 FAIR STREET, GUILFORD CT 06437
1941-068 MACKIEWICZ, FELIX THADDEUS.........................D. DECEMBER 20, 1993, OLIVETTE, MO.
1953-052 MACKINSON, JOHN JOSEPH..............................D. OCTOBER 17, 1989, RESEDA, CALIF.
1979-071 MACKO, STEVEN JOSEPH...................................D. NOVEMBER 15, 1981, ARLINGTON, TEXAS
2001-110 MACKOWIAK, ROBERT WILLIAM........................26742 SHOREGRASS DRIVE, WESLEY CHAPEL FL 33543
1962-079 MACLEOD, WILLIAM DANIEL..............................14 HERITAGE WAY, MARBLEHEAD MA 01945
1993-111 MACLIN, LONNIE LEE..9635 MEEKS, SAINT LOUIS MO 63132
1938-057 MACON, MAX CULLEN..D. AUGUST 5, 1989, JUPITER, FLA.
1922-079 MACPHEE, WALTER SCOTT 'WADDY'..................D. JANUARY 20, 1980, CHARLOTTE, N.C.
1944-080 MACPHERSON, HARRY WILLIAM.......................971 BAY VISTA BLVD, ENGLEWOOD FL 33533
2001-111 MACRAE, SCOTT PATRICK..................................1164 FOREST BROOK COURT, MARIETTA GA 30068
1980-084 MACWHORTER, KEITH..9 MANNING DRIVE, PROVIDENCE RI 02915
1983-094 MADDEN, MICHAEL ANTHONY............................4733 FRANKFORT WAY, DENVER CO 80239
1987-084 MADDEN, MORRIS DEWAYNE.............................105 JENNINGS, LAURENS SC 29360
1946-066 MADDERN, CLARENCE JAMES............................D. AUGUST 9, 1986, TUCSON, ARIZ.
1999-115 MADDON, JOSEPH JOHN....................................2560-32 NORTH LINDSAY ROAD, MESA AZ 85213
1970-083 MADDOX, ELLIOTT...980 CORAL RIDGE DRIVE #104, CORAL SPRINGS FL 33071
1972-065 MADDOX, GARRY LEE...C/O IMG, 1360 EAST 9TH STREET #1300, CLEVELAND OH 44114
1978-077 MADDOX, JERRY GLENN.....................................20647 THUNDERSKY CIRCLE, RIVERSIDE CA 92508
1986-091 MADDUX, GREGORY ALAN..................................4132 SOUTH RAINBOW BLVD, LAS VEGAS NV 89103
1986-092 MADDUX, MICHAEL AUSLEY...............................3172 NORTH RAINBOW BLVD #225, LAS VEGAS NV 89108
1985-069 MADISON, CHARLES SCOTT 'SCOTTI'................5397 THORNAPPLE LANE NW, ACWORTH GA 30101
1950-056 MADISON, DAVID PLEDGER................................D. DECEMBER 9, 1985, MACON, MISS.
1932-046 MADJESKI, EDWARD WILLIAM...........................D. NOVEMBER 11, 1994, MONTGOMERY, OHIO
1973-080 MADLOCK, BILL..104 PRAIRIE AVENUE, HIGHWOOD IL 60040
1987-085 MADRID, ALEXANDER..PO BOX 1974, SAINT JOHNS AZ 85936
1947-062 MADRID, SALVADOR..D. FEBRUARY 24, 1977, FORT WAYNE, IND.
2004-127 MADRITSCH, ROBERT A. 'BOBBY'.......................8628 LINDER AVENUE, BURBANK IL 60459
2003-099 MADSON, RYAN MICHAEL..................................12904 FOREMAN AVENUE, MORENO VALLEY CA 92553

1996-110	MADURO, CALVIN GREGORY	OLD ADD: SANTA CRUZ ARUBA
1960-062	MAESTRI, HECTOR ANIBAL	581 SW 89TH COURT, MIAMI FL 33174
1986-093	MAGADAN, DAVID JOSEPH	3733 JOHNATHAN AVENUE, PALM HARBOR FL 34685
1991-113	MAGALLANES, EVERARDO 'EVER'	834 GOVERNOR STREET, COSTA MESA CA 92627
1996-111	MAGEE, WENDELL ERROL	927 SPENCER STREET, HATTIESBURG MS 39401
1938-058	MAGGERT, HARL WARREN	D. JULY 10, 1986, CITRUS HEIGHTS, CALIF.
1945-064	MAGLIE, SALVATORE ANTHONY	D. DECEMBER 28, 1992, NIAGARA FALLS, N.Y.
1991-114	MAGNANTE, MICHAEL ANTHONY	5305 VIA QUINTO, NEWBURY PARK CA 91320
1970-084	MAGNUSON, JAMES ROBERT	D. MAY 30, 1991, GREEN BAY, WISC.
1987-086	MAGRANE, JOSEPH DAVID	705 GUISANDO DE AVILA, TAMPA FL 33613
1989-077	MAGRANN, THOMAS JOSEPH	910 NORTH 31ST COURT, HOLLYWOOD FL 33021
1966-057	MAGRINI, PETER ALEXANDER	2402 RANCHO CABEZA DRIVE, SANTA ROSA CA 95404
2001-112	MAGRUDER, CHRISTOPHER JAMES	1740 LEISURE LANE, YAKIMA WA 98908
1922-080	MAGUIRE, FRED EDWARD	D. NOVEMBER 3, 1961, BOSTON, MASS.
1950-057	MAGUIRE, JACK	D. SEPTEMBER 28, 2001, KERRVILLE, TEXAS
1921-057	MAHADY, JAMES BERNARD	D. AUGUST 9, 1936, CORTLAND, N.Y.
1960-063	MAHAFFEY, ARTHUR	PO BOX 1212, ALLENTOWN PA 18105
1926-052	MAHAFFEY, LEE ROY	D. JULY 23, 1969, ANDERSON, S.C.
1940-052	MAHAN, ARTHUR LEO	418 GLENMORE AVENUE, ELKINS PARK PA 19027
1995-129	MAHAY, RONALD MATTHEW	19 SUTTON PLACE, HIGHTSTOWN NJ 08520
1978-078	MAHLBERG, GREGORY JOHN	5100 NORTH PLACITA DEL LAZO, TUCSON AZ 85715
1977-085	MAHLER, MICHAEL JAMES 'MICKEY'	7911 QUIRT, SAN ANTONIO TX 78227
1979-072	MAHLER, RICHARD KEITH 'RICK'	D. MARCH 2, 2005, JUPITER, FLA.
2005-113	MAHOLM, PAUL G	PO BOX 5542, HOLLY SPRINGS MS 38634
1992-075	MAHOMES, PATRICK LAVON	PO BOX 1025, LINDALE TX 75771
1930-048	MAHON, ALFRED GWINN	D. DECEMBER 26, 1977, NEW HAVEN, CONN.
1959-050	MAHONEY, JAMES THOMAS	644 LAFAYETTE AVENUE #R19, HAWTHORNE NJ 07506
2000-102	MAHONEY, MICHAEL JOHN	4412 98TH STREET, URBANDALE IA 50322
1951-057	MAHONEY, ROBERT PAUL	D. AUGUST 27, 2000, LINCOLN, NEB.
2006-106	MAIER, MITCHELL WILLIAM	14942 WEST DAHLIA DRIVE, SURPRISE AZ 85379
1945-065	MAIER, ROBERT PHILIP	D. AUGUST 4, 1993, SOUTH PLAINFIELD, N.J.
1936-050	MAILHO, EMIL PIERRE	D. MARCH 7, 2007, HAYWARD, CALIF.
1948-062	MAIN, FORREST HARRY 'WOODY'	D. JUNE 27, 1992, WHITTIER, CALIF.
2004-128	MAINE, JOHN K.	129 RICHARDS FERRY ROAD, FREDERICKSBURG VA 22406
1943-080	MAINS, JAMES ROYAL	D. MARCH 17, 1969, PORTLAND, MAINE
2000-103	MAIRENA, OSWALDO ANTONIO	OLD ADD: CHINANDEGA NICARAGUA
1939-072	MAJESKI, HARRY 'HANK'	D. AUGUST 9, 1991, STATEN ISLAND, N.Y.
2004-129	MAJEWSKI, GARY WAYNE	1103 CHAMBOARD, HOUSTON TX 77018
2004-130	MAJEWSKI, WALTER V. 'VAL'	890 OAKLEY DRIVE, FREEHOLD NJ 07728
1937-068	MAKOSKY, FRANK	D. JANUARY 10, 1987, STROUDSBURG, PA.
1975-069	MAKOWSKI, THOMAS ANTHONY	E6686 OMPHIS ROAD #2, COLDEN NY 14033
1992-076	MAKSUDIAN, MICHAEL BRYANT	12148 EAST SAN SIMEON DRIVE, SCOTTSDALE AZ 85259
2003-100	MALASKA, DENNIS MARK 'MARK'	612 CLEARMOUNT DRIVE, YOUNGSTOWN OH 44511
1996-112	MALAVE, JOSE FRANCISCO	OLD ADD: CUMANA VENEZUELA
1933-040	MALAY, JOSEPH CHARLES	D. MARCH 19, 1989, BRIDGEPORT, CONN.
1981-077	MALDONADO, CANDIDO 'CANDY'	HCO2 BOX 16800, ARECIBO PR 00612
1990-094	MALDONADO, CARLOS CESAR	CASA #1835 CHEPO, PANAMA
2006-107	MALDONADO, CARLOS LUIS	OLD ADD: MARACAIBO VENEZ UCLA
1981-078	MALER, JAMES MICHAEL	1758 NE 177TH STREET, NORTH MIAMI BEACH FL 33162
1937-069	MALINOSKY, ANTHONY JOSEPH 'TONY'	5540 WEST FIFTH STREET #60, OXNARD CA 93030
1934-064	MALIS, CYRUS SOL	D. JANUARY 12, 1971, NORTH HOLLYWOOD, FLA.
1957-045	MALKMUS, ROBERT EDWARD	400 WALLINGFORD TER, UNION NJ 07083
1959-051	MALLETT, GERALD GORDON	7610 FOREST PARK DR, BEAUMONT TX 77707
2002-116	MALLETTE, BRIAN DREW	3012 GILDER ROAD, GLENWOOD GA 30428
1950-058	MALLETTE, MALCOLM FRANCIS	D. NOVEMBER 25, 2005, DURHAM, N.C.
1987-087	MALLICOAT, ROBBIN DALE	13025 NE 70TH DRIVE, KIRKLAND WA 98033
1931-050	MALLON, LESLIE CLYDE 'CLYDE'	D. APRIL 17, 1991, GRANBURY, TEXAS
1921-058	MALLONEE, HOWARD BENNETT 'BEN'	D. FEBRUARY 19, 1978, BALTIMORE, MD.
1925-068	MALLONEE, JULIUS NORRIS	D. DECEMBER 26, 1934, CHARLOTTE, N.C.
1940-053	MALLORY, JAMES BAUGH	D. AUGUST 6, 2001, GREENVILLE, N.C.
1977-086	MALLORY, SHELDON	21353 OLD NORTH CHURCH ROAD, FRANKFORT IL 60423
1998-113	MALLOY, MARTIN THOMAS	PO BOX 1644, CHIEFLAND FL 32644
1943-081	MALLOY, ROBERT PAUL	D. FEBRUARY 20, 2007, CINCINNATI, OHIO
1987-088	MALLOY, ROBERT WILLIAM	1904 SAN CARLOS AVENUE, ALLEN TX 75002
1955-076	MALMBERG, HARRY WILLIAM	D. OCTOBER 29, 1976, SAN FRANCISCO, CALIF.
1990-095	MALONE, CHARLES RAY	310 LIBERTY STREET, MARKED TREE AR 72365
1949-047	MALONE, EDWARD RUSSELL	D. JUNE 1, 2006, LAGUNA HILLS, CALIF.
1928-062	MALONE, PERCE LEIGH 'PAT'	D. MAY 13, 1943, ALTOONA, PA.
1960-064	MALONEY, JAMES WILLIAM	7027 NORTH TEILMAN AVE #102, FRESNO CA 93711
1997-105	MALONEY, SEAN PATRICK	167 PINECREST DRIVE, NORTH KINGSTOWN RI 02852
1943-082	MALTZBERGER, GORDON RALPH	D. DECEMBER 11, 1974, RIALTO, CALIF.
1955-077	MALZONE, FRANK JAMES	16 ALETHA RD, NEEDHAM MA 02192
1928-063	MANCUSO, AUGUST RODNEY 'GUS'	D. OCTOBER 26, 1984, HOUSTON, TEXAS
1944-081	MANCUSO, FRANK OCTAVIUS	5126 CRIPPLE CREEK, HOUSTON TX 77017
1941-069	MANDERS, HAROLD CARL	PO BOX 149, DALLAS CENTER IA 50063
1952-071	MANGAN, JAMES DANIEL	6878 TRINIDAD, SAN JOSE CA 95120
1969-106	MANGUAL, ANGEL LUIS	OLD ADD: 1406 R. DEL VALLE, PONCE PR 00728
1972-066	MANGUAL, JOSE MANUEL 'PEPE'	2325 CALLE TABONUCO, PONCE PR 00731
1924-073	MANGUM, LEON ALLEN	D. JULY 9, 1974, LIMA, OHIO
1920-079	MANION, CLYDE JENNINGS	D. SEPTEMBER 4, 1967, DETROIT, MICH.
1976-058	MANKOWSKI, PHILIP ANTHONY	2280 SOUTHWESTERN BLVD, BUFFALO NY 14224
1944-082	MANN, BEN GARTH 'GARTH'	D. SEPTEMBER 11, 1980, ITALY, TEXAS
2000-104	MANN, JAMES JOSEPH	32 LANTERN ROAD, HOLBROOK MA 02343
1928-064	MANN, JOHN LEO	D. MARCH 31, 1977, TERRE HAUTE, IND.
1989-078	MANN, KELLY JOHN	PO BOX 34296, LOS ANGELES CA 90034
2003-101	MANNING, DAVID ANTHONY	OLD ADD: WEST PALM BEACH FL 33406

1962-080 MANNING, JAMES BENJAMIN....41 FOX RUN DRIVE, WEAVERVILLE NC 28787
1975-070 MANNING, RICHARD EUGENE....12151 NEW MARKET, CHESTERLAND OH 44026
1940-054 MANNO, DONALD....D. MARCH 11, 1995, WILLIAMSPORT, PA.
2003-102 MANON, JULIO ALBERTO....4726 15TH AVENUE SOUTH, SAINT PETERSBURG FL 33711
1990-096 MANON, RAMON (REYES)....OLD ADD: CALLE 18 #113 SABANA PERDIDA, SANTO DOMINGO DOM REP
1981-079 MANRIQUE, FRED ELOI....OLD ADD: URB. PEDREGAL, BARQUISIMETO VENEZUELA
1995-130 MANTEI, MATTHEW BRUCE....4709 CHICAGO PATH, STEVENSVILLE MI 49127
1956-055 MANTILLA, FELIX....6973 NORTH TACOMA ST, MILWAUKEE WI 53224
1951-058 MANTLE, MICKEY CHARLES....D. AUGUST 13, 1995, DALLAS, TEXAS
1990-097 MANTO, JEFFREY PAUL....725 RADCLIFFE STREET, BRISTOL PA 19007
1991-115 MANUEL, BARRY PAUL....805 OAK STREET, MAMOU LA 70554
1969-107 MANUEL, CHARLES FUQUA....2931 PLANTATION ROAD, WINTER HAVEN FL 33884
1975-071 MANUEL, JERRY....4023 GREENVIEW DRIVE, EL DORADO HILLS CA 95762
1923-085 MANUSH, HENRY EMMETT 'HEINIE'....D. MAY 12, 1971, SARASOTA, FLA.
1950-059 MANVILLE, RICHARD WESLEY....1436 LAKE FRANCIS DRIVE, APOPKA FL 32712
1987-089 MANWARING, KURT DEAN....20 PROSPECT RIDGE, HORSEHEADS NY 14845
1991-116 MANZANILLO, JOSIAS....OLD ADD: 18641 SW 41ST STREET, MIRAMAR FL 33029
1988-085 MANZANILLO, RAVELO....ULISES ESPAILLAT #7 SAN PEDRO DE MACORIS, DOM REP
1948-063 MAPES, CLIFFORD FRANKLIN....D. DECEMBER 5, 1996, CLAREMORE, OKLA.
1932-047 MAPLE, HOWARD ALBERT....D. NOVEMBER 9, 1970, PORTLAND, ORE.
1990-098 MARAK, PAUL PATRICK....1211 COMANCHE TRAIL, ALAMOGORDO NM 88310
1960-065 MARANDA, GEORGES HENRI....D. JULY 14, 2000, LEVIS, QUE.
1923-086 MARBERRY, FREDRICK 'FIRPO'....D. JUNE 30, 1976, MEXIA, TEXAS
1940-055 MARCHILDON, PHILIP JOSEPH....D. JANUARY 10, 1997, TORONTO, ONT.
1933-041 MARCUM, JOHN ALFRED....D. SEPTEMBER 10, 1984, LOUISVILLE, KY.
2005-114 MARCUM, SHAUN M....1413 JILL LANE, EXCELSIOR SPRINGS MO 64024
1965-069 MARENTETTE, LEO JOHN....33606 BEECHWOOD STREET, WESTLAND MI 48185
1956-056 MARGONERI, JOSEPH EMANUEL....341 TURKEYTOWN ROAD, WEST NEWTON PA 15089
1960-066 MARICHAL, JUAN ANTONIO SANCHEZ....9458 NW 54 DORAL CIRCLE LANE, MIAMI FL 33128
1935-065 MARION, JOHN WYETH 'RED'....D. MARCH 13, 1975, SAN JOSE, CALIF.
1940-056 MARION, MARTIN WHITEFORD 'SLATS'....8 FORCEE LANE, SAINT LOUIS MO 63124
1957-046 MARIS, ROGER EUGENE....D. DECEMBER 14, 1985, HOUSTON, TEXAS
2006-108 MARKAKIS, NICHOLAS WILLIAM....7002 HUNTERS RIDGE, WOODSTOCK GA 30189
1951-059 MARKELL, HARRY DUQUESNE 'DUKE'....D. JUNE 14, 1984, FORT LAUDERDALE, FLA.
1950-060 MARKLAND, CLENETH EUGENE 'GENE'....D. JUNE 15, 1999, BAREFOOT BAY, FLA.
1951-060 MARLOWE, RICHARD BURTON....D. DECEMBER 30, 1968, TOLEDO, OHIO
2006-109 MARMOL, CARLOS AGUSTIN....OLD ADD: BONAO DOM REP
1940-057 MARNIE, HARRY SYLVESTER 'HAL'....D. JANUARY 7, 2002, PHILADELPHIA, PA.
1953-053 MAROLEWSKI, FRED DANIEL....15705 WEST WATERFORD LANE, MANHATTAN IL 60442
1969-108 MARONE, LOUIS STEPHEN....10851 CARBET PLACE, SAN DIEGO CA 92124
2002-117 MAROTH, MICHAEL WARREN....909 JOHNS POINTE DRIVE, OAKLAND FL 34787
1931-051 MARQUARDT, ALBERT LUDWIG 'OLLIE'....D. FEBRUARY 7, 1968, PORT CLINTON, OHIO
1972-067 MARQUEZ, GONZALO ENRIQUE....D. DECEMBER 20, 1984, CAGUA, ARAGUA, VENEZUELA
1995-131 MARQUEZ, ISIDRO ESPINOZA....OLD ADD: NAVAJOA SONORA MEXICO
1951-061 MARQUEZ, LUIS ANGEL....D. MARCH 1, 1988, AGUADILLA, P.R.
1925-069 MARQUIS, JAMES MILBURN....D. AUGUST 5, 1992, JACKSON, CALIF.
2000-105 MARQUIS, JASON SCOTT....300 VOGEL AVENUE, STATEN ISLAND NY 10309
1953-054 MARQUIS, ROBERT RUDOLPH....3766 DELAWARE STREET #303, BEAUMONT TX 77706
1955-078 MARQUIS, ROGER JULIAN....D. JULY 19, 2004, HOLYOKE, MASS.
1950-061 MARRERO, CONRADO EUGENIO RAMOS....129 GORDON STREET, PERTH AMBOY NJ 08861
1997-106 MARRERO, ELIESER 'ELI'....10230 SW 64TH STREET, MIAMI FL 33173
1993-112 MARRERO, ORESTE VILATO (VAZQUEZ)....OLD ADD: URQUAY ST T703, FOREST HILL, BAYAMON PR 00618
1932-048 MARROW, CHARLES KENNON 'BUCK'....D. NOVEMBER 21, 1982, NEWPORT NEWS, VA.
1949-048 MARSH, FRED FRANCIS....D. OCTOBER 26, 2006, CORRY, PA.
1992-077 MARSH, THOMAS OWEN....9140 SUMMERFIELD ROAD, TEMPERANCE MI 48182
1941-070 MARSHALL, CHARLES ANDREW....D. APRIL 15, 2007, WILMINGTON, DEL.
1946-067 MARSHALL, CLARENCE WESTLY....27642-I SUSAN BETH WAY, SAUGUS CA 91350
1967-069 MARSHALL, DAVID LEWIS....4802 EAST CENTRALIA STREET, LONG BEACH CA 90808
1929-068 MARSHALL, EDWARD HARBERT 'DOC'....D. SEPTEMBER 1, 1999, LAKE SAN MARCOS, CALIF.
1958-058 MARSHALL, JIM RUFE....19700 NORTH 76TH STREET #1119, SCOTTSDALE AZ 85255
1973-081 MARSHALL, KEITH ALAN....RURAL ROUTE 1, WOODHULL NY 14898
1981-080 MARSHALL, MICHAEL ALLEN....OLD ADD: 12 MADOCH COURT, DEER PARK IL 60010
1967-070 MARSHALL, MICHAEL GRANT....38313 VINSON AVENUE, ZEPHYRHILLS FL 33541
1942-066 MARSHALL, MILO MAX 'MAX'....D. SEPTEMBER 6, 1993, SALEM, ORE.
2006-110 MARSHALL, SEAN CHRISTOPHER....OLD ADD: CHESTERFIELD, VA
1942-067 MARSHALL, WILLARD WARREN....D. NOVEMBER 5, 2000, NORWOOD, N.J.
1931-052 MARSHALL, WILLIAM HENRY....D. MAY 5, 1977, SACRAMENTO, CALIF.
2004-131 MARSONEK, SAMUEL R.....712 WELTON ROAD, LUTZ FL 33549
2005-115 MARTE, ANDY M....OLD ADD: TAPIA DOM REP
1999-116 MARTE, DAMASO SABINON....2869 GRAND CONCOURSE, BRONX NY 10468
1992-078 MARTIN, ALBERT SCALES....11028 WEST DURANGO, CASHION AZ 85329
1950-062 MARTIN, ALFRED MANUEL 'BILLY'....D. DECEMBER 25, 1989, JOHNSON CITY, N.Y.
1953-055 MARTIN, BARNEY ROBERT....D. OCTOBER 30, 1997, COLUMBIA, S.C.
1944-083 MARTIN, BORIS MICHAEL 'BABE '....114 NORTH HOLLOWAY ROAD, BALLWIN MO 63011
1979-073 MARTIN, DONALD RENIE 'RENIE'....509 LITTLE EAGLE COURT, VALRICO FL 33594
1946-068 MARTIN, FRED TURNER....D. JUNE 11, 1979, CHICAGO, ILL.
1937-070 MARTIN, HERSHEL RAY....D. NOVEMBER 17, 1980, CUBA, MO.
1974-079 MARTIN, JERRY LINDSEY....109 CHELTON COURT, COLUMBIA SC 29212
1928-065 MARTIN, JOHN LEONARD ROOSEVELT 'PEPPER'..D. MARCH 5, 1965, MCALESTER, OKLA.
1980-085 MARTIN, JOHN ROBERT....2037 SW STRATFORD WAY, PALM CITY FL 34990
1959-052 MARTIN, JOSEPH CLIFTON 'JC'....112 OAKMONT COURT, ADVANCE NC 27006
1986-094 MARTIN, JOSEPH MICHAEL 'MIKE'....7904 WATERFALLS AVENUE, LAS VEGAS NV 89128
1949-049 MARTIN, MORRIS WEBSTER....1786 POTTERY ROAD, WASHINGTON MO 63090
1993-113 MARTIN, NORBERTO EDONAL 'PACO'....GENERAL DUBERGE 109 SAN PEDRO DE MACORIS, DOM REP
1955-079 MARTIN, PAUL CHARLES 'JAKE'....1529 33RD STREET, SAN DIEGO CA 92102
1943-083 MARTIN, RAYMOND JOSEPH....107 PELLANA ROAD, NORWOOD MA 02062

2006-111	MARTIN, RUSSELL NATHAN COLTRANE	OLD ADD: CHELSEA QUEBEC
1936-051	MARTIN, STUART MCGUIRE	D. JANUARY 11, 1997, SEVERN, N.C.
1997-107	MARTIN, THOMAS EDGAR	8001 SURF DRIVE, PANAMA CITY FL 32408
1968-057	MARTIN, THOMAS EUGENE 'GENE'	133 WINCHESTER DRIVE, LEESBURG GA 31763
1936-052	MARTIN, WILLIAM JOSEPH 'JOE'	D. SEPTEMBER 28, 1960, BUFFALO, N.Y.
1924-074	MARTINA, JOSEPH JOHN	D. MARCH 22, 1962, NEW ORLEANS, LA.
1980-086	MARTINEZ, ALFREDO	2346 THOMAS, LOS ANGELES CA 90031
2004-132	MARTINEZ, ANASTACIO EUCLIDES	OLD ADD: SANTO DOMINGO DOM REP
1995-132	MARTINEZ, ANGEL SANDY 'SANDY'	HERMANA MIRABEL #166, SANTA CRUZ SANTO DOMINGO, DOM REP
1988-086	MARTINEZ, CARLOS ALBERTO ESCOBAR	D. JANUARY 24, 2006, VARGAS, VENEZUELA
2006-112	MARTINEZ, CARLOS M.	OLD ADD: VILLA VASQUEZ DOM REP
1983-095	MARTINEZ, CARMELO	BRISAS DE PLATA #32, DORADO PR 00646
1990-099	MARTINEZ, CONSTANTINO 'TINO'	324 BLANCA AVENUE, TAMPA FL 33606
1986-095	MARTINEZ, DAVID	3315 ENTERPRISE ROAD EAST, SAFETY HARBOR FL 34695
1992-079	MARTINEZ, DOMINGO EMILIO	LA ISABELA, LOS ALCARRIZZO#35 RD SANTO DOMINGO, DOM REP
1987-090	MARTINEZ, EDGAR	PO BOX 53490, BELLEVUE WA 98015
1974-080	MARTINEZ, FELIX ANTHONY 'TIPPY'	1524 DELLSWAY RD, TOWSON MD 21204
1997-108	MARTINEZ, FELIX MATA	OLD ADD: NAGUA DOM REP
1963-075	MARTINEZ, GABRIEL ANTONIO 'TONY'	D. AUGUST 24, 1991, MIAMI, FLA.
1998-114	MARTINEZ, GREGORY ALFRED	1596 PALORA AVENUE, LAS VEGAS NV 89109
1998-115	MARTINEZ, JAVIER ANTONIO	OLD ADD: BAYAMON PR 00958
1969-109	MARTINEZ, JOHN ALBERT 'BUCK'	OLD ADD: 212 RAINTREE DRIVE, LEES SUMMIT MO 64130
1969-110	MARTINEZ, JOSE AZCUIZ	14601 SW 33RD COURT, MIRAMAR FL 33027
1976-059	MARTINEZ, JOSE DENNIS 'DENNIS'	9400 SW 63RD COURT, MIAMI FL 33156
1994-069	MARTINEZ, JOSE MIGUEL (MARTINEZ)	OLD ADD: 7971 PARK DRIVE, FAIR OAKS CA 95628
2003-103	MARTINEZ, LUIS	OLD ADD: BOCA CHICA DOM REP
1996-113	MARTINEZ, MANUEL DEJESUS	OLD ADD: SAN PEDRO DE MACORIS DOM REP
1962-082	MARTINEZ, ORLANDO OLIVO 'MARTY'	D. MARCH 15, 2007, SANTO DOMINGO, DOM REP
1996-114	MARTINEZ, PABLO VALERA	OLD ADD: TAMPA FL 33601
1993-114	MARTINEZ, PEDRO AQUINO	VILLA MELA EL VONITO #121 SANTO DOMINGO, DOM REP
1992-080	MARTINEZ, PEDRO JAIME	186 FAIRMONT AVENUE, HYDE PARK MA 02136
1998-116	MARTINEZ, RAMON E	OLD ADD: TOA ALTA PR 00953
1988-087	MARTINEZ, RAMON JAIME	BO. SAN MIGUEL #9, MANAGUAYABA SANTO DOMINGO, DOM REP
1991-117	MARTINEZ, REYENALDO IGANCIO 'CHITO'	1205 OAK CREEK DRIVE, COLLIERVILLE TN 38017
1962-081	MARTINEZ, RODOLFO HECTOR	D. DECEMBER 1, 1999, CUBA
1950-063	MARTINEZ, ROGELIO ULLOA	OLD ADD: 209 NICHOLS AVENUE, BROOKLYN NY 11208
1977-087	MARTINEZ, SILVIO RAMON	8321 CORNISH AVENUE #2, ELMHURST NY 11373
1970-085	MARTINEZ, TEODORO NOEL 'TEDDY'	J. CONTRERAS #194, ENS. LAPAZ, SANTO DOMINGO, DOM REP
2002-118	MARTINEZ, VICTOR JESUS	OLD ADD: BOLIVAR VENEZUELA
2000-106	MARTINEZ, WILLIAM JOSE 'WILLIE'	OLD ADD: BARQUISIMETO VENEZUELA
1935-066	MARTINI, GUIDO JOE 'WEDO'	D. OCTOBER 28, 1970, PHILADELPHIA, PA.
1937-071	MARTY, JOSEPH ANTON	D. OCTOBER 4, 1984, SACRAMENTO, CALIF.
1957-047	MARTYN, ROBERT GORDON	PO BOX 778 7350 SUMMITT, PACIFIC CITY OR 97135
1975-072	MARTZ, GARY MARTZ	525 SAGE HILL DRIVE, WENATCHEE WA 98801
1980-087	MARTZ, RANDY CARL	211 HI POINTE PLAZA, EAST ALTON IL 62024
1987-091	MARZANO, JOHN ROBERT	1224 SOUTH 11TH STREET, PHILADELPHIA PA 19147
1999-117	MASAOKA, ONAN KAINOA SATOSHI	1323 AUWAE ROAD, HILO HI 96720
1969-111	MASHORE, CLYDE WAYNE	590 VALMORE PLACE, BRENTWOOD CA 94513
1996-115	MASHORE, DAMON WAYNE	7923 TERRAZA DISOMA, CARLSBAD CA 92009
1939-073	MASI, PHILIP SAMUEL	D. MARCH 29, 1990, MOUNT PROSPECT, ILL.
1966-058	MASON, DONALD STETSON	8 FAWN ROAD, SOUTH YARMOUTH MA 02664
1958-059	MASON, HENRY	3801 BROOK ROAD, RICHMOND VA 23227
1971-066	MASON, JAMES PERCY	11410 QUEENS WAY, THEODORE AL 36582
1982-081	MASON, MICHAEL PAUL	2711 PIPER RIDGE LANE, EXCELSIOR MN 55331
1984-073	MASON, ROGER LEROY	4587 STOVER ROAD, BELLAIRE MI 49615
1957-048	MASSA, GORDON RICHARD	8255 BONANZA LANE, CINCINNATI OH 45255
2006-113	MASSET, NICHOLAS ALLEN	12559 70TH STREET, LARGO FL 33773
1995-133	MASTELLER, DAN PATRICK	159111 ALDERSYDE DRIVE, SHAKER HEIGHTS OH 44120
1931-053	MASTERS, WALTER THOMAS	D. JULY 10, 1992, OTTAWA, ONT.
1940-058	MASTERSON, PAUL NICKALIS	D. NOVEMBER 27, 1997, CHICAGO, ILL.
1939-074	MASTERSON, WALTER EDWARD	421 MILLSPRING DRIVE, DURHAM NC 27705
2006-114	MASTNY, THOMAS RAYMOND	130 LEXINGTON COURT, ZIONSVILLE IN 46077
1984-074	MATA, VICTOR JOSE	JUAN PABLO PINA, #16, ALTO SANTO DOMINGO, DOM REP
1952-072	MATARAZZO, LEONARD	2715 CARLISLE STREET, NEW CASTLE PA 16105
1967-071	MATCHICK, JOHN THOMAS 'TOM'	7700 PILLIOD ROAD, HOLLAND OH 43528
2001-113	MATEO, HENRY ANTONIO (VALERA)	OLD ADD: SANTURCE PR
2006-115	MATEO, JUAN MANUEL	OLD ADD: BANI DOM REP
2002-119	MATEO, JULIO CESAR	OLD ADD: BANI DOM REP
1999-118	MATEO, RUBEN AMAURYS	OLD ADD: SAN CRISTOBAL DOM REP
1994-070	MATHENY, MICHAEL SCOTT	2034 JOES WAY, CHESTERFIELD MO 63005
1952-073	MATHEWS, EDWIN LEE	D. FEBRUARY 18, 2001, LAJOLLA, CALIF.
1986-096	MATHEWS, GREGORY INMAN	1752 CRAIG ROAD, SAINT LOUIS MO 63146
1960-067	MATHEWS, NELSON ELMER	211 CRESTVIEW, COLUMBIA IL 62236
1991-118	MATHEWS, TERRY ALAN	1132 BELGARD BEND, BOYCE LA 71409
1995-134	MATHEWS, TIMOTHY JAY 'T.J.'	211 CRESTVIEW DRIVE, COLUMBIA IL 62236
1960-068	MATHIAS, CARL LYNWOOD	567 LONG LANE, OLEY PA 19567
2006-116	MATHIESON, SCOTT WILLIAM	OLD ADD: ALDERGROVE BC
2005-116	MATHIS, JEFFREY STEPHEN	4420 SPRING VALLEY DRIVE, MARIANNA FL 32448
1985-070	MATHIS, RONALD VANCE	10118 EAST CHEVELON STREET, TUCSON AZ 85748
1970-086	MATIAS, JOHN ROY	98-1616 HOOLAUAE ST, AIEA HI 96701
1971-067	MATLACK, JONATHAN TRUMPBOUR	192 CLEVELAND ROAD, JOHNSBURG NY 12843
1994-071	MATOS, FRANCISCO AGUIRRE (MANCEBO)	C/O DUARTE #14 ESTEBANIA ANZA, DOM REP
2002-120	MATOS, JULIUS	12823 VALIMAR ROAD, NEW PORT RICHEY FL 34654
2000-107	MATOS, LUIS DAVID	OLD ADD: BAYAMON PR
1999-119	MATOS, PASCUAL	OLD ADD: BARAHONA DOM REP
2003-104	MATRANGA, DAVID MICHAEL	6 CHESTNUT DRIVE, ALISO VIEJO CA 92656

2003-105	MATSUI, HIDEKI	845 UNITED NATIONS PLAZA #52C, NEW YORK NY 10017
2004-133	MATSUI, KAZUO	OLD ADD: OSAKA JAPAN
2001-114	MATTES, TROY WALTER	2932 LEXINGTON STREET, SARASOTA FL 34231
1972-068	MATTHEWS, GARY NATHANIEL	1542 WEST JACKSON BLVD, CHICAGO IL 60607
1999-120	MATTHEWS, GARY NATHANIEL	OLD ADD: 4222 NORTHVALE, HOUSTON TX 77014
1922-081	MATTHEWS, JOHN JOSEPH	D. FEBRUARY 8, 1968, HAGERSTOWN, MD.
2000-108	MATTHEWS, MICHAEL SCOTT	12493 HEDGES RUN DRIVE, WOODBRIDGE VA 22192
1923-087	MATTHEWS, WID CURRY	D. OCTOBER 5, 1965, HOLLYWOOD, CALIF.
1943-084	MATTHEWSON, DALE WESLEY	D. FEBRUARY 20, 1984, BLAIRSVILLE, GA.
1938-059	MATTICK, ROBERT JAMES	D. DECEMBER 16, 2004, SCOTTSDALE, ARIZ.
1982-082	MATTINGLY, DONALD ARTHUR	11825 DARMSTADT ROAD, EVANSVILLE IN 47725
1931-054	MATTINGLY, LAURENCE EARL	D. SEPTEMBER 8, 1993, BROOKVILLE, MD.
1929-069	MATTOX, CLOY MITCHELL	D. AUGUST 3, 1985, DANVILLE, VA.
1922-082	MATTOX, JAMES POWELL	D. OCTOBER 12, 1973, MYRTLE BEACH, S.C.
1979-074	MATULA, RICHARD CARLTON 'RICK'	1817 CHAPEL HEIGHTS DRIVE, WHARTON TX 77488
1981-081	MATUSZEK, LEONARD JAMES	10326 DEERFIELD ROAD, CINCINNATI OH 45242
1934-065	MATUZAK, HARRY GEORGE	D. NOVEMBER 26, 1978, HOPE, ALA.
1944-084	MAUCH, EUGENE WILLIAM	D. AUGUST 8, 2005, RANCHO MIRAGE, CALIF.
2004-134	MAUER, JOSEPH PATRICK	10508 WASHINGTON PALM WAY #4525, FORT MYERS FL 33912
1934-066	MAULDIN, MARSHALL REESE	D. SEPTEMBER 2, 1990, UNION CITY, GA.
1924-075	MAUN, ERNEST GERALD	D. JANUARY 1, 1987, CORPUS CHRISTI, TEXAS
1945-066	MAUNEY, RICHARD	D. FEBRUARY 6, 1970, ALBEMARLE, N.C.
2000-109	MAURER, DAVID CHARLES	15013 STEVENS AVENUE, BURNSVILLE MN 55306
1991-119	MAURER, ROBERT JOHN 'ROB'	6240 OAK HILL ROAD, EVANSVILLE IN 47711
1958-060	MAURIELLO, RALPH	4241 PERSIMMON STREET, MOORPARK CA 93021
1948-064	MAURO, CARMEN LOUIS	D. DECEMBER 19, 2003, CARMICHAEL, CALIF.
1991-120	MAUSER, TIMOTHY EDWARD	1321 SAXONY ROAD, FORT WORTH TX 76116
1949-050	MAVIS, ROBERT HENRY	D. MARCH 1, 2005, LITTLE ROCK, ARK.
1995-135	MAXCY, DAVID BRIAN 'BRIAN'	982 COBBLE CREEK DRIVE, BIRMINGHAM AL 35226
1969-112	MAXIE, LARRY HANS	296 VERDUGO WAY, UPLAND CA 91786
1962-083	MAXVILL, CHARLES DALLAN 'DAL'	1115 EAGLE CREEK ROAD, CHESTERFIELD MO 63005
1950-064	MAXWELL, CHARLES RICHARD	730 MAPLEVIEW AVENUE, PAW PAW MI 49079
1998-117	MAXWELL, JASON RAMOND	1113 OLDE CAMERTON LANE, FRANKLIN TN 37067
1968-058	MAY, CARLOS	6102 AMHERST PLACE, MATTESON IL 60443
1995-136	MAY, DARRELL KEVIN	747 MENTHORNE, ROGUE RIVER OR 97537
1967-072	MAY, DAVID LAFRANCE	4619 BIG ROCK DRIVE, WILMINGTON DE 19802
1990-100	MAY, DERRICK BRANT	2 JAYMAR BLVD, NEWARK DE 19702
1964-068	MAY, JERRY LEE	D. JUNE 30, 1996, SWOOPE, VA.
1965-070	MAY, LEE ANDREW	2272 4TH PLACE CIRCLE NE, BIRMINGHAM AL 35215
1939-075	MAY, MERRILL GLEND 'PINKY'	D. SEPTEMBER 4, 2000, CORYDON, IND.
1970-087	MAY, MILTON SCOTT	2200 MANATEE AVENUE WEST, BRADENTON FL 34205
1965-071	MAY, RUDOLPH	8090 NORTH AUGUSTA STREET, FRESNO CA 93720
1988-088	MAY, SCOTT FRANCIS	1630 RAVEN CIRCLE #H, ESTES PARK CO 80517
1924-076	MAY, WILLIAM HERBERT 'BUCKSHOT'	D. MARCH 15, 1984, BAKERSFIELD, CALIF.
1968-059	MAYBERRY, JOHN CLAIBORN	11115 WEST 121ST TERRACE, OVERLAND PARK KS 66213
1959-053	MAYE, ARTHUR LEE 'LEE'	D. JULY 17, 2002, RIVERSIDE, CALIF.
1957-049	MAYER, EDWIN DAVID	440 OAKDALE AVE, CORTE MADERA CA 94925
1940-059	MAYNARD, JAMES WALTER	D. SEPTEMBER 7, 1977, DURHAM, N.C.
1922-083	MAYNARD, LEROY EVANS 'CHICK'	D. JANUARY 31, 1957, BANGOR, MAINE
1990-101	MAYNE, BRENT DANEM	16909 EAST 51ST TERRACE CT SOUTH, INDEPENDENCE MO 64055
1936-053	MAYO, EDWARD JOSEPH	D. NOVEMBER 27, 2006, BANNING, CALIF.
1948-065	MAYO, JOHN LEWIS 'JACKIE '	450 BOARDMAN POLAND ROAD, YOUNGSTOWN OH 44512
1999-121	MAYS, JOSEPH EMERSON	6935 WINNERS CIRCLE, BRADENTON FL 34202
1951-062	MAYS, WILLIE HOWARD	51 MOUNT VERNON LANE, ATHERTON CA 94025
1992-081	MAYSEY, MATTHEW SAMUEL	OLD ADD: 428 CRESCENT BLVD, LOMBARD IL 60148
1956-057	MAZEROSKI, WILLIAM STANLEY	281 WALTON TEA ROOM ROAD, GREENSBURG PA 15601
1935-067	MAZZERA, MELVIN LEONARD	D. DECEMBER 19, 1997, STOCKTON, CALIF.
1976-060	MAZZILLI, LEE LOUIS	67 STONEHEDGE DRIVE SOUTH, GREENWICH CT 06831
1930-049	MCAFEE, WILLIAM FORT	D. JULY 8, 1958, CULPEPPER, VA.
1971-068	MCANALLY, ERNEST LEE	PO BOX 942, MOUNT PLEASANT TX 75456
1958-061	MCANANY, JAMES	11518 PEOMA PLACE #102, CHATSWORTH CA 91311
1995-137	MCANDREW, JAMES BRIAN	17917 NORTH 93RD STREET, SCOTTSDALE AZ 85255
1968-060	MCANDREW, JAMES CLEMENT	16540 EAST EL LAGO BLVD #41, FOUNTAIN HILLS AZ 85268
2005-117	MCANULTY, PAUL MICHAEL	835 TRINIDAD WAY, OXNARD CA 93033
1960-069	MCAULIFFE, RICHARD JOHN	32 WORTHINGTON DRIVE, FARMINGTON CT 06032
1959-054	MCAVOY, THOMAS JOHN	CLINTON COURT, STILLWATER NY 12118
1961-072	MCBEAN, ALVIN ONEAL	BOX 4475, SAINT THOMAS VI 00801
1926-053	MCBEE, PRYOR EDWARD	D. APRIL 19, 1963, ROSEVILLE, CALIF.
1973-082	MCBRIDE, ARNOLD RAY 'BAKE'	4077 RELIANT CIRCLE, OWENSBORO KY 42301
2005-118	MCBRIDE, JOSEPH MACAY 'MACAY'	608 MCDONALD ROAD, SYLVANIA GA 30467
1959-055	MCBRIDE, KENNETH FAYE	3446 CYPRESS CIRCLE, WESTLAKE OH 44145
1943-085	MCBRIDE, THOMAS RAYMOND	D. DECEMBER 26, 2001, WICHITA FALLS, TEXAS
1964-069	MCCABE, JOE ROBERT	3003 GULF SHORE BLVD N. #904, NAPLES FL 34103
1946-069	MCCABE, RALPH HERBERT	D. MAY 4, 1974, WINDSOR, ONT.
1946-070	MCCAHAN, WILLIAM GLENN	D. JULY 3, 1986, FORT WORTH, TEXAS
1962-084	MCCALL, BRIAN ALLEN	105 UNION ST, ALEXANDRIA VA 22314
1948-066	MCCALL, JOHN WILLIAM 'WINDY'	8043 EAST RAGWEED DRIVE, TUCSON AZ 85710
1977-088	MCCALL, LARRY STEPHEN	354 JUSTICE RIDGE ROAD, CANDLER NC 28715
1948-067	MCCALL, ROBERT LEONARD	D. JANUARY 8, 1996, LITTLE ROCK, ARK.
1927-057	MCCALLISTER, JOHN	D. OCTOBER 18, 1946, COLUMBUS, OHIO
1989-079	MCCAMENT, LARRY RANDALL 'RANDY'	17338 NORTH DEL WEBB BLVD, SUN CITY AZ 85373
2005-119	MCCANN, BRIAN MICHAEL	OLD ADD: SATELLITE BEACH FL
1920-080	MCCANN, ROBERT EMMETT	D. APRIL 15, 1937, PHILADELPHIA, PA.
1959-056	MCCARDELL, ROGER MORTON	D. NOVEMBER 13, 1996, WILMINGTON, DEL.
1923-088	MCCARREN, WILLIAM JOSEPH	D. SEPTEMBER 11, 1983, DENVER, COLO.
2005-120	MCCARTHY, BRANDON PATRICK	5050 PIKES PEAK HIGHWAY, CASCADE CO 80809

1996-116	MCCARTHY, GREGORY ONEIL	56 WAKELEE AVENUE EXT., SHELTON CT 06484
1948-068	MCCARTHY, JEROME FRANCIS	D. OCTOBER 3, 1965, OCEANSIDE, N.Y.
1934-067	MCCARTHY, JOHN JOSEPH	D. SEPTEMBER 13, 1973, MUNDELEIN, ILL.
1926-054	MCCARTHY, JOSEPH VINCENT	D. JANUARY 13, 1978, BUFFALO, N.Y.
1985-071	MCCARTHY, THOMAS MICHAEL	PO BOX 38, LIMINGTON ME 04049
1993-115	MCCARTY, DAVID ANDREW	635 GILBERT AVENUE, MENLO PARK CA 94025
1959-057	MCCARVER, JAMES TIMOTHY 'TIM'	5825 RIEGELS HARBOR ROAD, SARASOTA FL 34242
1985-072	MCCASKILL, KIRK EDWARD	PO BOX 451, RANCHO SANTA FE CA 92067
1977-089	MCCATTY, STEVEN EARL	1075 WOODBRIAR DRIVE, OXFORD MI 48371
1961-073	MCCLAIN, JOE FRED	1370 MILLIGAN HWY, JOHNSON CITY TN 37601
1998-118	MCCLAIN, SCOTT MICHAEL	660 GOLDEN GATE POINT #61, SARASOTA FL 34236
1931-055	MCCLANAHAN, ROBERT HUGH 'PETE'	D. OCTOBER 28, 1987, MONT BELVIEU, TEXAS
1990-102	MCCLELLAN, PAUL WILLIAM	1648 ANDOVER LANE, LINCOLN CA 95648
1987-092	MCCLENDON, LLOYD GLENN	1082 MISSION HILLS COURT, CHESTERTON IN 46304
1936-054	MCCLOSKEY, JAMES ELLWOOD	D. AUGUST 18, 1971, JERSEY CITY, N.J.
2003-106	MCCLUNG, MICHAEL SETH	206 DWYER LANE, LEWISBURG WV 24901
1975-073	MCCLURE, ROBERT CRAIG	PO BOX 628, ISLAMORADA FL 33034
1933-042	MCCOLL, ALEXANDER BOYD	D. FEBRUARY 6, 1991, KINGSVILLE, OHIO
2004-135	MCCONNELL, JOHN SAMUEL 'SAM'	3635 KOHN DRIVE #4303, FAIRFIELD OH 45014
1964-070	MCCOOL, WILLIAM JOHN	9250 SE 121ST LOOP, SUMMERFIELD FL 34491
1980-088	MCCORMACK, DONALD ROSS	OLD ADD: 2331 AZALEA DRIVE, PALM HARBOR FL 34683
1934-068	MCCORMICK, FRANK ANDREW	D. NOVEMBER 21, 1982, MANHASSET, N.Y.
1956-058	MCCORMICK, MICHAEL FRANCIS	1600 MORGANTON ROAD #U9, PINEHURST NC 28374
1940-060	MCCORMICK, MYRON WINTHROP 'MIKE'	D. APRIL 14, 1976, LOS ANGELES, CALIF.
1939-076	MCCOSKY, WILLIAM BARNEY 'BARNEY'	D. SEPTEMBER 6, 1996, VENICE, FLA.
1959-058	MCCOVEY, WILLIE LEE	PO BOX 620342, WOODSIDE CA 94062
1938-060	MCCOY, BENJAMIN JENISON	3932 EAST OMAHA DRIVE SW, GRANDVILLE MI 49418
1939-077	MCCRABB, LESTER WILLIAM	433 SOUTH KINZER AVENUE #26 GS, NEW HOLLAND PA 17557
1995-138	MCCRACKEN, QUINTON ANTOINE	11308 EAST AUMTUMN SAGE DRIVE, SCOTTSDALE AZ 85255
1963-076	MCCRAW, TOMMY LEE	3142 SE MONTE VISTA COURT, PORT SAINT LUCIE FL 34952
1990-103	MCCRAY, RODNEY DUNCAN	45365 HORSESHOE CIRCLE, CANTON MI 48187
1925-070	MCCREA, FRANCIS WILLIAM	D. FEBRUARY 25, 1981, DOVER, N.J.
1922-084	MCCUE, FRANK ALOYSIUS	D. JULY 5, 1953, EVERGREEN PARK, ILL.
1985-073	MCCULLERS, LANCE GRAYE	4036 PRIORY CIRCLE, TAMPA FL 33618
1940-061	MCCULLOUGH, CLYDE EDWARD	D. SEPTEMBER 18, 1982, SAN FRANCISCO, CALIF.
1929-070	MCCULLOUGH, PAUL WILLARD	D. NOVEMBER 7, 1970, NEWCASTLE, PA.
1942-068	MCCULLOUGH, PHILIP LAMAR	D. JANUARY 16, 2003, DECATUR, GA.
1922-085	MCCURDY, HARRY HENRY	D. JULY 21, 1972, HOUSTON, TEXAS
1995-139	MCCURRY, JEFFREY DEE	3635 UNDERWOOD STREET, HOUSTON TX 77025
1955-080	MCDANIEL, LYNDALL DALE	1095 MEDAOW HILL DRIVE, LAVON TX 75166
1957-050	MCDANIEL, MAX VON 'VON'	D. AUGUST 20, 1995, LAWTON, OKLA.
1991-121	MCDANIEL, TERRENCE KEITH	OLD ADD: 537 NW 55TH TERRACE, KANSAS CITY MO 64118
1994-072	MCDAVID, RAY DARNELL	1245 MARKET STREET #1348, SAN DIEGO CA 92101
1948-069	MCDERMOTT, MAURICE JOSEPH 'MICKEY'	D. AUGUST 7, 2003, PHOENIX, ARIZ.
1972-069	MCDERMOTT, TERRENCE MICHAEL	7205 SUNLIGHT PEAK DRIVE NE, RIO RANCHO NM 87124
1957-051	MCDEVITT, DANIEL EUGENE	PO BOX 561, HALLSTEAD PA 18822
1997-109	MCDILL, ALLEN GABRIEL	1024 EVERGREEN DRIVE, ARKADELPHIA AR 71923
2004-136	MCDONALD, DARNELL T.	OLD ADD: 553 SOUTH FOREST STREET, DENVER CO 80246
1969-113	MCDONALD, DAVID BRUCE	2545 SE THIRD STREET, POMPANO BEACH FL 33062
2001-115	MCDONALD, DONZELL	2020 PARK PLACE, DENVER CO 80205
1931-056	MCDONALD, HENRY MONROE	D. OCTOBER 17, 1982, HEMET, CALIF.
1997-110	MCDONALD, JASON ADAM	OLD ADD: 6320 STONERIDGE MALL ROAD, PLEASNTON CA 94588
1950-065	MCDONALD, JIMMIE LEROY	600 LINDEN WAY, BREA CA 92821
1999-122	MCDONALD, JOHN JOSEPH	11 NELSON DRIVE, EAST LYME CT 06333
1989-080	MCDONALD, LARRY BENARD 'BEN'	1650 GARDNER STREET, DENHAM SPRINGS LA 70726
2000-110	MCDONALD, WILLIAM KEITH 'KEITH'	5162A EAST GREENSBORO LANE, ANAHEIM CA 92807
1943-086	MCDONNELL, JAMES JOSEPH	D. APRIL 24, 1993, DETROIT, MICH.
1951-063	MCDOUGALD, GILBERT JAMES	2005 MILL POND COURT, WALL NJ 07719
2005-121	MCDOUGALL, MARSHALL JAMES	4523 HAWKSLEY PLACE, WESLEY CHAPEL FL 33544
1987-093	MCDOWELL, JACK BURNS	2875 CALLE RANCHO VISTA, ENCINITAS CA 92024
1985-074	MCDOWELL, ODDIBE	5240 SW 18TH STREET, HOLLYWOOD FL 33023
1985-075	MCDOWELL, ROGER ALAN	58 ROBINWOOD PLACE, JACKSON MS 39211
1961-074	MCDOWELL, SAMUEL EDWARD	12902 BROWN BARK TRAIL, CLERMONT FL 34711
1989-081	MCELROY, CHARLES DWAYNE	1049 NEDERLAND AVENUE, PORT ARTHUR TX 77640
1942-069	MCELYEA, FRANK	D. APRIL 19, 1987, EVANSVILLE, IND.
1974-081	MCENANEY, WILLIAM HENRY 'WILL'	1055 SW THIRD STREET, BOCA RATON FL 33486
1930-050	MCEVOY, LOUIS ANTHONY	D. DECEMBER 16, 1953, WEBSTER GROVE, MO.
1998-119	MCEWING, JOSEPH EARL	2622 BALFOUR AVENUE, BRISTOL PA 19007
1968-061	MCFADDEN, LEON	8617 10TH AVENUE, INGLEWOOD CA 90305
1945-067	MCFARLAND, HOWARD ALEXANDER	D. APRIL 7, 1993, WICHITA, KAN.
1962-085	MCFARLANE, ORLANDO DE JESUS	2102 LAKEVIEW DRIVE WEST, ROYAL PALM BEACH FL 33411
1981-082	MCGAFFIGAN, ANDREW JOSEPH	6243 FORESTWOOD DRIVE EAST, LAKELAND FL 33811
1946-071	MCGAH, EDWARD JOSEPH	D. SEPTEMBER 30, 2002, OAKLAND, CALIF.
1962-086	MCGAHA, FRED MELVIN 'MEL'	D. FEBRUARY 3, 2002, TULSA, OKLA.
1934-069	MCGEE, DANIEL ALOYSIUS	D. DECEMBER 4, 1991, LAKEHURST, N.J.
1925-071	MCGEE, FRANCIS D. 'TUBBY'	D. JANUARY 30, 1934, COLUMBUS, OHIO
1935-068	MCGEE, WILLIAM HENRY	D. FEBRUARY 11, 1987, ST. LOUIS, MO.
1982-083	MCGEE, WILLIE DEAN	65 PLEASANT KNOLL COURT, ALAMO CA 94507
1993-116	MCGEHEE, GEORGE KEVIN	131 HOOD ROAD, POLLOCK LA 71467
1950-066	MCGHEE, WARREN EDWARD 'ED'	D. FEBRUARY 13, 1986, MEMPHIS, TENN.
1944-085	MCGHEE, WILLIAM MAC	D. MARCH 10, 1984, DECATUR, GA.
1977-090	MCGILBERRY, RANDALL KENT	2011 RIDGELINE DRIVE, MOBILE AL 36695
1944-086	MCGILLEN, JOHN JOSEPH	D. AUGUST 11, 1987, UPLAND, PA.
1968-062	MCGINN, DANIEL MICHAEL	1340 SOUTH 163RD ST, OMAHA NE 68120
1992-082	MCGINNIS, RUSSELL BRENT	1110 NORTH JUDD PLACE, CHANDLER AZ 85226
1999-123	MCGLINCHY, KEVIN MICHAEL	101 WEST STREET, MALDEN MA 02148

1972-070	MCGLOTHEN, LYNN EVERATT	D. AUGUST 14, 1984, DUBACH, LA.
1949-051	MCGLOTHIN, EZRA MAC 'PAT'	1454 KENESAW AVENUE, KNOXVILLE TN 37919
1965-072	MCGLOTHLIN, JAMES MILTON	D. DECEMBER 23, 1975, UNION, KY.
2005-122	MCGOWAN, DUSTIN MICHAEL	PO BOX 1281, LUDOWICI GA 31316
1922-086	MCGOWAN, FRANK BERNARD 'BEAUTY'	D. MAY 6, 1982, HAMDEN, CONN.
1948-070	MCGOWAN, TULLIS EARL 'MICKEY'	D. MARCH 8, 2003, WAYCROSS, GA.
1965-073	MCGRAW, FRANK EDWIN 'TUG'	D. JANUARY 5, 2004, BRENTWOOD, TENN.
1997-111	MCGRAW, THOMAS VIRGIL	11300 NE 379TH STREET, LA CENTER WA 98629
1976-061	MCGREGOR, SCOTT HOUSTON	1514 PROVIDENCE ROAD #A, TOWSON MD 21286
1922-087	MCGREW, WALTER HOWARD 'SLIM'	D. AUGUST 21, 1967, PORT ARTHUR, TEXAS
1986-097	MCGRIFF, FREDERICK STANLEY	16314 MILLAN DE AVILA, TAMPA FL 33613
1987-094	MCGRIFF, TERENCE ROY	2905 LANGSTON DRIVE, FORT PIERCE FL 33450
1962-087	MCGUIRE, M.C. ADOLFUS 'MICKEY'	OLD ADD: 1537 VANCOUVER DRIVE, DAYTON OH 45406
1997-112	MCGUIRE, RYAN BYRON	23656 MARTHA STREET, WOODLAND HILLS CA 91367
1988-089	MCGUIRE, WILLIAM PATRICK	17209 I STREET, OMAHA NE 68135
1986-098	MCGWIRE, MARK DAVID	OLD ADD: 3 REDBIRD, IRVINE CA 92603
1943-087	MCHALE, JOHN JOSEPH	2014 ROYAL FERN COURT, PALM CITY FL 34990
1981-083	MCHENRY, VANCE LOREN	2396 BROWN ST, DURHAM CA 95938
1921-059	MCILREE, VANCE ELMER	D. MAY 6, 1959, KANSAS CITY, MO.
1957-052	MCILWAIN, WILLIAM STOVER 'STOVER'	D. JANUARY 15, 1966, BUFFALO, N.Y.
1974-082	MCINTOSH, JOSEPH ANTHONY	9120 SE 54TH STREET, MERCER ISLAND WA 98040
1990-104	MCINTOSH, TIMOTHY ALAN	10662 CHANTEL LANE, STOCKTON CA 95212
1937-072	MCKAIN, ARCHIE RICHARD	D. MAY 21, 1985, SALINA, KAN.
1927-058	MCKAIN, HAROLD LEROY	D. JANUARY 24, 1970, SACRAMENTO, CALIF.
2002-121	MCKAY, CODY DEAN	9702 EAST LA POSADA CIRCLE, SCOTTSDALE AZ 85255
1975-074	MCKAY, DAVID LAWRENCE	9702 EAST LA POSADA CIRCLE, SCOTTSDALE AZ 85255
1972-071	MCKEE, JAMES MARION	D. SEPTEMBER 14, 2002, PICKAWAY COUNTY, OHIO
1943-088	MCKEE, ROGERS HORNSBY	409 FOREST HILL DRIVE, SHELBY NC 28150
1996-117	MCKEEL, WALTER THOMAS	7637 NC HIGHWAY 58 NORTH, STANTONSBURG NC 27883
1932-049	MCKEITHAN, EMMETT JAMES 'TIM'	D. AUGUST 20, 1969, FOREST CITY, N.C.
1986-099	MCKEON, JOEL JACOB	1901 PIERCE STREET #7, HOLLYWOOD FL 33020
1973-083	MCKEON, JOHN ALOYSIUS 'JACK'	1529 CHARLEIGH COURT, ELON COLLEGE NC 27244
1970-088	MCKINNEY, CHARLES RICHARD 'RICH'	2495 EAST PETERSON ROAD, TROY OH 45373
1960-070	MCKNIGHT, JAMES ARTHUR	D. FEBRUARY 24, 1994, VAN BUREN COUNTY, ARK.
1989-082	MCKNIGHT, JEFFERSON ALAN	3296 HIGHWAY 92 WEST, BEE BRANCH AR 72013
2000-111	MCKNIGHT, TONY MARK	303 ARTESIAN, TEXARKANA AR 71854
1963-077	MCLAIN, DENNIS DALE	4889 MERCER ROAD, PINCKNEY MI 48169
1932-050	MCLARNEY, ARTHUR JAMES	D. DECEMBER 20, 1984, SEATTLE, WASH.
1977-091	MCLAUGHLIN, BYRON SCOTT	OLD ADD: 3464 SWEETWATER MESA, MALIBU CA 92154
1932-051	MCLAUGHLIN, JAMES ROBERT	D. DECEMBER 15, 1968, MOUNT VERNON, ILL.
1977-092	MCLAUGHLIN, JOEY RICHARD	1611 SOUTH TROOST, TULSA OK 74120
1931-057	MCLAUGHLIN, JUSTIN THEODORE 'JUD'	D. SEPTEMBER 27, 1964, CAMBRIDGE, MASS.
1976-062	MCLAUGHLIN, MICHAEL DUANE 'BO'	536 NORTH GRAND, MESA AZ 85201
1937-073	MCLAUGHLIN, PATRICK ELMER	D. NOVEMBER 1, 1999, HOUSTON, TEXAS
1935-069	MCLEAN, ALBERT ELDON 'ELDON'	D. SEPTEMBER 29, 1990, ASHEBORO, N.C.
2004-137	MCLEARY, MARTY LEE	2120 LONG MEADOW DRIVE, SPRING HILL TN 37174
1951-064	MCLELAND, WAYNE GAFFNEY	D. MAY 8, 2004, HOUSTON, TEXAS
1986-100	MCLEMORE, MARK TREMELL	PO BOX 92819, SOUTHLAKE TX 76092
1938-061	MCLEOD, RALPH ALTON	541 RALPH TALBOT STREET, SOUTH WEYMOUTH MA 02190
1930-051	MCLEOD, SOULE JAMES 'JIM'	D. AUGUST 3, 1981, LITTLE ROCK, ARK.
1944-087	MCLISH, CALVIN COOLIDGE	639 TIMBER LANE, EDMOND OK 73034
2005-123	MCLOUTH, NATHAN RICHARD	140 LITTLETON ROAD #100, PARSIPPANY NJ 07054
1956-059	MCMAHAN, JACK WALLY	131 FOREST VIEW CIRCLE, HOT SPRINGS AR 71913
1957-053	MCMAHON, DONALD JOHN	D. JULY 22, 1987, LOS ANGELES, CALIF.
1960-071	MCMANUS, JAMES MICHAEL	2352 HOPKINS MILL ROAD, DULUTH GA 30096
1920-081	MCMANUS, MARTIN JOSEPH	D. FEBRUARY 18, 1966, ST. LOUIS, MO.
1968-063	MCMATH, JIMMY LEE	3321 22ND STREET, TUSCALOOSA AL 35401
1993-117	MCMICHAEL, GREGORY WINSTON	11072 PEACHCOVE COURT, SUWANEE GA 30024
1922-088	MCMILLAN, NORMAN ALEXIS	D. SEPTEMBER 28, 1969, LATTA, S.C.
1951-065	MCMILLAN, ROY DAVID	D. NOVEMBER 2, 1997, BONHAM, TEXAS
1977-093	MCMILLAN, THOMAS ERWIN	712 SPRING LAKE ROAD, THOMASVILLE GA 31792
1996-118	MCMILLION, WILLIAM EDWARD	130 K STREET, SUMTER SC 29150
1925-072	MCMULLEN, HUGH RAPHAEL	D. MAY 23, 1986, WHITTIER, CALIF.
1962-088	MCMULLEN, KENNETH LEE	10 ESTABAN, CAMARILLO CA 93010
1983-096	MCMURTRY, JOE CRAIG 'CRAIG'	2600 SOUTH FIRST STREET, TEMPLE TX 76504
1945-068	MCNABB, CARL MAC	PO BOX 203, JASPER TN 37347
1929-071	MCNAIR, DONALD ERIC 'ERIC'	D. MARCH 11, 1949, MERIDIAN, MISS.
1962-089	MCNALLY, DAVID ARTHUR	D. DECEMBER 1, 2002, BILLINGS, MONT.
1922-089	MCNAMARA, GEORGE FRANCIS	D. JUNE 12, 1990, HINSDALE, ILL.
1992-083	MCNAMARA, JAMES PATRICK	15317 SURREY HOUSE WAY, CENTREVILLE VA 20120
1969-114	MCNAMARA, JOHN FRANCIS	1206 BEECH HILL, BRENTWOOD TN 37027
1927-059	MCNAMARA, JOHN RAYMOND	D. DECEMBER 20, 1963, ARLINGTON, TEXAS
1939-078	MCNAMARA, ROBERT MAXEY	4764 DALEA PLACE, OCEANSIDE CA 92057
1922-090	MCNAMARA, THOMAS HENRY	D. MAY 5, 1974, DANVERS, MASS.
1922-091	MCNAMARA, TIMOTHY AUGUSTINE	D. NOVEMBER 5, 1994, NORTH SMITHFIELD, R.I.
1932-052	MCNAUGHTON, GORDON JOSEPH	D. AUGUST 6, 1942, CHICAGO, ILL.
1983-097	MCNEALY, ROBERT LEE	3301 BOZEMAN STREET, SACRAMENTO CA 95838
1924-077	MCNEELY, GEORGE EARL 'EARL'	D. JULY 16, 1971, SACRAMENTO, CALIF.
1993-118	MCNEELY, JEFFREY LAVERNE	405 EVERETTE STREET, MONROE NC 28110
1964-071	MCNERTNEY, GERALD EDWARD 'JERRY'	1124 TENTH STREET, NEVADA IA 50201
1999-124	MCNICHOL, BRIAN DAVID	2 BLUEFIELD LANE, FREDERICKSBURG VA 22406
1922-092	MCNULTY, PATRICK HOWARD	D. MAY 4, 1963, HOLLYWOOD, CALIF.
1969-115	MCNULTY, WILLIAM FRANCIS	12210 172ND STREET EAST #G101, PUYALLUP WA 98374
2004-138	MCPHERSON, DALLAS LYLE	307 SWAIM STREET, RANDLEMAN NC 27317
1923-089	MCQUAID, HERBERT GEORGE	D. APRIL 5, 1966, RICHMOND, CALIF.
1934-070	MCQUAIG, GERALD JOSEPH	D. FEBRUARY 5, 2001, BUFORD, GA.

1969-116	MCQUEEN, MICHAEL ROBERT	3206 CAMEO DR, HOUSTON TX 77055
1938-062	MCQUILLEN, GLENN RICHARD	D. JUNE 8, 1989, GARDENVILLE, MD.
1936-055	MCQUINN, GEORGE HARTLEY	D. DECEMBER 24, 1978, ALEXANDRIA, VA.
1990-105	MCRAE, BRIAN WESLEY	500 NORTH 13TH STREET #8C, SAINT LOUIS MO 63103
1968-064	MCRAE, HAROLD ABRAHAM 'HAL'	500 NORTH 13TH STREET #8C, SAINT LOUIS MO 63103
1969-117	MCRAE, NORMAN	D. JULY 25, 2003, GARLAND, TEXAS
1983-098	MCREYNOLDS, WALTER KEVIN 'KEVIN'	7 WITRY COURT, LITTLE ROCK AR 72223
1921-060	MCWEENY, DOUGLAS LAWRENCE	D. JANUARY 1, 1953, MELROSE PARK, ILL.
1978-079	MCWILLIAMS, LARRY DEAN	4102 BECKLEY COURT, COLLEYVILLE TX 76034
1931-058	MCWILLIAMS, WILLIAM HENRY	D. JANUARY 21, 1997, GARLAND, TEXAS
1983-099	MEACHAM, ROBERT ANDREW	7079 SOUTH COLUMBINE WAY, LITTLETON CO 80122
1991-122	MEACHAM, RUSSELL LOREN 'RUSTY'	1906 EDEN GLEN LANE, PEARLAND TX 77581
1943-089	MEAD, CHARLES RICHARD	7482 SVL BOX, VICTORVILLE CA 92392
1920-082	MEADOR, JOHN DAVIS	D. APRIL 11, 1970, WINSTON-SALEM, N.C.
1998-120	MEADOWS, MATTHEW BRIAN 'BRIAN'	208 PALOS VERDES DRIVE, TROY AL 36079
1986-101	MEADOWS, MICHAEL RAY	110 HEAVENS LANE, MAYSVILLE NC 28555
1926-055	MEADOWS, RUFUS RIVERS	D. MAY 10, 1970, WICHITA, KAN.
1987-095	MEADS, DAVID DONALD 'DON'	3220 CYPRESS WAY, SANTA ROSA CA 95405
1993-119	MEARES, PATRICK JAMES	8405 BRIDLEWOOD STREET, WICHITA KS 67206
2003-107	MEARS, CHRISTOPHER PETER	OLD ADD: VICTORIA BC
1999-125	MECHE, GILBERT ALLEN	PO BOX 392, SCOTT LA 70583
1995-140	MECIR, JAMES MASON	21219 WEST CREEKSIDE DRIVE, LAKE ZURICH IL 60047
2005-124	MEDDERS, BRANDON EDWARD	9732 CHAROLAIS DRIVE, TUSCALOOSA AL 35405
1945-069	MEDEIROS, RAY ANTON	D. JUNE 6, 2003, SAN MATEO, CALIF.
1972-072	MEDICH, GEORGE FRANCIS 'DOC'	2206 RIDGEVIEW AVENUE, ALIQUIPPA PA 15001
1988-090	MEDINA, LUIS MAIN	16015 SOUTH FIRST STREET, PHOENIX AZ 85048
1998-121	MEDINA, RAFAEL EDUARDO	OLD ADD: PANAMA CITY PANAMA
1949-052	MEDLINGER, IRVING JOHN	D. SEPTEMBER 3, 1975, WHEELING, ILL.
1988-091	MEDVIN, SCOTT HOWARD	22900 CENTER RIDGE ROAD #419, CLEVELAND OH 44116
1932-053	MEDWICK, JOSEPH MICHAEL	D. MARCH 21, 1975, ST. PETERSBURG, FLA.
1923-090	MEEKER, CHARLES ROY 'ROY'	D. MARCH 25, 1929, ORLANDO, FLA.
1948-071	MEEKS, SAMUEL MACK	4963 HELENE, MEMPHIS TN 38117
1972-073	MEELER, CHARLES PHILIP 'PHIL'	102 PINE STREET, KNIGHTDALE NC 27545
1941-071	MEERS, RUSSELL HARLAN	D. NOVEMBER 16, 1994, LANCASTER, PA.
1984-075	MEIER, DAVID KEITH	523 WEST STUART, FRESNO CA 93704
1922-093	MEINE, HENRY WILLIAM 'HEINIE'	D. MARCH 18, 1968, ST. LOUIS, MO.
1996-119	MEJIA, MIGUEL	OLD ADD: SAN PEDRO DE MACORIS DOM REP
1993-120	MEJIA, ROBERTO ANTONIO (DIAZ)	30 DEMAYO #20 HATO MAYOR, DOM REP
1955-081	MEJIAS, ROMAN GEORGE	3242 WEST 59TH ST, LOS ANGELES CA 90043
1976-063	MEJIAS, SAMUEL ELLIS	OLD ADD: CALLE HARVEY #73, L CAICAZGOS, SANTO DOMINGO DOM REP
1937-074	MELE, ALBERT ERNEST 'DUTCH'	D. FEBRUARY 12, 1975, HOLLYWOOD, FLA.
1947-063	MELE, SABATH ANTHONY 'SAM'	340 ADAMS STREET, QUINCY MA 02169
1984-076	MELENDEZ, FRANCISCO	OLD ADD: RURAL ROUTE 3 BOX 590, RIO PIEDRAS PR 00928
1990-106	MELENDEZ, JOSE LUIS	OLD ADD: BO. DAGUAO NAGUABO #264, BAGUABO PR 00718
1970-089	MELENDEZ, LUIS ANTONIO	EXT. SAN JOSE D-2, AIBONITO PR 00609
2000-112	MELHUSE, ADAM MICHAEL	245 ALMOND STREET, SAN LUIS OBISPO CA 93405
1926-056	MELILLO, OSCAR DONALD	D. NOVEMBER 14, 1963, CHICAGO, ILL.
1927-060	MELLANA, JOSEPH PETER	D. NOVEMBER 1, 1969, SAN RAFAEL, CALIF.
2000-113	MELO, JUAN ESTEBAN	OLD ADD: BANI DOM REP
1937-075	MELTON, CLIFFORD GEORGE	D. JULY 28, 1986, BALTIMORE, MD.
1956-060	MELTON, DAVID OLIN	10253 RICHWOOD DR, CUPERTINO CA 95014
1941-072	MELTON, REUBEN FRANKLIN	D. SEPTEMBER 11, 1971, GREER, S.C.
1968-065	MELTON, WILLIAM EDWIN	3639 NORTH PINE GROCE #14G, CHICAGO IL 60613
1998-122	MELUSKEY, MITCHELL WADE	26 MEADOWBROOK ROAD, YAKIMA WA 98903
1985-076	MELVIN, ROBERT PAUL	5637 EAST CANYON RIDGE NORTH DR, CAVE CREEK AZ 85331
2002-122	MENCH, KEVIN FORD	414 SAINT REGIS DRIVE, NEWARK DE 19711
2003-108	MENDEZ, CARLOS ALBERTO (CASTILLO)	OLD ADD: CARACAS VENEZ
2001-116	MENDEZ, DONALDO ALFONSO	OLD ADD: BARQUISIMETO VENEZ
1997-113	MENDOZA, CARLOS RAMON	OLD ADD: BOLIVAR VENEZUELA
1970-090	MENDOZA, CRISTOBAL RIGOBERTO 'MINNIE'	701 SAMUEL ADAMS CIRCLE, CONCORD NC 28027
1974-083	MENDOZA, MARIO	NO. RE-ELECION Y ROSALES #501, NAVAJOA SONORA, MEXICO
1979-075	MENDOZA, MICHAEL JOSEPH	14207 SOUTH 20TH STREET, PHOENIX AZ 85048
1996-120	MENDOZA, RAMIRO	OLD ADD: LOS SANTOS PANAMA
1999-126	MENECHINO, FRANK	522 ARLENE STREET, STATEN ISLAND NY 10314
1992-084	MENENDEZ, ANTONIO GUSTAVO	18730 NW 48TH COURT, CAROL CITY FL 33055
1995-141	MENHART, PAUL GERARD	RAMSEY CENTER, WCU, CULLOWHEE NC 28723
1962-090	MENKE, DENIS JOHN	1246 BERKSHIRE LANE, TARPON SPRINGS FL 34689
1933-043	MEOLA, EMILE MICHAEL 'MIKE'	D. SEPTEMBER 1, 1976, FAIR LAWN, N.J.
1971-069	MEOLI, RUDOLPH BARTHOLOMEW	8150 EAST OAK RIDGE CIRCLE, ANAHEIM HILLS CA 92807
2000-114	MERCADO, HECTOR LUIS	OLD ADD: DORADO PR
1982-084	MERCADO, ORLANDO (RODRIGUEZ)	PO BOX 1465, ARECIBO PR 00613
1990-107	MERCED, ORLANDO LUIS (VILLANUEVA)	3115 WEST CHERRY STREET, TAMPA FL 33607
1992-085	MERCEDES, HENRY FELIPE (PEREZ)	OLD ADD: 1217 BOARDWALK STREET, ARLINGTON TX 76011
1994-073	MERCEDES, JOSE MIGUEL	SECCION ANAMA DEL SEYBO LAS PALMILLAS, DOM REP
1991-123	MERCEDES, LUIS ROBERTO	OLD ADD: SAN PEDRO DE MACORIS, DOM REP
1981-084	MERCER, MARK KENNETH	10607 PENN AVENUE SOUTH, MINNEAPOLIS MN 55431
1975-075	MERCHANT, JAMES ANDERSON 'ANDY'	BATES LAKE ROAD, MALCOLM AL 36556
1989-083	MERCKER, KENT FRANKLIN	5340 MUIRFIELD COURT, DUBLIN OH 43017
2005-125	MEREDITH, OLISE C. 'CLA'	PO BOX 2922, CHESTERFIELD VA 23832
1934-071	MERENA, JOHN JOSEPH	D. MARCH 9, 1977, BRIDGEPORT, CONN.
1922-094	MEREWETHER, ARTHUR FRANCIS	D. FEBRUARY 2, 1997, BAYSIDE, N.Y.
1984-077	MERIDITH, RONALD KNOX	308 VIA PROMESA, SAN CLEMENTE CA 92673
1998-123	MERLONI, LOUIS WILLIAM	103 MELLEN STREET, FRAMINGHAM MA 01702
1990-108	MERRILL, CARL HARRISON 'STUMP'	18 MERRYMEETING ROAD, TOPSHAM ME 04086
1993-121	MERRIMAN, BRETT ALAN	907 NORTH COBBLESTONE STREET, GILBERT AZ 85234
1949-053	MERRIMAN, LLOYD ARCHER	D. JANUARY 20, 2004, FRESNO, CALIF.

1921-061	MERRITT, HERMAN G.	D. MAY 26, 1927, KANSAS CITY, MO.
1965-074	MERRITT, JAMES JOSEPH	833 SANDWAGON CIRCLE, HEMET CA 92544
1957-054	MERRITT, LLOYD WESLEY	4703 WILD IRIS DRIVE #301, MYRTLE BEACH SC 29577
1951-066	MERSON, JOHN WARREN	D. APRIL 28, 2000, ELK RIDGE, MD.
1943-090	MERTZ, JAMES VERLIN	D. FEBRUARY 4, 2003, WAYCROSS, GA.
1941-073	MERULLO, LEONARD RICHARD	159 SUMMER AVENUE, READING MA 01867
1989-084	MERULLO, MATTHEW BATES	8 FOX RUN ROAD, MADISON CT 06443
1987-096	MESA, JOSE ROMAN	13173 SW 51ST STREET, MIRAMAR FL 33027
1938-063	MESNER, STEPHEN MATHIAS	D. APRIL 6, 1981, SAN DIEGO, CALIF.
1924-078	MESSENGER, ANDREW WARREN 'BUD'	D. NOVEMBER 4, 1971, LANSING, MICH.
2005-126	MESSENGER, RANDALL JEROME	OLD ADD: 2110 18TH STREET, SPARKS NV 89431
1968-066	MESSERSMITH, JOHN ALEXANDER 'ANDY'	200 LAGUNITA DR, SOQUEL CA 95073
1963-078	METCALF, THOMAS JOHN	1390 WISCONSIN RIVER DRIVE, PORT EDWARDS WI 54469
1998-124	METCALFE, MICHAEL HENRY	9 COTTAGE STREET, ASHLAND NH 03217
1940-062	METHA, FRANK JOSEPH 'SCAT'	D. MARCH 2, 1975, FOUNTAIN VALLEY, CALIF.
1943-091	METHENY, ARTHUR BEAUREGARD 'BUD'	D. JANUARY 2, 2003, VIRGINIA BEACH, VA.
1922-095	METIVIER, GEORGE DEWEY	D. MARCH 2, 1947, CAMBRIDGE, MASS.
1943-092	METKOVICH, GEORGE MICHAEL 'CATFISH'	D. MAY 17, 1995, COSTA MESA, CALIF.
1943-093	METRO, CHARLES	7890 INDIANA STREET, ARVADA CO 80007
1923-091	METZ, LEONARD RAYMOND	D. FEBRUARY 24, 1953, DENVER, COLO.
1974-084	METZGER, CLARENCE EDWARD 'BUTCH'	PO BOX 22037, SACRAMENTO CA 95822
1970-091	METZGER, ROGER HENRY	3560 BLUEBONNET BLVD, BRENHAM TX 77833
1944-088	METZIG, WILLIAM ANDREW	D. MARCH 12, 2006, LUBBOCK, TEXAS
1925-073	METZLER, ALEXANDER	D. NOVEMBER 30, 1973, FRESNO, CALIF.
1989-085	MEULENS, HENSLEY FILEMON	OLD ADD: 11801 NW 12TH DRIVE, POMPANO BEACH FL 33071
1920-083	MEUSEL, ROBERT WILLIAM	D. NOVEMBER 28, 1977, DOWNEY, CALIF.
1988-092	MEYER, BRIAN SCOTT	33 BANK STREET, MEDFORD NJ 08051
2004-139	MEYER, DANIEL LIVINGSTON	OLD ADD: MICKLETON NJ
1974-085	MEYER, DANIEL THOMAS	9610 DAVONA DRIVE, SAN RAMON CA 94583
2006-117	MEYER, DREW EDWARD	OLD ADD: CHARLESTON SC
1938-064	MEYER, GEORGE FRANCIS	D. JANUARY 3, 1992, HOFFMAN ESTATES, ILL.
1955-082	MEYER, JOHN ROBERT 'JACK'	D. MARCH 9, 1967, PHILADELPHIA, PA.
1937-076	MEYER, LAMBERT DALTON 'DUTCH'	D. JANUARY 19, 2003, FORT WORTH, TEXAS
1964-072	MEYER, ROBERT BERNARD	PO BOX 3024, MISSION VIEJO CA 92690
1946-072	MEYER, RUSSELL CHARLES	D. NOVEMBER 16, 1997, OGLESBY, ILL.
1978-080	MEYER, SCOTT WILLIAM	OLD ADD: 15243 SOUTH HAMLIN AVE, MIDLOTHIAN IL 60445
1988-093	MEYER, TANNER JOE	392 KAIMAKE LOOP, KAILUA HI 96734
1999-127	MEYERS, CHAD WILLIAM	1804 WINDCREST AVENUE, PAPILLION NE 68133
2001-117	MIADICH, JOHN BARTON 'BART'	17841 HILLSIDE DRIVE, LAKE OSWEGO OR 97034
1993-122	MICELI, DANIEL	1013 HART BRANCH DRIVE, OVIEDO FL 32765
1954-066	MICELOTTA, ROBERT PETER 'MICKEY'	3266 JOG PARK DRIVE #11, GREENACRES FL 33467
1966-059	MICHAEL, EUGENE RICHARD	49 UNION AVENUE, UPPER SADDLE RIVER NJ 07458
1943-094	MICHAELS, CASIMIR EUGENE	D. NOVEMBER 12, 1982, GROSSE POINTE, MICH.
2001-118	MICHAELS, JASON DREW	10412 CARROLL COVE PLACE, TAMPA FL 33612
1932-054	MICHAELS, JOHN JOSEPH	D. NOVEMBER 18, 1996, SEBRING, FLA.
1924-079	MICHAELS, RALPH JOSEPH	D. AUGUST 5, 1988, MONROEVILLE, PA.
1921-062	MICHAELSON, JOHN AUGUST	D. APRIL 16, 1968, WOODRUFF, WISC.
1998-125	MICHALAK, CHRISTIAN MATTHEW	1108 MOCKINGBIRD LANE, KELLER TX 76248
1950-067	MICKELSON, EDWARD ALLEN	1532 CHARLEMONT DRIVE, CHESTERFIELD MO 63017
1953-056	MICKENS, GLENN ROGER	5920 KINI PLACE, KAPAA HI 96746
2001-119	MIDDLEBROOK, JASON DOUGLAS	3309 GLENVIEW, AUSTIN TX 78703
1922-096	MIDDLETON, JOHN WAYNE	D. NOVEMBER 3, 1986, AMARILLO, TEXAS
1938-065	MIDKIFF, RICHARD JAMES	D. OCTOBER 30, 1956, TEMPLE, TEXAS
1987-097	MIELKE, GARY ROGER	1718 ORCHID DRIVE SOUTH, NORTH MANKATO MN 56003
1998-126	MIENTKIEWICZ, DOUGLAS ANDREW	13550 SW 67TH CIRCLE, MIAMI FL 33156
1945-070	MIERKOWICZ, EDWARD FRANK	7530 MACOMB #1-A, GROSSE ILE MI 48138
1993-123	MIESKE, MATTHEW TODD	2199 EAST BOMBAY ROAD, MIDLAND MI 48642
1948-072	MIGGINS, LAWRENCE EDWARD 'LARRY'	2405 KINGSTON DRIVE, HOUSTON TX 77019
1935-070	MIHALIC, JOHN MICHAEL	D. APRIL 24, 1987, FORT OGLETHORPE, GA.
1964-073	MIKKELSEN, PETER JAMES	D. NOVEMBER 29, 2006, MABTON, WASH.
1944-089	MIKLOS, JOHN JOSEPH	D. MARCH 29, 2000, ADRIAN, MICH.
1944-090	MIKSIS, EDWARD THOMAS	D. APRIL 8, 2005, HUNTINGTON VALLEY, PA.
1988-094	MILACKI, ROBERT	1873 MARTINIQUE DRIVE, LAKE HAVASU CITY AZ 86406
1974-086	MILBOURNE, LAWRENCE WILLIAM	9020 HILLCREST AVENUE, PITTSBURGH PA 15237
1996-121	MILCHIN, MICHAEL WAYNE	13651 GLYNSHEL DRIVE, WINTER GARDEN FL 34787
2003-109	MILES, AARON WADE	1716 SAN JOSE DRIVE, ANTIOCH CA 94509
1940-063	MILES, CARL THOMAS	5 MILLER DRIVE, COLUMBIA MO 65201
1958-062	MILES, DONALD RAY	22335 BANEBERRY ROAD, MAGNOLIA TX 77355
1968-067	MILES, JAMES CHARLIE	RURAL ROUTE 2 BOX 708B, MABEN MS 39750
1935-071	MILES, WILSON DANIEL 'DEE'	D. NOVEMBER 2, 1976, BIRMINGHAM, ALA.
2003-110	MILEY, DAVID ALLEN	9304 FOREST HILLS DRIVE, TAMPA FL 33612
1975-076	MILEY, MICHAEL WILFRED	D. JANUARY 6, 1977, BATON ROUGE, LA.
1992-086	MILITELLO, SAM SALVATORE	3217 WEST SAINT JOHN STREET, TAMPA FL 33607
1966-060	MILLAN, FELIX BERNARDO	G16 CALLE CAMARERO PARC ECUESTRE, CAROLINA PR 00987
1998-127	MILLAR, KEVIN CHARLES	5290 BERWICK DRIVE, BEAUMONT TX 77706
2006-118	MILLEDGE, LASTINGS DARNELL	11114 SAILBROOKE DRIVE, RIVERVIEW FL 33569
2001-120	MILLER, ABRAHAM PHILIP 'CORKY'	1115 SEVENTH STREET, CALIMESA CA 92320
2006-119	MILLER, ANDREW MARK	OLD ADD: GAINESVILLE FL
1973-084	MILLER, CHARLES BRUCE 'BRUCE'	2126 PARKLAND DR, FORT WAYNE IN 46825
1997-114	MILLER, DAMIAN DONALD	450 WEST FRANKLIN STREET, WEST SALEM WI 54669
1984-078	MILLER, DARRELL KEITH	21159 VIA ALISA, YORBA LINDA CA 92686
1975-077	MILLER, DYAR K.	8816 ADMIRAL BAY DRIVE, INDIANAPOLIS IN 46236
1921-063	MILLER, EDMUND JOHN 'BING'	D. MAY 7, 1966, PHILADELPHIA, PA.
1977-094	MILLER, EDWARD LEE	1819 ALFREDA STREET, SAN PABLO CA 94806
1936-056	MILLER, EDWARD ROBERT	D. JULY 31, 1997, LAKE WORTH, FLA.
1929-072	MILLER, ELMER JOSEPH	D. JANUARY 8, 1987, MIRA LOMA, CALIF.

1922-097	MILLER, JACOB GEORGE	D. AUGUST 24, 1974, TOWSON, MD.
1924-080	MILLER, JACOB WALTER 'JAKE'	D. AUGUST 20, 1975, VENICE, FLA.
1944-091	MILLER, JAMES ELDRIDGE 'HACK'	D. NOVEMBER 21, 1966, DALLAS, TEXAS
1966-061	MILLER, JOHN ALLEN	20 SWIFT COURT, NEWPORT BEACH CA 92663
1943-095	MILLER, JOHN ANTHONY 'OX'	1890 NORTH HWY 37 ACCESS, GEORGE WEST TX 78022
1962-091	MILLER, JOHN ERNEST	13443 OLD ANNAPOLIS ROAD, MOUNT AIRY MD 21771
2002-123	MILLER, JUSTIN MARK	22715 ANZA AVENUE, TORRANCE CA 90505
1987-098	MILLER, KEITH ALAN	1161 ST. ANDREWS, HIGHLAND MI 48357
1944-092	MILLER, KENNETH ALBERT	D. APRIL 3, 1991, ST. LOUIS, MO.
1994-074	MILLER, KURT EVERETT	1511 IROQUOIS CIRCLE, CARROLLTON TX 75007
1964-074	MILLER, LARRY DON	10045 NORTH 36TH STREET, PHOENIX AZ 85028
1984-079	MILLER, LEMMIE EARL	OLD ADD: 1234 EAST COTTONWOOD LANE, PHOENIX AZ 85048
1923-092	MILLER, LEO ALPHONSO 'RED'	D. OCTOBER 20, 1973, ORLANDO, FLA.
2003-111	MILLER, MATT JACOB	OLD ADD: GREENVILLE MS 48838
2001-121	MILLER, MATTHEW LINCOLN	4501 83RD STREET, LUBBOCK TX 79424
1988-095	MILLER, NEAL KEITH 'KEITH'	1831 WEST ALAMOSA DRIVE, TERRELL TX 75160
1965-075	MILLER, NORMAN CALVIN	43 COLUMBIA CREST PLACE, SPRING TX 77382
1994-075	MILLER, ORLANDO SALMON (DIXON)	OLD ADD: APTDO 6-2638 ESTAFETA, EL DORADO PANAMA
1927-061	MILLER, OTIS LOUIS 'OTTO'	D. JULY 26, 1959, BELLEVILLE, ILL.
1991-124	MILLER, PAUL ROBERT	252 REDBUN LANE, BATAVIA IL 60510
1921-064	MILLER, RALPH HENRY	D. FEBRUARY 18, 1967, WHITE BEAR LAKE, MINN.
1920-084	MILLER, RALPH JOSEPH	D. MARCH 18, 1939, FORT WAYNE, IND.
1977-095	MILLER, RANDALL SCOTT	22523 OAK MIST LANE, KATY TX 77494
1985-077	MILLER, RAYMOND ROGER	PO BOX 41, NEW ATHENS OH 43981
1971-070	MILLER, RICHARD ALAN 'RICK'	28548 FB FOWLER COURT, BONITA SPRINGS FL 34135
1953-057	MILLER, ROBERT GERALD	1702 KEIM TRAIL, SAINT CHARLES IL 60174
1949-054	MILLER, ROBERT JOHN	17397 GLENMORE, DETROIT MI 48240
1957-055	MILLER, ROBERT LANE	D. AUGUST 6, 1993, RANCHO BERNARDO, CALIF.
1957-056	MILLER, RODNEY CARTER	40 MOGUL MOUNTAIN DRIVE, RENO NV 89523
1974-087	MILLER, ROGER WESLEY	D. APRIL 26, 1993, MILL RUN, PA.
1941-074	MILLER, ROLLAND ARTHUR 'RONNIE'	D. JANUARY 6, 1998, FERGUSON, MO.
1929-073	MILLER, RUDEL CHARLES	D. JANUARY 22, 1994, KALAMAZOO, MICH.
1927-062	MILLER, RUSSELL LEWIS	D. AUGUST 30, 1962, BUCYRUS, OHIO
1952-074	MILLER, STUART LEONARD	3701 OCASO COURT, CAMERON PARK CA 95682
1996-122	MILLER, TRAVIS EUGENE	51 WHISPER WAY, EATON OH 45320
1996-123	MILLER, TREVER DOUGLAS	5852 COUNT TURF LANE, WESLEY CHAPEL FL 33544
1999-128	MILLER, WADE T.	12 WOODS WAY, READING PA 19610
1937-077	MILLER, WILLIAM FRANCIS	D. FEBRUARY 26, 1982, HANNIBAL, MO.
1952-075	MILLER, WILLIAM PAUL	D. JULY 1, 2003, LITITZ, PA.
1992-087	MILLETTE, JOSEPH ANTHONY	759 SOLANA DRIVE, LAFAYETTE CA 94549
1996-124	MILLIARD, RALPH GREGORY	5600 STADIUM PKWY, MELBOURNE FL 32940
1934-072	MILLIES, WALTER LOUIS	D. FEBRUARY 28, 1995, OAK LAWN, ILL.
1928-066	MILLIGAN, JOHN ALEXANDER	D. MAY 15, 1972, FORT PIERCE, FLA.
1987-099	MILLIGAN, RANDY ANDRE	OLD ADD: 3300 NORTH RIDGE ROAD, ELLICOTT CITY MD 21043
1953-058	MILLIKEN, ROBERT FOGLE	D. JANUARY 4, 2007, CLEARWATER, FLA.
1990-109	MILLS, ALAN BERNARD	1811 BELLGROVE STREET, LAKELAND FL 33805
1927-063	MILLS, ARTHUR GRANT	D. JULY 23, 1975, UTICA, N.Y.
1934-073	MILLS, COLONEL BUSTER 'BUSTER'	D. DECEMBER 1, 1991, ARLINGTON, TEXAS
1934-074	MILLS, HOWARD ROBINSON 'LEFTY'	D. SEPTEMBER 23, 1982, RIVERSIDE, CALIF.
1980-089	MILLS, JAMES BRADLEY 'BRAD'	3025 EAST BIRCH AVENUE, VISALIA CA 93292
1970-092	MILLS, RICHARD ALAN	11445 EAST VIA LINDA #2, SCOTTSDALE AZ 85259
1944-093	MILLS, WILLIAM HENRY	4344 COMMERCIAL STREET, PORT CHARLOTTE FL 33953
1997-115	MILLWOOD, KEVIN AUSTIN	2828 GREY MOSS PASS, DULUTH GA 30097
1936-057	MILNAR, ALBERT JOSEPH	D. JUNE 3, 2005, CLEVELAND, OHIO
1948-073	MILNE, WILLIAM JAMES 'PETE'	D. APRIL 11, 1999, MOBILE, ALA.
1978-081	MILNER, BRIAN TATE	1202 THISTLE HILL TRAIL, WEATHERFORD TX 76087
1980-090	MILNER, EDDIE JAMES	491 STAMBAUGH, COLUMBUS OH 43207
1971-071	MILNER, JOHN DAVID	D. JANUARY 4, 2000, EAST PAOINT, GA.
1944-094	MILOSEVICH, MICHAEL	D. FEBRUARY 3, 1966, EAST CHICAGO, IND.
1924-081	MILSTEAD, GEORGE EARL	D. AUGUST 9, 1977, CLEBURNE, TEXAS
1998-128	MILTON, ERIC ROBERT	14581 JONATHAN HARBOR DRIVE, FORT MYERS FL 33908
1995-142	MIMBS, MICHAEL RANDALL	2761 MIMBS ROAD, ALAMO GA 30411
1955-083	MINARCIN, RUDY ANTHONY	37 NORTH FIRST ST, NORTH VANDERGRIFT PA 15690
1960-072	MINCHER, DONALD RAY	5605 CRINER ROAD SE, HUNTSVILLE AL 35802
1993-124	MINCHEY, NATHAN DEREK	1212 RAMBLE CREEK DRIVE, PFLUGERVILLE TX 78660
1921-065	MINER, RAYMOND THEADORE	D. SEPTEMBER 15, 1963, GLENRIDGE SAN., N.Y.
2006-120	MINER, ZACHARY CHARLES	242 BARBADOS DRIVE, JUPITER FL 33458
1978-082	MINETTO, CRAIG STEPHEN	1809 LAKESHORE DRIVE, LODI CA 95240
1970-093	MINGORI, STEPHEN BERNARD	8841 NORTH CONGRESS AVENUE #637, KANSAS CITY MO 64153
1946-073	MINNER, PAUL EDISON	D. MARCH 28, 2006, LEMOYNE, PA.
1957-057	MINNICK, DONALD ATHEY	215 BERNARD ROAD, ROCKY MOUNT VA 24151
1992-088	MINOR, BLAS	7139 NORTH DEAN STREET, WINTON CA 95388
2000-115	MINOR, DAMON REED	3909 BELLWOOD DRIVE, NORMAN OK 73072
1998-129	MINOR, RYAN DALE	3909 BELLWOOD DRIVE, NORMAN OK 73072
1949-055	MINOSO, SATURNINO ORESTES 'MINNIE'	3700 NORTH LAKE SHORE DRIVE, CHICAGO IL 60613
1974-088	MINSHALL, JAMES EDWARD	225 MARY ENGLES HWY, MELBOURNE KY 41059
1975-078	MINTON, GREGORY BRIAN	4434 EAST CAMELBACK ROAD #127, PHOENIX AZ 85018
1995-143	MINTZ, STEPHEN WAYNE	128 FOREST HILLS DRIVE, LELAND NC 28451
1990-110	MINUTELLI, GINO MICHAEL	3305 FOXTROT COURT, SPRING HILL TN 37174
1978-083	MIRABELLA, PAUL THOMAS	15 JENKS ROAD, MORRISTOWN NJ 07960
1996-125	MIRABELLI, DOUGLAS ANTHONY	9788 EDGEWOOD AVENUE, TRAVERSE CITY MI 49684
1993-125	MIRANDA, ANGEL LUIS	CALLE B BUZON 50 FACTOR 1, ARECIBO PR 00612
1951-067	MIRANDA, GUILLERMO PEREZ 'WILLIE'	D. SEPTEMBER 8, 1996, BALTIMORE, MD.
2006-121	MISCH, PATRICK THEODORE JOSEPH	2635 CRABTREE LANE, NORTH BROOK IL 60062
1997-116	MISURACA, MICHAEL WILLIAM	27601 SUN CITY BLVD #330, SUN CITY CA 92586
1984-080	MITCHELL, CHARLES ROSS	5017 HASTY DR, NASHVILLE TN 37211

1975-079	MITCHELL, CRAIG SETON	BOX 174, ELK CA 95432
1921-066	MITCHELL, JOHN FRANKLIN	D. NOVEMBER 4, 1965, OAKLAND CO., MICH.
1986-102	MITCHELL, JOHN KYLE	5017 HASTY DR, NASHVILLE TN 37211
1991-125	MITCHELL, KEITH ALEXANDER	731 SOUTH 42ND STREET, SAN DIEGO CA 92113
1984-081	MITCHELL, KEVIN DARNELL	OLD ADD: 3867 OCEAN VIEW BLVD, SAN DIEGO CA 92113
1996-126	MITCHELL, LARRY PAUL	1040 PRESTON AVENUE, CHARLOTTESVILLE VA 22903
1946-074	MITCHELL, LOREN DALE 'DALE'	D. JANUARY 5, 1987, TULSA, OKLA.
1923-093	MITCHELL, MONROE BARR	D. SEPTEMBER 4, 1976, VALDOSTA, GA.
1975-080	MITCHELL, PAUL MICHAEL	23 CARR ROAD, BERLIN MA 01503
1980-091	MITCHELL, ROBERT VAN	19522 SENECA ROAD, APPLE VALLEY CA 92307
1970-094	MITCHELL, ROBERT VANCE	38 ELM STREET, NORRISTOWN PA 19401
2003-112	MITRE, SERGIO ARMANDO	230 COTTONWOOD ROAD #8, SAN YSIDRO CA 92173
1966-062	MITTERWALD, GEORGE EUGENE	1721 MURDOCK BLVD, ORLANDO FL 32807
1936-058	MIZE, JOHN ROBERT	D. JUNE 2, 1993, DEMOREST, GA.
1952-076	MIZELL, WILMER DAVID 'VINEGAR BEND'	D. FEBRUARY 21, 1999, KERRVILLE, TEXAS
1983-100	MIZEROCK, JOHN JOSEPH	PO BOX 5, PUNXSUTAWNEY PA 15767
1923-094	MIZEUR, WILLIAM FRANCIS	D. AUGUST 27, 1976, DANVILLE, ILL.
1992-089	MLICKI, DAVID JOHN	5350 RESERVE DRIVE, DUBLIN OH 43017
1989-086	MMAHAT, KEVIN PAUL	5500 ERLANGER ROAD, KENNER LA 70065
1974-089	MOATES, DAVID ALLAN	7924 24TH AVENUE WEST, BRADENTON FL 34209
1945-071	MODAK, MICHAEL JOSEPH ALOYSIUS	D. DECEMBER 12, 1995, LAKELAND, FLA.
1996-127	MOEHLER, BRIAN MERRITT	4492 BELVEDERE PLACE SE, MARIETTA GA 30067
2000-116	MOELLER, CHAD EDWARD	11058 EAST RAINTREE DRIVE, SCOTTSDALE AZ 85255
1992-090	MOELLER, DENNIS MICHAEL	2324 RIDGEMONT DRIVE, BIRMINGHAM AL 35244
1962-092	MOELLER, JOSEPH DOUGLAS	1505 AVENIDA DE NOGALES, SAN CLEMENTE CA 92672
1956-061	MOELLER, RONALD RALPH	683 BRIDLE PATH, CINCINNATI OH 45231
1972-074	MOFFITT, RANDALL JAMES	1725 BALTIC AVENUE, PRESCOTT AZ 86301
1955-084	MOFORD, HERBERT	D. DECEMBER 3, 2005, CINCINNATI, OHIO
1922-098	MOHARDT, JOHN HENRY	D. NOVEMBER 24, 1961, SAN DIEGO, CALIF.
1920-085	MOHART, GEORGE BENJAMIN	D. OCTOBER 2, 1970, SILVER CREEK, N.Y.
1993-126	MOHLER, MICHAEL ROSS	15241 RYAN AVENUE, PRAIRIEVILLE LA 70769
1986-103	MOHORCIC, DALE ROBERT	15501 ROCKSIDE ROAD, MAPLE HEIGHTS OH 44137
2001-122	MOHR, DUSTAN KYLE	103 PARKWOODS DRIVE, HATTIESBURG MS 39402
1953-059	MOISAN, WILLIAM JOSEPH	BOX 41, NEWTON NH 03858
1921-067	MOKAN, JOHN LEE	D. FEBRUARY 10, 1985, BUFFALO, N.Y.
1949-056	MOLE, FENTON LEROY	738 GLEN EAGLE COURT, DANVILLE CA 94526
1999-130	MOLINA, BENJAMIN JOSE 'BENJIE'	OLD ADD: VEGA ALTA PR 00762
1999-129	MOLINA, CRUZ GABRIEL 'GABE'	2181 EAST 119TH PLACE, NORTHGLENN CO 80233
1996-128	MOLINA, ISLAY 'IZZY'	9979 NW 25TH STREET, MIAMI FL 33172
1998-130	MOLINA, JOSE BENJAMIN	OLD ADD: VEGA ALTA PR 00692
2004-140	MOLINA, YADIER B.	OLD ADD: 7745 KINGSBURY BLVD #32, SAINT LOUIS MO 63105
1975-081	MOLINARO, ROBERT JOSEPH	1 HARBOURSIDE DRIVE #2312, DELRAY BEACH FL 33483
1978-084	MOLITOR, PAUL LEO	748 LAKE POINT DRIVE, CHANHASSEN MN 55317
1970-095	MOLONEY, RICHARD HENRY	125 MALLARD WAY, WALTHAM MA 02452
1937-078	MONACO, BLAS	D. FEBRUARY 10, 2000, SAN ANTONIO, TEXAS
1953-060	MONAHAN, EDWARD FRANCIS	D. JULY 27, 2003, BROOKLYN, N.Y.
1998-131	MONAHAN, SHANE HARTLAND	63 WEATHERSTONE PARKWAY, MARIETTA GA 30068
1958-063	MONBOUQUETTE, WILLIAM CHARLES	46 DOONAN STREET, MEDFORD MA 02155
1928-067	MONCEWICZ, FRED ALFRED	D. APRIL 23, 1969, BROCKTON, MASS.
1940-064	MONCHAK, ALEX	7414 8TH AVENUE WEST, BRADENTON FL 34209
1966-063	MONDAY, ROBERT JAMES 'RICK'	811 GAYFEATHER LANE, VERO BEACH FL 32967
1993-127	MONDESI, RAUL RAMON	8012 WILES ROAD, POMPANO BEACH FL 33067
1968-068	MONEY, DONALD WAYNE	282 OLD FOREST ROAD, VINELAND NJ 08360
1975-082	MONGE, ISIDRO PEDROZA 'SID'	716 5TH AVENUE, CHULA VISTA CA 91910
2001-123	MONROE, CRAIG KEYSTONE	4123 LYNN DRIVE, TEXARKANA TX 75503
1921-068	MONROE, JOHN ALLEN	D. JUNE 19, 1956, CONROE, TEXAS
1976-064	MONROE, LAWRENCE JAMES	725 NORTH HUNDLEY STREET, HOFFMAN ESTATES IL 60169
1958-064	MONROE, ZACHARY CHARLES	1 SANDALWOOD LN, BARTONVILLE IL 61607
1928-068	MONTAGUE, EDWARD FRANCIS	D. JUNE 17, 1988, DALY CITY, CALIF.
1973-085	MONTAGUE, JOHN EVANS	6001 VINEYARD LANE, MONTGOMERY AL 36117
1986-104	MONTALVO, RAFAEL EDGARDO	C/O CAOBA, LOS COLOBOS PARK #206, CAROLINA PR 00985
1966-064	MONTANEZ, GUILLERMO NARANJO 'WIILIE'	HC-05 BOX 52020, CAGUAS PR 00725
1963-079	MONTEAGUDO, AURELIO FAUNTINI	D. NOVEMBER 10, 1990, SALTILLO, MEXICO
1938-066	MONTEAGUDO, RENE MIRANDA	D. SEPTEMBER 14, 1973, HIALEAH, FLA.
1974-090	MONTEFUSCO, JOHN JOSEPH	PO BOX 3508, LAKE HAVASU CITY AZ 86405
1961-075	MONTEJO, MANUEL	OLD ADD: CALLE 28 #4115 MUNICIPIO PLAYA, HAVANA CUBA
1987-100	MONTELEONE, RICHARD	441 LUCERNE AVENUE, TAMPA FL 33606
1953-061	MONTEMAYOR, FELIPE ANGEL	TORREON #308, MITRAS CENTRO, MONTERREY NUEVO, LAREDO, MEXICO
2006-123	MONTERO, AGUSTIN ALCANTARA	OLD ADD: SAN PEDRO DE MACORIS DOM REP
2006-122	MONTERO, MIGUEL ANGEL	OLD ADD: CARACAS VENEZ
1941-075	MONTGOMERY, ALVIN ATLAS	D. APRIL 26, 1942, WAVERLY, VA.
1987-101	MONTGOMERY, JEFFREY THOMAS	2713 WEST 116TH STREET, LEAWOOD KS 66211
1971-072	MONTGOMERY, MONTY BRYSON	807 CORN TASSEL TRAIL, MARTINSVILLE VA 24112
1996-129	MONTGOMERY, RAYMOND JAMES	3107 SOUTH WEBBER COURT, PEARLAND TX 77584
1970-096	MONTGOMERY, ROBERT EDWARD	2 PARKWAY DR, SAUGUS MA 01906
1996-130	MONTGOMERY, STEVEN LEWIS	3262 AVENIDA DEL ALBA, CARLSBAD CA 92009
1993-128	MONTOYO, JOSE CARLOS 'CHARLIE'	84 EAST CALLE DEL RONDADOR, SAHUARITA AZ 85629
1972-075	MONTREUIL, ALLAN ARTHUR	2016 LAUREL ST, GRETNA LA 70053
1954-067	MONZANT, RAMON SEGUNDO	D. AUGUST 10, 2001, MARACAIBO, VENEZUELA
1972-076	MONZON, DANIEL FRANCISCO	D. JANUARY 21, 1996, SANTO DOMINGO, DOM REP
1967-073	MOOCK, JOSEPH GEOFFREY	12432 PECOS AVE, GREENWELL LA 70739
1997-117	MOODY, ERIC LANE	336 GLENEAGLE CIRCLE, IRMO SC 29063
1932-055	MOON, LEO	D. AUGUST 25, 1970, NEW ORLEANS, LA.
1954-068	MOON, WALLACE WADE	702 ELLEN LEE COURT, BRYAN TX 77802
1931-059	MOONEY, JAMES IRVING	D. APRIL 27, 1979, JOHNSON CITY, TENN.
1986-105	MOONEYHAM, WILLIAM CRAIG	5731 WHITE CRANE ROAD, MERCED CA 95340

1925-074	MOORE, ALBERT JAMES	D. NOVEMBER 29, 1974, ATLANTIC OCEAN
1976-065	MOORE, ALVIN EARL 'JUNIOR'	3728 WALL AVENUE, RICHMOND CA 94804
1946-075	MOORE, ANSEL WINN	D. OCTOBER 29, 1993, PEARL, MISS.
1964-075	MOORE, ARCHIE FRANCIS	201 COURTLAND ROAD, INDIANA PA 15701
1970-097	MOORE, BALOR LILBON	901 WEST VIEJO DRIVE, FRIENDSWOOD TX 77546
1988-096	MOORE, BRADLEY ALAN	3135 CHALLENGER POINT DRIVE, LOVELAND CO 80538
1930-052	MOORE, CARLOS WHITMAN	D. JULY 2, 1958, NEW ORLEANS, LA.
1973-086	MOORE, CHARLES WILLIAM	342 COUNTY ROAD 276, CULLMAN AL 35057
1936-059	MOORE, D.C. 'DEE'	D. JULY 2, 1997, WILLISTON, N.D.
1975-083	MOORE, DONNIE RAY	D. JULY 18, 1989, ANAHEIM, CALIF.
1934-075	MOORE, EUEL WALTON	D. FEBRUARY 12, 1989, TISHOMINGO, OKLA.
1931-060	MOORE, EUGENE, JR.	D. MARCH 12, 1978, JACKSON, MISS.
1970-098	MOORE, GARY DOUGLAS	7985 ROUNDROCK ROAD, DALLAS TX 75248
1923-095	MOORE, GRAHAM EDWARD 'EDDIE'	D. FEBRUARY 10, 1976, FORT MYERS, FLA.
1965-076	MOORE, JACKIE SPENCER	2721 LAUREL VALLEY LANE, ARLINGTON TX 76006
1928-069	MOORE, JAMES STANFORD	D. MAY 19, 1973, SEATTLE, WASH.
1930-053	MOORE, JAMES WILLIAM	D. MAY 7, 1986, MEMPHIS, TENN.
1928-070	MOORE, JOHN FRANCIS	D. APRIL 4, 1991, BRADENTON, FLA.
1930-054	MOORE, JOSEPH GREGG	D. APRIL 1, 2001, BRYAN, TEXAS
1981-085	MOORE, KELVIN ORLANDO	OLD ADD: 918 UNION DRIVE, PARK FOREST IL 60466
1996-131	MOORE, KERWIN LAMAR	18137 GODDARD STREET, DETROIT MI 48234
1936-060	MOORE, LLOYD ALBERT 'WHITEY'	D. DECEMBER 10, 1987, CANTON, OHIO
1993-129	MOORE, MARCUS RAYMOND	OLD ADD: 1044 83RD AVENUE, OAKLAND CA 94621
1982-085	MOORE, MICHAEL WAYNE	1472 EAST CALLE DE CABALLOS, TEMPE AZ 85284
1927-064	MOORE, RANDOLPH EDWARD	D. JUNE 12, 1992, MOUNT PLEASANT, TEXAS
1952-077	MOORE, RAYMOND LEROY	D. MARCH 2, 1995, CLINTON, MD.
1965-077	MOORE, ROBERT BARRY 'BARRY'	6702 CONIFER CIRCLE, INDIAN TRAIL NC 28079
1985-078	MOORE, ROBERT DEVELL	2500 WELLINGTON ROAD, LOS ANGELES CA 90016
1991-126	MOORE, ROBERT VINCENT	3703 HYDE PARK AVENUE, CINCINNATI OH 45209
1920-086	MOORE, ROY DANIEL	D. APRIL 5, 1951, SEATTLE, WASH.
2006-124	MOORE, SCOTT ALANBOYD	OLD ADD: LONG BEACH CA
1935-072	MOORE, TERRENCE BLUFORD	D. MARCH 29, 1995, COLLINSVILLE, ILL.
1972-077	MOORE, TOMMY JOE	PO BOX 336, PIONEERTOWN CA 92268
1998-132	MOORE, WARREN NEAL 'TREY'	5128 BELLERIVE BEND DRIVE, COLLEGE STATION TX 77845
1929-074	MOORE, WILLIAM AUSTIN 'CY'	D. MARCH 28, 1972, AUGUSTA, GA.
1925-075	MOORE, WILLIAM CHRISTOPHER	D. JANUARY 24, 1984, CORNING, N.Y.
1926-057	MOORE, WILLIAM HENRY	D. MAY 24, 1972, KANSAS CITY, MO.
1986-106	MOORE, WILLIAM ROSS	419 NORTH ASTELL AVENUE, WEST COVINA CA 91790
1927-065	MOORE, WILLIAM WILCY 'WILCY'	D. MARCH 29, 1963, HOLLIS, OKLA.
1962-093	MOORHEAD, CHARLES ROBERT 'BOB'	D. DECEMBER 3, 1986, LEMOYNE, PA.
1967-074	MOOSE, ROBERT RALPH	D. OCTOBER 9, 1976, MARTINS FERRY, OHIO
1936-061	MOOTY, J.T. 'JAKE'	D. APRIL 20, 1970, FORT WORTH, TEXAS
1976-066	MORA, ANDRES	MARCIAL ORDONEZ #172 OTE. LOS MOCHIS SINALOA, MEXICO
1999-131	MORA, MELVIN	2205 WARWICK WAY #200, MARRIOTTSVILLE MD 21104
2000-117	MORAGA, DAVID MICHAEL	62 TERRY LANE, SUISUN CITY CA 94585
1973-087	MORALES, JOSE MANUEL	17411 FOSGATE ROAD, MONTVERDE FL 34756
1969-118	MORALES, JULIO RUBEN 'JERRY'	OLD ADD: VILLA NUEVA CALLE #16 VALUE, CAGUAS PR 00625
2006-125	MORALES, KENDRYS	OLD ADD: SANTO DOMINGO DOM REP
1967-075	MORALES, RICHARD ANGELO	1650 ROSITA ROAD, PACIFICA CA 94044
2000-118	MORALES, WILLIAM ANTHONY 'WILLIE'	5001 WEST CAMINO DEL DESIERTO, TUCSON AZ 85745
1938-067	MORAN, ALBERT THOMAS 'HIKER'	D. JANUARY 7, 1998, SARATOGA SPRINGS, N.Y.
1974-091	MORAN, CARL WILLIAM 'BILL'	200 SHORE DRIVE, PORTSMOUTH VA 23701
1963-080	MORAN, RICHARD ALAN 'AL'	34134 BANBURY, FARMINGTON HILLS MI 48331
1958-065	MORAN, WILLIAM NELSON	107 EMERLING LANE, PEACHTREE CITY GA 30269
1990-111	MORANDINI, MICHAEL ROBERT 'MICKEY'	290 EAST TRATEBAS ROAD, CHESTERTON IN 46304
2003-113	MORBAN, JOSE	OLD ADD: SANTIAGO DOM REP
1994-076	MORDECAI, MICHAEL HOWARD	10 CROSS CREEK LANE, DOTHAN GA 36303
1924-082	MOREHART, RAYMOND ANDERSON	D. JANUARY 13, 1989, DALLAS, TEXAS
1963-081	MOREHEAD, DAVID MICHAEL	13872 GLENMERE DRIVE, SANTA ANA CA 92705
1957-058	MOREHEAD, SETH MARVIN	D. JANUARY 17, 2006, SHREVEPORT, LA.
1958-066	MOREJON, DANIEL TORRES	22625 SW 207TH AVENUE, MIAMI FL 33170
1995-144	MOREL, RAMON RAFAEL	CLE DUARTE #29, PALM. V. GONZALES SANTIAGO, DOM REP
1978-085	MORELAND, BOBBY KEITH 'KEITH'	4209 HIDDEN CANYON, AUSTIN TX 78746
1981-086	MORENO, ANGEL	GOMEZ FARIAZ #604 AGUASCALIENTES AGUAS., MEXICO
1980-092	MORENO, JOSE DE LOS SANTOS	CORREA Y CIDRON 9 SANTO DOMINGO, DOM REP
2001-124	MORENO, JUAN CARLOS (VEGAS)	OLD ADD: CAGUA VENEZ
1950-068	MORENO, JULIO GONZALES	D. JANUARY 2, 1987, MIAMI, FLA.
1975-084	MORENO, OMAR	OLD ADD: APARTADO #5 BALBOA, NCON, PANAMA CITY PANAMA
1999-132	MORENO, ORBER	2102 NE 23RD PLACE, CAPE CORAL FL 33909
1970-099	MORET, ROGELIO 'ROGER'	HC-01 BOX 5225, GUAYNABO PR 00671
1935-073	MORGAN, CHESTER COLLINS	D. SEPTEMBER 20, 1991, PASADENA, TEXAS
1921-069	MORGAN, CYRIL ARLON	D. SEPTEMBER 11, 1946, LAKEVILLE, MASS.
1928-071	MORGAN, EDWARD CARRE	D. APRIL 9, 1980, NEW ORLEANS, LA.
1936-062	MORGAN, EDWIN WILLIS	D. JUNE 27, 1982, LAKEWOOD, OHIO
1963-082	MORGAN, JOSEPH LEONARD	3239 DANVILLE BLVD #A, ALAMO CA 94507
1959-059	MORGAN, JOSEPH MICHAEL	15 OAK HILL DRIVE, WALPOLE MA 02081
1997-118	MORGAN, KEVIN LEE	YEARLING ROAD A, DUSON LA 70529
1978-086	MORGAN, MICHAEL THOMAS	PO BOX 681130, PARK CITY UT 84068
1950-069	MORGAN, ROBERT MORRIS 'BOBBY'	3004 STONEYBROOK ROAD, OKLAHOMA CITY OK 73120
1951-068	MORGAN, TOM STEPHEN	D. JANUARY 13, 1987, ANAHEIM, CALIF.
1954-069	MORGAN, VERNON THOMAS	D. NOVEMBER 8, 1975, MINNEAPOLIS, MINN.
1961-076	MORHARDT, MEREDITH GOODWIN 'MOE'	PO BOX 563, WINSTED CT 06098
1935-074	MORIARTY, EDWARD JEROME	D. SEPTEMBER 29, 1991, HOLYOKE, MASS.
2002-124	MORIARTY, MICHAEL THOMAS	5 EAST OLEANDER DRIVE, MOUNT LAUREL NJ 08054
2006-126	MORILLO, JUAN BAUTISTA	OLD ADD: SAN DEDRO DE MACORIS DOM REP
1973-088	MORLAN, JOHN GLEN	2348 SALEM AVE, GROVE CITY OH 43123

1996-132	MORMAN, ALVIN	117 PHILADELPHIA DRIVE, ROCKINGHAM NC 28379
1986-107	MORMAN, RUSSELL LEE	34W002 CHERRY LANE, GENEVA IL 60134
2003-114	MORNEAU, JUSTIN ERNEST GEORGE	OLD ADD: 598 EAST RANCH ROAD, GILBERT AZ 85296
1983-101	MOROGIELLO, DANIEL JOSEPH	99 DISTILLERY ROAD, WHITEHOUSE STATION NJ 08889
1984-082	MORONKO, JEFFREY ROBERT	3903 BARTONS COURT, SUGAR LAND TX 77479
1926-058	MORRELL, WILLARD BLACKMER	D. AUGUST 5, 1975, BIRMINGHAM, ALA.
1968-069	MORRIS, DANNY WALKE	OLD ADD: 216 WILSON STREET, GREENVILLE KY 42345
1937-079	MORRIS, DOYT THEODORE	D. JULY 4, 1984, GASTONIA, N.C.
1999-133	MORRIS, JAMES SAMUEL	1031 HART ROAD, MCKINNEY TX 75069
1986-108	MORRIS, JOHN DANIEL	2645 ELM DRIVE, NORTH BELLMORE NY 11710
1977-096	MORRIS, JOHN SCOTT 'JACK'	7993 100TH STREET NORTH, SAINT PAUL MN 55110
1966-065	MORRIS, JOHN WALLACE	5538 E. PARADISE LN, SCOTTSDALE AZ 85254
1997-119	MORRIS, MATTHEW CHRISTIAN	397 OLD JUPITER BEACH ROAD, JUPITER FL 33477
1922-100	MORRIS, WALTER EDWARD	D. MARCH 3, 1932, CENTURY, FLA.
1999-134	MORRIS, WARREN RANDALL	401 WEST DEM DRIVE, ALEXANDRIA LA 71303
1988-097	MORRIS, WILLIAM HAROLD 'HAL'	C/O J. CLARK, 9145 N. HAMLIN AVENUE, PORTLAND OR 97217
1977-097	MORRISON, JAMES FOREST	8715 11TH AVENUE PLACE NW, BRADENTON FL 34209
1920-087	MORRISON, JOHN DEWEY	D. MARCH 20, 1966, LEXINGTON, KY.
1921-070	MORRISON, PHILIP MELVIN	D. JANUARY 18, 1955, LEXINGTON, KY.
1927-066	MORRISON, WALTER GUY 'GUY'	D. AUGUST 14, 1934, GRAND RAPIDS, MICH.
1932-056	MORRISSEY, JOSEPH ANSELM 'JO-JO'	D. MAY 2, 1950, WORCESTER, MASS.
2005-127	MORSE, MICHAEL JOHN	417 NW 97TH AVENUE, FORT LAUDERDALE FL 33324
1929-075	MORSE, NEWELL OBEDIAH 'BUD'	D. APRIL 6, 1987, SPARKS, NEV.
1969-119	MORTON, CARL WENDLE	D. APRIL 12, 1983, TULSA, OKLA.
1954-070	MORTON, GUY	567 FERNDALE AVENUE, VERMILION OH 44089
1991-127	MORTON, KEVIN JOSEPH	26 GLEN AVENUE, NORWALK CT 06850
1961-077	MORTON, WYCLIFFE NATHAN 'BUBBA'	D. JANUARY 14, 2006, SEATTLE, WASH.
1954-071	MORYN, WALTER JOSEPH 'MOOSE'	D. JULY 21, 1996, WINFIELD, ILL.
1965-078	MOSCHITTO, ROSAIRO ALLEN 'ROSS'	PO BOX 61, TUCKAHOE NY 10707
1980-093	MOSEBY, LLOYD ANTHONY	9140 LOS LAGOS CIRCLE SOUTH, GRANITE BAY CA 95746
2006-127	MOSELEY, DUSTIN AARON	3500 PINE STREET, TEXARKANA TX 75503
1937-080	MOSER, ARNOLD ROBERT	D. AUGUST 15, 2002, HOUSTON, TEXAS
1965-079	MOSES, GERALD BRAHEEN 'JERRY'	9 RAYMOND COURT, GEORGETOWN MA 01833
1982-086	MOSES, JOHN WILLIAM	2133 E. LAKE SAMMAMISH PLACE SE, ISSAQUAH WA 98029
1935-075	MOSES, WALLACE	D. OCTOBER 10, 1990, VALDOSTA, GA.
1977-098	MOSKAU, PAUL RICHARD	5041 NORTH APACHE HILLS TRAIL, TUCSON AZ 85750
1929-076	MOSOLF, JAMES FREDERICK	D. DECEMBER 28, 1979, DALLAS, ORE.
1996-133	MOSQUERA, JULIO ALBERTO	2168 GREENBRIAR BLVD, CLEARWATER FL 33763
1934-076	MOSS, CHARLES CROSBY	D. OCTOBER 9, 1991, MERIDIAN, MISS.
1930-055	MOSS, CHARLES MALCOLM 'MAL'	D. FEBRUARY 5, 1983, SAVANNAH, GA.
2001-125	MOSS, DAMIAN JOSEPH	OLD ADD: SADLER AUSTRALIA
1942-070	MOSS, HOWARD GLENN	D. MAY 7, 1989, BALTIMORE, MD.
1946-076	MOSS, JOHN LESTER 'LES'	420 TULLIS AVENUE, LONGWOOD FL 32750
1926-059	MOSS, RAYMOND EARL	D. AUGUST 9, 1998, CHATTANOOGA, TENN.
1954-072	MOSSI, DONALD LOUIS	23250 CANYON LANE, CALDWELL ID 83607
1951-069	MOSSOR, EARL DALTON	D. DECEMBER 29, 1988, BATAVIA, OHIO
1991-128	MOTA, ANDRES ALBERTO	1875 CLUB DRIVE, POMONA CA 91768
2000-119	MOTA, DANIEL	6436 LARIBA WAY, LOS ANGELES CA 90042
1999-135	MOTA, GUILLERMO	OLD ADD: SAN PEDRO DE MACORIS DOM REP
1991-129	MOTA, JOSE MANUEL (MATOS)	OLD ADD: 2040 COBBLEFIELD WAY, GLENDORA CA 91740
1962-094	MOTA, MANUEL RAFAEL	19058 EAST LACROSSE STREET, GLENDORA CA 91741
1981-087	MOTLEY, DARRYL DEWAYNE	2543 NORTH ALAFAYA TRAIL #81, ORLANDO FL 32826
1945-072	MOTT, ELISHA MATTHEW 'BITSY'	D. FEBRUARY 24, 2001, BRANDON, FLA.
1996-134	MOTTOLA, CHARLES EDWARD 'CHAD'	6479 LAKE PEMBROKE PLACE, ORLANDO FL 32829
1967-076	MOTTON, CURTELL HOWARD	19903 QUIET VALLEY COURT, PARKTON MD 21120
1946-077	MOULDER, GLEN HUBERT	D. NOVEMBER 27, 1994, DECATUR, GA.
2003-115	MOUNCE, ANTHONY DAVID	3812 WEST 19TH COURT, KENNEWICK WA 99338
1994-077	MOUTON, JAMES RALEIGH	3490 ASTORIA STREET, SACRAMENTO CA 95838
1995-145	MOUTON, LYLE JOSEPH	4101 AUSTIN WAY, PALM HARBOR FL 34685
1933-044	MOWRY, JOSEPH ALOYSIUS	D. FEBRUARY 9, 1994, ST.LOUIS, MO.
1986-109	MOYER, JAMIE	2550 40TH AVENUE WEST, SEATTLE WA 98199
2006-128	MOYLAN, PETER MICHAEL	OLD ADD: ATTADALE AUSTRALIA
1954-073	MROZINSKI, RONALD FRANK	D. OCTOBER 19, 2005, WASHINGTON, N.J.
1963-083	MUDROCK, PHILIP RAY	2548 EAST 6600 SOUTH, SALT LAKE CITY UT 84121
1920-088	MUELLER, CLARENCE FRANCIS 'HEINIE'	D. JANUARY 23, 1975, DESOTO, MO.
1948-074	MUELLER, DONALD FREDERICK	12102 AUTUMN LAKES DRIVE, MARYLAND HEIGHTS MO 63043
1938-068	MUELLER, EMMETT JEROME 'HEINIE'	D. OCTOBER 3, 1986, ORLANDO, FLA.
1950-070	MUELLER, JOSEPH GORDON 'GORDY'	D. SEPTEMBER 7, 2006, BALTIMORE, MD.
1941-076	MUELLER, LESLIE CLYDE	PO BOX 294, MILLSTADT IL 62260
1935-076	MUELLER, RAY COLEMAN	D. JUNE 29, 1994, LOWER PAXTON TWP., PA.
1922-101	MUELLER, WALTER JOHN	D. AUGUST 16, 1971, ST. LOUIS, MO.
1978-087	MUELLER, WILLARD LAWRENCE 'WILLIE'	2320 TOLBERT LANE, WEST BEND WI 53090
1942-071	MUELLER, WILLIAM LAWRENCE	D. OCTOBER 24, 2001, GLENVIEW, ILL.
1996-135	MUELLER, WILLIAM RICHARD	11868 CHARLEMAGNE DRIVE, MARYLAND HEIGHTS MO 63043
1957-059	MUFFETT, BILLY ARNOLD	1145 FINKS HIDEAWAY ROAD, MONROE LA 71203
1924-083	MUICH, IGNATIUS ANDREW	D. JULY 2, 1993, ST. LOUIS, MO.
1951-070	MUIR, JOSEPH ALLEN	D. JUNE 25, 1980, BALTIMORE, MD.
2006-129	MUJICA, EDWARD JOSE	OLD ADD: YAGUA VENEZ
1935-077	MULCAHY, HUGH NOYES	D. OCTOBER 19, 2001, ALIQUIPPA, PA.
2000-120	MULDER, MARK ALAN	OLD ADD: 12095 EAST CHOLLA STREET, SCOTTSDALE AZ 85260
1986-110	MULHOLLAND, TERENCE JOHN	4011 EAST CLAREMONT STREET, PARADISE VALLEY AZ 85253
1930-056	MULLEAVY, GREGORY THOMAS	D. FEBRUARY 1, 1980, ARCADIA, CALIF.
1944-095	MULLEN, FORD PARKER	1841 TROSPER ROAD SW #8, TUMWATER WA 98512
2000-121	MULLEN, KENNETH SCOTT 'SCOTT'	96 WADE HAMPTON, BEAUFORT SC 29902
1920-089	MULLEN, WILLIAM JOHN	D. MAY 4, 1971, ST. LOUIS, MO.
1933-045	MULLER, FREDERICK WILLIAM	D. OCTOBER 20, 1976, DAVIS, CALIF.

1934-077 MULLIGAN, JOSEPH IGNATIUS ....D. JUNE 5, 1986, WEST ROXBURY, MASS.
1941-077 MULLIGAN, RICHARD CHARLES ....D. DECEMBER 15, 1992, VICTORIA, TEXAS
1996-136 MULLIGAN, SEAN PATRICK ....24474 EASTGATE DRIVE, DIAMOND BAR CA 91765
1940-065 MULLIN, PATRICK JOSEPH ....D. AUGUST 14, 1999, BROWNSVILLE, PA.
1977-099 MULLINIKS, STEVEN RANCE 'RANCE'..................2614 SOUTH PEPPERTREE, VISALIA CA 93277
1980-094 MULLINS, FRANCIS JOSEPH ....9226 RITENOUR COURT, LONE TREE CO 80124
1998-133 MULLINS, GREGORY E. ....PO BOX 443, FLORAHOME FL 32140
1921-071 MULRENAN, DOMINICK JOSEPH ....D. JULY 27, 1964, MELROSE, MASS.
1930-057 MULRONEY, FRANCIS JOSEPH ....D. NOVEMBER 11, 1985, ABERDEEN, WASH.
1974-092 MUMPHREY, JERRY WAYNE ....7709 FM 850, TYLER TX 75705
1937-081 MUNCRIEF, ROBERT CLEVELAND..........................D. FEBRUARY 6, 1996, DUNCANVILLE, TEXAS
1943-096 MUNGER, GEORGE DAVID 'RED'..........................D. JULY 23, 1996, HOUSTON, TEXAS
1931-061 MUNGO, VAN LINGLE ....D. FEBRUARY 12, 1985, PAGELAND, S.C.
1971-073 MUNIZ, MANUEL..PO BOX 6301, CAGUAS PR 00625
1980-095 MUNNINGHOFF, SCOTT ANDREW........................866 LAVERTY LANE, CINCINNATI OH 45230
1934-078 MUNNS, LESLIE ERNEST.......................................D. FEBRUARY 28, 1997, CEDAR RAPIDS, IOWA
2004-141 MUNOZ, ARNALDO RAFEL....................................OLD ADD: MAO DOM REP
1996-137 MUNOZ, JOSE LUIS ....OLD ADD: YABUCOA PR 00767
1995-146 MUNOZ, JUAN OSCAR 'OSCAR' ....14161 LEANING PINE DRIVE, HIALEAH FL 33014
1989-087 MUNOZ, MICHAEL ANTHONY ....1000 CARROLL MEADOWS COURT, SOUTHLAKE TX 76092
1995-147 MUNOZ, NOE...OLD ADD: LOS MOCHIS SINOLOA MEXICO
1990-112 MUNOZ, PEDRO JAVIER ....OLD ADD: RIOCANA STREET 10-1-5, PONCE PR 00731
1993-130 MUNOZ, ROBERTO...OLD ADD: 227 TOUCHDOWN DRIVE, IRVING TX 75063
1999-136 MUNRO, PETER DANIEL ....4025 GRAMERCY STREET, HOUSTON TX 77025
2000-122 MUNSON, ERIC WALTER ....1574 WEST YELLOWSTONE WAY, CHANDLER AZ 85248
1925-076 MUNSON, JOSEPH MARTIN NAPOLEON ....D. FEBRUARY 24, 1991, DREXEL HILL, PA.
1969-120 MUNSON, THURMAN LEE.....................................D. AUGUST 2, 1979, AKRON-CANTON AIRPORT, OHIO
2005-128 MUNTER, SCOTT MICHAEL ....13024 JESSEE AVENUE, OMAHA NE 68164
1978-088 MURA, STEPHEN ANDREW ....31892 OLD OAK ROAD, TRABUCO CANYON CA 92679
1964-076 MURAKAMI, MASANORI...1-4-15-1506, NISHO OHI SHINAGAWA-KU, TOKYO 140-0015 JAPAN
1965-080 MURCER, BOBBY RAY ....77153 CALLE MAZATLAN, LAQUINTA CA 92253
1956-062 MURFF, JOHN ROBERT 'RED' ....5401 HOLLYTREE DRIVE #1301, TYLER TX 75703
1976-067 MURPHY, DALE BRIAN ....CHURCH SECURITIES CORP., 605 CLAIREMONT AVENUE, DECATUR GA 30030
1960-073 MURPHY, DANIEL FRANCIS..................................5030 CHAMPION BLVD #6226, BOCA RATON FL 33496
1989-088 MURPHY, DANIEL LEE ....19661 SYMERON ROAD, APPLE VALLEY CA 92307
2006-130 MURPHY, DAVID MATTHEW ....OLD ADD: SPRING TX
2004-142 MURPHY, DONALD REX...OLD ADD: ANAHEIM CA
1978-089 MURPHY, DWAYNE KEITH ....1811 SOUTH KAREN DRIVE, CHANDLER AZ 85248
1942-072 MURPHY, EDWARD JEROME.................................D. DECEMBER 10, 1991, JOLIET, ILL.
1932-057 MURPHY, JOHN JOSEPH ....D. JANUARY 14, 1970, NEW YORK, N.Y.
1954-074 MURPHY, RICHARD LEE ....10200 FAIRMOUNT, AVON IN 46123
1985-079 MURPHY, ROBERT ALBERT ....PO BOX 1996, STUART FL 34995
1968-070 MURPHY, THOMAS ANDREW ....1175 KELLER WAY, LAGUNA BEACH CA 92651
2006-131 MURPHY, THOMAS CHRISTIAN............................221 SE FIRST AVENUE, BOYNTON BEACH FL 33435
1931-062 MURPHY, WALTER JOSEPH..................................D. MARCH 23, 1976, HOUSTON, TEXAS
1966-066 MURPHY, WILLIAM EUGENE ....5309 66TH AVENUE COURT WEST, UNIVERSITY PLACE WA 98467
1923-096 MURRAY, ANTHONY JOHN ....D. MARCH 19, 1974, CHICAGO, ILL.
1999-137 MURRAY, CALVIN DUANE ....17434 COURTNEY PINE CIRCLE, SPRING TX 77379
1974-093 MURRAY, DALE ALBERT ....RR 2 BOX 1850, YORKTOWN TX 78164
1999-138 MURRAY, DANIEL SAFFLE ....5412 SANTA CATALINA AVENUE, GARDEN GROVE CA 92845
1977-100 MURRAY, EDDIE CLARENCE ....26911 TRIUMPH AVENUE, CANYON COUNTRY CA 91351
1922-102 MURRAY, GEORGE KING.....................................D. OCTOBER 18, 1955, MEMPHIS, TENN.
1996-138 MURRAY, GLENN EVERETT.................................OLD ADD: END STREET BOX 189, MANNING SC 29101
1997-120 MURRAY, HEATH ROBERTSON ....2605 GREENLAWN DRIVE, TROY OH 45373
1922-103 MURRAY, JAMES FRANCIS..................................D. JULY 15, 1973, NEW YORK , N.Y.
1950-071 MURRAY, JOSEPH AMBROSE...............................D. OCTOBER 19, 2001, SAN CLEMENTE, CALIF.
1936-063 MURRAY, JOSEPH AMBROSE 'AMBY'..................D. FEBRUARY 6, 1997, PORT SALERNO, FLA.
1974-094 MURRAY, LARRY ....3200 ROUND HILL DRIVE, HAYWOOD CA 94562
1995-148 MURRAY, MATTHEW MICHAEL.............................109 GREENWOOD AVENUE, SWAMPSCOTT MA 01907
1948-075 MURRAY, RAYMOND LEE ....D. APRIL 9, 2003, FORT WORTH, TEXAS
1980-096 MURRAY, RICHARD DALE....................................435 EAST 108TH ST, LOS ANGELES CA 90061
1923-097 MURRAY, ROBERT HAYES ....D. JANUARY 4, 1979, NASHUA, N.H.
1963-084 MURRELL, IVAN AUGUSTE..................................D. OCTOBER 8, 2006, STUART, FLA.
1941-078 MURTAUGH, DANIEL EDWARD ....D. DECEMBER 2, 1976, CHESTER PA.
2005-129 MURTON, MATTHEW HENRY...............................OLD ADD: 2304 SILVER PALM DRIVE, KISSIMMEE FL 34747
1969-121 MUSER, ANTHONY JOSEPH ....11222 MARTHA ANN DR, LOS ALAMITOS CA 90720
1965-081 MUSGRAVES, DENNIS EUGENE...........................RR FOUR, CENTRALIA MO 65240
1941-079 MUSIAL, STANLEY FRANK...................................85 TRENT DRIVE, LADUE MO 63124
1986-111 MUSSELMAN, JEFFREY JOSEPH ....1842 PORT TIFFIN PLACE, NEWPORT BEACH CA 92660
1982-087 MUSSELMAN, RALPH RICHARD ....5313 AUTUMN DR, WILMINGTON NC 28401
1932-058 MUSSER, WILLIAM DANIEL 'DANNY'...................D. MARCH 2, 2000, UPPER SANDUSKY, OHIO
1944-096 MUSSILL, BERNARD JAMES 'BARNEY'.................912 MOORLAND DRIVE, GROSSE POINTE WOODS MI 48236
1991-130 MUSSINA, MICHAEL COLE ....1302 SPRUCE STREET, MONTOURSVILLE PA 17754
1940-066 MUSTAIKIS, ALEXANDER DOMINICK ....D. JANUARY 17, 1970, SCRANTON, PA.
1991-131 MUTIS, JEFFREY THOMAS ....630 EAST WYOMING STREET, ALLENTOWN PA 18103
1938-069 MYATT, GEORGE EDWARD ....D. SEPTEMBER 14, 2000, ALTAMONTE SPRINGS, FLA.
1920-090 MYATT, GLENN CALVIN.......................................D. AUGUST 9, 1969, HOUSTON, TEXAS
1925-077 MYER, CHARLES SOLOMON 'BUDDY'...................D. OCTOBER 31, 1974, BATON ROUGE, LA.
2002-125 MYERS, BRETT ALLEN ....2 WATERSMEET CIRCLE, GLEN MILLS PA 19342
1987-102 MYERS, GREGORY RICHARD ....2525 CROSS STREET, RIVERSIDE CA 92503
1996-139 MYERS, JAMES XAVIER ....OLD ADD: 2705 STANBERRY DRIVE, SHREVEPORT LA 71118
1938-070 MYERS, LINNWOOD LINCOLN ....D. JANUARY 19, 2000, HARRISBURG, PA.
1995-149 MYERS, MICHAEL STANLEY ....337 HIGH RIDGE WAY, CASTLE ROCK CO 80086
1985-080 MYERS, RANDALL KIRK......................................15525 NE CAPLES ROAD, BRUSH PRAIRIE WA 98606
1956-063 MYERS, RICHARD..521 PONY TRAIL, MOUNT SHASTA CA 96067
1996-140 MYERS, RODERICK DEMOND..............................1816 SOUTH THIRD, CONROE TX 77301

1996-141	MYERS, RODNEY LUTHER	OLD ADD: 1422 EAST SHANNON STREET, CHANDLER AZ 85225
1935-078	MYERS, WILLIAM HARRISON	D. APRIL 10, 1995, CARLISLE, PA.
1999-139	MYETTE, AARON KENNETH	14277 101A AVENUE SURREY BC, V0B 2G2 CANADA
1976-068	MYRICK, ROBERT HOWARD	22 TROON CIRCLE, HATTIESBURG MS 39401
2005-130	MYROW, BRIAN SHAWN	809 SILVERBROOK DRIVE, FORT WORTH TX 76179

N

1990-113	NABHOLZ, CHRISTOPHER WILLIAM	602 KENWOOD DRIVE, POTTSVILLE PA 17901
2000-123	NADY, XAVIER D.	1195 LOYOLA DRIVE, SALINAS CA 93901
1990-114	NAEHRING, TIMOTHY JAMES	7300 PINEHURST DRIVE, CINCINNATI OH 45244
1939-079	NAGEL, WILLIAM TAYLOR	D. OCTOBER 8, 1981, FREEHOLD, N.J.
1968-071	NAGELSON, RUSSELL CHARLES 'RUSTY'	4 CARRIAGE COURT, LITTLE ROCK AR 72211
2004-143	NAGEOTTE, CLINTON SCOTT	4703 SPOKANE AVENUE #1, CLEVELAND OH 44144
1990-115	NAGY, CHARLES HARRISON	75 DENISE TERRACE, FAIRFIELD CT 06430
1969-122	NAGY, MICHAEL TIMOTHY	8 INDIAN TRAIL, BRONX NY 10465
1947-064	NAGY, STEPHEN	9450 NORTH 94TH PLACE #102, SCOTTSDALE AZ 85258
1938-071	NAHEM, SAMUEL RALPH	D. APRIL 19, 2004, BERKELEY, CALIF.
1976-069	NAHORODNY, WILLIAM GERARD	1948 RAINBOW DRIVE, CLEARWATER FL 33765
2003-116	NAKAMURA, MICHAEL YOSHIHIDE	OLD ADD: FERNFREE GULLY AUSTRALIA
2005-131	NAKAMURA, NORIHIRO	OLD ADD: OSAKA JAPAN
1936-064	NAKTENIS, PETER ERNEST	5200 NORTH OCEAN DRIVE #19D, SINGER ISLAND FL 33404
1924-084	NALEWAY, FRANK	D. JANUARY 28, 1949, CHICAGO, ILL.
2002-126	NANCE, JOSEPH SHANE 'SHANE'	3403 HARBOUR BREEZE LANE, PEARLAND TX 77584
1949-057	NAPLES, ALOYSIUS FRANCIS	99 NICKERSON ROAD, ORLEANS MA 02653
1965-082	NAPOLEON, DANIEL	D. APRIL 26, 2003, TRENTON, N.J.
2006-132	NAPOLI, MICHAEL ANTHONY	OLD ADD: COOPER CITY FL
1951-071	NARAGON, HAROLD RICHARD	1521 HAGEY DRIVE, BARBERTON OH 44203
1956-064	NARANJO, LAZARO RAMON GONZALO 'GONZALO'	6541 SW 25TH TERRACE, MIAMI FL 33155
1954-075	NARLESKI, RAYMOND EDMOND	1183 CHEWS LANDING ROAD, LAUREL SPRINGS NJ 08021
1929-077	NARLESKI, WILLIAM EDWARD	D. JULY 22, 1964, LAUREL SPRINGS, N.J.
1979-076	NARRON, JERRY AUSTIN	206 FRIENDSWOOD DRIVE, GOLDSBORO NC 27530
2004-144	NARRON, SAMUEL FRANKLIN	101 MILL PLACE, GOLDSBORO NC 27530
1935-079	NARRON, SAMUEL WOODY	D. DECEMBER 31, 1996, RALEIGH, N.C.
1963-085	NARUM, LESLIE FERDINAND 'BUSTER'	D. MAY 17, 2004, CLEARWATER, FLA.
2006-133	NARVESON, CHRISTOPHER GREGG	PO BOX 907, SKYLAND NC 28776
1967-077	NASH, CHARLES FRANCIS 'COTTON'	600 SUMMERSHADE CIR, LEXINGTON KY 40502
1966-067	NASH, JAMES EDWIN	ROSWELL STREET BAPTIST CHURCH, 774 ROSWELL STREET NE, MARIETTA GA 30060
1978-090	NASTU, PHILIP	119 AUSTIN ST, BRIDGEPORT CT 06604
1992-091	NATAL, ROBERT MARCEL	3913 COCKRILL DRIVE, MCKINNEY TX 75070
1999-140	NATHAN, JOSEPH MICHAEL	4360 SOUTH OLEANDER DRIVE, CHANDLER AZ 85248
2000-124	NATION, JOSEPH PAUL 'JOEY'	7009 NORTH ROFF AVENUE, OKLAHOMA CITY OK 73116
1953-062	NATON, PETER ALPHONSUS	4136 SPLIT ROCK RD, CAMILLUS NY 13031
1996-142	NAULTY, DANIEL DONOVAN	17811 BEARD LANE, HUNTINGTON BEACH CA 92647
2004-145	NAVARRO, DIONER FAVIAU	OLD ADD: CARACAS VENEZ
1989-089	NAVARRO, JAIME	8100 OAK PARK ROAD, ORLANDO FL 32819
1962-095	NAVARRO, JULIO VENTURA	CALLE 3, BLOQUE 10, #32 SANTA ROSA, BAYAMON PR 00619
1993-131	NAVARRO, NORBERTO RODRIGUEZ 'TITO'	556 CALLE CREUZ, SAN JUAN PR 00923
2006-134	NAVARRO, OSWALDO RAMSES	OLD ADD: MARACAY VENEZ
1942-073	NAYLOR, EARL EUGENE	D. JANUARY 16, 1990, WINTER HAVEN, FLA.
1939-080	NAYMICK, MICHAEL JOHN	D. OCTOBER 12, 2005, STOCKTON, CALIF.
1991-132	NEAGLE, DENNIS EDWARD	945 WAUGH CHAPEL ROAD, GAMBRILLS MD 80465
2001-126	NEAL, BLAINE	256 DOWDY DRIVE, GIBBSTOWN NJ 08027
1956-065	NEAL, CHARLES LENARD	D. NOVEMBER 10, 1996, DALLAS, TEXAS
1952-078	NECCIAI, RONALD ANDREW	2024 HIGHVIEW, BELLE VERNON PA 15012
1992-092	NEEL, TROY LEE	PO BOX 1582, EL CAMPO TX 77437
1957-060	NEEMAN, CALVIN AMANDUS	93 CHAMPAGNE, LAKE SAINT LOUIS MO 63367
1952-079	NEGRAY, RONALD ALVIN	587 WEST NIMISILA ROAD, AKRON OH 44319
1969-123	NEIBAUER, GARY WAYNE	146 DELTA AVENUE, BISMARCK ND 58504
1990-116	NEIDLINGER, JAMES LLEWELLYN	139 SUNSET DRIVE, BURLINGTON VT 05408
1960-074	NEIGER, ALVIN EDWARD	213 PINEHURST RD, WILMINGTON DE 19803
1939-081	NEIGHBORS, ROBERT OTIS	D. AUGUST 8, 1952, NORTH KOREA
1998-134	NEILL, MICHAEL ROBERT	17 CAPEMAY POINTE, GREENSBORO NC 27455
1946-078	NEILL, THOMAS WHITE	D. SEPTEMBER 22, 1980, HOUSTON, TEXAS
1920-091	NEIS, BERNARD EDMUND	D. NOVEMBER 29, 1972, INVERNESS, FLA.
1929-078	NEKOLA, FRANCIS JOSEPH 'BOTS'	D. MARCH 11, 1987, ROCKVILLE CENTRE, N.Y.
2002-127	NELSON, BRYANT LAWRENCE	OLD ADD: 502 BYRD STREET, CROSSETT AR 71635
1968-072	NELSON, DAVID EARL	12213 CLUBHOUSE DRIVE, BRADENTON FL 34202
1935-080	NELSON, GEORGE EMMETT	D. AUGUST 25, 1967, SIOUX FALLS, S.D.
1949-058	NELSON, GLENN RICHARD 'ROCKY'	D. OCTOBER 31, 2006, PORTSMOUTH, OHIO
1970-100	NELSON, JAMES LORIN	D. AUGUST 22, 2004, SACRAMENTO, CALIF.
1983-102	NELSON, JAMES VICTOR	OLD ADD: 18411 PLUMMER STREET, NORTHRIDGE CA 91325
1992-093	NELSON, JEFFREY ALLAN	323 289TH PLACE NE, CARNATION WA 98014
2006-135	NELSON, JOHN CLARK	OLD ADD: DENTON TX
2001-127	NELSON, JOSEPH GEORGE	1816 SAN ANTONIO, ALAMEDA CA 94501
1930-058	NELSON, LYNN BERNARD	D. FEBRUARY 15, 1955, KANSAS CITY, MO.
1960-075	NELSON, MELVIN FREDERICK	27420 FISHER ST, HIGHLAND CA 92346
1983-103	NELSON, RICKY LEE	16441 SOUTH 46TH PLACE, PHOENIX AZ 85048
1986-112	NELSON, ROBERT AUGUSTUS	312 ALTA VISTA AVENUE, SOUTH PASADENA CA 91030
1955-085	NELSON, ROBERT SIDNEY	10248 SANDY WILLOWS COVE, SANDY UT 84070
1967-078	NELSON, ROGER EUGENE	OLD ADD: 14650 SANTA FE TRAIL, LENEXA KS 66118
1945-073	NELSON, TOM COUSINEAU	D. SEPTEMBER 24, 1973, SAN DIEGO, CALIF.
1981-088	NELSON, WAYLAND EUGENE 'GENE'	PO BOX 1197, SAN ANTONIO FL 33576
1963-086	NEN, RICHARD LEROY	6152 KILLARNEY AVENUE, GARDEN GROVE CA 92845
1993-132	NEN, ROBERT ALLEN 'ROBB'	48 VIA BARCAZA, COTO DE CAZA CA 92679

2006-136	NESHEK, PATRICK J.	3632 DUNBAR KNOLL, BROOKLYN PARK MN 55443
1967-079	NETTLES, GRAIG	OLD ADD: 11217 CARMEL CREEK ROAD #2, SAN DIEGO CA 92130
1970-101	NETTLES, JAMES WILLIAM	4632 DARIEN DR, TACOMA WA 98407
1974-095	NETTLES, MORRIS	551 1/2 SAN JUAN, VENICE CA 90291
2003-117	NEU, MICHAEL DAVID	406 FRAGA COURT, MARTINEZ CA 94553
1925-078	NEUBAUER, HAROLD CHARLES	D. SEPTEMBER 9, 1949, PROVIDENCE, R.I.
2001-128	NEUGEBAUER, NICKOLAS DONALD	101 SOUTH SAHUARO DRIVE, GILBERT AZ 85233
1972-078	NEUMEIER, DANIEL GEORGE	N2635 CITY HIGHWAY U, LODI WI 53555
1925-079	NEUN, JOHN HENRY	D. MARCH 28, 1990, BALTIMORE, MD.
1950-072	NEVEL, ERNIE WYRE	D. JULY 10, 1988, SPRINGFIELD, MO.
1926-060	NEVERS, ERNEST ALONZO	D. MAY 3, 1976, SAN RAFAEL, CALIF.
1995-150	NEVIN, PHIL JOSEPH	18795 HERITAGE DRIVE, POWAY CA 92064
1949-059	NEWCOMBE, DONALD	2555 PLAZA DE AMO #H, TORRANCE CA 90503
1987-103	NEWELL, THOMAS DEAN	9525 CORDOBA BLVD, SPARKS NV 89441
1993-133	NEWFIELD, MARC ALEXANDER	5591 SELKIRK DRIVE, HUNTINGTON BEACH CA 92649
1999-141	NEWHAN, DAVID MATTHEW	2678 HARVEST CREST LANE, CORONA CA 92881
1972-079	NEWHAUSER, DONALD LOUIS	321 SHERYL DR, DELTONA FL 32738
1939-082	NEWHOUSER, HAROLD 'HAL'	D. NOVEMBER 10, 1998, DETROIT, MICH.
1934-079	NEWKIRK, FLOYD ELMO	D. APRIL 15, 1976, CLAYTON, MO.
1940-067	NEWLIN, MAURICE MILTON	D. AUGUST 14, 1978, HOUSTON, TEXAS
1999-142	NEWMAN, ALAN SPENCER	24 RICE LANE, DRY PRONG LA 71423
1985-081	NEWMAN, ALBERT DWAYNE	3676 WYNDCREST DRIVE, ELKO MN 55020
1962-096	NEWMAN, FREDERICK WILLIAM	D. JUNE 24, 1987, FRAMINGHAM, MASS.
1976-070	NEWMAN, JEFFREY LYNN	10133 NORTH 103RD STREET, SCOTTSDALE AZ 85258
1971-074	NEWMAN, RAYMOND FRANCIS	1260 MALIBU LANE, MYRTLE BEACH SC 29577
1929-079	NEWSOM, NORMAN LOUIS 'BOBO'	D. DECEMBER 7, 1962, ORLANDO, FLA.
1941-080	NEWSOME, HEBER HAMPTON 'DICK'	D. DECEMBER 15, 1965, AHOSKIE, N.C.
1935-081	NEWSOME, LAMAR ASHBY 'SKEETER'	D. AUGUST 31, 1989, COLUMBUS, GA.
1991-133	NEWSON, WARREN DALE	1839 ALSACE AVENUE, LOS ANGELES CA 90019
1946-079	NIARHOS, CONSTANTINE GREGORY 'GUS'	D. DECEMBER 29, 2004, HARRISONBURG, VA.
1952-080	NICHOLAS, DONALD LEIGH	12311 CHASE, GARDEN GROVE CA 92645
1986-113	NICHOLS, CARL EDWARD	OLD ADD: 4351 SOUTH VAN NESS AVE, LOS ANGELES CA 90062
1951-072	NICHOLS, CHESTER RAYMOND 'CHET'	D. MARCH 27, 1995, LINCOLN, R.I.
1926-061	NICHOLS, CHESTER RAYMOND, SR.	D. JULY 11, 1982, PAWTUCKET, R.I.
1958-067	NICHOLS, DOLAN LEVON	D. NOVEMBER 20, 1969, TUPELO, MISS.
1988-098	NICHOLS, RODNEY LEA	1570 ELK TRAIL, HELENA MT 59601
1944-097	NICHOLS, ROY	D. APRIL 3, 2002, HOT SPRINGS, ARK.
1980-097	NICHOLS, THOMAS REID 'REID'	OLD ADD: 1610 SPRING CREEK COURT, KELLER TX 76248
1960-076	NICHOLSON, DAVID LAWRENCE	527 SOUTH SPRINGINGSGUTH ROAD, SCHAUMBURG IL 60193
2000-125	NICHOLSON, KEVIN RONALD	OLD ADD: SURREY BRITISH COLUMBIA
1936-065	NICHOLSON, WILLIAM BECK	D. MARCH 8, 1996, CHESTERTOWN, MD.
1995-151	NICHTING, CHRISTOPHER THOMAS	7151 GRACELY DRIVE, CINCINNATI OH 45233
2000-126	NICKLE, DOUGLAS ALAN	19440 VICTORIA COURT, SONOMA CA 95476
1978-091	NICOSIA, STEVEN RICHARD	1401 NW 103RD AVENUE, PLANTATION FL 33322
1921-073	NIEBERGALL, CHARLES ARTHUR 'NIG'	D. AUGUST 29, 1982, HOLIDAY, FLA.
1992-094	NIED, DAVID GLEN	PO BOX 836, GRAND PRAIRIE TX 75050
1981-089	NIEDENFUER, THOMAS EDWARD	10212 MILLPORT DRIVE, TAMPA FL 33626
1925-080	NIEHAUS, ALBERT BERNARD	D. OCTOBER 14, 1931, CINCINNATI, OHIO
1967-080	NIEKRO, JOSEPH FRANKLIN	D. OCTOBER 27, 2006, TAMPA, FLA.
2003-118	NIEKRO, LANCE JOSEPH	2707 FAIRWAY DRIVE SOUTH, PLANT CITY FL 33567
1964-077	NIEKRO, PHILIP HENRY	6382 NICHOLS ROAD, FLOWERY BRANCH GA 30542
1992-095	NIELSEN, GERALD ARTHUR 'JERRY'	4631 KEWANEE STREET, FAIR OAKS CA 95628
1986-114	NIELSEN, JEFFREY SCOTT 'SCOTT'	2898 VALLEY VIEW AVENUE, SALT LAKE CITY UT 84117
1949-060	NIELSEN, MILTON ROBERT	D. AUGUST 1, 2005, MANKATO, MINN.
1943-097	NIEMAN, ELMER LEROY 'BUTCH'	D. NOVEMBER 2, 1993, TOPEKA, KAN.
1951-073	NIEMAN, ROBERT CHARLES	D. MARCH 10, 1985, CORONA, CALIF.
1979-077	NIEMANN, RANDAL HAROLD	1585 SW HARBOUR ISLES CIRCLE, PORT SAINT LUCIE FL 34986
1943-098	NIEMES, JACOB LELAND 'JACK'	D. MARCH 4, 1966, HAMILTON, OHIO
1934-080	NIEMIEC, ALFRED JOSEPH	D. OCTOBER 29, 1995, KIRKLAND, WASH.
1964-078	NIESON, CHARLES BASSETT	14408 EDGEWOOD AVENUE, SAVAGE MN 55378
1984-083	NIETO, THOMAS ANDREW	22446 EAGLES WATCH DRIVE, LAND O'LAKES FL 34639
1921-072	NIETZKE, ERNEST FREDRICH	D. APRIL 27, 1977, SYLVANIA, OHIO
2006-137	NIEVE, FERNANDO ALEXIS	OLD ADD: SAN FELIPE VENEZ
1998-135	NIEVES, JOSE MIGUEL	OLD ADD: GUACARA VENEZUELA
1986-115	NIEVES, JUAN MANUEL	2280 DEERFIELD DRIVE, FORT MILL SC 29715
1992-096	NIEVES, MELVIN	PO BOX 87, SOUTHERN PINES NC 28388
2002-128	NIEVES, WILBERT	OLD ADD: SANTURCE PR 00936
1938-072	NIGGELING, JOHN ARNOLD	D. SEPTEMBER 16, 1963, LEMARS, IOWA
1992-097	NILSSON, DAVID WAYNE	OLD ADD: 601 S. MESA HILLS DRIVE #611, EL PASO TX 79912
1983-104	NIPPER, ALBERT SAMUEL	401 WHITE BIRCH VALLEY CT, CHESTERFIELD MO 63017
2005-132	NIPPERT, DUSTIN DAVID	51304 SWITZERLAND TWP. ROAD 185, BEALLSVILLE OH 43716
1962-097	NIPPERT, MERLIN LEE	1015 NORTH MICHIGAN STREET, MANGUM OK 73554
1961-078	NISCHWITZ, RONALD LEE	1390 CIMARRON CIRCLE, FAIRBORN OH 45324
1945-074	NITCHOLAS, OTHO JAMES	D. SEPTEMBER 11, 1986, MCKINNEY, TEXAS
1995-152	NITKOWSKI, CHRISTOPHER JOHN 'C.J.'	205 TOWNSEND LANE, ALPHARETTA GA 30004
2003-119	NIVAR, RAMON A.	OLD ADD: SAN CRISTOBAL DOM REP
2003-120	NIX, LAYNCE MICHAEL	1506 PRINCETON, MIDLAND TX 79701
1996-143	NIXON, CHRISTOPHER TROTMAN 'TROT'	1023 OCEAN RIDGE DRIVE, WILMINGTON NC 28405
1983-105	NIXON, OTIS JUNIOR	1304 MORNINGSIDE PARK DRIVE, ALPHARETTA GA 30022
1987-104	NIXON, ROBERT DONELL 'DONELL'	6401 CHADBOURNE WHY, CHADBOURN NC 28431
1957-061	NIXON, RUSSELL EUGENE	4265 TEE TEE LANE, LAS VEGAS NV 89129
1950-073	NIXON, WILLARD LEE	D. DECEMBER 10, 2000, ROME, GA.
1951-074	NOBLE, RAFAEL MIGUEL 'RAY'	D. MAY 9, 1998, BROOKLYN, N.Y.
1984-084	NOBOA, MILCIADES ARTURO 'JUNIOR'	401 EAST JEFFERSON, PHOENIX AZ 85004
1987-105	NOCE, PAUL DAVID	942 WEST MAUMEE, ADRIAN MI 49221
1985-082	NOKES, MATTHEW DODGE	OLD ADD: 16127 RIMSTONE LANE, SAN DIEGO CA 92127

1967-081	NOLAN, GARY LYNN	97 ACACIA AVENUE, OROVILLE CA 95666
1972-080	NOLAN, JOSEPH WILLIAM	9515 ALIX DR, MEHLVILLE MO 63123
2006-138	NOLASCO, CARLOS ENRIQUE	OLD ADD: RIALTO CA
1967-082	NOLD, RICHARD LOUIS	715 ATHENS STREET, SAN FRANCISCO CA 94112
1979-078	NOLES, DICKIE RAY	51 HIDDEN VALLEY ROAD, ASTON PA 19014
1987-106	NOLTE, ERIC CARL	682 SEVILLE DRIVE, HEMET CA 92343
1995-153	NOMO, HIDEO	OLD ADD: 10380 WILSHIRE BLVD #202, LOS ANGELES CA 90024
2002-129	NOMURA, TAKAHITO	OLD ADD: KOUCHI JAPAN
1933-046	NONNENKAMP, LEO WILLIAM 'RED'	D. DECEMBER 3, 2000, LITTLE ROCK, ARK.
1974-096	NORDBROOK, TIMOTHY CHARLES	14018 BLENHEIM ROAD NORTH, PHOENIX MD 21131
1976-071	NORDHAGEN, WAYNE OREN	25538 BAKER PLACE, STEVENSON RANCH CA 91381
1950-074	NOREN, IRVING ARNOLD	3154 CAMINO CREST, OCEANSIDE CA 92056
1969-124	NORIEGA, JOHN ALAN	D. SEPTEMBER 29, 2001, BOUNTIFUL, UTAH
1977-101	NORMAN, DANIEL EDMUND	2011 BORREGO DRIVE #27, BARSTOW CA 92311
1962-098	NORMAN, FREDIE ROBERT	5921 MONNETT ROAD, JULIAN NC 27283
1931-063	NORMAN, HENRY WILLIS PATRICK 'BILL'	D. APRIL 21, 1962, MILWAUKEE, WISC.
1995-154	NORMAN, LESLIE EUGENE	1401 DOGWOOD STREET, GREENWOOD MO 64034
1978-092	NORMAN, NELSON AUGUSTO	OLD ADD: 3282 FAIRFAX AVENUE NE, PALM BAY FL 32905
1977-102	NORRIS, JAMES FRANCIS	6375 OAK HOLLOW DRIVE, BURLESON TX 76028
1936-066	NORRIS, LEO JOHN	D. FEBRUARY 13, 1987, ZACHARY, LA.
1975-085	NORRIS, MICHAEL KELVIN	20910 LITTLE CANYON LANE, YORBA LINDA CA 92886
1971-075	NORTH, WILLIAM ALEX	5523 106TH AVENUE NE, KIRKLAND WA 98033
1942-074	NORTHEY, RONALD JAMES	D. APRIL 16, 1971, PITTSBURGH, PA.
1969-125	NORTHEY, SCOTT RICHARD	9920 BANKSIDE DRIVE, ROSWELL GA 30076
1964-079	NORTHRUP, JAMES THOMAS	29508 SOUTHFIELD ROAD, SOUTHFIELD MI 48076
1996-144	NORTON, GREGORY BLAKEMOOR	312 WINDCHIME DRIVE, DANVILLE CA 94506
2000-127	NORTON, PHILLIP DOUGLAS	677 COUNTY ROAD 3772, QUEEN CITY TX 75572
1972-081	NORTON, THOMAS JOHN	4900 SOUTHWOOD, SHEFFIELD LAKES OH 44054
1977-103	NORWOOD, WILLIE	225 GUNSMOKE DRIVE, DIAMOND BAR CA 91765
1989-090	NOSEK, RANDALL WILLIAM	15485 KNOBHILL DRIVE, LINDER MI 48451
1964-080	NOSSEK, JOSEPH RUDOLPH	630 SUNRISE DRIVE, AMHERST OH 44001
1960-077	NOTTEBART, DONALD EDWARD	219 ROUND POND ROAD, EAST WAKEFIELD NH 03830
1941-081	NOVIKOFF, LOUIE ALEXANDER	D. SEPTEMBER 30, 1970, SOUTH GATE, CALIF.
1990-117	NOVOA, RAFAEL ANGEL	320 WEST 47TH STREET, NEW YORK NY 10036
2004-146	NOVOA, ROBERTO	OLD ADD: SANTO DOMINGO DOM REP
1949-061	NOVOTNEY, RALPH JOSEPH	D. JULY 16, 1987, REDONDO BEACH, CALIF.
2002-130	NUNEZ, ABRAHAM	OLD ADD: HAINA DOM REP
1997-121	NUNEZ, ABRAHAM ORLANDO	OLD ADD: SANTO DOMINGO DOM REP
1982-088	NUNEZ, EDWIN	2481 EAST STEPHENS PLACE, CHANDLER AZ 85225
2004-147	NUNEZ, FRANKLIN	OLD ADD: RINCON DOM REP
1987-107	NUNEZ, JOSE	OLD ADD: MAURICIO BAEZ #40 VILLA JUANA, SANTO DOMINGO DOM REP
2001-129	NUNEZ, JOSE ANTONIO	OLD ADD: MONTECRISTI DOM REP
2005-133	NUNEZ, LEONEL	OLD ADD: BONAO DOM REP
1998-136	NUNEZ, VLADIMIR	18053 SW 139TH PLACE, MIAMI FL 33177
1959-060	NUNN, HOWARD RALPH	204 DEPOT STREET, PILOT MOUNTAIN NC 27041
1995-155	NUNNALLY, JONATHAN KEITH	1380 OLD QUARRY ROAD #2, RINGGOLD VA 24586
2000-128	NUNNARI, TALMADGE RAPHAEL	7101 JOY STREET #A8, PENSACOLA FL 32504
1944-098	NUXHALL, JOSEPH HENRY	5706 LINENWOOD LANE, FAIRFIELD OH 45014
1966-068	NYE, RICHARD RAYMOND	7510 WEST NORTH AVENUE, ELMWOOD PARK IL 60707
1997-122	NYE, RYAN CRAIG	637 WEST NEWBERRY ROAD, ALMA AR 72921
1982-089	NYMAN, CHRISTOPHER CURTIS	1700 HAPPY CREEK ROAD, FRONT ROYAL VA 22630
1968-073	NYMAN, GERALD SMITH	76 SUNDANCE LANE, AFTON WY 83110
1974-097	NYMAN, NYLS WALLACE REX	1304 4TH STREET, SUSANVILLE CA 96130

O

1934-081	OANA, HENRY KAUHANE 'PRINCE'	D. JUNE 19, 1976, AUSTIN, TEXAS
1970-102	OATES, JOHNNY LANE	D. DECEMBER 24, 2004, RICHMOND, VA.
1993-134	OBANDO, SHERMAN OMAR	7037 CORAL COVE DRIVE, ORLANDO FL 32818
1977-104	OBERKFELL, KENNETH RAY	1335 WEST WELSFORD DRIVE, SPRING TX 77386
2002-131	OBERMUELLER, WESLEY MITCHELL	2191 PORT TALBOT PLACE, CORALVILLE IA 52241
1979-079	OBERRY, PRESTON MICHAEL 'MIKE'	5647 LAKE TRACE DRIVE, HOOVER AL 35244
1978-093	OBRADOVICH, JAMES THOMAS	1101 SOUTH MIRAMAR NORTH #203, INDIALANTIC FL 32903
1985-083	OBRIEN, CHARLES HUGH	4932 EAST 38TH PLACE, TULSA OK 74135
1978-094	OBRIEN, DANIEL JOGUES	8223 FOREST HILLS BLVD, DALLAS TX 75218
1953-063	OBRIEN, EDWARD JOSEPH	522 ALDER STREET #101, EDMONDS WA 98020
1923-098	OBRIEN, FRANK ALOYSIUS 'MICKEY'	D. NOVEMBER 4, 1971, MONTEREY PARK, CALIF.
1953-064	OBRIEN, JOHN THOMAS	7712 18TH AVENUE NE, SEATTLE WA 98115
1982-090	OBRIEN, PETER MICHAEL	5509 MONTCLAIR STREET, COLLEYVILLE TX 76034
1971-076	OBRIEN, ROBERT ALLEN	2303 EAST ACACIA, FRESNO CA 93726
1969-126	OBRIEN, SYDNEY LLOYD	6570 RICHARD AVENUE, PLACERVILLE CA 95667
1943-099	OBRIEN, THOMAS EDWARD	D. NOVEMBER 5, 1978, ANNISTON, ALA.
1995-156	OCHOA, ALEX	17490 SW 22ND STREET, MIRAMAR FL 33029
1935-082	OCK, HAROLD DAVID 'WHITEY'	D. MARCH 18, 1975, MOUNT KISCO, N.Y.
1944-099	OCKEY, WALTER ANDREW	D. DECEMBER 4, 1971, STATEN ISLAND, N.Y.
1950-075	OCONNELL, DANIEL FRANCIS	D. OCTOBER 2, 1969, CLIFTON, N.J.
1923-099	OCONNELL, JAMES JOSEPH	D. NOVEMBER 11, 1976, BAKERSFIELD, CALIF.
1928-072	OCONNELL, JOHN CHARLES	D. OCTOBER 17, 1992, CANTON, OHIO
2000-129	OCONNOR, BRIAN MICHAEL	1743 KEITH DRIVE, CINCINNATI OH 45215
1981-090	OCONNOR, JACK WILLIAM	BOX 430, YUCCA VALLEY CA 92284
2006-139	OCONNOR, MICHAEL PATRICK	4637 OLD DRAGON PATH, ELLICOTT CITY MD 21042
1935-083	ODEA, JAMES KENNETH 'KEN'	D. DECEMBER 17, 1985, LIMA, N.Y.
1944-100	ODEA, PAUL	D. DECEMBER 11, 1978, CLEVELAND, OHIO
1954-076	ODELL, WILLIAM OLIVER	225 O'DELL ROAD, NEWBERRY SC 29108
1921-074	ODENWALD, THEODORE JOSEPH	D. OCTOBER 23, 1965, SHAKOPEE, MINN.

1943-100	ODOM, DAVID EVERETT	D. NOVEMBER 19, 1987, MYRTLE BEACH, S.C.
1925-081	ODOM, HERMAN BOYD 'HEINIE'	D. AUGUST 31, 1970, RUSK, TEXAS
1964-081	ODOM, JOHN LEE 'BLUE MOON'	10343 SLATER #204, FOUNTAIN VALLEY CA 92708
1954-077	ODONNELL, GEORGE DANA	70 CRUSADER ROAD, SPRINGFIELD IL 62704
1927-067	ODONNELL, HARRY HERMAN	D. JANUARY 31, 1958, PHILADELPHIA, PA.
1963-087	ODONOGHUE, JOHN EUGENE	5246 FAR OAK CIRCLE, SARASOTA FL 34238
1993-135	ODONOGHUE, JOHN PRESTON	5246 FAR OAK CIRCLE, SARASOTA FL 34238
1983-106	OELKERS, BRYAN ALOIS	3404 TAYLOR AVENUE, BRIDGETON MO 63044
1958-068	OERTEL, CHARLES FRANK	D. OCTOBER 4, 2000, ROYAL OAK, MICH.
1978-095	OESTER, RONALD JOHN	3780 NINEMILE ROAD, CINCINNATI OH 45255
1990-118	OFFERMAN, JOSE ANTONIO (DONO)	ED.B1 URB ANACAONO MOSCOSO SAN PEDRO DE MACORIS, DOM REP
1972-082	OFFICE, ROWLAND JOHNNIE	1028 LAKE GLEN WAY, SACRAMENTO CA 95822
2006-140	OFLAHERTY, ERIC GEORGE	128 MERRIAM STREET, WALLA WALLA WA 99362
1922-104	OGDEN, WARREN HARVEY 'CURLY'	D. AUGUST 6, 1964, CHESTER, PA.
1994-078	OGEA, CHAD WAYNE	418 BONABRIDGE DRIVE, BATON ROUGE LA 70808
1936-067	OGLESBY, JAMES DORN	D. SEPTEMBER 1, 1955, TULSA, OKLA.
1971-077	OGLIVIE, BENJAMIN AMBROSIO	1012 EAST SANDPIPER DRIVE, TEMPE AZ 85283
1936-068	OGRODOWSKI, AMBROSE FRANCIS 'BRUSIE'	D. MARCH 5, 1956, SAN FRANCISCO, CALIF.
1925-082	OGRODOWSKI, JOSEPH ANTHONY	D. JUNE 24, 1959, ELMIRA, N.Y.
1994-079	OHALLORAN, GREGORY JOSEPH	1021 HEDGE DRIVE MISSISSAUGA ON, L4Y 1G3 CANADA
1999-143	OHKA, TOMOKAZU	OLD ADD: KYOTO JAPAN
2000-130	OHMAN, WILLIAM MCDANIEL 'WILL'	8939 EAST NORWOOD CIRCLE, MESA AZ 85207
2003-121	OHME, KEVIN ARTHUR	806 STARLIFTER LANE, VALRICO FL 33594
1997-123	OJALA, KIRT STANLEY	1902 FOREST LAKE DRIVE SE, GRAND RAPIDS MI 49546
2003-122	OJEDA, MIGUEL ARTURO	OLD ADD: SONORA MEX
2000-131	OJEDA, OCTAVIO 'AUGIE'	9402 DOROTHY AVENUE, SOUTH GATE CA 90280
1980-098	OJEDA, ROBERT MICHAEL	2736 EAST TULARE AVENUE, VISALIA CA 93292
1920-092	OKRIE, FRANK ANTHONY	D. OCTOBER 16, 1959, DETROIT, MICH.
1948-076	OKRIE, LEONARD JOSEPH	2636 BURKE LANE, FAYETTEVILLE NC 28306
1991-134	OLANDER, JAMES BENTLEY	8421 SOUTH TRIANGLE R RANCH PLACE, VAIL AZ 85641
1956-066	OLDHAM, JOHN HARDIN	1845 ANNE WAY, SAN JOSE CA 95124
1953-065	OLDIS, ROBERT CARL	306 VIRGINIA DRIVE, IOWA CITY IA 52246
1993-136	OLEARY, TROY FRANKLIN	1105 EAST THUNDERHILL PLACE, PHOENIX AZ 85048
1989-091	OLERUD, JOHN GARRETT	8629 LAKE WASHINGTON BLVD NE, MEDINA WA 98039
1989-092	OLIN, STEPHEN ROBERT	D. MARCH 22, 1993, LITTLE LAKE NELLIE, FLA.
1994-080	OLIVA, JOSE (GALVEZ)	D. DECEMBER 22, 1997, SAN CRISTOBAL, DOM REP
1962-099	OLIVA, PEDRO 'TONY'	212 SPRING VALLEY DRIVE, BLOOMINGTON MN 55420
1960-078	OLIVARES, EDWARD BALZAC	PO BOX 1328, SAN GERMAN PR 00683
1990-119	OLIVARES, OMAR (PALQU)	HC 02 BOX 12887 CARR. 330 K2, SAN GERMAN PR 00753
1968-074	OLIVER, ALBERT	PO BOX 1466, PORTSMOUTH OH 45662
1993-137	OLIVER, DARREN CHRISTOPHER	1804 LARKSPUR COURT, SOUTHLAKE TX 76092
1977-105	OLIVER, DAVID JACOB	1709 TIMBERLAKE CIRCLE, LODI CA 95242
1959-061	OLIVER, EUGENE GEORGE	D. MARCH 3, 2007, ROCK ISLAND, ILL.
1989-093	OLIVER, JOSEPH MELTON	4137 BOUNCE DRIVE, ORLANDO FL 32812
1963-088	OLIVER, NATHANIEL 'NATE'	4403 OAK HILL ROAD, OAKLAND CA 94605
1965-083	OLIVER, ROBERT LEE	1716 G STREET, RIO LINDA CA 95673
1930-059	OLIVER, THOMAS NOBLE	D. FEBRUARY 16, 1988, MONTGOMERY, ALA.
1989-094	OLIVERAS, FRANCISCO JAVIER	OLD ADD: BAJO K1H3 BUZON 1476, RIO PIEDRAS PR 00928
1960-079	OLIVO, DIOMEDES ANTONIO	D. FEBRUARY 15, 1977, SANTO DOMINGO, DOM REP
1961-079	OLIVO, FEDERICO EMILIO 'CHI-CHI'	D. FEBRUARY 3, 1977, GUAYUBIN, DOM REP
2002-132	OLIVO, MIGUEL EDUARDO PENA	3112 LARRYNELL DRIVE, CERES CA 95307
1966-069	OLLOM, JAMES DONALD	1517 3RD PLACE, KIRKLAND WA 98033
2003-123	OLMEDO, RAINER GUSTAVO	OLD ADD: MARACAY VENEZUELA
1943-101	OLMO, LUIS FRANCISCO RODRIGUEZ	620 FIGUEROA STREET, SANTURCE PR 00907
1980-099	OLMSTED, ALAN RAY	1008 PINECONE TRAIL, FLORISSANT MO 63031
1922-105	OLSEN, ARTHUR 'OLE'	D. SEPTEMBER 12, 1980, NORWALK, CONN.
1941-082	OLSEN, BERNARD CHARLES	D. MARCH 30, 1977, EVERETT, MASS.
2001-130	OLSEN, KEVIN GARY	3353 DALES DRIVE, NORCO CA 92860
2005-134	OLSEN, SCOTT MATTHEW	OLD ADD: LAKE IN THE HILLS IL
1939-083	OLSEN, VERN JARL	D. JULY 13, 1989, MAYWOOD, ILL.
1988-099	OLSON, GREGGORY WILLIAM	1996 PORT NELSON PLACE, NEWPORT BEACH CA 92660
1989-095	OLSON, GREGORY WILLIAM	18592 ST. MELLION PLACE, EDEN PRAIRIE MN 55347
1951-075	OLSON, KARL ARTHUR	PO BOX 1897, ZEPHYR COVE NV 89448
1931-064	OLSON, MARVIN CLEMENT	D. FEBRUARY 5, 1998, TYNDALL, S.D.
1936-069	OLSON, THEODORE OTTO	D. DECEMBER 9, 1980, WEYMOUTH, MASS.
2004-148	OLSON, TIMOTHY LANE	5416 PEBBLE COURT, MCKINNEY TX 75070
1986-116	OLWINE, EDWARD R.	223 SPANISH LAKES DRIVE, NOKOMIS FL 34275
2006-141	OMALLEY, RYAN JOSEPH	OLD ADD: SPRINGFIELD IL
1982-091	OMALLEY, THOMAS PATRICK	10 CARRIAGE SQUARE, MONTOURSVILLE PA 17754
1925-083	ONEAL, ORAN HERBERT 'SKINNY'	D. JUNE 2, 1981, SPRINGFIELD, MO.
1984-085	ONEAL, RANDALL JEFFREY	524 E. RAMBLING DR, WEST PALM BEACH FL 33411
1946-080	ONEIL, JOHN FRANCIS	220 SOUTHWESTERN DRIVE #131, LAKEWOOD NY 14750
1939-084	ONEILL, HARRY MINK	D. MARCH 8, 1945, IWO JIMA, MARIANAS IS.
1920-093	ONEILL, JAMES LEO	D. SEPTEMBER 5, 1976, CHAMBERSBURG, PA.
1922-106	ONEILL, JOSEPH HENRY 'HARRY'	D. SEPTEMBER 5, 1969, RIDGETOWN, ONT.
1985-084	ONEILL, PAUL ANDREW	7785 HARTFORD HILL LANE, CINCINNATI OH 45242
1943-103	ONEILL, ROBERT EMMETT 'EMMETT'	D. OCTOBER 11, 1993, SPARKS NV
1935-084	ONIS, MANUEL DOMINGUEZ	D. JANUARY 4, 1995, TAMPA, FLA.
1985-085	ONTIVEROS, STEVEN	9970 EAST CHARTER OAK ROAD, SCOTTSDALE AZ 85260
1973-089	ONTIVEROS, STEVEN ROGERS	OLD ADD: 20 LIGGET STREET, BAKERSFIELD CA 93307
1983-107	OQUENDO, JOSE MANUEL	13219 SELMA ROAD, DE SOTO MO 63020
1993-138	OQUIST, MICHAEL LEE	1910 RATON, LAJUNTA CO 81050
1955-086	ORAVETZ, ERNEST EUGENE	D. DECEMBER 3, 2006, TAMPA, FLA.
1997-124	ORDAZ, LUIS JAVIER	OLD ADD: MARACAIBO VENEZUELA
1943-104	ORDENANA, ANTONIO RODRIGUEZ	D. SEPTEMBER 29, 1988, MIAMI, FLA.
1997-125	ORDONEZ, MAGGLIO	181 NURMI DRIVE, FORT LAUDERDALE FL 33301

1996-145 ORDONEZ, REYNALDO ....1000 SE 9TH AVENUE, HIALEAH FL 33010
1939-085 ORENGO, JOSEPH CHARLES....................D. JULY 24, 1988, SAN FRANCISCO, CALIF.
1997-126 ORIE, KEVIN LEONARD....................190 SHADOW RIDGE DRIVE, PITTSBURGH PA 15238
1969-127 ORILEY, DONALD LEE....................D. MAY 2, 1997, KANSAS CITY, MO.
1920-094 ORME, GEORGE WILLIAM....................D. MARCH 16, 1962, INDIANAPOLIS, IND.
2001-131 OROPESA, EDILBERTO 'EDDIE'....................15757 SW 102ND STREET, MIAMI FL 33196
1979-080 OROSCO, JESSE RUSSELL....................15795 EL CAMINO ENTRADA, POWAY CA 92064
1959-062 OROURKE, JAMES PATRICK....................N 15612 LITTLE SPOKANE DRIVE, SPOKANE WA 99208
1929-080 OROURKE, JOSEPH LEO....................D. JUNE 27, 1990, PHILADELPHIA, PA.
2005-135 ORR, PETERSON T....................6102 SEAWALL BLVD, GALVESTON TX 77551
1943-105 ORRELL, FORREST GORDON....................D. JANUARY 12, 1993, CHULA VISTA, CALIF.
1927-068 ORSATTI, ERNEST RALPH....................D. SEPTEMBER 4, 1968, CANOGA PARK, CALIF.
1961-080 ORSINO, JOHN JOSEPH....................6141 TERRE MERE CIRCLE, BOYNTON BEACH FL 33437
1983-108 ORSULAK, JOSEPH MICHAEL....................29 KEANSBURG RD, PARSIPPANY NJ 07054
1972-083 ORTA, JORGE....................1201 HEATHER HILL CRESCENT, FLOSSMOOR IL 60422
1960-080 ORTEGA, FILOMENO CORONADO 'PHIL'....................3071 VIA REAL, CARPINTERIA CA 93013
2001-132 ORTEGA, WILLIAM (BOBADILLA)....................OLD ADD: 8121 NW 197TH STREET, HIALEAH FL 33015
1973-090 ORTENZIO, FRANK JOSEPH....................2357 OAK CREST, JACKSONVILLE BEACH FL 32250
1982-092 ORTIZ, ADALBERTO 'JUNIOR'....................OLD ADD: PO BOX 213, HUMACAO PR 00792
1997-127 ORTIZ, DAVID AMERICO....................OLD ADD: HAINA DOM REP
1998-137 ORTIZ, HECTOR....................OLD ADD: CANOVANOS PR 00729
1990-120 ORTIZ, JAVIER VICTOR....................3725 SOUTH OCEAN DRIVE #1005, HOLLYWOOD FL 33019
2000-132 ORTIZ, JOSE DANIEL....................OLD ADD: SANTO DOMINGO DOM REP
1969-128 ORTIZ, JOSE LUIS....................OLD ADD: CALLE 14 HH-57, VILLA DEL CARME, PLAYA PONCE PR 00731
1993-139 ORTIZ, LOUIS ALBERTO JOCHY....................9012 MARTIN DRIVE, NORTH RICHLAND HILLS TX 76180
1944-101 ORTIZ, OLIVRIO NUNEZ 'BABY'....................D. MARCH 27, 1984, CENTRAL SENADO, CAMAGUEY, CUBA
1999-144 ORTIZ, RAMON DIOGENES....................OLD ADD: COTUI DOM REP
1941-083 ORTIZ, ROBERTO GONZALO NUNEZ....................D. SEPTEMBER 15, 1971, MIAMI, FLA.
1998-138 ORTIZ, RUSSELL REID....................3906 WAVERLY DRIVE, NORMAN OK 73072
2005-136 ORTMEIER, DANIEL D....................2121 FAIRMOUNT DRIVE, FLOWER MOUND TX 75029
1989-096 ORTON, JOHN ANDREW....................1437 SOUTH 58TH STREET, MESA AZ 85206
2005-137 ORVELLA, CHAD ROBERT....................3327 SAHALEE DRIVE WEST, SAMMAMISH WA 98074
1928-073 ORWOLL, OSWALD CHRISTIAN....................D. MAY 8, 1967, DECORAH, IOWA
1975-086 OSBORN, DANNY LEON....................7620 KNOX CT, WESTMINSTER CO 80030
1925-084 OSBORN, ROBERT....................D. APRIL 19, 1960, PARIS, ARK.
1992-098 OSBORNE, DONOVAN ALAN....................1651 BRIGHTSTONE, RENO NV 89521
1922-107 OSBORNE, ERNEST PRESTON 'TINY'....................D. JANUARY 5, 1969, ATLANTA, GA.
1957-062 OSBORNE, LAWRENCE SIDNEY....................3309 ROUGH CREEK DRIVE, WOODSTOCK GA 31089
1935-085 OSBORNE, WAYNE HAROLD....................D. MARCH 13, 1987, VANCOUVER, WASH.
1974-098 OSBURN, LARRY PAT 'PAT'....................208 64TH STREET COURT NW, BRADENTON FL 34209
1944-102 OSGOOD, CHARLES BENJAMIN....................3 SOUTH MEADOW VLG #22, CARVER MA 02330
1996-146 OSIK, KEITH RICHARD....................5 PAL COURT, SHOREHAM NY 11786
1962-100 OSINSKI, DANIEL....................9723 WEST AMBER TRAIL DRIVE, SUN CITY AZ 85351
2005-138 OSORIA, FRANQUELIS ANTONIO....................OLD ADD: SANTIAGO DOM REP
1957-063 OSTEEN, CLAUDE WILSON....................624 BRENT DRIVE, ARLINGTON TX 76012
1965-084 OSTEEN, MILTON DARRELL 'DARRELL'....................69902 VAN GOGH ROAD, CATHEDRAL CITY CA 92234
1954-078 OSTER, WILLIAM CHARLES....................56 LITTLE RECK ROAD, CENTERPORT NY 11721
1921-075 OSTERGARD, ROY LUND 'RED'....................D. JANUARY 13, 1977, HEMET, CALIF.
1934-082 OSTERMUELLER, FREDERICK RAYMOND....................D. DECEMBER 17, 1957, QUINCY, ILL.
2001-133 OSTING, JAMES MICHAEL....................927 LAKESIDE DRIVE, TAYLORSVILLE KY 40071
1973-091 OSTROSSER, BRIAN LEONARD....................27 CHELSEA CRESCENT STONEY CREEK ON, L8E 5R7 CANADA
1943-106 OSTROWSKI, JOHN THADDEUS....................D. NOVEMBER 13, 1992, CHICAGO, ILL.
1948-077 OSTROWSKI, JOSEPH PAUL....................D. JANUARY 3, 2003, WILKES-BARRE, PA.
1990-121 OSUNA, ALFONSO....................8256 VIA ROSA, ORLANDO FL 32835
1995-157 OSUNA, PEDRO ANTONIO 'ANTONIO'....................CALLE 11 AVE MEXICO #436 JUAN JOSE RIOS SINALOA, MEXICO
2001-134 OSWALT, ROY EDWARD....................PO BOX 98, WEIR MS 39772
1998-139 OTANEZ, WILLIS ALEXANDER....................66 VERMILYEA AVENUE #41, NEW YORK NY 10034
1945-075 OTERO, REGINO JOSE GOMEZ 'REGGIE'....................D. OCTOBER 21, 1988, HIALEAH, FLA.
1995-158 OTERO, RICARDO FIGUEROA....................33 ELEVENTH AVENUE, HUNTINGTON STATION NY 11746
1967-083 OTIS, AMOS JOSEPH....................568 PREAKNESS STAKES STREET, HENDERSON NV 89015
1969-129 OTOOLE, DENNIS JOSEPH....................3453 RIDGEWOOD DR, ERLANGER KY 41018
1958-069 OTOOLE, JAMES JEROME....................1010 LANETTE DR, CINCINNATI OH 45230
2004-149 OTSUKA, AKINORI....................OLD ADD: SAN DIEGO CA
1926-062 OTT, MELVIN THOMAS....................D. NOVEMBER 21, 1958, NEW ORLEANS, LA.
1974-099 OTT, NATHAN EDWARD 'ED'....................OLD ADD: 1511 WEST HAMILTON STREET, ALLENTOWN PA 18102
1962-101 OTT, WILLIAM JOSEPH....................C/O COUNTY LOCK, 132 WEST NYACK WAY, WEST NYACK NY 10994
1974-100 OTTEN, JAMES EDWARD....................1417 NORTH FOREST, MESA AZ 85203
1987-108 OTTO, DAVID ALAN....................1383 SHADY LANE, WHEATON IL 60187
1986-117 OUELLETTE, PHILIP ROLAND....................7421 POPPY STREET, CORONA CA 92881
1933-047 OULLIBER, JOHN ANDREW....................D. DECEMBER 26, 1980, NEW ORLEANS, LA.
1933-048 OUTEN, WILLIAM AUSTIN 'CHICK'....................D. SEPTEMBER 11, 1961, DURHAM, N.C.
1937-082 OUTLAW, JAMES PAULUS....................D. APRIL 9, 2006, JACKSON, ALA.
2001-135 OVERBAY, LYLE STEFAN....................3114 RUSSELL ROAD, CENTRALIA WA 98531
1943-107 OVERMIRE, FRANK 'STUBBY'....................D. MARCH 3, 1977, LAKELAND, FLA.
1976-072 OVERY, HARRY MICHAEL 'MIKE'....................3010 NORTH 152ND AVENUE, GOODYEAR AZ 85338
1976-073 OWCHINKO, ROBERT DENNIS....................14000 NORTH 94TH STREET #1033, SCOTTSDALE AZ 85260
1937-083 OWEN, ARNOLD MALCOLM 'MICKEY'....................D. JULY 13, 2005, MOUNT VERNON, MO.
1983-109 OWEN, DAVE....................1921 FM 3136, CLEBURNE TX 76031
1981-091 OWEN, LAWRENCE THOMAS....................804 WHITE PINE ST, NEW CARLISLE OH 45344
1931-065 OWEN, MARVIN JAMES....................D. JUNE 22, 1991, MOUNTAIN VIEW, CALIF.
1983-110 OWEN, SPIKE DEE....................121 TELLUS STREET, AUSTIN TX 78734
1993-140 OWENS, CLAUDE JAYHAWK 'JAYHAWK'....................2085 KAY ROAD, SARDINIA OH 45171
1995-159 OWENS, ERIC BLAKE....................22431 NORTH 54TH STREET, PHOENIX AZ 85054
1935-086 OWENS, FURMAN LEE 'JACK'....................D. NOVEMBER 14, 1958, GREENVILLE, S.C.
2006-142 OWENS, HENRY JAY....................4944 SW 140TH COURT, MIAMI FL 33175
1955-087 OWENS, JAMES PHILIP....................1426 RAMADA DRIVE, HOUSTON TX 77062

2006-143	OWENS, JERRY LEE	OLD ADD: NEWHALL CA
1972-084	OWENS, PAUL FRANCIS	D. DECEMBER 26, 2003, WOODBURY, N.J.
1982-093	OWNBEY, RICHARD WAYNE	1178 NEWCASTLE COURT, OCEANSIDE CA 92056
2005-139	OXSPRING, CHRIS ANDREW	OLD ADD: LABRADOR AUSTRALIA
1965-085	OYLER, RAYMOND FRANCIS	D. JANUARY 26, 1981, REDMOND, WASH.
1973-092	OZARK, DANIEL LEONARD	BOX 6666, VERO BEACH FL 32960
1923-100	OZMER, HORACE ROBERT 'DOC'	D. DECEMBER 28, 1970, ATLANTA, GA.
2000-133	OZUNA, PABLO JOSE	OLD ADD: SANTO DOMINGO DOM REP

P

1977-106	PACELLA, JOHN LEWIS	1500 ABBOTSFORD GREEN DRIVE, POWELL OH 43065
1996-147	PACHECHO, ALEXANDER MELCHOR	OLD ADD: CARACAS VENEZUELA
1987-109	PACILLO, PATRICK MICHAEL	8 ROCKY GLEN WAY, LEBANON NJ 08833
1987-110	PACIOREK, JAMES JOSEPH	5385 QUAIL RUN, BLAINE WA 98230
1963-089	PACIOREK, JOHN FRANCIS	8400 HUNTINGTON DR, SAN GABRIEL CA 91775
1970-103	PACIOREK, THOMAS MARIAN	2389 BROAD CREEK DRIVE, STONE MOUNTAIN GA 30087
1949-062	PACK, FRANKIE	D. JANUARY 26, 2000, HENDERSONVILLE, N.C.
1975-087	PACTWA, JOSEPH MARTIN	OLD ADD: 961 LAWRENCE PLACE, LAKE STSTION IN 46405
1932-059	PADDEN, THOMAS FRANCIS	D. JUNE 11, 1973, MANCHESTER, N.H.
1937-084	PADGETT, DON WILSON	D. DECEMBER 9, 1980, HIGH POINT, N.C.
1923-101	PADGETT, ERNEST KITCHEN	D. APRIL 15, 1957, EAST ORANGE, N.J.
2004-150	PADILLA, JUAN MIGUEL	OLD ADD: LEVITTOWN PR
1999-145	PADILLA, VICENTE DE LA CRUZ	OLD ADD: MANAGUA NICARAGUA
1969-130	PAEPKE, DENNIS RAE	4560 TRIESTE DRIVE, CARLSBAD CA 92008
1943-108	PAFKO, ANDREW	1420 BLACKHAWK DRIVE, MOUNT PROSPECT IL 60056
2006-144	PAGAN, ANGEL ANTHONY	OLD ADD: RIO PIEDRAS PR
1973-093	PAGAN, DAVID PERCY	BOX 1819 NIPAWIN SK, S0E 1E0 CANADA
1959-063	PAGAN, JOSE ANTONIO	425 MAPLE LANE, SEBRING FL 33876
1944-103	PAGE, JOSEPH FRANCIS	D. APRIL 21, 1980, LATROBE, PA.
1968-075	PAGE, MICHAEL RANDY	599 BRIARCLIFF DRIVE, WOODRUFF SC 29388
1977-107	PAGE, MITCHELL OTIS	484 LAKE PARK AVENUE #162, OAKLAND CA 94610
1928-074	PAGE, PHILIPPE RAUSAC	D. JUNE 27, 1958, SPRINGFIELD, MASS.
1939-086	PAGE, SAMUEL WALTER	D. MAY 29, 2002, GREENVILLE, S.C.
1938-073	PAGE, VANCE LINWOOD	D. JULY 14, 1951, WILSON, N.C.
1978-096	PAGEL, KARL DOUGLAS	2698 NORTH ELLIS STREET, CHANDLER AZ 85224
1955-088	PAGLIARONI, JAMES VINCENT	10388 PARTRIDGE DR, GRASS VALLEY CA 95945
1984-086	PAGLIARULO, MICHAEL TIMOTHY	11 FIELDSTONE DRIVE, WINCHESTER MA 01890
1987-111	PAGNOZZI, THOMAS ALAN	2319 NORTH HEATHER COVE, FAYETTEVILLE AR 72701
1948-078	PAIGE, LEROY 'SATCHEL'	D. JUNE 8, 1982, KANSAS CITY, MO.
1951-076	PAINE, PHILLIPS STEERE	D. FEBRUARY 19, 1978, LEBANON, PA.
1993-141	PAINTER, LANCE TELFORD	2683 EAST PINTO DRIVE, GILBERT AZ 85296
1988-100	PALACIOS, ROBERT REY 'REY'	160 HEBERTON AVENUE #4H, STATEN ISLAND NY 10302
1987-112	PALACIOS, VICENTE	DOMICILIO CONOCIDO MATALOMA VERACRUZ, MEXICO
1939-087	PALAGYI, MICHAEL RAYMOND	167 14TH ST REET, CONNEAUT OH 44030
1945-076	PALICA, ERVIN MARTIN	D. MAY 29, 1982, HUNTINGTON BEACH, CALIF.
1988-101	PALL, DONN STEVEN	154 WELLINGTON AVENUE, BLOOMINGDALE IL 60108
1948-079	PALM, RICHARD PAUL	21 RIVERVIEW PLACE, SCITUATE MA 02066
1995-160	PALMEIRO, ORLANDO	11991 SW 103RD TERRACE, MIAMI FL 33186
1986-118	PALMEIRO, RAFAEL CORRALES	5216 REIMS COURT, COLLEYVILLE TX 76034
1978-097	PALMER, DAVID WILLIAM	61 SHERMAN AVENUE, GLENS FALLS NY 12801
1989-097	PALMER, DEAN WILLIAM	3907 WEST MILLERS BRIDGE ROAD, TALLAHASSEE FL 32312
1965-086	PALMER, JAMES ALVIN	239 SANFORD AVENUE, PALM BEACH FL 33480
1969-131	PALMER, LOWELL RAYMOND	PO BOX 5253, EL DORADO HILLS CA 95762
1931-066	PALMISANO, JOSEPH	D. NOVEMBER 5, 1971, ALBUQUERQUE, N.M.
1960-081	PALMQUIST, EDWIN LEE	250 THE VILLAGE #314, REDONDO BEACH CA 90277
1953-066	PALYS, STANLEY FRANCIS	RURAL ROUTE 6 BOX 6119, MOSCOW PA 18444
1996-148	PANIAGUA, JOSE LUIS SANCHEZ	OLD ADD: SANTO DOMINGO DOM REP
1984-087	PANKOVITS, JAMES FRANKLIN	2337 COMMONWEALTH AVENUE, CHICAGO IL 60614
1971-078	PANTHER, JAMES EDWARD	7936 TIGER PALM WAY, FORT MYERS FL 33912
1961-081	PAPA, JOHN PAUL	29 PHILLIPS DR, SHELTON CT 06484
1948-080	PAPAI, ALFRED THOMAS	D. SEPTEMBER 7, 1995, SPRINGFIELD, ILL.
1976-074	PAPE, KENNETH WAYNE	2617 GREEN CREEK STREET, SAN ANTONIO TX 78232
2005-140	PAPELBON, JONATHAN R	1739 HAWKINS COVE DRIVE EAST, JACKSONVILLE FL 32246
1974-101	PAPI, STANLEY GERARD	1111 WEST SIERRA MADRE, FRESNO CA 93705
1945-077	PAPISH, FRANK RICHARD	D. AUGUST 30, 1965, PUEBLO, COLO.
1991-135	PAPPAS, ERIK DANIEL	OLD ADD: 2545 WEST 111TH STREET, CHICAGO IL 60655
1957-064	PAPPAS, MILTON STEPHEN	502 HIGHLINGTON COURT, BEECHER IL 60401
1993-142	PAQUETTE, CRAIG HAROLD	1500 GARDEN VALLEY DRIVE, GLENCOE MO 63038
1985-086	PARDO, ALBERTO JUDAS	908 HILLARY CIRCLE, LUTZ FL 33549
1988-102	PAREDES, JOHNNY ALFONSO	OLD ADD: MARACAIBO VENEZUELA
1986-119	PARENT, MARK ALAN	PO BOX 591, COTTONWOOD CA 96022
1982-094	PARIS, KELLY JAY	1515 REDWOOD CIRCLE, THOUSAND OAKS CA 91360
1943-109	PARISSE, LOUIS PETER	D. JUNE 2, 1956, PHILADELPHIA, PA.
1994-081	PARK, CHAN HO	1800 O'HENRY COURT, ARLINGTON TX 76006
2001-136	PARKER, CHRISTIAN MICHAEL	10101 MESA ARRIBA NE, ALBUQUERQUE NM 87111
1937-085	PARKER, CLARENCE MCKAY 'ACE'	210 SNEAD'S FAIRWAY, PORTSMOUTH VA 23701
1973-094	PARKER, DAVID GENE	4036 OAK TREE COURT, LOVELAND OH 45140
1923-102	PARKER, DOUGLAS WOOLLEY 'DIXIE'	D. MAY 15, 1972, GREEN POND, ALA.
1936-070	PARKER, FRANCIS JAMES 'SALTY'	D. JULY 27, 1992, HOUSTON, TEXAS
1970-104	PARKER, HARRY WILLIAM	6049 HAVENVIEW DRIVE, MECHANICSVILLE VA 23111
1987-113	PARKER, JAMES CLAYTON 'CLAY'	6614 BRICKSTON STREET, HIXSON TN 37343
1964-082	PARKER, MAURICE WESLEY 'WES'	OLD ADD: 1237 VILLA WOODS DRIVE, PACIFIC PALISADES CA 90272
1990-122	PARKER, RICHARD ALAN	2641 NE 74TH STREET, GLADSTONE MO 64119
1971-079	PARKER, WILLIAM DAVID	D. FEBRUARY 9, 2003, SUN CITY WEST, ARIZ.

1921-076 PARKINSON, FRANK JOSEPH ....D. JULY 4, 1960, TRENTON, N.J.
1937-086 PARKS, ARTIE WILLIAM ....D. DECEMBER 6, 1989, LITTLE ROCK, ARK.
1992-099 PARKS, DEREK GAVIN ....6562 STARSTONE PLACE, RANCHO CUCAMONGA CA 91739
1921-077 PARKS, VERNON HENRY 'SLICKER' ....D. FEBRUARY 21, 1978, ROYAL OAK, MICH.
1929-081 PARMELEE, LEROY EARL ....D. AUGUST 31, 1981, MONROE, MICH.
1947-065 PARNELL, MELVIN LLOYD ....700 TURQUOISE STREET, NEW ORLEANS LA 70124
2001-137 PARONTO, CHAD MICHAEL ....617 BENEDICT ROAD, PITTSFIELD MA 01201
1998-140 PARQUE, JIM VO ....4109 CRYSTAL RIDGE DRIVE SE, PUYALLUP WA 98372
1995-161 PARRA, JOSE MIGUEL ....OLD ADD: SANTIAGO DOM REP
1986-120 PARRETT, JEFFREY DALE ....722 SEATTLE DRIVE, LEXINGTON KY 40503
1970-105 PARRILLA, SAMUEL ....D. FEBRUARY 9, 1994, BROOKLYN, N.Y.
1995-162 PARRIS, STEVEN MICHAEL ....22942 JUDITH DRIVE, PLAINFIELD IL 60544
2000-134 PARRISH, JOHN HENRY ....84 GARDEN CITY DRIVE, LANCASTER PA 17602
1977-108 PARRISH, LANCE MICHAEL ....19637 MERCER ROAD, BOWLING GREEN OH 43402
1974-102 PARRISH, LARRY ALTON ....234 GREEN HAVEN LANE WEST, DUNDEE FL 33838
1977-109 PARROTT, MICHAEL EVERETT ARCH ....PO BOX 1264, LYONS CO 80540
1981-092 PARSONS, CASEY ROBERT ....23014 EAST MOCHA LANE, LIBERTY LAKE WA 99019
1939-088 PARSONS, EDWARD DIXON 'DIXIE' ....D. OCTOBER 31, 1991, LONGVIEW, TEXAS
1963-090 PARSONS, THOMAS ANTHONY ....7106 LORRAINE AVENUE NW, NORTH CANTON OH 44720
1971-080 PARSONS, WILLIAM RAYMOND ....16209 SOUTH FIRST STREET, PHOENIX AZ 85048
1943-110 PARTEE, ROY ROBERT ....D. DECEMBER 26, 2000, EUREKA, CALIF.
1944-104 PARTENHEIMER, STANWOOD WENDELL ....D. JANUARY 28, 1989, WILSON, N.C.
1927-069 PARTRIDGE, JAMES BUGG 'JAY' ....D. JANUARY 4, 1974, NASHVILLE, TENN.
1978-098 PASCHALL, WILLIAM HERBERT ....7926 WINDSPRAY DRIVE, SUMMERFIELD NC 27358
1954-079 PASCUAL, CAMILO ALBERTO ....7741 SW 32ND ST, MIAMI FL 33155
1950-076 PASCUAL, CARLOS ALBERTO ....2540 SW 92ND COURT, MIAMI FL 33165
2004-151 PASCUCCI, VALENTINO MARTIN ....11163 JAMES PLACE, CERRITOS CA 90703
1933-049 PASEK, JOHN PAUL ....D. MARCH 13, 1976, NIAGARA FALLS, N.Y.
1982-095 PASHNICK, LARRY JOHN ....506 HIGHLAND, WYANDOTTE MI 48192
1974-103 PASLEY, KEVIN PATRICK ....2701 LANCASTER DRIVE, SUN CITY CENTER FL 33570
1985-087 PASQUA, DANIEL ANTHONY ....45 SILO RIDGE ROAD EAST, ORLAND PARK IL 60467
1935-087 PASSEAU, CLAUDE WILLIAM ....D. AUGUST 30, 2003, LUCEDALE, MISS.
1979-081 PASTORE, FRANK ENRICO ....1542 NORTH FRANCIS WAY, UPLAND CA 91786
1983-111 PASTORNICKY, CLIFFORD SCOT ....4815 50TH AVENUE WEST, BRADENTON FL 34210
1926-063 PATE, JOSEPH WILLIAM ....D. DECEMBER 26, 1948, FORT WORTH, TEXAS
1980-100 PATE, ROBERT WAYNE ....16834 SUPERIOR STREET, NORTH HILLS CA 91325
1968-076 PATEK, FREDERICK JOSEPH ....227 WILLOW STREET, SEALY TX 77474
1998-141 PATRICK, BRONSWELL DANTE ....3202 MORTON LANE, GREENVILLE NC 27834
1941-084 PATRICK, ROBERT LEE ....D. OCTOBER 6, 1999, FORT SMITH, ARK.
1996-149 PATTERSON, DANNY SHANE ....13944 EAST YUCCA STREET, SCOTTSDALE AZ 85259
1968-077 PATTERSON, DARYL ALAN ....20145 TOLLHOUSE RD, CLOVIS CA 93612
1979-082 PATTERSON, DAVID GLENN ....8425 EVANSTON AVENUE, RAYTOWN MO 64138
2000-135 PATTERSON, DONALD COREY 'COREY' ....1115 GORDON COMBS ROAD NW, MARIETTA GA 30064
1977-110 PATTERSON, GILBERT THOMAS ....3910 LITTLE EGRET COURT, LUTZ FL 33558
1932-060 PATTERSON, HENRY JOSEPH ....D. SEPTEMBER 30, 1970, PANORAMA CITY, CALIF.
2001-138 PATTERSON, JARROD LANE ....1995 COUNTY ROAD 701, CLANTON AL 35045
1995-163 PATTERSON, JEFFREY SIMMONS ....27825 TAMARA DRIVE, YORBA LINDA CA 92887
1992-100 PATTERSON, JOHN ALLEN ....2659 EAST JADE PLACE, CHANDLER AZ 85249
2002-133 PATTERSON, JOHN HOLLIS ....2709 COUNTRY CLUB DRIVE, ORANGE TX 77630
1988-103 PATTERSON, KENNETH BRIAN ....6723 FISH POND DRIVE, WACO TX 76710
1981-093 PATTERSON, MICHAEL LEE ....19306 CHAMBLEE AVENUE, CERRITOS CA 90703
1981-094 PATTERSON, REGINALD ALLEN ....7748 SOUTH CREST TRAIL, BESSEMER AL 35022
1985-088 PATTERSON, ROBERT CHARLES ....3106 47TH AVENUE LANE NE, HICKORY NC 28601
1921-078 PATTERSON, WILLIAM JENNINGS BRYAN ....D. OCTOBER 1, 1977, ST. LOUIS, MO.
1968-078 PATTIN, MARTIN WILLIAM ....3401 SWEETGRASS COURT, LAWRENCE KS 66049
1929-082 PATTISON, JAMES WELLS ....D. FEBRUARY 22, 1991, MELBOURNE, FLA.
1944-105 PATTON, GENE TUNNEY ....60 SOUTH 17TH AVENUE, COATESVILLE PA 19320
1935-088 PATTON, GEORGE WILLIAM ....D. MARCH 15, 1986, PHILADELPHIA, PA.
1957-065 PATTON, THOMAS ALLEN ....807 RESERVOIR, HONEY BROOK PA 19344
1999-146 PAUL, JOSHUA WILLIAM ....5682 DELANO AVENUE, SAN DIEGO CA 92120
1968-079 PAUL, MICHAEL GEORGE ....5121 CIRCULO SOBRIO, TUCSON AZ 85718
1954-080 PAULA, CARLOS (CONNILL) ....D. APRIL 25, 1983, MIAMI, FLA.
2006-145 PAULEY, DAVID WAYNE ....5150 NORTH 99TH AVENUE #1085, GLENDALE AZ 85305
2005-141 PAULINO, RONNY LEONEL ....OLD ADD: SANTO DOMINGO DOM REP
1925-085 PAULSON, GUILFORD PAUL HANS 'PAUL' ....D. APRIL 20, 1994, HARLAN, IOWA
1998-142 PAVANO, CARL ANTHONY ....7900 FAIRWAY LANE, WEST PALM BEACH FL 33412
1990-123 PAVLAS, DAVID LEE ....PO BOX 1224, SHINER TX 77984
1957-066 PAVLETICH, DONALD STEPHEN ....13645 ADELAIDE LANE, BROOKFIELD WI 53005
1992-101 PAVLIK, ROGER ALLEN ....622 BEAVER BEND, HOUSTON TX 77037
1946-081 PAWELEK, THEODORE JOHN ....D. FEBRUARY 12, 1964, CHICAGO HEIGHTS, ILL.
1955-089 PAWLOSKI, STANLEY WALTER ....413 MARYJOE WAY, WARRINGTON PA 18976
1987-114 PAWLOWSKI, JOHN ....257 MILL BRANCH WAY, NORTH AUGUSTA SC 29860
1977-111 PAXTON, MICHAEL DEWAYNE ....2514 WINDY OAKS, GERMANTOWN TN 38139
1920-095 PAYNE, GEORGE WASHINGTON ....D. JANUARY 24, 1959, BELLFLOWER, CALIF.
1984-088 PAYNE, MICHAEL EARL ....D. AUGUST 4, 2002, DUNELLON, FLA.
1998-143 PAYTON, JAYSON LEE ....OLD ADD: ZANESVILLE OH 43701
1975-088 PAZIK, MICHAEL JOSEPH ....8413 COMANCHE COURT, BETHESDA MD 20817
1937-087 PEACOCK, JOHN GASTON ....D. OCTOBER 17, 1981, WILSON, N.C.
1933-050 PEARCE, FRANKLIN THOMAS ....D. SEPTEMBER 3, 1950, VAN BUREN, N.Y.
1949-063 PEARCE, JAMES MADISON ....D. JULY 17, 2005, ZEBULON, N.C.
2002-134 PEARCE, JOSHUA RAY ....2607 DRAPER ROIAD, YAKIMA WA 98903
1958-070 PEARSON, ALBERT GREGORY 'ALBIE' ....55473 OAK HILL, LAQUINTA CA 92253
1939-089 PEARSON, ISSAC OVERTON 'IKE' ....D. MARCH 17, 1985, SARASOTA, FLA.
2002-135 PEARSON, JASON JOHN ....2373 SUNSET DRIVE, FREEPORT IL 61032
1932-061 PEARSON, MONTGOMERY MARCELLUS ....D. JANUARY 27, 1978, FRESNO, CALIF.
2002-136 PEARSON, TERRY BOBBY GENE ....3010 WISTERIA LANE, NORTHPORT AL 35473

2002-137	PEAVY, JACOB EDWARD	8124 BRANCH COURT, SEMMES AL 36575
1943-111	PECK, HAROLD ARTHUR 'HAL'	D. APRIL 13, 1995, MILWAUKEE, WISC.
1986-121	PECOTA, WILLIAM JOSEPH	332 NE WARRINGTON COURT, LEES SUMMIT MO 64064
1953-067	PEDEN, LESLIE EARL	D. FEBRUARY 11, 2002, JACKSONVILLE, FLA.
1985-089	PEDERSON, STUART RUSSELL	747 BERMUDA, SAN MATEO CA 94403
1991-136	PEDRE, JORGE ENRIQUE 'GEORGE'	7894 BELLFLOWER DRIVE, BUENA PARK CA 90620
1987-115	PEDRIQUE, ALFREDO JOSE	1702 EAST ST. APPOLLONIA STREET, TUCSON AZ 85713
2006-146	PEDROIA, DUSTIN LUIS	14 FISKE AVENUE, WOODLAND CA 95695
1941-085	PEEK, STEPHEN GEORGE	D. SEPTEMBER 20, 1991, SYRACUSE, N.Y.
1927-070	PEEL, HOMER HEFNER	D. APRIL 8, 1997, SHREVEPORT, LA.
1935-089	PEERSON, JACK CHILES	D. OCTOBER 23, 1966, FT. WALTON BEACH, FLA.
1927-071	PEERY, GEORGE A. 'RED'	D. MAY 6, 1985, SALT LAKE CITY, UTAH
1956-067	PEETE, CHARLES	D. NOVEMBER 27, 1956, CARACAS, VENEZ.
1992-102	PEGUERO, JULIO CESAR (SANTANA)	OLD ADD: EL TIO #25 SAN ISIDRO, SANTO DOMINGO DOM REP
1994-082	PEGUES, STEVEN ANTONE	362 PRESIDENT DRIVE, PONTOTOC MS 38863
2002-138	PELAEZ, ALEJANDRO	1501 OLEANDER AVENUE, CHULA VISTA CA 91911
2006-147	PELFREY, MICHAEL ALAN	OLD ADD: 8512 CRAIG DRIVE, WICHITA KS 67210
1946-082	PELLAGRINI, EDWARD CHARLES	D. OCTOBER 11, 2006, WEYMOUTH, MASS.
2002-139	PELLOW, KIT DONOVAN	925 EAST 14TH STREET #D1, LAWRENCE KS 66044
1992-103	PELTIER, DANIEL EDWAR	239 LAPP ROAD, CLIFTON PARK NY 12065
2002-140	PEMBER, DAVID JOSEPH	8832 MALLOW DRIVE, KNOXVILLE TN 37922
1974-104	PEMBERTON, BROCK	C/O CLIFF ROBERTSON, 1422 WINDSOR DRIVE, ARDMORE OK 73409
1995-164	PEMBERTON, RUDY HECTOR PEREZ	OLD ADD: 1620 TWIN OAKS DRIVE, TOLEDO OH 43615
1981-095	PENA, ADALBERTO	STA. ELVIRA, STA. ROSA K35, CAGUAS PR 00625
1981-096	PENA, ALEJANDRO	12635 ETRIS ROAD, ROSWELL GA 30075
1998-144	PENA, ANGEL MARIA	OLD ADD: SAN PEDRO DE MACORIS DOM REP
1980-101	PENA, ANTONIO FRANCISCO	COMP HAB 30 DEMARZO,MAN #1 ED 14 SANTIAGO, DOM REP
2005-142	PENA, BRAYAN EDUARDO	18020 SW 139TH COURT, MIAMI FL 33177
2001-139	PENA, CARLOS FELIPE	440 NORTH AVENUE #126, HAVERHILL MA 01830
2000-136	PENA, ELVIS	OLD ADD: SANTO DOMINGO DOM REP
1990-124	PENA, GERONIMO	KM 17 #7 PISTA DUARTE LOS ALCARRIZZOS,D.N., DOM REP
1986-122	PENA, HIPOLITO	OLD ADD: 6814 NORTH CHURCH AVENUE, TAMPA FL 33614
1992-104	PENA, JAMES PATRICK	3228 EAST SILVERWOOD DRIVE, PHOENIX AZ 85048
1999-147	PENA, JESUS	OLD ADD: SANTO DOMINGO DOM REP
1969-132	PENA, JOSE	A. FLORES #1116 NTE C. JIQUILPAN, LOS MOCHIS SINALOA, MEXICO
1999-148	PENA, JUAN FRANCISCO	OLD ADD: MIAMI FL 33101
1958-071	PENA, ORLANDO	1750 WEST 46TH STREET #416, HIALEAH FL 33012
2006-148	PENA, RAMON ANTONIO	OLD ADD: SANTO DOMINGO DOM REP
1989-098	PENA, RAMON ARTURO	OLD ADD: CALLE H ESQ. J. CERRO ALTO, SANTIAGO DOM REP
1965-087	PENA, ROBERT CESAR	D. JULY 23, 1982, SANTIAGO, DOM REP
2006-149	PENA, TONY FRANCISCO	OLD ADD: SANTIAGO DOM REP
2002-141	PENA, WILY MODESTO	OLD ADD: 3101 N. ROCKY POINT DRIVE EAST, TAMPA FL 33607
1922-108	PENCE, ELMER CLAIR	D. SEPTEMBER 17, 1968, SAN FRANCISCO, CALIF.
1921-079	PENCE, RUSSELL WILLIAM	D. AUGUST 11, 1971, HOT SPRINGS, ARK.
1953-068	PENDLETON, JAMES EDWARD	D. MARCH 20, 1996, HOUSTON, TEXAS
1984-089	PENDLETON, TERRY LEE	332 GRASSMEADE WAY, SNELLVILLE GA 30078
2005-143	PENN, HAYDEN ANDREW	9150 CANYON PARK TERRACE, SANTEE CA 92071
1995-165	PENN, SHANNON DION	3443 GREENLAWN AVENUE, CINCINNATI OH 45207
1993-143	PENNINGTON, BRAD LEE	7220 EAST STATE ROAD 160, SALEM IN 47167
2000-137	PENNY, BRADLEY WAYNE	14321 SOUTH 248TH EAST AVENUE, COWETA OK 74429
1992-105	PENNYFEATHER, WILLIAM NATHANIEL 'WILL'	333 RECTOR STREET #6D, PERTH AMBOY NJ 08861
1954-081	PENSON, PAUL EUGENE	D. MAY 3, 2006, MERRIAM, KAN.
1975-089	PENTZ, EUGENE DAVID	OLD ADD: 1203 HEENEY AVENUE, JOHNSTOWN PA 15904
1962-102	PEPITONE, JOSEPH ANTHONY	101 WEST SHORE DRIVE, MASSAPEQUA NY 11758
1929-083	PEPLOSKI, HENRY STEPHEN	D. JANUARY 28, 1982, DOVER, N.J.
1966-070	PEPPER, DONALD HOYTE	7 BRECKENHAM LANE, GREENVILLE SC 29609
1954-082	PEPPER, HUGH MCLAURIN 'LAURIN'	8932 DAVIS STREET, OCEAN SPRINGS MS 39564
1932-062	PEPPER, RAYMOND WATSON	D. MARCH 24, 1996, HUNTSVILLE, ALA.
2003-124	PERALTA, JHONNY ANTONIO	OLD ADD: SANTIAGO DOM REP
2005-144	PERALTA, JOEL	OLD ADD: BONAO DOM REP
1969-133	PERAZA, LUIS	CALLE 6 C.F. 13 RES. BAIROA, CAGUAS PR 00625
1988-104	PERAZA, OSWALDO JOSE	OLD ADD: BARBUAL #19-36, PUERTO CABELLO, CARABOBO VENEZUELA
1995-166	PERCIVAL, TROY EUGENE	2127 CENTURY AVENUE, RIVERSIDE CA 92506
1980-102	PERCONTE, JOHN PATRICK	6197 HINTERLONG COURT, LISLE IL 60532
2003-125	PEREZ, ANTONIO MIGUEL	OLD ADD: BANI DOM REP
1964-083	PEREZ, ATANASIO RIGAL 'TONY'	LAS FLORES 113, SANTURCE PR 00911
2006-150	PEREZ, BELTRAN OGILBIO	OLD ADD: SAN FRANCISCO DE MACORIS DOM REP
1995-167	PEREZ, CARLOS GROSS	CARRE TARA SANCHEZ K-M21 NIGUA SAN CRISTOBAL, DOM REP
1996-150	PEREZ, DANIEL	10511 CUESTA BRAVA LANE, EL PASO TX 79935
1993-144	PEREZ, EDUARDO ATANACIO	OLD ADD: 2302 MAKI ROAD #35, PLANT CITY FL 33566
1995-168	PEREZ, EDUARDO RAFAEL	615 ROSE CREEK CIRCLE, DULUTH GA 30097
1958-072	PEREZ, GEORGE THOMAS	711 SOUTH OLD STAGE ROAD, CAVE JUNCTION OR 97523
2006-151	PEREZ, JUAN P.	OLD ADD: EL IN DIO VILLARIVAS DOM REP
1969-134	PEREZ, MARTIN ROMAN	30 WILLOWICK DRIVE, LITHONIA GA 30038
1987-116	PEREZ, MELIDO TURPEN	NIGUA KM 21 1/2 SANTO DOMINGO, DOM REP
1990-125	PEREZ, MICHAEL IRVIN	OLD ADD: RURAL ROUTE 2 BOX 165-A, YAUCO PR 00768
2005-145	PEREZ, MIGUEL ANTONIO	OLD ADD: GUATIRE VENEZUELA
1996-151	PEREZ, NEIFI NEFTALI DIAZ	OLD ADD: 255 KING STREET, SAN FRANCISCO CA 94107
1998-145	PEREZ, ODALIS AMADOL	11509 GEMINI LANE, FORT WASHINGTON MD 20744
2002-142	PEREZ, OLIVER MARTINEZ	OLD ADD: CULIACAN MEX
1980-103	PEREZ, PASCUAL (GROSS)	SALVADOR, CUCURULO #105 SANTIAGO, DOM REP
2006-152	PEREZ, RAFAEL JEROME	OLD ADD: SANTO DOMINGO DOM REP
1994-083	PEREZ, ROBERT ALEXANDER (JIMENEZ)	VISTA EL SOL CASADO #62 EDO BOLIVAR, VENEZUELA
2000-138	PEREZ, SANTIAGO ALBERTO	OLD ADD: SANTO DOMINGO DOM REP
2000-139	PEREZ, TIMONIEL 'TIMO'	41 PEARSALL AVENUE, FREEPORT NY 11520
1995-169	PEREZ, TOMAS ORLANDO	U.L.CYEPUSCULO BLQ 17 #0102 BARQUISIMETO, VENEZUELA

1991-137	PEREZ, YORKIS MIGUEL	OLD ADD: 1431 SOUTH 14TH AVENUE, HOLLYWOOD FL 33020
1988-105	PEREZCHICA, ANTONIO LLAMAS	79220 VICTORIA DRIVE, LAQUINTA CA 92253
1997-128	PERISHO, MATTHEW ALAN	1462 WEST CARDINAL WAY, CHANDLER AZ 85248
1978-099	PERKINS, BRODERICK PHILLIP	10024 JACOBY ROAD, SPRING VALLEY CA 91977
1967-084	PERKINS, CECIL BOYCE	711 CUSHWA ROAD, MARTINSBURG WV 25401
1930-060	PERKINS, CHARLES SULLIVAN	D. MAY 25, 1988, SALEM, ORE.
1999-149	PERKINS, DANIEL LEE	7720 SW 61ST AVENUE, SOUTH MIAMI FL 33143
2006-153	PERKINS, GLEN WESTON	20728 HARTFORD WAY, LAKEVILLE MN 55044
1950-077	PERKOVICH, JOHN JOSEPH	D. SEPTEMBER 16, 2000, LITTLE ROCK, ARK.
1947-066	PERKOWSKI, HAROLD WALTER	211 MCGINNIS, BECKLEY WV 25801
1985-090	PERLMAN, JONATHAN SAMUEL	3225 BRYN MAWR, DALLAS TX 75225
1977-112	PERLOZZO, SAMUEL BENEDICT	18101 EMERALD BAY STREET, TAMPA FL 33647
1942-075	PERME, LEONARD JOSEPH	3350 D STREET, HAYWARD CA 94541
1961-082	PERRANOSKI, RONALD PETER	3805 INDIAN RIVER DRIVE, VERO BEACH FL 32963
1921-080	PERRIN, JOHN STEPHENSON	D. JUNE 24, 1969, DETROIT, MICH.
1934-083	PERRIN, WILLIAM JOSEPH	D. JUNE 30, 1974, NEW ORLEANS, LA.
1941-086	PERRY, BOYD GLENN	D. JUNE 29, 1990, BURLINGTON, N.C.
2000-140	PERRY, CHAN EVERETT	353 SW LINCOLN ROAD, MAYO FL 32066
1962-103	PERRY, GAYLORD JACKSON	PO BOX 489, SPRUCE PINE NC 28777
1983-112	PERRY, GERALD JUNE	1348 WATERFORD GREEN CLOSE, MARIETTA GA 30068
1994-084	PERRY, HERBERT EDWARD	353 SW LINCOLN ROAD, MAYO FL 32066
1959-064	PERRY, JAMES EVAN	155 PRINTERS LANE, NEW LONDON NC 28127
1963-091	PERRY, MELVIN GAY 'BOB'	621 FOX CHASE VILLAGE, NEW BERN NC 28560
1985-091	PERRY, WILLIAM PATRICK 'PAT'	1115 WEST FRANKLIN, TAYLORVILLE IL 62568
1995-170	PERSON, ROBERT ALAN	25 BELLERIVE ACRES, SAINT LOUIS MO 63121
1971-081	PERZANOWSKI, STANLEY	3250 173RD STREET, HAMMOND IN 46323
1942-076	PESKY, JOHN MICHAEL	375 MERRIMACK STREET, METHUEN MA 01844
1994-085	PETAGINE, ROBERTO ANTONIO (GUERRA)	1098 HUNTING LODGE DRIVE, MIAMI FL 33166
1989-099	PETEREK, JEFFREY ALLEN	1547 ECHO VALLEY DRIVE, NILES OH 49120
1942-077	PETERMAN, WILLIAM DAVID	D. MARCH 13, 1999, PHILADELPHIA, PA.
1996-152	PETERS, CHRISTOPHER MICHAEL	6091 IRISHTOWN ROAD, BETHEL PARK PA 15102
1959-065	PETERS, GARY CHARLES	7121 NORTH SEVENDA DRIVE, SARASOTA FL 34241
1970-106	PETERS, RAYMOND JAMES	106 CIFUENTES WAY, HOT SPRINGS VILLAGE AR 71909
1979-083	PETERS, RICHARD DEVIN 'RICKY'	OLD ADD: 1534 WEST COMSTOCK DRIVE, CHANDLER AZ 85224
1936-071	PETERS, RUSSELL DIXON 'RUSTY'	D. FEBRUARY 21, 2003, HARRISONBURG, VA.
1987-117	PETERS, STEVEN BRADLEY	1524 SW 123RD STREET, OKLAHOMA CITY OK 73170
1999-150	PETERSEN, CHRISTOPHER RONALD	348 CANOE TRAIL LANE, ORLANDO FL 32825
1987-118	PETERSON, ADAM CHARLES	6401 NE 144TH STREET, VANCOUVER WA 98666
2004-152	PETERSON, ADAM L	168 NORTH MAIN STREET, OCONTO FALLS WI 54154
1955-090	PETERSON, CARL FRANCIS 'BUDDY'	D. SEPTEMBER 19, 2006, SACRAMENTO, CALIF.
1962-104	PETERSON, CHARLES ANDREW 'CAP'	D. MAY 16, 1980, TACOMA, WASH.
1966-071	PETERSON, FRED INGELS 'FRITZ'	PO BOX 802, DUBUQUE IA 52004
1955-091	PETERSON, HARDING WILLIAM 'PETE'	2822C SHERBROOKE LANE, PALM HARBOR FL 34684
1931-067	PETERSON, JAMES NIELS	D. APRIL 8, 1975, PALM BEACH, FLA.
1944-106	PETERSON, KENT FRANKLIN	D. APRIL 27, 1995, HIGHLAND, UTAH
1999-151	PETERSON, KYLE JOHNATHAN	OLD ADD: 1880 ARAPAHOE STREET #3608, DENVER CO 80202
1943-112	PETERSON, SIDNEY HERBERT	D. AUGUST 29, 2001, WICHITA FALLS, TEXAS
2006-154	PETIT, YUSMEIRO ALBERTO	OLD ADD: MARACAIBO VENEZ
1991-138	PETKOVSEK, MARK JOESPH	5575 DUFF, BEAUMONT TX 77706
1934-084	PETOSKEY, FREDERICK LEE	D. NOVEMBER 30, 1996, ELGIN, S.C.
1982-096	PETRALLI, EUGENE JAMES	119 LASER LANE, WEATHERFORD TX 76087
1999-152	PETRICK, BENJAMIN WAYNE	5320 SE PINE STREET, HILLSBORO OR 97123
1963-092	PETROCELLI, AMERICO PETER 'RICO'	37 GREEN HERON LANE, NASHUA NH 03062
1979-084	PETRY, DANIEL JOSEPH	30715 MYSTIC FOREST DRIVE, FARMINGTON MI 48331
1983-113	PETTIBONE, HARRY JONATHAN 'JAM'	5112 VIA MARCOS, YORBA LINDA CA 92887
1980-104	PETTINI, JOSEPH PAUL	112 LOGAN COURT, BETHANY WV 26032
1982-097	PETTIS, GARY GEORGE	3129 CRESTLINE COURT, ANTIOCH CA 94509
1951-077	PETTIT, GEORGE WILLIAM PAUL 'PAUL'	928 SARAZEN STREET, HEMET CA 92543
1935-090	PETTIT, LEON ARTHUR	D. NOVEMBER 21, 1974, COLUMBIA, TENN.
1995-171	PETTITE, ANDREW EUGENE	2310 EAST LAWTHER DRIVE, DEER PARK TX 77536
1921-081	PETTY, JESSE LEE	D. OCTOBER 23, 1971, ST. PAUL, MINN.
2001-140	PETTYJOHN, ADAM CHRISTOPHER	717 WESTWOOD DRIVE, EXETER CA 93221
1989-100	PEVEY, MARTY ASHLEY	158 NIGHTWIND TRACE, ACWORTH GA 30101
1935-091	PEZZULLO, JOHN 'PRETZLES'	D. MAY 16, 1990, DALLAS, TEXAS
1969-135	PFEIL, ROBERT RAYMOND	2358 PHEASANT RUN CIRCLE, STOCKTON CA 95207
1961-083	PFISTER, DANIEL ALBIN	1436 NW 9TH STREET, DANIA FL 33004
1941-087	PFISTER, GEORGE EDWARD	D. AUGUST 14, 1997, SOMERSET, N.J.
1945-078	PFUND, LEROY HERBERT 'LEE'	130 WINDSOR PARK DRIVE #C214, CAROL STREAM IL 60188
1936-072	PHEBUS, RAYMOND WILLIAM 'BILL'	D. OCTOBER 11, 1989, BARTOW, FLA.
1931-068	PHELPS, ERNEST GORDON 'BABE'	D. DECEMBER 10, 1992, ODENTON, MD.
2000-141	PHELPS, JOSHUA LEE	1503 REGAL MIST LOOP, TRINITY FL 34655
1980-105	PHELPS, KENNETH ALLEN	6030 EAST FOOTHILLS DRIVE, PARADISE VALLEY AZ 85253
1930-061	PHELPS, RAYMOND CLIFFORD	D. JULY 7, 1971, FT. PIERCE, FLA.
2003-126	PHELPS, THOMAS ALLEN	4418 PAWNEE PATH, VALRICO FL 33594
2001-141	PHELPS, TRAVIS HOWARD	PO BOX 336, WHEATON MO 64874
1941-088	PHILLEY, DAVID EARL	1336 EAST POLK STREET, PARIS TX 75460
1964-084	PHILLIPS, ADOLFO EMILIO LOPEZ	10438 88TH AVENUE, RICHMOND HILL NY 11418
1930-062	PHILLIPS, ALBERT ABERNATHY 'BUZZ'	D. NOVEMBER 6, 1964, BALTIMORE, MD.
2002-143	PHILLIPS, BRANDON EMIL	OLD ADD: STONE MOUNTAIN GA 30086
1993-145	PHILLIPS, CLARENCE GENE 'J.R.'	OLD ADD: 11062 WEST FARGO DRIVE, SUN CITY AZ 85351
1934-085	PHILLIPS, CLARENCE LEMUEL 'RED'	D. FEBRUARY 1, 1988, WICHITA, KAN.
1942-078	PHILLIPS, DAMON RUSSELL 'DEE'	D. NOVEMBER 4, 2004, FORT WORTH, TEXAS
1924-085	PHILLIPS, EDWARD DAVID	D. JANUARY 26, 1968, BUFFALO, N.Y.
2004-153	PHILLIPS, GEORGE ANDREW 'ANDY'	420 RIVER RANCH ROAD, GALLION AL 36742
1969-136	PHILLIPS, HAROLD ROSS 'LEFTY	D. JUNE 12, 1972, FULLERTON, CALIF.
1953-069	PHILLIPS, HOWARD EDWARD 'ED'	8878 COUNTY ROAD 414, HANNIBAL MO 63401

1947-067	PHILLIPS, JACK DORN	721 MAY ROAD #2, POTSDAM NY 13676
1999-153	PHILLIPS, JASON CHARLES	265 KATIE LANE, MONTOURSVILLE PA 17754
2001-142	PHILLIPS, JASON LLOYD	16374 WOODSON VIEW ROAD, POWAY CA 92064
1945-079	PHILLIPS, JOHN	D. JUNE 16, 1958, ST. LOUIS, MO.
1955-092	PHILLIPS, JOHN MELVIN 'BUBBA'	D. JUNE 22, 1993, HATTIESBURG, MISS.
1982-098	PHILLIPS, KEITH ANTHONY 'TONY'	13341 EAST COCHISE ROAD, SCOTTSDALE AZ 85259
1973-095	PHILLIPS, MICHAEL DWAINE	3322 RIDGEFIELD, IRVING TX 75062
1970-107	PHILLIPS, NORMAN EDWIN 'EDDIE'	8211 CHICKENING WAY, LOUISVILLE KY 40228
2004-154	PHILLIPS, PAUL ANTHONY	6757 CENTER HILL ROAD, BAILEY MS 39320
1962-105	PHILLIPS, RICHARD EUGENE	D. MARCH 29, 1998, BURNABY, B.C.
1956-068	PHILLIPS, WILLIAM TAYLOR 'TAYLOR'	594 MEIN MITCHELL ROAD, HIRAM GA 30141
1966-072	PHOEBUS, THOMAS HAROLD	2822 SW LAKEMONT PLACE, PALM CITY FL 34990
1994-086	PHOENIX, STEVEN ROBERT	11212 HORIZON HILLS DRIVE, EL CAJON CA 92020
2000-142	PIATT, ADAM DAVID	1808 SE 37TH TERRACE, CAPE CORAL FL 33904
1991-139	PIATT, DOUGLAS WILLIAM	29 L STREET, BEAVER PA 15009
1992-106	PIAZZA, MICHAEL JOSEPH	3591 CHINNBERRY TERRACE, BOYNTON BEACH FL 33436
1977-113	PICCIOLO, ROBERT MICHAEL 'ROB'	11773 INVIERNO DRIVE, SAN DIEGO CA 92124
1945-080	PICCIUTO, NICHOLAS THOMAS	D. JANUARY 10, 1997, WINCHESTER, VA.
1992-107	PICHARDO, HIPOLITO ANTONIO	JICOME, ESPERANZA ESPERANZA, DOM REP
1960-082	PICHE, RONALD JACQUES	100 RUE DE GASPE #1208 VERDUN QC, H3E 1E5 CANADA
1923-103	PICK, EDGAR EVERETT	D. MAY 13, 1967, WEST LOS ANGELES, CALIF.
1998-146	PICKERING, CALVIN E.	1913 EAST BROAD STREET, TAMPA FL 33610
1931-069	PICKERING, URBANE HENRY 'DICK'	D. MAY 13, 1970, MODESTO, CALIF.
1998-147	PICKETT, CECIL LEE 'RICKY'	1017 WOOD RIDGE DRIVE, AZLE TX 76020
2002-144	PICKFORD, KEVIN PATRICK	6006 NORTH HARCOURT DRIVE, COEUR D'ALENE ID 83815
1933-051	PICKREL, CLARENCE DOUGLAS	D. NOVEMBER 4, 1983, ROCKY MOUNT, VA.
1988-106	PICO, JEFFREY MARK	3291 GRAPE WAY, CHICO CA 95973
1947-068	PICONE, MARIO PETER	8876 BAY 16, BROOKLYN NY 11214
1940-068	PIECHOTA, ALOYSIUS EDWARD	D. JUNE 13, 1996, CHICAGO, ILL.
2004-155	PIEDRA, JORGE MOISES	14748 BURBANK BLVD, VAN NUYS CA 91411
1992-108	PIERCE, EDWARD JOHN	543 CRESTVIEW DRIVE, GLENDORA CA 91741
1995-172	PIERCE, JEFFREY CHARLES	PO BOX 143, KNOTTS ISLAND NC 27950
1973-096	PIERCE, LAVERN JACK 'JACK'	1002 CORTEZ STREET, LAREDO TX 78040
1924-086	PIERCE, RAYMOND LESTER	D. MAY 4, 1963, DENVER, COLO.
1967-085	PIERCE, TONY MICHAEL	6119 BRITTANY COURT, COLUMBUS GA 31909
1945-081	PIERCE, WALTER WILLIAM 'BILLY'	1321 BAILEYS CROSSING DRIVE, LEMONT IL 60439
1945-082	PIERETTI, MARINO PAUL 'CHICK'	D. JANUARY 30, 1981, SAN FRANCISCO, CALIF.
1920-096	PIEROTTI, ALBERT FELIX	D. FEBRUARY 12, 1964, EVERETT, MASS.
2000-143	PIERRE, JUAN D'VAUGHN	240 RIVERSIDE BLVD #10P, NEW YORK NY 10069
1950-078	PIERRO, WILLIAM LEONARD	D. APRIL 1, 2006, BROOKLYN, N.Y.
1950-079	PIERSALL, JAMES ANTHONY	1105 OAKVIEW DRIVE, WHEATON IL 60187
2001-143	PIERSOLL, CHRISTOPHER EARL	4417 GROVELAND AVENUE, SARASOTA FL 34231
1998-148	PIERZYNSKI, ANTHONY JOHN 'A. J.'	8990 DARLENE AVENUE, ORLANDO FL 32836
1931-070	PIET, ANTHONY FRANCIS	D. DECEMBER 1, 1981, HINSDALE, ILL.
1957-067	PIGNATANO, JOSEPH BENJAMIN	150 78TH ST, BROOKLYN NY 11209
1946-083	PIKE, JAMES WILLARD	D. MARCH 28, 1984, SAN DIEGO, CALIF.
1956-069	PIKTUZIS, GEORGE RICHARD	D. NOVEMBER 28, 1993, LONG BEACH, CALIF.
1956-070	PILARCIK, ALFRED JAMES	BOX 185, SAINT JOHN IN 46373
1949-064	PILLETTE, DUANE XAVIER	404 LILY ANN WAY, SAN JOSE CA 95123
1936-073	PILNEY, ANDREW JAMES	D. SEPTEMBER 15, 1996, NEW ORLEANS, LA.
1968-080	PINA, HORACIO GARCIA	OLD ADD: VENUSTIANA CARRANZA 207, OAHUILA MEX
2001-144	PINEDA, LUIS A.	OLD ADD: SAN CRISTOBAL DOM REP
2000-144	PINEIRO, JOEL ALBERTO	5990 BRAEMER PLACE #101, ORLANDO FL 32802
1964-085	PINIELLA, LOUIS VICTOR	1005 TARAY DE AVILA, TAMPA FL 33613
1958-073	PINSON, VADA EDWARD	D. OCTOBER 21, 1995, OAKLAND, CALIF.
2006-155	PINTO, RENYEL ELIGIO	OLD ADD: CUPIRA VENEZ
1922-109	PINTO, WILLIAM LERTON 'LERTON'	D. MAY 13, 1983, OXNARD, CALIF.
1932-063	PIPGRAS, EDWARD JOHN	D. APRIL 13, 1964, CURRIE, MINN.
1923-104	PIPGRAS, GEORGE WILLIAM	D. OCTOBER 19, 1986, GAINESVILLE, FLA.
1936-074	PIPPEN, HENRY HAROLD 'COTTON'	D. FEBRUARY 15, 1981, WILLIAMS, CALIF.
1993-146	PIRKL, GREGORY DANIEL	6822 EMERALD BAY LANE, INDIANAPOLIS IN 46237
1978-100	PIRTLE, GERALD EUGENE	30306 EAST 59TH, BROKEN ARROW OK 74014
1997-129	PISCIOTTA, MARC GEORGE	867 VILLAGE GREENE NW, MARIETTA GA 30064
1953-070	PISONI, JAMES PETE	D. FEBRUARY 4, 2007, DALLAS, TEXAS
1938-074	PITKO, ALEXANDER	655 SOUTH 79TH WAY, MESA AZ 85208
1970-108	PITLOCK, LEE EDWARD 'SKIP'	C/O C. PITLOCK, 215 PROSPECT STREET, SEGUIN TX 78155
1985-092	PITTARO, CHRISTOPHER FRANCIS	42 PINTINALLI DRIVE, TRENTON NJ 08619
1921-082	PITTENGER, CLARKE ALONZO 'PINKY'	D. NOVEMBER 4, 1977, FORT LAUDERDALE, FLA.
1981-097	PITTMAN, JOSEPH WAYNE	809 MCKINNON DR, COLUMBUS GA 31907
1974-105	PITTS, GAYLEN RICHARD	214 ROCKY BLUFF LANE, MOUNTAIN HOME AR 72653
1995-173	PITTSLEY, JAMES MICHAEL	SOUTH OLD WOODS ROAD, DUBOIS PA 15801
1957-068	PITULA, STANLEY	D. AUGUST 16, 1965, HACKENSACK, N.J.
1957-069	PIZARRO, JUAN CORDOVA	2262 BORINQUEN AVENUE, SANTURCE PR 00912
1979-085	PLADSON, GORDON CECIL	19087 87 A AVENUE SURREY BC, V4N 3C5 CANADA
1931-071	PLANETA, EMIL JOSEPH	D. FEBRUARY 2, 1963, ROCKY HILL, CONN.
1978-101	PLANK, EDWARD ARTHUR	1816 BRIDGE STREET, ENGLEWOOD FL 34223
1993-147	PLANTENBERG, ERIK JOHN	9521 LA COSTA LANE, LITTLETON CO 80124
1990-126	PLANTIER, PHILLIP ALAN	16001 MARTINCOTT ROAD, POWAY CA 92064
1955-093	PLARSKI, DONALD JOSEPH	D. DECEMBER 29, 1981, ST. LOUIS, MO.
1962-106	PLASKETT, ELMO ALEXANDER	D. NOVEMBER 2, 1998, FREDERIKSTED, V.I.
1942-079	PLATT, MIZELL GEORGE 'WHITEY'	D. JULY 27, 1970, WEST PALM BEACH, FLA.
1961-084	PLEIS, WILLIAM	3835 LITTLE COUNTRY ROAD, PARRISH FL 34219
1986-123	PLESAC, DANIEL THOMAS	245 EAST WHITE THORNE LANE, VALPARAISO IN 46383
1956-071	PLESS, RANCE	5528 ASHEVILLE HWY, GREENEVILLE TN 37743
1956-072	PLEWS, HERBERT EUGENE	350 PONCA PLACE, BOULDER CO 80303
1972-085	PLODINEC, TIMOTHY ALFRED	23251 GILMORE STREET, WEST HILLS CA 91307

1968-081	PLUMMER, WILLIAM FRANCIS	5609 WEST ACACIA BLOSSOM PLACE, MARANA AZ 85653
1986-124	PLUNK, ERIC VAUGHN	9500 PATS POINT DRIVE, CORONA CA 92883
1991-140	PLYMPTON, JEFFREY HUNTER	8 ROBIN STREET, PLAINVILLE MA 02762
1942-080	POAT, RAYMOND WILLIS	D. APRIL 29, 1990, OAK LAWN, ILL.
1975-090	POCOROBA, BIFF BENEDICT	7002 DESHON RIDGE DRIVE, LITHONIA GA 30058
1949-065	PODBIELAN, CLARENCE ANTHONY 'BUD'	D. OCTOBER 26, 1982, SYRACUSE, N.Y.
1940-069	PODGAJNY, JOHN SIGMUND	D. MARCH 2, 1971, CHESTER, PA.
1953-071	PODRES, JOHN JOSEPH	1 COLONIAL COURT, QUEENSBURY NY 12804
2001-145	PODSEDNIK, SCOTT ERIC	176 BERGER ROAD, WEST TX 76691
1975-091	POEPPING, MICHAEL HAROLD	13047 230TH AVENUE, PIERZ MN 56364
1926-064	POETZ, JOSEPH FRANK	D. FEBRUARY 7, 1942, ST. LOUIS, MO.
1940-070	POFAHL, JAMES WILLARD	D. SEPTEMBER 14, 1984, OWATONNA, MINN.
1979-086	POFF, JOHN WILLIAM	2786 MISHLER ROAD, MIO MI 48647
1937-088	POFFENBERGER, CLETUS ELWOOD 'BOOTS'	D. SEPTEMBER 1, 1999, WILLIAMSPORT, MD.
1950-080	POHOLSKY, THOMAS GEORGE	D. JANUARY 6, 2001, KIRKWOOD, MO.
1936-075	POINDEXTER, CHESTER JENNINGS 'JINKS'	D. MARCH 3, 1983, NORMAN, OKLA.
1963-093	POINTER, AARON ELTON	4902 NORTH SCENIC VIEW LANE, TACOMA WA 98407
1998-149	POLANCO, PLACIDO ENRIQUE	9494 SW 125TH TERRACE, MIAMI FL 33176
1943-113	POLAND, HUGH REID	D. MARCH 29, 1984, GUTHRIE, KY.
1997-130	POLCOVICH, KEVIN MICHAEL	3 BEARDSLEY STREET, AUBURN NY 13021
1973-097	POLE, RICHARD HENRY	21012 WHITLOCK DRIVE, DEARBORN HEIGHTS MI 48127
1985-093	POLIDOR, GUSTAVO ADOLFO	D. APRIL 28, 1995, CARACAS, VENEZ.
1998-150	POLITTE, CLIFFORD ANTHONY	6306 SPRING OAK COURT #C, SAINT LOUIS MO 63128
1947-069	POLIVKA, KENNETH LYLE	D. JULY 23, 1988, AURORA, ILL.
1941-089	POLLET, HOWARD JOSEPH	D. AUGUST 8, 1974, HOUSTON, TEXAS
1996-153	POLLEY, EZRA DALE 'DALE'	107 REDDING ROAD, GEORGETOWN KY 40324
1932-064	POLLI, LOUIS AMERICO	D. DECEMBER 19, 2000, BERLIN, VT.
1937-089	POLLY, NICHOLAS JOSEPH	D. JANUARY 17, 1993, CHICAGO, ILL.
1977-114	POLONI, JOHN PAUL	1714 POLO CLUB DRIVE, TARPON SPRINGS FL 34689
1987-119	POLONIA, LUIS ANDREW	OLD ADD: 9 PROSPECT STREET, DEMAREST NJ 07627
1934-086	POMORSKI, JOHN LEON	D. DECEMBER 6, 1977, BRAMPTON, ONT.
1985-094	PONCE, CARLOS ANTONIO	590 KINGSBURY COURT, WELLINGTON FL 33414
2004-156	POND, SIMON EMILIO	OLD ADD: NORTH VANCOUVER BC
1998-151	PONSON, SIDNEY ALTON	OLD ADD: ARUBA NETHERLAND ANT.
1934-087	POOL, HARLIN WELTY	D. FEBRUARY 15, 1963, RODEO, CALIF.
1925-086	POOLE, JAMES RALPH	D. JANUARY 2, 1975, HICKORY, N.C.
1990-127	POOLE, JAMES RICHARD	OLD ADD: 40 CONNARD DRIVE, EASTON PA 18042
1941-090	POOLE, RAYMOND HERMAN	D. MARCH 1, 2006, BURLINGTON, N.C.
1952-081	POPE, DAVID	D. AUGUST 28, 1999, CLEVELAND, OHIO
1964-086	POPOVICH, PAUL EDWARD	2604 WOODLAWN, NORTHBROOK IL 60062
1969-137	POPOWSKI, EDWARD JOSEPH	D. DECEMBER 4, 2001, SAYREVILLE, N.J.
1973-098	POQUETTE, THOMAS ARTHUR	3411 RIDGEWAY DRIVE, EAU CLAIRE WI 54701
1981-098	PORTER, CHARLES WILLIAM	9321 SNYDER LN, PERRY HALL MD 21128
2003-127	PORTER, COLIN F.	1631 EAST SONORAN DESERT DRIVE, TUCSON AZ 85737
1951-078	PORTER, DANIEL EDWARD	7360 COWLES MT BLVD, SAN DIEGO CA 92119
1971-082	PORTER, DARRELL RAY	D. AUGUST 5, 2002, KANSAS CITY, MO.
1952-082	PORTER, J.W. 'JAY'	9677 HEATHER CIRCLE WEST, PALM BEACH GARDENS FL 33410
1999-154	PORTER, MARQUIS DONNELL 'BO'	1226 NORTH TEAL ESTATES CIRCLE, FRESNO TX 77545
1926-065	PORTER, NED SWINDELL	D. JUNE 30, 1968, GAINESVILLE, FLA.
1929-084	PORTER, RICHARD TWILLEY	D. SEPTEMBER 24, 1974, PHILADELPHIA, PA.
1981-099	PORTER, ROBERT LEE	2301 BUENA STREET, NAPA CA 94558
1948-081	PORTERFIELD, ERWIN COOLIDGE 'BOB'	D. APRIL 28, 1980, CHARLOTTE, N.C.
1948-082	PORTO, ALFRED	635 WEST AVENUE 514, PALMDALE CA 93551
1954-083	PORTOCARRERO, ARNOLD MARIO	D. JUNE 21, 1986, KANSAS CITY, KAN.
1985-095	PORTUGAL, MARK STEVEN	67 SERPENTINE ROAD, WARREN RI 02885
1999-155	PORZIO, LAWRENCE MICHAEL 'MIKE'	20 MEEKER, WESTPORT CT 06880
1995-174	POSADA, JORGE RAFAEL	16814 AVILA BLVD, TAMPA FL 33613
1960-083	POSADA, LEOPOLDO JESUS	8200 GRAND CANAL DRIVE, MIAMI FL 33144
1993-148	POSE, SCOTT VERNON	1216 KINTAIL DRIVE, RALEIGH NC 27613
1938-075	POSEDEL, WILLIAM JOHN	D. NOVEMBER 28, 1989, LIVERMORE, CALIF.
1932-065	POSER, JOHN FALK 'BOB'	D. MAY 21, 2002, COLUMBUS, WISC.
1946-084	POSSEHL, LOUIS THOMAS	D. OCTOBER 7, 1997, SARASOTA, FLA.
1922-110	POST, SAMUEL GILBERT	D. MARCH 31, 1971, PORTSMOUTH, VA.
1949-066	POST, WALTER CHARLES	D. JANUARY 6, 1982, SAINT HENRY, OHIO
1999-156	POTE, LOUIS WILLIAM	10601 ORCHARD LANE, CHICAGO RIDGE IL 60415
1922-111	POTT, NELSON ADOLPH	D. DECEMBER 3, 1963, MACK, OHIO
1938-076	POTTER, MARYLAND DYKES 'DYKES'	D. FEBRUARY 27, 2002, GREENUP, KY.
1976-075	POTTER, MICHAEL GARY	21582 ARCHER CIR, HUNTINGTON BEACH CA 92646
1936-076	POTTER, NELSON THOMAS	D. SEPTEMBER 30, 1990, MOUNT MORRIS, ILL.
1923-105	POTTER, SQUIRE	D. JANUARY 27, 1983, ASHLAND, KY.
1996-154	POTTS, MICHAEL LARRY	3560 STRICKLAND STREET, LITHIA SPRINGS GA 30057
1967-086	POULSEN, KEN STERLING	OLD ADD: 1644 MAYALL STREET, NORTH HILLS CA 91343
1987-120	POWELL, ALONZO SIDNEY	620 GARFIELD STREET, SAN FRANCISCO CA 94132
1930-063	POWELL, ALVIN JACOB 'JAKE'	D. NOVEMBER 4, 1948, WASHINGTON. D. C.
1985-096	POWELL, DENNIS CLAY	PO BOX 133, NORMAN PARK GA 31771
1963-094	POWELL, GROVER DAVID	D. MAY 21, 1985, RALEIGH, N.C.
1978-102	POWELL, HOSKEN	1289 TAMARA STREET, PENSACOLA FL 32503
1995-175	POWELL, JAMES WILLARD 'JAY'	106 COVE LANE, MADISON MS 39110
1998-152	POWELL, JEREMY ROBERT	2710 WEST VIA CALABRIA, PHOENIX AZ 85086
1961-085	POWELL, JOHN WESLEY 'BOOG'	333 WEST CAMDEN STREET, BALTIMORE MD 21201
1997-131	POWELL, LEJON DANTE 'DANTE'	6235 RIVIERA CIRCLE, LONG BEACH CA 90815
1971-083	POWELL, PAUL RAY	5254 EAST ENROSE STREET, MESA AZ 85205
1955-094	POWELL, ROBERT LEROY	4424 CRIMSON LEAF DRIVE, LAS VEGAS NV 89130
1993-149	POWELL, ROSS JOHN	605 BRISTLEWOOD DRIVE, MCKINNEY TX 75070
1998-153	POWELL, WILLIAM BRIAN 'BRIAN'	246 RIVER OAKS DRIVE, BAINBRIDGE GA 31717
1981-100	POWER, TED HENRY	544 SUTTON PLACE, LONGBOAT KEY FL 34228

1954-084	POWER, VICTOR PELLOT	D. NOVEMBER 29, 2005, BAYAMON, P.R.
1932-066	POWERS, ELLIS FOREE 'MIKE'	D. DECEMBER 2, 1983, LOUISVILLE, KY.
1955-095	POWERS, JOHN CALVIN	D. SEPTEMBER 25, 2001, BIRMINGHAM, ALA.
1927-072	POWERS, JOHN LLOYD 'IKE'	D. DECEMBER 22, 1968, HANCOCK, MD.
1938-077	POWERS, LESLIE EDWIN	D. NOVEMBER 13, 1978, SANTA MONICA, CALIF.
1957-070	POWIS, CARL EDGAR	D. MAY 10, 1999, HOUSTON, TEXAS
1995-176	POZO, ARQUIMEDEZ ORTIZ	CALLE VERSALLES #25 JARDINES SANTO DOMINGO, DOM REP
2006-156	PRADO, MARTIN MANUEL	OLD ADD: MARACAY VENEZUELA
1975-092	PRALL, WILFRED ANTHONY 'WILLIE'	3 PHEASANT RUN, KINNELON NJ 07405
1949-067	PRAMESA, JOHN STEVEN	D. SEPTEMBER 9, 1996, SIMI VALLEY, CALIF.
2002-145	PRATT, ANDREW ELIAS	OLD ADD: 2040 NORTH VAL VISTA DRIVE, CHINO VALLEY CA 86323
1921-083	PRATT, FRANCIS BRUCE	D. APRIL 8, 1974, CENTREVILLE, ALA.
1992-109	PRATT, TODD ALAN	5950 DORSET BRIDGE ROAD, DOUGLASVILLE GA 30135
1963-095	PREGENZER, JOHN ARTHUR	6314 104TH STREET EAST, PUYALLUP WA 98373
1940-071	PREIBISCH, MELVIN ADOLPHUS	D. APRIL 12, 1980, SEALY, TEXAS
1948-083	PRENDERGAST, JAMES BARTHOLOMOEW	D. AUGUST 23, 1994, AMHERST, N.Y.
1961-086	PRESCOTT, GEORGE BERTRAND 'BOBBY'	OLD ADD: ESTAFETA PARQUE LEFEVRE, PANAMA CITY PANAMA
1951-079	PRESKO, JOSEPH EDWARD	1612 NE 77TH TERRACE, KANSAS CITY MO 64118
1984-090	PRESLEY, JAMES ARTHUR	2449 BONANZA DRIVE, CANTONMENT FL 32533
1938-078	PRESSNELL, FOREST CHARLES 'TOT'	D. JANUARY 6, 2001, FINDLAY, OHIO
1967-087	PRICE, JIMMIE WILLIAM	57152 WILLOW WAY, WASHINGTON MI 48094
1946-085	PRICE, JOHN THOMAS REID 'JACKIE'	D. OCTOBER 2, 1967, SAN FRANCISCO, CALIF.
1928-075	PRICE, JOSEPH PRESTON	D. JANUARY 15, 1961, WASHINGTON. D.C.
1980-106	PRICE, JOSEPH WALTER	1874 ARABIAN COURT, HEBRON KY 41048
1939-090	PRICHARD, ROBERT ALEXANDER	D. SEPTEMBER 25, 1991, ABILENE, TEXAS
1941-091	PRIDDY, GERALD EDWARD	D. MARCH 3, 1980, NORTH HOLLYWOOD, CALIF.
1962-107	PRIDDY, ROBERT SIMPSON	136 SHINGESS STREET #214, MCKEES ROCKS PA 15136
1993-150	PRIDE, CURTIS JOHN	1288 LAKE BREEZE DRIVE, WEST PALM BEACH FL 33414
1998-154	PRIEST, EDDIE LEE	445 BALLARD ROAD, ALTOONA AL 35952
2003-128	PRIETO, ALEJANDRO ANTONIO 'ALEX'	5010 HARBORSIDE DRIVE, WICHITA KS 67204
1995-177	PRIETO, ARIEL	434 RIDGE DRIVE, NAPLES FL 34108
2005-146	PRIETO, CHRISTIAN MICHAEL	5801 BIRKDALE LANE, FONTANA CA 92336
1933-052	PRIM, RAYMOND LEE	D. APRIL 29, 1995, MONTE RIO, CALIF.
1962-108	PRINCE, DONALD MARK	11143 J.B. WHITE WHY SOUTH, WHITEVILLE NC 28472
1987-121	PRINCE, THOMAS ALBERT	6816 10TH AVENUE NW, BRADENTON FL 34209
2001-146	PRINZ, BRET RANDOLPH	15471 NORTH 88TH AVENUE, PEORIA AZ 85382
2002-146	PRIOR, MARK WILLIAM	3256 CASA BONITA DRIVE, BONITA CA 91902
1957-071	PRITCHARD, HAROLD WILLIAM 'BUDDY'	507 EAST SUNNY HILL ROAD, FULLERTON CA 92635
1996-155	PRITCHETT, CHRISTOPHER DAVIS	OLD ADD: MODESTO CA 95356
1959-066	PROCTOR, JAMES ARTHUR	2 WEST MORELAND, SAINT LOUIS MO 63108
1923-106	PROCTOR, NOAH RICHARD 'RED'	D. DECEMBER 17, 1954, RICHMOND, VA.
2004-157	PROCTOR, SCOTT CHRISTOPHER	1110 NE TOWN TERRACE, JENSEN BEACH FL 34957
2000-145	PROKOPEC, KENNETH LUKE 'LUKE'	OLD ADD: RENMARK AUSTRALIA
1976-076	PROLY, MICHAEL JAMES	2585 FRISCO DR, CLEARWATER FL 33519
1923-107	PROPST, WILLIAM JACOB 'JAKE'	D. FEBRUARY 24, 1967, COLUMBUS, MISS.
1920-097	PROTHRO, JAMES THOMPSON 'DOC'	D. OCTOBER 14, 1971, MEMPHIS, TENN.
1929-085	PRUDHOMME, JOHN OLGUS	D. OCTOBER 4, 1992, SHREVEPORT, LA.
1920-098	PRUESS, EARL HENRY 'GIBBY'	D. AUGUST 28, 1979, BRANSON, MO.
1922-112	PRUETT, HUBERT SHELBY	D. JANUARY 28, 1982, LADUE, MO.
1944-107	PRUETT, JAMES CALVIN	D. JULY 29, 2003, WAUKESHA, WISC.
1975-093	PRUITT, RONALD RALPH	3632 TURNBERRY DRIVE, MEDINA OH 44256
1976-077	PRYOR, GREGORY RUSSELL	9726 WEST 115TH TERRACE, OVERLAND PARK KS 66210
1930-064	PUCCINELLI, GEORGE LAWRENCE	D. APRIL 16, 1956, SAN FRANCISCO, CALIF.
1984-091	PUCKETT, KIRBY	D. MARCH 6, 2006, PHOENIX, ARIZ.
1970-109	PUENTE, MIGUEL ANTONIO	COBRE 106, COL MORALES SAN LUIS POTOSI SLP, MEXICO
2002-147	PUFFER, BRANDON DUANE	1701 MCKENZIE STREET, ROUND ROCK TX 78664
1992-110	PUGH, TIMOTHY DEAN	8015 NORTH 187TH EAST AVENUE, OWASSO OK 74055
1977-115	PUHL, TERRANCE STEPHEN	331 WEST ALKIRE LAKE DRIVE, SUGAR LAND TX 77478
1974-106	PUIG, RICHARD GERALD	4216 MILL VALLEY COURT, TAMPA FL 33618
2001-147	PUJOLS, JOSE ALBERT 'ALBERT'	13229 AUTUMN TRAILS COURT, SAINT LOUIS MO 63141
1977-116	PUJOLS, LUIS BIENVENIDO	OLD ADD: 3867 JONATHANS WAY, LAKE WORTH FL 33462
1981-101	PULEO, CHARLES MICHAEL	PO BOX 1032, LOUISVILLE TN 37777
1983-114	PULIDO, ALFONSO	H. RICARDO MERCADO, CASILLAS 26-27 TIERRA BLANCA, VERACRUZ MEXICO
1994-087	PULIDO, JUAN CARLOS 'CARLOS'	OLD ADD: 7411 67TH AVENUE, MIAMI FL 33143
1991-141	PULLIAM, HARVEY JEROME	2009 MOUNT HAMILTON DRIVE, ANTIOCH CA 94531
1995-178	PULSIPHER, WILLIAM THOMAS	1996 SW CERTOSA ROAD, PORT SAINT LUCIE FL 34953
1925-087	PUMPELLY, SPENCER ARMSTRONG	D. DECEMBER 5, 1973, SAYRE, PA.
2001-148	PUNTO, NICHOLAS PAUL	27756 SOLLER #35, MISSION VIEJO CA 92692
1964-087	PURDIN, JOHN NOLAN	4942 SOUTHGATE PKWY, MYRTLE BEACH SC 29579
1926-066	PURDY, EVERETT VIRGIL 'PID'	D. JANUARY 16, 1951, BEATRICE, NEB.
1954-085	PURKEY, ROBERT THOMAS	5559 STEEPLECHASE COURT, BETHEL PARK PA 15102
1976-078	PUTMAN, EDDY WILLIAM	PO BOX 3366, MESQUITE NV 89024
1977-117	PUTNAM, PATRICK EDWARD	2311 CARRELL ROAD, FORT MYERS FL 33901
2003-129	PUTZ, JOSEPH JASON 'J.J.'	4039 BUTLER COURT, TRENTON MI 48183
1955-096	PYBURN, JAMES EDWARD	259 LONGVIEW DRIVE, JASPER AL 35501
1994-088	PYE, ROBERT EDWARD 'EDDIE'	307 POLK STREET, COLUMBIA TN 38401
1954-086	PYECHA, JOHN NICHOLAS	107 NOTTINGHAM DRIVE, CHAPEL HILL NC 27514
1939-091	PYLE, EWALD	D. JANUARY 10, 2004, DUQUOIN, ILL.
1928-076	PYLE, HARLAN ALBERT	D. JANUARY 13, 1993, BEATRICE, NEB.
1932-067	PYTLAK, FRANK ANTHONY	D. MAY 8, 1977, BUFFALO, N.Y.
1986-125	PYZNARSKI, TIMOTHY MATTHEW	10716 SOUTH AUSTIN, CHICAGO RIDGE IL 60415

Q

2004-158	QUALLS, CHAD MICHAEL	1868 260TH STREET, LOMITA CA 90717

1969-138	QUALLS, JAMES ROBERT	410 NORTH COUNTY ROAD 950, SUTTER IL 62373
1953-072	QUALTERS, THOMAS FRANCIS	236 LAKE ROAD, SOMERSET PA 15501
1992-111	QUANTRILL, PAUL JOHN	334 EAST LAKE ROAD #117, PALM HARBOR FL 34685
1964-088	QUEEN, MELVIN DOUGLAS	430 QUINTANA #116, MORRO BAY CA 93442
1942-081	QUEEN, MELVIN JOSEPH	D. APRIL 4, 1982, FORT SMITH, ARK.
1954-087	QUEEN, WILLIAM EDDLEMAN	D. APRIL 23, 2006, GASTONIA, N.C.
1931-072	QUELLICH, GEORGE WILLIAM	D. AUGUST 31, 1958, JOHNSVILLE, CALIF.
2006-157	QUENTIN, CARLOS JOSE	1666 POINT CONCEPTION COURT, CHULA VISTA CA 91911
2000-146	QUEVEDO, RUBEN EDUARDO	OLD ADD: VALENCIA VENEZUELA
1939-092	QUICK, JAMES HAROLD	D. MARCH 9, 1974, SWANSEA, ILL.
1965-088	QUILICI, FRANK RALPH	3413 EAST 126TH STREET, BURNSVILLE MN 55337
2003-130	QUINLAN, ROBB MICHAEL	1271 BOBCAT LANE, MAPLEWOOD MN 55119
1990-128	QUINLAN, THOMAS RAYMOND	1061 SOUTH STERLING AVENUE, MAPLEWOOD MN 55119
1949-068	QUINN, FRANK WILLIAM	D. JANUARY 11, 1993, BOYNTON BEACH, FLA.
1999-157	QUINN, MARK DAVID	OLD ADD: WEST COVINA CA 91790
1941-092	QUINN, WELLINGTON HUNT 'WIMPY'	D. SEPTEMBER 1, 1954, LOS ANGELES, CALIF.
1983-115	QUINONES, LUIS RAUL	5821 CALLE SAN BRUNO, PONCE PR 00730
1986-126	QUINONES, REY FRANCISCO	OLD ADD: PO BOX 1323, SAINT JUST PR 00978
1988-107	QUINTANA, CARLOS NARCIS	OLD ADD: RIVER STREET NO. 558, MAPORAL MIRANDA VENEZ
1974-107	QUINTANA, LUIS JOAQUIN	OLD ADD: CASCRIO CATONI ED. 11 #70, VEGA BAJA PR 00763
2005-147	QUINTANILLA, OMAR	12457 PASEO DE ARCO COURT, EL PASO TX 79928
2003-131	QUINTERO, HUMBERTO	OLD ADD: MARACAIBO VENEZUELA
1996-156	QUIRICO, RAFAEL OCTAVIO DOTTIN	2901 NORTH DALE MABRY HWY #2415, TAMPA FL 33607
1962-109	QUIRK, ARTHUR LEONARD	3 ENSIGN LANE, STONINGTON CT 06378
1975-094	QUIRK, JAMES PATRICK 'JAMIE'	310 WEST 123RD TERRACE, KANSAS CITY MO 64145
2004-159	QUIROZ, GUILLERMO ANTONIO	OLD ADD: MARACAIBO VENEZUELA
1979-087	QUISENBERRY, DANIEL RAYMOND	D. SEPTEMBER 30, 1998, LEAWOOD, KAN.

R

1995-179	RAABE, BRIAN CHARLES	38760 KOST TRAIL, NORTH BRANCH MN 55056
1982-099	RABB, JOHN ANDREW	OLD ADD: 1321 WEST 106TH ST, LOS ANGELES CA 90044
1922-113	RABBITT, JOSEPH PATRICK	D. DECEMBER 5, 1969, NORWALK, CONN.
1957-072	RABE, CHARLES HENRY	6059 E. SIERRA BLANCA STREET, MESA AZ 85215
2006-158	RABE, JOSHUA WAYNE	1710 OAK STREET, QUINCY IL 62301
2006-159	RABELO, MICHAEL GREGORY	5813 NORTH 17TH STREET, TAMPA FL 33610
2004-160	RABURN, RYAN N.	6612 IKE SMITH ROAD, PLANT CITY FL 33565
1940-072	RACHUNOK, STEPHEN STEPANOVICH	D. MAY 11, 2002, CORONA, CALIF.
1947-070	RACKLEY, MARVIN EUGENE	512 SOUTH BIBB STREET, WESTMINSTER SC 29693
1992-112	RACZKA, MICHAEL	72 FOLEY DRIVE, SOUTHINGTON CT 06489
1962-110	RADATZ, RICHARD RAYMOND	D. MARCH 16, 2005, EASTON, MASS.
1934-088	RADCLIFF, RAYMOND ALLEN 'RIP'	D. MAY 23, 1962, ENID, OKLA.
1971-084	RADER, DAVID MARTIN	2620 SUNSET HILLS, ESCONDIDO CA 92025
1967-088	RADER, DOUGLAS LEE	PO BOX 2768, STUART FL 34995
1921-084	RADER, DREW LEON	D. JUNE 5, 1975, CATSKILL, N.Y.
1990-129	RADINSKY, SCOTT DAVID	2974 SANTIAGO STREET, WESTLAKE VILLAGE CA 91362
1995-180	RADKE, BRAD WILLIAM	907 OAKWOOD DRIVE, LARGO FL 33770
1999-158	RADLOSKY, ROBERT VINCENT	1219 WEST BROWARD STREET, LANTANA FL 33462
1998-155	RADMANOVICH, RYAN ASHLEY	205 337 SIXTH AVENUE NE CALGARY AB, T2E 0M1 CANADA
1936-077	RADTKE, JACK WILLIAM	D. OCTOBER 24, 2006, TWIN FALLS, IDAHO
1954-088	RAETHER, HAROLD HERMAN	230 OAK SHORE DRIVE, BURNSVILLE MN 55306
1939-093	RAFFENSBERGER, KENNETH DAVID	D. NOVEMBER 10, 2002, YORK, PA.
1969-139	RAFFO, ALBERT MARTIN	330 PLEASANT VIEW, JASPER TN 37347
1997-132	RAGGIO, BRADY JOHN	564 ZEPHYR CIRCLE, DANVILLE CA 94526
1932-068	RAGLAND, FRANK ROLAND	D. JULY 28, 1959, PARIS, MISS.
1971-085	RAGLAND, THOMAS	20201 GREENLAWN ST, DETROIT MI 48224
1975-095	RAICH, ERIC JAMES	3963 EDWARD DRIVE, BRUNSWICK OH 44212
1999-159	RAIN, STEVEN NICHOLAS	20320 EAST CRESTLINE DRIVE, WALNUT CA 91789
1957-073	RAINES, LAWRENCE GLENN HOPE	D. JANUARY 28, 1978, LANSING, MICH.
1979-088	RAINES, TIMOTHY	1242 ST. ALBANS LOOP, LAKE MARY FL 32746
2001-149	RAINES, TIMOTHY	1242 ST. ALBANS LOOP, LAKE MARY FL 32746
1979-089	RAINEY, CHARLES DAVID	6484 DEL CERRO BLVD, SAN DIEGO CA 92120
1978-103	RAJSICH, DAVID CHRISTOPHER	1605 NORTH MAIN STREET, FLAGSTAFF AZ 86004
1982-100	RAJSICH, GARY LOUIS	6510 CHARLESTON DRIVE, COLLEYVILLE TX 76034
2004-161	RAKERS, AARON JAMES	553 WEST 3RD STREET, TRENTON IL 62293
1998-156	RAKERS, JASON PAUL	845 RESERVE STREET, PITTSBURGH PA 15209
1960-084	RAKOW, EDWARD CHARLES	D. AUGUST 26, 2000, WEST PALM BEACH, FLA.
1946-086	RAMAZOTTI, ROBERT LOUIS	D. FEBRUARY 15, 2000, ALTOONA, PA.
1939-094	RAMBERT, ELMER DONALD 'PEP'	D. NOVEMBER 16, 1974, WEST PALM BEACH, FLA.
1926-067	RAMBO, WARREN DAWSON 'PETE'	D. JUNE 19, 1991, CAMDEN, N.J.
1998-157	RAMIREZ, ALEXANDER RAMON	PO BOX 880, WINTER HAVEN FL 33882
1998-158	RAMIREZ, ARAMIS NIN	OLD ADD: SANTO DOMINGO DOM REP
1983-116	RAMIREZ, DANIEL ALLAN 'ALLAN'	8 LINE DRIVE ROAD, VICTORIA TX 77905
2004-162	RAMIREZ, ELIZARDO	OLD ADD: SANTO DOMINGO DOM REP
2003-132	RAMIREZ, ERASMO	3605 SOUTH PARTON STREET, SANTA ANA CA 92707
2005-148	RAMIREZ, HANLEY	OLD ADD: SANTO DOMINGO DOM REP
1999-160	RAMIREZ, HECTOR BIENVENIDO	OLD ADD: EL SEIBO DOM REP
2003-133	RAMIREZ, HORACIO	OLD ADD: INGLEWOOD CA 90301
1999-161	RAMIREZ, JULIO CESAR	OLD ADD: SANTO DOMINGO DOM REP
1993-151	RAMIREZ, MANUEL ARISTIDES 'MANNY'	2666 PALMER PLACE, WESTON FL 33332
1980-107	RAMIREZ, MARIO	OLD ADD: HC03 BOX 14107, YAUCO PR 00698
1970-110	RAMIREZ, MILTON	7 TULIO LARRINAGA ST, MAYAGUEZ PR 00708
1974-108	RAMIREZ, ORLANDO	OLD ADD: SOCORRO MANZANO #9, G-1, CARTAGENA COLOMBIA
1980-108	RAMIREZ, RAFAEL EMILIO	OLD ADD: PO BOX 9, BUFORD GA 30515
2006-160	RAMIREZ, RAMON SANTO	OLD ADD: PUERTO PLATA DOM REP

1998-159 RAMIREZ, ROBERTO SANCHEZ............................6411 SOUTH 6TH AVENUE, PHOENIX AZ 85041
2006-161 RAMIREZ, SANTIAGO ....OLD ADD: BONAO DOM REP
1978-104 RAMOS, DOMINGO ANTONIO............................CARR DUARTE KM 8 1/2,LICEY AL MEDIO SANTIAGO, DOM REP
1997-133 RAMOS, EDGAR JOSE MALAVE............................OLD ADD: CUINANA VENEZUELA
1944-108 RAMOS, JESUS MANUEL GARCIA 'CHUCO'........D. SEPTEMBER 2, 1977, CARACAS, VENEZUELA
1991-142 RAMOS, JOHN JOSEPH............................4214 WEST LEONA STREET, TAMPA FL 33629
1997-134 RAMOS, KENNETH CECIL............................9 IRONBRIDGE LANE, PUEBLO CO 81001
2003-134 RAMOS, MARIO MARTIN............................107 LOYOLA DRIVE, PFLUGERVILLE TX 78660
1955-097 RAMOS, PEDRO............................OLD ADD: PO BOX 226504, MIAMI FL 33122
1978-105 RAMOS, ROBERTO 'BOBBY'............................15109 SW 62ND STREET, MIAMI FL 33139
1999-162 RAMSAY, ROBERT ARTHUR............................1122 NW 10TH AVENUE, CAMAS WA 98607
1947-071 RAMSDELL, JAMES WILLARD 'WILLIE'..............D. OCTOBER 8, 1969, WICHITA, KAN.
1992-113 RAMSEY, FERNANDO DAVID............................2501 SANDY TRAIL, KELLER TX 76248
1987-122 RAMSEY, MICHAEL JAMES............................PO BOX 262, HARLEM GA 30814
1978-106 RAMSEY, MICHAEL JEFFREY............................11564 92ND WAY NORTH, LARGO FL 34643
1945-083 RAMSEY, WILLIAM THRACE............................511 CENTER STREET, GALION OH 44833
1953-073 RAND, RICHARD HILTON............................D. JANUARY 22, 1996, MORENO VALLEY, CALIF.
1995-181 RANDA, JOSEPH GREGORY............................14512 MISSION ROAD, LEAWOOD KS 66224
1988-108 RANDALL, JAMES ODELL 'SAP'............................158 HEATHER LANE, RUSTON LA 71270
1976-079 RANDALL, ROBERT LEE............................UNIV. OF KANSAS, 220 ALLEN FIELDHOUSE, LAWRENCE KS 66045
2003-135 RANDALL, SCOTT PHILIP............................467 REED COURT, GOLETA CA 93117
1971-086 RANDLE, LEONARD SHENOFF 'LENNY'..............3332 GRAND AVENUE #116, CHINO HILLS CA 91710
2003-136 RANDOLPH, STEPHEN LECHARLES....................3706 APACHE FOREST DRIVE, AUSTIN TX 78739
1975-096 RANDOLPH, WILLIE LARRY............................715 JENNEY TRAIL, FRANKLIN LAKES NJ 07417
1962-111 RANEW, MERRITT THOMAS............................7611 SOUTH DUVAL ISLAND DRIVE, FLORAL CITY FL 34436
1949-069 RANEY, FRANK ROBERT DONALD 'RIBS'............D. JULY 7, 2003, WARREN, MICH.
2001-150 RANSOM, BRIAN CODY 'CODY'............................12217 EAST BLUEBIRD PLACE, CHANDLER AZ 85249
1981-102 RANSOM, JEFFERY DEAN............................2131 CURTIS ST, BERKELEY CA 94702
1949-070 RAPP, EARL WELLINGTON............................D. FEBRUARY 13, 1992, SWEDESBORO, N.J.
1921-085 RAPP, JOSEPH ALOYSIUS 'GOLDIE'....................D. JULY 1, 1966, LAMESA, CALIF.
1992-114 RAPP, PATRICK LELAND............................2771 SARA JANE DRIVE, SULPHUR LA 70663
1977-118 RAPP, VERNON FRED............................1559 REDWING LANE, BROOMFIELD CO 80020
1946-087 RASCHI, VICTOR JOHN ANGELO............................D. OCTOBER 14, 1988, GROVELAND, N.Y.
1983-117 RASMUSSEN, DENNIS LEE............................3402 GOLFVIEW BLVD, ORLANDO FL 32804
1975-097 RASMUSSEN, ERIC RALPH............................237 SW 45TH STREET, CAPE CORAL FL 33914
2005-149 RASNER, DARRELL W............................3994 WESTWOOD DRIVE, CARSON CITY NV 89703
1998-160 RATH, ALFRED GARY 'GARY'............................202 JAMES DRIVE, LONG BEACH MS 39560
1968-082 RATH, FRED HELSHER............................7308 PELICAN ISLAND DRIVE, TAMPA FL 33614
1998-161 RATH, FREDERICK HELSHER............................7308 PELICAN ISLAND DRIVE, TAMPA FL 33634
2000-147 RATLIFF, JON CHARLES............................289 BOUGHTON HILL ROAD, HONEOYE FALLS NY 14472
1965-089 RATLIFF, KELLY EUGENE 'GENE'............................3403 MILLERFIELD RD, MACON GA 31201
1963-096 RATLIFF, PAUL HAWTHORNE............................78 CAMPTON PLACE, LAGUNA NIGUEL CA 92677
1980-109 RATZER, STEVEN WAYNE............................1218 DELEON COURT, PALM HARBOR FL 34683
1972-086 RAU, DOUGLAS JAMES............................1615 TREASURE OAKS DRIVE, KATY TX 77450
2002-148 RAUCH, JON ERICH............................6535 JACOB DRIVE, WESTPORT KY 40077
1972-087 RAUCH, ROBERT JOHN............................3409 HEAD RIVER ROAD, VIRGINIA BEACH VA 23457
1966-073 RAUDMAN, ROBERT JOYCE 'SHORTY'................440 NORTH 300 WEST, TETONIA ID 83452
1977-119 RAUTZHAN, CLARENCE GEORGE 'LANCE'..........2472 COVINGTON DRIVE, MYRTLE BEACH SC 29579
1978-107 RAWLEY, SHANE WILLIAM............................4587 CHERRY BARK COURT, SARASOTA FL 34241
2005-150 RAY, CHRISTOPHER T............................15311 WINDING CREEK DRIVE, TAMPA FL 33613
1965-090 RAY, JAMES FRANCIS............................OLD ADD: 7530 PROMPTON, HOUSTON TX 77025
1981-103 RAY, JOHN CORNELIUS............................12470 SOUTH 432, CHOUTEAU OK 74337
1999-163 RAY, KENNETH ALAN............................65 HAMMOND HESTER ROAD, DAWSONVILLE GA 30534
1982-101 RAY, LARRY DOYLE............................8989 OAKMONT COURT, PLAINFIELD IN 46168
1958-074 RAYDON, CURTIS LOWELL............................OLD ADD: 242 PEACHTREE ROAD, JASPER TX 75951
1980-110 RAYFORD, FLOYD KINNARD............................11701 POINTE CIRCLE, FORT MYERS FL 33908
1959-067 RAYMOND, JOSEPH CLAUDE 'CLAUDE'..............3 DE LA CITIERE, B.P. 911, SAINT JEAN-SUR-RICHELIEU QC, J2W 1B8 CANADA
1973-099 RAZIANO, BARRY JOHN............................1315 4TH ST, KENNER LA 70062
1983-118 READY, RANDY MAX............................15835 EL CAMINO ENTRADA, POWAY CA 92064
2000-148 REAMES, WILLIAM BRITT 'BRITT'....................806 DALTON ROAD, SENECA SC 29678
1969-140 REAMS, LEROY............................6140 EAST 17TH STREET, OAKLAND CA 94621
1979-090 REARDON, JEFFREY JAMES............................5 MARLWOOD LN, PALM BEACH GARDENS FL 33410
1938-079 REBEL, ARTHUR ANTHONY............................D. JULY 10, 2004, TAMPA, FLA.
1968-083 REBERGER, FRANK BEALL............................439 SUNSET VIEW LANE, HOPE ID 83836
1992-115 REBOULET, JEFFREY ALAN............................3775 GRAND OAK TRAIL, DAYTON OH 45440
2001-151 REDDING, TIMOTHY J............................BENTLEY ROAD, CLYDE NY 14433
1932-069 REDER, JOHN ANTHONY............................D. APRIL 12, 1990, FALL RIVER, MASS.
1928-077 REDFERN, GEORGE HOWARD 'BUCK'................D. SEPTEMBER 8, 1964, ASHEVILLE, N.C.
1976-080 REDFERN, PETER IRVINE............................12516 HADDON AVENUE, SYLMAR CA 91342
1988-109 REDFIELD, JOSEPH RANDALL............................307 GLENVIEW CIRCLE, WOODWAY TX 76712
2000-149 REDMAN, JULIAN JAWONN 'TIKE'....................13838 VEAR CREEK ROAD, DUNCANVILLE AL 35456
1999-164 REDMAN, MARK ALLEN............................6818 EAST 109TH STREET, TULSA OK 74133
2003-137 REDMAN, PRENTICE MONTEZZ............................13814 BEAR CREEK ROAD, DUNCANVILLE AL 35456
1974-109 REDMON, GLENN VINCENT............................8509 DEE CIRCLE, RIVERVIEW FL 33569
1965-091 REDMOND, HOWARD WAYNE 'WAYNE'..............180 60 SUSSEX DRIVE, DETROIT MI 48235
1935-092 REDMOND, JACKSON MCKITTRICK....................D. JULY 28, 1968, GARLAND, TEXAS
1998-162 REDMOND, MICHAEL PATRICK............................13506 SOUTH BLUEGROUSE LANE, SPOKANE WA 99224
1982-102 REDUS, GARY EUGENE............................2202 MALLARD LANE SE, DECATUR AL 35601
1978-108 REECE, ROBERT SCOTT............................3106 CASTLEWOOD CIRCLE, POLLOCK PINES CA 95726
1990-130 REED, DARREN DOUGLAS............................161 NORTH CAESAR AVENUE, FRESNO CA 93727
2006-162 REED, ERIC SHANE............................OLD ADD: MONTICELLO AR
1958-075 REED, HOWARD DEAN............................D. DECEMBER 7, 1984, CORPUS CHRISTI, TEXAS
1984-092 REED, JEFF SCOTT............................259 SUNRISE, ELIZABETHTON TN 37643
2004-163 REED, JEREMY T............................977 HORMEL AVENUE, LAVERNE CA 91750
1981-104 REED, JERRY MAXWELL............................505 ENKA LAKE ROAD, CANDLER NC 28715
1987-123 REED, JODY ERIC............................17299 SOLIE ROAD, ODESSA FL 33556

1961-087	REED, JOHN BURWELL 'JACK'	PO BOX 728, TOUGALOO MS 39174
2005-151	REED, KEITH A.	1912 RED QUARTZ DRIVE, RALEIGH NC 27610
1988-110	REED, RICHARD ALLEN	9604 STATE ROUTE 7, PROCTORVILLE OH 45669
1969-141	REED, ROBERT EDWARD	42519 LAKE HOSPITALITY LN #L, ALTOONA FL 32702
1966-074	REED, RONALD LEE	2613 CLIFFVIEW DR, LILBURN GA 30247
1992-116	REED, STEVEN VINCENT	5335 PINE RIDGE ROAD, GOLDEN CO 80403
1952-083	REED, WILLIAM JOSEPH	D. DECEMBER 5, 2005, HOUSTON, TEXAS
1949-071	REEDER, WILLIAM EDGAR	D. MARCH 12, 2001, SULPHUR SPRINGS, TEXAS
1927-073	REESE, ANDREW JACKSON	D. JANUARY 10, 1966, TUPELO, MISS.
1997-135	REESE, CALVIN 'POKEY'	12416 SYLVAN OAK WAY, CHARLOTTE NC 28273
1940-073	REESE, HAROLD HENRY 'PEEWEE '	D. AUGUST 14, 1999, LOUISVILLE, KY.
1930-065	REESE, JAMES HYMIE	D. JULY 13, 1994, SANTA ANA, CALIF.
2005-152	REESE, KEVIN PATRICK	OLD ADD: SAN DIEGO CA
1964-089	REESE, RICHARD BENJAMIN 'RICH'	PO BOX 2339, CAREFREE AZ 85377
1926-068	REEVES, ROBERT EDWIN	D. JUNE 4, 1993, CHATTANOOGA, TENN.
1954-089	REGALADO, RUDOLPH VALENTINO	PO BOX 475, BORREGO SPRINGS CA 92004
1960-085	REGAN, PHILIP RAYMOND	1375 108TH ST, BYRON CENTER MI 49315
1926-069	REGAN, WILLIAM WRIGHT	D. JUNE 11, 1968, PITTSBURGH, PA.
2004-164	REGILIO, NICHOLAS D.	1700 FROGS LEAP COURT, PORT ORANGE FL 32128
1924-087	REGO, ANTONE 'TONY'	D. JANUARY 6, 1978, TULSA, OKLA.
1933-053	REIBER, FRANK BERNARD	D. DECEMBER 26, 2002, BRADENTON, FLA.
1949-072	REICH, HERMAN CHARLES	PO BOX 1292, BONSALL CA 92003
1964-090	REICHARDT, FREDERIC CARL 'RICK'	2605 NW 90TH TERRACE, GAINESVILLE FL 32606
1999-165	REICHERT, DANIEL ROBERT	445 CORNELL DRIVE, TURLOCK CA 95382
1922-114	REICHLE, RICHARD WENDELL	D. JUNE 13, 1967, ST. LOUIS, MO.
1946-088	REID, EARL PERCY	D. MAY 11, 1984, CULLMAN, ALA.
1987-124	REID, JESSIE THOMAS	2641 CAREY STATION ROAD, GREENSBORO GA 30642
1969-142	REID, SCOTT DONALD	OLD ADD: 4855 EAST WARREN ROAD, PHOENIX AZ 85044
1988-111	REIMER, KEVIN MICHAEL	OLD ADD: 1225 ENCLAVE CIRCLE #619, ARLINGTON TX 76011
1974-110	REINBACH, MICHAEL WAYNE	D. MAY 21, 1989, PALM DESERT, CALIF.
1928-078	REINHOLZ, ARTHUR AUGUST	D. DECEMBER 29, 1980, NEWPORT RICHEY, FLA.
1931-073	REIS, ROBERT JOSEPH THOMAS	D. MAY 1, 1973, ST. PAUL, MINN.
1938-080	REIS, THOMAS EDWARD	15456 SW 15TH TERRACE ROAD, OCALA FL 34473
1940-074	REISER, HAROLD PATRICK 'PETE'	D. OCTOBER 25, 1981, PALM SPRINGS, CALIF.
1932-070	REISS, ALBERT ALLEN	D. MAY 13, 1989, RED BANK, N.J.
2001-152	REITH, BRIAN ERIC	5515 40TH AVENUE EAST, BRADENTON FL 34208
2001-153	REITSMA, CHRISTOPHER MICHAEL	OLD ADD: 4920 NORTH LOCKWOOD RIDGE RD, SARASOTA FL 34234
1972-088	REITZ, KENNETH JOHN	2883 FAIRWAYS CIRCLE, SAINT CHARLES MO 63303
1995-182	REKAR, BRYAN ROBERT	4326 WATERVILLE AVENUE, WESLEY CHAPEL FL 33543
1996-157	RELAFORD, DESMOND LAMONT 'DESI'	12483 HIGHVIEW DRIVE, JACKSONVILLE FL 32225
1991-143	REMLINGER, MICHAEL JOHN	5320 EAST PALO VERDE DRIVE, PARADISE VALLEY AZ 85253
1979-091	REMMERSWAAL, WILHELMUS ABRAHAM	DOKTOR VAN PRAAG ST 16 WASSENAAR, HOLLAND
1975-098	REMY, GERALD PETER	33 VILES STREET, WESTON MA 02193
1991-144	RENFROE, COHEN WILLIAMS 'LADDIE'	236 HICKORY LANE, BATESVILLE MS 38606
1959-068	RENFROE, MARSHALL DALTON	D. DECEMBER 10, 1970, PENSACOLA, FLA.
1968-084	RENICK, WARREN RICHARD 'RICK'	7320 HAWKINS ROAD, SARASOTA FL 34241
1961-088	RENIFF, HAROLD EUGENE	D. SEPTEMBER 7, 2004, ONTARIO, CALIF.
1938-081	RENINGER, JAMES DAVID	D. AUGUST 23, 1993, NORTH FORT MYERS, FLA.
1969-143	RENKO, STEVEN	15812 WEST 136TH STREET, OLATHE KS 66062
1953-074	RENNA, WILLIAM BENEDITTO	1476 LESHER CT, SAN JOSE CA 95125
1930-066	RENSA, GEORGE ANTHONY 'TONY'	D. JANUARY 4, 1987, WILKES-BARRE, PA.
1996-158	RENTERIA, EDGAR ENRIQUE	12926 NW 20TH STREET, PEMBROKE PINES FL 33028
1986-127	RENTERIA, RICHARD AVINA	43310 CALLE NACIDO, TEMECULA CA 92592
1939-095	REPASS, ROBERT WILLIS	D. JANUARY 26, 2006, WETHERSFIELD, CONN.
2005-153	REPKO, JASON EDWARD	1186 TOMICH AVENUE, RICHLAND WA 99352
1978-109	REPLOGLE, ANDREW DAVID	8047 HIDDEN HILLS DRIVE, SPRING HILL FL 34606
1964-091	REPOZ, ROGER ALLEN	930 WHITEWATER DRIVE, FULLERTON CA 92633
1953-075	REPULSKI, ELDON JOHN 'RIP'	D. FEBRUARY 10, 1993, WAITE PARK, MINN.
1943-114	RESCIGNO, XAVIER FREDERICK	D. DECEMBER 24, 2005, SUN CITY WEST, ARIZ.
2005-154	RESOP, CHRISTOPHER PAUL	9622 BLUE STONE CIRCLE, FORT MYERS FL 33913
1949-073	RESTELLI, DINO PAOLO	D. AUGUST 8, 2006, SAN CARLOS, CALIF.
2002-149	RESTOVICH, MICHAEL JEROME	710 11TH STREET SW, ROCHESTER MN 55902
1968-085	RETTENMUND, MERVIN WELDON	655 INDIA STREET #123, SAN DIEGO CA 92101
1922-115	RETTIG, ADOLPH JOHN 'OTTO'	D. JUNE 16, 1977, STUART, FLA.
1961-089	RETZER, KENNETH LEO	746 HARVARD DRIVE, EDWARDSVILLE IL 62025
1975-099	REUSCHEL, PAUL RICHARD	106 CIRCLE DRIVE, AVON IL 61415
1972-089	REUSCHEL, RICKY EUGENE 'RICK'	PO BOX 143, RENFREW PA 16053
1969-144	REUSS, JERRY	1 LINE DRIVE, DES MOINES IA 50309
1992-117	REVENIG, TODD MICHAEL	2412 EAST PRESCOTT PLACE, CHANDLER AZ 85249
1978-110	REVERING, DAVID ALVIN	1039 SHADOW RIDGE COURT, WASHINGTON UT 84780
2005-155	REYES, ANTHONY L	OLD ADD: WHITTIER CA
1994-089	REYES, CARLOS ALBERTO	2811 BUTTERFLY LANDING DRIVE, LAND O'LAKES FL 34638
1997-136	REYES, DENNIS VELARDE	OLD ADD: HIGUERA DE ZARAGOVA MEXICO
1983-119	REYES, GILBERTO ROLANDO	CALLE 2DA. #7 LOS MAMEYES SANTO DOMINGO, DOM REP
2006-163	REYES, JOSE ARIEL (RAMIREZ)	OLD ADD: BARAHONA DOM REP
2003-138	REYES, JOSE BERNABE	OLD ADD: SANTIAGO DOM REP
1943-115	REYES, NAPOLEON AGUILERA	D. SEPTEMBER 15, 1995, MIAMI, FLA.
1995-183	REYES, RAFAEL ALBERTO 'AL'	OLD ADD: S.PEDRDIDA CLE 1A VICTORIA 115, SANTO DOMINGO DOM REP
2003-139	REYES, RENE	OLD ADD: MARGARITA VZ
1942-082	REYNOLDS, ALLIE PIERCE	D. DECEMBER 26, 1994, OKLAHOMA CITY, OKLA.
1968-086	REYNOLDS, ARCHIE EDWARD	1828 PINECREST DRIVE, TYLER TX 75701
1927-074	REYNOLDS, CARL NETTLES	D. MAY 29, 1978, HOUSTON, TEXAS
1945-084	REYNOLDS, DANIEL VANCE	D. FEBRUARY 18, 2007, STATESVILLE, N.C.
1978-111	REYNOLDS, DONALD EDWARD	6035 NE 35TH PLACE, PORTLAND OR 97211
1975-100	REYNOLDS, GORDON CRAIG 'CRAIG'	19 INVERNESS PARK WAY, HOUSTON TX 77055
1983-120	REYNOLDS, HAROLD CRAIG	2890 NW ANGELICA DRIVE, CORVALLIS OR 97330

1970-111	REYNOLDS, KENNETH LEE	182 GREENWOOD, MARLBOROUGH MA 01752
1992-118	REYNOLDS, RICHARD SHANE 'SHANE'	20 QUEEN MARY COURT, SUGAR LAND TX 77479
1969-145	REYNOLDS, ROBERT ALLEN	952 SW CAMPUS DRIVE #26D3, FEDERAL WAY WA 98023
1983-121	REYNOLDS, ROBERT JAMES	OLD ADD: 1411 T STREET #18, SACRAMENTO CA 95814
1982-103	REYNOLDS, RONN DWAYNE	OLD ADD: 6916 GARDEN RIDGE CIRCLE, WICHITA KS 67205
1963-097	REYNOLDS, THOMAS	1577 SAN ALTOS, LEMON GROVE CA 92045
1991-145	REYNOSO, ARMANDO MARTIN (GUTIERREZ)	OLD ADD: 3642 EAST AGAVE WAY, CHANDLER AZ 85225
1947-072	RHAWN, ROBERT JOHN	D. JUNE 9, 1984, DANVILLE, PA.
2006-164	RHEINECKER, JOHN PHILIP	7152 STATE HIGHWAY 156, WATERLOO IL 62298
1924-088	RHEM, CHARLES FLINT 'FLINT'	D. JULY 30, 1969, COLUMBIA, S.C.
1929-086	RHIEL, WILLIAM JOSEPH	D. AUGUST 16, 1946, YOUNGSTOWN, OHIO
1974-111	RHODEN, RICHARD ALAN 'RICK'	8009 WHISPER LAKE LANE EAST, PONTE VEDRA BEACH FL 32082
1991-146	RHODES, ARTHUR LEE	14114 PHOENIX ROAD, PHOENIX MD 21131
1952-084	RHODES, JAMES LAMAR 'DUSTY'	1047 MISTY ROSE AVENUE, HENDERSON NV 89074
1929-087	RHODES, JOHN GORDON 'GORDON'	D. MARCH 22, 1960, LONG BEACH, CALIF.
1990-131	RHODES, KARL DERRICK 'DUSTY'	234 FOREST AVENUE, CINCINNATI OH 45229
1982-104	RHOMBERG, KEVIN JAY	9692 EXECUTIVE COURT, MENTOR OH 44060
1926-070	RHYNE, HAROLD J.	D. JANUARY 7, 1971, ORANGEVALE, CALIF.
1964-092	RIBANT, DENNIS JOSEPH	46 SIDRA COVE, NEWPORT COAST CA 92657
1976-081	RICCELLI, FRANK JOSEPH	PO BOX 2102, SYRACUSE NY 13220
1995-184	RICCI, CHARLES MARK	1417 SKYLER DRIVE, WAXHAW NC 28173
1945-085	RICE, DELBERT	D. JANUARY 26, 1983, BUENA PARK, CALIF.
1948-084	RICE, HAROLD HOUSTON 'HAL'	D. DECEMBER 22, 1997, BLOOMINGTON, IND.
1923-108	RICE, HARRY FRANCIS 'SAM'	D. JANUARY 1, 1971, PORTLAND, ORE.
1974-112	RICE, JAMES EDWARD	35 BOBBY JONES DRIVE, ANDOVER MA 01810
1944-109	RICE, LEONARD OLIVER	D. JUNE 13, 1992, SONORA, CALIF.
1991-147	RICE, PATRICK EDWARD	4090 ZURICH DRIVE, COLORADO SPRINGS CO 80920
1926-071	RICE, ROBERT TURNBULL	D. FEBRUARY 20, 1986, ELIZABETHTOWN, PA.
1939-096	RICH, WOODROW EARL	D. APRIL 18, 1983, MORGANTON, N.C.
2000-150	RICHARD, CHRISTOPHER ROBERT	11389 IRONWOOD ROAD, SAN DIEGO CA 92131
1971-087	RICHARD, JAMES RODNEY 'J.R.'	11827 PEPPERDINE LANE, HOUSTON TX 77071
1971-088	RICHARD, LEE EDWARD 'BEE BEE'	1621 EAST 14TH ST, PORT ARTHUR TX 77640
1960-086	RICHARDS, DUANE LEE	PO BOX 54, PALESTINE OH 45352
1977-120	RICHARDS, EUGENE	6560 BUCKING HORSE LANE #103, HENDERSON NV 89011
1951-080	RICHARDS, FRED CHARLES	1760 DODGE NORTHWEST, WARREN OH 44485
1932-071	RICHARDS, PAUL RAPIER	D. MAY 5, 1986, WAXAHACHIE, TEXAS
1989-101	RICHARDS, RUSSELL EARL 'RUSTY'	OLD ADD: 805 FALLOW, MARBLE FALLS TX 78657
1929-088	RICHARDSON, CLIFFORD NOLEN 'NOLAN'	D. SEPTEMBER 25, 1951, ATHENS, GA.
1964-093	RICHARDSON, GORDON CLARK	23 ST. PAUL CHURCH ROAD, COLQUITT GA 31737
1989-102	RICHARDSON, JEFFREY SCOTT	47 KUESTER LAKE, GRAND ISLAND NE 68801
1990-132	RICHARDSON, JEFFREY SCOTT	922 BLUE ROSALIE PLACE, HENDERSON NV 89052
1942-083	RICHARDSON, KENNETH FRANKLIN	D. DECEMBER 7, 1987, WOODLAND HILLS, CALIF.
1955-098	RICHARDSON, ROBERT CLINTON	47 ADAMS, SUMTER SC 29150
1980-111	RICHARDT, MICHAEL ANTHONY	5286 WEST RICHERT AVENUE, FRESNO CA 93722
1921-086	RICHBOURG, LANCE CLAYTON	D. SEPTEMBER 10, 1975, CRESTVIEW, FLA.
1962-112	RICHERT, PETER GERARD	80 LA CERRA DRIVE, RANCHO MIRAGE CA 92270
1989-103	RICHIE, ROBERT EUGENE	1835 MEADOWDALE WAY, SPARKS NV 89431
1933-054	RICHMOND, BERYL JUSTICE	D. APRIL 24, 1980, CAMERON, W.VA.
1941-093	RICHMOND, DONALD LESTER	D. MAY 24, 1981, ELMIRA, N.Y.
1920-099	RICHMOND, RAYMOND SINCLAIR	D. OCTOBER 21, 1969, DESOTO, MO.
1951-081	RICHTER, ALLEN GORDON	PO BOX 41, VIRGINIA BEACH VA 23458
1942-084	RICKERT, MARVIN AUGUST	D. JUNE 3, 1978, OAKVILLE, WASH.
1963-098	RICKETTS, DAVID WILLIAM	12860 POLO PARC DRIVE, SAINT LOUIS MO 63146
1959-069	RICKETTS, RICHARD JAMES	D. MARCH 6, 1988, ROCHESTER, N.Y.
1969-146	RICO, ALFREDO CRUZ	7720 ENSIGN STREET, SUN VALLEY CA 91353
1923-109	RICONDA, HARRY PAUL	D. NOVEMBER 15, 1958, MAHOPAC, N.Y.
1939-097	RIDDLE, ELMER RAY	D. MAY 14, 1984, COLUMBUS, GA.
1930-067	RIDDLE, JOHN LUDY	D. DECEMBER 15, 1998, INDIANAPOLIS, IND.
1970-112	RIDDLEBERGER, DENNIS MICHAEL	35785 HUNTER AVENUE, WESTLAND MI 48185
1990-133	RIDDOCH, GREGORY LEE	703 WINDFLOWER DRIVE, LONGMONT CO 80501
1950-081	RIDZIK, STEPHEN GEORGE	7008 11TH AVENUE WEST, BRADENTON FL 34209
1942-085	RIEBE, HARVEY DONALD 'HANK'	D. APRIL 16, 2001, CLEVELAND, OHIO
2000-151	RIEDLING, JOHN RICHARD	14321 DRAFT HORSE LANE, WELLINGTON FL 33414
1991-148	RIESGO, DAMON NIKCO 'NIKCO'	29625 BERMUDA LANE, SOUTHFIELD MI 48076
1997-137	RIGBY, BRADLEY KENNETH	1317 BALLENTYNE PLACE, APOPKA FL 32703
2000-152	RIGDON, PAUL DAVID	3851 MAGILL ROAD, JACKSONVILLE FL 32220
2000-153	RIGGAN, JERROD ASHLEY	PO BOX 1019, BREWSTER WA 98812
2006-165	RIGGANS, SHAWN WILLIS	OLD ADD: FORT LAUDERDALE FL
1992-119	RIGGLEMAN, JAMES DAVID	14950 GULF BLVD #1003, MADEIRA BEACH FL 33708
1997-138	RIGGS, ADAM DAVID	OLD ADD: 1 SPRING LANE, STANHOPE NJ 07874
1934-089	RIGGS, LEWIS SIDNEY	D. AUGUST 12, 1975, DURHAM, N.C.
1979-092	RIGHETTI, DAVID ALLAN	552 MAGDALENA AVENUE, LOS ALTOS CA 94024
1995-185	RIGHTNOWAR, RONALD GENE	8926 STONYBROOK BLVD, SYLVANIA OH 43560
1922-116	RIGNEY, EMORY ELMO 'TOPPER'	D. JUNE 6, 1972, SAN ANTONIO, TEXAS
1937-090	RIGNEY, JOHN DUNGAN	D. OCTOBER 21, 1984, LOMBARD, ILL.
1946-089	RIGNEY, WILLIAM JOSEPH	D. FEBRUARY 20, 2001, WALNUT CREEK, CALIF.
1984-093	RIJO, JOSE ANTONIO	CENTRAL CABRAL #66 SAN CRISTOBAL, DOM REP
1941-094	RIKARD, CULLEY	D. FEBRUARY 25, 2000, MEMPHIS, TENN.
1985-097	RILES, ERNEST	RURAL ROUTE 1 BOX 38, WHIGHAM GA 31797
1979-093	RILEY, GEORGE MICHAEL	OLD ADD: 601 CARSONIA AVENUE #2, READING PA 19606
1921-087	RILEY, JAMES NORMAN	D. MAY 25, 1969, SEQUIN, TEXAS
1944-110	RILEY, LEON FRANCIS	D. SEPTEMBER 13, 1970, SCHENECTADY, N.Y.
1999-166	RILEY, MATTHEW PAUL	OLD ADD: OAKLEY CA 94561
1980-112	RINCON, ANDREW	5425 LOS TOROS, PICO RIVERA CA 90660
2001-154	RINCON, JUAN MANUEL	OLD ADD: MARACAIBO VENEZUELA
1997-139	RINCON, RICARDO	OLD ADD: VERACRUZ MEXICO

1979-094	RINEER, JEFFREY ALAN	325 WEST CHARLOTTE STREET, MILLERSVILLE PA 17551
1950-082	RINKER, ROBERT JOHN	D. DECEMBER 19, 2002, HAZELTON, PA.
2004-165	RIOS, ALEXIS ISRAEL	OLD ADD: GUAYNABO PR
1998-163	RIOS, ARMANDO	19361 SW 69TH STREET, FORT LAUDERDALE FL 33326
1997-140	RIOS, DANIEL	2523 WEST 9TH LANE, HIALEAH FL 33010
1969-147	RIOS, JUAN ONOFRE VELEZ	D. AUGUST 28, 1995, MAYAGUEZ, P.R.
1981-105	RIPKEN, CALVIN EDWIN, JR.	OLD ADD: 2330 WEST JOPPA ROAD #333, LUTHERVILLE MD 21093
1985-098	RIPKEN, CALVIN EDWIN, SR.	D. MARCH 25, 1999, BALTIMORE, MD.
1987-125	RIPKEN, WILLIAM OLIVER	900 MOUNT SOMA COURT, FALLSTON MD 21047
1978-112	RIPLEY, ALLEN STEVENS	OLD ADD: 55 WEST STREET, NORTH ATTLEBORO MA 02760
1935-093	RIPLEY, WALTER FRANKLIN	D. OCTOBER 7, 1990, ATTLEBORO, MASS.
1962-113	RIPPELMEYER, RAYMOND ROY	104 EAGLE COURT, WATERLOO IL 62298
1944-111	RIPPLE, CHARLES DAWSON	D. MAY 6, 1979, WILMINGTON, N.C.
1936-078	RIPPLE, JAMES ALBERT	D. JULY 16, 1959, GREENSBURG, PA.
1999-167	RISKE, DAVID RICHARD	2302 GREAT ELK DRIVE, HENDERSON NV 89052
1992-120	RISLEY, WILLIAM CHARLES	1160 PRIM ROSE CIRCLE, GREENWOOD AR 72936
1964-094	RITCHIE, JAY SEAY	8275 HWY 52, ROCKWELL NC 28138
1997-141	RITCHIE, TODD EVERETT	114 HULAN DRIVE, KERENS TX 75144
1987-126	RITCHIE, WALLACE REID	341 WONDERVIEW DRIVE, GLENDALE CA 91202
1986-128	RITTER, REGGIE BLAKE	1564 ESTEP ROAD, DONALDSON AR 71941
1970-113	RITTWAGE, JAMES MICHAEL	23931 COLUMBUS RD, BEDFORD HEIGHTS OH 44146
1989-104	RITZ, KEVIN D.	836 NORTH 6TH STREET, CAMBRIDGE OH 43725
2000-154	RIVAS, LUIS WILFREDO	OLD ADD: LA GUAIRA VENEZUELA
1992-121	RIVERA, BIENVENIDO 'BEN'	OLD ADD: CLE CLUB DE LEOWES #11, SAN PEDRO DE MACORIS DOM REP
2003-140	RIVERA, CARLOS ALBERTO	OLD ADD: RIO GRANDE PR 00721
1983-122	RIVERA, GERMAN	OLD ADD: VIALETICIA #4E4, V. FONTANA, CAROLINA PR 00630
1975-101	RIVERA, JESUS 'BOMBO'	5907 CALLE GUARINA, PONCE PR 00716
2001-155	RIVERA, JUAN LUIS	OLD ADD: GUARENAS VENEZUELA
1986-129	RIVERA, LUIS ANTONIO	LAZARO RAMOS #16, CIDRA PR 00639
2000-155	RIVERA, LUIS GUTIERREZ	OLD ADD: CHIHUAHUA MEXICO
1952-085	RIVERA, MANUEL JOSEPH 'JIM'	2311 ABBEY DRIVE #7, FORT WAYNE IN 46835
1995-186	RIVERA, MARIANO	CASA 3666 CALLE EL PUERTO, PUERTO CAIMITO, PANAMA
2001-156	RIVERA, MICHAEL R.	OLD ADD: BAYAMON PR
2006-166	RIVERA, RABELL SAUL	OLD ADD: RIO PIEDRAS PR
2004-166	RIVERA, RENE	OLD ADD: BAYAMON PR
1995-187	RIVERA, ROBERTO DIAZ	OLD ADD: BAYAMON PR 00988
1995-188	RIVERA, RUBEN MORENO	OLD ADD: CHORREA PANAMA
1970-114	RIVERS, JOHN MILTON 'MICKEY'	3507 LAKE CHAMPLAIN DRIVE, ARLINGTON TX 76016
1921-088	RIVIERE, ARTHUR BERNARD 'TINK'	D. SEPTEMBER 27, 1965, LIBERTY, TEXAS
1938-082	RIZZO, JOHN COSTA	D. DECEMBER 4, 1977, HOUSTON, TEXAS
1998-164	RIZZO, TODD MICHAEL	7 WILLIAMSBURG COURT, SEWELL NJ 08080
1941-095	RIZZUTO, PHILIP FRANCIS 'SCOOTER'	OLD ADD: 912 WESTMINSTER AVENUE, HILLSIDE NJ 07205
2006-167	RLEAL, SENDY (AQUINO)	OLD ADD: SAN PEDRO DE MACORIS DOM REP
1995-189	ROA, JOSEPH RODGER	46072 REX COURT, CHESTERFIELD MI 48051
2003-141	ROACH, JASON GLENN	11031 LOUSON PLACE, RALEIGH NC 27614
1953-076	ROACH, MELVIN EARL	4131 SOUTHAVEN ROAD, RICHMOND VA 23235
1961-090	ROARKE, MICHAEL THOMAS	11 ROSEVIEW DR, CRANSTON RI 02910
1979-095	ROBBINS, BRUCE DUANE	19311 MORRISON WAY, NOBLESVILLE IN 46060
2004-167	ROBBINS, PHILIP JACOB 'JAKE'	14704 BALLANTYNE GLEN WAY, CHARLOTTE NC 28277
1933-055	ROBELLO, THOMAS VARDASCO 'TOBY'	D. DECEMBER 25, 1994, FORT WORTH, TEXAS
1979-096	ROBERGE, BERTRAND ROLAND	267 SUNDERLAND DRIVE, AUBURN ME 04210
1941-096	ROBERGE, JOSEPH ALBERT 'SKIP'	D. JUNE 7, 1993, LOWELL, MASS.
2006-168	ROBERSON, CHRISTOPHER WILLIAM	2651 VALE ROAD, SAN PABLO CA 94806
1993-152	ROBERSON, KEVIN LYNN	1565 EAST NORTH PORT ROAD, DECATUR IL 62526
1995-190	ROBERSON, SIDNEY DEAN	132 TULIP TREE COURT, JUPITER FL 33458
2001-157	ROBERTS, BRIAN MICHAEL	3434 RUGBY ROAD, DURHAM NC 27707
1943-116	ROBERTS, CHARLES EMORY	D. DECEMBER 2, 1998, ATLANTA, GA.
1954-090	ROBERTS, CURTIS BENJAMIN	D. NOVEMBER 14, 1969, OAKLAND, CALIF.
1967-089	ROBERTS, DALE	206 BERRY AVE, VERSAILLES KY 40383
1969-148	ROBERTS, DAVID ARTHUR	10002 WINDOVER DRIVE, FORT ASHBY WV 26719
1962-114	ROBERTS, DAVID LEONARD	9705 SAM BASS TRAIL, KELLER TX 76248
1999-168	ROBERTS, DAVID RAY	3746 KELTON DRIVE, OCEANSIDE CA 92056
1972-090	ROBERTS, DAVID WAYNE	5509 MEADOW VALLEY DRIVE, FORT WORTH TX 76123
2000-156	ROBERTS, GRANT WILLIAM	1299 VISTA CAPITAN DRIVE, EL CAJON CA 92022
1924-089	ROBERTS, JAMES NEWSOM	D. JUNE 24, 1984, COLUMBUS, MISS.
1986-130	ROBERTS, LEON JOSEPH 'BIP'	3569 RUSINCRESS DRIVE, SAN RAMON CA 94583
1974-113	ROBERTS, LEON KAUFFMAN	PO BOX 170299, ARLINGTON TX 76003
1948-085	ROBERTS, ROBIN EVAN	504 TERRACE HILL DRIVE, TEMPLE TERRACE FL 33617
2006-169	ROBERTS, RYAN ALAN	OLD ADD: 2432 BRIDGETON LANE, BEDFORD TX 76021
1999-169	ROBERTS, WILLIS AUGUSTO	11476 EMUNESS ROAD, JACKSONVILLE FL 32218
1954-091	ROBERTSON, ALFRED JAMES 'JIM'	2515 109TH AVENUE SE, BELLEVUE WA 98004
1981-106	ROBERTSON, ANDRE LEVETT	2229 CROSS LN ST, ORANGE TX 77360
1962-115	ROBERTSON, DARYL BERDINE	52 WEST PRINCETON DRIVE, MIDVALE UT 84047
1954-092	ROBERTSON, DONALD ALEXANDER	3724 EAST SAHUARO DRIVE, PHOENIX AZ 85028
2002-150	ROBERTSON, JERIOME PAUL	OLD ADD: 1140 EAST 37TH STREET, DAVENPORT IA 52807
1969-149	ROBERTSON, JERRY LEE	D. MARCH 24, 1996, TOPEKA, KAN.
1996-159	ROBERTSON, MICHAEL FRANCIS	2626 EAST VIKING ROAD, LAS VEGAS NV 89121
2002-151	ROBERTSON, NATHAN DANIEL	621 WEST NESS STREET, VALLEY CENTER KS 67147
1966-075	ROBERTSON, RICHARD PAUL	1201 CRESCENT TERRACE, SUNNYVALE CA 94087
1993-153	ROBERTSON, RICHARD WAYNE 'RICH'	32202 SOUNDWEDGE DRIVE, WALLER TX 77484
1967-090	ROBERTSON, ROBERT EUGENE	RR 1 SHINNAMON DR, LAVALE MD 21502
1940-075	ROBERTSON, SHERRARD ALEXANDER 'SHERRY'	D. OCTOBER 23, 1970, HOUGHTON, S.D.
1985-099	ROBIDOUX, WILLIAM JOSEPH	2 KING GEORGE DRIVE, WARE MA 01082
1943-117	ROBINSON, AARON ANDREW	D. MARCH 9, 1966, LANCASTER, OHIO
1955-099	ROBINSON, BROOKS CALBERT	PO BOX 1168, BALTIMORE MD 21203
1978-113	ROBINSON, BRUCE PHILLIP	1310 DELLCREST LANE, LAJOLLA CA 92037

1972-091	ROBINSON, CRAIG GEORGE	648 PICKETTS MILL DRIVE, SHREVEPORT LA 71115
1970-115	ROBINSON, DAVID TANNER	6140 CAMINO DEL RINSON, SAN DIEGO CA 92120
1979-097	ROBINSON, DEWEY EVERETT	1388 COTTONWOOD TRAIL, SARASOTA FL 34232
1978-114	ROBINSON, DON ALLEN	1215 86TH COURT NW, BRADENTON FL 34209
1958-076	ROBINSON, EARL JOHN	6895 OAKWOOD DRIVE, OAKLAND CA 94611
1960-087	ROBINSON, FLOYD ANDREW	740 SOUTH 36TH STREET #226, SAN DIEGO CA 92113
1956-073	ROBINSON, FRANK	15557 AQUA VERDE DRIVE, LOS ANGELES CA 90077
1955-100	ROBINSON, HUMBERTO VALENTINO	1695 BROOKLYN AVE, BROOKLYN NY 11210
1947-073	ROBINSON, JACK ROOSEVELT	D. OCTOBER 24, 1972, STAMFORD, CONN.
1984-094	ROBINSON, JEFFREY DANIEL	27 WEBER LANE, TRABUCO CANYON CA 92679
1987-127	ROBINSON, JEFFREY MARK	5317 WEST 158TH PLACE, OVERLAND PARK KS 66224
1949-074	ROBINSON, JOHN EDWARD	D. MARCH 2, 2000, ORMOND BEACH, FLA.
1995-191	ROBINSON, KENNETH NEAL	D. FEBRUARY 28, 1999, TUCSON, ARIZ.
1998-165	ROBINSON, KERRY K.	639 EAGLESBRIDGE DRIVE, WILDWOOD MO 63021
1984-095	ROBINSON, RONALD DEAN	3128 EAST RACE STREET, VISALIA CA 93292
1942-086	ROBINSON, WILLIAM EDWARD 'EDDIE'	6104 CHOLLA, FORT WORTH TX 76112
1966-076	ROBINSON, WILLIAM HENRY	165 PITTMAN DOWNER ROAD, SEWELL NJ 08080
2005-157	ROBLES, OSCAR M.	OLD ADD: TIJUANA MEXICO
1969-150	ROBLES, RAFAEL RADAMES	D. AUGUST 13, 1998, NEW YORK, N.Y.
1972-092	ROBLES, SERGIO	CERRO CHIQUIHUITE #148 C. CHURUBUSCO, 21 MEXICO
1974-114	ROBSON, THOMAS JAMES	PO BOX 25978, TEMPE AZ 85285
1943-118	ROCCO, MICHAEL DOMINICK 'MICKEY'	D. JUNE 1, 1997, ST. PAUL, MINN.
1945-086	ROCHE, ARMANDO BAEZ	D. JUNE 26, 1997, CHICAGO, ILL.
1944-112	ROCHELLI, LOUIS JOSEPH	D. OCTOBER 23, 1992, VICTORIA, TEXAS
1988-112	ROCHFORD, MICHAEL JOSEPH	9478 PALOMINO DRIVE, LAKE WORTH FL 33467
1936-079	ROCK, LESTER HENRY	D. SEPTEMBER 9, 1991, DAVIS, CALIF.
1998-166	ROCKER, JOHN LOY	1223 MANOR OAKS COURT, ATLANTA GA 30338
1976-082	ROCKETT, PATRICK EDWARD	17107 EAGLE HOLLOW DRIVE, SAN ANTONIO TX 78248
1983-123	RODAS, RICHARD MARTIN 'RICK'	6877 BERGANO PLACE, ALTA LOMA CA 91701
1957-074	RODGERS, KENNETH ANDRE IAN 'ANDRE'	D. DECEMBER 13, 2004, NASSAU, BAHAMAS
1961-091	RODGERS, ROBERT LEROY 'BUCK'	5181 WEST KNOLL DR, YORBA LINDA CA 92686
1944-113	RODGERS, WILLIAM SHERMAN	D. MAY 13, 2004, WORCESTER, MASS.
1954-093	RODIN, ERIC CHAPMAN	D. JANUARY 4, 1991, SOMERVILLE, N.J.
2002-152	RODNEY, FERNANDO	OLD ADD: SANTO DOMINGO DOM REP
1994-090	RODRIGUEZ, ALEXANDER EMMANUEL	6018 SW 128TH COURT, MIAMI FL 33183
1967-091	RODRIGUEZ, AURELIO HUARTE	D. SEPTEMBER 23, 2000, DETROIT, MICH.
1991-149	RODRIGUEZ, CARLOS	2929 PRINCEVILLE DRIVE, PICKERINGTON OH 43147
2004-168	RODRIGUEZ, EDDY	OLD ADD: SAN PEDRO DE MACORIS DOM REP
1973-100	RODRIGUEZ, EDUARDO	OLD ADD: URB. CATALINA CALLE 4 #E34, BARCELONETA PR 00617
1982-105	RODRIGUEZ, EDWIN	OLD ADD: 7901 30TH AVENUE NORTH, SAINT PETERSBURG FL 33710
1968-087	RODRIGUEZ, ELISEO C. 'ELLIE'	OLD ADD: BOX 188, BAYAMON PR 00619
1995-192	RODRIGUEZ, FELIX ANTONIO	OLD ADD: MONTECRISTY DOM REP
1958-077	RODRIGUEZ, FERNANDO PEDRO 'FREDDY'	OLD ADD: 555 MAYIA RODRIGUEZ, HAVANA CUBA
1995-193	RODRIGUEZ, FRANCISCO 'FRANK'	OLD ADD: 1017 POND APPLE COURT, OVIEDO FL 32765
2002-153	RODRIGUEZ, FRANCISCO JOSE	OLD ADD: CARACAS VENEZUELA
1952-086	RODRIGUEZ, HECTOR ANTONIO	D. SEPTEMBER 1, 2003, CANCUN, QUINTANA ROO, MEXICO
1992-122	RODRIGUEZ, HENRY ANDERSON	295 WADSWORTH AVENUE #3F, NEW YORK NY 10040
1991-150	RODRIGUEZ, IVAN 'PUDGE'	OLD ADD: 5507 CLERMONT COURT, COLLEYVILLE TX 76034
2005-158	RODRIGUEZ, JOHN JOSEPH	OLD ADD: HOBOKEN NJ
2000-157	RODRIGUEZ, JOSE ILICH	OLD ADD: CAYEY PR
1999-170	RODRIGUEZ, LIUBIEMITHZ	OLD ADD: CARACAS VENEZUELA
1996-160	RODRIGUEZ, LUIS ANTONIO 'TONY'	OLD ADD: CIDRA PR 00739
2005-159	RODRIGUEZ, LUIS ORLANDO	OLD ADD: COJEDES VENEZUELA
1996-161	RODRIGUEZ, NERIO	OLD ADD: SANTO DOMINGO DOM REP
1986-131	RODRIGUEZ, RICARDO 'RICK'	106 O'NEILL COURT, FOLSOM CA 95630
2002-154	RODRIGUEZ, RICARDO ANTONIO	OLD ADD: GUAYUBIN DOM REP
1990-134	RODRIGUEZ, RICHARD ANTHONY	2164 AMBER AVENUE, EL MONTE CA 91733
1967-092	RODRIGUEZ, ROBERTO MUNOZ	OLD ADD: CORT. DESARRIAS, 8 CJN RECOBECO, CARACAS VENEZUELA
1989-105	RODRIGUEZ, ROSARIO ISABEL	OLD ADD: LOS MOCHIS SINALOA MEXICO
1986-132	RODRIGUEZ, RUBEN DARIO	10 #17 ENSANCHE LUPERON SANTO DOMINGO, DOM REP
1995-194	RODRIGUEZ, STEVEN JAMES	10430 ORCHARD LANE, RIVERSIDE CA 92503
1984-096	RODRIGUEZ, VICTOR MANUEL	631 SE 9TH PLACE, CAPE CORAL FL 33990
2005-160	RODRIGUEZ, WANDY E.	OLD ADD: SANTIAGO DOM REP
2001-158	RODRIGUEZ, WILFREDO JOSE	OLD ADD: SAN FELIX VENEZ
1938-083	ROE, ELWIN CHARLES 'PREACHER'	204 WILDWOOD TERRACE, WEST PLAINS MO 65775
1923-110	ROE, JAMES CLAY	D. APRIL 3, 1956, CLEVELAND, MISS.
1955-101	ROEBUCK, EDWARD JACK	3434 WARWOOD RD, LAKEWOOD CA 90712
1976-083	ROENICKE, GARY STEVEN	11023 ROUGH & READY ROAD, ROUGH AND READY CA 95975
1981-107	ROENICKE, RONALD JON	2212 AVENIDA LAS RAMBLAS, CHINO HILLS CA 91709
1989-106	ROESLER, MICHAEL JOSEPH	12033 FALLEN LEAF COURT, FORT WAYNE IN 46845
1923-111	ROETTGER, OSCAR FREDERICK LOUIS	D. JULY 4, 1986, ST. LOUIS, MO.
1927-075	ROETTGER, WALTER HENRY	D. SEPTEMBER 14, 1951, CHAMPAIGN, ILL.
1929-089	ROETZ, EDWARD BERNARD	D. MARCH 16, 1965, PHILADELPHIA, PA.
1938-084	ROGALSKI, JOSEPH ANTHONY	D. NOVEMBER 20, 1951, ASHLAND, WISC.
1925-088	ROGELL, WILLIAM GEORGE	D. AUGUST 9, 2003, STERLING HEIGHTS, MICH.
2006-170	ROGERS, BRIAN ALAN	OLD ADD: 1150 SOUTH MARIETTA PKWY SE, MARIETTA GA 30060
1992-123	ROGERS, CHARLES KEVIN 'KEVIN'	604 DOUGLAS AVENUE, CLEVELAND MS 38732
2002-155	ROGERS, EDWARD ANTONIO	OLD ADD: SAN PEDRO DE MACORIS DR
1995-195	ROGERS, JAMES RANDALL	5513 SE 80TH STREET, OKLAHOMA CITY OK 73135
1989-107	ROGERS, KENNETH SCOTT	PO BOX 967, DURANT FL 33530
1938-085	ROGERS, LEE OTIS	D. NOVEMBER 23, 1995, LITTLE ROCK, ARK.
1935-094	ROGERS, ORLIN WOODROW 'BUCK'	D. FEBRUARY 20, 1999, WINSTON-SALEM. N. C.
1938-086	ROGERS, STANLEY FRANK 'PACKY'	D. MAY 15, 1998, ELMIRA, N.Y.
1973-101	ROGERS, STEPHEN DOUGLAS	2 LENAPE LANE, PRINCETON JUNCTION NJ 06550
1963-099	ROGGENBURK, GARRY EARL	35550 STREAMVIEW DRIVE, AVON OH 44011
1973-102	ROGODZINSKI, MICHAEL GEORGE	1 EMLYN COURT, LAUREL SPRINGS NJ 08021

1949-075	ROGOVIN, SAUL WALTER	D. JANUARY 23, 1995, NEW YORK, N.Y.
1990-135	ROHDE, DAVID GRANT	1707 PORT BARMOUTH, NEWPORT BEACH CA 92660
1983-124	ROHN, DANIEL JAY	2406 ARTHUR COURT, TRAVERSE CITY MI 49684
1967-093	ROHR, LESLIE NORVIN	OLD ADD: 2001 EAST KING AVENUE, DES MOINES IA 50320
1967-094	ROHR, WILLIAM JOSEPH	67545 SOUTH LAGUNA DRIVE, CATHEDRAL CITY CA 92234
1997-142	ROHRMEIER, DANIEL	4240 WEST FORD ROAD, CINCINNATI OH 45247
1921-089	ROHWER, RAY	D. JANUARY 24, 1988, DAVIS, CALIF.
1953-077	ROIG, ANTON AMBROSE	24125 EAST LAKERIDGE DRIVE, LIBERTY LAKE WA 99019
1990-136	ROJAS, MELQUIADES (MEDRANO)	OLD ADD: 15645 COLLINS AVENUE, NORTH MIAMI BEACH FL 33160
1966-077	ROJAS, MINERVINO ALEJANDRO 'MINNIE'	D. MARCH 23, 2002, LOS ANGELES, CALIF.
1962-116	ROJAS, OCTAVIO 'COOKIE'	19195 MYSTIC POINTE DRIVE BLDG 100 #LP2, MIAMI FL 33180
1942-087	ROJEK, STANLEY ANDREW	D. JULY 9, 1997, NORTH TONAWANDA, N.Y.
1962-117	ROLAND, JAMES IVAN	1802 ARBOR WAY DRIVE, SHELBY NC 28150
1996-162	ROLEN, SCOTT BRUCE	11711 N. PENNSYLVANIA STREET #250, CARMEL IN 46032
1931-074	ROLFE, ROBERT ABIAL 'RED'	D. JULY 8, 1969, GILFORD, N.H.
2000-158	ROLISON, NATHAN MARDIS	89 BRIDGEFIELD COURT, HATTIESBURG MS 39402
1927-076	ROLLINGS, WILLIAM RUSSELL 'RED'	D. DECEMBER 31, 1964, MOBILE, ALA.
2000-159	ROLLINS, JAMES CALVIN	1137 ROSEWOOD WAY, ALAMEDA CA 94501
1961-092	ROLLINS, RICHARD JOHN 'RICH'	4670 ROLLING VIEW DRIVE, AKRON OH 44333
2000-160	ROLLS, DAMIAN MICHAEL	2341 MESSENGER CIRCLE, SAFETY HARBOR FL 34695
1984-097	ROMAN, JOSE RAFAEL	VISTA ALEGRE #10 SANCHES LUPERON PUERTO PLATA, DOM REP
1964-095	ROMAN, WILLIAM ANTHONY	1720 YALE COURT, LAKE FOREST IL 60045
1984-098	ROMANICK, RONALD JAMES	15709 EAST CERVANTES COURT, FOUNTAIN HILLS AZ 85268
1950-083	ROMANO, JAMES KING	D. SEPTEMBER 12, 1990, DEER PARK, N.Y.
2002-156	ROMANO, JASON ANTHONY	17620 GLENAPP DRIVE, LAND O'LAKES FL 34638
1958-078	ROMANO, JOHN ANTHONY	160 WEST PAGO PAGO DRIVE, NAPLES FL 34113
1999-171	ROMANO, MICHAEL DESPORT	3705 RIVERLAND DRIVE, CHALMETTE LA 70043
1987-128	ROMANO, THOMAS MICHAEL	1266 PENORA STREET, DEPEW NY 14043
1954-094	ROMBERGER, ALLEN IRVING	D. MAY 26, 1983, WEIKERT, PA.
1997-143	ROMERO, ARMANDO 'MANDY'	19280 SW 216TH STREET, MIAMI FL 33170
2006-171	ROMERO, DAVIS JAVIER (RODRIGUEZ)	OLD ADD: CUCLE PANAMA
1977-121	ROMERO, EDGARDO	1380 WOOD ROW WAY, WEST PALM BEACH FL 33414
1999-172	ROMERO, JUAN CARLOS 'J.C.'	OLD ADD: SAN JUAN PR 00901
1984-099	ROMERO, ROMAN	OLD ADD: CALLE U. ESPAILLOT #60, SAN PEDRO DE MACORIS DOM REP
1985-100	ROMINE, KEVIN ANDREW	8750 ROGUE RIVER AVE, FOUNTAIN VALLEY CA 92708
1920-100	ROMMEL, EDWIN AMERICUS	D. AUGUST 26, 1970, BALTIMORE, MD.
1977-122	ROMO, ENRIQUE	AVENIDA SN, CARLOS #923, TORREON COAHUILA, MEXICO
1968-088	ROMO, VICENTE	OLD ADD: GMO PRIETO 116 OTE, CD. OBREGON SONORA MEXICO
1953-078	ROMONOSKY, JOHN	5090 BIXBY ROAD, GROVEPORT OH 43125
1993-154	RONAN, EDWARD MARCUS 'MARC'	104 EVONSHIRE DRIVE, ARKADELPHIA AR 71923
1976-084	RONDON, GILBERT	OLD ADD: 1000 BALLPARK WAY, ARLINGTON TX 76011
2003-142	RONEY, MATTHEW STEPHEN	1809 NIGHTHAWK COURT, EDMOND OK 73034
2005-156	RONG, ROGER ROYCE 'ROYCE'	OLD ADD: LA MESA CA
1981-108	ROOF, EUGENE LAWRENCE	175 SPRING VALLEY DRIVE, PADUCAH KY 42001
1961-093	ROOF, PHILLIP ANTHONY	7350 US HIGHWAY 45, BOAZ KY 42047
1968-089	ROOKER, JAMES PHILIP	1684 CITATION DR, LIBRARY PA 15129
1988-113	ROOMES, ROLANDO AUDLEY	11520 EAST PRATT AVENUE, MESA AZ 85212
1981-109	ROONEY, PATRICK EUGENE	4825 LIGHTHOUSE DRIVE, RACINE WI 53402
1923-112	ROOT, CHARLES HENRY	D. NOVEMBER 5, 1970, HOLLISTER, CALIF.
1993-155	ROPER, JOHN CHRISTOPHER	6273 UPPER BURNINGTON ROAD, FRANKLIN NC 28734
1970-116	ROQUE, JORGE	OLD ADD: BO. SAN ANTON #135, PONCE PR 00731
1998-167	ROQUE, RAFAEL ANTONIO	OLD ADD: SANTO DOMINGO DOM REP
1996-163	ROSADO, JOSE ANTONIO	OLD ADD: DORADO PR 00646
1977-123	ROSADO, LUIS (ROBLES)	CALLE 508 B-213 #13 5TH, CAROLINA PR 00630
1939-098	ROSAR, WARREN VINCENT 'BUDDY'	D. FEBRUARY 13, 1994, ROCHESTER, N.Y.
1971-089	ROSARIO, ANGEL RAMON 'JIMMY'	OLD ADD: CALLE 1 #421 HERNANDES DAVILA, BAYAMON PR 00619
2006-172	ROSARIO, FRANCISCO ALBERTO (DIVISON)	OLD ADD: SAN RAFAEL DOM REP
1997-144	ROSARIO, MELVIN GREGORIO	2000 NW 29TH STREET #5, MIAMI FL 33142
2003-143	ROSARIO, RODRIGO	OLD ADD: LA ROMANA DOM REP
1965-092	ROSARIO, SANTIAGO	OLD ADD: HC1 BUZON #7982, GUAYANILLA PR 00656
1990-137	ROSARIO, VICTOR MANUEL	AVE. CIRCUM VALACION #36 SAN PEDRO DE MACORIS, DOM REP
1997-145	ROSE, BRIAN LEONARD	5 ASHLAND STREET, SOUTH DARTMOUTH MA 02748
1971-090	ROSE, DONALD GARY	16254 PALOMINO MESA WAY, SAN DIEGO CA 92127
2004-169	ROSE, MICHAEL JOHN	12031 CRESTHILL DRIVE, ELK GROVE CA 95624
1963-100	ROSE, PETER EDWARD	8144 WEST GLADES ROAD, BOCA RATON FL 33434
1997-146	ROSE, PETER EDWARD, JR.	1032 CORONADO AVENUE, CINCINNATI OH 45238
1989-108	ROSE, ROBERT RICHARD	OLD ADD: 2406 COSTA DEL SOL, LAVERNE CA 91750
1957-075	ROSEBORO, JOHN JUNIOR	D. AUGUST 19, 2002, LOS ANGELES, CALIF.
1995-196	ROSELLI, JOSEPH DONALD	OLD ADD: 6281 LESAGE AVE, WOODLAND HILLS CA 91367
1955-102	ROSELLI, ROBERT EDWARD	100 CLYDESDALE WAY, ROSEVILLE CA 95678
1972-093	ROSELLO, DAVID	PAZ 160 BO PARIS, MAYAGUEZ PR 00708
1947-074	ROSEN, ALBERT LEONARD	15 MAYFAIR DRIVE, RANCHO MIRAGE CA 92270
1937-091	ROSEN, GOODWIN GEORGE	D. APRIL 6, 1994, TORONTO, ONT.
1930-068	ROSENBERG, HARRY	D. APRIL 13, 1997, SAN MATEO, CALIF.
1923-113	ROSENBERG, LOUIS	D. SEPTEMBER 8, 1991, SAN FRANCISCO, CALIF.
1988-114	ROSENBERG, STEVEN ALLEN	8425 FOREST HILLS DRIVE #104, CORAL SPRINGS FL 33065
1931-075	ROSENFELD, MAX	D. MARCH 10, 1969, MIAMI, FLA.
1936-080	ROSENTHAL, LAWRENCE JOHN	D. MARCH 4, 1992, WOODBURY, MINN.
1925-089	ROSENTHAL, SIMON	D. APRIL 7, 1969, BOSTON, MASS.
1991-151	ROSENTHAL, WAYNE SCOTT	OLD ADD: 5336 WILLOW CLIFF ROAD #320, OKLAHOMA CITY OK 73122
1944-114	ROSER, EMERSON COREY	D. FEBRUARY 8, 2002, UTICA, N.Y.
1922-118	ROSER, JOHN JOSEPH 'BUNNY'	D. MAY 6, 1979, ROCKY HILL, CONN.
1998-168	ROSKOS, JOHN EDWARD	PO BOX 45515, RIO RANCHO NM 87174
1924-090	ROSS, CHESTER FRANKLIN 'BUSTER'	D. APRIL 24, 1982, MAYFIELD, KY.
1939-099	ROSS, CHESTER JAMES	D. FEBRUARY 21, 1989, BUFFALO, N.Y.
1954-095	ROSS, CLIFFORD DAVID	D. APRIL 13, 1999, PHILADELPHIA, PA.

2003-144	ROSS, CODY JOSEPH	1030 NORTH EDDY STREET, CARLSBAD NM 88220
2002-157	ROSS, DAVID WADE	2604 ANTIETAM TRAIL, TALLAHASSEE FL 32312
1938-087	ROSS, DONALD RAYMOND	D. APRIL 4, 1996, ARCADIA, CALIF.
1950-084	ROSS, FLOYD ROBERT 'BOB'	862 BERGAMO AVENUE, SAN JACINTO CA 92583
1968-090	ROSS, GARY DOUGLAS	1729 CUADRO VISTA, SAN MARCOS CA 92078
1936-081	ROSS, LEE RAVON 'BUCK'	D. NOVEMBER 23, 1978, CHARLOTTE, N.C.
1982-106	ROSS, MARK JOSEPH	1747 NORTH WILD HYACINTH DRIVE, TUCSON AZ 85715
1952-087	ROSSI, JOSEPH ANTHONY	D. FEBRUARY 20, 1999, OAKLAND, CALIF.
1944-115	ROSSO, FRANCIS JAMES	D. JANUARY 26, 1980, SPRINGFIELD, MASS.
1991-152	ROSSY, ELAM JOSE 'RICO'	7551 WEST SAND LAKE ROAD, ORLANDO FL 32819
1948-086	ROTBLATT, MARVIN	8501 LOTUS #103, SKOKIE IL 60077
1945-087	ROTHEL, ROBERT BURTON	D. MAY 21, 1984, HURON, OHIO
1925-090	ROTHROCK, JOHN HOUSTON 'JACK'	D. FEBRUARY 2, 1980, SAN BERNARDINO, CALIF.
1981-110	ROTHSCHILD, LAWRENCE LEE	4508 WEST CULBREATH AVENUE, TAMPA FL 33609
2006-173	ROTTINO, VINCENT ANTONIO	OLD ADD: 1811 EAST WALNUT STREET, CARBONDALE IL 62901
1970-117	ROUNSAVILLE, VIRL GENE 'GENE'	2901 LONE TREE WAY #A, ANTIOCH CA 94509
2006-174	ROUSE, MICHAEL GREGORY	569 CHURHILL PARK DRIVE, SAN JOSE CA 95136
2001-159	ROWAND, AARON RYAN	1301 KINGDOM STREET, LAS VEGAS NV 89117
1984-100	ROWDON, WADE LEE	230 CROOKED TREE TRAIL, DELAND FL 32724
1963-101	ROWE, DONALD HOWARD	D. OCTOBER 15, 2005, NEWPORT BEACH, CALIF.
1963-102	ROWE, KENNETH DARRELL	347 PRINCETON DRIVE, DALLAS GA 30157
1933-056	ROWE, LYNWOOD THOMAS 'SCHOOLBOY'	D. JANUARY 8, 1961, EL DORADO, ARK.
1939-100	ROWELL, CARVEL WILLIAM 'BAMA'	D. AUGUST 16, 1993, CITRONELLE, ALA.
1923-114	ROWLAND, CHARLES LELAND	D. JANUARY 21, 1992, RALEIGH, N.C.
1980-113	ROWLAND, MICHAEL EVAN	12104 EAST MESCAL STREET, SCOTTSDALE AZ 85259
1990-138	ROWLAND, RICHARD GARNET	593 EAST FIRST STREET, CLOVERDALE CA 95425
1933-057	ROY, EMILE ARTHUR	D. JANUARY 5, 1997, CRYSTAL RIVER, FLA.
1946-090	ROY, JEAN PIERRE	418 S.M. CHARTRAND, SAINT NICHOLAS QC, G7A 3K3 CANADA
1924-091	ROY, LUTHER FRANKLIN	D. JULY 24, 1963, GRAND RAPIDS, MICH.
1950-085	ROY, NORMAN BROOKS	2 AUTUMN LEAF DRIVE #15, NASHUA NH 03060
1991-153	ROYER, STANLEY DEAN	9301 CHRISTOPHER LAKE DRIVE, COLUMBIA IL 62236
1973-103	ROYSTER, JERON KENNIS 'JERRY'	OLD ADD: 9 SHELDRAKE LANE, PALM BEACH GARDENS 33418
1981-111	ROYSTER, WILLIE A.	229 55TH STREET NORTHEAST, WASHINGTON DC 20019
1950-086	ROZEK, RICHARD LOUIS	D. SEPTEMBER 27, 2001, LAQUINTA, CALIF.
1977-124	ROZEMA, DAVID SCOTT	1560 NORTH RENARD AVENUE, GROSSE POINTE MI 48236
1964-096	ROZNOVSKY, VICTOR JOSEPH	1686 WEST BULLARD, FRESNO CA 93711
2002-158	RUAN, WILKIN CHAL	OLD ADD: GUAYMATE DOM REP
1940-076	RUBELING, ALBERT WILLIAM	D. JANUARY 28, 1988, BALTIMORE, MD.
1969-151	RUBERTO, JOHN EDWARD 'SONNY'	13208 LAUREL LAKE COURT, SAINT LOUIS MO 63131
1966-078	RUBIO, JORGE JESUS	OLD ADD:1001 LERDO AVE, MEXICALI BAJA CALIFORNIA
1927-077	RUBLE, WILLIAM ARTHUR 'ART'	D. NOVEMBER 1, 1983, MARYVILLE, TENN.
1981-112	RUCKER, DAVID MICHAEL	PO BOX 559, PINION HILLS CA 92372
1940-077	RUCKER, JOHN JOEL	D. AUGUST 7, 1985, MOULTRIE, GA.
1967-095	RUDI, JOSEPH ODEN	17667 DEER PARK LOOP, BAKER CITY OR 97814
1945-088	RUDOLPH, ERNEST WILLIAM	D. JANUARY 13, 2003, BLACK RIVER FALLS, WISC.
1957-076	RUDOLPH, FREDERICK DONALD 'DON'	D. SEPTEMBER 12, 1968, ENCINO, CALIF.
1969-152	RUDOLPH, KENNETH VICTOR	14989 NORTH ZAPATA DRIVE, FOUNTAIN HILLS AZ 85268
1996-164	RUEBEL, MATTHEW ALEXANDER	2709 SW 116TH STREET, MOORE OK 73170
1993-156	RUETER, KIRK WESLEY	PO BOX 147, HOYLETON IL 62803
1949-076	RUFER, RUDOLPH JOSEPH	649 CORNWELL AVENUE, MALVERNE NY 11565
1993-157	RUFFCORN, SCOTT PATRICK	2137 BARTON HILLS DRIVE, AUSTIN TX 78704
1986-133	RUFFIN, BRUCE WAYNE	3410 PAWNEE PASS SOUTH, AUSTIN TX 78738
1993-158	RUFFIN, JOHNNY RENANDO	314 SOUTH CHURCH STREET, ADAMS TN 37016
1924-092	RUFFING, CHARLES HERBERT 'RED'	D. FEBRUARY 17, 1986, MAYFIELD HEIGHTS, OHIO
1974-115	RUHLE, VERNON GERALD	D. JANUARY 20, 2007, HOUSTON, TEXAS
2006-175	RUIZ, CARLOS JOAQUIN	OLD ADD: DAVID CHIRIQUI PANAMA
1964-097	RUIZ, HIRALDO SABLON 'CHICO'	D. FEBRUARY 9, 1972, SAN DIEGO, CALIF.
1978-115	RUIZ, MANUEL 'CHICO'	TAPIA 267, SANTURCE PR 00912
1943-119	RULLO, JOSEPH VINCENT	D. OCTOBER 28, 1969, PHILADELPHIA, PA.
1981-113	RUNGE, PAUL WILLIAM	1719 WEST COMMUNITY DRIVE, JUPITER FL 33458
1985-101	RUNNELLS, THOMAS WILLIAM	6045 SETTLERS RIDGE CIRCLE, SYLVANIA OH 43560
1951-082	RUNNELS, JAMES EDWARD 'PETE'	D. MAY 20, 1991, PASADENA, TEXAS
1998-169	RUNYAN, SEAN DAVID	4105 77TH STREET, URBANDALE IA 50322
2005-161	RUPE, JOSHUA MATTHEW	OLD ADD: 911 INDIAN RIDGE DRIVE, LYNCHBURG VA 24502
1999-173	RUPE, RYAN KITTMAN	9723 SPRINGVIEW LANE, HOUSTON TX 77080
1997-147	RUSCH, GLENDON JAMES	6428 CHAFFEE STREET, TUJUNGA CA 91042
1925-091	RUSH, JESS HOWARD 'ANDY'	D. MARCH 16, 1969, FRESNO, CALIF.
1948-087	RUSH, ROBERT RANSOM	4330 SOUTHEASTERN AVENUE #164, LAS VEGAS NV 891A9
2002-159	RUSHFORD, JAMES THOMAS	6000 BOB STREET, LAMESA CA 91942
1990-139	RUSKIN, SCOTT DREW	387 ST. JOHNS GOLF DRIVE, SAINT AUGUSTINE FL 32092
1939-101	RUSSELL, GLEN DAVID 'RIP'	D. SEPTEMBER 26, 1976, LOS ANGELES CAL.
1926-072	RUSSELL, JACK ERWIN	D. NOVEMBER 3, 1990, CLEARWATER, FLA.
1942-088	RUSSELL, JAMES WILLIAM	D. NOVEMBER 24, 1987, PITTSBURGH, PA.
1983-125	RUSSELL, JEFFREY LEE	2325 OAK KNOLL DRIVE, COLLEYVILLE TX 76034
1984-101	RUSSELL, JOHN WILLIAM	6212 WEST PAPAW STREET, ODESSA TX 79763
1938-088	RUSSELL, LOYD OPAL	D. MAY 24, 1968, WACO, TEXAS
1969-153	RUSSELL, WILLIAM ELLIS	27982 RED PINE COURT, VALENCIA CA 91354
1939-102	RUSSO, MARIUS UGO	D. MARCH 26, 2005, FORT MYERS, FLA.
1966-079	RUSTECK, RICHARD FRANK	6302 NORTH 87TH STREET, SCOTTSDALE AZ 85250
1944-116	RUSZKOWSKI, HENRY ALEXANDER	D. MAY 31, 2000, CLEVELAND, OHIO
1952-088	RUTHERFORD, JOHN WILLIAM	765 BRIAR HILL LANE, BLOOMFIELD HILLS MI 48304
1973-104	RUTHVEN, RICHARD DAVID	13480 PROVIDENCE LAKE DRIVE, ALPHARETTA GA 30004
1947-075	RUTNER, MILTON MICKEY	277 TRAIL OF THE FLOWERS, GEORGETOWN TX 78628
1982-107	RYAL, MARK DWAYNE	PO BOX 190, HENRYETTA OK 74437
1942-089	RYAN, CORNELIUS JOSEPH 'CONNIE'	D. JANUARY 3, 1996, NEW ORLEANS, LA.
1999-174	RYAN, JASON PAUL	1232 ROCKY RIVER ROAD WEST, CHARLOTTE NC 28213

1930-069	RYAN, JOHN COLLINS 'BLONDY'	D. NOVEMBER 28, 1959, SWAMPSCOTT, MASS.
1929-090	RYAN, JOHN FRANCIS	D. SEPTEMBER 2, 1967, ROCHESTER, MINN.
1992-124	RYAN, KENNETH FREDERICK	45 TANAGER ROAD, SEEKONK MA 02771
1966-080	RYAN, LYNN NOLAN 'NOLAN'	2925 SOUTH LOOP 35, ALVIN TX 77511
1964-098	RYAN, MICHAEL JAMES	592 STONEHAM ROAD, WOLFEBORO NH 03894
2002-160	RYAN, MICHAEL SEAN	PO BOX 12, INDIANA PA 15701
1999-175	RYAN, ROBERT JAMES	914 EAST GOLDEN COURT, SPOKANE WA 99208
1999-176	RYAN, ROBERT VICTOR 'B. J.'	4014 WISTERIA LANE, BENTON LA 71006
1935-095	RYBA, DOMINIC JOSEPH 'MIKE'	D. DECEMBER 13, 1971, SPRINGFIELD, MO.
1931-076	RYE, EUGENE RUDOLPH 'HALF-PINT'	D. JANUARY 21, 1980, PARK RIDGE, ILL.
1972-094	RYERSON, GARY LAWRENCE	1059 TERRACE COURT, EL CAJON CA 92019
2006-176	RYU, JAE KUK	OLD ADD: SEOUL SOUTH KOREA

S

2002-161	SAARLOOS, KIRK CRAIG	2497 200TH AVENUE SE, SAMMAMISH WA 98075
2001-160	SABATHIA, CARSTEN CHARLES 'C.C.'	130 DEININGER STREET, VALLEJO CA 94589
1999-177	SABEL, ERIK DOUGLAS	3113 NORTH 400 WEST, WEST LAFAYETTE IN 47906
1984-102	SABERHAGEN, BRET WILLIAM	22817 VENTURA BLVD #474, WOODLAND HILLS CA 91364
1936-082	SABO, ALEXANDER	D. JANUARY 3, 2001, TUCKERTOWN, N.J.
1988-115	SABO, CHRISTOPHER ANDREW	7455 STONEMEADOW LANE, CINCINNATI OH 45242
1951-083	SACKA, FRANK	D. DECEMBER 7, 1994, DEARBORN, MICH.
1996-165	SACKINSKY, BRIAN WALTER	1820 EDWARD DRIVE, LIBRARY PA 15129
1960-088	SADECKI, RAYMOND MICHAEL	4237 EAST CLOVIS AVENUE, MESA AZ 85206
1973-105	SADEK, MICHAEL GEORGE	6741 QUARTZ MINE ROAD, MOUNTAIN RANCH CA 95246
1998-170	SADLER, DONNIE LAMONT	802 SADLER ROAD, VALLEY MILLS TX 76689
2005-162	SADLER, RAYMOND LEE	2112 JOEY DRIVE, WACO TX 76711
2002-162	SADLER, WILLIAM CARL 'CARL	202 SOUTH HENDRY AVENUE, PERRY FL 32347
2006-177	SADLER, WILLIAM HENRY	2361 INVERNESS DRIVE, PENSACOLA FL 32503
1960-089	SADOWSKI, EDWARD RAMON	D. NOVEMBER 6, 1993, GARDEN GROVE, CALIF.
1974-116	SADOWSKI, JAMES MICHAEL	537 FIELDCREST DRIVE, PITTSBURGH PA 15209
1963-103	SADOWSKI, ROBERT	26 BARRINGTON COURT, SHARPSBURG GA 30277
1960-090	SADOWSKI, ROBERT FRANK	1465 CREEKSIDE DRIVE, HIGH RIDGE MO 63049
1960-091	SADOWSKI, THEODORE	D. JULY 18, 1993, SHALER TWP., PA.
2004-170	SAENZ, CHRISTOPHER ANDREW	7919 NORTH RONDURE LOOP, TUCSON AZ 85243
1994-091	SAENZ, OLMEDO (SANCHEZ)	AMINTA BURGOS AMADO #2027 CHITRE HERRERA, PANAMA
1949-077	SAFFELL, THOMAS JUDSON	1503 CLOWER CREEK DRIVE #HA262, SARASOTA FL 33581
1994-092	SAGER, ANTHONY JOSEPH 'A.J.'	235 NORTH FOURTH, KIRKERSVILLE OH 43033
1997-148	SAGMOEN, MARC RICHARD	19715 FIRST PLACE SW, NORMANDY PARK WA 98166
1942-090	SAIN, JOHN FRANKLIN	D. NOVEMBER 7, 2006, DOWNERS GROVE, ILL.
1951-084	SAINTCLAIRE, EDWARD JOSEPH 'EBBA'	D. AUGUST 22, 1982, WHITEHALL, N.Y.
1984-103	SAINTCLAIRE, RANDY ANTHONY	52 CHAMPLAIN AVENUE, WHITEHALL NY 12887
1998-171	SAIPE, MIKE ERIC	4191 COMBE WAY, SAN DIEGO CA 92122
2006-178	SAITO, TAKASHI	OLD ADD: MIYAGI JAPAN
1977-125	SAKATA, LENN HARUKI	467 HALEMAUMAU STREET, HONOLULU HI 96821
2006-179	SALAS, JUAN	OLD ADD: SANTO DOMINGO DJM REP
1984-104	SALAS, MARK BRUCE	1302 6TH STREET SE, RUSKIN FL 33570
1983-126	SALAZAR, ARGENIS ANTONIO 'ANGEL'	RODRIGUEZ DOMINGUES MANZANA G#7 VARINA, VENEZUELA
2006-180	SALAZAR, JEFFREY DEWAN	OLD ADD: PORT BOLIVAR TX
1980-114	SALAZAR, LUIS ERNESTO	21218 ST. ANDREWS BLVD, BOCA RATON FL 33433
2002-163	SALAZAR, OSCAR ENRIQUE	OLD ADD: MARACAY VENEZUELA
1924-093	SALE, FREDERICK LINK	D. MAY 27, 1956, HERMOSA BEACH, CALIF.
1993-159	SALKELD, ROGER WILLIAM	27824 RIDGEGROVE DRIVE, SANTA CLARITA CA 91350
1945-089	SALKELD, WILLIAM FRANKLIN	D. APRIL 22, 1967, LOS ANGELES, CALIF.
1964-099	SALMON, RUTHERFORD EDUARDO 'CHICO'	D. SEPTEMBER 17, 2000, BOCAS DEL TORO, PANAMA
1992-125	SALMON, TIMOTHY JAMES	6061 EAST SUNNYSIDE DRIVE, SCOTTSDALE AZ 85254
1932-072	SALTZGAVER, OTTO HAMLIN 'JACK'	D. FEBRUARY 2, 1978, KEOKUK, IOWA
1933-058	SALVESON, JOHN THEODORE	D. DECEMBER 28, 1974, NORWALK, CALIF.
1939-103	SALVO, MANUEL	D. FEBRUARY 7, 1997, VALLEJO, CALIF.
1976-085	SAMBITO, JOSEPH CHARLES	23 MODESTO, IRVINE CA 92602
1951-085	SAMCOFF, EDWARD WILLIAM	8153 MADEIRA PORT LANE, FAIR OAKS CA 95628
1954-096	SAMFORD, RONALD EDWARD	2174 KESLER COURT, DALLAS TX 75208
1990-140	SAMPEN, WILLIAM ALBERT	11 CARNABY COURT, BROWNSBURG IN 46112
1978-116	SAMPLE, WILLIAM AMOS	10 PASCOCK ROAD, TWP. OF WASHINGTON NJ 07676
1998-172	SAMPSON, BENJAMIN DAMON	8312 FLAT ROCK COURT, NORTH RICHLAND HILLS TX 76180
2006-181	SAMPSON, CHRISTOPHER KEITH	OLD ADD: 5302 11TH STREET, LUBBOCK TX 79416
1962-118	SAMUEL, AMADO RUPERTO	1931 YALE DR, LOUISVILLE KY 40205
1983-127	SAMUEL, JUAN MILTON	OLD ADD: 20520 ROOKERY DRIVE, ESTERO FL 33928
1930-070	SAMUELS, JOSEPH JONES	D. OCTOBER 28, 1996, BATH, N.Y.
1988-116	SAMUELS, ROGER HOWARD	4865 TAMPICO WAY, SAN JOSE CA 95118
2006-182	SANCHES, BRIAN LEE	1131 LULING AVENUE, NEDERLAND TX 77627
1982-108	SANCHEZ, ALEJANDRO	BOCA CHICA GATEY GAUTIR SANTO DOMINGO, DOM REP
1989-109	SANCHEZ, ALEJANDRO ANTHONY	2015 ALPHA WAY, ANTIOCH CA 94509
2001-161	SANCHEZ, ALEXIS	OLD ADD: 1920 NW 119TH STREET #603, MIAMI FL 33167
2006-184	SANCHEZ, ANGEL LUIS	OLD ADD: LAS PIEDRAS PR
2006-183	SANCHEZ, ANIBAL ALEJANDRO	OLD ADD: MARACAY VENEZ
1972-095	SANCHEZ, CELERINO (PEREZ)	D. MAY 1, 1992, LEON, GUANAJUNTO, MEXICO
2002-164	SANCHEZ, DUANER	OLD ADD: COTUI DOM REP
2003-145	SANCHEZ, FELIX ANTONIO	OLD ADD: PUERTA PLATA DOM REP
2002-165	SANCHEZ, FREDERICK PHILLIP 'FREDDY'	335 EAST DELAWARE ROAD, BURBANK CA 91504
1988-117	SANCHEZ, ISRAEL	5444 NORTH SPAULDING AVENUE, CHICAGO IL 60625
1998-173	SANCHEZ, JESUS PAULINO	OLD ADD: BANI DOM REP
2006-185	SANCHEZ, JONATHAN O.	OLD ADD: SABANA GRANDE PR
1981-114	SANCHEZ, LUIS MERCEDES ESCO	D. FEBRUARY 4, 2005, LAGUAIRA, VENEZUELA
1981-115	SANCHEZ, ORLANDO	OLD ADD: BOX SAN ISODRO P52, CANOVANOS PR 00629

1952-089	SANCHEZ, RAUL GUADALUPE	D. JUNE 13, 2002, PEMBROKE PINES, FLA.
1991-154	SANCHEZ, REY FRANCISCO	OLD ADD: 8084 PRICE, PUNTA GORDA FL 33949
1923-116	SAND, JOHN HENRY 'HEINIE'	D. NOVEMBER 3, 1958, SAN FRANCISCO, CALIF.
1923-115	SANDBERG, GUSTAVE E.	D. FEBRUARY 3, 1930, LOS ANGELES, CALIF.
2001-162	SANDBERG, JARED LAWRENCE	OLD ADD: OLYMPIA WA
1981-116	SANDBERG, RYNE DEE	26 BILTMORE ESTATES, PHOENIX AZ 85016
1999-178	SANDERS, ANTHONY MARCUS	7881 EAST MCGEE MOUNTAIN ROAD, TUCSON AZ 85750
2003-146	SANDERS, DAVID ANDREW	1330 HILLTOP ROAD, DERBY KS 67037
1945-090	SANDERS, DEE WILMAN	1312 COUNTRY CLUB ROAD, MCALESTER OK 74501
1989-110	SANDERS, DEION LUWYNN	10200 DEER RUN FARMS ROAD, FORT MYERS FL 33912
1965-093	SANDERS, JOHN FRANK	3004 CHESHIRE COURT, WOODSTOCK GA 30189
1964-100	SANDERS, KENNETH GEORGE	12141 PARKVIEW LN, HALES CORNERS WI 53130
1942-091	SANDERS, RAYMOND FLOYD	D. OCTOBER 28, 1983, WASHINGTON, MO.
1974-117	SANDERS, REGINALD JEROME	PO BOX 241454, DETROIT MI 48224
1991-155	SANDERS, REGINALD LAVERNE	1764 WILLIAMSBURG CIRCLE, FLORENCE SC 29501
1993-160	SANDERS, SCOTT GERALD	15910 VENTURA BLVD #1701, ENCINO CA 91436
1978-117	SANDERSON, SCOTT DOUGLAS	945 NEWCASTLE DRIVE, LAKE FOREST IL 60033
1942-092	SANDLOCK, MICHAEL JOSEPH	81 BIBLE STREET, COS COB CT 06807
2005-163	SANDOVAL, DANNY E.	OLD ADD: LARA VENEZUELA
1967-096	SANDS, CHARLES DUANE	28940 BERMUDA POINTE CIRCLE #103, BONITA SPRINGS FL 34134
1975-102	SANDT, THOMAS JAMES	3723 ELAENOR STREET, LAKE OSWEGO OR 97035
1998-174	SANFORD, CHANCE STEVEN	14576 TEAKWOOD DRIVE, FRISCO TX 75035
1940-078	SANFORD, JOHN DOWARD	D. JANUARY 4, 2005, GREENSBORO, N.C.
1943-120	SANFORD, JOHN FREDERICK 'FRED'	1046 WEST 600 NORTH, SALT LAKE CITY UT 84116
1956-074	SANFORD, JOHN STANLEY 'JACK'	D. MARCH 7, 2000, BECKLEY, W.VA.
1991-156	SANFORD, MEREDITH LEROY 'MO'	2800 HWY 389, STARKVILLE MS 39759
1967-097	SANGUILLEN, MANUEL DEJESUS 'MANNY'	2838 4TH STREET, BOYNTON BEACH FL 33435
1949-078	SANICKI, EDWARD ROBERT	D. JULY 6, 1998, OLD BRIDGE, N.J.
1929-091	SANKEY, BENJAMIN TURNER	D. OCTOBER 14, 2001, WASHINGTON, GA.
2005-164	SANTANA, ERVIN RAMON	OLD ADD: SAN CRISTOBAL DOM REP
1990-141	SANTANA, ANDRES CONFESOR (BELONIS)	CALLE 1 327 QUISQUEYA, SAN PEDRO DE MACORIS, DOM REP
2000-161	SANTANA, JOHAN ALEXANDER	OLD ADD: TOVAR VENEZUELA
1997-149	SANTANA, JULIO FRANKLIN	OLD ADD: SAN PEDRO DE MACORIS DOM REP
1998-175	SANTANA, MARINO CASTRO	OLD ADD: SANTO DOMINGO DOM REP
2001-163	SANTANA, PEDRO	OLD ADD: SAN PEDRO DE MACORIS DR
1983-128	SANTANA, RAFAEL FRANCISCO	3220 SE FIRST AVENUE, CAPE CORAL FL 33904
1995-197	SANTANGELLO, FRANK PAUL 'F.P.'	3602 ROCKY RIDGE WAY, EL DORADO HILLS CA 95762
1986-134	SANTIAGO, BENITO	12503 NW 23RD STREET, PEMBROKE PINES FL 33028
1954-097	SANTIAGO, JOSE GUILLERMO	56-SE-NO. 1167, RIO PIEDRAS PR 00921
1963-104	SANTIAGO, JOSE RAFAEL	YAGRUMO STREET Z-12 VALLE ARRIBA HEIGHTS, CAROLINA PR 00893
1997-150	SANTIAGO, JOSE RAFAEL	OLD ADD: 11618 TOMAHAWK CREEK PKWY, LEAWOOD KS 66211
2002-166	SANTIAGO, RAMON D.	OLD ADD: LAS MATAS DOM REP
1960-092	SANTO, RONALD EDWARD	1721 MEADOW LANE, BANNOCKBURN IL 60015
1979-098	SANTODOMINGO, RAFAEL	PO BOX 21, OROCOVIS PR 00720
1968-091	SANTORINI, ALAN JOEL	26 ARTHUR ROAD, HILLSBOROUGH NJ 08844
2001-164	SANTOS, ANGEL RAMON 'RAMON'	OLD ADD: CAYEY PR
2006-186	SANTOS, CHAD ROQUE	OLD ADD: KANEOHE HI
2003-147	SANTOS, FRANCISCO	OLD ADD: SANTO DOMINGO DOM REP
2001-165	SANTOS, VICTOR IRVING	OLD ADD: 22 PORTLAND AVENUE, CLIFTON NJ 07011
1987-129	SANTOVENIA, NELSON GIL	14642 SW 141ST COURT, MIAMI FL 33186
2003-148	SARDINHA, DANE K.	156 KUULEI ROAD, KAILUA HI 96734
2006-187	SARFATE, DENNIS SCOTT	886 WEST DESERT CANYON DRIVE, QUEEN CREEK AZ 85243
1921-090	SARGENT, JOSEPH ALEXANDER	D. JULY 5, 1950, ROCHESTER, N.Y.
1976-086	SARMIENTO, MANUEL EDUARDO	SABANA LARGA #70 ARAGUA, VENEZUELA
1951-086	SARNI, WILLIAM FLORINE	D. APRIL 15, 1983, CREVE COEUR, MO.
2000-162	SASAKI, KAZUHIRO	6542 OCEAN CREST DRIVE, RANCHO PALOS VERDES CA 90275
1987-130	SASSER, MACK DANIEL	1200 DARTMOUTH DRIVE, DOTHAN AL 36303
1998-176	SASSER, ROBERT DOFFELL	2284 EAST 17TH STREET #4, OAKLAND CA 94606
1961-094	SATRIANO, THOMAS VICTOR	11661 SAN VICENTE BLVD #615, LOS ANGELES CA 90049
2000-163	SATURRIA, LUIS ARTURO	OLD ADD: 201 FIFTH STREET SOUTH, SAINT PETERSBURG FL 33701
1951-087	SAUCIER, FRANCIS FIELD	1615 BRYAN PLACE #9, AMARILLO TX 79102
1978-118	SAUCIER, KEVIN ANDREW	2316 SILVERSIDES LOOP, PENSACOLA FL 32526
1943-121	SAUER, EDWARD	D. JULY 1, 1988, THOUSAND OAKS, CALIF.
1941-097	SAUER, HENRY JOHN	D. AUGUST 24, 2001, BURLINGAME, CALIF.
1999-179	SAUERBECK, SCOTT WILLIAM	3570 CHESTNUT PARK, CLEVES OH 45002
1997-151	SAUNDERS, ANTHONY SCOTT	PO BOX 166, ARNOLD MD 21012
1970-118	SAUNDERS, DENNIS JAMES	OLD ADD: 19971 AVENIDA DEL REY, ROWLAND HEIGHTS CA 91745
1993-161	SAUNDERS, DOUGLAS LONG	5791 MOUNTAIN VIEW, YORBA LINDA CA 92686
2005-165	SAUNDERS, JOSEPH FRANCIS	409 HILLMOOR DRIVE, SILVER SPRING MD 20901
1927-078	SAUNDERS, RUSSELL COLLIER 'RUSTY'	D. NOVEMBER 24, 1967, DOVER TWP., OCEAN CO., N.J.
1986-135	SAUVEUR, RICHARD DANIEL	3312 47TH AVENUE EAST, BRADENTON FL 34203
1944-117	SAVAGE, DONALD ANTHONY	D. DECEMBER 25, 1961, MONTCLAIR, N.J.
1987-131	SAVAGE, JOHN JOSEPH 'JACK'	9920 WHITE BLOSSOM BLVD, LOUISVILLE KY 40241
1942-093	SAVAGE, JOHN ROBERT 'BOB'	95 RAYCREST DRIVE, RANDOLPH NH 03593
1962-119	SAVAGE, THEODORE EPHESIAN	1510 MALLARD LANDING COURT, CHESTERFIELD MO 63017
1959-070	SAVERINE, ROBERT PAUL	228 SLICE DR, STAMFORD CT 06907
1929-092	SAVIDGE, DONALD SNYDER	D. MARCH 22, 1983, SANTA BARBARA, CALIF.
1954-098	SAVRANSKY, MORRIS 'MOE'	4550 WEST SAHARA AVENUE #1235, LAS VEGAS NV 89102
1948-088	SAWATSKI, CARL ERNEST	D. NOVEMBER 24, 1991, LITTLE ROCK, ARK.
1948-089	SAWYER, EDWIN MILBY	D. SEPTEMBER 22, 1997, PHOENIXVILLE, PA.
1974-118	SAWYER, RICHARD CLYDE	7727 STONY RIVER COURT, BAKERSFIELD CA 93308
1982-109	SAX, DAVID JOHN	3352 EATON DRIVE, ROSEVILLE CA 95661
1928-079	SAX, ERIK OLIVER 'OLLIE'	D. MARCH 21, 1982, NEWARK, N.J.
1981-117	SAX, STEPHEN LOUIS	201 WESLEY COURT, ROSEVILLE CA 95661
1939-104	SAYLES, WILLIAM NISBETH	D. NOVEMBER 20, 1996, LINCOLN CITY, ORE.
1948-090	SCALA, GERARD MICHAEL 'JERRY'	D. DECEMBER 14, 1993, FALLSTON, MD.

1939-105	SCALZI, FRANK JOHN 'SKEETER'	D. AUGUST 25, 1984, PITTSBURGH, PA.
1931-077	SCALZI, JOHN ANTHONY	D. SEPTEMBER 27, 1962, PORT CHESTER, N.Y.
1991-157	SCANLAN, ROBERT GUY	2150 CHARDON LANE, EL CAJON CA 92019
1974-119	SCANLON, JAMES PATRICK 'PAT'	7400 PORTLAND AVE SOUTH, RICHFIELD MN 55423
1956-075	SCANTLEBURY, PATRICIO ATHELSTAN	D. MAY 24, 1991, GLEN RIDGE, N.J.
1979-099	SCARBERY, RANDY JAMES	5010 EAST LEWIS, FRESNO CA 93727
1942-094	SCARBOROUGH, RAY WILSON	D. JULY 1, 1982, MOUNT OLIVE NC
1972-096	SCARCE, GUERRANT MCCURDY 'MAC'	1010 RICHMOND GLEN CIRCLE, ALPHARETTA GA 30004
1929-093	SCARRITT, STEPHEN RUSSELL MALLORY 'RUSS'	D. DECEMBER 4, 1994, PENSACOLA, FLA.
1935-096	SCARSELLA, LESLIE GEORGE	D. DECEMBER 16, 1958, SAN FRANCISCO, CALIF.
1992-126	SCARSONE, STEVEN WAYNE	23946 NORTH 77TH WAY, SCOTTSDALE AZ 85255
1964-101	SCHAAL, PAUL	17520 SOUTH CODY STREET, OLATHE KS 66062
1950-087	SCHACHT, SIDNEY	D. MARCH 30, 1991, FORT LAUDERDALE, FLA.
1945-091	SCHACKER, HAROLD	4609 NORTH MATANZAS AVENUE, TAMPA FL 33614
1989-111	SCHAEFER, JEFFREY SCOTT	2110 WOODBEND TRAIL, FORT MILL SC 29708
1991-158	SCHAEFER, ROBERT WALDEN	9070 OLD HICKORY CIRCLE, FORT MYERS FL 33912
1952-090	SCHAEFFER, HARRY EDWARD	412 WHEATLAND AVENUE, SHILLINGTON PA 19607
1972-097	SCHAEFFER, MARK PHILIP	18261 PARTHENIA ST, NORTHRIDGE CA 91324
1961-095	SCHAFFER, JIMMIE RONALD	655 BIRCH TER, COOPERSBURG PA 18036
1959-071	SCHAFFERNOTH, JOSEPH ARTHUR	20 MARIAN AVE, BERKLEY HEIGHTS NJ 07922
1958-079	SCHAIVE, JOHN EDWARD	8000 WILSON TERRACE, SPRINGFIELD IL 62707
1932-073	SCHALK, LEROY JOHN	D. MARCH 11, 1990, GAINESVILLE, TEXAS
1995-198	SCHALL, EUGENE DAVID	2702 DILLIE CIRCLE, JAMISON PA 18929
1951-088	SCHALLOCK, ARTHUR LAWRENCE	749 CROCUS DRIVE, SONOMA CA 95476
1944-118	SCHANZ, CHARLES MURRELL	D. MAY 28, 1992, SACRAMENTO, CALIF.
1932-074	SCHAREIN, ARTHUR OTTO	D. JULY 3, 1969, SAN ANTONIO, TEXAS
1937-092	SCHAREIN, GEORGE ALBERT	D. DECEMBER 22, 1981, DECATUR, ILL.
1981-118	SCHATTINGER, JEFFERY	PO BOX 134, LAKE ARROWHEAD CA 92352
1977-126	SCHATZEDER, DANIEL ERNEST	26W020 KLEIN CREEK DRIVE, WINFIELD IL 60190
1922-119	SCHEER, HENRY 'HEINIE'	D. MARCH 21, 1976, NEW HAVEN, CONN.
1943-122	SCHEETZ, OWEN FRANKLIN	D. SEPTEMBER 28, 1994, PICKERINGTON, OHIO
1999-180	SCHEFFER, AARON ALVIN MARCUS	1351 SHARON STREET, WESTLAND MI 48185
1941-098	SCHEFFING, ROBERT BODEN	D. OCTOBER 26, 1985, PHOENIX, ARIZ.
1943-123	SCHEIB, CARL ALVIN	2922 OLD RANCH ROAD, SAN ANTONIO TX 78217
1992-127	SCHEID, RICHARD PAUL	402 GRANT AVENUE, HIGHTSTOWN NJ 08520
1965-094	SCHEINBLUM, RICHARD ALAN 'RICHIE'	1308 WOODSTOCK DRIVE, PALM HARBOR FL 34684
1954-099	SCHELL, CLYDE DANIEL 'DANNY'	D. MAY 11, 1972, MAYVILLE, MICH.
1939-106	SCHELLE, GERARD ANTHONY 'JIM'	D. MAY 4, 1990, WEYMOUTH, MASS.
1923-117	SCHEMANSKE, FREDERICK GEORGE	D. FEBRUARY 18, 1960, DETROIT, MICH.
1945-092	SCHEMER, MICHAEL 'LEFTY'	D. APRIL 22, 1983, MIAMI, FLA.
1946-091	SCHENZ, HENRY LEONARD 'HANK'	D. MAY 12, 1988, CINCINNATI, OHIO
1950-088	SCHERBARTH, ROBERT ELMER	7971 EAST BAY ROAD, PRESQUE ISLE WI 54557
1969-154	SCHERMAN, FREDERICK JOHN	7454 SOUTH TIPP COWLESVILLE ROAD, TIPP CITY OH 45371
1982-110	SCHERRER, WILLIAM JOSEPH	222 FAREWAY LANE, GRAND ISLAND NY 14072
1931-078	SCHESLER, CHARLES 'DUTCH'	D. NOVEMBER 19, 1953, HARRISBURG, PA.
1961-096	SCHILLING, CHARLES THOMAS	7 WOODRIDGE ROAD, MEDFIELD MA 02052
1988-118	SCHILLING, CURTIS MONTAGUE	7 WOODRIDGE ROAD, MEDFIELD MA 02052
1922-120	SCHILLINGS, ELBERT ISAIAH 'RED'	D. JANUARY 7, 1954, OKLAHOMA CITY, OKLA.
1920-101	SCHINDLER, WILLIAM GIBBONS	D. FEBRUARY 6, 1979, PERRYVILLE, MO.
1984-105	SCHIRALDI, CALVIN DREW	9108 TWEED BERWICK DRIVE, AUSTIN TX 78750
1965-095	SCHLESINGER, WILLIAM CORDES	5708 ABELIA COURT, CINCINNATI OH 45213
1923-118	SCHLIEBNER, FREDERICK PAUL 'DUTCH'	D. APRIL 15, 1975, TOLEDO, OHIO
1971-091	SCHLUETER, JAYD	5232 EAST SHAW BUTTE DRIVE, SCOTTSDALE AZ 85254
1938-089	SCHLUETER, NORMAN JOHN	D. OCTOBER 6, 2004, BELLEVILLE, ILL.
2003-149	SCHMACK, BRIAN ROBERT	504 EAST WYE MESA, BROOKINGS SD 57006
1952-091	SCHMEES, GEORGE EDWARD	D. OCTOBER 30, 1998, SAN JOSE , CALIF.
1967-098	SCHMELZ, ALAN GEORGE	7406 EAST CAMINO RAYO DE LUZ, SCOTTSDALE AZ 85262
1995-199	SCHMIDT, CURTIS ALLEN	4025 CHARA LANE, BILLINGS MT 59105
1981-119	SCHMIDT, DAVID FREDERICK	22636 PORTALES, MISSION VIEJO CA 92691
1981-120	SCHMIDT, DAVID JOSEPH	7172 NORTH SERENOA DRIVE, SARASOTA FL 34241
1944-119	SCHMIDT, FREDERICK ALBERT	128 CONSTITUTION AVENUE, WIND GAP PA 18091
1995-200	SCHMIDT, JASON DAVID	35 VIEW RIDGE CIRCLE, LONGVIEW WA 98632
1996-166	SCHMIDT, JEFFREY THOMAS	1028 SEMINOLE HWY, MADISON WI 53711
1972-098	SCHMIDT, MICHAEL JACK	373 EAGLE DRIVE, JUPITER FL 33477
1958-080	SCHMIDT, ROBERT BENJAMIN	9 HARDWOOD ST, SAINT CHARLES MO 63301
1952-092	SCHMIDT, WILLARD RAYMOND	D. MARCH 29, 2007, NEWCASTLE, OKLA.
1941-099	SCHMITZ, JOHN ALBERT	526 EAST UNION AVENUE, WAUSAU WI 54401
2005-166	SCHMOLL, STEPHEN JOHN	4758 CHASTAIN DRIVE, MELBOURNE FL 32940
1943-124	SCHMULBACH, HENRY ALRIVES	D. MAY 3, 2001, BELLEVILLE, ILL.
1972-099	SCHNECK, DAVID LEE	3891 LEHIGH DR, NORTHAMPTON PA 18067
2000-164	SCHNEIDER, BRIAN DUNCAN	OLD ADD: 1030 EAST LANCASTER AVENUE, BRYN MAWR PA 19010
1963-105	SCHNEIDER, DANIEL LOUIS	PO BOX 2421, TABAC AZ 85646
1981-121	SCHNEIDER, JEFFERY THEODORE	268 PIN OAK DRIVE, GENESEO IL 61254
1922-121	SCHNELL, KARL OTTO	D. MAY 31, 1992, PALO ALTO, CALIF.
1968-092	SCHOEN, GERALD THOMAS	OLD ADD: 900 PECAN STREET, HAMMOND LA 70401
1945-093	SCHOENDIENST, ALBERT FRED 'RED'	1105 JO CARR DRIVE, TOWN AND COUNTRY MO 63017
1999-181	SCHOENEWEIS, SCOTT DAVID	15380 NORTH 100TH STREET #2126, SCOTTSDALE AZ 85260
1953-079	SCHOFIELD, JOHN RICHARD 'DICK'	138 CIRCLE DR, SPRINGFIELD IL 62703
1983-129	SCHOFIELD, RICHARD CRAIG	PO BOX 5341, MORTON IL 61550
1988-119	SCHOOLER, MICHAEL RALPH	519 NORTH BUTTONWOOD STREET, ANAHEIM CA 92805
1955-103	SCHOONMAKER, JERALD LEE	8343 SCHREIDER AVE, MUNSTER IN 46321
1935-097	SCHOTT, ARTHUR EUGENE	D. NOVEMBER 16, 1992, SUN CITY CENTER, FLA.
1991-159	SCHOUREK, PETER ALAN	13256 MAPLE CREEK LANE, CENTREVILLE VA 20120
1953-080	SCHRAMKA, PAUL EDWARD	W180N9923 RIVERSBEND CIRCLE WEST, GERMANTOWN WI 53022
1922-122	SCHREIBER, PAUL FREDERICK	D. JANUARY 28, 1982, SARASOTA, FLA.
1963-106	SCHREIBER, THEODORE HENRY	116 NANTUCKET ISLAND, CENTERVILLE GA 31028

1999-182	SCHRENK, STEVEN WAYNE	OLD ADD: 5910 FORK HAMER ROAD, PARRISH FL 34219
2006-188	SCHRODER, CHRISTOPHER KEITH	OLD ADD: PO BOX 86, OKARCHE OK 73762
1965-096	SCHRODER, ROBERT JAMES	2810 JEFFERSON DRIVE, HATTIESBURG MS 39402
1983-130	SCHROEDER, ALFRED WILLIAM 'BILL'	575W17724 HARBOR CIRCLE, MUSKEGO WI 53150
1958-081	SCHROLL, ALBERT BRINGHURST	D. NOVEMBER 30, 1999, ALEXANDRIA, LA.
1980-115	SCHROM, KENNETH MARVIN	1002 BLACK DIAMOND COURT, PORTLAND TX 78374
1984-106	SCHU, RICK SPENCER	11862 MARJON DRIVE, NEVADA CITY CA 95959
1927-079	SCHUBLE, HENRY GEORGE 'HEINE'	D. OCTOBER 2, 1990, BAYTOWN, TEXAS
1972-100	SCHUELER, RONALD RICHARD	3201 EAST CAMINO SIN NUMBRE, PARADISE VALLEY AZ 85253
1979-100	SCHULER, DAVID PAUL	5348 NW 122ND DRIVE, POMPANO BEACH FL 33076
1994-093	SCHULLSTROM, ERIK PAUL	1425 COURT STREET, ALAMEDA CA 94501
1931-079	SCHULMERICH, EDWARD WESLEY 'WES'	D. JUNE 26, 1985, CORVALLIS, ORE.
1953-081	SCHULT, ARTHUR WILLIAM	9225 SW 90TH STREET, OCALA FL 34481
1927-080	SCHULTE, FRED WILLIAM	D. [illegible], BELVIDERE, ILL.
[illegible]	SCHULTE, HERMAN JOSEPH	D. DECEMBER 21, 1993, SAINT CHARLES, MO.
1923-119	SCHULTE, JOHN CLEMENT	D. JUNE 28, 1978, ST. LOUIS, MO.
1944-120	SCHULTE, LEONARD WILLIAM	D. MAY 6, 1986, ORLANDO, FLA.
1975-103	SCHULTZ, CHARLES BUDD 'BUDDY'	5629 EAST THUNDERBIRD ROAD, SCOTTSDALE AZ 85254
1955-104	SCHULTZ, GEORGE WARREN 'BARNEY'	790 WOODLANE RD, BEVERLY NJ 08010
1943-125	SCHULTZ, HOWARD HENRY	1333 MCKUSICK ROAD LANE WEST, STILLWATER MN 55082
1939-107	SCHULTZ, JOSEPH CHARLES	D. JANUARY 10, 1996, SAINT LOUIS, MO.
1951-089	SCHULTZ, ROBERT DUFFY	D. MARCH 31, 1979, NASHVILLE, TENN.
1924-094	SCHULTZ, WEBB CARL	D. JULY 26, 1986, DELAVAN, WISC.
1947-076	SCHULTZ, WILLIAM MICHAEL 'MIKE'	D. AUGUST 2, 2004, EAST SYRACUSE, N.Y.
1989-112	SCHULZ, JEFFREY ALAN	OLD ADD: 1167 SOUTH STOCKWELL ROAD, EVANSVILLE IN 47715
1920-102	SCHULZ, WALTER FREDERICK	D. FEBRUARY 27, 1928, PRESCOTT, ARIZ.
1983-131	SCHULZE, DONALD ARTHUR	1851 NORTH BRINTON AVENUE, DIXON IL 61021
1931-080	SCHUMACHER, HAROLD HENRY	D. APRIL 21, 1993, COOPERSTOWN, N.Y.
2005-167	SCHUMAKER, JARED MICHAEL 'SKIP'	19054 DELAWARE STREET, HUNTINGTON BEACH CA 92649
1964-102	SCHURR, WAYNE ALLEN	10030 WEST 500 SOUTH, HUDSON IN 46747
1937-093	SCHUSTER, WILLIAM CHARLES	D. JUNE 28, 1987, EL MONTE, CALIF.
1996-167	SCHUTZ, CARL JAMES	PO BOX 162, FRENCH SETTLEMENT LA 70733
1989-113	SCHWABE, MICHAEL SCOTT	13341 PRESIDIO PLACE, TUSTIN CA 92782
1961-097	SCHWALL, DONALD BERNARD	2000 LAKE MARSHALL DRIVE, GIBSONIA PA 15044
1948-091	SCHWAMB, RALPH RICHARD	D. DECEMBER 21, 1989, LANCASTER, CALIF.
1965-097	SCHWARTZ, DOUGLAS RANDALL 'RANDY'	757 EL RANCHO DR, EL CAJON CA 92019
1993-162	SCHWARZ, JEFFREY WILLIAM	912 CLUB DRIVE, PALM BEACH GARDENS FL 33418
1955-105	SCHYPINSKI, GERALD ALBERT	28014 SHADOWOOD LANE, SELFRIDGE MI 48045
1980-116	SCIOSCIA, MICHAEL LORRI	1915 FALLING STAR AVENUE, WESTLAKE VILLAGE CA 91362
1936-083	SCOFFIC, LOUIS	D. AUGUST 28, 1997, HERRIN, ILL.
1981-122	SCONIERS, DARYL ANTHONY	16775 PAINE STREET, FONTANA CA 92336
1955-106	SCORE, HERBERT JUDE	15142 PORTSIDE DRIVE, FORT MYERS FL 33908
1973-106	SCOTT, ANTHONY	PO BOX 1893, SPARTANBURG SC 29304
1993-163	SCOTT, DARRYL NELSON	4026 EAST HAMBLIN DRIVE, PHOENIX AZ 85050
1983-132	SCOTT, DONALD MALCOLM	6042 114TH TERRACE NORTH, PINELLAS PARK FL 34666
1926-073	SCOTT, FLOYD JOHN 'PETE'	D. MAY 3, 1953, DALY CITY, CALIF.
1991-160	SCOTT, GARY THOMAS	OLD ADD: 50 LINDEN AVENUE, PELHAM NY 10803
1966-081	SCOTT, GEORGE	1316 GOODRICH STREET, GREENVILLE MS 38701
1920-103	SCOTT, GEORGE WILLIAM	D. DECEMBER 3, 1962, PHILOMATH, ORE.
1974-120	SCOTT, JOHN HENRY	917 SOUTH PEARL AVENUE, COMPTON CA 90221
1939-108	SCOTT, LEGRANT EDWARD	D. NOVEMBER 12, 1993, BIRMINGHAM, ALA.
2005-168	SCOTT, LUKE BRANDON	1245 ARREDONDO GRANT ROAD, DELEON SPRINGS FL 32130
1945-094	SCOTT, MARSHALL 'LEFTY'	D. MARCH 3, 1964, HOUSTON, TEXAS
1979-101	SCOTT, MICHAEL WARREN	28355 CHAT DRIVE, LAGUNA NIGUEL CA 92677
1972-101	SCOTT, RALPH ROBERT 'MICKEY'	1134 VESTAL AVE, BINGHAMTON NY 13903
1989-114	SCOTT, RICHARD EDWARD	10 GLENDALE DRIVE, SCARBOROUGH ME 04074
1963-107	SCOTT, RICHARD LOUIS	PO BOX 525, THOMASVILLE GA 31799
1975-104	SCOTT, RODNEY DARRELL	OLD ADD: 4206 PRISCILLA, INDIANAPOLIS IN 46226
1991-161	SCOTT, TIMOTHY DALE	4866 KENSINGTON DRIVE, SAN DIEGO CA 92116
1984-107	SCRANTON, JAMES DEAN	27519 HAMMACK AVENUE, PERRIS CA 92570
1975-105	SCRIVENER, WAYNE ALLISON	1766 HAZEL, BIRMINGHAM MI 48009
1991-162	SCRUGGS, ANTHONY RAYMOND	OLD ADD: 11621 BRADDOCK DRIVE, CULVER CITY CA 90230
1989-115	SCUDDER, WILLIAM SCOTT 'SCOTT'	943 FARM ROAD 1499, PARIS TX 75460
1980-117	SCURRY, RODNEY GRANT	D. NOVEMBER 5, 1992, RENO, NEV.
2002-167	SCUTARO, MARCOS	OLD ADD: SAN FELIPE VENEZUELA
2001-166	SEABOL, SCOTT ANTHONY	2880 WASHINGTON BLVD, MCKEESPORT PA 15133
1964-103	SEALE, JOHNNIE RAY	1941 COUNTY RD 207, DURANGO CO 81301
1979-102	SEAMAN, KIM MICHAEL	3106 CANTY STREET, PASCAGOULA MS 39567
1989-116	SEANEZ, RUDY CABALLERO	1422 MCCABE COVE ROAD, EL CENTRO CA 92243
1981-123	SEARAGE, RAYMOND MARK	9737 PINE LAKE TRAIL, SAINT PETERSBURG FL 33708
1988-120	SEARCY, WILLIAM STEPHEN 'STEVE'	5112 GOUFFON ROAD, KNOXVILLE TN 37918
1943-126	SEARS, KENNETH EUGENE	D. JULY 17, 1968, BRIDGEPORT, TEXAS
2002-168	SEARS, TODD ANDREW	513 NW CHAPEL DRIVE, ANKENY IA 50021
1940-080	SEATS, THOMAS EDWARD	D. MAY 10, 1992, SAN RAMON, CALIF.
1967-099	SEAVER, GEORGE THOMAS 'TOM'	1761 DIAMOND MOUNTAIN ROAD, CALISTOGA CA 94515
2001-167	SEAY, ROBERT MICHAEL 'BOBBY'	1591 OAK CIRCLE NORTH, SARASOTA FL 34232
1985-102	SEBRA, ROBERT BUSH	20 MISNERS TRAIL, ORMOND BEACH FL 32174
1940-081	SECORY, FRANK EDWARD	D. APRIL 7, 1995, PORT HURON, MICH.
1969-155	SECRIST, DONALD LAVERNE	5851 PARK ROAD, PINCKNEYVILLE IL 62274
1921-091	SEDGEWICK, HENRY KENNETH 'DUKE'	D. DECEMBER 4, 1982, CLEARWATER, FLA.
2002-169	SEDLACEK, SHAWN PATRICK	OLD ADD: CEDAR RAPIDS IA 52401
1986-136	SEE, RALPH LAURENCE 'LARRY'	1913 WEST REMINGTON DRIVE, CHANDLER AZ 85248
1930-071	SEEDS, IRA ROBERT 'BOB'	D. OCTOBER 28, 1993, ERICK, OKLA.
1971-092	SEELBACH, CHARLES FREDERICK	13800 FAIRHILL #501, SHAKER HEIGHTS OH 44120
2000-165	SEELBACH, CHRISTOPHER DON	700 WILLOW BEND DRIVE, LUFKIN TX 75901
1943-127	SEEREY, JAMES PATRICK 'PAT'	D. APRIL 28, 1986, JENNINGS, MO.

1995-201	SEFCIK, KEVIN JOHN	16921 STEEPLECHASE PKWY, ORLAND PARK IL 60467
1982-111	SEGELKE, HERMAN NEILS	1833 KERN MOUNTAIN WAY, ANTIOCH CA 94509
1952-093	SEGRIST, KAL HILL	3813 55TH STREET, LUBBOCK TX 79413
1990-142	SEGUI, DAVID VINCENT	13421 LEAVENWORTH ROAD, KANSAS CITY KS 66109
1962-120	SEGUI, DIEGO PABLO	13421 LEAVENWORTH RD, KANSAS CITY KS 66109
1998-177	SEGUIGNOL, FERNANDO ALFREDO	OLD ADD: 1244 SOUTH MILITARY TRAIL, DEERFIELD BEACH FL 33442
1988-121	SEGURA, JOSE ALTAGRACIA	CALLE COLON #8 FUNDACION, BARAHONA, DOM REP
2004-171	SEIBEL, PHILIP MATTHEW	351 WOODLAND DRIVE, AUSTIN TX 78719
1979-103	SEIBERT, KURT ELLIOTT	95 AMBERWOOD CIRCLE, IRMO SC 29063
1980-118	SEILHEIMER, RICKY ALLEN	401 HICKORY HOLLOW LANE, BRENHAM TX 77833
1986-137	SEITZER, KEVIN LEE	16005 KESSLER STREET, STILWELL KS 66085
1996-168	SELBY, WILLIAM FRANK	PO BOX 686, SOUTHERN MS 38671
1993-164	SELE, AARON HELMER	11 HONORS DRIVE, NEWPORT BEACH CA 92660
2005-169	SELF, TODD DOUGLAS	OLD ADD: 407 WEST 38TH STREET, AUSTIN TX 78705
1934-090	SELKIRK, GEORGE ALEXANDER	D. JANUARY 19, 1987, FORT LAUDERDALE, FLA.
1922-123	SELL, ELWOOD LESTER 'EPP'	D. FEBRUARY 20, 1961, READING, PA.
1985-103	SELLERS, JEFFREY DOYLE	4158 NIPOMO AVENUE, LAKEWOOD CA 90713
1972-102	SELLS, DAVID WAYNE	700 BLUE RIDGE LANE, VACAVILLE CA 95688
1965-098	SELMA, RICHARD JAY	D. AUGUST 29, 2001, CLOVIS, CALIF.
1929-094	SELPH, CAREY ISOM	D. FEBRUARY 24, 1976, HOUSTON, TEXAS
1977-127	SEMBER, MICHAEL DAVID	OLD ADD: 7272 EAST GAINEY ROAD, SCOTTSDALE AZ 85258
1965-099	SEMBERA, CARROLL WILLIAM	D. JUNE 14, 2005, SHINER, TEXAS
1992-128	SEMINARA, FRANK PETER	C/O SMITH BARNEY, PO BOX 1924, MORRISTOWN NJ 07962
1943-128	SEMINICK, ANDREW WASAL	D. FEBRUARY 22, 2004, MELBOURNE, FLA.
1958-082	SEMPROCH, ROMAN ANTHONY 'RAY'	4220 BUECHNER AVE, CLEVELAND OH 44109
1952-094	SENERCHIA, EMANUEL ROBERT 'SONNY'	D. NOVEMBER 1, 2003, FREEHOLD, N.J.
1982-112	SENTENEY, STEPHEN LEONARD	D. JUNE 19, 1989, COLUSA, CALIF.
2002-170	SEO, JAE WEONG	OLD ADD: 4622 LA CANADA BLVD, LA CANADA CA 91011
1977-128	SEOANE, MANUEL MODESTO	4703 NORTH ROME AVENUE, TAMPA FL 33603
1942-095	SEPKOWSKI, THEODORE WALTER	D. MARCH 8, 2002, SEVERNA PARK, MD.
1996-169	SERAFINI, DANIEL JOSEPH	430 ALAMOSA DRIVE, SPARKS NV 89441
1949-079	SERENA, WILLIAM ROBERT	D. APRIL 17, 1996, HAYWARD, CALIF.
1981-124	SERNA, PAUL DAVID	1375 CAMINO VERDE, HOLTVILLE CA 92250
2004-172	SERRANO, JAMES 'JIMMY'	2943 EAST ERIKA COURT, GRAND JUNCTION CO 81504
2001-168	SERRANO, WASCAR RADAMES	OLD ADD: BANI DOM REP
1977-129	SERUM, GARY WAYNE	10525 HIDDEN OAKS LANE NORTH, CHAMPLIN MN 55316
1991-163	SERVAIS, SCOTT DANIEL	OLD ADD: 4515 JAMAICA DRIVE, SUGAR LAND TX 77479
1988-122	SERVICE, SCOTT DAVID	14713 WALMER STREET, OVERLAND PARK KS 66223
1941-100	SESSI, WALTER ANTHONY	D. APRIL 18, 1998, MOBILE, ALA.
1928-080	SETTLEMIRE, EDGAR MERLE 'MERLE'	D. JUNE 12, 1988, RUSSELL POINT, OHIO
1965-100	SEVCIK, JOHN JOSEPH	3518 BARRINGTON STREET, SAN ANTONIO TX 78217
1969-156	SEVERINSEN, ALBERT HENRY	133 WARREN AVENUE, MYSTIC CT 06355
1970-119	SEVERSON, RICHARD ALLEN	1036 NORTH 145TH CIRCLE, OMAHA NE 68154
1943-129	SEWARD, FRANK MARTIN	D. APRIL 12, 2004, ELMIRA, N.Y.
1921-092	SEWELL, JAMES LUTHER 'LUKE'	D. MAY 14, 1987, AKRON, OHIO
1920-104	SEWELL, JOSEPH WHEELER	D. MARCH 3, 1990, MOBILE, ALA.
1927-081	SEWELL, THOMAS WESLEY	D. JULY 30, 1956, MONTGOMERY, ALA.
1932-075	SEWELL, TRUETT BANKS 'RIP'	D. SEPTEMBER 3, 1989, PLANT CITY, FLA.
1948-092	SEXAUER, ELMER GEORGE	12401 NORTH 22ND STREET #H601, TAMPA FL 33612
1997-152	SEXSON, RICHMOND LOCKWOOD 'RICHIE'	6539 170TH PLACE SE, BELLEVUE WA 98006
1999-183	SEXTON, CHRISTOPHER PHILIP	7030 BAYTOWNE DRIVE, CINCINNATI OH 45247
1977-130	SEXTON, JIMMY DALE	2680 BAXTER ROAD, WILMER AL 36587
1963-108	SEYFRIED, GORDON CLAY	56428 LOWE AVENUE, YUCCA VALLEY CA 92284
2005-170	SHABALA, ADAM JASON	6 M STREET, STREATOR IL 61364
2005-171	SHACKELFORD, BRIAN WESLEY	821 JONA KAY TERRACE, NORMAN OK 73069
1965-101	SHAMSKY, ARTHUR LEWIS	OLD ADD: 58 BLANCHARD ROAD, SOUTH ORANGE NJ 07079
1973-107	SHANAHAN, PAUL GREGORY 'GREG'	PO BOX 6488, EUREKA CA 95502
1923-120	SHANER, WALTER DEDAKER	D. NOVEMBER 13, 1992, LAS VEGAS, NEV.
1970-120	SHANK, HARVEY TILLMAN	201 EAST JEFFERSON STREET, PHOENIX AZ 85004
1920-105	SHANNER, WILFRED WILLIAM 'BILL'	D. DECEMBER 18, 1986, EVANSVILLE, IND.
1962-121	SHANNON, THOMAS MICHAEL 'MIKE'	3104 SOUTHWICK DRIVE, SAINT CHARLES MO 63301
1959-072	SHANNON, WALTER CHARLES 'WALLY'	D. FEBRUARY 8, 1992, CREVE COUER, MO.
1949-080	SHANTZ, ROBERT CLAYTON	152 MOUNT PLEASANT AVENUE, AMBLER PA 19002
1954-100	SHANTZ, WILMER EBERT 'BILL'	D. DECEMBER 13, 1993, LAUDERHILL, FLA.
1973-108	SHARON, RICHARD LOUIS	PO BOX 349, DILLON MT 59725
1973-109	SHARP, WILLIAM HOWARD	2244 THORNWOOD, WILMETTE IL 60091
1987-132	SHARPERSON, MICHAEL TYRONE	D. MAY 26, 1996, LAS VEGAS, NEV.
2006-189	SHARPLESS, JOSHUA DAVID	1116 ROOSEVELT STREET, CONWAY PA 15027
1922-124	SHAUTE, JOSEPH BENJAMIN	D. FEBRUARY 21, 1970, SCRANTON, PA.
1993-165	SHAVE, JONATHAN TAYLOR	1801 PARKWAY, FERNANDINA BEACH FL 32034
1988-123	SHAVER, JEFFREY THOMAS	9651 EAST CLINTON, SCOTTSDALE AZ 85260
1967-100	SHAW, DONALD WELLINGTON	1225 SAINT CHARLES STREET #5A, SAINT LOUIS MO 63103
1990-143	SHAW, JEFFREY LEE	1215 STORYBROOK DRIVE, WASHINGTON COURT HOUSE OH 43160
1957-077	SHAW, ROBERT JOHN	222 US HWY ONE #208, TEQUESTA FL 33469
1947-077	SHEA, FRANCIS JOSEPH 'SPEC'	D. JULY 19, 2002, NEW HAVEN, CONN.
1928-081	SHEA, JOHN MICHAEL JOSEPH	D. NOVEMBER 30, 1956, MALDEN, MASS.
1927-082	SHEA, MERVYN DAVID JOHN	D. JANUARY 27, 1953, SACRAMENTO, CALIF.
1968-093	SHEA, STEVEN FRANCIS	1 SHEPHERDS LANE, NORTH HAMPTON NH 03862
1987-133	SHEAFFER, DANNY TODD	165 SAVANNAH LANE, MOUNT AIRY NC 27030
1928-082	SHEALY, ALBERT BERLEY	D. MARCH 7, 1967, HAGERSTOWN, MD.
2005-172	SHEALY, RYAN NELSON	2168 NE 63RD COURT, FORT LAUDERDALE FL 33308
1957-078	SHEARER, RAY SOLOMON	D. FEBRUARY 21, 1982, YORK, PA.
1936-084	SHEEHAN, JAMES THOMAS	D. DECEMBER 2, 2003, NEW HAVEN, CONN.
1920-106	SHEEHAN, JOHN THOMAS	D. MAY 29, 1987, WEST PALM BEACH, FLA.
1921-093	SHEELY, EARL HOMER	D. SEPTEMBER 16, 1952, SEATTLE, WASH.
1951-090	SHEELY, HOLLIS KIMBALL 'BUD'	D. OCTOBER 17, 1985, SACRAMENTO, CALIF.

1936-085 SHEERIN, CHARLES JOSEPH ....D. SEPTEMBER 27, 1986, VALLEY STREAM, N.Y.
1996-170 SHEETS, ANDREW MARK..............................45399 JOHN SHEETS ROAD, SAINT AMANT LA 70774
2001-169 SHEETS, BEN M. ....PO BOX 147, SAINT AMANT LA 70774
1984-108 SHEETS, LARRY KENT..............................1413 LYLE AVENUE, STAUNTON VA 24401
1988-124 SHEFFIELD, GARY ANTONIAN ....6731 30TH STREET SOUTH, SAINT PETERSBURG FL 33712
1981-125 SHELBY, JOHN T. ....2232 BROADHEAD LANE, LEXINGTON KY 40515
1974-121 SHELDON, BOB MITCHELL..............................42340 OREGON TRAIL, MURRIETA CA 92562
1961-098 SHELDON, ROLAND FRANK..............................614 NE CORONADO, LEES SUMMIT MO 64063
1997-153 SHELDON, SCOTT PATRICK..............................306 ROBIN HILL DRIVE, ALTAMONTE SPRINGS FL 32701
1966-082 SHELLENBACK, JAMES PHILIP ....189 WILL BOMAR ROAD, GREER SC 29651
1935-098 SHELLEY, HUBERT LENEIRRE 'HUGH'..............................D. JUNE 16, 1978, BEAUMONT, TEXAS
1993-166 SHELTON, BENJAMIN DAVIS ....OLD ADD: 2207 PRENTISS DRIVE, DOWNERS GROVE IL 60516
2004-173 SHELTON, CHRISTOPHER BOB..............................6382 SHADY GROVE CIRCLE, SALT LAKE CITY UT 84121
1944-121 SHEMO, STEPHEN MICHAEL ....D. APRIL 13, 1992, EDEN, N.C.
1945-095 SHEPARD, BERT ROBERT..............................8014 BANGOR AVENUE, HESPERIA CA 92345
1953-082 SHEPARD, JACK LEROY ....D. DECEMBER 31, 1993, ATHERTON, CALIF.
1968-094 SHEPARD, LAWRENCE WILLIAM 'LARRY' ....5610 PIONEERS BLVD #294, LINCOLN NE 68506
1924-095 SHEPHARDSON, RAYMOND FRANCIS..............................D. NOVEMBER 8, 1975, LITTLE FALLS, N.Y.
1992-129 SHEPHERD, KEITH WAYNE..............................6130 WEST 300 NORTH, WABASH IN 46992
1984-109 SHEPHERD, RONALD WAYNE..............................5821 FARM 349, KILGORE TX 75662
1929-095 SHERID, ROYDEN RICHARD..............................D. FEBRUARY 28, 1982, PARKER FORD, PA.
1948-093 SHERIDAN, NEILL RAWLINS ....150 CHAUCER DRIVE, PLEASANT HILL CA 94523
1981-126 SHERIDAN, PATRICK ARTHUR ....31654 TAFT, WAYNE MI 48184
1924-096 SHERLING, EDWARD CREECH..............................D. NOVEMBER 16, 1965, ENTERPRISE, ALA.
1930-072 SHERLOCK, JOHN CLINTON 'MONK'..............................D. NOVEMBER 26, 1985, BUFFALO, N.Y.
1935-099 SHERLOCK, VINCENT THOMAS..............................D. MAY 11, 1997, CHEEKTOWAGA, N.Y.
1993-167 SHERMAN, DARRELL EDWARD..............................20695 AZALEA TERRACE ROAD, RIVERSIDE CA 92508
1978-119 SHERRILL, DENNIS LEE ....1691 TOLLEY TERRACE SE, PALM BAY FL 32909
2004-174 SHERRILL, GEORGE FRIEDERICH ....2092 LEE PLACE, MEMPHIS TN 38104
1990-144 SHERRILL, TIMOTHY SHAWN ....PO BOX 812, HARRISON AR 72601
1958-083 SHERRY, LAWRENCE..............................D. DECEMBER 17, 2006, MISSION VIEJO, CALIF.
1959-073 SHERRY, NORMAN BURT ....4383-89 NOBEL DRIVE, SAN DIEGO CA 92122
1959-074 SHETRONE, BARRY STEVAN ....D. JULY 18, 2001, BOWIE, MD.
1930-073 SHEVLIN, JAMES CORNELIUS..............................D. OCTOBER 30, 1974, FORT LAUDERDALE, FLA.
1924-097 SHIELDS, BENJAMIN COWAN ....D. JANUARY 24, 1982, WOODRUFF, S.C.
2006-190 SHIELDS, JAMES ANTHONY..............................24631 SAINT DENIS COURT, VALENCIA CA 91355
2001-170 SHIELDS, ROBERT SCOT 'SCOT' ....3021 NW 68TH STREET, FORT LAUDERDALE FL 33309
1985-104 SHIELDS, STEPHEN MACK ....4969 LEONARD DRIVE, GADSDEN AL 35903
1992-130 SHIELDS, THOMAS CHARLES ....518 NORTH ELM STREET, LITITZ PA 17543
1924-098 SHIELDS, VINCENT WILLIAM..............................D. NOVEMBER 24, 1952, PLASTER ROCK, NEB.
2002-171 SHIELL, JASON ALEXANDER..............................301 STING RAY COURT, GUYTON GA 31312
1957-079 SHIFFLETT, GARLAND JESSIE ....1095 CODY, LAKEWOOD CO 80215
1992-131 SHIFFLETT, STEVEN EARL ....24004 EAST 172ND STREET, PLEASANT HILL MO 64080
1939-109 SHILLING, JAMES ROBERT ....D. SEPTEMBER 12, 1986, TULSA, OKLA.
1993-168 SHINALL, ZAKARY SEBASTIAN 'ZAK'..............................16605 SELL CIRCLE, HUNTINGTON BEACH CA 92649
1921-094 SHINAULT, ENOCH ERSKINE 'GINGER'..............................D. DECEMBER 29, 1930, DENVER, COLO.
1983-133 SHINES, ANTHONY RAYMOND 'RAZOR'..............................11508 HERB COVE, AUSTIN TX 78750
2001-171 SHINJO, TSUYOSHI ....OLD ADD: FUKUOKA JAPAN
1922-125 SHINNERS, RALPH PETER ....D. JULY 23, 1962, MILWAUKEE, WISC.
1985-105 SHIPANOFF, DAVID NOEL..............................3 SALINA DRIVE SAINT ALBERT AB, T8N 0L1 CANADA
1986-138 SHIPLEY, CRAIG BARRY..............................52 BEAMISH ROAD NORTHMEAD, NEW SOUTH WALES, 2152 AUSTRALIA
1958-084 SHIPLEY, JOSEPH CLARK..............................23 PARK DRIVE, SAINT CHARLES MO 63303
1928-083 SHIRES, CHARLES ARTHUR 'ART' ....D. JULY 13, 1967, ITALY, TEXAS
1920-107 SHIREY, CLAIR LEE 'DUKE'..............................D. SEPTEMBER 1, 1962, HAGERSTOWN, MD.
1941-101 SHIRLEY, ALVIS NEWMAN 'TEX'..............................D. NOVEMBER 7, 1993, DESOTO, TEXAS
1964-104 SHIRLEY, BARTON ARVIN..............................5757 SOUTH STAPLES STREET #4208, CORPUS CHRISTI TX 78413
1924-099 SHIRLEY, ERNEST RAEFORD 'MULE' ....D. AUGUST 3, 1955, GOLDSBORO, N.C.
1977-131 SHIRLEY, ROBERT CHARLES..............................761 WEST 13TH STREET, TULSA OK 74127
1982-113 SHIRLEY, STEVEN BRIAN ....9200 JAMES PLACE NE, ALBUQUERQUE NM 87111
1931-081 SHIVER, IVEY MERWIN ....D. AUGUST 31, 1972, SAVANNAH, GA.
1964-105 SHOCKLEY, JOHN COSTEN..............................405 WALTER ST, GEORGETOWN DE 19947
1961-099 SHOEMAKER, CHARLES LANDIS..............................D. MAY 31, 1990, MOUNT PENN, PA.
1929-096 SHOFFNER, MILBURN JAMES 'MILT' ....D. JANUARY 19, 1978, MADISON, OHIO
1947-078 SHOFNER, FRANK STRICKLAND 'STRICK' ....D. OCTOBER 10, 1998, CRAWFORD, TEXAS
1941-102 SHOKES, EDWARD CHRISTOPHER ....D. SEPTEMBER 14, 2002, WINCHESTER, VA.
1959-075 SHOOP, RONALD LEE..............................D. MARCH 14, 2003, RURAL VALLEY, PA.
1967-101 SHOPAY, THOMAS MICHAEL ....10145 NW 19TH STREET, DORAL FL 33172
2005-173 SHOPPACH, KELLY BRIAN..............................8517 GIBBS DRIVE, FORT WORTH TX 76108
1946-092 SHORE, RAYMOND EVERETT ....D. AUGUST 13, 1996, SAINT LOUIS, MO.
1928-084 SHORES, WILLIAM DAVID..............................D. FEBRUARY 19, 1984, PURCELL, OKLA.
1959-076 SHORT, CHRISTOPHER JOSEPH..............................D. AUGUST 1, 1991, WILMINGTON, DEL.
1940-082 SHORT, DAVID ORVIS..............................D. NOVEMBER 22, 1983, SHREVEPORT, LA.
2005-174 SHORT, RICHARD RYAN ....3021 FORYSYTHE COURT, PEORIA IL 61614
1960-093 SHORT, WILLIAM ROSS ....2975 57TH STREET, SARASOTA FL 33580
1935-100 SHOUN, CLYDE MITCHELL ....D. MARCH 20, 1968, MOUNTAIN HOME, TENN.
1993-169 SHOUSE, BRIAN DOUGLAS ....1616 MAGNOLIA, WASHINGTON IL 61571
1981-127 SHOW, ERIC VAUGHN..............................D. MARCH 16, 1994, DULZURA, CALIF.
1992-132 SHOWALTER, WILLIAM NATHANIEL 'BUCK' ....9736 HATHAWAY STREET, DALLAS TX 75220
1922-126 SHRIVER, HARRY GRAYDON..............................D. JANUARY 21, 1970, MORGANTOWN, W.VA.
1948-094 SHUBA, GEORGE THOMAS 'SHOTGUN'..............................3421 BENT WILLOW LANE, YOUNGSTOWN OH 44511
1994-094 SHUEY, PAUL KENNETH..............................5252 MILL DAM ROAD, WAKE FOREST NC 27587
1999-184 SHUMAKER, ANTHONY WARREN..............................109 WEST 4TH STREET, BREMEN IN 46506
1942-096 SHUMAN, HARRY ....D. OCTOBER 25, 1996, PHILADELPHIA, PA.
1990-145 SHUMPERT, TERRANCE DARNELL..............................8432 FAIRVIEW COURT, LITTLETON CO 80124
1945-096 SHUPE, VINCENT WILLIAM..............................D. APRIL 5, 1962, CANTON, OHIO
1993-170 SIDDALL, JOSEPH TODD ....2785 SIERRA DRIVE, WINDSOR ON, N9E 2Y9 CANADA

1956-076	SIEBERN, NORMAN LEROY	2006 PALO ALTO AVENUE, LADY LAKE FL 32159
1974-122	SIEBERT, PAUL EDWARD	1711 ACKER STREET, ORLANDO FL 32837
1932-076	SIEBERT, RICHARD WALTHER	D. DECEMBER 9, 1978, MINNEAPOLIS, MINN.
1964-106	SIEBERT, WILFRED CHARLES 'SONNY'	2555 BRUSH CREEK, SAINT LOUIS MO 63129
1963-109	SIEBLER, DWIGHT LEROY	11565 SOUTH 204TH, GRETNA NE 68028
1925-092	SIEMER, OSCAR SYLVESTER	D. DECEMBER 5, 1959, ST. LOUIS, MO.
1986-139	SIERRA, RUBEN ANGEL	12355 SW 51ST STREET, MIAMI FL 33175
1988-125	SIERRA, ULISSES 'CANDY'	OLD ADD: BO. TORRECILLA, BAJA BUZ. 108, LOIZA PR 00672
1949-081	SIEVERS, ROY EDWARD	11505 BELLEFONTAINE ROAD, SPANISH LAKE MO 63138
1926-074	SIGAFOOS, FRANCIS LEONARD	D. APRIL 12, 1968, INDIANAPOLIS, IND.
1929-097	SIGMAN, WESLEY TRIPLETT 'TRIPP'	D. MARCH 8, 1971, AUGUSTA, GA.
1943-130	SIGNER, WALTER DONALD ALOYSIUS	D. JULY 23, 1974, GREENWICH, CONN.
2000-166	SIKORSKI, BRIAN PATRICK	17930 WEXFORD STREET, ROSEVILLE MI 48056
1937-094	SILBER, EDWARD JAMES	D. OCTOBER 26, 1976, DUNEDIN, FLA.
2002-172	SILVA, CARLOS	OLD ADD: BOLIVAR VENEZUELA
1996-171	SILVA, JOSE LEONEL	OLD ADD: SAN DIEGO CA 92101
1955-107	SILVERA, AARON ALBERT 'AL'	D. JULY 24, 2002, LOS ANGELES, CALIF.
1948-095	SILVERA, CHARLES ANTHONY RYAN	1240 MANZANITA DRIVE, MILLBRAE CA 94030
1978-120	SILVERIO, LUIS PASCUAL	OLD ADD: 3130 89TH TERRACE, KANSAS CITY MO 64154
1970-121	SILVERIO, TOMAS ROBERTO	OLD ADD: CALLE 914 COLINAS, SANTO DOMINGO DOM REP
1992-133	SILVESTRI, DAVID JOSEPH	1888 SCHOETTLER VALLEY DRIVE, CHESTERFIELD MO 63017
1939-110	SILVESTRI, KENNETH JOSEPH	D. MARCH 31, 1992, TALLAHASSEE, FLA.
1950-089	SIMA, ALBERT	D. AUGUST 17, 1993, SUFFERN, N.Y.
1995-202	SIMAS, WILLIAM ANTHONY	6084 MILLERTON ROAD, FRIANT CA 93626
1924-100	SIMMONS, ALOYSIUS HARRY	D. MAY 26, 1956, MILWAUKEE, WISC.
1998-178	SIMMONS, BRIAN LEE	226 VILLAGE DRIVE, CANONSBURG PA 15317
1947-079	SIMMONS, CURTIS THOMAS	200 PARK ROAD, PROSPECTVILLE PA 19002
1949-082	SIMMONS, JOHN EARL	9 LEE DRIVE, FARMINGDALE NY 11735
1984-110	SIMMONS, NELSON BERNARD	OLD ADD: 610 NORTH TWEEDT STREET, KENNEWICK WA 99336
1928-085	SIMMONS, PATRICK CLEMENT	D. JULY 3, 1968, ALBANY, N.Y.
1968-095	SIMMONS, TED LYLE	PO BOX 26, CHESTERFIELD MO 63006
1990-146	SIMMS, MICHAEL HOWARD	OLD ADD: 5951 SUMMIT, YORBA LINDA CA 92686
1997-154	SIMON, RANDALL CARLITO	OLD ADD: WILLEMSTAD CURACAO
1923-121	SIMON, SYLVESTER ADAM	D. FEBRUARY 28, 1973, CHANDLER, IND.
1991-164	SIMONS, DOUGLAS EUGENE	1988 MOUNT OLIVE ROAD, LOOKOUT MOUNTAIN GA 30750
1931-082	SIMONS, MELBERN ELLIS 'TEX'	D. OCTOBER 11, 1974, PADUCAH, KY.
2002-173	SIMONTACCHI, JASON WILLIAM	3419 LAGUNA COURT, SANTA CLARA CA 95051
1951-091	SIMPSON, HARRY LEON	D. APRIL 3, 1979, AKRON, OHIO
1975-106	SIMPSON, JOE ALLEN	4681 JEFFERSON TWP LANE, MARIETTA GA 30066
2004-175	SIMPSON, LARRY ALLAN 'ALLAN'	OLD ADD: 3255 EAST DESERT INN ROAD, LAS VEGAS NV 89121
1962-122	SIMPSON, RICHARD CHARLES	PO BOX 3593, CULVER CITY CA 90231
1972-103	SIMPSON, STEVEN EDWARD	D. NOVEMBER 2, 1989, OMAHA, NEB.
1953-083	SIMPSON, THOMAS LEO	78369 KISTLER WAY, PALM DESERT CA 92211
1970-122	SIMPSON, WAYNE KIRBY	330 COLLAMER DR, CARSON CA 90744
1964-107	SIMS, DUANE B. 'DUKE'	10509 SHOALHAVEN DRIVE, LAS VEGAS NV 89134
1966-083	SIMS, GREGORY EMMETT	6700 RANCHO PICO WAY, SACRAMENTO CA 95828
1981-128	SINATRO, MATTHEW STEPHEN	2619 239TH AVENUE SE, SAMMAMISH WA 98075
1998-179	SINCLAIR, STEVEN SCOTT	OLD ADD: 147 JOSEPH STREET, VICTORIA BC V8S 3H6 CANADA
1964-108	SINGER, WILLIAM ROBERT	1119 MALLARD MARSH DRIVE, OSPREY FL 34229
1945-097	SINGLETON, BERT ELMER	D. JANUARY 5, 1996, OGDEN, UTAH
1999-185	SINGLETON, CHRISTOPHER VERDELL	2038 TOWN MANOR COURT, DACULA GA 30019
1994-095	SINGLETON, DUANE EARL	OLD ADD: 16 BOND STREET, STATEN ISLAND NY 10302
1922-127	SINGLETON, JOHN EDWARD	D. OCTOBER 23, 1937, DAYTON, OHIO
1970-123	SINGLETON, KENNETH WAYNE	10 SPARKS FARM ROAD, SPARKS MD 21152
1934-091	SINGTON, FREDERIC WILLIAM	D. AUGUST 20, 1998, BIRMINGHAM, ALA.
1945-098	SIPEK, RICHARD FRANCIS	D. JULY 17, 2005, QUINCY, ILL.
1969-157	SIPIN, JOHN WHITE	455 PONZA LANE, SOQUEL CA 95073
1995-203	SIROTKA, MICHAEL ROBERT	4812 LABRANCH STREET #4, HOUSTON TX 77004
2005-175	SISCO, ANDREW FRANK	7800 EAST LINCOLN DRIVE, SCOTTSDALE AZ 85250
2000-167	SISCO, STEVEN MICHAEL	630 SAN DOVAL PLACE, THOUSAND OAKS CA 91359
1982-114	SISK, DOUGLAS RANDALL	3610 42ND AVENUE NE, TACOMA WA 98422
1962-123	SISK, TOMMIE WAYNE	164 EAST 4635 NORTH, PROVO UT 84604
1956-077	SISLER, DAVID MICHAEL	11 HACIENDA DR, SAINT LOUIS MO 63124
1946-093	SISLER, RICHARD ALLEN 'DICK'	D. NOVEMBER 20, 1998, NASHVILLE, TENN.
1939-111	SISTI, SEBASTIAN DANIEL 'SIBBY'	D. APRIL 24, 2006, BUFFALO, N.Y.
1936-086	SIVESS, PETER	D. JUNE 1, 2003, CANDLER, N.C.
1982-115	SIWY, JAMES GERARD	6919 APRIL WIND AVENUE, LAS VEGAS NV 89131
2004-176	SIZEMORE, GRADY	14323 27TH DRIVE SE, BOTHELL WA 98012
1969-158	SIZEMORE, TED CRAWFORD	14030 CONWAY ROAD, CHESTERFIELD MO 63017
1935-101	SKAFF, FRANCIS MICHAEL	D. APRIL 12, 1988, TOWSON, MD.
1977-132	SKAGGS, DAVID LINDSEY	11131 ARLINGTON AVENUE, RIVERSIDE CA 92505
1989-117	SKALSKI, JOSEPH DOUGLAS	630 114TH, WHITING IN 46394
1957-080	SKAUGSTAD, DAVID WENDALL	16222 MONTEREY LANE #274, HUNTINGTON BEACH CA 92649
1942-097	SKETCHLEY, HARRY CLEMENT 'BUD'	D. DECEMBER 19, 1979, LOS ANGELES, CALIF.
1970-124	SKIDMORE, ROBERT ROE 'ROE'	964 MARLIN DRIVE, DECATUR IL 62521
1921-095	SKIFF, WILLIAM FRANKLIN	D. DECEMBER 25, 1976, BRONXVILLE, N.Y.
1922-128	SKINNER, ELISHA HARRISON 'CAMP'	D. AUGUST 4, 1944, DOUGLASVILLE, GA.
1983-134	SKINNER, JOEL PATRICK	OLD ADD: 24310 LAKE DRIVE, BAY VILLAGE OH 44140
1954-101	SKINNER, ROBERT RALPH	1576 DIAMOND ST, SAN DIEGO CA 92109
1956-078	SKIZAS, LOUIS PETER	2101 WEST WHITE STREET #118, CHAMPAIGN IL 61821
1973-110	SKOK, CRAIG RICHARD	981 SLASH PINE WAY NW, LAWRENCEVILLE GA 30243
1954-102	SKOWRON, WILLIAM JOSEPH 'MOOSE'	1118 BEACHCOMBER DR, SCHAUMBURG IL 60193
2000-168	SKRMETTA, MATTHEW LELAND	827 POINSETTIA DRIVE, INDIAN HARBOUR BEACH FL 32937
1982-116	SKUBE, ROBERT JACOB	8456 WEST TETHER TRAIL, PEORIA AZ 85383
1930-074	SLADE, GORDON LEIGH	D. JANUARY 2, 1974, LONG BEACH, CALIF.
1979-104	SLAGLE, ROGER LEE	536 WEST 3RD STREET, LARNED KS 67550

1920-108	SLAPPEY, JOHN HENRY	D. JUNE 10, 1957, MARIETTA, GA.
2006-191	SLATEN, DOUGLAS	233 RENNIE AVENUE, VENICE CA 90291
1971-093	SLATON, JAMES MICHAEL	4082 NORTH ARBOR LANE, BUCKEYE AZ 85396
1982-117	SLAUGHT, DONALD MARTIN	27 MIDDLERIDGE LANE SOUTH, ROLLING HILLS CA 90274
1938-090	SLAUGHTER, ENOS BRADSHER 'COUNTRY'	D. AUGUST 12, 2002, DURHAM, N.C.
1964-109	SLAUGHTER, STERLING FEORE	742 EAST AVE SIERRA MADRE, GILBERT AZ 85234
1926-075	SLAYBACK, ELBERT 'SCOTTIE'	D. NOVEMBER 30, 1979, CINCINNATI, OHIO
1972-104	SLAYBACK, WILLIAM GROVER	41421 SANDALWOOD PLACE, LANCASTER CA 93536
1928-086	SLAYTON, FOSTER HERBERT 'STEVE'	D. DECEMBER 20, 1984, MANCHESTER, N.H.
1950-090	SLEATER, LOUIS MORTIMER	12 BANDON COURT #102, TIMONIUM MD 21093
2004-177	SLEDGE, TERRMEL	30041 MEDFORD PLACE, CASTAIC CA 91384
1944-122	SLOAN, BRUCE ADAMS	D. SEPTEMBER 24, 1973, OKLAHOMA CITY, OKLA.
1948-096	SLOAT, DWAIN CLIFFORD	D. APRIL 18, 2003, SAINT PAUL, MINN.
2006-192	SLOCUM, BRIAN JOHN	OLD ADD: EAST CHESTER NY
1969-159	SLOCUM, RONALD REECE	OLD ADD: 1240 28TH STREET, SAN DOEGO CA 92101
1991-165	SLOCUMB, HEATHCLIFF	1045 ARTHUR STREET, UNIONDALE NY 11553
1991-166	SLUSARSKI, JOSEPH ANTHONY	25 MUSTANG LANE, SAINT ROSE LA 70087
1988-126	SMAJSTRLA, CRAIG LEE	4606 HONEY CREEK COURT, PEARLAND TX 77584
1994-096	SMALL, AARON JAMES	1427 WEST BADILLO, WEST COVINA CA 91790
1930-075	SMALL, CHARLES ALBERT	D. JANUARY 14, 1953, LEWISTON, MAINE
1978-121	SMALL, GEORGE HENRY 'HANK'	4715 MILLBROOK DRIVE, ATLANTA GA 30327
1955-108	SMALL, JAMES ARTHUR	7960 ISLAND COURT, STANWOOD MI 49346
1996-172	SMALL, MARK ALLEN	20088 WOODEN COURT NE, POULSBO WA 98370
1948-097	SMALLEY, ROY FREDERICK	922 NORTH KENNETH DRIVE, GREEN VALLEY AZ 85614
1975-107	SMALLEY, ROY FREDERICK III	6319 TIMBER TRAIL, EDINA MN 55439
1999-186	SMART, JON DAVID 'J.D.'	1325 LOST CREEK, AUSTIN TX 78746
1946-094	SMAZA, JOSEPH PAUL	D. MAY 30, 1979, ROYAL OAK, MICH.
1986-140	SMILEY, JOHN PATRICK	208 WEST THIRD AVENUE, TRAPPE PA 19426
1934-092	SMITH, ALFRED JOHN	D. APRIL 28, 1977, BROWNSVILLE, TEXAS
1926-076	SMITH, ALFRED KENDRICKS	D. AUGUST 11, 1995, SAN DIEGO, CALIF.
1953-084	SMITH, ALPHONSE EUGENE	D. JANUARY 3, 2002, CHICAGO, ILL.
1932-077	SMITH, ARTHUR LAIRD	D. NOVEMBER 22, 1995, NORWALK, CONN.
1975-108	SMITH, BILLY ED	5304 VICKSBURG DRIVE, ARLINGTON TX 76017
1981-129	SMITH, BILLY LAVERN	8407 NEFF, HOUSTON TX 77036
1957-081	SMITH, BOBBY GENE	22323 AUTUMNWOOD COURT SE, YELM WA 98597
1987-134	SMITH, BRICK DUDLEY	4743 AMITY PLACE, CHARLOTTE NC 28212
1981-130	SMITH, BRYN NELSON	1239 HIGHWAY 1, SANTA MARIA CA 93455
1970-125	SMITH, CALVIN BERNARD 'BERNIE'	BOX 513, LUTCHER LA 70071
1966-084	SMITH, CARL REGINALD 'REGGIE'	22239 1/2 ERWIN STREET, WOODLAND HILLS CA 91367
2000-169	SMITH, CHARLES EDWARD 'CHUCK'	OLD ADD: HILLSIDE IL
1960-094	SMITH, CHARLES WILLIAM	D. NOVEMBER 29, 1994, RENO, NEV.
1981-131	SMITH, CHRISTOPHER WILLIAM	1404 NORTH TUSTIN AVENUE #R3, SANTA ANA CA 92705
1938-091	SMITH, CLAY JAMIESON	D. MARCH 5, 2002, CAMBRIDGE, KAN.
1999-187	SMITH, DANIEL CHARLES	133 VAN HOOSER BLVD, CARL JUNCTION MO 64834
1992-134	SMITH, DANIEL SCOTT	2305 HARVARD DRIVE, FLOWER MOUND TX 75022
1990-147	SMITH, DARYL CLINTON	OLD ADD: PO BOX 22033, BALTIMORE MD 21203
1938-092	SMITH, DAVID MERWIN	D. APRIL 1, 1998, WHITEVILLE, N.C.
1980-119	SMITH, DAVID STANLEY	1729 GERANIUM STREET, CARLSBAD CA 92009
1984-111	SMITH, DAVID WAYNE	16330 JERSEY DR, HOUSTON TX 77040
1955-109	SMITH, EARL CALVIN	2764 NORTH LEONARD, FRESNO CA 93727
1936-087	SMITH, EDGAR	D. JANUARY 2, 1994, WILLINGBORO, N.J.
1945-099	SMITH, EDWARD MAYO 'MAYO'	D. NOVEMBER 24, 1977, BOYNTON BEACH, FLA.
1926-077	SMITH, ELWOOD HOPE 'MIKE'	D. MAY 31, 1981, CHESAPEAKE, VA.
1923-122	SMITH, EMANUEL CARR 'CARR'	D. APRIL 14, 1989, MIAMI, FLA.
1930-076	SMITH, ERNEST HENRY	D. APRIL 6, 1973, BROOKLYN, N.Y.
1950-091	SMITH, FRANK THOMAS	D. SEPTEMBER 24, 2005, MALONE, FLA.
1963-110	SMITH, GEORGE CORNELIUS	D. JUNE 15, 1987, ST. PETERSBURG, FLA.
1926-078	SMITH, GEORGE SELBY	D. MAY 26, 1981, RICHMOND, VA.
1989-118	SMITH, GREGORY ALAN	27435 HANES ROAD EAST, DAVENPORT WA 99122
1932-078	SMITH, HAROLD LAVERNE	D. SEPTEMBER 27, 1992, FORT LAUDERDALE, FLA.
1956-079	SMITH, HAROLD RAYMOND	9514 LONDONDERRY COURT, FORT SMITH AR 72908
1955-110	SMITH, HAROLD WAYNE	637 HOUSTON STREET, COLUMBUS TX 78934
1962-124	SMITH, JACK HATFIELD	250 DOUBLES DRIVE, COVINGTON GA 30016
1982-118	SMITH, JAMES LORNE	OLD ADD: 4452 MISTY WAY, YORBA LINDA CA 92686
2001-172	SMITH, JASON WILLIAM	OLD ADD: 6350 GOLDEN ACRES DRIVE, COTTONDALE AL 35453
1989-119	SMITH, JOHN DWIGHT 'DWIGHT'	PO BOX 98, VARNVILLE SC 29944
1931-083	SMITH, JOHN MARSHALL	D. MAY 9, 1982, SILVER SPRING, MD.
1977-133	SMITH, KEITH LAVARNE	5823 13TH STREET, BRADENTON FL 34203
1981-132	SMITH, KENNETH EARL	100 LANDSDOWNE BLVD, YOUNGSTOWN OH 44506
1920-109	SMITH, LAWRENCE PATRICK 'PADDY'	D. DECEMBER 2, 1990, NEW ROCHELLE, N.Y.
1980-120	SMITH, LEE ARTHUR	2124 HWY 507, CASTOR LA 71016
1984-112	SMITH, LEROY PURDY 'ROY'	472 GRAMATON AVE #G2, MOUNT VERNON NY 10552
1978-122	SMITH, LONNIE	OLD ADD: 110 SOUTHPORT ROAD #111, SAPRTANBURG SC 29306
1983-135	SMITH, MARK CHRISTOPHER	658 BUZZARDS POINT ROAD, REEDVILLE VA 22539
1994-097	SMITH, MARK EDWARD	1312 ELMHURST LANE, FLOWER MOUND TX 75028
1925-093	SMITH, MARVIN HAROLD 'RED'	D. FEBRUARY 19, 1961, LOS ANGELES, CALIF.
2006-193	SMITH, MATTHEW JOEL	OLD ADD: HENDERSON NV
1984-113	SMITH, MICHAEL ANTHONY	3226 LIVINGSTON ROAD, JACKSON MS 39213
2002-174	SMITH, MICHAEL ANTHONY	6 WILLETT POND DRIVE, WESTWOOD MA 02090
1989-120	SMITH, MICHAEL ANTHONY 'TEXAS'	OLD ADD: 7605 ANTIQUE OAK, SAN ANTONIO TX 78233
1955-111	SMITH, MILTON	D. APRIL 11, 1997, SAN DIEGO, CALIF.
1962-125	SMITH, NATHANIEL BEVERLY 'NATE'	6365 TAHOE DRIVE, ATLANTA GA 30349
1978-123	SMITH, OSBORNE EARL 'OZZIE'	PO BOX 164, SAINT ALBANS MO 63073
1984-114	SMITH, PATRICK KEITH 'KEITH'	15710 ADA STREET, CANYON COUNTRY CA 91351
1953-085	SMITH, PAUL LESLIE	711 TREVINO LANE, CONROE TX 77302
1987-135	SMITH, PETER JOHN	10030 HALSTEAD DRIVE, SUWANEE GA 30024

1962-126	SMITH, PETER LUKE	3512 DIXON LANE, THE VILLAGES FL 32162
2000-170	SMITH, RANDALL BRIAN 'BRIAN'	203 BO HOWARD ROAD, TONEY AL 35773
1981-133	SMITH, RAYMOND EDWARD	163 OLD MILLIGAN HWY, JOHNSON CITY TN 37601
1963-111	SMITH, RICHARD ARTHUR	6850 DOWNING ROAD #35, CENTRAL OR 97502
1951-092	SMITH, RICHARD HARRISON	1926 NORWOOD LANE, STATE COLLEGE PA 16803
1969-160	SMITH, RICHARD KELLY	2615 GATES ROAD, LINCOLNTON NC 28092
1927-083	SMITH, RICHARD PAUL 'RED'	D. MARCH 8, 1978, TOLEDO, OHIO
2001-173	SMITH, ROBERT ALLAN 'BUD'	5923 EAST WARDLOW ROAD, LONG BEACH CA 90809
1923-123	SMITH, ROBERT ELDRIDGE	D. JULY 19, 1987, WAYCROSS, GA.
1998-180	SMITH, ROBERT EUGENE	OLD ADD: OAKLAND CA 94601
1955-112	SMITH, ROBERT GILCHRIST	221 HACKBERRY LANE, AIKEN SC 29803
1958-085	SMITH, ROBERT WALKAY 'RIVERBOAT'	D. JUNE 23, 2003, CLARENCE, MO.
1927-084	SMITH, RUFUS FRAZIER	D. AUGUST 21, 1984, AIKEN, S.C.
1973-111	SMITH, TOMMIE ALEXANDER	1299 EAST CANNON AVE, ALBEMARIE NC 28001
1998-181	SMITH, TRAVIS WILLIAM	635 NE KEARNEY AVENUE, BEND OR 97701
1941-103	SMITH, VINCENT AMBROSE	D. DECEMBER 14, 1979, VIRGINIA BEACH, VA.
2001-174	SMITH, WALTER ROY 'ROY'	7200 59TH STREET, PINELLAS PARK FL 33781
1958-086	SMITH, WILLIAM GARLAND	D. MARCH 30, 1997, CLINTON, MD.
1963-112	SMITH, WILLIE	D. JANUARY 23, 2006, ANNISTON, ALA.
1994-098	SMITH, WILLIE EVERETT	1330 EAST 68TH STREET, SAVANNAH GA 31404
1984-115	SMITH, ZANE WILLIAM	420 WINDSHIP PLACE, ATLANTA GA 30327
1993-171	SMITHBERG, ROGER CRAIG	21 WHITE OAK LANE, ELGIN IL 60123
2003-150	SMITHERMAN, STEPHEN LYDELL	HC 74 BOX 240-010, HARTSHORNE OK 74547
1982-119	SMITHSON, BILLY MIKE 'MIKE'	2540 SWAN CREEK ROAD, CENTERVILLE TN 37033
1940-083	SMOLL, CLYDE HETRICK	D. AUGUST 31, 1985, QUAKERTOWN, PA.
1988-127	SMOLTZ, JOHN ANDREW	700 FOXHOLLOW RUN, ALPHARETTA GA 30004
1944-123	SMYRES, CLARENCE MELVIN 'CLANCY'	11470 ORCAS AVENUE, SAN FERNANDO CA 91342
2002-175	SMYTH, STEVEN DELTON	44005 NORTHGATE AVENUE, TEMECULA CA 92592
1929-098	SMYTHE, WILLIAM HENRY 'HARRY'	D. AUGUST 28, 1980, AUGUSTA, GA.
2004-178	SNARE, RYAN DELBERT	2671 DERBY WALK NE, ATLANTA GA 30319
2002-176	SNEAD, ESIX	6110 SW 8TH LANE, GAINESVILLE FL 32696
2004-179	SNELL, IAN DANTE	OLD ADD: 1514 TENTH AVENUE WEST, BRADENTON FL 34205
1984-116	SNELL, NATHANIEL	7299 OLD STATE ROAD, HOLLY HILL SC 29059
2002-177	SNELLING, CHRISTOPHER DOYLE	OLD ADD: GOROKAN AUSTRALIA
1947-080	SNIDER, EDWIN DONALD 'DUKE'	3037 LAKEMONT DRIVE, FALLBROOK CA 92028
1988-128	SNIDER, VAN VOORHEES	1615 WINDSOR DRIVE, CLEVELAND OH 44124
1923-124	SNIPES, WYATT EURE 'DUTCH'	D. MAY 1, 1941, FAYETTEVILLE, N.C.
1973-112	SNOOK, FRANK WALTER	2580 ELYSUM, EUGENE OR 97401
1995-204	SNOPEK, CHRISTOPHER CHARLES	103 BRADFORD DRIVE, CYNTHIANA KY 41031
1992-135	SNOW, JACK THOMAS 'J.T.'	15 BRIDLE COURT, HILLSBOROUGH CA 94010
1935-102	SNYDER, BERNARD AUSTIN	D. APRIL 15, 1999, HAVERTOWN, PA.
1985-106	SNYDER, BRIAN ROBERT	14834 WOOD HOME ROAD, CENTERVILLE VA 20120
2004-180	SNYDER, CHRISTOPHER RYAN	15017 SOUTH 47TH STREET, PHOENIX AZ 85044
2002-178	SNYDER, EARL CLIFFORD	58 DIAMOND AVENUE, PLAINVILLE CT 06062
1959-077	SNYDER, GENE WALTER	D. JUNE 2, 1996, YORK, PA.
1986-141	SNYDER, JAMES CORY 'CORY'	1684 RENAISSANCE WAY, SPRINGVILLE UT 84663
1961-100	SNYDER, JAMES ROBERT	7516 DUNBRIDGE DRIVE, ODESSA FL 33556
1952-095	SNYDER, JERRY GEORGE	29603 IMPERIAL CREEK DRIVE, TOMBALL TX 77377
1998-182	SNYDER, JOHN MICHAEL	17729 WEST PORT ROYALE LANE, SURPRISE AZ 85379
2003-151	SNYDER, KYLE EHREN	1008 BEN FRANKLIN DRIVE, SARASOTA FL 34236
1959-078	SNYDER, RUSSELL HENRY	PO BOX 264, NELSON NE 68961
2001-175	SOBKOWIAK, SCOTT	817 SYMPHONY DRIVE, AURORA IL 60504
1937-095	SODD, WILLIAM	D. MAY 14, 1998, FORT WORTH, TEXAS
1971-094	SODERHOLM, ERIC THANE	10 SOUTH 360 HAMPSHIRE LN WEST, HINSDALE IL 60521
1996-173	SODERSTROM, STEPHEN ANDREW	301 NORTH FAITH HOME, TURLOCK CA 95380
1995-205	SODOWSKY, CLINT REA	2801 TROPICANA AVENUE, NORMAN OK 73071
1986-142	SOFF, RAYMOND JOHN	9015 RODESILER HIGHWAY, RIGA MI 49276
1979-105	SOFIELD, RICHARD MICHAEL 'RICK'	18811 BIG CYPRESS DRIVE, JUPITER FL 33458
1990-148	SOJO, LUIS BELTRAN (SOJO)	18455 MIRAMAR PKWY #128, MIRAMAR FL 33029
1968-096	SOLAITA, TOLIA TONY	D. FEBRUARY 10, 1990, TAFUNA, AMERICAN SAMOA
1983-136	SOLANO, JULIO CESAR	OLD ADD: VILLA ESPANA C.O. 31, LAROMANA DOM REP
2006-194	SOLER, ALAIN	OLD ADD: MIAMI FL
1958-087	SOLIS, MARCELINO	D. JUNE 15, 2001, MONTERREY, MEXICO
1973-113	SOLOMON, EDDIE BUDDY	D. JANUARY 12, 1986, MACON, GA.
1923-125	SOLOMON, MOSES HIRSCH	D. JUNE 25, 1966, MIAMI, FLA.
1934-093	SOLTERS, JULIUS JOSEPH 'MOOSE'	D. SEPTEMBER 28, 1975, PITTSBURGH, PA.
1950-092	SOMMERS, WILLIAM DUNN	D. SEPTEMBER 22, 2000, PALM CITY, FLA.
1924-101	SONGER, DON	D. OCTOBER 3, 1962, KANSAS CITY, MO.
1977-134	SORENSEN, LARY ALAN	42515 NORTHVILLE DRIVE #406, NORTHVILLE MI 48167
2003-152	SORENSON, ZACH HART	OLD ADD: PO BOX 845, MESQUITE NV 89024
1999-188	SORIANO, ALFONSO G.	1512 PALISADE AVENUE #2H, FORT LEE NJ 07024
2002-179	SORIANO, RAFAEL	OLD ADD: SAN JOSE DOM REP
1928-087	SORRELL, VICTOR GARLAND	D. MAY 4, 1972, RALEIGH, N.C.
1965-102	SORRELL, WILLIAM	12299 RANCH HOUSE RD, SAN DIEGO CA 92128
1922-129	SORRELLS, RAYMOND EDWIN 'CHICK'	D. JULY 20, 1983, TERRELL, TEXAS
1989-121	SORRENTO, PAUL ANTHONY	7709 142ND WAY SE, NEWCASTLE WA 98059
1972-105	SOSA, ELIAS	3126 SUMMERFIELD RIDGE LANE, MATTHEWS NC 28105
2002-180	SOSA, JORGE BOLIVAR	OLD ADD: SAN JOSE DOM REP
1975-109	SOSA, JOSE YNOCENCIO	OLD ADD: HAINA KN12 CARRETERA SANCHEZ, SANTO DOMINGO DOM REP
1999-189	SOSA, JUAN LUIS	OLD ADD: SAN FRANCISCO DE MACORIS DOM REP
1989-122	SOSA, SAMUEL 'SAMMY'	OLD ADD: 505 NORTH LAKE SHORE DR #5502, CHICAGO IL 60611
1926-079	SOTHERN, DENNIS ELWOOD	D. DECEMBER 7, 1977, DURHAM, N.C.
2005-176	SOTO, GEOVANY	6319 PERCH CREEK DRIVE, HOUSTON TX 77049
1977-135	SOTO, MARIO MELVIN	JOACHS LACHAUSTEGUI #42 SUR BANI, DOM REP
1946-095	SOUCHOCK, STEPHEN	D. JULY 28, 2002, WESTLAND, MICH.
1964-110	SOUTHWORTH, WILLIAM FREDERICK	320 DOBBEN RD, WEBSTER GROVES MO 63119

1980-121	SOUZA, KENNETH MARK 'MARK'	10001 WOODCREEK OAKS BLVD #817, ROSEVILLE CA 95747
2006-195	SOWERS, JEREMY BRYAN	26700 ALSACE COURT #305, BEACHWOOD OH 44122
1942-098	SPAHN, WARREN EDWARD	D. NOVEMBER 24, 2003, BROKEM ARROW, OKLA.
1927-085	SPALDING, CHARLES HARRY 'DICK'	D. FEBRUARY 3, 1950, PHILADELPHIA, PA.
1959-079	SPANGLER, ALBERT DONALD	27202 AFTON WAY, HUFFMAN TX 77336
1964-111	SPANSWICK, WILLIAM HENRY	1200 COMMONWEALTH CIRCLE #202, NAPLES FL 34116
1999-190	SPARKS, JAMES JEFFREY 'JEFF'	714 WEST 42ND STREET, HOUSTON TX 77018
2000-171	SPARKS, STEPHEN LANIER	23378 WILSON DRIVE, LOXLEY AL 36551
1995-206	SPARKS, STEVEN WILLIAM	4019 COLONY OAKS DRIVE, SUGAR LAND TX 77479
1964-112	SPARMA, JOSEPH BLASE	D. MAY 14, 1986, COLUMBUS, OHIO
1955-113	SPEAKE, ROBERT CHARLES	4742 SW URISH RD, TOPEKA KS 66604
1986-143	SPECK, ROBERT CLIFFORD 'CLIFF'	823 SOUTH NUEVA VISTA DR, PALM SPRINGS CA 92264
1924-102	SPEECE, BYRON FRANKLIN	D. SEPTEMBER 29, 1974, ELGIN, ORE.
1975-110	SPEED, HORACE ARTHUR	6821 STATE BLVD EXT., MERIDIAN MS 39305
1943-131	SPEER, ERNIE FLOYD 'FLOYD'	D. MARCH 22, 1969, LITTLE ROCK, ARK.
1991-167	SPEHR, TIMOTHY JOSEPH	8524 BRIAR GROVE DRIVE, WACO TX 76712
1971-095	SPEIER, CHRIS EDWARD	OLD ADD: 3102 NORTH MIAMI DRIVE WEST, PHOENIX AZ 85014
1998-183	SPEIER, JUSTIN JAMES	OLD ADD: 9405 SOUTH 51ST STREET, PHOENIX AZ 85044
2005-177	SPEIER, RYAN ANDREW	7616 BERTITO LANE, SPRINGFIELD VA 22153
1969-161	SPENCE, JOHN ROBERT 'BOB'	3081 BONITA WOODS DRIVE, BONITA CA 91902
1940-084	SPENCE, STANLEY ORVILLE	D. JANUARY 9, 1983, KINSTON, N.C.
1952-096	SPENCER, DARYL DEAN	2740 LARKIN DRIVE, WICHITA KS 67216
1950-093	SPENCER, GEORGE ELWELL	8160 HICKORY AVENUE, GALENA OH 43021
1928-088	SPENCER, GLENN EDWARD	D. DECEMBER 30, 1958, BINGHAMTON, N.Y.
1978-124	SPENCER, HUBERT THOMAS 'TOM'	2021 EAST CONNER STREET, TUCSON AZ 85719
1968-097	SPENCER, JAMES LLOYD	D. FEBRUARY 12, 2002, FORT LAUDERDALE, FLA.
1998-184	SPENCER, MICHAEL SHANE 'SHANE'	2890 CONESTOGA CIRCLE, ALPINE CA 91901
1925-094	SPENCER, ROY HAMPTON	D. FEBRUARY 8, 1973, PORT CHARLETTE, FLA.
1999-191	SPENCER, SEAN JAMES	3584 EAST CALISTOGA COURT, PORT ORCHARD WA 98366
1998-185	SPENCER, STANLEY ROGER	3100 NE 188TH STREET, RIDGEFIELD WA 98642
1920-110	SPENCER, VERNON MURRAY	D. JUNE 3, 1971, WIXOM, MICH.
1920-111	SPERAW, PAUL BACHMAN	D. FEBRUARY 22, 1962, CEDAR RAPIDS, IOWA
1924-103	SPERBER, EDWIN GEORGE	D. JANUARY 5, 1976, CINCINNATI, OHIO
1974-123	SPERRING, ROBERT WALTER	13302 CHRISWOOD DRIVE, CYPRESS TX 77429
1936-088	SPERRY, STANLEY KENNETH	D. SEPTEMBER 27, 1962, EVANSVILLE, WISC.
1955-114	SPICER, ROBERT OBERTON	423 MCPHEE DR, FAYETTEVILLE NC 28305
1989-123	SPIERS, WILLIAM JAMES	9233 OLD STATE ROAD, CAMERON SC 29030
1964-113	SPIEZIO, EDWARD WAYNE	2027 TALLER ROAD, MORRIS IL 60450
1996-174	SPIEZIO, SCOTT EDWARD	2027 TALLER ROAD, MORRIS IL 60450
1972-106	SPIKES, LESLIE CHARLES 'CHARLIE'	531 NORTH BORDER DRIVE, BOGALUSA LA 70427
2005-178	SPILBORGHS, RYAN A.	2220 ELISE WAY, SANTA BARBARA CA 93109
1974-124	SPILLNER, DANIEL RAY	18505 SE NEWPORT WAY #C113, ISSAQUAH WA 98027
1978-125	SPILMAN, WILLIAM HARRY 'HARRY'	4423 ST. PHILLIPS ROAD, MOUNT VERNON IN 47620
1939-112	SPINDEL, HAROLD STEWART	D. JULY 28, 2002, SAN CLEMENTE, CALIF.
1969-162	SPINKS, SCIPIO RONALD	11422 ROCK BRIDGE LANE, SUGAR LAND TX 77478
2001-176	SPIVEY, ERNEST LEE 'JUNIOR'	PO BOX 82621, OKLAHOMA CITY OK 73148
1970-126	SPLITTORFF, PAUL WILLIAM	4204 HICKORY LANE, BLUE SPRINGS MO 64015
1932-079	SPOGNARDI, ANDREA ETTORE	D. JANUARY 1, 2000, DEDHAM, MASS.
1928-089	SPOHRER, ALFRED RAY	D. JULY 21, 1972, CARMEL, N.Y.
1994-099	SPOLJARIC, PAUL NIKOLA	OLD ADD: 13261 NORTH 73RD AVENUE, PEORIA AZ 85381
1954-103	SPOONER, KARL BENJAMIN	D. APRIL 10, 1984, VERO BEACH, FLA.
2001-177	SPOONEYBARGER, TIMOTHY FLOYD	6041 SPANISH OAK DRIVE, PENSACOLA FL 32526
1930-077	SPOTTS, JAMES RUSSELL	D. JUNE 15, 1964, MEDFORD, N.J.
1993-172	SPRADLIN, JERRY CARL	2824 EAST DIANA AVENUE, ANAHEIM CA 92806
1947-081	SPRAGINS, HOMER FRANK	D. OCTOBER 2, 2002, MINTER CITY, MISS.
1968-098	SPRAGUE, EDWARD MARTIN	19015 NORTH DAVIS ROAD, LODI CA 95242
1991-168	SPRAGUE, EDWARD NELSON	4677 PINE VALLEY CIRCLE, STOCKTON CA 95219
1965-103	SPRIGGS, GEORGE HERMAN	77 WEST BAY FRONT ROAD #A, LOTHIAN MD 20711
1955-115	SPRING, JACK RUSSELL	PO BOX 118, COLBERT WA 99005
1925-095	SPRINGER, BRADFORD LOUIS	D. JANUARY 4, 1970, BIRMINGHAM, MICH.
1995-207	SPRINGER, DENNIS LEROY	205 WEST DANTPN AVENUE, FRESNO CA 93705
1992-136	SPRINGER, RUSSELL PAUL	PO BOX 185, POLLOCK LA 71467
1990-149	SPRINGER, STEVEN MICHAEL	6962 CARLA CIRCLE, HUNTINGTON BEACH CA 92647
1930-078	SPRINZ, JOSEPH CONRAD	D. JANUARY 11, 1994, FREMONT, CALIF.
1945-100	SPROULL, CHARLES WILLIAM	D. JANUARY 13, 1980, ROCKFORD, ILL.
1961-101	SPROUT, ROBERT SAMUEL	213 GLENWOOD LANE#D, ENTERPRISE AL 36330
1978-126	SPROWL, ROBERT JOHN	4711 LEEWARD AVENUE, NORTHPORT AL 35476
1924-104	SPURGEON, FRED	D. NOVEMBER 5, 1970, KALAMAZOO, MICH.
2000-172	SPURGEON, JAY AARON	5820 AL FRESCO AVENUE, PAHRUMP NV 89061
2003-153	SPURLING, CHRISTOPHER MICHAEL	8401 MARYLAND DRIVE #A, RICHMOND VA 23294
1975-111	SQUIRES, MICHAEL LYNN	9548 AUTUMNWOOD CIRCLE, KALAMAZOO MI 49009
1980-122	STABLEIN, GEORGE CHARLES	6 STONEBROOK, IRVINE CA 92626
1964-114	STAEHLE, MARVIN GUSTAVE	19421 CROMWELL COURT #208, FORT MYERS FL 33912
1960-095	STAFFORD, BILL CHARLES	D. SEPTEMBER 19, 2001, CANTON TWP., MICH.
1977-136	STAGGS, STEPHEN ROBERT	4021 KENT STREET, NORMAN OK 73072
1964-115	STAHL, LARRY FLOYD	1506 EAST MAIN STREET #A, BELLEVILLE IL 62221
1993-173	STAHOVIAK, SCOTT EDMUND	507 BALMORAL COURT, GRAYSLAKE IL 60030
1975-112	STAIGER, ROY JOSEPH	1233 TYLER DRIVE, LEBANON MO 65536
1934-094	STAINBACK, GEORGE TUCKER 'TUCK'	D. NOVEMBER 29, 1992, CAMARILLO, CALIF.
1992-137	STAIRS, MATTHEW WADE	79 SKYLINE ROAD, BANGOR ME 04401
1925-096	STALEY, GEORGE GAYLORD 'GALE'	D. APRIL 19, 1989, WALNUT CREEK, CALIF.
1947-082	STALEY, GERALD LEE	2517 NE 100TH STREET, VANCOUVER WA 98686
1960-096	STALLARD, EVAN TRACY 'TRACY'	PO BOX 905, WISE VA 24293
1947-083	STALLCUP, THOMAS VIRGIL 'VIRGIL'	D. MAY 2, 1989, GREENVILLE, S.C.
1943-132	STALLER, GEORGE WALBORN	D. JULY 3, 1992, HARRISBURG, PA.
1941-104	STANCEU, CHARLES	D. APRIL 3, 1969, CANTON, OHIO

1925-097	STANDAEART, JEROME JOHN	D. AUGUST 4, 1964, CHICAGO, ILL.
2001-178	STANDRIDGE, JASON WAYNE	6228 CARDINAL DRIVE, PINSON AL 35126
1963-113	STANEK, AL	96 ALLYN STREET, HOLYOKE MA 01040
1979-106	STANFIELD, KEVIN BRUCE	7565 NEWCOMB ST, SAN BERNARDINO CA 92410
2003-154	STANFORD, JASON JOHN	4505 WEST MESQUITAL DEL ORO, TUCSON AZ 85742
1961-102	STANGE, ALBERT LEE 'LEE'	436 DOLPHIN STREET, MELBOURNE BEACH FL 32951
1972-107	STANHOUSE, DONALD JOSEPH	4 CREEKMORE DRIVE, ROANOKE TX 76262
1987-136	STANICEK, PETER LOUIS	525 WILSON STREET, DOWNERS GROVE IL 60515
1987-137	STANICEK, STEPHEN BLAIR	16354 LANFEAR DRIVE, LOCKPORT IL 60441
1997-155	STANIFER, ROBERT WAYNE	10618 PARK PLACE DRIVE, LARGO FL 33778
1959-080	STANKA, JOE DONALD	32718 WEYMOUTH COAST, FULSHEAR TX 77441
1992-138	STANKIEWICZ, ANDREW NEAL	1807 EAST COMMERCE AVENUE, GILBERT AZ 85234
1943-133	STANKY, EDWARD RAYMOND	D. JANUARY 6, 1999, FAIRHOPE, ALA.
1969-163	STANLEY, FREDRICK BLAIR	11627 EAST ONYX AVENUE, SCOTTSDALE AZ 85259
1964-116	STANLEY, MITCHELL JACK 'MICKEY'	6370 CUNNINGHMA LAKE ROAD, BRIGHTON MI 48116
1986-144	STANLEY, ROBERT MICHAEL	1108 NORTHEAST 10TH AVENUE, FORT LAUDERDALE FL 33304
1977-137	STANLEY, ROBERT WILLIAM	19 WILLIAM FAIRFIELD DRIVE, WENHAM MA 01984
1931-084	STANTON, GEORGE WASHINGTON 'BUCK'	D. JANUARY 1, 1992, SAN ANTONIO, TEXAS
1970-127	STANTON, LEROY BOBBY	1751 NORWOOD LN, FLORENCE SC 29501
1975-113	STANTON, MICHAEL THOMAS	1229 SEAGATE DRIVE, PALM HARBOR FL 34675
1989-124	STANTON, WILLIAM MICHAEL 'MIKE'	19602 INDIGO LAKE DRIVE, MAGNOLIA TX 77355
1987-138	STAPLETON, DAVID EARL	GRAND CANYON BASEBALL PO BOX 11097, PHOENIX AZ 85017
1980-123	STAPLETON, DAVID LESLIE	51 NORTH BAYVIEW STREET, FAIRHOPE AL 36532
1962-127	STARGELL, WILVER DORNEL 'WILLIE'	D. APRIL 9, 2001, WILMINGTON, N.C.
1999-192	STARK, DENNIS JAMES	213 NORTH ELM STREET, EDGERTON OH 43517
1987-139	STARK, MATTHEW SCOTT	OLD ADD: 7846 EAST PORTOBELLO AVENUE, MESA AZ 85212
1932-080	STARR, RAYMOND FRANCIS	D. FEBRUARY 9, 1963, BAYLISS, ILL.
1947-084	STARR, RICHARD EUGENE	613 NORTH CRESCENT DRIVE, KITTANNING PA 16201
1935-103	STARR, WILLIAM 'CHICK'	D. AUGUST 12, 1991, LAJOLLA, CALIF.
1963-114	STARRETTE, HERMAN PAUL	103 HOWARD POND LOOP, STATESVILLE NC 28625
1993-174	STATON, DAVID ALLEN	2175 ARNOLD DRIVE, ROCKLIN CA 95765
1972-108	STATON, JOSEPH	2929 76TH AVENU SE, MERCER ISLAND WA 98040
1963-115	STAUB, DANIEL JOSEPH 'RUSTY'	C/O WWOR RADIO, 9 BROADCAST PLAZA, SECAUCUS NJ 07094
1923-126	STAUFFER, CHARLES EDWARD 'ED'	D. JULY 2, 1979, ST PETERSBURG, FLA.
2005-179	STAUFFER, TIMOTHY JAMES	OLD ADD: 88 VAN DAM STREET, SARATOGA SPRINGS NY 12866
1974-125	STEARNS, JOHN HARDIN	OLD ADD: 4240 PIN OAK DRIVE, LOVELAND CO 80531
2000-173	STECHSCHULTE, GENE URBAN	206 WELLINGTON PLACE, FINDLAY OH 45840
1987-140	STEELS, JAMES EARL	1654 VIA RICO, SANTA MARIA CA 93454
1924-105	STEENGRAFE, MILTON HENRY	D. JUNE 2, 1977, OKLAHOMA CITY, OKLA.
1998-186	STEENSTRA, KENNETH GREGORY	1228 PHEASANT COURT, LIBERTY MO 64068
1962-128	STEEVENS, MORRIS DALE 'MOE'	14465 CADILLAC DRIVE, SAN ANTONIO TX 78248
1983-137	STEFERO, JOHN ROBERT	529 MICHELLE ROAD, ODENTON MD 21113
1978-127	STEGMAN, DAVID WILLIAM	3234 SIMMONS DRIVE, GROVE CITY OH 43123
1932-081	STEIN, IRVIN MICHAEL	D. JANUARY 7, 1981, COVINGTON, LA.
1938-093	STEIN, JUSTIN MARION	D. MAY 1, 1992, CREVE COEUR, MO.
1972-109	STEIN, WILLIAM ALLEN	2935 WHIRLAWAY COURT, GREEN COVE SPRINGS FL 32043
1998-187	STEIN, WILLIAM BLAKE 'BLAKE'	115 FORMOSA DRIVE, BRANDON MS 39047
1978-128	STEIN, WILLIAM RANDOLPH	505 HOLIDAY HILLS DRIVE, MINERAL WELLS TX 76067
1986-145	STEINBACH, TERRY LEE	6936 OAK RIDGE ROAD, CORCORAN MN 55340
1937-096	STEINBACHER, HENRY JOHN	D. APRIL 3, 1977, SACRAMENTO, CALIF.
1931-085	STEINECKE, WILLIAM ROBERT	D. JULY 20, 1986, SAINT AUGUSTINE, FLA.
1923-127	STEINEDER, RAYMOND	D. AUGUST 25, 1982, VINELAND, N.J.
1945-101	STEINER, BENJAMIN SAUNDERS	D. OCTOBER 27, 1988, VENICE, FLA.
1945-102	STEINER, JAMES HARRY 'RED'	D. NOVEMBER 16, 2001, GARDENA, CALIF.
1982-120	STEIRER, RICKY FRANCIS	1015 HAVERHILL ROAD, BALTIMORE MD 21229
1971-096	STELMASZEK, RICHARD FRANCIS	2734 EAST 97TH ST, CHICAGO IL 60617
1980-124	STEMBER, JEFFREY ALAN	25H NOBHILL, ROSELAND NJ 07068
2005-180	STEMLE, STEPHEN J	OLD ADD: 3118 GREEN VALLEY ROAD, NEW ALBANY IN 47150
1962-129	STENHOUSE, DAVID ROTCHFORD	70 WOODBURY RD, CRANSTON RI 02905
1982-121	STENHOUSE, MICHAEL	70 WOODBURY RD, CRANSTON RI 02905
1971-097	STENNETT, RENALDO ANTONIO 'RENNIE'	5075 NW 57TH WAY, CORAL SPRINGS FL 33067
2003-155	STENSON, DERNELL RENAULD	D. NOVEMBER 5, 2003, CHANDLER, ARIZ.
1968-099	STEPHEN, LOUIS ROBERTS 'BUZZ'	15512 SYCAMORE, PORTERVILLE CA 93257
1947-085	STEPHENS, BRYAN MARIS	D. NOVEMBER 21, 1991, SANTA ANA, CALIF.
1990-150	STEPHENS, CARL RAY 'RAY'	1065 COUNCIL ROAD NE, CHARLESTON TN 37310
1952-097	STEPHENS, GLEN EUGENE 'GENE'	6504 CIRCO DRIVE, GRANBURY TX 76049
2002-181	STEPHENS, JOHN M	OLD ADD: BERALA AUSTRALIA
1941-105	STEPHENS, VERNON DECATUR	D. NOVEMBER 4, 1968, LONG BEACH, CALIF.
1971-098	STEPHENSON, CHESTER EARL 'EARL'	4043 ZACKS MILL ROAD, ANGIER NC 27501
1996-175	STEPHENSON, GARRETT CHARLES	3075 WEST BALATA COURT, MERIDIAN ID 83642
1921-096	STEPHENSON, JACKSON RIGGS 'RIGGS'	D. NOVEMBER 15, 1985, TUSCALOOSA, ALA.
1963-116	STEPHENSON, JERRY JOSEPH	1425 MARELEN DR, FULLERTON CA 92635
1964-117	STEPHENSON, JOHN HERMAN	7 MAROUNER DRIVE, HAMMOND LA 70401
1943-134	STEPHENSON, JOSEPH CHESTER	D. SEPTEMBER 20, 2000, LOS ANGELES, CALIF.
1989-125	STEPHENSON, PHILLIP RAYMOND	1307 HANCOCK STREET, DODGE CITY KS 67801
1955-116	STEPHENSON, ROBERT LOYD	1518 BROOKHAVEN BLVD, NORMAN OK 73072
1935-104	STEPHENSON, WALTER MCQUEEN	D. JULY 4, 1993, SHREVEPORT, LA.
1974-126	STERLING, RANDALL WAYNE	2516 LINDA AVE, KEY WEST FL 33040
2005-181	STERN, ADAM JAMES	OLD ADD: 1401 NORTH NINTH STREET, LINCOLN NE 68508
1941-106	STEVENS, CHARLES AUGUSTUS	12591 GEORGE REYBURN ROAD, GARDEN GROVE CA 92645
1994-100	STEVENS, DAVID JAMES	2630 CANDLEWOOD WAY, LAHABRA CA 90631
1990-151	STEVENS, DEWAIN LEE 'LEE'	9157 BUCK HILLS DRIVE, HIGHLANDS RANCH CO 80126
1945-103	STEVENS, EDWARD LEE	6211 SOUTH BRAESWOOD, HOUSTON TX 77096
1958-088	STEVENS, R.C.	1405 MOUND ST, DAVENPORT IA 52803
1931-086	STEVENS, ROBERT JORDAN	D. DECEMBER 30, 2005, FREDERICK, MD.
1995-208	STEVERSON, TODD ANTHONY	109 WEST GLENHAVEN DRIVE, PHOENIX AZ 85045

1997-156	STEWART, ANDREW DAVID	2603 WEST 17TH STREET, WILMINGTON DE 19806
2006-196	STEWART, CHRISTOPHER DAVID	OLD ADD: MORENO VALLEY CA
1978-129	STEWART, DAVID KEITH	17762 VINEYARD LANE, POWAY CA 90264
1941-107	STEWART, EDWARD PERRY	D. JUNE 21, 2000, PALO ALTO, CALIF.
1927-086	STEWART, FRANK	D. APRIL 30, 2001, STILLWATER, MINN.
1940-085	STEWART, GLEN WELDON	D. FEBRUARY 11, 1997, MEMPHIS, TENN.
1963-117	STEWART, JAMES FRANKLIN	15644 EAST BOURN DRIVE, ODESSA FL 33556
2003-156	STEWART, JOSHUA CRAIG	182 STEWART LANE, LEDBETTER KY 42058
1978-130	STEWART, SAMUEL LEE	231 KING DAVID LANE, GASTONIA NC 28056
2001-179	STEWART, SCOTT EDWARD	5243 HICKORY KNOLL LANE, MOUNT HOLLY NC 28120
1995-209	STEWART, SHANNON HAROLD	14348 SW 156TH AVENUE, MIAMI FL 33196
1952-098	STEWART, VESTON GOFF 'BUNKY'	200 CAROLINA BEACH AVENUE, CAROLINA BEACH NC 28428
1921-097	STEWART, WALTER CLEVELAND 'LEFTY'	D. SEPTEMBER 26, 1974, KNOXVILLE, TENN.
1940-086	STEWART, WALTER NESBITT	D. JUNE 8, 1990, LONDON, OHIO
1944-124	STEWART, WILLIAM MACKLIN 'MACK'	D. MARCH 21, 1960, MACON, GA.
1955-117	STEWART, WILLIAM WAYNE	302 RUMFORD ROAD, LITITZ PA 17543
1994-101	STIDHAM, PHILLIP WAYNE	5025 MALABAR BLVD, MELBOURNE BEACH FL 32951
1979-107	STIEB, DAVID ANDREW	10860 SHAY LANE, RENO NV 89511
1929-099	STIELY, FRED WARREN	D. JANUARY 6, 1981, VALLEY VIEW, PA.
1960-097	STIGMAN, RICHARD LEWIS	12914 5TH AVE SOUTH, BURNSVILLE MN 55337
1930-079	STILES, ROLLAND MAYS 'ROLLIE'	2535 OAKMONT DRIVE #334, SAINT LOUIS MO 63129
1975-114	STILLMAN, ROYLE ELDON	580 JB COURT, GLENWOOD SPRINGS CO 81601
1986-146	STILLWELL, KURT ANDREW	1105 LASSEN VIEW DRIVE, LAKE ALMANOR CA 96137
1961-103	STILLWELL, RONALD ROY	1105 LASSEN VIEW DRIVE, LAKE ALMANOR CA 96137
1980-125	STIMAC, CRAIG STEVEN	334 SHERIDAN DRIVE, CLARENDON HILLS IL 60514
1923-128	STIMSON, CARL REMUS	D. NOVEMBER 9, 1936, OMAHA, NEB.
1934-095	STINE, LEE ELBERT	D. MARCH 6, 2005, HEMET, CALIF.
1994-102	STINNETT, KELLY LEE	PO BOX 21736, MESA AZ 85277
1969-164	STINSON, GORRELL ROBERT 'BOB'	1309 BANDO LANE, THE VILLAGES FL 32162
1943-135	STIRNWEISS, GEORGE HENRY 'SNUFFY'	D. SEPTEMBER 15, 1958, NEWARK, N.J.
1947-086	STOBBS, CHARLES KLEIN 'CHUCK'	1731 RIVIERA CIRCLE, SARASOTA FL 34232
1959-081	STOCK, WESLEY GAY	PO BOX 1309, ALLYN WA 98524
1993-175	STOCKER, KEVIN DOUGLAS	OLD ADD: PO BOX 58685, PHILADELPHIA PA 19102
2006-197	STOCKMAN, PHILLIP MATTHEW	OLD ADD: BRISBANE AUSTRALIA
1981-134	STODDARD, ROBERT LYLE	15760 SUNNYSIDE AVE, MORGAN HILL CA 95037
1975-115	STODDARD, TIMOTHY PAUL	C/O NORTHWESTERN U., 1501 CENTRAL STREET, EVANSTON IL 60208
1925-098	STOKES, ALBERT JOHN	D. DECEMBER 10, 1986, GRANTHAM, N.H.
1925-099	STOKES, ARTHUR MELTON	D. JUNE 3, 1962, TITUSVILLE, PA.
2006-198	STOKES, BRIAN ALEXANDER	OLD ADD: RIVERSIDE CA
1945-104	STONE, CHARLES RICHARD 'DICK'	D. FEBRUARY 18, 1980, OKLAHOMA CITY, OKLA.
1953-086	STONE, DARRAH DEAN 'DEAN'	213 13TH STREET, SILVIS IL 61282
1923-129	STONE, EDWIN ARNOLD 'ARNIE'	D. JULY 29, 1948, HUDSON FALLS N. Y.
1969-165	STONE, EUGENE DANIEL	OLD ADD: 6897 HWY 262 SE, OTHELLO WA 99344
1967-102	STONE, GEORGE HEARD	1304 FAIRFIELD DRIVE, RUSTON LA 71270
1966-085	STONE, HARRY RONALD 'RON'	11720 NW LOVEJOY, PORTLAND OR 97229
1983-138	STONE, JEFFREY GLEN	RURAL ROUTE 2 BOX 392, PORTAGEVILLE MO 63873
1928-090	STONE, JOHN THOMAS	D. NOVEMBER 30, 1955, SHELBYVILLE, TENN.
1943-136	STONE, JOHN VERNON 'VERN'	D. NOVEMBER 12, 1986, FOUNTAIN VALLEY, CALIF.
2001-180	STONE, RICKY L.	PO BOX 3, AMLIN OH 43002
1971-099	STONE, STEVEN MICHAEL	9261 NORTH 128TH WAY, SCOTTSDALE AZ 85259
1923-130	STONE, WILLIAM ARTHUR 'TIGE'	D. JANUARY 1, 1960, JACKSONVILLE, FLA.
1933-059	STONEHAM, JOHN ANDREW	D. JANUARY 1, 2004, OWASSO, OKLA.
1967-103	STONEMAN, WILLIAM HAMBLY	2519 NORTH SAN MIGUEL DRIVE, ORANGE CA 92867
1922-130	STONER, ULYSSES SIMPSON GRANT 'LIL'	D. JUNE 26, 1966, ENID, OKLA.
1998-188	STOOPS, JAMES WELLINGTON	OLD ADD: 14435 SOUTH 48TH STREET, PHOENIX AZ 85044
1931-087	STORIE, HOWARD EDWARD	D. JULY 27, 1968, PITTSFIELD, MASS.
1930-080	STORTI, LINDO IVAN	D. JULY 24, 1982, ONTARIO, CALIF.
1964-118	STOTTLEMYRE, MELVIN LEON	26004 SE 27TH STREET, ISSAQUAH WA 98029
1990-152	STOTTLEMYRE, MELVIN LEON, JR.	3314 MEADOW LARK DRIVE, LEWISTON ID 83501
1988-129	STOTTLEMYRE, TODD VERNON	6918 EAST BRONCO DRIVE, PARADISE VALLEY AZ 85253
1931-088	STOUT, ALLYN MCCLELLAND	D. DECEMBER 22, 1974, SIKESTON, MO.
1998-189	STOVALL, DAROND TYRONE	1107 GOELZ DRIVE, EAST SAINT LOUIS IL 62203
1938-094	STOVIAK, RAYMOND THOMAS	D. FEBRUARY 23, 1998, NICOYA, COSTA RICA
1960-098	STOWE, HAROLD RUDOLPH	1361 UNION NEW HOPE ROAD, GASTONIA NC 28056
1999-193	STOWERS, CHRISTOPHER JAMES	3633 HIGH GREEN DRIVE, MARIETTA GA 30068
1970-128	STRAHLER, MICHAEL WAYNE	8 CANYON DRAW, ALAMOGORDO NM 88310
1954-104	STRAHS, RICHARD BERNARD	D. MAY 26, 1988, LAS VEGAS, NEV.
1979-108	STRAIN, JOSEPH ALLEN	8668 EAST OTERO CIRCLE, ENGLEWOOD CO 80112
1987-141	STRAKER, LESTER PAUL	OLD ADD: URB. MARIO BRICENO IRRAGRY CAL, MARACAY VENEZUELA
1972-110	STRAMPE, ROBERT EDWIN	SOUTH 24720 LANCE HILL ROAD, CHENEY WA 99004
1934-096	STRANGE, ALAN COCHRANE	D. JUNE 27, 1994, SEATTLE, WASH.
1989-126	STRANGE, JOSEPH DOUGLAS 'DOUG'	435 HEIGHTS DRIVE, GIBSONIA PA 15044
2002-182	STRANGE, PATRICK MARTIN	156 MILL STREET, SPRINGFIELD MA 01108
1934-097	STRATTON, MONTY FRANKLIN PIERCE	D. SEPTEMBER 29, 1982, GREENVILLE, TEXAS
1983-139	STRAWBERRY, DARRYL EUGENE	2550 BRROKFOREST DRIVE, WESLEY CHAPEL FL 33543
2005-182	STREET, HUSTON LOWELL	107 WOOD TRAIL, AUSTIN TX 78746
1928-091	STRELECKI, EDWARD HAROLD	D. JANUARY 9, 1968, NEWARK, N.J.
1954-105	STREULI, WALTER HERBERT	1107 WESTMINSTER, GREENSBORO NC 27410
1950-094	STRICKLAND, GEORGE BEVAN	6328 CONSTANCE STREET, NEW ORLEANS LA 70118
1971-100	STRICKLAND, JAMES MICHAEL	2139 EQUESTRIAN ROAD, PASO ROBLES CA 93446
1999-194	STRICKLAND, SCOTT MICHAEL	415 ENCHANTED RIVER DRIVE, SPRING TX 77301
1937-097	STRICKLAND, WILLIAM GOSS	D. JANUARY 26, 2000, LAKELAMD, FLA.
1959-082	STRIKER, WILBUR SCOTT 'JAKE'	1963 SE GREGORY DRIVE, DALLAS OR 97338
1940-087	STRINCEVICH, NICHOLAS MIHAILOVICH	1308 CAMELOT MANOR, PORTAGE IN 46368
1941-108	STRINGER, LOUIS BERNARD	23442 EL TORO ROAD #W139, LANCASTER CA 92630
1928-092	STRIPP, JOSEPH VALENTINE	D. JUNE 10, 1989, ORLANDO, FLA.

1998-190	STRITTMATTER, MARK ARTHUR	10230 WOODROSE COURT, HIGHLANDS RANCH CO 07506
1970-129	STROHMAYER, JOHN EMERY	1825 CROSBY LANE, REDDING CA 96003
1972-111	STROM, BRENT TERRY	6115 EAST SAN CRISTOBAL STREET, TUCSON AZ 85715
1939-113	STROMME, FLOYD MARVIN	D. FEBRUARY 7, 1993, WENATCHEE, WASH.
1929-100	STRONER, JAMES MELVIN	D. DECEMBER 6, 1975, TARBORO, N.C.
2003-157	STRONG, JAMAL NAJAR	300 NEWLAND STREET #12, LOS ANGELES CA 90042
2000-174	STRONG, JOSEPH BENJAMIN	1340 CORCOARN AVENUE, VALLEJO CA 94591
1966-086	STROUD, EDWIN MARVIN	1696 OAK ST, WARREN OH 44485
1982-122	STROUGHTER, STEPHEN LOUIS	323 NE 2ND, VISALIA CA 93277
1934-098	STRUSS, CLARENCE HERBERT 'STEAMBOAT'	D. SEPTEMBER 12, 1985, GRAND RAPIDS, MICH.
1924-106	STRYKER, STERLING ALPA 'DUTCH'	D. NOVEMBER 5, 1964, RED BANK, N.J.
1922-131	STUART, JOHN DAVIS	D. MAY 13, 1970, CHARLESTON, W.VA.
1921-098	STUART, LUTHER LANE 'LUKE'	D. JUNE 15, 1947, WINSTON-SALEM, N.C.
1949-083	STUART, MARLIN HENRY	D. JUNE 16, 1994, PARAGOULD, ARK.
1958-089	STUART, RICHARD LEE	D. DECEMBER 15, 2002, REDWOOD CITY, CALIF.
1984-117	STUBBS, FRANKLIN LEE	PO BOX 325, GOSHEN KY 40026
1967-104	STUBING, LAWRENCE GEORGE 'MOOSE'	10821 SOUTH LACONIA DRIVE, VILLA PARK CA 92861
1921-099	STUELAND, GEORGE ANTON	D. SEPTEMBER 9, 1964, ONAWA, IOWA
1950-095	STUFFEL, PAUL HARRINGTON	25501 TRUST BLVD, BONITA SPRINGS FL 34135
1997-157	STULL, EVERETT JAMES	1667 FIELDGREEN OVERLOOK, STONE MOUNTAIN GA 30088
2006-199	STULTS, ERIC WILLIAM	18509 GUMWOOD ROAD, MISHAWAKA IN 46501
1957-082	STUMP, JAMES GILBERT	7432 CREEKSIDE DRIVE, LANSING MI 48917
1931-089	STUMPF, GEORGE FREDERICK	D. MARCH 6, 1993, METAIRIE, LA.
1982-123	STUPER, JOHN ANTON	38 LAKE STREET, HAMDEN CT 06517
1955-118	STURDIVANT, THOMAS VIRGIL	1324 SW 71ST, OKLAHOMA CITY OK 73159
1927-087	STURDY, GUY R.	D. MAY 4, 1965, MARSHALL, TEXAS
1940-088	STURGEON, ROBERT HARWOOD	D. MARCH 10, 2007, SAN DIMAS, CALIF.
1941-109	STURM, JOHN PETER JOSEPH	D. OCTOBER 8, 2004, SAINT LOUIS, MO.
1995-210	STURTZE, TANYON JAMES	501 KNIGHTS RUN AVENUE #2316, TAMPA FL 33602
1926-080	STUTZ, GEORGE	D. DECEMBER 29, 1930, PHILADELPHIA, PA.
1995-211	STYNES, CHRISTOPHER DESMOND	1980 NE 77TH STREET, DEERFIELD BEACH FL 33441
1966-087	SUAREZ, KENNETH RAYMOND	6000 FOREST LANE, FORT WORTH TX 76112
1944-125	SUAREZ, LUIS ABELARDO	D. JUNE 5, 1991, HAVANA, CUBA
1970-130	SUCH, RICHARD STANLEY	7614 DIVOT DRIVE, SANFORD NC 27332
1938-095	SUCHE, CHARLES MORRIS	D. FEBRUARY 11, 1984, SAN ANTONIO, TEXAS
1950-096	SUCHECKI, JAMES JOSEPH	D. JULY 20, 2000, CROFTON, MD.
1968-100	SUDAKIS, WILLIAM PAUL	44054 ELKHORN TRAIL, INDIAN WELLS CA 92210
1941-110	SUDER, PETER	D. NOVEMBER 14, 2006, ALIQUIPPA, PA.
1992-139	SUERO, WILLIAMS	D. NOVEMBER 30, 1995, SANTO DOMINGO, DOM REP
1930-081	SUHR, AUGUST RICHARD 'GUS'	D. JANUARY 15, 2004, SCOTTSDALE, ARIZ.
1926-081	SUKEFORTH, CLYDE LEROY	D. SEPTEMBER 5, 2000, WALDOBORO, MAINE
1964-119	SUKLA, EDWARD ANTHONY	16 PERCH, IRVINE CA 92714
1980-126	SULARZ, GUY PATRICK	10818 NORTH 83RD STREET, SCOTTSDALE AZ 85260
1936-089	SULIK, ERNEST RICHARD	D. MAY 31, 1963, OAKLAND, CALIF.
1944-126	SULLIVAN, CARL MANUEL 'JACK'	D. OCTOBER 15, 1992, DALLAS, TEXAS
1928-093	SULLIVAN, CHARLES EDWARD	D. MAY 28, 1935, MAIDEN, N.C.
2005-183	SULLIVAN, CORY	OLD ADD: EVANSTON WY
1953-087	SULLIVAN, FRANKLIN LEAL	BOX 1873, LIHUE HI 96766
1955-119	SULLIVAN, HAYWOOD COOPER	D. FEBRUARY 12, 2003, FORT MYERS, FLA.
1921-100	SULLIVAN, JAMES RICHARD	D. FEBRUARY 12, 1972, BURTONSVILLE, MD.
1935-105	SULLIVAN, JOE	D. APRIL 8, 1985, SEQUIM, WASH.
1920-112	SULLIVAN, JOHN LAWRENCE	D. APRIL 1, 1966, UNION CO., PA.
1942-099	SULLIVAN, JOHN PETER	2301 183RD STREET #403A, HOMEWOOD IL 60430
1963-118	SULLIVAN, JOHN PETER	24 HIGHLAND ST, DANSVILLE NY 14437
1982-124	SULLIVAN, MARC COOPER	2038 WEST FIRST STREET #100, FORT MYERS FL 33901
1939-114	SULLIVAN, PAUL THOMAS 'LEFTY'	D. NOVEMBER 1, 1988, SCOTTSDALE, ARIZ.
1951-093	SULLIVAN, RUSSELL GUY H	1701 HILL-N-DALE DRIVE, FREDERICKSBURG VA 22401
1922-132	SULLIVAN, THOMAS AUGUSTIN	D. SEPTEMBER 23, 1962, BOSTON, MASS.
1925-100	SULLIVAN, THOMAS BRANDON	D. AUGUST 16, 1944, SEATTLE, WASH.
1931-090	SULLIVAN, WILLIAM JOSEPH, JR.	D. JANUARY 4, 1994, SARASOTA, FLA.
1995-212	SULLIVAN, WILLIAM SCOTT 'SCOTT'	100 MARVIN CHAPEL ROAD, CARROLLTON AL 35447
1920-113	SUMMA, HOMER WAYNE	D. JANUARY 29, 1966, LOS ANGELES, CALIF.
1974-127	SUMMERS, JOHN JUNIOR 'CHAMP'	13708 SW 111TH AVENUE, DUNNELLON FL 34432
1928-094	SUMNER, CARL RINGDAHL	D. FEBRUARY 8, 1999, CHATHAM, MASS.
1974-128	SUNDBERG, JAMES HOWARD	2308 NEWFOREST COURT, ARLINGTON TX 76017
1956-080	SUNDIN, GORDON VINCENT	15600 OLD 41 NORTH, NAPLES FL 34110
1936-090	SUNDRA, STEPHEN RICHARD	D. MARCH 23, 1952, CLEVELAND, OHIO
1937-098	SUNKEL, THOMAS JACOB	D. APRIL 6, 2002, PARIS, ILL.
1995-213	SUPPAN, JEFFREY SCOT	PMB 164 19350 RINALDI STREET, PORTER RANCH CA 91326
1985-107	SURHOFF, RICHARD CLIFFORD	1839 WHITE OAK DRIVE, READING PA 19608
1987-142	SURHOFF, WILLIAM JAMES 'B.J.'	2205 PINE HILL FARMS LANE, COCKEYSVILLE MD 21030
1949-084	SURKONT, MATTHEW CONSTANTINE 'MAX'	D. OCTOBER 8, 1986, LARGO, FLA.
1929-101	SUSCE, GEORGE CYRIL METHODIUS, SR.	D. FEBRUARY 25, 1986, SARASOTA, FLA.
1955-120	SUSCE, GEORGE DANIEL	2852 VELMA STREET, MATLACHER FL 33909
1934-099	SUSKO, PETER JONATHAN	D. MAY 22, 1978, JACKSONVILLE, FLA.
1938-096	SUTCLIFFE, CHARLES INIGO	D. MARCH 2, 1994, FALL RIVER, MASS.
1976-087	SUTCLIFFE, RICHARD LEE 'RICK'	616 NE SEABROOK COURT, LEES SUMMIT MO 64064
1964-120	SUTHERLAND, DARRELL WAYNE	1011 NW JEFFREY PLACE, BEAVERTON OR 97006
1966-088	SUTHERLAND, GARY LYNN	338 NORTH OAK CLIFF, MONROVIA CA 91016
1921-101	SUTHERLAND, HARVEY SCOTT 'SUDS'	D. MAY 11, 1972, PORTLAND, ORE.
1949-085	SUTHERLAND, HOWARD ALVIN 'DIZZY'	D. AUGUST 26, 1979, WASHINGTON, D.C.
1980-127	SUTHERLAND, LEONARDO CANTIN	12082 NIETO DRIVE, GARDEN GROVE CA 92640
1990-153	SUTKO, GLENN EDWARD	4475 SETTLES BRIDGE ROAD, SUWANEE GA 30024
1976-088	SUTTER, HOWARD BRUCE 'BRUCE'	510 SADDLE BROOKE DRIVE, DALLAS GA 30132
1966-089	SUTTON, DONALD HOWARD	120 CALLE DE LOS ROSAS, RANCHO MIRAGE CA 92270
1977-138	SUTTON, JOHNNY IKE	536 BLUEBERRY BLVD, DALLAS TX 75217

1997-158	SUTTON, LARRY JAMES	14209 WOODWARD STREET, OVERLAND PARK KS 66223
2001-181	SUZUKI, ICHIRO	OLD ADD: KASUGAI JAPAN
1996-176	SUZUKI, MAKOTO 'MAC'	OLD ADD: KOBE JAPAN
1986-147	SVEUM, DALE CURTIS	13483 EAST ESTRELLA AVENUE, SCOTTSDALE AZ 85259
1983-140	SWAGGERTY, WILLIAM DAVID	34 SPRENKLE AVENUE, HANOVER PA 17331
1973-114	SWAN, CRAIG STEVEN	296 SOUND BEACH AVENUE, OLD GREENWICH CT 06870
1989-127	SWAN, RUSSELL HOWARD	D. APRIL 26, 2006, LAS VEGAS, NEV.
2000-175	SWANN, PEDRO MAURICE	PO BOX 184, TOWNSEND DE 19734
1955-121	SWANSON, ARTHUR LEONARD	1139 CHIPPENHAM DRIVE, BATON ROUGE LA 70808
1929-102	SWANSON, ERNEST EVAR 'EVAR'	D. JULY 17, 1973, GALESBURG, ILL.
1928-095	SWANSON, KARL EDWARD	D. APRIL 3, 2002, MOLINE, ILL.
1971-101	SWANSON, STANLEY LAWRENCE	OLD ADD: 1705 EAST WHALEY STREET, LONGVIEW TX 75601
1947-087	SWARTZ, SHERWIN MERLE	D. JUNE 24, 1991, LOS ANGELES, CALIF.
1920-114	SWARTZ, VERNON MONROE 'DAZZY'	D. JANUARY 13, 1980, GERMANTOWN, OHIO
1995-214	SWARTZBAUGH, DAVID THEODORE	113 ORCHARD STREET, MIDDLETOWN OH 45044
2003-158	SWEENEY, BRIAN EDWARD	111 OLD COACH ROAD, CLIFTON PARK NY 12065
1944-127	SWEENEY, HENRY LEON	D. MAY 6, 1980, COLUMBIA, TENN.
1995-215	SWEENEY, MARK PATRICK	32 HEMLOCK DRIVE, HOLLISTON MA 01746
1995-216	SWEENEY, MICHAEL JOHN	OLD ADD: 2802 TAM O'SHANTER, ONTARIO CA 91761
2006-200	SWEENEY, RYAN JOSEPH	6941 WATERVIEW DRIVE SW, CEDAR RAPIDS IA 52404
1928-096	SWEENEY, WILLIAM JOSEPH	D. APRIL 18, 1957, SAN DIEGO, CALIF.
1978-131	SWEET, RICHARD JOE 'RICK'	1503 NE 89TH COURT, VANCOUVER WA 98664
1927-088	SWEETLAND, LESTER LEO	D. MARCH 4, 1974, MELBOURNE, FLA.
1922-133	SWENTOR, AUGUST WILLIAM	D. NOVEMBER 10, 1969, WATERBURY, CONN.
1929-103	SWETONIC, STEPHEN ALBERT	D. APRIL 22, 1974, CANONSBURG, PA.
1940-089	SWIFT, ROBERT VIRGIL	D. OCTOBER 17, 1966, DETROIT, MICH.
1985-108	SWIFT, WILLIAM CHARLES	5880 EAST SAPPHIRE LANE, PARADISE VALLEY AZ 85253
1932-082	SWIFT, WILLIAM VINCENT	D. FEBRUARY 23, 1969, BARTOW, FLA.
1939-115	SWIGART, OADIS VAUGHN	D. AUGUST 8, 1997, ST. JOSEPH, MO.
1986-148	SWINDELL, FOREST GREGORY 'GREG'	6601 DOGWOOD CREEK DRIVE, AUSTIN TX 78746
1993-176	SWINGLE, PAUL CHRISTOPHER	6844 SOUTH WHETSTON PLACE, CHANDLER AZ 85249
2004-181	SWISHER, NICHOLAS THOMPSON	1905 WASHINGTON AVENUE, PARKERSBURG WV 26101
1974-129	SWISHER, STEVEN EUGENE	1905 WASHINGTON AVENUE, PARKERSBURG WV 26101
2003-159	SWITZER, JON MICHAEL	15722 STONEHAVEN DRIVE, HOUSTON TX 77059
1965-104	SWOBODA, RONALD ALAN	315 ALONZO STREET, NEW ORLEANS LA 70115
1977-139	SYKES, ROBERT JOSEPH	509 WEST MAIN ST, CARMI IL 62821
1953-088	SZEKELY, JOSEPH	D. OCTOBER 16, 1995, PARIS, TEXAS
1970-131	SZOTKIEWICZ, KENNETH JOHN	133 HAZELWOOD DRIVE, STATESBORO GA 30458
2004-182	SZUMINSKI, JASON ERNEST	15326 PEBBLE PEAK, SAN ANTONIO TX 78232

T

1994-103	TABAKA, JEFFREY JON	1481 NORVIEW DRIVE, CLINTON OH 44216
1976-089	TABB, JERRY LYNN	18 EAST ELM STREET #612, CHICAGO IL 60611
1926-082	TABER, EDWARD TIMOTHY 'LEFTY'	D. NOVEMBER 5, 1983, LINCOLN, NEB.
1981-135	TABLER, PATRICK SEAN	OLD ADD: 8715 BLOME ROAD, CINCINNATI OH 45243
1987-143	TABOR, GREGORY STEPHEN	29317 WHALE BONE WAY, HAYWARD CA 94544
1938-097	TABOR, JAMES REUBIN	D. AUGUST 22, 1953, SACRAMENTO, CALIF.
1991-169	TACKETT, JEFFERY WILSON	1574 FRAZIER STREET, CAMARILLO CA 93012
2004-183	TADANO, KAZUHITO	OLD ADD: 8 SLATE CREEK DRIVE, BUFFALO NY 14227
2002-183	TAGUCHI, SO	OLD ADD: NISHONOMIYA JAPAN
1928-097	TAITT, DOUGLAS JOHN	D. DECEMBER 12, 1970, PORTLAND, ORE.
2004-184	TAKATSU, SHINGO	OLD ADD: TOKYO JAPAN
1963-119	TALBOT, FREDERICK LEALAND	7701 LUNSEFORD LANE, FALLS CHURCH VA 22043
1953-089	TALBOT, ROBERT DALE	608 WEST KAWEAH, VISALIA CA 93277
1943-137	TALCOTT, LEROY EVERETT 'ROY'	D. DECEMBER 6, 1999, MIAMI, FLA.
2002-184	TALLET, BRIAN CURTIS	3167 MCCLENDON COURT, BATON ROUGE LA 70810
1966-090	TALTON, MARION LEE 'TIM'	130 HARDY TALTON ROAD, PIKEVILLE NC 27863
1998-191	TAM, JEFFREY EUGENE	8535 BASS AVENUE, PALM BAY FL 32909
1976-090	TAMARGO, JOHN FELIX	19018 FERN MEADOW LOOP, LUTZ FL 33548
1934-100	TAMULIS, VITAUTIS CASIMIRUS	D. MAY 5, 1974, NASHVILLE, TENN.
1973-115	TANANA, FRANK DARYL	28492 SOUTH HARWICH, FARMINGTON HILLS MI 48334
2002-185	TANKERSLEY, DENNIS LEE	1313 STONE CREEK VALLEY CIRCLE, O'FALLON MO 63366
1925-101	TANKERSLEY, LAWRENCE WILLIAM 'LEO'	D. SEPTEMBER 18, 1980, DALLAS, TEXAS
2006-201	TANKERSLEY, TAYLOR MARK	1406 BAUM STREET, VICKSBURG MS 39180
1985-109	TANNER, BRUCE MATTHEW	324 HEARTHSTONE DRIVE, NEW CASTLE PA 16105
1955-122	TANNER, CHARLES WILLIAM 'CHUCK'	34 MAITLAND LN EAST, NEW CASTLE PA 16101
1989-128	TAPANI, KEVIN RAY	781 FERNDALE ROAD NORTH, WAYZATA MN 55391
1954-106	TAPPE, ELVIN WALTER	D. OCTOBER 10, 1998, QUINCY, ILL.
1950-097	TAPPE, THEODORE NASH	D. FEBRUARY 13, 2004, WENATCHEE, WASH.
1993-177	TARASCO, ANTHONY GIACINTO	3528 MAPLEWOOD AVENUE, LOS ANGELES CA 90066
1927-089	TARBERT, WILBER ARLINGTON 'ARLIE'	D. NOVEMBER 27, 1946, CLEVELAND, OHIO
1984-118	TARTABULL, DANILO	24341 ASTOR RACING COURT, VALENCIA CA 91354
1962-130	TARTABULL, JOSE	1658 WEST 72ND STREET, HIALEAH FL 33014
1986-149	TARVER, LASCHELLE	4410 NORTH EMERSON AVENUE, FRESNO CA 93705
1958-090	TASBY, WILLIE	PO BOX 623, SAN LEANDRO CA 94577
2005-184	TASCHNER, JACK GERARD	1375 COOKE ROAD, NEENAH WI 54956
2006-202	TATA, JORDAN ARTHUR	OLD ADD: 10504 ROBINDALE DRIVE, DALLAS TX 75238
1946-096	TATE, ALVIN WALTER	D. MAY 8, 1993, BOUNTIFUL, UTAH
1924-107	TATE, HENRY BENNETT 'BENNIE'	D. OCTOBER 27, 1973, FRANKFORT, ILL.
1958-091	TATE, LEE WILLIE	32338 OAK PARK DRIVE, LEESBURG FL 34748
1975-116	TATE, RANDALL LEE	106 KING STREET, MUSCLE SHOALS AL 35661
1989-129	TATE, STUART DOUGLAS	695 LIBERTY HILL ROAD, TONEY AL 35773
1997-159	TATIS, FERNANDO	OLD ADD: SAN PEDRO DE MACORIS DOM REP
1997-160	TATIS, RAMON FRANCISCO	OLD ADD: GUAYABIN DOM REP

1992-140	TATUM, JAMES RAY	7433 INDIAN WELLS COVE, LITTLETON CO 80124
1968-101	TATUM, JARVIS	D. JANUARY 6, 2003, LOS ANGELES, CALIF.
1969-166	TATUM, KENNETH RAY	19 OAKDALE ROAD, MONTEVALLO AL 35115
1941-111	TATUM, THOMAS VEE TEE	D. NOVEMBER 7, 1989, OKLAHOMA CITY, OKLA.
2006-203	TAUBENHEIM, TY ANDREW	OLD ADD: 134 EAST GROVER STREET, LYNDEN WA 98264
1991-170	TAUBENSEE, EDWARD KENNETH	2234 FOUNTAIN KEY CIRCLE, WINDERMERE FL 34786
1935-106	TAUBY, FRED JOSEPH	D. NOVEMBER 23, 1955, CONCORDIA, CALIF.
1928-098	TAUSCHER, WALTER EDWARD	D. NOVEMBER 27, 1992, WINTER HAVEN, FLA.
1958-092	TAUSSIG, DONALD FRANKLIN	1111 OCEAN DUNES CIRCLE, JUPITER FL 33477
1994-104	TAVAREZ, JESUS RAFAEL	CALLE YZ #39 LOS MINAS SANTO DOMINGO, DOM REP
1993-178	TAVAREZ, JULIAN	11138 ARIES DRIVE, ORLANDO FL 32837
1921-102	TAVENER, JOHN ADAM	D. SEPTEMBER 14, 1969, FT. WORTH, TEXAS
1976-091	TAVERAS, ALEJANDRO ANTONIO 'ALEX'	CALLE 7B #18, REPARTO PERELLO SANTIAGO, DOM REP
1971-102	TAVERAS, FRANKLIN CRISOSTOMO	OLD ADD: CALLE 31 - #16, LOS COLINAS, SANTIAGO DOM REP
2004-185	TAVERAS, WILLY	OLD ADD: TENARES DOM REP
2002-186	TAYLOR, AARON WADE	4520 GEORGIA HWY 23 SOUTH, MILLEN GA 30442
1958-093	TAYLOR, ANTONIO 'TONY'	8415 NW 165TH TERRACE, HIALEAH FL 33016
1921-103	TAYLOR, ARLAS WALTER	D. SEPTEMBER 10, 1958, DADE CITY, FLA.
1977-140	TAYLOR, BRUCE BELL	PO BOX, RUTLAND MA 01543
1925-102	TAYLOR, C. L. 'CHINK'	D. JULY 7, 1980, TEMPLE, TEXAS
1968-102	TAYLOR, CARL MEANS	2356 RIVIERA DRIVE, SARASOTA FL 34232
1969-167	TAYLOR, CHARLES GILBERT 'CHUCK'	1535 GEORGETOWN LANE, MURFREESBORO TN 37129
1926-083	TAYLOR, DANIEL TURNEY	D. OCTOBER 11, 1972, LATROBE, PA.
1987-144	TAYLOR, DONALD CLYDE 'DORN'	OLD ADD: 2536 LAMOTT AVENUE, WILLOW GROVE PA 19090
1986-150	TAYLOR, DWIGHT BERNARD	5163 QUEEN MARY LANE, JACKSON MS 39209
1926-084	TAYLOR, EDWARD JAMES	D. JANUARY 30, 1992, CHULA VISTA, CALIF.
1951-094	TAYLOR, EUGENE BENJAMIN 'BEN'	D. MAY 1, 1999, ALMA, OKLA.
1950-098	TAYLOR, FREDERICK RANKIN	D. JANUARY 6, 2002, COLUMBUS, OHIO
1969-168	TAYLOR, GARY WILLIAM	995 BEAUMONT ROAD, HIGHLAND MI 48356
1957-083	TAYLOR, HARRY EVANS	2125 COOKS LANE, FORT WORTH TX 76120
1932-083	TAYLOR, HARRY WARREN	D. APRIL 27, 1969, TOLEDO, OHIO
1946-097	TAYLOR, JAMES HARRY 'HARRY'	D. NOVEMBER 5, 2000, TERRE HAUTE, IND.
1920-115	TAYLOR, JAMES WREN 'ZACK'	D. SEPTEMBER 19, 1974, ORLANDO, FLA.
1954-107	TAYLOR, JOE CEPHUS	D. MARCH 18, 1993, PITTSBURGH, PA.
1993-179	TAYLOR, KERRY THOMAS	239 VINEYARD STREET, HOT SPRINGS AR 71913
1923-131	TAYLOR, LEO THOMAS	D. MAY 20, 1982, SEATTLE, WASH.
2000-176	TAYLOR, REGINALD TREMAIN	OLD ADD: PO BOX 290152, COLUMBIA SC 29229
1957-084	TAYLOR, ROBERT DALE 'HAWK'	136 SKYWAY DRIVE, MURRAY KY 42071
1970-132	TAYLOR, ROBERT LEE	27 SUNNYBROOK RD, SPRINGFIELD MA 01109
1992-141	TAYLOR, RODNEY SCOTT 'SCOTT'	926 INDIAN BRIDGE LANE, DEFIANCE OH 43512
1962-131	TAYLOR, RONALD WESLEY	19 ALVIN AVENUE TORONTO ON, M4T 2A7 CANADA
1958-094	TAYLOR, SAMUEL DOUGLAS	OLD ADD: 9093 HARRISON OOLTEWAH ROAD, HARRISON TN 37341
1995-217	TAYLOR, SCOTT MICHAEL	1113 NORTH SUMMITLAWN STREET, WICHITA KS 67212
1988-130	TAYLOR, TERRY DERRELL	743 WEST WALNUT AVENUE, CRESTVIEW FL 32536
1924-108	TAYLOR, THOMAS LIVINGSTONE CARLTON	D. APRIL 5, 1956, GREENVILLE, MISS.
1952-099	TAYLOR, VERNON CHARLES 'PETE'	D. NOVEMBER 17, 2003, ANNAPOLIS, MD.
1991-171	TAYLOR, WADE ERIC	6 SLEEPY HOLLOW COVE, LONGWOOD FL 32750
1994-105	TAYLOR, WILLIAM HOWELL	201 WASHINGTON PLACE, THOMASVILLE GA 31792
1954-108	TAYLOR, WILLIAM MICHAEL	PO BOX 146, ACTON CA 93510
1930-082	TEACHOUT, ARTHUR JOHN 'BUD'	D. MAY 11, 1985, LAGUNA BEACH, CALIF.
2005-185	TEAHEN, MARK THOMAS	13679 MESA VERDE DRIVE, YUCAIPA CA 92399
1936-091	TEBBETTS, GEORGE ROBERT 'BIRDIE'	D. MARCH 24, 1999, MANATEE, FLA.
1953-090	TEED, RICHARD LEROY	45 TAYLOR STREET, WINDSOR CT 06095
2003-160	TEIXEIRA, MARK CHARLES	1100 SHADY LANE, SOUTHLAKE TX 76092
1997-161	TEJADA, MIGUEL ORDALIS MARTINEZ	OLD ADD: BANI DOM REP
1986-151	TEJADA, WILFREDO ARISTIDES	CALLE CLUB DE LEONES #84 ENSANCHE OZAMA, SANTO DOMINGO DOM REP
2005-186	TEJEDA, ROBINSON GARCIA	7 COUNTRY PINE LANE, EGG HARBOR TOWNSHIP NJ 08234
1999-195	TEJERA, MICHAEL	14271 SW 18TH STREET, MIAMI FL 33175
1974-130	TEKULVE, KENTON CHARLES	1531 SEQUOIA, PITTSBURGH PA 15241
1996-177	TELEMACO, AMAURY REGALADO	OLD ADD: 830 SOUTH WEBSTER AVENUE, SCRANTON PA 18505
1990-154	TELFORD, ANTHONY CHARLES	3109 CYPRESS KEEP LANE, ODESSA FL 33556
1993-180	TELGHEDER, DAVID WILLIAM	50 ORCHARD CREST DRIVE, WESTTOWN NY 10998
1979-109	TELLMANN, THOMAS JOHN	445 EASTBURN ROAD, KING OF PRUSSIA PA 19406
1952-100	TEMPLE, JOHN ELLIS	D. JANUARY 9, 1994, ANDERSON, S.C.
1955-123	TEMPLETON, CHARLES SHERMAN 'CHUCK'	D. OCTOBER 9, 1997, IRVING, TEXAS
1976-092	TEMPLETON, GARRY LEWIS	13552 DEL PONIENTE ROAD, POWAY CA 92064
1969-169	TENACE, FURY GENE 'GENE'	2650 CLIFF HAWK COURT, REDMOND OR 97756
1929-104	TENNANT, JAMES MCDONNELL	D. APRIL 16, 1967, TRUMBULL, CONN.
1967-105	TEPEDINO, FRANK RONALD	1231 STONYBROOK ROAD, LAKE GROVE NY 11755
1946-098	TEPSIC, JOSEPH JOHN	RURAL ROUTE 3 BOX 285, TYRONE PA 16686
1972-112	TERLECKI, ROBERT JOSEPH	113 SHADY BROOK DRIVE, LANGHORNE PA 19047
1975-117	TERLECKY, GREGORY JOHN	2130 CAMINO LAUREL, SAN CLEMENTE CA 92673
1974-131	TERPKO, JEFFREY MICHAEL	RR 1 BOX 156, SAYRE PA 18840
1982-125	TERRELL, CHARLES WALTER 'WALT'	1304 OXLEY COURT, UNION KY 41091
1973-116	TERRELL, JERRY WAYNE	1301 SUNNY CREEK LN, BLUE SPRINGS MO 64015
2003-161	TERRERO, LUIS ENRIQUE	OLD ADD: BARAHONA DOM REP
1940-090	TERRY, LANCELOT YANK 'YANK'	D. NOVEMBER 4, 1979, BLOOMINGTON, IND.
1956-081	TERRY, RALPH WILLARD	801 PARK STREET, LARNED KS 67550
1986-152	TERRY, SCOTT RAY	7503 CHRISTOPHER RIDGE COURT, SAINT LOUIS MO 63129
1923-132	TERRY, WILLIAM HAROLD	D. JANUARY 9, 1989, JACKSONVILLE, FLA.
1932-084	TERWILLIGER, RICHARD MARTIN	D. JANUARY 21, 1969, GREENVILLE, MICH.
1949-086	TERWILLIGER, WILLARD WAYNE 'WAYNE'	1909 CLEAR CREEK DRIVE, WEATHERFORD TX 76087
1998-192	TESSMER, JAY WELDON	6071 NW FARIAN AVENUE, PORT SAINT LUCIE FL 34986
1958-095	TESTA, NICHOLAS	4324 KEPLER AVENUE, BRONX NY 10470
1955-124	TETTELBACH, RICHARD MORLEY	D. JANUARY 26, 1995, EAST HARWICH, MASS.
1984-119	TETTLETON, MICKEY LEE	346 WEST FRANKLIN ROAD, NORMAN OK 73069

1983-141	TEUFEL, TIMOTHY SHAWN	PO BOX 3517, JUPITER FL 33469
2002-187	TEUT, NATHAN MARK	14523 SUMMIT DRIVE, CLIVE IA 50325
1986-153	TEWKSBURY, ROBERT ALAN	63 RIDGE ROAD, CONCORD NH 03301
1958-096	THACKER, MORRIS BENTON 'MOE'	D. NOVEMBER 13, 1997, LOUISVILLE, KY.
2002-188	THAMES, MARCUS MARKLEY	101 MOUNT MARIAH CIRCLE, LOUISVILLE MS 39339
1978-132	THAYER, GREGORY ALLEN	1000 3RD ST NORTH, SAUK RAPIDS MN 56379
1920-116	THEIS, JOHN LOUIS	D. JULY 6, 1941, GEORGETOWN, OHIO
1977-141	THEISS, DUANE CHARLES	66 JUNIPER AVENUE, WESTERVILLE OH 43081
1971-103	THEOBALD, RONALD MERRILL	319 WEST JACARANDA, FULLERTON CA 92632
1973-117	THEODORE, GEORGE BASIL	1388 PRINCETON AVENUE, SALT LAKE CITY UT 84105
2005-187	THERIOT, RYAN STEWART	8531 TRAILWOOD AVENUE, BATON ROUGE LA 70810
1944-128	THESENGA, ARNOLD JOSEPH 'JUG '	D. DECEMBER 3, 2002, WICHITA, KAN.
1924-109	THEVENOW, THOMAS JOSEPH	D. JULY 28, 1957, MADISON, IND.
1952-101	THIEL, MAYNARD BERT 'BERT'	W11077 COUNTY ROAD D, MARION WI 54950
1963-120	THIES, DAVID ROBERT	7250 LEWIS RIDGE PKWY #206, MINNEAPOLIS MN 55439
1954-109	THIES, VERNON ARTHUR 'JAKE'	4 CORNFLOWER COURT, FLORISSANT MO 63033
1986-154	THIGPEN, ROBERT THOMAS	1857 BRIGHTWATER BLVD, SAINT PETERSBURG FL 33704
1995-218	THOBE, JOHN JOSEPH 'J.J.'	902 GROVEMONT STREET, SANTA ANA CA 92706
1995-219	THOBE, THOMAS NEAL	OLD ADD: 10471 SHUMARK DRIVE, CHESTER VA 23831
1967-106	THOENEN, RICHARD CRISPIN	PO BOX 364, HARRISBURG OR 97446
1926-085	THOMAS, ALPHONSE THOMAS 'TOMMY'	D. APRIL 27, 1988, YORK COUNTY, PA.
1985-110	THOMAS, ANDRES PERES	35 DUARTE #35 BOCA CHICA, DOM REP
2001-182	THOMAS, BRADLEY RICHARD	OLD ADD: SEVEN HILLS AUSTRALIA
1960-099	THOMAS, CARL LESLIE	4525 NORTH 66TH STREET #99, SCOTTSDALE AZ 85251
2004-186	THOMAS, CHARLES WESLEY	OLD ADD: ASHEVILLE NC
1925-103	THOMAS, CLARENCE FLETCHER 'LEFTY'	D. MARCH 21, 1952, CHARLOTTESVILLE, VA.
1976-093	THOMAS, DANNY LEE	D. JUNE 12, 1980, MOBILE, ALA.
1971-104	THOMAS, DERREL OSBON	7908 WISTERIA COURT, HIGHLAND CA 92346
1927-090	THOMAS, FAY WESLEY	D. AUGUST 16, 1990, CHATSWORTH, CALIF.
1990-155	THOMAS, FRANK EDWARD	OLD ADD: 875 NORTH MICHIGAN AVENUE, CHICAGO IL 60611
1951-095	THOMAS, FRANK JOSEPH	118 DORAY DRIVE, PITTSBURGH PA 15237
1957-085	THOMAS, GEORGE EDWARD	803 121ST STREET #10, AMERY WI 54001
1924-110	THOMAS, HERBERT MARK	D. DECEMBER 4, 1991, STARKE, FLA.
1973-118	THOMAS, JAMES GORMAN 'GORMAN'	759 TALLWOOD RD, CHARLESTON SC 29412
1961-104	THOMAS, JAMES LEROY 'LEE'	14260 MANDERLEIGH WOODS DR, CHESTERFIELD MO 63017
1951-096	THOMAS, JOHN TILLMAN 'BUD'	2475 WOODLAND DRIVE, SEDALIA MO 65301
1952-102	THOMAS, KEITH MARSHALL 'KITE'	D. JANUARY 7, 1995, ROCKY MOUNT, N.C.
1995-220	THOMAS, LARRY WAYNE	3825 GRAHAM LANE, EIGHT MILE AL 36613
1950-099	THOMAS, LEO RAYMOND	D. MARCH 5, 2001, CONCORD, CALIF.
1932-085	THOMAS, LUTHER BAXTER 'BUD'	D. MAY 20, 2001, CHARLOTTESVILLE, VA.
1995-221	THOMAS, MICHAEL STEVEN	4808 GREGORY DRIVE, JONESBORO AR 72401
1926-086	THOMAS, MYLES LEWIS	D. DECEMBER 12, 1963, TOLEDO, OHIO
1938-098	THOMAS, RAYMOND JOSEPH	D. DECEMBER 6, 1993, WILSON, N.C.
1921-104	THOMAS, ROBERT WILLIAM 'RED'	D. MARCH 29, 1962, FREMONT, OHIO
1977-142	THOMAS, ROY JUSTIN	OLD ADD: 6514 WEST ROBIN LANE, GLENDALE AZ 85310
1974-132	THOMAS, STANLEY BROWN	16149 REDMOND WAY, REDMOND WA 98052
1957-086	THOMAS, VALMY	CHRISTIANSTED PO BOX 811, SAINT CROIX VI 00821
1974-133	THOMASON, MELVIN ERSKINE 'ERSKINE'	932 DIAL PLACE, LAURENS SC 29360
1972-113	THOMASSON, GARY LEAH	8300 NORTH 53RD STREET, PARADISE VALLEY AZ 85253
1991-172	THOME, JAMES HOWARD	125 EAST 8TH STREET, HINSDALE IL 60521
2000-177	THOMPSON, ANDREW JOHN	OLD ADD: 18701 CHOPIN DRIVE, LUTZ FL 33558
1978-133	THOMPSON, BOBBY LARUE	OLD ADD: 919 RHYNE ROAD, CHARLOTTE NC 28214
2005-188	THOMPSON, BRADLEY JOSEPH	3650 SOUTH EASTERN AVENUE, LAS VEGAS NV 89109
1954-110	THOMPSON, CHARLES LEMOINE	536 SUMMIT DRIVE, LEWISTOWN PA 17044
1970-133	THOMPSON, DANNY LEON	D. DECEMBER 10, 1976, ROCHESTER, MINN.
1948-098	THOMPSON, DAVID FORREST	D. FEBRUARY 26, 1979, CHARLOTTE, N.C.
2005-189	THOMPSON, DEREK R	4935 GULF STREAM PLACE, LAND O'LAKES FL 34639
1949-087	THOMPSON, DONALD NEWLIN	PO BOX 8218, ASHEVILLE NC 28814
1939-116	THOMPSON, EUGENE EARL	D. AUGUST 24, 2006, SCOTTSDALE, ARIZ.
1920-117	THOMPSON, FRANK E.	D. JUNE 27, 1940, JASPER CO., MINERAL TWP., MO.
1947-088	THOMPSON, HENRY CURTIS 'HANK'	D. SEPTEMBER 30, 1969, FRESNO, CALIF.
1976-094	THOMPSON, JASON DOLPH	4056 SUMMERFIELD DRIVE, TROY MI 48085
1996-178	THOMPSON, JASON MICHAEL	427 SOUTH WRIGHTWOOD STREET, ORANGE CA 92869
1921-105	THOMPSON, JOHN DUDLEY 'LEE'	D. FEBRUARY 17, 1965, SANTA BARBARA, CALIF.
1948-099	THOMPSON, JOHN SAMUEL 'JOCKO'	D. FEBRUARY 3, 1988, OLNEY, MD.
1996-179	THOMPSON, JUSTIN WILLARD	37111 EDGEWATER DRIVE, PINEHURST TX 77362
2006-204	THOMPSON, KEVIN DESHAWN	9808 WESTPARK DRIVE, FORT WORTH TX 76126
1925-104	THOMPSON, LAFAYETTE FRESCO 'FRESCO'	D. NOVEMBER 20, 1968, FULLERTON, CALIF.
1994-106	THOMPSON, MARK RADFORD	5951 SOUTH WRIGHT COURT, LITTLETON CO 80127
2006-205	THOMPSON, MICHAEL PAUL	OLD ADD: LAMAR CO
1971-105	THOMPSON, MICHAEL WAYNE	7565 TURNER DR, DENVER CO 80221
1984-120	THOMPSON, MILTON BERNARD	PO BOX 663, WILLIAMSTOWN NJ 08094
2004-187	THOMPSON, RICHARD CHARLES	RURAL ROUTE 1, NEW MILFORD PA 18834
1985-111	THOMPSON, RICHARD NEIL	7 CHAMBERS COURT, HUNTINGTON STATION NY 11746
1986-155	THOMPSON, ROBERT RANDALL	4438 GUN CLUB ROAD, WEST PALM BEACH FL 33406
1933-060	THOMPSON, RUPERT LUCKHART 'TOMMY'	D. MAY 24, 1971, AUBURN, CALIF.
1992-142	THOMPSON, RYAN ORLANDO	918 WOODCREST DRIVE, DOVER DE 19904
1978-134	THOMPSON, VERNON SCOT 'SCOT'	110 BEACON RD, RENFREW PA 16053
1997-162	THOMSON, JOHN CARL	1414 EAST KENT STREET, SULPHUR LA 70663
1946-099	THOMSON, ROBERT BROWN	95 SKIDAWAY ISLAND PARK RD #7, SAVANNAH GA 31411
1979-110	THON, RICHARD WILLIAM 'DICKIE'	URB. DORADO DEL MAR C17 CALLE LIVIO DEL MAR, DORADO PR 00646
2006-206	THORMAN, SCOTT ROBERT	OLD ADD: CAMBRIDGE ONTARIO
1977-143	THORMODSGARD, PAUL GAYTON	7752 EAST ROSE LANE, SCOTTSDALE AZ 85250
1973-119	THORNTON, ANDRE	BOX 395, CHAGRIN FALLS OH 44022
1985-112	THORNTON, LOUIS	233 HENDERSON ROAD, HOPE HULL AL 36043
2004-188	THORNTON, MATTHEW J	6831 JOAL STREET, ALLENDALE MI 49401

1973-120	THORNTON, OTIS BENJAMIN	4312 AVENUE L, BIRMINGHAM AL 35208
1951-097	THORPE, BENJAMIN ROBERT	D. OCTOBER 30, 1996, WAVELAND, MISS.
1955-125	THORPE, ROBERT JOSEPH	D. MARCH 17, 1960, SAN DIEGO, CALIF.
1955-126	THRONEBERRY, MARVIN EUGENE	D. JUNE 23, 1994, FISHERVILLE, TENN.
1952-103	THRONEBERRY, MAYNARD FAYE 'FAYE'	D. APRIL 26, 1999, MEMPHIS, TENN.
1975-118	THROOP, GEORGE LYNFORD	239 WINDWOOD LANE, SIERRA MADRE CA 91024
1939-117	THUMAN, LOUIS CHARLES FRANK	D. DECEMBER 19, 2000, BALTIMORE, MD.
2002-189	THURMAN, COREY LAMAR	1524 COUNTY ROAD 371, MARBLE HILL MO 63764
1987-145	THURMAN, GARY MONTEZ	3143 ARTHINGTON BLVD, INDIANAPOLIS IN 46218
1997-163	THURMAN, MICHAEL RICHARD	6130 SW GRAND OAKS DRIVE, CORVALLIS OR 97333
1955-127	THURMAN, ROBERT BURNS	D. OCTOBER 31, 1998, WICHITA, KAN.
1983-142	THURMOND, MARK ANTHONY	1614 KINGS CASTLE DRIVE, KATY TX 77450
1923-133	THURSTON, HOLLIS JOHN 'SLOPPY'	D. SEPTEMBER 14, 1973, LOS ANGELES, CALIF.
2002-190	THURSTON, JOSEPH WILLIAM	1424 MAGAZINE STREET, VALLEJO CA 94591
1964-121	TIANT, LUIS CLEMENTE	24 SOUTHWOOD DRIVE, SOUTHBOROUGH MA 01772
1984-121	TIBBS, JAY LINDSEY	905 SMITH ROAD, ONEONTA AL 35121
1972-114	TIDROW, RICHARD WILLIAM	324 NE WARRINGTON COURT, LEES SUMMIT MO 64064
1952-104	TIEFENAUER, BOBBY GENE	D. JUNE 13, 2000, DESLOGE, MO.
1962-132	TIEFENTHALER, VERLE MATHEW	1852 QUINT AVE, CARROLL IA 51401
1920-118	TIERNEY, JAMES ARTHUR 'COTTON'	D. APRIL 18, 1953, KANSAS CITY, MO.
1933-061	TIETJE, LESLIE WILLIAM	D. OCTOBER 2, 1996, ROCHESTER, MINN.
2004-189	TIFFEE, TERRY R.	2620 CALICO CREEK DRIVE, NORTH LITTLE ROCK AR 72116
1957-087	TIGHE, JOHN THOMAS 'JACK'	D. AUGUST 1, 2002, POMPANO BEACH, FLA.
1962-133	TILLMAN, JOHN ROBERT 'BOB'	D. JUNE 23, 2000, GALLATIN, TENN.
1982-126	TILLMAN, KERRY JEROME 'RUSTY'	8343 HOGAN ROAD #25, JACKSONVILLE FL 32216
1967-107	TILLOTSON, THADDEUS ASA	6450 NORTH WINTON WAY #44, WINTON CA 95388
1969-170	TIMBERLAKE, GARY DALE	14016 WATERS EDGE DRIVE, LOUISVILLE KY 40245
1991-173	TIMLIN, MICHAEL AUGUST	2734 MEADOWVIEW COURT, TARPON SPRINGS FL 34688
1969-171	TIMMERMANN, THOMAS HENRY	197 COYOTE COURT, PICKNEY MI 48169
1995-222	TIMMONS, OSBORNE LLEWELLYN 'OZZIE'	4901 83RD STREET, TAMPA FL 33619
1982-127	TINGLEY, RONALD IRVIN	349 OMNI DRIVE, SPARKS NV 89436
1932-086	TINNING, LYLE FORREST 'BUD'	D. JANUARY 17, 1961, EVANSVILLE, IND.
1993-181	TINSLEY, LEE OWEN	237 TENOR STREET, SHELBYVILLE KY 40065
1939-118	TIPTON, ERIC GORDON	D. AUGUST 29, 2001, NEWPORT NEWS, VA.
1948-100	TIPTON, JOSEPH JOHN	D. MARCH 1, 1994, BIRMINGHAM, ALA.
1969-172	TISCHINSKI, THOMAS ARTHUR	2607 NE 68TH TER, GLADSTONE MO 64119
1936-092	TISING, JOHNNIE JOSEPH	D. SEPTEMBER 5, 1967, LEADVILLE, COLO.
1978-135	TOBIK, DAVID VANCE	848 CHANCELLOR HEIGHTS DRIVE, BALLWIN MO 63011
1937-099	TOBIN, JAMES ANTHONY	D. MAY 19, 1969, OAKLAND, CALIF.
1932-087	TOBIN, JOHN MARTIN	D. AUGUST 8, 1983, RHINEBECK, N.Y.
1945-105	TOBIN, JOHN PATRICK	D. JANUARY 18, 1982, OAKLAND, CALIF.
1941-112	TOBIN, MARION BROOKS 'PAT'	D. JANUARY 21, 1975, SHREVEPORT, LA.
1999-196	TOCA, JORGE LUIS	7940 167 TERRACE, HIALEAH FL 33016
1932-088	TODD, ALFRED CHESTER	D. MARCH 8, 1985, ELMIRA, N.Y.
1977-144	TODD, JACKSON	8958 EAST 76TH, TULSA OK 74133
1974-134	TODD, JAMES RICHARD	21639 HILL GAIL WAY, PARKER CO 80138
1924-111	TODT, PHILIP JULIUS	D. NOVEMBER 15, 1973, ST. LOUIS, MO.
1947-089	TOENES, WILLIAM HARRELL 'HAL'	D. JUNE 28, 2004, TAMPA, FLA.
1965-105	TOLAN, ROBERT 'BOBBY'	804WOODSTOCK STREET, BELLAIRE TX 77401
2000-178	TOLAR, KEVIN ANTHONY	1117 DEARDON DRIVE, VENICE FL 34292
1991-174	TOLENTINO, JOSE FRANCO	24681 VIA SAN FERNANDO, MISSION VIEJO CA 92692
1984-122	TOLIVER, FREDDIE LEE	7903 ELM AVENUE #120, RANCHO CUCAMONGA CA 91730
2000-179	TOLLBERG, BRIAN PATRICK	2104 39TH STREET, BRADENTON FL 34205
1981-136	TOLLESON, JIMMY WAYNE 'WAYNE'	313 MASSYCUP OAK COURT, SPARTANBURG SC 29306
1981-137	TOLMAN, TIMOTHY LEE	11425 NORTH INGOTLOOP, TUCSON AZ 85737
1925-105	TOLSON, CHESTER JULIUS 'CHICK'	D. APRIL 16, 1965, WASHINGTON, D.C.
1953-091	TOMANEK, RICHARD CARL	165 DUFF DRIVE, AVON LAKE OH 44012
1949-088	TOMASIC, ANDREW JOHN	439D WILLOW CIRCLE, ALLENTOWN PA 18102
1993-182	TOMBERLIN, ANDY LEE	7411 CROOKED CREEK ROAD, MONROE NC 28110
1997-164	TOMKO, BRETT DANIEL	14008 LAKE POWAY ROAD, POWAY CA 92064
1972-115	TOMLIN, DAVID ALLEN	2020 CLAYTON ROAD, MANCHESTER OH 45144
1990-156	TOMLIN, RANDY LEON	153 RIDGEVIEW LANE, MADISON HEIGHTS VA 24572
1965-106	TOMPKINS, RONALD EVERETT	25072 LEUCADIA #G, LAGUNA NIGUEL CA 92677
1975-119	TOMS, THOMAS HOWARD	126 LEADBETTER ROAD, WAYNE ME 04284
2004-190	TONIS, MICHAEL TIMOTHY	8708 THETFORD COURT, ELK GROVE CA 95624
1921-106	TOPORCER, GEORGE 'SPECS'	D. MAY 17, 1989, HUNTINGTON STATION, N.Y.
1962-134	TOPPIN, RUPERTO	PO BOX 25724, MIAMI FL 33102
1964-122	TORBORG, JEFFREY ALLEN	5208 SIESTA COVE DRIVE, SARASOTA FL 34242
2002-191	TORCATO, ANTHONY DALE	21 WEST HAYS STREET, WOODLAND CA 95695
1947-090	TORGESON, CLIFFORD EARL 'EARL'	D. NOVEMBER 8, 1990, EVERETT, WASH.
1920-119	TORPHY, WALTER ANTHONY 'RED'	D. FEBRUARY 11, 1980, FALL RIVER, MASS.
1956-082	TORRE, FRANK JOSEPH	13901 PALM GROVE PLACE, PALM BEACH GARDENS FL 33418
1960-100	TORRE, JOSEPH PAUL	20 LAWRENCE LANE, HARRISON NY 10528
1975-120	TORREALBA, PABLO ARNOLDO	EL MANANTIAL,APT L.CORDONES PISO 5, APTOS 52, BARQUISIMETO, VENEZUELA
2001-183	TORREALBA, STEVEN ALEXANDER	OLD ADD: BARQUISIMETO VENEZUELA
2001-184	TORREALBA, YORVIT ADOLFO	OLD ADD: GUARENAS VENEZUELA
2002-192	TORRES, ANDRES VUNGO FELICIANO	OLD ADD: AGUADILLA PR 00605
1977-145	TORRES, ANGEL RAFAEL	SECCIM LACIENGA CASA 40 AZUA, DOM REP
1995-223	TORRES, DILSON DARIO	OLD ADD: 6241 NORTH WINTHROP AVENUE, CHICAGO IL 60660
1940-091	TORRES, DON GILBERTO (NUNEZ) 'GIL'	D. JANUARY 10, 1983, REGLA, HAVANA CUBA
1962-135	TORRES, FELIX	HC01 BOX 6424, SANTA ISABEL PR 00757
1968-103	TORRES, HECTOR EPITACIO	662 LEXINGTON STREET, DUNEDIN FL 34698
1920-120	TORRES, RICARDO J.	D. APRIL 17, 1960, REGLA, HAVANA, CUBA
1971-106	TORRES, ROSENDO 'RUSTY'	250 NORTH CEDAR STREET, MASSAPEQUA NY 11758
1993-183	TORRES, SALOMON RAMIREZ	PROL. CARLOS ORDONEZ 53, SAN PEDRO DE MACORIS, DOM REP
1967-108	TORREZ, MICHAEL AUGUSTINE	1015 FRANCES COURT, NAPERVILLE IL 60563

1988-131	TORVE, KELVIN CURTIS	18701 HAMMOCK LANE, DAVIDSON NC 28036
2002-193	TOSCA, CARLOS	2831 TIMBER KNOLL DRIVE, VALRICO FL 33594
1942-100	TOST, LOUIS EUGENE	D. FEBRUARY 22, 1967, SANTA CLARA, CALIF.
1962-136	TOTH, PAUL LOUIS	D. MARCH 20, 1999, TOLEDO, OHIO
1928-099	TOUCHSTONE, CLAYLAND MAFFITT	D. APRIL 28, 1949, BEAUMONT, TEXAS
1965-107	TOVAR, CESAR LEONARDO	D. JULY 14, 1994, CARACAS, VENEZUELA
2001-185	TOWERS, JOSHUA ERIC	853 BUSSORA ROSE DRIVE, HENDERSON NV 89015
1920-121	TOWNSEND, IRA DANCE	D. JULY 21, 1965, SCHULENBERG, TEXAS
1920-122	TOWNSEND, LEO ALPHONSE	D. DECEMBER 3, 1976, MOBILE, ALA.
1984-123	TRABER, JAMES JOSEPH	SPORTS ANIMAL RADIO 4045 NW 64TH, OKLAHOMA CITY OK 73116
2003-162	TRABER, WILLIAM HENRY	836 LOMITA STREET, EL SEGUNDO CA 90245
1962-137	TRACEWSKI, RICHARD JOHN	5 FLORA DR, PECKVILLE PA 18452
2006-207	TRACEY, SEAN PATRICK	1747 FERNBROOK AVENUE, UPLAND CA 91784
1993-184	TRACHSEL, STEPHEN CHRISTOPHER	1301 NW 55TH STREET, FORT LAUDERDALE FL 33309
2000-180	TRACY, ANDREW MICHAEL	1048 NORTH MAIN STREET, BOWLING GREEN OH 43402
2004-191	TRACY, CHAD AUSTIN	6021 FOX CROSSING DRIVE, CHARLOTTE NC 28216
1980-128	TRACY, JAMES EDWIN	7112 WOOHDALL COURT, PRESTO PA 15142
1940-092	TRAMBACK, STEPHEN JOSEPH 'RED'	D. DECEMBER 28, 1979, BUFFALO, N.Y.
1977-146	TRAMMELL, ALAN STUART	5852 BOX CANYON ROAD, LAJOLLA CA 92037
1997-165	TRAMMELL, THOMAS BUBBA 'BUBBA'	4680 ST. CROIX LANE, NAPLES FL 34109
1988-132	TRAUTWEIN, JOHN HOWARD	882 BEACH ROAD, SANIBEL FL 33957
1974-135	TRAVERS, WILLIAM EDWARD	10 SHORELINE DR, FOXBORO MA 02035
1933-062	TRAVIS, CECIL HOWELL	D. DECEMBER 16, 2006, RIVERDALE, GA.
1990-157	TRAXLER, BRIAN LEE	D. NOVEMBER 19, 2004, SAN ANTONIO, TEXAS
1920-123	TRAYNOR, HAROLD JOSEPH 'PIE'	D. MARCH 16, 1972, PITTSBURGH, PA.
1930-083	TREADAWAY, EDGAR RAYMOND 'RAY'	D. OCTOBER 12, 1935, CHATTANOOGA, TENN.
1987-146	TREADWAY, HUGH JEFFERY 'JEFF'	1150 RIVER WALK, FORSYTH GA 31029
1944-129	TREADWAY, THADFORD LEON 'RED'	D. MAY 26, 1994, ATLANTA, GA.
2004-192	TREANOR, MATTHEW AARON	11508 SPRINGWOOD COURT, RIVERSIDE CA 92505
1986-156	TREBELHORN, THOMAS LYNN	4344 SE 26TH AVENUE, PORTLAND OR 97202
1937-100	TRECHOCK, FRANK ADAM	D. JANUARY 16, 1989, MINNEAPOLIS, MINN.
1934-101	TREMARK, NICHOLAS JOSEPH	D. SEPTEMBER 7, 2000, TOMBALL, TEXAS
1954-111	TREMEL, WILLIAM LEONARD	315 EAST 23RD AVE, ALTOONA PA 16601
1995-224	TREMIE, CHRISTOPHER JAMES 'JIM'	48 MARION LANE, NEW WAVERLY TX 77358
1927-091	TREMPER, CARLTON OVERTON 'OVERTON'	D. JANUARY 8, 1996, CLEARWATER, FLA.
1938-099	TRESH, MICHAEL	D. OCTOBER 1, 1966, DETROIT, MICH.
1961-105	TRESH, THOMAS MICHAEL	1751 WAXWING CIRCLE, VENICE FL 34293
1978-136	TREVINO, ALEJANDRO 'ALEX'	PO BOX 288, HOUSTON TX 77001
1968-104	TREVINO, CARLOS CASTRO 'BOBBY'	OLD ADD: ALONDRA #102, COL. CUANHTEMON, MONTERREY MEXICO
1953-092	TRIANDOS, CONSTANDIN GUS 'GUS'	PO BOX 5642, SAN JOSE CA 95150
1953-093	TRICE, ROBERT LEE	D. SEPTEMBER 16, 1988, WEIRTON, W.VA.
1973-121	TRILLO, JESUS MANUEL 'MANNY'	CALLE 724 AVE 3AM ED. EVEREST #14 MARACAIBO, VENEZUELA
1955-128	TRIMBLE, JOSEPH GERARD	14 FAIR OAKS DRIVE, LINCOLN RI 02865
1943-138	TRINKLE, KENNETH WAYNE	D. MAY 10, 1976, PAOLI, ILL.
1938-100	TRIPLETT, HERMAN COAKER 'COAKER'	D. JANUARY 30, 1992, BOONE, N.C.
1992-143	TRLICEK, RICHARD ALAN 'RICK'	PO BOX 1109, LAGRANGE TX 78945
1973-122	TROEDSON, RICHARD LAMONTE	899 BOWEN AVENUE, SAN JOSE CA 95123
1992-144	TROMBLEY, MICHAEL SCOTT	15800 GLENISLE WAY, FORT MYERS FL 33912
1958-097	TROSKY, HAROLD ARTHUR	1414 NE CURTIS BRIDGE ROAD, SWISHER IA 52338
1933-063	TROSKY, HAROLD ARTHUR, SR. 'HAL'	D. JUNE 18, 1979, CEDAR RAPIDS, IOWA
1937-101	TROTTER, WILLIAM FELIX	D. AUGUST 26, 1984, ARLINGTON, MASS.
1952-105	TROUPPE, QUINCY THOMAS	D. AUGUST 10, 1993, CREVE COEUR, MO.
1939-119	TROUT, PAUL HOWARD 'DIZZY'	D. FEBRUARY 28, 1972, HARVEY, ILL.
1978-137	TROUT, STEVEN RUSSELL	OLD ADD: 1808 EAST RAINBOW LANE, CRETE IL 60417
1956-083	TROWBRIDGE, ROBERT	D. APRIL 3, 1980, HUDSON, N.Y.
2000-181	TRUBY, CHRISTOPHER JOHN	12244 SILVERADO DRIVE, FISHERS IN 46038
1941-113	TRUCKS, VIRGIL OLIVER 'FIRE'	1016 WATERFORD TRAIL, CALERA AL 35040
2002-194	TRUJILLO, JUAN MANUEL 'J. J.'	1329 YORK AVENUE, CORPUS CHRISTI TX 78415
1985-113	TRUJILLO, MICHAEL ANDREW	2019 SOUTH TOWNSEND, MONTROSE CO 81401
1993-185	TSAMIS, GEORGE ALEX	12 SWEETBRIAR COURT, COLCHESTER CT 06415
2003-163	TSAO, CHIN-HUI	OLD ADD: HUALIEN TAIWAN
1957-088	TSITOURIS, JOHN PHILIP	5207 AUSTIN ROAD, MONROE NC 28112
1993-186	TUBBS, GREGORY ALAN	114 HUNTER, COOKEVILLE TN 38501
1992-145	TUCKER, EDDIE JACK 'SCOOTER'	PO BOX 764, BOYLE MS 38730
1995-225	TUCKER, MICHAEL ANTHONY	OLD ADD: 407 NORTH MAPLE NORTH, LEHIGH ACRES FL 33972
1927-092	TUCKER, OSCAR DINWIDDIE	D. JULY 13, 1940, RADIANT, VA.
2000-182	TUCKER, THOMAS J. 'TJ'	6616 RIDGE TOP DRIVE, NEW PORT RICHEY FL 34655
1942-101	TUCKER, THURMAN LOWELL	D. MAY 7, 1993, OKLAHOMA, OKLA.
1979-111	TUDOR, JOHN THOMAS	5 NATHAN LANE, MIDDLETON MA 01949
1981-138	TUFTS, ROBERT MALCOLM	67-38 108TH STREET #A27, FOREST HILLS NY 11375
2006-208	TULOWITZKI, TROY TREVER	1615 XIMENO AVENUE, LONG BEACH CA 90804
1982-128	TUNNELL, BYRON LEE 'LEE'	6000 KINGSBRIDGE DRIVE, OKLAHOMA CITY OK 73162
1993-187	TURANG, BRIAN CRAIG	3014 MCNAB AVENUE, LONG BEACH CA 90808
1935-107	TURBEVILLE, GEORGE ELKINS	D. OCTOBER 5, 1983, SALISBURY, N.C.
1943-139	TURCHIN, EDWARD LAWRENCE	D. FEBRUARY 8, 1982, BROOKHAVEN, N.Y.
1923-134	TURGEON, EUGENE JOSEPH 'PETE'	D. JANUARY 24, 1977, WICHITA FALLS, TEXAS
1922-134	TURK, LUCAS NEWTON	D. JANUARY 11, 1994, HOMER, GA.
1951-098	TURLEY, ROBERT LEE	3327 DULIUTH HWY 120 #101, DULUTH GA 30096
2000-183	TURNBOW, THOMAS DERRICK	45120 HWY 69, SALTILLO TN 38370
1993-188	TURNER, CHRISTOPHER WAN	258 WARREN WAY, BOWLING GREEN KY 42101
1948-101	TURNER, EARL EDWIN	D. OCTOBER 20, 1999, LEE, MASS.
1937-102	TURNER, JAMES RILEY	D. NOVEMBER 29, 1998, NASHVILLE, TENN.
1974-136	TURNER, JOHN WEBBER 'JERRY'	1935 18TH STREET #B, SANTA MONICA CA 90404
1967-109	TURNER, KENNETH CHARLES	PO BOX 252, SAN MARCOS CA 92079
1977-162	TURNER, ROBERT EDWARD 'TED'	1050 TECHWOOD AVENUE, ATLANTA GA 30318
1988-133	TURNER, SHANE LEE	13104 GLENN COURT #20, CHINO HILLS CA 91709

1920-124	TURNER, THEODORE HOLTOP	D. FEBRUARY 4, 1958, LEXINGTON, KY.
1940-093	TURNER, THOMAS RICHARD	D. MAY 14, 1986, KENNEWICK, WASH.
1993-189	TURNER, WILLIAM MATTHEW 'MATT'	829 DELLA DRIVE, LEXINGTON KY 40504
1952-106	TUTTLE, WILLIAM ROBERT	D. JULY 27, 1998, ANOKA, MINN.
1928-100	TUTWILER, ELMER STRANGE	D. MAY 3, 1976, PENSACOLA, FLA.
1970-134	TWITCHELL, WAYNE LEE	5719 SW BRUGGR STREET, PORTLAND OR 97219
1980-129	TWITTY, JEFFREY DEAN	812 WILLOW COVE ROAD, CHAPIN SC 29036
1920-125	TWOMBLY, CLARENCE EDWARD 'BABE'	D. NOVEMBER 23, 1974, SAN CLEMENTE, CALIF.
1921-107	TWOMBLY, EDWIN PARKER 'CY'	D. DECEMBER 3, 1974, SAVANNAH, GA.
1943-140	TYACK, JAMES FRED	D. JANUARY 3, 1995, BAKERSFIELD, CALIF.
1934-102	TYLER, JOHN ANTHONY	D. JULY 11, 1972, MOUNT PLEASANT, PA.
2000-184	TYNER, JASON RENYT	5535 SUL ROSS LANE, BEAUMONT TX 77706
1962-138	TYRIVER, DAVID BURTON	D. OCTOBER 28, 1988, OSHKOSH, WISC.
1972-116	TYRONE, JAMES VERNON	505 TISH CIRCLE, ARLINGTON TX 76006
1976-095	TYRONE, OSCAR WAYNE 'WAYNE'	505 TISH CIRCLE #404, ARLINGTON TX 76006
1926-087	TYSON, ALBERT THOMAS 'TY'	D. AUGUST 16, 1953, BUFFALO, N.Y.
1944-130	TYSON, CECIL WASHINGTON 'CY'	D. FEBRUARY 17, 2000, ELM CITY, N.C.
1972-117	TYSON, MICHAEL RAY	479 THUNDERHEAD CANYON DR, BALLWIN MO 63011

U

1926-088	UCHRINSCKO, JAMES EMERSON 'EMERSON'	D. MARCH 17, 1995, MOUNT PLEASANT, PA.
1962-139	UECKER, ROBERT GEORGE	W131 N7867 COUNTRY, MENOMONEE FALLS WI 53051
2006-209	UGGLA, DANIEL COOLEY	1400 JEWELL DRIVE, COLUMBIA TN 38401
2002-195	UGUETO, LUIS ENRIQUE	OLD ADD: 6009 188TH LANE NE, REDMOND WA 98052
1934-103	UHALT, BERNARD BARTHOLOMEW 'FRENCHY'	D. SEPTEMBER 3, 2004, WALNUT CREEK, CALIF.
1965-108	UHLAENDER, THEODORE OTTO	60 COUNTY ROAD 3080, PARSHALL CO 80468
1938-101	UHLE, ROBERT EDWARD	D. AUGUST 21, 1990, SANTA ROSA, CALIF.
1934-104	UHLIR, CHARLES KAREL	D. JULY 9, 1984, SPIRIT LAKE, IOWA
1980-130	UJDUR, GERALD RAYMOND	112 RIVENESS ROAD, DULUTH MN 55811
1945-106	ULISNEY, MICHAEL EDWARD	D. SEPTEMBER 22, 2005, NEW SMYRNA BEACH, FLA.
1983-143	ULLGER, SCOTT MATTHEW	4149 WEST RUSSELL AVENUE, VISALIA CA 93277
1944-131	ULLRICH, CARLOS SANTIAGO CASTELLO	D. APRIL 21, 2001, MIAMI, FLA.
1925-106	ULRICH, FRANK W. 'DUTCH'	D. FEBRUARY 11, 1929, BALTIMORE, MD.
1964-123	UMBACH, ARNOLD WILLIAM	760 MOORES MILL ROAD, AUBURN AL 36830
1975-121	UMBARGER, JAMES HAROLD	3083 MARITIME FOREST DRIVE, JOHNS ISLAND SC 29455
1959-083	UMBRICHT, JAMES	D. APRIL 8, 1964, HOUSTON, TEXAS
1953-094	UMPHLETT, THOMAS MULLEN	104 BERKELEY ROAD, AHOSKIE NC 27910
1927-093	UNDERHILL, WILLIE VERN	D. OCTOBER 26, 1970, BAY CITY, TEXAS
1979-112	UNDERWOOD, PATRICK JOHN	708 RIVERVIEW DRIVE, KOKOMO IN 46901
1974-137	UNDERWOOD, THOMAS GERALD	13595 83RD LANE NORTH, WEST PALM BEACH FL 33412
1995-226	UNROE, TIMOTHY BRIAN	2719 SOUTH JOPLIN, MESA AZ 85212
1942-102	UNSER, ALBERT BERNARD	D. JULY 7, 1995, DECATUR, ILL.
1968-105	UNSER, DELBERT BERNARD	33516 NORTH 79TH WAY, SCOTTSDALE AZ 85262
1935-108	UPCHURCH, JEFFERSON WOODROW 'WOODY'	D. OCTOBER 23, 1971, BUIES CREEK, N.C.
1967-110	UPHAM, JOHN LESLIE	1502 PIERRE AVENUE WINDSOR ON, N8X 4P5 CANADA
1953-095	UPRIGHT, ROY T. 'DIXIE'	D. NOVEMBER 13, 1986, CONCORD, N.C.
1966-091	UPSHAW, CECIL LEE	D. FEBRUARY 7, 1995, LAWRENCEVILLE, GA.
1978-138	UPSHAW, WILLIE CLAY	193 OSBORNE LANE, SOUTHPORT CT 06490
2004-193	UPTON, MELVIN EMMANUEL 'B.J.'	844 GREENFIELD LANE, CHESAPEAKE VA 23322
1950-100	UPTON, THOMAS HERBERT	OLD ADD: 306 MAY STREET, BISHOP CA 93514
1954-112	UPTON, WILLIAM RAY	D. JANUARY 2, 1987, SAN DIEGO, CALIF.
1957-089	URBAN, JACK ELMER	D. JUNE 26, 2006, OMAHA, NEB.
1927-094	URBAN, LOUIS JOHN 'LUKE'	D. DECEMBER 7, 1980, SOMERSET, MASS.
1993-190	URBANI, THOMAS JAMES	12378 INCLINE DRIVE, AUBURN CA 95603
1931-091	URBANSKI, WILLIAM MICHAEL	D. JULY 12, 1973, PERTH AMBOY, N.J.
1995-227	URBINA, UGUETH URTAIN	ROJAS CONJ RES LAS ACA LIAS #2 OCUMARE DEL TOY, VENEZUELA
2004-194	URDANETA, LINO	OLD ADD: GUARENAS VENEZUELA
1984-124	URIBE, JOSE ALTAGRACIA	D. DECEMBER 1, 2006, DOM REP
2001-186	URIBE, JUAN C. (TENA)	OLD ADD: SAN CRISTOBAL DOM REP
1977-147	URREA, JOHN GODBY	9312 PALM STEEET, BELLFLOWER CA 90706
1946-100	USHER, ROBERT ROYCE	1022 NORTH FIFTH STREET, SAN JOSE CA 95112
1925-107	USSAT, WILLIAM AUGUST 'DUTCH'	D. MAY 29, 1959, DAYTON, OHIO
2003-164	UTLEY, CHASE CAMERON	OLD ADD: LAS VEGAS NV 89125

V

1925-108	VACHE, ERNEST LEWIS 'TEX'	D. JUNE 11, 1953, LOS ANGELES, CALIF.
1975-122	VAIL, MICHAEL LEWIS	PO BOX 777626, HENDERSON NV 89077
2003-165	VALDERRAMA, CARLOS ALBERTO (CORDERO)	OLD ADD: MARACAIBO VENEZUELA
1994-107	VALDES, ISMAEL	4001 26TH STREET, VERO BEACH FL 32960
1995-228	VALDES, MARC CHRISTOPHER	7519 PAULA DRIVE, TAMPA FL 33615
1996-180	VALDES, PEDRO JOSE MANZO	OLD ADD: LOIZA PR 00772
1957-090	VALDES, RENE GUTIERREZ	AVENIDA 7A,14511 ALTURAS MANANA, HAVANA, CUBA
1944-132	VALDES, ROGELIO LAZARO 'ROY'	D. DECEMBER 3, 2005, MIAMI, FLA.
1965-109	VALDESPINO, HILARIO 'SANDY'	434 SE 3RD STREET, DANIA FL 33004
1995-229	VALDEZ, CARLOS LUIS LORENZO	OLD ADD: NIZAO BANI DOM REP
1990-158	VALDEZ, EFRAIN ANTONIO	K NUM 118 EN NIZAO DE BANI BANI, DOM REP
1980-131	VALDEZ, JULIO JULIAN CASTILLO	MAXIMO GOMEZ #3 NIZAO BANI, DOM REP
1997-166	VALDEZ, MARIO ANTONIO	OLD ADD: 7145 BALBOA ROAD, JACKSONVILLE FL 32217
2004-195	VALDEZ, MERKIN R.	OLD ADD: SAN CRISTOBAL DOM REP
1990-159	VALDEZ, RAFAEL EMILIO (DIAZ)	MAXIMO GOMEZ #5 NIZAO DE BANI, DOM REP
1986-157	VALDEZ, SERGIO SANCHEZ	OLD ADD: CAL LA PAZ #14, HERRERA, SANTO DOMINGO DOM REP
2004-196	VALDEZ, WILSON ANTONIO	OLD ADD: NIZAO DOM REP

1955-129	VALDIVIELSO, JOSE LOPEZ	14 RITA DR, MOUNT SINAI NY 11766
2001-187	VALENT, ERIC CHRISTIAN	5949 EAST CAMINO MANZANO, ANAHEIM CA 92807
1992-146	VALENTIN, JOHN WILLIAM	86 VILLAGE GREEN, HAZLET NJ 07730
1992-147	VALENTIN, JOSE ANTONIO (ROSARIO)	OLD ADD: 915 EAST LYON STREET, MILWAUKEE WI 53202
1997-167	VALENTIN, JOSE JAVIER ROSARIO 'JAVIER'	OLD ADD: MANATI PR 00674
1975-123	VALENTINE, ELLIS CLARENCE	44746 LESLIE COURT, LANCASTER CA 93535
1959-084	VALENTINE, FRED LEE	4838 BLAGDEN AVE NW, WASHINGTON DC 20011
1954-113	VALENTINE, HAROLD LEWIS 'CORKY'	D. JANUARY 21, 2005, ROSWELL, GA.
2003-166	VALENTINE, JOSEPH JOHN	4168 CHIFFON LANE, NORTH PORT FL 34287
1969-173	VALENTINE, ROBERT JOHN	71 WYNNEWOOD LANE, STAMFORD CT 06903
1954-114	VALENTINETTI, VITO JOHN	271 SUMMIT AVE, MOUNT VERNON NY 10552
1958-098	VALENZUELA, BENJAMIN BELTRAN	BAHIA SAN ESTEBAN #267 SUR LOS MOCHIS SINALOA, MEXICO
1980-132	VALENZUELA, FERNANDO	2123 NORTH BEACHWOOD DRIVE, HOLLYWOOD CA 90068
1990-160	VALERA, JULIO ENRIQUE	OLD ADD: 9-H-12, SEBASTIAN PR 00755
2000-185	VALERA, YOHANNY	PO BOX 716, TOANO VA 23168
1984-125	VALLE, DAVID	2260 95TH AVENUE NE, BELLEVUE WA 98004
1965-110	VALLE, HECTOR JOSE	PO BOX 5909 COLLEGE STATION, MAYAGUEZ PR 00708
1940-094	VALO, ELMER WILLIAM	D. JULY 19, 1998, PALMERTON, PA.
2003-167	VALVERDE, JOSE RAFAEL	OLD ADD: EL SEIBO DOM REP
2002-196	VAN HEKKEN, ANDREW WILLIAM	4742 64TH STREET, HOLLAND MI 49423
1927-095	VANALSTYNE, CLAYTON EMERY	D. JANUARY 5, 1960, HUDSON, N.Y.
1933-064	VANATTA, RUSSELL	D. OCTOBER 10, 1986, ANDOVER, N.J.
2004-197	VANBENSCHOTEN, JOHN WESLEY	10246 EAST LOMITA AVENUE, MESA AZ 85212
1954-115	VANBRABANT, CAMILLE OSCAR 'OSSIE'	5389 WILLIAM DRIVE, LEXINGTON MI 48450
2005-190	VANBUREN, JERMAINE RUSSELL	209 WEST RAY DRIVE, HATTIESBURG MS 39402
1993-191	VANBURKLEO, TYLER LEO	19681 RABON VALLEY ROAD, GRASS VALLEY CA 95949
1928-101	VANCAMP, ALBERT JOSEPH	D. FEBRUARY 2, 1981, DAVENPORT, IOWA
2002-197	VANCE, CORY WADE	1321 SURREY ROAD, VANDALIA OH 45377
1970-135	VANCE, GENE COVINGTON 'SANDY'	5863 CHELTON DRIVE, OAKLAND CA 94611
1935-109	VANCE, JOSEPH ALBERT	D. JULY 4, 1978, DEVINE, TEXAS
1950-101	VANCUYK, CHRISTIAN GERALD	D. NOVEMBER 3, 1992, HUDSON, FLA.
1947-091	VANCUYK, JOHN HENRY	2096 11TH AVENUE SE #A, ROCHESTER MN 55904
1982-129	VANDEBERG, EDWARD JOHN	4903 SOUTH MEADOWS PLACE, CHANDLER AZ 85248
1935-110	VANDENBURG, HAROLD HARRIS 'HY'	D. JULY 31, 1994, BLOOMINGTON, MINN.
1937-103	VANDERMEER, JOHN SAMUEL	D. OCTOBER 6, 1997, TAMPA, FLA.
1991-175	VANDERWAL, JOHN HENRY	5142 ABBEYDALE DRIVE SE, GRAND RAPIDS MI 49546
1955-130	VANDUSEN, FREDERICK WILLIAM	331 GILLETTE DRIVE, FRANKLIN TN 37069
1994-108	VANEGMOND, TIMOTHY LAYNE	8839 CALLAWAY RAOD, GAY GA 30218
1982-130	VANGORDER, DAVID THOMAS	212 BLACK EAGLE AVENUE, HENDERSON NV 89015
1994-109	VANLANDINGHAM, WILLIAM JOSEPH	3023 OLD HILLSBORO ROAD, FRANKLIN TN 37064
1951-099	VANNOY, JAY LOWELL	1092 NORTH 1700 EAST, LOGAN UT 84321
1991-176	VANPOPPEL, TODD MATTHEW	PO BOX 190, MERIDIAN TX 76665
1939-120	VANROBAYS, MAURICE RENE	D. MARCH 1, 1965, DETROIT, MICH.
1996-181	VANRYN, BENJAMIN ASHLEY	PO BOX 672572, CHUGIAK AK 99567
1983-144	VANSLYKE, ANDREW JAMES	710 SOUTH PRICE ROAD, SAINT LOUIS MO 63124
1950-102	VARGA, ANDREW WILLIAM	D. NOVEMBER 4, 1992, ORLANDO, FLA.
2003-168	VARGAS, CLAUDIO (ALMONTE)	OLD ADD: SANTIAGO DOM REP
1982-131	VARGAS, HEDIBERTO	BOX 1172, GUANICA PR 00653
2005-191	VARGAS, JASON M.	14775 KEOTA ROAD, APPLE VALLEY CA 92307
1955-131	VARGAS, ROBERT ENRIQUE	OLD ADD: URB. M.RIVERA, 24 CLE BRISAIDA, GUAYNABO PR 09969
1925-109	VARGUS, WILLIAM FAY	D. FEBRUARY 12, 1979, HYANNIS, MASS.
1997-168	VARITEK, JASON ANDREW	78 WABAN AVENUE, WABAN MA 02468
1952-107	VARNER, GLEN GANN	D. APRIL 29, 2000, CHATTANOOGA, TENN.
1973-123	VARNEY, RICHARD FRED 'PETE'	BRANDEIS BASEBALL 415 SOUTH STREET, WALTHAM MA 02254
1988-134	VARSHO, GARY ANDREW	11921 LINDSEY DRIVE, CHILI WI 54420
2004-198	VASQUEZ, JORGE LUIS	OLD ADD: NAGUA DOM REP
1979-113	VASQUEZ, RAFAEL (SANTIAGO)	CALLE JULIO A JARSIA #29 LA ROMANA, DOM REP
1990-161	VATCHER, JAMES ERNEST	16039 NORTHFIELD STREET, PACIFIC PALISADES CA 90272
1940-095	VAUGHAN, CECIL PORTER 'PORTER'	2931 POLO PKWY, MIDLOTHIAN VA 23113
1966-092	VAUGHAN, CHARLES WAYNE	5717 BRAZILWOOD COURT, HARLINGEN TX 78552
1963-121	VAUGHAN, GLENN EDWARD	D. DECEMBER 18, 2004, HOUSTON, TEXAS
1932-089	VAUGHAN, JOSEPH FLOYD 'ARKY'	D. AUGUST 30, 1952, EAGLEVILLE, CALIF.
1934-105	VAUGHN, CLARENCE LEROY	D. MARCH 1, 1937, MARTINSVILLE, VA.
1988-135	VAUGHN, DEWAYNE MATHEW	5501NW 37TH STREET, OKLAHOMA CITY OK 73122
1944-133	VAUGHN, FREDERICK THOMAS	D. MARCH 2, 1964, LAKE WALES, FLA.
1989-130	VAUGHN, GREGORY LAMONT	10830 SHELDON WOODS WAY, ELK GROVE CA 95624
1991-177	VAUGHN, MAURICE SAMUEL 'MO'	2740 AIRPORT DRIVE #170, COLUMBUS OH 43219
1998-193	VAZQUEZ, JAVIER CARLOS	OLD ADD: PONCE PR 00731
2001-188	VAZQUEZ, RAMON LUIS	OLD ADD: CAYEY PR
1935-111	VEACH, ALVIS LINDELL	D. SEPTEMBER 6, 1990, CHARLOTTE, N.C.
1958-099	VEAL, ORVILLE INMAN 'COOT'	238 STONE GABLES DRIVE, GRAY GA 31032
1962-140	VEALE, ROBERT ANDREW	2833 BUSH BLVD, BIRMINGHAM AL 35208
1920-126	VEDDER, LOUIS EDWARD	D. MARCH 9, 1990, LAKE PLACID, FLA.
1979-114	VEGA, JESUS ANTONIO	OLD ADD: MAGOLY CENTRAL NH22, LEVITTOWN PR 00632
1939-121	VEIGEL, ALLEN FRANCIS	1907 DOVER AVENUE, DOVER OH 44622
1997-169	VELANDIA, JORGE LUIS MACIAS	OLD ADD: CARACAS VENEZUELA
1987-147	VELARDE, RANDY LEE	4902 THAMES COURT, MIDLAND TX 79705
1992-148	VELASQUEZ, GUILLERMO	13577 FERN PINE ROAD, VICTORVILLE CA 92392
1973-124	VELAZQUEZ, CARLOS	OLD ADD: BO MEDINA ALTA, LUIZA ALDEA PR 00672
1969-174	VELAZQUEZ, FEDERICO ANTONIO 'FREDDIE'	JOSE AMADO SOLER NO. 70 SANTO DOMINGO, DOM REP
1973-125	VELEZ, OTONIEL 'OTTO'	OLD ADD: LOS CAOBOS CALLE #35 T2, PONCE PR 00731
1926-089	VELTMAN, ARTHUR PATRICK	D. OCTOBER 1, 1980, SAN ANTONIO, TEXAS
1979-115	VENABLE, WILLIAM MCKINLEY 'MAC'	107 CLARK STREET, SAN RAFAEL CA 94901
1999-197	VENAFRO, MICHAEL ROBERT	PMB 131 16970C SAN CARLOS BLVD, FORT MYERS FL 33908
2005-192	VENTO, MICHAEL	821 EAST PEARSON STREET, MILWAUKEE WI 53202
1989-131	VENTURA, ROBIN MARK	1088 NEWSOM SPRINGS ROAD, ARROYO GRANDE CA 93420

1945-107	VENTURA, VINCENT	D. SEPTEMBER 11, 2001, LAKE WORTH, FLA.
1996-182	VERAS, DARIO ANTONIO	OLD ADD: VILLA VASQUEZ DOM REP
2006-210	VERAS, JOSE ENGER	OLD ADD: SANTO DOMINGO DOM REP
1995-230	VERAS, QUILVIO ALBERTO PEREZ	OLD ADD: 9 POST AVENUE, NEW YORK NY 10034
1999-198	VERAS, WILTON ANDRES	OLD ADD: SANTO DOMINGO DOM REP
1944-134	VERBAN, EMIL MATTHEW 'THE ANTELOPE'	D. JUNE 8, 1989, QUINCY, ILL.
1966-093	VERBANIC, JOSEPH MICHAEL	85462 LORANE HWY, EUGENE OR 97405
1951-100	VERBLE, GENE KERMIT	633 CAMROSE CIRCLE NE, CONCORD NC 28025
1944-135	VERDEL, ALBERT ALFRED	D. APRIL 16, 1991, SARASOTA, FLA.
1953-096	VERDI, FRANK MICHAEL	10961 PEPPERTREE LANE, PORT RICHEY FL 34668
1994-110	VERES, DAVID SCOTT	871 DIAMOND RIDGE CIRCLE, CASTLE ROCK CO 80104
1989-132	VERES, RANDOLPH RUHLAND	9213 WEST FRANK AVENUE, PEORIA AZ 85382
1931-092	VERGEZ, JOHN LOUIS	D. JULY 15, 1991, DAVIS, CALIF.
1976-096	VERHOEVEN, JOHN C.	20805 PASEO DE LA RAMBLA, YORBA LINDA CA 92887
2005-193	VERLANDER, JUSTIN B.	1501 GRASSLANDS BLVD, LAKELAND FL 33803
1939-122	VERNON, JAMES BARTON 'MICKEY'	1343 WEST BALTIMORE PIKE #E417, MEDIA PA 19063
1959-085	VERSALLES, ZOILO 'ZORRO'	D. JUNE 9, 1995, BLOOMINGTON, MINN.
1973-126	VERYZER, THOMAS MARTIN	41 UNION AVE, ISLIP NY 11751
1980-133	VESELIC, ROBERT MICHAEL	D. DECEMBER 26, 1995, LOS ANGELES, CALIF.
1922-135	VICK, HENRY ARTHUR 'ERNIE'	D. JULY 16, 1980, ANN ARBOR, MICH.
1948-102	VICO, GEORGE STEVE	D. JANUARY 13, 1994, REDONDO BEACH, CALIF.
2003-169	VICTORINO, SHANE PATRICK	498 SOUTH ALU ROAD, WAILUKU HI 96793
1966-094	VIDAL, JOSE NICOLAS	OLD ADD: JUAN ERAZO, 152 SANTO DOMINGO DOM REP
1997-170	VIDRO, JOSE ANGEL CETTY	OLD ADD: 4657 MAIN STREET, JUPITER FL 33458
2004-199	VILLACIS, EDUARDO ENRIQUE	OLD ADD: MIRANDA VENEZ
2000-186	VILLAFUERTE, BRANDON PAUL	17265 PEAK AVENUE, MORGAN HILL CA 95037
2006-211	VILLANUEVA, CARLOS MANUEL (PAULINO)	OLD ADD: SANTO DOMINGO DOM REP
1990-162	VILLANUEVA, HECTOR (BALASQUIDE)	OLD ADD: 2 AMBESE 156 R.P.H., RIO PIEDRAS PR 00926
2003-170	VILLAREAL, OSCAR EDUARDO	376 WEST LINDBERGH AVENUE, COOLIDGE AZ 85228
2000-187	VILLEGAS, ISMAEL	OLD ADD: CAGUAS PR
1995-231	VILLONE, RONALD THOMAS	49 WEST MADISON AVENUE, DUMONT NJ 07628
1993-192	VINA, FERNANDO	11703 COLONY ROAD, GALT CA 95632
1924-112	VINES, ROBERT EARL	D. OCTOBER 18, 1982, ORLANDO, FLA.
1964-124	VINEYARD, DAVID KENT	1850 TARIFF ROAD, LEFT HAND WV 25251
2001-189	VINING, KENNETH EDWARD	1819 LELA AVENUE, CHARLOTTE NC 28208
1966-095	VINSON, CHARLES ANTHONY	3821 WALTERS LN, FORESTVILLE MD 20747
1982-132	VIOLA, FRANK JOHN	9868 KILGORE ROAD, ORLANDO FL 32836
1955-132	VIRDON, WILLIAM CHARLES	1311 RIVER RD, SPRINGFIELD MO 65804
1980-134	VIRGIL, OSVALDO JOSE	5444 WEST CREEDANCE BLVD, GLENDALE AZ 85310
1956-084	VIRGIL, OSVALDO JOSE 'OZZIE'	4316 WEST MESCAL ST, GLENDALE AZ 85301
1944-136	VITELLI, ANTONIO JOSEPH 'JOE'	D. FEBRUARY 7, 1967, PITTSBURGH, PA.
1995-232	VITIELLO, JOSEPH DAVID	13615 OLD EL CAMINO REAL, SAN DIEGO CA 92130
1992-149	VITKO, JOSEPH JOHN	1853 FRANKSTOWN ROAD #1, JOHNSTOWN PA 15902
1989-133	VIZCAINO, JOSE LUIS	1702 MONARCH RIDGE CIRCLE, EL CAJON CA 92019
1999-199	VIZCAINO, LUIS	OLD ADD: BANI DOM REP
1989-134	VIZQUEL, OMAR ENRIQUE	26630 SE ISSAQUAH FALL CITY ROAD, ISSAQUAH WA 98029
1923-135	VOGEL, OTTO HENRY	D. JULY 19, 1969, IOWA CITY, IOWA
2000-188	VOGELSONG, RYAN ANDREW	370 WEST MAIN STREET, KUTZTOWN PA 19530
1992-150	VOIGT, JOHN DAVID 'JACK'	1759 BAYSHORE ROAD, NOKOMIS FL 34275
1924-113	VOIGT, OLEN EDWARD	D. APRIL 7, 1970, SCOTTSDALE, ARIZ.
1942-103	VOISELLE, WILLIAM SYMNES	D. JANUARY 31, 2005, GREENWOOD, S.C.
1942-104	VOLLMER, CLYDE FREDERICK	D. OCTOBER 2, 2006, FLORENCE, KY.
2005-194	VOLQUEZ, EDISON	OLD ADD: LA SEGUNDA DOM REP
1965-111	VONHOFF, BRUCE FREDERICK	423 RIVER HILLS DRIVE, TEMPLE TERRACE FL 33617
1983-145	VONOHLEN, DAVID	653 WINDMILL AVENUE, WEST BABYLON NY 11704
1986-158	VOSBERG, EDWARD JOHN	7839 EAST MARQUISE DRIVE, TUCSON AZ 85715
1930-084	VOSMIK, JOSEPH FRANKLIN	D. JANUARY 27, 1962, CLEVELAND, OHIO
1965-112	VOSS, WILLIAM EDWARD	10625 EAST OAK TRAIL, CORNVILLE AZ 86325
2001-190	VOYLES, BRADLEY ROY	341 EAST AVENUE, CASCO WI 54205
1929-105	VOYLES, PHILIP VANCE	D. NOVEMBER 3, 1972, MARLBORO, MASS.
1975-124	VUCKOVICH, PETER DENNIS	86 LEONARD STREET, JOHNSTOWN PA 15902
1980-135	VUKOVICH, GEORGE STEPHEN	6060 FOXBERRY LANE, ROSWELL GA 30075
1970-136	VUKOVICH, JOHN CHRISTOPHER	D. MARCH 8, 2007, PHILADELPHIA, PA.

W

1984-126	WADDELL, THOMAS DAVID	10171 ACHI STREET, TUCSON AZ 85748
1931-093	WADDEY, FRANK ORUM	D. OCTOBER 21, 1990, KNOXVILLE, TENN.
1948-103	WADE, BENJAMIN STYRON	D. DECEMBER 2, 2002, LOS ANGELES, CALIF.
1955-133	WADE, GALEARD LEE	10240 NC 226 SOUTH, NEBO NC 28761
1995-233	WADE, HAWATHA TERRELL 'TERRELL'	OLD ADD: 1451 RAINTREE DRIVE, ROSWELL GA 30076
1936-093	WADE, JACOB FIELDS	D. FEBRUARY 1, 2006, WILDWOOD, CALIF.
1923-136	WADE, RICHARD FRANK	D. JUNE 16, 1957, DULUTH, MINN.
2003-171	WAECHTER, DOUGLAS MICHAEL	8059 31ST AVENUE NORTH, SAINT PETERSBURG FL 33710
1938-102	WAGNER, CHARLES THOMAS	D. AUGUST 31, 2006, READING, PA.
1965-113	WAGNER, GARY EDWARD	3145 SUMAC COURT, COLUMBUS IN 47203
1937-104	WAGNER, HAROLD EDWARD	D. AUGUST 7, 1979, RIVERSIDE NJ
1990-163	WAGNER, HECTOR RAUL	SEGUNDA CASA #114, LOS MAMEYE SANTO DOMINGO, DOM REP
1958-100	WAGNER, LEON LAMAR	D. JANUARY 3, 2004, LOS ANGELES, CALIF.
1976-097	WAGNER, MARK DUANE	1838 WILLOW ARMS DRIVE, ASHTABULA OH 44004
1996-183	WAGNER, MATTHEW WILLIAM	1112 LILAC DRIVE, CEDAR FALLS IA 50613
1992-151	WAGNER, PAUL ALAN	N1960 STATE ROAD 67, NEOSHO WI 53059
2003-172	WAGNER, RYAN SCOTT	59 COUNTY ROAD #311, YOAKUM TX 77995
1995-234	WAGNER, WILLIAM EDWARD 'BILLY'	5066 JONES MILL ROAD, CROZET VA 22932
1944-137	WAHL, KERMIT EMERSON	D. SEPTEMBER 16, 1987, TUCSON, ARIZ.

1991-178	WAINHOUSE, DAVID PAUL	6101 85TH PLACE SOUTHEAST, MERCER ISLAND WA 98040
2005-195	WAINWRIGHT, ADAM P.	401 PEBBLE TRACE, SAINT SIMONS ISLAND GA 31522
1941-114	WAITKUS, EDWARD STEPHEN	D. SEPTEMBER 16, 1972, BOSTON, MASS.
1973-127	WAITS, MICHAEL RICHARD 'RICK'	12012 EAST CLAIM JUMPER SQUARE, TUCSON AZ 85749
1991-179	WAKAMATSU, WILBUR DONALD 'DON'	8740 RAMBLEWOOD COURT, NORTH RICHLAND HILLS TX 76180
1941-115	WAKEFIELD, RICHARD CUMMINGS	D. AUGUST 26, 1985, REDFORD TWP., WAYNE CO., MICH.
1992-152	WAKEFIELD, TIMOTHY STEPHEN	241 LANSING ISLAND DRIVE, INDIAN HARBOUR BEACH FL 32937
1964-125	WAKEFIELD, WILLIAM SUMNER	1 BAYPOINT VILLAGE DRIVE, SAN RAFAEL CA 94901
2001-191	WAKELAND, CHRISTOPHER ROBERT	60997 LUTTRELL LANE, SAINT HELENS OR 97051
1993-193	WALBECK, MATTHEW LOVICK	8216 OLIVE AVENUE, FAIR OAKS CA 95628
1923-137	WALBERG, GEORGE ELVIN 'RUBE'	D. OCTOBER 27, 1978, TEMPE, ARIZ.
1945-108	WALCZAK, EDWIN JOSEPH	D. MARCH 10, 1998, NORWICH, CONN.
1987-148	WALEWANDER, JAMES	7427 EAST RUSTLING PASS, SCOTTSDALE AZ 85255
1980-136	WALK, ROBERT VERNON	PO BOX 7000, PITTSBURGH PA 15212
1948-104	WALKER, ALBERT BLUFORD 'RUBE'	D. DECEMBER 12, 1992, MORGANTON, N.C.
1986-159	WALKER, ANTHONY BRUCE	2724 MORGAN DRIVE, SAN RAMON CA 94583
1980-137	WALKER, CLEOTHA 'CHICO'	6 ATHENA COURT, TINLEY PARK IL 60477
1982-133	WALKER, DUANE ALLEN	2509 GEORGIA AVENUE, DEER PARK TX 77536
1931-094	WALKER, FRED 'DIXIE'	D. MAY 17, 1982, BIRMINGHAM, ALA.
1931-095	WALKER, GERALD HOLMES 'GEE'	D. MARCH 20, 1981, WHITFIELD, MISS.
1982-134	WALKER, GREGORY LEE	530 NORTH LAKE SHORE DRIVE #1009, CHICAGO IL 60611
1940-096	WALKER, HARRY WILLIAM 'THE HAT'	D. AUGUST 8, 1999, PASCAGOULA, ALA.
1931-096	WALKER, HARVEY WILLOS 'HUB'	D. NOVEMBER 26, 1982, SAN JOSE, CALIF.
1965-114	WALKER, JAMES LUKE 'LUKE'	316 LOMA LINDA, WAKE VILLAGE TX 75501
1997-171	WALKER, JAMIE ROSS	12137 CRAIG LANE, OVERLAND PARK KS 66213
1957-091	WALKER, JERRY ALLEN	2015 COLLINS BLVD, ADA OK 74820
1923-138	WALKER, JOSEPH RICHARD	D. JUNE 20, 1959, WEST MIFFLIN, PA.
2000-189	WALKER, KEVIN MICHAEL	1387 HIGHWAY 144 SOUTH, GLEN ROSE TX 76043
1989-135	WALKER, LARRY KENNETH ROBERT	1667 FLAGLER PKWY, WEST PALM BEACH FL 33411
1928-102	WALKER, MARTIN VAN BUREN	D. APRIL 24, 1978, PHILADELPHIA, PA.
1992-153	WALKER, MICHAEL AARON	24616 MARKS ROAD, SPLENDORA TX 77372
1988-136	WALKER, MICHAEL CHARLES	23195 TANKERSLEY ROAD, BROOKSVILLE FL 34601
1995-235	WALKER, PETER BRIAN	2 WHITE OAK LANE, QUAKER HILL CT 06375
1972-118	WALKER, ROBERT THOMAS 'TOM'	817 WHIPPOORWILL HILL ROAD, GIBSONIA PA 15044
1996-184	WALKER, TODD ARTHUR	212 MADONNA DRIVE, BENTON LA 71006
2002-198	WALKER, TYLER LANIER	1533 4TH AVENUE WEST #OFC, BRADENTON FL 34205
1927-096	WALKER, WILLIAM HENRY	D. JUNE 14, 1966, EAST ST. LOUIS, ILL.
1934-106	WALKUP, JAMES ELTON	D. FEBRUARY 7, 1997, DANVILLE, ARK.
1927-097	WALKUP, JAMES HUEY	D. JUNE 12, 1990, DUNCAN, OKLA.
1995-236	WALL, DONNELL LEE 'DONNE'	116 RIVER BREEZE WAY, SAINT LOUIS MO 63129
1950-103	WALL, MURRAY WESLEY	D. OCTOBER 8, 1971, LONE OAK, TEXAS
1975-125	WALL, STANLEY ARTHUR	9907 E. 80TH ST, RAYTOWN MO 64138
1973-128	WALLACE, DAVID WILLIAM	82 WHIPPLE BROOK ROAD, WRENTHAM MA 02093
1996-185	WALLACE, DEREK ROBERT	2950 OLD FORD ROAD, PASO ROBLES CA 93446
1967-111	WALLACE, DONALD ALLEN	23 KRIS LN, MANITOU SPRINGS CO 80829
1942-105	WALLACE, JAMES HAROLD 'LEFTY'	D. JULY 28, 1982, EVANSVILLE, IND.
1997-172	WALLACE, JEFFREY ALLEN	2904 FEDERAL AVENUE, ALLIANCE OH 44601
1973-129	WALLACE, MICHAEL SHERMAN	12483 ELK RUN ROAD, MIDLAND VA 22728
1980-138	WALLACH, TIMOTHY CHARLES	40375 CHAPPARAL DRIVE, TEMECULA CA 92592
1940-097	WALLAESA, JOHN	D. DECEMBER 27, 1986, EASTON, PA.
1945-109	WALLEN, NORMAN EDWARD	D. JUNE 20, 1994, MILWAUKEE, WISC.
1980-139	WALLER, ELLIOTT TYRONE 'TYE'	16963 SILVER CREST DRIVE, SAN DIEGO CA 92127
1975-126	WALLING, DENNIS	BOX 1312, WAYNESBORO VA 22980
1975-127	WALLIS, HAROLD JOSEPH 'JOE'	155 CASTLEWOOD DRIVE, BALLWIN MO 63021
1952-108	WALLS, RAYMOND LEE 'LEE'	D. OCTOBER 11, 1993, LOS ANGELES, CALIF.
2003-173	WALROND, LESLIE DALE	113 AUTUMN OAKS COURT, BRENTWOOD TN 37027
1927-098	WALSH, AUGUST SOTHLEY	D. NOVEMBER 12, 1985, SAN RAFAEL, CALIF.
1990-164	WALSH, DAVID PETER	500 CONCORD LANE, EDMOND OK 73003
1928-103	WALSH, EDWARD ARTHUR	D. OCTOBER 31, 1937, MERIDEN, CONN.
1946-101	WALSH, JAMES GERALD	D. NOVEMBER 12, 1990, OLYPHANT, PA.
1921-108	WALSH, JAMES THOMAS	D. MAY 13, 1967, BOSTON, MASS.
1938-103	WALSH, JOSEPH PATRICK	D. OCTOBER 5, 1996, BOSTON, MASS.
1920-127	WALSH, WALTER WILLIAM	D. JANUARY 15, 1966, NEPTUNE, N.J.
1985-114	WALTER, GENE WINSTON	C/O AG EDWARDS, 101 BULLITT LANE #110, LOUISVILLE KY 40222
1930-085	WALTER, JAMES BERNARD 'BERNIE'	D. OCTOBER 30, 1988, NASHVILLE, TENN.
1969-175	WALTERS, CHARLES LEONARD	1717 SUTTON LANE, MENDOTA HEIGHTS MN 55118
1992-154	WALTERS, DANIEL GENE	298 PICNIC VIEW LANE, OCEANSIDE CA 92056
1945-110	WALTERS, JAMES FREDERICK 'FRED'	D. FEBRUARY 1, 1980, LAUREL, MISS.
1960-101	WALTERS, KENNETH ROGERS	9545 BELLE MEADE DR, SAN RAMON CA 94583
1983-146	WALTERS, MICHAEL CHARLES	79480 MANDEVILLE ROAD, INDIO CA 92201
1931-097	WALTERS, WILLIAM HENRY 'BUCKY'	D. APRIL 20, 1991, ABINGTON, PA.
1991-180	WALTON, BRUCE KENNETH	10625 TIVOLI COURT, BAKERSFIELD CA 93311
1968-106	WALTON, DANIEL JAMES	765 SOUTH 7900 EAST, HUNTSVILLE UT 84317
1989-136	WALTON, JEROME O'TERRELL	459 COUNTRY CLUB ROAD, NEWNAN GA 30263
1980-140	WALTON, REGINALD SHERARD	1142 SOUTH CURSON AVE, LOS ANGELES CA 90019
1927-099	WANER, LLOYD JAMES	D. JULY 22, 1982, OKLAHOMA CITY, OKLA.
1926-090	WANER, PAUL GLEE	D. AUGUST 29, 1965, SARASOTA, FLA.
2005-196	WANG, CHIEN-MING	OLD ADD: TAMPA FL
1925-110	WANNINGER, PAUL LOUIS 'PEE WEE'	D. MAY 7, 1981, NORTH AUGUSTA, S.C.
1965-115	WANTZ, RICHARD CARTER	D. MAY 13, 1965, INGLEWOOD, CALIF.
1990-165	WAPNICK, STEVEN LEE	29795 KINGS CANYON COURT SOUTH, COARSEGOLD CA 93614
1998-194	WARD, BRYAN MATTHEW	OLD ADD: MOUNT HOLLY NJ 08060
1972-119	WARD, CHRIS GILBERT	12858 WILLIAMS RANCH ROAD, MOORPARK CA 93021
1985-115	WARD, COLIN NORVAL	3701 EAST BASELINE ROAD, GILBERT AZ 85234
1998-195	WARD, DARYLE LAMAR	18073 GRANITE AVENUE, RIVERSIDE CA 92508
1979-116	WARD, GARY LAMELL	18073 GRANITE AVENUE, RIVERSIDE CA 92508

1963-122	WARD, JOHN FRANCIS 'JAY'	PMB 184 918 IDAHO AVENUE, LIBBY MT 59923
1991-181	WARD, KEVIN MICHAEL	133 F AVENUE, CORONADO CA 92118
1962-141	WARD, PETER THOMAS	575 SOUTHWEST G, LAKE OSWEGO OR 97034
1948-105	WARD, PRESTON MEYER	4371 DE SILVA PLACE, LAS VEGAS NV 89121
1934-107	WARD, RICHARD OLE	D. JUNE 1, 1966, FREELAND, WASH.
1990-166	WARD, ROBERT COLBY 'COLBY'	1508 EAST HOBBLECREEK, SPRINGVILLE UT 84663
1986-160	WARD, ROY DUANE 'DUANE'	8205 TAOS PASCO AVENUE, LAS VEGAS NV 89128
1990-167	WARD, TURNER MAX	232 AUTUMN DRIVE, SARALAND AL 36571
1968-107	WARDEN, JONATHAN EDGAR	6575 OASIS DRIVE, LOVELAND OH 45140
1984-127	WARDLE, CURTIS RAY	13900 PHEASANT KNOLL LANE, MORENO VALLEY CA 92553
1995-237	WARE, JEFFREY ALLEN	OLD ADD: 4861 RIDGEMOOR CIRCLE, CLEARWATER FL 33755
1930-086	WARNEKE, LONNIE 'LON'	D. JUNE 23, 1976, HOT SPRINGS, ARK.
1962-142	WARNER, JACK DYER	5938 WEST CALLE LEJOS, GLENDALE AZ 85310
1966-096	WARNER, JOHN JOSEPH	19136 HIGHWAY 18 NORTH, APPLE VALLEY CA 92307
1925-111	WARNER, JOHN RALPH 'JACK'	D. MARCH 13, 1986, MOUNT VERNON, ILL.
1935-112	WARNOCK, HAROLD CHARLES	D. FEBRUARY 8, 1997, TUCSON, ARIZ.
1939-123	WARREN, BENNIE LOUIS	D. MAY 11, 1994, OKLAHOMA CITY, OKLA.
1983-147	WARREN, MICHAEL BRUCE	12281 DIANE STREET, GARDEN GROVE CA 92640
1944-138	WARREN, THOMAS GENTRY	D. JANUARY 2, 1968, TULSA, OKLA.
1930-087	WARSTLER, HAROLD BURTON 'RABBIT'	D. MAY 31, 1964, NORTH CANTON, OHIO
1975-128	WARTHEN, DANIEL DEAN	3933 SOUTHWEST WAPATO AVENUE, PORTLAND OR 97201
1961-106	WARWICK, CARL WAYNE	14102 BONNEY BRIER, HOUSTON TX 77069
1921-109	WARWICK, FIRMAN NEWTON 'BILL'	D. DECEMBER 19, 1984, SAN ANTONIO, TEXAS
1937-105	WASDELL, JAMES CHARLES	D. AUGUST 6, 1983, NEWPORT RICHEY, FLA.
1995-238	WASDIN, JOHN TRUMAN	2676 RIVERPORT DRIVE SOUTH, JACKSONVILLE FL 32223
1937-106	WASEM, LINCOLN WILLIAM 'LINK'	D. MARCH 6, 1979, SOUTH LAGUNA, CALIF.
1941-116	WASHBURN, GEORGE EDWARD	D. JANUARY 5, 1979, BATON ROUGE, LA.
1969-176	WASHBURN, GREGORY JAMES	1685 E. STELLON ST, COAL CITY IL 60416
1998-196	WASHBURN, JARROD MICHAEL	10003 OLINGER ROAD, WEBSTER WI 54893
1961-107	WASHBURN, RAY CLARK	19001 131ST DRIVE SE, SNOHOMISH WA 98296
1974-138	WASHINGTON, CLAUDELL	OLD ADD: 4067 HARDWICK STREET, LAKEWOOD CA 90712
1974-139	WASHINGTON, HERBERT	642 EAST AUSTIN STREET, FLINT MI 48505
1978-139	WASHINGTON, LARUE	6323 RESEDA BLVD #16, TARZANA CA 91335
1977-148	WASHINGTON, RONALD	OLD ADD: 7365 PERTH STREET, NEW ORLEANS LA 70126
1935-113	WASHINGTON, SLOAN VERNON 'VERN'	D. FEBRUARY 17, 1985, LINDEN, TEXAS
1977-149	WASHINGTON, U.L.	BOX 164, STRINGTOWN OK 74569
1986-161	WASINGER, MARK THOMAS	18021 CARSON DRIVE, EL PASO TX 79928
1967-112	WASLEWSKI, GARY LEE	1799 EAST TERRESTRIAL PLACE, TUCSON AZ 85737
2000-190	WASZGIS, ROBERT MICHAEL 'B.J.'	2708 DOVER LANE, ALBANY GA 31701
1976-098	WATERBURY, STEVEN CRAIG	710 N. GARFIELD, MARION IL 62958
1955-134	WATERS, FRED WARREN	D. AUGUST 28, 1989, PENSACOLA, FLA.
2002-199	WATHAN, DUSTIN JAMES	1354 NE TODD GEORGE ROAD, LEES SUMMIT MO 64086
1976-099	WATHAN, JOHN DAVID	1354 NE TODD GEORGE ROAD, LEES SUMMIT MO 64086
1969-177	WATKINS, DAVID ROGER	506 RIDGEWOOD ROAD, LOUISVILLE KY 40207
1930-088	WATKINS, GEORGE ARCHIBALD 'WATTY'	D. JUNE 1, 1970, HOUSTON, TEXAS
1969-178	WATKINS, ROBERT CECIL	4417 WEST 58TH PLACE, LOS ANGELES CA 90043
1995-239	WATKINS, SCOTT ALLEN	14577 WEST 19TH STREET, SAND SPRINGS OK 74063
2004-200	WATKINS, STEPHEN DOUGLAS	3408 EVANSTON AVENUE, LUBBOCK TX 79407
1997-173	WATKINS, WILLIAM PATRICK 'PAT'	1205 FOWLER DRIVE, GARNER NC 27529
1953-097	WATLINGTON, JULIUS NEAL 'NEAL'	BOX 418, YANCEYVILLE NC 27379
1993-194	WATSON, ALLEN KENNETH	61-44 65TH STREET, MIDDLE VILLAGE NY 11379
2005-197	WATSON, BRANDON ERIC	OLD ADD: INGLEWOOD CA
1930-089	WATSON, JOHN THOMAS	D. APRIL 29, 1965, HUNTINGTON, W.VA.
2000-191	WATSON, MARK BRADFORD	555 SPENDER TRACE, ATLANTA GA 30301
2003-174	WATSON, MATTHEW KYLE	141 AMERICAN AVENUE, LANCASTER PA 17602
1966-097	WATSON, ROBERT JOSE	18103 DARLING POINT COURT, CYPRESS TX 77429
1920-128	WATT, ALBERT BAILEY	D. MARCH 15, 1968, NORFOLK, VA.
1966-098	WATT, EDDIE DEAN	PO BOX 7, NORTH BEND NE 68649
1931-098	WATT, FRANK MARION	D. AUGUST 31, 1956, GLEN COVE, MD.
1929-106	WATWOOD, JOHN CLIFFORD	D. MARCH 1, 1980, GOODWATER, ALA.
1952-109	WAUGH, JAMES ELDEN	501 BOURLAND ROAD #3106, KELLER TX 76248
1927-100	WAY, ROBERT CLINTON	D. JUNE 20, 1974, PITTSBURGH, PA.
1924-114	WAYENBERG, FRANK	D. APRIL 16, 1975, ZANESVILLE, OHIO
1989-137	WAYNE, GARY ANTHONY	5762 WEST ASBURY PLACE, DENVER CO 80227
2002-200	WAYNE, JUSTIN MORGAN	302 MUIRFIELD COURT, JUPITER FL 33458
1936-094	WEAFER, KENNETH ALBERT	D. JUNE 4, 2005, GUILDERLAND, N.Y.
1936-095	WEATHERLY, CYRIL ROY 'ROY'	D. JANUARY 19, 1991, WOODVILLE, TEXAS
1991-182	WEATHERS, JOHN DAVID 'DAVE'	979 LEXINGTON HWY, LORETTO TN 38469
1962-143	WEAVER, DAVID FLOYD 'FLOYD'	93 COUNTY ROAD 35930, POWDERLY TX 75473
1968-108	WEAVER, EARL SIDNEY	501 CYPRESS POINTE DRIVE WEST, PEMBROKE PINES FL 33027
1967-113	WEAVER, JAMES BRIAN	276 RHODA DR, LANCASTER PA 17601
1928-104	WEAVER, JAMES DEMENT	D. DECEMBER 12, 1983, LAKELAND, FLA.
1998-197	WEAVER, JAMES ERIC 'ERIC'	2641 WAEVER ROAD, ILLIOPOLIS IL 62539
1985-116	WEAVER, JAMES FRANCIS	6916 8TH AVENUE WEST, BRADENTON FL 34209
1999-200	WEAVER, JEFFREY CHARLES	2246 BIRCHGLEN STREET #125, SIMI VALLEY CA 93063
2006-212	WEAVER, JERED DAVID	OLD ADD: NORTHRIDGE CA
1931-099	WEAVER, MONTE MORTON	D. JUNE 14, 1994, ORLANDO, FLA.
1980-141	WEAVER, ROGER EDWARD	65 MOYER STREET, CANAJOHARIE NY 13317
2003-175	WEBB, BRANDON TYLER	8814 EAST ANN WAY, SCOTTSDALE AZ 85260
1972-120	WEBB, HENRY GAYLON	4527 LAKE VALANCIA BLVD WEST, PALM HARBOR FL 34684
1932-090	WEBB, JAMES LEVERNE 'SKEETER'	D. JULY 8, 1986, MERIDIAN, MISS.
2004-201	WEBB, JOHN FLOYD	OLD ADD: PENSACOLA FL
1948-106	WEBB, SAMUEL HENRY 'RED'	D. FEBRUARY 7, 1996, HYATTSVILLE, MD.
1925-112	WEBB, WILLIAM EARL	D. MAY 22, 1965, JAMESTOWN, TENN.
1943-141	WEBB, WILLIAM FRANKLIN	D. JUNE 1, 1994, MABLETON, GA.
1942-106	WEBBER, LESTER ELMER	D. NOVEMBER 13, 1986, SANTA MARIA, CALIF.

2000-192	WEBER, BENJAMIN EDWARD	5550 BAIRD STREET, GROVES TX 77619
1998-198	WEBER, NEIL AARON	1 MORNING VIEW, IRVINE CA 92612
1989-138	WEBSTER, LEONARD IRELL 'LENNY'	323 WEIL STREET (PO BOX 811), LUTCHER LA 70071
1983-148	WEBSTER, MITCHELL DEAN	5260 TIMBER CREEK ROAD, GREAT BEND KS 67530
1967-114	WEBSTER, RAMON ALBERTO	PO BOX 6-5790 EL DORADO, PANAMA
1959-086	WEBSTER, RAYMOND GEORGE	311 5TH STREET, MARYSVILLE CA 95901
1991-183	WEDGE, ERIC MICHAEL	31422 SAINT ANDREWS, WESTLAKE OH 44145
1962-144	WEEKLY, JOHN	D. NOVEMBER 24, 1974, WALNUT CREEK, CALIF.
2003-176	WEEKS, RICKIE DARNELL	550 BIRCH COURT, ALTAMONTE SPRINGS FL 32714
1969-179	WEGENER, MICHAEL DENIS	1507 BENNETT ROAD, MADISON OH 44057
1985-117	WEGMAN, WILLIAM EDWARD	20521 HEATHER COURT, LAWRENCEBURG IN 47025
1930-090	WEHDE, WILBUR 'BIGGS'	D. SEPTEMBER 21, 1970, SIOUX FALLS, S.D.
1945-111	WEHMEIER, HERMAN RALPH	D. MAY 21, 1973, DALLAS, TEXAS
1991-184	WEHNER, JOHN PAUL	105 AVERYS WAY, CRANBERRY TWP PA 16066
1976-100	WEHRMEISTER, DAVID THOMAS	4216 DUBHE COURT, CONCORD CA 94521
1946-102	WEIGEL, RALPH RICHARD	D. APRIL 15, 1992, MEMPHIS, TENN.
1948-107	WEIK, RICHARD HENRY	D. APRIL 21, 1991, HARVEY, ILL.
1940-098	WEILAND, EDWIN NICHOLAS	D. JULY 12, 1972, CHICAGO, ILL.
1928-105	WEILAND, ROBERT GEORGE	D. NOVEMBER 9, 1988, CHICAGO, ILL.
1945-112	WEINGARTNER, ELMER WILLIAM	13604 LORAIN, CLEVELAND OH 44111
1933-065	WEINTRAUB, PHILIP	D. JUNE 21, 1987, PALM SPRINGS, CALIF.
1936-096	WEIR, WILLIAM FRANKLIN	D. SEPTEMBER 30, 1989, ANAHEIM, CALIF.
1962-145	WEIS, ALBERT JOHN	902 SOUTH POPLAR, ELMHURST IL 60126
1922-136	WEIS, ARTHUR JOHN	D. MAY 4, 1997, SAINT LOUIS, MO.
1980-142	WEISS, GARY LEE	1700 WEISS LANE, BRENHAM TX 77833
1987-149	WEISS, WALTER WILLIAM	1275 CASTLEPOINT CIRCLE, CASTLE ROCK CO 80104
1939-124	WELAJ, JOHN LUDWIG	D. SEPTEMBER 13, 2003, ARLINGTON, TEXAS
1925-113	WELCH, HERBERT M.	D. APRIL 13, 1967, MEMPHIS, TENN.
1926-091	WELCH, JOHN VERNON	D. SEPTEMBER 2, 1940, ST. LOUIS, MO.
1998-199	WELCH, MICHAEL PAUL	6 FOREST PARK DRIVE, NASHUA NH 03060
1945-113	WELCH, MILTON EDWARD	818 JANNETTE COURT, SPRINGFIELD OR 97477
1978-140	WELCH, ROBERT LYNN	11055 EAST GOLD DUST AVENUE, SCOTTSDALE AZ 85259
1982-135	WELCHEL, DONALD RAY	21518 PATTON AVENUE, LEANDER TX 78645
2003-177	WELLEMEYER, TODD ALLEN	8402 WESTOVER DRIVE, PROSPECT KY 40059
1982-136	WELLMAN, BRAD EUGENE	733 GRAHAM COURT, DANVILLE CA 94526
1948-108	WELLMAN, ROBERT JOSEPH	D. DECEMBER 20, 1994, VILLA HILLS, KY.
1987-150	WELLS, DAVID LEE	2519 N. MCMULLEN BOOTH #510-198, CLEARWATER FL 33761
1923-139	WELLS, EDWIN LEE	D. MAY 1, 1986, BIRMINGHAM, ALA.
1981-139	WELLS, GREGORY DEWAYNE 'BOOMER'	RR 1 BOX 98, MCINTOSH AL 36553
1944-139	WELLS, JOHN FREDERICK	D. OCTOBER 23, 1993, OLEAN, N.Y.
1942-107	WELLS, LEO DONALD	D. JUNE 23, 2006, SAINT PAUL, MINN.
1999-201	WELLS, ROBERT KIP 'KIP'	3063 TAM O SHANTER LANE, MISSOURI CITY TX 77459
1994-111	WELLS, ROBERT LEE	154 WILCOX ROAD, COWICHE WA 98923
1990-168	WELLS, TERRY	OLD ADD: 5445 SOUTH CORNELL #3, CHICAGO IL 60615
1999-202	WELLS, VERNON M.	1025 DEER HOLLOW BLVD, SOUTHLAKE TX 76092
1981-140	WELSH, CHRISTOPHER CHARLES	12640 HUEY LANE, WALTON KY 41094
1925-114	WELSH, JAMES DANIEL	D. OCTOBER 30, 1970, OAKLAND, CALIF.
1948-109	WELTEROTH, RICHARD JOHN	122 ELDRED STREET, WILLIAMSPORT PA 17701
1926-092	WELZER, ANTON FRANK	D. MARCH 18, 1971, MILWAUKEE, WISC.
1993-195	WENDELL, STEVEN JOHN 'TURK'	1053 SOUTH STREET, DALTON MA 01226
1995-240	WENGERT, DONALD PAUL	C/O WJ WENGERT, 3822 VINE AVENUE, SIOUX CITY IA 51106
1943-142	WENSLOFF, CHARLES WILLIAM 'BUTCH'	D. FEBRUARY 18, 2001, SAN RAFAEL, CALIF.
1945-114	WENTZEL, STANLEY AARON	D. NOVEMBER 28, 1991, ST. LAWRENCE, PA.
1968-109	WENZ, FREDERICK CHARLES	1 CIRCLE DR, SOMERVILLE NJ 08876
1927-101	WERA, JULIAN VALENTINE	D. DECEMBER 12, 1975, ROCHESTER, MINN.
1930-091	WERBER, WILLIAM MURRAY	VILLA 5732A 5800 OLD PROVIDENCE ROAD, CHARLOTTE NC 28226
1964-126	WERHAS, JOHN CHARLES	23705 VIA DEL RIO, YORBA LINDA CA 92887
1949-089	WERLE, WILLIAM GEORGE	833 WEST 28TH AVENUE, SAN MATEO CA 94403
1956-085	WERLEY, GEORGE WILLIAM	1374 CLARKSON CLAYTON CIR, BALLWIN MO 63011
1975-129	WERNER, DONALD PAUL	2204 BRIARWOOD, ARLINGTON TX 76013
1963-123	WERT, DONALD RALPH	647 SAW MILL ROAD, MECHANICSBURG PA 17051
1979-117	WERTH, DENNIS DEAN	2505 TARTAN WAY, SPRINGFIELD IL 62711
2002-201	WERTH, JAYSON RICHARD GOWAN	2713 TARTANWAY, SPRINGFIELD IL 62711
1926-093	WERTZ, HENRY LEVI 'JOHNNY'	D. AUGUST 24, 1990, NEWBERRY, S.C.
1947-092	WERTZ, VICTOR WOODROW	D. JULY 7, 1983, DETROIT, MICH.
1993-196	WERTZ, WILLIAM CHARLES	26514 MINGO DRIVE, PERRYSBURG OH 43551
1979-118	WESSINGER, JAMES MICHAEL	4275 ALTAIR COURSE, LIVERPOOL NY 13090
2002-202	WESSON, BARRY JARVIS	OLD ADD: GLEN ALLAN MS 38744
1988-137	WEST, DAVID LEE	OLD ADD: 1571 CROSSING DRIVE, NESBIT MS 38651
1938-104	WEST, MAX EDWARD	D. DECEMBER 31, 2003, SIERRA MADRE, CALIF.
1938-105	WEST, RICHARD THOMAS	D. MARCH 13, 1996, FORT WAYNE, IND.
1927-102	WEST, SAMUEL FILMORE	D. NOVEMBER 23, 1985, LUBBOCK, TEXAS
1928-106	WEST, WALTER MAXWELL 'MAX'	D. APRIL 25, 1971, HOUSTON, TEXAS
1944-140	WEST, WELDON EDISON 'LEFTY'	D. JULY 23, 1979, HENDERSONVILLE, N.C.
2000-193	WESTBROOK, JACOB CAUTHEN	3136 BOOGER HILL ROAD, DANIELSVILLE GA 30633
1955-135	WESTLAKE, JAMES PATRICK	D. JANUARY 3, 2003, SACRAMENTO, CALIF.
1947-093	WESTLAKE, WALDON THOMAS 'WALLY'	3800 61ST, SACRAMENTO CA 95820
1929-107	WESTON, ALFRED JOHN	D. NOVEMBER 13, 1997, SAN DIEGO, CALIF.
1989-139	WESTON, MICHAEL LEE 'MICKEY'	819 LYDIA STREET, WARSAW IN 46580
1947-094	WESTRUM, WESLEY NOREEN	D. MAY 28, 2002, CLEARBROOK, MINN.
1989-140	WETHERBY, JEFFREY BARRETT	28410 GREAT BEND PLACE, WESLEY CHAPEL FL 33543
1989-141	WETTELAND, JOHN KARL	1229 KENTUCKY DERBY DRIVE, BARTONVILLE TX 76226
1927-103	WETZEL, CHARLES EDWARD 'BUZZ'	D. MARCH 7, 1941, GLOBE, ARIZ.
1920-129	WETZEL, FRANKLIN BURTON 'BUZZ'	D. MARCH 5, 1942, BURBANK, CALIF.
1982-137	WEVER, STEFAN MATTHEW	186 JORDAN AVENUE, SAN FRANCISCO CA 94118
1923-140	WHALEY, WILLIAM CARL	D. MARCH 3, 1943, INDIANAPOLIS, IND.

1954-116 WHEAT, LEROY WILLIAM 'LEE' ....4010 GALT OCEAN DRIVE #1406, FORT LAUDERDALE FL 33308
1943-143 WHEATON, ELWOOD PIERCE 'WOODY' ....D. DECEMBER 11, 1995, LANCASTER, PA.
1999-203 WHEELER, DANIEL MICHAEL ....OLD ADD: 1018 MAIN STREET, HOPE VALLEY RI 02832
1949-090 WHEELER, DONALD WESLEY ....D. DECEMBER 10, 2003, BLOOMINGTON, MINN.
1945-115 WHEELER, EDWARD RAYMOND ....D. AUGUST 4, 1983, CENTRALIA, WASH.
1921-110 WHEELER, FLOYD CLARK 'RIP' ....D. SEPTEMBER 18, 1968, MARION, KY.
1976-101 WHEELOCK, GARY RICHARD ....25537 WEST PRIMROSE LANE, BUCKEYE AZ 85326
1920-130 WHELAN, THOMAS JOSEPH ....D. JUNE 26, 1957, BOSTON, MASS.
1971-107 WHILLOCK, JACK FRANKLIN ....2118 RIVER RIDGE ROAD, ARLINGTON TX 76017
1997-174 WHISENANT, MATTHEW MICHAEL ....1035 FAIRVIEW DRIVE, LA CANADA CA 91011
1952-110 WHISENANT, THOMAS PETER 'PETE' ....D. MARCH 22, 1996, PORT CHARLOTTE, FLA.
1977-150 WHISENTON, LARRY ....524 MAIN STREET, CANTON MS 39046
1977-151 WHITAKER, LOUIS RODMAN ....4781 HIGHLAND PLACE CIRCLE, LAKELAND FL 33813
1966-099 WHITAKER, STEVE EDWARD ....OLD ADD: 37123 SUWANEE WAY, DADE CITY FL 33523
1964-127 WHITBY, WILLIAM EDWARD ....13926 HUNTERSVILLE CONCORD RD, HUNTERSVILLE NC 28078
1945-116 WHITCHER, ROBERT ARTHUR ....D. MAY 8, 1997, AKRON, OHIO
1937-107 WHITE, ADEL 'ABE' ....D. OCTOBER 1, 1978, ATLANTA, GA.
1940-099 WHITE, ALBERT EUGENE 'FUZZ ' ....D. APRIL 24, 2003, SPRINGFIELD, MO.
1954-117 WHITE, CHARLES ....D. MAY 26, 1998, SEATAC, WASH.
1993-197 WHITE, DERRICK RAMON ....3524 DERBY SHIRE CIRCLE, GWYNN OAK MD 21244
1985-118 WHITE, DEVON MARKES ....6440 EAST SIERRA VISTA DRIVE, PARADISE VALLEY AZ 85253
1948-110 WHITE, DONALD WILLIAM ....D. JUNE 15, 1987, CARLSBAD, CALIF.
1955-136 WHITE, EDWARD PERRY ....D. SEPTEMBER 28, 1982, LAKELAND, FLA.
1962-146 WHITE, ELDER LAFAYETTE ....919 COLONY AVE, AHOSKIE NC 27910
1940-100 WHITE, ERNEST DANIEL ....D. MAY 22, 1974, AUGUSTA, GA.
1973-130 WHITE, FRANK ....412 NE PARKS EDGE DRIVE, LEES SUMMIT MO 64064
1994-112 WHITE, GABRIEL ALLEN ....1571 LAKEVIEWVIEW DRIVE, SEBRING FL 33870
1941-117 WHITE, HAROLD GEORGE ....D. APRIL 21, 2001, VENICE, FLA.
1974-140 WHITE, JEROME CARDELL ....581 GLEN DRIVE, SAN LEANDRO CA 94577
1927-104 WHITE, JOHN PETER ....D. JUNE 19, 1971, FLUSHING, N.Y.
1932-091 WHITE, JOYNER CLIFFORD 'JO-JO' ....D. OCTOBER 9, 1986, TACOMA, WASH.
1963-124 WHITE, JOYNER MICHAEL 'MIKE' ....26438 SOUTH JARDIN DRIVE, SUN LAKE AZ 85248
1983-149 WHITE, LARRY DAVID ....12601 VAN NUYS BLVD #210, PACOIMA CA 91331
2003-178 WHITE, MATTHEW J. ....535 MAIN STREET, DALTON MA 01226
1978-141 WHITE, MYRON ALAN ....OLD ADD: 3005 BELLAIRE RANCH DRIVE, FORT WORTH TX 76109
1994-113 WHITE, RICHARD ALLEN 'RICK' ....2860 WINDY RIDGE DRIVE, SPRINGFIELD OH 45502
1993-198 WHITE, RONDELL BERNARD ....407 CREEKSIDE DRIVE, GRAY GA 31032
1965-116 WHITE, ROY HILTON ....306 GREEN VIEW WAY, TOMS RIVER NJ 08753
1951-101 WHITE, SAMUEL CHARLES ....D. AUGUST 4, 1991, HANALEI, HAWAII
1945-117 WHITE, WILLIAM BARNEY ....D. JULY 24, 2002, TYLER, TEXAS
1956-086 WHITE, WILLIAM DEKOVA ....PO BOX 199, UPPER BLACK EDDY PA 18972
1989-142 WHITED, EDWARD MORRIS ....2613 DAWN RIDGE DRIVE, WESTFIELD IN 46074
1933-066 WHITEHEAD, BURGESS URQUHART 'WHITEY' ...D. NOVEMBER 25, 1993, WINDSOR, N.C.
1935-114 WHITEHEAD, JOHN HENDERSON ....D. OCTOBER 20, 1964, BONHAM, TEXAS
1923-141 WHITEHILL, EARL OLIVER ....D. OCTOBER 22, 1954, OMAHA, NEB.
1981-141 WHITEHOUSE, LEONARD JOSEPH ....300 SHORE ROAD, BURLINGTON VT 05401
1989-143 WHITEHURST, WALTER RICHARD 'WALLY' ....NEW ORLEANS BASEBALL LAKEFRONT ARENA, NEW ORLEANS LA 70148
1990-169 WHITEN, MARK ANTHONY ....5810 JEFFERSON PARK DRIVE, TAMPA FL 33625
1995-241 WHITESIDE, DAVID SEAN 'SEAN' ....3506 NORTH HILLS DRIVE, HALEYVILLE AL 35565
2005-198 WHITESIDE, DUSTIN ELI 'ELI' ....PO BOX 467, NEW ALBANY MS 38652
1992-155 WHITESIDE, MATTHEW CHRISTOPHER ....255 PALISADES RIDGE COURT, EUREKA MO 63025
1962-147 WHITFIELD, FRED DWIGHT ....RR 1 BOX 91, VANDIVER AL 35176
1974-141 WHITFIELD, TERRY BERTLAND ....9921 EAST 11TH AVENUE, BLYTHE CA 92225
1946-103 WHITMAN, DICK CORWIN ....D. FEBRUARY 12, 2003, PEORIA, ARIZ.
1946-104 WHITMAN, WALTER FRANKLIN 'FRANK' ....D. FEBRUARY 6, 1994, MARYVILLE, ILL.
1980-143 WHITMER, DANIEL CHARLES ....823 ROBINHOOD LN, REDLANDS CA 92373
1993-199 WHITMORE, DARRELL LAMONT ....301 EAST 15TH STREET, FRONT ROYAL VA 22630
1928-107 WHITNEY, ARTHUR CARTER 'PINKY' ....D. SEPTEMBER 2, 1987, CENTER, TEXAS
1977-152 WHITSON, EDDIE LEE ....10473 MACKENZIE WAY, DUBLIN OH 43017
1976-102 WHITT, ERNEST LEO ....37370 MORAVIAN, CLINTON TOWNSHIP MI 48036
1989-144 WICKANDER, KEVIN DEAN ....4319 WEST BANFF LANE, GLENDALE AZ 85306
1968-110 WICKER, FLOYD EULISS ....1758 W. GREENSBORO CHAPEL HILL RD, SNOW CAMP NC 27349
1936-097 WICKER, KEMP CASWELL ....D. JUNE 11, 1973, KERNERSVILLE, N.C.
1960-102 WICKERSHAM, DAVID CLIFFORD ....9118 WEST 104TH TER, OVERLAND PARK KS 66212
1992-156 WICKMAN, ROBERT JOE ....6568 CHEYENNE DRIVE, ABRAMS WI 54101
1995-242 WIDGER, CHRISTOPHER JON ....95 FORT MOTT ROAD, PENNSVILLE NJ 08070
1947-095 WIDMAR, ALBERT JOSEPH ....D. OCTOBER 15, 2005, TULSA, OKLA.
1958-101 WIEAND, FRANKLIN DELANO ROOS. 'TED' ....216 WALNUT ST, SLATINGTON PA 18080
1934-108 WIEDEMEYER, CHARLES JOHN ....D. OCTOBER 27, 1979, LAKE GENEVA, FLA.
1979-119 WIEDENBAUER, THOMAS JOHN ....1460 KILRUSH DRIVE, ORMOND BEACH FL 32174
1981-142 WIEGHAUS, THOMAS ROBERT ....9724 EAST 800 NORTH ROAD, GRANT PARK IL 60940
1921-111 WIENEKE, JOHN ....D. MARCH 16, 1933, PLEASANT RIDGE, MICH.
1951-102 WIESLER, ROBERT GEORGE ....2325 INDIAN CUP DRIVE, FLORISSANT MO 63031
1939-125 WIETELMANN, WILLIAM FREDERICK 'WHITEY' ..D. MARCH 26, 2002, SAN DIEGO, CALIF.
1981-143 WIGGINS, ALAN ANTHONY ....D. JANUARY 6, 1991, LOS ANGELES, CALIF.
2002-203 WIGGINS, SCOTT JOSEPH ....18 16TH STREET, NEWPORT KY 41071
2002-204 WIGGINTON, TY ALLEN ....237 I STREET, CHULA VISTA CA 91910
1946-105 WIGHT, WILLIAM ROBERT ....6247 MEADOW VISTA DRIVE, CARMICHAEL CA 95608
1923-142 WIGINGTON, FREDERICK THOMAS ....D. MAY 8, 1980, MESA, ARIZ.
1979-120 WIHTOL, ALEXANDER AMES 'SANDY' ....195 SOUTH SAN ANTONIO ROAD, LOS ALTOS CA 94022
1946-106 WILBER, DELBERT QUENTIN ....D. JULY 18, 2002, ST. PETERSBURG, FLA.
1940-101 WILBORN, CALUDE EDWARD ....D. NOVEMBER 13, 1992, ROXBORO, N.C.
1979-121 WILBORN, THADDEAUS IGLEHART 'TED' ....6671 POCKET ROAD, SACRAMENTO CA 95831
1970-137 WILCOX, MILTON EDWARD ....10064 VERNON AVENUE, HUNTINGTON WOODS MI 48070
1977-153 WILES, RANDALL ....3716 LAKE CATHERINE DRIVE, HARVEY LA 70058
1975-130 WILEY, MARK EUGENE ....22273 VISTA LOGO DRIVE, BOCA RATON FL 33428

1977-154	WILFONG, ROBERT DONALD 'ROB'	126 MAVERICK DRIVE, SAN DIMAS CA 91773
1953-098	WILHELM, CHARLES ERNEST 'SPIDER'	D. OCTOBER 20, 1992, VENICE, FLA.
1952-111	WILHELM, JAMES HOYT 'HOYT'	D. AUGUST 23, 2002, SARASOTA, FLA.
1978-142	WILHELM, JAMES WEBSTER	348 LAUREL WAY, MILL VALLEY CA 94941
1927-105	WILKE, HARRY JOSEPH	D. JUNE 21, 1991, HAMILTON, OHIO
1983-150	WILKERSON, CURTIS VERNON	PO BOX 182993, ARLINGTON TX 76096
2001-192	WILKERSON, STEPHEN BRADLEY 'BRAD'	6076 STATE ROUTE 144, OWENSBORO KY 42303
1941-118	WILKIE, ALDON JAY	D. AUGUST 5, 1992, TUALATIN, ORE.
1989-145	WILKINS, DEAN ALLAN	10212 ROCKWOOD DRIVE, SAN DIEGO CA 92131
1979-122	WILKINS, ERIC LAMOINE	2233 EAST MILLER STREET, SEATTLE WA 98112
1996-186	WILKINS, MARC ALLEN	1636 STATE ROUTE 314 NORTH, MANSFIELD OH 44903
1991-185	WILKINS, RICHARD DAVID 'RICK'	12766 LONGVIEW DRIVE WEST, JACKSONVILLE FL 32223
1944-141	WILKINS, ROBERT LINWOOD	357 JANIE LANE, SHREVEPORT LA 71106
1985-119	WILKINSON, WILLIAM CARL	3738 YUHAS AVENUE, HELENA MT 59602
1944-142	WILKS, THEODORE 'TED'	D. AUGUST 21, 1989, HOUSTON, TEXAS
1957-092	WILL, ROBERT LEE	PO BOX 997, WOODSTOCK IL 60098
1984-128	WILLARD, GERALD DUANE	1421 KUMQUAT PLACE, OXNARD CA 93036
1958-102	WILLEY, CARLTON FRANCIS	BOX 64, CHERRYFIELD ME 04622
1963-125	WILLHITE, JON NICHOLAS 'NICK'	4619 QUAIL VISTA LANE #G, SALT LAKE CITY UT 84117
1980-144	WILLIAMS, ALBERT HAMILTON	PEARL LAGOON, DEPOT ZELOYA, NICARAGUA
1937-108	WILLIAMS, ALMON EDWARD	D. JULY 19, 1969, GROVES, TEXAS
1991-186	WILLIAMS, BERNABE (FIGUEROA)	PO BOX 203, VEGA ALTA PR 00762
1970-138	WILLIAMS, BERNARD	6214 MARKET STREET, EMERYVILLE CA 94608
1959-087	WILLIAMS, BILLY LEO	586 PRINCE EDWARD ROAD, GLEN ELLYN IL 60137
1991-187	WILLIAMS, BRIAN O'NEAL	OLD ADD: RURAL ROUTE 4, KINGSFREE SC 29556
1971-108	WILLIAMS, CHARLES PROSEK	5898 KENDREW DRIVE, PORT ORANGE FL 32127
1981-144	WILLIAMS, DALLAS MCKINLEY	7638 ALLENWOOD CIRCLE, INDIANAPOLIS IN 46208
1989-146	WILLIAMS, DANA LAMOUNT	121 ARLENE DRIVE, NORTH VERSAILLES PA 15137
2001-193	WILLIAMS, DAVID AARON	157 CARTER LANE, CAMDEN DE 19934
1949-091	WILLIAMS, DAVID CARLOUS	14802 ENTERPRISE DRIVE #30C, FARMER'S BRANCH TX 75234
1996-187	WILLIAMS, DAVID KEITH 'KEITH'	1756 NORTH ARIGNON LANE, CLOVIS CA 93619
1944-143	WILLIAMS, DEWEY EDGAR	D. MARCH 19, 2000, WILLISTON, N.D.
1958-103	WILLIAMS, DONALD FRED	2114 CHRISTIANSBURG PIKE NE, FLOYD VA 24091
1963-126	WILLIAMS, DONALD REID	D. DECEMBER 20, 1991, LAJOLLA, CALIF.
1928-108	WILLIAMS, EARL BAXTER	D. MARCH 10, 1958, KNOXVILLE, TENN.
1970-139	WILLIAMS, EARL CRAIG	61 WINSTON DRIVE, SOMERSET NJ 08873
1986-162	WILLIAMS, EDWARD LAQUAN	OLD ADD: 4196 MILL VALLEY COURT, LA MESA CA 91941
1930-092	WILLIAMS, EDWIN DIBRELL 'DIB'	D. APRIL 2, 1992, SEARCY, ARK.
1921-112	WILLIAMS, EVON DANIEL	D. MARCH 23, 1929, SAN CLEMENTE, CALIF.
1984-129	WILLIAMS, FRANK LEE	OLD ADD: 2470 VALLEYVIEW DRIVE, CLARKSTON WA 99403
1945-118	WILLIAMS, FREDERICK 'PAP'	D. NOVEMBER 2, 1993, MERIDIAN, MISS.
1961-108	WILLIAMS, GEORGE	26090 SUMMERDALE DRIVE, SOUTHFIELD MI 48033
1995-243	WILLIAMS, GEORGE ERIK	N 5250 COUNTY ROAD M, WEST SALEM WI 54669
1992-157	WILLIAMS, GERALD FLOYD	PO BOX 47, LA PLACE LA 70068
2005-199	WILLIAMS, GLENN DAVID	OLD ADD: WATTLE GROVE AUSTRALIA
1993-200	WILLIAMS, GREGORY SCOTT 'WOODY'	5110 NEWPOINT DRIVE, FRESNO TX 77545
1969-180	WILLIAMS, JAMES ALFRED	OLD ADD: 1200 SOUTH HIGHLAND AVE #142, FULLERTON CA 92632
1966-100	WILLIAMS, JAMES FRANCIS 'JIMY'	1401 OLDE POST ROAD, PALM HARBOR FL 34683
1999-204	WILLIAMS, JEFFREY F.	OLD ADD: PAGE AUSTRALIA
2003-179	WILLIAMS, JEROME LEE	OLD ADD: LAS VEGAS NV 89125
1986-163	WILLIAMS, KENNETH ROYAL	6430 EAST SIERRA VISTA DRIVE, PARADISE VALLEY AZ 85253
1926-094	WILLIAMS, LEON THEO	D. NOVEMBER 20, 1984, ATLANTA, GA.
1977-155	WILLIAMS, MARK WESTLEY	1453 TRUMANSBURG ROAD, ITHACA NY 14850
1987-151	WILLIAMS, MATTHEW DERRICK	4400 NORTH SCOTTSDALE RD #381, SCOTTSDALE AZ 85251
1983-151	WILLIAMS, MATTHEW EVAN	205 TEAROSE LANE, LAKE JACKSON TX 77566
2000-194	WILLIAMS, MATTHEW TAYLOR	OLD ADD: ATLANTA GA
1992-158	WILLIAMS, MICHAEL DARREN	240 HORSESHOE FARM ROAD, PEMBROKE VA 24136
1986-164	WILLIAMS, MITCHELL STEVEN	67 HIGHBRIDGE BLVD, MEDFORD NJ 08055
2004-202	WILLIAMS, RANDALL DUANE	4500 CYPRESSWOOD DRIVE #828, SPRING TX 77379
1992-159	WILLIAMS, REGINALD BERNARD	10 PERCY STREET, CHARLESTON SC 29403
1985-120	WILLIAMS, REGINALD DEWAYNE	9300 CLEARSTON COVE, COLLIERVILLE TN 38017
1978-143	WILLIAMS, RICHARD ALLEN	1217 WESSMITH, MADERA CA 93638
1951-103	WILLIAMS, RICHARD HIRSCHFIELD	1526 VIA SALARIA COURT, HENDERSON NV 89052
1940-102	WILLIAMS, ROBERT FULTON 'ACE'	D. SEPTEMBER 16, 1999, FORT MYERS, FLA.
1996-188	WILLIAMS, SHAD CLAYTON	4682 EAST CORNELL, FRESNO CA 93703
1958-104	WILLIAMS, STANLEY WILSON	4702 HAYTER AVE, LAKEWOOD CA 90712
1939-126	WILLIAMS, THEODORE SAMUEL	D. JULY 5, 2002, INVERNESS, FLA.
1995-244	WILLIAMS, TODD MICHAEL	16707 WHISPERING GLEN DRIVE, LUTZ FL 33558
1964-128	WILLIAMS, WALTER ALLEN	2417 MONTEREY DR, BROWNWOOD TX 76801
1969-181	WILLIAMS, WILLIAM	3227 RANDOLPH AVENUE, OAKLAND CA 94602
1938-106	WILLIAMS, WOODROW WILSON	D. FEBRUARY 24, 1995, APPOMATTOX, VA.
1997-175	WILLIAMSON, ANTHONY JOSEPH 'ANTONE'	OLD ADD: TEMPE AZ 85282
1987-152	WILLIAMSON, MARK ALAN	OLD ADD: 1983 FAIRHAVEN STREET, LEMON GROVE CA 91945
1928-109	WILLIAMSON, NATHANIEL HOWARD 'HOWIE'	D. AUGUST 15, 1969, TEXARKANA, ARK.
1999-205	WILLIAMSON, SCOTT RYAN	OLD ADD: 1104 MIDDLE CREEK STREET, FRIENDSWOOD TX 77546
1928-110	WILLIAMSON, SILAS ALBERT	D. NOVEMBER 29, 1978, HOT SPRINGS, ARK.
2004-203	WILLINGHAM, JOSHUA DAVID	OLD ADD: FLORENCE AL
1930-093	WILLINGHAM, THOMAS HUGH 'HUGH'	D. JUNE 15, 1988, EL RENO, OKLA.
1984-130	WILLIS, CARL BLAKE	6811 LIPSCOMB DRIVE, DURHAM NC 27712
1925-115	WILLIS, CHARLES WILLIAM 'LEFTY'	D. MAY 10, 1962, BETHESDA, MD.
1963-127	WILLIS, DALE JEROME	3415 HAYES BAYOU DRIVE, RUSKIN FL 33570
2003-180	WILLIS, DONTRELLE WAYNE	2805 SAN LEANDRO BLVD #106, SAN LEANDRO CA 94578
1953-099	WILLIS, JAMES GLADDEN	BOX 35, BOYCE LA 71409
1947-096	WILLIS, LESTER EVANS	D. JANUARY 22, 1982, JASPER, TEXAS
1977-156	WILLIS, MICHAEL HENRY	6234 TAGGART, HOUSTON TX 77007
1966-101	WILLIS, RONALD EARL	D. NOVEMBER 21, 1977, MEMPHIS, TENN.

2006-213	WILLITS, REGGIE GENE	RURAL ROUTE 1, FORT COBB OK 73038
1925-116	WILLOUGHBY, CLAUDE WILLIAM	D. AUGUST 14, 1973, MCPHERSON, KAN.
1971-109	WILLOUGHBY, JAMES ARTHUR	PO BOX 707, EUFAULA OK 74432
1977-157	WILLS, ELLIOTT TAYLOR 'BUMP'	1124 SOUTH ROBINHOOD STREET, SPOKANE VALLEY WA 99206
1983-152	WILLS, FRANK LEE	733 GEN. PERSHING ST, NEW ORLEANS LA 70115
1959-088	WILLS, MAURICE MORNING	5 DALTON VALLEY DRIVE, SAINT PETERS MO 63376
1959-089	WILLS, THEODORE CARL	10585 EAST DUCKPOINT WAY, CLOVIS CA 93611
1989-147	WILMET, PAUL RICHARD	PO BOX 330074, NASHVILLE TN 37203
1934-109	WILSHERE, VERNON SPRAGUE 'WHITEY'	D. MAY 23, 1985, COOPERSTOWN, N.Y.
1973-131	WILSHUSEN, TERRY WAYNE	D. DECEMBER 1, 2000, LOMITA, CALIF.
1951-104	WILSON, ARCHIE CLIFTON	1620 WOODLAND STREET SE, DECATUR AL 35601
1951-105	WILSON, ARTHUR LEE	2226 NE TENTH AVENUE, PORTLAND OR 97212
2006-214	WILSON, BRIAN PATRICK	OLD ADD: 43 ROYAL CREST DRIVE, NASHUA NH 03060
1931-100	WILSON, CHARLES WOODROW	D. DECEMBER 19, 1970, ROCHESTER, N.Y.
2005-200	WILSON, CHRISTOPHER JOHN 'C. J.'	OLD ADD: HUNTINGTON BEACH CA
1989-148	WILSON, CRAIG	8241 DRYBANK DRIVE, HUNTINGTON BEACH CA 92646
2001-194	WILSON, CRAIG ALAN	OLD ADD: HUNTINGTON BEACH CA
1998-200	WILSON, CRAIG FRANKLIN	OLD ADD: PHOENIX AZ 85001
1992-160	WILSON, DANIEL ALLEN	2161 EAST INTERLAKEN BLVD, SEATTLE WA 98112
1996-189	WILSON, DESI BERNARD	OLD ADD: GLEN COVE NY 11542
1966-102	WILSON, DONALD EDWARD	D. JANUARY 5, 1975, HOUSTON, TEXAS
1958-105	WILSON, DUANE LEWIS	735 SOUTH VINE STREET, WICHITA KS 67213
1959-090	WILSON, EARL LAWRENCE	D. APRIL 23, 2005, DETROIT, MICH.
1936-098	WILSON, EDWARD FRANCIS	D. APRIL 11, 1979, HAMDEN, CONN.
1997-176	WILSON, ENRIQUE MARTES	OLD ADD: 1310 BOBBY LANE, WESTLAKE OH 44145
1924-115	WILSON, FRANCIS EDWARD	D. NOVEMBER 25, 1974, LEICESTER, MASS.
1995-245	WILSON, GARY MORRIS	1021 GLENDALE DRIVE, ARCATA CA 95521
1979-123	WILSON, GARY STEVEN	713 OUACHITA ROAD 64, CAMDEN AR 71701
1934-110	WILSON, GEORGE PEACOCK 'ICEHOUSE'	D. OCTOBER 13, 1973, MORAGA, CALIF.
1952-112	WILSON, GEORGE WASHINGTON	D. OCTOBER 29, 1974, GASTONIA, N.C.
1982-138	WILSON, GLENN DWIGHT	7123 DIAMOND FALLS LANE, SPRING TX 77389
1924-116	WILSON, GOMER RUSSELL 'TEX'	D. SEPTEMBER 15, 1946, SULPHUR SPRINGS, TEXAS
1948-111	WILSON, GRADY HERBERT	D. JULY 23, 2003, COLUMBUS, GA.
2001-195	WILSON, JACK EUGENE	1750 EAST AVENUE DE LAS ORES, THOUSAND OAKS CA 91359
1923-143	WILSON, JAMES	D. JUNE 1, 1947, PALMETTO, FLA.
1945-119	WILSON, JAMES ALGER	D. SEPTEMBER 2, 1986, NEWPORT BEACH, CALIF.
1985-121	WILSON, JAMES GEORGE	8112 NW BACON ROAD, VANCOUVER WA 98665
1934-111	WILSON, JOHN FRANCIS 'BLACK JACK'	D. APRIL 19, 1995, EDMONDS, WASH.
1927-106	WILSON, JOHN SAMUEL	D. AUGUST 27, 1980, CHATTANOOGA, TENN.
2005-201	WILSON, JOSHUA AARON	OLD ADD: PITTSBURGH PA
2000-195	WILSON, KRISTOPHER KYLE	219 HEMINGWAY DRIVE, OLDSMAR FL 34677
1923-144	WILSON, LEWIS ROBERT 'HACK'	D. NOVEMBER 23, 1948, BALTIMORE, MD.
1940-103	WILSON, MAX	D. JANUARY 2, 1977, GREENSBORO, N.C.
1983-153	WILSON, MICHAEL 'TACK'	1089 OLDE HINGE WAY, SNELLVILLE GA 30078
1993-201	WILSON, NIGEL EDWARD	110 BURCHR ROAD AJAX ON, L1S 2R2 CANADA
1996-190	WILSON, PAUL ANTHONY	113 DUNCAN TRAIL, LONGWOOD FL 32779
1998-201	WILSON, PRESTON JAMES RICHARD	C/O FMP, 8001 FORYSTH BLVD #2, CLAYTON MO 63105
1958-106	WILSON, ROBERT	D. APRIL 23, 1985, DALLAS, TEXAS
1951-106	WILSON, ROBERT JAMES 'RED'	806 CABOT LANE, MADISON WI 53711
1928-111	WILSON, ROY EDWARD	D. DECEMBER 3, 1969, CLARION, IOWA
1960-103	WILSON, SAMMY ONEIL 'NEIL'	4300 HIGHWAY 412 WEST, LEXINGTON TN 38351
1921-113	WILSON, SAMUEL MARSHALL 'MIKE'	D. MAY 16, 1978, BOYNTON BEACH, FLA.
1988-138	WILSON, STEPHEN DOUGLAS	OLD ADD: 8446 AQUA DRIVE, VANCOUVER BC V5P 4S2 CANADA
2001-196	WILSON, THOMAS LEROY	2679 TANGLEWOOD COURT, LAKE HAVASU CITY AZ 86403
1988-139	WILSON, TREVOR KIRK	11857 SOUTH WHITE LANE, OREGON CITY OR 97045
1999-206	WILSON, VANCE ALLEN	6368 ELIZABETH AVENUE, SPRINGDALE AR 72762
1945-120	WILSON, WALTER WOOD	D. APRIL 17, 1994, BREMEN, GA.
1920-131	WILSON, WILLIAM CLARENCE 'MUTT'	D. AUGUST 31, 1962, WILDWOOD, FLA.
1950-104	WILSON, WILLIAM DONALD	64245 DORAL DRIVE, DESERT HOT SPRINGS CA 92240
1969-182	WILSON, WILLIAM HARLAN	D. AUGUST 11, 1993, PHILADELPHIA, PA.
1980-145	WILSON, WILLIAM HAYWARD 'MOOKIE'	OLD ADD: 127 ROSA WILSON ROAD, EASTOVER SC 29044
1976-103	WILSON, WILLIE JAMES	14 PEGALLY COURT, SCARSBORO ON M1L 4L9 CANADA
1926-095	WILTSE, HAROLD JAMES	D. NOVEMBER 2, 1983, BUNKIE, LA.
1956-087	WINCENIAK, EDWARD JOSEPH	10828 SOUTH AVENUE O, CHICAGO IL 60617
1997-177	WINCHESTER, SCOTT JOSEPH	4705 OAKRIDGE DRIVE, MIDLAND MI 48640
1959-091	WINDHORN, GORDON RAY	145 BENT CREEK RD, DANVILLE VA 24540
1928-112	WINDLE, WILLIS BREWER	D. DECEMBER 8, 1981, CORPUS CHRISTI TX.
2006-215	WINDSOR, JASON DAVID	40091 NORTH WESTRAY WAY, QUEEN CREEK AZ 85242
1960-104	WINE, ROBERT PAUL	2614 WOODLAND AVENUE, NORRISTOWN PA 19403
1986-165	WINE, ROBERT PAUL, JR. 'ROBBIE'	OKLAHOMA STATE BASEBALL, ALLIE REYNOLDS STADIUM, STILLWATER OK 74078
1929-108	WINEAPPLE, EDWARD	D. JULY 23, 1996, DELRAY BEACH, FLA.
1930-094	WINEGARNER, RALPH LEE	D. APRIL 14, 1988, WICHITA, KAN.
1973-132	WINFIELD, DAVID MARK	2235 STRATFORD CIRCLE, LOS ANGELES CA 90077
1932-092	WINFORD, JAMES HEAD	D. DECEMBER 16, 1970, MIAMI, OKLA.
1924-117	WINGARD, ERNEST JAMES	D. JANUARY 17, 1977, PRATTVILLE, ALA.
1923-145	WINGFIELD, FREDERICK DAVIS 'TED'	D. JULY 18, 1975, JOHNSON CITY, TENN.
1920-132	WINGO, EDMOND ARMAND	D. DECEMBER 5, 1964, LACHINE, QUE.
1999-207	WINKELSAS, JOSEPH	OLD ADD: 4001 GAELIC LANE, GLEN ALLEN VA 23060
1973-133	WINKLES, BOBBY BROOKS	78452 CALLE HUERTA, LAQUINTA CA 92253
1998-202	WINN, DWIGHT RANDOLPH 'RANDY'	59 LEEDS COURT EAST, DANVILLE CA 94526
1983-154	WINN, JAMES FRANCIS	3440 SOUTH DELAWARE #123, SPRINGFIELD MO 65804
1984-131	WINNINGHAM, HERMAN SON	1542 BELLEVILLE ROAD, ORANGEBURG SC 29115
1930-095	WINSETT, JOHN THOMAS 'TOM'	D. JULY 20, 1987, MEMPHIS, TENN.
1997-178	WINSTON, DARRIN ALEXANDER	14 CALDWELL ROAD, EDISON NJ 08817
1933-067	WINSTON, HENRY RUDOLPH	D. FEBRUARY 7, 1974, JACKSONVILLE, FLA.
1924-118	WINTERS, CLARENCE JOHN	D. JUNE 29, 1945, DETROIT, MICH.

1989-149	WINTERS, MATTHEW LITTLETON	1201 FOXFIRE DRIVE, GREENSBORO NC 27410
1978-144	WIRTH, ALAN LEE	2858 EAST JASMINE STREET, MESA AZ 85213
1921-114	WIRTS, ELWOOD VERNON 'KETTLE'	D. JULY 12, 1968, SACRAMENTO, CALIF.
1932-093	WISE, ARCHIBALD EDWIN	D. FEBRUARY 2, 1978, WAXAHACHIE, TEXAS
1930-096	WISE, HUGH EDWARD	D. JULY 21, 1987, PLANTATION, FLA.
1957-093	WISE, KENDALL COLE 'CASEY'	D. FEBRUARY 20, 2007, NAPLES, FLA.
2000-196	WISE, LARRY DEWAYNE 'DEWAYNE'	709 OLD LEXINGTON WAY, CHAPIN SC 29036
2000-197	WISE, MATTHEW JOHN	11627 EAST TWILIGHT COURT, CHANDLER AZ 85249
1964-129	WISE, RICHARD CHARLES 'RICK'	8235 SW 184TH AVENUE, BEAVERTON OR 97007
1944-144	WISE, ROY OGDEN 'OGDEN '	14851 JEFFREY ROAD, IRVINE CA 92618
1964-130	WISSMAN, DAVID ALVIN	PO BOX 38, DERBY VT 05829
1934-112	WISTERT, FRANCIS MICHAEL 'WHITEY'	D. APRIL 23, 1985, PAINESVILLE, OHIO
1996-191	WITASICK, GERALD ALPHONSE 'JAY'	923 EAST BROADWAY, BEL AIR MD 21014
1940-104	WITEK, NICHOLAS JOSEPH 'MICKEY'	D. AUGUST 24, 1990, KINGSTON, PA.
1998-203	WITHEM, SHANNON BOLT	39668 DORCHESTER CIRCLE, CANTON MI 48188
1920-133	WITHROW, FRANK BLAINE	D. SEPTEMBER 5, 1966, OMAHA, NEB.
1963-128	WITHROW, RAYMOND WALLACE 'CORKY'	6225 SUTHERLIN LANE, UTICA KY 42376
1991-188	WITMEYER, RONALD HERMAN	ATH. DEPT.,STANFORD UNIV., STANFORD CA 94305
1957-094	WITT, GEORGE ADRIAN	2209 CATALINA ST, LAGUNA BEACH CA 92651
1998-204	WITT, KEVIN JOSEPH	6350 CONCO BAY DRIVE, HOUSTON TX 77041
1981-145	WITT, MICHAEL ATWATER	37 POPPY HILLS ROAD, LAGUNA NIGUEL CA 92677
1986-166	WITT, ROBERT ANDREW	4601 WINEWOOD COURT, COLLEYVILLE TX 76034
1946-107	WITTE, JEROME CHARLES	D. APRIL 27, 2002, HOUSTON, TEXAS
1938-107	WITTIG, JOHN CARL	D. FEBRUARY 24, 1999, NASSAWADOX, VA.
1974-142	WOCKENFUSS, JOHN BILTON	26 WALLAMSEY LANE, CHESAPEAKE CITY MD 21915
1923-146	WOEHR, ANDREW EMIL	D. JULY 24, 1990, FORT WAYNE, IND.
1991-189	WOHLERS, MARK EDWARD	OLD ADD: 6115 ABBOTS BRIDGE ROAD, DULUTH GA 30097
1972-121	WOHLFORD, JAMES EUGENE	24186 LOMITAS DRIVE, WOODLAKE CA 93286
1995-246	WOJCIEHOWSKI, STEVEN JOSEPH	OLD ADD: 1033 BURNHAM 3304, CALUMET CITY IL 60409
1962-148	WOJCIK, JOHN JOSEPH	1072 EASTERN PARKWAY, LOUISVILLE KY 40217
1954-118	WOJEY, PETER PAUL	D. APRIL 23, 1991, MOBILE, ALA.
1985-122	WOJNA, EDWARD DAVID	225 SUSSEX PLACE, CARSON CITY NV 89703
1995-247	WOLCOTT, ROBERT WILLIAM	3323 BRYSON WAY, MEDFORD OR 97504
1999-208	WOLF, RANDALL CHRISTOPHER	8054 ROYER AVENUE, CANOGA PARK CA 91304
1927-107	WOLF, RAYMOND BERNARD	D. OCTOBER 6, 1979, FORT WORTH, TEXAS
1969-183	WOLF, WALTER BECK	PO BOX 9, YORBA LINDA CA 92686
1921-115	WOLF, WALTER FRANCIS 'LEFTY'	D. SEPTEMBER 25, 1971, NEW ORLEANS, LA.
1923-147	WOLFE, CHARLES HENRY	D. NOVEMBER 27, 1957, SCHELLSBURG, PA.
1952-113	WOLFE, EDWARD ANTHONY	470 LABRANT ROAD, KALISPELL MT 59901
1977-158	WOLFE, LAURENCE MARCH	24949 SMOKEWOOD WAY, STEVENSON RANCH CA 91381
1941-119	WOLFF, ROGER FRANCIS	D. MARCH 23, 1994, CHESTER, ILL.
1993-202	WOMACK, ANTHONY DARRELL 'TONY'	OLD ADD: 3619 EAST NAMBE COURT, PHOENIX AZ 85044
1966-103	WOMACK, HORACE GUY 'DOOLEY'	209 WEEPING CHERRY LANE, COLUMBIA SC 29212
1926-096	WOMACK, SIDNEY KIRK	D. AUGUST 28, 1958, JACKSON, MISS.
1930-097	WOOD, CHARLES ASHER 'SPADES'	D. MAY 18, 1986, WICHITA, KAN.
1923-148	WOOD, CHARLES SPENCER 'DOC'	D. NOVEMBER 3, 1974, NEW ORLEANS, LA.
1991-190	WOOD, EDWARD ROBERT 'TED'	OLD ADD: 4102 DAUPHINE STREET, NEW ORLEANS LA 70117
1961-109	WOOD, JACOB	9129 DAYTONA DRIVE, PENSACOLA FL 32506
1998-205	WOOD, JASON WILLIAM	9899 NORTH CASCADE DRIVE, FRESNO CA 93720
1944-145	WOOD, JOE FRANK	D. OCTOBER 10, 2002, OLD SAYBROOK, CONN.
1943-144	WOOD, JOSEPH PERRY	D. MARCH 25, 1985, HOUSTON, TEXAS
1948-112	WOOD, KENNETH LANIER	600A 10TH AVENUE SOUTH, NORTH MYRTLE BEACH SC 29582
1998-206	WOOD, KERRY LEE	400 RANDAL WAY #106, SPRING TX 77388
2003-181	WOOD, MICHAEL BURTON	1199 CHERLYNN TERRACE, WEST PALM BEACH FL 33406
1961-110	WOOD, WILBUR FORRESTER	3 ELMSBROOK ROAD, BEDFORD MA 01730
1920-134	WOODALL, CHARLES LAWRENCE 'LARRY'	D. MAY 6, 1963, CAMBRIDGE, MASS.
1994-114	WOODALL, DAVID BRADLEY 'BRAD'	3539 JOHN MUIR DRIVE, MIDDLETON WI 53562
1978-145	WOODARD, DARRELL LEE	1227 EAST 69TH STREET, LOS ANGELES CA 90001
1985-123	WOODARD, MICHAEL CARY	PO BOX 35, MAYWOOD IL 60153
1997-179	WOODARD, STEVEN LARRY	800 FROST COURT SW, HARTSELLE AL 35640
1944-146	WOODEND, GEORGE ANTHONY	D. FEBRUARY 6, 1980, HARTFORD, CONN.
1956-088	WOODESHICK, HAROLD JOSEPH	803 WYCLIFFE DR, HOUSTON TX 77079
1943-145	WOODLING, EUGENE RICHARD	D. JUNE 2, 2001, BARBERTON, OHIO
1977-159	WOODS, ALVIS	2518 60TH AVE, OAKLAND CA 94605
1976-104	WOODS, GARY LEE	PO BOX 151, SOLVANG CA 93464
1943-146	WOODS, GEORGE ROWLAND 'PINKY'	D. OCTOBER 30, 1982, LOS ANGELES, CALIF.
2005-202	WOODS, JACOB THOMAS	OLD ADD: KINGSBURG CA
1957-095	WOODS, JAMES JEROME	4509 GARDENIA AVENUE, KEYES CA 95328
1924-119	WOODS, JOHN FULTON	D. OCTOBER 4, 1946, NORFOLK, VA.
1969-184	WOODS, RONALD LAWRENCE	5209 DESERT STAR DRIVE, LAS VEGAS NV 89130
1969-185	WOODSON, RICHARD LEE	27879 PANORAMA HILLS DRIVE, MENIFEE CA 92584
1987-153	WOODSON, TRACY MICHAEL	1559 BYFIELD PKWY, VALPARAISO IN 46385
1992-161	WOODSON, WALTER BROWNE 'KERRY'	19392 LA SERENA DRIVE, FORT MYERS FL 33967
1999-209	WOODWARD, CHRISTOPHER MICHAEL	15049 HOWELLHURST DRIVE, BALDWIN PARK CA 91706
1985-124	WOODWARD, ROBERT JOHN	HCR 63 BOX 43A EASTMAN HILL, LEBANON NH 03766
1963-129	WOODWARD, WILLIAM FREDERICK 'WOODY'	10 SAN MARCO COURT, PALM COAST FL 32137
2005-203	WOODYARD, MARK ANTHONY	PO BOX 833, GRAND BAY AL 36541
1955-137	WOOLDRIDGE, FLOYD LEWIS	214 BARBER ST, GREENFIELD MO 65661
1947-097	WOOTEN, EARL HAZELL	D. AUGUST 12, 2006, WILLIAMSTON, N.C.
2000-198	WOOTEN, WILLIAM SHAWN 'SHAWN'	7966 LEUCITE AVENUE, RANCHO CUCAMONGA CA 91730
1938-108	WORKMAN, CHARLES THOMAS	D. JANUARY 3, 1953, KANSAS CITY, MO.
1924-120	WORKMAN, HARRY HALL 'HOGE'	D. MAY 20, 1972, FORT MYERS, FLA.
1950-105	WORKMAN, HENRY KILGARIFF	307 19TH STREET, SANTA MONICA CA 90402
1993-203	WORRELL, TIMOTHY HAROLD	4719 WEST CORTEZ PLACE, GLENDALE AZ 85310
1985-125	WORRELL, TODD ROLAND	13320 BUCKLAND HILL ROAD, SAINT LOUIS MO 63131
1978-146	WORTHAM, RICHARD COOPER	10247 MISSEL THRUSH DRIVE, AUSTIN TX 78750

1953-100	WORTHINGTON, ALLAN FULTON	12070 HIGHWAY 55, STERRETT AL 35147
1988-140	WORTHINGTON, CRAIG RICHARD	10019 MATTOCK AVENUE, DOWNEY CA 90240
1931-101	WORTHINGTON, ROBERT LEE 'RED'	D. DECEMBER 8, 1963, LOS ANGELES, CALIF.
1983-155	WOTUS, RONALD ALLAN	1902 STRAYHORN ROAD, PLEASANT HILL CA 94523
1933-068	WRIGHT, ALBERT EDGAR	D. NOVEMBER 13, 1998, OAKLAND, CALIF.
1935-115	WRIGHT, ALBERT OWEN 'AB'	D. MAY 23, 1995, MUSKOGEE, OKLA.
1966-104	WRIGHT, CLYDE	528 JEANINE AVENUE, ANAHEIM CA 92806
2004-204	WRIGHT, DAVID ALLEN	1017 ENGLISH OAK DRIVE, SUFFOLK VA 23434
1924-121	WRIGHT, FOREST GLENN 'GLENN'	D. APRIL 6, 1984, OLATHE, KAN.
1982-139	WRIGHT, GEORGE DEWITT	4228 NE 18TH STREET, OKLAHOMA CITY OK 73121
1945-121	WRIGHT, HENDERSON EDWARD 'ED'	D. NOVEMBER 19, 1995, DYERSBURG, TENN.
1927-108	WRIGHT, JAMES	D. APRIL 12, 1963, OAKLAND, CALIF.
1978-147	WRIGHT, JAMES CLIFTON	549 EAST RANDALL STREET, COOPERSVILLE MI 49404
1981-146	WRIGHT, JAMES LEON	513 WEST WYNDERMERE COURT, PEORIA IL 61614
1982-140	WRIGHT, JAMES RICHARD 'RICKY'	2502 CLARK LANE, PARIS TX 75460
1996-192	WRIGHT, JAMEY ALAN	12801 LORIEN WAY, OKLAHOMA CITY OK 73170
1997-180	WRIGHT, JARET SAMUEL	1423 SANTIAGO DRIVE, NEWPORT BEACH CA 92660
2001-197	WRIGHT, JONATHAN DANIEL 'DAN'	PO BOX 55, CAVE SPRINGS AR 72718
1970-140	WRIGHT, KENNETH WARREN	1651 ORA DRIVE, PENSACOLA FL 32506
1954-119	WRIGHT, MELVIN JAMES	D. MAY 16, 1983, HOUSTON, TEXAS
2002-205	WRIGHT, RONALD WADE	310 SOUTH 2100 EAST, SAINT GEORGE UT 84790
1956-089	WRIGHT, ROY EARL	331 PINEHURST CIR, CHICKAMAUGA GA 30707
1938-109	WRIGHT, TAFT SHEDRON	D. OCTOBER 22, 1981, ORLANDO, FLA.
1948-113	WRIGHT, THOMAS EVERETT	1116 POPLAR SPRINGS CH ROAD, SHELBY NC 28152
1920-135	WRIGHTSTONE, RUSSELL GUY	D. MARCH 1, 1969, HARRISBURG, PA.
1988-141	WRONA, RICHARD JAMES 'RICK'	2946 EAST 57TH STREET, TULSA OK 74105
2004-205	WUERTZ, MICHAEL JAMES	3840 WEST 67TH PLACE, CHICAGO IL 60629
1929-109	WUESTLING, GEORGE 'YATS'	D. APRIL 26, 1970, ST. LOUIS, MO.
2000-199	WUNSCH, KELLY DOUGLAS	11613 HUNTERS GREEN TRAIL, AUSTIN TX 78732
1944-147	WURM, FRANK JAMES	D. SEPTEMBER 19, 1993, GLENS FALLS, N.Y.
1961-111	WYATT, JOHN	D. APRIL 6, 1998, OMAHA, NEB.
1929-110	WYATT, JOHN WHITLOW 'WHIT'	D. JULY 17, 1999, BUCHANAN, GA.
1924-122	WYATT, LORAL JOHN 'JOE'	D. DECEMBER 5, 1970, OBLONG, ILL.
1976-105	WYNEGAR, HAROLD DELANO 'BUTCH'	PO BOX 915811, LONGWOOD FL 32791
1939-127	WYNN, EARLY	D. APRIL 4, 1999, VENICE, FLA.
1963-130	WYNN, JAMES SHERMAN	5507 SANDY FIELD COURT, ROSHARON TX 77583
1983-156	WYNNE, MARVELL	39640 DEL VAL DRIVE, MURRIETA CA 92562
1967-115	WYNNE, WILLIAM VERNON	7722 GREENWICH COURT WEST, JACKSONVILLE FL 32216
1942-108	WYROSTEK, JOHN BARNEY	D. DECEMBER 12, 1986, ST.LOUIS, MO.
1942-109	WYSE, HENRY WASHINGTON	D. OCTOBER 22, 2000, PRYOR, OKLA.
1930-098	WYSONG, HARLIN 'BIFF'	D. AUGUST 7, 1951, XENIA, OHIO

Y

2005-204	YABU, KEIICHI	796 VESPUCCI LANE, FOSTER CITY CA 94404
1996-193	YAN, ESTEBAN LUIS	OLD ADD: LA HIGUERA DOM REP
1972-122	YANCY, HUGH	2743 18TH STREET, SARASOTA FL 34234
1942-110	YANKOWSKI, GEORGE EDWARD	12 POTTER ROAD, LEXINGTON MA 02421
1999-210	YARNALL, HARVEY EDWARD 'ED'	9837 VOUVRAY DRIVE, BATON ROUGE LA 70817
1926-097	YARNALL, WALDO WARD 'RUSTY'	D. OCTOBER 9, 1985, LOWELL, MASS.
1922-137	YARRISON, BYRON WARDSWORTH 'RUBE'	D. APRIL 22, 1977, WILLIAMSPORT, PA.
1921-116	YARYAN, CLARENCE EVERETT 'YAM'	D. NOVEMBER 16, 1964, BIRMINGHAM, ALA.
1961-112	YASTRZEMSKI, CARL MICHAEL	255 STATE STREET, BOSTON MA 02109
1971-110	YATES, ALBERT ARTHUR	999 INLET CIRCLE #A104, VENICE FL 34285
2004-206	YATES, TYLER KALI	3718 OMAO ROAD, KOLOA HI 96756
1924-123	YDE, EMIL OGDEN	D. DECEMBER 4, 1968, LEESBURG, FLA.
1972-123	YEAGER, STEPHEN WAYNE	PO BOX 34184, GRANADA HILLS CA 91394
1922-138	YEARGIN, JAMES ALMOND	D. MAY 8, 1937, GREENVILLE, S.C.
1989-150	YELDING, ERIC GIRARD	PO BOX 325, MONTROSE AL 36559
1963-131	YELLEN, LAWRENCE ALLEN	3886 TOCCOA FALLS DRIVE, DULUTH GA 30097
1921-117	YELLOW HORSE, MOSES J. 'CHIEF'	D. APRIL 10, 1964, PAWNEE, OKLA.
1927-109	YERKES, CHARLES CARROLL	D. DECEMBER 20, 1950, OAKLAND, CALIF.
1985-126	YETT, RICHARD MARTIN	5840 EAST FAIRBROOK CIRCLE, MESA AZ 85205
1957-096	YEWCIC, THOMAS	31 CHEORKEE RD, ARLINGTON MA 02174
1951-107	YOCHIM, LEONARD JOSEPH	316 NELSON DRIVE, NEW ORLEANS LA 70123
1948-114	YOCHIM, RAYMOND AUSTIN ALOYSIUS	D. JANUARY 26, 2002, NEW ORLEANS, LA.
1970-141	YORK, JAMES HARLAN	31262 VIA DEL VERDE, SAN JUAN CAPISTRANO CA 92675
1990-170	YORK, MICHAEL DAVID	8001 SOUTH 84TH COURT, JUSTICE IL 60458
1934-113	YORK, RUDOLPH PRESTON	D. FEBRUARY 5, 1970, ROME, GA.
1944-148	YORK, TONY BATTEN	D. APRIL 18, 1970, HILLSBORO, TEXAS
1998-207	YOSHII, MASATO	OLD ADD: TOKYO JAPAN
1980-146	YOST, EDGAR FREDERICK 'NED'	111 TRAILWAY DRIVE, CLINTON MS 39056
1944-149	YOST, EDWARD FRED JOSEPH	48 OAKRIDGE ROAD, WELLESLEY MA 02181
1921-118	YOTER, ELMER ELLSWORTH	D. JULY 26, 1966, CAMP HILL, PA.
2004-207	YOUKILIS, KEVIN E.	11661 CEDARVIEW DRIVE, CINCINNATI OH 45249
2006-216	YOUMAN, SHANE DEMOND	PO BOX 14125, NEW IBERIA LA 70562
1985-127	YOUMANS, FLOYD EVERETT	1915 EAST NOEL STREET, TAMPA FL 33610
1991-191	YOUNG, ANTHONY WAYNE	13107 ELLESMERE DRIVE, HOUSTON TX 77015
1992-162	YOUNG, BRYAN OWEN 'PETE'	PO BOX 95, SUMMIT MS 39666
2006-217	YOUNG, CHRISTOPHER BRANDON	OLD ADD: HOUSTON TX
2004-208	YOUNG, CHRISTOPHER RYAN	7248 LA COSA DRIVE, DALLAS TX 75248
1990-171	YOUNG, CLIFFORD RAPHAEL	D. NOVEMBER 4, 1993, MONTGOMERY COUNTY, TEXAS
1983-157	YOUNG, CURTIS ALLEN	10800 EAST CACTUS ROAD #2, SCOTTSDALE AZ 85259
2000-200	YOUNG, DANIEL BRACEY	OLD ADD: WOODBURY TN
1937-109	YOUNG, DELMER EDWARD	D. DECEMBER 8, 1979, SAN FRANCISCO, CALIF.

2006-218	YOUNG, DELMON DAMARCUS	OLD ADD: CAMARILLO CA
2006-219	YOUNG, DELWYN RUDY	OLD ADD: LOS ANGELES CA
1996-194	YOUNG, DMITRI DELL	3823 PINE LAKE DRIVE, FORT LAUDERDALE FL 33332
1965-117	YOUNG, DONALD WAYNE	OLD ADD: 8105 WEST US HWY 34, LOVELAND CO 80537
1992-163	YOUNG, ERIC ORLANDO	2205 WARWICK WAY #200, MARRIOTTSVILLE MD 21104
1994-115	YOUNG, ERNEST WESLEY	999 EAST INDIAN WELLS PLACE, CHANDLER AZ 85249
1987-154	YOUNG, GERALD ANTHONY	10014 RAIN CLOUD DRIVE, HOUSTON TX 77095
2003-182	YOUNG, JASON KARIYA	OLD ADD: BODEGA CA 94922
1971-111	YOUNG, JOHN THOMAS	OLD ADD: 849 NAPOLEON RD #28, BOWLING GREEN OH 43402
1992-164	YOUNG, KEVIN STACEY	4793 EAST CHARLES DRIVE, PARADISE VALLEY AZ 85253
1978-148	YOUNG, KIP LANE	OLD ADD: 2570 US HWY 62, WINCHESTER OH 45697
1933-069	YOUNG, LEMUEL FLOYD 'PEP'	D. JANUARY 14, 1962, JAMESTOWN, N.C.
1983-158	YOUNG, MATTHEW JOHN	471 MAYLIN STREET, PASADENA CA 91105
2000-201	YOUNG, MICHAEL BRIAN	4685 NORTH EDENFIELD AVENUE, COVINA CA 91723
1982-141	YOUNG, MICHAEL DARREN	5 NORTHWICH COURT, SACRAMENTO CA 95832
1936-099	YOUNG, NORMAN ROBERT 'BABE'	D. DECEMBER 25, 1983, EVERETT, MASS.
1951-108	YOUNG, RICHARD ENNIS	2311 SOUTH FARNSWORTH DRIVE #64, MESA AZ 85208
1948-115	YOUNG, ROBERT GEORGE	D. JANUARY 28, 1985, BALTIMORE, MD.
1931-102	YOUNG, RUSSELL CHARLES	D. MAY 13, 1984, ROSEVILLE, CALIF.
1998-208	YOUNG, TIMOTHY R	20730 SE SHERRY AVENUE, BLOUNTSTOWN FL 32424
2005-205	YOUNG, WALTER EARNEST	134 CENTER STREET, PURVIS MS 39475
1922-139	YOUNGBLOOD, ARTHUR CLYDE 'CHIEF'	D. JULY 6, 1968, AMARILLO, TEXAS
1976-106	YOUNGBLOOD, JOEL RANDOLPH	4446 EAST CAMELBACK ROAD #113, PHOENIX AZ 85018
1937-110	YOUNT, FLOYD EDWIN 'EDDIE'	D. OCTOBER 26, 1973, NEWTON, N.C.
1971-112	YOUNT, LAWRENCE KING	5040 EAST SHEA #254, SCOTTSDALE AZ 85254
1974-143	YOUNT, ROBIN R.	5001 EAST ARABIAN WAY, PARADISE VALLEY AZ 85253
1924-124	YOWELL, CARL COLUMBUS	D. JULY 27, 1985, JACKSONVILLE, TEXAS
1952-114	YUHAS, JOHN EDWARD 'EDDIE'	D. JULY 6, 1986, WINSTON-SALEM, N.C.
1978-149	YURAK, JEFFREY LYNN	18024 26TH STREET COURT EAST, SUMMER WA 98390
1947-098	YVARS, SALVADOR ANTHONY	1 ALLEN STREET, VALHALLA NY 10595

Z

1945-122	ZABALA, ADRIAN RODRIGUEZ	D. JANUARY 4, 2002, JACKSONVILLE, FLA.
1944-150	ZACHARY, ALBERT MYRON 'CHINK '	D. JUNE 24, 2006, ROME, N.Y.
1963-132	ZACHARY, WILLIAM CHRIS	D. APRIL 19, 2003, KNOXVILLE, TENN.
1976-107	ZACHRY, PATRICK PAUL	7611 BOSQUE BLVD, WACO TX 76712
1973-134	ZAHN, GEOFFREY CLAYTON	6536 WALSH ROAD, DEXTER MI 48130
1923-149	ZAHNISER, PAUL VERNON	D. SEPTEMBER 26, 1964, KLAMATH FALLS, ORE.
1944-151	ZAK, FRANK THOMAS	D. FEBRUARY 6, 1972, PASSAIC, N.J.
2001-198	ZAMBRANO, CARLOS ALBERTO	OLD ADD: PUERTO CABELLO VENEZ
1993-204	ZAMBRANO, EDUARDO JOSE	166 N. 44-147 COROMOTO MARACAIBO, VENEZUELA
2001-199	ZAMBRANO, VICTOR MANUEL	OLD ADD: VALENCIA VENEZUELA
1974-144	ZAMORA, OSCAR JOSE	OLD ADD: 1612 SW FIRST STREET, MIAMI FL 33135
1958-107	ZANNI, DOMINICK THOMAS	7 SUSSEX AVE NORTH, MASSAPEQUA NY 11758
1933-070	ZAPUSTAS, JOSEPH JOHN	D. JANUARY 14, 2001, RANDOLPH, MASS.
1945-123	ZARDON, JOSE ANTONO SANCHEZ	7261 NW FIRST MANOR, PLANTATION FL 33317
1943-147	ZARILLA, ALLEN LEE 'ZEKE'	D. AUGUST 28, 1996, HONOLULU, HAWAII
1984-132	ZASKE, LLOYD JEFFREY 'JEFF'	2404 185TH PLACE SE, BOTHELL WA 98012
1951-109	ZAUCHIN, NORBERT HENRY 'NORM'	D. JANUARY 31, 1999, BIRMINGHAM, ALA.
1995-248	ZAUN, GREGORY OWEN	9595 WILSHIRE BLVD #1010, BEVERLY HILLS CA 90212
1989-151	ZAVARAS, CLINTON WAYNE	9675 SOUTH THIMBLEBERRY WAY, PARKER CO 80134
1977-160	ZDEB, JOSEPH EDWARD	5717 GREENWOOD, SHAWNEE KS 66216
1977-161	ZEBER, GEORGE WILLIAM	18826 WINNWOOD LANE, SANTA ANA CA 92705
1989-152	ZEILE, TODD EDWARD	2138 NARSHBROOK ROAD, WESTLAKE VILLAGE CA 91361
1970-142	ZELLER, BARTON WALLACE	13885 EAST LUPINE DRIVE, SCOTTSDALE AZ 85259
1969-186	ZEPP, WILLIAM CLINTON	15000 FARMBROOK DRIVE, PLYMOUTH MI 48170
2000-202	ZERBE, WILLIAM CHAD 'CHAD'	7248 PALOMINO STREET, HIGHLAND CA 92346
1949-092	ZERNIAL, GUS EDWARD	687 COVENTRY AVENUE, CLOVIS CA 93611
1954-120	ZICK, ROBERT GEORGE	12028 SOUTH 45TH STREET, PHOENIX AZ 85044
1987-155	ZIEM, STEVEN GRAELING	1309 AVALON AVENUE, BEAUMONT CA 92223
1941-120	ZIENTARA, BENEDICT JOSEPH	D. APRIL 16, 1985, LAKE ELSINORE, CALIF.
1954-121	ZIMMER, DONALD WILLIAM	7069 KEY HAVEN ROAD #201, SEMINOLE FL 33777
1961-113	ZIMMERMAN, GERALD ROBERT	D. SEPTEMBER 9, 1998, NESKOWIN, ORE.
1999-211	ZIMMERMAN, JEFFREY ROSS	3930 GLADE ROAD #108, COLLEYVILLE TX 76034
1999-212	ZIMMERMAN, JORDAN WILLIAM	2426 AIRLINE DRIVE, BRENHAM TX 77833
1945-124	ZIMMERMAN, ROY FRANKLIN	D. NOVEMBER 22, 1991, PINE GROVE, PA.
2005-206	ZIMMERMAN, RYAN WALLACE	OLD ADD: WASHINGTON NC
1921-119	ZINK, WALTER NOBLE	D. JUNE 12, 1964, QUINCY, MASS.
1944-152	ZINSER, WILLIAM FREDERICK	D. FEBRUARY 16, 1993, ENGLEWOOD, FLA.
2002-206	ZINTER, ALAN MICHAEL	12143 NORTH SEASONS LOOP, ORO VALLEY AZ 85737
1961-114	ZIPFEL, MARION SYLVESTER 'BUD'	57 WHITESIDE DR, BELLEVILLE IL 62221
1971-113	ZISK, RICHARD WALTER 'RICHIE'	4231 NORTHEAST 26TH TERRACE, LIGHTHOUSE POINT FL 33064
2000-203	ZITO, BARRY WILLIAM	16627 GILMORE STREET, VAN NUYS CA 91406
2006-220	ZOBRIST, BENJAMIN T.	RURAL ROUTE 1, EUREKA IL 61530
2003-183	ZOCCOLILLO, PETER J	5 SPRUCE DRIVE, WHITE PLAINS NY 10605
1944-153	ZOLDAK, SAMUEL WALTER	D. AUGUST 25, 1966, MINEOLA, N.Y.
1991-192	ZOSKY, EDWARD JAMES	13535 DITTMAR DRIVE, WHITTIER CA 90605
1996-195	ZUBER, JON EDWARD	197 FERNWOOD DRIVE, MORAGA CA 94556
1936-100	ZUBER, WILLIAM HENRY	D. NOVEMBER 2, 1982, CEDAR RAPIDS, IOWA
2000-204	ZULETA, JULIO ERNESTO	140 LITTLETON ROAD #100, PARSIPPANY NJ 07054
2006-221	ZUMAYA, JOEL MARTIN	1060 CAMINO ESPUELAS, CHULA VISTA CA 91910
1991-193	ZUPCIC, ROBERT	5409 SILVER CREEK DRIVE, WAXHAW NC 28173
1957-097	ZUPO, FRANK JOSEPH	D. MARCH 25, 2005, BURLIGAME, CALIF.
1982-142	ZUVELLA, PAUL	2040 CANYON CREST AVENUE, SAN RAMON CA 94583
1951-110	ZUVERINK, GEORGE	1027 EAST MCNAIR DRIVE, TEMPE AZ 85283

COACHES WITH NO MAJOR LEAGUE PLAY DEBUTING FROM 1930 TO 2006

C1935-01	ABBOTT, SPENCER ARTHUR	D. DECEMBER 18, 1951, WASHINGTON, D.C.
C2000-01	ACOSTA, OSCAR CARLOS	D. APRIL 19, 2006, DOM REP
C2002-01	ACTA, MANUEL ELIAS	3428 CYPRESS POINT CIRCLE, SAINT CLOUD FL 34772
C1992-01	ADAIR, MICHAEL RICHARD 'RICK'	141 BENNETT CIRCLE, SPARTANBURG SC 29302
C1997-01	ALEJO, ROBERT KEVIN	3724 PORTOFINO WAY #A, SANTA BARBARA CA 93105
C1992-02	ALFONSO, CARLOS	PO BOX 8773, NAPLES FL 34101
C1992-03	ARSENAULT, PIERRE JEAN	17942 AMALFI PIERREFONDS QC, H9K 1M2 CANADA
C1973-01	AUFERIO, ANTHONY PATRICK 'TONY'	35 BEECH TERRACE, WAYNE NJ 07470
C2000-02	BAILEY, WELBY SHELDON	190 HILLTOP DRIVE, MADISON HEIGHTS VA 24572
C2004-01	BALSLEY, DARREN W	9958 KIKA COURT #5818, SAN DIEGO CA 92129
C2002-02	BARNETT, MICHAEL LEE	PO BOX 53625, KNOXVILLE TN 37950
C2006-01	BEASLEY, ANTHONY W 'TONY'	13155 COURTLAND LANE, RUTHER GLEN VA 22546
C1989-01	BERARDINO, RICHARD J.	37 EMMELINE AVENUE, WALTHAM MA 02154
C1967-01	BERINGER, CARROLL JAMES 'C.B.'	4917 GRANITE SHOALS, FORT WORTH TX 76103
C1998-01	BERNHARDT, CARLOS	CALLE DUVERGE #196, SAN PEDRO DE MACORIS, DOM REP
C2003-01	BERRY, MARK	1086 LONGMORE STREET, CHANDLER AZ 85224
C1992-04	BIAGINI, GREGORY PETER	D. OCTOBER 3, 2003, OKLAHOMA CITY, OKLA.
C1993-01	BIALAS, DAVID BRUCE	14080 NORTH BAYSHORE DRIVE, MADEIRA BEACH FL 33708
C1963-01	BLACKBURN, WAYNE CLARK	D. FEBRUARY 16, 2000, PORTSMOUTH, OHIO
C1974-01	BLOOMFIELD, GORDON LEIGH 'JACK'	1310 IRIS, MCALLEN TX 78501
C1996-01	BOMBARD, MARC	8612 BARKWOOD COURT, TAMPA FL 33615
C1967-02	BRAGAN, JAMES ALTON	D. JUNE 2, 2001, STERRETT, ALA.
C1986-01	BREEDEN, HAROLD SCOTT	D. FEBRUARY 21, 2006, TAMPA, FLA.
C1995-01	BREEDEN, JOSEPH THOMAS	1305 BONAVENTURE, MELBOURNE FL 32940
C1998-02	BUNDY, CHARLES LORENZO 'LORENZO'	1401 SOUTH DAKOTA SKY COURT, TUCSON AZ 85748
C1994-02	BUTTERFIELD, BRIAN JAMES	PO BOX 1538, STANDISH ME 04084
C1969-01	CAMACHO, JOSEPH GOMES	48 MASSASOIT AVENUE, FAIRHAVEN MA 02719
C1997-02	CAREY, PETER JOSEPH 'P.J.'	10810 NORTH DE LA TIERRA CAMINO, TUCSON AZ 85742
C1996-02	CARLUCCI, DAVID MARIO	4 YAWKEY WAY, BOSTON MA 02215
C1970-01	CARNEVALE, DANIEL JOSEPH	D. DECEMBER 29, 2005, BUFFALO, N.Y.
C1988-01	CARRION, LEONEL SANTIAGO	SAN JACINTO, SEC 7, VER 5#1, MARACAIBO, VENEZUELA
C1959-01	CARTER, RICHARD JOSEPH	D. SEPTEMBER 11, 1969, PHILADELPHIA, PA.
C2006-02	CHAVES, RAFAEL	OLD ADD: ISABELA PR 00662
C1991-01	CHITI, HARRY DOMINIC 'DOM'	1943 FOX HOLLOW DRIVE, AUBURNDALE FL 33823
C1976-01	CLEAR, ELWOOD ROBERT 'BOB'	120 EAST 234TH STREET, CARSON CA 90745
C1979-02	CLUCK, ROBERT ALTON	6192 BALTIMORE DRIVE, LAMESA CA 92042
C1984-01	CONNOR, MARK PETER	7312 WHEATFIELD PLACE, KNOXVILLE TN 37919
C2005-01	CONTI, GUY	448 53RD SQUARE, VERO BEACH FL 32968
C1953-01	CRANDALL, JAMES MARK 'JIMMIE	D. FEBRUARY 1, 1983, BULLHEAD CITY, ARIZ.
C1977-01	CRESSE, MARK EMERY	89 AVENIDO LIRIO BLANCO, RANCHO MIRAGE CA 92270
C2005-02	DANCY, WILLIAM WOODRUFF	651 NORTH OLD COACHMAN ROAD, CLEARWATER FL 33765
C1995-02	DEARMAS, ROLANDO JESUS 'ROLY'	2840 VALENCIA LANE WEST, PALM HARBOR FL 34684
C2005-03	DEBUS, JON	355 29TH COURT SW, VERO BEACH FL 32968
C1989-02	DEMERRITT, MARTIN GORDON	8317 LAKELAND DRIVE, GRANITE BAY CA 95746
C2001-01	DENBO, GARY BRIAN	27740 WATER ASH DRIVE, WESLEY CHAPEL FL 33543
C1979-01	DEWS, ROBERT WALTER	423 AUDUBON, ALBANY GA 31707
C1964-01	DIXON, WALTER EDWARD	505 PINECROFT DRIVE, RALEIGH NC 27609
C1980-01	DONNELLY, RICHARD FRANCIS	47899 ANNAPOLIS ROAD, HOPEDALE OH 43976
C2005-04	DORANTE, LUIS	4400 MUNSON COURT, PALM BEACH GARDENS FL 33410
C1961-01	DOUGLAS, OTIS WHITFIELD	D. MARCH 21, 1989, KILMARNOCK, PA.
C1987-01	DOWN, RICHARD JOHN 'RICK'	8311 NORTH WASHBURN ROAD, LAS VEGAS NV 89149
C1998-03	DUBEE, RICHARD PETER	4702 THOMAS HOBY PLACE, SARASOTA FL 34241
C1969-02	DUNLOP, HARRY ALEXANDER	5605 LAGUNA QUAIL WAY, ELK GROVE CA 95758
C1983-01	DUSAN, EUGENE PAUL	2241 SE PLIATOS LANE, BEND OR 97702
C2006-03	EBEL, DINO ALEX	5012 MARTINEZ BAY AVENUE, LAS VEGAS NV 89131
C2003-02	ESPY, DUANE G	9032 EAST HANNIBAL STREET, MESA AZ 85207
C2006-04	EVERS, WILLIAM JOSEPH	11955 ROSELAND DRIVE, NEW PORT RICHEY FL 34654
C1983-02	EZELL, GLENN WAYNE	14257 WEST 151ST TERRACE #1603, OLATHE KS 66062
C1996-03	FISCHER, BRADLEY JAMES	6103 FOREST RIDGE COURT, MCFARLAND WI 53558
C1947-01	FITZGERALD, JOSEPH PATRICK	D. AUGUST 29, 1967, ORLANDO, FLA.
C1953-02	FITZPATRICK, JOHN ARTHUR	D. NOVEMBER 19, 1990
C1998-04	GAMBOA, THOMAS HAROLD	318 LOCH LOMOND ROAD, RANCHO MIRAGE CA 92270
C1994-03	GLYNN, EUGENE PATRICK	15329 SNAKE TRAIL, WASECA MN 56093
C2005-05	GOFF, MICHAEL ROGER	7320 WEST SURREY AVENUE, PEORIA AZ 85381
C1991-02	GOMEZ, JUAN ALEJANDRO 'ORLANDO'	C-1 URB. LAS FLORES, JUANA DIAZ PR 00795
C1999-01	GONZALEZ, FREDI J.	2368 NETHERSTONE DRIVE NE, MARIETTA GA 30066
C1999-02	GRAHAM, J. BRIAN	612 TOFTREE DRIVE, CRANBERRY TWP PA 16066
C1998-05	GREGSON, GLENN	719 BRIDGEVIEW COURT, HELENA MT 59601
C1981-01	GUERRERO, EPIFANIO OBDULIO (ABUD) 'EPY'	RES. LA ROTONDA #19, ARROYO HONDO, SANTO DOMINGO, DOM REP
C2002-03	HALE, DEMARLO	4560 WOODLANDS VILLAGE DRIVE, ORLANDO FL 32835
C1991-03	HANSEN, GUY CHRISTOPHER	3876 RED ROCK STREET, LAS VEGAS NV 89103
C1992-05	HANSEN, ROGER CHRISTIAN	14618 KAYAK POINT ROAD, STANWOOD WA 98292
C1982-01	HARMON, THOMAS HAROLD	6101 BON TERRA DRIVE, AUSTIN TX 78731
C1998-06	HENDERSON, RAMON GASPAR	276 OAK LANE, PHOENIXVILLE PA 19460
C1992-06	HERNANDEZ, CARLO AMADO 'CHUCK'	3113 WEST RIVER COVE DRIVE, TAMPA FL 33614
C2004-02	HICKEY, JAMES W.	4297 SASHA TRAIL, SAINT CLOUD FL 34772
C1992-07	HILL, PERRY WENDELL	6101 LONG PRAIRIE ROAD #744-10, FLOWER MOUND TX 75028
C1984-02	HINES, BENJAMIN THORTAN	2709 SECOND STREET, LAVERNE CA 91750
C1991-04	HINES, BRUCE EDWIN	4155 EAST FAIRFIELD STREET, MESA AZ 85205
C1994-04	HOLMBERG, DENNIS NELS	2079 MONICA COURT, PALM HARBOR FL 34683

C1984-03	HOLMQUIST, DOUGLAS LEONARD	D. FEBRUARY 27, 1988, ALTAMONTE SPRINGS, FLA.
C1948-01	HOLT, GOLDEN DESMOND 'GOLDIE'	D. JUNE 11, 1991, SHERMAN OAKS, CALIF.
C1968-01	HOSCHEIT, VERNARD ARTHUR	PO BOX 36, PLAINVIEW NE 68769
C1993-02	HUBBARD, JOHN H. 'JACK'	10239 SORENSTAM DRIVE, NEW PORT RICHEY FL 34655
C1987-02	ISAAC, LUIS (APONTE)	2401 ONTARIO STREET, CLEVELAND OH 44115
C1990-01	JARAMILLO, RUDOLFO A.	3855 ECHO BROOK LANE, DALLAS TX 75229
C1997-03	JAUSS, DAVID PATRICK	56 LANDSEER STREET, WEST ROXBURY MA 02132
C2001-02	JEWETT, PHILIP TRENT 'TRENT'	PO BOX 914, COPPELL TX 75019
C1998-07	JONES, GARY WAYNE	11 WOODBOX DRIVE, HENDERSON TX 75652
C1987-03	JONES, JOSEPH CARMACK	2411 CARLISLE PLACE, SARASOTA FL 34231
C2004-03	JONES, THOMAS M	6812 EAST MONTERRA WAY, SCOTTSDALE AZ 85262
C1955-01	KAHN, LOUIS	D. MARCH 13, 2002, ALBANY, GA.
C1930-01	KELLY, BERNARD FRANCIS 'MIKE'	D. OCTOBER 23, 1968, INDIANAPOLIS, IND.
C1989-03	KIM, WENDELL KEALOHAPAUOLE	4732 EAST SOURWOOD RIVE, GILBERT AZ 85297
C1969-03	KISSELL, GEORGE MARSHALL	9878 34TH WAY, PINELLAS PARK FL 33782
C1971-01	KITTLE, HUBERT MILTON 'HUB'	D. FEBRUARY 10, 2004, YAKIMA, WASH.
C2002-04	KNIFFIN, CHARLES E.	PO BOX 259, FLORISSANT CO 80816
C1970-02	KOENIG, FRED CARL	D. JANUARY 12, 1993, CHOTEAU, OKLA.
C2002-05	KRANITZ, RICHARD ALAN 'RICK'	6344 WEST BUCKSKIN TRAIL, GLENDALE AZ 85310
C1995-03	LACHEMANN, WILLIAM CHARLES	208 RIVERVIEW LANE, GREAT FALLS MT 59404
C1988-02	LETT, JAMES CURTIS	STAR ROUTE 34 BOX 5751, WINFIELD WV 25213
C1957-01	LEVY, LEONARD HOWARD	D. FEBRUARY 2, 1993, PALM DESERT, CALIF.
C2002-06	LIDDLE, STEVEN MICHAEL	437 HEATH PLACE, SMYRNA TN 37167
C1994-05	LINARES, JULIO MARIENU (RIJO)	PO BOX 62 SAN PEDRO DE MACORIS, DOM REP
C1951-01	LOBE, WILLIAM CHARLES	D. JANUARY 7, 1969, CLEVELAND, OHIO
C1999-03	LOPEZ, JUAN ENRIQUE 'PORKY'	RURAL ROUTE 1 BOX 12690, TOA ALTA PR 00953
C2002-07	LOPEZ, JUAN ISAAC	OLD ADD: CAROLINA PR
C1972-01	LOWE, Q.V.	125 PALAMINO LANE, WETUMPKA AL 36093
C1964-02	MACKO, JOSEPH JOHN	2219 TEMPLETON COURT, ARLINGTON TX 76006
C1988-03	MAJTYKA, LEROY WALTER 'ROY'	2082 ORANGESIDE ROAD, PALM HARBOR FL 34683
C1990-02	MALOOF, JACK GARTH	3140 SOUTH VISTA DRIVE, CHANDLER AZ 85248
C1992-08	MANSOLINO, DOUGLAS	891 JULIANA COVE, COLLIERVILLE TN 38017
C2000-03	MASON, MARTIN LEE	1876 GATEWOOD DRIVE, MONTGOMERY AL 36106
C1993-03	MATHEWS, RICK RAY	837 DRAKE AVENUE, CENTERVILLE IA 52544
C1985-01	MAZZONE, LEO DAVID	4518 MYSTIQUE WAY NE, ROSWELL GA 30075
C1951-02	MCDONNELL, ROBERT A. 'MAJE'	7423 REVERE STREET, PHILADELPHIA PA 19152
C1947-02	MCKEE, JOHN R. 'J.R.'	
C1986-02	MCLAREN, JOHN LOWELL	4385 WEST BELL ROAD, GLENDALE AZ 85308
C1977-02	MOZZALI, MAURICE JOSEPH 'MO'	D. MARCH 2, 1987, LAKELAND, FLA.
C1985-02	MULL, JACK LEROY	2361 MCCLEARY, CHAMBERSBURG PA 17221
C2001-03	MYERS, DAVID K	4221 71ST AVENUE COURT NW, GIG HARBOR WA 98335
C1983-03	NAPOLEON, EDWARD GEORGE	1312 73RD STREET NORTHWEST, BRADENTON FL 34209
C1983-04	NOTTLE, EDWARD WILLIAM	416 KINGS PATH, EVANSVILLE IN 47711
C1958-01	OCEAK, FRANK JOHN	D. MARCH 19, 1983, JOHNSTOWN, PA.
C1994-06	OLIVERAS, MAX 'MAKO'	16TH STREET NN #8 JARDINES CAPARRA, BAYAMON PR 00959
C1962-01	ONEIL, JOHN JORDAN 'BUCK'	D. OCTOBER 6, 2006, KANSAS CITY, MO.
C1963-02	OSBORN, DONALD EDWIN	D. MARCH 23, 1979, TORRANCE, CALIF.
C1974-02	PACHECO, ANTONIO ARISTIDES 'TONY'	D. MARCH 23, 1987, MIAMI, FLA.
C1961-02	PAEPKE, JACK	4560 TRIESTE DRIVE, CARLSBAD CA 92008
C1946-01	PATKIN, MAX O.	D. OCTOBER 30, 1999, PAOLI, PA.
C1985-03	PAVLICK, GREGORY MICHAEL	936 PINELLAS BAYWAY SOUTH #T8, TIERRA VERDE FL 33715
C1996-04	PENTLAND, JEFFREY WILLIAM	1032 NORTH CHERRY, MESA AZ 85201
C1984-04	PETERSON, ERIC HARDING 'RICK'	1905 VINCENT COURT, WALL NJ 07719
C1969-04	PLAZA, RONALD CHARLES	2083 69TH AVENUE SOUTH, SAINT PETERSBURG FL 33712
C2004-04	POLDBERG, BRIAN JON	1119 CACHELIN DRIVE, CARTER LAKE IA 51510
C2000-04	PRICE, BRYAN	10897 NORTH 122ND STREET, SCOTTSDALE AZ 85259
C2000-05	QUADE, GREGORY MIKE 'MIKE'	212 68TH STREET NW, BRADENTON FL 34209
C1993-04	RADISON, DANIEL JOHN	116 SE 20TH AVENUE, DEERFIELD BEACH FL 33441
C1950-01	REDYS, EDWARD	4105 JOHN PAUL COURT, WARREN MI 48091
C1966-01	RESINGER, GROVER S.	D. JANUARY 11, 1986, ST. LOUIS, MO.
C1981-02	REYES, BENJAMIN (CHAVEZ) 'CANANEA'	D. DECEMBER 10, 1991, HERMOSILLO, SONORA, MEXICO
C1995-04	RIGGINS, MARK ALAN	1536 OXFORD DRIVE, MURRAY KY 42071
C1996-05	RIGOLI, JOSEPH M.	94 CHAMPIONSHIP #2, AUGUSTA NJ 07822
C1992-09	ROBERTS, MELVIN HENRY	86 BRANDERMILL ROAD, SPARTANBURG SC 29301
C1964-03	ROBINSON, WARREN GRANT 'SHERIFF'	D. APRIL 5, 2002, CAMBRIDGE, MD.
C1996-06	RODRIGUEZ, EDUARDO	4320 NORTH STREET ELIAS, MESA AZ 85215
C2000-06	ROESSLER, PATRICK ALAN	4910 HIDDEN OAKS TRAIL, SARASOTA FL 34232
C2003-03	ROJAS, EUCLIDES 'EUKY'	14777 SW 80TH STREET, MIAMI FL 33193
C1973-02	ROSENBAUM, GLEN OTIS	PO BOX 1, UNION MILLS IN 46382
C1972-02	ROWE, RALPH EMANUEL	D. FEBRUARY 29, 1996, NEWBERRY, S.C.
C1975-01	SAUL, JAMES ALLEN	2405 OSBORNE STREET, BRISTOL VA 23201
C1970-03	SCHERGER, GEORGE RICHARD	701 SAIN T JULIEN, CHARLOTTE NC 28205
C2005-06	SHELTON, DEREK LEE	750 PROSPECT AVENUE EAST #403, CLEVELAND OH 44115
C1998-08	SHERLOCK, GLENN PATRICK	5908 EAST BERYL AVENUE, PARADISE VALLEY CA 85253
C1987-04	SLIDER, RACHEL W. 'RAC'	123 COUNTY EOAD 3306, DEKALB TX 75559
C1984-05	SMITH, BILLY FRANKLIN	191 WINDEMERE POINT, MOUNT GILEAD NC 27306
C1996-07	SMITH, STEVEN JOHN	2224 VILLAGE CENTER DRIVE, ENCINITAS CA 92024
C1985-04	SNITKER, BRIAN GERALD	3148 PINE NEEDLE COURT, LILBURN GA 30241
C1977-03	SOMMERS, DENNIS JAMES	PO BOX 133, HORTONVILE WI 54944
C1979-03	SPARKS, JOSEPH EVERETT	3915 EAST CHOLLA STREET, PHOENIX AZ 85028
C1985-05	TORCHIA, ANTHONY LOUIS 'TONY'	9980 NORTH OUTLAW TRAIL, TUCSON AZ 85742
C1995-05	TREUEL, RALPH MARTIN	15 MIDDLETON ROAD, WOLFEBORO NH 03894
C2006-05	TUCK, GARY ROBERT	2196 GRANDMA BARNES ROAD, NASHVILLE IN 47448

C1980-02	VANORNUM, JOHN CLAYTON	40193 ROAD 222, BASS LAKE CA 93604
C2006-06	VAVRA, JOSEPH ALAN	E4640 483RD AVENUE, MENOMONIE WI 54751
C1943-01	VINCENT, ALBERT LINDER	D. DECEMBER 14, 2000, BEAUMONT, TEXAS
C1961-03	WALKER, VERLON LEE 'RUBE'	D. MARCH 24, 1971, CHICAGO, ILL.
C1973-03	WALTON, JAMES ROBERT	PO BOX 787, SHATTUCK OK 73858
C1977-04	WARNER, HARRY CLINTON	JACKSON HEIGHTS, REEDERS PA 18352
C2004-05	WHISLER, RANDY K	1708 NORTH CYPRESS AVENUE, BROKEN ARROW OK 74012
C1995-06	WILLIAMS, DANIEL LAWRENCE	3006 GREENWICH LANE, BRUNSWICK OH 44212
C1977-05	WILLIAMS, DONALD ELLIS	5597 GREENE ROAD #125, PARAGOULD AR 72450
C1994-07	WILLIAMS, DONALD RAY 'SPIN'	4470 270TH STREET, STOCKTON IA 52769
C1975-02	WILLIAMS, JAMES BERNARD	4 OLD SOUND ROAD, JOPPA MD 21085
C1995-07	WILLIAMS, RICHARD ANTHONY	501 KNIGHTS RUN AVENUE #5104, TAMPA FL 33602
C1931-01	WOLGAMOT, CLINTON EARL 'EARL'	D. APRIL 25, 1970, INDEPENDENCE, IOWA
C1976-02	ZIMMER, THOMAS JEFFREY	4219 28TH AVENUE NORTH, SAINT PETERSBURG FL 33713

UMPIRES DEBUTING FROM 1930 TO 2006

U1969-01	ANTHONY, GEORGE MERLYN 'MERLYN'	D. FEBRUARY 2, 1993, YUBA CITY, CALIF.
U2004-01	ARMENDARIZ, RAMON	OLD ADD: 550 LOS ARBOLITOS BLVD #99, OCEANSIDE CA 92054
U2003-01	ASCHWEGE, DAVID PAUL	2824 LAWSON DRIVE, LINCOLN NE 68516
U1965-01	ASHFORD, EMMETT LITTLETON	D. MARCH 1, 1980, MARINA DEL REY, CALIF.
U1969-02	AVANTS, NICK	3914 MOUNT CARMEL ROAD, BRYANT AR 72022
U1936-01	BALLANFANT, EDWARD LEE 'LEE'	D. JULY 15, 1987, DALLAS, TEXAS
U2000-01	BARKSDALE, ROBERT LANCE 'LANCE'	4507 PINE LAKE DRIVE, TERRY MS 39170
U1940-01	BARLICK, ALBERT JOSEPH	D. DECEMBER 27, 1995, SPRINGFIELD, ILL.
U1990-01	BARNES, RONALD E.	130 CARMEL AVENUE, EL CERRITO CA 94530
U1968-01	BARNETT, LAWRENCE ROBERT	6464 HUGHES ROAD, PROSPECT OH 43342
U1931-01	BARR, GEORGE MCKINLEY	D. JULY 26, 1974, SULPHUR, OKLA.
U1994-01	BARRETT, EDWARD GEORGE 'TED'	4380 EAST SUNDANCE COURT, GILBERT AZ 85297
U1992-01	BARRON, MARK	110 NORTH RANDOLPH AVENUE, CLARKSVILLE IN 47129
U2006-01	BARRY, SCOTT ADAM	148 LUKESPORT DRIVE, QUINCY MI 49082
U1936-02	BASIL, STEPHEN JOHN	D. JUNE 24, 1962, GILCHRIST, TEXAS
U1994-02	BEAN, EDDIE	1827 THIRD COURT SOUTHEAST, WINTER HAVEN FL 33880
U1992-02	BELL, WALLACE ROBERT	3825 VILLA ROSA DRIVE, CANFIELD OH 44406
U1942-01	BERRY, CHARLES FRANCIS	D. SEPTEMBER 6, 1972, EVANSTON, ILL.
U1976-01	BETCHER, RALPH	153 PARKFEL AVENUE, PITTSBURGH PA 15237
U1970-01	BLANDFORD, FRED	D. JULY 19, 1997, HILTON, N.Y.
U1944-01	BOGGESS, LYNTON ROSS 'DUSTY'	D. JULY 8, 1968, DALLAS, TEXAS
U1984-01	BONIN, GREGORY LOUIS	403 COBBLESTONE ROAD, LAFAYETTE LA 70508
U1944-02	BOYER, JAMES MURRY	D. JULY 25, 1959, FINKSBURG, MD.
U1973-01	BREMIGAN, NICHOLAS GREGORY	D. MARCH 29, 1989, GARLAND, TEXAS
U1973-02	BRINKMAN, JOSEPH NORBERT	10551 NW 70TH STREET, CHIEFLAND FL 32626
U1979-01	BROCKLANDER, FRED WILLIAM	317 EAGLES LANDING COURT #K, ODENTON MD 21113
U1998-01	BUCHANAN, WILLIAM	94 TWILL VALLEY DRIVE, SAINT PETERS MO 63376
U1996-01	BUCKNOR, C.B.	46 MIDWOOD STREET, BROOKLYN NY 11225
U1957-01	BURKHART, WILLIAM KENNETH 'KEN'	D. DECEMBER 29, 2004, KNOXVILLE, TENN.
U1999-01	CARLSON, MARK CHRISTOPHER	10 EMERY STREET, JOLIET IL 60436
U1961-01	CARRIGAN, HERVE SAMUEL 'SAM'	607 SUNRISE AVENUE, ALAMOGORDO NM 88310
U2006-02	CAUSEY, KEVIN MICHAEL	5719 HERALD GREEN DRIVE, CHESTERFIELD VA 23832
U1989-01	CEDERSTROM, GARY L.	755 WHIDBEY STREET, MELBOURNE FL 32904
U1954-01	CHYLAK, NESTOR L.	D. FEBRUARY 17, 1982, DUNMORE, PA.
U1976-02	CLARK, ALAN MARSHALL	16 INDEPENDENCE PLACE, NEWTOWN PA 18940
U1930-01	CLARKE, ROBERT	
U1982-01	COBLE, GEORGE DREW 'DREW'	205 80TH AVENUE NORTH, MYRTLE BEACH SC 29572
U1976-03	COHEN, ALFRED	113 LESLIE ROAD, MONROEVILLE PA 15146
U1968-02	COLOSI, NICHOLAS	D. FEBRUARY 25, 2005, NEW YORK, N.Y.
U1941-01	CONLAN, JOHN BERTRAND 'JOCKO'	D. APRIL 16, 1989, SCOTTSDALE, ARIZ.
U1998-02	CONNORS, PATRICK	1075 MARICOPA DRIVE, OSHKOSH WI 54904
U1999-02	COOK, ROBERT	179 ROYAL FARM EAST, BLACKLICK OH 43004
U1975-01	COONEY, TERRANCE JOSEPH	3205 FILBERT AVENUE, CLOVIS CA 93612
U1996-02	COOPER, ERIC RICHARD	5404 LONGVIEW COURT, JOHNSTON IA 50131
U1983-01	COSTELLO, PERRY	814 ANDREW DRIVE, DEWITT MI 48820
U1979-02	COUSINS, DERRYL	78136 DESERT MOUNTAIN CIRCLE, INDIO CA 92201
U1987-01	CRAFT, TERRY LEE	10009 CHERRY HILLS AVENUE CIRCLE, BRADENTON FL 34202
U1975-02	CRAWFORD, GERALD JOSEPH	111 NINTH STREET EAST, SAINT PETERSBURG FL 33715
U1956-01	CRAWFORD, HENRY CHARLES 'SHAG'	242 BALTIMORE PIKE #207, GLEN MILLS PA 19342
U1993-01	CULBRETH, FIELDIN HENRY	205 LAKE LENNOX DRIVE, SIMPSONVILLE SC 29681
U1991-01	CUZZI, PHILIP	32 MAPES AVENUE, NUTLEY NJ 07110
U1970-02	DALE, JERRY PARKER	2112 MIDDLEWOOD DRIVE, MARYVILLE TN 37803
U1991-02	DANLEY, KERWIN JOSEPH	3789 EAST LIBRA PLACE, CHANDLER AZ 85249
U1986-01	DARLING, GARY RICHARD	16422 SOUTH 36TH PLACE, PHOENIX AZ 85044
U1948-01	DASCOLI, FRANK	D. AUGUST 11, 1990, DANIELSON, CONN.
U1969-03	DAVIDSON, DAVID LEROY 'SATCH'	2400 WESTHEIMER STREET #209W, HOUSTON TX 77098
U1982-02	DAVIDSON, ROBERT ALLAN	91 DEERWOOD DRIVE, LITTLETON CO 81027
U1982-03	DAVIS, GERALD SIDNEY	2440 STROEBE ISLAND DRIVE, APPLETON WI 54915
U1970-03	DEEGAN, WILLIAM EDWARD JOHN	8392 77TH AVENUE, LARGO FL 34647
U2005-01	DELLINGER, DUSTIN EUGENE	OLD ADD: 5203 GRIST MILL LANE, GRANITE FALLS NC 28630
U1956-02	DELMORE, VICTOR	D. JUNE 10, 1960, SCRANTON, PA.
U1983-02	DEMUTH, DANA ANDREW	1156 WEST WAGNER DRIVE, GILBERT AZ 85234
U1968-03	DENKINGER, DONALD ANTON	3505 KINGSWOOD PLACE, WATERLOO IA 50701
U1966-01	DEZELAN, FRANK JOHN	7423 LIGHTHOUSE POINT, PITTSBURGH PA 15221
U1995-01	DIAZ, LAZARO ANTONIO	13557 MEADOW BAY LOOP, ORLANDO FL 32824
U1963-01	DIMURO, LOUIS JOHN	D. JUNE 7, 1982, ARLINGTON, TEXAS
U1997-01	DIMURO, MICHAEL RYAN	OLD ADD: 2321 NORTH ESSEL DRIVE, TUCSON AZ 85715
U1996-03	DIMURO, RAYMOND JOHN	9625 NORTH 33RD STREET, PHOENIX AZ 85028
U1953-01	DIXON, HAL HAYWORTH	D. JULY 28, 1966, CHURNEE, S.C.
U1950-01	DONATELLI, AUGUST JOSEPH 'AUGIE'	D. MAY 24, 1990, ST. PETERSBURG, FLA.
U1931-02	DONNELLY, CHARLES	D. DECEMBER 13, 1968, LAKE WORTH, FLA.
U1930-02	DONOHUE, MICHAEL	D. AUGUST 7, 1968, ST. LOUIS, MO.
U2002-01	DOWDY, ADAM MATTHEW	909 EAST CHESTNUT STREET, PONTIAC IL 61764
U1963-02	DOYLE, WALTER JAMES	D. MARCH 2, 1988, TAMPA, FLA.
U1999-03	DRAKE, ROBERT PAUL	5409 BARRETT CIRCLE, BUENA PARK CA 90621
U1996-04	DRECKMAN, BRUCE MICHAEL	110 NORTH MAPLE, MARCUS IA 51035
U1960-01	DRUMMOND, CALVIN TROY 'TROY'	D. MAY 2, 1970, DES MOINES, IOWA
U1951-01	DUFFY, JAMES FRANCIS	D. NOVEMBER 29, 2003, PORTSMOUTH, R.I.
U1998-03	DUNCAN, R. DENNIS	8 NORDELL, BLACK JACK MO 63033
U1939-01	DUNN, THOMAS PATRICK	D. JANUARY 20, 1976, PRINCE GEORGES CO., MD.

U2005-02	DURFEE, PETER KEITH	54 LOBELIA COURT, CHICO CA 95973
U1998-04	EDDINGS, DOUGLAS LEON	OLD ADD: 1501 MONTARA DRIVE, LOS LUNAS NM 87031
U1999-04	EMMEL, PAUL LEWIS	8462 IDLEWOOD COURT, BRADENTON FL 34202
U1965-02	ENGEL, ROBERT ALLEN	3500 HARMONY LANE, BAKERSFIELD CA 93306
U1952-01	ENGELN, WILLIAM RAYMOND	D. APRIL 17, 1968, PALO ALTO, CALIF.
U2006-03	ESTABROOK, MICHAEL JOSEPH	502 TITUS ROAD, LAMBERTVILLE NJ 08530
U1971-01	EVANS, JAMES BREMOND	OLD ADD: 1801 ROGGE LANE, AUSTIN TX 78723
U1996-05	EVERITT, MIKE G.	4215 162ND STREET, URBANDALE IA 50323
U2004-02	FAIRCHILD, CHADWICK JARRETT	2745 50TH AVENUE WEST #117, BRADENTON FL 34207
U1999-05	FICHTER, MICHAEL JAMES	8821 JACKSON COURT, MUNSTER IN 46321
U1979-03	FIELDS, STEPHEN HAROLD	8306 WICKHAM ROAD, SPRINGFIELD VA 22152
U1979-04	FITZPATRICK, MICHAEL	262 LODGE LANE, KALAMAZOO MI 49009
U1953-02	FLAHERTY, JOHN FRANCIS 'RED'	D. APRIL 1, 1999, FALMOUTH, MASS.
U1999-06	FLETCHER, ANDREW JAY	3282 KINDERHILL LANE, GERMANTOWN TN 38138
U1975-03	FORD, ROBERT DALE 'DALE'	678 BRETHERN CHURCH ROAD, JONESBOROUGH TN 37659
U1961-02	FORMAN, ALLEN SANFORD	219B WEST TATEWAY, KITTY HAWK NC 27949
U1996-06	FOSTER, MARTIN ROBERT	319 WEST 5TH AVENUE, DENVER CO 80204
U1968-04	FRANTZ, ARTHUR FRANK	7000 NORTH NEWARK AVENUE, NILES IL 60714
U1971-02	FROEMMING, BRUCE NEAL	702 WEST HADDONSTONE PLACE, THIENSVILLE WI 53092
U1952-02	FROESE, GROVER	D. JULY 20, 1982, BAY SHORE, N.Y.
U1998-05	FUGERE, JOSEPH	1150 HILLSBORO MILE #404, HILLSBORO BEACH FL 33062
U2004-03	FULLWOOD, TROY ALEXANDER	317 MANNING LANE, HAMPTON VA 23666
U1975-04	GARCIA, RICHARD RAUL	PO BOX 3276, CLEARWATER FL 33767
U1994-03	GIBBONS, BRIAN	51785 WHITESTABLE LANE, SOUTH BEND IN 46637
U1997-02	GIBSON, GREGORY ALLAN	20305 COUNTRY CLUB DRIVE, CATLETTSBURG KY 41129
U1936-03	GOETZ, LAWRENCE JOHN	D. OCTOBER 31, 1962, CINCINNATI, OHIO
U1968-05	GOETZ, RUSSELL LEWIS	937 FAWCETT AVENUE, MCKEESPORT PA 15132
U1946-01	GORE, ARTHUR JOSEPH 'ARTIE'	D. SEPTEMBER 29, 1986, WOLFEBORO, N.H.
U1991-03	GORMAN, BRIAN	PO BOX 1208, SOMIS CA 93066
U1951-02	GORMAN, THOMAS DAVID	D. AUGUST 11, 1986, CLOSTER, N.J.
U1976-04	GREGG, ERIC EUGENE	D. JUNE 5, 2006, PHILADELPHIA, PA.
U1938-01	GRIEVE, WILLIAM TURNER	D. AUGUST 17, 1979, YONKERS, N.Y.
U1970-04	GRIMSLEY, JOHN WILLIAM	D. OCTOBER 23, 1992
U1983-03	GRINDER, SCOTT	1323 14TH AVENUE SOUTH, BIRMINGHAM AL 35205
U1970-05	GRYGIEL, GEORGE R.	451 WEST BAZILLE WAY, GREEN VALLEY AZ 85614
U2000-02	GUCCIONE, CHRISTOPHER GENE	88 PALOMA AVENUE, BRIGHTON CO 80601
U1976-05	GUCKERT, ELMER	1212 BALMORAL DRIVE, PITTSBURGH PA 15237
U1952-03	GUGLIELMO, ANGELO AUGIE	D. FEBRUARY 28, 1996, WATERBURY, CONN.
U1961-03	HALLER, WILLIAM EDWARD	RURAL ROUTE 2 BOX 82C, BROWNSTOWN IL 62418
U1985-01	HALLION, THOMAS FRANCIS	4040 ORMOND ROAD, LOUISVILLE KY 40207
U1979-05	HARRIS, LANNY DEAN	D. JUNE 16, 1991
U1962-01	HARVEY, HAROLD DOUGLAS 'DOUG'	32398 RIVER ISLAND DRIVE, SPRINGVILLE CA 93265
U1977-01	HENDRY, EUGENE 'TED'	14740 NORTH 90TH PLACE, SCOTTSDALE AZ 85260
U1945-01	HENLINE, WALTER JOHN 'BUTCH'	D. OCTOBER 9, 1957, SARASOTA, FLA.
U1993-02	HENRICHS, JEFF	OLD ADD: 1901 MORNINGSTAR DR, LINCOLN NE 68506
U1991-04	HERNANDEZ, ANGEL	501 CYPRESS CROSSING, WELLINGTON FL 33414
U1990-02	HICKOX, EDWIN W.	2001 STEAMBOAT RIDGE COURT, DAYTONA BEACH FL 32124
U2000-03	HIGGINS, SCOTT EDWARD	3591 INDIAN CLOVER STREET, PLUMAS LAKE CA 95961
U1983-04	HIRSCHBECK, JOHN FRANCIS	8730 RAINTREE RUN, POLAND OH 44514
U1987-02	HIRSCHBECK, MARK	15 BLACKBERRY LANE, SHELTON CT 06484
U1999-07	HODGES, MORRIS	404 PARK LAKE TERRACE, HELENA AL 35080
U1987-03	HOHN, WILLIAM JOHN	50 ARROW DRIVE, GILBERTSVILLE PA 19525
U1997-03	HOLBROOK, SAMUEL WOODFORD	2620 SUNGATE COURT, LEXINGTON KY 40513
U2000-04	HOLLOWELL, MATTHEW STUART	8 OLDWICK ROAD, WHITEHOUSE STATION NJ 08889
U1949-01	HONOCHICK, GEORGE JAMES 'JIM'	D. MARCH 10, 1994, ALLENTOWN, PA.
U2003-02	HOYE, JAMES PATRICK	12838 PATRICIA DRIVE, NORTH ROYALTON OH 44133
U1936-04	HUBBARD, ROBERT CAL 'CAL'	D. OCTOBER 16, 1977, ST. PETERSBURG, FLA.
U1998-06	HUDSON, MARVIN LEE	542 METASVILLE ROAD, WASHINGTON GA 30673
U1983-05	HUMPHREY, RICHARD	26 PLAYER GREEN PLACE, SPRING TX 77382
U1947-01	HURLEY, EDWIN HENRY	D. NOVEMBER 12, 1969, BOSTON, MASS.
U1999-08	IASSOGNA, DANIEL RALPH	1501 BAILEY FARM COURT SW, MARIETTA GA 30064
U1952-04	JACKOWSKI, WILLIAM ANTHONY	D. JULY 29, 1996, SPRINGFIELD, VT.
U2006-04	JOHNSON, ADRIAN ANDRE	8102 MEADVILLE DRIVE, HOUSTON TX 77061
U1984-02	JOHNSON, MARK STEPHEN	OLD ADD: 1210 AUAHI STREET, HONOLULU HI 96814
U1936-05	JOHNSTON, CHARLES EDWARD	D. SEPTEMBER 1, 1974, MIAMI, FLA.
U1944-03	JONES, NICHOLAS ITTNER 'RED'	D. MARCH 19, 1987, MIAMI, FLA.
U2004-04	JOST, MICHAEL LEWIS	11312 EAST PETERSON AVENUE, MESA AZ 85212
U1989-02	JOYCE, JAMES A.	9785 SW 167TH PLACE, BEAVERTON OR 97007
U1977-02	KAISER, KENNETH JOHN	56 HOLLY SUE LANE, ROCHESTER NY 14626
U1999-09	KATZENMAYER, TRAVIS DEAN	OLD ADD: 562 NORTH OVERLAND, MESA AZ 85207
U2001-01	KELLEY, KEVIN WAYNE	1311 QUARTERPATH COURT, RICHMOND TX 77469
U1991-05	KELLOGG, JEFFREY	22900 CHERRY HILL COURT, MATTAWAN MI 49071
U1963-03	KIBLER, JOHN WILLIAM	2701 EL CAMINO REAL #205, PALO ALTO CA 94306
U1960-02	KINNAMON, WILLIAM ERVIN	8211 ANNWOOD ROAD, SEMINOLE FL 33777
U2000-05	KLEMM, JUSTIN FRANCIS 'JAY'	47 CHOCTAW RIDGE ROAD, BRANCHBURG NJ 08875
U2001-02	KNIGHT, BRIAN MICHAEL	1123 STUART STREET, HELENA MT 59601
U1933-01	KOLLS, LOUIS CHARLES	D. FEBRUARY 23, 1941, HOOPPOLE, ILL.
U1976-06	KOSC, GREGORY JOHN	3465 HUNTING RUN ROAD, MEDINA OH 44256
U1998-07	KULPA, RONALD CLARENCE	1958 PARKLAND WOODS DRIVE, MARYLAND HEIGHTS MO 63043
U1968-06	KUNKEL, WILLIAM GUSTAVE JAMES	D. MAY 4, 1985, RED BANK, N.J.
U2000-06	LAMPLUGH, IAN MICHAEL	1830 FAIRBURN DRIVE, VICTORIA BC, V8N 1P9 CANADA
U1955-01	LANDES, STANLEY ALBERT	D. JANUARY 23, 1994, PEORIA, ARIZ.
U1979-06	LAWSON, WILLIAM	8800 EAST MCCLELLAN STREET, TUCSON AZ 85710

U1989-03	LAYNE, JERRY BLAKE	2323 CYPRESS GARDEN BLVD, WINTER HAVEN FL 33884
U1985-02	LEPPERD, THOMAS	5962 WISTFUL VISTA DRIVE, WEST DES MOINES IA 50266
U1961-04	LINSALATA, JOSEPH	4017 WASHINGTON STREET, HOLLYWOOD FL 33021
U1968-07	LUCIANO, RONALD MICHAEL	D. JANUARY 18, 1995, ENDICOTT, N.Y.
U1970-06	MALONEY, GEORGE PATRICK	D. JULY 29, 2003, BARSTOW, CALIF.
U1935-01	MARBERRY, FRED 'FIRPO'	D. JUNE 30, 1976, MEXIA, TEXAS
U1999-10	MARQUEZ, ALFONSO	271 MONTANA DEL LAGO DRIVE, RANCHO SANTA MARGARITA CA 92688
U1981-01	MARSH, RANDALL GILBERT	3023 WINTERBORNE ROAD, COVINGTON KY 41017
U2004-05	MCARDLE, JOHN E.	6640 LYNFORD STREET, PHILADELPHIA PA 19149
U1983-06	MCCLELLAND, TIMOTHY REID	5405 WOODLAND AVENUE, WEST DES MOINES IA 50266
U1970-07	MCCOY, LARRY SANDERS	5758 HIGHWAY 139, GREENWAY AR 72450
U1930-03	MCGREW, HARRY HANCOCK 'TED'	D. JUNE 29, 1969, BEDFORD, VA.
U1974-01	MCKEAN, JAMES GILBERT	740 SAND PIKE DRIVE NE, SAINT PETERSBURG FL 33703
U1946-02	MCKINLEY, WILLIAM FRANCIS	D. AUGUST 1, 1980, MOUNT PLEASANT, PA.
U1971-03	MCSHERRY, JOHN PATRICK	D. APRIL 1, 1996, CINCINNATI, OHIO
U1992-04	MEALS, GERALD WILLIAM	2164 SHAMROCK ARBOR DRIVE, SALEM OH 44460
U1987-04	MERIWETHER, JULIUS EDWARD 'CHUCK'	2409 SEIFRIED STREET, NASHVILLE TN 37208
U1977-03	MERRILL, EDWIN DURWOOD 'DURWOOD'	D. JANUARY 11, 2003, TEXARKANA, TEXAS
U1997-04	MILLER, WILLIAM SCOTT	174 VIA LANTANA, APTOS CA 95003
U1974-02	MONTAGUE, EDWARD MICHAEL	1521 CHERRYWOOD DRIVE, SAN MATEO CA 94402
U1970-08	MORGENWECK, HENRY CHARLES	33 BOGERT STREET, TEANECK NJ 07666
U1983-07	MORRISON, DANIEL G.	14220 SUNSHINE COURT, LARGO FL 34644
U2005-03	MOSER, CASEY RYAN	9013 FM 368 NORTH, IOWA PARK TX 76367
U2006-05	MUCHLINSKI, MICHAEL WILLIAM	2266 CHERRY BLOSSOM DRIVE, EPHRATA WA 98823
U1951-03	NAPP, LARRY ALBERT	D. JULY 7, 1993, PLANTATION, FLA.
U1995-02	NAUERT, PAUL EDWARD	1201 STEEPLE RUN, LAWRENCEVILLE GA 30243
U1997-05	NELSON, JEFFREY BRIAN	c/o MLB, 245 PARK AVENUE, NEW YORK NY 10167
U1979-07	NELSON, RICHARD	OLD ADD: 123 MONTGOMERY LANE, PERRYVILLE AR 72126
U2001-03	NELSON, SCOTT WRIGHT	811 OVERLOOK DRIVE, COSHOCTON OH 43812
U1965-03	NEUDECKER, JEROME 'JERRY'	D. JANUARY 11, 1997, FORT WALTON BEACH, FLA.
U1964-01	ODOM, JAMES CECIL	D. JANUARY 18, 1989, BENNETTSVILLE, S.C.
U1966-02	ODONNELL, JAMES MICHAEL	OLD ADD: 3026 WEST QUEEN LANE #1B, PHILADELPHIA PA 19129
U1968-08	OLSEN, ANDREW HOLGER	451 93RD AVENUE NORTH, SAINT PETERSBURG FL 33702
U1992-05	ONORA, BRIAN	4294 MAUREEN DRIVE, YOUNGSTOWN OH 44511
U2000-07	PACKARD, SCOTT RICHARD	135 EASTVIEW DRIVE, HORSEHEADS NY 14845
U1977-04	PALERMO, STEPHEN MICHAEL	5102 WEST 143RD TERRACE, OVERLAND PARK KS 66224
U1979-08	PALLONE, DAVID MICHAEL	201 ARNO STREET NE #303, ALBUQUERQUE NM 87102
U1946-03	PAPARELLA, JOSEPH JAMES	D. OCTOBER 17, 1994, SEBASTIAN, FLA.
U1936-06	PARKER, GEORGE LAMBACH	D. MAY 22, 1984, HOMESTEAD, FLA.
U1979-09	PARKS, DALLAS FINNEY	3353 PITTMAN GROVE CHURCH ROAD, RAEFORD NC 28376
U1941-02	PASSARELLA, ARTHUR MATTHEW	D. OCTOBER 12, 1981, HEMET, CALIF.
U1960-03	PELEKOUDAS, CHRISTOS GEORGE	D. NOVEMBER 30, 1984, SUNNYVALE, CALIF.
U1970-09	PHILLIPS, DAVID ROBERT	12 UPPER WHITMOUR DRIVE, SAINT CHARLES MO 63304
U1935-02	PINELLI, RALPH ARTHUR 'BABE'	D. OCTOBER 22, 1984, DALY CITY, CALIF.
U1938-02	PIPGRAS, GEORGE WILLIAM	D. OCTOBER 19, 1986, GAINESVILLE, FLA.
U1985-03	PONCINO, LARRY	2954 NORTH CALLE LADERA, TUCSON AZ 85715
U1991-06	POTTER, SCOTT A.	1637 CORDOVA AVENUE, DAYTONA BEACH FL 32117
U1961-05	PRYOR, JOHN PAUL 'PAUL'	D. DECEMBER 15, 1995, ST. PETERSBURG, FLA.
U1972-01	PULLI, FRANK VICTOR	1981 DOWNING PLACE, PALM HARBOR FL 34683
U1976-07	PUSKARIC, JOSEPH	201 WEST DRIVE NORTH #63, MARSHALL MI 49068
U1974-03	QUICK, JAMES EDWARD	6061 KEEBLE LANE, CAMINO CA 95709
U1935-03	QUINN, JOHN ALOYSIUS	D. JULY 4, 1968, PHILADELPHIA, PA.
U1999-11	RANDAZZO, ANTHONY JOHN	2462 LOS ALAMOS COURT, LAS CRUCES NM 88011
U1990-03	RAPUANO, EDWARD S.	10815 JAPONICA COURT, BOCA RATON FL 33498
U1979-10	REED, RICK ALAN	4938 CRESTONE WAY, ROCHESTER HILLS MI 48306
U1977-05	REILLY, MICHAEL EUGENE	131 SMITHFIELD ROAD, BATTLE CREEK MI 49015
U2005-04	REININGER, TRAVIS	453 VOILES DRIVE, BRIGHTON CO 80601
U1989-04	RELIFORD, CHARLES HAROLD	1509 CYPRESS STREET, ASHLAND KY 41101
U1973-03	RENNERT, LAURENCE HARVEY	WALKERS GLEN 2560 46TH ROAD, VERO BEACH FL 32966
U1999-12	REYNOLDS, JAMES NORRIS	708 HIGHPOINT DRIVE, ROCKY HILL CT 06067
U1955-02	RICE, JOHN LA CLAIRE	2666 EAST 73RD STREET #A12W, CHICAGO IL 60649
U1992-06	RIEKER, RICHARD	4130 WHIPPOORWILL DRIVE, SAINT LOUIS MO 63123
U1983-08	RIPPLEY, THOMAS STEVEN	3900 GALT OCEAN DRIVE #1406, FORT LAUDERDALE FL 33308
U1947-02	ROBB, DOUGLAS W. 'SCOTTY'	D. APRIL 10, 1969, MONTCLAIR, N.J.
U1953-03	ROBERTS, LEONARD WYATT	1027 WATERFORD, DALLAS TX 75218
U1974-04	RODRIGUEZ, ARMANDO HUMBERTO	OLD ADD: INDEPENCIA 1375, VERACRUZ, VERACRUZ MEXICO
U1980-01	ROE, JOHN A. 'ROCKY'	2033 STEFANO COURT, MOUNT DORA FL 32757
U1938-03	ROMMEL, EDWIN AMERICUS	D. AUGUST 26, 1970, BALTIMORE, MD.
U1938-04	RUE, JOSEPH WILLIAM	D. DECEMBER 1, 1984, LAGUNA HILLS, CALIF.
U1999-13	RUNGE, BRIAN EDWARD	1333 VIA ISIDRO, OCEANSIDE CA 92056
U1954-02	RUNGE, EDWARD PAUL	D. JULY 25, 2002, SAN DIEGO, CALIF.
U1972-02	RUNGE, PAUL EDWARD	8225 EAST COUNTY DRIVE, EL CAJON CA 92021
U1946-04	RYAN, WALTER	D. JUNE 16, 1981
U1961-06	SALERNO, ALEX JOSEPH	21 ROSEMARY STREET, UTICA NY 13501
U2001-04	SAMUELS, JOHN RAYMOND 'JACK'	16040 LEFFINGWELL ROAD #25, WHITTIER CA 90603
U1970-10	SATCHELL, DAROLD	D. DECEMBER 10, 1997, SAN DIEGO, CALIF.
U1997-06	SCHRIEBER, PAUL WARREN	10350 EAST DESERT COVE AVENUE, SCOTTSDALE AZ 85260
U1960-04	SCHWARTS, HARRY CLARK	D. FEBRUARY 22, 1963, CLEVELAND, OHIO
U1985-04	SCOTT, DALE ALLAN	1283 SW CARDINELL DRIVE, PORTLAND OR 97201
U1930-04	SCOTT, JAMES 'DEATH VALLEY JIM'	D. APRIL 7, 1957, PALM SPRINGS, CALIF.
U1934-01	SEARS, JOHN WILLIAM 'ZIGGY'	D. DECEMBER 16, 1956, HOUSTON, TEXAS
U1952-05	SECORY, FRANK EDWARD	D. APRIL 7, 1995, PORT HURON, MICH.
U1979-11	SHULOCK, JOHN RICHARD	4180 5TH STREET SW, VERO BEACH FL 32968

U1957-02	SMITH, VINCENT AMBROSE	D. DECEMBER 14, 1979, VIRGINIA BEACH, VA.
U1960-05	SMITH, WILLIAM ALARIC 'AL'	1101 OGLIVIE STREET, BOSSIER CITY LA 71111
U1950-02	SOAR, ALBERT HENRY 'HANK'	D. DECEMBER 24, 2001, PAWTUCKET, R.I.
U2002-02	SPAGNARDI, DARREN JOHN	2364 WEST CENTER STREET EAST, LEXINGTON NC 27295
U1977-06	SPENN, FREDERICK CHARLES	5201 DESOTO ROAD, SARASOTA FL 34235
U2000-08	SPIELER, PATRICK MERLE	6635 SOUTH 108TH AVENUE, OMAHA NE 68137
U1966-03	SPRINGSTEAD, MARTIN JOHN	5164 FLICKER FIELD CIRCLE, SARASOTA FL 33581
U1961-07	STEINER, MELVIN JAMES	D. MAY 6, 1997
U1968-09	STELLO, RICHARD JACK	D. NOVEMBER 18, 1987, LAKELAND, FLA.
U1948-02	STEVENS, JOHN WILLIAM	D. SEPTEMBER 9, 1981, PHILADELPHIA PA.
U1941-03	STEWART, ERNEST DRAPER	D. NOVEMBER 15, 2001, OCEANSIDE, CALIF.
U1959-01	STEWART, ROBERT WILLIAM	D. DECEMBER 1, 1981, WOONSOCKET, R.I.
U1933-02	STEWART, WILLIAM JOSEPH	D. FEBRUARY 18, 1964, JAMAICA PLAIN, MASS.
U1957-03	SUDOL, EDWARD LAWRENCE	D. DECEMBER 10, 2004, DAYTONA BEACH, FLA.
U1933-03	SUMMERS, WILLIAM REED	D. SEPTEMBER 12, 1966, UPTON, MASS.
U1956-03	TABACCHI, FRANK TULE	D. OCTOBER 26, 1983, HOBOKEN, N.J.
U1972-03	TATA, TERRY ANTHONY	23 STONEGATE CIRCLE, CHESHIRE CT 06410
U1999-14	TIMMONS, TIMOTHY FORBES	PO BOX 574, NEW ALBANY OH 43054
U1970-11	TREMBLAY, RICHARD HENRY	D. JUNE 12, 1987, LITTLETON, N.H.
U1985-05	TSCHIDA, TIMOTHY	274 15 1/2 AVENUE, TURTLE LAKE WI 54889
U1954-03	UMONT, FRANK WILLIAM	D. JUNE 20, 1991, FORT LAUDERDALE, FLA.
U1963-04	VALENTINE, WILLIAM TERRY	15 BLUE RIDGE CIRCLE, LITTLE ROCK AR 72207
U1991-07	VANOVER, LARRY W.	3037 STERLING COURT, OWENSBORO KY 42303
U2000-09	VANVLEET, MICHAEL EDWARD	118 CREAMFIELD DRIVE, BATTLE CREEK MI 49014
U1960-06	VARGO, EDWARD PAUL	101 FREEDOM ROAD, BUTLER PA 16001
U1957-04	VENZON, ANTHONY	D. SEPTEMBER 20, 1971, PITTSBURGH, PA.
U1977-07	VOLTAGGIO, VITO HENRY 'VIC'	1049 FLORIAN WAY, SPRING HILL FL 34609
U1961-08	WALSH, FRANCIS D. 'FRANK'	D. JULY 1, 1985
U1949-02	WARNEKE, LONNIE 'LON'	D. JUNE 23, 1976, HOT SPRINGS, ARK.
U1943-01	WEAFER, HAROLD LEON	D. AUGUST 23, 1978, RICHMOND, VA.
U1998-08	WEGNER, MARK PATRICK	2607 LAKEVIEW WAY, PLANT CITY FL 33566
U1983-09	WELKE, TIMOTHY JAMES	7790 DOUBLETREE COURT, KALAMAZOO MI 49009
U1999-15	WELKE, WILLIAM ANTHONY	54 COUNTRY HILLS, MARSHALL MI 49068
U1966-04	WENDELSTEDT, HARRY HUNTER	88 SOUTH ST ANDREWS DRIVE, ORMOND BEACH FL 32174
U1998-09	WENDELSTEDT, HARRY HUNTER 'HUNTER'	88 SOUTH ST ANDREWS DRIVE, ORMOND BEACH FL 32174
U1976-08	WEST, JOSEPH HENRY	114 NORTH EASTERN STREET, GREENVILLE NC 27834
U1961-09	WEYER, LEE HOWARD	D. JULY 4, 1988, SAN MATEO, CALIF.
U1990-04	WICKHAM, DANIEL	3221 EAST MOUNTAIN VISTA DRIVE, PHOENIX AZ 85044
U1972-04	WILLIAMS, ARTHUR	D. FEBRUARY 8, 1979, BAKERSFIELD, CALIF.
U1978-01	WILLIAMS, CHARLES HERMAN	D. SEPTEMBER 15, 2005, CHICAGO, ILL.
U1963-05	WILLIAMS, WILLIAM GEORGE 'BILLY'	D. SEPTEMBER 22, 1998, DEERFIELD BEACH, FLA.
U1994-04	WINANS, MATTHEW	21 ST. GEORGE PLACE, SANDY HOOK CT 06482
U1988-01	WINTERS, MICHAEL JOHN	OLD ADD: 321 14TH STREET, DEL MAR CA 92014
U1999-16	WOLF, JAMES MICHAEL	8054 ROYER AVENUE, WEST HILLS CA 91304
U1983-10	YOUNG, LARRY EUGENE	PO BOX 255, ROSCOE IL 61073

DEATHS IN 2005, 2006 AND 2007

1952-001	ABERNATHIE, WILLIAM EDWARD	D. FEBRUARY 19, 2006, YUCAIPA, CALIF.
C2000-01	ACOSTA, OSCAR CARLOS	D. APRIL 19, 2006, DOMINICAN REPUBLIC
1941-001	ADAMS, ACE TOWNSEND	D. FEBRUARY 26, 2006, ALBANY, GA.
1937-002	ALLEN, ROBERT EARL 'EARL'	D. OCTOBER 30, 2005, CHESAPEAKE, VA.
1933-002	AUKER, ELDEN LEROY	D. AUGUST 4, 2006, VERO BEACH, FLA.
1946-007	BAHR, EDSON GARFIELD	D. APRIL 6, 2007, SEATTLE, WASH.
1953-004	BAILEY, LONAS EDGAR 'ED'	D. MARCH 29, 2007, KNOXVILLE, TENN.
1940-001	BAKER, WILLIAM PRESLEY	D. APRIL 13, 2006, MYRTLE BEACH, S.C.
1947-009	BANTA, JOHN KAY	D. SEPTEMBER 17, 2006, HUTCHINSON, KAN.
1960-004	BARBER, STEPHEN DAVID	D. FEBRUARY 4, 2007, HENDERSON, NEV.
1945-003	BARTOSCH, DAVID ROBERT	D. APRIL 30, 2006, NASHVILLE, TENN.
1948-007	BASGALL, ROMANUS 'MONTY'	D. SEPTEMBER 22, 2005, SIERRA VISTA, ARIZ.
1948-008	BAUER, HENRY ALBERT 'HANK'	D. FEBRUARY 9, 2007, KANSAS CITY, MO.
1977-010	BERNAL, VICTOR HUGO	D. SEPTEMBER 2, 2006, ARCADIA, CALIF.
1934-007	BERRES, RAYMOND	D. FEBRUARY 1, 2007, KENOSHA, WISC.
1952-010	BLACK, WILLIAM CARROLL	D. OCTOBER 2, 2005, ST. LOUIS, MO.
1955-014	BLASINGAME, DONALD LEE	D. APRIL 13, 2005, FOUNTAIN HILLS, ARIZ.
1933-005	BOCEK, MILTON FRANK	D. APRIL 29, 2007, BROOKFIELD, ILL.
1935-006	BOWERS, STEWART COLE 'DOC'	D. DECEMBER 14, 2005, HAVERTOWN, PA.
1938-010	BOYLES, HARRY	D. JANUARY 7, 2005, MCALLEN, TEXAS
C1986-01	BREEDEN, HAROLD SCOTT	D. FEBRUARY 21, 2006, TAMPA, FLA.
1960-013	BREEDING, MARVIN EUGENE	D. DECEMBER 30, 2006, DECATUR, ALA.
1965-014	BRILES, NELSON KELLEY	D. FEBRUARY 13, 2005, ORLANDO, FLA.
1984-011	BROWN, JOHN CHRISTOPHER 'CHRIS'	D. DECEMBER 26, 2006, HOUSTON, TEXAS
1950-014	BURDETTE, SELVA LEWIS 'LOU'	D. FEBRUARY 6, 2007, WINTER GARDEN, FLA.
1943-019	BUTKA, EDWARD LUKE	D. APRIL 21, 2005, PITTSBURGH, PA.
1950-018	CALDERONE, SAMUEL FRANCIS	D. NOVEMBER 28, 2006, BEVERLY, N.J.
1958-017	CALLISON, JOHN WESLEY	D. OCTOBER 12, 2006, ABINGTON, PA.
1941-013	CAMPBELL, PAUL MCLAUGHLIN	D. JUNE 22, 2006, CHARLOTTE, N.C.
1951-009	CAMPOS, FRANCISCO JOSE LOPEZ 'FRANK'	D. JANUARY 28, 2006, MIAMI, FLA.
C1970-01	CARNEVALE, DANIEL JOSEPH	D. DECEMBER 29, 2005, BUFFALO, N.Y.
1940-009	CARPENTER, ROBERT LOUIS	D. OCTOBER 19, 2005, EVERGREEN PARK, ILL.
1950-019	CARRASQUEL, ALFONSO COLON 'CHICO'	D. MAY 26, 2005, CARACAS, VENEZ.
1931-011	CARTER, SOLOMON MOBLEY	D. DECEMBER 23, 2006, EL DORADO, ARK.
1938-012	CHAPMAN, SAMUEL BLAKE	D. DECEMBER 22, 2006, TIBURON, CALIF.
1961-022	CLENDENON, DONN ALVIN	D. SEPTEMBER 17, 2005, SIOUX FALLS, S.D.
1943-031	CLYDE, THOMAS KNOX	D. OCTOBER 1, 2005, DALLAS, TEXAS
U1968-02	COLOSI, NICHOLAS	D. FEBRUARY 25, 2005, NEW YORK, N.Y.
1937-027	CONNORS, MERVYN JAMES	D. JANUARY 8, 2006, SAN FRANCISCO, CALIF.
1950-023	CONSUEGRA, SANDALIO SIMEON 'SANDY'	D. NOVEMBER 16, 2005, MIAMI, FLA.
1931-020	CUNNINGHAM, RAYMOND LEE	D. JULY 30, 2005, PEARLAND, TEXAS
1960-026	CURRY, GEORGE ANTHONY 'TONY'	D. OCTOBER 16, 2006, NASSAU, BAHAMAS
1956-025	DAHLKE, JEROME ALEXANDER	D. SEPTEMBER 2, 2006, BATESVILLE, MISS.
1945-022	DANIELS, FREDERICK CLINTON	D. JULY 23, 2005, STATESVILLE, N.C.
1965-025	DAVIDSON, THOMAS EUGENE 'TED'	D. SEPTEMBER 1, 2006, BULLHEAD CITY, ARIZ.
1952-023	DAVIS, ROBERT BRANDON 'BRANDY'	D. JUNE 12, 2005, NEWARK, DEL.
1935-022	DEDEAUX, RAOUL MARTIAL 'ROD'	D. JANUARY 5, 2006, GLENDALE, CALIF.
1943-038	DELSAVIO, GARTON ORVILLE 'GAR'	D. NOVEMBER 9, 2006, BLAUVELT, N.Y.
1948-031	DELSING, JAMES HENRY	D. MAY 4, 2006, CHESTERFIELD, MO.
1951-023	DEMPSEY, CORNELIUS FRANCIS 'CON'	D. AUGUST 5, 2006, REDWOOD CITY, CALIF.
1965-027	DENNIS, DONALD RAY	D. MARCH 22, 2007, FORT SCOTT, KAN.
1966-028	DIETZ, RICHARD ALLEN	D. JUNE 28, 2005, DILLARD, GA.
1967-025	DOBSON, PATRICK EDWARD	D. NOVEMBER 22, 2006, SAN DIEGO, CALIF.
1947-029	DOZIER, WILLIAM JOSEPH 'BUZZ'	D. NOVEMBER 24, 2005, WACO, TEXAS
1956-028	DRABOWSKY, MYRON WALTER 'MOE'	D. JUNE 10, 2006, LITTLE ROCK, ARK.
2001-055	ENCARNACION, MARIO (GONZALEZ)	D. OCTOBER 3, 2005, DANSHUEI TAIWAN
1943-044	EYRICH, GEORGE LINCOLN	D. JUNE 25, 2006, READING, PA.
1934-033	FEHRING, WILLIAM PAUL 'DUTCH'	D. APRIL 14, 2006, PALO ALTO, CALIF.
1947-034	FINE, THOMAS MORGAN	D. JANUARY 10, 2005, LITTLE ELM, TEXAS
1948-036	FLEITAS, ANGEL FELIX HUSTA	D. JULY 10, 2006, MIAMI, FLA.
1940-021	FLEMING, LESLIE FLETCHERD 'BILL'	D. JUNE 4, 2006, RENO, NEV.
1954-028	FOWLER, JOHN ARTHUR 'ART'	D. JANUARY 29, 2007, SPARTANBURG, S.C.
1959-028	FREEMAN, MARK PRICE	D. FEBRUARY 21, 2006, RANCHO MIRAGE, CALIF.
1942-041	GALLE, STANLEY JOSEPH	D. JANUARY 28, 2006, MOBILE, ALA.
1945-035	GARDELLA, ALFRED STEVE	D. SEPTEMBER 10, 2006, CORAL SPRINGS, FLA.
1944-046	GARDELLA, DANIEL LEWIS	D. MARCH 6, 2005, YONKERS, N.Y.
1947-038	GEBRIAN, PETER	D. MAY 6, 2005, STUART, FLA.
1945-038	GETTEL, ALLEN JAMES	D. APRIL 8, 2005, NORFOLK, VA.
1957-024	GRAFF, MILTON EDWARD	D. AUGUST 2, 2005, ROCKDALE, TEXAS
1966-039	GRAHAM, WILLIAM ALBERT	D. OCTOBER 26, 2006, FLEMINGSBURG, KY.
U1976-04	GREGG, ERIC EUGENE	D. JUNE 5, 2006, PHILADELPHIA, PA.
1956-038	GRIGGS, HAROLD LLOYD	D. MAY 10, 2005, TUCSON, ARIZ.
1946-039	GRISSOM, MARVIN EDWARD	D. SEPTEMBER 19, 2005, RED BLUFF, CALIF.
1930-028	GROSKLOSS, HOWARD HOFFMAN 'HOWDIE'	D. JULY 15, 2006, VERO BEACH, FLA.
1967-040	GUTIERREZ, CESAR DARIO	D. JANUARY 22, 2005, MARACIBO, VENEZ.
1958-041	HADLEY, KENT WILLIAM	D. MARCH 10, 2005, POCATELLO. IDAHO
1941-042	HAJDUK, CHESTER	D. JULY 4, 2006, CHICAGO, ILL.
1943-056	HALL, IRVIN GLADSTONE	D. DECEMBER 12, 2006, BALTIMORE, MD.
1940-032	HANCKEN, MORRIS MEDLOCK 'BUDDY'	D. FEBRUARY 15, 2007, ORANGE, TEXAS
2002-076	HANCOCK, JOSHUA MORGAN	D. APRIL 29, 2007, SAINT LOUIS, MO.

1944-058	HAYWORTH, MYRON CLAUDE 'RED'	D. NOVEMBER 2, 2006, HIGH POINT, N.C.
1960-047	HEIST, ALFRED MICHAEL	D. OCTOBER 2, 2006, TAHLEQUAH, OKLA.
1968-037	HENDRICKS, ELROD JEROME	D. DECEMBER 21, 2005, GLEN BURNIE, MD.
1958-045	HERRERA, JUAN FRANCISCO 'FRANK'	D. APRIL 28, 2005, MIAMI, FLA.
1942-050	HITCHCOCK, WILLIAM CLYDE	D. APRIL 9, 2006, OPELIKA AL
1946-047	HODKEY, ALOYSIUS JOSEPH 'ELI'	D. AUGUST 30, 2005, LORAIN, OHIO
1952-050	HOGUE, CALVIN GREY	D. AUGUST 5, 2005, KETTERING, OHIO
1950-036	HOUSE, HENRY FRANKLIN 'FRANK'	D. MARCH 13, 2005, BIRMINGHAM, ALA.
1980-057	HOWE, STEVEN ROY	D. APRIL 28, 2006, COACHELLA, CALIF.
1937-053	HUFFMAN, BENNIE FRANKLIN	D. FEBRUARY 22, 2005, LURAY, VA.
1968-044	JAMES, JEFFREY LYNN	D. MAY 7, 2006, INDIANAPOLIS, IND.
1941-052	JOHNSON, ADAM RANKIN 'RANK '	D. FEBRUARY 11, 2006, WILLIAMSPORT, PA.
1944-065	JOHNSON, VICTOR OSCAR	D. MAY 10, 2005, EAU CLAIRE, WISC.
1943-067	JOHNSON, WILLIAM RUSSEL	D. JUNE 20, 2006, AUGUSTA, GA.
1988-073	JONES, RONALD GLEN	D. JUNE 4, 2006, HOUSTON, TEXAS
1960-056	JONES, SHERMAN JARVIS	D. FEBRUARY 21, 2007, KANSAS CITY, KAN.
1965-054	JOYCE, RICHARD EDWARD	D. JANUARY 23, 2007, CARY, N.C.
1952-060	KELLNER, WALTER JOSEPH	D. JUNE 19, 2006, TUCSON, ARIZ.
1967-057	KELLY, HAROLD PATRICK 'PAT'	D. OCTOBER 2, 2005, CHAMBERSBURG, PA.
1939-061	KENNEDY, ROBERT DANIEL	D. APRIL 7, 2005, MESA, ARIZ.
1943-070	KERR, JOHN JOSEPH 'BUDDY'	D. NOVEMBER 7, 2006, NEW YORK, N.Y.
1953-046	KIPPER, THORNTON JOHN	D. MARCH 29, 2006, SCOTTSDALE, ARIZ.
1952-061	KLAUS, WILLIAM JOSEPH	D. DECEMBER 3, 2006, SARASOTA, FLA.
1958-053	KOPPE, JOSEPH	D. SEPTEMBER 27, 2006, ANN ARBOR, MICH.
1938-047	KOY, ERNEST ANYZ	D. JANUARY 1, 2007, BELLVILLE, TEXAS
1949-044	KRYHOSKI, RICHARD DAVID	D. APRIL 10, 2007, BEVERLY HILLS, MICH.
1973-072	KUSICK, CRAIG ROBERT	D. SEPTEMBER 27, 2006, SAINT PAUL. MINN.
1950-045	LABINE, CLEMENT WALTER	D. MARCH 2, 2007, VERO BEACH, FLA.
1938-050	LANIER, HUBERT MAX 'MAX'	D. JANUARY 30, 2007, LOCANTO, FLA.
1958-054	LARKER, NORMAN HOWARD	D. MARCH 12, 2007, LONG BEACH, CALIF.
1936-047	LARSEN, ERLING ADELI	D. OCTOBER 8, 2005, TUCSON, ARIZ.
1938-052	LEFEBVRE, WILFRID HENRY 'BILL'	D. JANUARY 19, 2007, LARGO, FLA.
1965-063	LEJOHN, DONALD EVERETT	D. FEBRUARY 25, 2005, CALIFORNIA, PA.
1950-050	LEMON, JAMES ROBERT	D. MAY 14, 2006, BRANDON, MISS.
1954-062	LENNON, ROBERT ALBERT	D. JUNE 14, 2005, DIX HILLS, N.Y.
1997-098	LIDLE, CORY FULTON	D. OCTOBER 11, 2006, NEW YORK, N.Y.
1951-052	LIMMER, LOUIS	D. APRIL 1, 2007, BOCA RATON, FLA.
1965-064	LINDBLAD, PAUL ANTON	D. JANUARY 1, 2006, ARLINGTON, TEXAS
1954-063	LINT, ROYCE JAMES	D. APRIL 3, 2006, PORTLAND, ORE.
1945-061	LOPATKA, ARTHUR JOSEPH	D. MARCH 10, 2007, ELK GROVE VILLAGE, ILL.
1928-060	LOPEZ, ALFONSO RAMON	D. OCTOBER 30, 2005, TAMPA, FLA.
1958-057	MABE, ROBERT LEE	D. JANUARY 9, 2005, DANVILLE, VA.
1979-072	MAHLER, RICHARD KEITH 'RICK'	D. MARCH 2, 2005, JUPITER, FLA.
1936-050	MAILHO, EMIL PIERRE	D. MARCH 7, 2007, HAYWARD, CALIF.
1950-058	MALLETTE, MALCOLM FRANCIS	D. NOVEMBER 25, 2005, DURHAM, N.C.
1943-081	MALLOY, ROBERT PAUL	D. FEBRUARY 20, 2007, CINCINNATI, OHIO
1949-047	MALONE, EDWARD RUSSELL	D. JUNE 1, 2006, LAGUNA HILLS, CALIF.
1949-048	MARSH, FRED FRANCIS	D. OCTOBER 26, 2006, CORRY, PA.
1941-070	MARSHALL, CHARLES ANDREW	D. APRIL 15, 2007, WILMINGTON, DEL.
1988-086	MARTINEZ, CARLOS ALBERTO ESCOBAR	D. JANUARY 24, 2006, VARGAS, VENEZ.
1962-082	MARTINEZ, ORLANDO OLIVO 'MARTY'	D. MARCH 15, 2007, SANTO DOMINGO, DOM REP
1944-084	MAUCH, EUGENE WILLIAM	D. AUGUST 8, 2005, RANCHO MIRAGE, CALIF.
1949-050	MAVIS, ROBERT HENRY	D. MARCH 1, 2005, LITTLE ROCK, ARK.
1936-053	MAYO, EDWARD JOSEPH	D. NOVEMBER 27, 2006, BANNING, CALIF.
1944-088	METZIG, WILLIAM ANDREW	D. MARCH 12, 2006, LUBBOCK, TEXAS
1964-073	MIKKELSEN, PETER JAMES	D. NOVEMBER 29, 2006, MABTON, WASH.
1944-090	MIKSIS, EDWARD THOMAS	D. APRIL 8, 2005, HUNTINGTON VALLEY, PA.
1953-058	MILLIKEN, ROBERT FOGLE	D. JANUARY 4, 2007, CLEARWATER, FLA.
1936-057	MILNAR, ALBERT JOSEPH	D. JUNE 3, 2005, CLEVELAND, OHIO
1946-073	MINNER, PAUL EDISON	D. MARCH 28, 2006, LEMOYNE, PA.
1955-084	MOFORD, HERBERT	D. DECEMBER 3, 2005, CINCINNATI, OHIO
1957-058	MOREHEAD, SETH MARVIN	D. JANUARY 17, 2006, SHREVEPORT, LA.
1961-077	MORTON, WYCLIFFE NATHAN 'BUBBA'	D. JANUARY 14, 2006, SEATTLE, WASH.
1954-073	MROZINSKI, RONALD FRANK	D. OCTOBER 19, 2005, WASHINGTON, N.J.
1950-070	MUELLER, JOSEPH GORDON 'GORDY'	D. SEPTEMBER 7, 2006, BALTIMORE, MD.
1963-084	MURRELL, IVAN AUGUSTE	D. OCTOBER 8, 2006, STUART, FLA.
1939-080	NAYMICK, MICHAEL JOHN	D. OCTOBER 12, 2005, STOCKTON, CALIF.
1949-058	NELSON, GLENN RICHARD 'ROCKY'	D. OCTOBER 31, 2006, PORTSMOUTH, OHIO
1967-080	NIEKRO, JOSEPH FRANKLIN	D. OCTOBER 27, 2006, TAMPA, FLA.
1949-060	NIELSEN, MILTON ROBERT	D. AUGUST 1, 2005, MANKATO, MINN.
1959-061	OLIVER, EUGENE GEORGE	D. MARCH 3, 2007, ROCK ISLAND, ILL.
C1962-01	ONEIL, JOHN JORDAN 'BUCK'	D. OCTOBER 6, 2006, KANSAS CITY, MO.
1955-086	ORAVETZ, ERNEST EUGENE	D. DECEMBER 3, 2006, TAMPA, FLA.
1937-082	OUTLAW, JAMES PAULUS	D. APRIL 9, 2006, JACKSON, ALA.
1937-083	OWEN, ARNOLD MALCOLM 'MICKEY'	D. JULY 13, 2005, MOUNT VERNON, MO.
1949-063	PEARCE, JAMES MADISON	D. JULY 17, 2005, ZEBULON, N.C.
1946-082	PELLAGRINI, EDWARD CHARLES	D. OCTOBER 11, 2006, WEYMOUTH, MASS.
1954-081	PENSON, PAUL EUGENE	D. MAY 3, 2006, MERRIAM, KAN.
1955-090	PETERSON, CARL FRANCIS 'BUDDY'	D. SEPTEMBER 19, 2006, SACRAMENTO, CALIF.
1950-078	PIERRO, WILLIAM LEONARD	D. APRIL 1, 2006, BROOKLYN, N.Y.
1953-070	PISONI, JAMES PETE	D. FEBRUARY 4, 2007, DALLAS, TEXAS
1941-090	POOLE, RAYMOND HERMAN	D. MARCH 1, 2006, BURLINGTON, N.C.
1954-084	POWER, VICTOR PELLOT	D. NOVEMBER 29, 2005, BAYAMON, P.R.

1984-091	PUCKETT, KIRBY	D. MARCH 6, 2006, PHOENIX, ARIZ.
1954-087	QUEEN, WILLIAM EDDLEMAN	D. APRIL 23, 2006, GASTONIA, N.C.
1962-110	RADATZ, RICHARD RAYMOND	D. MARCH 16, 2005, EASTON, MASS.
1936-077	RADTKE, JACK WILLIAM	D. OCTOBER 24, 2006, TWIN FALLS, IDAHO
1952-083	REED, WILLIAM JOSEPH	D. DECEMBER 5, 2005, HOUSTON, TEXAS
1939-095	REPASS, ROBERT WILLIS	D. JANUARY 26, 2006, WETHERSFIELD, CONN.
1943-114	RESCIGNO, XAVIER FREDERICK	D. DECEMBER 24, 2005, SUN CITY WEST, ARIZ.
1949-073	RESTELLI, DINO PAOLO	D. AUGUST 8, 2006, SAN CARLOS, CALIF.
1945-084	REYNOLDS, DANIEL VANCE	D. FEBRUARY 18, 2007, STATESVILLE, N.C.
1963-101	ROWE, DONALD HOWARD	D. OCTOBER 15, 2005, NEWPORT BEACH, CALIF.
1974-115	RUHLE, VERNON GERALD	D. JANUARY 20, 2007, HOUSTON, TEXAS
1939-102	RUSSO, MARIUS UGO	D. MARCH 26, 2005, FORT MYERS, FLA.
1942-090	SAIN, JOHN FRANKLIN	D. NOVEMBER 7, 2006, DOWNERS GROVE, ILL.
1981-114	SANCHEZ, LUIS MERCEDES ESCO	D. FEBRUARY 4, 2005, LAGUAIRA, VENEZUELA
1940-078	SANFORD, JOHN DOWARD	D. JANUARY 4, 2005, GREENSBORO, N.C.
1952-092	SCHMIDT, WILLARD RAYMOND	D. MARCH 29, 2007, NEWCASTLE, OKLA.
1965-099	SEMBERA, CARROLL WILLIAM	D. JUNE 14, 2005, SHINER, TEXAS
1958-083	SHERRY, LAWRENCE	D. DECEMBER 17, 2006, MISSION VIEJO, CALIF.
1945-098	SIPEK, RICHARD FRANCIS	D. JULY 17, 2005, QUINCY, ILL.
1939-111	SISTI, SEBASTIAN DANIEL 'SIBBY'	D. APRIL 24, 2006, BUFFALO, N.Y.
1950-091	SMITH, FRANK THOMAS	D. SEPTEMBER 24, 2005, MALONE, FLA.
1963-112	SMITH, WILLIE	D. JANUARY 23, 2006, ANNISTON, ALA.
1931-086	STEVENS, ROBERT JORDAN	D. DECEMBER 30, 2005, FREDERICK, MD.
1934-095	STINE, LEE ELBERT	D. MARCH 6, 2005, HEMET, CALIF.
1940-088	STURGEON, ROBERT HARWOOD	D. MARCH 10, 2007, SAN DIMAS, CALIF.
1941-110	SUDER, PETER	D. NOVEMBER 14, 2006, ALIQUIPPA, PA.
1989-127	SWAN, RUSSELL HOWARD	D. APRIL 26, 2006, LAS VEGAS, NEV.
1939-116	THOMPSON, EUGENE EARL	D. AUGUST 24, 2006, SCOTTSDALE, ARIZ.
1933-062	TRAVIS, CECIL HOWELL	D. DECEMBER 16, 2006, RIVERDALE, GA.
1945-106	ULISNEY, MICHAEL EDWARD	D. SEPTEMBER 22, 2005, NEW SMYRNA BEACH, FLA.
1957-089	URBAN, JACK ELMER	D. JUNE 26, 2006, OMAHA, NEB.
1984-124	URIBE, JOSE ALTAGRACIA	D. DECEMBER 1, 2006, DOMINICAN REPUBLIC
1944-132	VALDES, ROGELIO LAZARO 'ROY'	D. DECEMBER 3, 2005, MIAMI, FLA.
1954-113	VALENTINE, HAROLD LEWIS 'CORKY'	D. JANUARY 21, 2005, ROSWELL, GA.
1942-103	VOISELLE, WILLIAM SYMNES	D. JANUARY 31, 2005, GREENWOOD, S.C.
1942-104	VOLLMER, CLYDE FREDERICK	D. OCTOBER 2, 2006, FLORENCE, KY.
1970-136	VUKOVICH, JOHN CHRISTOPHER	D. MARCH 8, 2007, PHILADELPHIA, PA.
1936-093	WADE, JACOB FIELDS	D. FEBRUARY 1, 2006, WILDWOOD, CALIF.
1938-102	WAGNER, CHARLES THOMAS	D. AUGUST 31, 2006, READING, PA.
1936-094	WEAFER, KENNETH ALBERT	D. JUNE 4, 2005, GUILDERLAND, N.Y.
1942-107	WELLS, LEO DONALD	D. JUNE 23, 2006, SAINT PAUL, MINN.
1947-095	WIDMAR, ALBERT JOSEPH	D. OCTOBER 15, 2005, TULSA, OKLA.
U1978-01	WILLIAMS, CHARLES HERMAN	D. SEPTEMBER 15, 2005, CHICAGO, ILL.
1959-090	WILSON, EARL LAWRENCE	D. APRIL 23, 2005, DETROIT, MICH.
1957-093	WISE, KENDALL COLE 'CASEY'	D. FEBRUARY 20, 2007, NAPLES, FLA.
1947-097	WOOTEN, EARL HAZELL	D. AUGUST 12, 2006, WILLIAMSTON, N.C.
1944-150	ZACHARY, ALBERT MYRON 'CHINK'	D. JUNE 24, 2006, ROME, N.Y.
1957-097	ZUPO, FRANK JOSEPH	D. MARCH 25, 2005, BURLIGAME, CALIF.

STATE-BY-STATE PLAYER LIST

UNITED STATES

ALASKA

CHUGIAK AK
VANRYN, BENJAMIN

SOLDOTNA AK
MABEUS, CHRISTOPHER

ALABAMA

ALTOONA AL
PRIEST, EDDIE

ATHENS AL
HEINKEL, DONALD

ATTALIA AL
JONES, JOSEPH

AUBURN AL
BECKWITH, THOMAS
GROSS, GABRIEL
JACKSON, ROY
UMBACH, ARNOLD

BESSEMER AL
PATTERSON, REGINALD

BIRMINGHAM AL
BAUMGARTNER, JOHN
BEAN, RANDALL
GRAMMAS, ALEXANDER
GREASON, WILLIAM
GRINDER, SCOTT
GUERRIER, MATTHEW
HALL, ALBERT
HELMS, WESLEY
MAXCY, DAVID
MAY, LEE
MOELLER, DENNIS
THORNTON, OTIS
VEALE, ROBERT

CALERA AL
TRUCKS, VIRGIL

CARROLLTON AL
SULLIVAN, WILLIAM

CENTRE AL
JELKS, GREGORY

CLANTON AL
PATTERSON, JARROD

COTTONWOOD AL
COACHMAN, BOBBY

CULLMAN AL
ATKINS, JAMES
MOORE, CHARLES

DAPHNE AL
BATTLE, ALLEN

DECATUR AL
BRITO, JORGE
KNOTTS, GARY
REDUS, GARY
WILSON, ARCHIE

DOTHAN AL
SASSER, MACK

DUNCANVILLE AL
REDMAN, JULIAN
REDMAN, PRENTICE

EIGHT MILE AL
THOMAS, LARRY

ENTERPRISE AL
SPROUT, ROBERT

FAIRHOPE AL
STAPLETON, DAVID

FAYETTE AL
FULTZ, RICHARD

FLORENCE AL
GRBA, ELI

GADSDEN AL
SHIELDS, STEPHEN

GALLION AL
PHILLIPS, GEORGE

GARDENDALE AL
KEEDY, CHARLES

GRAND BAY AL
HENLEY, ROBERT
WOODYARD, MARK

GULF SHORES AL
BLOOMFIELD, CLYDE

HALEYVILLE AL
WHITESIDE, DAVID

HARTSELLE AL
WOODARD, STEVEN

HELENA AL
HODGES, MORRIS

HIGDON AL
LACY, KERRY

HOOVER AL
OBERRY, PRESTON

HOPE HULL AL
THORNTON, LOUIS

HUEYTOWN AL
DAVIS, RUSSELL

HUNTSVILLE AL
LIVELY, EVERETT
MINCHER, DONALD

IRONDALE AL
BAKER, JACK

JASPER AL
PYBURN, JAMES

LIVINGSTON AL
BOWLIN, LOIS

LOXLEY AL
BREEDEN, DANNY
SPARKS, STEPHEN

MADISON AL
DUNCAN, COURTNEY

MALCOLM AL
MERCHANT, JAMES

MCINTOSH AL
WELLS, GREGORY

MOBILE AL
BOLLING, FRANK
BOLLING, MILTON
HOWELL, PATRICK
JOHNSON, KENNETH
JONES, CLEON
LIEBER, JONATHAN
MCGILBERRY, RANDALL

MONTEVALLO AL
TATUM, KENNETH

MONTGOMERY AL
BRAZELL, CRAIG
BURNSIDE, SHELDON
COMPTON, ROBERT
GAMBLE, OSCAR
HUNT, JAMES
MASON, MARTIN
MONTAGUE, JOHN

MONTROSE AL
YELDING, ERIC

MUSCLE SHOALS AL
TATE, RANDALL

NORTHPORT AL
BRUNEY, BRIAN
LARY, FRANK
PEARSON, TERRY BOBBY
SPROWL, ROBERT

ONEONTA AL
TIBBS, JAY

OPELIKA AL
BRYAN, BILLY
LINDSEY, RODNEY

PELL CITY AL
JONES, TODD

PHENIX CITY AL
INGRAM, GAREY

PIKE ROAD AL
LONG, TERRENCE

PINSON AL
STANDRIDGE, JASON

PRATTVILLE AL
KOCH, ALAN

PRINCETON AL
BURNS, TODD

SARALAND AL
WARD, TURNER

SEMMES AL
ADAMS, TERRY
DAVIS, THOMAS
PEAVY, JACOB

STERRETT AL
WORTHINGTON, ALLAN

THEODORE AL
CARBO, BERNARDO
MASON, JAMES

TONEY AL
SMITH, RANDALL
TATE, STUART

TROY AL
MEADOWS, MATTHEW

TRUSSVILLE AL
LATHAM, WILLIAM

TUSCALOOSA AL
KUBISZYN, JACK
MCMATH, JIMMY
MEDDERS, BRANDON

VANDIVER AL
WHITFIELD, FRED

WEDOWEE AL
ANDREWS, FRED
HAMMOND, CHRISTOPHER

WETUMPKA AL
FERGUSON, ROBERT
LOWE, Q.V.

WILMER AL
SEXTON, JIMMY

ARKANSAS

ALMA AR
NYE, RYAN

ARKADELPHIA AR
MCDILL, ALLEN
RONAN, EDWARD

BEE BRANCH AR
MCKNIGHT, JEFFERSON

BENTON AR
CROUSHORE, RICHARD
GARDNER, WESLEY
KUROSAKI, RYAN
LEE, CLIFTON

BRYANT AR
AVANTS, NICK

CAMDEN AR
WILSON, GARY

CAVE SPRINGS AR
WRIGHT, JONATHAN

CONWAY AR
KELL, EVERETT

DES ARC AR
CAMPBELL, KEVIN

DONALDSON AR
RITTER, REGGIE

ELKINS AR
KING, JAMES

EUDORA AR
ETHERIDGE, BOBBY

FAYETTEVILLE AR
PAGNOZZI, THOMAS

FORT SMITH AR
COLEMAN, MICHAEL
SMITH, HAROLD

GREENWAY AR
MCCOY, LARRY

GREENWOOD AR
RISLEY, WILLIAM

HARRISON AR
SHERRILL, TIMOTHY

HOT SPRINGS AR
DANIEL, CHARLES
MCMAHAN, JACK
TAYLOR, KERRY

HOT SPRINGS VILLAGE AR
PETERS, RAYMOND

JONESBORO AR
BETHEA, WILLIAM
KESSINGER, ROBERT
THOMAS, MICHAEL

LITTLE ROCK AR
BEARD, MICHAEL
HANNAHS, GERALD
MCREYNOLDS, WALTER
NAGELSON, RUSSELL
VALENTINE, WILLIAM

LOCUST GROVE AR
GRILLI, GUIDO

LOWELL AR
COCANOWER, JAMES

MARKED TREE AR
MALONE, CHARLES

MARMADUKE AR
FAHR, GERALD

MAUMELLE AR
JONES, WILLIAM

MOUNTAIN HOME AR
PITTS, GAYLEN

NORTH LITTLE ROCK AR
ABBOTT, WILLIAM
GATEWOOD, AUBREY
TIFFEE, TERRY

PARAGOULD AR
WILLIAMS, DONALD

ROGERS AR
LISI, RICCARDO

SPRINGDALE AR
CARPENTER, CHARLES
WILSON, VANCE

STEPHENS AR
HUGHES, RICHARD

SWIFTON AR
KELL, GEORGE

TEXARKANA AR
MCKNIGHT, TONY

ARIZONA

BUCKEYE AZ
SLATON, JAMES

WHEELOCK, GARY

BULLHEAD CITY AZ
BUTCHER, MICHAEL

CAREFREE AZ
REESE, RICHARD

CASA GRANDE AZ
ENDERS, TREVOR

CASHION AZ
MARTIN, ALBERT

CAVE CREEK AZ
DUROCHER, JAYSON
MELVIN, ROBERT

CHANDLER AZ
ACRE, MARK
BARRETT, MARTIN
BARRETT, THOMAS
BELL, DAVID
BELL, DAVID
BELL, ERIC
BELLINGER, CLAYTON
BERRY, MARK
BREWINGTON, JAMIE
BROW, SCOTT
CONTI, STANLEY
DANLEY, KERWIN
DAVANON, JEFFREY
DONNELLY, BRENDAN
EDDY, STEVEN
ETHIER, ANDRE
FALTEISEK, STEVEN
FETTERS, MICHAEL
FRAZIER, ARTHUR
GINTER, KEITH
GORDON, DONALD
HANSELL, GREGORY
HIGUERA, TEODORO
HUCKABY, KENNETH
KENNEDY, TERRENCE
LEZCANO, CARLOS
MALOOF, JACK
MCGINNIS, RUSSELL
MUNSON, ERIC
MURPHY, DWAYNE
NATHAN, JOSEPH
NUNEZ, EDWIN
PAGEL, KARL
PATTERSON, JOHN
PERISHO, MATTHEW
RANSOM, BRIAN
REVENIG, TODD
SEE, RALPH
SWINGLE, PAUL
VANDEBERG, EDWARD
WISE, MATTHEW
YOUNG, ERNEST

COOLIDGE AZ
VILLAREAL, OSCAR

CORNVILLE AZ
VOSS, WILLIAM

EL MIRAGE AZ
AKERFELDS, DARREL

FLAGSTAFF AZ
BOURQUE, PATRICK
RAJSICH, DAVID

FOUNTAIN HILLS AZ
KUEHL, KARL
MCANDREW, JAMES
ROMANICK, RONALD
RUDOLPH, KENNETH

GILBERT AZ
BARRETT, EDWARD
BOUCHEE, EDWARD
BURBA, DAVID
CHRISTENSON, GARY
DEMUTH, DANA
DURBIN, JOSEPH
HILLENBRAND, SHEA
HURST, BRUCE
JENSEN, LARRY
KIM, WENDELL
LOPEZ, ALBERT
LOUX, SHANE
LYDY, DONALD
MERRIMAN, BRETT
NEUGEBAUER, NICKOLAS
PAINTER, LANCE
SLAUGHTER, STERLING
STANKIEWICZ, ANDREW
WARD, COLIN

GLENDALE AZ
BARTEE, KIMERA
BATES, CHARLES
DOWLING, DAVID
DUFFY, CHRISTOPHER
EASLEY, DAMION
FOULKE, KEITH
HOWRY, BOBBY
KRANITZ, RICHARD
MCLAREN, JOHN
PAULEY, DAVID
VIRGIL, OSVALDO
VIRGIL, OSVALDO
WARNER, JACK
WICKANDER, KEVIN
WORRELL, TIMOTHY

GOLD CANYON AZ
FUNK, FRANKLIN

GOODYEAR AZ
BLANCO, HENRY
FALKENBORG, BRIAN
JACKSON, DARRIN
OVERY, HARRY

GREEN VALLEY AZ
GRYGIEL, GEORGE
SMALLEY, ROY

LAKE HAVASU CITY AZ
BAKER, CHARLES
CHRISTENSEN, JOHN
CORKINS, MICHAEL
LEE, ROBERT
MILACKI, ROBERT
MONTEFUSCO, JOHN
WILSON, THOMAS

LAVEEN AZ
GARCIA, LEONARDO

LITCHFIELD PARK AZ
GURA, LARRY
KING, RAYMOND

MARANA AZ
PLUMMER, WILLIAM

MARICOPA AZ
BERGMAN, DUSTIN

MESA AZ
ACCARDO, JEREMY
ARROYO, FERNANDO
BANKS, BRIAN
BURDA, EDWARD
CASSINI, JACK
CHRISTIANSEN, JASON
COREY, BRYAN
COUCHEE, MICHAEL
ESPY, DUANE
GRAHAM, DANIEL
HAAS, ROBERT
HEIDEMANN, JACK
HEINTZELMAN, THOMAS
HINES, BRUCE
HYZDU, ADAM
JOHNSON, RICHARD
JOST, MICHAEL
KIM, BYUNG-HYUN
LACEY, ROBERT
LIND, JACKSON
LOPATA, STANLEY
MACDOUGAL, ROBERT
MADDON, JOSEPH
MCLAUGHLIN, MICHAEL
OHMAN, WILLIAM
ORTON, JOHN
OTTEN, JAMES
PENTLAND, JEFFREY
PITKO, ALEXANDER
POWELL, PAUL
RABE, CHARLES
RODRIGUEZ, EDUARDO
ROOMES, ROLANDO
SADECKI, RAYMOND
STINNETT, KELLY
UNROE, TIMOTHY
VANBENSCHOTEN, JOHN
WIRTH, ALAN
YETT, RICHARD
YOUNG, RICHARD

ORO VALLEY AZ
ZINTER, ALAN

PARADISE VALLEY AZ
BANNISTER, FLOYD
BARAJAS, RODRIGO
BRUSKE, JAMES
CHAVEZ, ERIC
DYE, JERMAINE
ESTES, AARON
FASSERO, JEFFREY
GAGNE, ERIC
GRACE, MARK
JENKINS, GEOFFREY
MULHOLLAND, TERENCE
PHELPS, KENNETH
REMLINGER, MICHAEL
SCHUELER, RONALD
STOTTLEMYRE, TODD
SWIFT, WILLIAM
THOMASSON, GARY
WHITE, DEVON
WILLIAMS, KENNETH
YOUNG, KEVIN
YOUNT, ROBIN

PEORIA AZ
BLOOMQUIST, WILLIAM
CAMPILLO, JORGE
COSGROVE, MICHAEL
GOFF, MICHAEL
LITTELL, MARK
PRINZ, BRET
SKUBE, ROBERT
VERES, RANDOLPH

PHOENIX AZ
ADAMSON, JOEL
ALLEN, RODERICK
ALSTON, GARVIN
AURILIA, RICHARD
BANDO, SALVATORE
BELL, JAY
BLACKABY, ETHAN
BLANCO, GILBERT
BLANKS, LARVELL
BOOTCHECK, CHRISTOPHER
BUTLER, BRETT
CARLOS, FRANCISCO
COLBERN, MICHAEL
CRON, CHRISTOPHER
DARLING, GARY
DESSENS, ELMER
DIGGINS, BENJAMIN
DIMURO, RAYMOND
DOUMIT, RYAN
DYER, DONALD
EGAN, RICHARD
GARAGIOLA, JOSEPH
GENTRY, GARY
GEREN, ROBERT
GILSON, HAROLD
HAAS, BRYAN
HAYES, WILLIAM
JENKINS, FERGUSON
JOHNSON, RANDALL
JONES, CHRISTOPHER
KELLY, MICHAEL
KNOOP, ROBERT
KRYNZEL, DAVID
LAROSE, VICTOR
LEFTWICH, PHILLIP
MEDINA, LUIS
MENDOZA, MICHAEL
MILLER, LARRY
MINTON, GREGORY
NELSON, RICKY
NOBOA, MILCIADES
OLEARY, TROY
OWENS, ERIC
PARSONS, WILLIAM
PENA, JAMES
POWELL, JEREMY
RAMIREZ, ROBERTO
ROBERTSON, DONALD
SANDBERG, RYNE
SCOTT, DARRYL
SHANK, HARVEY
SNYDER, CHRISTOPHER
SPARKS, JOSEPH
STAPLETON, DAVID
STEVERSON, TODD
WICKHAM, DANIEL
YOUNGBLOOD, JOEL
ZICK, ROBERT

PRESCOTT AZ
MOFFITT, RANDALL

QUEEN CREEK AZ
BANDO, CHRISTOPHER
BENJAMIN, MICHAEL
DEHAAN, KORWIN
HOLDRIDGE, DAVID
SARFATE, DENNIS
WINDSOR, JASON

SAFFORD AZ
ALLRED, DALE
CARRASCO, DANIEL

SAHUARITA AZ
MONTOYO, JOSE

SAINT JOHNS AZ
MADRID, ALEXANDER

SCOTTSDALE AZ
BANNISTER, ALAN
BEAM, THEODORE
BECK, RODNEY
BELLE, ALBERT
BOONE, AARON
BOROWSKI, JOSEPH
BOSKIE, SHAWN
BOURJOS, CHRISTOPHER
BRENLY, ROBERT
BROSS, TERRANCE
BURWELL, RICHARD
CAMPANERIS, DAGOBERTO
CANDIOTTI, THOMAS
CASTILLO, FRANK
COLEMAN, VINCENT
COMSTOCK, KEITH
COX, JAMES
DAUGHERTY, JOHN
DAVIS, MARK
DAVIS, RONALD
DEER, ROBERT
DELOSSANTOS, VALERIO
DRISCOLL, JAMES
HARPER, BRIAN
HENDRY, EUGENE
HERMANSON, DUSTIN
HILTON, JOHN
HINCH, ANDREW
HUDGENS, DAVID
JACKSON, CONOR
JACOBY, BROOK
JAMES, JOHN
JENSEN, MARCUS
JESTADT, GARRY
JONES, THOMAS
KEOUGH, RICHARD
KERSHNER, JASON
KILLEBREW, HARMON
KOBEL, KEVIN
KONERKO, PAUL
KROON, MARC
LACHEMANN, RENE

LAGROW, LERRIN
LAYTON, LESTER
LEFEBVRE, JAMES
LEIPER, DAVID
LOCKMAN, CARROLL
LYNCH, EDWARD
MAKSUDIAN, MICHAEL
MARSHALL, JIM
MCANDREW, JAMES
MCCRACKEN, QUINTON
MCKAY, CODY
MCKAY, DAVID
MILLS, RICHARD
MOELLER, CHAD
MORRIS, JOHN
NAGY, STEPHEN
NEWMAN, JEFFREY
ONTIVEROS, STEVEN
OWCHINKO, ROBERT
PATTERSON, DANNY
PHILLIPS, KEITH
PRICE, BRYAN
ROWLAND, MICHAEL
RUSTECK, RICHARD
SALMON, TIMOTHY
SCARSONE, STEVEN
SCHLUETER, JAYD
SCHMELZ, ALAN
SCHOENEWEIS, SCOTT
SCHRIEBER, PAUL
SCHULTZ, CHARLES
SHAVER, JEFFREY
SISCO, ANDREW
STANLEY, FREDRICK
STONE, STEVEN
SULARZ, GUY
SVEUM, DALE
THOMAS, CARL
THORMODSGARD, PAUL
UNSER, DELBERT
WALEWANDER, JAMES
WEBB, BRANDON
WELCH, ROBERT
WILLIAMS, MATTHEW
YOUNG, CURTIS
YOUNT, LAWRENCE
ZELLER, BARTON

SEDONA AZ
AMALFITANO, JOHN

SIERRA VISTA AZ
LOUCKS, SCOTT

SUN CITY AZ
GROTT, MATTHEW
MCCAMENT, LARRY
OSINSKI, DANIEL

SUN CITY WEST AZ
BUDASKA, MARK

SUN LAKE AZ
WHITE, JOYNER

SURPRISE AZ
ARNOLD, JAMES
DAVID, ANDRE
EBERT, DERRIN
GONZALEZ, ADRIAN
HOLBERT, RAY
MAIER, MITCHELL
SNYDER, JOHN

TABAC AZ
SCHNEIDER, DANIEL

TEMPE AZ
ALLEN, JAMES
BROWN, LEON
CEDENO, RONNY
EGAN, THOMAS
HARTGRAVES, DEAN
KLIMCHOCK, LOUIS
MOORE, MICHAEL
OGLIVIE, BENJAMIN
ROBSON, THOMAS
ZUVERINK, GEORGE

TOLLESON AZ
BROWNE, BYRON

TUCSON AZ
ANDERSON, BRIAN
ARIAS, GEORGE
ARNDT, LARRY
BARCELO, LORENZO
BATHE, WILLIAM
BUNDY, CHARLES
BURPO, GEORGE
CAREY, PETER
DARCY, PATRICK
DICKSON, LANCE
DUFFY, FRANK
HAIRSTON, JERRY
HAIRSTON, JERRY
HAIRSTON, SCOTT
HARDY, JAMES
HASSEY, RONALD
HEREDIA, GILBERT
HOWELL, JACK
JACOME, JASON
JOHNSON, BRIAN
KHALIFA, SAM
KINDALL, GERALD
KINSLER, IAN
LAWSON, WILLIAM
LEE, DONALD
LEON, EDUARDO
LOFTON, KENNETH
MAHLBERG, GREGORY
MATHIS, RONALD
MCCALL, JOHN
MORALES, WILLIAM
MOSKAU, PAUL
PAUL, MICHAEL
PEDRIQUE, ALFREDO
PONCINO, LARRY
PORTER, COLIN
ROSS, MARK
SAENZ, CHRISTOPHER
SANDERS, ANTHONY
SPENCER, HUBERT
STANFORD, JASON
STROM, BRENT
TOLMAN, TIMOTHY
TORCHIA, ANTHONY
VOSBERG, EDWARD
WADDELL, THOMAS
WAITS, MICHAEL
WASLEWSKI, GARY

VAIL AZ
BAJENARU, JEFFREY
OLANDER, JAMES

WADDELL AZ
LAKE, STEPHEN

CALIFORNIA

ACTON CA
TAYLOR, WILLIAM

AGOURA CA
BOISCLAIR, BRUCE

AGUANGA CA
HOLMAN, GARY

ALAMEDA CA
NELSON, JOSEPH
ROLLINS, JAMES
SCHULLSTROM, ERIK

ALAMO CA
ANDERSON, DWAIN
BLANKENSHIP, LANCE
FAZIO, ERNEST
LARUSSA, ANTHONY
MCGEE, WILLIE
MORGAN, JOSEPH

ALISO VIEJO CA
KRAWCZYK, RAYMOND
MATRANGA, DAVID

ALPINE CA
GILES, MARCUS
KOONCE, GRAHAM
SPENCER, MICHAEL

ALTA LOMA CA
ADAMS, RICKY
BLUM, GEOFFREY
DAVIS, HERMAN
GWYNN, CHRISTOPHER
RODAS, RICHARD

ALTADENA CA
BOOKER, RODERICK

ANAHEIM CA
FORSCH, KENNETH
GRAY, RICHARD
HOFFMAN, GLENN
MCDONALD, WILLIAM
SCHOOLER, MICHAEL
SPRADLIN, JERRY
VALENT, ERIC
WRIGHT, CLYDE

ANAHEIM HILLS CA
JONES, GARY
MEOLI, RUDOLPH

ANGELS CAMP CA
HEISE, ROBERT

ANTELOPE CA
BROWN, STEPHEN
GARLAND, JON

ANTIOCH CA
MILES, AARON
PETTIS, GARY
PULLIAM, HARVEY
ROUNSAVILLE, VIRL
SANCHEZ, ALEJANDRO
SEGELKE, HERMAN

APPLE VALLEY CA
FERRARESE, DONALD
MITCHELL, ROBERT
MURPHY, DANIEL
VARGAS, JASON
WARNER, JOHN

APTOS CA
EICHHORN, MARK
HALE, WALTER
KRAMER, RANDALL
MILLER, WILLIAM

ARCADIA CA
ARNOLD, CHRISTOPHER
BELTRE, ADRIAN
DUKES, THOMAS

ARCATA CA
WILSON, GARY

ARLETA CA
HERNANDEZ, JEREMY

AROMAS CA
DILLARD, GORDON

ARROYO GRANDE CA
ANDERSON, LAWRENCE
VENTURA, ROBIN

ATHERTON CA
JOHNSON, GERALD
MAYS, WILLIE

AUBURN CA
URBANI, THOMAS

AZUSA CA
EPPARD, JAMES
LITTLEFIELD, JOHN

BAKERSFIELD CA
BARNES, LARRY
BROWN, BRANT
CAIRO, MIGUEL
CULVER, GEORGE
DEMERY, LAWRENCE
ENGEL, ROBERT
HALE, JOHN
HARRELSON, WILLIAM
HOBSON, CLELL
KENNEDY, JUNIOR
LEWIS, COLBY
LITTLEJOHN, DENNIS
LOMAN, DOUGLAS
SAWYER, RICHARD
WALTON, BRUCE

BALDWIN PARK CA
WOODWARD, CHRISTOPHER

BANNING CA
BERUMEN, ANDRES

BARSTOW CA
NORMAN, DANIEL

BASS LAKE CA
LILLY, THEODORE
VANORNUM, JOHN

BEAUMONT CA
ZIEM, STEVEN

BELLFLOWER CA
URREA, JOHN

BENICIA CA
BOHNET, JOHN
CULLEN, TIMOTHY

BERKELEY CA
FELDER, MICHAEL
RANSOM, JEFFERY

BEVERLY HILLS CA
DURRINGTON, TRENT
ZAUN, GREGORY

BLYTHE CA
WHITFIELD, TERRY

BONITA CA
PRIOR, MARK
SPENCE, JOHN

BONSALL CA
REICH, HERMAN

BORREGO SPRINGS CA
CRAIG, ROGER
REGALADO, RUDOLPH

BOULDER CREEK CA
BURRELL, PATRICK

BOULEVARD CA
BYRD, JEFFREY

BREA CA
HOUGH, CHARLES
MCDONALD, JIMMIE

BRENTWOOD CA
HANCOCK, LELAND
MASHORE, CLYDE

BUENA PARK CA
BROWN, OLLIE
DRAKE, ROBERT
HATCHER, MICHAEL
PEDRE, JORGE

BURBANK CA
DAVIS, WILLIAM
SANCHEZ, FREDERICK

BURLINGAME CA
CLEMENTE, EDGARD

CALABASAS CA
AUERBACH, FREDERICK
DAVIS, ERIC

CALIMESA CA
MILLER, ABRAHAM

CALISTOGA CA
SEAVER, GEORGE

CAMARILLO CA
BORCHARD, JOSEPH
MCMULLEN, KENNETH
TACKETT, JEFFERY

CAMERON PARK CA
CODIROLI, CHRISTOPHER
MILLER, STUART

CAMINO CA
QUICK, JAMES

CAMP CONNELL CA
BRIGGS, JOHN

CAMPBELL CA
HAHN, DONALD

CANOGA PARK CA
WOLF, RANDALL

CANYON COUNTRY CA
DILLINGER, ROBERT
ESSEGIAN, CHARLES
JAMES, ROBERT
MURRAY, EDDIE
SMITH, PATRICK

CARLSBAD CA
BEVACQUA, KURT
CHRISTENSON, RYAN
KARL, RANDALL
LYNN, FREDRIC
MASHORE, DAMON
MONTGOMERY, STEVEN
PAEPKE, DENNIS
PAEPKE, JACK
SMITH, DAVID

CARMICHAEL CA
BARRAGAN, FACUNDO
KNUDSEN, KURT
WIGHT, WILLIAM

CARPINTERIA CA
ORTEGA, FILOMENO

CARSON CA
BROWN, OSCAR
BULLOCK, ERIC
CLEAR, ELWOOD
SIMPSON, WAYNE

CASTAIC CA
SLEDGE, TERRMEL

CASTRO VALLEY CA
MAAS, KEVIN

CATHEDRAL CITY CA
OSTEEN, MILTON
ROHR, WILLIAM

CERES CA
OLIVO, MIGUEL EDUARDO

CERRITOS CA
BARBERIE, BRET
BOSLEY, THADDIS
DARWIN, ARTHUR
PASCUCCI, VALENTINO
PATTERSON, MICHAEL

CHATSWORTH CA
GRUNWALD, ALFRED
GUBICZA, MARK
HILJUS, ERIK
LOE, KAMERON
MCANANY, JAMES

CHICO CA
BITKER, JOSEPH
CLEMENTS, PATRICK
DURFEE, PETER
KERFELD, CHARLES
PICO, JEFFREY

CHINO HILLS CA
BILLINGSLEY, BRETT
BRADLEY, RYAN
CLEAR, MARK
GOMEZ, PRESTON
RANDLE, LEONARD
ROENICKE, RONALD
TURNER, SHANE

CHULA VISTA CA
MONGE, ISIDRO
PELAEZ, ALEJANDRO
QUENTIN, CARLOS
WIGGINTON, TY
ZUMAYA, JOEL

CITRUS HEIGHTS CA
GOMEZ, PATRICK
INGLETT, JOSEPH
LINCOLN, MICHAEL

CLAREMONT CA
CLARK, JAMES
GERMANO, JUSTIN
GIAMBI, JASON
GIAMBI, JEREMY
GROSS, KEVIN
HOLTON, BRIAN
JAECKEL, PAUL

CLOVERDALE CA
ROWLAND, RICHARD

CLOVIS CA
ASADOOR, RANDALL
COONEY, TERRANCE
PATTERSON, DARYL
WILLIAMS, DAVID
WILLS, THEODORE
ZERNIAL, GUS

COARSEGOLD CA
WAPNICK, STEVEN

COMPTON CA
DANIELS, BENNIE
DAVIS, RICHARD
GRAY, LORENZO
JOHNSON, RONALD
SCOTT, JOHN

CONCORD CA
ANDREWS, ROBERT
WEHRMEISTER, DAVID

CORONA CA
CAREW, RODNEY
DARR, MICHAEL
DAVIS, BRYSHEAR
GLAUS, TROY
HINSHAW, GEORGE
NEWHAN, DAVID
OUELLETTE, PHILIP
PLUNK, ERIC

CORONA DEL MAR CA
ABBOTT, JAMES
ARDELL, DANIEL

CORONADO CA
WARD, KEVIN

CORTE MADERA CA
MAYER, EDWIN

COSTA MESA CA
AMARAL, RICHARD
COLE, RICHARD
COLUCCIO, ROBERT
LEWIS, SCOTT
MAGALLANES, EVERARDO

COTO DE CAZA CA
GRICH, ROBERT
LIDDELL, DAVID
NEN, ROBERT

COTTONWOOD CA
PARENT, MARK

COVINA CA
BIDDLE, LEE
BOWERS, SHANE
GONZALES, RENE
JONES, DOUGLAS
YOUNG, MICHAEL

CRESTLINE CA
GROTEWOLD, JEFFREY

CULVER CITY CA
SIMPSON, RICHARD

CUPERTINO CA
LEONARD, MARK
MELTON, DAVID

CYPRESS CA
ADLESH, DAVID
CROSBY, ROBERT

DALY CITY CA
JOHNSON, STANLEY

DANA POINT CA
ETHERTON, SETH

DANVILLE CA
CRUDALE, MICHAEL
GROSS, WAYNE
KOLB, BRANDON
KUIPER, DUANE
MOLE, FENTON
NORTON, GREGORY
RAGGIO, BRADY
WELLMAN, BRAD
WINN, DWIGHT

DAVIS CA
CHILES, RICHARD

DEL MAR CA
AUSMUS, BRADLEY
HOFFMAN, TREVOR
HOUSE, THOMAS

DESERT HOT SPRINGS CA
CRISP, COVELLI
WILSON, WILLIAM

DIABLO CA
FOSSE, RAYMOND

DIAMOND BAR CA
BURNS, MICHAEL
HARKEY, MICHAEL
MULLIGAN, SEAN
NORWOOD, WILLIE

DOVE CANYON CA
BOTTING, RALPH
COCHRANE, DAVID

DOWNEY CA
JACKSON, DARRELL
WORTHINGTON, CRAIG

DURHAM CA
MCHENRY, VANCE

EAST PALO ALTO CA
BEAMON, CHARLES

EL CAJON CA
BOONE, DANIEL
BRUCKER, EARLE
ELLIOTT, HARRY
FORDHAM, THOMAS
GEARY, GEOFFREY
HARTLEY, MICHAEL
JONES, CHRISTOPHER
LOCKLEAR, GENE
PHOENIX, STEVEN
ROBERTS, GRANT
RUNGE, PAUL
RYERSON, GARY
SCANLAN, ROBERT
SCHWARTZ, DOUGLAS
VIZCAINO, JOSE

EL CENTRO CA
SEANEZ, RUDY

EL CERRITO CA
BARNES, RONALD
GREEN, ELIJAH

EL DORADO HILLS CA
LEE, DERREK
LOPEZ, FELIPE
MANUEL, JERRY
PALMER, LOWELL
SANTANGELLO, FRANK

EL MONTE CA
ALVAREZ, GABRIEL
RODRIGUEZ, RICHARD

EL SEGUNDO CA
TRABER, WILLIAM

ELK CA
MITCHELL, CRAIG

ELK GROVE CA
CARRITHERS, DONALD
DUNLOP, HARRY
FORTUGNO, TIMOTHY
HOTTMAN, KENNETH
JIMENEZ, JASON
ROSE, MICHAEL
TONIS, MICHAEL

VAUGHN, GREGORY

EMERYVILLE CA
WILLIAMS, BERNARD

ENCINITAS CA
BANE, EDWARD
BEANE, WILLIAM
MCDOWELL, JACK
SMITH, STEVEN

ENCINO CA
BYRNES, ERIC
LOVULLO, SALVATORE
SANDERS, SCOTT

ESCONDIDO CA
AFENIR, MICHAEL
HELFAND, ERIC
HINZO, THOMAS
JACKSON, DAMIAN
JOHNSON, RANDALL
JONES, RANDALL
RADER, DAVID

EUREKA CA
SHANAHAN, PAUL

EXETER CA
PETTYJOHN, ADAM

FAIR OAKS CA
FOX, ANDREW
NIELSEN, GERALD
SAMCOFF, EDWARD
WALBECK, MATTHEW

FAIRFIELD CA
CEPEDA, ORLANDO

FALLBROOK CA
ADAMS, RICHARD
BAKER, DOUGLAS
DAPPER, CLIFFORD
HOWARD, LEE
LEE, MICHAEL
SNIDER, EDWIN

FOLSOM CA
CATHER, MICHAEL
FITZGERALD, EDWARD
GARVIN, THEODORE
RODRIGUEZ, RICARDO

FONTANA CA
CRUZ, TODD
HARRIS, ALONZO
KINGMAN, BRIAN
PRIETO, CHRISTIAN
SCONIERS, DARYL

FORT BRAGG CA
DESILVA, JOHN

FORT JONES CA
BOSCH, DONALD

FOSTER CITY CA
KMAK, JOSEPH
YABU, KEIICHI

FOUNTAIN VALLEY CA
AMELUNG, EDWARD
HUDSON, LUKE
ODOM, JOHN
ROMINE, KEVIN

FREMONT CA
DEBARR, DENNIS
HAUGHEY, CHRISTOPHER

FRESNO CA
BERRY, SEAN
DALENA, PETER
DUPREE, MICHAEL
ELLSWORTH, RICHARD
ESTRADA, JOHNNY
GILBERT, ALBERT
GREGORY, GROVER
HINDS, SAMUEL
HOOVER, JOHN
HOSEY, STEVEN
JONES, ROBERT
MALONEY, JAMES
MAY, RUDOLPH

MEIER, DAVID
OBRIEN, ROBERT
PAPI, STANLEY
REED, DARREN
RICHARDT, MICHAEL
ROZNOVSKY, VICTOR
SCARBERY, RANDY
SMITH, EARL
SPRINGER, DENNIS
TARVER, LASCHELLE
WILLIAMS, SHAD
WOOD, JASON

FRIANT CA
GARDNER, MARK
SIMAS, WILLIAM

FULLERTON CA
ABBOTT, PAUL
GILES, BRIAN
LASORDA, THOMAS
PRITCHARD, HAROLD
REPOZ, ROGER
STEPHENSON, JERRY
THEOBALD, RONALD

GALT CA
VINA, FERNANDO

GARDEN GROVE CA
CROSBY, EDWARD
KIEFER, MARK
KIEFER, STEVEN
LAIRD, GERALD
MURRAY, DANIEL
NEN, RICHARD
NICHOLAS, DONALD
STEVENS, CHARLES
SUTHERLAND, LEONARDO
WARREN, MICHAEL

GARDENA CA
BOYD, GARY

GILROY CA
GOMEZ, RANDALL
LACORTE, FRANK

GLENDALE CA
RITCHIE, WALLACE

GLENDORA CA
BURRIGHT, LARRY
COOPER, BRIAN
MOTA, MANUEL
PIERCE, EDWARD

GOLD RIVER CA
CROWE, GEORGE

GOLETA CA
RANDALL, SCOTT

GRANADA HILLS CA
CIAS, DARRYL
YEAGER, STEPHEN

GRAND TERRACE CA
FERREIRA, ANTHONY

GRANITE BAY CA
DEMERRITT, MARTIN
LEE, LERON
MOSEBY, LLOYD

GRASS VALLEY CA
PAGLIARONI, JAMES
VANBURKLEO, TYLER

GREENBRAE CA
FERRARI, ANTHONY

GROVELAND CA
HARDTKE, JASON

HANFORD CA
LANDIS, WILLIAM

HAWTHORNE CA
LAW, RUDY

HAYWARD CA
IRELAND, TIMOTHY
JIMERSON, CHARLTON
PERME, LEONARD
TABOR, GREGORY

HAYWOOD CA
MURRAY, LARRY

HEMET CA
MERRITT, JAMES
NOLTE, ERIC
PETTIT, GEORGE

HERCULES CA
DOZIER, THOMAS

HERMOSA BEACH CA
ENSBERG, MORGAN
LYONS, STEPHEN

HESPERIA CA
BROOKS, HUBERT
SHEPARD, BERT

HIGHLAND CA
ALLEN, KIM
NELSON, MELVIN
THOMAS, DERREL
ZERBE, WILLIAM

HILLSBOROUGH CA
SNOW, JACK

HOLLISTER CA
BARONE, RICHARD

HOLLYWOOD CA
GENOVESE, GEORGE
VALENZUELA, FERNANDO

HOLTVILLE CA
SERNA, PAUL

HORNBROOK CA
COLEMAN, RAYMOND

HUNTINGTON BEACH CA
CASTILLO, ANTHONY
DOYLE, PAUL
ELSTER, KEVIN
KNACKERT, BRENT
KUBSKI, GILBERT
LEICESTER, JONATHAN
NAULTY, DANIEL
NEWFIELD, MARC
POTTER, MICHAEL
SCHUMAKER, JARED
SHINALL, ZAKARY
SKAUGSTAD, DAVID
SPRINGER, STEVEN
WILSON, CRAIG

INDIAN WELLS CA
FAIRLY, RONALD
GARVEY, STEVEN
SUDAKIS, WILLIAM

INDIO CA
COUSINS, DERRYL
WALTERS, MICHAEL

INGLEWOOD CA
BASS, NORMAN
BROWN, JOPHERY
MCFADDEN, LEON

IRVINE CA
ANDERSON, GARRET
ATKINS, GARRETT
BOOTY, JOSHUA
BRUNETTE, JUSTIN
GOMEZ, CHRIS
GRIFFIN, DOUGLAS
LANGSTON, MARK
SAMBITO, JOSEPH
STABLEIN, GEORGE
SUKLA, EDWARD
WEBER, NEIL
WISE, ROY

KEYES CA
WOODS, JAMES

LA CANADA CA
WHISENANT, MATTHEW

LA HABRA CA
DERRINGTON, CHARLES

LADERA HEIGHTS CA
BRADFORD, CHARLES

LADERA RANCH CA
HAMPTON, ISAAC
HOULTON, DENNIS

LAFAYETTE CA
BOCHTE, BRUCE
FARIES, PAUL
LOCKER, ROBERT
MILLETTE, JOSEPH

LAGUNA BEACH CA
DECINCES, DOUGLAS
MURPHY, THOMAS
WITT, GEORGE

LAGUNA HILLS CA
CONATSER, CLINTON

LAGUNA NIGUEL CA
BERRYHILL, DAMON
CUMMINGS, JOHN
GREBECK, CRAIG
HILL, DONALD
KIRKPATRICK, EDGAR
RATLIFF, PAUL
SCOTT, MICHAEL
TOMPKINS, RONALD
WITT, MICHAEL

LAHABRA CA
ANDREWS, JOHN
BURLESON, RICHARD
HENRICH, ROBERT
STEVENS, DAVID

LAJOLLA CA
COLEMAN, GERALD
ROBINSON, BRUCE
TRAMMELL, ALAN

LAKE ALMANOR CA
BOWMAN, ROBERT
STILLWELL, KURT
STILLWELL, RONALD

LAKE ARROWHEAD CA
SCHATTINGER, JEFFERY

LAKE ELSINORE CA
CRAM, GERALD

LAKE FOREST CA
HEATHCOCK, RONALD

LAKE ISABELLA CA
KLUTTS, GENE

LAKEWOOD CA
CHIFFER, FLOYD
ELLINGSEN, HAROLD
HUNTER, BRIAN
ROEBUCK, EDWARD
SELLERS, JEFFREY
WILLIAMS, STANLEY

LAMESA CA
CLUCK, ROBERT
ERAUTT, EDWARD
FOSTER, ALAN
JUDD, MICHAEL
RUSHFORD, JAMES

LAMIRADA CA
ADAMS, WILLIAM

LANCASTER CA
SLAYBACK, WILLIAM
STRINGER, LOUIS
VALENTINE, ELLIS

LAPALMA CA
GARCIA, RALPH

LAPUENTE CA
LANDREAUX, KENNETH

LAQUINTA CA
BAYLOR, DON
MURCER, BOBBY
PEARSON, ALBERT
PEREZCHICA, ANTONIO
WINKLES, BOBBY

LATHROP CA
HART, JAMES

LAVERNE CA
CORCORAN, TIMOTHY
HENLEY, GAIL
HINES, BENJAMIN
REED, JEREMY

LEMON COVE CA
LACOSS, MICHAEL

LEMON GROVE CA
REYNOLDS, THOMAS

LEMOORE CA
BILLINGSLEY, CHAD

LEUCADIA CA
FLANNERY, TIMOTHY

LIDO ISLE CA
CAREY, ANDREW

LINCOLN CA
BRYANT, RONALD
HENGEL, DAVID
MCCLELLAN, PAUL

LLANO CA
ADAMS, ROBERT

LODI CA
BARTLETT, JASON
BURKE, STEVEN
HITTLE, LLOYD
MINETTO, CRAIG
OLIVER, DAVID
SPRAGUE, EDWARD

LOMITA CA
QUALLS, CHAD

LOMPOC CA
CHURCH, RYAN
HARGIS, GARY

LONG BEACH CA
BURROUGHS, JEFFREY
CONNELLY, STEVEN
EVANS, DARRELL
FITZGERALD, MICHAEL
FROST, CARL
GALLO, MICHAEL
GONZALEZ, GABRIEL
MARSHALL, DAVID
POWELL, LEJON
SMITH, ROBERT
TULOWITZKI, TROY
TURANG, BRIAN

LOS ALAMITOS CA
HARRISON, THOMAS
JOHNSTON, REX
MUSER, ANTHONY

LOS ALTOS CA
CAMPBELL, JAMES
DACQUISTO, JOHN
RIGHETTI, DAVID
WIHTOL, ALEXANDER

LOS ALTOS HILLS CA
GABRIELSON, LEONARD

LOS ANGELES CA
ALEXANDER, GARY
CASTILLO, ROBERT
CHRIS, MICHAEL
CLAREY, DOUGLAS
DRAKE, SAMUEL
DRAKE, SOLOMON
ELLIS, DOCK
GRANT, JAMES
HARRIS, VICTOR
HUGHES, JAMES
JOHNSON, LOUIS
JONES, HAROLD
LOFTON, JAMES
LYONS, HERSCHEL
MANN, KELLY
MARTINEZ, ALFREDO
MEJIAS, ROMAN
MOORE, ROBERT
MOTA, DANIEL
MURRAY, RICHARD
NEWSON, WARREN

ROBINSON, FRANK
SATRIANO, THOMAS
STRONG, JAMAL
TARASCO, ANTHONY
WALTON, REGINALD
WATKINS, ROBERT
WINFIELD, DAVID
WOODARD, DARRELL

LOS GATOS CA
BOITANO, DANNY
HENDERSON, KENNETH

LOS MOLINOS CA
COX, GLENN

MADERA CA
CLARK, BRYAN
WILLIAMS, RICHARD

MALIBU CA
CLAYTON, ROYCE

MANHATTAN BEACH CA
BOWLES, BRIAN
GARCIAPARRA, ANTHONY
KENDALL, FRED

MARINA DEL REY CA
BANKS, ERNEST

MARTINEZ CA
GARCIA, ALFONSO
NEU, MICHAEL

MARYSVILLE CA
WEBSTER, RAYMOND

MENIFEE CA
LUULOA, KEITH
WOODSON, RICHARD

MENLO PARK CA
BREWER, MICHAEL
MCCARTY, DAVID

MERCED CA
FUENTES, BRIAN
MOONEYHAM, WILLIAM

MILL VALLEY CA
BAXES, MICHAEL
KUHN, KENNETH
WILHELM, JAMES

MILLBRAE CA
BOCKMAN, JOSEPH
JEFFERIES, GREGORY
SILVERA, CHARLES

MILPITAS CA
HARRELL, JOHN

MISSION VIEJO CA
ACOSTA, EDUARDO
AUGUST, DONALD
DYER, MICHAEL
GASPAR, RODNEY
KEMP, STEVE
MEYER, ROBERT
PUNTO, NICHOLAS
SCHMIDT, DAVID
TOLENTINO, JOSE

MODESTO CA
BRINK, BRADFORD
KOSKI, WILLIAM

MONROVIA CA
SUTHERLAND, GARY

MONTEREY CA
HEYDEMAN, GREGORY

MOORPARK CA
MAURIELLO, RALPH
WARD, CHRIS

MORAGA CA
ZUBER, JON

MORENO VALLEY CA
DAWLEY, JOSEPH
EDWARDS, MICHAEL
GARCIA, MICHAEL
JAMES, CLEO
KIELTY, ROBERT
MADSON, RYAN
WARDLE, CURTIS

MORGAN HILL CA
LERCH, RANDY
STODDARD, ROBERT
VILLAFUERTE, BRANDON

MORRO BAY CA
QUEEN, MELVIN

MOUNT SHASTA CA
MYERS, RICHARD

MOUNTAIN RANCH CA
SADEK, MICHAEL

MOUNTAIN VIEW CA
ARROYO, RUDOLPH
CHIAMPARINO, SCOTT
DALTON, MICHAEL
KEYSER, BRIAN

MURRIETA CA
BARTON, ROBERT
BATTON, CHRISTOPHER
SHELDON, BOB
WYNNE, MARVELL

NAPA CA
BRUSSTAR, WARREN
LANDIS, JAMES
LODIGIANI, DARIO
PORTER, ROBERT

NATIONAL CITY CA
HERNANDEZ, RODOLFO

NEVADA CITY CA
SCHU, RICK

NEWBERRY SPRINGS CA
KEENER, JOSEPH

NEWBURY PARK CA
DALEY, PETER
JOHNSON, TYLER
LAMB, DAVID
MAGNANTE, MICHAEL

NEWHALL CA
ANDERSON, JAMES
FLAVIN, JOHN
KREUTER, CHAD

NEWPORT BEACH CA
GARDNER, JEFFREY
HANDLEY, EUGENE
HASEGAWA, SHIGETOSHI
MILLER, JOHN
MUSSELMAN, JEFFREY
OLSON, GREGGORY
ROHDE, DAVID
SELE, AARON
WRIGHT, JARET

NEWPORT COAST CA
HARRISON, RORIC
RIBANT, DENNIS

NIPOMO CA
BOWSFIELD, EDWARD
LILLARD, WILLIAM

NORCO CA
HARLOW, LARRY
OLSEN, KEVIN

NORTH HILLS CA
PATE, ROBERT

NORTHRIDGE CA
LOMBARDI, PHILIP
SCHAEFFER, MARK

NOVATO CA
BARNES, JOHN
DEMAESTRI, JOSEPH
GOFF, JERRY

OAK VIEW CA
HOVLEY, STEPHEN

OAKDALE CA
HERRIAGE, WILLIAM

OAKLAND CA
DRESE, RYAN
GAINES, ARNESTA
HENDERSON, RICKEY
HOWARD, STEVEN
LACY, LEONDAUS
OLIVER, NATHANIEL
PAGE, MITCHELL
REAMS, LEROY
ROBINSON, EARL
SASSER, ROBERT
VANCE, GENE
WILLIAMS, WILLIAM
WOODS, ALVIS

OCEANSIDE CA
BRAUN, JOHN
LITTLETON, WES
MCNAMARA, ROBERT
NOREN, IRVING
OWNBEY, RICHARD
ROBERTS, DAVID
RUNGE, BRIAN
WALTERS, DANIEL

OJAI CA
LOWRY, NOAH

ORANGE CA
BUCKELS, GARY
GIPSON, CHARLES
HOCKING, DENNIS
STONEMAN, WILLIAM
THOMPSON, JASON

ORANGEVALE CA
COQUILLETTE, TRACE
JONES, TIMOTHY

OROVILLE CA
CAMPBELL, JAMES
NOLAN, GARY

OXNARD CA
CRUZ, JACOB
HILTON, HOWARD
MALINOSKY, ANTHONY
MCANULTY, PAUL
WILLARD, GERALD

PACIFIC PALISADES CA
DREIFORT, DARREN
FULLMER, BRADLEY
HORTON, ANTHONY
KENDALL, JASON
LEARY, TIMOTHY
VATCHER, JAMES

PACIFICA CA
DIAZ, MICHAEL
MORALES, RICHARD

PACOIMA CA
BUFORD, DONALD
WHITE, LARRY

PALM DESERT CA
BARNES, LUTHER
BROHAMER, JOHN
COHEN, HYMAN
SIMPSON, THOMAS

PALM SPRINGS CA
HARGAN, STEVEN
SPECK, ROBERT

PALMDALE CA
ALLANSON, ANDREW
EVELAND, DANA
JONES, ODELL
KUBEL, JASON
KUTCHER, RANDY
PORTO, ALFRED

PALO ALTO CA
KIBLER, JOHN

PALO CEDRO CA
CADARET, GREGORY

PALOS VERDES ESTATES CA
COWAN, BILLY

PALOS VERDES PENINSULA CA
BORDLEY, WILLIAM

PARADISE CA
LOHSE, KYLE

PARADISE VALLEY CA
SHERLOCK, GLENN

PASADENA CA
DAVIS, MARK
JOHNSTONE, JOHN
LITTLE, WILLIAM
YOUNG, MATTHEW

PASO ROBLES CA
LARSON, DANIEL
STRICKLAND, JAMES
WALLACE, DEREK

PEBBLE BEACH CA
INCAVIGLIA, PETER

PENRYN CA
LACHEMANN, MARCEL

PERRIS CA
CLARK, ROBERT
SCRANTON, JAMES

PICO RIVERA CA
BRADLEY, FREDERICK
GONZALES, DANIEL
RINCON, ANDREW

PINION HILLS CA
RUCKER, DAVID

PIONEERTOWN CA
MOORE, TOMMY

PISMO BEACH CA
HOWELL, ROY

PLACENTIA CA
GREER, BRIAN

PLACERVILLE CA
OBRIEN, SYDNEY

PLEASANT HILL CA
DAVIS, DOUGLAS
SHERIDAN, NEILL
WOTUS, RONALD

PLEASANTON CA
BLUE, VIDA

PLUMAS LAKE CA
HIGGINS, SCOTT

POLLOCK PINES CA
REECE, ROBERT

POMONA CA
MOTA, ANDRES

PORT HUENEME CA
HOLLY, JEFFREY

PORTER RANCH CA
SUPPAN, JEFFREY

PORTERVILLE CA
CLEVENGER, TRUMAN
LABANDEIRA, JOHN
STEPHEN, LOUIS

PORTOLA VALLEY CA
GALL, JOHN

POWAY CA
ANDERSON, BRADY
BEARE, GARY
BOCHY, BRUCE
BRUNANSKY, THOMAS
BURNITZ, JEROMY
EICHELBERGER, JUAN
GRIFFIN, THOMAS
GWYNN, ANTHONY
GWYNN, ANTHONY
HERRMANN, EDWARD
JOHNSON, JERRY
NEVIN, PHIL
OROSCO, JESSE
PHILLIPS, JASON
PLANTIER, PHILLIP
READY, RANDY
STEWART, DAVID
TEMPLETON, GARRY
TOMKO, BRETT

RAMONA CA
KUBIAK, THEODORE

RANCHO CORDOVA CA
BOSIO, CHRISTOPHER
CONVERSE, JAMES
HORGAN, JOSEPH

RANCHO CUCAMONGA CA
HOSEY, DWAYNE
PARKS, DEREK
TOLIVER, FREDDIE
WOOTEN, WILLIAM

RANCHO MIRAGE CA
CRESSE, MARK
GAMBOA, THOMAS
RICHERT, PETER
ROSEN, ALBERT
SUTTON, DONALD

RANCHO MURIETA CA
ADAMS, CHARLES

RANCHO PALOS VERDES CA
IRABU, HIDEKI
SASAKI, KAZUHIRO

RANCHO SANTA FE CA
AGUILERA, RICHARD
BLACK, HARRY
BOONE, BRET
FINLEY, STEVEN
GRUDZIELANEK, MARK
LORETTA, MARK
MCCASKILL, KIRK

RANCHO SANTA MARGARITA CA
LAMP, DENNIS
MARQUEZ, ALFONSO

REDDING CA
BERNERO, ADAM
BOSETTI, RICHARD
STROHMAYER, JOHN

REDLANDS CA
GROSS, KIP
WHITMER, DANIEL

REDONDO BEACH CA
BRADLEY, MILTON
PALMQUIST, EDWIN

REDWOOD CITY CA
GILE, DONALD

REDWOOD VALLEY CA
CHAPMAN, KELVIN

RICHMOND CA
BABITT, MACK
CAIN, LESLIE
MOORE, ALVIN

RIO LINDA CA
OLIVER, ROBERT

RIVERSIDE CA
BLOMDAHL, BENJAMIN
CHANT, CHARLES
DAVIS, ALVIN
EDWARDS, DAVID
EDWARDS, MARSHALL
FORD, DARNELL
HALL, THOMAS
HEMAN, RUSSELL
HOUSIE, WAYNE
KENNEDY, ADAM
MADDOX, JERRY
MYERS, GREGORY
PERCIVAL, TROY
RODRIGUEZ, STEVEN
SHERMAN, DARRELL
SKAGGS, DAVID
TREANOR, MATTHEW
WARD, DARYLE
WARD, GARY

ROCKLIN CA
BLANKENSHIP, KEVIN
STATON, DAVID

ROHNERT PARK CA
BORDI, RICHARD

ROLLING HILLS CA
SLAUGHT, DONALD

ROSEVILLE CA
BARR, JAMES
BESANA, FREDERICK
HEMPHILL, BRET
ROSELLI, ROBERT
SAX, DAVID
SAX, STEPHEN
SOUZA, KENNETH

ROUGH AND READY CA
ROENICKE, GARY

SACRAMENTO CA
BAUER, RICHARD
BROWN, CURTIS
CHARLES, FRANKLIN
CROUCH, ZACHARY
DOWELL, KENNETH
EDGE, CLAUDE
FLENER, GREGORY
FREEMAN, LAVEL
HAZEWOOD, DRUNGO
HOWELL, JAMES
JAMES, DION
JOHNSON, NICHOLAS
JORDAN, PAUL
LINTZ, LARRY
MCNEALY, ROBERT
METZGER, CLARENCE
MOUTON, JAMES
OFFICE, ROWLAND
SIMS, GREGORY
WESTLAKE, WALDON
WILBORN, THADDEAUS
YOUNG, MICHAEL

SALIDA CA
BALDWIN, RICK

SALINAS CA
ALDRETE, MICHAEL
CAMACHO, ERNIE
NADY, XAVIER

SAN BERNARDINO CA
GERBER, CRAIG
STANFIELD, KEVIN

SAN BRUNO CA
BAKER, JOHNNIE

SAN CARLOS CA
DAVENPORT, JAMES
GRIEVE, BENJAMIN

SAN CLEMENTE CA
LAMB, RAYMOND
LENTINE, JAMES
MERIDITH, RONALD
MOELLER, JOSEPH
TERLECKY, GREGORY

SAN DIEGO CA
ARLIN, STEPHEN
BALAZ, JOHN
BALSLEY, DARREN
BLACKWELL, TIMOTHY
BURROUGHS, SEAN
CANNIZZARO, CHRISTOPHER
CIANFROCCO, ANGELO
CLARK, ANTHONY
CORREIA, KEVIN
ELLIOT, LAWRENCE
ENGLE, RALPH
ESPY, CECIL
GARCIA, DAVID
GILES, BRIAN
GLYNN, WILLIAM
GRABER, RODNEY
HAMELS, COLBERT
HARANG, AARON
HENSLEY, MATTHEW
HORN, SAMUEL
JACOBS, MICHAEL
JONES, JACQUE
JONES, RUPPERT
KARROS, ERIC
KLAUS, ROBERT
KROEGER, JOSHUA
LYSANDER, RICHARD
MARONE, LOUIS
MARTIN, PAUL
MCDAVID, RAY
MITCHELL, KEITH
PAUL, JOSHUA
PICCIOLO, ROBERT
PORTER, DANIEL
RAINEY, CHARLES
RETTENMUND, MERVIN
RICHARD, CHRISTOPHER
ROBINSON, DAVID
ROBINSON, FLOYD
ROSE, DONALD
SAIPE, MIKE
SCOTT, TIMOTHY
SHERRY, NORMAN
SKINNER, ROBERT
SORRELL, WILLIAM
VITIELLO, JOSEPH
WALLER, ELLIOTT
WILKINS, DEAN

SAN DIMAS CA
WILFONG, ROBERT

SAN FERNANDO CA
SMYRES, CLARENCE

SAN FRANCISCO CA
ARDIZOIA, RINALDO
CIMOLI, GINO
CLARK, JERMAINE
COSEY, DONALD
FRANKLIN, MICAH
JONES, ALFORNIA
LEAGUE, BRANDON
NOLD, RICHARD
POWELL, ALONZO
WEVER, STEFAN

SAN GABRIEL CA
GRABOW, JOHN
PACIOREK, JOHN

SAN JACINTO CA
CAMPER, CARDELL
CRIPE, DAVID
ROSS, FLOYD

SAN JOSE CA
BONGIOVANNI, ANTHONY
BROGLIO, ERNEST
CAPILLA, DOUGLAS
DAVIS, STEVEN
DUNN, RONALD
DURAN, DANIEL
GIOVANALA, EDWARD
KOLSTAD, HAROLD
LOHRKE, JACK
MANGAN, JAMES
OLDHAM, JOHN
PILLETTE, DUANE
RENNA, WILLIAM
ROUSE, MICHAEL
SAMUELS, ROGER
TRIANDOS, CONSTANDIN
TROEDSON, RICHARD
USHER, ROBERT

SAN JUAN CAPISTRANO CA
FULLER, JOHN
JANESKI, GERALD
YORK, JAMES

SAN LEANDRO CA
GOODWIN, CURTIS
TASBY, WILLIE
WHITE, JEROME
WILLIS, DONTRELLE

SAN LORENZO CA
KLEVEN, JAY

SAN LUIS OBISPO CA
CANDAELE, CASEY
ESTRADA, CHARLES
KRUKOW, MICHAEL
KUBINSKI, TIMOTHY
MELHUSE, ADAM

SAN MARCOS CA
BURICH, WILLIAM
LATMAN, ARNOLD
LINIAK, COLE
ROSS, GARY
TURNER, KENNETH

SAN MARINO CA
GOTT, JAMES

SAN MATEO CA
BREINING, FRED
MONTAGUE, EDWARD
PEDERSON, STUART
WERLE, WILLIAM

SAN PABLO CA
MILLER, EDWARD
ROBERSON, CHRISTOPHER

SAN PEDRO CA
JURAK, EDWARD

SAN RAFAEL CA
BOCCABELLA, JOHN
FOPPERT, JESSE
VENABLE, WILLIAM
WAKEFIELD, WILLIAM

SAN RAMON CA
BRESSOUD, EDWARD
DAVIS, MICHAEL
HAMILTON, DAVID
JACKSON, MICHAEL
JOHNSON, ERIK
KIRRENE, JOSEPH
MEYER, DANIEL
ROBERTS, LEON
WALKER, ANTHONY
WALTERS, KENNETH
ZUVELLA, PAUL

SAN YSIDRO CA
MITRE, SERGIO

SANTA ANA CA
MOREHEAD, DAVID
RAMIREZ, ERASMO
SMITH, CHRISTOPHER
THOBE, JOHN
ZEBER, GEORGE

SANTA BARBARA CA
ALEJO, ROBERT
SPILBORGHS, RYAN

SANTA CLARA CA
LANSFORD, JOSEPH
SIMONTACCHI, JASON

SANTA CLARITA CA
CRIM, CHARLES
DELAMAZA, ROLAND
SALKELD, ROGER

SANTA CRUZ CA
GALLAGHER, ROBERT
HAMM, PETER
HILL, GLENALLEN

SANTA MARIA CA
BISHOP, MICHAEL
DINEEN, KERRY
SMITH, BRYN
STEELS, JAMES

SANTA MONICA CA
CACEK, CRAIG
HAYNES, HEATH
TURNER, JOHN
WORKMAN, HENRY

SANTA PAULA CA
COOKSON, BRENT

SANTA ROSA CA
BRANT, MARSHALL
CHILDRESS, RODNEY
DRAHMAN, BRIAN
JOOST, EDWIN
MAGRINI, PETER
MEADS, DAVID

SANTA YNEZ CA
ASSELSTINE, BRIAN

SANTEE CA
DAVENPORT, JOSEPH
FORSTER, TERRY
PENN, HAYDEN

SAUGUS CA
MARSHALL, CLARENCE

SEASIDE CA
JACKSON, REGINALD

SEBASTOPOL CA
LANE, JASON

SELMA CA
CERDA, JAIME

SEPULVEDA CA
ANDREW, KIM
EDWARDS, WAYNE

SHERMAN OAKS CA
BUFORD, DAMON
FANZONE, CARMEN
GOOSSEN, GREGORY
JUSTICE, DAVID
LESLEY, BRADLEY

SIERRA MADRE CA
THROOP, GEORGE

SILVERADO CA
CHAMPION, ROBERT

SIMI VALLEY CA
FRANCO, MATTHEW
KING, ERIC
LAKER, TIMOTHY
WEAVER, JEFFREY

SOLVANG CA
BONHAM, WILLIAM
KELLEHER, MICHAEL
WOODS, GARY

SOMIS CA
ELLIOTT, RANDY
GORMAN, BRIAN

SONOMA CA
BRIGGS, DANIEL
NICKLE, DOUGLAS
SCHALLOCK, ARTHUR

SONORA CA
ENDICOTT, WILLIAM

SOQUEL CA
MESSERSMITH, JOHN
SIPIN, JOHN

SOUTH GATE CA
OJEDA, OCTAVIO

SOUTH PASADENA CA
NELSON, ROBERT

SPRING VALLEY CA
PERKINS, BRODERICK

SPRINGVILLE CA
HARVEY, HAROLD

STANFORD CA
WITMEYER, RONALD

STEVENSON RANCH CA
NORDHAGEN, WAYNE
WOLFE, LAURENCE

STOCKTON CA
BURTT, DENNIS
GARIBALDI, BOB
JACQUEZ, PATRICK
JACQUEZ, THOMAS
JOHNSON, FRANK
JOHNSON, KEITH
MCINTOSH, TIMOTHY
PFEIL, ROBERT
SPRAGUE, EDWARD

STRATHMORE CA
COX, CHARLES

STUDIO CITY CA
BARRY, RICHARD

SUISUN CITY CA
BOWIE, JAMES
MORAGA, DAVID

SUN CITY CA
MISURACA, MICHAEL

SUN VALLEY CA
RICO, ALFREDO

SUNNYVALE CA
DUKES, JAN
ERICKSON, SCOTT
LANDRITH, HOBERT
ROBERTSON, RICHARD

SURFSIDE CA
CHAMBERLAIN, CRAIG

SUSANVILLE CA
ERNAGA, FRANK
NYMAN, NYLS

SYLMAR CA
REDFERN, PETER

TARZANA CA
WASHINGTON, LARUE

TEMECULA CA
GLEASON, ROY
HOWARD, MATTHEW
JOHNSON, REED
RENTERIA, RICHARD
SMYTH, STEVEN
WALLACH, TIMOTHY

THOUSAND OAKS CA
ANDERSON, GEORGE
ASHLEY, BILLY
COMBE, GEOFFREY
DYKSTRA, LENNY
FICK, ROBERT
LIEBERTHAL, MICHAEL
PARIS, KELLY
SISCO, STEVEN
WILSON, JACK

TORRANCE CA
BARGAR, GREG
DAVISON, SCOTTY
DEDMON, JEFFREY
DEMARIA, CHRIS
LEEPER, DAVID
MILLER, JUSTIN
NEWCOMBE, DONALD

TRABUCO CANYON CA
DONNELS, CHRIS
FLORA, KEVIN
FYHRIE, MICHAEL
HUMPHREY, TERRYAL
KEOUGH, MATTHEW
MURA, STEPHEN
ROBINSON, JEFFREY

TUJUNGA CA
RUSCH, GLENDON

TULARE CA
ELLIS, JAMES

TURLOCK CA
REICHERT, DANIEL
SODERSTROM, STEPHEN

TUSTIN CA
BANEY, RICHARD
DUNNING, STEVEN
GUARDADO, EDWARD
HUDLER, REX
LARKIN, PATRICK
SCHWABE, MICHAEL

UNION CITY CA
LEDESMA, AARON

UPLAND CA
COGGIN, DAVID
FRANK, STEPHEN
MAXIE, LARRY
PASTORE, FRANK
TRACEY, SEAN

VACAVILLE CA
SELLS, DAVID

VALENCIA CA
DOWNING, ALPHONSO
LORRAINE, ANDREW
RUSSELL, WILLIAM
SHIELDS, JAMES
TARTABULL, DANILO

VALLEJO CA
HOLLINS, DAMON
SABATHIA, CARSTEN
STRONG, JOSEPH
THURSTON, JOSEPH

VAN NUYS CA
KENDERS, ALBERT
PIEDRA, JORGE
ZITO, BARRY

VENICE CA
NETTLES, MORRIS
SLATEN, DOUGLAS

VENTURA CA
COLBORN, JAMES
HIBBS, JAMES
KNIGHT, BRANDON
LANG, DONALD

VICTORVILLE CA
HART, JON
MEAD, CHARLES
VELASQUEZ, GUILLERMO

VILLA PARK CA
BOONE, ROBERT
HANSEN, DAVID
STUBING, LAWRENCE

VISALIA CA
COSTA, SHANE
HILL, AARON
LEEK, EUGENE
MILLS, JAMES
MULLINIKS, STEVEN
OJEDA, ROBERT
ROBINSON, RONALD
STROUGHTER, STEPHEN
TALBOT, ROBERT
ULLGER, SCOTT

VISTA CA
DUNLAP, GRANT

WALNUT CA
GARKO, RYAN
RAIN, STEVEN

WALNUT CREEK CA
ANDRADE, STEPHEN
BRYE, STEPHEN

WATSONVILLE CA
HART, BODHI

WEST COVINA CA
COX, JEFFREY
DEVEREAUX, MICHAEL
HAREN, DANIEL
LEHR, CHARLES
MOORE, WILLIAM
SMALL, AARON

WEST HILLS CA
BIRKINS, KURT
PLODINEC, TIMOTHY
WOLF, JAMES

WEST HOLLYWOOD CA
CANSECO, JOSE

WEST SACRAMENTO CA
LEACH, JALAL
LOWERY, QUENTON

WESTLAKE VILLAGE CA
CONSOLO, WILLIAM
DEMPSEY, JOHN
RADINSKY, SCOTT
SCIOSCIA, MICHAEL
ZEILE, TODD

WESTMINSTER CA
BURTON, ELLIS
HESSMAN, MICHAEL

WHITTIER CA
SAMUELS, JOHN
ZOSKY, EDWARD

WILDOMAR CA
KRUG, EVERETT
MACK, SHANE

WINDSOR CA
FIMPLE, JOHN

WINNETKA CA
BROCK, TARRIK

WINTON CA
MINOR, BLAS
TILLOTSON, THADDEUS

WOODLAKE CA
WOHLFORD, JAMES

WOODLAND CA
GRIFFIN, MICHAEL
PEDROIA, DUSTIN
TORCATO, ANTHONY

WOODLAND HILLS CA
AUDE, RICHARD
BRAGGS, GLENN
BROUHARD, MARK
CEY, RONALD
MCGUIRE, RYAN
SABERHAGEN, BRET
SMITH, CARL

WOODSIDE CA
MCCOVEY, WILLIE

YORBA LINDA CA
AASE, DONALD
CAMPANIS, JAMES
GALLEGO, MICHAEL
JONES, MARCUS
LUKE, MATTHEW
MILLER, DARRELL
NORRIS, MICHAEL
PATTERSON, JEFFREY
PETTIBONE, HARRY
RODGERS, ROBERT
SAUNDERS, DOUGLAS
VERHOEVEN, JOHN
WERHAS, JOHN
WOLF, WALTER

YREKA CA
BENNETT, DAVID
BENNETT, ERIK

YUBA CITY CA
DECKER, DEE

YUCAIPA CA
GARCIA, DANIEL
TEAHEN, MARK

YUCCA VALLEY CA
OCONNOR, JACK
SEYFRIED, GORDON

COLORADO

ARVADA CO
METRO, CHARLES

AURORA CO
ANGELINI, NORMAN
EPSTEIN, MICHAEL
FISHER, BRIAN
JOHNSON, BOBBY
LERSCH, BARRY

BOULDER CO
PLEWS, HERBERT

BRIGHTON CO
GUCCIONE, CHRISTOPHER
HELTON, TODD
REININGER, TRAVIS

BROOMFIELD CO
DEIDEL, JAMES
RAPP, VERNON

CASCADE CO
MCCARTHY, BRANDON

CASTLE ROCK CO
GIVENS, BRIAN
MYERS, MICHAEL

VERES, DAVID
WEISS, WALTER

COLORADO SPRINGS CO
COCKRELL, ATLEE
DRAVECKY, DAVID
GOSSAGE, RICHARD
HAJEK, DAVID
KRUG, GARY
LEE, MARK
RICE, PATRICK

CRAIG CO
HERNDON, HARRY

DENVER CO
BARD, JOSHUA
BLATERIC, STEPHEN
EGLOFF, BRUCE
FOSTER, MARTIN
HILLMAN, JOHN
KOSTRO, FRANK
MADDEN, MICHAEL
MCDONALD, DONZELL
THOMPSON, MICHAEL
WAYNE, GARY

DURANGO CO
CARLTON, STEVEN
SEALE, JOHNNIE

ENGLEWOOD CO
CHOUINARD, ROBERT
STRAIN, JOSEPH

ERIE CO
HALLADAY, HARRY
HENSLEY, CHARLES

ESTES PARK CO
MAY, SCOTT

EVERGREEN CO
KOUZMANOFF, KEVIN

FLORISSANT CO
KNIFFIN, CHARLES

FORT COLLINS CO
DRAGO, RICHARD
DYBZINSKI, JEROME

FRUITA CO
ELDER, GEORGE

GLENWOOD SPRINGS CO
STILLMAN, ROYLE

GOLDEN CO
LOLLAR, WILLIAM
REED, STEVEN

GRAND JUNCTION CO
SERRANO, JAMES

GREELEY CO
CHACON, SHAWN

HIGHLANDS RANCH CO
COREY, MARK
HOLZEMER, MARK
LANSING, MICHAEL
LIDGE, BRADLEY
STEVENS, DEWAIN
STRITTMATTER, MARK

LAJUNTA CO
OQUIST, MICHAEL

LAKEWOOD CO
GLINATSIS, GEORGE
SHIFFLETT, GARLAND

LITTLETON CO
BAILEY, CHARLES
BOVEE, MICHAEL
BURKE, JOHN
BURKE, TIMOTHY
CASTILLA, VINICIO
DAVIDSON, ROBERT
GEBHARD, ROBERT
GOLDY, PURNAL
HURDLE, CLINTON
MEACHAM, ROBERT
PLANTENBERG, ERIK
SHUMPERT, TERRANCE
TATUM, JAMES
THOMPSON, MARK

LONE TREE CO
MULLINS, FRANCIS

LONGMONT CO
BEHNEY, MELVIN
CRAIN, JESSE
HARDY, CARROLL
RIDDOCH, GREGORY

LOVELAND CO
BROCK, GREGORY
MOORE, BRADLEY

LYONS CO
PARROTT, MICHAEL

MANITOU SPRINGS CO
WALLACE, DONALD

MONTROSE CO
TRUJILLO, MICHAEL

MONUMENT CO
ADAMSON, JOHN

NORTHGLENN CO
KNUDSON, MARK
MOLINA, CRUZ

PARKER CO
HUSON, JEFFREY
TODD, JAMES
ZAVARAS, CLINTON

PARSHALL CO
UHLAENDER, THEODORE

PUEBLO CO
LOWN, OMAR
RAMOS, KENNETH

PUEBLO WEST CO
BROCAIL, DOUGLAS

THORNTON CO
COX, JAMES

VILLA GROVE CO
ELARTON, VINCENT

WESTMINSTER CO
JESTER, VIRGIL
OSBORN, DANNY

WHEAT RIDGE CO
JUTZE, ALFRED

CONNECTICUT

BRIDGEPORT CT
NASTU, PHILIP

BRISTOL CT
DIBBLE, ROBERT

CHESHIRE CT
TATA, TERRY

COLCHESTER CT
TSAMIS, GEORGE

COS COB CT
SANDLOCK, MICHAEL

DEEP RIVER CT
DAYETT, BRIAN

EAST LYME CT
MCDONALD, JOHN

FAIRFIELD CT
NAGY, CHARLES

FARMINGTON CT
MCAULIFFE, RICHARD

GREENWICH CT
BONILLA, ROBERTO
FOSTER, GEORGE
MAZZILLI, LEE

GUILFORD CT
GREENBERG, ADAM
MACKENZIE, KENNETH

HAMDEN CT
STUPER, JOHN

JEWETT CITY CT
LAFRANCOIS, ROGER

LISBON CT
DAWLEY, WILLIAM

MADISON CT
MERULLO, MATTHEW

MYSTIC CT
SEVERINSEN, ALBERT

NAUGATUCK CT
CANEIRA, JOHN

NEW BRITAIN CT
DEJOHN, MARK

NEW PRESTON CT
LAHOUD, JOSEPH

NIANTIC CT
CHIASSON, SCOTT
KELLY, ROBERT

NORWALK CT
GRABOWSKI, JASON
MORTON, KEVIN

OLD GREENWICH CT
SWAN, CRAIG

OLD SAYBROOK CT
ELLIS, JOHN

ORANGE CT
CECCARELLI, ARTHUR

OXFORD CT
KEPSHIRE, KURT

PLAINVILLE CT
SNYDER, EARL

QUAKER HILL CT
WALKER, PETER

ROCKY HILL CT
BOTTALICO, RICHARD
REYNOLDS, JAMES

SANDY HOOK CT
WINANS, MATTHEW

SHARON CT
LAMB, JOHN

SHELTON CT
HIRSCHBECK, MARK
MCCARTHY, GREGORY
PAPA, JOHN

SIMSBURY CT
KOBACK, NICHOLAS

SOUTHBURY CT
FLEMING, DAVID

SOUTHINGTON CT
DENORFIA, CHRISTOPHER
RACZKA, MICHAEL

SOUTHPORT CT
UPSHAW, WILLIE

STAMFORD CT
LINZ, PHILIP
SAVERINE, ROBERT
VALENTINE, ROBERT

STONINGTON CT
QUIRK, ARTHUR

TRUMBULL CT
BRESLOW, CRAIG

WATERBURY CT
DIORIO, RONALD

WATERFORD CT
GARDNER, WILLIAM

WATERTOWN CT
BROGNA, RICO

WESTPORT CT
PORZIO, LAWRENCE

WINDSOR CT
TEED, RICHARD

WINSTED CT
MORHARDT, MEREDITH

DISTRICT OF COLUMBIA

WASHINGTON DC
HINTON, CHARLES
ROYSTER, WILLIE
VALENTINE, FRED

DELAWARE

CAMDEN DE
WILLIAMS, DAVID

CLAYMONT DE
CRIMIAN, JOHN

DOVER DE
THOMPSON, RYAN

GEORGETOWN DE
SHOCKLEY, JOHN

MIDDLETOWN DE
HENRY, DWAYNE

MILFORD DE
JACOBS, FORREST

NEWARK DE
LESHER, BRIAN
MAY, DERRICK
MENCH, KEVIN

TOWNSEND DE
SWANN, PEDRO

WILMINGTON DE
EDDY, CHRISTOPHER
GRAFFANINO, ANTHONY
HARMAN, WILLIAM
MAY, DAVID
NEIGER, ALVIN
STEWART, ANDREW

FLORIDA

ALTAMONTE SPRINGS FL
SHELDON, SCOTT
WEEKS, RICKIE

ALTOONA FL
REED, ROBERT

ALVA FL
GREENWELL, MICHAEL

APOPKA FL
COLEMAN, CLARENCE
GORYL, JOHN
MANVILLE, RICHARD
RIGBY, BRADLEY

AUBURNDALE FL
CHITI, HARRY
DAVIS, JOHNNY

AVENTURA FL
BERENYI, BRUCE

AVON PARK FL
GORDON, THOMAS

BARTOW FL
BARR, STEVEN

BELLEVIEW FL
BENTON, ALFRED

BLOUNTSTOWN FL
YOUNG, TIMOTHY

BOCA RATON FL
BELLIARD, RAFAEL
FERNANDEZ, OCTAVIO
FINNVOLD, ANDERS
GILBERT, MARK
GRAY, JOHN
HOLMES, THOMAS
JENNINGS, JAMES
LYTTLE, JAMES
MCENANEY, WILLIAM
MURPHY, DANIEL
RAPUANO, EDWARD
ROSE, PETER
SALAZAR, LUIS

WILEY, MARK

BOKEELIA FL
AUST, DENNIS

BONITA SPRINGS FL
LUZINSKI, GREGORY
MILLER, RICHARD
SANDS, CHARLES
STUFFEL, PAUL

BOYNTON BEACH FL
ALOU, FELIPE
DENT, RUSSELL
MURPHY, THOMAS
ORSINO, JOHN
PIAZZA, MICHAEL
SANGUILLEN, MANUEL

BRADENTON FL
AGOSTO, JUAN
ALVAREZ, WILSON
ANDRES, ERNEST
BARTIROME, ANTHONY
BRICE, ALAN
CARDENAL, JOSE
CARTER, LANCE
CLAY, KENNETH
CLINES, EUGENE
CRAFT, TERRY
DIAZ, EINAR
EMMEL, PAUL
EYRE, SCOTT
FAIRCHILD, CHADWICK
FISK, CARLTON
GORZELANNY, THOMAS
GREEN, CHRISTOPHER
KISON, BRUCE
KORCHECK, STEPHEN
LANGFORD, JAMES
LAVALLIERE, MICHAEL
MACKANIN, PETER
MAY, MILTON
MAYS, JOSEPH
MOATES, DAVID
MONCHAK, ALEX
MORRISON, JAMES
NAPOLEON, EDWARD
NELSON, DAVID
OSBURN, LARRY
PASTORNICKY, CLIFFORD
PRINCE, THOMAS
QUADE, GREGORY
REITH, BRIAN
RIDZIK, STEPHEN
ROBINSON, DON
SAUVEUR, RICHARD
SMITH, KEITH
TOLLBERG, BRIAN
WALKER, TYLER
WEAVER, JAMES

BRISTOL FL
DAVIS, TIMOTHY

BROOKSVILLE FL
ARROYO, BRONSON
CLEMONS, LANCE
FORSCH, ROBERT
FRASCATORE, JOHN
WALKER, MICHAEL

CANTONMENT FL
HIATT, PHILIP
LEWIS, JOHNNY
PRESLEY, JAMES

CAPE CORAL FL
ALLENSON, GARY
BIRD, JAMES
CASTILLO, MARTIN
COLEMAN, JOSEPH
COLETTA, CHRISTOPHER
DWYER, JAMES
JOHNSON, RONTREZ
LOMASNEY, STEVEN
MORENO, ORBER
PIATT, ADAM
RASMUSSEN, ERIC

RODRIGUEZ, VICTOR
SANTANA, RAFAEL

CAROL CITY FL
ALVAREZ, ROGELIO
MENENDEZ, ANTONIO

CHIEFLAND FL
BRINKMAN, JOSEPH
MALLOY, MARTIN

CLEARWATER FL
ANDERSON, MARLON
BRUMMER, GLENN
COX, JOSEPH
DANCY, WILLIAM
DEMARS, WILLIAM
GARCIA, RICHARD
GOOD, ANDREW
HORSMAN, VINCENT
KNOWLES, DAROLD
KOCH, WILLIAM
MOSQUERA, JULIO
NAHORODNY, WILLIAM
PROLY, MICHAEL
WELLS, DAVID

CLERMONT FL
CONLEY, DONALD
KORONKA, JOHN
MCDOWELL, SAMUEL

COCOA FL
BUSSE, RAYMOND

COOPER CITY FL
FERNANDEZ, ALEXANDER

CORAL GABLES FL
IBANEZ, RAUL

CORAL SPRINGS FL
FORD, MATTHEW
MADDOX, ELLIOTT
ROSENBERG, STEVEN
STENNETT, RENALDO

CRESTVIEW FL
BALE, JOHN
BONILLA, JUAN
TAYLOR, TERRY

DADE CITY FL
ELLIS, SAMUEL
HEPLER, WILLIAM

DANIA FL
CHAPPAS, HARRY
PFISTER, DANIEL
VALDESPINO, HILARIO

DAVENPORT FL
BATISTA, LEOCADIO

DAVIE FL
FLOYD, CORNELIUS
FUENTES, MICHAEL
LEYRITZ, JAMES

DAYTONA BEACH FL
BAUTA, EDUARDO
HICKOX, EDWIN
POTTER, SCOTT

DEBARY FL
FOSNOW, GERALD

DEERFIELD BEACH FL
RADISON, DANIEL
STYNES, CHRISTOPHER

DELAND FL
BOROS, STEPHEN
GLOVER, JOHN
ROWDON, WADE

DELEON SPRINGS FL
SCOTT, LUKE

DELRAY BEACH FL
BELTRAN, RIGOBERTO
GRAY, THEODORE
HOUSEHOLDER, PAUL
KUTYNA, MARION
MOLINARO, ROBERT

DELTONA FL
BROWN, ANDREW
CAMPBELL, DAVID
CONCEPCION, ONIX
NEWHAUSER, DONALD

DORAL FL
SHOPAY, THOMAS

DUNDEE FL
PARRISH, LARRY

DUNEDIN FL
ADAMS, RUSS
TORRES, HECTOR

DUNNELLON FL
ANDERSON, NORMAN
SUMMERS, JOHN

DURANT FL
ROGERS, KENNETH

ENGLEWOOD FL
BECKERT, GLENN
MACPHERSON, HARRY
PLANK, EDWARD

ESTERO FL
FREY, JAMES

FERNANDINA FL
CORBETT, DOUGLAS

FERNANDINA BEACH FL
SHAVE, JONATHAN

FLORAHOME FL
MULLINS, GREGORY

FLORAL CITY FL
HAWBLITZEL, RYAN
RANEW, MERRITT

FORT LAUDERDALE FL
BRITTON, CHRISTOPHER
CONINE, JEFFREY
FORD, EDWARD
GIL, TOMAS
HAMMONDS, JEFFREY
HOPE, JOHN
JUDEN, JEFFREY
LYDEN, MITCHELL
MORSE, MICHAEL
ORDONEZ, MAGGLIO
RIOS, ARMANDO
RIPPLEY, THOMAS
SHEALY, RYAN
SHIELDS, ROBERT
STANLEY, ROBERT
TRACHSEL, STEPHEN
WHEAT, LEROY
YOUNG, DMITRI

FORT MYERS FL
BLYLEVEN, RIKALBERT
BUCHANAN, BRIAN
CABRERA, ORLANDO
CLIBURN, STEWART
CUYLER, MILTON
DUVALL, MICHAEL
EVANS, DWIGHT
JOHNSON, ADAM
LOONEY, BRIAN
LOWE, DEREK
MAUER, JOSEPH
MILTON, ERIC
PANTHER, JAMES
PUTNAM, PATRICK
RAYFORD, FLOYD
RESOP, CHRISTOPHER
SANDERS, DEION
SCHAEFER, ROBERT
SCORE, HERBERT
STAEHLE, MARVIN
SULLIVAN, MARC
TROMBLEY, MICHAEL
VENAFRO, MICHAEL
WOODSON, WALTER

FORT PIERCE FL
HUDSON, HAL
MCGRIFF, TERENCE

FRUITLAND PARK FL
HOLT, ROGER
MACKENZIE, HENRY

GAINESVILLE FL
REICHARDT, FREDERIC
SNEAD, ESIX

GOLDEN BEACH FL
GUILLEN, OSWALDO

GREEN COVE SPRINGS FL
STEIN, WILLIAM

GREENACRES FL
MICELOTTA, ROBERT

GULFPORT FL
HERNANDEZ, ROBERTO

HAINES CITY FL
DAVIDSON, CLEATUS

HIALEAH FL
DIAZ, EDDY
GANDARILLAS, GUSTAVO
HARRIS, LEONARD
HEREDIA, FELIX
MUNOZ, JUAN
ORDONEZ, REYNALDO
PENA, ORLANDO
RIOS, DANIEL
TARTABULL, JOSE
TAYLOR, ANTONIO
TOCA, JORGE

HIGH SPRINGS FL
DINARDO, LEONARD

HILLSBORO BEACH FL
FUGERE, JOSEPH

HOBE SOUND FL
JOHNSON, HOWARD

HOLIDAY FL
JOHNSON, DANE

HOLLYWOOD FL
ARIAS, ALEJANDRO
AVEN, DAVID
BAUTISTA, JOSE
GALVEZ, BALVINO
JONES, ANDRUW
KLINK, JOSEPH
LINSALATA, JOSEPH
MAGRANN, THOMAS
MCDOWELL, ODDIBE
MCKEON, JOEL
ORTIZ, JAVIER

HOMOSASSA FL
HAMPTON, MICHAEL
HERMANSKI, EUGENE

HUDSON FL
DELLAERO, JASON
LOPEZ, HECTOR

INDIALANTIC FL
OBRADOVICH, JAMES

INDIAN HARBOUR BEACH FL
SKRMETTA, MATTHEW
WAKEFIELD, TIMOTHY

INDIAN ROCK BEACH FL
BOYER, CLETIS

ISLAMORADA FL
MCCLURE, ROBERT

JACKSONVILLE FL
BARNWELL, CHRISTOPHER
BRYANT, DONALD
DAVIS, JOEL
DUNN, TODD
FREEL, RYAN
HATHAWAY, HILLARY
JASTER, LARRY
JONES, MICHAEL
JONES, THOMAS
KELLER, KRISTOPHER
PAPELBON, JONATHAN
RELAFORD, DESMOND
RIGDON, PAUL
ROBERTS, WILLIS

TILLMAN, KERRY
WASDIN, JOHN
WILKINS, RICHARD
WYNNE, WILLIAM

JACKSONVILLE BEACH FL
ORTENZIO, FRANK

JENSEN BEACH FL
PROCTOR, SCOTT

JUPITER FL
ABAD, FAUSTO
ANKIEL, RICHARD
ARMSTRONG, JACK
BOTTENFIELD, KENT
BUMP, NATHAN
ESSER, MARK
JOHNSON, MICHAEL
KINGSALE, EUGENE
MINER, ZACHARY
MORRIS, MATTHEW
ROBERSON, SIDNEY
RUNGE, PAUL
SCHMIDT, MICHAEL
SOFIELD, RICHARD
TAUSSIG, DONALD
TEUFEL, TIMOTHY
WAYNE, JUSTIN

KEY WEST FL
STERLING, RANDALL

KISSIMMEE FL
BROWN, DERMAL
CEDENO, CESAR
EUSEBIO, RAUL
FARNSWORTH, KYLE
KARKOVICE, RONALD
LUGO, JULIO

LADY LAKE FL
CHURN, CLARENCE
SIEBERN, NORMAN

LAKE MARY FL
BUTERA, SALVATORE
RAINES, TIMOTHY
RAINES, TIMOTHY

LAKE PARK FL
GRAHE, JOSEPH

LAKE SUZY FL
GINSBERG, MYRON

LAKE WALES FL
BORDERS, PATRICK
DUREN, RINOLD

LAKE WORTH FL
DEGERICK, MICHAEL
EATON, CRAIG
ENRIGHT, GEORGE
GAILLARD, JULIAN
KOZAR, ALBERT
ROCHFORD, MICHAEL

LAKELAND FL
BOURNIGAL, RAFAEL
CRAWFORD, STEVE
DIAZ, MATTHEW
DUSTAL, ROBERT
MCGAFFIGAN, ANDREW
MILLS, ALAN
VERLANDER, JUSTIN
WHITAKER, LOUIS

LAND O'LAKES FL
CHOATE, RANDOL
NIETO, THOMAS
REYES, CARLOS
ROMANO, JASON
THOMPSON, DEREK

LANTANA FL
RADLOSKY, ROBERT

LARGO FL
ANDREWS, CLAYTON
CLARK, RONALD
DEEGAN, WILLIAM
HUFF, AUBREY
MASSET, NICHOLAS
MORRISON, DANIEL
RADKE, BRAD
RAMSEY, MICHAEL
STANIFER, ROBERT

LEESBURG FL
FRASER, WILLIAM
TATE, LEE

LEHIGH ACRES FL
FOSTER, JOHN

LIGHTHOUSE POINT FL
ZISK, RICHARD

LONGBOAT KEY FL
POWER, TED

LONGWOOD FL
LESKANIC, CURTIS
MOSS, JOHN
TAYLOR, WADE
WILSON, PAUL
WYNEGAR, HAROLD

LOXAHATCHEE FL
ALICEA, LUIS

LUTZ FL
CONTRERAS, ARNALDO
CUMBERLAND, JOHN
EVERETT, CARL
FIORE, ANTHONY
KELLY, KENNETH
MARSONEK, SAMUEL
PARDO, ALBERTO
PATTERSON, GILBERT
TAMARGO, JOHN
WILLIAMS, TODD

MADEIRA BEACH FL
BIALAS, DAVID
RIGGLEMAN, JAMES

MARGATE FL
HAAD, YAMID

MARIANNA FL
MATHIS, JEFFREY

MARY ESTHER FL
JAMES, MICHAEL

MATLACHER FL
SUSCE, GEORGE

MAYO FL
PERRY, CHAN
PERRY, HERBERT

MELBOURNE FL
BREEDEN, JOSEPH
CEDERSTROM, GARY
HENNIS, RANDALL
LARKIN, ANDREW
LUDWICK, ERIC
MILLIARD, RALPH
SCHMOLL, STEPHEN

MELBOURNE BEACH FL
STANGE, ALBERT
STIDHAM, PHILLIP

MERRITT ISLAND FL
CLAPINSKI, CHRISTOPHER

MIAMI FL
ALFONSECA, ANTONIO
ALVAREZ, CLEMENTE
ALVAREZ, JUAN
ARCIA, JOSE
ARIAS, RODOLFO
AROCHA, RENE
BAEZ, DANYS
BARRIOS, JOSE
BELLIARD, RONALD
BETANCOURT, YUNIESKY
BOGLE, WARREN
CASANOVA, RAUL
CHULK, CHARLES
CRUZ, NELSON
DAWSON, ANDRE
DELAHOZ, MIGUEL
FABREGAS, JORGE
FERNANDEZ, LORENZO
GARRIDO, GIL
GONZALEZ, ALEXANDER
GONZALEZ, ANDRES
GONZALEZ, ORLANDO
GRATE, DONALD
GRIFFIN, ALFREDO
HERNANDEZ, EISLER
HERNANDEZ, GREGORIO
HERNANDEZ, JACINTO
HERNANDEZ, LEONARDO
HERTZ, STEPHEN
HURST, WILLIAM
ISALES, ORLANDO
IZQUIERDO, HANSEL
JOHNSON, RANDALL
LANDESTOY, RAFAEL
LOPEZ, RAYMOND
LOWELL, MICHAEL
MAESTRI, HECTOR
MARICHAL, JUAN
MARRERO, ELIESER
MARTINEZ, JOSE
MIENTKIEWICZ, DOUGLAS
MOLINA, ISLAY
MOREJON, DANIEL
NARANJO, LAZARO
NUNEZ, VLADIMIR
OROPESA, EDILBERTO
OWENS, HENRY
PALMEIRO, ORLANDO
PASCUAL, CAMILO
PASCUAL, CARLOS
PENA, BRAYAN
PETAGINE, ROBERTO
POLANCO, PLACIDO
POSADA, LEOPOLDO
RAMOS, ROBERTO
RODRIGUEZ, ALEXANDER
ROJAS, EUCLIDES
ROJAS, OCTAVIO
ROMERO, ARMANDO
ROSARIO, MELVIN
SANTOVENIA, NELSON
SIERRA, RUBEN
STEWART, SHANNON
TEJERA, MICHAEL
TOPPIN, RUPERTO

MIAMI BEACH FL
AQUINO, LUIS

MIDDLEBURG FL
BYNUM, MICHAEL

MINNEOLA FL
CUELLAR, MIGUEL

MIRAMAR FL
AMOR, VINCENTE
MARTINEZ, JOSE
MESA, JOSE
OCHOA, ALEX
SOJO, LUIS

MIRAMAR BEACH FL
CARY, CHARLES

MOLINO FL
FRYMAN, DAVID

MONTVERDE FL
MORALES, JOSE

MOUNT DORA FL
KELLY, BRYAN
ROE, JOHN

NAPLES FL
ALFONSO, CARLOS
BROWN, MICHAEL
BRUCKBAUER, FRED
CALI, CARMEN
CARMAN, DONALD
DELOCK, IVAN
HART, JAMES
JAVIER, MANUEL
KOECHER, RICHARD
LEPPERT, DONALD
MCCABE, JOE
PRIETO, ARIEL
ROMANO, JOHN
SPANSWICK, WILLIAM
SUNDIN, GORDON
TRAMMELL, THOMAS

NEW PORT RICHEY FL
CREEK, PAUL
EVERS, WILLIAM
HUBBARD, JOHN
MATOS, JULIUS
TUCKER, THOMAS

NEW SMYRNA FL
BILLINGHAM, JOHN

NEW SMYRNA BEACH FL
FANOVICH, FRANK

NOBLETON FL
HARRIS, CHARLES

NOKOMIS FL
ETCHEBARREN, ANDREW
KNOTT, JONATHAN
OLWINE, EDWARD
VOIGT, JOHN

NORTH LAUDERDALE FL
FALLON, ROBERT

NORTH MIAMI BEACH FL
ABREU, BOB
CROMARTIE, WARREN
MALER, JAMES

NORTH PORT FL
VALENTINE, JOSEPH

OAKLAND FL
MAROTH, MICHAEL

OCALA FL
DICKEN, PAUL
LEDEE, RICARDO
REIS, THOMAS
SCHULT, ARTHUR

OCEAN RIDGE FL
DIMAGGIO, DOMINIC

ODESSA FL
CASH, DAVID
ELIA, LEE
HALL, TOBY
REED, JODY
SNYDER, JAMES
STEWART, JAMES
TELFORD, ANTHONY

OKEECHOBEE FL
BALLINGER, MARK

OLDSMAR FL
DAMICO, JEFFREY
WILSON, KRISTOPHER

ORLANDO FL
BROWN, EDWIN
CLARK, PHILLIP
COLE, DAVID
CRESPO, FELIPE
DEJESUS, IVAN
DIAZ, LAZARO
DIXON, THOMAS
GREINKE, DONALD
GRIFFEY, GEORGE
GRILLI, JASON
HALE, DEMARLO
HEISE, JAMES
LARKIN, BARRY
LEWIS, JAMES
LEZCANO, SIXTO
LILLIS, ROBERT
MITTERWALD, GEORGE
MOTLEY, DARRYL
MOTTOLA, CHARLES
NAVARRO, JAIME
OBANDO, SHERMAN
OLIVER, JOSEPH
OSUNA, ALFONSO
PETERSEN, CHRISTOPHER
PIERZYNSKI, ANTHONY
PINEIRO, JOEL
RASMUSSEN, DENNIS

ROSSY, ELAM
SIEBERT, PAUL
TAVAREZ, JULIAN
VIOLA, FRANK

ORMOND BEACH FL
HOUSE, JAMES
SEBRA, ROBERT
WENDELSTEDT, HARRY
WENDELSTEDT, HARRY
WIEDENBAUER, THOMAS

OSPREY FL
SINGER, WILLIAM

OVIEDO FL
BELLHORN, MARK
CHRISTMAS, STEPHEN
KING, HAROLD
MICELI, DANIEL

PALM BAY FL
SHERRILL, DENNIS
TAM, JEFFREY

PALM BAY GARDENS FL
JACKSON, ROLAND

PALM BEACH FL
BROBERG, PETER
GROTH, JOHN
KINER, RALPH
PALMER, JAMES

PALM BEACH GARDENS FL
CORNELIUS, JONATHAN
DORANTE, LUIS
GULLICKSON, WILLIAM
HUTTON, THOMAS
KEY, JAMES
PORTER, J.W.
REARDON, JEFFREY
SCHWARZ, JEFFREY
TORRE, FRANK

PALM CITY FL
BARK, BRIAN
MARTIN, JOHN
MCHALE, JOHN
PHOEBUS, THOMAS

PALM COAST FL
BOZE, MARSHALL
KARSAY, STEFAN
WOODWARD, WILLIAM

PALM HARBOR FL
ABERNATHY, MICHAEL
BAILOR, ROBERT
BOSMAN, RICHARD
DEARMAS, ROLANDO
DIFELICE, MICHAEL
FOLEY, THOMAS
HEATH, KELLY
HOLMBERG, DENNIS
LLOYD, GRAEME
MAGADAN, DAVID
MAJTYKA, LEROY
MOUTON, LYLE
PETERSON, HARDING
PULLI, FRANK
QUANTRILL, PAUL
RATZER, STEVEN
SCHEINBLUM, RICHARD
STANTON, MICHAEL
WEBB, HENRY
WILLIAMS, JAMES

PALMETTO FL
DAVIS, TRENCH
HUME, THOMAS
JACOBS, LAMAR

PANAMA CITY FL
GAINER, JONATHAN
MARTIN, THOMAS

PARRISH FL
PLEIS, WILLIAM

PEMBROKE PINES FL
ALMONTE, HECTOR
ALOU, MOISES
BUSHING, CHRISTOPHER
GUTIERREZ, RICARDO
HARDY, JOHN
RENTERIA, EDGAR
SANTIAGO, BENITO
WEAVER, EARL

PENSACOLA FL
CANNON, JOSEPH
HANNA, PRESTON
HUTTO, JAMES
LEWALLYN, DENNIS
LITTON, JON
NUNNARI, TALMADGE
POWELL, HOSKEN
SADLER, WILLIAM
SAUCIER, KEVIN
SPOONEYBARGER, TIMOTHY
WOOD, JACOB
WRIGHT, KENNETH

PERRY FL
SADLER, WILLIAM

PINELLAS PARK FL
BONSER, BOOF
KISSELL, GEORGE
LEFLORE, RONALD
SCOTT, DONALD
SMITH, WALTER

PLANT CITY FL
NIEKRO, LANCE
RABURN, RYAN
WEGNER, MARK

PLANTATION FL
FOSSAS, EMILIO
JOHNS, DOUGLAS
JOHNSON, CHARLES
NICOSIA, STEVEN
ZARDON, JOSE

POMPANO BEACH FL
BAHNSEN, STANLEY
BROWN, CURTIS
CASTIGLIONE, PETER
DOTEL, OCTAVIO
MCDONALD, DAVID
MONDESI, RAUL
SCHULER, DAVID

PONTE VEDRA BEACH FL
RHODEN, RICHARD

PORT CHARLOTTE FL
MILLS, WILLIAM

PORT ORANGE FL
REGILIO, NICHOLAS
WILLIAMS, CHARLES

PORT RICHEY FL
VERDI, FRANK

PORT SAINT LUCIE FL
ALFONZO, EDGARDO
APODACA, ROBERT
BELL, HEATH
BRANTLEY, MICHAEL
CASTILLO, ALBERTO
ESPINOZA, ALVARO
ESTRELLA, LEONCIO
FLOYD, ROBERT
GARDNER, CHRISTOPHER
JACKSON, ALVIN
KLASSEN, DANIEL
MCCRAW, TOMMY
NIEMANN, RANDAL
PULSIPHER, WILLIAM
TESSMER, JAY

PORT SALERNO FL
KAAT, JAMES

PUNTA GORDA FL
FRANKLIN, GARY

RIVERVIEW FL
MILLEDGE, LASTINGS
REDMON, GLENN

ROCKLEDGE FL
BURNS, ROBERT
FIORENTINO, JEFFREY
FOUCAULT, STEVEN

ROTUNDA WEST FL
EISCHEN, JOSEPH

ROYAL PALM BEACH FL
MCFARLANE, ORLANDO

RUSKIN FL
CRAWFORD, CARLOS
SALAS, MARK
WILLIS, DALE

SAFETY HARBOR FL
COLES, DARNELL
CONNORS, WILLIAM
DIAZ, CARLOS
MACDONALD, ROBERT
MARTINEZ, DAVID
ROLLS, DAMIAN

SAINT AUGUSTINE FL
BRADY, JAMES
CHEADLE, DAVID
RUSKIN, SCOTT

SAINT CLOUD FL
ACTA, MANUEL
HICKEY, JAMES
LANIER, HAROLD

SAINT PETERSBURG FL
ARROJO, LUIS
BERGERON, PETER
BIERBRODT, NICHOLAS
CRAWFORD, GERALD
FOLKERS, RICHARD
HAYES, BEN
HAYES, VON
HOLBERT, AARON
KLINE, JOHN
MANON, JULIO
MCKEAN, JAMES
OLSEN, ANDREW
PLAZA, RONALD
SEARAGE, RAYMOND
SHEFFIELD, GARY
THIGPEN, ROBERT
WAECHTER, DOUGLAS
ZIMMER, THOMAS

SAINT PETERSBURG BEACH FL
CAMPISI, SALVATORE

SAN ANTONIO FL
NELSON, WAYLAND

SANFORD FL
BROCK, TERRENCE
ECKSTEIN, DAVID

SANIBEL FL
TRAUTWEIN, JOHN

SARASOTA FL
ALLEN, NEIL
AYRAULT, JOSEPH
BLOSSER, GREGORY
BROWER, JAMES
BROWN, MARTY
CACERES, EDGAR
CAREY, PAUL
CARROLL, CLAY
COOPER, DONALD
DEPASTINO, JOSEPH
DUBEE, RICHARD
FOLEY, MARVIS
FRAILING, KENNETH
GARRETT, RONALD
GUTHRIE, MARK
HINTON, RICHARD
HOWARD, BRUCE
JACKSON, RYAN
JOHNSTONE, JOHN
JONES, JOSEPH
KELLY, DALE
KRAVEC, KENNETH
KUSNYER, ARTHUR
LAMONT, GENE
LUTZ, ROLLIN
MATTES, TROY
MCCARVER, JAMES
MCCLAIN, SCOTT
ODONOGHUE, JOHN
ODONOGHUE, JOHN
PETERS, GARY
PIERSOLL, CHRISTOPHER
RAWLEY, SHANE
RENICK, WARREN
ROBINSON, DEWEY
ROESSLER, PATRICK
SAFFELL, THOMAS
SCHMIDT, DAVID
SEAY, ROBERT
SHORT, WILLIAM
SNYDER, KYLE
SPENN, FREDERICK
SPRINGSTEAD, MARTIN
STOBBS, CHARLES
TAYLOR, CARL
TORBORG, JEFFREY
YANCY, HUGH

SEBASTIAN FL
ESTOCK, GEORGE

SEBRING FL
HURST, JAMES
KNOTT, ERIC
PAGAN, JOSE
WHITE, GABRIEL

SEFFNER FL
FIGGINS, DESMOND
HITCHCOCK, STERLING

SEMINOLE FL
JONES, GREG
KINNAMON, WILLIAM
KOTCHMAN, CASEY
KOZLOWSKI, BENJAMIN
ZIMMER, DONALD

SINGER ISLAND FL
NAKTENIS, PETER

SOUTH MIAMI FL
PERKINS, DANIEL

SPRING HILL FL
BELL, MICHAEL
REPLOGLE, ANDREW
VOLTAGGIO, VITO

STUART FL
ABBOTT, KURT
FORDYCE, BROOK
LEACH, TERRY
MURPHY, ROBERT
RADER, DOUGLAS

SUMMERFIELD FL
JATA, PAUL
MCCOOL, WILLIAM

SUN CITY CENTER FL
PASLEY, KEVIN

SUNRISE FL
FERNANDEZ, HUMBERTO

TALLAHASSEE FL
FIGUEROA, BIENVENIDO
GREENE, CHARLES
JEFFERSON, REGINALD
PALMER, DEAN
ROSS, DAVID

TAMARAC FL
LEVY, EDWARD

TAMPA FL
ADKINS, STEVEN
BOGGS, WADE
BOLES, CARL
BOMBARD, MARC
CASH, RONALD
COMPTON, MICHAEL
CORT, BARRY
EDEN, EDWARD
FAEDO, LEONARDO
FIGGA, MICHAEL
FOGG, JOSHUA
GOODEN, DWIGHT

GRAY, JEFFREY
HENDERSON, STEPHEN
HERNANDEZ, CARLO
JAY, JOSEPH
JEFFCOAT, HAROLD
JOHNSON, LARRY
KNORR, RANDY
LITWHILER, DANIEL
LOVELACE, VANCE
MAGRANE, JOSEPH
MARTINEZ, CONSTANTINO
MCCULLERS, LANCE
MCGRIFF, FREDERICK
MERCED, ORLANDO
MICHAELS, JASON
MILEY, DAVID
MILITELLO, SAM
MONTELEONE, RICHARD
NIEDENFUER, THOMAS
PERLOZZO, SAMUEL
PICKERING, CALVIN
PINIELLA, LOUIS
POSADA, JORGE
PUIG, RICHARD
QUIRICO, RAFAEL
RABELO, MICHAEL
RAMOS, JOHN
RATH, FRED
RATH, FREDERICK
RAY, CHRISTOPHER
ROTHSCHILD, LAWRENCE
SCHACKER, HAROLD
SEOANE, MANUEL
SEXAUER, ELMER
STURTZE, TANYON
TIMMONS, OSBORNE
VALDES, MARC
WHITEN, MARK
WILLIAMS, RICHARD
YOUMANS, FLOYD

TARPON SPRINGS FL
ARCHER, JAMES
CUMMINGS, MIDRE
DAVIS, OTIS
DUCEY, ROBERT
FREGOSI, JAMES
ISRINGHAUSEN, JASON
MENKE, DENIS
POLONI, JOHN
TIMLIN, MICHAEL

TEMPLE TERRACE FL
ROBERTS, ROBIN
VONHOFF, BRUCE

TEQUESTA FL
BELLA, JOHN
SHAW, ROBERT

THE VILLAGES FL
LINES, RICHARD
SMITH, PETER
STINSON, GORRELL

TIERRA VERDE FL
PAVLICK, GREGORY

TRINITY FL
PHELPS, JOSHUA

UMATILLA FL
LEMON, CHESTER

VALRICO FL
CARTER, JEFFREY
GRAVES, DANIEL
HANCOCK, RONALD
HEATH, MICHAEL
HERMIDA, JEREMY
MARTIN, DONALD
OHME, KEVIN
PHELPS, THOMAS
TOSCA, CARLOS

VENICE FL
GUINDON, ROBERT
TOLAR, KEVIN
TRESH, THOMAS
YATES, ALBERT

VERO BEACH FL
BALL, JEFFERY
BILARDELLO, DANN
CAMILLI, DOUGLAS
CONTI, GUY
COSTELLO, JOHN
DEBUS, JON
GABBARD, KASON
LILLIQUIST, DEREK
MONDAY, ROBERT
OZARK, DANIEL
PERRANOSKI, RONALD
RENNERT, LAURENCE
SHULOCK, JOHN
VALDES, ISMAEL

WELLINGTON FL
BROWNSON, MARK
BURNETT, SEAN
CORMIER, RHEAL
HERNANDEZ, ANGEL
PONCE, CARLOS
RIEDLING, JOHN

WESLEY CHAPEL FL
DENBO, GARY
EILAND, DAVID
MACKOWIAK, ROBERT
MCDOUGALL, MARSHALL
MILLER, TREVER
REKAR, BRYAN
STRAWBERRY, DARRYL
WETHERBY, JEFFREY

WEST MELBOURNE FL
BOLES, JOHN

WEST PALM BEACH FL
ANDINO, ROBERT
BARNES, RICHARD
BROWN, LARRY
BRUNSON, WILLIAM
CARTER, GARY
FISCHER, JEFFREY
GALARRAGA, ANDRES
GARCIA, GUILLERMO
IZQUIERDO, ENRIQUE
LAUZERIQUE, GEORGE
ONEAL, RANDALL
PAVANO, CARL
PRIDE, CURTIS
ROMERO, EDGARDO
THOMPSON, ROBERT
UNDERWOOD, THOMAS
WALKER, LARRY
WOOD, MICHAEL

WESTON FL
AMARO, RUBEN
COLON, BARTOLO
DAAL, OMAR
GUZMAN, JUAN
JONES, ROSS
LEITER, ALOIS
RAMIREZ, MANUEL

WILDWOOD FL
BRANDT, JOHN

WINDERMERE FL
CAPPUZZELLO, GEORGE
DAMON, JOHNNY
HAMMOND, STEVEN
HART, JOHN
TAUBENSEE, EDWARD

WINTER GARDEN FL
BARBER, BRIAN
MILCHIN, MICHAEL

WINTER GARDENS FL
GRIFFEY, GEORGE

WINTER HAVEN FL
BEAN, EDDIE
DOYLE, BRIAN
DOYLE, ROBERT
GIBSON, DERRICK
HOUK, RALPH
HOWARD, FRED
JUDSON, HOWARD
LAYNE, JERRY
MANUEL, CHARLES
RAMIREZ, ALEXANDER

WINTER PARK FL
BICHETTE, ALPHONSE
DILLMAN, WILLIAM
JOHNSON, DAVID

ZEPHYRHILLS FL
ALDRED, SCOTT
ENYART, TERRY
HUPPERT, DAVID
MARSHALL, MICHAEL

GEORGIA

ACWORTH GA
EVERETT, JEFFREY
MADISON, CHARLES
PEVEY, MARTY

ALAMO GA
MIMBS, MICHAEL

ALBANY GA
BURDETTE, FREDDIE
DEWS, ROBERT
KNIGHT, CHARLES
WASZGIS, ROBERT

ALPHARETTA GA
ASSENMACHER, PAUL
BARRETT, MICHAEL
BEARD, CHARLES
BOEVER, JOSEPH
BYRD, PAUL
CHAMBLISS, CARROLL
GLAVINE, THOMAS
GRAPENTHIN, RICHARD
GREENE, TODD
HOFFMAN, RAYMOND
HOWELL, JAY
JORDAN, BRIAN
LEIBRANDT, CHARLES
NITKOWSKI, CHRISTOPHER
NIXON, OTIS
RUTHVEN, RICHARD
SCARCE, GUERRANT
SMOLTZ, JOHN

ARLINGTON GA
CURRIE, WILLIAM

ATHENS GA
ARMSTRONG, MICHAEL
JACKSON, RANSOM
JONES, RICKY

ATLANTA GA
AARON, HENRY
AIKENS, WILLIE
BENSON, KRISTEN
BRIZZOLARA, ANTHONY
CORRALES, PATRICK
DAVIES, HIRAM
HARTS, GREGORY
JONES, CLARENCE
JORDAN, SCOTT
LANKFORD, FRANK
LOMBARD, GEORGE
LUM, MICHAEL
ROCKER, JOHN
SMALL, GEORGE
SMITH, NATHANIEL
SMITH, ZANE
SNARE, RYAN
TURNER, ROBERT
WATSON, MARK

AUBURN GA
KEPPINGER, JEFFREY

AUGUSTA GA
CHILDERS, MATTHEW
GLENN, JOHN

BAINBRIDGE GA
POWELL, WILLIAM

BUFORD GA
HAMMOCK, ROBERT

CANTON GA
BUSKEY, MICHAEL
EDMONDSON, BRIAN

CENTERVILLE GA
SCHREIBER, THEODORE

CHATSWORTH GA
GREENGRASS, JAMES

CHICKAMAUGA GA
WRIGHT, ROY

COLLEGE PARK GA
HARPER, TERRY

COLQUITT GA
RICHARDSON, GORDON

COLUMBUS GA
ABERCROMBIE, REGINALD
BESWICK, JAMES
DAVIS, GLENN
JACKSON, EDWIN
PIERCE, TONY
PITTMAN, JOSEPH

CONYERS GA
DAWKINS, TRAVIS
ELDER, DAVID

COVINGTON GA
HYERS, TIMOTHY
KLESKO, RYAN
SMITH, JACK

CRAWFORDSVILLE GA
IVIE, MICHAEL

CUMMING GA
HILL, MILTON
INNIS, JEFFREY
JOHNSON, ERNEST

DACULA GA
BARNES, BRIAN
DAVIS, GEORGE
LOCKHART, KEITH
SINGLETON, CHRISTOPHER

DALLAS GA
BUTLER, CECIL
ROWE, KENNETH
SUTTER, HOWARD

DANIELSVILLE GA
WESTBROOK, JACOB

DAWSONVILLE GA
RAY, KENNETH

DECATUR GA
MURPHY, DALE

DOTHAN GA
MORDECAI, MICHAEL

DOUGLAS GA
CHILDERS, JASON
DUFFIE, JOHN

DOUGLASVILLE GA
FURCAL, RAFAEL
PRATT, TODD

DULUTH GA
COGGINS, FRANKLIN
HAMILTON, JOHNS
HIGGINS, MARK
MCMANUS, JAMES
MILLWOOD, KEVIN
PEREZ, EDUARDO
TURLEY, ROBERT
YELLEN, LAWRENCE

DUNWOODY GA
LYNCH, GERALD

EAST ELLIJAY GA
HARTSFIELD, ROY

FAIRBURN GA
DESHIELDS, DELINO
GRISSOM, MARQUIS

FAYETTEVILLE GA
FLETCHER, SCOTT

JACKSON, RONNIE

FLOWERY BRANCH GA
NIEKRO, PHILIP

FORSYTH GA
TREADWAY, HUGH

FORT OGLETHORPE GA
HONEYCUTT, FREDERICK

GAINESVILLE GA
CARPENTER, CRIS
DAVIS, JODY
ESCHEN, LAWRENCE

GAY GA
VANEGMOND, TIMOTHY

GLENWOOD GA
MALLETTE, BRIAN

GRAY GA
VEAL, ORVILLE
WHITE, RONDELL

GREENSBORO GA
FISCHLIN, MICHAEL
REID, JESSIE

GUYTON GA
SHIELL, JASON

HAHIRA GA
DREW, DAVID
DREW, STEPHEN
DREW, TIMOTHY

HARLEM GA
RAMSEY, MICHAEL

HIRAM GA
PHILLIPS, WILLIAM

JACKSON GA
CAMERON, MICHAEL

JASPER GA
FISCHER, HENRY

JONESBORO GA
EVANS, BARRY

LA GRANGE GA
HAYNES, JIMMY
KELTON, DAVID

LAWRENCEVILLE GA
DEES, CHARLES
DEVINE, PAUL
GOMEZ, LUIS
GREEN, NICHOLAS
NAUERT, PAUL
SKOK, CRAIG

LEESBURG GA
BREEDEN, HAROLD
MARTIN, THOMAS

LILBURN GA
CAVARRETTA, PHILIP
FRANCOEUR, JEFFREY
GILBREATH, RODNEY
INGRAM, RICCARDO
LEMASTER, DENVER
REED, RONALD
SNITKER, BRIAN

LITHIA SPRINGS GA
POTTS, MICHAEL

LITHONIA GA
BOSTON, DARYL
PEREZ, MARTIN
POCOROBA, BIFF

LOOKOUT MOUNTAIN GA
SIMONS, DOUGLAS

LUDOWICI GA
MCGOWAN, DUSTIN

MABLETON GA
JAMES, CHARLES

MACON GA
BRENNAN, WILLIAM
BROWN, JAMES
GAUDET, JAMES
HENDLEY, CHARLES
RATLIFF, KELLY

MARIETTA GA
BLASINGAME, WADE
BOYER, BLAINE
BYRD, MARLON
COX, ROBERT
ESASKY, NICHOLAS
GONZALEZ, FREDI
HEARRON, JEFFREY
IASSOGNA, DANIEL
MACRAE, SCOTT
MOEHLER, BRIAN
MONAHAN, SHANE
NASH, JAMES
PATTERSON, DONALD
PERRY, GERALD
PISCIOTTA, MARC
SIMPSON, JOE
STOWERS, CHRISTOPHER

MILLEN GA
TAYLOR, AARON

NEWNAN GA
WALTON, JEROME

NORMAN PARK GA
POWELL, DENNIS

PEACHTREE CITY GA
CANDELARIA, JOHN
CARROLL, THOMAS
HUDSON, TIMOTHY
MORAN, WILLIAM

PERRY GA
CORRELL, VICTOR

RINGGOLD GA
HAWES, ROY

ROSWELL GA
ABBOTT, JEFFREY
BLOMBERG, RONALD
BRAGG, DARREN
MAZZONE, LEO
NORTHEY, SCOTT
PENA, ALEJANDRO
VUKOVICH, GEORGE

SAINT SIMONS ISLAND GA
WAINWRIGHT, ADAM

SAUTEE NACOOCHEE GA
CHANEY, DARREL

SAVANNAH GA
BELLOIR, ROBERT
COOPER, GARY
HUTSON, GEORGE
SMITH, WILLIE
THOMSON, ROBERT

SENOIA GA
BEDROSIAN, STEPHEN

SHARPSBURG GA
BEHENNA, RICHARD
COLLINS, DONALD
GREGG, WILLIAM
SADOWSKI, ROBERT

SMYRNA GA
JONES, JASON

SNELLVILLE GA
BULGER, JASON
PENDLETON, TERRY
WILSON, MICHAEL

SOCIAL CIRCLE GA
ALLEN, LUCAS

STATESBORO GA
SZOTKIEWICZ, KENNETH

STONE MOUNTAIN GA
BLOCKER, TERRY
GOODWIN, DANNY
HUBBARD, GLENN
LITTLETON, LARRY
PACIOREK, THOMAS
STULL, EVERETT

SUWANEE GA
BRITTON, JAMES
MCMICHAEL, GREGORY

SMITH, PETER
SUTKO, GLENN

SYLVANIA GA
MCBRIDE, JOSEPH

TEMPLE GA
BRYANT, RALPH

THOMASVILLE GA
MCMILLAN, THOMAS
SCOTT, RICHARD
TAYLOR, WILLIAM

TUCKER GA
JARVIS, ROBERT

TYRONE GA
BEAUCHAMP, JAMES

WARNER ROBINS GA
COX, DANNY
DANIELS, KALVOSKI
JOHNSON, MARK

WASHINGTON GA
HUDSON, MARVIN

WAYNESBORO GA
BROXTON, JONATHAN

WHIGHAM GA
RILES, ERNEST

WOODSTOCK GA
CASANOVA, ORTIZ
GANT, RONALD
MARKAKIS, NICHOLAS
OSBORNE, LAWRENCE
SANDERS, JOHN

HAWAII

AIEA HI
MATIAS, JOHN

HILO HI
MASAOKA, ONAN

HONOLULU HI
JOHNSON, MARK
KOMINE, SHANE
SAKATA, LENN

KAILUA HI
FERNANDEZ, CHARLES
MEYER, TANNER
SARDINHA, DANE

KANEOHE HI
DIAZ, CARLOS

KAPAA HI
MICKENS, GLENN

KOLOA HI
YATES, TYLER

LIHUE HI
SULLIVAN, FRANKLIN

NANAKULI HI
KUHAULUA, FRED

WAIALUA HI
AGBAYANI, BENNY

WAILUKU HI
VICTORINO, SHANE

IOWA

AMANA IA
KIMM, BRUCE

ANKENY IA
SEARS, TODD

AUDUBON IA
HATCHER, CHRISTOPHER

BURLINGTON IA
BOTELHO, DEREK

CAMANCHE IA
HILGENDORF, THOMAS

CARROLL IA
TIEFENTHALER, VERLE

CARTER LAKE IA
POLDBERG, BRIAN

CEDAR FALLS IA
WAGNER, MATTHEW

CEDAR RAPIDS IA
BUCHANAN, ROBERT
ELDRED, CALVIN
FORD, BENJAMIN
SWEENEY, RYAN

CENTERVILLE IA
MATHEWS, RICK

CLIVE IA
TEUT, NATHAN

CORALVILLE IA
OBERMUELLER, WESLEY

COUNCIL BLUFFS IA
FISCHER, WILLIAM

DALLAS CENTER IA
MANDERS, HAROLD

DAVENPORT IA
STEVENS, R.C.

DES MOINES IA
EINERTSON, DARRELL
REUSS, JERRY

DUBUQUE IA
PETERSON, FRED

ELDON IA
BUSCH, MICHAEL

ELKADER IA
DITTMER, JOHN

FAIRFIELD IA
BIANCALANA, ROLAND

GLENWOOD IA
KAUFMAN, CURT

GRINNELL IA
COLLUM, JACK

HAWARDEN IA
CERV, ROBERT

INDIANOLA IA
BLAKE, WILLIAM

IOWA CITY IA
OLDIS, ROBERT

JOHNSTON IA
COOPER, ERIC
DREYER, STEVEN

LACONA IA
BAKER, DAVID

MARCUS IA
DRECKMAN, BRUCE

NEVADA IA
MCNERTNEY, GERALD

NEW LONDON IA
DUNEGAN, JAMES

POCAHONTAS IA
BIITTNER, LARRY

ROCKWELL IA
EDDY, DONALD

SIOUX CITY IA
WENGERT, DONALD

STOCKTON IA
WILLIAMS, DONALD

SWISHER IA
TROSKY, HAROLD

URBANDALE IA
EVERITT, MIKE
MAHONEY, MICHAEL
RUNYAN, SEAN

WATERLOO IA
DENKINGER, DONALD

WEST DES MOINES IA
LEPPERD, THOMAS
MCCLELLAND, TIMOTHY

IDAHO

BOISE ID
BUCKNER, WILLIAM

CALDWELL ID
GARMAN, MICHAEL
MOSSI, DONALD

COEUR D'ALENE ID
BRIDGES, EVERETT
PICKFORD, KEVIN

EAGLE ID
CHAMBERS, CLIFFORD

HAILEY ID
HARTZELL, PAUL

HAYDEN ID
FREY, LINUS

HAYDEN LAKE ID
LARSEN, DON

HOPE ID
REBERGER, FRANK

KOOSKIA ID
GATES, MICHAEL

LEWISTON ID
FOSTER, JOHN
STOTTLEMYRE, MELVIN

MERIDIAN ID
HOUSE, PATRICK
STEPHENSON, GARRETT

POST FALLS ID
CAMPBELL, DAVID

SANDPOINT ID
KRESS, CHARLES

TETONIA ID
RAUDMAN, ROBERT

TWIN FALLS ID
EASLEY, KENNETH

ILLINOIS

ARLINGTON HEIGHTS IL
BOKELMANN, RICHARD
HARGESHEIMER, ALAN
LUND, GORDON

ATLANTA IL
LINDSTROM, CHARLES

AURORA IL
SOBKOWIAK, SCOTT

AVON IL
REUSCHEL, PAUL

BANNOCKBURN IL
SANTO, RONALD

BARTONVILLE IL
MONROE, ZACHARY

BATAVIA IL
MILLER, PAUL

BEECHER IL
PAPPAS, MILTON

BELLE RIVE IL
BERNARD, DWIGHT

BELLEVILLE IL
BLAKE, EDWARD
BUSH, HOMER
FIALA, NEAL
HACKER, RICHARD
LEVINE, ALAN
STAHL, LARRY
ZIPFEL, MARION

BENSENVILLE IL
HUISMAN, RICHARD

BLOOMINGDALE IL
PALL, DONN

BOLINGBROOK IL
FURMANIAK, JASON

BRAIDWOOD IL
DUBOIS, BRIAN

BREESE IL
HOLTGRAVE, LAVERN

BROWNSTOWN IL
HALLER, WILLIAM

BURBANK IL
MADRITSCH, ROBERT

BURR RIDGE IL
JACKSON, VINCENT

CARMI IL
SYKES, ROBERT

CAROL STREAM IL
PFUND, LEROY

CARPENTERSVILLE IL
ACEVEDO, JUAN
DONAHUE, JOHN

CHAMPAIGN IL
HERGES, MATTHEW
HYDE, RICHARD
SKIZAS, LOUIS

CHICAGO IL
BROWN, EMIL
BRUETT, JOSEPH
COLLIER, LOUIS
DEMPSTER, RYAN
DIAZ, VICTOR
FARMER, EDWARD
FRENCH, RICHARD
GLANVILLE, DOUGLAS
GRUNDT, KENNETH
HICKEY, KEVIN
MATTHEWS, GARY
MELTON, WILLIAM
MINOSO, SATURNINO
PANKOVITS, JAMES
RICE, JOHN
SANCHEZ, ISRAEL
STELMASZEK, RICHARD
TABB, JERRY
WALKER, GREGORY
WINCENIAK, EDWARD
WUERTZ, MICHAEL

CHICAGO HEIGHTS IL
GRANDERSON, CURTIS

CHICAGO RIDGE IL
POTE, LOUIS
PYZNARSKI, TIMOTHY

CLARENDON HILLS IL
STIMAC, CRAIG

COAL CITY IL
WASHBURN, GREGORY

COLUMBIA IL
MATHEWS, NELSON
MATHEWS, TIMOTHY
ROYER, STANLEY

DANVILLE IL
ANDERSON, JASON

DECATUR IL
KOSLOFSKI, KEVIN
ROBERSON, KEVIN
SKIDMORE, ROBERT

DES PLAINES IL
LINDEMAN, JAMES

DIXON IL
SCHULZE, DONALD

DOWNERS GROVE IL
BINKS, GEORGE
STANICEK, PETER

EAST ALTON IL
MARTZ, RANDY

EAST SAINT LOUIS IL
GETTIS, BYRON
STOVALL, DAROND

EDWARDSVILLE IL
BOYD, JASON
LITTLE, MARK
RETZER, KENNETH

ELGIN IL
SMITHBERG, ROGER

ELMHURST IL
WEIS, ALBERT

ELMWOOD PARK IL
NYE, RICHARD

EUREKA IL
ZOBRIST, BENJAMIN

EVANSTON IL
FOSTER, KEVIN
STODDARD, TIMOTHY

FAIRVIEW HEIGHTS IL
CHOATE, DONALD

FITHIAN IL
FLETCHER, DARRIN

FLOSSMOOR IL
ORTA, JORGE

FRANKFORT IL
DUNCAN, JEFFREY
LEE, DEREK
MALLORY, SHELDON

FRANKLIN PARK IL
FASANO, SALVATORE

FREEPORT IL
PEARSON, JASON

GENESEO IL
SCHNEIDER, JEFFERY

GENEVA IL
MORMAN, RUSSELL

GLEN ELLYN IL
WILLIAMS, BILLY

GLENCOE IL
BAUMGARTEN, ROSS

GLENVIEW IL
HUNDLEY, TODD

GRANITE CITY IL
LINHART, CARL

GRANT PARK IL
WIEGHAUS, THOMAS

GRAYSLAKE IL
STAHOVIAK, SCOTT

HARVARD IL
LOISELLE, RICHARD

HAZEL CREST IL
HUBBARD, TRENIDAD

HEYWORTH IL
LYONS, WILLIAMS

HIGHLAND PARK IL
COGAN, ANTHONY

HIGHWOOD IL
MADLOCK, BILL

HINSDALE IL
SODERHOLM, ERIC
THOME, JAMES

HOFFMAN IL
EVERSGERD, BRYAN

HOFFMAN ESTATES IL
CAPRA, LEE
HISER, GENE
MONROE, LAWRENCE

HOMEWOOD IL
CHAMBERLAIN, WESLEY
SULLIVAN, JOHN

HOYLETON IL
RUETER, KIRK

ILLIOPOLIS IL
WEAVER, JAMES

INVERNESS IL
HOLLANDSWORTH, TODD

JACKSONVILLE IL
BRADY, STEPHEN

JOLIET IL
CARLSON, MARK
GRACE, MICHAEL
GRANT, MARK

JUSTICE IL
YORK, MICHAEL

KEWANEE IL
LINDBECK, EMERIT

KILBOURNE IL
CLARK, MARK

LAKE FOREST IL
GIRARDI, JOSEPH
ROMAN, WILLIAM
SANDERSON, SCOTT

LAKE VILLA IL
ECKENSTAHLER, ERIC

LAKE ZURICH IL
MECIR, JAMES

LASALLE IL
BECKER, RICHARD

LEBANON IL
COTTS, NEAL

LEMONT IL
PIERCE, WALTER

LISLE IL
PERCONTE, JOHN

LOCKPORT IL
BYRDAK, TIMOTHY
GORECKI, RICHARD
STANICEK, STEPHEN

LOMBARD IL
GERUT, JOSEPH

MACOMB IL
DISTASO, ALEC

MANHATTAN IL
MAROLEWSKI, FRED

MARION IL
BAILEY, PHILIP
WATERBURY, STEVEN

MATTESON IL
MAY, CARLOS

MATTOON IL
BRADLEY, STEVEN

MAYWOOD IL
WOODARD, MICHAEL

MILLSTADT IL
MUELLER, LESLIE

MOKENA IL
BOWERS, BRENT
LOVRICH, PETER

MORRIS IL
DRANSFELDT, KELLY
SPIEZIO, EDWARD
SPIEZIO, SCOTT

MORTON IL
SCHOFIELD, RICHARD

MORTON GROVE IL
BROSNAN, JAMES

MOUNT PROSPECT IL
PAFKO, ANDREW

MURPHYSBORO IL
KEENER, JEFFREY

NAPERVILLE IL
TORREZ, MICHAEL

NILES IL
FRANTZ, ARTHUR

NORMAL IL
HOFFMAN, GUY

NORTH BROOK IL
MISCH, PATRICK

NORTH RIVERSIDE IL
CISAR, GEORGE

NORTHBROOK IL
ASTACIO, PEDRO

POPOVICH, PAUL

O'FALLON IL
DAUBACH, BRIAN

OAK FOREST IL
FRASOR, JASON

OAK LAWN IL
ADDUCI, JAMES

OAKLAWN IL
JOHNSON, CLAIR

OAKWOOD IL
FLETCHER, THOMAS

OLYMPIA FIELDS IL
FREEMAN, MARVIN

ORLAND PARK IL
BRENNAN, THOMAS
CANGELOSI, JOHN
KOPACZ, GEORGE
PASQUA, DANIEL
SEFCIK, KEVIN

PALATINE IL
CAMPBELL, WILLIAM
HUNDLEY, CECIL

PALOS HEIGHTS IL
LOOPER, BRADEN

PARK RIDGE IL
HALE, ROBERT

PEORIA IL
DUNNE, MICHAEL
GARBEY, BARBARO
GILLES, THOMAS
SHORT, RICHARD
WRIGHT, JAMES

PINCKNEYVILLE IL
SECRIST, DONALD

PLAINFIELD IL
DALESANDRO, MARK
PARRIS, STEVEN

PONTIAC IL
BOGAR, TIMOTHY
DOWDY, ADAM

PRAIRIE VIEW IL
FREDERICK, KEVIN ALBERT

QUINCY IL
RABE, JOSHUA

RAMSEY IL
HOBBIE, GLEN

ROSCOE IL
YOUNG, LARRY

SAINT CHARLES IL
MILLER, ROBERT

SCHAUMBURG IL
NICHOLSON, DAVID
SKOWRON, WILLIAM

SILVIS IL
STONE, DARRAH

SKOKIE IL
ROTBLATT, MARVIN

SPRING GROVE IL
FELSKE, JOHN

SPRINGFIELD IL
ERICKSON, DON
ERICKSON, ROGER
FRY, JERRY
KNOEDLER, JUSTIN
ODONNELL, GEORGE
SCHAIVE, JOHN
SCHOFIELD, JOHN
WERTH, DENNIS
WERTH, JAYSON

STREATOR IL
SHABALA, ADAM

SUTTER IL
QUALLS, JAMES

TAYLORVILLE IL
PERRY, WILLIAM

TINLEY PARK IL
ERICKS, JOHN
WALKER, CLEOTHA

TRENTON IL
BREDE, BRENT
RAKERS, AARON

WASHINGTON IL
SHOUSE, BRIAN

WATERLOO IL
RHEINECKER, JOHN
RIPPELMEYER, RAYMOND

WAUKEGAN IL
BENNETT, GARY

WESTERN SPRINGS IL
LINDEN, WALTER

WHEATON IL
JOYCE, MICHAEL
OTTO, DAVID
PIERSALL, JAMES

WILMETTE IL
BURNSIDE, PETER
SHARP, WILLIAM

WINFIELD IL
SCHATZEDER, DANIEL

WOODSTOCK IL
WILL, ROBERT

WORDEN IL
HAMPSON, JUSTIN

INDIANA

ALBION IN
GAFF, BRENT

ALEXANDRIA IN
CLOSSER, JEFFREY

ANDERSON IN
ALLENSWORTH, JERMAINE
ERSKINE, CARL
LIND, ADAM

AURORA IN
BARRETT, TIMOTHY

AVON IN
MURPHY, RICHARD

BREMEN IN
SHUMAKER, ANTHONY

BROWNSBURG IN
SAMPEN, WILLIAM

CARMEL IN
ALLEN, BERNARD
ROLEN, SCOTT

CENTERVILLE IN
JONES, BARRY

CHESTERTON IN
KITTLE, RONALD
MCCLENDON, LLOYD
MORANDINI, MICHAEL

CLARKSVILLE IN
BARRON, MARK

COLUMBUS IN
WAGNER, GARY

EVANSVILLE IN
CARROLL, JAMEY
DANIELS, HAROLD
HANSEN, ROBERT
MATTINGLY, DONALD
MAURER, ROBERT
NOTTLE, EDWARD

FISHERS IN
BEARD, CRAMER
TRUBY, CHRISTOPHER

FORT WAYNE IN
DOSTER, DAVID
KINZER, MATTHEW
MILLER, CHARLES
RIVERA, MANUEL
ROESLER, MICHAEL

GARY IN
FARMER, HOWARD
GATES, JOSEPH
JOHNSON, WALLACE

HAMMOND IN
PERZANOWSKI, STANLEY

HOBART IN
BIGBIE, LARRY

HUDSON IN
SCHURR, WAYNE

INDIANAPOLIS IN
BARNES, WILLIAM
HARRISON, ROBERT
KEMMERER, RUSSELL
KENWORTHY, RICHARD
MILLER, DYAR
PIRKL, GREGORY
THURMAN, GARY
WILLIAMS, DALLAS

KOKOMO IN
DUMOULIN, DANIEL
UNDERWOOD, PATRICK

LAFAYETTE IN
BRUNTLETT, ERIC
GICK, GEORGE

LAWRENCEBURG IN
KOELLING, BRIAN
WEGMAN, WILLIAM

LOGANSPORT IN
HEILMAN, AARON

LOSANTVILLE IN
LEWIS, RICHIE

MCCORDSVILLE IN
EARL, WILLIAM

MISHAWAKA IN
EDGERTON, WILLIAM
STULTS, ERIC

MONROEVILLE IN
HISNER, HARLEY

MOUNT VERNON IN
SPILMAN, WILLIAM

MUNSTER IN
FICHTER, MICHAEL
LAZAR, JOHN
SCHOONMAKER, JERALD

NASHVILLE IN
TUCK, GARY

NEWBURGH IN
BROWN, KEVIN
LIS, JOSEPH

NOBLESVILLE IN
GRAMAN, ALEX
ROBBINS, BRUCE

PLAINFIELD IN
RAY, LARRY

PORTAGE IN
STRINCEVICH, NICHOLAS

SAINT JOHN IN
PILARCIK, ALFRED

SALEM IN
PENNINGTON, BRAD

SCHERERVILLE IN
HUISMAN, JUSTIN

SELLERSBURG IN
LOZADO, WILLIAM

SOUTH BEND IN
FODGE, EUGENE
GIBBONS, BRIAN

TERRE HAUTE IN
DORSETT, BRIAN

UNION MILLS IN
ROSENBAUM, GLEN

VALPARAISO IN
CROWELL, JAMES
PLESAC, DANIEL
WOODSON, TRACY

WABASH IN
SHEPHERD, KEITH

WARSAW IN
HICKERSON, BRYAN
WESTON, MICHAEL

WEST HARRISON IN
DAY, STEPHEN

WEST LAFAYETTE IN
DUNWOODY, TODD
SABEL, ERIK

WESTFIELD IN
WHITED, EDWARD

WHITING IN
FRITZ, LAURENCE
SKALSKI, JOSEPH

ZIONSVILLE IN
MASTNY, THOMAS

KANSAS

ABILENE KS
KEALEY, STEVEN

ARKANSAS CITY KS
DAULTON, DARREN

COLUMBUS KS
CHRISTIANSEN, CLAY

CONCORDIA KS
BRUMMETT, GREGORY

COTTONWOOD FALLS KS
KOHLMEIER, RYAN

DERBY KS
SANDERS, DAVID

DODGE CITY KS
ANDREWS, HERBERT
STEPHENSON, PHILLIP

FORT SCOTT KS
LAROCHE, DAVID
LAROCHE, DAVID

GODDARD KS
BERBLINGER, JEFFREY

GREAT BEND KS
WEBSTER, MITCHELL

HOLSINGTON KS
FIELD, NATHAN

HUTCHINSON KS
BROWER, ROBERT

JUNCTION CITY KS
DEVINE, JOSEPH

KANSAS CITY KS
SEGUI, DAVID
SEGUI, DIEGO

KINGMAN KS
LOCK, DONALD

LARNED KS
SLAGLE, ROGER
TERRY, RALPH

LAWRENCE KS
JELTZ, LARRY
PATTIN, MARTIN
PELLOW, KIT
RANDALL, ROBERT

LEAWOOD KS
HALTER, SHANE
MONTGOMERY, JEFFREY
RANDA, JOSEPH

LENEXA KS
DIPOTO, GERARD
MACFARLANE, MICHAEL

OLATHE KS
EZELL, GLENN
FITZMORRIS, ALAN
RENKO, STEVEN
SCHAAL, PAUL

OVERLAND PARK KS
AZCUE, JOSE
BLUMA, JAMES
BODDICKER, MICHAEL
BURGMEIER, THOMAS
CONE, DAVID
GABLER, JOHN
JAMES, PHILIP
KIPP, FRED
KRSNICH, ROCCO
MAYBERRY, JOHN
PALERMO, STEPHEN
PRYOR, GREGORY
ROBINSON, JEFFREY
SERVICE, SCOTT
SUTTON, LARRY
WALKER, JAMIE
WICKERSHAM, DAVID

PAOLA KS
APPIER, ROBERT

PITTSBURG KS
GUTTERIDGE, DONALD

PRAIRIE VILLAGE KS
BRETT, GEORGE
GEORGE, ALEX

SHAWNEE KS
HEARN, EDWARD
ZDEB, JOSEPH

SHAWNEE MISSION KS
JACKSON, DANNY
LACOCK, RALPH

STILWELL KS
SEITZER, KEVIN

TOPEKA KS
BERRY, ALLEN
DEHART, RICHARD
GOLDEN, JAMES
SPEAKE, ROBERT

VALLEY CENTER KS
ROBERTSON, NATHAN

WELLINGTON KS
CORNEJO, NATHAN
CORNEJO, NEIVES

WICHITA KS
DINGMAN, CRAIG
FORBES, PATRICK
FOSS, LAWRENCE
FRIEND, OWEN
HILL, KOYIE
HOLMAN, BRADLEY
HOOPER, KEVIN
LEMAY, RICHARD
MEARES, PATRICK
PRIETO, ALEJANDRO
SPENCER, DARYL
TAYLOR, SCOTT
WILSON, DUANE

KENTUCKY

ASHLAND KY
RELIFORD, CHARLES

BELLEVUE KY
JONES, TRACY

BOAZ KY
ROOF, PHILLIP

BOWLING GREEN KY
BLANTON, JOSEPH
CAMPBELL, JOSEPH
KILGUS, PAUL
TURNER, CHRISTOPHER

CATLETTSBURG KY
GIBSON, GREGORY

COVINGTON KY
FLANIGAN, THOMAS
MARSH, RANDALL

CRESTWOOD KY
LITTRELL, JACK

CYNTHIANA KY
SNOPEK, CHRISTOPHER

EDGEWOOD KY
BROWNING, THOMAS

ERLANGER KY
OTOOLE, DENNIS

EWING KY
FRYMAN, WOODROW

FLORENCE KY
HOOK, CHRISTOPHER

FORT WRIGHT KY
BUNNING, JAMES

FRANKFORT KY
LUEBBERS, LARRY

GEORGETOWN KY
POLLEY, EZRA

GOSHEN KY
STUBBS, FRANKLIN

HEBRON KY
BERGER, BRANDON
PRICE, JOSEPH

LAKSIDE PARK KY
LONG, JEOFFREY

LEDBETTER KY
STEWART, JOSHUA

LEXINGTON KY
ARNOLD, SCOTT
FLYNN, ROBERT
GREEN, ANDREW
HENDERSON, RODNEY
HOLBROOK, SAMUEL
KEARNS, AUSTIN
MACK, TONY
NASH, CHARLES
PARRETT, JEFFREY
SHELBY, JOHN
TURNER, WILLIAM

LOUISVILLE KY
ANDERSON, MATTHEW
BURKE, CHRISTOPHER
DIXON, STEVEN
DOWNS, SCOTT
GREEN, SEAN
HALL, ANDREW
HALLION, THOMAS
PHILLIPS, NORMAN
SAMUEL, AMADO
SAVAGE, JOHN
TIMBERLAKE, GARY
WALTER, GENE
WATKINS, DAVID
WOJCIK, JOHN

MADISONVILLE KY
HINRICHS, PAUL

MELBOURNE KY
MINSHALL, JAMES

MURRAY KY
RIGGINS, MARK
TAYLOR, ROBERT

NEWPORT KY
WIGGINS, SCOTT

NICHOLASVILLE KY
COWLEY, JOSEPH

OWENSBORO KY
BRUBAKER, BRUCE
MCBRIDE, ARNOLD
VANOVER, LARRY
WILKERSON, STEPHEN

PADUCAH KY
HAAS, GEORGE
ROOF, EUGENE

PIKEVILLE KY
BLAIR, WILLIAM
LEMASTER, JOHNNIE

PROSPECT KY
WELLEMEYER, TODD

SHELBYVILLE KY
TINSLEY, LEE

SHEPHERDVILLE KY
DAVIS, JOHN

SOUTH SHORE KY
GULLETT, DONALD

TAYLORSVILLE KY
OSTING, JAMES

UNION KY
BRANSON, JEFFREY
TERRELL, CHARLES

UTICA KY
WITHROW, RAYMOND

VERSAILLES KY
ROBERTS, DALE

WALTON KY
WELSH, CHRISTOPHER

WATER VALLEY KY
BRADLEY, MARK

WESTPORT KY
RAUCH, JON

WILDER KY
BOULDIN, CARL

WINCHESTER KY
GINTER, MATTHEW

LOUISIANA

ALEXANDRIA LA
FALCONE, PETER
MORRIS, WARREN

BASTROP LA
EAVE, GARY

BATON ROUGE LA
AINSWORTH, KURT
BATTS, MATTHEW
BROWN, THOMAS
DELLUCCI, DAVID
DURBIN, CHAD
ELLIS, ROBERT
HAMILTON, DARRYL
LAMABE, JOHN
OGEA, CHAD
SWANSON, ARTHUR
TALLET, BRIAN
THERIOT, RYAN
YARNALL, HARVEY

BENTON LA
RYAN, ROBERT
WALKER, TODD

BOGALUSA LA
SPIKES, LESLIE

BOSSIER CITY LA
SMITH, WILLIAM

BOYCE LA
MATHEWS, TERRY
WILLIS, JAMES

CASTOR LA
SMITH, LEE

CHALMETTE LA
ROMANO, MICHAEL

CROWLEY LA
HETZEL, ERIC

DENHAM SPRINGS LA
DEJEAN, MICHAEL
JOHNSON, WILLIAM
LAXTON, BRETT
MCDONALD, LARRY

DEQUINCY LA
BROWN, SCOTT

DONALDSONVILLE LA
ALEXANDER, GERALD

DRY PRONG LA
NEWMAN, ALAN

DUSON LA
MORGAN, KEVIN

FRENCH SETTLEMENT LA
SCHUTZ, CARL

GREENWELL LA
MOOCK, JOSEPH

GRETNA LA
MONTREUIL, ALLAN

HAMMOND LA
BRUMFIELD, JACOB
STEPHENSON, JOHN

HARVEY LA
WILES, RANDALL

HOUMA LA
HAYDEL, JOHN

KENNER LA
MMAHAT, KEVIN
RAZIANO, BARRY

LA PLACE LA
GATHRIGHT, JOEY
GRAY, GARY
WILLIAMS, GERALD

LAFAYETTE LA
BAKO, GABOR
BONIN, GREGORY
CORMIER, LANCE
FONTENOT, JOSEPH
GRIMSLEY, JASON

LAKE CHARLES LA
BURROWS, TERRY
CLARK, HOWARD
FONTENOT, SILTON
LAWRENCE, JOSEPH

LUTCHER LA
SMITH, CALVIN
WEBSTER, LEONARD

MAMOU LA
MANUEL, BARRY

MANDEVILLE LA
CANNIZARO, ANDREW
CRESSEND, JOHN

MANSFIELD LA
HUDSON, JESSIE

METAIRIE LA
BULLINGER, JAMES
BULLINGER, KIRK
CABALLERO, RALPH
FREESE, EUGENE

MONROE LA
MUFFETT, BILLY

MORGAN CITY LA
DOHMANN, CHRISTOPHER

NATCHITOCHES LA
LISTACH, PATRICK

NEW IBERIA LA
FOX, TERRENCE
YOUMAN, SHANE

NEW ORLEANS LA
BUSH, ROBERT
GAUDIN, CHAD
PARNELL, MELVIN
STRICKLAND, GEORGE
SWOBODA, RONALD
WHITEHURST, WALTER
WILLS, FRANK
YOCHIM, LEONARD

PAULINA LA
BOURGEOIS, STEVEN

PINEVILLE LA
HICKMAN, JESSE
JOHNSON, KENNETH

POLLOCK LA
MCGEHEE, GEORGE
SPRINGER, RUSSELL

PRAIRIEVILLE LA
BATISTE, KIMOTHY

CLARK, WILLIAM
MOHLER, MICHAEL

QUITMAN LA
BORLAND, TOBY

RUSTON LA
CAGE, WAYNE
CAUSEY, JAMES
RANDALL, JAMES
STONE, GEORGE

SAINT AMANT LA
SHEETS, ANDREW
SHEETS, BEN

SAINT ROSE LA
SLUSARSKI, JOSEPH

SCOTT LA
GUIDRY, RONALD
MECHE, GILBERT

SHREVEPORT LA
ALEXANDER, MATTHEW
BAKER, TIMOTHY
GARRELTS, SCOTT
HULETT, TIMOTHY
JETER, JOHN
ROBINSON, CRAIG
WILKINS, ROBERT

SLAUGHTER LA
CORCORAN, ROY
CORCORAN, TIMOTHY

SLIDELL LA
FONTENOT, MICHAEL
KEISLER, RANDY

SULPHUR LA
DAIGLE, SEAN
RAPP, PATRICK
THOMSON, JOHN

VILLE PLATTE LA
ARDOIN, DANIEL

ZACHARY LA
FELTON, TERRY

MASSACHUSETTS

ANDOVER MA
RICE, JAMES

ARLINGTON MA
YEWCIC, THOMAS

BEDFORD MA
WOOD, WILBUR

BERLIN MA
MITCHELL, PAUL

BEVERLY MA
LEONHARD, DAVID

BILLERICA MA
DISARCINA, GARY

BOSTON MA
ANDREWS, MICHAEL
CARLUCCI, DAVID
YASTRZEMSKI, CARL

BRAINTREE MA
BUCKLEY, KEVIN
GIGGIE, ROBERT

BROCKTON MA
GORDON, MICHAEL
KIELY, JOHN

CARVER MA
OSGOOD, CHARLES

CHESTNUT HILL MA
FRANCONA, TERRY

DALTON MA
WENDELL, STEVEN
WHITE, MATTHEW

DEDHAM MA
LEPCIO, THADDEUS

FAIRHAVEN MA
CAMACHO, JOSEPH

FALMOUTH MA
ALLIETTA, ROBERT

FOXBORO MA
TRAVERS, WILLIAM

FRAMINGHAM MA
GEDMAN, RICHARD
MERLONI, LOUIS

GEORGETOWN MA
MOSES, GERALD

HANOVER MA
GARDINER, MICHAEL

HARWICH MA
BENJAMIN, ALFRED

HAVERHILL MA
PENA, CARLOS

HOLBROOK MA
MANN, JAMES

HOLDEN MA
JOHNSON, ARTHUR

HOLLISTON MA
SWEENEY, MARK

HOLYOKE MA
HEALY, FRANCIS
STANEK, AL

HOPKINTON MA
CORSI, JAMES

HUNTINGTON MA
GRANGER, WAYNE

HYDE PARK MA
DELCARMEN, MANUEL
MARTINEZ, PEDRO

IPSWICH MA
ECKERSLEY, DENNIS

LEOMINSTER MA
LAPALME, PAUL

LEXINGTON MA
YANKOWSKI, GEORGE

MALDEN MA
MCGLINCHY, KEVIN

MANCHESTER MA
BRODOWSKI, RICHARD

MARBLEHEAD MA
MACLEOD, WILLIAM

MARLBOROUGH MA
REYNOLDS, KENNETH

MEDFIELD MA
SCHILLING, CHARLES
SCHILLING, CURTIS

MEDFORD MA
MONBOUQUETTE, WILLIAM

MENDON MA
GRANT, THOMAS

METHUEN MA
PESKY, JOHN

MIDDLETON MA
CONIGLIARO, WILLIAM
TUDOR, JOHN

MILFORD MA
LUMENTI, RAPHAEL

MILLBURY MA
DARLING, RONALD

MILTON MA
HILL, RICHARD

NAHANT MA
HOWARD, CHRISTIAN

NEEDHAM MA
MALZONE, FRANK

NORTH ANDOVER MA
BERE, JASON
HRINIAK, WALTER

NORTH ATTLEBORO MA
CORREIA, RONALD

NORTH BILLERICA MA
GLAVINE, MICHAEL

NORTH EDGEMONT MA
BOUTON, JAMES

NORTH READING MA
KENNEY, ARTHUR

NORTHBORO MA
FIDRYCH, MARK

NORTHBRIDGE MA
LUCIER, LOUIS

NORWOOD MA
MARTIN, RAYMOND

ORLEANS MA
HARRIS, GREG
NAPLES, ALOYSIUS

PEABODY MA
DROPO, WALTER

PITTSFIELD MA
PARONTO, CHAD

PLAINVILLE MA
JOHNSON, JOSEPH
PLYMPTON, JEFFREY

PLYMOUTH MA
BRANDON, DARRELL

QUINCY MA
MELE, SABATH

READING MA
DOHERTY, JOHN
GOHR, GREGORY
MERULLO, LEONARD

ROWLEY MA
DAGRES, ANGELO

RUTLAND MA
TAYLOR, BRUCE

SAUGUS MA
MONTGOMERY, ROBERT

SCITUATE MA
LONBORG, JAMES
PALM, RICHARD

SEEKONK MA
DORSEY, JAMES
RYAN, KENNETH

SHARON MA
HARPER, THOMAS

SOMERSET MA
BOMBACK, MARK
GAGNE, GREGORY

SOUTH DARTMOUTH MA
ROSE, BRIAN

SOUTH WEYMOUTH MA
MCLEOD, RALPH

SOUTH YARMOUTH MA
MASON, DONALD

SOUTHBOROUGH MA
TIANT, LUIS

SPRINGFIELD MA
STRANGE, PATRICK
TAYLOR, ROBERT

STONEHAM MA
BARKER, RICHARD

SWAMPSCOTT MA
MURRAY, MATTHEW

SWANSEA MA
GIBSON, JOHN

WABAN MA
VARITEK, JASON

WALPOLE MA
HEBNER, RICHARD
MORGAN, JOSEPH

WALTHAM MA
BERARDINO, RICHARD
MOLONEY, RICHARD
VARNEY, RICHARD

WARE MA
ROBIDOUX, WILLIAM

WELLESLEY MA
YOST, EDWARD

WELLESLEY HILLS MA
AINGE, DANIEL

WENHAM MA
STANLEY, ROBERT

WEST NEWBURY MA
EASTWICK, RAWLINS

WEST PEABODY MA
KENNEDY, JOHN

WEST ROXBURY MA
JAUSS, DAVID

WEST SPRINGFIELD MA
CAPUANO, CHRISTOPHER

WESTON MA
REMY, GERALD

WESTPORT MA
LEVRAULT, ALLEN

WESTWOOD MA
SMITH, MICHAEL

WILLIAMSTOWN MA
BAYLISS, JONAH

WINCHESTER MA
PAGLIARULO, MICHAEL

WRENTHAM MA
LOCKWOOD, CLAUDE
WALLACE, DAVID

MARYLAND

ANNAPOLIS MD
KREUTZER, FRANKLIN

ARNOLD MD
SAUNDERS, ANTHONY

BALDWIN MD
HANSEN, RONALD

BALTIMORE MD
ALSTON, WENDELL
BEATTIE, JAMES
BORDICK, MICHAEL
CHRISTOPHER, JOSEPH
CLOUDE, KENNETH
GRASMICK, LOUIS
HEISER, LEROY
POWELL, JOHN
ROBINSON, BROOKS
STEIRER, RICKY

BEL AIR MD
WITASICK, GERALD

BELTSVILLE MD
CARTER, STEVEN

BERLIN MD
FILE, LAWRENCE

BETHESDA MD
CASTIGLIA, JAMES
PAZIK, MICHAEL

BOONSBORO MD
DRAPER, MICHAEL

BOWIE MD
LOPEZ, ARTURO

CHESAPEAKE CITY MD
WOCKENFUSS, JOHN

CHURCH HILL MD
KURTZ, HAROLD

COCKEYSVILLE MD
CROWLEY, TERRENCE
SURHOFF, WILLIAM

CONOWINGO MD
GREEN, GEORGE

CROWNSVILLE MD
BIELECKI, MICHAEL

ELLICOTT CITY MD
OCONNOR, MICHAEL
FALLSTON MD
RIPKEN, WILLIAM
FEDERALSBURG MD
DETWEILER, ROBERT
FINKSBURG MD
DOPSON, JOHN
FORESTVILLE MD
VINSON, CHARLES
FORT WASHINGTON MD
PEREZ, ODALIS
GAMBRILLS MD
NEAGLE, DENNIS
GRANTVILLE MD
LEHEW, JAMES
GWYNN OAK MD
WHITE, DERRICK
HAGERSTOWN MD
BARNHART, VICTOR
HYATTSVILLE MD
BRADLEY, THOMAS
JOPPA MD
BOSWELL, DAVID
WILLIAMS, JAMES
KINGSVILLE MD
JOHNSON, DAVID
LAPLATA MD
DRUMMOND, TIMOTHY
LAVALE MD
ROBERTSON, ROBERT
LOTHIAN MD
SPRIGGS, GEORGE
LUTHERVILLE MD
BUMBRY, ALONZO
HUNTER, GORDON
MARRIOTTSVILLE MD
MORA, MELVIN
YOUNG, ERIC
MONKTON MD
BURNETT, ALLAN
MOUNT AIRY MD
MILLER, JOHN
NORTH EAST MD
BRUMBAUGH, CLIFFORD
ODENTON MD
BROCKLANDER, FRED
STEFERO, JOHN
OLNEY MD
GORDON, KEITH
OWINGS MILLS MD
BLAIR, PAUL
GIBBONS, JAY
GRIMSLEY, ROSS
KOWITZ, BRIAN
PARKTON MD
MOTTON, CURTELL
PERRY HALL MD
HOWARD, DAVID
PORTER, CHARLES
PHOENIX MD
NORDBROOK, TIMOTHY
RHODES, ARTHUR
RANDALLSTOWN MD
DURHAM, JOSEPH
SAINT MICHAELS MD
BAINES, HAROLD
SALISBURY MD
BROWN, THOMAS
CORBETT, EUGENE
GUTH, CHARLES
SEVERNA PARK MD
FLOYD, GAVIN
SILVER SPRING MD
SAUNDERS, JOSEPH
SPARKS MD
FLANAGAN, MICHAEL
SINGLETON, KENNETH
TIMONIUM MD
HALL, RICHARD
SLEATER, LOUIS
TOWSON MD
MARTINEZ, FELIX
MCGREGOR, SCOTT
UPPER MARLBORO MD
ALLEN, HAROLD
WESTMINSTER MD
HERSH, EARL
WOOLFORD MD
BROHAWN, MICHAEL

MAINE

AUBURN ME
GOWELL, LAWRENCE
ROBERGE, BERTRAND
BANGOR ME
KINNEY, MATTHEW
STAIRS, MATTHEW
CHERRYFIELD ME
WILLEY, CARLTON
LIMINGTON ME
MCCARTHY, THOMAS
SCARBOROUGH ME
LADD, PETER
SCOTT, RICHARD
STANDISH ME
BUTTERFIELD, BRIAN
TOPSHAM ME
MERRILL, CARL
WAYNE ME
TOMS, THOMAS

MICHIGAN

ADA MI
CURTIS, CHAD
GATES, BRENT
ADRIAN MI
NOCE, PAUL
ALLEN PARK MI
GULLIVER, GLENN
ALLENDALE MI
THORNTON, MATTHEW
ALPENA MI
ILSLEY, BLAISE
ANN ARBOR MI
LUND, DONALD
BATTLE CREEK MI
HOWITT, DANN
KENNEDY, JOSEPH
REILLY, MICHAEL
VANVLEET, MICHAEL
BAY CITY MI
KONUSZEWSKI, DENNIS
BELLAIRE MI
MASON, ROGER
BENTON HARBOR MI
HOPKINS, DONALD
BIRMINGHAM MI
SCRIVENER, WAYNE
BLOOMFIELD HILLS MI
HIGGINSON, ROBERT
HORTON, WILLIAM
INGE, CHARLES
KALINE, ALBERT
RUTHERFORD, JOHN
BRIGHTON MI
STANLEY, MITCHELL
BRONSON MI
CARY, SCOTT
BYRON CENTER MI
REGAN, PHILIP
CANTON MI
MCCRAY, RODNEY
WITHEM, SHANNON
CHESTERFIELD MI
ROA, JOSEPH
CLARKSTON MI
BIRTSAS, TIMOTHY
FIFE, DANNY
CLAWSON MI
HINCHCLIFFE, BRETT
KIRKWOOD, DONALD
CLINTON TOWNSHIP MI
WHITT, ERNEST
CLIO MI
GROSS, DONALD
COLDWATER MI
FELLER, JACK
COOPERSVILLE MI
WRIGHT, JAMES
DAVISBURG MI
GRACE, MICHAEL
DEARBORN MI
AVERY, STEVEN
DEARBORN HEIGHTS MI
POLE, RICHARD
DETROIT MI
BALDWIN, REGINALD
BLESSITT, ISAIAH
BROWN, WILLIAM
COLLINS, DAVID
FIELDS, BRUCE
GREENE, ALTAR
JAMES, ARTHUR
JOHNSON, ALEXANDER
KIRKLAND, WILLIE
MILLER, ROBERT
MOORE, KERWIN
RAGLAND, THOMAS
REDMOND, HOWARD
SANDERS, REGINALD
DEWITT MI
COSTELLO, PERRY
DEXTER MI
ZAHN, GEOFFREY
EDWARDSBURG MI
FINCH, JOEL
FAIRVIEW MI
DAVIE, GERALD
FARMINGTON MI
HOWELL, KENNETH
PETRY, DANIEL
FARMINGTON HILLS MI
MORAN, RICHARD
TANANA, FRANK
FENTON MI
HAMILTON, JEFFREY
FLINT MI
WASHINGTON, HERBERT
GARDEN CITY MI
LERCHEN, GEORGE
GLADWIN MI
KAZANSKI, THEODORE
GOODRICH MI
KAMIENIECKI, SCOTT
GRAND BLANC MI
LEACH, RICHARD
GRAND RAPIDS MI
COMMAND, JAMES
ELLIS, ROBERT
OJALA, KIRT
VANDERWAL, JOHN
GRANDVILLE MI
MCCOY, BENJAMIN
GROSSE ILE MI
BOLLO, GREGORY
KAISER, JEFFREY
MIERKOWICZ, EDWARD
GROSSE POINTE MI
GIBSON, KIRK
ROZEMA, DAVID
GROSSE POINTE WOODS MI
BERGMAN, DAVID
MUSSILL, BERNARD
HARTLAND MI
GARDNER, TERRENCE
HIGHLAND MI
MILLER, KEITH
TAYLOR, GARY
HOLLAND MI
VAN HEKKEN, ANDREW
HUNTINGTON WOODS MI
WILCOX, MILTON
IRON MOUNTAIN MI
HILLER, JOHN
JENISON MI
HOWE, CALVIN
KREUGER, RICHARD
KALAMAZOO MI
BERRY, CORNELIUS
FITZPATRICK, MICHAEL
JACKSON, RONALD
SQUIRES, MICHAEL
WELKE, TIMOTHY
KENTWOOD MI
EADDY, DONALD
LAMBERTVILLE MI
HENNESSEY, BRAD
LANSING MI
STUMP, JAMES
LEXINGTON MI
VANBRABANT, CAMILLE
LINDER MI
NOSEK, RANDALL
MAPLE CITY MI
HOOK, JAMES
MARSHALL MI
PUSKARIC, JOSEPH
WELKE, WILLIAM
MATTAWAN MI
KELLOGG, JEFFREY
MCMILLAN MI
HAMLIN, KENNETH
MIDLAND MI
MIESKE, MATTHEW
WINCHESTER, SCOTT
MILFORD MI
CLUTTERBUCK, BRYAN
MIO MI
POFF, JOHN
NEW ERA MI
DEWEY, MARK
NORTHVILLE MI
SORENSEN, LARY
NOVI MI
COLLINS, TERRY
OAKLAND TOWNSHIP MI
LUSADER, SCOTT
OKEMOS MI
LOOK, DEAN
OXFORD MI
HARE, SHAWN
MCCATTY, STEVEN

PAW PAW MI
MAXWELL, CHARLES

PETOSKEY MI
FREEHAN, WILLIAM

PICKNEY MI
TIMMERMANN, THOMAS

PIGEON MI
COLLINS, KEVIN

PINCKNEY MI
MCLAIN, DENNIS

PLYMOUTH MI
DAVEY, THOMAS
HAEGER, CHARLES
ZEPP, WILLIAM

PORT HURON MI
GOSGER, JAMES

QUINCY MI
BARRY, SCOTT

RIGA MI
SOFF, RAYMOND

ROCHESTER HILLS MI
REED, RICK

ROSEVILLE MI
SIKORSKI, BRIAN

ROYAL OAK MI
HAVENS, BRADLEY

SAGINAW MI
LUPLOW, ALVIN

SAINT JOSEPH MI
KNAPP, ROBERT

SAINT LOUIS MI
LEISTER, JOHN

SALINE MI
IGNASIAK, MICHAEL

SELFRIDGE MI
SCHYPINSKI, GERALD

SOUTH HAVEN MI
GUMPERT, DAVID

SOUTH LYON MI
JOSHUA, VON

SOUTHFIELD MI
NORTHRUP, JAMES
RIESGO, DAMON
WILLIAMS, GEORGE

STANWOOD MI
HERBERT, RAYMOND
HOEFT, WILLIAM
SMALL, JAMES

STERLING HEIGHTS MI
BORKOWSKI, DAVID
LANE, MARVIN
LANGE, RICHARD

STEVENSVILLE MI
MACHEMER, DAVID
MANTEI, MATTHEW

TAYLOR MI
FEDEROFF, ALFRED

TEMPERANCE MI
MARSH, THOMAS

THREE RIVERS MI
FENWICK, ROBERT

TRAVERSE CITY MI
MIRABELLI, DOUGLAS
ROHN, DANIEL

TRENTON MI
PUTZ, JOSEPH

TROY MI
ESSIAN, JAMES
GOETZ, JOHN
THOMPSON, JASON

UTICA MI
COLPAERT, RICHARD
HENTGEN, PATRICK

WARREN MI
REDYS, EDWARD

WASHINGTON MI
LOLICH, MICHAEL
PRICE, JIMMIE

WATERFORD MI
IGNASIAK, GARY

WAYNE MI
SHERIDAN, PATRICK

WEST OLIVE MI
BAILEY, HOWARD

WESTLAND MI
MARENTETTE, LEO
RIDDLEBERGER, DENNIS
SCHEFFER, AARON

WHITEHALL MI
FOSTER, LARRY

WILLIAMSBURG MI
LOOK, BRUCE

WYANDOTTE MI
JONES, JEFFREY
KUZAVA, ROBERT
PASHNICK, LARRY

MINNESOTA

APPLE VALLEY MN
JUREWICZ, MICHAEL

BLOOMINGTON MN
HRBEK, KENT
OLIVA, PEDRO

BROOKLYN PARK MN
NESHEK, PATRICK

BURNSVILLE MN
MAURER, DAVID
QUILICI, FRANK
RAETHER, HAROLD
STIGMAN, RICHARD

CARVER MN
GULDEN, BRADLEY

CHAMPLIN MN
SERUM, GARY

CHANHASSEN MN
BARNOWSKI, EDWARD
BERENGUER, JUAN
MOLITOR, PAUL

CHASKA MN
BUTCHER, JOHN
COMER, STEVEN

COON RAPIDS MN
BRUNSBERG, ARLO

CORCORAN MN
STEINBACH, TERRY

COTTAGE GROVE MN
ARLICH, DONALD

DULUTH MN
UJDUR, GERALD

EAGAN MN
KIECKER, DANA

EDEN PRAIRIE MN
COOMER, RONALD
DREES, THOMAS
GLADDEN, CLIFTON
LARKIN, EUGENE
OLSON, GREGORY

EDINA MN
SMALLEY, ROY

ELK RIVER MN
BOHN, THOMAS

ELKO MN
NEWMAN, ALBERT

EXCELSIOR MN
HELLING, RICKY
MASON, MICHAEL

FERGUS FALLS MN
GOLTZ, DAVID

GROVE CITY MN
KINGERY, MICHAEL

HAMEL MN
LAUDNER, TIMOTHY

HAZEL MN
CASTINO, JOHN

HUTCHINSON MN
DAVISON, MICHAEL

INVER GROVE HEIGHTS MN
LIGTENBERG, KERRY

LAKEVILLE MN
PERKINS, GLEN

LITTLE CANADA MN
GARDENHIRE, RONALD

MAPLEWOOD MN
KELLY, JAY
QUINLAN, ROBB
QUINLAN, THOMAS

MEDINA MN
KOSKIE, CORDEL

MENDOTA HEIGHTS MN
WALTERS, CHARLES

MINNEAPOLIS MN
BECQUER, JULIO
DAVIS, ARTHUR
LEIUS, SCOTT
MERCER, MARK
THIES, DAVID

NEW HOPE MN
HENDRICKSON, BENJAMIN

NORTH BRANCH MN
RAABE, BRIAN

NORTH MANKATO MN
MIELKE, GARY

PIERZ MN
POEPPING, MICHAEL

RICHFIELD MN
SCANLON, JAMES

ROCHESTER MN
RESTOVICH, MICHAEL
VANCUYK, JOHN

SAINT PAUL MN
ANDERSON, RICHARD
BROSSEAU, FRANKLIN
HANNAHAN, JOHN
JOHNSON, ROBERT
JOHNSON, THOMAS
MORRIS, JOHN

SAUK RAPIDS MN
THAYER, GREGORY

SAVAGE MN
NIESON, CHARLES

STILLWATER MN
SCHULTZ, HOWARD

WASECA MN
GLYNN, EUGENE

WAYZATA MN
BLANCHARD, JOHN
KNOBLAUCH, EDWARD
TAPANI, KEVIN

MISSOURI

AFFTON MO
JENNINGS, WILLIAM

ARNOLD MO
GABLER, WILLIAM

BALLWIN MO
DETTMER, JOHN
JOHNS, ROBERT
LAWLESS, THOMAS
MARTIN, BORIS
TOBIK, DAVID

TYSON, MICHAEL
WALLIS, HAROLD
WERLEY, GEORGE

BELLE MO
FASZHOLZ, JOHN

BLACK JACK MO
DUNCAN, R.

BLUE SPRINGS MO
BROWN, MARK
LEONARD, DENNIS
SPLITTORFF, PAUL
TERRELL, JERRY

BRIDGETON MO
OELKERS, BRYAN

BROOKFIELD MO
AUSTIN, RICK

CARL JUNCTION MO
DETHERAGE, ROBERT
SMITH, DANIEL

CENTRALIA MO
MUSGRAVES, DENNIS

CHESTERFIELD MO
BLATTNER, ROBERT
DAYLEY, KENNETH
GILKEY, OTIS
HORTON, RICKY
KEPPEL, ROBERT
MATHENY, MICHAEL
MAXVILL, CHARLES
MICKELSON, EDWARD
NIPPER, ALBERT
SAVAGE, THEODORE
SILVESTRI, DAVID
SIMMONS, TED
SIZEMORE, TED
THOMAS, JAMES

CLAYTON MO
WILSON, PRESTON

COLUMBIA MO
BRADLEY, PHILIP
MILES, CARL

DE SOTO MO
OQUENDO, JOSE

ELSBERRY MO
HILL, MARC

EUREKA MO
CEPICKY, MATTHEW
WHITESIDE, MATTHEW

EXCELSIOR SPRINGS MO
MARCUM, SHAUN

FENTON MO
BOEHRINGER, BRIAN
JORGENSEN, MICHAEL

FLORISSANT MO
OLMSTED, ALAN
THIES, VERNON
WIESLER, ROBERT

FULTON MO
JAMES, CHARLES

GLADSTONE MO
PARKER, RICHARD
TISCHINSKI, THOMAS

GLENCOE MO
PAQUETTE, CRAIG

GRAIN VALLEY MO
BONNER, ROBERT

GREENFIELD MO
WOOLDRIDGE, FLOYD

GREENWOOD MO
HANKINS, JAY
NORMAN, LESLIE

GROVER MO
HOLTZMAN, KENNETH

HANNIBAL MO
PHILLIPS, HOWARD

HIGH RIDGE MO
SADOWSKI, ROBERT
HOLLISTER MO
GAGLIANO, PHILIP
HOLT MO
KRAUSSE, LEWIS
INDEPENDENCE MO
BUSCHHORN, DONALD
EISENREICH, JAMES
HERNANDEZ, RUNELVYS
MAYNE, BRENT
JACKSON MO
LITTLE, DENNIS
JASPER MO
BOYER, CLOYD
JEFFERSON CITY MO
HENKE, THOMAS
HIGGINS, DENNIS
JOPLIN MO
LUEBBER, STEPHEN
KANSAS CITY MO
BETHKE, JAMES
DOBSON, CHARLES
FUNK, THOMAS
KELSO, WILLIAM
MINGORI, STEPHEN
PRESKO, JOSEPH
QUIRK, JAMES
KIMBERLING CITY MO
BUCHEK, GERALD
DUNCAN, DAVID
KOSHKONONG MO
CUNNINGHAM, JOSEPH
LADUE MO
MUSIAL, STANLEY
LAKE SAINT LOUIS MO
NEEMAN, CALVIN
LEBANON MO
CARNETT, EDWIN
STAIGER, ROY
LEES SUMMIT MO
CORNELL, JEFFERY
DERNIER, ROBERT
HEGMAN, ROBERT
HUISMANN, MARK
PECOTA, WILLIAM
SHELDON, ROLAND
SUTCLIFFE, RICHARD
TIDROW, RICHARD
WATHAN, DUSTIN
WATHAN, JOHN
WHITE, FRANK
LIBERTY MO
STEENSTRA, KENNETH
MALDEN MO
BLAYLOCK, GARY
MARBLE HILL MO
THURMAN, COREY
MARYLAND HEIGHTS MO
KULPA, RONALD
MUELLER, DONALD
MUELLER, WILLIAM
MEHLVILLE MO
NOLAN, JOSEPH
NIXA MO
EVANS, BART
O'FALLON MO
ALTMAN, GEORGE
GREEN, BERTRUM
TANKERSLEY, DENNIS
PALMYRA MO
BOGENER, TERRY
PLEASANT HILL MO
SHIFFLETT, STEVEN
POPLAR BLUFF MO
LOCKE, CHARLES
PORTAGEVILLE MO
STONE, JEFFREY
RAYTOWN MO
PATTERSON, DAVID
WALL, STANLEY
RIDGEDALE MO
HAMILTON, JACK
SAINT ALBANS MO
SMITH, OSBORNE
SAINT CHARLES MO
BROCK, LOUIS
BUEHRLE, MARK
BURKHART, MORGAN
COOPER, SCOTT
PHILLIPS, DAVID
REITZ, KENNETH
SCHMIDT, ROBERT
SHANNON, THOMAS
SHIPLEY, JOSEPH
SAINT LOUIS MO
BAUMANN, FRANK
BENES, ALAN
BENES, ANDREW
BRANCH, ROY
BYERLY, ELDRED
DIERING, CHARLES
DONOHUE, JAMES
EDMONDS, JAMES
FORD, CURTIS
GOODWIN, JAMES
HERZOG, DORREL
HRABOSKY, ALAN
LANKFORD, RAYMOND
LENHARDT, DONALD
MABRY, JOHN
MACLIN, LONNIE
MARION, MARTIN
MATHEWS, GREGORY
MCRAE, BRIAN
MCRAE, HAROLD
PERSON, ROBERT
POLITTE, CLIFFORD
PROCTOR, JAMES
PUJOLS, JOSE
RICKETTS, DAVID
RIEKER, RICHARD
RUBERTO, JOHN
SHAW, DONALD
SIEBERT, WILFRED
SISLER, DAVID
STILES, ROLLAND
TERRY, SCOTT
VANSLYKE, ANDREW
WALL, DONNELL
WORRELL, TODD
SAINT PETERS MO
BUCHANAN, WILLIAM
CALERO, ENRIQUE
COLYER, STEPHEN
WILLS, MAURICE
SAINTE GENEVIEVE MO
BIESER, STEVEN
SEDALIA MO
THOMAS, JOHN
SPANISH LAKE MO
SIEVERS, ROY
SPRINGFIELD MO
BAILES, SCOTT
DRUMRIGHT, KEITH
HART, JASON
LUMPE, JERRY
VIRDON, WILLIAM
WINN, JAMES
TOWN AND COUNTRY MO
SCHOENDIENST, ALBERT
WASHINGTON MO
MARTIN, MORRIS
WEBSTER GROVES MO
SOUTHWORTH, WILLIAM
WENTZVILLE MO
BOEHMER, LEONARD
HUNT, RONALD
WEST PLAINS MO
ROE, ELWIN
WESTPHALIA MO
CREDE, JOSEPH
WHEATON MO
PHELPS, TRAVIS
WILDWOOD MO
ROBINSON, KERRY

MISSISSIPPI

ALLIGATOR MS
DUFF, MATTHEW
BAILEY MS
PHILLIPS, PAUL
BATESVILLE MS
RENFROE, COHEN
BILOXI MS
BATTLE, HOWARD
LYONS, BARRY
BOYLE MS
TUCKER, EDDIE
BRANDON MS
BUKVICH, RYAN
HOLMAN, RANDY
STEIN, WILLIAM
CANTON MS
WHISENTON, LARRY
CLEVELAND MS
FERRISS, DAVID
ROGERS, CHARLES
CLINTON MS
BRANTLEY, JEFFREY
YOST, EDGAR
COLLINSVILLE MS
BROWN, JAMIE
COLUMBUS MS
HACKMAN, LUTHER
GREENVILLE MS
BARNES, FRANK
SCOTT, GEORGE
GULFPORT MS
HOWARTH, JAMES
LAWTON, MARCUS
HATTIESBURG MS
HARRINGTON, CHARLES
MAGEE, WENDELL
MOHR, DUSTAN
MYRICK, ROBERT
ROLISON, NATHAN
SCHRODER, ROBERT
VANBUREN, JERMAINE
HOLLY SPRINGS MS
MAHOLM, PAUL
IUKA MS
DEAN, TOMMY
JACKSON MS
CLIBURN, STANLEY
GRZANICH, MICHAEL
MCDOWELL, ROGER
SMITH, MICHAEL
TAYLOR, DWIGHT
LIBERTY MS
JONES, JAMES
LONG BEACH MS
RATH, ALFRED
LOUISVILLE MS
THAMES, MARCUS
LYON MS
LASSETTER, DONALD
MABEN MS
MILES, JAMES
MADISON MS
POWELL, JAMES
MERIDIAN MS
BAKER, FRANK
BOYD, DENNIS
BUSBY, PAUL
SPEED, HORACE
NETTLETON MS
HALL, WILLIAM
NEW ALBANY MS
WHITESIDE, DUSTIN
NEWTON MS
GIBBON, JOSEPH
OCEAN SPRINGS MS
PEPPER, HUGH
OXFORD MS
GIBBS, JERRY
KESSINGER, DONALD
PASCAGOULA MS
SEAMAN, KIM
PONTOTOC MS
PEGUES, STEVEN
PURVIS MS
YOUNG, WALTER
RAYMOND MS
BRADFORD, CHADWICK
ROXIE MS
BROWN, ADRIAN
SALTILLO MS
DILLARD, STEPHEN
SAUCIER MS
LAWTON, MATTHEW
SENATOBIA MS
CASTLE, DONALD
SOUTHAVEN MS
LEPPERT, DON
SOUTHERN MS
SELBY, WILLIAM
SOUTHHAVEN MS
LUNSFORD, JAMES
STARKVILLE MS
SANFORD, MEREDITH
SUMMIT MS
CARREON, MARK
YOUNG, BRYAN
TERRY MS
BARKSDALE, ROBERT
TOUGALOO MS
REED, JOHN
VICKSBURG MS
BROWN, ROOSEVELT
TANKERSLEY, TAYLOR
WALNUT GROVE MS
GARDNER, ARTHUR
WEIR MS
OSWALT, ROY

MONTANA

BILLINGS MT
BALLARD, JEFFREY
SCHMIDT, CURTIS
DILLON MT
SHARON, RICHARD
GREAT FALLS MT
LACHEMANN, WILLIAM
HELENA MT
GREGSON, GLENN
KNIGHT, BRIAN
NICHOLS, RODNEY
WILKINSON, WILLIAM
KALISPELL MT
WOLFE, EDWARD

LIBBY MT
WARD, JOHN

WISDOM MT
KING, JEFFREY

NORTH CAROLINA

ADVANCE NC
BUDDIE, MICHAEL
MARTIN, JOSEPH

AHOSKIE NC
UMPHLETT, THOMAS
WHITE, ELDER

ALBEMARIE NC
SMITH, TOMMIE

ANDREWS NC
BRISTOL, JAMES

ANGIER NC
STEPHENSON, CHESTER

ARDEN NC
HOLMES, DARREN

ASHEBORO NC
BANKHEAD, MICHAEL

ASHEVILLE NC
HATHAWAY, RAY
HOLCOMBE, KENNETH
THOMPSON, DONALD

BOONVILLE NC
FLETCHER, VANOIDE

BREVARD NC
COAN, GILBERT

CANDLER NC
MCCALL, LARRY
REED, JERRY

CAROLINA BEACH NC
STEWART, VESTON

CARY NC
AUTRY, ALBERT

CASHIERS NC
KELLER, RONALD

CATAWBA NC
HARVEY, BRYAN

CHADBOURN NC
NIXON, ROBERT

CHAPEL HILL NC
PYECHA, JOHN

CHARLOTTE NC
BARMES, BRUCE
BONIKOWSKI, JOSEPH
BURTON, JIM
COLE, STEWART
CUETO, DAGOBERTO
DIETZEL, LEROY
DIXON, JOHN
DONALDSON, JOHN
DUNBAR, MATTHEW
DURHAM, RAY
FLINN, JOHN
FUNDERBURK, MARK
HILL, GARRY
JOHN, THOMAS
LEMONDS, DAVID
REESE, CALVIN
ROBBINS, PHILIP
RYAN, JASON
SCHERGER, GEORGE
SMITH, BRICK
TRACY, CHAD
VINING, KENNETH
WERBER, WILLIAM

CLEMMONS NC
CARDWELL, DONALD
LYONS, EDWARD

CONCORD NC
CALLAHAN, BENJAMIN
HAMELIN, ROBERT
MENDOZA, CRISTOBAL
VERBLE, GENE

COUNCIL NC
GODWIN, CARLTON

CULLOWHEE NC
MENHART, PAUL

DAVIDSON NC
TORVE, KELVIN

DENVER NC
CLONINGER, TONY

DURHAM NC
BUTTERS, THOMAS
CHADWICK, RAY
GRIFFETH, LEON
HENRY, RONALD
MASTERSON, WALTER
ROBERTS, BRIAN
WILLIS, CARL

ELM CITY NC
HALL, JIMMIE

ELON COLLEGE NC
BOOKER, GREGORY
MCKEON, JOHN

FAYETTEVILLE NC
OKRIE, LEONARD
SPICER, ROBERT

FRANKLIN NC
CASH, KEVIN
CORBIN, ALTON
ROPER, JOHN

GARNER NC
DAVIS, WALLACE
HARRINGTON, WILLIAM
WATKINS, WILLIAM

GASTONIA NC
LEWIS, JOHN
STEWART, SAMUEL
STOWE, HAROLD

GOLDSBORO NC
KING, CLYDE
NARRON, JERRY
NARRON, SAMUEL

GRAHAM NC
HOLT, JAMES

GRANITE FALLS NC
CURTIS, JACK

GRANITE QUARRY NC
BENSON, VERNON

GREENSBORO NC
BROWN, HECTOR
GAKELER, DANIEL
HARTSOCK, JEFFREY
HODGIN, ELMER
NEILL, MICHAEL
STREULI, WALTER
WINTERS, MATTHEW

GREENVILLE NC
BRILEY, GREGORY
PATRICK, BRONSWELL
WEST, JOSEPH

HENDERSONVILLE NC
HILL, DAVID

HICKORY NC
BARKLEY, JEFFREY
LUNDQUIST, DAVID
PATTERSON, ROBERT

HUBERT NC
DOUGLAS, CHARLES

HUNTERSVILLE NC
WHITBY, WILLIAM

INDIAN TRAIL NC
MOORE, ROBERT

JULIAN NC
NORMAN, FREDIE

KITTY HAWK NC
FARR, STEVEN
FORMAN, ALLEN

KNIGHTDALE NC
MEELER, CHARLES

KNOTTS ISLAND NC
PIERCE, JEFFREY

LAURINBURG NC
BUTLER, JUSTIN

LELAND NC
MINTZ, STEPHEN

LEXINGTON NC
SPAGNARDI, DARREN

LINCOLNTON NC
SMITH, RICHARD

LUMBERTON NC
FOWLKES, ALAN

MATTHEWS NC
SOSA, ELIAS

MAYSVILLE NC
MEADOWS, MICHAEL

MIDWAY PARK NC
FONVILLE, CHAD

MONROE NC
MCNEELY, JEFFREY
TOMBERLIN, ANDY
TSITOURIS, JOHN

MOORESVILLE NC
BRAUN, RYAN

MOUNT AIRY NC
SHEAFFER, DANNY

MOUNT GILEAD NC
SMITH, BILLY

MOUNT HOLLY NC
STEWART, SCOTT

NEBO NC
WADE, GALEARD

NEW BERN NC
PERRY, MELVIN

NEW LONDON NC
PERRY, JAMES

PIKEVILLE NC
TALTON, MARION

PILOT MOUNTAIN NC
NUNN, HOWARD

PINEHURST NC
BALDWIN, JAMES
MCCORMICK, MICHAEL

RAEFORD NC
PARKS, DALLAS

RALEIGH NC
CALDWELL, RALPH
CRAIG, PETER
DIXON, WALTER
ESPOSITO, SAMUEL
POSE, SCOTT
REED, KEITH
ROACH, JASON

RANDLEMAN NC
MCPHERSON, DALLAS

ROCKINGHAM NC
MORMAN, ALVIN

ROCKWELL NC
RITCHIE, JAY

RUTHERFORDTON NC
HODGE, HAROLD

SANFORD NC
SUCH, RICHARD

SHELBY NC
MCKEE, ROGERS
ROLAND, JAMES
WRIGHT, THOMAS

SKYLAND NC
NARVESON, CHRISTOPHER

SMITHFIELD NC
LEE, COREY

SNOW CAMP NC
WICKER, FLOYD

SOUTHERN PINES NC
NIEVES, MELVIN

SPENCER NC
KELLY, VAN

SPRUCE PINE NC
PERRY, GAYLORD

STANTONSBURG NC
BYNUM, FREDDIE
MCKEEL, WALTER

STATESVILLE NC
DAVIDSON, JOHN
STARRETTE, HERMAN

SUMMERFIELD NC
PASCHALL, WILLIAM

TROUTMAN NC
HERTWECK, NEAL

TRYON NC
ALYEA, BRANT

WAKE FOREST NC
BYRNE, THOMAS
SHUEY, PAUL

WAXHAW NC
GIALLOMBARDO, ROBERT
RICCI, CHARLES
ZUPCIC, ROBERT

WAYNESVILLE NC
BEVERLIN, JASON

WEAVERVILLE NC
MANNING, JAMES

WHITEVILLE NC
PRINCE, DONALD

WILMINGTON NC
FOOTE, BARRY
HARRIS, JAMES
MUSSELMAN, RALPH
NIXON, CHRISTOPHER

WILSON NC
FLOWERS, BENNETT

YANCEYVILLE NC
WATLINGTON, JULIUS

NORTH DAKOTA

BISMARCK ND
NEIBAUER, GARY

FARGO ND
COSTE, CHRISTOPHER
ERSTAD, DARIN

SYKESTON ND
HAFNER, TRAVIS

NEBRASKA

BEAVER CITY NE
HUGHES, TRAVIS

BELLEVUE NE
CARLYLE, EARL
GIBSON, ROBERT

GRAND ISLAND NE
RICHARDSON, JEFFREY

GRETNA NE
SIEBLER, DWIGHT

KEARNEY NE
ANDERSON, DREW

LINCOLN NE
ASCHWEGE, DAVID
SHEPARD, LAWRENCE

NELSON NE
SNYDER, RUSSELL

NORTH BEND NE
WATT, EDDIE

OMAHA NE
HEISERMAN, RICHARD
HUNTER, WILLARD
MCGINN, DANIEL
MCGUIRE, WILLIAM
MUNTER, SCOTT
SEVERSON, RICHARD
SPIELER, PATRICK

PAPILLION NE
MEYERS, CHAD

PLAINVIEW NE
HOSCHEIT, VERNARD

PLATTSMOUTH NE
HUNTER, HAROLD

SUPERIOR NE
HEIM, VAL

NEW HAMPSHIRE

ASHLAND NH
METCALFE, MICHAEL

CONCORD NH
TEWKSBURY, ROBERT

DERRY NH
DEPAULA, SEAN

EAST WAKEFIELD NH
NOTTEBART, DONALD

HOLLIS NH
FULCHINO, JEFFREY

HOOKSETT NH
LEFEBVRE, JOSEPH

LEBANON NH
WOODWARD, ROBERT

LEE NH
LUBRATICH, STEVEN

NASHUA NH
PETROCELLI, AMERICO
ROY, NORMAN
WELCH, MICHAEL

NEW BOSTON NH
FLORENCE, DONALD

NEWTON NH
MOISAN, WILLIAM

NORTH HAMPTON NH
SHEA, STEVEN

RANDOLPH NH
SAVAGE, JOHN

RAYMOND NH
CARPENTER, CHRISTOPHER

WOLFEBORO NH
RYAN, MICHAEL
TREUEL, RALPH

NEW JERSEY

AUDUBON NJ
LAXTON, WILLIAM

AUGUSTA NJ
RIGOLI, JOSEPH

BERKLEY HEIGHTS NJ
SCHAFFERNOTH, JOSEPH

BEVERLY NJ
SCHULTZ, GEORGE

BRANCHBURG NJ
KLEMM, JUSTIN

BRIDGETON NJ
BYERS, RANDELL

BRIDGEWATER NJ
LUKACHYK, ROBERT

BUTLER NJ
BORGMANN, GLENN

CARLSTADT NJ
DEROSA, MARK

CHERRY HILL NJ
HOBBS, JOHN

CLARKSBURG NJ
GALLAGHER, DAVID

COLONIA NJ
CITARELLA, RALPH

COLTS NECK NJ
HARNISCH, PETER

CRANBURY NJ
KARP, RYAN

DUMONT NJ
VILLONE, RONALD

EDISON NJ
WINSTON, DARRIN

EGG HARBOR TOWNSHIP NJ
TEJEDA, ROBINSON

ELIZABETH NJ
BAEZ, JOSE

ENGLISHTOWN NJ
BERGMANN, JASON

FLEMINGTON NJ
CUST, JOHN

FORT LEE NJ
SORIANO, ALFONSO

FRANKLIN LAKES NJ
RANDOLPH, WILLIE

FREEHOLD NJ
GLAUBER, KEITH
MAJEWSKI, WALTER

GIBBSTOWN NJ
NEAL, BLAINE

HADDON HEIGHTS NJ
JONES, JEFFERY

HAWTHORNE NJ
MAHONEY, JAMES

HAZLET NJ
VALENTIN, JOHN

HIGHTSTOWN NJ
MAHAY, RONALD
SCHEID, RICHARD

HILLSBOROUGH NJ
BORIS, PAUL
SANTORINI, ALAN

HILLSDALE NJ
KUCKS, JOHN

HOWELL NJ
BEARSE, KEVIN

JERSEY CITY NJ
BANKS, WILLIE

KINNELON NJ
PRALL, WILFRED

LAMBERTVILLE NJ
ESTABROOK, MICHAEL

LANOKA HARBOR NJ
LEITER, MARK

LAUREL SPRINGS NJ
NARLESKI, RAYMOND
ROGODZINSKI, MICHAEL

LEBANON NJ
PACILLO, PATRICK

MAHWAH NJ
GIGON, NORMAN

MEDFORD NJ
HARMON, TERRY
HUDSON, JOSEPH
MEYER, BRIAN
WILLIAMS, MITCHELL

MEDFORD LAKES NJ
CIHOCKI, ALBERT

MIDDLETOWN NJ
HUNTER, JAMES

MONTCLAIR NJ
BERRA, DALE
BERRA, LAWRENCE

MORRISTOWN NJ
MIRABELLA, PAUL
SEMINARA, FRANK

MOUNT LAUREL NJ
GARAGOZZO, KEITH
MORIARTY, MICHAEL

MURRAY HILL NJ
BALBONI, STEPHEN

NEW BRUNSWICK NJ
DEJESUS, DAVID

NUTLEY NJ
CULLEN, JOHN
CUZZI, PHILIP

PALMYRA NJ
FILE, ROBERT

PARSIPPANY NJ
MCLOUTH, NATHAN
ORSULAK, JOSEPH
ZULETA, JULIO

PATERSON NJ
ALBA, GIBSON
BRIGGS, JOHN
JACKSON, MICHAEL

PENNINGTON NJ
BRADLEY, SCOTT

PENNSVILLE NJ
WIDGER, CHRISTOPHER

PERTH AMBOY NJ
MARRERO, CONRADO
PENNYFEATHER, WILLIAM

PISCATAWAY NJ
CIARDI, MARK

POINT PLEASANT NJ
ESTELLE, RICHARD

PRINCETON JUNCTION NJ
ROGERS, STEPHEN

ROSELAND NJ
STEMBER, JEFFREY

RUTHERFORD NJ
JONES, ROBERT

SEASIDE HEIGHTS NJ
EUFEMIA, FRANK

SECAUCUS NJ
MACCORMACK, FRANK
STAUB, DANIEL

SEWELL NJ
KEEGAN, EDWARD
RIZZO, TODD
ROBINSON, WILLIAM

SHORT HILLS NJ
LOYND, MICHAEL

SOMERSET NJ
WILLIAMS, EARL

SOMERVILLE NJ
WENZ, FREDERICK

SOUTH AMBOY NJ
CLARK, ALFRED

SPRING LAKE NJ
FITZGERALD, JOHN

TEANECK NJ
MORGENWECK, HENRY

TOMS RIVER NJ
GLYNN, EDWARD
WHITE, ROY

TRENTON NJ
BRAUN, STEPHEN
DAVIS, GERALD
HOEY, JAMES
PITTARO, CHRISTOPHER

TWP. OF WASHINGTON NJ
SAMPLE, WILLIAM

UNION NJ
MALKMUS, ROBERT

UPPER SADDLE RIVER NJ
MICHAEL, EUGENE

VINELAND NJ
MONEY, DONALD

VOORHEES NJ
KOPLOVE, MICHAEL
LYLE, ALBERT

WALL NJ
MCDOUGALD, GILBERT
PETERSON, ERIC

WAYNE NJ
AUFERIO, ANTHONY

WEST PATERSON NJ
CERONE, RICHARD

WHITEHOUSE STATION NJ
HOLLOWELL, MATTHEW
MOROGIELLO, DANIEL

WHITING NJ
CONLEY, ROBERT

WILLIAMSTOWN NJ
THOMPSON, MILTON

WOODBRIDGE NJ
ALUSIK, GEORGE

YARDVILLE NJ
DREW, CAMERON

NEW MEXICO

ALAMOGORDO NM
CARRIGAN, HERVE
MARAK, PAUL
STRAHLER, MICHAEL

ALBUQUERQUE NM
ADAMS, ROBERT
CAMILLI, LOUIS
KEKICH, MICHAEL
LANDRUM, TERRY
LOCKLIN, STUART
PALLONE, DAVID
PARKER, CHRISTIAN
SHIRLEY, STEVEN

CARLSBAD NM
ANDREWS, DARRELL
ROSS, CODY

HOBBS NM
CLAUSSEN, BRANDON
HARPER, BRANDON

LAS CRUCES NM
CALLOWAY, RONALD
HINSLEY, JERRY
RANDAZZO, ANTHONY

RIO RANCHO NM
MCDERMOTT, TERRENCE
ROSKOS, JOHN

ROSWELL NM
JORDAN, THOMAS

RUIDOSO NM
BROWNING, CALVIN

SEDAN NM
ADAMS, GLENN

NEVADA

CARSON CITY NV
RASNER, DARRELL
WOJNA, EDWARD

GARDNERVILLE NV
KESTER, RICHARD

GLENBROOK NV
KINGMAN, DAVID

HENDERSON NV
BARBER, STEVEN
COLBERT, NATHAN
CORDOVA, MARTIN
HERMANSEN, CHAD

HOUSTON, TYLER
JOHNSON, TIMOTHY
LEE, TRAVIS
OTIS, AMOS
RHODES, JAMES
RICHARDS, EUGENE
RICHARDSON, JEFFREY
RISKE, DAVID
TOWERS, JOSHUA
VAIL, MICHAEL
VANGORDER, DAVID
WILLIAMS, RICHARD

INCLINE VILLAGE NV
BUICE, DEWAYNE

LAS VEGAS NV
ALLEN, DUSTIN
BAILEY, ROBERT
CHITREN, STEPHEN
CLARK, RICKEY
COLBERT, CRAIG
DALLIMORE, BRIAN
DARENSBOURG, VICTOR
DEWITT, MATTHEW
DOWN, RICHARD
EBEL, DINO
FERRARO, MICHAEL
FINGERS, ROLAND
FLORES, RANDY
FLORES, RONALD
GARLAND, MARCUS
HANSEN, GUY
HAUSMAN, THOMAS
HENDRICK, GEORGE
HIGGINS, KEVIN
HIRSH, JASON
KAYE, JUSTIN
KIRBY, WAYNE
LANE, RICHARD
LATHAM, CHRISTOPHER
LOWENSTEIN, JOHN
LUDWICK, RYAN
MADDUX, GREGORY
MADDUX, MICHAEL
MARTIN, JOSEPH
MARTINEZ, GREGORY
NIXON, RUSSELL
POWELL, ROBERT
ROBERTSON, MICHAEL
ROWAND, AARON
RUSH, ROBERT
SAVRANSKY, MORRIS
SIMS, DUANE
SIWY, JAMES
THOMPSON, BRADLEY
WARD, PRESTON
WARD, ROY
WOODS, RONALD

MESQUITE NV
PUTMAN, EDDY

NORTH LAS VEGAS NV
CARDINAL, CONRAD
EASLER, MICHAEL

PAHRUMP NV
SPURGEON, JAY

RENO NV
AGUILA, CHRISTOPHER
AYRAULT, ROBERT
FUENTES, ROGOBERTO
GAMBLE, JOHN
HALICKI, EDWARD
KOTSAY, MARK
MILLER, RODNEY
OSBORNE, DONOVAN
STIEB, DAVID

SPARKS NV
JOHNSON, JOHN
NEWELL, THOMAS
RICHIE, ROBERT
SERAFINI, DANIEL
TINGLEY, RONALD

ZEPHYR COVE NV
OLSON, KARL

NEW YORK

ALBANY NY
BARKER, GLEN
HARRELL, WILLIAM

AMITYVILLE NY
GIORDANO, THOMAS

ARMONK NY
GARCIA, GUSTAVO

AUBURN NY
LOMBARDOZZI, STEPHEN
POLCOVICH, KEVIN

BALDWINSVILLE NY
ALBERTS, FRANCIS
GRILLI, STEPHEN

BAY SHORE NY
BALSAMO, ANTHONY

BEACON NY
CASALE, JERRY

BINGHAMTON NY
SCOTT, RALPH

BRONX NY
JEFFERSON, STANLEY
MARTE, DAMASO
NAGY, MICHAEL
TESTA, NICHOLAS

BROOKLYN NY
BUCKNOR, C.
DUNSTON, SHAWON
HALAMA, JOHN
LOPEZ, LUIS
PICONE, MARIO
PIGNATANO, JOSEPH
ROBINSON, HUMBERTO

BUFFALO NY
DENMAN, BRIAN
MANKOWSKI, PHILIP

CAMILLUS NY
DIPINO, FRANK
NATON, PETER

CANAJOHARIE NY
WEAVER, ROGER

CAZENOVIA NY
BARLOW, MICHAEL

CENTER MORICHES NY
GIBSON, PAUL

CENTERPORT NY
OSTER, WILLIAM

CLARENCE NY
LANCELLOTTI, RICHARD

CLARENCE CENTER NY
BIRRER, WERNER

CLAY NY
CASSIDY, SCOTT
LUKASIEWICZ, MARK

CLIFTON PARK NY
PELTIER, DANIEL
SWEENEY, BRIAN

CLYDE NY
REDDING, TIMOTHY

COLDEN NY
MAKOWSKI, THOMAS

CORAM NY
CARMEL, LEON

DANSVILLE NY
SULLIVAN, JOHN

DEPEW NY
GARCIA, CARLOS
ROMANO, THOMAS

EAST AURORA NY
HESKETH, JOSEPH

EAST HAMPTON NY
GLOAD, ROSS

EAST ISLIP NY
LOVIGLIO, JOHN

EAST PATCHOGUE NY
HEATON, NEAL

EAST WANEAUGH NY
ANDERSON, KARL

ELMHURST NY
MARTINEZ, SILVIO

FARMINGDALE NY
LIPETRI, MICHAEL
SIMMONS, JOHN

FOREST HILLS NY
TUFTS, ROBERT

FRANKLIN SQUARE NY
BRUHERT, MICHAEL

FREDONIA NY
CRISCIONE, DAVID

FREEPORT NY
PEREZ, TIMONIEL

GARDEN CITY NY
CHLUPSA, ROBERT

GLENS FALLS NY
PALMER, DAVID

GRAND ISLAND NY
SCHERRER, WILLIAM

GREAT NECK NY
AKER, JACK

HARRISON NY
TORRE, JOSEPH

HAUPPAUGE NY
DEMOLA, DONALD
HARRELSON, DERREL

HIGHLAND MILLS NY
BERTOTTI, MICHAEL

HOLBROOK NY
BAEZ, KEVIN

HONEOYE FALLS NY
RATLIFF, JON

HORSEHEADS NY
KEAGLE, GREGORY
MANWARING, KURT
PACKARD, SCOTT

HUNTINGTON STATION NY
OTERO, RICARDO
THOMPSON, RICHARD

ISLIP NY
VERYZER, THOMAS

ITHACA NY
WILLIAMS, MARK

JAMAICA NY
HERNANDEZ, PEDRO

JERICHO NY
GARCIA, DANIEL
KRANEPOOL, EDWARD

JOHNSBURG NY
MATLACK, JONATHAN

JOHNSON CITY NY
KRALY, STEVEN

KINGSTON NY
AUSANIO, JOSEPH

LAKE GROVE NY
TEPEDINO, FRANK

LAKEWOOD NY
ONEIL, JOHN

LINDENHURST NY
GIANNELLI, RAYMOND

LIVERPOOL NY
WESSINGER, JAMES

MALVERNE NY
FIORE, MICHAEL
RUFER, RUDOLPH

MARLBORO NY
BELL, ROBERT

MASSAPEQUA NY
PEPITONE, JOSEPH
TORRES, ROSENDO
ZANNI, DOMINICK

MASSAPEQUA PARK NY
ERARDI, JOSEPH

MIDDLE VILLAGE NY
WATSON, ALLEN

MONTGOMERY NY
HUMMEL, TIMOTHY

MOUNT SINAI NY
VALDIVIELSO, JOSE

MOUNT VERNON NY
SMITH, LEROY
VALENTINETTI, VITO

NESCONSET NY
BIANCO, THOMAS
HABYAN, JOHN

NEW YORK NY
BERROA, GERONIMO
CHARLES, EDWIN
HERNANDEZ, KEITH
JETER, DEREK
KENNEDY, KEVIN
MATSUI, HIDEKI
NELSON, JEFFREY
NOVOA, RAFAEL
OTANEZ, WILLIS
PIERRE, JUAN
RODRIGUEZ, HENRY

NORTH BELLMORE NY
MORRIS, JOHN

NORTHPORT NY
CAMBRIA, FREDERICK

OLD FORGE NY
BARRY, KEVIN

ONEONTA NY
CHRISTMAN, TIMOTHY

ORANGEBURG NY
FLAHERTY, JOHN

ORCHARD PARK NY
HOLLINS, DAVID

ORIENT NY
HANDS, WILLIAM

PITTSFORD NY
ANTONELLI, JOHN

POTSDAM NY
PHILLIPS, JACK

PUTNAM VALLEY NY
GARBOWSKI, ALEXANDER

QUEENS VILLAGE NY
JERZEMBECK, MICHAEL

QUEENSBURY NY
HARRIS, BRENDAN
LAPOINT, DAVID
PODRES, JOHN

RICHMOND HILL NY
PHILLIPS, ADOLFO

ROCHESTER NY
ALTOBELLI, JOSEPH
KAISER, KENNETH
LINTON, DOUGLAS

ROCKVILLE CENTRE NY
LEMANCZYK, DAVID

RYE NY
BRANCA, RALPH
JOHNSON, MARK
JUNGE, ERIC

SAUGERTIES NY
KOEGEL, PETER

SCOTIA NY
KUCZEK, STANISLAW

SHOREHAM NY
OSIK, KEITH
STATEN ISLAND NY
BRANTLEY, CLIFFORD
BROOKS, FRANK
FERNANDEZ, FRANK
FRANCO, JOHN
GALANTE, MATTHEW
GREGORIO, THOMAS
MARQUIS, JASON
MENECHINO, FRANK
PALACIOS, ROBERT
STILLWATER NY
MCAVOY, THOMAS
SYOSSET NY
KLIMKOWSKI, RONALD
SYRACUSE NY
RICCELLI, FRANK
TUCKAHOE NY
DOHERTY, JOHN
MOSCHITTO, ROSAIRO
UNIONDALE NY
SLOCUMB, HEATHCLIFF
UTICA NY
SALERNO, ALEX
VALHALLA NY
YVARS, SALVADOR
WATERVLIET NY
HOLLE, GARY
WEST BABYLON NY
VONOHLEN, DAVID
WEST NYACK NY
CUNNANE, WILLIAM
OTT, WILLIAM
WEST SENECA NY
CIPRIANI, FRANK
WESTBURY NY
DONOHUE, THOMAS
WESTHAMPTON BEACH NY
KILLEEN, EVANS
WESTTOWN NY
TELGHEDER, DAVID
WHITE PLAINS NY
CATO, JOHN
ZOCCOLILLO, PETER
WHITEHALL NY
SAINTCLAIRE, RANDY
WHITESBORO NY
LEMKE, MARK
WINDSOR NY
BENNETT, JOEL
WOODHULL NY
MARSHALL, KEITH
WOODSIDE NY
CASTRO, BERNABEL
YONKERS NY
DILLON, STEPHEN

OHIO

AKRON OH
BALDWIN, ROBERT
NEGRAY, RONALD
ROLLINS, RICHARD
ALLIANCE OH
WALLACE, JEFFREY
AMELIA OH
ARRIGO, GERALD
AMHERST OH
NOSSEK, JOSEPH
AMLIN OH
STONE, RICKY
ANDOVER OH
KUME, JOHN
ASHTABULA OH
WAGNER, MARK
AURORA OH
FULLER, VERN
AVON OH
ROGGENBURK, GARRY
AVON LAKE OH
GRIFFITHS, JEREMY
TOMANEK, RICHARD
BARBERTON OH
NARAGON, HAROLD
BEACHWOOD OH
SOWERS, JEREMY
BEALLSVILLE OH
NIPPERT, DUSTIN
BEDFORD HEIGHTS OH
RITTWAGE, JAMES
BLACKLICK OH
COOK, ROBERT
BOWLING GREEN OH
PARRISH, LANCE
TRACY, ANDREW
BRUNSWICK OH
RAICH, ERIC
WILLIAMS, DANIEL
BRYAN OH
BERGMAN, SEAN
BRINKMAN, CHARLES
FIREOVID, STEPHEN
GARVER, NED
HELD, MELVIN
BURTON OH
BRANYAN, RUSSELL
CAMBRIDGE OH
RITZ, KEVIN
CANFIELD OH
BELL, WALLACE
KUCEK, JOHN
CELINA OH
CISCO, GALEN
CHAGRIN FALLS OH
BURKS, ELLIS
THORNTON, ANDRE
CHARDON OH
BARKER, LEONARD
FANOK, HARRY
CHESTERLAND OH
MANNING, RICHARD
CHILLICOTHE OH
HERRNSTEIN, JOHN
CINCINNATI OH
BAIR, CHARLES
BENCH, JOHN
BOLGER, JAMES
BRINKMAN, EDWIN
CARDENAS, LEONARDO
CASTLEMAN, FOSTER
DENSON, ANDREW
DURHAM, LEON
EARLEY, WILLIAM
FOSTER, LEONARD
HANSON, ERIK
HARMON, CHARLES
HATCHER, WILLIAM
HELMS, TOMMY
KEETON, RICKEY
KLINGENBECK, SCOTT
KRAMER, THOMAS
LARKIN, STEPHEN
LONG, WILLIAM
MASSA, GORDON
MATUSZEK, LEONARD
MOELLER, RONALD
MOORE, ROBERT
MUNNINGHOFF, SCOTT
NAEHRING, TIMOTHY
NICHTING, CHRISTOPHER
OCONNOR, BRIAN
OESTER, RONALD
ONEILL, PAUL
OTOOLE, JAMES
PENN, SHANNON
RHODES, KARL
ROHRMEIER, DANIEL
ROSE, PETER
SABO, CHRISTOPHER
SCHLESINGER, WILLIAM
SEXTON, CHRISTOPHER
YOUKILIS, KEVIN
CLEVELAND OH
COLBERT, VINCENT
DEMETER, STEVEN
FARRELL, JOHN
FORD, DAVID
GRAHAM, LEE
ISAAC, LUIS
LANIER, LORENZO
MADDOX, GARRY
MEDVIN, SCOTT
NAGEOTTE, CLINTON
SEMPROCH, ROMAN
SHELTON, DEREK
SNIDER, VAN
WEINGARTNER, ELMER
CLEVES OH
SAUERBECK, SCOTT
CLINTON OH
TABAKA, JEFFREY
COLUMBUS OH
CLAY, DANNY
COURTRIGHT, JOHN
CROZIER, ERIC
JETER, SHAWN
LESHNOCK, DONALD
MILNER, EDDIE
VAUGHN, MAURICE
CONNEAUT OH
PALAGYI, MICHAEL
CONOVER OH
LONG, JOEY
CORTLAND OH
CHAPIN, DARRIN
HAWKINS, WYNN
COSHOCTON OH
NELSON, SCOTT
CUYAHOGA FALLS OH
HOOVER, PAUL
DAYTON OH
BELL, TERENCE
BORKOWSKI, ROBERT
COLEMAN, DAVID
DURNBAUGH, ROBERT
HENRICH, THOMAS
REBOULET, JEFFREY
DEFIANCE OH
TAYLOR, RODNEY
DOVER OH
VEIGEL, ALLEN
DUBLIN OH
BORK, FRANK
DEVORE, DOUG
DURANT, MICHAEL
MERCKER, KENT
MLICKI, DAVID
WHITSON, EDDIE
EATON OH
MILLER, TRAVIS
EDGERTON OH
STARK, DENNIS
FAIRBORN OH
NISCHWITZ, RONALD
FAIRFIELD OH
MCCONNELL, JOHN
NUXHALL, JOSEPH
FINDLAY OH
STECHSCHULTE, GENE
FREDERICKTOWN OH
FISHER, MAURICE
FREMONT OH
GALLAGHER, DOUGLAS
GAHANNA OH
FISHEL, JOHN
GALENA OH
BAKENHASTER, DAVID
SPENCER, GEORGE
GALION OH
RAMSEY, WILLIAM
GATES MILLS OH
FELLER, ROBERT
GENEVA OH
ANDERSON, BRIAN
GENOA OH
LITTLE, DONALD
GROVE CITY OH
MORLAN, JOHN
STEGMAN, DAVID
GROVEPORT OH
ROMONOSKY, JOHN
HAMILTON OH
COOK, AARON
ENGEL, STEVEN
LEWIS, MARK
HILLSBORO OH
CRAWFORD, JOSEPH
HINCKLEY OH
DAUER, RICHARD
HOLLAND OH
MATCHICK, JOHN
HOPEDALE OH
DONNELLY, RICHARD
KIRKERSVILLE OH
SAGER, ANTHONY
LANCASTER OH
ANDERSON, ALLAN
LORAIN OH
BAILEY, STEVEN
LOVELAND OH
BENZINGER, TODD
PARKER, DAVID
WARDEN, JONATHAN
MADISON OH
WEGENER, MICHAEL
MAINEVILLE OH
DORAN, WILLIAM
MALVERN OH
DILAURO, JACK
MANCHESTER OH
TOMLIN, DAVID
MANSFIELD OH
WILKINS, MARC
MAPLE HEIGHTS OH
MOHORCIC, DALE
MARENGO OH
BELCHER, TIMOTHY
MASSILLON OH
HERSHBERGER, NORMAN
MEDINA OH
KOSC, GREGORY
PRUITT, RONALD
MENTOR OH
ADDIS, ROBERT
ENGLE, RICHARD
RHOMBERG, KEVIN
MIDDLETOWN OH
HOWARD, THOMAS
SWARTZBAUGH, DAVID
NEW ALBANY OH
TIMMONS, TIMOTHY

NEW ATHENS OH
MILLER, RAYMOND

NEW CARLISLE OH
OWEN, LAWRENCE

NEW RICHMOND OH
DOTSON, RICHARD

NILES OH
PETEREK, JEFFREY

NORTH CANTON OH
PARSONS, THOMAS

NORTH RIDGEVILLE OH
CHARBONEAU, JOSEPH

NORTH ROYALTON OH
HOYE, JAMES

ORIENT OH
GEDDES, JAMES

ORRVILLE OH
BIRKBECK, MICHAEL

PALESTINE OH
RICHARDS, DUANE

PARMA OH
HETKI, JOHN

PERRYSBURG OH
WERTZ, WILLIAM

PICKERINGTON OH
RODRIGUEZ, CARLOS

POLAND OH
HIRSCHBECK, JOHN
KOSCO, ANDREW

PORTSMOUTH OH
OLIVER, ALBERT

POWELL OH
PACELLA, JOHN

PROCTORVILLE OH
REED, RICHARD

PROSPECT OH
BARNETT, LAWRENCE

RICHFIELD OH
HARGROVE, DUDLEY

ROCKY RIVER OH
HUNTZ, STEPHEN

SALEM OH
MEALS, GERALD

SARDINIA OH
OWENS, CLAUDE

SHAKER HEIGHTS OH
MASTELLER, DAN
SEELBACH, CHARLES

SHEFFIELD LAKES OH
NORTON, THOMAS

SPRINGFIELD OH
JOURNELL, JAMES
WHITE, RICHARD

STEUBENVILLE OH
GULAN, MICHAEL

SYLVANIA OH
RIGHTNOWAR, RONALD
RUNNELLS, THOMAS

TALLMADGE OH
BOCKUS, RANDY

TIPP CITY OH
SCHERMAN, FREDERICK

TOLEDO OH
CLARKE, STANLEY
FISHER, FREDERICK
LASKEY, WILLIAM

TORONTO OH
COULTER, THOMAS

TROY OH
MCKINNEY, CHARLES
MURRAY, HEATH

UNION OH
DEMPSEY, MARK

VANDALIA OH
VANCE, CORY

VERMILION OH
MORTON, GUY

WADSWORTH OH
DATZ, JEFFREY

WARREN OH
CAFFIE, JOSEPH
RICHARDS, FRED
STROUD, EDWIN

WASHINGTON COURT HOUSE OH
SHAW, JEFFREY

WAYNE OH
HOILES, CHRISTOPHER

WEST FARMINGTON OH
FEIERABEND, RYAN

WESTERVILLE OH
KOMMINSK, BRAD
THEISS, DUANE

WESTLAKE OH
MCBRIDE, KENNETH
WEDGE, ERIC

WOOSTER OH
CHANCE, WILMER

YOUNGSTOWN OH
ALLEN, RONALD
MALASKA, DENNIS
MAYO, JOHN
ONORA, BRIAN
SHUBA, GEORGE
SMITH, KENNETH

OKLAHOMA

ADA OK
KAISER, CLYDE
WALKER, JERRY

ALTUS OK
FISHER, EDDIE

ANADARKO OK
GRIFFITH, ROBERT

APACHE OK
HUSKEY, ROBERT

ARDMORE OK
PEMBERTON, BROCK

BRAGGS OK
KING, KEVIN

BROKEN ARROW OK
CALVERT, MARK
EMERY, CALVIN
FRAZIER, JOSEPH
PIRTLE, GERALD
WHISLER, RANDY

CAMERON OK
LOMON, KEVIN

CHOCTAW OK
HAUGHT, GARY

CHOUTEAU OK
RAY, JOHN

COALGATE OK
HUDSON, CHARLES

COWETA OK
LINZY, FRANK
PENNY, BRADLEY

EDMOND OK
BRONKEY, JACOB
GENTILE, JAMES
MCLISH, CALVIN
RONEY, MATTHEW
WALSH, DAVID

ENID OK
KRETLOW, LOUIS

EUFAULA OK
WILLOUGHBY, JAMES

FORT COBB OK
WILLITS, REGGIE

GROVE OK
DODSON, PATRICK
FOSTER, ROY

HARTSHORNE OK
SMITHERMAN, STEPHEN

HENRYETTA OK
RYAL, MARK

HOBART OK
GELNAR, JOHN

HOLDENVILLE OK
BROWN, JACKIE
BROWN, PAUL

HOLLIS OK
COLSON, LOYD

JENKS OK
BOWLING, STEPHEN
FRAZIER, GEORGE

JONES OK
GILMORE, LEONARD

LAWTON OK
BASS, RANDY
BYRD, JAMES

LEEDEY OK
FARISS, MONTY

LOCUST GROVE OK
DAVIS, ROBERT

MANGUM OK
NIPPERT, MERLIN

MCALESTER OK
SANDERS, DEE

MOORE OK
RUEBEL, MATTHEW

MULDROW OK
BLAYLOCK, ROBERT

NORMAN OK
CAPRA, NICK
HAYWARD, RAYMOND
MINOR, DAMON
MINOR, RYAN
ORTIZ, RUSSELL
SHACKELFORD, BRIAN
SODOWSKY, CLINT
STAGGS, STEPHEN
STEPHENSON, ROBERT
TETTLETON, MICKEY

OKLAHOMA CITY OK
COX, WILLIAM
DEAL, ELLIS
DEMETER, DONALD
MORGAN, ROBERT
NATION, JOSEPH
PETERS, STEVEN
ROGERS, JAMES
SPIVEY, ERNEST
STURDIVANT, THOMAS
TRABER, JAMES
TUNNELL, BYRON
VAUGHN, DEWAYNE
WRIGHT, GEORGE
WRIGHT, JAMEY

OWASSO OK
PUGH, TIMOTHY

PRAGUE OK
DENNEY, KYLE

SAND SPRINGS OK
WATKINS, SCOTT

SHATTUCK OK
WALTON, JAMES

SHAWNEE OK
FRANKLIN, RYAN
LOOPER, AARON

STILLWATER OK
BORLAND, THOMAS
WINE, ROBERT

STILWELL OK
GUINN, DRANNON

STRINGTOWN OK
WASHINGTON, U.

TULSA OK
ADAMS, HERBERT
ANDERSON, ROBERT
BURCHART, LARRY
CALMUS, RICHARD
FREEMAN, JIMMY
JONES, ROBERT
KREMERS, JAMES
KROLL, GARY
KUNTZ, RUSSELL
MCLAUGHLIN, JOEY
OBRIEN, CHARLES
REDMAN, MARK
SHIRLEY, ROBERT
TODD, JACKSON
WRONA, RICHARD

WASHINGTON OK
EDELEN, BENNY

WAYNE OK
KERNEK, GEORGE

OREGON

AGNESS OR
DOERR, ROBERT

BAEVERTON OR
KENNEDY, JAMES

BAKER OR
LANSFORD, CARNEY

BAKER CITY OR
LEY, TERRENCE
RUDI, JOSEPH

BEAVERTON OR
BAPTIST, TRAVIS
BOYLAND, DORIAN
COOKE, STEVEN
JOYCE, JAMES
SUTHERLAND, DARRELL
WISE, RICHARD

BEND OR
DUSAN, EUGENE
SMITH, TRAVIS

CANBY OR
KLINE, STEVEN

CAVE JUNCTION OR
JOHNSON, ROBERT
PEREZ, GEORGE

CENTRAL OR
SMITH, RICHARD

COOS BAY OR
HOOTEN, MICHAEL

COQUILLE OR
HIATT, JACK

CORVALLIS OR
DOYLE, JEFFREY
GREGG, KEVIN
REYNOLDS, HAROLD
THURMAN, MICHAEL

DALLAS OR
STRIKER, WILBUR

EUGENE OR
BAKER, STEVEN
LEE, TERRY
SNOOK, FRANK
VERBANIC, JOSEPH

FOREST GROVE OR
DRESSLER, ROBERT
JANSEN, LAWRENCE

GOLD BEACH OR
DALRYMPLE, CLAYTON

GRESHAM OR
CARLSON, DAN

HAPPY VALLEY OR
BETTENDORF, JEFFREY

HARRISBURG OR
THOENEN, RICHARD

HERMISTON OR
JACOBSEN, LARRY

HILLSBORO OR
BEALL, ROBERT
PETRICK, BENJAMIN

HOOD RIVER OR
LAHTI, JEFFREY

JACKSONVILLE OR
BARRY, JEFFREY

KEIZER OR
DECKER, STEVEN

KLAMATH FALLS OR
BENNETT, DENNIS

LAKE OSWEGO OR
ANDERSON, SCOTT
MIADICH, JOHN
SANDT, THOMAS
WARD, PETER

MCMINNVILLE OR
BROSIUS, SCOTT

MEDFORD OR
WOLCOTT, ROBERT

MILWAUKIE OR
BASINSKI, EDWIN

MOUNT ANGEL OR
BLADT, RICHARD

OREGON CITY OR
WILSON, TREVOR

PACIFIC CITY OR
MARTYN, ROBERT

PORTLAND OR
BAUGHMAN, JUSTIN
COLTON, LAWRENCE
DOBBEK, DANIEL
DODD, THOMAS
FREESE, GEORGE
GORMAN, THOMAS
HAIRSTON, JOHN
JOHNSON, DONALD
KINKADE, MICHAEL
LOLICH, RONALD
MORRIS, WILLIAM
REYNOLDS, DONALD
SCOTT, DALE
STONE, HARRY
TREBELHORN, THOMAS
TWITCHELL, WAYNE
WARTHEN, DANIEL
WILSON, ARTHUR

PRINEVILLE OR
BACKMAN, WALTER

REDMOND OR
TENACE, FURY

ROGUE RIVER OR
MAY, DARRELL

ROSEBURG OR
BURKE, JAMES
CORNUTT, TERRY

SAINT HELENS OR
WAKELAND, CHRISTOPHER

SALEM OR
CASIAN, LAWRENCE

SPRINGFIELD OR
WELCH, MILTON

WALTERVILLE OR
CLARK, BRADY

WARRENTON OR
DICKSON, JAMES

YACHATS OR
BALDWIN, DAVID

PENNSYLVANIA

ALIQUIPPA PA
MEDICH, GEORGE

ALLENTOWN PA
HEFFNER, ROBERT
KERN, WILLIAM
MAHAFFEY, ARTHUR
MUTIS, JEFFREY
TOMASIC, ANDREW

ALTOONA PA
TREMEL, WILLIAM

AMBLER PA
SHANTZ, ROBERT

ARCHBALD PA
LEGG, GREGORY

ASTON PA
NOLES, DICKIE

AUSTIN PA
COREY, MARK

BEAVER PA
BURKETT, JOHN
LONNETT, JOSEPH
PIATT, DOUGLAS

BEAVER FALLS PA
DAMASKA, JACK

BELLE VERNON PA
NECCIAI, RONALD

BELLWOOD PA
BLAZIER, RONALD

BENSALEM PA
AMARO, RUBEN

BERWICK PA
KARCHNER, MATTHEW

BETHEL PARK PA
PETERS, CHRISTOPHER
PURKEY, ROBERT

BETHLEHEM PA
DUSER, CARL

BIRDSBORO PA
BAMBERGER, HAROLD

BLOOMSBURG PA
DAVIS, DOUGLAS

BOLIVAR PA
GROAT, RICHARD

BRISTOL PA
CIMINO, PETER
MANTO, JEFFREY
MCEWING, JOSEPH

BROOKHAVEN PA
CHISM, THOMAS

BUTLER PA
CLEMENT, MATTHEW
VARGO, EDWARD

CALUMET PA
GORINSKI, ROBERT

CANONSBURG PA
DETTORE, THOMAS
SIMMONS, BRIAN

CARNEGIE PA
DAL CANTON, JOHN

CATASAUQUA PA
KELLY, PATRICK

CHALFONT PA
ASTROTH, JOSEPH

CHAMBERSBURG PA
MULL, JACK

COATESVILLE PA
PATTON, GENE

CONNEAUTVILLE PA
JONES, LYNN

CONNELLSVILLE PA
GALASSO, ROBERT

CONWAY PA
SHARPLESS, JOSHUA

COOPERSBURG PA
SCHAFFER, JIMMIE

CRANBERRY TWP PA
BEIMEL, JOSEPH
ERDOS, TODD
GRAHAM, J.
JACKSON, ZACHARY
WEHNER, JOHN

CUDDY PA
JELIC, CHRISTOPHER

DEVON PA
BUSH, DAVID

DILLSBURG PA
LEREW, ANTHONY

DOUGLASSVILLE PA
GUMPERT, RANDALL

DUBOIS PA
DUFFALO, JAMES
PITTSLEY, JAMES

DUNBAR PA
LOCKE, LAWRENCE

DUSHORE PA
KRAVITZ, DANIEL

EASTON PA
FISHER, JOHN

ELIZABETHTOWN PA
GARBER, HENRY
KIRK, WILLIAM

ELKINS PARK PA
MAHAN, ARTHUR

EXPORT PA
FULTON, WILLIAM
MACHA, KENNETH

FAYETTEVILLE PA
BROOKENS, EDWARD
BROOKENS, THOMAS

FLOURTOWN PA
FORSTER, SCOTT

FOLSOM PA
FILSON, WILLIAM

FORD CITY PA
HOBAUGH, EDWARD

FORT WASHINGTON PA
LEVIS, JESSE

FOX CHAPEL PA
FRIEND, ROBERT

GEIGERTOWN PA
BYSTROM, MARTIN

GIBSONIA PA
SCHWALL, DONALD
STRANGE, JOSEPH
WALKER, ROBERT

GILBERTSVILLE PA
HOHN, WILLIAM

GLEN MILLS PA
CRAWFORD, HENRY
MYERS, BRETT

GLENSIDE PA
CARTER, ANDREW

GOULDSBORO PA
GRZENDA, JOSEPH

GREENSBURG PA
FROBEL, DOUGLAS
MAZEROSKI, WILLIAM

HALLSTEAD PA
MCDEVITT, DANIEL

HANOVER PA
SWAGGERTY, WILLIAM

HARRISBURG PA
CHAMBERS, ALBERT

HAVERTOWN PA
HUGHES, KEITH

HILLER PA
DASCENZO, DOUGLAS

HONEY BROOK PA
PATTON, THOMAS

INDIANA PA
MOORE, ARCHIE
RYAN, MICHAEL

IRWIN PA
KRIVDA, RICK

JAMISON PA
SCHALL, EUGENE

JOHNSTOWN PA
VITKO, JOSEPH
VUCKOVICH, PETER

KING OF PRUSSIA PA
TELLMANN, THOMAS

KITTANNING PA
HARRIGER, DENNIS
STARR, RICHARD

KUTZTOWN PA
VOGELSONG, RYAN

LAFAYETTE HILL PA
HOFFMAN, WILLIAM
JORDAN, KEVIN

LANCASTER PA
DAUGHERTY, HAROLD
HERR, THOMAS
PARRISH, JOHN
WATSON, MATTHEW
WEAVER, JAMES

LANGHORNE PA
FILER, THOMAS
TERLECKI, ROBERT

LEWISTOWN PA
THOMPSON, CHARLES

LIBRARY PA
ROOKER, JAMES
SACKINSKY, BRIAN

LINCOLN UNIVERSITY PA
JOHNSTON, MICHAEL

LITITZ PA
SHIELDS, THOMAS
STEWART, WILLIAM

MACENGIE PA
DOZIER, WILLIAM

MALVERN PA
CHRISTENSON, LARRY
GILLIFORD, PAUL

MCKEES ROCKS PA
PRIDDY, ROBERT

MCKEESPORT PA
GOETZ, RUSSELL
SEABOL, SCOTT

MEADVILLE PA
JONES, DARRYL

MECHANICSBURG PA
EDWARDS, MICHAEL
WERT, DONALD

MEDIA PA
GEISEL, JOHN
VERNON, JAMES

MILLERSVILLE PA
RINEER, JEFFREY

MONACA PA
GRATER, MARK

MONROEVILLE PA
COHEN, ALFRED
CONROY, TIMOTHY

MONTOURSVILLE PA
FARLEY, ROBERT
MUSSINA, MICHAEL
OMALLEY, THOMAS
PHILLIPS, JASON

MOSCOW PA
PALYS, STANLEY

NEW BRIGHTON PA
FRANCONA, JOHN

NEW CASTLE PA
MATARAZZO, LEONARD
TANNER, BRUCE
TANNER, CHARLES

NEW HOLLAND PA
MCCRABB, LESTER

NEW HOPE PA
CLEMENS, DOUGLAS

NEW MILFORD PA
THOMPSON, RICHARD

NEWTOWN PA
CLARK, ALAN

NORRISTOWN PA
HARRIS, WALTER
MITCHELL, ROBERT
WINE, ROBERT

NORTH VANDERGRIFT PA
MINARCIN, RUDY

NORTH VERSAILLES PA
FACE, ELROY
WILLIAMS, DANA

NORTHAMPTON PA
SCHNECK, DAVID

NORTHERN CAMBRIA PA
HOLTZ, MICHAEL

OLEY PA
MATHIAS, CARL

PAICINES PA
BOLICK, FRANK

PALMYRA PA
DORTA, MELVIN

PECKVILLE PA
TRACEWSKI, RICHARD

PHILADELPHIA PA
ANDERSEN, LARRY
DIMICHELE, FRANK
HOLDSWORTH, FREDRICK
KERRIGAN, JOSEPH
LEONARD, JEFFREY
MARZANO, JOHN
MCARDLE, JOHN
MCDONNELL, ROBERT

PHOENIXVILLE PA
GUBANICH, CREIGHTON
HENDERSON, RAMON

PITTSBURGH PA
BETCHER, RALPH
BLASS, STEPHEN
CASEY, SEAN
DELGRECO, ROBERT
DEZELAN, FRANK
GEORGE, CHRISTOPHER
GIUSTI, DAVID
GREEN, GARY
GUCKERT, ELMER
KING, NELSON
LANG, ROBERT
LEE, DAVID
LEYLAND, JAMES
MILBOURNE, LAWRENCE
ORIE, KEVIN
RAKERS, JASON
SADOWSKI, JAMES
TEKULVE, KENTON
THOMAS, FRANK
WALK, ROBERT

PITTSTON PA
ASHBY, ANDREW

POTTSTOWN PA
BEDELL, HOWARD
JOHNSTON, JOEL

POTTSVILLE PA
NABHOLZ, CHRISTOPHER

PRESTO PA
TRACY, JAMES

PROSPECTVILLE PA
SIMMONS, CURTIS

PUNXSUTAWNEY PA
MIZEROCK, JOHN

RADNOR PA
BOWA, LAWRENCE

READING PA
BALLER, JAY
BARTON, SHAWN
DELUCIA, RICHARD
GERNERT, RICHARD
MILLER, WADE
SURHOFF, RICHARD

REEDERS PA
WARNER, HARRY

RENFREW PA
REUSCHEL, RICKY
THOMPSON, VERNON

RIMERSBURG PA
CALIGIURI, FREDERICK

SAYLORSBURG PA
BITTIGER, JEFFREY

SAYRE PA
TERPKO, JEFFREY

SCHNECKSVILLE PA
KINNEY, DENNIS

SCRANTON PA
LIPSKI, ROBERT

SEWICKLEY PA
COSMAN, JAMES
HOLMAN, SHAWN

SHILLINGTON PA
SCHAEFFER, HARRY

SHOHOLA PA
LAGA, MICHAEL

SLATINGTON PA
WIEAND, FRANKLIN

SOMERSET PA
QUALTERS, THOMAS

SOUTH FORK PA
HILLEGAS, SHAWN

SOUTHAMPTON PA
FREY, STEVEN

SPRINGFIELD PA
BUCHHOLZ, TAYLOR
GIBSON, ROBERT

STATE COLLEGE PA
BELINDA, STANLEY
SMITH, RICHARD

TRAPPE PA
SMILEY, JOHN

TYRONE PA
TEPSIC, JOSEPH

UPPER BLACK EDDY PA
WHITE, WILLIAM

UPPER DARBY PA
BRANCATO, ALBERT

UPPER SAINT CLAIR PA
JACKSON, GRANT

WAMPUM PA
ALLEN, RICHARD

WARRINGTON PA
FLETCHER, EDWARD
HASENMAYER, DONALD
PAWLOSKI, STANLEY

WAYNE PA
LEYVA, NICHOLAS

WEST CHESTER PA
DAVIS, MARK
EDELMAN, JOHN
GROSS, GREGORY

WEST NEWTON PA
MARGONERI, JOSEPH

WEST PITTSTON PA
DULIBA, ROBERT

WEST SUNBURY PA
BABCOCK, ROBERT

WILKES-BARRE PA
GRYBOSKI, KEVIN

WILLIAMSPORT PA
DANEKER, PATRICK
WELTEROTH, RICHARD

WIND GAP PA
SCHMIDT, FREDERICK

YARDLEY PA
KATA, MATTHEW

YORK PA
BARRANCA, GERMAN
CRUMLING, EUGENE
HAMULACK, TIMOTHY

ZELIENOPE PA
BREAM, SIDNEY

RHODE ISLAND

CRANSTON RI
ROARKE, MICHAEL
STENHOUSE, DAVID
STENHOUSE, MICHAEL

CUMBERLAND RI
BALDELLI, ROCCO
LAROSE, HENRY

EAST GREENWICH RI
ALMON, WILLIAM

LINCOLN RI
TRIMBLE, JOSEPH

NORTH KINGSTOWN RI
MALONEY, SEAN

NORTH SCITUATE RI
LICKERT, JOHN

PROVIDENCE RI
IANNETTA, CHRISTOPHER
LOPES, DAVID
MACWHORTER, KEITH

SMITHFIELD RI
JARVIS, RAYMOND

WARREN RI
PORTUGAL, MARK

WEST KINGSTON RI
LOCKE, RONALD

SOUTH CAROLINA

AIKEN SC
DUNBAR, THOMAS
SMITH, ROBERT

BEAUFORT SC
MULLEN, KENNETH

BELTON SC
LECROY, MATTHEW

BLACKSBURG SC
GILFILLAN, JASON

CAMERON SC
SPIERS, WILLIAM

CHAPIN SC
TWITTY, JEFFREY
WISE, LARRY

CHARLESTON SC
CLINE, TYRONE
THOMAS, JAMES
WILLIAMS, REGINALD

CHERAW SC
BREWER, THOMAS
GAINEY, TELMANCH

CLEMSON SC
FAIREY, JAMES

COLUMBIA SC
CROMER, ROY
HOYT, DEWEY
LANDRUM, JOSEPH
LANDRUM, THOMAS
MARTIN, JERRY
WOMACK, HORACE

CONWAY SC
CHRISLEY, BARBRA

DANIEL ISLAND SC
GALE, RICHARD

DARLINGTON SC
HUDSON, ORLANDO

EASLEY SC
BOLIN, BOBBY
CLARY, MARTIN
DARK, ALVIN

FLORENCE SC
HOOD, DONALD
SANDERS, REGINALD
STANTON, LEROY

FORT MILL SC
CROW, DONALD
DUCKWORTH, JAMES
NIEVES, JUAN
SCHAEFER, JEFFREY

GREENVILLE SC
ABREU, WINSTON
ALVAREZ, JOSE
BUDDIN, DONALD
PEPPER, DONALD

GREENWOOD SC
JOHNSON, BENJAMIN

GREER SC
GREENE, KHALIL
KIPPER, ROBERT
SHELLENBACK, JAMES

HARTSVILLE SC
BATCHELOR, RICHARD

HILTON HEAD ISLAND SC
DRIESSEN, DANIEL
HEGAN, JAMES
HENRY, WILLIAM

HOLLY HILL SC
SNELL, NATHANIEL

INMAN SC
CHAMPION, BUFORD

IRMO SC
CHEN, BRUCE
JOHNSON, JONATHAN
MOODY, ERIC
SEIBERT, KURT

JOHNS ISLAND SC
UMBARGER, JAMES

LAMAR SC
CAMPBELL, JAMES

LANCASTER SC
CLYBURN, DANNY
HARRIS, HERNANDO

LAURENS SC
MADDEN, MORRIS
THOMASON, MELVIN

LEXINGTON SC
CROMER, DAVID
DERRICK, JAMES
JODIE, BRETT
KEATLEY, GREGORY

MOORE SC
HOSLEY, TIMOTHY

MOUNT PLEASANT SC
COLBRUNN, GREGORY
FLORIE, BRYCE

MYRTLE BEACH SC
COBLE, GEORGE
DITMAR, ARTHUR
MERRITT, LLOYD
NEWMAN, RAYMOND

PURDIN, JOHN
RAUTZHAN, CLARENCE

NEWBERRY SC
ODELL, WILLIAM

NORTH AUGUSTA SC
BRISSIE, LELAND
PAWLOWSKI, JOHN

NORTH MYRTLE BEACH SC
HAYWOOD, WILLIAM
WOOD, KENNETH

ORANGEBURG SC
WINNINGHAM, HERMAN

PROSPERITY SC
BUZHARDT, JOHN
LANCE, GARY

RIDGELAND SC
BUNKER, WALLACE

ROCK HILL SC
CURRENCE, DELANCY

SENECA SC
REAMES, WILLIAM

SIMPSONVILLE SC
CULBRETH, FIELDIN

SPARTANBURG SC
ADAIR, MICHAEL
HUGHES, TERRY
HURST, JONATHAN
ROBERTS, MELVIN
SCOTT, ANTHONY
TOLLESON, JIMMY

SUMTER SC
MCMILLION, WILLIAM
RICHARDSON, ROBERT

TIMMONSVILLE SC
ANDERSON, KENT

VARNVILLE SC
SMITH, JOHN

WATERLOO SC
DILLARD, DAVID

WESTMINSTER SC
RACKLEY, MARVIN

WOODRUFF SC
PAGE, MICHAEL

SOUTH DAKOTA

BROOKINGS SD
LAWSON, STEVEN
SCHMACK, BRIAN

PIERRE SD
BRUNO, THOMAS

RAPID CITY SD
ELLIS, MARK
GREEN, RICHARD

TENNESSEE

ADAMS TN
RUFFIN, JOHNNY

ARLINGTON TN
HERNDON, LARRY

BEAN STATION TN
HARVILLE, CHAD

BLOUNTVILLE TN
KISER, GARLAND

BRENTWOOD TN
BOWEN, SAMUEL
BROWN, THOMAS
DESTRADE, ORESTES
MCNAMARA, JOHN
WALROND, LESLIE

BRISTOL TN
GENTRY, HARVEY
GOBBLE, BILLY

BRUSH CREEK TN
BENNETT, DAVID

CENTERVILLE TN
SMITHSON, BILLY

CHAPEL HILL TN
BICKNELL, CHARLES

CHARLESTON TN
BRUMLEY, DUFF
DAVIS, JASON
STEPHENS, CARL

CHATTANOOGA TN
ERMER, CALVIN

CLEVELAND TN
CAMPBELL, RONALD

COLLIERVILLE TN
BEVINGTON, TERRY
CLARK, DAVID
GOZZO, MAURO
LEA, CHARLES
MANSOLINO, DOUGLAS
MARTINEZ, REYENALDO
WILLIAMS, REGINALD

COLUMBIA TN
PYE, ROBERT
UGGLA, DANIEL

COOKEVILLE TN
DALE, JAMES
TUBBS, GREGORY

COVINGTON TN
ASHFORD, THOMAS

ELIZABETHTON TN
REED, JEFF

FRANKLIN TN
EWING, SAMUEL
HAMRICK, RAYMOND
JARVIS, KEVIN
MAXWELL, JASON
VANDUSEN, FREDERICK
VANLANDINGHAM, WILLIAM

GERMANTOWN TN
FLETCHER, ANDREW
HIBBARD, JAMES
PAXTON, MICHAEL

GREENEVILLE TN
HEMOND, SCOTT
PLESS, RANCE

HARRIMAN TN
CHARTON, FRANK

HENDERSONVILLE TN
CHITTUM, NELSON
GOGGIN, CHARLES

HENNING TN
HICKMAN, JAMES

HIXSON TN
PARKER, JAMES

JACKSON TN
HOWARD, BENJAMIN

JASPER TN
MCNABB, CARL
RAFFO, ALBERT

JOHNSON CITY TN
BOWMAN, ERNEST
BURBACH, WILLIAM
HODGE, ED
MCCLAIN, JOE
SMITH, RAYMOND

JONESBOROUGH TN
FORD, ROBERT

KINGSPORT TN
HILLMAN, DARIUS

KNOXVILLE TN
BARNETT, MICHAEL
CONNOR, MARK
CRADLE, RICKEY
EDENFIELD, KENNETH
GILBERT, DREW
HAMMAKER, CHARLTON
JONES, STEVEN
MCGLOTHIN, EZRA
PEMBER, DAVID
SEARCY, WILLIAM

LENOIR CITY TN
FOLI, TIMOTHY
GUETTERMAN, ARTHUR

LEXINGTON TN
WILSON, SAMMY

LORETTO TN
WEATHERS, JOHN

LOUISVILLE TN
PULEO, CHARLES

MARYVILLE TN
BOCHTLER, DOUGLAS
DALE, JERRY

MEMPHIS TN
ANDERSON, DAVID
BRANCH, HARVEY
CALLAWAY, MICHAEL
COOK, ANDREW
DENNY, JOHN
GAGLIANO, RALPH
HOUSE, CRAIG
KARNUTH, JASON
MEEKS, SAMUEL
SHERRILL, GEORGE

MERCER TN
COLE, VICTOR

MOUNT JULIET TN
BELL, JERRY
KIRBY, JAMES

MURFREESBORO TN
BRADEY, DONALD
GERHART, HAROLD
TAYLOR, CHARLES

NASHVILLE TN
BROWN, KEITH
DICKEY, ROBERT
DURHAM, DONALD
FOSSUM, CASEY
HEFLIN, BRONSON
MERIWETHER, JULIUS
MITCHELL, CHARLES
MITCHELL, JOHN
WILMET, PAUL

NOLENSVILLE TN
BOLTON, THOMAS

OOLTEWAH TN
BOLTON, RODNEY

PARIS TN
KING, CHARLES

POWELL TN
GLADDING, FRED

SALTILLO TN
TURNBOW, THOMAS

SEVIERVILLE TN
CZAJKOWSKI, JAMES

SIGNAL MOUNTAIN TN
COSTO, TIMOTHY
LAYNE, IVORIA

SMYRNA TN
LIDDLE, STEVEN

SPRING HILL TN
FOYTACK, PAUL
MCLEARY, MARTY
MINUTELLI, GINO

TEN MILE TN
BAILEY, JAMES

TULLAHOMA TN
BRAZELTON, DEWON

UNIONVILLE TN
FISCHER, TODD

TEXAS

ABILENE TX
ALDRIDGE, CORY
GILBRETH, WILLIAM
HARRISON, CHARLES
JOHNSON, DAVID
LACKEY, JOHN

ALEDO TX
HENN, SEAN

ALICE TX
CUELLAR, BOBBY

ALLEN TX
MALLOY, ROBERT

ALTO TX
JAMES, DONALD

ALVIN TX
RYAN, LYNN

AMARILLO TX
LEE, MARK
SAUCIER, FRANCIS

ANNA TX
CLEVELAND, REGINALD

ARGYLE TX
ABBOTT, LAWRENCE

ARLINGTON TX
ALEXANDER, DOYLE
ARNSBERG, BRADLEY
BACSIK, MICHAEL
BACSIK, MICHAEL
BILLINGS, RICHARD
BUECHELE, STEVEN
CONNALLY, FRITZIE
COOK, RAYMOND
GRABARKEWITZ, BILLY
GRANGER, JEFFREY
GRIEVE, THOMAS
HEDLUND, MICHAEL
HOSTETLER, DAVID
JEFFCOAT, JAMES
JOHNSON, LAMAR
KELLY, ROBERTO
KERN, JAMES
LANDRUM, CEDRIC
MACKO, JOSEPH
MOORE, JACKIE
OSTEEN, CLAUDE
PARK, CHAN
RIVERS, JOHN
ROBERTS, LEON
SMITH, BILLY
SUNDBERG, JAMES
TYRONE, JAMES
TYRONE, OSCAR
WERNER, DONALD
WHILLOCK, JACK
WILKERSON, CURTIS

AUSTIN TX
BELISLE, MATTHEW
BOGGS, THOMAS
CULP, RAY
FLANNERY, JOHN
GIDEON, JAMES
GORIN, CHARLES
GREIF, WILLIAM
GRUBER, KELLY
HARMON, THOMAS
HARTENSTEIN, CHARLES
MIDDLEBROOK, JASON
MORELAND, BOBBY
OWEN, SPIKE
RANDOLPH, STEPHEN
RUFFCORN, SCOTT
RUFFIN, BRUCE
SCHIRALDI, CALVIN
SEIBEL, PHILIP
SHINES, ANTHONY
SMART, JON
STREET, HUSTON
SWINDELL, FOREST

WORTHAM, RICHARD
WUNSCH, KELLY

AZLE TX
HARRAH, COLBERT
PICKETT, CECIL

BARTONVILLE TX
WETTELAND, JOHN

BASTROP TX
AHEARNE, PATRICK

BAY CITY TX
BREAZEALE, JAMES

BEAUMONT TX
AMBRES, RAYMOND
BROUSSARD, BENJAMIN
CORBIN, ARCHIE
MALLETT, GERALD
MARQUIS, ROBERT
MILLAR, KEVIN
PETKOVSEK, MARK
TYNER, JASON

BELLAIRE TX
CROSBY, RICHARD
HEMUS, SOLOMON
TOLAN, ROBERT

BOERNE TX
KENSING, LOGAN

BONHAM TX
DARWIN, JEFFREY

BRENHAM TX
EILERS, DAVID
MACHEMEHL, CHARLES
METZGER, ROGER
SEILHEIMER, RICKY
WEISS, GARY
ZIMMERMAN, JORDAN

BROWNWOOD TX
WILLIAMS, WALTER

BRUCEVILLE TX
HAWKINS, MELTON

BRYAN TX
LITTLE, RICHARD
MOON, WALLACE

BURLESON TX
KUNKEL, JEFFREY
NORRIS, JAMES

CARRIZO SPRINGS TX
JONES, LARRY

CARROLLTON TX
MILLER, KURT

CARTHAGE TX
DAVIS, JACKE
HUMBER, PHILIP

CEDAR HILL TX
FREEMAN, RAPHAEL

CELINA TX
DOWNING, BRIAN

CENTER TX
HENNIGAN, PHILLIP

CENTER POINT TX
BEENE, RAMON

CLEBURNE TX
OWEN, DAVE

COLLEGE STATION TX
MOORE, WARREN

COLLEYSVILLE TX
COOLBAUGH, SCOTT

COLLEYVILLE TX
BLALOCK, HANK
CRABTREE, TIMOTHY
DUCHSCHERER, JUSTIN
GREER, THURMAN
LUCCHESI, FRANK
MCWILLIAMS, LARRY
OBRIEN, PETER
PALMEIRO, RAFAEL
RAJSICH, GARY
RUSSELL, JEFFREY
WITT, ROBERT
ZIMMERMAN, JEFFREY

COLUMBUS TX
SMITH, HAROLD

CONROE TX
MYERS, RODERICK
SMITH, PAUL

CONVERSE TX
JOHNSON, CLIFFORD

COPPELL TX
CHALK, DAVID
HOLT, CHRISTOPHER
JEWETT, PHILIP

CORPUS CHRISTI TX
FLORES, JOSE
SHIRLEY, BARTON
TRUJILLO, JUAN

CROCKETT TX
EASTERLY, JAMES

CYPRESS TX
ASHBY, ALAN
BLANK, CLARENCE
KAZMIR, SCOTT
SPERRING, ROBERT
WATSON, ROBERT

DALLAS TX
ALLEN, JOHN
BEAMON, CLIFFORD
BOROM, EDWARD
BOWEN, RYAN
BRISCOE, JOHN
CLARK, GLEN
DIMMEL, MICHAEL
FAHEY, BRANDON
FAHEY, WILLIAM
GIBRALTER, STEPHEN
GREEN, SHAWN
HENSON, DREW
HERRSCHER, RICHARD
HERSHISER, OREL
HILL, JEREMY
JARAMILLO, RUDOLFO
JONES, JAMES
JOSEPH, KEVIN
MOORE, GARY
OBRIEN, DANIEL
PERLMAN, JONATHAN
ROBERTS, LEONARD
SAMFORD, RONALD
SHOWALTER, WILLIAM
SUTTON, JOHNNY
YOUNG, CHRISTOPHER

DEER PARK TX
ELLIOTT, DONALD
GONZALEZ, MICHAEL
HENRY, WILLIAM
HUGHES, THOMAS
PETTITE, ANDREW
WALKER, DUANE

DEKALB TX
SLIDER, RACHEL

DENTON TX
CARTER, LARRY
CHAMBLEE, JAMES

DESOTO TX
HUMPHREYS, MICHAEL

DICKINSON TX
COOK, DENNIS
DUES, HAL

DUNCANVILLE TX
BARTOSCH, CLIFFORD
CREEL, STEVEN

EARLY TX
GLEATON, JERRY

EL CAMPO TX
GERBERMAN, GEORGE
NEEL, TROY

EL PASO TX
ALMANZA, ARMANDO
BOTZ, ROBERT
COPPINGER, JOHN
HENRY, FLOYD
PEREZ, DANIEL
QUINTANILLA, OMAR
WASINGER, MARK

FARMER'S BRANCH TX
WILLIAMS, DAVID

FLOWER MOUND TX
HALL, MICHAEL
HILL, PERRY
ORTMEIER, DANIEL
SMITH, DANIEL
SMITH, MARK

FORT WORTH TX
ALFARO, JASON
BARTLEY, BOYD
BERINGER, CARROLL
BRAGAN, ROBERT
BRONSTAD, JAMES
BROWN, ROBERT
BURRIS, BERTRAM
FRYE, JEFFREY
GOLDSTEIN, LESLIE
HAND, RICHARD
HAWPE, BRADLEY
MAUSER, TIMOTHY
MYROW, BRIAN
ROBERTS, DAVID
ROBINSON, WILLIAM
SHOPPACH, KELLY
SUAREZ, KENNETH
TAYLOR, HARRY
THOMPSON, KEVIN

FREER TX
ACKER, JAMES

FRESNO TX
PORTER, MARQUIS
WILLIAMS, GREGORY

FRIENDSWOOD TX
MOORE, BALOR

FRISCO TX
BROOKS, JEROME
CLARK, JACK
DODD, ROBERT
HAWKINS, LATROY
SANFORD, CHANCE

FULSHEAR TX
BAILEY, JOHN
STANKA, JOE

GALVESTON TX
BATISTE, KEVIN
ORR, PETERSON

GEORGE WEST TX
MILLER, JOHN

GEORGETOWN TX
ANDERSON, MICHAEL
GIDEON, BYRON
HARSHMAN, JOHN
RUTNER, MILTON

GLEN ROSE TX
WALKER, KEVIN

GRANBURY TX
STEPHENS, GLEN

GRAND PRAIRIE TX
NIED, DAVID

GRAPEVINE TX
BUSBY, STEVEN
GOODWIN, THOMAS

GROVES TX
WEBER, BENJAMIN

HARLINGEN TX
VAUGHAN, CHARLES

HENDERSON TX
JONES, GARY

HOUSTON TX
ASPROMONTE, KENNETH
ASPROMONTE, ROBERT
BAGWELL, JEFFREY
BELK, TIMOTHY
BERKMAN, WILLIAM
BEVIL, BRIAN
BIGGIO, CRAIG
BOHANON, BRIAN
BORBON, PEDRO
BUBELA, JAIME
BURK, MACK
CALHOUN, JEFFREY
CLEMENS, WILLIAM
COOMBS, DANIEL
CRAWFORD, CARL
CROW, PAUL
CUMMINGS, STEVEN
DAVANON, FRANK
DAVIDSON, DAVID
DIERKER, LAWRENCE
DUBOSE, ERIC
FOOR, JAMES
GARR, RALPH
GRAHAM, WAYNE
HARTMAN, J.
HICKS, JAMES
HOWARD, CHRISTOPHER
HOWARD, WILBUR
HOWE, ARTHUR
IRVIN, MONFORD
JOHNSON, ADRIAN
KAINER, DONALD
LAMPARD, CHRISTOPHER
LUECKEN, RICHARD
MAJEWSKI, GARY
MANCUSO, FRANK
MCCURRY, JEFFREY
MCQUEEN, MICHAEL
MIGGINS, LAWRENCE
MUNRO, PETER
OWENS, JAMES
PAVLIK, ROGER
REYNOLDS, GORDON
RICHARD, JAMES
RUPE, RYAN
SIROTKA, MICHAEL
SMITH, BILLY
SMITH, DAVID
SOTO, GEOVANY
SPARKS, JAMES
STEVENS, EDWARD
SWITZER, JON
TREVINO, ALEJANDRO
WARWICK, CARL
WILLIS, MICHAEL
WITT, KEVIN
WOODESHICK, HAROLD
YOUNG, ANTHONY
YOUNG, GERALD

HUFFMAN TX
SPANGLER, ALBERT

HUMBLE TX
AUSTIN, JEFFREY
BOURN, MICHAEL
BRANDENBURG, MARK
GARNER, PHILIP

IOWA PARK TX
MOSER, CASEY

IRVING TX
HORNER, JAMES
PHILLIPS, MICHAEL

JASPER TX
ALVIS, ROY
GILBERT, JOE

JOHNSON CITY TX
BOSWELL, KENNETH

KATY TX
CAPEL, MICHAEL
COOPER, CECIL
DALEY, BUDDY

FIELDER, PRINCE
MILLER, RANDALL
RAU, DOUGLAS
THURMOND, MARK

KELLER TX
ATCHISON, SCOTT
BRUMLEY, ANTHONY
BRUMLEY, TONY
GIL, ROMAR
MICHALAK, CHRISTIAN
RAMSEY, FERNANDO
ROBERTS, DAVID
WAUGH, JAMES

KERENS TX
RITCHIE, TODD

KILGORE TX
SHEPHERD, RONALD

KILLEEN TX
KENT, STEVEN

KINGWOOD TX
JORGENSEN, RYAN

LAGRANGE TX
TRLICEK, RICHARD

LAKE JACKSON TX
WILLIAMS, MATTHEW

LAREDO TX
BENAVIDES, ALFREDO
PIERCE, LAVERN

LAVON TX
MCDANIEL, LYNDALL

LEAGUE CITY TX
BANISTER, JEFFERY
COOK, GLEN

LEANDER TX
CLEVLEN, BRENT
WELCHEL, DONALD

LEWISVILLE TX
FORD, JON
JONES, CALVIN

LINDALE TX
MAHOMES, PATRICK

LINDEN TX
LAWRENCE, BRIAN

LONGVIEW TX
COOK, RONALD

LUBBOCK TX
MILLER, MATTHEW
SEGRIST, KAL
WATKINS, STEPHEN

LUFKIN TX
SEELBACH, CHRISTOPHER

MAGNOLIA TX
EDWARDS, JOHN
MILES, DONALD
STANTON, WILLIAM

MANCHACA TX
GARRETT, HENRY

MANSFIELD TX
LACHOWICZ, ALLEN

MCALLEN TX
BLOOMFIELD, GORDON

MCKINNEY TX
ARNOLD, TONY
BRAY, WILLIAM
GRAMLY, BERT
HENNEMAN, MICHAEL
MORRIS, JAMES
NATAL, ROBERT
OLSON, TIMOTHY
POWELL, ROSS

MERIDIAN TX
VANPOPPEL, TODD

MESQUITE TX
JENNINGS, JASON
LOWE, JONATHAN

MIDLAND TX
HUDSON, REX
NIX, LAYNCE
VELARDE, RANDY

MINERAL WELLS TX
STEIN, WILLIAM

MISSION TX
CANTU, JORGE

MISSOURI CITY TX
BREWER, ANTHONY
CABELL, ENOS
DISTEFANO, BENITO
LONEY, JAMES
WELLS, ROBERT

MOUNT PLEASANT TX
MCANALLY, ERNEST

NACOGDOCHES TX
JAMES, DELVIN

NAVASOTA TX
CONDREY, CLAYTON

NEDERLAND TX
CAMMACK, ERIC
SANCHES, BRIAN

NEW BRAUNFELS TX
BOWIE, MICAH

NEW LONDON TX
GERHARDT, ALLEN

NEW WAVERLY TX
TREMIE, CHRISTOPHER

NORTH RICHLAND HILLS TX
CRAWFORD, RUFUS
ORTIZ, LOUIS
SAMPSON, BENJAMIN
WAKAMATSU, WILBUR

OAKHURST TX
BEENE, FREDERICK

OAKWOOD TX
HUDSON, CHARLES

ODESSA TX
BRADY, BRIAN
CORNETT, BRAD
RUSSELL, JOHN

ORANGE TX
PATTERSON, JOHN
ROBERTSON, ANDRE

OVILLA TX
GROOM, WEDSEL

PARIS TX
PHILLEY, DAVID
SCUDDER, WILLIAM
WRIGHT, JAMES

PASADENA TX
FREISLEBEN, DAVID
FULLER, JAMES

PEARLAND TX
CRUZ, JOSE
CRUZ, JOSE
DRESSENDORFER, KIRK
GWOSDZ, DOUGLAS
HENSLEY, CLAYTON
LONG, RYAN
MEACHAM, RUSSELL
MONTGOMERY, RAYMOND
NANCE, JOSEPH
SMAJSTRLA, CRAIG

PFLUGERVILLE TX
BECKETT, ROBERT
MINCHEY, NATHAN
RAMOS, MARIO

PINEHURST TX
THOMPSON, JUSTIN

PLANO TX
BJORKMAN, GEORGE
BRAND, RONALD
CATER, DANNY
KNOX, JOHN

PORT ARTHUR TX
MCELROY, CHARLES
RICHARD, LEE

PORTLAND TX
SCHROM, KENNETH

POTTSBORO TX
HENNINGER, RICHARD

POWDERLY TX
WEAVER, DAVID

PROSPER TX
HUNTER, TORII

QUEEN CITY TX
NORTON, PHILLIP

REFUGIO TX
FIROVA, DANIEL

RICHARDSON TX
BEECH, LUCAS
BLAIR, DENNIS

RICHMOND TX
COMBS, PATRICK
HEATH, WILLIAM
KELLEY, KEVIN

ROANOKE TX
BERG, DAVID
DOTTER, GARY
STANHOUSE, DONALD

ROBINSON TX
CLEMONS, CHRISTOPHER

ROBSTOWN TX
GARCIA, JESUS

ROCKPORT TX
CHARLTON, NORMAN

ROCKWALL TX
LAZORKO, JACK

ROSHARON TX
WYNN, JAMES

ROUND ROCK TX
DRISKILL, TRAVIS
FIKAC, JEREMY
LANGERHANS, RYAN
PUFFER, BRANDON

SAN ANGELO TX
EDWARDS, HOWARD
HULSE, DAVID

SAN ANTONIO TX
ABREGO, JOHNNY
ALLIE, GAIR
BELL, WILBUR
BRUCE, ROBERT
COOLBAUGH, MICHAEL
CORBETT, SHERMAN
CURRIN, PERRY
DAVIS, ODIE
DUNN, SCOTT
FREDRICKSON, SCOTT
GIBBONS, JOHN
GROTE, GERALD
HEEP, DANIEL
HOOTON, BURT
HORLEN, JOEL
KEARNEY, ROBERT
KIESCHNICK, MICHAEL
LAMACCHIA, ALFRED
LARSON, BRANDON
LODUCA, PAUL
MAHLER, MICHAEL
PAPE, KENNETH
ROCKETT, PATRICK
SCHEIB, CARL
SEVCIK, JOHN
STEEVENS, MORRIS
SZUMINSKI, JASON

SANGER TX
DARWIN, DANIEL

SCHULENBERG TX
KUBENKA, JEFFREY

SEALY TX
PATEK, FREDERICK

SEGUIN TX
PITLOCK, LEE

SHAVANO PARK TX
KEOUGH, JOSEPH

SHINER TX
PAVLAS, DAVID

SINTON TX
ADAMS, JON
HARTUNG, CLINTON

SOUTHLAKE TX
HILL, KENNETH
HUFF, MICHAEL
LIVINGSTONE, SCOTT
LOAIZA, ESTEBAN
MCLEMORE, MARK
MUNOZ, MICHAEL
OLIVER, DARREN
TEIXEIRA, MARK
WELLS, VERNON

SPLENDORA TX
WALKER, MICHAEL

SPRING TX
BARFIELD, JESSE
BARFIELD, JOSHUA
BATES, WILLIAM
BECKETT, JOSHUA
BEIRNE, KEVIN
CANIZARO, JASON
ESHELMAN, VAUGHN
FOX, CHAD
GEORGE, CHRISTOPHER
HODGES, KEVIN
HODGES, TREY
HUMPHREY, RICHARD
KLAGES, FRED
KONIECZNY, DOUGLAS
MILLER, NORMAN
MURRAY, CALVIN
OBERKFELL, KENNETH
STRICKLAND, SCOTT
WILLIAMS, RANDALL
WILSON, GLENN
WOOD, KERRY

SPRING BRANCH TX
LARUE, MICHAEL

SUGAR LAND TX
ANTHONY, ERIC
BASS, KEVIN
HERNANDEZ, FRANCIS
HUDEK, JOHN
MORONKO, JEFFREY
PUHL, TERRANCE
REYNOLDS, RICHARD
SPARKS, STEVEN
SPINKS, SCIPIO

SUGARLAND TX
BALES, WESLEY
BARZILLA, PHILIP
JONES, GROVER

TATUM TX
ALLEN, ROBERT

TAYLOR TX
LINEBRINK, SCOTT

TEMPLE TX
MCMURTRY, JOE

TERRELL TX
MILLER, NEAL

TEXARKANA TX
BUNCH, MELVIN
MONROE, CRAIG
MOSELEY, DUSTIN

TEXAS CITY TX
BACKE, BRANDON

THE WOODLANDS TX
AARDSMA, DAVID
DESHAIES, JAMES

DRABEK, DOUGLAS

TOMBALL TX
CLYDE, DAVID
HAYES, CHARLES
SNYDER, JERRY

TROPHY CLUB TX
HARDY, HOWARD

TYLER TX
CHICK, TRAVIS
MUMPHREY, JERRY
MURFF, JOHN
REYNOLDS, ARCHIE

VALLEY MILLS TX
SADLER, DONNIE

VICTORIA TX
BEATTY, GORDON
COFFMAN, KEVIN
MACHA, MICHAEL
RAMIREZ, DANIEL

WACO TX
BARKLEY, BRIAN
BREWER, WILLIAM
HANEY, TODD
HARRIS, DONALD
HUDSON, SIDNEY
PATTERSON, KENNETH
SADLER, RAYMOND
SPEHR, TIMOTHY
ZACHRY, PATRICK

WAKE VILLAGE TX
WALKER, JAMES

WALLER TX
ROBERTSON, RICHARD

WARREN TX
HATTON, GRADY

WASKOM TX
JACKSON, KENNETH

WAXAHACHIE TX
CRONE, RAYMOND
FOSTER, STEPHEN

WEATHERFORD TX
MILNER, BRIAN
PETRALLI, EUGENE
TERWILLIGER, WILLARD

WEST TX
PODSEDNIK, SCOTT

WHARTON TX
MATULA, RICHARD

WILLIS TX
HOLLINS, JESSIE

WOODWAY TX
REDFIELD, JOSEPH

YOAKUM TX
WAGNER, RYAN

YORKTOWN TX
MURRAY, DALE

UTAH

ALPINE UT
COOPER, GARY

BOUNTIFUL UT
DOWNS, DAVID

CENTERVILLE UT
DOWNS, KELLY

DRAPER UT
HANCOCK, RYAN

HUNTSVILLE UT
WALTON, DANIEL

KEARNS UT
DUCKWORTH, BRANDON

LEHI UT
CHRISTENSEN, MCKAY

LOGAN UT
VANNOY, JAY

MAPLETON UT
JOYNER, WALLACE

MIDVALE UT
ROBERTSON, DARYL

MORGAN UT
HUNT, KENNETH

MORONI UT
CHRISTENSEN, BRUCE

OGDEN UT
ERICKSON, HAROLD

PARK CITY UT
CROSBY, KENNETH
JENNINGS, ROBIN
MORGAN, MICHAEL

PAROWAN UT
EYRE, WILLIAM

PLEASANT GROVE UT
IORG, DANE

PROVO UT
LAW, VANCE
LAW, VERNON
SISK, TOMMIE

RIVERTON UT
HEIMUELLER, GORMAN

SAINT GEORGE UT
HICKS, CLARENCE
WRIGHT, RONALD

SALT LAKE CITY UT
FRANKS, HERMAN
HOWARD, DOUGLAS
MUDROCK, PHILIP
NIELSEN, JEFFREY
SANFORD, JOHN
SHELTON, CHRISTOPHER
THEODORE, GEORGE
WILLHITE, JON

SANDY UT
NELSON, ROBERT

SANTA CLARA UT
JOHNSON, JASON
LYON, BRANDON

SPRINGVILLE UT
SNYDER, JAMES
WARD, ROBERT

WASHINGTON UT
REVERING, DAVID

WEST JORDAN UT
COX, TERRY

WEST VALLEY UT
FERNANDEZ, JARED

VIRGINIA

ALDIE VA
HOWARD, FRANK

ALEXANDRIA VA
MCCALL, BRIAN

ANNANDALE VA
HANNAN, JAMES

BARBOURSVILLE VA
HANEY, CHRISTOPHER
HANEY, WALLACE

BEDFORD VA
HUMPHREYS, ROBERT

BIG ISLAND VA
BOWYER, TRAVIS

BOWLING GREEN VA
BEASLEY, LEWIS

BRISTOL VA
SAUL, JAMES

BROOKNEAL VA
BOOKER, RICHARD

CENTERVILLE VA
SNYDER, BRIAN

CENTREVILLE VA
MCNAMARA, JAMES
SCHOUREK, PETER

CHARLOTTESVILLE VA
HICKS, WILLIAM
MITCHELL, LARRY

CHESAPEAKE VA
ANDERSON, JAMES
BROWN, ROGERS
CUDDYER, MICHAEL
UPTON, MELVIN

CHESTER VA
GRUBB, JOHN

CHESTERFIELD VA
CAUSEY, KEVIN
MEREDITH, OLISE

CHURCH ROAD VA
CHRISTOPHER, MICHAEL

COBBS CREEK VA
ATHERTON, KEITH

CROZET VA
WAGNER, WILLIAM

CULPEPER VA
HASH, HERBERT

DANVILLE VA
WINDHORN, GORDON

DAYTON VA
KNICELY, ALAN

DUBLIN VA
DAILEY, WILLIAM

DUMFRIES VA
BAKER, JEFFREY

FAIRFAX VA
CAMP, SHAWN

FALLS CHURCH VA
GREISINGER, SETH
TALBOT, FREDERICK

FLOYD VA
WILLIAMS, DONALD

FREDERICKSBURG VA
MAINE, JOHN
MCNICHOL, BRIAN
SULLIVAN, RUSSELL

FRONT ROYAL VA
NYMAN, CHRISTOPHER
WHITMORE, DARRELL

GALAX VA
GOODSON, JAMES

GLEN ALLEN VA
ALLEY, LEONARD
BUDZINSKI, MARK
GREENE, IRA

HAMILTON VA
CARROLL, THOMAS

HAMPTON VA
FULLWOOD, TROY
GOMES, WAYNE

KESWICK VA
CUBBAGE, MICHAEL

LANCASTER VA
COATES, JAMES

LEESBURG VA
FERRIS, ROBERT

LOCUST GROVE VA
HEFFERNAN, BERTRAM

LYNCHBURG VA
HALL, JOSHUA

MADISON HEIGHTS VA
BAILEY, WELBY
BIBBY, JAMES
TOMLIN, RANDY

MANASSAS VA
COLANGELO, MICHAEL
HARRIS, BOYD

MARTINSVILLE VA
MONTGOMERY, MONTY

MECHANICSVILLE VA
PARKER, HARRY

MIDDLETOWN VA
ALLISON, DANA

MIDLAND VA
WALLACE, MICHAEL

MIDLOTHIAN VA
FITZMAURICE, SHAUN
JEFFERSON, JESSE
VAUGHAN, CECIL

PATRICK SPRINGS VA
CLONTZ, JOHN

PEMBROKE VA
WILLIAMS, MICHAEL

PORTSMOUTH VA
MORAN, CARL
PARKER, CLARENCE

PRINCE GEORGE VA
BRADSHAW, TERRY

REEDVILLE VA
SMITH, MARK

RICHMOND VA
CARPIN, FRANK
CHAKALES, ROBERT
CLOSTER, ALAN
HUBBARD, MICHAEL
KASKO, EDWARD
MASON, HENRY
ROACH, MELVIN
SPURLING, CHRISTOPHER

RINER VA
BURKE, LEO

RINGGOLD VA
NUNNALLY, JONATHAN

ROANOKE VA
CANALE, GEORGE
HOLLAND, ALFRED

ROCKY MOUNT VA
HODGES, RONALD
MINNICK, DONALD

RUTHER GLEN VA
BEASLEY, ANTHONY
FITZGERALD, BRIAN

SHENANDOAH VA
COMER, HARRY

SPRINGFIELD VA
FIELDS, STEPHEN
SPEIER, RYAN

STAUNTON VA
SHEETS, LARRY

STUARTS DRAFT VA
ACKER, THOMAS

SUFFOLK VA
WRIGHT, DAVID

TOANO VA
VALERA, YOHANNY

VIENNA VA
LOUN, DONALD

VIRGINIA BEACH VA
BROWN, ALTON
DUBOIS, JASON
FOILES, HENRY
LAVELLE, GARY
RAUCH, ROBERT
RICHTER, ALLEN

WARRENTON VA
FRANKLIN, JOHN

WAYNESBORO VA
HARRIS, REGINALD
WALLING, DENNIS

WILLIAMSBURG VA
FARR, JAMES

WISE VA
STALLARD, EVAN
WOODBRIDGE VA
MATTHEWS, MICHAEL

VERMONT

BURLINGTON VT
NEIDLINGER, JAMES
WHITEHOUSE, LEONARD
CRAFTSBURY VT
LEE, WILLIAM
DERBY VT
WISSMAN, DAVID
MORETOWN VT
LAROCCA, GREGORY
RUTLAND VT
BENTZ, CHAD

WASHINGTON

ALLYN WA
STOCK, WESLEY
AUBURN WA
AVERILL, EARL
BAINBRIDGE ISLAND WA
DAMICO, JEFFREY
BELLEVUE WA
DAVIS, CHARLES
HENDERSON, DAVID
MARTINEZ, EDGAR
ROBERTSON, ALFRED
SEXSON, RICHMOND
VALLE, DAVID
BLAINE WA
PACIOREK, JAMES
BOTHELL WA
CASKEY, CRAIG
HOLMAN, BRIAN
SIZEMORE, GRADY
ZASKE, LLOYD
BREMERTON WA
LINDEN, TODD
BREWSTER WA
RIGGAN, JERROD
BRUSH PRAIRIE WA
MYERS, RANDALL
CAMAS WA
EMBREE, ALAN
GUNDERSON, ERIC
HUNTER, BRIAN
JAHA, JOHN
RAMSAY, ROBERT
CARNATION WA
NELSON, JEFFREY
CENTRALIA WA
FAST, DARCY
OVERBAY, LYLE
CHENEY WA
STRAMPE, ROBERT
CLARKSTON WA
BRYDEN, THOMAS
EDENS, THOMAS
CLYDE HILL WA
CRUZ, JULIO
COLBERT WA
ALLARD, BRIAN
BELITZ, TODD
SPRING, JACK
COWICHE WA
WELLS, ROBERT
DAVENPORT WA
SMITH, GREGORY
EDMONDS WA
COTTIER, CHARLES
OBRIEN, EDWARD
ELLENSBURG WA
EATON, ADAM
EPHRATA WA
MUCHLINSKI, MICHAEL
EVERETT WA
DEDRICK, JAMES
FALL CITY WA
KRUEGER, WILLIAM
FEDERAL WAY WA
DIDIER, ROBERT
JOHNSON, RONDIN
REYNOLDS, ROBERT
FOX ISLAND WA
HANSEN, JED
GIG HARBOR WA
HATTEBERG, SCOTT
MYERS, DAVID
ISSAQUAH WA
BUHNER, JAY
ELLISON, JASON
EVANS, THOMAS
MOSES, JOHN
SPILLNER, DANIEL
STOTTLEMYRE, MELVIN
VIZQUEL, OMAR
KENNEWICK WA
BENARD, MARVIN
HARRIS, WILLIAM
MOUNCE, ANTHONY
KENT WA
HAGEN, KEVIN
KIRKLAND WA
BATES, DELBERT
CAUDILL, WILLIAM
MALLICOAT, ROBBIN
NORTH, WILLIAM
OLLOM, JAMES
LA CENTER WA
KRAEMER, JOSEPH
MCGRAW, THOMAS
LIBERTY LAKE WA
PARSONS, CASEY
ROIG, ANTON
LONGVIEW WA
SCHMIDT, JASON
MEDICAL LAKE WA
AFFELDT, JEREMY
MEDINA WA
OLERUD, JOHN
MERCER ISLAND WA
MCINTOSH, JOSEPH
STATON, JOSEPH
WAINHOUSE, DAVID
MOSES LAKE WA
HEAVERLO, DAVID
MOUNT VERNON WA
ATCHLEY, JUSTIN
HENDRICKSON, MARK
NEWCASTLE WA
SORRENTO, PAUL
NEWPORT WA
BULLING, TERRY
NORMANDY PARK WA
SAGMOEN, MARC
OLYMPIA WA
BAEK, CHA-SEUNG
GAJKOWSKI, STEPHEN
PASCO WA
BONDERMAN, JEREMY
PORT ORCHARD WA
HAMMEL, JASON
SPENCER, SEAN
POULSBO WA
SMALL, MARK
PUYALLUP WA
BARRON, ANTHONY
LESTER, JONATHAN
MCNULTY, WILLIAM
PARQUE, JIM
PREGENZER, JOHN
REDMOND WA
BONNELL, ROBERT
THOMAS, STANLEY
RENTON WA
HASELMAN, WILLIAM
JACKSON, CHARLES
RICHLAND WA
REPKO, JASON
RIDGEFIELD WA
SPENCER, STANLEY
SAMMAMISH WA
ORVELLA, CHAD
SAARLOOS, KIRK
SINATRO, MATTHEW
SEATTLE WA
CAMPBELL, MICHAEL
KINNUNEN, MICHAEL
MOYER, JAMIE
OBRIEN, JOHN
WILKINS, ERIC
WILSON, DANIEL
SEDRO-WOOLLEY WA
JORDAN, NILES
LEHMAN, KENNETH
SEQUIM WA
KELLER, HAROLD
SNOHOMISH WA
BEST, KARL
WASHBURN, RAY
SPANAWAY WA
BLOWERS, MICHAEL
SPOKANE WA
BARBIERI, JAMES
BECK, RICHARD
DAVEY, MICHAEL
KREMMEL, JAMES
OROURKE, JAMES
REDMOND, MICHAEL
RYAN, ROBERT
SPOKANE VALLEY WA
WILLS, ELLIOTT
STANWOOD WA
HANSEN, ROGER
SUMMER WA
YURAK, JEFFREY
TACOMA WA
ISHIKAWA, TRAVIS
NETTLES, JAMES
POINTER, AARON
SISK, DOUGLAS
TUMWATER WA
MULLEN, FORD
UNIVERSITY PLACE WA
DADE, LONNIE
MURPHY, WILLIAM
VANCOUVER WA
CHOI, HEE
COUGHTRY, JAMES
GISSELL, CHRISTOPHER
HAMBRIGHT, ROGER
PETERSON, ADAM
STALEY, GERALD
SWEET, RICHARD
WILSON, JAMES
WALLA WALLA WA
OFLAHERTY, ERIC
WENATCHEE WA
DASSO, FRANCIS
MARTZ, GARY
YAKIMA WA
DIPIETRO, ROBERT
EDLER, DAVID
MAGRUDER, CHRISTOPHER
MELUSKEY, MITCHELL
PEARCE, JOSHUA
YELM WA
SMITH, BOBBY

WISCONSIN

ABRAMS WI
WICKMAN, ROBERT
AMERY WI
THOMAS, GEORGE
APPLETON WI
DAVIS, GERALD
GASSNER, DAVID
HIETPAS, JOSEPH
KUBEK, ANTHONY
BELOIT WI
KENNEY, GERALD
KRENCHICKI, WAYNE
BOSCOBEL WI
CLARK, WILLIAM
BROOKFIELD WI
PAVLETICH, DONALD
CASCO WI
VOYLES, BRADLEY
CHILI WI
VARSHO, GARY
EAU CLAIRE WI
POQUETTE, THOMAS
EDEN WI
GANTNER, JAMES
EPHRAIM WI
LAWRENCE, SEAN
LUNDSTEDT, THOMAS
FRANKLIN WI
ALDRICH, JAY
CASTRO, WILLIAMS
GERMANTOWN WI
SCHRAMKA, PAUL
GREEN BAY WI
BALDSCHUN, JACK
GREENVILLE WI
HARIKKALA, TIMOTHY
GREENWOOD WI
BUKER, CYRIL
HALES CORNERS WI
SANDERS, KENNETH
HARTLAND WI
HENRY, RICHARD
HORTONVILE WI
SOMMERS, DENNIS
JANESVILLE WI
ADAMS, HAROLD
KENOSHA WI
BROWN, JARVIS
HARTMAN, ROBERT
KUTZLER, JERRY
LACROSSE WI
GHELFI, ANTHONY
LODI WI
NEUMEIER, DANIEL
LUXEMBURG WI
JORGENSEN, TERRY
MADISON WI
SCHMIDT, JEFFREY
WILSON, ROBERT
MARION WI
THIEL, MAYNARD
MCFARLAND WI
FISCHER, BRADLEY
MENASHA WI
HINSKE, ERIC

MENOMONEE FALLS WI
UECKER, ROBERT

MENOMONIE WI
VAVRA, JOSEPH

MEQUON WI
HISLE, LARRY

MERRILLAN WI
LASHER, FREDERICK

MIDDLETON WI
WOODALL, DAVID

MILWAUKEE WI
CIMORELLI, FRANK
COUNSELL, CRAIG
KRSNICH, MICHAEL
LOGAN, JOHN
MANTILLA, FELIX
VENTO, MICHAEL

MUSKEGO WI
AUGUSTINE, GERALD
SCHROEDER, ALFRED

NEENAH WI
TASCHNER, JACK

NEOSHO WI
WAGNER, PAUL

NEW BERLIN WI
HART, MICHAEL

OCONTO FALLS WI
PETERSON, ADAM

ONALASKA WI
HOCKENBERY, CHARLES

OSCEOLA WI
KOOSMAN, JERRY

OSHKOSH WI
CONNORS, PATRICK
GOGOLEWSKI, WILLIAM
KOPLITZ, HOWARD

PORT EDWARDS WI
METCALF, THOMAS

PORT WASHINGTON WI
DEMERIT, JOHN

PRESQUE ISLE WI
SCHERBARTH, ROBERT

RACINE WI
ROONEY, PATRICK

RICE LAKE WI
LUCAS, GARY

RICHLAND CENTER WI
GEISHERT, VERNON

THIENSVILLE WI
FROEMMING, BRUCE

TURTLE LAKE WI
TSCHIDA, TIMOTHY

TWIN LAKES WI
CLANCY, JAMES

UNION GROVE WI
KOLB, DANIEL

WAUKESHA WI
FROHWIRTH, TODD

WAUSAU WI
SCHMITZ, JOHN

WEBSTER WI
WASHBURN, JARROD

WEST BEND WI
MUELLER, WILLARD

WEST SALEM WI
MILLER, DAMIAN
WILLIAMS, GEORGE

WEST VIRGINA

BECKLEY WV
GODDARD, JOSEPH
PERKOWSKI, HAROLD

BERKELEY SPRINGS WV
BUTLER, WILLIAM

BETHANY WV
PETTINI, JOSEPH

CHAPMANVILLE WV
GODBY, DANNY

CHARLESTON WV
CHANCE, ROBERT
CURTIS, JOHN

CROSS LANES WV
KOLB, GARY

ELKINS WV
FANSLER, STANLEY

FORT ASHBY WV
ROBERTS, DAVID

KENOVA WV
BALDWIN, JEFFREY

KEYSER WV
KRUK, JOHN

LEFT HAND WV
VINEYARD, DAVID

LEWISBURG WV
MCCLUNG, MICHAEL

MARTINSBURG WV
BARKER, RAYMOND
BULLETT, SCOTT
PERKINS, CECIL

PARKERSBURG WV
HOPKINS, GAIL
SWISHER, NICHOLAS
SWISHER, STEVEN

REEDY WV
DAVIS, KANE

SAINT ALBANS WV
AUGUSTINE, DAVID

WEST COLUMBIA WV
CLARK, MELVIN

WINFIELD WV
LETT, JAMES

YAWKEY WV
HARPER, TRAVIS

WYOMING

AFTON WY
NYMAN, GERALD

ALPINE WY
LOEWER, CARLTON

DUBOIS WY
HELD, WOODSON

PUERTO RICO

AGUADA PR
HERNANDEZ, GUILLERMO

AGUADILLO PR
DELGADO, CARLOS

AIBONITO PR
MELENDEZ, LUIS

ARECIBO PR
MALDONADO, CANDIDO
MERCADO, ORLANDO
MIRANDA, ANGEL

ARROYO PR
CRUZ, CIRILO
CRUZ, HECTOR

BAYAMON PR
NAVARRO, JULIO
OLIVERAS, MAX

CAGUAS PR
BERNAZARD, ANTONIO
CORA, JOSE
GARCIA, PEDRO
MONTANEZ, GUILLERMO
MUNIZ, MANUEL
PENA, ADALBERTO
PERAZA, LUIS

CAROLINA PR
BENIQUEZ, JUAN
CORREA, EDWIN
HERNAIZ, JESUS
LABOY, JOSE
MILLAN, FELIX
MONTALVO, RAFAEL
ROSADO, LUIS
SANTIAGO, JOSE

CIDRA PR
DEJESUS, JOSE
RIVERA, LUIS

DORADO PR
LIND, JOSE
MARTINEZ, CARMELO
THON, RICHARD

FAJARDO PR
CRUZ, HENRY

GUANICA PR
VARGAS, HEDIBERTO

GUAYAMA PR
BONES, RICARDO

GUAYNABO PR
MORET, ROGELIO

JUANA DIAZ PR
CONDE, RAMON
GOMEZ, JUAN

MANATI PR
AVILES, RAMON

MAYAGUEZ PR
RAMIREZ, MILTON
ROSELLO, DAVID
VALLE, HECTOR

OROCOVIS PR
SANTODOMINGO, RAFAEL

PENUELAS PR
ARROYO, LUIS

PONCE PR
MANGUAL, JOSE
QUINONES, LUIS
RIVERA, JESUS

RIO GRANDE PR
ALVAREZ, JESUS

RIO PIEDRAS PR
ALCARAZ, ANGEL
BENITEZ, YAMIL
SANTIAGO, JOSE

SALINAS PR
ALOMAR, ROBERTO
ALOMAR, SANTOS
ALOMAR, SANTOS

SAN GERMAN PR
OLIVARES, EDWARD
OLIVARES, OMAR

SAN JUAN PR
BOCACHICA, HIRAM
NAVARRO, NORBERTO

SANTA ISABEL PR
TORRES, FELIX

SANTA JUANITA PR
FIGUEROA, EDUARDO

SANTURCE PR
OLMO, LUIS
PEREZ, ATANASIO
PIZARRO, JUAN
RUIZ, MANUEL

TOA ALTA PR
LOPEZ, JUAN

TOA BAJA PR
AYALA, BENIGNO

VEGA ALTA PR
HERNANDEZ, JOSE
WILLIAMS, BERNABE

VEGA BAJA PR
GONZALEZ, JUAN

VIRGIN ISLANDS

CHRISTIANSTED VI
BROWNE, JEROME

FREDERIKSTED VI
CLARKE, HORACE

SAINT CROIX VI
THOMAS, VALMY

SAINT THOMAS VI
MCBEAN, ALVIN

CANADA

ALBERTA

CALGARY AB
RADMANOVICH, RYAN

EDMONTON AB
COVINGTON, JOHN

SAINT ALBERT AB
SHIPANOFF, DAVID

BRITISH COLUMBIA

BURNABY BC
CHAVARRIA, OSWALDO

SURREY BC
MYETTE, AARON
PLADSON, GORDON

VICTORIA BC
LAMPLUGH, IAN

ONTARIO

AJAX ON
WILSON, NIGEL

BRIGHT GROVE ON
MACKENZIE, ERIC

CALEDONIA ON
LAWRENCE, JAMES

CARDINAL ON
HOY, PETER

CHATHAM ON
ATKINSON, WILLIAM

DORCHESTER ON
FANNING, WILLIAM

LONDON ON
BURGESS, THOMAS

MISSISSAUGA ON
OHALLORAN, GREGORY

STEVENSVILLE ON
KORINCE, GEORGE

STONEY CREEK ON
OSTROSSER, BRIAN

STRATFORD ON
LANDRETH, LARRY

TORONTO ON
GASTON, CLARENCE
TAYLOR, RONALD

WINDSOR ON
BERTOIA, RENO
SIDDALL, JOSEPH
UPHAM, JOHN

PRINCE EDWARD ISLAND

CHARLOTTETOWN PE
HANDRAHAN, JAMES

QUEBEC

LACHINE QC
BOUCHER, DENIS

PIERREFONDS QC
ARSENAULT, PIERRE

POINTES AUX TREMBLES QC
DAVIAULT, RAYMOND

SAINT JEAN-SUR-RICHELIEU QC
RAYMOND, JOSEPH

SAINT NICHOLAS QC
ROY, JEAN

VERDUN QC
PICHE, RONALD

SASKATCHEWAN

NIPAWIN SK
PAGAN, DAVID

SPRING TRAINING 2007

Mike Boddicker and Matt Smalling holding his daughter, MaKenzie. Royals Minor League Complex, March 22, 2007, Surprise, Ariz.

David Smalling, John Mayberry and Jack Smalling. Royals Minor League Complex, March 22, 2007, Surprise, Ariz.

BATTING AGAINST SATCHEL PAIGE

July 1964, Brookside Park, Ames, Iowa. Jack Smalling faces Hall of Famer Satchel Paige in the first inning of the Ames Merchants game against the traveling Kansas City Monarchs. The result was a line drive single to right center.

Two big events in my life occurred ten days apart in the summer of 1964. I batted against Satchel Paige and got married. The game against Paige takes a little more explanation. Read on.

I organized and played on a semi-pro baseball team in Ames from 1960 to 1971. For those twelve years I was always the business manager, caught and played outfield (couldn't pick up a ground ball), and served as field manager about half of those twelve years. We played about 30 to 35 games each summer and I would relive those days in a minute if I could.

In the late spring of 1964, Ted Rasberry of the Kansas City Monarchs contacted me about playing a game in Ames. They billed themselves as the Kansas City Monarchs although the Negro Leagues were not organized at that time. They traveled from town to town and featured the immortal Satchel Paige. Mr. Rasberry and I met, set up a deal and scheduled a game for July 29, 1964.

A local television station wanted to interview Satchel Paige, so we set up an interview for late afternoon the day of the game. About 4 o'clock a big green Cadillac rolled to a stop in front of our home in Ames. Out stepped Ted Rasberry followed by Satchel Paige. They walked slowly up the slope of our front yard. Rasberry said, "Mr. Smalling, this is Leroy." We shook hands. This was my first introduction to Satchel

Paige. I'd seen him before at a minor league game in Burlington, Iowa, a few years before. But this was my first time to meet him personally.

Paige was supposed to pitch three innings to start the game. And he did. We really didn't do much damage to him or the Monarchs as they beat us 5-1. However, my at-bat in the first inning was unforgettable. Paige didn't throw hard. At age 55, his motion was somewhere between side arm and underhand and deceptive. He threw me one that I drilled one hop off the right centerfield fence. And with my great speed I got a single out of it. But it was a clean hit. I could tell my boys that I batted against Hall of Famer Satchel Paige just like my dad told me about the time he batted against Hall of Famer Grover Cleveland Alexander.

That summer I also batted against two other major leaguers. Jackie Collum, who last had played in the majors in 1962, pitched for Grinnell. He was still pretty crafty and dispatched me on strikes with ease. However, I homered off of Larry Biittner. He later played first base and outfield in the majors for a number of years. Satchel Paige pitched again in the majors in 1965 and threw three scoreless innings. It must have been his motion. But, to this day I've always wondered if ol' Satch laid one in there for the opposing manager to hit. I'll never know.

Ten days after the game with the Monarchs, on August 8, 1964, Marge and I were married in Rochester, Minnesota. Together we had 33 years of wedded bliss and raised four fine sons.

Margaret Smalling

1942–1997

Navy Pre-Flight School, Chapel Hill, N.C., 1943. Ray Smalling (father of Jack) and Cornelius "Dutch" Warmerdam demonstrate boxing before a class of young Naval officers. Warmerdam was the first to pole vault fifteen feet and at the time the world record holder at 15 feet, 7¾ inches. He was the last to set a record with a bamboo pole.